Riding the Video Range

*The Rise and Fall of
the Western on Television*

RIDING THE VIDEO RANGE

The Rise and Fall of the Western on Television

by GARY A. YOGGY

McFarland & Company, Inc., Publishers
Jefferson, North Carolina, and London

Frontispiece: William Boyd as Hopalong Cassidy,
television's first cowboy hero.

British Library Cataloguing-in-Publication data are available

Library of Congress Cataloguing-in-Publication Data

Yoggy, Gary A.
   Riding the video range : the rise and fall of the western on
television / by Gary A. Yoggy.
     p. cm.
   Includes bibliographical references and index.
   ISBN 0-7864-0021-8 (lib. bdg. : 50# alk. paper) ∞
   1. Westerns (Television programs) — United States — History and
criticism. I. Title.
PN1992.8.W4Y64 1995
791.45'6278 — dc20   94-37472
                                     CIP

Manufactured in the United States of America

McFarland & Company, Inc., Publishers
  Box 611, Jefferson, North Carolina 28640

For Anna Jean,
without whose support and patience
this book would not have been possible

Table of Contents

Introduction

No television genre, not even the situation comedy, has ever been so dominant as the Western. Nor has any other format produced so many movie stars, from Steve McQueen, Clint Eastwood and Charles Bronson to Burt Reynolds, James Garner and Roger Moore. Eighteen new Westerns appeared on the home screen in 1958 when 12 of the top 25 Nielsen-rated shows were Westerns, including a phenomenal seven of the top ten. There were so many popular and well made Westerns that in 1959 the industry gave the genre its own Emmy, placing it on an equal footing with comedies and dramas. (ABC's *Maverick* won.)

On any given week in the fall of 1959 one could spend almost twenty hours of prime television viewing time watching Westerns. On Sundays: ABC offered *Colt .45*, *Maverick*, *The Lawman*, *The Rebel* and *The Alaskans*, while NBC provided *Riverboat*; Mondays: ABC gave us *Cheyenne*, CBS broadcast *The Texan*, and NBC offered *Tales of Wells Fargo*; Tuesdays: *Sugarfoot* and *Bronco* alternated on ABC followed by *The Life and Legend of Wyatt Earp* and *The Rifleman*, while NBC was offering *Laramie*; Wednesdays (a light night for Westerns): NBC broadcast *Wagon Train* and *Wichita Town*; Thursdays: CBS offered *Johnny Ringo* and *Dick Powell's Zane Grey Theatre*, while NBC provided *Law of the Plainsman* and *Bat Masterson*; Fridays: CBS aired *Rawhide* and *Hotel de Paree*, and ABC had *Black Saddle* and *Walt Disney Presents* (with frequent appearances from Elfego Baco, Texas John Slaughter and other Western heros); and Saturdays offered five of the best: *Bonanza* and *The Deputy* on NBC; *Wanted: Dead or Alive*, *Gunsmoke* and *Have Gun Will Travel* on CBS. It was truly a golden age of television Westerns.

No other type of program has ever disappeared so quickly and completely from the home screen: from 32 Westerns broadcast each week in prime time in 1959 to but a single network horse opera in 1984. In the mid–1990s, with few exceptions, Westerns can only be found on cable channels like the Family Channel, TBS and TNT, where the best of the old oaters still ride the video range.

In 1988, when I began work on this book, very little serious research had been done on this genre. Why had the Western enjoyed such enormous popularity in the fifties and sixties only to fall completely from public favor in little more than a decade? And how does the rise and fall of the television Western reflect changing American ethical values and cultural interests? In other words, what do Westerns tell us about ourselves — our past and our present?

It has been my intent not only to examine the cultural impact of the Western genre on television, but to provide a detailed behind-the-scenes look at some of the most popular and critically acclaimed programs. What made them successful and significant? I have not attempted to include every Western ever broadcast. The number would be in excess of two hundred, depending on how one defines "Western."

At this point, let me explain my definition of Western. Time *and* place are both important criteria. A program should be considered a Western if it takes place west of the Mississippi in the continental United States prior to 1900, in a *rural* setting west of the Mississippi *after* 1900, or east of the Mississippi prior to 1800. Furthermore, comedies that meet these time and place criteria also should be considered a part of the genre. (How can you include *Maverick*, but exclude *F Troop*, as one author has recently done?) Obviously this is a very broad definition and leads to the inclusion of programs that are set in the contemporary West (on a ranch or farm) like *Empire*, *The Yellow Rose* and even *Dallas*. While this is the definition I have used in categorizing television programs, the emphasis of this study has been the Western set in the trans–Mississippi West prior to 1900.

Frequently, during the course of my research I have been asked by colleagues and friends what my favorite television Westerns are. As I near the end of my task, I have given considerable thought to this question. I tried to list 10, quickly expanded it to 20 and finally concluded with 25. (If Nielsen can do it, why not me?) Here they are, roughly in order of preference:

1. *Gunsmoke*	14. *The Rifleman*
2. *Lonesome Dove* (miniseries)	15. *The Lone Ranger*
3. *Maverick*	16. *The Big Valley*
4. *Have Gun, Will Travel*	17. *Cheyenne*
5. *Rawhide*	18. *Wagon Train*
6. *Ned Blessing—The Story of My Life and Times*	19. *The Outcasts*
7. *Bonanza*	20. *The Westerner*
8. *The Life and Legend of Wyatt Earp*	21. *The Young Riders*
9. *Little House on the Prairie*	22. Disney's *Davy Crockett*
10. *Paradise (Guns of Paradise)*	23. *Wildside*
11. *Dr. Quinn, Medicine Woman*	24. *Kung Fu*
12. *The Wild, Wild West*	25. Disney's *Zorro* (tie)
13. *The Adventures of Brisco County, Jr.*	25. *The Virginian* (tie)

These are all programs that I have viewed extensively in the course of researching this book and many that I enjoyed when they were originally broadcast. In fact, the major portion of my research has involved the viewing of hundreds of hours of old shows on video—a few episodes of the more popular series were purchased commercially (e.g., *Gunsmoke*, *Bonanza*, *Rawhide* and *Wanted: Dead or Alive*); others were obtained from collectors, like David Miller (M&M Enterprises, Allen, Texas) and Bill Epler (The Old Prospector Video, Quarryville, Pennsylvania), whose assistance in locating specific episodes of a series was invaluable; most, however, were taped from cable television.

Anyone pursuing research on television Westerns will find very few secondary sources of value. Prior to 1982 only Ralph Brauer had done any substantial research on the genre (and his documentation is very limited). Since then, Rita Parks and J. Fred MacDonald have made significant contributions to the general study of television Westerns, and SuzAnne and Gabor Barabas have completed what is undoubtedly the definitive work on *Gunsmoke*.

Primary materials, in addition to the shows themselves, abound, but considerable effort must be expended in searching them out. Probably the single most valuable printed source of information is *TV Guide*. Also extremely useful, for its extensive reviews, is *Variety*. In addition, popular periodicals of the era from *Time* to *Life* frequently featured articles on the genre, stars and specific shows.

The Thousand Oaks Library in Thousand Oaks, California, has a very useful collection of television and radio materials, including many scripts. (Brad Miller, director of special collections, and his assistant, Martin Getzler, were unusually helpful.) The Margaret Herrick Library of the Academy of Motion Picture Arts and Sciences in Beverly Hills, California, has extensive clippings files on virtually every major film star. The Library of Congress in Washington, D.C., is a valuable source of scripts. The Library of the Performing Arts in New York City has a wide variety of printed and photographic materials relating to television in general and television Westerns in particular.

In addition to the staffs at these fine institutions I would like to hereby publicly express my appreciation to Ray White, professor of history at Ball State University in Muncie, Indiana, for his encouragement and support; to Archie P. McDonald, Regent's Professor of History at Stephen F. Austin State University in Nacogdoches, Texas, for publishing my first article on the subject; to Donald Voorhees, librarian at the Arthur A. Houghton, Jr., Library at Corning Community College, for his assistance in obtaining materials through interlibrary loan; to Francis M. (Mike) Nevins, Jr., of St. Louis University, for supplying me with program logs and other valuable information; to author Tim Kelly, story editor on *The High Chaparral*, for supplying me with scripts and storylines; to Ed and Jackie Solomon for their hospitality while visiting libraries in California; to Anthony and Adrienne Tollin for their hospitality while visiting libraries in New York City; to Louise Faulisi, my secretary, for her patience and typing; and most of all to my wife, Anna Jean, who spent countless hours at the computer processing my rough manuscript.

A further debt of gratitude is, of course, owed to all those performers and technicians who brought to life these wonderful shows. Let us especially remember those who have passed on to that great range in the sky: Doug McClure, Cameron Mitchell, Barry Sullivan, Chuck Connors, Michael Landon, Lorne Greene, Dan Blocker, Amanda Blake, Milburn Stone, Ken Curtis, Glenn Strange, Richard Boone, Steve McQueen, Eric Fleming, Ward Bond, John McIntire, Barbara Stanwyck, Richard Long, Ross Martin, Jay Silverheels, William Boyd, Lee J. Cobb, Leif Erickson, Jock Mahoney, Duncan Renaldo, Leo Carrillo, Dick Powell, John Russell, Forrest Tucker, Henry Fonda, Kirby Grant, Peter Deuel, Victor Sen Yung, Edgar Buchanan, Jim Davis, Jackie Coogan, Richard Eagan, Gabby Hayes, Walter Brennan, Neville Brand, Frank Silvera, Andrew Duggan, Victor French, Paul Fix, Tom Tryon, Joel McCrea, Andy Devine, Michael Dunn, Henry Calvin, Guy Williams, John Ireland et al.

I take full responsibility for any mistakes and errors of judgment.

GARY A. YOGGY
Corning, New York
January 1995

I. Hoppy, The Ranger, Gene and Roy Ride In

THE ARRIVAL OF JUVENILE WESTERNS ON THE HOME SCREEN

In the summer of 1949, television sets were large and television screens were small; wrestling, quiz shows and test patterns dominated the air waves, and Milton Berle was the undisputed king of the medium. Onto that video range rode television's first cowboy hero, Hopalong Cassidy, on Friday evening, June 24. During the years that followed nearly two hundred horse operas galloped into countless millions of American living rooms.

Hoppy broke the trail and the Lone Ranger, Gene Autry and Roy Rogers soon followed his successful lead, as Westerns slowly began to dominate home viewing. As historian J. Fred MacDonald has pointed out, they "captured the imagination of a nation of neophyte TV viewers" and "drew audiences to the infant entertainment medium ... insuring that television would be a cultural and financial success."[1]*

Early television Westerns were made with a juvenile audience in mind. The plots were simple and to the point. Good always triumphed over evil, crime did not pay and the hero was invariably brave, just, kind, smart and tough. Television shows modeled after the old B (for "budget") Westerns that were such an important part of those Saturday matinees of the forties became a sensation on television in the fifties. The "good guys" never shot first and rarely killed the "bad guys." They simply incapacitated them by expertly shooting the pistols out of their hands and then turned them over to the law for punishment.

Their stories about the winning of the West with examples of justice prevailing were both culturally and politically compatible with an America caught up in the East-West confrontation of the Cold War. They offered a simplistic and direct solution to virtually every problem, and adults, as well as children, could appreciate that. *Time Magazine* proclaimed:

> The western helps people to get away from the complexities of modern life and back to the "restful absolutes" of the past.... In the cowboy's world justice is the result of

Chapter Notes begin on page 653.

5

direct action not of elaborate legality. A man's fate depends on his own choices and capacities, not on the vast impersonal forces of society or science.... The western is the American morality play in which Good and Evil, Spirit and Nature, Christian and Pagan fight to the finish on the vast stage of the unbroken prairie. The hero is a Galahad with a six-gun, a Perseus of the purple sage.[2]

Over thirty years later, Pulitzer Prize–winning critic William A. Henry III agreed:

> The public was attracted to the heroic dimensions of those earlier and simpler times, to the pioneer values on which the nation had been built (and to which, politicians kept proclaiming, a wayward land should revert) and to that era's seeming moral clarity. By the western's conventions after all the good guys in white hats could be distinguished at a glance from the bad guys in black. In a modern world that sensed itself obligated to a cold war of perplexing tolerance rather than a hot war of righteous obliteration, this older world seemed seductively straight forward.[3]

The Western hero in many ways resembled a medieval knight. He was a champion of the oppressed, the weak, the less fortunate, and those in need of help such as widows, orphans and the elderly. He brought law, order and justice to the frontier. He was a model of honesty, integrity, fairness, courage, hard work, mental alertness, mercy, tolerance and patriotism, and he attempted to instill these qualities in his young viewers.

Such a hero was Hopalong Cassidy. But he had not always been that way. Cassidy was the creation of a former marriage license clerk from Brooklyn named Clarence E. Mulford who dreamed of the West he had never visited. In 1905 he sold his first Western story about a handsome stalwart cowhand he called Buck Peters. Peters had a profane, tobacco-chewing pal who limped and hence had been nicknamed Hopalong Cassidy. Cassidy, a near-illiterate who spoke only in Western lingo (e.g., "shore," "git," "purty," "plum loco"), was vaguely on the side of Good but managed to reduce the population by anywhere from two to twelve "varmits" per story. He could drop a man while swigging raw whisky from a bottle and pause after "ventilatin'" another "owlhoot" to pinpoint a fly on a nearby wall with a stream of tobacco juice.

Actor Bill Boyd was chosen by Harry "Pop" Sherman to play Buck Peters in the first Cassidy film. Boyd found Peters dull and talked Sherman into letting him play the foul-mouthed, mustachioed sidekick instead. It was Boyd who transformed Cassidy into the clean-shaven, sarsaparilla-swigging character destined for immortality.

William Boyd was born in Cambridge (or Hedrysburg), Ohio, in 1898 (or 1895 depending on what source is consulted).[4] As a youngster, he moved with his family to Tulsa, Oklahoma, where his father was killed in an explosion on a construction job. At the age of 13, Boyd quit school, and over the next few years worked his way back East to Akron and then went West again. He dreamed of becoming an engineer, but settled instead for such odd jobs as grocery clerk, surveyor, car salesman, rubber plant worker, lumberjack, oilfield laborer and hotelkeeper. He finally reached California in 1918 where he became an orange picker and a chauffeur. Tall, with chiseled features and platinum hair (which appeared silver under film lights), he married an heiress, developed a taste for expensive clothes and got his first acting job as a bit player in Cecil B. DeMille's *Why Change Your Wife?* in 1920.

Boyd caught DeMille's eye and was signed by Famous Players–Lasky to a $30 a week contract. Under DeMille's direction, he became a silent-movie matinee idol, in such films as *The Volga Boatman, King of Kings* (he played Simon of Cyrene who carried Christ's cross to Golgotha), *The Yankee Clipper* and *Two Arabian Knights.* When sound came along, he went to Pathé, where his resonant voice earned him $2500 a week in such popular films as *The Leatherneck* and *The Painted Desert* (his first Western). All the time, Boyd was enjoying the Hollywood high life, with a Beverly Hills mansion, a Malibu beach house, and a ranch in the hills. When he was not working, he was gambling, drinking, and partying. By the time he was 40 he had been married and divorced four times.

Then in 1930 a case of mistaken identity derailed his career. His photo was printed with a newspaper account of a drug and gambling party that had been thrown by a New York stage actor with the same name. Although the newspaper later printed a retraction, the damage had been done. Worried about bad publicity, RKO Films invoked a morals clause in a multipicture contract Boyd had just signed, voiding it and leaving the actor broke and unemployed.

After four years of surviving on bit parts in Gower Gulch Westerns, Boyd was approached by Sherman to play Buck Peters. James Gleason had already been tentatively cast to play the old gimpy-legged reprobate Cassidy. Sherman agreed to take a chance on the change, although he got a rude shock on the first day of shooting when Boyd confessed he could barely stay on a horse. (Supposedly, a double was used in the riding close-ups for the first few films until Boyd learned how to ride properly.)

Boyd would turn Cassidy into the prototypical cowboy hero. He would dress Hoppy all in black (in contradiction to convention), arm him with two pearl-handled six-shooters and have him ride a pure-white horse, Topper. He would present a "picture of gallantry, chivalry, honesty, justice, morality, and good-natured Christian decency."[5] He would also be quick on the draw and walk on two good legs. (The limp-producing wound which he had received in the first film would heal by the second.) Boyd would portray Cassidy as a soft-spoken paragon of rangeland virtue who did not smoke, drink, swear or kiss girls. And true to that unwritten code of the West, he would try to capture outlaws instead of killing them and he would always let the villain draw first if gunplay was necessary.

The public certainly approved. Between 1935 and 1948 Boyd made 66 Hoppy movies (54 for Sherman and 12 on his own) which earned him a large, loyal following. He was among the top five "Western Money-Making Stars" from 1937 to 1945, in 1947, and in 1948, and in the top ten for 1949, 1950 and 1952.

No less a character change overtook William Boyd himself during this same period. He gave up drinking and quit going to wild parties. Then he met a beautiful blond woman, Grace Bradley, 23, who had fallen in love with Boyd, the matinee idol, ten years earlier. In three weeks she became his fifth (and last) wife, to whom he was married for over thirty-five years. Playing the clean-cut, straight-shooting hero had transformed Boyd's personal life, and revitalized his screen career. Bill Boyd *became* Hopalong Cassidy. As Boyd later explained to columnist Hedda Hopper:

> ... the fellow is real to me. Often when working in pictures I'd object to certain directions, saying, "But the man wouldn't do that." The irritated directors would reply, "Who wouldn't do that?" And I'd say, "Hopalong."
>
> You may call it irony, but I worked under some of the greatest directors in the business; then spent sixteen years and more than $400,000 to be myself. I simply appropriated a name and did what I think Bill Boyd would have done had he lived in the West during Hoppy's era — the 1890s. Thus Hopalong Cassidy is Bill Boyd. I took Bill Boyd and made him into Hopalong Cassidy.[6]

In a recent interview, Boyd's widow explained the transformation of her husband this way:

> With Hopalong, Bill felt he was contributing something. He became totally concentrated on doing something good with his life. Bill, himself, once described his conversion this way: "In 1935 I met a man I admired. I became that man. Hopalong is the good side of Bill Boyd."[7]

It would be the longest-running continuous characterization in Hollywood history. There have been 16 different Tarzans, six different Lone Rangers, seven different Cisco Kids, three Supermen, four Batmen and a dozen or so Lassies. But there has been only one Hopalong Cassidy. Film historian Kalton C. Lahue has assessed Boyd's contributions to the genre in his *Riders of the Range: The Sagebrush Heroes of the Sound Screen*:

> Only one of the B Western stars ever became so closely identified with his screen character that his personal identity was almost totally submerged in the alter ego. Bill Boyd has one other qualification which he shared only with Randolph Scott and a select few of the other program Western heroes—he could really act and the series that brought him lasting fame and a good-sized fortune allowed him to do just that.[8]

Boyd's virtuous transformation was accompanied by an increased business acumen, as well as a desire to protect the image of the character he had created. Foreseeing the coming impact of television, Boyd sensed the medium's need for ready-made programs. Over the years, he quietly made a series of contracts for television rights to the Cassidy films with Mulford's publishers. He also gradually rounded up all the negatives of the Sherman films. In order to finance the project Boyd was forced to sell his ranch and Grace's car, mortgage his own automobile, sell Grace's jewels and furs and rent a four-room cottage where Grace did her own cooking and Hoppy mowed the lawn. They borrowed every penny they could get their hands on and even cut down on meals. Boyd gambled everything he had to save Hopalong. It cost him over $350,000 and left him completely broke.

What happened next was one of the most amazing developments in the history of the entertainment business. In November 1948, Boyd talked Los Angeles television station KNBH (KNBC's forerunner) into showing one of his films at a rental of $200. This telecast was given one of the most enthusiastic receptions of early television. Hoppy became a household word with a new generation of youngsters. Within a year, over 60 stations were carrying his films. NBC paid him $250,000 for the weekly showings. In January 1950, the clamor for more Hopalong Cassidy led to a Hoppy radio show broadcast over 500 Mutual Network stations. According to radio historian John Dunning:

> Boyd had one of radio's perfect voices. His voice could do anything—comfort a bereaved widow one moment, scare the boots off her husband's killers the next. It was strong, virile, and straight to the point. And that Hoppy bellylaugh became famous. It was one of his trademarks, as indispensable as his all-black outfit and his horse Topper.[9]

The radio series was followed by a comic strip carried in 125 newspapers. There were also two record albums. ("Hopalong Cassidy and the Singing Bandit" had pre-release sales of $200,000.)

Boyd's biggest bonanza was the fact that every manufacturer wanted Hoppy's endorsement for their product. Soon stores were selling Hopalong Cassidy–Bar 20 cowboy and cowgirl outfits, bathrobes, raincoats, pajamas, lunch boxes, six-gun and holster sets, table model radios, wastebaskets, wallets, two-gun bicycles, neckties, wristwatches, jack knives, animated lamps, spur roller skates, bars of soap, latex masks, cookies, candy bars, wallpaper, bedspreads, towels, and blankets, as well as books and comic books. In order to maintain some sort of control over the quality of the Hoppy products, Boyd set a limit of 100 manufactures. He refused to license bubble gum (of which he disapproved) and sharply pointed objects. Indeed, he rejected nine out of every ten products on which he had been asked to put his name. He insisted on reasonable prices and good quality. He forced one manufacturer to remove shiny gold and silver fringes from leather jackets, saying, "What cowhand would wear those?"[10]

William Boyd as Hopalong Cassidy.

In addition, he criss-crossed the country on personal appearance tours to meet his fans. In January 1950, a crowd of New Yorkers estimated at 350,000 lined up for twenty-five blocks to shake his hand in Macy's. In May 1950, he drew the largest circus audience (18,700) ever to pack the Chicago Stadium. And he was invited to ride with the President of the United States in the annual "I Am an American Day" parade in Washington, D.C. Feeling that it was his duty "to strengthen the fiber of American Youth," Boyd established the Hopalong Cassidy Troopers Clubs, whose two million members rivaled the Boy Scouts. Hoppy's Troopers wore badges, had secret code words and membership cards and practiced the principles of honesty and fair play. Every youngster was asked to swear allegiance to an eight-point creed when he became a member:

To be kind to birds and animals	To be careful when crossing streets
To always be truthful and fair	To avoid bad habits
To keep yourself neat and clean	To study and learn your lessons
To always be courteous	To obey your parents[11]

By 1952 the 54 Sherman Cassidys were becoming stale and Boyd decided to augment them with a series of 52 half-hour films made expressly for television. Twenty-six episodes of *Hopalong Cassidy* were broadcast on NBC during the 1952-53 season and another 26 during 1953-54. The first dozen, however, were cut down versions of the 12 Cassidy features Boyd had produced himself between 1946 and 1948. They were supplemented with voice-over narration to bridge the gaps in the storylines. Thus, Boyd only had to make 14 new shows for the first season.

Boyd, of course, starred as Hoppy and still looked good on screen even though he was already approaching his late fifties. For budgetary reasons he eliminated the traditional role of a younger romantic sidekick and brought in pudgy, gravel-voiced Edgar Buchanan for comedy relief in the role of Red Connors (instead of his film sidekick Andy Clyde, who wanted more money).

Many of the plots were tried and true and could easily have been interchanged with most of the other juvenile Westerns then beginning to proliferate the airwaves. In "The Trap," Hoppy helps an ex-convict who is trying to go straight but who is being blackmailed into joining a plot to rob the Cattleman's Association. In "The Feud," Hoppy saves an innocent man from hanging and tracks down a murderer who is manipulating a feud between two rival ranches. In "The Devil's Idol," Hoppy and a young minister try to convince a boy who has just committed his first holdup that his gunman idol has feet of clay. In "Black Sheep," Hoppy and Red try to settle a dispute between cattle ranchers and sheep grazers. In "The Last Laugh," Hoppy poses as a cattle buyer in order to break up a ring of thieves who are stealing gold from a smelter. In "Double Trouble," Hoppy tries to help a young Mexican laborer whose knife was found in a banker's back.[12] What did the critics think of the new Cassidy shows? *Variety* (September 29, 1952) said after the first episode aired:

> Boyd is still a striking figure in the sharp contrast of his dark accoutrements to his full head of grey hair. It may have been implied by the tube's distortion that he's getting a little portly around the middle, but there's more twilight than spring in his gait. It's too early to tell whether time has slowed the draw on his side arms.
>
> Even though the action was temperate for a western, it had all the skilled touches of production, direction and camera of an experienced crew. Hoppy will still be headman with the young shavers as long as he can throw a slowing leg across the saddle.

Even during the final season of 30 minute Cassidy shows *Variety* (March 26, 1954) was still praising Boyd's strengths while minimizing his shortcomings. Writing nearly thirty-five years later, however, Francis M. Nevins, author of the definitive study of Hopalong Cassidy, assesses the television series much more harshly:

> Of all the Western series on the small tube during the early fifties, "Hopalong Cassidy" was just about the worst. Scripts were standard issue, outdoor locations dreary-looking, action sequences minimal or non-existent. The only saving grace of the series was that all exterior scenes were actually shot outdoors, not on the cheap and phony-looking stage sets that had become a staple of rival TV shows.... Each episode featured a huge amount of Boyd's voice-over narration and was capped by a mini-sermon in which Hoppy offered counsel to kids.... The theme song by Nacio Herb Brown and L. Wolfe Gilbert—"Here He Comes" ...—was the absolute pits.[13]

Why then was the series so successful? What made Hoppy the first big Western star on television? What made him the idol of American children *and* their parents? (Surveys showed that 65 percent of Hoppy's fans were adults.) Why was he the first cowboy television star to have his picture on the covers of *Time*, *Life* and *Look* magazines? In 1951, the man who had "discovered" William Boyd and helped launch his career, Cecil B. DeMille, explained it this way:

> Hopalong Cassidy is as much an American character now as George Washington, Abe Lincoln or Daniel Boone. He is the power of good always trying to down the power of evil.[14]

In 1957, British television historian F. Maurice Speed commented on Boyd's significance:

> Boyd is much more than a mere cowboy. He embodies much that is desirable, reassuring and exciting in life. He is a good samaritan, a pal to children and popular with adults, too.... Legions of Hopalong fans of every age believe he can do no wrong. He's chivalrous with women, affectionate with children and kind to animals. He's law, order, honor and frontier bravery personified.[15]

Writing thirty years later J. Fred MacDonald assessed the Hopalong Cassidy phenomenon:

> As with most popular cultural phenomena, Hoppy embodied strategic, relevant social issues. His character communicated more than a simple story of cowboys versus outlaws ... in a time of Cold War tensions ... Hoppy was a patriot.
> ... Hoppy operated in a black-and-white moral world: One was either good or bad, and Cassidy was uncompromising with those who were bad.... He followed the good course; and like a moral force on horse back, he led a generation of youngsters—and often those parents who approvingly watched with their children—toward realization of what the good person or society could be.[16]

Some three months after Hopalong Cassidy's television debut, *The Lone Ranger* joined him on the video range. Another hero from the B-Western mold, but one created especially for radio, *The Lone Ranger* had first premiered on Detroit radio station WXYZ in late January or early February 1933. (There is some dispute over the date. January 30 had long been given as the correct date. In 1976, however, David Rothel determined that January 20 was the actual date. Fran Striker, Jr., thinks it is January 31 and David Holland's most recent—1988—and thorough research indicates that February 2 is probably the real date of the first broadcast.[17])

The radio series was created to solve a financial problem at WXYZ which, as an independent station, was unable to compete successfully with the "high-priced" entertainment being offered by the networks. Businessman George W. Trendle, owner of the station, discovered that the Western which had been so successful on the movie screen had not yet been adapted for radio. He also believed that there was a lack of wholesome, well written and appealing programs for children. Influenced by the assumption that children are less critical and can coax their parents into buying the sponsor's product, Trendle decided to develop a Western drama for children.

The creation of a "hero" for Trendle's proposed series was a cooperative effort involving Buffalo, New York, script writer Fran Striker and WXYZ staff director Jim Jewell. Trendle originally conceived of the hero of his Western drama as combining the traits of Robin Hood and Zorro. Gradually, the concept took on the familiar characteristics of the Ranger as he is known today: a Texas Ranger, sole survivor of an ambush; wearing a mask to conceal his true identity; riding a great white horse, eventually named Silver; silver bullets as his "calling card"; an Indian companion (Tonto) to talk to.

The Lone Ranger program was designed to be both practical and educational. Practically, the program was designed to make money. Educationally, the program was designed to communicate a message which would teach patriotism, tolerance, fairness, and a sympathetic understanding of one's fellow men and their rights and privileges. The creators felt that their message could be effectively communicated through the character of the Lone Ranger whose actions would be imitated by children who listened. Thus, the Lone Ranger was conceived to have all the desirable virtues of men who uphold the law. The agency responsible for promoting the series, Trendle, Campbell, and Mewrer, Inc., developed, with the assistance of Striker, a brochure for freelance writers who wished to submit scripts for the series. This can be considered the definitive description of the Ranger and his qualities:

> *Patriotism*: The Lone Ranger is motivated by love of country—a desire to help those who are building the West. . . . Patriotism means service to a community; voting . . . the development of schools and churches. Patriotism includes also an obligation to maintain a home in which good citizens may be reared. Patriotism means respect for law and order, and the selection of officials who merit such respect. Patriotism consists of the preservation of the things for which our ancestors fought and died. The preservation of the rights of freedom of speech and religion.
>
> *Fairness*: The Lone Ranger never attacks from behind, or takes unfair advantage of an adversary. The Lone Ranger registers disapproval of bullets—of men who take unfair advantage—of men who, even though within their legal rights, step beyond the bounds of fair play. . . . The Lone Ranger advocates the American Tradition, which gives each man the right to chose his work and to profit in proportion to his effort; and to retain for himself a fair proportion of his profits. The Lone Ranger also advocates the right to possess and hold worldly goods.
>
> *Tolerance*: The Lone Ranger's friend is an Indian. If the Lone Ranger accepts the Indian as his closest companion, it is obvious to the child listener that great men have no racial or religious prejudice. Nowhere in the stories is any minority group referred to in a derogatory manner.
>
> *Sympathy*: The Lone Ranger is a specific example of a man who can be strong, yet tender—a man who can fight hard, yet show mercy and compassion. . . . The Lone Ranger chooses the side of the oppressed—the underdog—the little man in need of help. The Lone Ranger can see the other fellow's point of view. He understands men's frailties. He knows no man is perfect and does not expect the impossible from anyone. He is of a forgiving nature.
>
> *Religion*: The Lone Ranger is not shown to be a member of any specific church, but he is definitely a respecter of all creeds. He is generally visualized as a Protestant, but one of his most beloved friends—in fact the only man aside from Tonto in whom he puts complete confidence—is the Catholic Padre of a Mission. He shows respect for preachers and worshippers of any denomination, including the Indian's veneration of their own Great Spirits.
>
> *Pure Speech*: The Lone Ranger by example, hopes to teach the strength and importance of pure speech. Easily the strongest character in every story, he is able to register in pure speech a greater impact than some of the characters whose limited understanding causes them at times to resort to slang and colloquialisms. The Lone Ranger is able to be forceful without swearing and emphatic without shouting.
>
> *Brutality, Gore and Sex*: The relationship of the sexes in the stories is kept wholesome. The Lone Ranger has no love interest. Romance in other characters is clean. Triangle situations, faithlessness and sex in lurid form are never used. The sanctity of the home is emphasized. Blood and brutality are eliminated except where plot definitely demands them. In these cases they are held to a minimum. Drinking, gambling and smoking are not done by the Lone Ranger and are kept to a minimum with the other characters and avoided entirely unless needed for plot.[18]

The first opportunity to test the new program's popularity came on May 15, 1933, when the Lone Ranger announced that a free popgun would be sent to the first 300 children who wrote in for it. The offer drew over 24,000 replies. At the end of July, just six months after the first broadcast, when the Detroit Department of Recreation staged its annual "School Field Day" with the Lone Ranger as special guest, over 70,000 children turned out to see the masked man in person. The show's fame and popularity grew steadily. In November, Silvercup Bread became the show's sponsor. Shortly thereafter WGN (Chicago) and WOR (New York) joined with WXYZ to broadcast the series and gave listeners outside of Michigan their first opportunity to hear *The Lone Ranger* over the new Mutual Network. Before long the program was being heard coast to coast.

From the beginning, the Ranger was destined to become one of the most successfully merchandised fictional characters in history, but only, as Fran Striker, Jr., points out, "in concert with the high standards and traditions that the character represented to his young fans."[19] An early example was the start of the Lone Ranger Safety Club in October 1935. The Club was introduced by a special broadcast that started with the Ranger talking directly to the audience. He explained that the purpose of the Club was to help the Lone Ranger do everything possible to reduce the many terrible accidents, deaths, and crippling injuries caused by automobiles. The first of several different versions of the Lone Ranger Safety Scout Pledge read:

I solemnly promise:
Not to play in the streets   To be careful when crossing streets
To always tell the truth   To keep out of bad company
To be honest and upright in all of my acts   To form no bad habits
To be kind to birds and animals   To keep myself neat and clean
To study hard and learn all that I can   To obey my father and mother[20]

The Lone Ranger, first on radio, and later on television, was in the forefront of the movement to promote high moral values and standards among young people. During the war, "The Lone Ranger Victory Corps" was established. Members received a personally signed letter from the Lone Ranger that read:

> You are now a full-fledged member of THE LONE RANGER VICTORY CORPS. Let me congratulate you on your willingness to do your share for our great country!
> Enclosed is your official "Victory Corps" material, including the membership-identification card, your instructions and the official insignia which will identify you as a full-fledged member of the "Victory Corps."
> Ours is a serious responsibility that can and will make a real contribution to our country's all-out Victory effort. There are many jobs that the Lone Ranger Victory Corps can and will do to help, such as:
> SALVAGE OF WASTEPAPER, SALVAGE OF RUBBER, SALVAGE OF METALS, DISTRIBUTION OF GOVERNMENT LITERATURE, GARDENING, CONSERVATION OF FOOD AND POWER, AIR RAID PRECAUTIONS IN YOUR OWN HOME, ETC., ETC.
> Special messages will be given on these and other jobs. So be sure to keep tuned to the Lone Ranger for your official instructions.[21]

In April 1949, CBS and General Mills established a National Lone Ranger Council of Honor "to encourage America's Youth to adhere to the principles of good citizenship and clean living." Included among its charter members were Dr. Norman Vincent Peale, Father John J. Cavanaugh (president of Notre Dame University), Dr. J. Robert Oppenheimer, Jane Froman, Gene Tunney, Robert Ripley, Bob Hope and Eddie Cantor.[22]

In 1958, "The Peace Patrol," a nationwide organization of boys and girls who bought U.S. Savings Stamps and Bonds, was established by the Treasury Department. The leader of the Peace Patrol was the Lone Ranger, whose likeness appeared on the Savings Stamp. The Lone Ranger, according to a CBS television press release dated August 7, 1958, was riding "on a mission of thrift and patriotism [in] to the classrooms and homes of America." Children were told that buying the stamps and bonds would "help build the economic and military strength required to preserve our freedom and insure the peace." The Lone Ranger launched the Peace Patrol in Washington, D.C., June 17 with a big youth rally. Then, he visited some thirty major cities, carrying his patriotic thrift story to thousands of young people and enrolling them in the ranks of the Peace Patrol. After the school year began, special Lone Ranger Peace Patrol posters were distributed to thousands of schools across the country. The Peace Patrol was also featured on *The Lone Ranger* television series.

Not content to merely serve as a role model, the Lone Ranger issued a glowing call to his young listeners to prepare for responsible adulthood on that program's twentieth anniversary radio broadcast in January 1953. Dan Reid, the Ranger's nephew, had been left in his care. The boy was to attend school in the East for part of each year. The rest of the time he would travel with the Lone Ranger to learn the ways of the West and the great heritage bequeathed him. On one such Western visit, the Ranger explained to Dan (and all his young listeners):

> When you're a man there'll be law and order in the West—and great cities, like those in the East. There will always be bad men, but they'll be different than the kind we know. To combat them you'll need weapons—and strength—and courage, but these must be backed by knowledge and education to handle them intelligently. Our great country will progress only so long as there are leaders. You and young people like you must educate yourselves to be the leaders. Son, I want you to go to college, to study science and law, history and the problems of government. I want you to learn the many things required so you'll be ready to take your place as a good citizen and carry on where we leave off. Knowing you're in school preparing for the future, I'll be content to continue helping others bring law and order to the West until you young men can take over.

The extent to which the program had affected the national consciousness is reflected in the way the media reacted to the death of Earle Graser, who had been playing the Ranger on radio since April 1933. On April 9, 1941, Graser was killed in an automobile accident. On the day following Graser's death the *New York Times* ran an editorial on the death of the Ranger which read in part:

> Earl H. Graser was killed in an automobile wreck early Tuesday morning, but the rumor that the Lone Ranger is dead is unfounded. It was a man who died.... But he didn't take the Lone Ranger with him. The Lone Ranger doesn't die, and Silver, his horse, will never get broken winded.... He still [lives], and his trusty steed waits to carry him on his errands across the face of the wondrous West where the air is crystal and virtue never lacks for its reward. Listen! There is a beating of hoofs as, in the nick of time, he swings into action. Ride, Tonto, ride Lone Ranger, "Hi Yo Silver!"[23]

The twentieth anniversary broadcast was recognized by Michigan Senator Homer Ferguson who placed a tribute to Trendle and the program into the *Congressional Record*. The statement concluded:

> ... every program came to a successful conclusion with the moral or message to be learned from the Ranger's adventures....
> In designing the Lone Ranger, George Trendle built in characteristics that would endear the Lone Ranger to the young and at the same time teach them the principles of good citizenship. In every program the Ranger has illustrated the basic tenets of honesty, patriotism, fair play, tolerance, and a sympathetic understanding of people and their rights and privileges.
> The Lone Ranger himself is a model of American manhood. One that can be used as an example of every father's son. The Ranger neither smokes, drinks intoxicating beverages, nor uses profanity. With his famous horse, Silver, his faithful Indian companion Tonto, and his oral signature of "Hi Yo Silver," the Lone Ranger continues to play to a third generation of youngsters, molding their thoughts along constructive American ideals.[24]

In his 1955 study, David Wilson Parker made some interesting discoveries about the world of the Lone Ranger through a careful analysis of 120 scripts:

> The period of the Lone Ranger stories is generally thought to lie between 1860 and 1890, the span so favored by writers of Western stories. But while the West of the Lone Ranger has a great deal in common with the West pictured in other frontier fiction, it is different in some significant respects.
>
> One distinctive characteristic of the Lone Ranger's West is that it so thoroughly subordinates the cattle culture and the cowboy. Lone Ranger stories are not cowboy stories in any sense. There is scant mention of trail herds, round-ups, cattle empires, and big drives to Northern railheads. . . . Instead, the Lone Ranger programs picture and approve themes of expansion, settlement, home-building, and law-bringing. In fact, almost anything connected with pushing back the frontier is viewed sympathetically in the world of the Lone Ranger.
>
> The railroads, which have been frequently shown unfavorably in Western literature, emerge as good in the West of the Lone Ranger. The sod busters, nesters, and sheep-men who are traditionally pictured as rather deplorable characters in the west of the cowboy and unfenced ranges, are viewed as solid citizens in the Lone Ranger episodes. . . .
>
> The frontier virtues of thrift, courage, hard work, cheerfulness, and the rest are given much greater approval in the world of the Lone Ranger than are frivolity or just plain having a good time. . . .
>
> In short, the West of the Lone Ranger . . . is a place of opportunity [as well as] a place of toil and hardship.[25]

Within five years of its inception, the adventures of the Lone Ranger were being released in novels, comic strips, comic books and motion pictures. The Ranger was first adapted for the screen in 1938's 15-chapter serial, *The Lone Ranger,* in which Lee Powell played the title role. A year later, another serial, *The Lone Ranger Rides Again,* was released with Bob Livingston as "the masked rider of the plains." The films ignored the radio mythology and angered Trendle. However, he had no legal recourse. He had assigned film rights to Republic Pictures without stipulating that the movie plots had to remain faithful to the origins and characteristics presented on radio. The only saving grace of the serials was the sound track, according to David Rothel. The score, composed by Alberto Colombo, was eventually incorporated into the radio and television series.[26]

Filming for the television version began on June 21, 1949, a full 16 years after the Ranger's radio debut. Casting the television series was the responsibility of Trendle. Brace Beemer, the radio Ranger after Earl Graser's death, reportedly wanted the part. He certainly had the physical build at six-feet, two-inches tall and 200 pounds and a magnificent deep voice as well. Indeed, he had made countless personal appearances as the Ranger even while Graser was still alive. (Graser was short and of slight build, with a moustache.) Trendle, however, felt Beemer was getting too old (46 at the time the Ranger was ready to move to television) and began the search for a new Ranger. When word spread that Beemer would not appear in the television series, Clayton Moore's agent forwarded a few of his client's Westerns to Trendle and Jack Chertok who would produce the new series. The agent believed that Moore's presence on camera, splendid physique and resonant voice would help him to land the role. The casting office saw the films and sent for Moore.

Moore was born in Chicago in 1914 (or 1908 or 1918 depending on the source consulted). He began his show business career as a trapeze aerialist with a circus that traveled throughout the United States. Moore claims he appeared in the youngest aerial act at the time, the first flying troupe to work on the high bars without a net, and the first to work over water. After leaving the circus, he took jobs modeling in New York and finally went to Hollywood in 1938. For some years he worked as an extra and stunt man in B Westerns and serials supplementing his income by digging ditches, mixing cement and pouring foundations. His big break came when Republic Studios cast him opposite the "Queen of the Serials," Kay Aldridge, in a jungle serial, *The Perils of Nyoka*, in 1942. With his great athletic abilities, Moore was able to handle the many hazardous and difficult stunts that were demanded of him. This led to starring roles in other chapter films for Republic and Columbia: *The Crimson Ghost* (1946), *Jesse James Rides Again* (1947), *The Adventures of Frank and Jesse James* (1948), *G-Men Never Forget* (1948), and *Ghost of Zorro* (1949).

Moore was signed to play the Lone Ranger, and Jay Silverheels, a full-blooded Mohawk from Ontario, Canada, became television's Tonto. General Mills, radio sponsor of the series, also underwrote the video version at an average production cost of $12,500 for each of the first 52 episodes. The outdoor scenes were filmed at locations in Utah and in California at Corriganville, Iverson's Ranch, Big Bear and Sonora, first for Hal Roach Studios and later for General Services Studios.

The series debuted on the home screen for ABC on September 15, 1949, and was carried by 90 stations coast-to-coast. The first three episodes presented the familiar story of how the Lone Ranger had received his name and his mission in life at Bryant's Gap. In an October 22 review for *The New York Times*, critic Jack Gould wrote, "*The Lone Ranger* is just another Western, and not a notable good one at that." He also took ABC, General Mills and Trendle to task for:

> ... keeping children emotionally hopped up and trying to capitalize on the normal anxiety and sensitiveness of youngsters by presenting unresolved, continuing stories. Use of the old cliff-hanging technique should be abandoned promptly.... Everyone concerned with the TV version of "The Lone Ranger" should stop and think what they are doing.[27]

Of course, *The Lone Ranger* was never intended to run as a serial and ABC officials advised Gould on October 4, 1949, that the program would no longer end on a note of suspense. *Variety* (September 14, 1949) also made mention of the "dyed-in-the-wool cliffhanger endings," although the review was much more favorable than that of the *Times*:

> General Mills, which backs the AM edition of "The Lone Ranger" has a good bet in the television version of the cowpoke classic ... the prem vidpic showed the slick touch of Coast westerns....
> Technically the acting is good and the editing fast-paced. Fact that the LR doesn't shoot to kill, but only to capture, tones down the element of violence and characterization of Tonto as an Indian Dr. Watson is acceptable.

Regardless of what the critics thought, within a year the Thursday night show was in the Nielsen top ten with a viewing audience of some five million people. It was ABC's highest rated program all season and the highest rated television Western up to that time.

After the 1950-51 season, Moore reportedly threatened to quit unless he received a substantial raise. (He was earning about $500 per show.) Trendle balked at his demands and hired John Hart to replace him, apparently believing the audience would not realize a switch had been made under the mask. Actually, audiences did notice that there was a new actor playing the Ranger, but many did not recognize Clayton Moore in the films he did while out of the mask: *Radar Men from the Moon* (1952), *Son of Geronimo* (1952), *Jungle Drums of Africa* (1953), *Gunfighters of the Northwest* (1954) and *Buffalo Bill in Tomahawk Territory* (1954).

Meanwhile, John Hart could be described as little more than adequate as the Ranger although he remained in the role for two seasons, filming 52 episodes. Although he had appeared in secondary roles in a score of films made both before and after World War II, his only lead had been in the Columbia serial *Jack Armstrong* in 1947. Hart is better remembered for his appearances in other television Westerns (after his stint as the Ranger) like *Tales of the Texas Rangers, Sky King, Rawhide, Rin Tin Tin* and *Sergeant Preston*. In 1982 he played the Ranger once again on an episode of *Happy Days* and had a small role in the disastrous film *The Legend of the Lone Ranger* in 1981.

In 1954 Trendle wisely rehired Moore and he played the Ranger in the final 91 episodes filmed between 1954 and 1957. After August 3, 1954, however, Moore rode for a new boss. On that date Trendle sold complete rights to the character, commercial tie-ins, radio scripts and shows, and television episodes to industrialist Jack Wrather. *Variety* called it the biggest television deal since NBC acquired ownership of *Hopalong Cassidy*. In 1956, the Wrather Corporation filmed 39 new installments in color. Wrather told the press that the show, costing approximately $25,000 per episode, would employ three "distinguished" novelists to help the screenwriters "retain *The Lone Ranger* precepts and teachings." The new owner was obviously concerned, however, that the children's show might not be able to compete favorably with the adult Western programs coming to television. Consequently, there was talk of "redesigning" the Ranger to appeal to older viewers. General Mills' advertising agency, Dancer Fitzgerald Sample, approved the plan, stating that "adults eat cereal too." Trendle, although not directly associated with the show any longer, argued that the Lone Ranger should not be changed:

> For years our ratings indicated that half our listeners and viewers were adults and this, without the blood and thunder of the "adult Westerns." The fights today seem more grue-some. If your scripts are good, you can have a hero who doesn't go around spitting tobacco juice. Nowadays, they don't glorify the leads—they're not enough inspiration for children. You don't need a lot of bloodshed to get fans—children or adults.[28]

After due consideration it was decided to leave the Lone Ranger on his tried-and-true path. He and Tonto did, however, venture into films. Moore and Silverheels appeared in two color Ranger films, *The Lone Ranger* (1956) and *The Lone Ranger and the Lost City of Gold* (1958).

Through much of the fifties, the series had the distinction of being broadcast on two major networks. ABC aired the prime time broadcasts and CBS owned the Saturday afternoon rerun rights. In 1960, NBC telecast *The Lone Ranger* on Saturday mornings. The network telecasts ended September 23, 1961, and thereafter episodes have been syndicated. At this very moment an episode is no doubt being rerun on a station somewhere in the world.

Like Hopalong Cassidy, the Lone Ranger produced a plentiful quantity of merchandise, and novelties, including clothing, hats, games, toys, cutlery, displays, school pencils, pens, boys' shoes, gun and holster sets, raincoats, musical instruments, candy, chains, badges, and buttons. Unlike Cassidy, the Ranger pioneered the use of premiums tied to the sponsor and promoted them on the radio and television programs. Among these items were a silver bullet with a secret compartment, a silver bullet with a compass, a flashlight ring, a telescope ring, an atomic bomb ring, a pedometer, a model Frontier town, a six-gun ring, a saddle ring, a movie ring and a deputy sheriff's badge with a secret compartment.

The Lone Ranger was also the recipient of numerous awards. In 1938 the program was given the Showmanship Award from *Variety*. Two years later the Radio Guild selected the series as the "Best Children's Program." In 1943 the Radio Editors chose *The Lone Ranger* as the best program in the nation. That same year listeners also picked the Ranger as the best show in the *Radio Daily* poll (an honor it received again in 1944 and 1945) and the National Safety Council presented Trendle and General Mills its

Distinguished Service Award. Between 1950 and 1955 the program was voted "Best Network Program for Children" by the Federation of Women's Clubs, the *Radio-TV Mirror* award for "Favorite Western TV Program" and the prestigious "1st Place in Children's Programming" by the Academy of Television Arts and Sciences. And, of course, in 1953 on the twentieth anniversary, *The Lone Ranger* was honored on the floors of both the United States Senate and the House of Representatives.[29]

More important than awards and profits generated has been the continued respect accorded the masked rider of the plains. Clayton Moore, who made countless personal appearance tours, criss-crossing the country in the years after he first appeared on the home screen, repeatedly expressed his pleasure in portraying the Ranger. In a 1961 interview he explained that he was "honored and proud" to be the Lone Ranger:

> And the kids regard him as a real hero. In all my years of personal appearances before hundreds of thousands of them, never once has one of them tried to grab my mask ... as some of them try to "unmask" Santa Claus. They have complete respect for the mask, costume and silver bullets, all of which symbolize justice to them.... And fair play.... There is action in the show, but the Ranger ... never kills anyone. And in fights we never use dirty tactics or hit anybody when they're down. I always wait until my opponent gets up before I strike him again.[30]

Moore has not appeared as another character since *The Lone Ranger* ended production. After a 1977 appearance in Decatur, Georgia, he said, "I just never wanted to do anything else after 'The Lone Ranger.' I fell in love with the character."[31] Years later, after a much publicized dispute during which Moore was ordered by the court to make no more appearances in his Lone Ranger mask, he still retained his reverence for the role:

> The Lone Ranger never shot to kill, always to wound. He stayed away from brutality but believed in fighting for that which is right. He never hit a man while he was down. He never swore, or drank and never kissed the heroine.... There are no longer any heroes on the screen or TV. The cowboy is sort of Americana, always has been, myth or not. The Lone Ranger programs always tried to deliver the message of the history of our country... and fair play.
>
> I've gone through generations of kids, but I'm ready to tackle the role again ... if they are serious about filming a new Ranger series. From what I've heard, plans are in the mill. I'd love to play the role again before I get too old.[32]

Alas, such a revival has yet to occur and Moore is considerably past his seventieth birthday by even the most generous estimate. Still the Lone Ranger has ridden the video range longer than any other Western hero and, along with Hoppy, broke the trail for the coming of those great singing cowboys, Gene Autry and Roy Rogers.

Gene Autry is considered to have been the first established star to enter the new medium. His distributors looked on this move as a betrayal. They insisted that the public would not pay to see an Autry film if television brought him into their homes for free. Autry, however, saw television as the last outlet left for the cheap Western. The major studios had already sold off their inventories, either to the networks or for syndication.[33] Autry's ride to stardom had been a long one. He was born Orvon Gene Autry in Tioga, Texas, on September 29, 1907. His family later moved to Oklahoma where he grew up on a small ranch near Ravia. There riding became as natural to him as walking and he learned to rope a steer and bust a bronco with the best of the cowhands. At the age of 12 he ordered his first guitar from a Sears-Roebuck catalogue for eight dollars. His grandfather was a Baptist preacher and Gene learned to sing in the church choir. At 15, he traveled with a medicine show called the Field Brothers Marvelous Medicine Show. Gene

Clayton Moore as the Lone Ranger, astride Silver.

provided entertainment with the simple songs of his homeland, while his employers were hawking patent medicines.

As a youngster Gene had aspired to be a baseball player and actually won a spot as an outfielder on one of the semipro teams in Oklahoma. However, his parents wanted him to learn a trade so he took up telegraphy. While still in his teens, he qualified for a job as a relief operator on the St. Louis-San Francisco line in Chelsea, Oklahoma. It was there that a chance meeting with famed humorist Will Rogers set him on the path to a career in show business. When his key was quiet and there were no messages to send, it was Gene's custom to while away his time by singing and strumming his guitar. Will Rogers came into the station to send a message, heard Gene practicing and told him, "You're good, young fella. Stick to it and you'll make something of yourself." Railroading was pretty slow and such encouragement was all Gene needed to try something else. He took his railroad pass and headed for New York where he thought he could make a record.

A hit record was a quick way to stardom, but New York was not ready for young Autry and vice versa. He heeded the advice of a kindly recording executive and returned home to gain some poise and experience. He concentrated on making as many local personal appearances as he could and eventually got a job (for no pay) on station KVOO in Tulsa. There he was billed as "Oklahoma's Yodelling Cowboy" and he became something of a regional sensation. The following year he returned to New York where he made his first hit record, "That Silverhaired Daddy of Mine." It sold a million copies and led Autry to Chicago where he joined the *National Barn Dance* broadcast nationally over radio station WLS.

In 1934, Autry went to Hollywood, where producer Nat Levine gave him his first opportunity to appear in a film. He was given a supporting role in Ken Maynard's *In Old Santa Fe*. Then Autry received top billing in an unusual serial called *The Phantom Empire*, which was part Western and part science fiction. The following year (1934) Autry signed with Republic and made that studio's first Western, *Tumbling Tumbleweeds*. With that film, which included several Autry songs, the "horse opera" was born and Gene became a bona fide movie star. In almost all of his films, he appeared as himself and thus began the trend of cowboy stars using their own names in their films. (The producers wanted to take advantage of the publicity Autry had received for his hit records and radio appearances.) Author James Horwitz explains Autry's overnight success in films:

> His popularity was astounding, incredible, enormous. Republic couldn't turn out Autry films fast enough. It hardly mattered what they were called. or even what they were about. As long as Gene Autry continued to pluck that guitar . . . and sing a few cowboy songs before and after he rounded up the bad guys. . . .
>
> Autry's pictures were a strange mixture of elements, Wild West Tales out of time. There were cowboys and horses chasing Zephyrs, Hudson Hornets, and Studebakers and being buzzed by low-flying aircraft. They were crossbreeds of the Old West and the day before yesterday. With the Cowboy Hero playing anything from a radio cowboy to a ranch foreman with 500 head of cattle to drive to market. But always singing.[34]

By 1940, Autry ranked fourth among all Hollywood stars (after Mickey Rooney, Spencer Tracy and Clark Gable). In many of his films, Autry chose subjects that were of concern to him personally. His pictures spoke strongly about issues of the times—the rights of Indians, the dust bowl, the harnessing of power. Autry also championed the rights of minorities and the underprivileged. For example in *The Strawberry Roan* (1948), when a new Mexican-American student is prevented from speaking in a class about American history by a Caucasian student, Autry interjects:

Your friend Pedro has a right to speak here too.... Pedro's not new here, Lefty. He may be new to this school or this ranch, but so are you. And he has a right to be here, just the same as you and I have. Sure you're an American, so am I. We were born here. So were our parents. But if you trace history far enough back Lefty, you'll find that some of our ancestors were new here too, like Pedro. A man named Columbus discovered America with three ships. He was new here, but the Indians were here ahead of him ... and after the Indians came settlers, even before your family and mine. The early Spaniards brought some things to the West we can never forget. Not just horses and cattle ... they also brought their missions and their faith. That's history, Lefty. So stand up and shake hands with a fella whose ancestors date back farther than ours. Shake hands with Pedro Gonzales.

In 1940, Autry branched out into network radio with a 30 minute adventure-variety series for CBS called *Melody Ranch* (after one of his films). *Melody Ranch*, "where the pavement ends and the West begins," was sponsored by Wrigley Gum and ran for 16 years. Autry, who was always introduced as "the boss man himself, America's favorite cowboy" by announcer Charlie Lyons, mixed Western songs with comedy (mainly by Pat Buttram) and a short dramatic segment. As in his films, Autry was a model of courage, strength, honesty and fairness. His character, charisma and style, on and off the screen, made him one of a kind.

When Autry was not making movies or doing his radio broadcasts, he was traveling the country with a musical Western show, getting to know the theater owners who showed his films and the fans who came to see them. In 1939, he even made a tour of the British Isles, where millions of fans came out to see him. On November 4, 1941, the little town of Berwyn, Oklahoma, officially changed its name to Gene Autry in recognition of Autry's Oklahoma heritage.

When war broke out in 1941, Autry, at first, was put to use recruiting, entertaining the troops and selling war bonds. However, he wanted a more direct role in the war effort, so he enlisted and was sworn in during a broadcast of his *Melody Ranch* radio program. After earning his pilot's wings on his own time, Autry was finally placed in the Air Ferry Command copiloting huge cargo planes of men and materials to such far outposts as North Africa, India, China, and Burma. When Autry returned home from service, his popularity was only slightly diminished. (From 1937 to 1942, he had placed first in the "Top Money-making Western Stars." From 1947 to 1954 he placed second only to Roy Rogers.) After a contractual dispute with Republic, he left that studio and signed a more favorable agreement with Columbia Pictures in 1947. In the meantime, he resumed his recording career. Two of his biggest hits, "Rudolph, the Red-Nosed Reindeer" and "Here Comes Santa Claus" were recorded during this period.[35]

Gene Autry, like William Boyd and George Trendle before him, saw the commercial value of product endorsements and celebrity licensed merchandise. The first Gene Autry endorsed product was the "Official Gene Autry Guitar." By the late thirties Autry was marketing comic books, cowboy outfits, cap gun and holster sets, hats, games, spurs, chaps and sweatshirts. Within ten years, at the peak of his popularity, Autry was earning nearly $100,000 a year from such items as wristwatches, boots, belts, jeans, bicycles, lunch boxes, billfolds, coloring books, kerchiefs, horseshoe nail rings and Whitman novels.[36]

In 1950 Gene Autry became the first motion picture star to make movies expressly for television. His production company, Flying A Productions, made 91 episodes of *The Gene Autry Show*, 13 of which were filmed in color. The series premiered on July 23, 1950, and remained on CBS until August 7, 1956. Autry tried to continue the high production standards of his theatrical films and each 30 minute episode was filled with songs, action and adventure. With titles like "Gold Dust Charlie" (Gene is arrested as a homicide

Gene Autry was the most successful B Western star to try television.

suspect), "Hot Lead" (a young bank robber sees the error of his ways), "Doublecross Valley" (Gene discovers a rich cache of gold), "Killer's Trail" (Gene chases a mysterious bandit chief), "The Poisoned Waterhole" (Indians are accused of poisoning a waterhole), and "Melody Mesa" (Gene poses as a music teacher), each episode was a mini Autry movie. In each Autry would ride the video range on his trusty steed Champion, assist a rancher or damsel in distress, right a wrong or expose a corrupt town official, and then warble a few bars of some classic Western ballad before jumping back in the saddle again. Pat Buttram provided the comic relief in all but a couple of the shows (when he was injured). Almost alone among juvenile programs, the story was uninterrupted by commercials. Autry would appear before and after the drama with on-camera pitches for Wrigley chewing gum.

For once the critics agreed with the show's young fans. *Billboard* called *The Gene Autry Show* "slick and competent" and said the show "should make Autry one of TV's big guns."[37] *Variety* (July 26, 1950) concurred:

> Gene Autry, whose position as the No. 1 cowboy star has been in question since video latched onto Hopalong Cassidy, is now being introduced to the newer medium in a series of half-hour films specifically made for television. As juvenile fodder, the series measures up to the requirements for school-age audiences.... The initial story ... displayed ... Autry's sterling qualities....
>
> The initial program provides a good selling point for outdoor films made for television.... A greater note of realism is possible in the riding scenes when the horsemen gallop toward the camera.
>
> Autry, of course, indicates that he can hold his own on video. He's transplanted his screen personality to this medium in a manner that will continue to hold a high degree of favor with the moppet trade and the adult segment of western fans.

Several years after the series had ended, Autry was interviewed by *TV Guide* writer Dwight Whitney regarding the evolution of the Western. Whitney asked Autry how he thought his Westerns compared with the newer adult Westerns. He responded:

> The so-called adult Western is not a bit different from the Western of Bill Hart. Personally, I miss the action. Adult Westerns drive me nuts! Too slow.
>
> Course that's where the emphasis is these days. On acting. But it means you've got to have a good story. And there're not that many stories kicking around these days. I admire a good actor—but the fact he's got boots on doesn't make him a cowboy....
>
> What Roy [Rogers] and I have got is box office draw—and showmanship.[38]

Nearly two decades later, Autry was even more critical of the changes that had taken place. He wrote in his autobiography, *Back in the Saddle Again*:

> The gore and crude sex of later westerns, what might be called the knee-in-the-groin school of westerns, left me cold. Had I attempted only a fraction of the Clint Eastwood dirty tricks in my films, in my day, I would have been arrested or horsewhipped. Until I quit, most movie fans thought dance hall girls actually danced. But the 1960s brought on the age of the anti-hero....
>
> It may not stretch a point to say that we lost a little more of our innocence with the passing of the "B" Western. Sportsmanship was the cloth we peddled. The good guys always won, but how he won and by what rules counted too.[39]

Autry, like Hoppy and the Ranger, had a code by which he lived. His movies and radio and television shows all reflected this code. It has been the most widely reproduced of all the so-called "Cowboy Codes" and, perhaps, was the most influential. It went like this:

1. The cowboy must never shoot first, hit a smaller man, or take unfair advantage.
2. He must never go back on his word, or a trust confided in him.
3. He must always tell the truth.
4. He must be gentle with children, the elderly, and animals.
5. He must not advocate or possess racially or religiously intolerant ideas.
6. He must help people in distress.
7. He must be a good worker.
8. He must keep himself clean in thought, speech, action and personal habits.
9. He must respect women, parents, and his nation's laws.
10. The cowboy is a patriot.

Autry concluded:

> Under this code, some have said, the cowboy became a sort of adult boy scout. Maybe so. I am aware that sophisticated people might snicker at such sentiments.... But I didn't exactly move in sophisticated circles. I never felt there was anything wrong with striving to be better than you are.[40]

Perhaps, the ultimate compliment was paid to Autry (who is one of only two entertainers to be honored with four stars in the Hollywood Walk of Fame, one for his records, one for his films, one for radio and one for television) by President Ronald Reagan as part of the Nashville Network's special, *Gene Autry: An American Legend*, televised in 1988:

> Over the years Gene has done more for his country and for his fellowman than just about anyone I know. While he was in the film business, Gene knew that he was serving as a role model for millions of young Americans and he always strived for the highest standards. Through his career, he used his musical and acting talents to promote decency and human kindness.

At the same time Autry was filming episodes of *The Gene Autry Show*, his company, Flying A Productions, was developing and producing four additional Western series for television in which he did not appear: *The Range Rider, Annie Oakley, Buffalo Bill, Jr.* and *The Adventures of Champion*. These were all filmed at Gene Autry's Melody Ranch in Newhall, California, about forty miles out in picturesque San Fernando Valley. In fact, some 75 percent of all outdoor Western dramas being filmed during the fifties were filmed at this location. (In addition to Autry's own productions, the ranch was rented out to other companies including those who made *Gunsmoke, Hopalong Cassidy* and *The Life and Legend of Wyatt Earp*.) The "ranch" was a ranch only in the Hollywood sense. The only cattle that grazed there were Autry's prize herd of 12 Texas longhorns and the only horses, Champion, Jr., and Little Champion. The main function of the ranch was to provide authentic looking exterior backgrounds for movie scenes. Scattered over the 78 acres were a Western village, an old-time railroad depot complete with engines and trains, a Mexican village, an Indian reservation plus some wild and rugged terrain which appeared to be a hundred miles from the nearest civilization but was only a hop, skip and gallop from the saloon on the Western Main Street.

Autry made his first feature film at the ranch in 1935 and bought it in the early fifties from Monogram Studios. There was only one permanent set interior—a fully stocked old-time general store used frequently as a setting for *Buffalo Bill, Jr.* As many as four different companies could film at the ranch at one time and the rent Autry charged averaged about $250 a day. *The Range Rider* was clearly a clone of *The Lone Ranger* developed by Autry to take advantage of the tremendous popularity of that series. He did not wear a mask but in every other way he was like "the masked rider of the plains." The show opened to the strains of "Home on the Range" and Autry's announcer, Charlie Lyon's narration:

> ... and who could be more at home on the range than "The Range Rider" with his thrilling adventures of the great outdoors, his exciting experiences rivaling those of Davy Crockett, Daniel Boone, Buffalo Bill and other Pioneers of this wonderful country of ours?

Without a name and with his faithful companion, young Dick West (whom he met in the premier episode after helping to rehabilitate West's gambling ex-con father), he rode the video range righting wrongs and helping everyone from the Arizona Navajos to the Canadian Mounties. The Rider's trusty steed was Rawhide, while Dick's mount was called Lucky. There was plenty of action and violence, but actually not a great deal of gunplay.

In answer to critics, the show's star, Jock Mahoney, explained that children were motivated by ideals and not by the ways in which they were manifested. He felt that

> Psychologically, children are looking for and should have security. If they can find a hero that they can put their trust and faith in, they will try to emulate and live up to his teachings, by their actions [in] dealing with their playmates and their parents.[41]

Although he lacked a degree in child psychology, the best thing about *The Range Rider* was Mahoney himself. Born Jacques O'Mahoney, he allowed Autry to "Americanize" the first name to Jock and drop the "O'." Tall and rugged, he was a standout gymnast and diving champion at the University of Iowa. After serving as a fighter pilot in World War II, he entered films in 1945, performing stunts for Errol Flynn, Gregory Peck, Randolph Scott, Gene Autry and others. He became the best stunt man in the business. He would take 47 foot dives into six-foot tanks of water, leap over a cattle fence, fall forty feet into a moat, and vault thirty feet from a rooftop into a net. Clayton Moore described him as "fearless." Guy Madison called him "an antelope—the best jumper in the world." Indeed, there was a saying in Hollywood that if Jacko (as he was nicknamed) walked away from a stunt, no one else wanted any part of it."[42] Over the years he broke every one of his ribs, suffered numerous broken noses and split kneecaps and had his leg run through by a sword. Mahoney and Dick Jones (Dick West on the show) performed all their own stunt work—even the dangerous transfers from horses to stagecoaches and wagons and all the fights. In fact, their stunt work was so popular with the fans that Mahoney and West took a ten minute stunt-fight demonstration on the rodeo circuit where they were a top draw.

The 78 *The Range Rider* episodes were syndicated during the 1952-53 season. Autry's company made a tidy profit from the shows as well as buckskin shirts and other Range Rider gear tie-ins. In a later interview, Mahoney was philosophical about the demise of the show:

> I was learning my trade at that point. TV was a marvelous school where I could try things and immediately see what the public reaction was.[43]

Several years later Mahoney was given the opportunity of starring in *Yancy Derringer* (1958-59). Set in New Orleans immediately after the Civil War, Derringer related the adventures of an ex–Confederate soldier turned cardsharp. He was a special agent who worked for the civilian administrator of the city, John Colton. His job was to prevent crimes when possible and apprehend criminals when it was not. Part policeman, part detective, as well as part secret agent, Derringer was smooth and dapper and a hit with the ladies. Of course, he always carried the tiny pistol that bore his name inside his fancy hat. The series, which was a cut above the typical Western of its day was canceled after only one season as the result of a contractual dispute between Mahoney and CBS.

Mahoney continued to work on television as a stunt man, primarily in Westerns like *Rawhide*, *Laramie* and *Kung Fu*. He also played Tarzan in three low budget films during the sixties. It was on the set of *Kung Fu* that he suffered a stroke in the early 1970s. Still he continued to work at his trade, making guest appearances on shows like *B.J. and the Bear*. In Burt Reynold's *The End* (1978) he played an old man who topples over a hill in a wheelchair. This led to further work with Reynolds as an advisor on *Hooper* (1978), a film about a stunt man costarring Brian Keith as a character named Jocko. In later years Mahoney took up hot air ballooning and flew with the Blue Angels precision team. He died in 1990.

Autry's second Flying A series was one of the most unusual juvenile Westerns on television. Utilizing the name and reputation of Phoebe Ann Oakley Moses, the famous sharpshooter featured in Buffalo Bill's Wild West show, *Annie Oakley* was a five-foot, two-inch, 95 pound heroine with pigtails. There, however, all similarities between the two ended. Television's Annie lived in Diablo, Arizona; the real Annie came from Ohio and saw the West only on tours. On television Annie put fear in the hearts of bad men who caused trouble around the town where she lived with her kid brother, Tagg. The tall and handsome deputy sheriff Lofty Craig was her friend and shy suitor. Annie's uncle, Luke MacTavish, made an occasional appearance as the town sheriff.

Annie could shoot the gun out of an outlaw's hand, sever a rope with a bullet and shatter practically any weapon raised against her with one shot from her trusty six-shooter. (Like her male counterparts, she never killed any of her adversaries.) Still, she left fisticuffs and other physical violence to the men (usually when her guns were useless, the fearless Lofty would come to her rescue) and demonstrated other feminine character-istics, like cooking the best apple pie in town. Once again Charlie Lyon did the voice-over opening: "Annie Oakley hits the entertainment bullseye every week with her hard ridin', straight shootin' and suspense."

Twenty-five year old Gail Davis starred as Annie. Born Betty Jean Grayson in Little Rock, Arkansas, Gail took to riding and shooting as naturally as most girls take to playing with dolls. She also developed an early flair for show business, having been named the "Most Beautiful Baby in Arkansas" at the age of 3. A graduate of Harcum Junior College in Bryn Mawr, Pennsylvania, and the University of Texas, where she majored in drama-tics, Gail went to Hollywood in 1947. In her first film, *The Romance of Rosy Ridge* (1947), she said, "Hello there," six times to Van Johnson.

Davis's first big break came when Columbia Studios gave her a routine assignment in *Cow Town* in 1950, the first of 15 Autry films in which she was destined to appear. Autry had long wanted to develop a cowgirl star, and had been searching for someone who could play Annie Oakley with some credibility. He later explained:

> There are lots of girls who can ride and shoot, and lots of girls who can act, but the girl who could do both just couldn't be found. Then this kid comes along and I didn't have any more problems.[44]

Davis, who also appeared in 30 episodes of *The Gene Autry Show*, began filming her own series on September 10, 1952, and continued through 1956 for 80 black and white programs. In the course of a day's work, Gail, who performed her own stunts would vault on and off her horse, ride him at full gallop, scramble over rocks and boulders, chase up steep and dusty trails and leap on and off wagons. She was also required to buy her own horse (she used three identically colored palominos named Target) and her wardrobe of some 75 Annie Oakley outfits.

Tagg was played by Jimmy Hawkins (Billy Grey in the pilot) and Brad John was Lofty Craig. The plots were mostly typical shoot-'em-ups although one episode, "Sure Shot Annie," purported to tell the true story of how Annie got her nickname and another, "Annie and the First Phone," told an imaginative story of Annie and the coming of the telephone to the West.

Autry held up the airdate of *Annie Oakley* while arranging for more sponsors and more stations to carry the show. The series finally premiered in 100 markets in January 1954, for Canada Dry and TV Time Popcorn. Both the *Variety* and *TV Guide* critics took special note of the feminine orientation of the series. *Variety* (January 20, 1954) said:

> How the kiddies are going to take a gal bullying the baddies is a good question for the sponsors of "Annie Oakley" to grapple with....
> Called on to ride like the wind, she also handles a gun with the practiced precision of a Dodge marshal. It all must be silly to the adult western fan, that she can outdraw any man and shoot the pistol out of his hand. She can even hit her mark on the ricochet ... [but] the film had good pace and fast action.

TV Guide (May 7, 1954) was even more favorable:

Gail Davis as Annie Oakley was television's first female Western star.

The idea of a cowgirl heroine may be new but the story ideas in the telefilms are not. Our gal Annie, like countless cowboys before her, is upholding law and justice in the best traditions of "they-went-that-a-way" drama and she does a fine job....

... Each episode is packed with enough action to satisfy even the most avid pistol-packin' viewer....

Miss Davis is a natural for the title role. Besides being a beauty, she's a fair little actress and can ride and shoot with the best of them.

The kids seemed to like the show too. It was number two on the 1954 list of children's shows.

In later years, Gail, who was an excellent horsewoman and trick shot, toured with Autry's rodeo. From the back of her galloping horse, she would light a series of six matches with well-placed shots from her .22 revolver. Davis once expressed her enjoyment of the role with the statement, "So far as I'm concerned I'm going to be Annie Oakley for the rest of my born days."[45]

In the final analysis, *Annie Oakley* was most significant for giving us our first real television heroine. Not until Barbara Stanwyck created the fiery matriarch Victoria Barkley some ten years later would television get another Western heroine. Writer Jeff Rovin has made this perceptive assessment:

> One must assume, that to have kept "Annie Oakley" on the air ... if the boys couldn't identify with her, they at least enjoyed her galloping escapades. That a lot of young girls who secretly dreamed of being the no-nonsense, gun-toting cowgirl were watching; and that a number of fathers tuned in to see the attractive Miss Davis in action.[46]

For his third series, *Buffalo Bill, Jr.*, Autry borrowed only the name of a famous American hero. (The two were not related, but Autry correctly thought this would be a highly marketable title.) The show was filmed across the lot from *Annie Oakley* and starred Dick Jones from *The Range Rider* in the title role. Bill and his kid sister, Calamity (Nancy Gilbert), were orphans adopted by an old judge named Ben Wiley (Harry Chesire), who was the founder of the pioneer community of Wileyville, Texas. Aided by Calamity, Bill chased villains, saved the judge from being bilked, broke bucking broncos and even lent a hand to the government from time to time.

Jones, who was born in Texas, had been a trick rider and roper in rodeos when he was only 5 (he was billed as "The World's Youngest"). He had ridden with Hoot Gibson and appeared in such films as *Wonder Bar* (1934) with Al Jolson, *Stella Dallas* (1937) with Barbara Stanwyck, *Renfrew of the Mounted* (1937), *Destry Rides Again* (1939) and *Heaven Can Wait* (1943). Autry saw his work and used him in a number of his films beginning with *The Strawberry Roan* (1948). Like Mahoney, West did all his own stunts and enjoyed touring with Autry's Western shows. The series ran for four years in syndication, but Jones had by this time become typecast and did very few films after *Buffalo Bill, Jr.* ended.

The critics were mildly receptive to the show, which broke no new ground in the development of the television Western. *Variety* (March 30, 1955) said:

> [This] half-hour vidfilm was absolute in following the standard pattern of juve hoss mellers.... The "Bill, Jr." production had just enough guns, blundering and fisticuffs to satisfy most juve video viewers.

Again *TV Guide* (May 15, 1955) was more lavish in its praise:

> Any youngster who gets a vicarious kick from watching cowboy movies should get an even more powerful wallop from "Buffalo Bill, Jr." Its hero is a teen-ager, and what's more, he has a kid sister who participates in all his exploits.... Jones is fine as the youthful Buffalo Bill.
> ... Autry apparently has spared neither the horses nor the budget. The sets, supporting players and stories are good, capturing much of what we've come to accept as the flavor of the Old West.

The Adventures of Champion, the final Flying A Western, featured Autry's "wonder horse" Champion. Autry, however, did not appear in the show. Instead, the horse was owned by 12 year old Ricky North, the only person, according to the story, that Champion would allow to ride him. Ricky also owned a German shepherd named Rebel, and he lived on a ranch owned by his Uncle Sandy. Whenever, Ricky got mixed up in some dangerous situation, Champion and Rebel would come to his rescue by performing some feat not normally associated with horses or dogs. Young Barry Curtis played Ricky, and Jim Bannon, who had starred in a series of Red Ryder B movies, was Sandy North.

The real star of the series was, of course, a handsome chestnut stallion who stood 15 hands high, weighed 1200 pounds, and was distinguished by his beautiful markings, four pure white stockings and a blazed face. Champion had been personally trained by Gene and could kneel, march, waltz, bow, hula, rhumba, untie knots with his teeth, laugh, kiss and even do the Charleston. Autry claimed that Champion could assume almost any pose known to educated horses and a few known only to him. He had appeared in Madison Square Garden and on Fifth Avenue in New York and had his hoofprints preserved in the forecourt of Grauman's Chinese Theater in Hollywood.

The show featured a theme song sung by Frankie Laine (several years before he did the *Rawhide* theme). It had been written by Marilyn Keith and Norman Lubof and exalted the equine star of the series with a great deal of gusto. The critics were not too impressed with his show, however, and it lasted only four months (September 30, 1955, to February 3, 1956) on CBS. *Variety* (October 5, 1955) even claimed Rebel stole the show:

> ...apparently there just weren't enough things a horse could do by itself, because the writers of the initial vidcast relied on a canine to carry the horse's workload.
> A German shepherd, Rebel by name, not only forefronted more than Autry's handsome stallion, but it got in final licks as hero of the initialer, without horsey help and, for that matter, without human aid either.

The show, perhaps, suffered from a lack of good stories, the result of Autry's trying to produce too many similar juvenile Westerns at the time. Autry believed the secret for making successful Westerns lay in a simple formula: "Keep it simple, keep it moving, keep it close and make it fast."[47] Nowhere did he say it had to be original or believable.

Roy Rogers rode onto the video range nearly eighteen months after Autry and the trail was considerably more rocky. Born Leonard Slye in Cincinnati, Ohio, he spent his early years on a houseboat near Portsmouth. His great-great-grandmother was a member of the Choctaw Indian tribe. As a boy he wanted to become a dentist, but the family could not afford to send him to college. His first horse, a mare named Babe, was a gift from his father. Young Leonard taught himself to play the guitar and became a caller for neighborhood square dances.

In 1931, at the age of 19, Slye headed for California, where he supported himself with a variety of odd jobs including truck driver, road construction worker and fruit picker. His first professional act was with his cousin Stanley Slye. They called themselves the Slye Brothers and sang for a dollar a performance in a Los Angeles theater. Slye's first radio appearance was with Uncle Tom Murray's Hollywood Hillbillies. Later he sang with the Rocky Mountaineers and finally organized the Sons of the Pioneers, who were signed to sing in several Gene Autry, Charles Starrett and Dick Foran Westerns (Slye appeared under the name Dick Weston in several of these Republic films).

Slye heard that Republic was looking for a new singing cowboy and he tried to sneak into the studio entrance. While he was arguing with the guard, a Republic executive, Sol Siegel, overheard the commotion, took one look at Slye and gave him an audition. Siegel and Herbert Yates helped Slye come up with a catchy new name for his new career—Roy Rogers. The "Rogers" came from Will Rogers and "Roy" was used because it went well with the last name.[48]

With his first film, *Under Western Stars* (1938), Rogers took the B Western market by storm. By the end of his first year as a star, he ranked third in the movie exhibitors poll of Top Money-Making Western Stars (behind Autry and William Boyd) and stayed third through 1940 and 1941. In 1942 he moved to second place behind Autry and from 1943 until the poll was discontinued in 1954, Rogers was the number one Western box office star. He made 88 films for Republic and every one was a money-maker. Costarring with Rogers in every picture was the golden palomino Trigger (billed as the "Smartest Horse in the Movies"), whom he had purchased in 1938 for $2500.

Many of Rogers' earlier films differed from Autry's. They were more "historical," with Rogers cast as a real character from the past such as Billy the Kid, Wild Bill Hickok, Buffalo Bill and Jesse James. There was also less music in his early films.[49] In 1943, he made a film entitled *King of the Cowboys* and Republic decided to use that description in all future Rogers publicity. (After all, Rogers was king of the box office.)

In 1944, Rogers followed Autry into radio with *The Roy Rogers Show* over Mutual. The show featured Bob Nolan and the Sons of the Pioneers and female vocalist Pat Friday. Each episode included Western songs and a dramatic sketch with a weekly guest star. Canceled after one season, *The Roy Rogers Show* moved to NBC in 1946 and included Gabby Hayes, Pat Buttram and Dale Evans. (Rogers married his leading lady on New Year's Eve, 1947.) In 1948 the series returned to Mutual with Foy Willing and the Riders of the Purple Sage replacing the Sons of the Pioneers. In 1951 it switched back to NBC, with Pat Brady added as Roy's sidekick, plus Dale, Trigger and a dog named Bullet (modeled after the television series which was just being developed).

Meanwhile, Rogers was earning a good income from his records. He never surpassed Autry in the vocal department, but he had many successful albums and was still recording in 1991 when *Tribute* was released on CD. Furthermore, Rogers, in the words of expert David Rothel, "turned self-merchandising into what could almost be called a new art form. No single show business performer, before or since, has ever been able to corral the tie-in market as successfully as he did in the 1940s and 1950s."[50] And Rogers guaranteed his merchandise. Over a replica of his signature, Rogers ran his "Roy Rogers Pledge to Parents" in numerous ads:

> Any item of merchandise, bearing my name, has been tested in one of the nation's largest testing bureaus and, in our judgement, equals in quality merchandise selling in the same price range. You pay no premium for my name. Rather, it is your assurance that the item is an authentic value.

Rogers surpassed even Autry and Boyd with the diversity of his products. In 1957 more than 56 manufacturers were producing some four hundred items bearing his or Dale Evans' name including a wide variety of clothing and hats, gloves, belts, boots, pajamas, comic books, Whitman books, coloring books, flashlights, binoculars, cap guns, rocking horses, bedspreads and drapes, tents, watches and clocks, toy jeeps, lunch boxes, and cups and plates. In addition Rogers endorsed countless products for adults like Magic Chef gas ranges, Auto-Lite original service parts, Friskies dog food and Kodacolor film.

Dale Evans, Western filmdom's most famous leading lady, was born Frances Octavia Smith in Uvalde, Texas, on October 31, 1912. She was raised in Arkansas and began singing at the age of 9. Her first professional entertainment job was as a singer on a small radio station in Memphis, Tennessee. While working at station WHAS in Louisville, Kentucky, the station's program director changed Smith's name to Dale Evans. Later, Dale became a big band singer with several touring orchestras and played bit parts in several films for 20th Century–Fox. She also worked as a vocalist on the Edgar Bergen–Charlie McCarthy Radio Show. In 1943, she signed a contract with Republic Pictures and was given roles in several musical comedies. Her first Western was *In Old Oklahoma* (1943), with John Wayne.

In 1944 she costarred with Roy in *The Cowboy and the Senorita*. Rogers was already a superstar and audiences liked the two together so much that they made four more Westerns that same year. By 1945 the Rogers-Evans duo was the B Western's most popular male-female team. Between 1944 and 1947 Roy and Dale made 20 films together. When Roy's first wife, Arlene, died from complications after the birth of their son, Dusty, Roy and Dale's on-screen romance blossomed off screen as well, ultimately leading to the marriage altar.

By 1951 the time seemed right for Rogers to make his move to television. However, his studio boss, Herbert Yates, had other plans. The studio did not want a Rogers television show to compete against their movies. Rogers' contract with Republic had expired and he refused to sign a new one unless Republic granted him the right to do television. However, Yates, aware of the fortune Boyd had made on his old films, was quietly editing 57 of Rogers' films down to 54 minutes of running time to fit the television format and informing advertising agencies of their availability. As soon as Rogers and his manager, Art Rush, discovered the studio's plans, they sought an immediate injunction against Yates and Republic to prevent them from selling the films to television. They based their case on a unique clause in Rogers' contract, stating that he retained the rights to his name, voice and likeness for any and all commercial ventures.

Quaker Oats, concerned that the Rogers movies would eventually turn up on television under the sponsorship of someone other than themselves, did not renew the contract for the weekly Roy Rogers radio show. Suddenly, after eight years as the motion picture industry's top-drawing Western star, Roy Rogers had no movie contract, no radio contract, and no television contract. Still Rogers decided to take the gamble and went ahead with plans for a television series. While waiting for the court's decision, he organized a production company (Frontier Productions, Inc.) and began filming a number of 24 minute shows that could be marketed for television. Rush, after some initial difficulty, landed a sponsor for the proposed series, Post Cereals, a division of General Foods. However, the contract Rogers signed contained an escape clause for the sponsor in the event he lost his court battle with Republic.

Rogers decided to follow the well-established pattern from his popular movies for the new television show. As Roy described it in *Happy Trails*:

> Each episode would be a new story, with only the setting and characters the same. Mineral City, located in Paradise Valley, would be our mythical TV home. I would play the prosperous owner of the Double R Bar Ranch, and Dale would be the proprietor of the local Eureka Cafe. As in our movies, there would be no real romance—just friendship and a combining of efforts to solve the problems and right the wrongs the scriptwriters came up with.[51]

The permanent members of the cast would include Dale, Trigger, Bullet, and Pat Brady, who had played Rogers' movie sidekick in several films after Gabby Hayes had left. Instead of riding his horse Phoebe, Brady would drive an old army jeep called Nellybelle, which was rigged up to do crazy and funny stunts. There was also a problem with Dale's mode of transportation. She rode a palomino named Pal in her rodeo and film appearances with Roy so he bought her a buckskin gelding with a black mane and tail whom she named Buttermilk. Exteriors for the television show were filmed on the old Iverson Ranch, where Westerns had been made since the days of silent pictures, and used an old Western street on the Goldwyn Studios lot for the Mineral City scenes.

Four episodes had already been filmed when U.S. Judge Pierson M. Hall handed

down a ruling that granted Rogers a permanent injunction restraining Republic from selling the Rogers films to television. Republic subsequently appealed the case and on June 9,
1954, the Ninth United States Circuit Court rendered a split decision, effectively reversing the previous decision. Confident that he could win, Rogers appealed the case all the
way to the Supreme Court. Four months later the highest tribunal in the land refused to
review the case, in effect, thereby, upholding the lower court's decision. Republic was
now free to syndicate Rogers' movies. By this time, however, Roy's television series was
already a big success, so the issue had actually become moot.

   The Roy Rogers Show debuted Sunday evening, December 30, 1951, on NBC. The
network made the premiere a special event by starting the hour long program with a live
30 minute comedy-variety segment featuring all the cast members plus special guest Bob
Hope. (This gave Bob and Roy a chance to plug their new film, *Son of Paleface*.) The show
was telecast live from the El Capitán Theatre in Los Angeles. In the second half-hour,
the first filmed episode of the regular series was broadcast. While the ratings were highly
favorable, the reviews were mixed. *Variety* (January 9, 1952) was enthusiastic:

> Roy Rogers' entry into TV ... was a holiday high spot....
> If anything, the live introduction served to strengthen Rogers' hold on the affection of
> his fans. He occasionally muffed a line but this was more than offset by his winsome per-
> sonality and spirit of wholesomeness that have always pervaded his pictures. These qualities
> appeared even stronger on TV.
> ... despite a trite story, the initialer had to its credit a breezy pacing from director John
> English and excellent camera work. Rogers was his sterling self and supporting players were
> good.

On the other hand, *The New York Times* (January 2, 1952) critic Jack Gould really
blasted the show:

> Mr. Rogers is billed as "the king of the cowboys"—but on the basis of the first film, he's
> got a piece to travel before catching up with his rivals—Bill Boyd and Gene Autry. Rogers
> could easily carry greater forcefulness if he spoke his lines with greater enthusiasm and a more
> genuine sense of participation. As it is his heroism leans to debauched efficiency, which sug-
> gests that he is walking through, rather than living, his part.

Obviously, television viewers thought otherwise—or simply did not care. If anything, the
weekly television series broadened Roy and Dale's audience considerably from their films
and undoubtedly extended their professional careers, making them household names. In
the opinion of their biographer, Carlton Stowers:

> Now it was no longer just the youngsters who were following their Western heroics, but
> entire families seated in living rooms across the country. To mom and dad, they were
> refreshing—a team whose show was not only entertaining but also taught their children high
> morals and made them aware of the high price of wrongdoing. To the kids, they were still
> Roy and Dale, good always triumphing over evil with a song and a smile or two along the way.
> And rather than voicing displeasure over the fact that their cowboy hero was married to
> his leading lady, youngsters began looking up to Roy and Dale as the kind of parents every
> kid would like to have....[52]

   In addition to increased popularity, the series brought Roy and Dale recognition
from their peers. In 1953, they were chosen Best Actor and Best Actress in a network
Western series.

   In the late fifties, Rogers bought out the NBC-TV interest in his series and, with total
ownership, turned the 100 episodes into a small fortune. He resold the show to CBS in
1960 and later repackaged it again for syndication.

   There was some interesting casting done on the series. Several future television stars

Roy Rogers continued the trend from B Westerns to the home screen.

appeared in episodes of *The Roy Rogers Show*: Ellen Corby (who became Grandma Walton on *The Waltons*), Stuart Whitman (who later starred in *Cimarron Strip*), Robert "Bobby" Blake (who would later become *Baretta*), and Charles Bronson (who appeared on a number of television Westerns before emerging as a major motion picture star). Dale and Roy also utilized their own children on several shows. Cheryl, their oldest daughter, appeared in "Outlaws of Paradise Valley," while Roy Rogers, Jr. ("Dusty"), acted in "Junior Outlaw" and "Three Masked Men." Their youngest child, "Dodi" or Little Doe, played the role of an Indian baby in "Little Dynamite." There were also many veterans of B Westerns who had worked in Rogers or Autry films, like Raymond Hatton, Chuck Roberson, William Fawcett, Denver Pyle, John Doucette and Dub Taylor.

Most episodes of *The Roy Rogers Show* were traditional adventure stories about bank robberies, land grabbing, Indians, cattle rustling and gold mining. Many of these stories included a moral lesson and several actually presented a Christian message. Professor Ray White, author of the most recent and comprehensive examination of Roy Rogers' career, offers some important observations about the roles Roy and Dale depicted in the series.

> Roy Rogers' image fit that of the stereotypical western hero, except for the fact that he was not a rootless wandering cowboy who moved from place to place dealing with the problems of society. Rather, he was a prominent settled rancher and citizen of Paradise Valley who was ever ready to help someone in need. . . . As with most western heroes Rogers was peaceful and slow to anger, but if the situation required it, he used his fists and guns handily, usually two or three times in an episode. . . . The fist fights in the series were often prolonged and brutal, and the villains on occasion battered and subdued Rogers.[53]

The violence in Rogers' television show was the subject of some controversy at the time. *Chicago Daily News* critic Jack Mabley complained after seeing an episode:

> It's frightening to see five and six year old tots sitting spellbound before TV sets soaking up this sadism. In a single episode, two men beat an old man . . . the old man is permanently blinded by the attack. Two men beat a dog [Bullet] about the head with a pistol. . . . The men again attack the dog as he is leading the old man on a mountain trail. The old man cries for help, plunges over a cliff to his death. . . . A veterinarian who is a thief kills an injured companion with an injection of poison. . . . The dog is doped but attacks a man. Two men kidnap a girl, then beat her.[54]

Rogers justified the violence in the shows by referring to history:

> . . . the Westerns I make come right out of the history books. In those old days, pioneers packed a six-shooter whether they were ploughing or riding herd. . . . The frontiersmen were blazing new trails, pioneering in new territory and [they] didn't let any gang of outlaws or ambushing Indians get the drop on them. . . . We only fire our guns when necessary. But, there's an evil force that always is challenging. And when that challenge comes you have to meet it with spirit and fire.[55]

As White says, "turning the other cheek" was a Christian virtue that was never practiced on *The Roy Rogers Show*.

While Rogers' image reflected the traditional Western hero, that of Dale Evans was less conventional and sometimes contradictory. Her relationship with Roy in the series was depicted as purely platonic. Roy and Dale were just good friends who talked problems over together, but never kissed or did anything "mushy." In White's opinion:

> . . . Dale was a kind of innocent Miss Kitty who owned a cafe and served Roy coffee, food and conversation when he was in Mineral City. In some ways Dale Evans was the traditional helpmate western heroine as she supported Roy Rogers in his masculine activities. She usually deferred to him in decision making and expressed her womanly nurturing instincts in the stories when she cared for children, the elderly and the sick. On the other hand, she shattered that mold by being an independent business woman who had ideas of her own and who on occasion took independent action. Rogers always tried to protect her in hazardous situations, but she was capable of using a gun and frequently came to the hero's rescue with her revolver blazing (e.g., in "Ghosttown Gold" and "Brady's Bonanza"). . . . Even more ironic is the fact that Dale Evans accepted that image despite the fact that she was a remarkably resourceful and independent woman off the screen.[56]

Another strong, continuing theme in the series was the importance of law and order in a civilized society. Yet it is significant to note that Rogers and his pals sometimes winked at the law themselves. Audiences seemed to accept his violations of the law because they were done to right an obvious wrong. It was understandable and acceptable to break the law if the violation insured justice.

The most distinctive characteristic of the series was its emphasis on religion. The decision (largely Dale's) to incorporate religious expressions and themes into the show resulted in part from the fact that Christianity became an increasingly important force in the lives of Roy and Dale during the late forties and early fifties. This emphasis was deliberate and sincere, and it seemed to fit the national mood. It also reflected their personal beliefs and coincided with their own religious development. They felt a moral responsibility to their young fans to set a Christian example and instill Christian values. All the other juvenile Western heroes professed a belief in God and emphasized the importance of religion, but Roy and Dale's religion was specifically Christian. In "Born Fugitive," Dale explains to a young girl she is caring for:

> Sunday School is a wonderful place. That's the place they teach children to live as God wants them to, where they teach them to love and to trust each other, and to do unto others as they would have others do unto them.

"The Ginger Horse" episode includes a direct reference to the Bible and a song composed by Dale that is sung by Roy and Dale in the show. Dale wrote "The Bible Tells Me So" in just twenty minutes. The song became a popular hit, being featured on *Your Hit Parade* and climbing to seventh place on the *BillBoard* charts with a recording by Don Cornell.

Members of the Roy Rogers Riders Club were asked to pray Roy's Cowboy Prayer:

> Oh Lord, I reckon I'm not much just by myself. I fail to do a lot of things I ought to do. But Lord, when trails are steep and passes high, help me to ride it straight the whole way through. And in the falling dusk, when I get the final call, I do not care how many flowers they send. Above all else the happiest trail would be for you to say to me, let's ride my friend. Amen.

Rogers was interviewed by *TV Guide*'s Dwight Whitney in 1959 at the same time as Gene Autry. In a philosophical mood, he reminisced about his career and recent changes in the Western:

> I don't think today's Westerns are that different. They're more psychological maybe. I see some pretty rugged things on TV. Sometimes the hero gets it in the belly—we always stayed away from that. Dress is more realistic.... And there's more killing. But the stories are similar.... I figure this adult Western stuff is just another cycle.[57]

In 1962 Roy and Dale hosted a musical-variety program, *The Roy Rogers and Dale Evans Show* for ABC. Less exciting and less popular, it was canceled after only three months. In 1976 Roy made his first theatrical film in three decades, *Mackintosh and T.J.* Unfortunately it was not a box office success. In the years since, Roy and Dale have been content to make guest appearances on other shows. Roy made two appearances on *The Fall Guy* (one in 1983 and one in 1984) with several other television cowboy heroes from the fifties. His son Dusty appeared with him in the 1984 episode. During the eighties, Roy and Dale hosted a series of their early films for cable television's Nashville Network on *Happy Trails Theatre*. After repeated personal tragedies involving members of their family, Roy and Dale's lives have taken an increasingly evangelical emphasis. Roy, of course, had closed his radio and television shows for years with "Good-bye, good luck, and may the good Lord take a likin' to ya!"

While the Ranger, Hoppy, Gene and Roy took the lead in establishing virtuous, upright and chaste role models for youngsters to emulate, *The Cisco Kid* was more of

a romantic rogue who occasionally broke the rules of the West's mythical code. He had been around longer than even the Lone Ranger. Created by William Sidney Porter (O. Henry), the Kid first appeared in *Heart of the West*, a collection of Western short stories published in 1904. In "The Caballero's Way" he was a scruffy bandito who victimized the rich and helped the poor.

The Kid turned up in several silent films and then in many B Westerns. He was the hero of Raoul Walsh's early talkie, *In Old Arizona* (1929), a picture that cost Walsh his eye and won Warner Baxter the Academy Award for Best Actor. Baxter was so good that he was promoted to "first class" films, but he had established the Cisco Kid as a cowboy hero to be reckoned with. There followed 23 motion pictures featuring O. Henry's "Robin Hood of the Old West." Cesar Romero, Gilbert Roland and Duncan Renaldo each took their turn at playing the macho caballero. It was Renaldo that really put charm and style into the character and who is best remembered as the broad humored swashbuckler. Renaldo played the role in 12 films for Monogram and later United Artists and finally the 156 television episodes. His interpretation of the popular character (who had his own comic strip and radio program) fell somewhere between jolly jester and gunslinging avenger: a man who liked to talk to his horse (Diablo), joke with his sidekick Pancho (Leo Carrillo) and flirt with women. Cisco was usually a friendly fellow, unless provoked by some act of gross injustice. Certainly every bit as heroic as the Ranger, Hoppy, Gene and Roy, he simply was not as serious.

While Renaldo is the Cisco Kid everyone remembers, his ride to screen and television immortality was a long and difficult one. He had been in the film business since the early twenties, playing his first big role in *The Bridge of San Luis Rey* in 1929. He then spent two years in Africa making *Trader Horn* with Harry Carey. On January 17, 1931, on the verge of the gala premier of *Trader Horn*, Duncan Renaldo was arrested and charged with being an illegal immigrant and of making false statements about his birthplace to obtain a passport. It was the beginning of a terrible ordeal for the future Cisco Kid. During the next six years, he was indicted by a grand jury, hauled into court for trial, then hounded out of the country by immigration authorities who wanted to deport him to Romania. This resulted in his having to live on a friend's houseboat out beyond the three-mile limit because neither the United States nor Mexico would let him land. Finally in 1936, he was given an unconditional pardon by President Roosevelt.

The problem had been caused by the fact that Renaldo had never known his parents nor his place of birth. Apparently, his father was Scotch and his mother Romanian. Raised as a foundling in various parts of Europe, he shipped out as a seaman while a young man and arrived in the United States in the early twenties. He drifted to Hollywood and eventually obtained work as an actor. During this time, however, he got into a feud with movie mogul Louis B. Mayer, who had engineered his arrest.

After his pardon, he spent some time doing menial jobs around Republic studios. Then Renaldo was put into Westerns by Herbert Yates and for the next five years he played in B oaters for Republic. In 1941, full of fresh ideas about the Cisco Kid and how he should be portrayed, and having picked up the rights to the character from Doubleday, O. Henry's publisher, Renaldo went to Monogram and became the Cisco Kid. Dressed immaculately in a highly embroidered black outfit, and possessing a surplus of Latin charm, he usually swept some señorita off her feet (after bringing the bad men to justice).

Opposite: Duncan Renaldo (center) and Leo Carrillo brought O. Henry's "Robin Hood of the West," the Cisco Kid, and his sidekick Pancho to television. The actress at left is unidentified.

All he gave the beautiful lady, however, was a kiss and a dashing sweep of the sombrero, before riding off into the night with Pancho. There was usually a lot of action, but relatively little gunplay. Cisco, in the best tradition of the Code of the West, would shoot the gun out of the outlaw's hand with his faster draw.

Even though there was lots of action in *The Cisco Kid* films and television shows, Renaldo consistently took a stand against excessive violence. In a mid-seventies interview with author Jim Harmon, Renaldo said:

> I didn't believe in my heart if you are going to play in television, particularly, and go into people's homes, you ever have to let the protagonist become a killer.... I only used *one* gun—that's enough for anybody.... Any time you point a gun at anybody you only have one meaning to the gesture—"I want to take your life."
>
> It's a dastardly thing to paint our people who worked so hard to leave us this beautiful West as criminals and brigands.... They were not that. They were hard-working people.... We have killed more people on television than populated the Old West.[58]

Renaldo was almost 50 when *The Cisco Kid* premiered in 1951 and he became identified with that character for the rest of his life. In later years he made many personal appearances as the Kid and was active in the annual Santa Barbara "Old Spanish Days" festival. He lived out his life at his Rancho mi Amigo near there, white-haired, charming, and forever the embodiment of the chivalrous tradition represented by the character for which he will always be known.

The syndicated series was popular for over a decade. In 1950, a year before it aired, three NBC owned and operated stations in New York, Washington and Cleveland paid Ziv-Television $1,000,000 for five year rights to the show. Within three years it was airing on 75 more stations and earning over $40,000 per week profit. In 1956, the show was dubbed and distributed to 20 countries including France, Italy, Belgium, Cuba and Argentina. By 1959 it had grossed a total of $11,000,000 in domestic sales.

The Cisco Kid was successful partly because it was the first Western series to be filmed entirely in color. Another reason for the show's popularity was the good-natured, fun-loving camaraderie between Cisco and Pancho. Fat old Pancho, who loved food and sleep more than anything else, was, with the possible exception of Andy Devine, the best comedy sidekick on television. He was always ready with a crack in fractured English that kids loved to imitate. ("Ceesco? Let's went! The shereef, he ees getting closer!") Still he was brave and could use his fists, as well as his six-guns. He was also an expert with a bull-whip. Leo Carrillo was in his seventies when the television series was made, but he did most of his own stunts and hard riding (on his stalwart steed Loco). Born to one of California's oldest Spanish families and descended from the state's first governor, Carrillo first appeared on stage doing dialect comedy in the second decade of this century. He launched a long and successful film career in the late thirties appearing in such films as *Love Me Forever* (1935), *History Is Made at Night* (1937), and *Lillian Russell* (1940).

Kids, parents and even the critics fell under *The Cisco Kid*'s spell. *Variety* (October 12, 1954) wrote:

> Far be it from this reviewer to asperse the derring-do of Cisco, who is Duncan Renaldo, or the comicalities of Leo Carrillo, who is Pancho, lest a gang war be incited. Kids, they're both fine so put away your slingshots....
>
> These Robin Hoods of the range are good for young minds. They preach good over evil in their own adventurous way and at the same time keep them out of mischief.

Writing in 1989, years after the program had virtually disappeared (except for a couple of episodes available on videocassette), Castleman and Podrazik offered this assessment of *The Cisco Kid*:

Much like his Anglo-compadre, the Lone Ranger, the Mexican-bred Cisco Kid is always polite, ever chivalrous, never gets dirty even after battling bad guys on the plains, and hardly, if ever, kills anyone. He and portly Pancho roam the Mexican-American border regions in the late 1880s righting wrongs, subduing evildoers, and charming the ladies. Much like the Lone Ranger, Cisco is viewed by local law enforcement officials as an outlaw of some type, so he must keep a low profile and vamoose pronto after doing his good deed for the day, in order not to be detained by any nosy federales. Of course, Cisco is no outlaw at all, but the added threat of capture by lawmen as well as banditos adds some spice to the plots.

They conclude that only the masked rider of the plains and Tonto surpassed the Cisco Kid and Pancho "for pure Western quality."[59]

In February 1994, Ted Turner attempted to revive the Cisco Kid with a new film starring former *L.A. Law* star Jimmy Smits as the Mexican Robin Hood and Cheech Marin as his sidekick. Shown repeatedly on Turner's cable channel, TNT, it was touted as the pilot for a possible new series. The new *Kid*, however, failed to generate any enthusiasm from viewers or critics. Jeff Jarvis of *TV Guide* (February 5, 1994) was the kindest:

Inline citation

The stars bring charm to their dusty fight, dance and rodeo scenes, but the movie tells its story flatly, without surprise or excitement. My score: 5.

Riding close on the heels of the Cisco Kid and Pancho were Wild Bill Hickok and Jingles. Also a syndicated series, *Wild Bill Hickok* paired the television West's most unusual duo. Tall, lean and handsome Guy Madison, who spoke in a quiet tenor voice was teamed with the overweight, ever-giggling, raspy-voiced Andy Devine.

Madison was born in Bakersfield, California, in 1923 and grew up on a nearby ranch. Serving in the Navy during World War II, he got his big break when a female Hollywood talent agent spotted his face on the cover of a Navy magazine. She got him a bit role in *Since You Went Away* (1944), which he filmed during a two-week leave. Bobby-soxers fell in love with the six-foot, one-inch Madison, and he became one of Hollywood's young rising stars. Roles in *Till the End of Time* (1946), *Honeymoon* (1947), and *Massacre River* (1949) followed and his success was assured.

During the years he wore Wild Bill's buckskin outfit and rode the video range on his loyal mount Buckskin, Madison also appeared in *The Charge at Feather River* (1953), *The Command* (1953), *The Last Frontier* (1956) and *On the Threshold of Space* (1956) among others. Unfortunately, typecasting almost ruined his career. After a few guest roles in the late fifties, mostly in television Westerns, he virtually disappeared. He spent the sixties in Europe making spaghetti Westerns and acted only occasionally after that (e.g., in an episode of *Fantasy Island*).

Devine's career had begun years earlier. Actually, it was almost over before it began due to a teenage accident when he fell with a stick in his mouth. This permanently damaged his vocal cords and left him with the raspy, gravelly voice for which he later became famous. In the silent era, Universal planned to make him a romantic star. When talkies replaced silent films, however, there seemed to be no place for a leading man with such a strange voice. One director decided to try him in a comedy, opening up a whole new career for Devine.

Thereafter, he appeared in hundreds of motion pictures including *We Americans* (1928), *The Spirit of Notre Dame* (1931), *Yellow Jack* (1938), *Torrid Zone* (1940), *Ali Baba and the Forty Thieves* (1944) and *Sudan* (1945). Most critics and fans agree, however, that Devine's best roles were in Westerns — as the stage driver in John Ford's *Stagecoach* (1939) and (in Ford's much later Western) as the cowardly sheriff in *The Man Who Shot Liberty Valance* (1962). He seemed right at home in Westerns and appeared as Roy Rogers'

Guy Madison (left) and Andy Devine played Wild Bill Hickok and Jingles on both radio and television.

sidekick in a number of mid-forties outings for Republic. In 1954, Devine replaced Smilin' Ed McConnell in his hit television show for kids which was then renamed *Andy's Gang*. He had been previously heard as a frequent guest on *The Jack Benny Show* on radio ("Hi-ya, Buck!"). Still, it is as Wild Bill's friend and companion, Jingles P. Jones, announcing, "That's Wild Bill Hickok, Mister, the bravest, fightingest U.S. marshal in the whole West!" or puffing along behind on his horse, Joker, yelling, "Hey, Wild Bill, wait for me!" that Devine is best remembered.

The idea for the series was developed by several advertising executives representing a group of department stores who decided that if Hopalong Cassidy could successfully merchandise products for kids on television, there ought to be room for other Western heroes, as well. They, like Autry, saw the appeal in giving the lead character the name of a genuine historical Western figure.

There had been a real Wild Bill Hickok in the nineteenth century who had, at various times in his life, served as a Pony Express rider, a Union scout during the Civil War, a scout for General Custer, and marshal of Abilene, Kansas. (He was also a notorious gambler who ran a bordello in Deadwood, Dakota Territory.) However, he definitely did not look like Guy Madison. Madison decided to do the series for a percentage of the profits. (The same arrangement was made by Devine.)

Wild Bill Hickok, relating the adventures of a U.S. marshal and his sidekick roaming the West to bring outlaws to justice, was launched in April 1951, and during the next seven years, 113 episodes (about half in color) were produced. Beginning as a syndicated program, the show was also seen on CBS from 1955 to 1958 and on ABC in 1957-58. At the same time, a radio series starring Madison and Devine and using substantially the same scripts was broadcast over the Mutual Broadcasting System (1951–1956). Two years after its premiere, *Wild Bill Hickok* was so successful that one New York station ran it a second time each week without charging the sponsor for air time. Station officials realized that if they could cut one minute from each episode and fill it with a new commercial, they would still make a profit. During its time period, the show pulled in as much as 80 percent of the viewing audience. Madison later tried to re-release the show with new introductions, but as yet has been unsuccessful. At the time, he explained:

> It had a very simple format; lots of action and comedy. We wanted to show a little bit of the West and with Andy, add some comedy.... Even now adults come up to me and say "You know, Guy, you showed me the difference between right and wrong while I was watching." It amazes me, but people remember it as a clean show, and I think it would be excellent for kids today.[60]

Still another juvenile Western hero from the real American West was Kit Carson. However, *The Adventures of Kit Carson* was even further removed from historical fact than *Wild Bill Hickok.* The famous frontier scout (as played by Bill Williams) roamed the Old West with his Mexican sidekick, El Toro (Don Diamond), in 104 episodes released for syndication between 1951 and 1955.

The handsome, blond Williams had been born in Brooklyn, New York. A superb athlete in his teens, he got his start in show business as a professional swimmer in aquatic reviews during the thirties. Moving into films in the mid-forties, he appeared in such action movies as *Thirty Seconds over Tokyo* (1944), which starred Van Johnson. During the early days of live television, Williams hosted several music shows before donning the buckskin apparel of Kit Carson. Later, he costarred as Betty White's husband in the domestic comedy, *A Date with the Angels.* He purportedly turned down the lead in *Sea Hunt* because he did not think an underwater show would work on television. Williams ended his television career playing guest roles on shows like *Lassie, Perry Mason* and *Police Woman.* Although Williams is still remembered for his portrayal of the crusading Western hero, he later remarked that he was sick of dusty trails and six-guns and "never want[ed] to see or hear of Kit Carson again!"[61]

Don Diamond was also born in Brooklyn. His comedic talents, however, were used to better advantage later as Corporal Reyes on *Zorro* and Crazy Cat on *F Troop.*

According to *Variety,* the MCA-TV Western reached more children's homes than any other series in 1954. Three and a half million households were estimated to be tuned in to the weekly exploits of Kit and El Toro.

Another juvenile television Western which made its debut in 1951 was *Sky King.* The hero of this show differed in a significant way from those who had blazed the trail before. *Sky King,* set in the contemporary West, used a Cessna 310-B twin-engine airplane called the Songbird, instead of a horse, to chase down crooks and evildoers. With the aid of his teenage niece, Penny, and nephew, Clipper, Schuyler King patrolled the vast Flying Crown Ranch from the air. The television series was a transplant from radio. The radio series premiered on October 28, 1946, when "America's favorite flying cowboy" first came zooming down from the skies over ABC for a quarter-hour of daily serialized action. By 1947 *Sky King* had moved into a Tuesday and Thursday 30 minute format for Peter

Bill Williams as television's Kit Carson.

Pan Peanut Butter (who also sponsored the television version). The stories were set in the modern American West for the most part, but occasionally they would visit such exotic locales as France and South America. In 1950 the series switched to Mutual where it remained until leaving the air in 1954. The show also helped launch the careers of Earl Nightingale (Sky in the 30 minute version) and announcer Mike Wallace.

Kirby Grant, who played Sky on television, was uniquely qualified for the role. Born in Montana, he was a real cowboy. In World War II, he spent considerable time as an Air Force flight instructor and was well qualified to fly the Songbird. Although he was considered a musical prodigy on the violin, Grant's interests shifted to baseball and acting as he grew older. After performing with a Midwest stock company in 1937, he entered a *Gateway to Hollywood* radio talent contest and won the first prize of a six-month RKO film contract. Grant appeared in the forties in a string of musicals, comedies, singing-cowboy films and Canadian Mounted Police features before taking the controls of the Songbird. His credits included *Blondie Goes Latin* (1941), *Hello, Frisco, Hello* (1943) and *Ghost Catchers* (1944). Grant won the television role for which he will always be remembered as the result of a screen test.

Gloria Winters, fresh from her role as Babs on *The Life of Riley* was cast as Penny. Unknown Ron Haggerty played Clipper for one season until he enlisted in the army.

A wide variety of subjects was utilized in the stories ranging from the typical cops 'n' robbers plots to issue-oriented scripts dealing with ecological concerns. The show also focused on the development and application of the latest electronic gadgetry such as

Geiger counters, tape recorders, dish antennas, and many devices that are commonly used today. In all, 130 episodes were filmed and later packed away in a New York film library. The 35mm negatives, the masters, and the 16mm release prints were all in one room when a fire broke out. Only 72 of the episodes were salvaged. *Sky King* was one of the more popular juvenile Westerns on television and hundreds of children would line the airfields whenever Grant flew in for a personal appearance. Grant, like most of television's cowboy-heroes, took the role seriously and totally believed that he could be a model for young viewers. In a 1958 newspaper interview, he confessed:

> I'm not so naive as to think that "goody goody" television programs are going to solve any world issue or even make a big dent in the problem of juvenile delinquency, but I sincerely feel that anything I can do to instill the idea of settling disputes peacefully in the minds of my young audience is of paramount importance. In my actions on the screen I try to crystalize that belief.[62]

In a much later interview, Grant expanded:

> ... I did enjoy a drink, but I never took one in front of kids. I never smoked near them and I watched my language. It all had a tendency of making a better person out of me. I tried to live up to the character that I portrayed.

On the subject of violence, he explained:

> We only used what violence was necessary to bring a culprit to justice. In fact, no heavy—regardless of how ruthless he was—was ever pistol-whipped or clubbed in any episodes.

He concluded with great satisfaction:

> If I never do anything else in my life, at least I know I've accomplished something good with "Sky King."[63]

Yet another successful crossover from radio starred one of the most famous canines ever to grace the silver screen. *The Adventures of Rin Tin Tin* premiered on ABC on October 15, 1954, starring the great-grandson of the original silent movie Rinty. Actually, the dog seen in the series might be any one of three animals including the great-grandson and great-great-grandson of the first Rin Tin Tin, who died in 1932. The original German shepherd puppy was discovered in a French farmhouse where he had been abandoned by Kaiser Wilhelm's departing troops at the close of World War I. Lee Duncan, a 29 year old noncommissioned-officer Air Corps pilot and sporting goods salesman from Los Angeles decided to take the puppy home with him. He also taught the dog (whom he had named Rin Tin Tin) the tricks that later made him famous after a reviewer for a dog breeders' journal criticized the animal's clumsiness during a dog show. Lavishing patience, affection and rewards on his eager pupil, he soon had a pet that was smarter than any other animal of its kind.

Rin Tin Tin I made his silent film debut in 1923 in *Where the North Begins*, and eventually appeared in 22 movies. The dog is said to have received as many as a million letters a year, and starred in hundreds of vaudeville shows. Duncan became a professional dog trainer and followed the same techniques with all the subsequent Rin Tin Tins. The fourth and fifth sons of the original Rinty, used by Duncan in the television series were both full-blooded German Shepherds. Rin Tin Tin IV was used mainly with horses, since scenes with animals were his specialty. Rin Tin Tin V was fierce by nature and a virtuoso growler, so he got utilized in all the fight sequences. The third dog on the show was Flame, Jr., the son of Flame, the canine star of 36 motion pictures. Flame, Jr., responded

Lee Aaker was Rusty, young master of Rin Tin Tin.

intelligently and efficiently to both voice and hand signals and was used for some of the more complicated stunts.

Herbert B. Leonard brought the famous canine film hero to television after determining that the animal had a ready-made audience. He conducted a survey, asking people if they knew who Rin Tin Tin was and discovered that well over 60 percent did. The show was sold as soon as news of the production was announced and the series went on the air within 60 days of shooting.

The stories were set in the Old West and were full of action involving gunfights, rampaging Indians and nasty outlaws. Rusty, a 10 year old orphan, and Rinty, according to the pilot episode, had survived a brutal Indian attack that left everyone else in their wagon train dead. Upon being discovered by the U.S. Cavalry (under the command of Lieutenant Rip Masters), the boy and his dog were made honorary soldiers of Fort Apache in Arizona Territory and spent most of their time helping the cavalry and townspeople of nearby Mesa Grande establish law and order on the frontier. The courageous acts of Rinty, Rusty and Masters also helped maintain the tenuous peace which existed between the Apaches and United States Army.

Besides the predictable stories in which Rinty had to struggle across the desert, brave a mountain lion's attack, or escape from a locked boxcar, the show presented dramatized moral lessons for its young viewers. In one episode, Rusty learned about government corruption; in another, he learned that former criminals can become honest citizens. As James Brown, who played Lieutenant Masters, later explained:

> We tried to preach without preaching. Our stories simply taught that right was right and wrong was wrong. You don't get those kinds of values on television anymore....
>
> I liked the story line and the chemistry between Lee Aaker [Rusty] and me.... Our popularity was reinforced by the mail we immediately received. The majority of the letters came from grownups, who wrote that they enjoyed watching the show with their children.[64]

A onetime teenage tennis star, James Brown had broken into movies in B action films during the forties including *Air Force* (1943), *Objective Burma!* (1945), *Sands of Iwo Jima* (1949), and *Chain Lightning* (1950). He had appeared in over 45 movies when he got the role of Masters over a hundred and fifty other candidates. Aaker was a former child star who had appeared in 15 films between 1947 and 1954 including the popular *Benji* (1947). Critics generally liked the show. *TV Guide* (March 26, 1955) said:

> The Rin Tin Tin telefilm series is crammed with the action, gunplay and chase scenes of premusical—cowpoke Westerns. It makes fine viewing for kids and nostalgic viewing for grownups.

On the other hand, the usually more critical *Variety* (October 20, 1954) commented on the pilot episode:

> This filmed stanza has few redeeming aspects. Aaker is precocious in the part of the bright and brave young orphan [but] he's not helped much by the direction.... The dog does nothing exceptional either, except look faithful at proper times, tear at an Indian's throat and run dozens of exhausting miles to warn the post of danger.

Variety's reservations notwithstanding, the series' popularity endured a highly popular five year run on ABC. Reruns of *The Adventures of Rin Tin Tin* aired on ABC late afternoons for two more years and on CBS's Saturday Morning lineup from September 1962 to September 1964. A two-part episode was released in Europe and Mexico as a feature film after additional footage was shot and tons of Rin Tin Tin merchandise was sold in stores from coast to coast. During production breaks the cast toured in a rodeo show and Brown issued six records for MGM including the highly successful "The Legend of the White Buffalo," which became the subject of an entire episode.

Because the show had enjoyed such popularity in the fifties it seemed to Stan Moger, executive vice president of SFM Media Service Corporation of New York, that Rin Tin Tin should be repackaged and re-released in the seventies. James Brown was brought in to host new introductions for each story with Rin Tin Tin VII lying alertly at his feet. The episodes, which had been filmed in black and white, were tinted sepia in order to give them an historical appearance. The rebroadcasts were not successful, however, due to the poor scheduling practice of local stations and the series can be seen today only on cable.

A review of juvenile television Westerns would be incomplete without including that champion of all animal series, *Fury*. This "story of a horse and the boy who loved him" was set in the contemporary West. The star of the show was a wild black stallion that had

Richard Simmons as Sergeant Preston, with Yukon King.

been captured by Jim Newton, a widower and ranch owner. In town for supplies, Jim clears a young orphan named Joey of breaking a window, and takes him home as his adopted son. Together with a grizzled old hand named Pete, Jim, Joey and Fury face all kinds of trouble, from forest fires to kidnappings to one memorable episode in which Joey falls from the horse and lies unconscious in the mountains. No matter how brave and resourceful the humans were, the horse was the hero and always outshone them all.

Each episode dramatized a simple lesson about some issue of importance for young audiences like civil defense, bicycle safety, wildlife preservation, freedom of the press, family responsibility and fire prevention. The show was the most honored juvenile pro-gram on television in the mid-fifties, winning awards from the National Education Association, the Junior Achievement program, the U.S. Civil Defense Agency, the United Fund, the Red Cross, the Boy Scouts and the National PTA.

Much of the credit for the show's success belonged to Beauty, the beautiful, 15 hands high, coal-black stallion that "played" Fury. He had appeared in a number of movies before gaining stardom on the small screen. The stallion carried Clark Gable in *Lone Star* (1952), Joan Crawford in *Johnny Guitar* (1954) and Elizabeth Taylor in *Giant* (1956).

Peter Graves, brother of *Gunsmoke*'s James Arness, was cast as Jim Newton. (He had changed his last name to avoid confusion.) Like his older brother, Peter grew up in Min-neapolis, served in World War II, and drifted to Hollywood after the war. A bit part in a live television play won him his first movie role in 1950 (a Western called *Rogue River*). Thereafter, he appeared in a number of action films, gaining recognition as the treacher-ous German spy in *Stalag 17* (1953). *Fury* was his first big break and he made 114 episodes of the show over a five year period. After several less successful television series (*Whiplash* and *Court-Martial*), he finally hit the big time as M.I.F. leader Jim Phelps in the highly popular and long running *Mission: Impossible* (1967–1973; 1988.1990).

Bobby Diamond, who played Joey (the only person who could ride Fury), had begun his show biz career as a toddler gracing the covers of such national magazines as *Collier's* and *Parade*. He appeared in his first film *The Mating of Millie* (1948) at age 4. His other screen credits included *The Greatest Show on Earth* (1952), *The Glass Slipper* (1955), *Un-tamed* (1955) and *To Hell and Back* (1955). After appearing in a number of early television dramas (*The Loretta Young Show, Cavalcade of Stars*), he was selected for the role on *Fury* that would make him famous. When the series ended production in 1960, Bobbie moved on to other roles for a while. However, he passed up the chance to become one of Fred MacMurray's sons on *My Three Sons* for a role in a show that lasted only six months and today he is a practicing attorney in Los Angeles.

Fury, which was filmed at the Iverson Ranch facilities in Chatsworth, California, became one of the most popular shows on Saturday morning television. It earned an average 17.8 Nielsen rating over the first four seasons (1955–1959) on NBC. (This meant that an estimated 17.8 percent of the nation's television sets were tuned in to the show, giving it a better rating than many prime time series.) In 1959 it was retitled *Brave Stallion* and distributed for non-network syndication. Even the *Variety* (October 19, 1955) critic liked *Fury*, writing:

> ... instead of a story of a boy and his dog, this time it's a tale of a boy and a horse....
> Graves scored nicely as the forthright rancher, young Diamond portrayed the boy with finesse ... while Gypsy[?], a black stallion, ran away with thesping honors in the title role....
> The production and direction plus the overall technical quality combine to make this a solid entry for the moppet market.

And so it was, with 12 consecutive years on the air.

Graves recently tried to explain *Fury*'s significance and popularity:

> "Fury" had a lot to offer a whole generation of young people. Every story was sort of a moral tale without attendant violence.
> We taught them something about animals, life, parental authority, growing up, getting an education—basic values that we sometimes lose sight of in this country.
> It was sometime during the first year that our line producer Leon Fromkess said to me, "Peter, do you know that as long as black and white half-hour series play anywhere on televi-sion, *Fury* will be seen. It's a classic. It's timeless." He's certainly been born out. It's still telecast all over the world.

Civil War veterans Peter Whitney (left), Kent Taylor and Jan Merlin join forces in *The Rough Riders*.

I think it was an all around excellent show for kids and for families, and today I look back on it very proudly.[65]

Sergeant Preston of the Yukon was another popular children's series that had been originally developed for radio. He was the third major hero created by George W. Trendle, Fran Striker and the staff of WXYZ, Detroit (following in the tradition of *The Lone Ranger* and *The Green Hornet*). Animals Yukon King, the wonder dog, and Rex, Preston's noble black horse, figured prominently in the stories. When the show debuted over ABC in 1947, it was known as *The Challenge of the Yukon*, but that title was later replaced by the name of its human hero. Children sometimes referred to it as Yukon King after "the swiftest and strongest lead dog in the Northwest" who was constantly mauling bushwhackers, chewing guns out of the hands of crooks and knocking down one villain while Preston himself finished off the other. The stories were set at the turn of the century in Canada's Yukon Territory, where thieves and scoundrels preyed upon the gold miners and settlers who had come to make their fortune on the frozen frontier.

The program came packaged to classical music: the *Donna Diana Overture* theme, though not as well-known as the Ranger's *William Tell Overture* and the Hornet's *Flight of the Bumblebee*, was perfect for evoking a northerly Canadian setting. Sergeant Preston (he never had a first name) upheld the finest tradition of the Northwest Mounted Police by always getting his man (with the help of King). Paul Sutton's deep voice exhorted the dogs each week with "On King! On, you huskies!" He was replaced during the final season by Brace Beemer (after the Ranger had been canceled) and Fred Foy took over for announcer Jay Michael. The show sustained itself on ABC for a year, then was picked up by Quaker Oats and in 1950 moved to Mutual where it remained until the radio version left the air in 1955.

The television series was filmed in color in mountainous areas of California and Colorado, against a spectacularly scenic background. Richard Simmons cut a splendid figure as the intrepid sergeant in his smart red broadcloth suit, broad-brimmed hat and pencil-thin mustache. The remarkably intelligent Malamute who played Yukon King and the beautiful black horse Rex added to the striking visual impression of the show. Back in 1940, Simmons was a rugged young six-footer who flew planes for a living. Among his hobbies were swimming, fencing, and breaking wild horses. His career in acting happened purely by chance. Simmons explained in a 1956 interview for *TV Guide*:

> I never intended to be an actor. I was happy being a pilot. One time I spent my vacation at a dude ranch near Palm Springs. The fellows that owned the place had an Arabian stallion that hadn't been broken. Since I was riding in rodeos when I was in high school, I got on and broke him in an hour.[66]

One of the guests at the ranch watching Simmons break the stallion was M-G-M's Louis B. Mayer. Simmons was offered a contract at twice his pilot's salary, and was guaranteed "outdoor roles." That Simmons was perfect for the role is illustrated by a little-known incident that occurred during the second season. Sixteen sled dogs needed for a studio sequence in Hollywood arrived by air with no one at the airport qualified to remove 1600 pounds of tired, nervous Malamutes from the plane. Word reached Simmons, who was giving a dinner party at his home. He slipped over and unloaded them without incident. Early reviews of the series were mixed. The *Variety* (October 5, 1955) critic wrote:

> "Sergeant Preston" doesn't stack up as a particularly well-produced series. First off, Skinner may have made a mistake in spreading the glory too thin. For in giving both the

dog and the horse so great a role, Skinner deprives Richard Simmons, as the Mountie, of the
impact he should have. . . .
    The kiddies need a strong hero and the first script . . . stressed the canine angle far
too strongly.

Still, the show ran for three seasons on CBS (1955–1958). It was widely seen in reruns and was broadcast on Saturday afternoons over NBC in 1963-64.

Two other juvenile Westerns deserve mention: *Cowboy G-Men* and *The Rough Riders*.
Trying to be unique, *Cowboy G-Men* combined the cops 'n' robbers and Western genres.
Actually, this series was a forerunner of a much more popular and longer running series,
The Wild Wild West, without the sophisticated humor and modern gadgets. The stories
concerned the adventures of two "hard-riding, fast-shooting" government agents, Pat
Gallagher and his bumbling partner Stony Crocket, who "worked undercover on danger-
ous, special assignments" in the Old West.

Former *Hopalong Cassidy* sidekick Russell Hayden starred as the upright and handsome Gallagher, while his comic sidekick Crocket was played by former child actor Jackie
Coogan. Film historian Don Miller points out that the series "was happily without the
condescending attitude that becomes the bane of the majority of juvenile programming."
This, and the fact that "Hayden and Coogan worked smoothly as a team with the latter's
comedy not too broad and astutely valued,"[67] made *Cowboy G-Men* one of the better
Westerns on television at the time.

The Rough Riders represented an attempt to bring the popular "trigger trio" B
Western to the home screen. Set in the West at the end of the Civil War, the series related
the adventures of three soldiers who join forces for companionship and protection. Each
had decided to start a new life in the West. Two of the soldiers, Captain Jim Flagg and
Sergeant Buck Sinclair, were veterans of the Union Army, while the third, Lieutenant
Kirby, had served the Confederacy. On their journey, they encounter outlaws, renegade
Indians and deserters from both armies. In one episode the heroes thwart an attempt by
the renegade Quantrill and his raiders to assassinate the President. In another they break
up a slave-labor camp operated by a land commissioner. In still another they rescue a
farm girl who has been kidnapped by a gang of outlaws. Veteran B movie actor Kent
Taylor, fresh from two seasons as television's *Boston Blackie*, played Flagg. Long time
Western villain Peter Whitney was cast as Sinclair and Jan Merlin, costar of *Tom Corbett,
Space Cadet*, was Kirby.

The critics panned the show. *TV Guide* called it "just another Western" and *Variety*
(October 8, 1958) said:

> "Roughriders" is hardly different from other video cowboy packages which sustain their
> action by loading the screen with an abundance of horses' hoofs, horses' neighs and con-
> siderable dust.
>   Scripting was . . . pedestrian (and) full of cliches. . . . Best performance was given by the
> Rocky Mountains.

The series was not particularly popular with viewers either and was canceled after just
one season (1958-59) on ABC.

Although each juvenile Western hero attracted his (or her) own loyal following, it
was Hoppy, Gene, and Roy, along with the Lone Ranger, who had the greatest impact on the development of the television Western. To paraphrase some lines from
Snuff Smith's hit song "Hoppy, Gene and Me"—it seems like only yesterday, they rode
the range together, Hoppy, Gene and Roy. They taught us how to shoot straight and

that a cowboy never cries. Lessons learned on the television screen from Hoppy, Gene and Roy will never be forgotten.

There was, however, another television pioneer who would leave his mark on the television Western. His shows would help to bridge the gap between juvenile and adult Westerns. That man was Walt Disney.

II. Walt Disney Rides West

OR, HOW DAVY CROCKETT FOUND
ZORRO ON THE VIDEO FRONTIER

Although Walt Disney is remembered chiefly for his films, his television series was one of the most successful, and remarkable, in the history of broadcasting. It was aired on all three commercial networks under several different titles, but actually was one continuous series—and considered as such, was television's longest-running prime time series, lasting 29 seasons (1954–1983).[1] Furthermore, it was not only the first prime time anthology series for children, it was the first series to utilize the miniseries (although the term itself was not coined until much later). Since a number of the most popular of these miniseries focused on a Western character and setting, and as such mark a transition between juvenile and adult Westerns, it is important at this point to consider Disney's contributions to that genre.

Walter Elias Disney was born in Chicago in 1901, and began making cartoons in Kansas City in the twenties. In 1926 he moved to Los Angeles and formed a production company with his older brother, Roy. Two years later Disney's most famous cartoon character, Mickey Mouse, came to the screen. Among his other early achievements were some of the first sound cartoons and the first animated film in full technicolor (in 1932). Before the thirties had ended, Donald Duck had made his appearance and Disney had produced the first feature length animated film, *Snow White and the Seven Dwarfs* (1937). Other early Disney successes included *Pinocchio* (1940), *Fantasia* (1940) and *Bambi* (1942). By the end of the forties, he had begun his famous nature documentaries, "True Life Adventures." (*The Living Desert*, 1953, was the first feature length "True Life Adventure.") About this time Disney also began experimenting with live action and partially live action, partially animated films. (*Song of the South*, 1946, and *Fun and Fancy Free*, 1947, fall into the latter category; *Treasure Island*, 1950, and *20,000 Leagues Under the Sea*, 1954, into the former.)

Meanwhile, Disney turned his attention to the new medium of television. In 1950, he had turned down an offer of $1,000,000 for the television rights to 350 cartoon shorts. He later explained, "The television people want to buy my films, but I'm not selling. Why should I? They're still good for the movie theaters. And because they're timeless, they always will be."[2] Disney, however, finally agreed to produce a one-hour television special to be broadcast on NBC during the 1950 Christmas season. Walt acted as a guide through the Disney Studios for ventriloquist Edgar Bergen and his dummies, Charlie McCarthy and Mortimer Snerd (who had worked with Walt in *Fun and Fancy Free*). Disney's two daughters also appeared on the show. Disney insisted that there be no commercial messages interrupting the fun, just an announcement of the sponsor's name at the beginning and end of the program. He called the constant interruptions on most programs "bad showmanship."[3] Everything was filmed at the studio taking all the time necessary to obtain the perfection always demanded by Disney. The show attracted such a large audience that Disney decided to produce another Christmas special in 1951. The reaction, both critical and popular, was phenomenal and Walt was impressed with the potential value of television as a public relations tool for the studio's theatrical products. Disney also foresaw a future for educational films on television, and he reactivated the studio's educational division.[4]

By 1954, Disney had decided to develop a weekly network series. When the show premiered in October, it was an historic event. It marked the first big plunge by a major Hollywood movie studio into television production. The big studios had been afraid of competition from the new medium and not only refused to produce any new programming, but denied television the use of any of their latest or best films.[5] In fact the announcement that Walt Disney was entering television with a weekly show stirred a rumble of controversy from the film industry, who feared that this collaboration would cause a further decline in the theater business. Theater owners bolstered that opinion with threats to boycott the product of any studio that released its movies to television. In an interview Disney explained: "Television makes lots of friends. It's just good policy. When four million people see your television show, they carry away with them an image of what you're doing."[6]

Luring Disney into television was a major coup for struggling ABC. Neither CBS or NBC could agree to his seemingly exorbitant terms. Among other things, Disney wanted the network to help finance his proposed amusement park in Anaheim, California. Only ABC was willing to pay the unheard of sum of a half million dollars per episode. (In fact, because Disney was unwilling to cut corners, the cost of producing his hour long television films often exceeded the amount he earned on them.)

The series, broadcast on Wednesday evenings (from 1954 to 1958), was called *Disneyland* and, in keeping with the format of the new amusement park, the show was divided into four rotating segments: Fantasyland, Adventureland, Tomorrowland and Frontierland. Disney used the series not only to promote the park, but to publicize upcoming theatrical features from Disney Studios as well. The first season set the pace for the weekly series: a combination of cartoon shorts, true-life nature films, multiepisode adventures (miniseries), old Disney feature films (divided into hour-long segments), and constant updates on the development of the Disneyland Park.

The shows were introduced by Walt himself. He agreed to appear after the network and advertising executives convinced him his presence was necessary to provide continuity and identification. He admitted to being "scared to death" when he had to face the camera, and he found fault with his performance, especially his voice. Furthermore, only on rare occasions would Disney agree to deliver commercials. He would talk about the sponsor's product only if he believed in it.[7] (After his first season, Disney was nominated for an Emmy Award as "Most Outstanding New Personality," but lost to George Gobel. The second season he won an Emmy for "Best Producer of a Filmed Series.")

It was out of the Frontierland segment ("tall tales and true from our legendary past") of the series that *Disneyland* was to make its contribution to the television Western. Disney had been contemplating a series of shows based on legendary American heroes like Johnny Appleseed, Daniel Boone, Mike Fink, Davy Crockett, Kit Carson and others. He decided to tell the story of Davy Crockett first, in three hour-long episodes, and asked studio writer Tom Blackburn to develop the storyline. Walt liked the saga, which took Crockett from the frontier to Congress and finally to his heroic death at the Alamo.

A tall, lanky actor named James Arness was recommended for the role, so Disney viewed his most recent film, *Them!*, a 1954 Warner Bros. science fiction movie about giant ants. A brief scene in the film included a six-foot, five-inch actor with a pleasant Texas accent and a face that appeared both likable and heroic. "That's Davy Crockett," Disney exclaimed, pointing not at Arness but another giant, Fess Parker.[8] Fess Parker, whose first name means "proud" in old English, grew up in San Angelo, Texas. Active in sports while in high school, he planned to play football at the University of Texas, but an injury kept him out of college sports. Instead, Parker became interested in music and drama. While majoring in American history, he played trumpet with local dance bands to help finance his college expenses. He intended to become a history teacher, but that changed when he happened to meet screen actor Adolphe Menjou, who urged Parker to try his luck in Hollywood after finishing college. With that in mind, he joined the University's dramatic society, "The Curtain Club." (This group also provided valuable experience for Rip Torn, Pat Hingle, Jayne Mansfield and a number of other future Hollywood stars.)

Following his graduation in 1950, Parker enrolled at the University of Southern California to obtain a master's degree in the history of the theater. Before long, however, he signed for a role in the national company of *Mister Roberts*, starring Henry Fonda, during the last weeks of its West Coast run, and his college life was over. Soon after his professional stage debut, Parker made his film debut in *Untamed Frontier* (1952), starring Shelley Winters. In rapid succession he played minor roles in a number of pictures, including *Springfield Rifle* (1952) and *Battle Cry* (1954). He also appeared on such television shows as *Dragnet, Death Valley Days, Stories of the Century, City Detective* and *My Little Margie* before being asked to test for the part of Davy Crockett. His career did not appear to be going any place in particular and it was not much of a gamble for him to accept the part of the "King of the Wild Frontier." He was hired, signed to a long-term Disney contract, taught to ride a horse and sent off to film *Davy Crockett* in North Carolina.

When the film was finally assembled, it fell short of the desired length. Disney first tried spacing out the gaps with additional sketches, but was unhappy with the result. One morning while visiting the office of George Bruns, a new composer at the studio, he mentioned the problem he was having bridging from one adventure to another. "George, can you get a little throwaway melody under the narration some way?" Walt asked. In half an hour, Bruns had composed a song that not only fit the lines in Blackburn's script but perpetuated many of the myths of Crockett's life (e.g., that he had killed a bear at the age of 3).[9] The demand for "The Ballad of Davy Crockett" began when a small part of it was heard in the preview portion of the first *Disneyland* show. After the first episode aired on December 5, 1954, as the eighth installment of *Disneyland*, the avalanche began. Seventeen different versions of the song were recorded, selling over ten million records making it number one on the *Hit Parade* for 13 weeks.[10]

Fess Parker became a star virtually overnight and Buddy Ebsen, who played Davy's sidekick, George Russell, found his career suddenly rejuvenated. Ebsen had started out as a dancer—first in such Broadway shows as *Whoopee* and later with his sister Vilma in Hollywood musicals of the thirties. By the 1950s Ebsen had switched to straight acting and although he was well established, he was hardly famous. He did television work early in the decade on several dramatic anthologies before his friend Walt Disney tapped him to play Davy's weather-beaten partner. (Ebsen had been one of those first considered to play Crockett, but was rejected primarily because of his age. In any case, this fortunate television exposure eventually led Ebsen to superstardom on *The Beverly Hillbillies* and *Barnaby Jones*.)

Probably no one, including Disney himself, realized the cultural revolution his three-part *Davy Crockett* series was going to produce on that mid–December evening in 1954 when Davy, wearing his buckskin outfit, his coonskin cap and clutching a rifle capable of making the truest shot on the frontier, made his first television appearance during the Creek Indian War. General Andrew Jackson, realizing that he and his cavalry needed some superheroics to defeat the Creeks who wanted to keep their land, sent for the legendary Davy Crockett. When his soldiers found Davy, he was busy with more important matters—like "grinnin' down a b'ar." Interrupted by Norton and his men, the bear snapped out of the trance caused by Davy's powerful grin and he was forced to finish off the critter with a more conventional weapon—his knife. This was certainly a most impressive introduction to "Davy Crockett, Indian Fighter" (December 15, 1954). The episode went on to relate how Davy and his friend George Russell tried to convince Chief Red Stick to give up his war against the settlers and join the other tribes in a peace treaty.

Red Stick was the fierce leader of the Creeks who could almost defeat the "white eyes" with his terrible scowl alone. Of course, Red Stick had never encountered a frontier hero like Davy Crockett, whose grin could stifle that scowl. When Jackson's aide, Major Tobias Norton, blunders into a Creek ambush, Davy and Russell come to their rescue, making so much noise that the Indians think they are being attacked by an entire regiment. Later Davy proves that he does not need an army or even his trusty rifle, Betsy, to show Red Stick the error of his ways. When Georgie is captured and tied to a stake, Davy walks boldly into Red Stick's camp and challenges him to hand-to-hand combat according to "Injun law." Since Davy made the challenge, Red Stick gets to pick the weapons—tomahawks. Red Stick, who could handle tomahawks the way Davy handled rifles, charges his adversary, but Davy soon gets the upper hand. He is, however, unwilling to kill his opponent; life to him is too precious to destroy unless there is no other alternative. Instead, Davy convinces Red Stick to make peace:

> DAVY: Now maybe you'll listen to reason... Turn my friend loose and go home. Sign
>   the treaty. Do that ... and I promise the government will let you keep your land.
> RED STICK: Government lies!
> DAVY: Davy Crockett don't lie. Here's my hand on it.
> RED STICK: I believe. We go home. We make peace.

Thus was the Creek savage transformed from a bloodthirsty cutthroat into a noble Redman of honor.

The Davy Crockett craze had begun! The second and third episodes of the series were even more successful. "Davy Crockett Goes to Congress" appeared on January 26, 1955, and "Davy Crockett at the Alamo" concluded the trilogy on February 23. Television historian J. Fred MacDonald flatly states that "no program before or since has captured the imagination of the nation in so short a period."[11] Nielson ratings placed the number of viewers of the second program at more than half of all the people who were watching television.

It resulted in a merchandising bonanza for Disney. The real Davy Crockett may have lived from 1786 to 1836, but 1954-55 was the year of television's Davy Crockett. Within a short while, toy and department stores were spilling over with Davy Crockett items. Of course, the hottest item was coonskin hats. Manufacturers (Disney-licensed and otherwise) worked around the clock to produce the furry headgear. When raccoon skins

Walt Disney's most popular frontier hero, Davy Crockett, was played by Fess Parker
(right), while Buddy Ebsen was his sidekick, Georgie Russell.

disappeared, hat makers used anything from Australian rabbit to mink. More than ten million Crockett hats were sold. The Disney merchandising division quickly recovered from its initial surprise at the enormity of the Davy Crockett boom. Telegrams were sent to major department stores warning that they would be liable for damages if they sold unauthorized merchandise. It was a bluff, but it gave Disney time to enfranchise manufacturers for products bearing the title "Walt Disney's Davy Crockett" along with a picture of Fess Parker. Posters of Parker with rifle and frontier outfit were dispatched to stores everywhere.[12]

Disney's competitors, however, reasoned that Davy Crockett was an American hero, and Walt Disney could not *own* an honest-to-goodness American hero. So they started selling hats despite Disney's warnings. When Disney took the case to court, his counsel argued that Davy Crockett coonskin caps were in demand nationwide only because the Disney Studio had popularized them in its new Davy Crockett television series. Disney won the case—the court ruled that, from then on, anyone who wanted to sell coonskin caps had to obtain permission from Walt Disney.[13] Besides the coonskin hats and buckskin outfits, coloring books, powder horns, bows and arrows, comic books and magazines and even bedspreads and wallpaper and toys of virtually every conceivable kind that could possibly be tied in with the television hero, sold by the millions. It was the greatest merchandising sweep in history. Disney offices in New York were so besieged by offers from hopeful licensees that the telephones had to be shut off for a time.

When another popular item turned out to be a wooden Davy Crockett rifle, the Disney merchandisers suggested a Davy Crockett Colt .45. "Absolutely not," Walt declared. "They didn't have Colt pistols in Crockett's time." Disney paid little attention to merchandising but he insisted on two things: "All articles must be authentic to the period: and the products had to be of good quality."[14]

The second installment, "Davy Crockett Goes to Congress," though extremely popular, was a little disappointing to kids who wanted to see their hero tangling with "b'ars and Injuns." The program related the story of Davy's journey to Washington to represent his home state of Tennessee in the United States House of Representatives. After overcoming a local bully named Bigfoot and learning of the sudden death of his wife, Polly, Davy decides to serve his country by running for Congress. His decision was based in part on the urging of his friend and fellow Tennessean, Andrew Jackson, who was planning to run for President. Davy, however, explained to Jackson at the outset that if he were elected to Congress, "I wouldn't be takin' orders from you, General. I'd be takin' 'em from them that elected me."

Davy later gets a chance to prove his independence and integrity when he opposes a bill being pushed by Jackson that would seize Indian lands in violation of several treaties Washington had signed with the Redmen. "Expansion," he declared to his fellow Congressmen, "ain't no excuse for persecutn' a whole part of our people because their skin is red and they're uneducated to our ways." In a subtle way, Disney was launching his own crusade for civil rights, years before such a stand would become popular, and was providing youngsters (and their parents, as well) with a painless, but valuable, lesson in American democracy.

As a political philosopher, Davy was a simple backwoods democrat who believed unequivocally in the principles upon which our government was based: "We got a responsibility to this strappin', fun-lovin', britches-bustin' young b'ar cub of a country ... to help it grow into the kind of a nation the Good Lord meant it to be." Davy's maiden speech to Congress (taken from Crockett's *Journals*) was a masterpiece of homespun rhetoric:

> I'm Davy Crockett, fresh from the backwoods. I'm half horse, half alligator, and a little touched with snappin' turtle. I got the fastest horse, the prettiest sister, the surest rifle, and the ugliest dog in Tennessee. My father can lick any man in Kentucky, and I can lick my father. I can hug a bear too close for comfort, and eat any man alive opposed to Andy Jackson. Now, some Congressmen take a lot of pride in sayin' a lot about nothin', like I'm doing right now. . . . Others don't do nothin' for their pay but just listen day in and day out. I wish I may be shot if I don't do more than listen.

At the end of this episode, Davy walked out of Congress in favor of the frontier life, which seemed only fitting and proper. Davy just was not Davy wearing fancy clothes and sitting among the politicians.

Davy and Russell returned to more conventional frontier action again in "Davy Crockett at the Alamo" which dramatized the heroic struggle of a couple of hundred men attempting to defend the Texas Alamo (an old mission serving as a fortress) against thousands of Mexican troops. After learning that Texas was fighting Mexico for her independence, Davy and his partner team up with a confidence artist named Thimblerig (played by Hans Conried) and an outcast Comanche rechristened Busted Luck and ride for the Alamo. The Alamo was under the command of injured Jim Bowie with Colonel William Travis second in command. Neither of them had much confidence in their survival if reinforcements did not arrive soon. History records that Bowie and Travis were slain by Mexican troops at the Alamo, but scholars remain uncertain as to the exact manner of Crockett's death. (There is some recent evidence that he may have survived the attack and been executed later.) Georgie Russell is shown being killed by a Mexican bullet, but Disney does not *show* Crockett's death. Davy, himself, is last seen out of ammunition and heroically swinging Old Betsy at the onrushing swarm of enemy soldiers, clearly *about* to die in the fight for American expansion.

Many years later, Parker explained in an interview, "They were ready to have Davy die on screen, but the Disney people, worried about the impact his dying might have on all the young children, decided to modify the ending."[15] Thus, before the premiere of the so-called adult Westerns in the fall of 1955, Disney had depicted a Western hero facing certain death (something that had never happened on a juvenile Western) — unquestionably a mature theme for what has been considered as basically a children's program.

Television historian J. Fred MacDonald describes the Davy Crockett programs as "transitional" in the history of the television Western, pointing out that although they were designed for children, they depicted adult values and relatively mature emotions. Davy displayed such juvenile characteristics as a trusty sidekick, a rifle named "Old Betsy" and a set of moral values that dealt only in "black-and-white" issues. At the same time, Davy possessed several "grownup" qualities. The death of his wife produced grief and gave Crockett an air of vulnerability. Furthermore, Davy was both a patriot and a political philosopher. Finally, no television Western to date had depicted death and violence to such an extent, nor had the hero been allowed to die.[16]

Disney had spent over $700,000 on the three Crockett films, even though he was assured of less than half that amount in revenue from television. The gamble paid off, however, in other ways besides merchandising. The Walt Disney Music Company, which had been formed in 1949 to sell sheet-music, thrived for the first time. The success of "The Ballad of Davy Crockett" lead to the formation of another subsidiary for phonograph records. Then, in a practice that was to become standard procedure for his television multipart dramas, Disney edited together the three episodes into a feature-length film, *Davy Crockett, King of the Wild Frontier*, for release to theaters. To charge money

Davy Crockett (Fess Parker, right) with archrival Mike Fink as played by Jeff York.

for an attraction that had already been seen free by 90,000,000 people was almost inconceivable. Yet the film earned a theatrical profit of nearly a quarter of a million dollars.[17]

Disney was faced with having killed off the most phenomenally popular hero in television history. Unable to resist the public clamor for more of Davy Crockett, he could only revive him in adventures purported to he based on the *legend*, rather than the life, of Davy Crockett. As Walt explained to his television audience at the beginning of the next adventure:

> Davy Crockett's death at the Alamo did not mean the end of the yarns about this fabulous frontiersman. His legendary adventures with the Mighty Mike Fink, self-styled "King

of the River" were kept alive in paperback almanacs ... forerunners of the old time dime novels. According to these tall tales Mike Fink was a fabulous character, a crack rifle shot and the biggest bully in the history of the river. In this program Mike Fink tangles with Davy Crockett in a series of fights, the likes of which has never been seen before or since.

Two more hour-long Crockett stories were shown on *Disneyland*. The first of these "Davy Crockett's Keelboat Race" (November 16, 1955), pitted Davy and Georgie against the boastful riverboat captain, Mike Fink. When Mike learns that Davy is hiring an old river salt to take him and Georgie down to New Orleans instead of paying Mike's outrageous fees, he gets Georgie drunk and challenges him to a race with the prize being the shipment of furs. Davy refuses to let Georgie go back on his word, so the next day the race is on. Mike and his men cheat at every opportunity while Davy and his men are continually beset by problems; but in the end Davy beats Fink to New Orleans. Instead of taking any bounty from Fink, however, he only insists that he make good on one part of this bet—eating his hat. This episode is essentially a comedy, centered around Jeff York's broad characterization of Mike Fink. The fights between the two crews are basically slapstick in nature, with a lot of falling into the water, sliding on molasses, ducking so someone else gets hit and so on.

The second sequel, "Davy Crockett and the River Pirates" (December 14, 1955), had Davy and Mike the best of friends working together to thwart a gang of thieves preying on riverboats plying their trade on the Ohio River. Davy and Georgie discover that a conniving white man is having his men dress as Indians and raid various boats sailing downstream. They enlist Fink's help in setting up a decoy, spreading the word along the river ports that they are carrying a cargo of gold down to New Orleans. When the "Indians" attack, Davy and Mike are ready for them and succeed in licking them soundly. Then they track down the ring leaders in their cave hideout. After a fierce battle, the thugs are captured and peace is restored to the river.

The sequels drew large numbers of viewers, but the Davy Crockett fad was mysteriously disappearing almost as quickly as it had begun. The two hour-long stories were again combined and released to theaters as a full-length movie, *Davy Crockett and the River Pirates*, but it was not nearly as popular as the original film. Thus fans were treated to a final view of their hero, Davy, and his faithful companion Georgie, biding farewell to Mike and his cronies as they pole down the broad river.

Fess Parker was undoubtedly relieved that Davy was no longer the national hero he had once been, for he was getting terribly typecast as the King of the Wild Frontier. If he had not been given different parts quickly, he might have found his career at a premature end. Disney starred him in four more feature films, all of which were box-office hits: *The Great Locomotive Chase* (1956), *Westward Ho the Wagons* (1956), *Old Yeller* (1957) and *The Light in the Forest* (1958). (All of these were eventually shown in hour-long segments on the Disney television show, reversing the procedure used with the Crockett films.) Disney also produced a series of successful record albums for Parker as tie-ins to the films (e.g., *Three Adventures of Davy Crockett*, *Westward Ho the Wagons* and *Old Yeller*).

Parker later returned to television in 1962 as a modern-day homespun politician in *Mr. Smith Goes to Washington*, but it was canceled after only one season. Soon thereafter, Parker approached Disney studios about a new series based on Davy Crockett but they were not interested. At first he proceeded with the project on his own, but fearing a legal suit by Disney he finally dropped the idea. He did, however, don his buckskins once again in 1964 to portray the Kentucky frontiersman Daniel Boone. *Daniel Boone* brought Parker renewed popularity and the series ran on NBC for six highly successful years, ranking twenty-fifth in the Nielsen ratings in 1966-67 and seventeenth in 1968-69.

In 1989 Parker was offered the opportunity of recreating the role of Davy Crockett, when Disney studio decided to revive the frontier hero for several segments of *The Magical World of Disney*. Parker would have played a 50-year-old Crockett who introduced each episode by recalling past exploits while Tim Dunigan played the younger Davy in "flashback" fashion. Parker, however, turned down the offer on the grounds that since Crockett had been killed at the Alamo, he could not have been alive to recall such past adventures. The role was consequently given to country music star Johnny Cash, who apparently felt no such concern about historical reality. (For a fuller discussion of Disney's attempted revival of Davy Crockett see Chapter XVI.)

Meanwhile Disney had turned his attention to a new weekly half-hour Western series, *Zorro*. Early in 1953 Disney purchased the film rights to the literary creation of writer Johnston McCulley, who had introduced the character in a serialized story, "The Curse of Capistrano," published in 1919 in the pulp magazine, *All-Story*. However, when he made his initial presentation to the television networks, each responded with: "You'll have to make a pilot film." "Look, I've been in the picture business for thirty years," Walt replied. "Don't you think I know how to make a film?" "But this is different; this is television," he was told. Disney argued that entertainment was the same in any medium, but the networks refused to budge. No pilot, no series.[18] So Walt set aside the *Zorro* project and did not return to it until after the phenomenal success of *Davy Crockett.*

Of all the masked heroes who graced the silver screen, none had been more durable than the masked avenger of the Old West, Zorro. As created by writer McCulley, Zorro was the son of a wealthy nobleman who went about Spanish California righting the wrongs committed upon the poor peons by an unscrupulous governor. In performing these acts of heroism, he wore a mask and, in fact, his identity was not revealed until the final installment of the story, although Don Diego de Vega was the only logical choice from nearly the beginning.

The story first came to the movie screen in 1920 as *The Mark of Zorro*, starring Douglas Fairbanks, Sr., and was "full of action and thrills in the well-known Fairbanks tradition." Five years later, the caped avenger was again brought to the silent screen in *Don Q, Son of Zorro* with Fairbanks playing Cesar De Vega, son of the original Zorro. Although in essence a sequel, it was not based on McCulley's work, but on a story written by K. and Hesheth Prichard that was adapted for the film.[19]

The first sound film featuring the "masked Robin Hood of Old California" was *The Bold Caballero*, produced by Republic in 1937 and starring the popular Western actor Robert Livingston (who would later play another masked hero, The Lone Ranger) as the "original" Zorro. The film was enhanced by being the first film to be photographed by the studio in "Natural Color." Finally, in 1937 Republic decided to feature the famous character in one of their serial adventures. Newcomer John Carroll played James Vega, great-grandson of the original Don Diego Vega, in *Zorro Rides Again*. (The serial was later edited into a feature version under the same title, and re-released in the late fifties to cash in on the interest generated by the television series.)[20]

Two years later another Zorro serial was released called *Zorro's Fighting Legion* starring Reed Hadley as the "original" Zorro. In 1947 yet another serial, *Son of Zorro*, brought back the popular hero once again with the title role being played by the unknown George Turner. Recalling that one of his ancestors had dressed as Zorro many years before to right wrongs, our hero decides to bring the masked man back once again. The final Zorro serial, *Ghost of Zorro*, was released in 1949. The lead was played this time by Clayton Moore who was just beginning his long-running role as television's Lone Ranger.[21]

Perhaps the best cinematic treatment of the Zorro character occurred in 1940 when

Guy Williams was perfectly cast as the title character in Walt Disney's *Zorro*.

the handsome young Tyrone Power starred in a more serious remake of *The Mark of Zorro* for 20th Century–Fox. In any case, while Disney's treatment of Zorro reflected the heritage of the B Westerns and the juvenile cowboy shows of early television (in that the stories were serialized, usually in 13-segment adventures, and the hero, a self-sacrificing Robin Hood, had a dual identity), Disney placed his own creative stamp on the lead role (e.g., Zorro now wore a flowing, black cape) and added a host of entertaining and well-defined supporting characters.

The Disney series debuted on September 19, 1957, to generally good ratings and reviews. *Variety* (September 20, 1959) characterized it as full of "vim, vigor and dash." Describing *Zorro* as "the 'Lone Ranger' with a cape and sword," the critic proclaimed that the show provided "no-girl horseplay in the grand tradition of the B Westerns."

Another Disney innovation involved continuing the plotline from episode to episode, in semiserial fashion (*without* the cliffhanging endings which characterized the old Saturday matinee serials). The stories were kept simple enough, however, that they could be joined at any point. He also utilized "teasers" at the end of each episode featuring dramatic scenes from the next adventure ("Next week suspense and action," proclaimed the voice of the off-screen narrator, "set a fast-moving pace! Watch the sinister Monastario use Garcia as bait for his biggest surprise—to unmask the elusive Zorro! Has the daring Zorro finally met his match? Be with us next week for the exciting action-filled answer, when the Disney Studio brings you *Zorro!*").

Disney was as fortunate in casting *Zorro* as he had been with *Davy Crockett*. Of the fifteen or so actors who initially tested for the title role, only Guy Williams knew how to fence. Born Armando Catalano in New York City, Williams had been taught how to fence when he was 7 by his father, who had been an expert fencer back in his native Italy. ("He'd once been forced into a duel to defend his honor.") Williams had embarked on an acting career when he was in his late teens, gone through the usual dramatic studies in New York and eventually wound up with a contract at Universal-International in 1952.[22]

Playing "anonymous men leaning in doorways with cigarettes dangling from their lips," Williams was forced to earn a living as a model, a worker in the Garment Center and a soda jerk. For the role of Zorro, the six-foot, three-inch Williams grew a mustache and sideburns, took guitar lessons from Vincente Gomez and received additional fencing training from Fred Caverns, who had earlier tutored both Fairbanks and Power for their screen portrayals as the masked swashbuckler. (Caverns had first staged fencing duels in Hollywood for *The Three Musketeers* and later trained a variety of knights, Don Juans and pirates to be dashing swordsmen.) Williams also learned how to stay on and ride Tornado, the 7 year old black quarter horse Zorro rode (alternately with a white stallion, Phantom).[23]

In addition to the lead, there were two other key roles in the Disney series—that of the fat, bumbling Sergeant Garcia, aide to the various evil commandants of "el pueblo de Los Angeles," and Bernado, Don Diego's mute servant. In both cases the roles were filled by actors with considerable comic expertise. The talented 340 pound Henry Calvin was cast as Garcia. At his audition it was feared that he was too fat to be agile enough for the part, so Calvin was forced to spend "fifteen or twenty minutes jumping around" before securing the role.

The Texas-born actor had studied opera on scholarships to North Texas State College and the University of Southern California, the Chicago Conservatory and Southern Methodist University. After serving in the armed forces during World War II (where he rose from private to first lieutenant in the artillery despite his bulk), he wound up as a soloist at Radio City Music Hall. He turned down an offer to sing secondary roles for the Met in favor of a major role in the hit Broadway musical *Kismet*. When the theatrical demand for king-sized bass vocalists dried up, radio, television and motion pictures welcomed him, in part because of his "growling, bearlike voice."[24]

Disney utilized Calvin's considerable vocal ability by inserting singing bits into *Zorro*. Fans deluged the studio with letters crying "encore, encore" and more songs were injected into the second season's episodes with equally favorable results. (Guy Williams also got to sing in a number of episodes.)

Gene Sheldon's comic timing was superb in the role of Bernardo, the only one who knew Don Diego's dual identity. He was mute and pretended to be deaf, enabling him to learn much valuable information for his master. Don Diego's father Don Alejandro was played by George Lewis, who had portrayed the hero in the Republic serial *Zorro's Black Whip* (1944).

Other "regulars" in the cast came and went—some lasting for several episodes, others for 13: Britt Lomand was appropriately villainous as Zorro's first adversary, Captain Monastario; Jan Arvan played escaped political prisoner and friend of Don Alejandro, Nacho Torres; Vinton Hayworth appeared as the despotic Magistrato Galindo. During the second season Don Diamond (from *The Adventures of Kit Carson*) was added in the continuing role of Corporal Reyes; as was Richard Anderson as Diego's friend and romantic rival, Ricardo Del Amo (Ricardo was also a compulsive practical joker who on one occasion was almost hanged for impersonating Zorro); and the veteran actor Edward Franz became Señor Gregorio Verdugo.

Beautiful señoritas were also plentiful: Eugenia Paul was Elena Torres, Lisa Gaye appeared for a few episodes as the Viceroy's daughter, Jolene Brand portrayed Anna Marie Verdugo, Don Diego's occasional sweetheart, and for several episodes Disney Mouseketeer Annette Funicello played Anita Cabrillo, who needed Zorro's help in finding her missing father. Her role was a birthday present from Walt, who even gave her a chance to sing a few songs on the show.

For two years *Zorro* was an exciting prime time series. The stories related the adventures of Don Diego de La Vega, the only son of wealthy landowner Don Alejando who returns home to California after three years of study in Spain. The year is 1820 and Monastario, a ruthless army officer, has become commandant of the Spanish Fortress in Los Angeles and is "taxing" the rancheros out of existence. Those who cannot pay are flogged and thrown into prison. The Indians are torn from their families and forced into slave labor.

Don Diego presents himself as a lazy, effete intellectual-playboy, much to his father's dismay. Secretly, however, he dons his mask, cape and sword and sets out "to aid the oppressed and foil the schemes of the evil Monastario." He takes the name of Zorro on these forays. ("When you cannot clothe yourself in the skin of a lion, put on that of a fox!"—*Zorro* means "fox" in Spanish.) In a note to the evil Monastario he proclaims: "Beware, commandante, my sword is a flame—to right every wrong. So heed well my name: Zorro!"

Thus, as J. Fred MacDonald so picturesquely describes, "with black cape flowing, his sword in hand and atop his surging black stallion, the intrepid Zorro rescues señoritas, defends the abused and thwarts the designs of villainous men. Adding delicious insult to the injury he inflicts upon the perpetrators of evil, Zorro leaves his monogram at the scene of all his victories, the letter 'Z' sliced ever so elegantly with the tip of his rapier."[25]

By the thirteenth episode of the first season, Zorro had thoroughly humiliated and discredited his first adversary, Monastario, to the point he was removed from his post by the Spanish Viceroy. For a brief period the rotund, ineffective and benign Garcia was made acting commandant, but he was soon replaced by a more formidable opponent for Zorro. Among the more durable villains who challenged Zorro during the 78 thirty-minute episodes of the series were Magistrato Galindo, whose brutal rule weighed heavily upon the common people, and a would-be dictator calling himself "The Eagle," who headed a secret society that was trying to take over Los Angeles.

Unlike the Davy Crockett programs, which were transitional—that is, designed for children, but displaying adult values and relatively mature perceptions—the *Zorro* shows were clearly aimed at a juvenile audience. If adults wanted to watch (as millions, no doubt, did), so much the better, but the show was scheduled at eight o'clock, when, Disney believed, grade-schoolers still controlled the television set. Naturally there were dramatic duels—up and down staircases, on the edge of cliffs, atop Spanish tables—until Zorro finally overcame the bad guys. Williams, himself, believed that the series "clicked"

Don Diego (i.e., Zorro, played by Guy Williams, right) converses with Sergeant Garcia (delightfully portrayed by Henry Calvin), while faithful servant Bernardo (Gene Sheldon) stands watch.

because "it combines some of the elements of a Western (like horsemanship, action and suspense) with that glamorous weapon—the sword."[26]

Although thousands of plastic capes and rubber-tipped swords were sold to youngsters bearing the Disney logo, the fad never caught on like the Crockett mania. The *Zorro* theme song (the music of which was also written by George Bruns) was recorded by Henry Calvin. However, the version which became a hit was done by the female group from the Arthur Godfrey show, the Chordettes.

In spite of the fact that *Zorro* had performed well in the ratings, ABC declined to renew it for a third season. The reason was economic: the network could make more money with shows which it owned, rather than those it bought from independent producers like Disney. In canceling the series, ABC contended that Disney was barred from offering *Zorro* or *Disneyland* (later called *Walt Disney Presents*) to other networks. Disney sued ABC and after lengthy negotiations, a settlement was reached. He would be able to take the shows to other networks, but he had to buy out ABC's one-third interest in the Disneyland amusement park for $7,500,000. This settlement galled Disney, but at least he was free. Although *Zorro* was not broadcast again until the eighties on the Disney Cable Channel, *Walt Disney Presents* eventually moved to NBC (as *Walt Disney's Wonderful World of Color*), and still later to CBS (as *Disney's Wonderful World*).[27]

(In what was to become another milestone in the history of Zorro's depiction, Gary Goodman and Barry Rosen of New World Television produced in 1989 what was to be the most thoroughly planned and elaborately developed *Zorro* project ever filmed. See Chapter XVI for more details regarding this interesting television version of McCulley's popular hero.)

Meanwhile, about the time *Zorro* was catching on with viewers, Disney decided to try "an entirely new kind of story of the American West never before told on television or in motion pictures" on *Disneyland*. Andy Burnett was the only Western hero depicted by Disney who was not based on an actual historical figure.

The six hour-long Burnett films (broadcast during the 1957-58 season) were based on the adult-oriented, historical stories of Stewart Edward White. They had been first serialized in the *Saturday Evening Post* and then published in four loosely sequential novels, *The Long Rifle* (1932), *Ranchero* (1933), *Folded Hills* (1934), and *Stampede* (1942). Intended by their author to be a "fictional history of the early years of the American fur trade," the Burnett stories were praised by critics for "White's fidelity to detail and historical fact."[28] Disney, himself, explained in the opening to the first Andy Burnett story that "Stewart Edward White was a master of the storyteller's art and a whole generation of Americans grew up with his stories. . . . His crowning work was not published in its entirety until 1947. . . . This epic novel created a legion of Andy Burnett fans whose loyalty remains as keen today as when they first read these exciting adventures of a young man on the frontiers of a young America. . . ."

"The Saga of Andy Burnett" dramatized the adventures of a young frontiersman from western Pennsylvania as he traveled west in the 1820s to become a mountain man. Armed with his grandfather's flintlock rifle (a gift from Daniel Boone), Andy meets Joe Crane and his fur trapper companions who are heading for the Colorado wilderness. With expert shooting, knife throwing and "wras'lin'," he earns a place in the party as they set out for the Rockies.

Subsequent episodes relate their adventures as they encounter the dangers and hardship of frontier life on their trek west. Eventually Burnett and his partners are captured by the Blackfoot Indians and Andy is forced to endure a number of painful ordeals. Ultimately, he wins their respect through the use of "white man's medicine" (using a glass lens to start a fire). Although Andy and his three friends remain captives of the Blackfoot, they assist them in finding buffalo to feed their starving tribe. Andy also saves the life of a brave's young son who is being dragged by a horse. Later the four trappers help the Blackfoot fight off an attack of their enemies the Assinibine in which Jack, the leader of the group, is mortally wounded. Andy, by now fully accepted by his partners as a mountain man, is selected to replace Jack as leader when he dies and they are all made honorary members of the tribe ("white brothers of the sun").

Disney, as usual, was most particular in his casting. To play the young frontiersman he selected Jerome Courtland. Despite his age, Courtland had extensive experience in films. He had played juvenile roles as a child in *The Man from Colorado* (1949), with Glenn Ford and William Holden, *The Walking Hills* (1949), with Randolph Scott, and *The Palomino* (1950), a children's movie. He had also played supporting roles in *Santa Fe* (1951), again with Randolph Scott, and in two George Montgomery Westerns, *The Texas Rangers* (1951) and *Cripple Creek* (1952). Following the Andy Burnett series, Disney used Courtland in a featured role in *Tonka* (1958). Later Courtland tried his hand at directing for the Disney Studios: *Run, Cougar, Run,* which was originally broadcast on *Walt Disney's Wonderful World of Color* and later released theatrically.

Other cast members of "The Saga of Andy Burnett" included Jeff York (who had played Mike Fink in the Davy Crockett series) as Andy's friend Joe Crane; newcomer Andrew Duggan (who was later to star in *Bourbon Street Beat, Room for One More, Twelve O'Clock High* and *Lancer*) as leader of the mountain men, Jack Kelly; veteran character actor Slim Pickens (who was later to appear as a regular in such Westerns as *The Outlaws* and *Custer*) as the grizzled trapper Old Bill Williams; and native American actor Iron Eyes Cody (who had appeared in dozens of forties' B Westerns) as the Blackfoot medicine man Mad Wolf.

The Burnett films used the same style and technique—a catchy theme song and musical narration to bridge gaps in the story. Artists also developed an animated map to depict the extensive travels of Andy and his friends. The series earned high ratings on Disney's television show, but never caught the public's fancy as Davy Crockett had.

Nevertheless, the series marked the first dramatic treatment of the trader-trapper frontier on film or television (long before the critically acclaimed Robert Redford film *Jeremiah Johnson* in 1972 and the Grizzly Adams television series in 1977-78). Screenwriter Tom Blackburn (who also scripted the Crockett series) declared later that the stories were not intended as typical Westerns but rather as "the dramatization of an historical novel ... and an attempt to recreate honestly the period of the mountain men."[29]

The television ratings war, however, was to push Disney further into the traditional format. After losing to *Disneyland* in the ratings for three years (1954 to 1957), NBC scheduled opposite the Disney show the most expensive series in television to date, an hour-long Western, *Wagon Train.* NBC lavishly promoted the show and it succeeded in toppling *Disneyland* from its number one ranking. ABC, which was having considerable success with its Hollywood-made Western series, *Cheyenne, Maverick* and *The Life and Legend of Wyatt Earp,* began imploring Disney: "Give us more Westerns! Give us more action!"[30] A meeting was scheduled with top ABC officials at the Disney Studio. Walt startled everyone by showing up in full cowboy regalia. He twirled two six-shooters and laid them down on the table. "Okay, you want Westerns? You're gonna get Westerns!" he exclaimed. He insisted, however, that he was going to do the Westerns "his way," depicting *authentic* heroes of the *real* West. He described the heroic adventures of such historical figures as Texas John Slaughter and Elfego Baca and the ABC executives were totally convinced.

Disney disliked turning out a product to a preconceived formula and now he found himself competing with some two dozen other television Westerns. That was not the Disney style and he argued that his product had always succeeded by its uniqueness, not in following trends. ABC, however, simply reiterated, "Just keep giving us Westerns."[31] The first of these true-life Westerns developed as a subseries of *Walt Disney Presents,* "The Nine Lives of Elfego Baca" premiered on October 3, 1958. It was to be the first of several episodes depicting the adventures of a man who brought law and order to late nineteenth-century New Mexico. There was plenty of action in that first episode as the brave, devil-may-care Baca fought off a lynch mob of eighty men who fired thousands of bullets into the flimsy shack in which he was hiding during a 36 hour siege; out-maneuvered a devious courtroom attorney, and won acquittal of trumped-up murder charges; showed up his snivelling greedy cousin; befriended a bunch of hardworking but rowdy miners; gave away a fortune in hard goods to his poor fellow Mexicans; captured with his bare hands a surly outlaw giant; outdrew all who raised a gun against him; was elected sheriff of Socorro County by acclamation; and was well on his way to becoming a lawyer who would not only stand up for the impoverished Mexican, but challenge the statutes of New Mexico that imprisoned the poor who could not pay their debts. It was an auspicious debut to say the least.

The critics loved it. *Variety* (October 4, 1958) wrote "the new show is likely to be very strong, not just with kids, but also with adults. Yet the show is with the pretensions . . . of the 'adult' Western"; it described Baca as "a man who, save for his chaps, could be Robin Hood, Zorro, Davy Crockett, et al.," being "their twin in deed and spirit." The only negative comment was that the story "offered a shade more violence than children deserve but will not reject. . . ."

Disney had pointed out in his introduction that Elfego Baca had really lived in the Old West as a "light-hearted adventurer and lightning fast gunfighter—but always on the side of justice." The Mexican Americans, whose cause he always defended, called him "the man who could not be killed. . . ." And, like Disney's other successful Western heroes, Elfego Baca had his own special theme song (written by Richard Dehr and Frank Miller) which stressed his ability to survive precarious situations in the manner of El Gato, the cat, with its legendary nine lives.

As in the case of Davy Crockett, Disney had selected for the hero of his series an historical figure whose real life exploits were legendary. And the opening episode had dramatized the most sensational events in his life. Elfego Baca (1865–1945) had grown up in the wilds of New Mexico Territory with a scant formal education. He had, however, learned well the hard lessons of survival on a virtually lawless frontier. In 1884 at the age of 19 he was employed by merchant José Baca of Cosoro. At that time Baca's brother-in-law, who was deputy sheriff of Frisco (now called Reserve), arrived complaining of crimes being committed by cowboys in his district. Most were Texans. In one instance they had castrated a Mexican in a public saloon and had used another man for target practice when he tried to intervene, wounding him in four places. Indignant over the recital of these and other misdeeds, young Baca borrowed the lawman's badge and as a self-made deputy rode out to set affairs straight in Frisco.

When he arrived, he found the townspeople cowering in fear. Several cowboys were riding the streets shooting at anything that moved, dogs, cats or people. When one of the rowdy crew removed Baca's hat with one well-placed shot, he was promptly arrested. On the following day eighty cowboys converged on the town to liberate their comrade and make an example of the self-styled deputy. After taking all the women and children to the church, Elfego Baca stood ready to face down his adversaries. Shooting began almost immediately and he sought cover in a small shack of poles chinked with adobe. During the ensuing day and a half an estimated 4000 shots were poured into the building. Baca killed four of the attackers and wounded eight others. He, himself, was unscathed. When two legitimate lawmen appeared, the cowboys withdrew and Baca was arrested and taken to Socorro. Later charged with murder in connection with the gunfight, Baca was tried in Albuquerque and found innocent.

Robert Loggia as Elfego Baca tries his hand at practicing law.

The historical courage of Baca had made him an overnight hero and he was looked upon as a champion of his people. It also launched him on a political career that lasted half a century. In later life he practiced law and operated a detective agency (his business card read "Discrete Shadowing Done") in Albuquerque, where he remained until his death. During his final years, Baca dictated his life story to writer Kyle Samuel Crichton, who in 1928 published *Law and Order, Ltd.: The Rousing Life of Elfego Baca of New Mexico*.[32]

Between October 1958 and March 1960, Disney presented nine more Elfego Baca stories on *Walt Disney Presents*, tracing Baca's life as he turned from six-guns to law books, becoming an accomplished lawyer with a flair for fighting and a perpetual sympathy for the underdog. He was certainly the first Latin lawman in television history. Only the juvenile Western *The Cisco Kid* had depicted Mexican-Americans in a favorable light before Disney and it would be almost another decade before *The High Chaparral* would do so for adult television viewers.

Once again Disney's casting was inspired. Robert Loggia was selected to play the dashing hero. Loggia, an agile "ethnic" actor of Sicilian descent, had been born and raised in the Little Italy section of New York City. His previous experience had been relegated to supporting roles in such films as *Cattle King* (1951) and *Somebody Up There Likes Me* (1956) and television appearances on dramatic anthologies like *Studio One*. The television exposure he received from the Disney series was to launch him on a long and distinguished career which included his own 1966-67 series *T.H.E. Cat* (about a reformed cat burglar) and a lengthy stint as a continuing character on the popular soap *The Secret Storm*. Well into his fifties he continued to play memorable supporting roles in such popular films as *An Officer and a Gentleman* (1982). In 1989-90 he starred in *Mancuso, FBI* for one season on NBC and was featured in the 1993 ABC miniseries *Wild Palms*. Like his predecessors in Disney Westerns, Fess Parker, Guy Williams and Jerome Courtland, Logia was called upon to sing occasionally, which he did with some credibility.

The marvelous character actor James Dunn played Elfego's senior law partner and later district attorney, J. Henry Newman. Dunn had won an Oscar for his outstanding performance as the alcoholic father in *A Tree Grows in Brooklyn* in 1945 and had played Uncle Earl on television's *It's a Great Life* (1954-56). Other veteran actors used in key roles for various episodes included Robert F. Simon, Jay C. Flippen, Audrey Dalton, Skip Homeier, Ramon Novarro, Beverly Garland, Arthur Hunnicutt and Brian Keith.

More popular than the Elfego Baca series was "Tales of Texas John Slaughter," which Disney introduced four weeks later on October 31, 1958. Perhaps the most "traditional" of all Disney Western heroes, Slaughter was a fast-draw sharpshooter who joined the Texas Rangers to help bring law and order to frontier Texas so that he could settle down on his own ranch, get married and raise a family. The early episodes are set in Friotown, Texas, during the 1880s and relate the exploits of Slaughter first as a Texas Ranger and then as a law-abiding rancher. Later the locale shifts as Slaughter becomes a large cattleman and finally sheriff of Tombstone, Arizona.

Directed by Harry Keller, a Republic Pictures Western veteran, on picturesque outdoor locations, with a budget of $300,000 per hour, the series benefited from tight pacing, beautiful scenery and above average acting. Furthermore, Disney had researched the character for ten years before starting production. Slaughter became the biggest success on the Disney television show since Davy Crockett and despite Disney's growing aversion to Westerns, he commented in an interview, "Every time it goes on the air, the rating goes up, so I guess we'll stick with it for a while."[33] With 17 episodes, the last of which aired on April 23, 1961, the series outlasted all other Disney Western miniseries.

Disney also had a personal interest in Slaughter as he explained in introducing the initial episode: "Our research department discovered that when Mrs. Slaughter died in 1942, among her personal effects were one hundred shares of Walt Disney Productions stocks.... That just goes to show that this old West we talk about is not so old after all.... It is only yesterday in this young country of ours...."

Once again Disney gave his hero a catchy theme song. It was written and performed on the show by composer Stan Jones and created the image Disney wanted projected of the real-life Civil War veteran, Texas Ranger, rancher, cattle baron, trailblazer, army scout and law enforcer with his white Stetson hat and pearl-handled revolver.

The real John Slaughter, "a true hero of the West," was born in the Republic of Texas in 1841. He was a member of a prominent cattle family. In the late 1860s he traveled to Arizona and in 1884 bought the famous San Bernardino land grant. The Mexican government had granted these 65,000 acres to the Mexican family of Ignacio Perez in 1822. After his purchase, Slaughter began grazing cattle on both sides of the international border. In 1886, Slaughter formed a partnership with the famous trail driver and rancher George W. Long. These two men operated a profitable ranching enterprise until 1890, when the partnership was dissolved. Saughter also profited from a packinghouse which he owned in Los Angeles. Slaughter became sheriff of Tombstone (Cochise County, Arizona) in 1886. He held the post for four years, retiring in 1890. Shortly thereafter, he was appointed honorary deputy sheriff of the county, a position he held until his death in 1922.[34]

Another key to the success of Disney's "Tales of Texas John Slaughter" was its charismatic star, Tom Tryon. Tryon, at six feet, two inches, with dark brown hair and eyes, had had previous stage, television and motion picture experience. After three years in the South Pacific as a Navy radio man, third class, Tryon had enrolled in Yale. He spent four years studying cartooning and earned money summers making caricatures of the audience at Richard Aldrich's Cape Cod Theater. When the director called for bit players to back up Paulette Goddard in *Caesar and Cleopatra*, Tryon became one of several spear carriers who stalked on stage to shout, "Hail, Caesar!" Unbelievable as it sounds, this led an agent to come backstage and ask Tryon if he would like to get into films. As the season progressed, he got larger parts and better lines and everyone began asking him why he did not take up acting.[35]

Tryon began to study acting with Sandy Meisner and reached Hollywood after understudying the star of *Wish You Were Here* and working in the chorus for a year and a half. Hal Wallis gave him a small part in *The Scarlet Hour* (1956) and then a larger supporting role in *Three Violent People* (1957), which starred Charlton Heston and Anne Baxter. This film brought Tryon some favorable attention as a one-armed Civil War veteran with deep emotional problems.

Meanwhile Tryon got some television experience when he played a young Abraham Lincoln on *The 20th Century-Fox Hour* production of "Young Man from Kentucky" (February 6, 1957). Then Tryon decided to test at Universal-International for casting director Jack Bower. When Bower went over to the Disney Studio, he told Walt he had just the man to play Texas John Slaughter. Tryon thought this part would lead to bigger and better things, but actually it is still the role for which he is best remembered. (Tryon was selected to play the title role in Otto Preminger's *The Cardinal* in 1963. However, the lavish, three-hour blockbuster bombed at the box office and Tryon's performance was widely panned by critics as "wooden" and "stoic.")[36]

When Tryon got his first script, he saw that there was plenty of action, so he spent two months training with Dick Farnsworth, one of the best stunt men in the business.

He wanted to do all his own stunts because he felt that kids would know when a double took over. Tryon was also given a chance to sing in the series (a capella). He proved he had a pleasant enough voice but singing was not one of his talents.

There were a number of roles in the Slaughter series which carried through several episodes. Texas Ranger "Ben Jenkins" was prominent in the first four episodes and later reappeared as an army scout (in "The End of the Trail"). For this key character, Disney cast veteran supporting actor Harry Carey, Jr., who had appeared in scores of Westerns with, for instance, John Wayne (*Red River*, 1948; *Three Godfathers*, 1948; *She Wore a Yellow Ribbon*, 1949; *Rio Grande*, 1950). Disney had previously used Carey in *The Great Locomotive Chase* in 1956.

Newcomer Norma Moore played Slaughter's first love and eventual wife Adeline ("Addie") during the first six episodes. After a long courtship, she marries John at the beginning of "Man from Bitter Creek," has two babies and dies at the conclusion of the next episode ("Slaughter Trail"). Slaughter thus (in keeping with historical fact) becomes a widower with two small children to raise—Addie, played by Annette Gorman, and Willie, played by Brian Corcoran.

In the seventh episode, "Robber Stallion," Slaughter meets Ashley, a wealthy young Easterner who has come West to become "a man." Played by Darryl Hickman, Ashley became a regular character, appearing intermittently through the last ten episodes as a sort of surrogate older son. Hickman was the older brother of Dwayne Hickman, who gained television fame as Dobie Gillis. Darryl had been groomed by his stage mother to become a star and had appeared as a child actor in a number of late thirties and forties films (*The Grapes of Wrath*, 1940, *The Star Maker*, *Rhapsody in Blue*, 1945). Darryl also played Dobie Gillis' brother for one season in *The Many Loves of Dobie Gillis*.

When Slaughter moves to Tombstone, Arizona, in the ninth episode ("Range War at Tombstone"), he meets Viola, the beautiful daughter of a local rancher. Their relationship is often stormy, but John eventually marries Viola (in "Kentucky Gunslick"), providing the series with frequent opportunities to depict the domestic life of a family living on the cattle frontier. Texas John Slaughter has the distinction of being the first television cowboy who has to discipline his children and take them on picnics as well as learn how to dance while tracking down rustlers and fighting off Indians.

Betty Lynn, an actress with some previous television experience (on *The Ray Bolger Show*, 1953-54 and *Love That Jill*, 1958), played the spunky, auburn-haired "Vi." She was later to become more famous as Barney's sweetheart, Thelma Lou, on *The Andy Griffith Show*.

In "Apache Friendship," a black character, John Raymond Beaumont ("Bat"), appears for the first time. He's the "best tracker in the West," who can also cook, wrangle horses and herd cattle. (According to the Slaughter children he could also "whittle, make taffy pull, tie fancy knots, cure warts, grow hair on bald people, swim underwater with his eyes open, and wrestle alligators.") Disney thus had the distinction of presenting the first television Western with a continuing black cowboy character. James Edwards, who had won plaudits in Stanley Kramer's war film about racial prejudice, *Home of the Brave* (1949), was cast as Bat. Bat was depicted as educated, articulate, self-confident, brave, and intelligent. In sum, he was a complicated and intriguing character who was, perhaps, not unlike thousands of real black cowboys who roamed the West. (It would not be until the final season of *Rawhide* that another black cowboy would become a regular in a television Western.)

A series of episodes chronicling John Slaughter's relationship with the Apaches introduces several new continuing, characters including Nachez, son of Cochise (played by

Tom Tryon "made 'em do what they oughter" as Texas John Slaughter.

Jay Siverheels following his retirement as Tonto), Geronimo (played by Pat Hogan), and General Miles (portrayed by Onslow Stevens, a former television regular on *This Is the Life*, 1952–1956). The final Geronimo episode dramatizes the true story of the role played by Slaughter in capturing the renegade Apache chief ("The End of the Trail").

Many other characters appear in a few episodes and then are killed off or disappear. They were usually played by established screen stars like Robert Middleton, Dan Duryea, Beverly Garland, Stephen McNally, Sidney Blackmer, Harold J. Stone, Jim Davis, Grant Williams, Bill Williams, Allan Lane and R.G. Armstrong.

The final three Texas John Slaughter episodes dealt with his exploits as sheriff of Tombstone.

Disney continued to feature Western heroes on *Walt Disney Presents* during the

1960-61 season. He began the year with back to back reruns of the Davy Crockett-Mike Fink adventures and then brought back *Zorro* for four brand new hour-long stories. Each episode featured the regulars from the old show (Williams, Calvin, Sheldon, Lewis and others) plus special guest stars like Gilbert Roland (in "El Bandido," October 30, 1960) and Ricardo Montalban (in "Auld Acquaintance," April 2, 1961). There was lots of action, plenty of humor and several new songs to provide rousing good entertainment. In the last "Zorro" segment, Don Diego even reveals his identity to an old rival from Spain—but, of course, to no consequence since no one will believe him.

Disney also introduced one new Western series on *Walt Disney Presents* during that season, featuring another frontier hero—one cut from the same pattern as Davy Crockett and perhaps even more famous, Daniel Boone. Boone, who lived from 1734 to 1820, had been an able woodsman, a diplomat in Indian dealings, a man of courage and a symbol of American pioneering, having wandered during his lifetime from Berks County, Pennsylvania, where he was born, via the North Carolina mountains to Kentucky, western Missouri and the Platte River. Walt introduced the first episode and set the stage for the three episodes that were to follow by comparing the activities of the frontier pathfinders to our modern astronauts, who in 1960 were just beginning their quest to reach the moon:

> Down through the ages man has been impelled for one reason or another to break away from the established order of things and push beyond the boundaries of civilization to find out what was on the other side of the mountain or the other side of the sea. The Norsemen set out for conquest; Columbus to prove a theory; Henry Hudson to find the Northwest Passage; and now modern astronauts to find out not what's on the other side of the mountain, but on the other side of the moon. These men were and are, the trailblazers—the first to venture into the realm of the unknown in their respective fields.
>
> Here in America we've had many famous trailblazers, Ponce de Leon, Cortez, La Salle, Lewis and Clark, but, perhaps the most famous trailblazer of them all was Daniel Boone.

As in the case of Elfego Baca, Disney selected Boone's most famous adventures for the first segment of his series, entitled "The Warriors' Path" and broadcast on December 4, 1960. In May of 1769, Boone with his old friend John Finley and a party of four companions, had crossed through Cumberland Gap into the upper reaches of the south fork of the Kentucky River and wandered down near the mouth of Station Camp Creek. For the next two years Boone had roamed about central Kentucky, most of the time alone. During this period he had had some trouble with the Indians, but it had given him an excellent opportunity to study the land, and fall in love with it. Disney took some dramatic liberties with this story. Finley and another of Boone's companions were killed in the first episode, but the historical context was essentially accurate. Subsequent episodes related the true story of Boone's role in opening the area to white settlement, developing the "Wilderness Road" and finally leading the movement west into "the promised land" of Missouri. Unlike Disney's other Western heroes, Daniel Boone was not given a theme song. He did, however, get to warble a love ballad from time to time.

To play the Fess Parker–type role, Disney selected the relatively unknown Dewey Martin. Martin had appeared in a minor role in *The Kansas Raiders* in 1950 with Audie Murphy and had graduated to the second male lead in Howard Hawks' 1952 filming of A.B. Guthrie, Jr.'s classic novel *The Big Sky*, starring Kirk Douglas. Martin's previous television experience included the pilot of an unsold series, *Doc*, in which he would have starred as Doc Holliday, telecast on *Dick Powell's Zane Grey Theater*, and guest appearances on other dramatic anthologies such as *Front Row Center*. Martin was both handsome and competent, but he did not have the charisma that Fess Parker obviously had and the Daniel Boone series never "took off." (Disney did later star Martin in a film sequel to *Old Yeller* called *Savage Sam* in 1963.)

The 1960-61 season was to mark Walt Disney's final use of Western heroes on his weekly television program. There were several reasons for this. One was that Disney had grown tired of Westerns. He felt that they were stifling his creativity. In an interview, Disney told author Leonard Maltin:

> I gave ABC their first full-hour Western series with my Davy Crockett shows and soon the network was flooded with other Westerns. They made so much money for ABC that before long I found myself in a straitjacket. I no longer had the freedom of action I enjoyed in those first three years. They kept insisting that I do more and more Westerns and my show became loaded with Elfego Baca, Texas John Slaughter and Daniel Boone. I found myself competing with *Maverick*, *Wyatt Earp* and every other Western myth. When I came up with a fresh idea in another field, the network executives would say no.[37]

(ABC used the Western episodes of *Walt Disney Presents* to promote its own Western series by inserting frequent "promos" for *Maverick*, *Cheyenne*, *Lawman* and others.) The other reason for the shelving of Western heroes was related to Disney's interest in color television. Even though ABC had telecast his show in black and white, all of the new material was filmed in color. Other Hollywood producers considered that an unwise extravagance, but Walt was certain that color would add future value to the shows. (Actually this proved profitable to the Disney Studio almost immediately as a number of the series were edited for theatrical release as feature films including the aforementioned two Crockett films, two Elfego Baca films and four Texas John Slaughter films.)

In order to make the change to color television, Disney felt it necessary to change networks. NBC seemed the obvious place for this since the network was already promoting color. (Its parent company, RCA, manufactured color television sets.) Part of the agreement with NBC involved a decision to abandon *all* previously established characters.[38] It meant good-bye to Davy Crockett, Zorro, Elfego Baca, Texas John Slaughter and Disney's other Western video heroes.

To make an accurate assessment of Disney's contribution to the development of the television Western, it is necessary to point out that he did not, as he later claimed, "invent" the adult Western. There were adult Westerns already in development: *Wyatt Earp* and *Cheyenne* were in the planning stages; *Death Valley Days* had been in syndication since 1952 and *Gunsmoke*, which had debuted on radio that same year, was already being adapted for television by Charles Marquis Warren. J. Fred MacDonald has explained the Disney contribution most succinctly:

> ...the commercial and cultural impact of *Davy Crockett*, and the attractive Western characters [Disney] developed on *Disneyland*, gave strong support to those who may have decided that the time was propitious to take the video Western out of its adolescence and introduce it as mature drama. The history of the genre during the next decade and a half is testimony to the soundness of such a business and cultural decision.[39]

Disney achieved this by making television Westerns of high technical and dramatic quality that would appeal to his traditional juvenile audience, but with a sufficiently "adult" orientation to attract a more mature audience as well. Furthermore, the Disney Westerns were unique in a number of ways: their emphasis on family life, realistically portraying the wives and children of Davy Crockett (although ignoring his second marriage), Texas John Slaughter and Daniel Boone; their use of Hispanic heroes like Elfago Baca and Zorro; the depiction of both "good" and "bad" whites as well as "good" and "bad"

Indians, especially in the Andy Burnett series; and finally and most significantly, their use of "dynamic" (developing) characters.

Film historian Douglas Brode has pointed out that while most literary characters are constantly growing and changing, this was rare in television Westerns where characters tended to be static and unchanging.[40] The Disney characters changed in virtually every episode, the only truly dynamic Western characters on television. For example, Don Diego's father finally discovers his son's secret identity as Zorro and then becomes part of his fight against tyranny, even impersonating Zorro himself at times. Furthermore, Davy Crockett's adjustment to the death of his first wife illustrates how characters are forced to adapt to changing situations and conditions. The Elfego Baca episodes not only portray his career change from lawman to lawyer, but the subsequent modification of his behavior (speaking more like an educated man in the later stories) and dress (going from jeans and chaps to suits and ties). It also shows him growing a moustache (perhaps a first for fifties television).

The most unusual example of a dynamically changing character was Disney's version of Texas John Slaughter, even though he perhaps appeared to be the most traditional: tall, handsome, white, with a big white hat and a pearl-handled six-gun strapped to his hip. The stories dealt with his various life cycles, from Texas Ranger in his youth to small rancher, to drifter (after the death of his first wife), to eventual cattle baron, to military scout (for General Miles), to lawman in Tombstone. With each of those changes, Slaughter became a different person.

The Disney Westerns also dealt in an educational way with such sensitive issues as racial and ethnic prejudice (toward Indians in the Davy Crockett and Andy Burnett episodes, toward blacks in the Texas John Slaughter episodes, and toward Hispanics in the Elfego Baca episodes) and death and dying (with the deaths of Davy Crockett and Georgie Russell at the Alamo, of Jack Kelly in the Andy Burnett series and of Texas John Slaughter's first wife). As Brode points out, the scene that perhaps best illustrates the Disney approach to real life in the real West is one showing the macho he-man hero Texas John Slaughter trying to diaper one of his babies (in "The Slaughter Trail"). In the Disney conception of life in the West, the hero was a man who did not simply kiss the girl and ride off into the sunset, but one who had to develop a lasting relationship with his wife and children.

Certainly Walt Disney had taken the television Western a long way from the Saturday matinee shoot-'em-ups. *Gunsmoke* would take it still further.

III. Television Westerns Grow Up
THE RISE OF "GUNSMOKE"
AND THE ADULT WESTERN

While Disney's Westerns were aimed primarily at children and youth, other programs were being developed that were designed for the prime time adult viewer. By the mid-fifties, the assumption that Westerns were just for kids began to change, as theatrical films such as *High Noon* (1952) and *Shane* (1953) placed more complex and serious themes in Western settings. These films, which were critical and commercial successes, became known as "adult Westerns." In its waning years, radio drama also had experimented with Western stories aimed at a mature audience and although, with the exception of *Gunsmoke*, the shows were short-lived, most critics agree that several were among the best quality dramatic programs ever broadcast (e.g., *The Six Shooter*, starring James Stewart as the frontier-drifting maverick Britt Ponsett; *Frontier Town*, relating stories about lawyer Chad Remington, played by Jeff Chandler and later Reed Hadley; *Frontier Gentleman*, with John Dehner as J.B. Kendall, a reporter for the *London Times* touring the West of the 1870s; and *Fort Laramie*, featuring Raymond Burr as Captain Lee Quince in dramas about life in the United States Cavalry).

The adult Western is a difficult genre to define. Ralph Brauer has concluded that the networks' idea of adultness simply meant that the shows must have more violence.[1] While Hoppy, Gene, Roy and the Lone Ranger merely shot the gun out of the villain's hand, the adult Western hero would usually kill him or at least beat him senseless. According to J. Fred MacDonald, the components of the adult Western include a distinct type of sponsor ("expensive, obviously adult products" like automobiles, beer, cigarettes and soap products); "characters that broke old stereotypes" (if they made mistakes, "they were compelled to suffer the consequences"); "attractive young men in starring roles" (e.g., James Garner, James Arness, Hugh O'Brian, Steve McQueen, Clint Walker); experienced and talented personnel behind the scenes, writing and directing (e.g., Charles Marques Warren, Sam Fuller, Budd Boetticher, Toy Garnett); in sum, a genre which blended "dramatic conflict, human insight, outdoor beauty, and subtle moralizing" without eliminating action.[2] The genre was defined during the golden age of television Westerns by *Time Magazine*:

> The new horse operas are generically known as adult Westerns, a term first used to
> describe the shambling, down-to-biscuits realism of "Gunsmoke", but there are numerous

subspecies. First came the psychological half-breeds, paranoid bluecoats, and amnesic prospectors. Then there was the Civil Rights Western and all the persecuted Piutes, molested
Mexicans, downtrodden Jewish drummers and tormented Chinese laundrymen had their
day. Scriptwriters are now riding farther from the train, rustling plots from De Maupassant,
Stevenson, even Aristophanes, introducing foreigners and dabbling in rape, incest, miscege-
nation, and cannibalism.[3]

Obviously, the characters in the adult Western had more substance than the stereotypical B Western variety. Here one found a hero who was more human and consequently
more believable than the one dimensional stars of the kiddie Westerns—a complex mixture of good and evil, strength and weakness. The hero of the adult Western could have
doubts, make mistakes, and have misgivings about what he had to do. The villains in
adult Westerns also were a different breed. There were no totally evil and cowardly
characters motivated solely by greed or a lust for power, as was so often the case in juvenile
Westerns; the villains could be the victims of circumstances beyond their control. Frequently psychological problems and social conditions were motivational factors influenc-
ing evildoers in adult Westerns. As sociologist Martin Nussbaum explained:

> . . . the authors of the "adult westerns" set about to humanize their characters. They ex-
> plained why Blackie was bad and that he wasn't all bad. They showed that the hero wasn't
> all good . . . and that he was capable of some costly mistakes. What they accomplished, in
> effect, was to graft on to western characters the emotions, fears, inadequacies, and psychoses
> of modern man. But problems that remain unsolved in life, must be solved in stories, so they
> salvaged the old good-evil concept and converted it to a concept of judicial right and wrong.
> Thus the western espouses that all men are a combination of good and evil, but that some,
> by their own volition or circumstances beyond their power, have placed themselves on the
> wrong side of the law, a law which transcends man's law and has overtones of moralistic law.
> It falls to the western hero, then, to judge the rightness and wrongness of an act and to satisfy
> the law if it has been violated. . . .[4]

Longtime *New York Herald Tribune* radio and television critic John Crosby described
the "adult Western" in considerably less scientific language:

> There have been a lot of changes out West since you and I were young, Maggie. The
> cowboy heroes are not only tall and handsome these days but now they have to have
> psychiatric training to understand the bad men. [And] when I was a child, the only good In-
> dian was a dead Indian. . . . Now Cochise . . . [is] a man whose word is never broken, whose
> honor is like stainless steel and who talks as if he graduated from Oxford. . . .
> . . . Back when I was a boy, the bad guy's sister never apologized for his conduct. Come
> to think of it, the bad guys never had a sister. They never had a mother, either. They were
> bad out of pure orneriness because they liked it that way. Now, of course, the bad guys have
> mothers and fathers too, and all that evil dates back to some childhood trauma. They're just
> crazy mixed-up kids and you feel sorry for them when the sheriff cuts them down.[5]

It was, consequently, not unusual to find in this new breed of Western the controversial themes that had been so scrupulously avoided in juvenile Westerns. In addition
to excessive violence, there were stories dealing with sex, religion, and racial discrimination—especially towards Native Americans—in most successful "adult Westerns."
There was also a much greater attempt at historical accuracy in these programs, although
literary license was taken whenever producers did not find truth to be more exciting than
fiction.

Most television historians cite 1955 as the year when the adult Western made its initial appearance on the home screen. However, *Death Valley Days* preceded that landmark
season's *Gunsmoke* and *Wyatt Earp* more than three years earlier. *Death Valley Days*, a
dramatic anthology of true stories of the old West, was one of radio's earliest and longest-

running adventure shows. It was broadcast over NBC Blue from 1930 until 1941 when it switched to CBS, where it aired until leaving radio in 1945.

Ruth Woodman, creator of the show, was working for the McCann-Erickson Advertising Agency in 1930 when one of their clients, then called Pacific Coast Borax Company, maker of 20 Mule Team Borax, requested assistance in increasing sales. The agency suggested that the then relatively new medium of radio be utilized to promote their product and proposed that some use should be made of Death Valley, the unique and little-known setting in which borax was produced. At the time Woodman, a former copywriter who had become a radio scriptwriter, was given the assignment of writing the audition script. Woodman, a longtime New Yorker who had graduated from Vassar and married a banker, knew nothing about the desert and even less about Death Valley. She wrote a story about the discovery of borax completely from reference books. The company liked the script and bought the concept. Woodman decided she had better visit Death Valley personally to become familiar with the area she was expected to write about. This was the first of many such trips she made not only to soak up the atmosphere, but to dig up actual stories about Death Valley.

The man who became her guide (named Wash Cahill) on these visits was a real desert rat with a broad Irish face who worked for the Borax Company. Wash knew almost everyone in the region and as he took Woodman around he would talk about the local history and introduce her to small town newspaper editors, old men who ran gas stations, proprietors of general stores, bartenders and others who had tales of their own to tell. All the while, she would be writing story ideas and information down in her notebook. Wash Cahill became her model for the character of the Old Ranger who was the host and narrator of the show. *Death Valley Days* was a radio hit and sales of Borax boomed. The opening bugle call became familiar to listeners as announcer Dresser Dahlstead intoned:

> As the early morning bugle call of covered wagon trains fades away among the echoes, another true *Death Valley Days* story is presented for your entertainment by the Pacific Coast Borax Company, producers of that famous family of products—20 Mule Team Borax, 20 Mule Team Borax Chips, and Boraxo. Well, Old Ranger, what's your story about tonight?

Jack MacBryde would then begin a vignette about some prospector, homesteader, bandit, saloon entertainer, lawman or the like whose life had been changed by his or her experiences in the Death Valley region.

In 1945, the Pacific Borax Company dropped the show in favor of a new series, *The Sheriff*, and *Death Valley Days* disappeared for almost eight years. When original material for television became hard to find, the show was revived for the new medium and it became even more successful than it had been on radio. For the opening television broadcast, Woodman selected the story of "How Death Valley Got Its Name." The dramatic tale of the exhausted, bedraggled group of Forty-niners, staggering blindly over the oven-hot desert in a desperate search for water, was brought to life. They found death instead of water, and months later, when a lone prospector stumbled across their bleached bones, turned chalky white in the 130-degree heat, Death Valley got its name. The story was syndicated in two parts and first broadcast on October 4, 1952. *Variety* (October 6, 1952) gave the series a favorable review:

> The transition has been made [from radio] with ease and the new series should enjoy a consistent, though not necessarily tremendous, following.
> Initial teleplay by Mrs. Ruth Woodman [is] told with an almost documentary fidelity that enhances the atmosphere.... Production by Dorrell McGowan takes full advantage of

the rugged country to enhance the grimness of the situation and Stuart McGowan's good direction paces a well-selected cast through better-than-average performances.

The series was filmed on location in the depths of Death Valley. The cast and crew flew in from Hollywood to film episodes about six times a year. (They did not, however, have to endure the hardships of the early settlers. Staying at the valley's Furnace Creek Inn, they enjoyed all the accommodations of a luxurious desert spa complete with swimming pool.) Most of the stories on *Death Valley Days* were of the human-interest variety, with the emphasis on gentle comedy and drama rather than violence and action. Nat Perin, the producer, asserted in a 1960 interview:

> We don't necessarily avoid violence, but we don't use it for the sake of violence alone. I think there's too much of it on TV. There are far too many shows featuring guys clutching their bellies and dying ... we are perfectly willing to let other westerns monopolize the gunplay-and-gore plots.... We feel that true stories have much more appeal.[6]

The educational flavor of the shows resulted in the series' being singled out for some 300 awards, including the prized Freedom Foundation's George Washington medal. The program also received the Southern California Historical Society's Award of Honor, the first time that award was ever presented to an entertainment medium. In contrast with other television Westerns, both juvenile and adult, *Death Valley Days* never presented a story without a solid basis in fact. Each program was carefully researched. Still, a few notable errors did creep in from time to time. The mistake which drew the largest amount of mail occurred in a story about a Mormon wagon train. In the tale, a member of the party was found unconscious in the desert. A fellow Mormon was depicted brewing a cup of coffee to revive him. Thousands of letters poured in pointing out that coffee is a stimulant and the Mormon religion specifically bans all stimulants. Another mistake occurred when General Custer was shown riding a bay at the Little Big Horn when in fact he rode a black stallion.

Although the stories on *Death Valley Days* clearly took precedence over the actors and actresses in them, a cast listing of the 558 episodes filmed reads like a Hollywood who's who. Many established stars like Cameron Mitchell, Jane Russell, Yvonne DeCarlo, Tony Martin, Ralph Bellamy, Jeffrey Hunter, Howard Keel, George Gobel, Forrest Tucker, Rory Calhoun, Gilbert Roland, Ronald Reagan, and Robert Taylor appeared, as well as newcomers soon to make their mark, like Fess Parker, Angie Dickinson, James Franciscus, Anne Francis, Robert Blake, Ken Curtis, James Caan, Clint Eastwood, Bethel Leslie, Carroll O'Connor, DeForrest Kelly, Robert Culp, David Janssen, Gavin MacLeod, Vic Morrow, Doug McClure, Mariette Hartley, Dabney Coleman, and Jamie Farr.

The most memorable feature of television's *Death Valley Days* was the host who introduced and closed each story. The first and longest running was Stanley Andrews, the Old Ranger (12 years), followed by Ronald Reagan (one year), Robert Taylor (two years), and Dale Robertson (four years). Later *Death Valley Days* was seen in reruns under a variety of titles and with different hosts including *Call of the West* (John Payne), *Frontier Adventure* (Dale Robertson), *The Pioneers* (Will Rogers, Jr.), *Trails West* (Ray Milland), and *Western Star Theatre* (Rory Calhoun).

Virtually every historical character associated with the Southwest was depicted over the years on the show—from Lotta Crabtree, Lola Montez, Joaquin Murrieta, and Black Bart to Pat Garrett, Samuel Clemens, Emperor Norton and Billy the Kid. Typical plots related the stories of the first woman judge fighting corruption in a rough and tumble

Maria Desti and Dale Robertson guest star on an episode of *Death Valley Days* entitled "The Biggest Post Office in the USA."

frontier town; an ex-cop from New York trying to maintain law and order in a rowdy Western town without a six-gun; a woman struggling to establish a medical practice in a dusty desert town; an honest state senator being killed in a duel by an unscrupulous judge; an eccentric inventer building the first prairie schooner; a frontier postman delivering the last letter in his sack to a young miner; a town moving its city limits to secure a railroad right-of-way, and hundreds of similar tales.

On December 27, 1960, Filmaster, producers of *Death Valley Days*, announced that a host of records had been set by the series:

> TV's longest running dramatic show nationally aired...;
>
> The TV version as probably giving work to more actors, 2,052 or more, than any other show since the start of commercial TV...;
>
> DVD has undoubtedly given more work to creative talent, writers and directors, than any other drama series in TV.
>
> Over 900 scripts have aired in the past 30 years representing 90,000 hours of script research and constituting some 3,000,000 words of dialog.
>
> [The series] has never been out of the Top 10 in the ratings for syndicated shows, playing to a cumulative audience of more than 2,000,000,000.
>
> It marks the longest association, unqualifiedly, of one person with one show in, quite possibly, the entire history of show business, but certainly in the history of broadcasting [Ruth Woodman since 1932]....
>
> It marks one of TV's longest running acting jobs [Stanley Andrews as the Old Ranger from 1952 to 1964]....
>
> And finally, it marks the longest association of one sponsor with one show [U.S. Borax, since 1932]....

(Many of these records would later be surpassed by *Gunsmoke*.) *TV Guide*, at about the same time, credited *Death Valley Days* with originating the adult Western:

> ... if the term adult western means a more mature western show than the standard goodies-and-baddies theme, then the syndicated "Death Valley Days" must be credited with having originated the idea several seasons before ["Gunsmoke"].

Although no new episodes were produced after 1972, the series was in continuous syndication until 1975. From 1975 to 1982, the show was seen in reruns on only a handful of local stations. Then Art Newberger, a former music promoter who had handled Stevie Wonder, Gladys Knight and Smokey Robinson among others, approached Borax with a deal giving him the distribution rights to *Death Valley Days* for seven years in exchange for sharing the profits with Borax. The renewed interest in the show was, of course, the result of Ronald Reagan's election to the Presidency. Reagan had appeared in 21 episodes (including 13 as host) just before he was elected governor of California. President Reagan's career definitely had moments of life imitating art, or at least of life imitating a good television Western. In fact, Reagan's life story might have provided material for an episode of *Death Valley Days*, if he had only lived a century earlier. One cannot get much more realistic than that.

Another adult Western anthology series, *Frontier*, debuted on September 25, 1955, for NBC, just 15 days after *Gunsmoke*. The series was quite good, with the emphasis, as in *Death Valley Days*, on the stories rather than the stars. Violence was minimized and life in the West was deglamorized on *Frontier*. Realism was stressed and most plots portrayed settlers coping with the harsh environment as well as the more typical villains, outlaws and Indians. Walter Coy, a real six-foot, two-inch Westerner who grew up in the rugged mining and cattle country of Great Falls, Montana, occasionally starred. His opening was simple, but memorable:

> This is the West. This is the land of beginning again. This is the story of men and women facing the frontier. This is the way it happened...

Although *Frontier* stressed human emotions and psychological influences, rather than gun duels and chases, it did not lack for action. In the initial episode, "Paper Gunman," for example, a village handyman (sensitively portrayed by John Smith) is falsely publicized as a vicious gunman by an imaginative newspaper reporter. (He is trying to prove that most gunslingers are the creation of publicity.) It works, as the newsman has predicted, but only as long as the handyman (now called "The Colfax Kid") is able to frighten his victims through his reputation. When the "Paper Gunman" begins to believe his own publicity, he is challenged by a legitimate gunman, who refuses to be scared and ends up killing him. The writers (Morton Fine and David Friedkin) delve into the mind of the handyman in an attempt to explain why he took his fabricated newspaper clippings seriously.

Perhaps the best story in the series was its third episode, "A Stillness in Wyoming," also by Fine and Friedkin. It is the story of a range war between sheepmen and cattlemen. The sons of the leaders of the two warring factions meet and become friends. When the cattleman's son attempts to help his friend drive his sheep out of harm's way, he is mistakenly shot and killed by his own father's hired killer. This tragedy brings the feud to an end and as Coy explains:

> To the South and West, clear to Wind River, the bloody war raged between sheepmen and cattlemen. But here, in this place the land was shared, and there was a stillness in Wyoming. It happened that way ... moving West.

The series drew outstanding reviews from the critics. *Variety* (September 22, 1955) wrote after the first broadcast:

> With "Paper Gunman," the new NBC-TV "Frontier" series made an auspicious debut into the video arena.... [I]f "Frontier" maintains the promise of the first presentation, it may prove a giant among the new crop of "adult" Westerns.

TV Guide, even more lavish in its praise, said:

> "Frontier," one of several new "adult" Western series, eschews the exploits of guntoting marshals and other popular heroes to concentrate on the more ordinary people who helped settle the West. The result is an absorbing telefilm show, well worth tuning in....
> ... The actors are good and the scripts are tautly written. The sets, costumes and other production trappings have been uniformly excellent.

Unfortunately the viewing audience did not agree and *Frontier* lasted only one season (30 episodes) and has not been seen since.

One other quality Western anthology series deserves mention: *Dick Powell's Zane Grey Theatre*. Although it premiered more than a year after *Frontier*, it was in several respects superior and certainly more popular. The program remained on the air for five seasons and produced 147 episodes.

The initial idea for the series came from radio. *The Zane Grey Radio Show* premiered on Mutual September 11, 1947, and ran one season presenting "tales of the old West — rugged frontier stories of a young nation, where strong men lived by the strong law of personal justice." Although the show owed little to the author after whom the program was named, the writers did occasionally deal with adult themes. In one broadcast, for example, the murderer, although apprehended in the end, was spared from hanging when the court found him criminally insane. Still the central character in most of the episodes was only one step removed from the traditional juvenile Western hero. Tex Thorne (played first by Vic Perrin, later by Don MacLaughlin) was Zane Grey's Pony Express rider who rode a trusty steed named Topaz. Accompanied by his sidekick, Sandy Fletcher, Thorne went around uttering such banalities as, "Don't throw lead at me unless you want your lead back with interest," and "I'm footloose and following the tumbleweed; no woman is dabbin' a rope on my carcass."[7]

The television version began as a legitimate attempt to dramatize adaptations of the short stories and novels of Zane Grey. In fact, the rights to at least forty such works were acquired by Four Star Films before shooting began on the first episode. Dick Powell, however, soon discovered that most of the novels were too bulky and complicated for 30 minute dramas. Thus, except for an occasional incident or character created by Grey, the scripts were all original. A number of the better stories were written by Aaron Spelling, Sterling Silliphant and Louis King, each of whom was to leave his mark later on the development of television drama.

Respected actor Dick Powell was the host and sometimes featured star on the series. He would present a factual and interesting commentary on some aspect of early Western history before each story began (e.g., on guns before "Trouble at Tres Cruces" and on hats before "The Long Shadow"). There was no shortage of talent that appeared in one or more episodes of *Zane Grey Theatre*, including many stars not usually associated with Westerns: Walter Pidgeon in "Pressure Point," Hedy Lamarr in "Proud Woman," Joan Crawford in "Rebel Ranger," Ginger Rogers in "Never Too Late," Mary Astor in "Black Is for Grief," Claudette Colbert in "So Young the Savage Land" and Esther Williams in "The Black Wagon." Other stars who appeared in the series, which ran between 1956 and 1961, included Robert Ryan, James Whitmore, Lew Ayres, Jack Palance, Lee J. Cobb,

Eddie Albert, Walter Brennan, John Ireland, Rory Calhoun, Ralph Bellamy, Lloyd Bridges, Stuart Whitman, Ernest Borgnine, Dean Jagger, Barbara Stanwyck, Mac-Donald Carey, Michael Rennie, Barry Sullivan, Thomas Mitchell, Gary Merrill, Van Johnson, Sammy Davis, Jr., Mel Ferrer, Cesar Romero, Danny and daughter Marlo Thomas (in her television debut), Raymond Massey, Burl Ives, Jack Lemmon, Art Linkletter and his son Jack, Edward G. Robinson and his son Edward, Jr., and future President Ronald Reagan and his wife Nancy Davis (in "The Long Shadow").

As Powell explained in an interview about the success of the show, "We cannot depend on the script alone; it must be complemented by the finest of actors and actresses."[8] No doubt Powell's long association with the motion picture industry was a great help in attracting such a formidable array of stars. Powell had been one of the most popular singing and dancing stars of Warner Bros.' lavish thirties musicals. He later became famous for his hard-boiled, wise-cracking detective roles during the late forties. When he entered television as one of the partners in Four Star Films, Inc., he wore many hats: actor, producer, director and narrator. His *Zane Grey Theatre* presented the pilot episodes for four other television Westerns subsequently produced by Four Star: *Trackdown*, with Robert Culp ("Badge of Honor"), *The Rifleman*, with Chuck Connors ("Sharpshooter"), *Johnny Ringo*, with Don Durant ("The Loner"), and *The Westerner*, with Brian Keith ("Trouble at Tres Cruces").

Critics liked the series too. *TV Guide* called it "an educated 20th century view of the Old West" and *Variety* (October 8, 1956) referred to the series as "interesting" and "well-produced," with Dick Powell as "a good host." After five seasons of original programs, CBS carried *Dick Powell's Zane Grey Theatre* for an extra season with reruns of the best previous episodes.

The contributions of dramatic anthologies to the development of the Western genre on television notwithstanding, the term "adult Western" itself had been used by Norman Macdonnell and John Meston as early as 1952. They were trying to create a radio series that was different from other Westerns. Since the American public was accustomed in 1952, with only a few exceptions in literature and film, to the Western as a form of entertainment geared for children, why not design a Western which adults would enjoy? To accomplish this Macdonnell, a director and producer, and Meston, a writer, sought to build a radio series that would rely on historical accuracy more than most other Westerns had done and that would be free from as many of the traditional Western clichés as possible. Their series would eliminate many of the things cowboys always did in Westerns, like heros always shooting better than anyone else, cowboys calling their horses by name, and heroes wearing white hats while villains wore black hats.

The key element was to be the fallibility of the hero. This was perhaps the most important innovation of Macdonnell and Meston: a hero who made mistakes. This fallibility would extend to all characters in the stories: a hotel owner who is more worried about cowboys' burning down his hotel than about a man who has pledged to shoot the marshal in the back; a doctor who cannot resist one more beer; the marshal's handyman, who can never make a decent cup of coffee; a saloon hostess who once explained that she broke her toe when a 16 year-old Texan tramped on it dancing.

One of the guiding principles of the new radio program, *Gunsmoke*, was the concept that in the early West the most hated man in town was usually the marshal. This idea was expressed week after week in the program's opening:

> DILLON: I'm that man... Matt Dillon... United States Marshal... The first man they look for and the last they want to meet... It's a chancy job and it makes a man watchful and a little lonely.

Much of the authenticity in *Gunsmoke* came from the wealth of reading both Meston and Macdonnell had done over the years in the Western genre. John Meston had an extensive Western library, to which he was constantly adding. Furthermore, he was a native of Pueblo, Colorado, and as a youngster had worked on cattle ranches and spent many hours listening to cowboys tell tall tales. Many of these later appeared, in different forms, on *Gunsmoke*.

This authenticity involved such seemingly minor considerations as only allowing five shots to be fired from any six-shooter, since in the 1870s, the pistol's hammer always rested on an empty chamber; keeping Kansas, Texas, Oklahoma, and Colorado geography straight; not using the names of Indian tribes which were not in the area; keeping horses to a lope instead of a full gallop except on rare occasions; and using authentic Western speech patterns and expressions. Still, this accuracy was never the only goal of the production. Macdonnell and Meston, like Zane Grey, never let accuracy hinder their storytelling. As Macdonnell later admitted in an interview in *TV Guide*:

> You have to temper honesty with showmanship. If we were completely honest, Kitty would be a heavily painted 58-year-old hag who bathed twice a month whether she needed to or not. And Dillon would go around wearing a derby hat and starched collars. You have to make compromises.[9]

Radio's *Gunsmoke* differed in one other significant way from other Westerns. Meston and Macdonnell experimented in the use of sound effects ("patterns") which other programs would have found objectionable or too subtle. For example, without using narration, they were able to change scenes by letting the character move from one location to another using only sounds to indicate movement. Macdonnell once explained:

> ... if we had to walk Matt from his office to the Long Branch, we'd walk him to the door, open the door, close the door, cross the broadwalk, clop, clop, clop, into the street, clop, clop, clop, up onto the other boardwalk, clunk, clunk, in the swinging door, bang, bang, bang.... You'd hear the boots and spurs come in, and then everybody would sort of quiet down. And you'd let that run for eight, ten, fifteen seconds, and you could just see Matt come up and stop at the bar. Well, they'd never done this before on radio; so it was a great picture painted right before your ears; great fun.... And he [Matt] wouldn't have said a word.[10]

John Meston's description of *Gunsmoke*'s hero bears little resemblance to juvenile radio heroes like Hopalong Cassidy or Gene Autry:

> Dodge at that time was the wildest town in America.... Consider this—the West just after the Civil War was in a sense a kind of arena for frustrated gladiators. Homicidal psychopaths gathered along the frontier and had themselves a real circus with little or nothing to stop them from happily mowing one another down. And that more men didn't die in this senseless slaughter may be laid to their comparatively primitive weapons and certainly not to any civilized tendencies on their part. It ended finally. The murderers killed one another off and gradually disappeared from this section of the American scene. But the end was partly hastened by a few strangers who happened to get their satisfaction from killing on the side of the law—sheriffs, marshals and the like. I'm sure a few of these men had a hazy sense of what the coming of law and order meant, but for the most part they looked on their role in the play of progress simply as a job. And, they went ahead and did their job-often in the face of unbelievable odds—and then picked up their paychecks and went their way.
>
> Heroes? To us now they were heroes, but to their contemporaries their biggest hero was he who, by what ever means, murdered the greatest number of men. The rules were childishly simple. If the other man went for his gun before you did, you were free to kill him with impunity. And, anyway, if there weren't too many unfriendly witnesses about, you could always claim he did and probably get by with it just as easily.
>
> Matt Dillon, because of obvious reasons, is a cut above the lawman I've described. But he's not, I trust, so far above the real thing as to be pure fiction.[11]

Marshal Matt Dillon was the only continuing role in the radio program when it first went on the air. For this role, Macdonnell and Meston picked William Conrad from among the actors who auditioned. Conrad was the narrator on *Escape*, a show which Macdonnell also produced and directed, and Conrad had worked for him on other programs as well. With his deep, dramatic voice, Conrad was often cast as a "heavy." While Matt Dillon was not supposed to be a villain, neither was he supposed to be a typical hero. Conrad projected just the right persona to convey this kind of trailworn and cynical, yet dedicated and upright, lawman. In an interview in the May 1958 *TV-Radio Mirror* Conrad, the only actor to play the role on radio, had this to say about the marshal:

> Matt Dillon is neither hero nor villain, but a human being. The best of us are sometimes ashamed of our thoughts, and there are times when the worst of us can be proud of our deeds. Matt Dillon is no different. He is a law-enforcement officer who doesn't like killings. He hates the thought of bloodshed. He's underpaid, never liked the job, but knows it has to be done. At times he's wanted to quit—has quit. But like most people who know the difference between right and wrong—and recognizing that justice could be done by him, probably better than by anyone else available—he has always come back to his responsibility. Matt Dillon isn't perfect but he's willing to try.[12]

Veteran radio actors were also cast in the other major roles, although there was no thought initially of who would or would not continue. Howard McNear was cast as a grumpy old doctor and Parley Baer played a rather foolish "hanger-on" named Chester. Georgia Ellis was selected for the part of a saloon prostitute called Kitty. After several months, it became evident that Chester, Doc and Kitty were marvelous continuing characters and Baer, McNear and Ellis joined Conrad in longterm contracts. Over the nine years *Gunsmoke* was on radio, all of these actors continued to work on other programs. They did, however, recognize that there was something different and special about *Gunsmoke* that was missing from any of the other productions on which they worked. Parley Baer later recalled:

> I think we recognized it as fine writing and as a sort of classic Western.... [B]asically it was a labor of love with everyone concerned.... I had worked on other series ... but I never quite felt about any other show, even shows that I had a running part in, like I did about *Gunsmoke*. And I know that was true with Howard McNear because he and I used to discuss it many times.... [I]t was an actor's show; it was very popular in the industry.... We were the last show, really at CBS that amounted to much, and what little red carpet treatment there was left, they gave us.[13]

The cast did a fine job delineating their characters. Matt Dillon was stern and forthright with a saving sense of irony as played by William Conrad. Doc Adams had no first name in the radio series. Based on the cartoonist Charles Adams, Doc shared Matt's dark sense of humor as well as his dedication to a job. Howard McNear as Doc shapes his sentences as carefully as he tends his patients. A well-educated Eastern doctor driven West by drink, he ministers to the people of Dodge with a blend of black humor and self-interest that keeps his character from becoming a cliché.

While Doc may have too few illusions, his friend Chester has too many. Parley Baer defined (and named) Chester Proudfoot, Matt's "helper," as an easy-going man grateful for the city comforts of Dodge. Good-natured Chester sprang from a line of hill folk who may have bred with kin one too many times. Bone-lazy, he did not have Matt's drive, but he also lacked Matt's quick temper and tendency to jump to conclusions. His embarrassment about his country relations and his desire to fit in with the townsfolk were characteristics that made Chester seem all the more human. Georgia Ellis played Kitty Russell in a Lauren Bacall style that gave her a hard-boiled edge while possessing a heart of gold. On radio, Kitty was never very sharply defined. She provided someone with whom Matt could talk out his problems. The character was much more fully developed in the television series.[14]

Gunsmoke made its first network appearance on CBS radio April 26, 1952. Cecil Smith, a columnist for *The Los Angeles Times*, described this history-making series as "the dramatization of the American epic legend of the West, our own *Iliad* and *Odyssey*, created from the standard elements of the dime novel and the pulp Western as romanticized by Buntline, Hart and Twain. It was ever the stuff of legends."[15] Those legends, facts and fantasies were brilliantly blended by John Meston in this portrayal of Dodge City, Kansas, in the 1870s. Meston's cow town was a microcosm of the American West. In the center of it was Marshal Matt Dillon. Listeners met and came to know him, his friends and his enemies, and learned of their life in a town referred to by historian Lucius Beebe as "a suburb of Hell." The picture that Meston painted of Kansas was remarkably accurate. There actually was a Front Street with a Long Branch Saloon in Dodge City. Most likely the buffalo steak served in the restaurants of the period did taste like shoe leather. And undoubtedly there were many Kittys in that "Babylon of the Plains."

Gunsmoke was hailed as the forerunner of a new breed of Western in which mature plot, fuller human characterization and intelligent theme, all enacted according to high dramatic standards, were combined to produce the most sophisticated Western drama in radio history. *Variety*'s (April 30, 1952) radio critic loved the show:

> The cactus vintage series is presented with top thespian and scripting values that pull it way ahead of the pack of AM radio westerns. It manages to dish out plenty of excitement and suspense without falling into the hokey sagebrush groove.

When the show had been on the air for almost eleven months, *Time* reported on the program:

> A "prestige program" in broadcasting circles is a show that abounds in a specific type of intelligence: it is intelligently conceived, intelligently produced and aimed at an audience with a reasonably high intelligence. It is seldom sponsored.... Such a program is *Gunsmoke*.... Producer-Director Norman Macdonnell, 36, describes *Gunsmoke* as "an adult western".... The things that happen, while exciting, are seldom contrived for the sake of violence or plot; they happen because Dillon and the people of Dodge City ... are merely people, who face human experiences.[16]

Jack Gould, *New York Times* critic, in his May 6, 1953 review also was lavish in his praise:

> Certainly as Westerns go on the air, be they on radio or television, "Gunsmoke" is different....
> The program ... is perhaps especially noteworthy because it believes the popular notion that anything radio can do television can do better. In the vividness of imagery "Gunsmoke" needs no pictures. The listener's imagination provides a far better setting....
> The production of "Gunsmoke" employs the emotional tautness and understatement that are more usually associated with the programming efforts of the British Broadcasting Corporation than with an American network. It is singularly effective.
> Norman Macdonnell, the producer and director of the series, can appreciate the drama inherent in moments of silence and keeps his cast attuned to a low-pressure key....
> The sound effects ... are handled by Tom Hanley and Ross Murray who do an unusually good job. Rex Koury's music also is imaginative without being intrusive. The principal cast members ... are thoroughly competent.
> For injecting a provocative and refreshing note in one of the oldest dramatic forms, "Gunsmoke" is an item of radio well off the beaten path.[17]

On July 7, 1954, John Crosby of the *New York Herald-Tribune* added his name to the list of critics who applauded the production:

> There seems to be a small trend ... toward a higher level of culture on radio these days.... Prime exhibit is "Gunsmoke" ... CBS's highly literate Western radio drama which has been called the "High Noon" of broadcasting.... "Gunsmoke," which is as far removed from the average Western as "Dragnet" is from the average cops-and-robbers epics, ... was fourth in the last Nielsen ratings, which goes to show that there are more eggheads around than you might suppose.[18]

Despite such critical acclaim, radio had passed its prime by the mid-fifties and ratings for all dramatic shows, including *Gunsmoke*, began to dwindle. In 1954 CBS decided that a television version of *Gunsmoke* should be developed, while they continued to air the radio series (for seven more years). This presented three immediate problems for CBS: selection of a producer, obtaining scripts, and the selection of a cast for the television version.

As producer-director of *Gunsmoke* on radio from the beginning, no one was better qualified to maintain the style and feel of the program than Norman Macdonnell. Television, however, was not Macdonnell's forte as he later admitted. So Charles Marquis Warren, a novelist, screenwriter, film director and producer, was hired to produce the television series. Macdonnell was chosen by Warren to be the program's associate producer. Thus Macdonnell served CBS in a double capacity, producer and director of the radio series and associate producer of the television series.

Warren was both a writer and a director of popular Westerns. As a novelist Warren had published two best selling novels, *Only the Valiant* (1943) and *Dead Head* (1949). His Western film credits included writing the stories for *Streets of Laredo* (1949), *Woman of the North Country* (1952), *Springfield Rifle* (1952), and *Pony Express* (1953); he coauthored the story, wrote the screenplay and directed *Hellgate* (1952); he wrote the stories for and directed *The Little Big Horn* (sometimes called *The Fighting Seventh*, 1951) and *Arrowhead* (1953); he wrote the story and the screenplay for *Oh, Susanna* (1951), which was based on his first novel, and he later directed *Seven Angry Men* (1958) and *Cattle Empire* (1958).

Unfortunately, Warren and Macdonnell never developed a working relationship. Macdonnell resented Warren for taking over what was his (and Meston's) creation, and Warren, sensing that resentment, thought, "They hired me to put my mark on it and make it mine." And, as SuzAnne and Gabor Barabas explain in their detailed and fascinating study of *Gunsmoke*, this he did with "enthusiasm" as director and producer of the first 26 episodes:

> He is the one who visually conjured the "Babylon of the West." He created its saloons, boardwalks, and jail. He brought before the audience in a concrete and material form what had been but an ephemeral place in their imagination for so many years on radio. He conjured the desolate prairies, the dust-swept plains, the lonely homesteads and ranches. Warren was painfully meticulous, and personally supervised everything from the sagebrush on the prairie to the wardrobes for his actors.[19]

One of his first tasks was the selection of material for scripts. From the standpoint of writing, *Gunsmoke* was chiefly the product of John Meston. Between the time when the radio show went on the air in 1952 and the filming of the television pilot in 1955, Meston had written 124 of the radio scripts. Thus it is not surprising that Warren asked Meston for scripts to use on the television series. The pilot for the television series was a Meston original and the first script of the television series was a Meston radio script which he adapted for television. Warren decided to make adaptations of Meston's radio material the rule rather that the exception. Through the first four seasons only 17 of the 155 scripts used were not Meston adaptations. Consequently, the television version of *Gunsmoke* required very few original television scripts during its early years.

A much bigger problem for Warren was casting the show's major characters. According to Parley Baer, the first the radio cast ever heard about the television version of *Gunsmoke* came from items appearing in the actors' trade magazines, *Variety* and *The Hollywood Reporter*. This was in 1955 and CBS had been making plans for the television show since 1954. It was not uncommon for a radio program that was converted into a television program to change casts. For example, on *The Lone Ranger*, Clayton Moore and Jay Silverheels had replaced radio's Brace Beemer and John Todd. Still, when the radio cast members were not called to test for the roles, they felt slighted. It was widely believed that William Conrad's weight and build worked against his selection. Ultimately Conrad, Baer and McNear were given screen tests, but none received any serious consideration by Warren.

In any case, fate was to determine that a relatively unknown actor, James Arness, would become television's quintessential Western hero. James Arness has been described as "the Virginian, Wyatt Earp, Gary Cooper, Shane and John Wayne all lumped into a single, definitive, towering good guy."[20] For more than three decades Arness personified the Western hero, towering head and shoulders—both physically and charismatically— over a multitude of television cowboy stars. First as Matt Dillon, the stoic and courageous marshal of Dodge City in *Gunsmoke* (1955–1975), and later as Zeb Macahan, the tough, free-spirited mountain man in *How the West Was Won* (1977–1979), Arness became the most filmed actor in the history of cinema and television. His later appearances were limited to made-for-television movies such as *The Alamo: 13 Days to Glory* (1987) and a remake of *Red River* (1988), and five *Gunsmoke* films (in 1989, 1990, 1992, 1993 and 1994), but his visage can be seen somewhere in the world at virtually any hour of the day in reruns of the ever popular *Gunsmoke*.

Of Norwegian descent, Arness was born James King Aurness on May 26, 1923, in Minneapolis, Minnesota. His ancestry was distinguished. His paternal grandfather, Dr. Peter Andrew Aurness, studied medicine at the Ohio University and later moved to Minnesota, where he was not only a surgeon but an inventor and sculptor of some renown. Fittingly, Arness' great-great-grandfather, William Pierce King, was a United States marshal during the 1840s in Wisconsin. Franklin Pierce, fourteenth president of the United States, was a relative.[21] Peter Graves, Arness' younger brother, was the star of the television adventure series *Mission: Impossible*.

Described by his mother as "a magnificent, sensitive primitive,"[22] Arness was a shy and withdrawn child. Self-conscious about his height, he was a loner in high school. Shunning team sports, he preferred hunting, fishing, and sailing to football or basketball. His only social activities involved singing in church and school choral groups, although he did appear in a supporting role in a school play, "The Gift of the Magi."

Drafted into the army during his freshman year (1942-43) at Beloit College (in Wisconsin), Arness was wounded in the leg on the Anzio beachhead in 1944. As a result, that leg was an inch shorter than the other and caused Arness to limp noticeably when tired. Receiving a medical discharge in 1945, he returned to Minneapolis, where he attended the University of Minnesota and became a substitute announcer at radio station WLOL.

Restless and uneasy, Arness drifted to Hollywood where he appeared in several amateur theatrical productions. This led to an unsuccessful screen test at Warner Bros. An agent named Leo Lance introduced Arness to film producer Dore Schary, who gave him a role as one of Loretta Young's three brothers in *The Farmer's Daughter* (1947). Although the film was successful, earning an Oscar for Young, it did not advance Arness' career. Discouraged, he beachcombed in Mexico and worked at various jobs while collecting veteran's benefits and unemployment insurance until Shary gave him the role of a corporal in M-G-M's blockbuster war film, *Battleground* (1949). (Amanda Blake, who later played Kitty on *Gunsmoke*, also had a minor role in the film.) *Battleground* helped establish Arness as an actor. In the next three years he appeared in more than twenty films. His first Western role was in *Wagonmaster* (1950), an RKO production, in which he played the fourth moronic brother in a family of killers. Although he did not have a line of dialogue, Arness effectively utilized all of his six-foot, six-inch frame to convey the menace and evil of his character. It also gave Arness a chance to work with master film director John Ford.

Other Westerns followed in which the hulking Arness usually was cast in a supporting role as an outlaw. He gained valuable experience by appearing with such established actors as Joel McCrea (*Stars in My Crown*, 1950, *The Lone Hand*, 1953), Rod Cameron (*Cavalry Scout*, 1951), Stephen McNally (*The Wyoming Mail*, 1950) and Robert Ryan (*Horizons West*, 1952). It was a non–Western role, however, that earned Arness his first critical attention. Playing the unjustly accused title character in *The People Against O'Hara* for MGM in 1951, he was described by New York *Herald Tribune* film critic James S. Barstow, Jr., as displaying "an authoritative blend of belligerence and fear surprising for a relative newcomer."[23] Because of the drawing power of stars Spencer Tracy and Pat O'Brien, the film did well at the box office and gave Arness valuable screen exposure. Still, time after time, he would be considered for a role but would lose the part when the film's star refused to work with him because, according to Arness, "I was just too damned big."[24]

Ironically Arness got his most publicized role of this period because of his size—as the giant vegetable-monster in Howard Hawks' science-fiction classic, *The Thing* (1951). Unfortunately, Arness was unrecognizable in a jumpsuit and puttied forehead, and had no dialogue whatever. Arness later appeared to better advantage in another science-fiction classic, *Them!* (1954), in which he played an FBI agent. Arness now could get work, but his roles offered little challenge or hope of stardom. Discouraged, Arness decided to return to the stage. He appeared as the warrior Ajax in the Greek play *Penelope*, at a small but well-known little theatre called the Player's Ring. Taking the part was a gamble. His salary had steadily risen to nearly $1,000 a week, but every casting director in Hollywood knew that the actors who worked in the Player's Ring did so for nothing. Taking the stage role could jeopardize his future in films.

Once again, luck was with Arness. Talent scouts from the newly formed Wayne-Fellows Company, a partnership formed by actor John Wayne and writer-producer Robert M. Fellows, which later became the Batjac Company when Wayne bought out his partner's interest in 1954, came to the play on opening night. Impressed with Arness' potential, they took him to meet Wayne's associates and within three weeks he was offered a contract. Wayne already was acquainted with Arness. They had met through Arness' agent and Wayne liked the younger man's size, his walk, and physical stature.

Wayne assisted Arness in obtaining his best role to date in his first film for Wayne-Fellows, *Big Jim McLain* (1952). In the title role, Wayne played an investigator who worked for the Committee on Un-American Activities of the House of Representatives to expose a Communist spy ring in Hawaii. Arness played Mal Baxter, a Korean War hero who worked with McLain for HUAC. An integral part of the first half of the film, Arness appears in a number of important scenes before his character is killed. While Arness did well in his role, the film was considered by most critics to be no more than "a shallow propaganda piece against the evils of Communism."[25] The public liked it, however, and it was much more commercially successful than most anti–Communist films of the 1950s, grossing close to $3,000,000 in the United States alone.

Arness was given roles in three more of Wayne's films. In *Island in the Sky* (1953), he played a pilot who helps rescue Wayne and the crew of his transport plane after it has crashed in a frozen area north of Labrador during World War II. The part gave Arness the chance to display a broad Southern accent and much more personality than any of his previous roles. He considered it the best role he had in pictures thus far and credited Wayne with giving him the opportunity to expand his acting abilities. His was to have been a smaller part, but Wayne said, "Doggone it, Jim's been around a while and we owe him a good role. Let's let him play this part."[26]

Arness was not as fortunate in the other two Wayne films. In *Hondo* (1953), considered by most critics to be one of the better Wayne Westerns, Arness only appeared in the final ten minutes of the film as Lennie, a rather unlikable Army scout. Although given only a few lines of dialogue, he did get to redeem himself by saving Wayne's life. *The Sea Chase* (1955), an adventure film set during World War II, provided Arness with another minor supporting role as a seaman loyal to Wayne, who played an anti–Nazi German captain. However with his blond locks cropped short, Arness was hardly distinguishable from half a dozen other supporting actors.

Meanwhile, Arness had married and now had a wife and three children to support. In 1948, while appearing at the Pasadena Playhouse in *Candida*, he had fallen in love with a brown-eyed, black-haired actress named Virginia Chapman. They had a daughter, Jenny Lee, and a son, Rolf, in addition to Craig, Virginia's son by a previous marriage, whom Arness adopted.

When *Gunsmoke* entered Arness' life, television was still a relatively new medium. His experience in that field had been limited to a supporting role in an episode of the popular juvenile Western *The Lone Ranger* ("A Matter of Courage") and a few minor parts on dramatic anthologies such as *Lux Video Theater*. Arness first learned about Charles Marquis Warren's efforts to bring *Gunsmoke* to television from his friend John Wayne. Wayne had been Warren's first choice to play the leading role of Matt Dillon, but considering himself a *"movie"* actor and not wanting to be tied down to a weekly show, Wayne rejected the offer and recommended Arness instead.[27] At Wayne's suggestion, *Them!* was screened by Warren, Macdonnell, Hubbell Robinson, vice-president of television programming for CBS in New York, and William Dozier, programming vice-president in Hollywood. Following the screening, according to Macdonnell, Dozier said, "That's it," and there was no further discussion of the matter: Arness would be asked to test for the role.[28] Warren had worked previously with Arness in the film *Hellgate*, which he had directed for Lippert in 1952.

Fearing that people "would get sick of seeing" his face so often and that he would be "typed," Arness initially refused to test for the role. Meanwhile, CBS began thinking of older men for the part, Randolph Scott and Van Heflin, among others. Eventually 26 actors tested for the role, including radio's Matt Dillon, William Conrad, and Raymond Burr, television's eventual Perry Mason, but none of them fit the Dillon image and Arness was approached again. This time Arness decided to discuss his doubts with Wayne. "The show is mine if I want it," he told him, "but I'm still dreaming of pictures." Wayne replied:

> Look, it's rough trying to compete in this movie business with guys like me or Gary Cooper or Greg Peck. We've been at it so long time and our names mean something at the

box office. But your name doesn't mean a thing—anyway not yet. Besides you're a tall galoot, and Coop's not going to play opposite you in a film unless you're the heavy. This means you're going to wind up playing character parts. Don't be a fool, Jim. Take the TV series.[29]

Convinced, Arness accepted the role that earned him television stardom.

Wayne believed so strongly in Arness that he agreed to introduce the first episode of *Gunsmoke* on the air despite the objections of a cigarette company with whom he had an endorsement contract because the program was sponsored by a competing tobacco company. Viewers who tuned to CBS on Saturday evening, September 10, 1955, saw the Duke make a prophesy, the truth of which even Wayne could not have realized:

> I'm here to tell you about a Western, a new television show called *Gunsmoke*.... I think it's the best thing of its kind that's come along. I hope you'll agree with me. It's honest, it's adult, it's realistic. When I first heard about the show *Gunsmoke*, I knew there was only one man to play in it—James Arness. He's a young fella and maybe new to some of you, but I've worked with him and I predict he'll be a big star. So you might as well get used to him like you've had to get used to me.

Wayne's image gave way to that of a tall, lean cowboy, silhouetted against the sky, as he strode up a hill lined with tombstones. In calm, thoughtful, but forceful tones, the deep voice that was to become so familiar to television viewers introduced the first *Gunsmoke* story:

> If some of these men had argued a little, they might not be here. Arguing doesn't fill any graves. Take me, I'm a U.S. marshal. How many times I'd rather have argued than gone for guns. Take Dodge City over there. "Gomorah of the plains," they call it . . . jump off spot. People coming and going all the time, good, bad and worse. Tempers high. A man'll draw his gun quicker to prove his point than he'll draw on his logic. That's where I come in, whether they like it or not. When they draw their gun, somebody's gotta be around— somebody on the law's side.

Western buffs settled back to watch what most thought would be just another 30 minute version of the routine "shoot 'em up" Westerns they had seen for years. They expected the marshal to be tough, and he was. They expected him to be a man of few words, and he was. They expected him to be tall, and he definitely was. The show seemed to follow the tried and true formula. Within the first few minutes, Marshal Dillon has a confrontation with a vicious killer named Dan Gratt. They face off on the main street of Dodge City in Kansas Territory.

"Ah'm bad," the killer announces as he steps over the body of a lawman he has just gunned down. "You want me, Marshal, you got to come git me. . . ." Dillon brushes aside the beautiful saloon girl Kitty, who tries to stop him, steps off the plank sidewalk and reaches for his trusty Colt. Then, violating every rule of the Western genre, the bad guy outdraws and outshoots the hero, leaving him writhing in the dust. In homes throughout America, men and women blinked in disbelief and pulled their chairs a little closer to the television set. Here was something unique: a Western hero who was not invincible; a Western story that was not predictable.

In the end Dillon recovered and got his man. Not, however, because he was faster or stronger or even braver, but because he was smarter: he figured out that Gratt maneuvered his adversaries into coming so close that he could fire without aiming and still not miss. From across a hotel lobby, Gratt fires first, but misses. The slower, but more accurate Dillon does not.

Viewers were intrigued. Dillon was clearly a hero, but he did not perform heroic acts in the conventional way. He seemed genuinely disturbed when he had to kill a man. In the words of a British journalist, "He appeared more trigger sorry than trigger happy."[30] *Variety* (September 14, 1955) liked the television version of *Gunsmoke* and gave much of the credit to Arness:

> ... James Arness, the U.S. Marshal of the vidversion quietly but firmly took command in an expert portrayal....
>
> The starter was rigged to the understated, leave-it-to-the-imagination pattern as reflected authoritatively by Hollywood's "High Noon" and "Shane".... Suspense was even with a designed intent to skirt the hair-raising level, ... and the heroics and gunplay, sans horses and chases, maintained a curious credibility rather than being pegged to orthodox do-or-die gallantry. Violence was conspicuously absent; the intensity was in the steady build up of story mated to an easy, natural pace that made the half-hour seem faster in the time span as the drama unfolded gracefully.

Each week more people tuned in to see this Western that broke all the traditional rules of the genre. There were few chases and even fewer barroom brawls. The hero did not go around warbling songs to beautiful damsels in distress. He did not ride a white steed that could fly like the wind and rescue his master when evildoers had gotten the best of him. Indeed, Arness wrote a press release for CBS in 1958 entitled "No Trick Horses for Me," in which he explained:

> When the occasion demands, I ride a big buckskin gelding named Buck, chosen not because of his intellect, nor his fidelity, but because he is very large and only a very large horse will fit me.... In the real old West, horses were cheap and a cowboy—or a U.S. marshal—seldom had a favorite. He didn't keep a horse that long. He'd swap him off on a long trip for a fresh horse, or sell him between jobs knowing he could buy another when he needed it to avoid stable bills.[31]

Dillon did not always wear a white hat; sometimes it was black, as in "Kite's Reward." And Dillon's permanently lame assistant, Chester, superbly played by Dennis Weaver, or the crusty, but dependable Doc Adams, a tour de force for Milburn Stone, were not traditional comedy sidekicks, though one might chuckle occasionally at their good-natured banter.

Gunsmoke also took the Western heroine down from her pedestal and brought her into the real world in the form of saloon "hostess" Kitty Russell (Amanda Blake filled the role perfectly), who could be both tough and tender with equal conviction. There was even the hint of an off-screen relationship between Matt and Kitty. Still, when Kitty accused him early in the series of not knowing much about women, he responded that "he hadn't made it his life's work." As Arness explained it:

> ... the man and woman relationship must be subtle. It had to be. As a hero, I represent law and order—authority. People look up to me.... I must be respected. I can't go too far in romancing Kitty. But I think on *Gunsmoke* we have shown that a frontier hero can sit with a girl and even kiss her—and get away with it.[32]

Amanda Blake had this to say about their relationship in an interview in 1958:

> Kitty is in love with Matt although she knows they will never marry. He faces death every day. He can't marry her because he doesn't want to leave her a widow.[33]

In less subtle ways Dillon differed from television's more traditional Western heroes. Almost every time he went to the Long Branch, he had a beer or a whiskey, but never enough to impair his capacity for sound reasoning or straight shooting. Most unorthodox of all, Dillon frequently violated the unwritten "code of the West" that had governed the actions of virtually all previous cowboy heroes: he did not always let his adversaries draw first. Sometimes he shot them from ambush or even in the back. Yet he retained his heroic image because, in the words of Arness, "Matt is very human and has all the failings and drives common to anyone who is trying to do a difficult job the best he knows how."[34]

According to Norman Macdonnell, all of the killing and violence was justifiable because "it arose out of the situation and was not employed for its own sake."[35] For example, in "Kitty Caught," Matt and Chester are forced to ambush two bank robbers who have taken Kitty hostage and sworn to kill her should anyone follow them. When Chester questions the fact that they are going to shoot these men in cold blood, the Marshal's only response is, "Can you think of any other way?" In "No Indians," Chester and Matt ambush a gang of rustlers who have been murdering and scalping the families they have robbed so Indians will be blamed. Again, the lawmen seem justified in gunning down these brutal killers.

In yet another departure from conventional heroics, Dillon goads a cowardly gunman, who will only draw on men he knows he can beat in a gunfight, so that he can eliminate this brutal killer ("The Killer"). Of course, when the man tries to shoot Matt in the back, the marshal is justified in killing him. Still, Dillon was not a violent man by nature and he sometimes even wondered if he was the right man to fill a marshal's job. Most other lawmen took a simple view of their work. They represented "good," while all lawbreakers represented "bad." For them, there was nothing in between.

To Matt Dillon, however, there was an in-between, and it was a sizeable one. He had jailed many men whom he did not consider a threat to society. Some had just gotten off to a bad start; others preferred to take the easy way rather than try to earn an honest living; still others probably liked the danger and excitement of a life outside the law. Most of these men were not basically vicious; to Dillon, just a few men were totally "bad," and not many were wholly "good." A man was considered "good" if he was reasonably honest and kept his word with others most of the time. If he slipped once in a while, no one would blame him—if he did not slip too badly. If he did make a serious mistake, Christian standards dictated that he should be forgiven. Thus was the moral side of Matt Dillon's world filled not with black and white but with various shades of gray. James Arness' Matt Dillon was a lawman more concerned with the whys of men's actions, more aware of the limitations that governed human beings, and more attuned to his moral than his legal responsibilities. All in all, he was more thoughtful and introspective than most Western men of action.

In "Hot Spell," Matt protects a cruel and arrogant gunfighter who has just been released from jail from a mob of righteous townsmen who want to lynch him. Siding with a potentially dangerous stranger against his friends and neighbors, while the stranger mocks him, is a real test for Dillon's conscience. He is able to hold his head high in the face of scorn and abuse because he knows he is protecting his fellow townsmen *from themselves* and, more importantly, he is defending the law against the onslaught of those who stand to lose the most if it is ignored.

On another occasion ("Gone Straight"), Dillon considers quitting rather than having to arrest a former outlaw with a questionable past who has reformed. After the man is killed in a gunfight protecting yet another reformed outlaw, Matt tells his widow that if he had decided to take her husband in "it would have been my last official act." Here he dispensed justice tempered with mercy, showing a greater concern for the spirit than for the letter of the law.

In "Cow Doctor," Matt is incensed when Doc is stabbed and seriously wounded by a farmer. He tells the man that if Doc dies, so will he—" ... if Doc doesn't come out of this all right—I'll quit being a Marshal—I'll come after you as a plain man—looking

James Arness (right) as Marshal Dillon and Dennis Weaver as Chester in the early years of _Gunsmoke_.

for revenge." Dillon is more that just a cold upholder of the law, he is a human being with real emotions.

There is also a gentle side to Matt Dillon. On several occasions he becomes so sick and tired of the killing that he resigns from his job. In "Bloody Hands," Matt kills three outlaws. The fourth, whom he captures alive, accuses him of being a "butcher." Matt suddenly feels disgust and shame for the blood that he has been forced to shed in carrying out his duties as a U.S. Marshal and turns in his badge.

Seeking peace, quiet, and escape from the responsibilities he has carried, Matt takes Kitty fishing. It is there that Chester tracks him down and begs him to take back his badge. Dodge City is again threatened with violence and there is no one else who can prevent the impending chaos and anarchy:

> CHESTER: I been thinkin' lately a whole lot about all this and there's just somethin' that you been forgettin'!
> DILLON: That so?
> CHESTER: Yeah, that's so. It's men like Stangler and Brand. Cause they gotta be stopped! That's all! They gotta be! I'd do it if I could, but I can't. I just ain't good enough. Most men ain't, but you are. It's kinda too bad for ya that ya are, but that's the way it is and there ain't a thing in the world ya can do about it.

The episode ends as Matt reluctantly, but decisively, straps on the gun Chester has brought for him.

In a much later episode, "Snap Decision," Matt again questions the purpose of his office. He has killed a horse thief, who was once his friend, when he mistakenly thought the man was about to shoot him. Actually, the man was trying to save Matt from a bounty hunter who was about to shoot him in the back. Matt ultimately has second thoughts about resigning when he disagrees with the peace-keeping methods of his successor.

Not all the stories on *Gunsmoke* conclude with conventional "happy endings." In "Kite's Reward," Matt tries to help a former outlaw reform by persuading him to stop wearing a gun. Later a bounty hunter shows up in Dodge looking for the young man, who forgets he has taken the gun off. When he instinctively reaches for it, the bounty hunter kills him. Rightly or wrongly, the marshal feels responsible for the young man's death. Perhaps Dillon's attitude toward death is best articulated in the Boot Hill opening to "How to Die for Nothing," written by Sam Peckinpah:

> MATT'S VOICE: Men die for a lot of reasons. I've even heard of worthy ones—like a man who's willing to face it for the good that might come after. But he's a far different breed than most of this Boot Hill trash. These people die for fools' reasons—a spilt drink . . . a wrong card . . . an imagined insult. But the worst is a man who dies for nothing . . . for no reason at all.

Television's *Gunsmoke* had the same simple basic premise as the radio version: a U.S. marshal trying to maintain law and order in Dodge City, Kansas, during the 1870s. Within this framework a wide variety of characters and situations evolved over a twenty-year period. The television series passed through three different stages: the first six years of 30 minute programs, which were based mostly upon the radio scripts of John Meston; the early hour-long episodes, which permitted characters to display several aspects of their personalities and move through a series of actions and reactions; and, finally the anthology format, which was instituted after the network demanded that the level of violence be reduced drastically. Since *Gunsmoke* always had relied more on characterization than action, the shift to more nonviolent story resolutions was possible. Furthermore, the introduction of guest stars to play featured roles moved responsibility away from the more action-oriented continuing characters such as Dillon.

Through all the changes Dillon remained the focal point, backbone, and protector of the community. Dodge City would revert to anarchy and chaos were it not for its lawman. The town had no security in laws; its only security was its lawman, for laws could be subverted but lawmen could not. This is the continuing message of *Gunsmoke*.[36]

It is apparent just how much Matt Dillon means to the town in an episode entitled, "Dead Man's Law." Here we see why people have put their faith in a lawman instead of "laws." When Matt is shot and left for dead by an outlaw, the town is left to police itself. Festus and Newley, the deputies, try to maintain order, but their authority is challenged by two men who organize a cattlemen's association and proceed to raise the ugly specter of vigilante justice. When Festus leaves to find Matt, the town falls into anarchy. The cattlemen convince the townspeople to hire a shotgun-toting killer as their acting marshal. Doc urges them to wait until Festus returns:

> For twelve years you've had law and order in Dodge City because one man enforced the law. Now that he's not here you're willing to give the town away to the first incompetent that comes along with a shotgun and is anxious to use it.

Unfortunately, that is just what happens as the killer is given full authority to enforce the law with his shotgun. Suspected lawbreakers are shot down, Doc is beaten, and Kitty is harassed for objecting to these strong-arm tactics. Eventually Matt, who has been nursed back to health by an Indian, returns and regains control of the town. Once again law and order prevail. It is clear that the limits and enforcement of the law lie with a man and not with the people who seem impotent without their lawman. What makes Matt Dillon unique is that he knows the people of his town, understands them, and is willing, in extenuating circumstances, to bend the law for them.

The people need to be reminded of their marshal's importance to them. In "The Wreckers," Matt is injured and taken prisoner by a gang of outlaws who demand a sizable ransom from the citizens of Dodge City. Doc and Kitty try to raise the money, even though they suspect that the outlaws will kill the marshal anyway. At a heated meeting held in the Long Branch, Doc describes what Matt has meant to the town:

> ... there's not a single person in this room that doesn't owe him a debt of some kind ... not one of ya! Now there's not enough money in the whole state of Kansas to pay another man to do what Matt's done, even if they could, and they couldn't. Now we built this town and we've seen it grow because Matt gave us the security of knowing that Tate Crocker and a hundred others like him can't come in here and burn it to the ground every time they think about it.... It may be his job, but who else would do it or who could? And what about the other debts you owe him?

Doc goes on to cite the debts individual citizens owe Matt. When Kitty delivers the money to the outlaws, she explains to Matt, "If you think they don't care, there's ten dollars on that table for every man, woman and child in Dodge City...." Matt, of course, eventually escapes and reaffirms the townspeople's confidence in him. But now they have been required to provide tangible proof of his value to them.

Except for a few more lines on his craggy face and the slight trace of a gray hair here and there, Matt Dillon changed little over the years. There is, perhaps, some discernable modification in his relationship toward women. In "Sarah," viewers learn about a girl that Dillon almost married long before coming to Dodge City when he was a young deputy in San Antonio. He even pretends to be her husband in a futile effort to protect her from the advances of several outlaws.

On September 24, 1973, an unprecedented situation occurred on *Gunsmoke*. In "Matt's Love Story," Matt falls in love—but not with Kitty. While suffering from amnesia after being ambushed by a gunman he is trailing, he is rescued by a widow who nurses him back to health. Their attraction to each other is shown, first through a series of looks and then with a passionate kiss. Finally, the inevitable happens—albeit off-screen during a commercial break. Matt disappears into the widow's bedroom and, presumably, her bed. All is back to normal by the end of the episode, for when Matt regains his memory he realizes he must return to his responsibilities in Dodge City, and to Kitty, of course. But another aspect of Dillon's character—perhaps the only one still hidden after 18 seasons—has been revealed.

As time went on, Arness the actor became more absorbed by and more protective of the character with whom he had become so closely identified. In an interview in 1957, he explained:

> There's a real sense of satisfaction in this. I wouldn't trade roles with anybody on TV. It has Quality. It has something to say. The man is somebody I can believe in. Dillon is a tragic figure. All those guys were. They died in the most ignominious ways. They had nothing.... That's what makes Dillon interesting.[37]

A couple of years later, Arness expanded his analysis of Dillon:

> Matt Dillon is a valid human being. On camera he shows the two sides of his personality that every human being has: his "on stage" character and his "off stage" side. When Dillon is working, he's stern and businesslike, as befits his job. When he's relaxing, taking a drink or eyeing Kitty, he's another kind of person.[38]

By 1971, interviewers were making reference to the obvious similarities between Arness and Dillon, to which Arness responded:

> Well, you know you can't live with a thing like this as closely as you have to over the years without it becoming part of the same thing.... Not entirely, obviously, but I mean the two have to blend together to a large extent....[39]

One of the key reasons for *Gunsmoke*'s popularity and consequent longevity was Arness. Through the years he received an increasingly favorable appraisal from the critics. Vernon Scot, United Press International correspondent, observed, "Arness is to television what William S. Hart, Tom Mix, and Ken Maynard were to the movies."[40] The *TV Guide* writer Dwight Whitney described Arness as "capable of great toughness and tenderness."[41] Gerald Nachman wrote in the New York *Daily News* that "Arness' slab-like face and massive outline merges all our memories of frontier lawmen.... [He] is still the all-time, all-star marshal, pure, square-shouldered square shooter...."[42]

Perhaps the most detailed analysis of Arness' acting style came from *New York Times* columnist Wallace Markfield in a loving tribute to *Gunsmoke* published after the series had left the air in 1975.

> ... none ... ever dominated a scene so easily and absolutely as James Arness.... The camera really loved his face, and with good reason: it was a face that would carry intimations of waste, loss and futility.... An enormous man—wearing a Stetson, he is said to stand 7 feet—Arness used every last ungainly line of his body to anchor an archetype in flesh and blood. If he looked good drawing his gun faster and shooting it straighter than anyone else, he looked even better when he did some humdrum piece of physical business—when he tried to shake sleep out of his eyes or trail-dust from his clothes; when he flinched, shuddered and tried to diminish himself under the full blast of sunlight, joint by joint, into a chair; when he battled out of a chair at the sound of a shot or scream. In these and other small ways, we were made to understand, for twenty years, that Matt Dillon's life was mostly labor and exhaustion, but that it was the only life possible to him.[43]

One of the most important decisions Charles Marquis Warren made in transferring the radio *Gunsmoke* to television was to develop a character with "romantic interest." Unless radical changes were made in the character of Matt and the relationship between Matt and Kitty altered, the lead character in the show was eliminated from such a possibility. Thus the decision was made to cast the role of Chester as a younger and more handsome man than the radio character of Chester would have suggested. On television Chester became a young man in his twenties instead of a middle-aged man in his late thirties.

When it came time to cast Chester, Warren already had Dennis Weaver in mind, having worked with him in *Seven Angry Men*. When he first read for the role, he played Chester "straight," but immediately realized that was not the way Warren wanted the character interpreted. Then, recalling an old Oklahoma accent he and a college friend had worked up, he asked for five minutes to rehearse. When he came in and read the part again with a twang, Warren hired him on the spot. Warren later explained in a *TV Guide* interview that Weaver simply got the part because he was "such a fine actor. In *Seven Angry Men* he had to go insane, and he did it so well that I knew he could do anything." Thus Weaver became the first actor to be signed for *Gunsmoke*.

The man who was to become television's Chester, was born Dennis Weaver on June 4, 1924, in Joplin, Missouri. Weaver was an outstanding athlete during his high school and college days and divided his time almost equally between dramatic studies and sports. His favorite movie stars were B cowboy heroes, Ken Maynard and Buck Jones. While attending school in Joplin, Weaver set many records in football and track and field, some of which remain unbroken to this day.

After a year at Joplin Junior College, Weaver left school to join the U.S. Naval Reserve. Discharged as an ensign after 27 months in the Naval Air Force, during which time he set several records as a member of the navy's track and field team, Weaver resumed his education by enrolling at the University of Oklahoma. It was the first time in seven years that institution had a student who could qualify for the decathlon. Weaver led his team to the national championships where it won first place honors in all competitions with other Midwestern universities. In 1948 the young athlete represented the university at the New Jersey tryouts for the Olympic games. After placing sixth out of 36 entrants, Weaver decided to pursue an acting career.

Accepted into New York's famous Actor's Studio, Weaver was ready for his Broadway debut in the spring of 1951 in William Inge's prize-winning *Come Back, Little Sheba*, starring Shirley Booth. He also played Stanley Kowalski in the Circle Theatre production of *A Streetcar Named Desire*, with Shelley Winters in Hollywood. It was there that he first met Winters, who praised him so highly to her studio, Universal-International, that he was signed to a contract by the company. However, Weaver was relegated to small roles in almost every Western the studio produced. He finally refused to be typed as a strictly Western actor and obtained his release from the contract. In 1954 and 1955, Weaver made four major films: *Dragnet, The Bridge at Toko-Ri, Ten Wanted Men* and *Seven Angry Men*. His television work to that time consisted of supporting roles on shows like *Dragnet* and *The Schlitz Playhouse*. Then he was offered the role of Chester and helped make television history.

During his years in the role Weaver would give the character a dimension far beyond the conception of its creators and in so doing earn for himself an Emmy Award as Best Supporting Actor in a Drama Series in 1959. On the whole, Chester was probably the most popular character on *Gunsmoke*. This was due partly to Dennis Weaver and partly to the revised interpretation of Chester as a character who brought an occasional romantic involvement to the show, in addition to humor. Chester was, of course, a close friend of the marshal but not an official deputy. The character was to be capable of wisdom which belied his youth and seemingly "country" exterior. He spoke in colloquialisms, brewed a nasty cup of coffee and fought with Doc on a daily basis. His television name finally became Chester Goode instead of Chester Proudfoot as it had been on radio.

The major problem which presented itself in regard to Chester was to devise a logical reason why this young man, who hung around the marshal's office, did not carry a gun as most able-bodied men of his age would have done in Dodge City during the 1870s. Warren, Macdonnell or Weaver (depending on which version you believe) came up with a limp for Chester as the solution to this dilemma. Macdonnell later recalled:

> We tried two or three things and Warren came up with the stiff leg idea. And I remember one night at Kelbo's ... right across the street from CBS in Hollywood, we had a drink and Dennis Weaver was out walking up and down Fairfax Avenue with the stiff leg, experimenting to see how it looked and how it worked.[44]

The limp, of course, worked fine and became one of the best remembered characteristics of Chester.

In the first two scripts aired, "Matt Gets It" and "Hot Spell," Chester was a somewhat neutral character as if the producers and writers did not know quite which way to go with him. In the second episode, Chester seems to lean a bit toward the "simpleness" that would make him both a favorite character and the subject of much of the humor in the scripts. When the chips were down, however, Chester was a no-nonsense, right-hand man to Matt. By the last half-hour episode, "Colorado Sheriff," he had become a very predictable—if entertaining and amusing—character:

CHESTER: I ain't et yet.
MATT: Oh...
CHESTER: I went and got the mail and then I been readying this place up and I ain't had time...
MATT: Well, that's fine, Chester...
CHESTER: Now doggone it, Mr. Dillon...
(Matt looks up surprised.)
MATT: What's the matter?
CHESTER: I been standing here trying to tell you I ain't had a bite to eat yet today and you ain't even listening to me.
MATT: Well, I ... I'm sorry, Chester. Don't you feel well?
(Disgusted, he picks the broom up.)
CHESTER: There ain't nobody around here appreciates nothing a body does for them... I'm going out to eat.

Another of these marvelous little exchanges between Matt and Chester takes place in "Custer":

CHESTER: All ready to go, Mr. Dillon... And I'm so hungry I could eat a whole hog.
MATT: This is all the hog you get this morning.
CHESTER: Is it done?
MATT: That depends on how hungry you are.
CHESTER: It's done.

While the conversations between Matt and Chester were humorous, those between Doc and Chester raised the art of comic dialogue to new heights—furthering the plot at times, while providing character insight and pure entertainment. In "Perce," Doc has just finished his dinner, when Chester comes in:

Doc:	If I'd known you were coming, I'd have left something, Chester.
CHESTER:	I was only trying to figure out what you had to eat.
DOC:	You could ask me.
CHESTER:	Oh ... Well, what was it?
DOC:	I don't know.
CHESTER:	What!
DOC:	I ordered beef stew, but what they brought me I couldn't say.

In "Old Yellow Boots," Doc and Chester have another one of their delightful exchanges:

Doc:	What's the matter with you this morning?
CHESTER:	I got a pain, Doc—right in there....
(He pokes himself just under the ribs.)	
Doc:	Oh, well, why didn't you come upstairs?
CHESTER:	Oh, no ... oh, no ... I wouldn't do that...
Doc:	No ... you'd rather stand out here in pain all day, wouldn't you? You'd rather hang around hoping to catch me on the fly than come up and make a regular visit.
CHESTER:	Doc, it ain't that. I just couldn't climb them stairs, the shape I'm in.
Doc:	And the pain ... it's so bad you couldn't bear to put your hand in your pocket for the two dollars you'll owe me, could you?

In many ways, Chester was *Gunsmoke*'s most "human" character. He was proud, vain, opinionated, and even a little "simple," but above all he was loyal, brave and kindhearted. Chester was accepted into viewers' homes as a welcome friend. Everyone dreamed of emulating the heroics of Matt Dillon, but in reality found themselves personally relating to the foibles of Chester. A number of episodes involved Chester as the central character during Weaver's nine years on the show. Several of these were romantic in nature. In "Chester's Mail Order Bride," Chester corresponds with Ann, a young woman from Philadelphia intent on finding a husband. When she arrives in Dodge, she discovers that Chester has sent her a photo of Matt rather than himself and it turns out she has sent Chester a picture of her sister. Still, Chester and Ann are attracted to each other. When Chester learns that Ann is only 17 years old and has run away from a wealthy and comfortable life in the East, he must decide whether or not to go through with the marriage. With Matt's help, he realizes that it is best for Ann that she return to her family. As his reward Chester receives his first on-screen kiss. It is a touching and poignant story and reveals Chester's need for feminine love.

Most of Chester's romances are ill-fated. In "Chester's Dilemma," Chester becomes infatuated with a pretty young woman. Unfortunately for Chester she is only interested in Chester's daily deliveries of Matt's official mail and is using him so she can steal a particular letter when it arrives.

"Chesterland," shown during the first season of hour long episodes (1961-62), is said to be one of Dennis Weaver's favorite episodes. It certainly is (as the Barabases note in their *Gunsmoke* episode guide) "a tour-de-force" for Weaver and offers considerable insight into the hopes and aspirations of Chester.[45] Chester falls in love with pretty Daisy Fair and proposes to her. Before she will consent she asks Chester to provide a home for her and prove that he can earn a decent living. The love-smitten Chester digs an underground home and takes up farming on a dry, barren piece of Kansas land. Daisy does not like living underground and Chester's plans for the future seem doomed until he strikes water. When it appears that Chester will become modestly prosperous, Daisy resumes her interest in him. Then the well dries up and Daisy dumps Chester. Accepting what seems to be his destiny, Chester returns to Dodge City and his job with Matt— knowing that there he is truly loved and appreciated for himself alone.

Another moving Chester episode is "He Learned about Women." This time Chester's love (for a beautiful half-breed) is returned. However, when the two of them are taken prisoner by a ruthless gang of comancheros, she sacrifices herself in order to save Chester's life.

Chester is almost forced into a "shot-gun wedding" in "Root Down" when a pretty, husband-hunting, young woman tells her father that Chester has spent the night with her. This episode is played for laughs and Chester ultimately escapes her clutches none the worse for wear.

Matters become much more serious in "Tell Chester," when Chester is romantically attracted to a woman who has her heart set on another man (who, unbeknownst to her, already had a wife). Chester almost ends up at the altar again, in "Daddy Went Away," when he becomes romantically involved with a penniless seamstress. He tries to help her financially and she reciprocates by making him a new suit and shirt. This leads Chester to think she is in love with him.

Although there is invariably some humor involved in virtually every Chester story, "Marshal Proudfoot" is a classic comedy episode. Based on a radio script of the same title, it was not retitled even though Chester's last name was now Goode. However, the story was slightly altered with Chester's *uncle* Wesley instead of his *father* Wesley suddenly arriving in Dodge for a visit. It seems Chester's letters have left his uncle with the impression that he is the marshal and Matt is his assistant. Chester is embarrassed, but he tries to keep his uncle from learning the truth. Meanwhile, Matt is sick in bed and Doc and Kitty decide to stage a "fake" holdup so Chester will look like a hero. Two real outlaws show up and attempt to rob the Dodge House. Chester, with a little help from his uncle, dispatches them both, winning the admiration of Uncle Wesley—and Matt.

Chester was the object of Matt's concern in a number of episodes. In "Chester's Murder," Chester is framed for murder and Matt must prevent a lynch mob of irate citizens from taking the law into their own hands before he can find the real murderer. In "A Gun for Chester," Matt risks his own life to prevent a man bent on revenge from killing Chester. It seems that years earlier Chester had been forced to shoot the man's brother for molesting a woman. In "Never Pester Chester," Weaver only appears in the opening and closing scenes, but is the focal point of the story. When Chester is dragged behind a horse and left for dead by two ruffians, Matt goes after the two men with a vengeance. While Chester struggles to survive, Matt metes out his own highly appropriate brand of justice. In "Chester's Hanging," two men threaten to hang Chester unless Matt agrees to release their imprisoned accomplice forcing Matt to concern himself with Chester's safety, while retaining custody of the murderer.

Despite Weaver's great success as Chester, he was restless and grew tired of a role that he felt did not give him sufficient opportunity to develop as an actor. He tried to leave the show twice for other projects but each time he returned when the proposed series fell through. The third time, however, the new series (*Kentucky Jones*) was approved and Weaver left *Gunsmoke* during the ninth season. Years later he explained to Lee Miller his decision to leave:

> I wanted to grow as an actor, to create, to expand and quitting "Gunsmoke" was the biggest decision I had to make in my life. In addition, I just couldn't see fit to make only one solitary character my entire life's work as an actor. Oh, from the standpoint of money, it couldn't be beat. Chester's remuneration grew beyond my expectations, in fact is still coming in every month from residuals. But money is a drag if you allow it to become an end instead of a means.... So I decided I'd have to make a clean break with Chester if I was ever going to fully accomplish what I wanted as an actor.[46]

Weaver was able to rise above typecasting and went on to create many other popular television roles. Besides, *Kentucky Jones* (1964-65), he did *Gentle Ben* (1967–1969), *McCloud* (1970–1977, his most successful series since *Gunsmoke*), *Emerald Point* (1983–1984), and *Buck James* (1987–1988), in addition to numerous made-for-television movies (e.g., *Duel*, 1971, *Duel at Diablo*, 1966, *The Great Man's Whiskers* as Lincoln, 1973, *Intimate Strangers*, 1977, *Centennial—The Longhorns*, 1979, *Ishi—The Last of His Tribe*, 1978, *The Islander*, 1978, *Get Patty Hearst*, 1979, *The Forgotten Man*, 1972, *The Rolling Man*, 1972, and *Female Artillery*, (1972). Still, most *Gunsmoke* fans would agree with the comments Milburn Stone made when Weaver left the show for the last time: "Dennis is a brilliant actor. But he's Chester and, whether he knows it or not, he'll always be Chester."[47]

The most experienced cast member selected for *Gunsmoke* was Milburn Stone. He, like Dennis Weaver, was known to Warren before casting began. Stone, a veteran of over 250 films, had worked for Warren in *Arrowhead* (1953). Warren made up his mind that Stone was the best possible person for the part of Doc Adams even though Stone had little television experience.

Milburn Stone was born on July 5, 1904, in Burton, Kansas, and grew up in Fort Larned only fifty miles from Dodge City. His uncle was Fred Stone, who had been a star on Broadway. Milburn began his acting career at the age of 18, earning $35 a week with a three-person tent show in Kansas. Later, he developed a vaudeville act with Smoky Strain called "Stone and Strain." They performed their song and dance routines in blazers and straw hats at various theaters in Denver. They also appeared on radio station KLZ. Then Stone moved to New York and was in two short-lived Broadway plays, *The Jayhawkers* and *Around the Corner*. Finally in 1935 Stone headed for Hollywood. There he earned a modest living while gaining experience as the villain in over 100 B Westerns. (Stone did play a doctor once: in *Gung Ho!*, he was a Navy doctor.) Stone played supporting roles on a few television shows (*Dragnet*, *Front Row Center*, *Climax*) during the fifties, but they have long since been overshadowed by the role of Doc Adams.

In response to a question about the character changes between the radio cast of *Gunsmoke* and the television cast, Norman Macdonnell once remarked that on radio Doc was more of a quack and spent more time in the Long Branch Saloon than did the character portrayed by Milburn Stone. In fact, Doc on radio and Doc on television were as different as the changes in the name would imply. On radio Howard McNear played Doctor Charles Adams while on television Milburn Stone was Doctor Galen Adams. Stone later explained in an interview that he had patterned his character after his paternal grandfather, Joseph Stone, and a "horse and buggy doctor" named Roger S. Hertzer whom Stone had known as a child in Kansas. The physical characteristics of Doc Adams were derived from Stone's grandfather who Stone described as being

> ... a little ol' fellow who was tough as a boot, and fiery as hell—he never smiled. If you ever saw him smile, he was having hysterics; he was just out of control. But he was laughing at everybody inside all the time. He'd say good morning to me ... he'd say it meaner than hell.... By the time I was eighteen, I could see that he was laughing at everybody. He just went through life laughing at everybody; he was a very, very contented man.[48]

It was Stone who came up with the idea for Doc's wardrobe. He believed that such a character would wear a vest in which he would carry his trusty pocket watch along with his glasses and a thermometer. Stone wanted Doc to look like he was just barely existing. (His clothes would be old and worn because he could not afford new ones.) When he began the role in 1955, Stone dyed his hair gray and wore a fake moustache. Later, of course, Stone grew his own moustache and nature took care of the color of his hair.

The extent of Stone's knowledge about his character can be found in the manuscript he wrote in which he created a fictional past for Doc. This biography (which was never published) reads in part:

> Doc was born Galen Adams in Boone County, Indiana, in 1822.... His mother, a gentle woman ... passed away during Galen's second year in high school....
> Galen always believed if there had been one more doctor in Boone, his mother's life might have been spared.... Admitted to William and Mary College in Williamsburg, Va. [sic], in 1840, he was graduated with honors and a medical degree five years later.... [When] the war between the States erupted with terrible violence in 1861, Doc Adams volunteered as a battlefield surgeon.
> The next four years were a nightmare of blood, carnage and utter frustration for Doc....
> When the war ended in 1865, Doc Adams was an old man at 43....
> The urge to move along hit Doc, ... and he boarded a stage in St. Louis and started toward San Francisco.... The stage stopped in Dodge City and while Doc was headed for the Long Branch Saloon, he witnessed an incident that changed his life.
> Marshal Matt Dillon walked alone to face three gunmen.... [W]hen the gunsmoke was cleared, no one seemed to care that in killing the three outlaws, Matt was himself near death from bullet wounds.... When told that there was no physician in Dodge City, Doc ... using what few crude implements he could find ... removed the bullets.
> While Matt convalesced from his ice-pack and jack-knife surgery, he and Doc became friends.... Doc insisted, however, that he was still going to San Francisco as soon as Matt was well.
> But Matt, too had found a friend.... Doc finally agreed to stay for a "little while," but as the weeks turned into months, Doc found two more friends, Kitty and Chester.
> Kitty ... Doc treats ... as if she were his daughter, and secretly he sort of hopes that someday she and Matt will marry.
> When Chester came to town, Doc said, "Matt made the mistake of feeding him and he's been here ever since." At first Doc resented Chester because of his association with Matt, but that has turned into a feeling of real affection.[49]

Stone wanted his character to be authentic. He once consulted his own personal physician and explained that he was about to do an episode where he would have to remove a bullet from Kitty ("Kitty Shot"). Stone wanted to know what he should say about Kitty's condition when Matt arrived.[50] Having thus formed the physical personality traits of Doc, Milburn Stone set in his mind a character with whom he would allow no tampering. The integrity of his portrayal was extremely important to him and he considered himself to be the chief authority on the character of Doc. Dee Phillips and Bev Copeland pointed out in an article they wrote for *TV Guide* in 1965 that over the years Stone had earned "respect and a grudging admiration for his pugnacious protection of Doc's image" and "his vehement insistence on [Doc's] professionalism." They explained:

> Perhaps years of immersion in the role have imbued him with—subliminally—the Doc-like traits he so admires. In person it becomes almost a moot point as to where Doc tapers off and the real Milburn Stone emerges.[51]

Claiming that he was "too old to scare, and too rich to care,"[52] Stone was not hesitant about suggesting changes in dialogue and once refused to appear in a scene he felt was out of character. Stone's work stands on its own merits. In 1968, he became the second member of the *Gunsmoke* cast to win an Emmy for his acting. He was also one of the few laymen ever to be given an honorary membership in the Kansas Medical Society. Rita Parks in *The Western Hero in Film and Television* describes Doc's changing function on *Gunsmoke*:

> ... As town physician, Doc provided several images that are a reflection of the heroic persona—images that are slightly inappropriate or limiting for the hero but still embody certain

values that need support for the audience. Doc played in turn the elder statesman, the mature friend, and the big brother, and came as close to a philosopher—clergyman as any continuing character in the series was allowed to do.[53]

A look at some of the stories featuring Doc helps to more clearly reveal the qualities he displayed for twenty years on *Gunsmoke*. Doc's word was his bond. In "Word of Honor," he is kidnapped by outlaws who want him to treat a boy they are holding for ransom. Doc removes the bullet, but the boy dies anyway. The outlaws want to kill him in order to silence him. In asking for his life, Doc says, "Right this minute there may be some woman having a baby and needing me real bad. There may be some man with gangrene of the leg—people needing help—right this minute." But Doc's humanitarianism is turned against him—the outlaws point out that if he does not give his word not to talk, that woman and that man are going to have to do without him because there will not be a *living* doctor for miles. So Doc promises. Later Doc tries to explain his actions to Matt:

> DOC: That's all I can tell you. And don't think it isn't driving me crazy. I can still see his face ... dying like that from a shot in the back.
> MATT: You've told me practically nothing about the killers, Doc.
> DOC: They didn't look like killers when they rode up to my office, and said a man's hurt real bad on a place out past Fort Dodge. I went with them.
> MATT: You must have known it was a shooting. All that hurry. You could have left word for me.
> DOC: My job's to take care of everybody—sinner and saved alike. A man was hurt bad and needed me. That's why I went with them—quick.
> MATT: Still won't tell me where?
> DOC: I promised not to—
> MATT: Or who they were?
> DOC: I've got to say I don't know, Matt. I gave my word—to save my life.

Doc's dedication to serve the ill is demonstrated again in "Cow Doctor." Doc is summoned to the home of a doctor-hating farmer and discovers that he has been called to treat an ailing cow. Doc is so angry that he strikes the man and is, in turn, knifed and seriously wounded. To add to Doc's resentment of the farmer, a patient who really needed his help has died while he was tending the cow. Later, while he is still recovering from his wounds, Doc is again summoned to the farmer's home by his son. It seems the farmer himself is seriously ill. Against the advice of Matt and Kitty, he hurries to help the stricken farmer. Ironically, although Doc saves the farmer's life, the man refuses to pay Doc because his cow has died.

Suspicion of doctors and distrust of medicine in general is again the problem confronted by Doc in "The Cast." Shell Tucker, a man who hates doctors, has so intimidated his wife that she waits too long before sending for Doc after swallowing a nail. Shell blames Doc for her death even though Doc tried valiantly to save her. He tries to kill Doc, but changes his mind when Doc is able to save his prize horse that has broken its leg. Doc applies a cast and the bone heals. Shell's transformation is completed when he asks Doc to pull his painful tooth.

Dodge City almost loses Doc's services in "Doc Quits." Another doctor arrives in Dodge and proposes a partnership with Doc. Doc refuses because he objects to the man's greed. When he quits his practice in anger, Doc's patients start going to the new physician. Only when the new doctor is exposed by Doc as a quack and a charlatan does Doc resume his rightful place in the community.

In "Apprentice Doc" Doc is kidnapped to treat a wounded outlaw. One of them befriends Doc. He is a bright young man named Pitt who wants to study medicine. Later after he has been released, Doc is approached by Pitt who wants to become his apprentice. Doc agrees and is impressed by Pitt's skill. When his former companions arrive on the scene, only Matt's intervention prevents tragedy. Here Doc is concerned with nurturing an interest in medicine in a capable young man. He realizes that new doctors must be trained to replace the old.

A potential rival appears on the scene in "Doctor's Wife." The ambitious wife of a newly arrived young doctor tries to steal Doc's patients away by spreading rumors that Doc drinks too much and is no longer capable of practicing medicine. First, Doc ignores the gossip and tries to befriend the young couple. When that fails, he pays a visit to the wife and teaches her a lesson. In so doing the viewer learns more about Dodge—and about Doc:

> JENNIFER (the young doctor's wife): There's nothing wrong with being important and making money.
> DOC: Not a thing. But, maybe, if that's all you want, you came to the wrong place. I'm here because I like this town. I like the people in it. Not because I'm getting rich on them.
> JENNIFER: Before we came, you were the only doctor here. You must have been making plenty of money.
> DOC: I think you've got the wrong idea about Dodge. You haven't seen the shacks, the dirt farmers bending their backs out of shape trying to get something—anything— to grow out of that dust and rock. The women looking fifteen years older than they are... You know my usual fee? A bunch of greens, maybe a skinned jackrabbit, sometimes a peck of potatoes. But usually it's just a handshake and "Sorry, Doc, but I'll pay you something soon as I can."
> (Jennifer is silent, staring down at the floor.)
> DOC: Look here, I've got a couple of calls to make outside of town. I'd like you to come with me.

On her travels with Doc she meets a woman who is 33, but looks 50. There is also a man with gangrene whose leg must be amputated or he will die. Jennifer, however, interferes, offering him the false hope that her husband (with more up to date methods) can save his leg. So he postpones the surgery and by the time her husband arrives, it is too late and the man dies. His son comes gunning for the young doctor and when he is critically wounded by the son, Doc saves his life. Only then does Jennifer begin to understand Doc's commitment and dedication. Her husband must make a name for himself without the interference of his wife. Jennifer tells Doc, that they will go to Denver, which was their original destination.

Several episodes featuring Doc are humorous in nature. In "Which Dr.," Doc and Festus are captured by a family of scruffy buffalo hunters while on a fishing trip. Not only do they want to keep Doc as their camp doctor, but they also think he would make a suitable husband for their leader's spinster daughter. In "Doctor Herman Schultz, M.D.," an episode written by guest star and vaudeville comic Benny Rubin, an old friend of Doc's arrives in Dodge. Unbeknownst to Doc, he wants to hypnotize Festus into stealing money for him. At first Doc goes along with his plans so that Festus can have a tooth removed without pain. Although later, as a joke, Dr. Schultz gets Festus to crow like a rooster, his plans to use Festus as an unwilling accomplice are thwarted in the end.

Of all the many episodes featuring Doc, the two which demonstrate Milburn Stone's greatest acting capacity are "Baker's Dozen" (which won him a 1968 Emmy for Best Supporting Actor in a Drama) and "Sam McTavish, M.D." "Baker's Dozen" was written by Milburn's brother Charles Joseph Stone. Originally entitled "The Triplets," it was conceived as a story for Chester in 1962, but never developed. In 1967 it was adapted for Doc. After a stage holdup, Doc delivers the triplets of one of the passengers. When the mother dies, he has his hands full taking care of the infant orphans. Matt, Kitty and Festus all try to help Doc find a suitable home for the babies. This is especially difficult when it is discovered that their father was an outlaw and the circuit judge decides to place them in the state orphanage. Finally they are taken in by a couple that already has ten children. Doc's kindness shines through in this delightful and unusual story.

"Sam McTavish, M.D." ends on a much more somber note. Doc has advertised for a temporary replacement so that he can attend a retirement dinner being held in the East for his former professor. The replacement he hires through a medical journal turns out to be a woman (Sam McTavish). At first hesitant at leaving a woman to handle what he considers to be a man's job, Doc soon learns that Dr. McTavish is not only an extremely competent professional, but also a very warm and loving woman. Before Doc can leave on his trip, a plague breaks out in Dodge and he must cancel his plans. The two doctors work together to stem the spread of the disease and discover that they have fallen in love. Unfortunately, Sam is felled by the plague. Her death leaves a void in Doc's life that he has never felt before. This is a beautiful, but sad, love story in which Stone and actress Vera Miles (in the role of Sam) sparkle. It makes Doc seem all the more human.

In the spring of 1971 Stone suffered a heart attack just shy of his sixty-seventh birthday. While he was recuperating from subsequent open heart surgery, a new doctor was brought to Dodge. He was played by veteran actor Pat Hingle in the role of Dr. John Chapman. Introduced in an episode entitled "New Doctor in Town," Dr. Chapman has been sent by Doc as his replacement while he is studying at Johns Hopkins Medical School in the East. It seems that Doc has left Dodge without even a good-bye because of the death of a little girl. Doc feels he could have saved her if he had been aware of recent medical progress. He sends a letter to his old friends with Dr. Chapman. Matt, Festus and Newly listen as Kitty reads:

> ... Living in Dodge has been the most rewarding experience of my life, but I've been so out of touch with modern medicine that when I arrived in Baltimore I felt like a schoolboy. I suddenly realized how little I know about medicine and how much has passed me by in the last twenty years ... and that's why I've decided to stay on here at the university.
>
> Please understand and forgive me, but I couldn't bear to face you all to say good-bye. We've been through so many years together, the pain would be too great.
>
> [Kitty, overcome with emotion, hands the letter to Newly.]
>
> This letter is the only way I know of to tell you my decision. I'll be gone from Dodge for a while. I don't know for how long, but it will not be forever. I will be back ... and I'll think of you very often.... I pray all of you will remember with affection, your old friend, Doc.

Unfortunately for Dr. Chapman most of the citizens of Dodge greet him with suspicion and mistrust, especially Festus. He is confronted with his first serious case when Newly is badly injured in a freak explosion. Forced into emergency surgery, Dr. Chapman saves Newly and wins the trust of Festus and the other townspeople. The story, which was written by Executive Story Consultant Jack Miller, effectively and movingly explains Doc's absence and introduces the new doctor into the story line.

Fortunately, Stone was able to return to the show in late 1971, after missing only nine episodes. (Hingle appeared in five of those episodes.) His return was marked by a special three-part story (the only one in the show's history) written by Jim Byrnes, "Gold Train: The Bullet." Matt is bushwhacked in Dodge and seriously wounded. He will either die or be paralyzed unless the bullet is removed from an area near the spine. It is too delicate an operation to be performed in Doc's office, so Matt is put on a train for Denver. Festus, Newly, and Kitty accompany Doc and Matt on this dangerous journey. While Matt lies helpless in a railroad car, a band of outlaws stops the train in an effort to steal an army gold shipment. A gun battle ensues involving Festus and Newly. Meanwhile, Doc is forced to operate on the train with Kitty's assistance. Doc's newly learned expertise comes in handy and the operation is a success. The Barabases explain the significance of an incident involving Stone which occurred during the filming:

> ... A sign of Stone's recovery was that he once again stood up for his character during the shooting of this story. Mantley (the executive producer) wanted Doc to hit the bottle to steady his nerves for the delicate operation, but Stone refused, saying that Doc would never jeopardize his efficiency by swilling down a few drinks.[54]

Stone (along with Arness) remained with *Gunsmoke* for its full 20 year run. Then he retired to his ranch in Santa Fe where he raised livestock until his death at the age of 75 in 1980. His portrayal of Doc Adams must rank as a monumental achievement, not only in the history of television Westerns, but in the history of television drama.

When the role of Kitty was being cast, Georgia Ellis was never considered, even though the other radio cast members were at least given screen tests. The part was eventually given to Amanda Blake, an actress who had been under contract first to M-G-M and later to Columbia Pictures. At the time casting for the television version of *Gunsmoke* began, Blake was working at CBS on such productions as *Lux Video Theatre*, *Climax*, *Playhouse 90*, *Professional Father*, *Schlitz Playhouse of Stars*, and *My Favorite Husband*. After she learned of the role, she insisted on an audition. It was her persistence as much as her acting ability that won her the part.

Born Beverly Louise Neill in 1929 in Buffalo, New York, Blake began acting in school plays when she was 7. Later she gained experience doing New England summer stock. Her first film work came with M-G-M, who christened her Amanda Blake and proclaimed her "the next Greer Garson." Among her earliest films were two (*Battleground*, 1949, and *Stars in My Crown*, 1950) in which James Arness also appeared. She was cast in such box office successes as *Lili* (1953), *A Star Is Born* (1954), and *The Glass Slipper* (1955). Among her major roles, Blake was Cameron Mitchell's girlfriend in *Smuggler's Gold* (1951) and in Warner Bros.' *Cattle Town* (1952) she competed with Rita Moreno for Dennis Morgan's affections. About this time Amanda Blake began appearing on television. Red Skelton liked her immediately, and years after her success on *Gunsmoke*, she would appear annually as a guest on his show. "Mandy," he said, "is the most underrated straight-woman in Hollywood. Besides, she breaks up at my nonsense faster than anyone I know."[55]

That Blake was a competent dramatic actress was demonstrated by her appearances in "Double Exposure" on *Schlitz Playhouse of Stars* (1952), "Crossroads," also on *Schlitz Playhouse of Stars* (1952), "Breakfast at Nancy's" on *Cavalcade of America* (1953), "Nine Quarts of Water" on *Fireside Theatre* (1954), and "Vote of Confidence" on *Four Star Playhouse* (1954).

Amanda Blake acknowledged that she had listened quite often to the radio version of *Gunsmoke*. She had, therefore, some conception in her mind of the character she was to portray. In fact, Blake's interpretation of Kitty Russell took shape over the first two seasons. Originally intended to be a saloon girl, like the character on radio, Kitty had to be changed on television to avoid offending viewers in the more broadly based medium. She could still sleep with Matt, but no longer with the general public. On radio, Kitty had always been a working girl who had a special relationship with Matt. They were close

Matt with Kitty Russell as played by Amanda Blake when *Gunsmoke* was just beginning its 20 year television run.

friends, but the fact that she stayed in Dodge and did not participate in most of the adventures that took place in the surrounding countryside placed limits on the sharing that was possible in their relationship. Creator Macdonnell explained the relationship in a *TV Guide* interview in 1958:

> The real reason for Kitty's presence on the show is that she gives Matt someone to talk to. He can express his inner feelings to her and know he'll be understood. Because of her, he takes on another dimension. But they aren't in love with each other. There's simply a tremendous underlying affection.[56]

In the same article, Arness voiced his disagreement. "Their relationship is not platonic," he proclaimed. "The extent of their affection is up to the viewer's imagination." Years later Blake re-emphasized the differences between radio and television's Kitty:

> It was much more sanitized for television. They got away with murder on the radio series. On radio, Matt and Miss Kitty would be having a conversation and he'd get up to leave and you'd hear bed springs squeaking! We couldn't do any of that. It was all very nervous in those days. Then Jim and I decided to leave the whole thing a mystery. We developed what we called our eyeballing scenes, doing everything with looks. It was great fun.[57]

During the early formative years of the television show, Blake worked out a biographical background for her character (in the same manner, but much less elaborate than Stone had done for Doc). Published in *TV Guide*, the biography explained how Kitty had come to be the kind of person she was, as well as her relationship with Matt:

> There was a man—isn't there always? He loved her and he left her and then they put a label on her. Kitty isn't the type to take in washing. Somehow I have the idea—don't ask me how I got it—that Kitty came from New Orleans. Let's just say that I think seaport cities are more feminine, that they bring out the woman—by jungle instinct. So she drifted, and she'd drift out of Dodge if it weren't for Matt Dillon. . . . She'd love Matt to say, "Kitty, let's buy a hunk o'land and raise some beans and kids." But then we'd have *I Love Lucy Out West*.[58]

In a 1958 interview for *The British Television Annual*, Blake further elaborated on her conception of Kitty. (*Gunsmoke* was seen in Great Britain under the title *Gun Law*.) She explained:

> Evidently all the "Kittys" of the old West gained themselves quite a reputation over the years—a bad one; and I'm here to say it's a shame! . . .
> In those days, the 1870s, it was more or less a foregone conclusion that soon after reaching her early teens a girl would get married, help with the ploughing, and have children. In fact early marriage was not only the accepted thing, but a girl who had reached her twenties still unmarried was considered 'over the hill' and held in rather questionable repute just for being single!
> A girl like Kitty, who had a mind of her own and didn't want to tie the knot with just any cowhand simply because she was at the age when it was the thing to do, found herself looked upon as being on the road to ruin. . . .
> So Kitty, a girl with responsibilities beyond her years, became a saloon hostess, a term which over the years has become synonymous with something quite apart from propriety. But this connotation is, in my opinion, unfair and unjustified. . . .
> Kitty is all woman; I like her breed and respect her for having the courage of her convictions. I consider her role one of the finest breaks of my career. We had trouble early in the series deciding just how I should play the part of Kitty. At first I was a bit on the sweet side. So I gradually grew tougher and finally reached a happy medium of sweetness and toughness.[59]

In attempting to redefine Kitty's role on the television series, a number of details were emphasized about her character that altered the viewer's reaction to Kitty Russell as a person. Younger and less world weary than Kitty on radio, she was also unwilling to settle for less than she wanted out of life. Ambitious and careful with a dollar, she saved her money in order to buy into the Long Branch.

In the opening scene of "Daddy-O," written by John Meston, Matt returns from a trip to find a new sign over the Long Branch: "Russell and Pence." Chester says to Matt, "She's been waiting real proud for you, Mr. Dillon." When asked by Doc what he thinks of this development, Matt replies: "That's mighty fine, but I'd better get some of the dust off before I start mixing with influential citizens." Later when Matt sees Kitty, he tells her: "I hear you're a big business woman now—congratulations, I hope you make a million ..." It is a loyal and supportive response to her new status in the community.

On radio, Sam the bartender had owned the saloon. Once on television, Kitty had to have a more acceptable profession. Being a madam apparently offended propriety less than being simply a prostitute. Kitty, as portrayed by Amanda Blake, was always a hardheaded business woman, careful with a dollar, who handled her own accounts and inventoried her shipments of liquor. While Matt, because of his occupation as marshal, lived day-to-day on his government pay and bunked at Ma Smalley's or the jail, Kitty roomed at the Long Branch and personally looked after her investments. It was not surprising that eventually she became sole owner of the Long Branch.

As Blake grew older, so did Kitty. She was so comfortable with the character that the evolutionary process "took care of itself." In addition to her relationship with Matt, she interacted with Doc as daughter to father and first with Chester and later with Festus, as sister to brother. As the first major continuing female character in an adult Western, Blake set the standard by which others would be judged. Rita Parks' assessment of Blake's contributions provides some insight:

> "Gunsmoke's" leading lady, Amanda Blake, matured gracefully in a role running the gamut of traditional female roles in the genre. As owner of the Long Branch Saloon, Miss Kitty's original character type suggested the seductress by implication but never by overt expression. Yet Kitty's (and Amanda Blake's) playing out of that character type added depth and complexity to what might have become mere stereotype. In her relationship with Matt, she played the role of an affectionate wife in a long-successful marriage. In her many and varied relationships with other members both of the repertory and guest casts, Kitty was sister and mother to those in need of either role. Finally, in an age of growing awareness of the liberated woman, Kitty remained her own person.[60]

In fact Kitty was so much like Blake herself that the question was often raised where did Kitty Russell end and Amanda Blake begin? Blake's bedroom, for example, might have been Kitty's boudoir. It was furnished in flamboyant cow-town decor, with old picture frames on the walls and heavy velour drapes. An ornate chandelier, circa 1870, hung in her adjoining bathroom. Blake once explained "I'd like to think that Kitty would feel at home here."[61] Amanda Blake was very much like Kitty Russell in her personal life as well. Despite her flaming red hair, she defiantly wore red, or a color related to it, every day. In the company of men, she unhesitatingly lit her own cigarettes and found her own ash trays. She was also known to down two or three scotch-and-waters before dinner. Furthermore, she could laugh at a good off-color story.

And off-camera Blake was close to her costars, especially Weaver (and later Ken Curtis) and Stone. Once a month the three would tour the hinterlands at fairs and rodeos with a song-and-patter act in which they remained steadfastly in character. When Blake would belt out the song written especially for Kitty by actor William Schallert, she would bring down the house. Entitled "The Long Branch Blues," it fit her like a glove.

Little by little, viewers learned about Kitty in the early episodes of *Gunsmoke*. In "Daddy-O," when her father shows up in Dodge to rescue his daughter from the unseemly profession of saloon owner, Kitty exclaims:

> You're too late. I'm not quitting for you or for anybody else. I've had it too rough to give up everything now that I've got a chance to live decently and to be somebody.... You offer me help the first time in my life that I don't need it.

In "Custer," Kitty tries to get Matt to retire from being marshal:

> KITTY: You going to Hays for the trial?
> MATT: I'll have to.
> KITTY: That'll take about a week, I suppose.
> MATT: About. Why?
> KITTY: Nothing. Only you've just been away for ten days.
> MATT: I have to earn a living, Kitty.
> KITTY: You could make more money gambling ... right here in Dodge.

Kitty's interest in Matt is revealed more fully, in "Perce," with this exchange involving Chester:

> KITTY: Well, it looks like another good night for us.
> CHESTER: Miss Kitty, You must be about the richest woman in the entire world.
> KITTY: You think I'd be working if I was rich?
> CHESTER: You'll always be working... You couldn't quit. Not even if you got married.
> KITTY: I'd like to have the choice, Chester. I'd like that much, at least.
> CHESTER: Why, you could get married anytime you wanted. Any man'd be a fool not to have you.
> KITTY: (looking up) Here comes one now.
> CHESTER: Huh? (looks up)
> (Matt has just entered the Long Branch)

As can be seen from this scene, Kitty occasionally expresses her need for love. She knows, as Chester has pointed out, that she is desirable to many men, but needs further assurances from the one man she cares for most—Matt. Over the 19 seasons Blake appeared on *Gunsmoke*, Kitty was tempted to find love elsewhere on only a couple of occasions.

Kitty seriously considers marriage with someone other than Matt in "Kitty's Love Affair." When Matt is called back to Dodge on business while on his way to St. Louis with Kitty for a vacation, she angrily decides to continue the trip alone. Gunfighter Will Stanbridge (well played by Richard Kiley) boards the stage and saves Kitty from being assaulted when the stage is held up. While recuperating in Dodge from the wounds he received in the gunfight, he is drawn to Kitty and she to him. Kitty begins to question her life with Matt:

> KITTY: I need some answers. The scales are getting all out of whack. It's hard to throw away eighteen years.
> MATT: Yeah.
> KITTY: I know what that badge means to you, to this town, to everyone. But I'm thinking of us. I was just a kid when we met, Matt, and I was gonna live forever. I knew how things had to be with us, and it was all right. But I thought that someday, some far off someday, that things would change. Well, Matt my somedays are almost gone. I guess what I'm asking is for you to tell me to say "no" to Will Stambridge.
> MATT: Kitty, you know how I feel. But that's a decision you're gonna have to make yourself.
> KITTY: I know, Matt. I know.

The story ends with Kitty not really having to make that choice. Stambridge, realizing that a man with his reputation can never settle down to a normal life, leaves Dodge. The episode closes as Matt and Kitty with their arms around each other walk toward the Long Branch while Doc and Festus look on with obvious satisfaction. All is right with the world once again, at least in Dodge.

Kitty was always willing to do anything when Matt's safety was concerned. In "The Wreckers," outlaws wreck a stage carrying Matt, Kitty and a convict. Matt is knocked unconscious and the convict appears dead. Kitty handcuffs Matt and pins his badge on the convict in an attempt to save Matt's life. Although the ruse ultimately fails, Kitty is instrumental in raising the ransom demanded by the outlaws for Matt's life. In "The Badge" she risks her own life to warn Matt of a sniper about to ambush him.

Intelligent, resourceful, as well as fearless, Kitty often takes the initiative in helping others who are injured or in trouble. In "Help Me Kitty," she protects an 18 year old expectant mother being terrorized by outlaws at a relay station. An old friend of Kitty's is the recipient of her assistance when she stops for an unexpected visit in "Thursday's Child." In "The Twisted Heritage" Kitty drives a stage across the plains in a desperate race to save the life of a wounded passenger after the driver has been killed.

Kitty's poker playing ability is utilized to good advantage in several episodes. She attempts to win the life of a young man who has saved her life in "The Prisoner." And in "Whalen's Men," Kitty challenges the ruthless leader of a band of outlaws to a card game, with Matt's life as the stakes.

The most common "Kitty scenario" over the years, however, is one in which Kitty's life has been placed in jeopardy and Matt is called upon to rescue her. In "Kittycaught," Kitty is taken hostage in a bank robbery and Matt and Chester must trail the robbers and ambush them or Kitty will be killed. In "Twenty Miles from Dodge," she is kidnapped from a stage by a band of outlaws and held for ransom. Kitty and Festus are kidnapped by a judge bent on revenge for the death of his son (in "The Avengers.") He plans to try them in a kangaroo court and then hang them. In "The Jailer," Kitty is kidnapped by the sons and widow (superbly played by Bette Davis) of a man who has been hanged for murder. The widow blames Matt for her husband's death and uses Kitty to lure him into a trap. In "The War Priest," Kitty is kidnapped and held hostage by a wounded Apache medicine man who is being pursued by a drunken cavalry sergeant. Kitty's safety in endangered by both the Apache and the inebriated army officer whose stretch in the Army is about to expire. A young man seeking revenge for his father's execution fifteen years earlier kidnaps Kitty in "The Noose."

Tough and resilient, Kitty is at her most vulnerable when Matt's life is at risk. Eleven times in fifteen years Doc has removed bullets from Matt after he has been seriously wounded. After threatening for years to sell the Long Branch, and leave Dodge, Kitty finally follows through with her threat when Matt is seriously wounded again in "The Badge." This scene holds the key to her pent up feelings:

> Doc: (After removing the bullet from Matt): Kitty, I know this has been harder on you than on anybody ... but, he's gonna be all right. I promise you.
>
> KITTY: (after downing a shot of whiskey): What about next time, Doc? What can you promise me about that?

Flashbacks were taken from this episode (as well as several from "Mannon") for *Gunsmoke: Return to Dodge* in 1987. They were used to explain why Kitty left Dodge and moved to New Orleans. In "The Badge," however, Kitty does return at the end of the episode.

Gunsmoke, of course, made Amanda Blake a star. Amanda Blake made Kitty Russell immortal. Blake was the first woman to be inducted into the Hall of Fame of Great Western Actors and Actresses in Oklahoma City. In 1959, she was nominated for an Emmy for Best Supporting Actress in a Dramatic Series, but lost the award to Barbara Hale of *Perry Mason*. At the end of *Gunsmoke*'s nineteenth season, Blake chose to leave the series. She later explained:

> I was very tired and had been commuting from Arizona for years. I was becoming a person I didn't like very much. It was a difficult decision to make. I shed a lot of tears.[62]

Her final *Gunsmoke* appearance (except for *Return to Dodge*) was in "Disciple" broadcast on April 1, 1974, in which she once again must worry about a serious injury to Matt. (He has been left without the use of his shooting arm and fearing he can no longer protect the residents of Dodge, he turns in his badge.) After *Gunsmoke*, Blake acted in television movies and game shows and appeared as a guest on such dramatic series as *Hart to Hart*, *The Loveboat*, and *The Quest*, as well as, the popular soap opera, *The Edge of Night*. She died in August 1989, at the age of 60.

Partly because of friction with cast members and partly because of the pressure of producing 52 half-hour *Gunsmoke* dramas during the first year (on a three-day filming schedule per show), Charles Marquis Warren left the show after completing the first 26 episodes. He had successfully transformed *Gunsmoke* from a radio to a television Western. He had also helped choose an entirely different cast while retaining the style of the radio program by making Norman Macdonnell associate producer and by using television adaptations of John Meston's radio scripts as his primary source of material. Macdonnell was the logical choice as successor to Warren and for the next eight years he guided *Gunsmoke* through its expansion to an hour long program. He was also responsible for adding two new continuing characters, Quint Asper and Festus Haggen.

The first new character to join the program was Quint Asper, a half-breed blacksmith. Played by 26 year old Burt Reynolds, the part was originally conceived as a new helper for Matt when Chester left. Dennis Weaver had planned to leave the show at the beginning of the 1962-63 season, but his plans fell through. Signed for eight episodes, Reynolds was kept even after Weaver returned. Reynolds was handsome and fun-loving with considerable sex appeal. He achieved some success on television in the sixties before reaching superstardom in motion pictures during the seventies. The son of a Florida police chief, Reynolds was born in Waycross, Georgia, in 1936 and grew up in Palm Beach Florida. He was an outstanding football prospect until an auto accident ended his plans to turn pro. Instead he became an actor, moving to New York in the mid-fifties and winning his first role on Broadway in a revival of *Mr. Roberts* in 1956.

Reynolds also was given small roles, usually as villains, on several television shows (e.g., *General Electric Theater*, *Schlitz Playhouse* and *M Squad*). His first major break came when he was selected to play opposite Darren McGavin in the 1959 adventure series *Riverboat*. He was dropped from the show after a year, but continued to get guest spots on shows like *Michael Shayne*, *Alfred Hitchcock Presents* and *Route 66*.

Because his grandmother was a full-blooded Cherokee, Reynolds had played other Indian roles prior to being cast as Quint Asper. Reynolds was chosen for the part from among 300 actors who applied. The Quint Asper character was the creation of John Meston and was introduced to television viewers in an episode called "Quint Asper Comes Home" broadcast on September 29, 1962. After white men slay his white father, Quint, whose mother is Comanche, joins her tribe so he can avenge his father's murder by killing more white men. Quint is subsequently wounded during a raid and is taken back to Dodge by Matt to recover. Suspicious of Matt because he is white, Quint is gradually won over by Matt's efforts to befriend him. Still, Quint is unacceptable to the townspeople and so he decides to return to his life as Comanche. After refusing to kill a white prisoner, Quint is relegated to women's work by the Comanche chief. Rejecting this existence, he helps the prisoner escape and later, with Matt's support, returns to Dodge and becomes the town's blacksmith.

Quint Asper quickly established himself as another strong, silent character like Dillon, a loner who did not need other characters in order to support a storyline himself. Often appearing bare-chested, Reynolds exuded a certain charisma and received over

The *Gunsmoke* cast circa 1965 with Burt Reynolds (second from left) as Quint Asper, Milburn Stone as Doc Adams and Ken Curtis as Festus Haggen joining Arness and Amanda Blake.

four thousand fan letters after his first appearance. During his second season on the show, Reynolds' role was included in 15 episodes. In "Quint's Indian," another Meston story, Quint is beaten up by some townsmen after being framed for horse stealing. Angered by the incident, he leaves town. After clearing Quint of the charges, Matt rides out to urge his return to Dodge. Instead of finding Quint, he is captured by a group of renegade Indians. After Quint secures his release, the friendship between the two men is strengthened and Quint again returns to Dodge.

Problems with Quint's character began to arise during the second season after he joined the cast. As Norman Macdonnell explained it, there were a limited number of stories which could be built around the fact that the blacksmith was a half-breed. They were called "Get your filthy hands off my daughter" type stores by Macdonnell.[63] And yet because the blacksmith was half Comanche, it was impossible to overlook this part of his character in the historical context of the 1870s. Several outstanding scripts dealing with bigotry toward half-breeds and Indians were written by Kathleen Hite ("Quint's Trail," "Comanches Is Soft," and "Quint-Cident"—a variation on that theme, where Quint must deal with the wrath of a woman spurned) and one by Les Crutchfield ("Crooked Mile").

A second problem arose from the fact that Quint did not in any way fill the comic void which the eventual departure of Weaver as Chester would leave. Thus, a second new character, Festus Haggen, was introduced and Quint was phased out. This phasing out was agreed upon by both Macdonnell and Reynolds. Reynolds had become dissatisfied with the potential for further development of this character. In a recent interview with SuzAnne Barabas he explained:

> You can't be a leading man when you're standing next to a guy six-foot-eight—and his name is Matt Dillon. I mean, I was the blacksmith and people used to call me a dirty half-breed and spit on me for fifty-eight minutes and then Arness would come back from Hawaii and beat 'em up. So it wasn't a terrific role in terms of really shining.[64]

So, by the end of the 1965-66 season Quint Asper had faded away and was never heard from again. Reynolds, of course, went on to star in two television series of his own, *Hawk* (1966) and *Dan August* (1970–1971), and then made the big time with such hit films as *Deliverance* (1972), *The Longest Yard* (1974), *Smokey and the Bandit* (1977), *Hooper* (1978), *Sharkey's Machine* (1981), *The Best Little Whorehouse in Texas* (1982), and *City Heat* (1984). He made a triumphant return to network television in 1989 with *B.L. Stryker*, which he followed with the even more successful *Evening Shade* (1990–1994).

To most television viewers, Festus was the name of the character on *Gunsmoke* who replaced Chester, not a Roman governor who was responsible for the apostle Paul's being sent to Rome in A.D. 60. Actually the character of Festus Haggen was the same character that had been called Monk on CBS's *Have Gun, Will Travel*. Both were the creation of writer Les Crutchfield. Crutchfield, a regular contributor to *Gunsmoke* since its third broadcast on radio and a freelance writer with numerous Western television credits, devised the character of Monk for an episode of *Have Gun, Will Travel* in which this comic character calls the program's hero "Mr. Palidin."

In the episode, "The Naked Gun," Monk almost gets Paladin hanged, hits him in the head with a log, kills two men and causes Paladin to kill another. The following season writer Jay Simms brought the character of Monk back in a purely comic episode entitled "Love's Young Dream" in which Monk inherits half interest in a fine dining establishment in San Francisco. The dirty bumpkin keeps getting thrown out until Paladin comes to his rescue. In the end Monk learns some manners, and wins the hand of the beautiful co-owner and hostess (with a little help from Paladin). Along the way, actor Ken Curtis got to show off his superb singing voice.

Ken Curtis was born Curtis Gates in the dry-lands of southeastern Colorado in a two room prairie cabin on July 2, 1916. He grew up in near by Lamar. His father was a homesteader and for a while sheriff of Las Animas, Colorado. The family lived in the jail, and at 10, young Curtis was substitute jailer when his father was out of town. He was blessed with a truly outstanding singing voice.

Although Curtis wanted to be a doctor, he was so successful as a songwriter in student productions at Colorado College that he left school and headed for Hollywood. There in 1939, he was assigned as a staff singer for NBC Radio. Later he sang briefly with the Tommy Dorsey Orchestra after Frank Sinatra left. It was Dorsey who changed his name to Ken Curtis. Before enlisting in the Army in 1942, Curtis sang with Shep Fields' band. After the war, his rendition of "Tumbling Tumbleweeds" on a radio program with Johnny Mercer landed him the costarring role in a series of Westerns of which he later said, "I'd stop in the middle of a gun fight and sing a song."[65] Curtis appeared in eight B Westerns for Columbia Pictures between 1945 and 1949 beginning with *Rhythm Roundup*. These films were more like Western jamborees than hard-hitting adventures with the songs always outnumbering the fights. In 1949 Curtis joined the Sons of the Pioneers, replacing original member Tim Spencer, and remained with them until 1953. Curtis also made one serial, *Don Daredevil Rides Again* for Republic Pictures in 1951 in which he played a masked Zorro-like hero.

During this period, Curtis met and married Barbara Ford, the daughter of famed movie director John Ford, and was given a small but memorable part in *The Searchers*. Curtis later believed that the character of Monk and Festus evolved out of that role. He recalled that it was supposed to be a serious part, "a kind of a Ralph Bellamy," but he got to "kidding around on the set," doing the dry-lands dialect he had picked up in Colorado. He did not realize that Ford was listening. When it came time to say his lines again, Ford had him play them that way.[66]

Other quality films in which Curtis appeared included such classics as *The Quiet Man* (1952), *The Wings of Eagles* (1957), *The Last Hurrah* (1958), *The Alamo* (1960), *How the West Was Won* (1963), and *Cheyenne Autumn* (1964). He was also cast as skydiver Jim Buckley in the syndicated television series *Ripcord* (1961–1963) and appeared in supporting roles on *Perry Mason* and *Rawhide*, as well as *Have Gun, Will Travel*. Curtis played several different characters on *Gunsmoke* (e.g., a villain, a victim and an Indian) before his first appearance as Festus on December 8, 1962, in "Us Haggens." In what was originally intended to be a single appearance, according to Norman Macdonnell, Festus was created. The *Gunsmoke* publicity release described the character as "a rascal of a drifter who is the only honest member of an outlaw family."[67] After his appearance during *Gunsmoke*'s eighth season, Macdonnell requested another script featuring Festus for the following year.

This time the story and script was written by John Dunkel and "Prairie Wolfer" was aired on January 18, 1964. (This is a rare *Gunsmoke* episode in which Matt, Chester, Doc, Kitty, Quint and Festus all appear.) The other members of the cast all liked Curtis and when it became clear that Weaver was finally leaving the show, Festus was phased in with spaced-out appearances during the rest of the season. Public reaction was not totally positive during this period. Commenting on fan mail, Macdonnell said at the time:

> The mail on Festus is either absolutely white or absolutely black. Some people say they can't stand him. Others say they like him better than Chester. They either love him or they hate him—but ninety percent say they love him.[68]

In "Us Haggens," Festus proves that his word, when sealed with a handshake, is as good as gold, as he helps Matt track down his Uncle Black Jack Haggen. It is obviously difficult for Festus as a Haggen to turn against his kin, but when the chips are down he backs Matt. He knows that Black Jack is a no-good, murderous scoundrel who was responsible for the painful death of one of Festus' brothers. In the script of "Prairie Wolfer," Dunkel gives this physical description of Festus:

> Festus Haggen is a wolfer, bewhiskered and unkempt, filthy of skin and clothes, he seems to be dressed in rags, actually it is buckskin so greasy and worn as to be nearly falling apart. He slouches on his big, rawboned mule, legs dangling, Hawken rifle across his thighs, ready for instant action.

Later in the same script we are given a glimpse of the townspeople's reaction to him:

> Festus comes riding down the street, trailing his pack horse. He presents such an out-landish figure that people turn to stare. [He stops at] a hitchrack, where he dismounts and ties his mule. Then he unties a pack of wolf pelts from the pack horse and slings them over his shoulder. A lady passes close and draws back from the obvious odor—he only gives her a grimace and goes on into a store.

The most striking aspect of Festus' personality is his humor which usually comes from his own special way of putting things. For example, in "Cattle Barons" this exchange takes place between Festus and a cattle rancher named Luke Cumberledge:

> FESTUS: Mr. Cumberledge, you don't know us Haggens 'r ya' wouldn't say sich a thing! Like Great-Unke Herkle said—'catch a Haggen in a lie, 'n a thunderbolt 'll hit him from th' clear blue sky!
> CUMBERLEDGE: What happened to Great-Uncle Herkle?
> FESTUS: Well—they's some say that this thunderstorm came up real suddenlike one time...

Carrying on in the tradition of Doc and Chester, Doc and Festus continued the verbal fencing that made both characters so human. Consider this discussion from "The Prodigal":

> (Festus is walking thoughtfully around Doc's buggy, glancing at the wheels. Doc impatiently watches him.)
> DOC: Well, for heaven's sake, I didn't ask for an estimate on a new buggy.
> FESTUS: Got t'see what sorta condition them wheels is in, Doc.
> DOC: I *know* what condition they're in! The spokes are loose!
> FESTUS: An' that there rein's about to fall off.
> DOC: I know that too! How much is it going to cost me to have 'em fixed?
> FESTUS: Shouldn't 'mount t'much; fifty cents 'll do. [sly look] Soakin' in the crik a few hours'll swell them spokes back tight as pin feathers on a prairie chicken's rump.
> DOC: Soaking in the crik?!
> FESTUS: Sure.
> DOC: And while you're sitting there, letting the wheels soak—I suppose you'll do a little fishing.
> FESTUS: Now that you mention it...
> DOC: So I end up paying you fifty-cents to fish!
> FESTUS: Well, Doc. I'm gonna have t'dig me some worms, catch me some grasshoppers. That's tirin'. If it wasn't for them wheels needin' soakin', I wouldn't have to...

Although the basic bumpkin humor of Chester and Festus was similar, the characters were quite different. Festus could be "cold and deadly." In "May Blossom" he kills a man in cold blood for raping his cousin. Festus was also occasionally seen kissing a girl (e.g., in "Now That April's Here"), something which would have been unthinkable for Chester. Furthermore, unlike Chester, Festus was a strong and independent man in his own right. Festus did not need the approval, permission or authority of Matt Dillon in order to take action on his own. Still, he was a friend of the marshal, like Chester, and addressed him with a name that no other character used ("Matthew," instead of Chester's "Mr. Dillon").

As Festus developed relationships with the other characters on *Gunsmoke,* he became a remarkable creation—a very alive, breathing character. The easiest relationship to

James Arness as an older and wiser Matt Dillon, circa 1970.

establish was that with Matt. He had proven his honesty and loyalty in their very first meeting, although Matt knew he was not above bending the law if the situation required it. Festus later claimed that Matthew had hired him "cuz I know more about four-legged critters than anybody you ever saw—and that goes special fer wolves" ("Clayton Thaddeus Greenwood"). In addition Festus was brave and dependable and could, when necessary, function as deputy. The friendship between Festus and Matt was therefore based on mutual trust and respect.

The most difficult relationship to establish was between Doc and Festus. As Milburn Stone later described the dilemma:

What was Doc, with all his education doing spending any amount of time with a messy, uneducated saddle tramp like Festus; the two men obviously had nothing in common.[69]

Jack Ross Stanley explains how this problem was resolved:

> The resolution came during the filming of one scene when Doc and Festus crossed the street from the Long Branch together and Festus attempted to help Doc make a high step up from the street to one of the boardwalks. Curtis tried to help Doc while Stone instinctively batted his arm away as if to say "don't you dare touch me." After the scene was over Stone explained that Doc would not let Festus touch him because as far as Doc was concerned Festus was "about one step up from the Neanderthal Man." . . . Doc, as Stone saw it, was unable to believe anybody like Festus really existed and so Doc was fascinated by this "throwback." Stone figured that at some point Doc would probably write a paper on Festus and submit it to a medical journal. For Festus' part he was content to have Doc observe him and at the same time Festus loved to see how far he could mislead Doc in his observations. Unlike Chester, Festus was able to give as good as he got from Doc, and often he would leave Doc mad and frustrated because Doc was unable to find an appropriate comeback for one of Festus's comments. The constant bickering and insulting between the two men was "the only way two grown men can make love to each other." Stone said, "You wouldn't think of insulting somebody you didn't like; he's liable to hit you." The relationship between Doc and Festus was more abrasive than that between Doc and Chester because, as Stone explained, "Chester was a little dog and you had to be careful or you'd hurt his feelings. But Festus is more than a match for Doc; you can't hurt his feelings and he gives it right back."[70]

On a personal level Curtis and Stone toured for several years making appearances together at rodeos and fairs. Curtis' favorite episode was one in which he and Doc were both featured, entitled "Wishbone." He and Stone had suggested the storyline to writer Paul Savage. It was based on an incident that happened to Curtis' mother when she was a young girl living in Arkansas. She was bitten by a copperhead and a farmhand killed and split open a chicken which he applied to the wound as a poultice. It saved her life. In the *Gunsmoke* story Festus uses prayer and a fresh-killed chicken to save Doc's life.[71]

Festus' relationship with Kitty evolved out of the fact that he was the friend of two mutual friends (Matt and Doc) of Kitty. Furthermore, Festus liked women and liquor, both of which were Kitty's stock and trade. And Kitty was always a pushover for a free beer.

Most episodes that feature Festus fall into one of three categories: comedies, usually involving other members of the Haggen family (e.g., "Deputy Festus" and "Hard Luck Henry"); life-threatening situations, where Festus is in mortal danger often because of mistaken identity (like "Rope Fever," "Alias Festus Haggen," and "Mad Dog") and stories involving selfless acts of heroism by Festus (like "Eleven Dollars" and "Trail of Bloodshed").

One particularly amusing episode (which did not involve other Haggens) was "Tycoon." Festus inherits $500 from a man he once helped. He uses the money to go into the freight business with an old friend. His friend, however, extravagantly spends money for a steam calliope, a circus wagon and two pairs of matched white horses. Then he encourages Festus to buy an elegant suit of clothes. When the two partners try to drive their wagon across a toll road they encounter the Fowler family. Ma sees Festus as a prime catch for her unmarried daughter and he has to fight off both the girl and the young farmer she is in love with. Festus almost becomes the victim of a "shotgun wedding," but by selling his share of the business to the young farmer, he is able to make Ma Fowler see that he, and not Festus, is the best mate for her daughter. "All's well, that ends well" as Festus explains to Doc that not only will he get his own money back (in installments) from the young man, but $50 extra as well.

The story "plays" better than it reads and is a delightfully funny tour de force for Ken Curtis and the others, especially Shug Fisher, who plays his partner Titus, and Nora Marlowe, who is Ma. It is an excellent example of how Festus was often utilized to bring humor into the series. Curtis remained with *Gunsmoke* until it left the air in 1975 — longer than any of the other major characters except Matt, Doc and Kitty.

As of September 1964 Norman Macdonnell had been the producer of television's *Gunsmoke* for nine years. Yet even under his experienced guidance the show had slipped from being ranked the number one show in the country to being twentieth at the end of the 1963-64 season. This was the third year that *Gunsmoke* had been an hour-long drama and the third year it had lost ground in the ratings. In an effort to reverse this trend, the CBS hierarchy decided to fire Macdonnell by instituting a new policy whereby no producer could stay with any CBS television program longer than four years. Macdonnell was replaced by director Philip Leacock. Although no stranger to television production (with work on *The Alfred Hitchcock Hour*, *Route 66*, and *The Defenders*), Leacock had never before sat in a producer's chair. His *Gunsmoke* assignment was made more difficult by his lack of rapport with the cast and crew brought on by Macdonnell's abrupt departure. Two of the major writers on the series, John Meston and Kathleen Hite, left in sympathy with Macdonnell. Furthermore, Leacock was British and had little experience with Westerns. (He had directed a couple of *Rawhide* episodes.) As producer for two seasons, Leacock was responsible for three major changes in the production of the television program: first, the institution of a guest star policy under which the regular cast was subordinated to the guest character each week; second, the change-over in filming from black and white to color; and third, the introduction of a new character, Thad Greenwood (as Quint disappeared).

In addition to Chester, every new, continuing character introduced in *Gunsmoke* after the first year was developed with the partial objective of providing "romantic interest." Both Chester and later Festus, however, were limited by their very natures in the type of women with whom they could become involved — neither man could financially support a genuinely refined lady. Therefore, women attracted to Chester and Festus had to be women of a low socioeconomic status. To some extent this was also true of the character of Quint because he was a half-breed. For this reason, primarily, Philip Leacock decided to introduce a new character to *Gunsmoke*, Thad Greenwood. A CBS publicity release dated August 29, 1966, describes Clayton Thaddeus (Thad) Greenwood as a shy young man who comes to Dodge City to avenge the death of his sheriff father and decides to remain. The release further announced that Roger Ewing would play Thad:

> Roger Ewing gives the character [Thad] a shy, boyish quality that marks the 24-year-old actor as a potential romantic interest for a generation of feminine fans who were hardly old enough to watch television when "Gunsmoke" first hit television 11 years ago.[72]

Ewing had made one prior appearance on *Gunsmoke* in an episode entitled "Song for Dying," with Theodore Bikel and Lee Majors. Prior to *Gunsmoke* he had appeared in small supporting roles in such films as *Ensign Pulver* (1964) and *None But the Brave* (1965), and in *Eleventh Hour, Room 222, Bewitched*, and *The Farmer's Daughter* on television. The part of Thad Greenwood was Ewing's first major role.

Thad was created by writer Calvin Clements and introduced to viewers in an episode called simply "Clayton Thaddeus Greenwood" on October 2, 1965. In the story four cowboys bully an elderly sheriff in a small town until he dies of a heart attack. Thad Greenwood, his son, follows the men to Dodge where he tries to arrest them. Since they have committed no crime in Kansas, Thad is unable to carry out his mission. He decides to wait in Dodge for them to commit a crime for which they can be punished. It turns out that they have been using trained dogs to steal cattle and with Matt's help all four are either killed or captured. At the close of the episode, Matt invites Thad to stay in Dodge as a deputy marshal at a salary eight times the one dollar a month he was making back home.

Ewing made eight more appearances that season, 1965-66, and was signed for a second season as he became one of Dodge City's leading citizens. One of his best episodes was undoubtedly "Quaker Girl," with guest star William Shatner. Shatner played an escaped convict and murderer whose identity is confused with that of Thad's when a group of Quakers rescue them on the desert where they have been stranded. Thad develops a romantic interest in a pretty, young Quaker girl. When he accidently injures her father, however, she chooses to believe that Thad is the criminal and the romance is squelched. This is exactly the kind of storyline for which Thad's character was created and Ewing's winsome smile and boyish good looks were well suited to this role. Furthermore, Ewing did project a pleasing personality which fit in nicely with the other regular *Gunsmoke* characters. Still, the character did not create as much interest among viewers as the producer had hoped and Thad was dropped from the series after only a year and a half. Years later Ewing described his role as

> ... an unofficial official deputy, or official unofficial deputy ... a very loose character.... He was just there.... With Thad's family gone, Matt, Kitty, Doc and Festus sort of adopted him.... Anything that needed to be done, you know, an extra hand here, and extra hand there, Thad was always around.... He fit in whenever necessary.[73]

After leaving *Gunsmoke*, Ewing gave up acting for photography, traveling extensively throughout Europe, Russia, Mexico and the South Pacific. The "romantic interest" on *Gunsmoke* soon shifted to another new character, Newly O'Brien.

Meanwhile, there had been another change at the top. In January 1967, Philip Leacock left *Gunsmoke* to assume the executive producership of another CBS Western, *Cimarron Strip*. During Leacock's two years with the series, the ratings had fallen still further to thirty-fourth and within two months of his departure *Gunsmoke* was cancelled. To the rescue came John Mantley, who would be *Gunsmoke*'s final executive producer. Mantley, who had begun as story editor under Leacock, was promoted to associate producer in 1965, to producer in 1966 and then to executive producer in 1967. Mantley was able to secure a one year renewal. Instead of cancellation, the program was moved from Saturday to Monday evenings at an earlier hour. Under Mantley, *Gunsmoke* returned to its earlier status as one of the top ten rated programs in the country. He was responsible for the program's evolution from a Western morality play to a dramatic anthology while operating under the network's severe violence restrictions. Mantley was also responsible for dropping Thad Greenwood and replacing that character with a new continuing character called Newly O'Brien.

Newly O'Brien, as created by writer Calvin Clements and played by Buck Taylor, was a handsome young gunsmith from the East who decided to settle down in Dodge City. He was honest, thrifty, single, slightly shy, but with a good eye for a pretty young girl. Unlike Quint, Newly was no second-class citizen. Although a second-generation Irishman, Newly was an American. Unlike Festus, he was educated. Unlike Chester, he was a skilled craftsman who was capable of earning a middle-class living. As a gunsmith, Newly had a trade which might call him away from Dodge to do work for the Army if the need arose in a story. His trade was also involved with the culture of the West—guns and their violence. Still, Newly was philosophical about the use of firearms, considering them only as tools like any other tool on the frontier. Yet this occupation also provided Newly with a reason to have more than average experience in handling pistols and rifles. Thus he was a logical choice to serve as part-time deputy for Matt and even fill in for the marshal when Matt had to be out of town.

John Mantley saw Newly filling the need for a character who would appeal to younger viewers. As Mantly explained, Newly was the embodiment of brash, impetuous youth, tempered with a complete willingness "to learn from his elders."[74] He was Matt Dillon as a young man; honest, open and dependable. Newley was capable of acting on his own and doing so in the spirit of youth or of newly acquired maturity.

Buck Taylor was born Walter Clarence Taylor III in Los Angeles. He was nicknamed by his father, veteran character actor and former vaudevillian Dub Taylor, because he weighed nine pounds at birth and "looked like a big buck."[75] His mother was a member of an acrobatic dance act called the Dean Sisters when she appeared on the same vaudeville bill with Dub (short for "W"), who played the xylophone and harmonica. (Dub appeared in scores of B Westerns as a comedy sidekick called "Cannonball" to Wild Bill Elliott, Russell Hayden, Charles Starrett, and Jimmy Wakely.) Young Taylor and his sister were raised on a small ranch in the San Fernando Valley. His first ambition was to be an illustrator and weekends, while he was in high school, he attended the Chouinard Art Institute. He was also an all-city gymnast which won him a scholarship to the University of Southern California. There he studied art, cinema and theater and tried out unsuccessfully for the United States Olympic team in 1960. He would have tried again in 1964, but a shoulder injury caused by a fall from a horse ended his gymnastics career. (The accident had occurred during the filming of a television show on which Taylor was serving as a stuntman.)

After serving a hitch in the Navy, Taylor decided to pursue a career as an actor. He supported himself between occasional acting jobs by driving a truck during the day and working as a parking lot attendant at night. Gradually, parts began to come his way. Before his role on *Gunsmoke*, Taylor had appeared a hundred or so television shows including *The Rebel*, *Ben Casey*, *The Fugitive*, *The Big Valley*, *Alfred Hitchcock Presents* and *Death Valley Days* (usually as a villain). His film experience included roles in *Ensign Pulver* (1964), *The Wild Angels* (1966) and *The Devil's Angels* (1967).

Buck Taylor made his first appearance on *Gunsmoke* not as good-guy Newly O'Brien, but as a killer named Leonard Parker in a two-part story entitled "Vengeance." Beneath his menacing exterior Mantley saw the young, rugged, but basically innocent quality that Taylor displayed later as Newly. (Unfortunately, his debut performance was later withheld from reruns because Mantley did not want to confuse viewers.) Taylor recalled that at first the producers were looking for a character named "Newly Jorgensen," but after he was cast in the role, the character was renamed O'Brien in keeping with Taylor's Irish background and dark appearance.

In "The Pillagers" broadcast on November 6, 1967, Newly O'Brien made his debut as a young gunsmith from Philadelphia traveling on a stage also carrying Kitty to Dodge. Newly and Kitty are abducted at gunpoint and taken to the hideout of the notorious bandit Julio Mañez (played by John Saxon). Because Newly carries gunsmith tools in the medical bag of his late uncle, Mañez is convinced that Newly is a doctor. Actually Newly has spent only six months in medical school before deciding to switch to engineering and become a gunsmith. Manez orders Newly, on threat of death to himself and Kitty, to extract a bullet from his seriously wounded brother Juan.

First, Newly is permitted to ride to Dodge (while Kitty remains a prisoner) in order to obtain the ether needed for the surgery. After the comanchero sent to keep an eye on him gets drunk, Newly reveals to Festus and Matt what has happened. They plan to sneak up on the outlaws' lair on foot after Newly has returned to carry out the surgery and see to the safety of Kitty. By constructing a gun out of some pipe, Newly is able to assist Matt and Festus in the destruction of the gang. Because of this experience and at the urging of his new found friends, Newly decides to remain in Dodge and open a gunsmith shop.

Newly is shown to good advantage with excellent scripts over the final eight seasons of *Gunsmoke*. He is the only major character to get married on the series. In the poignant episode "Patricia," Newly lives up to his "romantic interest" potential when he falls in love with and marries a beautiful young governess from the East named Patricia Colby. After meeting on a stage headed for Dodge, they work together helping victims of a Kansas tornado. Unfortunately their happiness is short lived. Patricia is stricken with leukemia and dies. Despondent, Newly vows to dedicate himself to medicine and to complete his studies with Doc's assistance. Newly is as much influenced in his decision to become a doctor by something Patricia said to him when he was ministering to the needs of the tornado victims as by Doc's plea for someone to whom he can pass on his medical knowledge. She told him: "Some men have a special gift, Newly. It's kind of an instinct for healing. I think you have it and I think it would be a shame if you didn't do anything with it." It was said that this episode was written because of Milburn Stone's health problems—in case Dodge needed a new physician.[76]

In a follow-up story the following season, Newly was given a chance to practice what he has learned in "The Hanging of Newly O'Brien." When Doc becomes overburdened with patients, he sends Newly out to check on some families in the back country. At first Newly is discouraged by the lack of confidence the people show in him. Following a boy whose grandfather is seriously ill to his home, Newly finds the man choking to death. He attempts a new medical procedure called a tracheotomy to save the old man's life, but he dies anyway. The superstitious hill people blame Newly and sentence him to hang for murder.

Doc and Festus arrive on the scene just as Newly is about to be hanged and in the struggle that ensues Doc is seriously wounded. Newly is permitted to operate on Doc in order to remove the bullet and stop the bleeding. By packing Doc in ice and thus lowering his body temperature, Newly tries to keep him conscious so that he can instruct Newly on the procedures he must follow in performing the operation. However, Doc lapses into unconsciousness and Newly must proceed on instinct with Festus' help. Newly saves Doc's life and the hill folk gain a new respect for the practice of medicine. It is not without significance that Doc addresses Newly as "Dr." O'Brien in the final scene.

Buck Taylor made Newly O'Brien the most popular and successful new character added to the *Gunsmoke* cast since Festus replaced Chester. Still it should be pointed out that the "romantic interest" approach is almost always short-lived. The audience is aware that any girl who falls in love with a continuing character must either die, prove false, or for some other reason disappear by the end of the program. This is necessary so that the continuing character is free to fall in love with someone new in the next week's episode.

Over the years, *Gunsmoke* was the recipient of many awards: *Look* Magazine's Annual Television Award in 1958 for Best Action Series; the *Radio Television Daily* All-American Favorite Western Show of the Year in 1958; Television Champions Award for Best Western in 1959 and again in 1969 and 1972. Many individuals—actors, writers, directors and technicians, were also recognized for their outstanding contributions. Two of the most important awards transcend the Western genre itself—the Mass Media Award from the National Conference of Christians and Jews for "This Golden Land" by Hal Sitowitz, for "the unusual and provocative concept of the universality of the Jewish traditions that the program depicted" in 1973, and an award from the President's Council on Mental Retardation for "The Deadly Innocent," by Calvin Clements, Sr., in 1974.

In "This Golden Land," a family of Jewish immigrants from Russia have purchased a farm in Kansas and have journeyed to the American frontier to escape from problems and harassment in their homeland. Unfortunately three drunken brothers come upon the settlers at prayer. The bullies amuse themselves by dragging off the younger son at the end of a rope. The boy is found shortly thereafter, fatally injured. Because the family members are Orthodox Jews, they are unwilling to identify the men who were responsible for the death of the boy. His father, Moshe Gorofsky (sensitively played by Paul Stevens), explains to Matt that he only saw his son being taken away—he did not see the actual murder. The Talmud does not permit circumstantial evidence.

The youngest of the two remaining sons (a moving portrayal by young Richard Dreyfuss) is ashamed of his father's timidity and goes after the ruffians with a shotgun, asking his father, "Where is the truth in letting a killer run loose?" The wife is torn between her son's anger and loyalty to her husband. But Gorofsky persists, asking, "What is it we fear most, offending the men who killed our son? Or offending ourselves, our traditions?" After overpowering the youngest son, the three bullies return to Gorofsky's farm and order the family to move out. Moved by Gorofsky's courage in refusing to leave and impressed with his steadfast devotion to his beliefs, the men agree to turn themselves over to the marshal. They claim that they released the rope and as the boy fled in panic the end of the rope caught on a rock, throwing him to the ground and causing the fatal injury. Gorofsky believes their story and will so testify in court. It is a simple, but unusual and well presented story, certainly a highlight from the final years of the series.

This is also true of "The Deadly Innocent," presented during *Gunsmoke's* nineteenth season which relates the moving story of Billy, a powerful young man with the mind of a child. He erupts into uncontrolled rage whenever he sees an animal being harmed. When he leaves the sheltered valley where he grew up and comes to Dodge to visit his friend Festus, trouble ensues. First he nearly kills a man who is tormenting a cat. Then he assaults Festus for killing a deer. Upon Doc's recommendation, the judge orders Billy incarcerated in the county asylum for the mentally disturbed. Festus reluctantly takes Billy to the asylum, but is unable to leave him there. Finally Festus arrives at a solution that will serve the best interests of everyone. Billy will live and work at the local orphanage since he has a real affinity for children and a gift for telling them stories. Doc and Matt concur and Billy has finally found a useful role in life. Russell Wiggins is excellent as Billy and Ken Curtis turns in what is perhaps his best (certainly most sensitive) performance as Festus. The script deservedly won a Golden Spur Award from the Western Writers of America in addition to the award from the President's Council.

In addition to its many other accomplishments, *Gunsmoke* also served as an important training ground for numerous actors who would eventually star in their own television Westerns. James Drury (*The Virginian*), Charles Bronson (*Empire, The Travels of Jaimie McPheeters*), Chuck Connors (*The Rifleman, Branded*), Stuart Whitman (*Cimarron Strip*), Andrew Duggan (*Lancer*), Jack Kelly (*Maverick*), Pernell Roberts (*Bonanza*), Pat Conway (*Tombstone Territory*), Dan Blocker (*Bonanza*), Jack Elam (*The Dakotas, Temple Houston*), and Alan Case (*The Deputy*) gained valuable experience on *Gunsmoke* before starring in their own series.

As a Saturday night series *Gunsmoke* ranked in the Nielsen top 20 shows from its second season until 1965, being first from 1957 through 1961. After being moved to Monday evenings in 1967, the series returned to the top 20 and remained there until its final season. It was an achievement unmatched by any other television program. Tim Brooks and Earle Marsh rank *Gunsmoke* as the number one television show of all time by a wide margin.[77] In 1960 the publishers of the magazine *Who's Who in Television* asked James Arness to explain the popularity of Westerns in general and of *Gunsmoke* in particular. He responded:

> The brief period on which today's Westerns are based is one of the great misunderstood eras of American history. In it the pioneers struggled to succeed against a hostile environment—as men always have and perhaps always will, but with one difference. Their environment happened to be unusually exciting and unusually romantic.
>
> Men pushed westward against vast wild land, against fearful climates. The romance came in conquering these elemental obstacles—and in conquering other elemental men.
>
> Men banded together in common purpose against real things they could see and feel. Right and wrong were clearly defined, as rarely happened in any other time. In such times men could make their noblest achievements.
>
> Who would not be affected by the story of these men? The story of the West will always be exciting as long as it is told well and honestly. I have often been asked why "Gunsmoke" is so popular. I believe it has one strong characteristic . . . everyone who is connected with "Gunsmoke" . . . has a sincere and honest respect for that period of American history. Great care is taken not to violate the spirit of that time—what the real old West stood for. All of us have the feeling, in telling its story, that we are actually a part of it.
>
> That is the X factor in "Gunsmoke." As long as one show has it or some part of it, there will be Westerns—and they'll be popular.[78]

SuzAnne and Gabor Barabas in their definitive study make this final assessment:

> "Gunsmoke" is inextricably linked to the Western genre, and was the result of an evolutionary process that encompassed pulp novels, film, radio and television. It is a luminescent point along this continuum, and perhaps is the greatest Western story ever told.[79]

James Arness' contribution to the development of the adult Western, however, did not end with *Gunsmoke*. In fact he did not have much time to lament the cancellation of *Gunsmoke*. A few days after the news became public, M-G-M contacted him about doing a telefilm called *The Macahans*. He fell in love with the script and told the people at M-G-M, "Forget about Matt Dillon. This Macahan guy's more colorful."[80] Arness was also pleased that John Mantley, who had produced *Gunsmoke* for its last 11 years, and as many from the old crew as were interested and available, would join the new show.

The Macahans was dedicated to "the courage of the simple people who pushed their wagons westward into the wilderness, a breed of people we'll never see again." Frontier scout Zeb Macahan decides after ten years that it is time to visit his family in Bull Run, Virginia. It is 1861 and the Civil War is about to begin. When Zeb reaches home, he sleeps out in the yard because he feels "closed in" by a roof over his head. He finds his brother Tim (Richard Kiley) and Tim's wife, Kate (Eva Marie Saint), yearning to go West and avoid the inevitable clash between North and South.

Shortly after Zeb and Tim leave for Oregon, the war breaks out and their elderly parents perish in the shelling of Bull Run. Tim, concerned for their safety, returns and finds their graves before he is captured by the Union Army and forced into service. Tim's son Seth (Bruce Boxleitner) turns back to look for his father and finds him dying at Shiloh. The rest of the Macahans reach Nebraska where they await Tim and Seth's return before pushing on to Oregon. Eventually Seth does join the family, but along the way he has been conscripted into the Army, fought in a bloody campaign, fled the battlefield, been branded a deserter, wounded a lawman, and stolen two horses.

The stage has been set for the development of a full-fledged series. That series, *How the West Was Won*, premiered to high ratings, being the most watched program of the week, as a six-hour miniseries in February 1979. Obviously happy that the television Western was being revived, one *New York Times* (February 4, 1977) critic wrote:

> For many of us, James Arness has been the American West for years.... Two decades of *Gunsmoke* on television ... tanned the hide of fiction into the leather of myth. We wore it, like a pair of boots, in a slow walk toward *High Noon*.... All right: imagine six hours of *Gunsmoke*. At the same time, imagine a James Arness, who wants to ride the high country and find places no white man has ever seen before ... in a permanent rage of impatience, Arness is just about perfect.

The story of the Macahans resumed with Zeb responsible for his dead brother's widow Kate and her four children: Luke (the eldest, the fugitive who had been called Seth in the original film), Laura, Josh (who had been called Jeb), and Jessie. After the six-hour miniseries, Kate dies and is replaced as the family mother-figure by Aunt Milly from Boston, played by Fionnula Flanagan. Both together and separately they face the dangers and hardships caused at various times by Indians, land barons, bigots, outlaws, nature, and the other perils of an untamed frontier. The series returned to the ABC schedule in September 1978, billed as "the longest motion picture ever made." More accurately it was the longest single-story television program produced to that time, surpassing *Roots* and *Washington: Behind Closed Doors* from the previous year.

During the 1978-79 season M-G-M presented 20 hours of connected plot beginning with two three-hour segments produced on a budget of $12 million. Filmed in Colorado, Utah, Arizona, and California, *How the West Was Won* utilized three Indian villages (one Sioux, one Arapaho, and one renegade), a Mexican town, a complete frontier town, an Army encampment, a robber's hideout, a cave, a mine, and Bent's Fort, a historical monument located in La Junta, Colorado. Over 1,700 animals were needed, including over 400 buffalo, a herd of cattle, oxen, mules, burros, pigs, goats, dogs, cats, and the standard quota of horses. It was truly an ambitious undertaking even by Hollywood standards. All the expense and attention to detail paid off. During its first season, *How the West Was Won* earned higher ratings than any recent television Western, finishing the year in seventeenth place on the Nielsen list. It was renewed for another season in a slightly altered format. Each story was completed in a two-hour weekly episode.

Arness insisted that only a Western could have lured him back to series television. "I like what Westerns mean," he explained in an interview. "It's more pleasant, looking back at a simpler time in our history. I even liked it better back in the thirties when I was growing up."[81] Regarding the character of Zeb Macahan, Arness claimed that he enjoyed portraying the freedom-loving mountain man even more than the straight-laced lawman of *Gunsmoke*:

> Zeb is an old-time frontier character who, I figure, came out to the West in the fur-trapping business in the early 1800's and saw the West when it was truly primitive. He's lived by his wits and experience and skill and that molded the man's character; he's pretty much of a free-spirit kind of a guy, doing what he wants, as opposed to living within the law, which is what Matt Dillon has to do. If there's a problem someplace, Zeb's tendency is to jump in and take over and resolve it by whatever means are available, without trying to work it through the law.... Matt was locked into a tighter framework. This guy has a broader scope of activity.[82]

As the critics had noted, Arness seemed "perfectly" cast. The series' creators obviously had him in mind when they developed this description of the series' lead character:

> Zeb Macahan was big. Had he been in the habit of standing straight, he'd have stood nearly seven feet tall in his boots. He seldom bothered to try. Thirty-odd years of survival

west of the Big Muddy had left Zeb bent out of shape, and too many men, red, and white, had taken a shot at that massive gray head for Zeb to be all that interested in carrying it any higher than he had to.... Not many men who'd tried to kill him were still around these days. The big man moved, when he had to, with the deceptive clumsy grace of a grizzly. When he didn't have to, Zeb moved slow.[83]

Arness' naturally blond hair had been darkened and closely cropped for *Gunsmoke*. For the role of Zeb Macahan of the 1860s, his silver-grey hair hung long and he grew a shaggy mustache. But Arness embodied the mountain man in far more than physical appearance. As the Macahan character, Arness was able to express the less restrained side of his nature—the outdoorsman who delighted in high surf and high slopes, fast cars, and wanderlust. Not many television heroes have possessed the raw strength of a Zeb Macahan, who once killed a trapper crony rather than allow him to be tortured by the Indians. Unlike Matt Dillon, his creed was "what's right is right and wrong is wrong; there are no grays." In his virtues—loyalty, honesty, humor—and in his protective, almost reclusive, nature, Zeb Macahan and James Arness were one and the same person.

Although the plots switched back and forth between the major characters, with one usually focusing on Zeb, one on Luke, and one on Aunt Molly and the other Macahan siblings, occasionally two or all three of the story lines would come together. The focal character, however, was always Zeb Macahan. Whether negotiating with the Indians for the release of a visiting Russian count, helping a mountain man rescue his son from the Indians, or trying to prevent a bloody war between the Army and the Indians, Arness dominated every scene in which he appeared.

An appreciation of the dignity and worth of the Indians the white man slaughtered when settling the West was a recurring theme in *How the West Was Won*. Zeb felt a genuine respect for Indian life and culture. He once had taken an Indian maiden for his bride, and she had given him a son. With both now dead, Zeb simply tried to keep the peace between the white men and the red men. Early in the series Zeb brought the dead body of his blood brother, Satangkoi, a Dakota chief, to General Philip Sheridan. Satangkoi had committed suicide rather than bring a war on his people that he knew they could not win. Later Zeb led a band of Arapaho braves on a long and dangerous cattle drive over the barren plains so that tribesmen would not starve. And always, when the need arose, Zeb pled the cause of the Indians.

Zeb Macahan had a more open attitude toward women than Matt Dillon. When Zeb found by accident the woman (Vera Miles) whom he had loved twenty years earlier, he had no reservations about going to bed with her. Here Arness had to overcome a natural shyness around women that was more typical of Dillon. In every other respect, Arness fit as comfortably into the role of Zeb Macahan, a man who was a law unto himself, as he had Matt Dillon, a man who not only had to see that the laws were carried out but live by them himself. As Dillon, he had to hold his own personal feelings or desires in restraint; as Macahan (for the most part), he could do what he felt like doing. There was however, one overriding similarity between the two characters: each always governed his actions by doing what he felt was right.

In the spring of 1979 *How the West Was Won* dropped to forty-sixth place in the Nielsen ratings and was canceled.[84] Arness was out of work for the first time in nearly twenty-five years. Arness' unemployment lasted but two years. In November 1981 he was back on the screen again—in *McClain*, his only non–Western role to date—as Jim McClain, a detective on the San Pedro, California, police department. Forced to retire from the force 13 years earlier due to a leg injury, McClain returned to duty when his friend and fishing partner was robbed and murdered. Convinced that only he could find the killer, he fought to have himself reinstated. McClain preferred the old-fashioned physical methods of combating crime, and he frequently came into conflict with his boss and his younger partner who and been trained in the modern high-tech methods of crime fighting. Although the "new" Arness, like the "old," was engaged in preserving law and order, he did not look comfortable driving a car and wearing a suit and tie. Viewers must have agreed; the series was canceled after only 16 episodes.

Westerns brought Arness out of retirement again in 1987. Between January 1987 and April 1988, Arness appeared in three made-for-television films, all Westerns. The first was a modified, three-hour remake of John Wayne's historical saga, *The Alamo*. When casting the original film in 1960, Wayne had tried to lure Arness away from *Gunsmoke* long enough to play Jim Bowie. Finally succumbing 27 years later to the urge to "play a role that counts for something," Arness appeared as the famous knife-wielding frontiersman in *The Alamo: 13 Days to Glory*.

Showing a few more wrinkles, Arness' Bowie was a mixture of Matt Dillon and Zeb Macahan. Putting duty and honor above personal safety, he fought with every means at his disposal until the inevitable end. Critics assessed the film, which was shot in Bracketville, Texas, on the same set that Wayne had used, as "a respectable addition to the Alamo repertory" full of "sweep and color." They found Arness "credible" but "forever stamped" as Marshal Dillon.[85] The role, while not stretching Arness' acting, did bring the star back to television.

Arness' second appearance was a *Gunsmoke* reunion film, which had been rumored for some time. It aired on Saturday, September 26, 1987, as *Gunsmoke: Return to Dodge*. Featuring plenty of action, a lot of plotting, some colorful new characters, and beautiful locations, it was a typical *Gunsmoke* story. In addition to Arness, his hair dark brown again, but longer, Amanda Blake, and Buck Taylor returned from the original series. Missing were Doc Adams (Milburn Stone was dead), Chester (Dennis Weaver was busy filming a new series) and Festus (problems of money and billing caused Ken Curtis' absence). Dillon had long since retired as marshal and become a trapper. Kitty had left Dodge City earlier for New Orleans, despairing that Matt would never put aside his badge and six-guns. Newly was now marshal of the apparently larger and more civilized Kansas community.

The choicest role went, however, to Steve Forrest, reprising his role as Mannon, one of the most evil screen "baddies" to come along since Jack Palance menaced Alan Ladd in *Shane*. Actually, Dillon had killed Mannon in an episode telecast on January 20, 1969. According to the new version, however, Mannon had only been sent to territorial prison. Now he is being released and is out to gain revenge on the ex-lawman and Kitty, who had spurned him. Flashbacks feature clips from old episodes to fill in background and provide viewers with the chance to see Doc and Festus again. Early in the story, Matt is knifed and, after a friendly trapper has brought him to Dodge, Kitty returns to nurse him ("old habits die hard"). The first scene between Matt and Kitty is electric:

> MATT: Glad ya came. Yer lookin' great.
> KITTY: You cut that out.
> MATT: What?
> KITTY: You listen ta me cowboy. I've got you out from underneath my fingernails and yer gonna stay out. Do ya hear me?
> MATT: Yes, ma'am... Kitty, I understand the rules and all, but it doesn't mean we can't still be friends does it?
> KITTY: Friends? Friends? I'm staying at the Long Branch while I'm in town, so when and if you feel up to it, I might even buy you a beer.

Later, when Matt leaves to find and save an old friend, he lets Kitty know that "it's really been good" seeing her again and "when all this is over and I get back. . ." Kitty answers, "I'll be here." After the door closes and he has gone, she poses the rhetorical question, "Aren't I always?" In the only other scene they play together, Matt and Kitty exchange meaningful glances after he has vanquished the brutal Mannon. Then Dillon walks alone down Front Street.

While the relationship between Kitty and Matt seems not to have changed in the least, Dillon appears to be less bound by the moral and legal restraints he faced as a lawman. He taunts Mannon as "fit only to beat up women" and goads him into a gunfight. Then he shoots the outlaw three times. There obviously is more than a bit of Zeb Macahan in the older Matt Dillon.

Viewers apparently enjoyed seeing the *Gunsmoke* gang again because the film ranked in the top ten shows for the week. This lead to four subsequent *Gunsmoke* television films, *Gunsmoke II: The Last Apache* (1990), *Gunsmoke III: To the Last Man* (1992), *Gunsmoke IV: The Long Ride* (1993), and *Gunsmoke V: One Man's Justice* (1994). In each, Arness was featured as Matt Dillon, but without any other cast members from the original series.

All three films, however, did feature guest stars who had appeared in a number of *Gunsmoke* episodes. In *Gunsmoke II*, Michael Learned, reprising her role as Mike Yardner in "Matt's Love Story," writes to Matt asking him to come to her ranch. In a flashback to the earlier show, Matt and Mike are shown kissing, while he is suffering from amnesia. Out of this brief romance came a child—a daughter, Beth, whom neither the television audience nor the marshal knew existed. She has been captured by Apaches, and Mike asks Matt to help rescue her.

With the assistance of an Army scout named Chalk Brighton, who is in love with Mike, they are successful in freeing Beth from the Indian warrior, Wolf, who has taken her for his bride. Richard Kiley, another *Gunsmoke* veteran, appears as Chalk, while Hugh O'Brian (television's Wyatt Earp) plays an Army general.

In the third *Gunsmoke* television movie, Matt finds himself swept up in a blood feud in Arizona Territory during the 1880s when one of his young drovers is murdered and his cattle rustled. With the help of a veteran lawman named Abel Rose, Matt tracks down and (in a bloody climactic gunfight) kills every member of the gang responsible. Morgan Woodard, who had appeared in 18 different roles during the 20-year run of the original series, plays Abel. Pat Hingle (who had been Doc's replacement during the season he missed because of heart surgery) is cast as the chief villain—a retired Army colonel and the tyrannical head of a family of rustlers and killers. In the film's only acknowledgement to *Gunsmoke II*, Amy Stock-Poynton again appears as Matt's daughter, Beth.

To the Last Man did not draw the high ratings (or favorable reviews) that the first two television films did. This may be due to an excessive amount of bloodshed and violence. In *Gunsmoke: The Long Ride* (shown on CBS, May 8, 1993), only Amy Stock-Poynton (again as Beth) returns with Arness from earlier *Gunsmoke*s. This time Dillon is framed for robbery and murder, and sets out, with the help of an itinerant preacher named John Parsley (likably played by television veteran James Brolin), to clear his name. He must apprehend the trio of baddies responsible before a posse of bounty hunters catch up with him. Ali MacGraw appears as a reformed prostitute-with-a-heart-of-gold. Shot partly on location in Santa Fe, New Mexico, the film is scenic—and violent.

Although *The Long Ride* did not pull in the high ratings that most of the earlier *Gunsmoke* made-for-television films had, it did win its time slot by a large margin, while pleasing most fans and critics. Jeff Jarvis of *TV Guide*, wrote:

> Thirty-eight years after he first rode out as Matt Dillon, James Arness returns in another movie, and that's a feat worth watching. He has a voice like a dusty old trail and a face that shows 20,000 sunsets; as an admiring sheriff says, "You got a lot of bark on you." Arness makes Jack Palance look like a pup.... The script creates more burial plots than plotlines—but who cares? Matt Dillon's back! My score [0 to 10]: 8.[86]

One Man's Justice (which aired on February 10, 1994) again earned respectable ratings. This time Bruce Boxleitner costars with Arness as a traveling salesman who joins Dillon on a search for a 15 year old boy chasing the robbers who killed his mother. Stock-Poynton reprises her role as Beth and Christopher Bradley returns as her husband Josh. Although the body count was high once again, most critics were pleased. Janette and Bob Anderson of *Trail Dust* (spring 1994), especially noted Boxleitner's contribution: "Bruce *literally* stole the show with as fine a performance as you're likely to see on a TV Western." As long as *Gunsmoke* films can produce that type of response, it seems likely that Matt Dillon will periodically continue to ride the video range.

Arness also appeared in a 1988 remake of Howard Hawks' classic Western, *Red River* (1948). The film dramatically recreated the first long drive from the plains of southern Texas to the railhead in Abilene, Kansas. It is also a story of the relationship between two strong-willed men—Tom Dunson, a tough old rancher, and his equally stubborn adopted son, Matthew Garth. Rated by many critics as the best Western ever made, the original *Red River* starred John Wayne and Montgomery Clift. Without doubt Arness was the best replacement for Wayne the producers could hope to get. The film had been one of Arness' favorites and he was eager to take on a role against type. The arrogant and tyrannical Dunson was basically an unsympathetic character.

While the role had won plaudits for Wayne twenty years earlier ("the best performance of his career to date"[87]), the best Arness could get from critics was "competent," and many felt that Bruce Boxleitner, Arness' capable costar in *How the West Was Won*, was miscast as the neurotic Matt. As John J. O'Connor of the *New York Times* wrote:

> Why not just do a brand new adventure about a cattle drive along the Chisholm Trail and leave *Red River* alone? ... Television is being forced to enter a new stage of awareness when it comes to tinkering with material that has already been produced with skill and imagination. Shabby imitations are likely to be increasingly rejected as more viewers are able—for prices that get lower and lower—to turn to the originals on video cassettes.[88]

The producers of the television version of *Red River* added a unique twist. Trying to make it a paean to television Westerns, they cast Robert Horton (*Wagon Train*), John Lupton (*Broken Arrow*), Guy Madison (*Wild Bill Hickock*), and Ty Hardin (*Bronco*) in small featured roles. The ratings indicated that many viewers did tune in to see what was becoming an increasingly rare phenomenon—an old-fashioned television Western adventure—and it was good to see James Arness in a role that differed from his previous roles.

Arness' place in the history of the Western, of course, has long been secure. In Matt Dillon, Arness created television's most enduring Western hero. Surely Matt Dillon is the standard against which all television cowboy heroes must be judged. And none—not Hopalong Cassidy, nor the Lone Ranger, nor Ben Cartwright, nor Paladin—has had a greater influence on the development of the genre. James Arness has deservedly earned immortality as television's quintessential Western hero.

There were, however, other Western heroes of some magnitude about to ride the video range during that September of 1955 when Matt Dillon vanquished his first foe. The stampede of adult Westerns was just beginning.

IV. Law and Order Arrive in the Video West

HERE COME THE LAWMEN, SHERIFFS, MARSHALS, DEPUTIES AND TEXAS RANGERS

If Matt Dillon was television's quintessential fictional Western lawman, then Wyatt Earp was most assuredly its quintessential historical one. Earp actually preceded Dillon on the home screen by four days when *The Life and Legend of Wyatt Earp* made its debut for ABC on September 6, 1955.

The American West has always been viewed as a region of lawlessness and violence, with the most distinguishing characteristic of the westward movement being the triumph of law and order. American frontiersmen used firearms for hunting, as well as self-defense and readily resorted to their fists, knives and rifles to settle disputes. Still, it was environmental and social conditions as much as willful lawlessness that prevented the easy establishment of law and order in the American West.

The earliest settlers moved west ahead of regular courts of law and peace officers. The first representatives of law and order on the frontier were army or militia units and Indian agents. As an area became better organized, responsibility for law enforcement rested more and more upon federal, territorial, state or local officials. Slowly the offices of public prosecutor, territorial attorney general, and United States district attorney became full-time jobs. United States marshals and deputy marshals served under the jurisdiction of federal district courts, while on a county level, the sheriff and his deputies were charged with enforcing local laws. Since frontier counties often were very large and the population sparse and scattered, the sheriff's job of law enforcement and the capture of criminals was a difficult one.[1]

Such lawmen usually came from the ranks of the West's gunfighters. Gunfighting was a socially and legally acceptable pursuit throughout the American West from the days of the mountain men to the 1890s, when it was gradually decreed that judges and juries would take over the functions of rendering justice from Kansas to California. The gunfighter was usually a young fellow—for obvious actuarial reasons—and almost always came from a farm or ranch where he had been handling firearms since he was old enough to lift, load, and shoot them. His skill in drawing a heavy .45 caliber revolver from its holster, aiming, and firing it in a matter of a split second could be acquired only after long hours of practice behind the barn or corral of his home. Later he sharpened that skill in buffalo hunting, Indian fighting, herding cattle, or scouting for the army. Thus seasoned, the gunfighter was much in demand. If he chose to employ his talents on the side of the law, he could work as one of the corps of gunmen employed by cattle barons to protect their vast ranges from homesteaders. Or he could become a lawman. As Bat Masterson's biographer, Richard O'Connor, explains:

> The property-owning citizens of the frontier towns realized the only way they could protect themselves and their interests was to pin the marshal's star or sheriff's badge on an expert whose skill and reputation could often stop gun battles and shooting sprees before they started. Naturally they did not inquire into ... the past records of their protector.[2]

Such a man was Wyatt Earp. Stuart N. Lake, Earp's biographer, glamorized Earp's life in a best-selling partly fictionalized account:

> Wyatt was a man of action. He was born, reared, and lived in an environment which held words and theories of small account, in which sheer survival often, and eminence invariably, might be achieved through deeds alone. Withal, Wyatt Earp was a thinking man, whose mental processes were as quick, as direct, as unflustered by circumstance and as effective as the actions they inspired.
> The man won from contemporaries who were his most competent judges—from intimates, from acquaintances, and from enemies, alike—frontier-wide recognition as the most proficient peace officer, the greatest gun-fighting marshal that the Old West knew. He attained this eminence through the only method his time and place might comprehend.[3]

It was, therefore, not surprising that such a hero became the subject of television's first historically-based adult Western. ABC executives made a careful, prolonged search for an actor to play their hero. He had to be tall, slim, steely-eyed and athletic. Most important he had to be totally acceptable to Lake, whose book, *The Life and Times of Wyatt Earp*, had turned Earp into the most famous lawman in Western folklore. Lake, who had known Earp personally, rejected actor after actor. As soon as he met Hugh O'Brian, however, and saw "the spring in his step, the firm slant to his jaw and those narrow hips,"[4] he knew he had found his man.

Born in Rochester, New York, in 1925, he was christened Hugh J. Krampe, Jr. He led somewhat of a nomadic existence throughout his early years. As a boy he went to grammar school with Marlon Brando and Wally Cox in Evanston, Illinois; attended New Trier High School in Winnetka, Illinois, with Rock Hudson; and transferred to the Kemper Military School in Missouri. Always a leader, Krampe's extracurricular interests included student government and athletics. After beginning coursework in English and political science at the University of Cincinnati, he decided to follow in the footsteps of his father by enlisting in the Marine Corps. In 1943, at the age of 18, Krampe became the youngest drill instructor in Marine history. In 1945, he was awarded a fleet appointment to the Naval Academy at Annapolis. Then he changed his mind about pursuing a military career and set his sights on becoming a lawyer. After finishing his hitch in the Marines, he enrolled at Yale for the fall of 1948.

It was summer, however, and Krampe decided to spend the few months before beginning college in sunny Southern California. He arrived in Hollywood and took a room in a boarding house known as the House of Seven Garbos because it was occupied primarily by aspiring young actresses (like Ruth Roman and Linda Christian). To pass the time Krampe joined a community theater group, and when one of the actors became ill, he was asked to assume the role. The play was Somerset Maugham's *Home and Beauty* and was important not only for providing Krampe with his first acting experience, but also a new name. By mistake, the mimeographed playbill dropped the "m" from Krampe, causing such jesting from the audience that the director decided the young man should change his last name. He suggested something Irish: "How about O'Brian—with an 'a', so your great body of fans won't confuse you with Pat O'Brien?"[5] O'Brian was the name he became known by and Yale was soon forgotten as he went on to star in several other community theater productions. This led to an apprenticeship in summer stock at Santa Barbara, where the rising actor appeared with such established players as Martha Scott, Wendell Cory and Sylvia Sidney.

Then O'Brian obtained a wholesale clothing license and went to work selling men's clothing out of a suitcase. At night, he continued his acting, by performing, gratis, in the first live television shows broadcast from the West Coast (e.g., *The Arch Obler Mystery Theater*). When television finally began to pay, O'Brian was one of the actors frequently hired—not out of gratefulness, but because he had the experience of some 30 live shows to his credit. During the day, O'Brian concentrated his solicitation for clothing orders in an area frequented by actors, agents, directors and producers. In this manner he met one of Hollywood's leading agents, Milo Frank, who was impressed enough with O'Brian to arrange an interview with the famous actress and producer Ida Lupino. After conducting screen tests, Miss Lupino signed O'Brian to appear in his first film, *Young Lovers* (1949).

In 1951, O'Brian was signed by Universal-International Studios where he appeared in 18 films over a three-year period. In the fourth year of his contract, the studio told him he would never be a leading man, but if he wanted to continue in supporting roles ("everything from old men to bald-headed Indians to Jerry Lewis–type comedian roles," he later explained), they would renew his agreement for three more years. O'Brian chose not to renew and in 1954 he became a freelance actor. This led to three major productions at 20th Century-Fox. O'Brian's most memorable films during this period were *Broken Lance* (1954) and *There's No Business Like Show Business* (also 1954). He also appeared in a number of dramatic productions on *The Loretta Young Show* as he gained further television experience playing roles which ran the gamut from comedy to heavy drama. It was during this period that O'Brian was selected to play the character for which he will always be remembered. Upon accepting the role, O'Brian began an intensive study of the man he was to portray. He explained in 1957:

> With the exception of Stuart Lake, who wrote the book upon which our story is based, I don't think anybody is closer to Wyatt than I am. Lake lived with Wyatt for four years before Earp died, but I know a lot about Wyatt too. I don't mean just facts, I mean what he stood for and what he'd do under certain circumstances.[6]

Writing later in *TV Guide*, O'Brian elaborated:

> In preparing myself for the role of Wyatt Earp, the famous frontier marshal of the late 1800's, I devoted seven months to reading about Earp. A controversial character, Earp has been depicted as being everything from saint to devil, lawman to bully, loquacious to taciturn.
>
> The problem was to hew close to the Earp line, while making the character entertaining, attractive and believable....
>
> I'm convinced that Earp was a thoroughly honest man, righteous, utterly fearless. He was just—in 200 gunfights, he killed only four men. He may not have been overly talkative, but a TV show requires dialog. He had a wonderfully subtle sense of humor. He was essentially an easy-moving type of guy—but he could tense up like a coiled spring, and he had fabulous reflexes. You stay alive through 200 gunfights and you've *got* to have fabulous reflexes.
>
> I do my best to play him as I understand him. No violence for violence's sake. No phony heroics. And enough humor to take the curse off what was a pretty rugged existence.[7]

Critics applauded *The Life and Legend of Wyatt Earp* from the very first telecast. *Variety* (September 14, 1955) said

> ... the first show was promising and the series has an approach and premise that offer standout potentialities.... [The] series ... is as the title indicates, semi-biographical in nature, and is based largely on the bio of Earp by Stuart N. Lake; ...
>
> [Hugh] O'Brian ... is a natural for the role—strong and lean-looking, a rugged but handsome face and a warm but casual approach to his part. He's got all the makings of a star, but more important, has the wherewithal to establish strong and immediate identity as Wyatt Earp ... there's a top-notch production crew on the series, with every foot turned out slick as a whistle. Photography is crystal-clear, sets and costumes are excellent, dialog is natural and the action is staged with crispness and authority.... O'Brian is backed by an excellent cast.

The show's theme song was written by Harry Warren (music) and Harold Adamson (lyrics) and sung by the Ken Darby Singers. Although the words and tune were catchy, "The Legend of Wyatt Earp" never caught on with the general public as had "The Ballad of Davy Crockett." A unique aspect of the series was the background music. All of the bridges, used whenever the scene changed, were sung by the Ken Darby Singers. Sometimes words were provided as narration for the story; at other times the balladeers simply provided melodious humming in harmony. When the show was at the peak of its popularity, Ken Darby, his singers and Hugh O'Brian collaborated on an album, "Hugh O'Brian Sings!" for ABC-Paramount. A full-scale presentation of the show's theme music was included as well as ten selections relating to Wyatt Earp written by Darby and one, "I'm Walkin' Away," written by O'Brian himself. The album was never a bestseller and did not lead to a recording career for O'Brian. Still O'Brian's voice is pleasant, the arrangements musically refreshing and the lyrics appropriately capture the spirit of both the man and his era.

How authentic was television's Wyatt Earp? This question was the subject of numerous articles and commentaries during the six seasons that Hugh O'Brian rode the video range. Because O'Brian chose not to duplicate Earp's fierce mustache, his appearance was criticized as bearing little resemblance to the real Earp. Actually, O'Brian once donned a "luxuriant" mustache like the one worn by Earp in all the known photos. He was photographed and the photo was published in *TV Guide* next to one of the real Earp.[8] O'Brian's appearance was remarkably similar to that of the marshal. A scar on O'Brian's lower lip, acquired in a childhood accident, was exactly the kind of souvenir that a veteran Western peace officer might have. O'Brian even learned Earp's facial mannerisms and his way of moving his mouth.

When O'Brian strode before the cameras as Wyatt Earp, he assumed the manner and confidence of the deadly lawman. He had studied old photos and donned the tight trousers with a narrow gray-on-black stripe, shiny gold vest with a daisy design, string tie, long-sleeved shirt, black sombrero and black boots that Earp commonly wore. To this he added a brown gun belt strapped across his hips at the correct professional height.

The most valid complaint about O'Brian's portrayal, according to Lake, was that he did not play Earp heroically *enough*. O'Brian had to play down the part so modern audiences would believe it. For example, the real Earp was fond of "buffaloing" lawbreakers. This meant that he laid the barrel of his revolver across the wrongdoer's skull and hauled him off to jail unconscious. Furthermore, Lake claimed that Earp, being a humane man as well as a tough one, seldom shot to kill if he could help it. In fact, he would not shoot at all unless he was forced to. It was not uncommon for him to buffalo twenty to thirty obstreperous cowboys on a single Saturday night. Buffaloing was not only painful but insulting for it implied that the recipient was not formidable enough to rate having a gun pulled on him.

Killers, of course, were a different matter. Lake discovered that at one time, organized outlaws made a standing offer of $1,000 to any gunfighter that killed Earp. The real Earp had to deal not only with these mercenaries but with young hotheads out to establish their reputations by outgunning Earp. Earp's speed on the draw was legendary. No less an authority than Bat Masterson personally told Lake:

> In a day when almost every man had, as a matter of course, the ability to get a six-gun into action with a rapidity that a later generation simply will not credit, Wyatt's speed was considered phenomenal by those who were marvels at the same feat.[9]

O'Brian spent long hours practicing Wyatt's fast draw. After over a hundred hours of repeated draw and fire action, he had the lightning motions down pat. He could whip both six-shooters out of their holsters and fire them in one-fifth of a second. These guns were replicas of the Buntline Specials with 12-inch barrels that Earp always carried. O'Brian took lessons from Arvo Ojola, who trained most of Hollywood's Western stars. In an interview for the Los Angeles *Courier-Journal* (February 26, 1956) O'Brian explained:

> Arvo could have held his own with the gun fighters of the 1870's. He probably could have fought on even terms with the real Earp, or with Bat Masterson, Billy the Kid, Johnny Slaughter and Johnny Ringo.
>
> These guys played for keeps, Ojala could have stayed with them for keeps, too. In fact he still does a lot of tricks using live ammunition. The rest of us, of course, use blanks.

In the same interview O'Brian also explained the role of gunplay in the contemporary television Western:

> ... the Western hero must be able to use his gun, and be able to use it effectively and with authority. Even if he doesn't shoot, he often saves his life and the lives of others by being in a position to shoot before his adversary.
>
> Early TV and movie gunmen were responsible for a lot of myths about gunmen. Tricks with guns look good on the screen. But the old-time gunmen who used them usually wound up very dead.
>
> Gunfighters who survived, for instance, did not "fan" their guns. While this got off a lot of shots in a short time, it destroyed accuracy. And an accurate shot a split second late was better than a faster shot which missed the mark....
>
> Most of the famous gunfighters were not above taking an unfair advantage. Most of them would shoot in the back, or from ambush. That the modern Western star cannot do. He must never take advantage of anyone, even an outlaw.

As skilled as he was with a six-shooter, O'Brian was not immune to the danger. While appearing in a touring Western show, he gave demonstrations of his fast draw in theaters and auditoriums in the South and Midwest. During a performance in Wilmington, North Carolina, one of his six-guns stuck in the holster. O'Brian triggered it accidently, detonating a blank cartridge. The explosion burned a hole in his trousers and singed an area of his skin the size of a silver dollar. The wound was painful, but after receiving first aid, O'Brian returned to the stage and finished the show.[10]

The real Wyatt Earp was also a superb tactician and psychologist. He knew how to neutralize an unruly mob by singling out its leader. Once such a one has been maneuvered into backing down, the whole crowd will disperse. According to Lake, there is no substantiated instance of Earp ever having "cited a hurdle" (backed down in a fight because of too-great odds). The gunfight at the O.K. Corral was the classic example. (The last five episodes of *The Life and Legend of Wyatt Earp* dramatized this momentous event.)

Hugh O'Brian played television's quintessential Western lawman, Wyatt Earp.

Stuart Lake concluded that "Wyatt was no saint. He was a man—and all things considered, one of probity, integrity and inherent human decency."[11] O'Brian agreed that Wyatt was "a lusty character, too lusty for television. He had to have faults to be human. And I try to play him that way—relaxed until he loses his temper, then all steel springs; capable of occasional errors in judgment, but humble about them."[12]

Wyatt Earp's producer explained to *Newsweek* in 1957 that "Earp gets slapped down occasionally. He's a very human person. We've got to slice the truth pretty close to make it last, but we stick closely to the biographical details."[13] Of course, it was not by chance that Lake's title, *The Life and Times...*, was modified for television, with "Legend" substituted for "Times." The series dealt with the ten year period in Earp's life (age 24 to 34) during which he served as a law officer, first in Ellsworth, Kansas, then Dodge City and finally, Tombstone, Arizona.

In the series opener "Mr. Earp Becomes a Marshal," Earp avenges the death of his friend Marshal Whitney by accepting his badge and bringing to justice his killer. During the first season, Earp's exploits in Ellsworth are depicted, including his encounters with Robert E. Lee ("Marshal Earp Meets General Lee"); killer and trick shot artist John Wesley Hardin (played convincingly by Philip Pine); the outlaw Thompson Brothers, Bill (Hal Baylor) and Ben (Denver Pyle); cattle king Shanghai Pierce (Roy Roberts); and Old Man Clanton, leader of the notorious "Ten Percent Gang" (a continuing role for Trevor Bardette), who would periodically plague Earp for six seasons.

Two friends and allies of Earp over the years are also introduced: young would-be gunfighter Bat Masterson (Alan Dinehart III—in a portrayal much different from Gene Barry's later tour de force) and famed dime novelist and showman, Ned Buntline (as engagingly performed by Lloyd Corrigan). In "The Buntline Special," Buntline, grateful to Earp for the material he had provided (for hundreds of yarns, few authentic, but still with a kernel of truth as their basis), decided to arm him as befitted his accomplishments. Buntline sent to the Colt factory for a pair of special .45 caliber six-guns of regulation single-action style, but with barrels four inches longer than standard—18 inches overall. Each was accompanied by a hand-tooled holster made especially for the weapon. They became part of Earp's trademark, although when he first saw them, he locked Buntline in jail for carrying "over-sized pistols." Their recoil was excessive, but their extra range and accuracy more than offset this inconvenience and they became Earp's favorite weapons. People called the Buntline Special, "the one-eyed jury," while Earp referred to it as his "unconverted friend," a "portable posse" and the "perfect persuader."

In "Bat Masterson Again," Wyatt provides Bat with some useful advice about gunfighting when he prepares to do battle with Sergeant King (whose "girl" Bat has been dating):

> You lose a lot of time reachin' up to it [your gun]. Now lower your holster until the grips just touch the palms of your hands as they hang naturally. . . .
>
> You're plenty fast enough, but you're telegraphing. A gunfighter who hasn't had too much experience usually starts the draw with his eyes. He either blinks 'em or narrows 'em and lets the order that his brain has given to his hand show in his face. And the shoulder muscles tense and his hand makes just a little move to get closer to that gun grip. . . .
>
> But your main fault is that you're watchin' my hand. . . . Never mind his hand, just keep your eye on the spot you want your bullet to go. . . .
>
> A shoulder shot is aimed just a hand's length from the breast bone. You hit just below the collar bone. Now the bullet paralyzes the brachial plexus nerve and the impact spins your man off balance and he falls. . . .
>
> Your eyes stay focused on this spot as your gunsight comes up. The instant that gunsight reaches the lower portion of this spot you fire, but not before. . . .
>
> Take your time. It's important to draw fast and get off the first shot, but it's much more important to have your bullet go where you want it to go. . . .
>
> If you're hit and you go down, you gotta kill him in the next instant or be killed. It's your life or his. . . . Aim right at his heart.

Needless to say, Masterson carefully followed Earp's advice, and although he was wounded by King's first shot, he killed King with his own first shot.

A number of subsequent episodes trace the friendship of Wyatt and Bat as Bat becomes Earp's deputy ("Bat Masterson Wins His Star"), is elected sheriff of Ford County ("Bat Masterson for Sheriff") and gets into difficulties ("Bat Jumps the Reservation").

During the first season, episodes are presented dealing with other problems Earp faced during that period, including the Pinkertons, the Suffragettes and members of the Jesse James gang. By the end of the year, however, Wichita and the surrounding environs are declared "civilized" and Earp moves to "the cowboy capital" in "Dodge City Gets a New

Wyatt (Hugh O'Brian, second from right) was joined by his two brothers, Morgan (Dirk London, second from left) and Virgil (John Anderson, on far right), and Doc Holliday (Douglas Fowley on the far left) at the end of the five year run of *The Life and Legend of Wyatt Earp* for a re-enactment of the gunfight at the OK Corral.

Marshal." (The real Earp had spent the better part of three years in the Ellsworth/Wichita area before moving on to Dodge—1873 to 1876.)

From the moment Earp hits Dodge City, the action is fast and furious. The marshal shoots a half dozen or so gunmen who try to kill him, bashes in the heads of ("buffaloes") a number of others, and rescues two local peace officers who are surrounded (by stampeding a herd of cattle down the main street of Dodge). There is even a bit of humor thrown in, when one townsman says to Earp, "You're the most violent peace officer I know."

made his life count for something eminently worthwhile beyond his accomplishments in the acting profession.

After leaving *Wyatt Earp*, O'Brian continued his career on television, Broadway and in feature films. Trying to create a new image for himself, he selected roles that were usually non–Western. He danced and sang on *Frances Langford Presents*, a variety show co-starring Bob Hope, Jerry Colonna and Edgar Bergen. In *Feathertop*, a television musical, O'Brian wore a scarecrow costume and sang a duet with Jane Powell. He portrayed Joseph, who wore the coat of many colors, on *Great Adventures from the Bible* and on *Bob Hope's Chrysler Theater* he was cast as a restaurant owner.

In 1972, O'Brian filmed a two-hour pilot for NBC called *Probe*, in which he played Hugh Lockwood, chief agent for a super-sophisticated detective agency that operated around the globe using elaborate equipment and fancy gadgets. The series which resulted was called *Search* and featured rotating leads, with Tony Franciosa and Doug McClure alternating with O'Brian. It did not, however, catch viewers' attention in significant numbers and was canceled after one season. O'Brian continued to make guest appearances on such shows as *Police Story* and *Fantasy Island* and in more than a dozen made-for-television films. He also occasionally made cameo appearances in theatrical films like *Twins* (1988). Still, to most television buffs over 40, he will always be Wyatt Earp. Happily for these viewers, O'Brian has in recent years returned to the role that won him fame and fortune. After appearing as Wyatt in three episodes of *Paradise*, he joined nearly a dozen other veterans of television's golden age of Westerns in recreating their original roles in Kenny Rogers' blockbuster television miniseries *The Gambler Returns: The Luck of the Draw* in 1991.

During the summer of 1994, O'Brian climbed back in the saddle again for CBS' *Wyatt Earp: Return to Tombstone*. The two-hour movie was made using a process called "featurization": The filmmakers pieced together shots from the original black and white series which were used as "flashback" scenes. The new scenes were also filmed in black and white. Finally, the old and new scenes were colorized together.

The story began in 1914 when Wyatt's return to Tombstone triggered memories of the famed gunfight at the O.K. Corral. The new cast members included such Western veterans as Bruce Boxleitner, Harry Carey, Jr., Paul Brinegar, Don Meredith and Bo Hopkins. The film's broadcast date was set to coincide with Kevin Costner's blockbuster (three hour) theatrical version of *Wyatt Earp* and the release of the earlier 1994 Earp movie, *Tombstone*, on videocassette. CBS could boast that unlike the other recent big-budget Wyatt remakes, their film was the only one that was shot on location in historic Tombstone.

Rob Word, who conceived the colorizing process, hoped that *Wyatt Earp* would develop into a series of television movies utilizing more footage from the original shows. Since the real Earp lived to be 80 years old, it could be expected that he would experience many "flashbacks" to his earlier adventures during his declining years.

Although critics were lukewarm about the first movie (*Entertainment Weekly*, June 24–July 1, 1994, said, "*Return* may not be better than Costner's big-screen spectacle, but at least it's shorter"), but it did moderately well in the ratings, winning its time slot and finishing in the top 30 shows for the week.

What is the place of *The Life and Legend of Wyatt Earp* in the development of the television Western? Harry Castleman and Walter J. Podrazik give it three stars:

> Much overlooked when discussions of the great adult westerns take place, "Wyatt Earp" is perhaps the most realistic western of the 1950s ... for quality serious western action

without some of the philosophical angst that crept into "Gunsmoke" over the years, "Wyatt Earp" withstands the passage of time quite well. It helped set the pattern for the adult western craze of the late 1950s and still stands as one of the best examples of the genre.[17]

The Life and Legend of Wyatt Earp established a pattern that was utilized by other television Westerns based on actual historical characters like *Bat Masterson, Jim Bowie*, and Pat Garrett in *The Tall Man*. In its quality of production and success in capturing the spirit of a man and his era, the series set a high standard for others to emulate.

Over three years passed before that other stalwart gunfighter-turned-lawman, *Bat Masterson*, was given his own television show. Premiering for NBC on October 5, 1958, *Bat Masterson* was based on Richard O'Connor's "official" biography and starred Gene Barry in the title role. Attired in black derby, polished boots, dark pin-striped suit with black string tie, gold vest, complete with gold-headed cane, Barry's Masterson looked like no other television Western hero before or since. In fact the real Masterson had actually dressed in similar apparel while working for Wyatt Earp in Tombstone. The derby and cane had been his trademarks.

If Bat Masterson had not carried a gold-headed cane, or worn a derby hat and polished boots, it is likely that Barry would have turned down the role. When Ziv's vice president in charge of talent approached him with the idea of starring in a Western series, Barry, who disdained *ordinary* cowboys, turned him down. "But, Gene," Gordon persisted, "this fellow carries a derby hat and a cane."[18] That convinced Barry, who as a young unemployed actor wore a navy-blue Homburg and black chesterfield coat while making the rounds of casting offices in New York City.

Born Eugene Klass in Manhattan in 1921, Barry was the son of a jeweler and oldest of five children. He grew up in Brooklyn where his father lost his jewelry business in the crash of 1929 and his home later during the Depression. A loner who liked to dress well, young Eugene started out to be a concert violinist, but changed his mind after he broke his arm playing football.

Then Barry decided to try singing. He rented a tuxedo for $12 and reported to a Paterson, New Jersey, nightclub for his first professional job at $30 a week. Although he was fired after a week, he persisted in pursuing a career as a baritone by singing in choirs, glee clubs and even with a small dance band. He also gained valuable experience singing in nightclubs. While in his senior year at New Utrecht High School, Barry won one of General Sarnoff's musical scholarships to the Chatham Square School of Music. After studying there for two years, he got a job singing on a weekly radio show and won a prize on Arthur Godfrey's *Talent Scouts*. He joined the road company of *Pins and Needles* in 1940. Following that show, Barry was given the role of a 35-year-old man known as "the Bat" (no relation to Masterson) in Max Reinhardt's Broadway production of *Rosalinda*. His subsequent Broadway credits included *The Merry Widow*; Michael Todd's production of *Catherine Was Great*, starring Mae West (he played a Cossack in tights); and the Jule Styne-Sammy Cahn musical *Glad to See You* and *The Would-Be Gentleman*. He also appeared in an off-Broadway production of *Idiot's Delight*.

Barry supplemented his stage endeavors by emceeing variety shows, performing in vaudeville and singing at state fairs. In the early fifties, Barry decided to concentrate on acting instead of pursuing a career as a singer. He signed a movie contract in 1951, and made some twenty films including *The Atomic City* (1952) and George Pal's widely acclaimed *War of the Worlds* (1953). He also became active in television with a variety of roles in such shows as *The Loretta Young Show, Science Fiction Theater, Alfred Hitchcock Presents* and *Ford Theatre*. In 1955-56 he appeared briefly on *Our Miss Brooks* as Gene Talbot, the object of Connie Brooks' affection while Philip Boynton was away. It was, of course, as

Bat Masterson, that Barry was to achieve his greatest fame. Barry later recalled in an interview for *TV Guide*:

> ... "Bat Masterson" certainly has been big for me. I, in turn, am crazy about him. He's
> elegant, dapper and colorful, with human failings and human attributes. Not just a one-
> dimensional saddle-type, but a sophisticated gentleman of the West.[19]

Barry, like O'Brian, studied the man he was to portray on the homescreen (and, like
O'Brian, chose to play the mustachioed Masterson clean-shaven). Describing him as a
"true adventurer," Barry explained:

> He didn't let society close in on him but he knew how to live in the framework of society.
> Bat's dress is a good clue to his character—he wouldn't have dared put on that fancy vest in
> Dodge City unless he had had great self-confidence.[20]

Masterson did, of course, occasionally wear "trail clothes" (modified derby, cartridge
belt, brown pants, gun, and cane in scabbard) when he was, for instance, driving cattle
between jobs as a lawman or gambler, but Barry much preferred his more familiar "town
costume."

Unlike *The Life and Legend of Wyatt Earp*, which dealt chronologically with only the
ten year period of Earp's life (age 24 to 34) during which he was a lawman, *Bat Masterson*
moves from year to year, occupation to occupation, and place to place in no particular
sequence. In one episode it is 1883 and Masterson is in Dodge City ("Sherman's March
Through Dodge City") serving as a special deputy responsible for the visiting General
Sherman's safety; in another it is 1878 and he is in Protection, Kansas ("Election Day"),
ensuring that there is an honest election for mayor in a small frontier town; in yet a third
episode it is 1885 and he is in Texas ("Deadline"), where he saves a beautiful young lady
from two murderers. In still another it is 1881, and he is in New Mexico Territory ("A
Personal Matter"), where he gains revenge on a notorious outlaw who has embarrassed
him by stealing his horse, gun and money. Such were the television exploits of the "man
who become a legend in his own time."

What kind of man was the real Bat Masterson and how close does the television series
come to depicting that man? According to biographer O'Connor, the real-life Bat was
never a deadly gunslinger. He could draw as fast and shoot as straight as the best. But
from all accounts he was also a man with a sense of humor that set him apart from most
other Western heroes. Writing in the preface to his official biography, O'Connor explains:

> A legendary figure of the American West gathers an amazing assortment of untruths. In
> every telling of his deeds he becomes more awesome—and unbelievable. Bat Masterson did
> not escape this hero-worshiping process of distortion. An example: he was widely credited
> with killing between twenty and thirty men in gunfights. The actual number was only three.
> Unable to dissuade the legend-makers, he sardonically handed out guns with twenty-odd
> notches to souvenir hunters who "wanted to buy the gun you killed all those men with," and
> took his friends out for a drink with the proceeds.[21]

Gary L. Roberts, writing in *The Readers Encyclopedia of the American West*, is somewhat more objective in his evaluation of Masterson:

> Gambler, lawman, and newspaperman, Masterson was neither a plaster saint nor dapper
> fop. He was simply a man who did good things and bad, won a reputation as a good lawman,
> and outlived his time.[22]

According to producers of the television series, Andy White and Frank Pitman:

> The TV presentation of Bat Masterson will be as authentic as we can make it. The plain
> facts of his life are too exciting to need embroidering. From the start Bat was an easy-going

Gene Barry was appropriately dapper as Bat Masterson.

enforcer of law and order, refusing to take a man in unless he was definitely out of hand and a menace to himself and others.

The reason for much of his popularity was that Bat didn't take himself too seriously. There was little of the grim killer about him. He proposed to relax between jobs of shooting it out with desperate characters or leading manhunts across the prairies. Bat was a familiar figure in all the bars and gambling establishments—and his numerous romances indicate he was not one to shun the ladies.[23]

The sources, however, cannot even agree on Bat's name. According to writer Damon Runyon, Bat's real name was William Barclay Masterson and his nickname was derived from one Baptiste Brown, "a mighty Nimrod of those days."[24] The television series, followed O'Connor's account, explaining that he was christened William Barclay Masterson, but because he carried a cane after he was wounded in the leg and often used it to subdue the unruly by batting them over the head with it, he became known as Bat. In the initial episode a young boy polishing Bat's boots, while watching Bat primp in a mirror, inquires:

SANDY: That's pretty fancy, Mr. Masterson. And I thought a gunfighter didn't care about his looks.
BAT: Gunfighter?
SANDY: My pa says you're the fastest draw between here and California.
BAT: That's a lot of territory.
(Bat twirls his cane.)
SANDY: That's why they call you Bat, isn't it?
BAT: Yeah. It was given to me by the grateful citizens of Dodge City when I was sheriff there.
SANDY: My pa says you can bat a man over the head faster than he can go for his gun.
(Bat adjusts his derby)
SANDY: You gonna wear that? . . . You *must* have a fast draw.

Still another source, *The Reader's Encyclopedia*, declares that Masterson was "born and christened Bartholomew Masterson, a name he later changed to William Barclay Masterson for reasons never explained." (Bat was apparently a shortened form of Bartholomew.)[25] In any case, Bat utilized his cane to disarm and incapacitate villains too numerous to count during his weekly ride across the video range. In one episode ("Deadline"), he even traded it to a friendly Indian chief for a horse when he and a young lady were left stranded in the wilderness by outlaws. (Bat later reclaimed his most prized possession from the chief in exchange for two horses he had taken from the outlaws.) Barry also used his cane to gesture and emphasize a point (by tapping it against his adversary's chest as he spoke). And it came in handy to collect the guns off the ruffians he disarmed.

One way in which the television series admittedly deviated from "the facts" of Masterson's life involved his relationship with Wyatt Earp. Bat explained in a series of magazine articles which he wrote in 1907, that Wyatt was one of his best friends. The producers, however, not wanting to invite comparison with O'Brian's Earp on ABC, carefully avoided any reference to Wyatt on their NBC show. Perhaps, if both shows had been telecast on the same network, Barry and O'Brian might have been permitted to ride together (as they did much later on CBS' *Paradise*).

Bat Masterson got off to a successful start with what was, possibly, the most interesting episode of the series, "Double Showdown." Masterson arrives in a small Arizona town in response to a saloon-owner friend's request for assistance. It seems that a rival saloon-owner is trying to corner the drinking and gambling trade by driving Bat's friend out of business. The rest of the story deals with Masterson's attempts to help his friend, finally culminating in one hand of showdown poker, after which the loser will leave town. One version of the showdown hand is shown, in which the baddie loses to Bat and quietly makes his exit. Then, in a move that was surely unprecedented among television's adult Western heroes, Gene Barry steps out of character and addresses viewers directly:

> I'm Gene Barry. You know this Bat Masterson fella was certainly an unpredictable and surprising kind of man. During his eventful life, he earns the reputation of being one of the west's most colorful marshals and gunfighters. Wherever there was excitement, wherever there was trouble, you'd find him. Indian fighter, army scout, buffalo hunter, at a later age, sports reporter, and as you first saw, professional gambler. His tools, his trademarks were his cane, his derby and his custom-built six-shooter.
>
> Bat Masterson was known to be an amiable fellow by nature and never killed when killing was unnecessary. But, he was considered a great threat at all times. He was liked by most men and certainly his enemies respected him. Stories about him are legion. As a matter of fact the incident you just saw has become legendary. Actually the are two versions of the now famous card game. You just saw one. What you are about to see is what other biographers believe really happened the night of the showdown hand.

There followed a second version of the incident in which, after winning the showdown hand, Bat is forced to kill the rival gambler, and two of his gunmen. The critics were impressed with this attempt to stick to the facts. *Variety* (October 15, 1958) wrote:

> Masterson on its own is a good western. It comes off well because of Gene Barry's quiet portrayal of the dandified Masterson who is equally adept with cane and short-barrelled colt, and the scripting of producers Pittman and White which didn't try for the extraordinary, but played it straight for believable results....
>
> [The double ending] gimmick is interesting and different and that's something for a western nowadays and puts the whole story on a more factual basis.

Castleman and Podrazik give *Bat Masterson* credit for "pretty good" stories while questioning Masterson's ability "to literally trip up 200 pound fleeing villains merely by tossing his cane" and asking "how someone swinging a stick can beat a fast draw."[26] Ned Brown, once a writer for *Ring Magazine*, explained the real Masterson's popular appeal by describing him as "the closest thing I know to our motion picture idea of a Western hero."[27] In spite of this historical acclaim, *Bat Masterson* soon became lost in the glut of television westerns and was canceled by NBC in 1961 after only three seasons. It never appeared in the Nielsen top 25.

One of the most important consequences of *Bat Masterson* was, of course, the broad exposure and new career opportunities it gave Gene Barry. While still playing Bat in the series, Barry managed to cut a record for Capitol, star in a stage version of *Kismet*, perform as a singer and dancer on a television variety show with Perry Como and Dinah Shore, and appear on a special with Sid Caesar. After *Bat Masterson*'s cancellation, Barry went on to his most famous role, that of Captain Amos Burke, the dapper and very rich police detective who arrived at the scene of the crime in his Rolls Royce, in *Burke's Law* (1963-66). This was followed by a three year stint as one of the three rotating leads on the 90 minute anthology series, *The Name of the Game* (1968-71). Still dapper and flamboyant, Barry played Glenn Howard, head of a huge publishing conglomerate that also solved crimes.

In the seventies and eighties, Barry worked mostly in big budget made-for-television movies and miniseries (like *Aspen* in 1977) and also made guest appearances on such anthologies as *The Love Boat* and *Fantasy Island*. He successfully returned to the Broadway stage in the hit musical *La Cage aux Folles* in 1983. In 1990, Barry at last got to ride the video range with Hugh O'Brian, when Bat Masterson and Wyatt Earp appeared together in a two-part episode of *Paradise*. Barry also played Bat in a memorable gambling sequence with Kenny Rogers in the second part of *The Gambler Returns* miniseries in 1991.

The cast of *Johnny Ringo* included Mark Goddard (left) as deputy Cully, Don Durant in the title role, and Karen Sharpe as Laura Thomas.

see before he died? Not his wife, not his kids, but you.... A man ought to be surrounded with love when he dies.

CASE: What started it, son?

RINGO: I don't know, it just grew. First time you felt like a big man. Everybody congratulating you. Then you try it again, just to see how good you really are. One day you find you're like a turkey in a shoot. Everybody wants to try their luck. You can't stop it. You wanna, but you can't. You run, they catch you. You hide, they find you. Sometimes you think it'd be better to lose. Be a little slower and get it over with. You think so, but you just can't slow down that hand. It's not even a part of you. It's learned its job too well.

CASE: Johnny, that badge—is it gonna change things for you?

RINGO: I don't know, Case. It won't make up for everything I've done, but it'll help. You know, Case, I'm kind of tired. I'd like to rest a while, settle down.

Dick Powell, impressed with Durant and the pilot, ordered a series from his Four Star Productions. The pilot, which aired on October 1, 1958, was called "The Arrival," and followed the script of "Man Alone" quite closely. This time, however, Durant got star billing. Beautiful Karen Sharpe was cast as Laura Thomas and Case, her reformed-drunk father, was played by the veteran Irish character actor, Terence de Marney. James Coburn appeared as the villain Taylor. One new gimmick was added to the story. It seems Case had invented a new-fangled, two-barreled pistol which he presented to Ringo:

> CASE: I got the idea from a French gunsmith name LeMat. Think of it, Johnny—a *seven-shooter!* One extra bullet that'll make all the difference!
> RINGO: How does it work?
> CASE: It looks like a regular six-shooter, but there's a separate barrel for an extra shell, not just a forty-five shell, mind you. But a 410 shotgun shell.

So now Johnny Ringo could not only outdraw his opponents, he could cut them in two with his shotgun pistol. Ringo uses it to save his life by killing Taylor and his henchmen in the climatic shoot-out of the first episode. (Taylor had counted Ringo's shots and thought his gun was empty after six.) Case is *not* killed in this version (as he had been in the pilot) and the townspeople ask Ringo to remain as sheriff of Velardi. *Variety* (October 5, 1959) was favorably impressed with the pilot:

> "Johnny Ringo" is as western a western as there is around. If ever a western epitomized what all the shooting is about on television, this is it. "Ringo" looks, sounds, feels, tastes, and smells western....
> To the show's credit, there is a crispness about its action and an authenticity about its sounds of violence.

In the second episode, "Cully," another regular character is added to the *Johnny Ringo* cast—the spirited and loyal young deputy, Cully, played by Mark Goddard. Another veteran character actor, Willis Bonchey, appears in most episodes as the mayor.

There was an actual gunman named Johnny Ringo who lived in Arizona during the late 1870s and early 1880s. Since only scattered records are available, he is more legendary than real. One historian has described him this way:

> Ringo emerges from the past as the idealized embodiment of the gentleman outlaw. Stories of his courage, honesty, and chivalry were common even in his own time. He was lionized by some who knew him in Tombstone, Arizona, and their recollections have dominated history's view of him. From these sources Ringo is characterized as an intellectual, a reserved and morose man who drank too much, an educated man obsessed with violence, yet possessed of a sense of honor straight out of Sir Walter Scott.[29]

The closest the real Johnny Ringo ever came to being a lawman was as a member of the sheriff's posse that pursued the Earp brothers after they left Tombstone for the last time following the gunfight at the O.K. Corral. Still, these legends are the stuff television Westerns are made of.

Don Durant sought a career in show business by moving to Hollywood after finishing high school. There he joined various theatrical groups and took vocal lessons. After making some appearances in Las Vegas, he was drafted by Uncle Sam in 1952. Upon his discharge, he resumed his acting career, landing roles in such films as *Battle Cry* (1954) and appearances on such television shows as *The Ray Anthony Show, The Red Skelton Show, The Jack Benny Show, Climax!* and *Maverick* before Dick Powell gave him his big break. In addition to his work on the screen, Durant also contributed the *Johnny Ringo* theme song, which he both wrote and sang in the first episode and beneath the closing credits of every episode.

Mark Goddard had appeared in college plays and studied at the American Theatre of Dramatic Arts before auditioning in Hollywood for the role of Cully. It was his first television role. (Goddard would go on to costar in *The Detectives* (1960–1962), with Robert Taylor, and *Lost in Space* (1965–1968), before his more recent work on soap operas like *General Hospital.*)

Johnny Ringo was canceled after only one season (38 episodes), yet it must be considered one of the better television Westerns of its day. One historian has written:

> This series was a mature, often despairing portrait of life in an Arizona town whose sheriff was once the celebrated gunslinger of the title. Producer Aaron Spelling has fashioned the series with extraordinary attention to character development and social conviction . . . while the sparse sets themselves magnify the moral sterility so many of those under Ringo's aegis display.[30]

Among the topics effectively covered by the series was that of the discrimination and mistreatment of various ethnic immigrant minorities like the Chinese (in "Single Debt") and the Italians (in "Shoot the Moon"). It is also noteworthy as the first series created and produced by Aaron Spelling, who went on to produce *The Mod Squad*, *The Love Boat*, *Fantasy Island*, *Charlie's Angels* and *Dynasty*, among others.

Wichita Town seemed to possess all of the ingredients for success. It was a Western broadcast at the peak of the cowboy craze on television, and starred one of Hollywood's best-liked old pros, Joel McCrea, and his 25 year old son, Jody, upon whom many of his father's winning qualities had apparently rubbed off. Yet the series achieved only mediocre ratings and lackluster reviews ("Unfortunately, except for the lead characters, this is nothing special"[31]) and was canceled after only 24 episodes.

The show focused on the efforts of Marshal Mike Dunbar at keeping law and order in Wichita, Kansas, during the turbulent decade following the Civil War. Wichita was the terminus of many great cattle drives of that era. Dunbar had led one of those cattle drives and decided to remain in the growing town assuming the duties of chief law enforcement officer. He was assisted by two deputies—Ben Matheson, the foreman at a nearby ranch, and Rico Rodriquez, a reformed Mexican gunfighter.

At the time he first ventured into series television, Joel McCrea had been a successful film star for nearly thirty years. The Western had always been McCrea's favorite genre and in 1933 (after marrying actress Frances Dee), he had purchased his own 2300-acre ranch in the San Fernando Valley. Not content to be merely a gentleman rancher, McCrea actually worked the ranch himself. McCrea's most memorable screen roles had come in such Westerns as *Wells Fargo* (1937), *Buffalo Bill* (1944), *The Virginian* (1946), *Union Pacific* (1939) *Ramrod* (1947), *Saddle Tramp* (1950), and *Border River* (1954). (He would cap his long career with Sam Peckinpah's superb *Ride the High Country* in 1967.) *Wichita Town* had evolved from another McCrea Western, Walter Mirisch's *Wichita* (1955). In the film, McCrea had played Wyatt Earp during the period he served as marshal of the lawless town of Wichita. It was Mirisch who persuaded McCrea to take the plunge into television, but television already had a Wyatt Earp, so the name of the character was changed to Mike Dunbar. McCrea later explained why, after so many years as a big box office draw in the comparatively easy business of movie-making, he decided to take on the hard work involved in a weekly television series:

> I loved making pictures. I was lucky and made some money. Then there came a time when you could make a good movie and nobody would go to see it. TV was booming. I like to keep active. Walter [Mirisch] broached [the idea] some time ago . . . a sort of "Our Town" laid in Wichita in the 1870s, with emphasis on character and story. We figured because of my, ahem, maturity, we needed a young and attractive guy. So why not make it someone we knew we liked? Later he'd be in a position to take over as the star. So we nabbed Jody coming out of the Army.[32]

Popular film star Joel McCrea tried his hand at television as Marshal Mike Dunbar in *Wichita Town.*

Jody had appeared in four films (two with his father) and played the lead in the *Studio One* production of "Babe in the Woods" before Uncle Sam got him. Later he gained some additional acting experience with small roles in *The Restless Years* (1958) and *Lafayette Escadrille* (1958) before joining his father in *Wichita Town*. He was, according to the elder McCrea, his father's equal on horseback and his superior at busting broncos. With Jody cast as Deputy Ben Matheson, the series premiered on November 30, 1959. A typical episode of *Wichita Town* like "The Long Night" opens with the elder McCrea's resonant voice-over narration:

> In 1872 there were those who thought a human life was about the cheapest thing you could either buy or sell. Of course, that wasn't true, but enough believed it to make a job for me and quite a number of others. Seth Johnson valued his own life so cheaply that he was willing to give it up for a horse—even kill to seal the bargain. When I delivered him to the sheriff in Salenus where he was wanted, he denied it. But then that was natural.

The plot involves the Marshal's desperate attempt to prevent the execution of an innocent young man, Seth Johnson, for murder and horse theft. Dunbar has discovered that another man committed the robbery and murder for which Johnson was to be executed the following morning in the distant town of Salenus. Working through the night to repair the telegraph, while at the same time being stalked by a killer, Dunbar succeeds in getting the message through moments before the scheduled hanging. During the long night,

Robert Culp began his television career as Texas Ranger Hoby Gilman in *Trackdown*.

he "could improve my knowledge of the men and the situations that they face, which, incidently, haven't changed so much since Hoby Gilman's time."[33] He lived with the Rangers and rode with them on several cases and he almost tied their fastest quick-draw expert. The Rangers were so impressed by Culp that Colonel Homer Garrison, head of the Rangers, told Bob, "We'd be proud to have you as one of our men!" and promptly offered his unqualified endorsement of *Trackdown*.[34]

Culp also put his own unique mark on the character he played. When he accepted the role of Hoby Gilman, Culp flatly refused to wear the usual Colt six-shooter, giving as a reason that all the other television cowboys were wearing them. Instead he wrote to the Smith and Wesson Company and asked them for an authentic weapon of the period. They promptly responded by sending him a fine 80 year old Smith and Wesson Second Model, .44 Russian revolver. He was somewhat startled to discover that three notches had been neatly carved on the grip which looked like the real thing.

"Smiths" were popular with many gunfighters of the Old West. Wild Bill Hickok carried a .32 caliber rimfire Smith and Wesson as a hideout gun, and he was wearing a large caliber Smith when he was fatally shot from behind by Jack McCall. Buffalo Bill Cody also used a Smith for shooting exhibitions in his Wild West Show because of its superior accuracy. Jesse James used a Schofield Model .45 Smith and Wesson and Belle Starr was another Smith fancier. Culp became very proficient with the gun, practicing long hours with live ammunition on a private target range behind his home. He even altered his gun by welding an extension onto the hammer and had the action hand tuned for smoothness. This made the pistol easier to cock. *Trackdown* premiered on October 4, 1957, to mixed reviews. *TV Guide* liked the series:

> [A]side from being a showcase for what is surely acting talent of lasting significance, *Trackdown* shows signs of rising a cut above the current herd of Westerns in another vital department: Many stories are good in themselves. . . .
> Culp makes Hoby Gilman human, vivid and memorable; a man with more trouble on his hands than anyone has a right to expect, and significantly who gets out of it the same way anyone else would—impulsively.

Variety (October 9, 1957), however, was not impressed (at least with the first episode):

> In the opener, Culp looked rather than acted the part of the town hero. . . . The material didn't give him much of a chance to display his acting prowess.

Unfortunately, the scripts were very uneven in quality. Among the best episodes were "Matter of Justice," where Gilman and a boy are left alone to battle a whole town in a story reminiscent of Carl Forman's classic *High Noon* scenario; "Right of Way," in which Gilman solves a murder and exonerates an innocent young man by comparing the caliber of bullets; and "Protector," where Gilman tracks down and kills a wanted outlaw who is using the daughter of the local sheriff to obtain protection. Some of the weaker episodes included "Sunday's Child," in which Gilman helps a reformed gunman win back his wife and infant daughter (the wife's motivation for returning to her husband makes no sense), and "The Schoolteacher," which includes a typically banal polemic on behalf of mandatory public education.

Still, *Trackdown*, which produced 67 episodes over two seasons, provided Culp with the opportunity for numerous roles on other shows, including *Ben Casey*, *The Outer Limits* and *87th Precinct*. This led Culp to refer to himself as "the highest paid actor still doing difficult character parts in other people's television series."[35] His biggest break, of course, came in 1965 when he was costarred with Bill Cosby in the highly popular adventure series, *I Spy*. Culp still appears from time to time on popular shows like *The Cosby Show* and *Columbo*.

Laredo presented the Texas Rangers in color for the first time and in a 60 minute format. Stories in *Laredo* stressed humor as well as action. The series, which made its debut over NBC on September 16, 1965, focused on three (four, the second season) members of company B of the Texas Rangers and their captain. The program was set in the vicinity of Laredo, Texas, in the 1870s. Laredo was the base of operations for the Ranger company whose 18 men comprised the only formal law between the Red River and the Rio Grande.

Not all of the Rangers were men whose earlier careers were open to scrutiny. Some were thieves, some even murderers. Within the Rangers, however, the slate of each was wiped clean and all were given a fresh start. Each man provided his own clothing, horse and six-shooter. In return, he received full amnesty within the state of Texas for his past crimes, plus $40 a month in cash—for as long as he lived to collect his pay.

The oldest of the Rangers, Reese Bennett, was already in his 40s when he joined the group, and his age was often the source of much amusement to the two or three younger Rangers who were his partners. As the son of the best sheriff El Paso ever had, Reese was brought up to know the difference between right and wrong. When he was only 12, he saw his father gunned down by three killers. Reese learned the names of the men, and bided his time. When he turned 18, Reese was appointed deputy U.S. marshal, swore out warrants for his father's killers and hunted them down. He brought one back alive, but the other two made the mistake of resisting arrest.

During the Civil War, Reese had fought for the Union because he believed that it was the right thing to do, just as Sam Houston, governor of Texas, had believed that the state should remain in the Union. After Appomattox, Reese returned to Texas and volunteered for the Rangers. He was accepted, in spite of strong objections from others in higher positions that he was a turncoat and a traitor. Occasionally this resentment generated friction between Reese and other Rangers in Company B. Most of the episodes were built around the deeds, misdeeds and personality of Reese Bennett. Reese's first appearance on *Laredo* finds him fighting a bull in the corral of a livery stable. The bull drapes him over a fence rail. In the same episode Reese knocks out a 240 pound bully who has been abusing a saloon girl. The girl thinks Reese is "wonderful, considerin' your age and all." Reese Bennett, in short, was not a typical Western hero—except, perhaps, in the exaggerated comic-strip sense.

To play the role, the producers of *Laredo* selected an actor who in no way resembled the star of a continuing television series. Neville Brand was 45 years old, with a broad nose, splayed nostrils, thick lips, uneven teeth, coarse hair and pockmarked face. In the past he had gained fame—and respect—as a heavy. The oldest of eight children, Brand was born in Kewanee, Illinois on August 13, 1920. His father, Leo Brand, built bridges, so the family had to keep moving up and down the Mississippi River to accommodate his work. As a teenager, Neville worked at a variety of part-time jobs—bootblack, soda jerk, waiter and even as a runner for a bookie joint. In 1939, after high school, Brand joined the army, intending to make a career of it. He became America's fourth most decorated GI of World War II. Included among his awards was the Silver Star, America's third highest combat decoration. He won it for single-handedly taking out a German machine-gun nest. Later, Brand was seriously wounded in the right upper arm and almost bled to death. This convinced him to pursue more peaceful pursuits and he entered acting school under the GI Bill of Rights following the war.

Soon Brand was being given some choice roles in Off Broadway productions. He also appeared on Broadway in Sidney Kingley's *Night Life*. Television provided him with the most work, however, as he appeared in literally dozens of roles during the fifties and early sixties. Invariably he was cast as the villain: on *The Untouchables*, he was Al Capone; on *Bonanza*, Hoss's ruthless uncle who kidnaps Little Joe; on *Rawhide*, he was a hired hand who tries to kill off the entire crew. The highlight of Brand's career, prior to *Laredo*, had been playing the Huey Long–like Willie Stark in the *Kraft Television Theatre*'s production of "All the King's Men" (for which he received a Sylvania Award) and his work as a prison guard in the theatrical film *Birdman of Alcatraz* (1962; starring Burt Lancaster) for which he received an Academy Award nomination as Best Supporting Actor. By portraying Reese Bennett in *Laredo*, Brand became one of the few actors to successfully make the switch from heavy roles to good guys (joining the likes of such screen legends as Humphrey Bogart and Wallace Beery).

Joining Reese Bennett in *Laredo*'s tales of Company B was the character of Chad Cooper. Cooper, a native of Boston and a graduate of West Point, had planned to make the Army his career. Then, as a lieutenant in command of a routine border patrol, he saw his men ambushed and wiped out by Mexican bandits armed with the latest U.S. weapons. Ordered by his commanding officer not to pursue his attackers into Mexico, he resigned his commission and joined the Rangers, so he could continue his search for the guilty American gunrunners, legally and with help.

Peter Brown, former costar of *Lawman*, played Chad Cooper. Brown had taken up acting while stationed in Alaska with the Army. He organized a base theatrical group to provide the men with an indoor activity to occupy their spare time. Following his discharge, Brown enrolled at UCLA to study acting and began getting small roles in television Westerns like *Wagon Train* and in a few action oriented movies. His big break came with the role of young Deputy Johnny McKay in *Lawman* in 1958.

The third member of the Ranger triumvirate during *Laredo*'s first season was Joe Riley. Cynical, worldly and a former gunfighter, Riley lived only for the present. He had joined the Rangers because the life appealed to him, and also because they afforded him sanctuary from lawmen in other territories who were after him. William Smith, who played Joe Riley, was a former Russian language major who decided to leave college and try acting in 1957. He won a screen test and was given supporting roles in several of television's most popular Westerns (e.g., *Wagon Train* and *The Virginian*). He also had bit parts in theatrical films like *The Mating Game* (1959), *Ask Any Girl* (1959) and *The Subterraneans* (1960). *Laredo* provided him with his first major American role, after he had appeared in a 1961 British series called *Zero-1*.

The Rangers of Company B were supervised by Captain Edward Parmalee. A widower, who had lost both his wife and his fortune during the Civil War, Parmalee now lived for the Rangers and his daughter, Jenny. As a Ranger, he had no equals and only one superior, the governor of Texas. His men respected him as an iron-willed leader with a straightforward, practical mind. Parmalee was both mentally and physically tough and he often chafed at the restraints forced upon him by his administrative duties. From time to time he would slip away from his desk to join his men on their dangerous missions.

Cast in the role of Captain Parmalee was Philip Carey. After seeing combat in World War II as a marine, Carey played his first major film role in *Operation Pacific* starring John Wayne in 1951. He appeared in many television shows during the fifties and sixties including the *Kraft Suspense Theatre*, *Walt Disney's Wonderful World of Color*, *Cheyenne*, *Ford Theatre* and *The Virginian*. He also starred in two short-lived series, as Lieutenant Michael Rhodes in *Tales of the 77th Bengal Lancers* (1956-57) and in the title role on *Philip Marlowe* (1959-60).

Erik Hunter was added to the cast during *Laredo*'s second season as a new Ranger. With his fancy jackets, vests and hats, he probably was the snappiest dresser in the Texas Rangers. He was played by Robert Wolders, who, according to NBC, was "the only Dutchman ever to be cast as a Texas lawman." He was also probably the only television actor who was a psychology graduate specializing in psychodrama.[36]

Developed by the producers of *The Virginian*, *Laredo* featured excellent color photography filmed on location in Utah, Arizona and Nevada (practically everywhere in the Southwestern U.S. *except* Texas). Initial reviews of *Laredo* were not, however, very encouraging. *Variety* (September 22, 1965) said:

> "Laredo" . . . seems betwixt and between judging by the initial opus. It tried hard to mix levity with standard sage action, but the tongue-in-cheek touch seemingly intended as dominant motif just didn't come off.

Despite such reviews, *Laredo* was ranked among the top 40 shows during most of the year and was renewed by NBC for a second season. The emphasis on humor became even more pronounced during the second season. Slapstick bits and pratfalls were incorporated into every story. Musical bridges and motifs were also used to enhance the comedic aspects. Such touches were especially effective in episodes directed by Ezra Stone (radio's Henry Aldrich) like "The Short, Happy Fatherhood of Reese Bennett." Still, the stories, photography and acting of Neville Brand separated this series from such "pure" Western comedies as *F Troop* and *Pistols 'n' Petticoats*.

A typical first season episode, "I See by Your Outfit," relates the adventures of the three Rangers when they are sent to a Texas border town to apprehend a gang of Mexican bandits. Reese is captured and taken hostage by the banditos and most of the story deals with Cooper and Riley's efforts to free him and capture the outlaws. There is a blazing gunfight and a raucous fistfight (between Reese and the bandit leader) at the conclusion of the episode.

In "Anybody Here Seen Billy?" the three Rangers tangle with the beautiful, but treacherous, girlfriend of a wanted outlaw. They finally track down and capture the outlaw and his gang in a blazing gunfight. Along the way, however, each tries a different approach on the girl to obtain her cooperation. Each fails, but learns a lesson about women. There is a good mixture of humor and Western adventure in the story.

"The Land Slickers," on the other hand, is heavy on comedy. Reese decides to take the reward money he has received for capturing a dangerous outlaw, invest it in a piece of land, resign from the Rangers and settle down to a life of ranching. The problem is that the land he has purchased lies beneath a pool of alkaline water and is worthless. The rest of the story depicts the Rangers' efforts to get Reese's money back while at the same time apprehending the two con artists, a beautiful girl and her uncle. Along the way Reese is locked in jail, tricked into re-enlisting in the Rangers and conked on the head innumerable times. Cooper even finds himself hanging over a cliff for a while before all is successfully resolved in the end.

Perhaps the most poignant episode is "The Short, Happy Fatherhood of Reese Bennett." Reese befriends a lonely young Comanche boy, Black Wing, whose parents have been murdered by a gang of outlaws. Later, after the boy has saved his life, Reese decides to take him home to Laredo. The two develop a genuine affection for each other and when the boy's uncle appears at the end of the episode, Reese knows that Black Wing will be better off with this own people. Their parting scene is very touching and is played by Brand with just the right amount of sentiment for his character.

In summation, while *Laredo* was not one of television's best Westerns, it was far from the worst. Its depiction of the Texas Rangers may have born little resemblance to reality, but it was, for the most part, great fun.

The show *26 Men* was to Arizona what *Tales of the Texas Rangers* had been to Texas. Presented as "dramatizations of historical material," only "the names were changed to protect the innocent." The only television Western at the time to be filmed "entirely in Arizona in the very places where the real Arizona Rangers risked their lives," *26 Men* was broadcast over ABC from 1957 to 1959.

Russell Gaylen, the show's creator and producer, tried to reinforce the show's authenticity by casting nonprofessional residents of Phoenix and Tucson in small supporting roles wherever possible. The lead roles of Captain Tom Rynning and Ranger Clint Travis were portrayed by real actors—Tris Coffin and Kelo Henderson respectively— but townspeople in the stories were played by housewives, teachers, clergymen, government employees, lawyers, businessmen, school children, and even policemen. Some were actual descendants of the original Rangers and three surviving Rangers, Oliver Parmer, 76, Clarence Beatty, 83, and John Redmond, 74, took turns introducing the cases upon which each episode was based.

In 1905, Joseph H. Kibbey, governor of Arizona Territory, sent a special report on the activities of the Arizona Rangers to the United States Secretary of the Interior. It read in part:

> Under an act of the legislature approved March 21, 1901 an armed force known as the Arizona Rangers is maintained for the preservation of law and order in the Territory. The force consists of 1 captain, 1 lieutenant, 4 sergeants and 20 privates, who provide at their own expense their arms, horses and equipment. The law was enacted to protect the frontier and preserve the peace and apprehend persons charged with crime. The members of the Ranger force are authorized and empowered to make arrests of criminals in any part of the Territory. Upon the arrest of criminals in the Territory, the Ranger effecting the arrest is required by law to deliver him to the nearest peace officer in the county where the crime was committed.[37]

Former Ranger Parmer explained in a 1958 *TV Guide* interview that "the only reason there was only 26 of us is because the Territory couldn't afford no more."[38]

Tris Coffin, who portrayed Captain Rynning, was a genuine Westerner, born and raised in a silver mining town in Utah's Wasatch Mountains. He became interested in theater while in high school and joined a resident stock company. After earning a degree in speech from the University of Washington, he was discovered by a talent scout who liked his accent. This led to a highly successful screen career for Coffin who appeared in over 300 Western films, usually playing a villain; *26 Men* gave him a chance to play the hero.

Kelo Henderson, who portrayed Ranger Travis, was also a native of the West. Born and raised on a ranch near Pueblo, Colorado, Henderson learned to ride at the age of 2. After a stint in the merchant marine, where he learned to perform six-gun tricks, he bought a horse and cattle ranch in California. In his spare time, Henderson became active in a local amateur theatrical group. Series producer Russell Hayden, a former Western star himself, met Henderson and cast him in *26 Men*, giving him his first television role.

Like *Tales of the Texas Rangers*, *26 Men* had its own catchy theme song. Written by Hayden, Hi Hoper and Gordon Zohler, it had a similar martial beat. The opening episode, "The Recruit," related the story of how Clint Travis was recruited into the band of 26 men. He is shown cleaning up a troubled Arizona town that was being terrorized by a ruthless criminal and his henchmen. The script gave Henderson ample opportunity to demonstrate some of his shooting skills. Another episode, "The Bells of St. Thomas," dramatized the capture of a brutal outlaw gang who were hiding in an Indian mission school. They are discovered by the Rangers when a brave Indian boy sends an SOS on the church bells. Most of the stories portrayed the bravery of the 26 men and the support they received from most of Arizona's citizens. The series, however, was too similar to many other television Westerns of the period to be successful for long. As *Variety* (October 16, 1957) explained:

> ... situations having ... similar plots have been seen so many times before, both in other series and in the lower double bill of theaters. Production values also appear on the weaker side, when compared to many network oaters.

The series was canceled after two seasons (78 episodes).

The peacekeeping and law enforcement activities of the United States Cavalry on the Western frontier were also depicted in several interesting television Westerns: The Fifth Cavalry in *Boots and Saddles* and the Fourth Cavalry in *MacKenzie's Raiders*.

Boots and Saddles was broadcast over NBC during the 1957-58 season and concerned the efforts of the troopers at Fort Lowell to keep the peace in an area being ravaged by Geronimo and various other lawless elements. Filmed almost entirely on location in Kanab, Utah, the series had an air of realism. According to veteran stuntman Neil Summers, "Life for the film company was in many ways the equivalent of life in the old Fifth Cavalry, since Kanab back in the fifties ... was known as 'the most inaccessible town in America.'"[39] The principal cast members included John Pickard as Captain Shank Adams; Michael Hinn as scout Luke Cummings; Gardner McKay as Lieutenant Kelly; John Alderson as Sergeant Bullock; Michael Emmett as Corporal Davis, and Patrick McVey as the commander, Colonel Wesley Hays.

Jack Pickard was born in Murfreesboro, Tennessee. Planning to be a singer, he studied at the Nashville Conservatory. Among other odd jobs, Pickard served as a model for U.S. Navy recruiting posters and then signed up for a four year hitch. In 1946, after leaving the service, Pickard decided to pursue an acting career. Small roles in films and television led to the biggest break of his career—being cast in the lead role of Captain Shank Adams on *Boots and Saddles*.

The following season (1958-59), 39 episodes of *MacKenzie's Raiders* were syndicated throughout the United States and Canada. As the opening title was flashed across the screen, narrator Art Gilmore intoned:

> From the archives of the U.S. Cavalry, the true stories of Col. Ronald Mackenzie and the cavalrymen he led—"Mackenzie's Raiders." His secret orders from the President of the United States: Clean up the Southwest. Make it a fit place for Americans to live. Wipe out the outlaws, renegades and murderers. If necessary, cross the Rio Grande knowing capture means hanging by the enemy, discovery, court-martial by the United States Army.

The series was based on a real person, Colonel Ronald S. MacKenzie, one of the most colorful figures in U.S. Army history, and most of the stories were taken from Colonel Russell Reeder's book, *The MacKenzie Raid*. MacKenzie was commander of the U.S. Fourth Cavalry and responsible for protecting the outlying settlers and stagecoaches from attack. Mexican bandits infested the territory he patrolled. These marauding banditos, as well as Apaches, made frequent raids onto American soil and then crossed the Rio Grande into Mexico for sanctuary. It seemed that the only way to bring an end to these attacks was to organize a secret Army unit that would be able to pursue these raiders across the border and attack them in their Mexican hideouts.

Since sending American cavalry into Mexico in pursuit of either outlaws or Apaches might result in an international incident, MacKenzie's activities had to be kept secret. Acting under secret orders from President Grant and General Sheridan, MacKenzie and his men were allowed to cross the Rio Grande in pursuit of these banditos and renegades. If they were caught, however, the United States government would disavow any knowledge of them.

Episodes of *MacKenzie's Raiders* dramatized their stealthy attacks across the border and their effect in bringing law and order to the area around Fort Clark, Texas, where they were stationed in the 1870s. The three major continuing characters were Colonel MacKenzie, played by Richard Carlson; his junior officer, portrayed by Jack Ging; and his capable sergeant, played by Riley Hill. Carlson, a phi beta kappa graduate of the University of Minnesota, was brought to Hollywood as a writer in 1942 by David O. Selznick. However, when Selznick saw the handsome young man, he put him in front of the cameras instead, which began a long screen career for Carlson in B films during the forties and early fifties. After serving in the U.S. Navy during World War II, he resumed his film career and decided to try television. Carlson appeared in many dramatic anthologies like *Studio One*, *Schlitz Playhouse* and *Climax!* His biggest break came when he was cast as the famous American undercover agent Herbert Philbrick in *I Led Three Lives* from 1953 to 1956. *MacKenzie's Raiders* was Carlson's only other continuing role.

Neil Summers describes *MacKenzie's Raiders* as "way above average television fare" and "well written with plenty of action highlights in each episode."[40] Other than in the comical *F Troop* and occasional dramatizations on anthology series like the *Zane Grey Theatre*, the U.S. Calvary did not draw much additional attention in television's version of the winning of the West. No television Western has even attempted to duplicate the majesty of the John Ford–John Wayne Cavalry trilogy. It is an oversight to be deeply deplored.

Perhaps the most realistic and believable lawman in the Video West was completely fictional—Marshal Dan Troop of ABC's *Lawman*. Personifying law and order in its purest, most unadulterated form, Troop was tall, rugged, deadly serious, single-minded, intelligent and dedicated. He could also be stubborn and unyielding in the face of duty. Troop might also have been the most self-confident lawman on television. He was assisted on *Lawman* by his young deputy, Johnny McKay, who always addressed the marshal as "Mr. Troop." He was respectful, hard-working, disciplined and above all, brave. He could also be restless and brash and was frequently heard to complain that nothing was happening. This was the team that maintained law and order in Laramie, Wyoming, during the 1870s.

When John Russell, who played the granite-jawed marshal, was asked what made *Lawman* different from other Westerns, he usually responded that *Lawman* was a "pure Western" that employed "standard weapons rather than gold-headed canes or tricked-up rifles. Its stories," he explained, "began with 'A,' proceeded straight to 'B,' and stopped neatly at 'C' without any fussy complications."[41] His costar, Peter Brown, put it somewhat more succinctly: "The only thing that makes *Lawman* different from other Westerns is how we do it."[42]

Undoubtedly, the two series stars, Russell and Brown, themselves were as much a reason for the show's success. Older viewers seemed to enjoy watching the stern-faced Marshal Troop stare down and, if necessary, gun down villains in Laramie; at the same time, the attempts of handsome Deputy McKay to avoid the distractions and temptations of youth while backing up Troop whenever the situation required it, appealed to the younger audience (especially females). Furthermore, Russell and Brown worked very well together. Brown later explained:

> ... When we started, he [Russell] sat down with me and said; "Look, we got ourselves a series. I don't know how you feel, but I think between us we can make it the best TV series in the country." I said, "I'm with you." That's why you never see us pull a gun we don't intend to use, take unnecessary risks like phony heroes, or stage any long-drawn-out fist fights.[43]

Descended from Western pioneer stock, John Russell was a California native. Born in Los Angeles, he had taken dramatics in high school because it was an easy credit. He was cast in his first film, *Frame-Up* (1937), at the age of 16. After serving in the Marines at Guadalcanal during the war, Russell returned to Hollywood in 1945. He was spotted in a restaurant and signed for a part in the highly acclaimed *A Bell for Adano* (1945). Russell was seldom out of work thereafter, appearing in at least one film a year, among them *Somewhere in the Night* (1946), *Forever Amber* (1947), *Yellow Sky* (1948), *Slattery's Hurricane* (1949), *Saddle Tramp* (1950), *The Fat Man* (1951), *Man in the Saddle* (1952), *Fair Wind to Java* (1953), *Hell's Outpost* (1954) and *The Last Command* (1955). In 1955,

feels McKay is too young. In rejecting McKay's request, Troop provides what may be one of television's best descriptions of what being a lawman on the Western frontier was really like:

> TROOP: What do you want with all this?
>
> McKAY: I wasn't cut out to be a rancher, marshal. Now the way I figure it, nowadays a fella's got about two ways he can go in order to amount to anything. The way Billy the Kid took . . . and your way.
>
> TROOP: Well, it's not a bad life . . . if you don't mind strapping one of these [six-guns] on every day and not knowing whether you're going to have to use it or somebody's going to use it on you. Course it's not much of a social life, either. You don't get invited to parties and such. People just naturally shy away from a paid gunman, badge or not. About the only time you really become popular is when some drunk cowboy starts shooting things up. Now that's one party you will be invited to. The way things go, the chances are pretty much against any lawman blowing out forty candles on his birthday cake. But, all in all, it's not a bad life, providing you can take it.

In the end, McKay earns Troop's respect and the job as deputy by backing the marshal when he must face down two of the murderous brothers in a climactic shoot-out. The supporting cast was excellent, with veteran film heavies Jack Elam and Lee Van Cleef and *77 Sunset Strip*'s Ed Byrnes as the three brothers. Like other Warner Bros. series, *Lawman* had an excellent theme song (written by Jerry Livington and Mack David, who had also written *Bronco*'s theme). The lyrics depicted the lonely, dangerous job of a lawman whose work began at sunrise and all he had to show for it was a badge and a gun.

At the beginning of the second season a new character was added to the regular cast—Lily Merrill as the owner of the Birdcage Saloon. She tolerated no nonsense from the cowpokes who frequented her saloon and she had a warm spot in her heart for Marshal Troop. Although Lily was in some ways similar to *Gunsmoke*'s Kitty, producers denied that they were copying the hit Western. Hugh Benson explained: "It is only natural that the lead should have a girlfriend, and the best place to put her is in the saloon."[46] Actually Troop, although obviously attracted to Lily, remained cautious in his relationship with her. He would not allow anything, including a woman, to come between him and his duty to the citizens of Laramie.

Peggie Castle was cast as Lily. Born Peggie Thomas Blair in Appalachia, Virginia, she later moved to California and attended Mills College in Oakland. After two years of college Peggie discontinued her studies to take a role on the popular radio soap opera, *Today's Children*. She also appeared on other shows like the *Lux Radio Theater*. Eventually she got a screen test at 20th Century–Fox where she read a scene from *Dinner at Eight* with a handsome young Fox contract player named John Russell. Castle's film debut came in *Mr. Belvedere Goes to Washington* in 1949. Her other film credits included *The Jury* (1953), *Two Gun Lady* (1956), and *Seven Hills of Rome* (1958). After landing a contract with Warner Bros., Castle appeared in several Warner television productions including *77 Sunset Strip* and *Cheyenne*.[47] It was this exposure that enabled her to secure the role of Lily Merrill when producers decided to provide a romantic interest for Marshal Troop in 1959.

"Lily" was the first episode of the second season. Troop is eager to close down the newly-opened saloon until he is won over by its beautiful owner. Castle also has a humorous scene with Peter Brown. Deputy McKay is assigned to guard Miss Merrill around the clock when she decides to take a bath. As Lily suds and sloshes, Johnny blushes and coughs, checks his ammunition and blushes, stares the other way and blushes some more. By episode's end the chemistry of the three stars has been effectively established.

The best episodes, however, are those which focused on Marshal Dan Troop. In "The Showdown," guest star James Coburn plays a professional gunman out for revenge on his former friend and mentor. Coburn falsely believes that he stole his girl years earlier and tries to goad the man, now married to the girl and leading a peaceful and respectable life, into a showdown gunfight. Troop tries to prevent the gunplay, but defends a man's right to wear a gun:

> If men are going to fight, they'll fight. Now you check their guns, they'll think you're afraid of them.... These aren't riffraff. They're honest men. If you go telling them they can't be trusted, things'll get way out of hand. Maybe some day men won't have to wear guns. The way things are now, they do.

Ultimately Troop is forced to kill the gunfighter to save his respectable friend who refuses to wear his gun.

Another interesting episode is "Left Hand of the Law." Several years earlier, Troop had severely wounded an outlaw in his gun arm. So bad was the wound that the arm had to be amputated. Now the man and his son have returned to Laramie bent on settling the score. He has trained his son in the fast draw and the young man has become as expert marksman. The father expects the son to wound Troop in the right arm and then he will face the marshal on equal terms. When Troop switches his gun to the left hand, the son refuses to draw on him. The crazed father takes the gun and Troop must kill him. The effect of this final confrontation is greatly enhanced by taking place in the pouring rain.

Another superior episode, "Thirty Minutes," involves action occurring in 30 real-time minutes—obviously appropriate for a half-hour show. A deranged gunman (played to perfection by television's best badman, Jack Elam) kills a cowboy, wounds Deputy McKay, and holds hostage four patrons of the Birdcage Saloon as well as Lily. He demands that Troop bring him a horse to make his getaway and vows to kill him when he does. Deputy McKay is able to distract him long enough for Troop to shoot him in the blazing finale.

All in all, *Lawman*, was a superior Western filled with adult situations, a minimum of dialogue and plenty of old-fashioned action. *Lawman* depicted the keeping of law and order on the video frontier as it could have been—indeed, as it must have been, if the lawman involved was honest and dedicated. Nevertheless, most critics were not very enthusiastic about *Lawman* at first. *Variety* (October 8, 1958) said:

> As for distinguishing marks on "Lawman", ... there are none, at least not of any importance. Yet the initialer was competent, even if the competence was partly in capturing the stylized terseness of the stock TV western.

By the beginning of the fourth (and final) season, however, *Variety* (September 23, 1961), gave a considerably more favorable review:

> ... Russell's serious handling of things seemed a little grim in spots but he's a competent actor who does a consistently solid job in the pivotal spot.... In all, "Lawman" is a usually entertaining concept for the horsey set.

The series would not have lasted four seasons had it not been popular with the viewers. During its second season, *Lawman* ranked sixteenth in the Nielsen ratings, making it the highest ranked Warner Bros. Western and second most watched ABC Western (after *The Rifleman*).

After *Lawman* was canceled in 1962, Russell did not lack for work either in films or on television. He made numerous television appearances mostly on adventure shows like *Alias Smith and Jones, McCloud, Police Story, Emergency, It Takes a Thief, The Fall Guy* and *Simon and Simon*. In 1979-80 he spent a season as the "commander" on the Saturday morning live-action series *Jason of Star Command*. His films consisted primarily of Westerns, most not particularly memorable, including *Hostile Guns* (1967), *Fort Utah* (1967), *Buckskin* (1968), and *The Frontiersman* (1971). Russell also made three quality films with Clint Eastwood, *The Outlaw Josey Wales* (1976), *Honky Tonk Man* (1982) and *Pale Rider* (1985). His portrayal of the professional gunman in the latter is positively chilling—a look at Dan Troop if he had changed sides in his later years. If Jim Arness is television's John Wayne then it is not stretching too much to liken John Russell's Dan Troop to Gary Cooper's Will Kane, the Western roles for which each is best remembered.

The Deputy was in many ways a clone of *Lawman*. What distinguished the series was the occasional presence of Henry Fonda. However, he actually "starred" in only six of the 39 episodes filmed during the first season and 13 of the 37 second-season episodes. Fonda did do the voice-over narration at the beginning and end of each episode and often appeared in the opening and closing scenes. The real star of the series was, however, as the title implies, *The Deputy*, Clay McCord, played by Allen Case.

Fonda played Simon Fry, the chief district marshal for Arizona Territory in the early 1880s. Clay McCord was a general store keeper in Silver City who also happened to be an expert shot. The catch was that McCord believed guns should be used only as a last resort and would rather let the judicial system deal with crime and criminals. Fry was able to persuade McCord, however, to serve as deputy while he was frequently out of town. After his store burned down, McCord became the town's full-time deputy. This gimmick was devised so that Fonda could be lured into a television series. Fonda later told *TV Guide*:

> Being able to do plays on Broadway and films in Hollywood is like having your cake and eating it too. My agents sort of talked me into doing television. . . . We looked at a lot of ideas, of course, but when I first saw the pilot script for "The Deputy" I figured this was the one I wanted to do. I liked the character . . .
>
> Now, while I star in only six of the 39 episodes, I appear briefly in all the rest. This sounds like cheating, but it really isn't. The brief appearances are done in such a way that you have the feeling that this marshal, my character, is actively involved all the time.[48]

The result of this approach is two distinctive levels of quality. The "Fonda episodes" are significantly better than the others. His charisma is apparent even on the home screen, and there is authority and integrity in his portrayal of the veteran Western lawman. Furthermore, the scenes between Fonda and Case are intense. Fry is depicted as totally dedicated to law and order with little mercy or compassion for wrongdoers. He would just as soon send them to Boot Hill as to try and reason with them. McCord, on the other hand, is genuinely reluctant to use violence to bring criminals to justice. The episodes which Case carries lack this tension and chemistry.

Born in Grand Island, Nebraska, and brought up in Omaha, Fonda always maintained that he blundered his way into acting. After two years at the University of Minnesota, he dropped out of school and got involved in the Omaha Community Playhouse. Fonda did some acting and worked backstage while supporting himself by working days as a clerk with a retail credit company. A few years later, he went to New York where he alternately worked and went hungry. Finally in 1934, he got the lead in Marc Connelly's *The Farmer Takes a Wife*. The following year, Fonda went to Hollywood to star in the film version.

Opposite: **Henry Fonda (left) appeared as Marshal Simon Fry with Allen Case in the title role of Clay McCord, *The Deputy*.**

By the time Fonda was ready to appear regularly in a television series, he had made some 50 films. Of these, only seven were Westerns but *The Ox-Bow Incident* (1943) and *My Darling Clementine* (1946) were among his best. Therefore, it was not surprising that Fonda decided to make a Western his first venture into series television. Obviously, the selection of the right costar to play the title character in *The Deputy*, was crucial to Fonda's willingness to enter the medium. Fonda explained:

> When we were casting for "The Deputy" I must have looked at hundreds of prospects. Then along came Allen. I can't tell you why this was our man any more than I can tell you why I like a play or a painting. You just have a feeling for people like him.... [He] did not only have looks, ease and naturalness, but an authority without seeming presumptuous.[49]

The son of a retail clothier, Allen Case was born in Dallas. As a young man he became familiar with the use of rifles (including the Winchester later used on the show). While attending Southern Methodist University, Case appeared in Dallas state fair musicals, sang on one Dallas radio station and announced on another. His singing led to five weeks as a regular on Arthur Godfrey's morning show in 1954. Later he sang in night clubs and appeared as the lead in the national company of *Damn Yankees*. After moving to Hollywood, he was given roles in several of the more popular television Westerns, including *Gunsmoke, Wagon Train, The Rifleman* and *Have Gun, Will Travel*. Case tested for the lead in *The Deputy* even though the part originally called for a much older man and Fonda picked him. While doing the series, Case became a recording star with his first album of standard ballads called *The Deputy Sings*.

The series premiered on September 12, 1959, to rave reviews, with Fonda dominating the story in the first episode. Some critics were concerned as to whether Case could carry the show on his own. *Variety* (September 14, 1959) loved the opening episode but wondered about those without Fonda:

> [The] opening segment of "The Deputy" is the pilot and it's a firecracker, as good a pilot as ever has been produced in Hollywood ...
>
> Here's the hitch, however, Fonda is so good in the pilot that one wonders if the rest of the series won't come as something of a letdown. On first impression, Case looks very good.... But Fonda so dominates this opening segment that Case is going to have to show an awful lot of strength to keep the audience happy in Fonda's absence.

In making the inevitable comparison of *The Deputy* to *Lawman*, on the positive side, there was considerably more humor in *The Deputy*. In the early episodes, Fry often tricked McCord into assisting him. Nor was McCord above using trickery himself on his boss. For example, in "The Challenger," McCord cleverly employs deception in getting Fry to give him a raise, even though he knows part of it ($10 a month) will come out of Fry's own pocket. During the second season a new character was added, "Sarge" Tasker (played by Read Morgan), to add humor. Tasker, an army sergeant assigned to set up a supply office in Silver City, has an easy-going jocular relationship with McCord, functioning almost like a comedy sidekick. (There, of course, was little humor of any kind in *Lawman*.)

Another strength of *The Deputy* was the use of promising young actors in key supporting roles, such as Robert Redford in "The Last Gunfight," Richard Crenna in "A Time to Sow," and Richard Chamberlain in "Edge of Doubt." On the negative side, the jazzy, modern-sounding background music seemed out of place in a Western.

Among the best Fonda episodes are "Three Brothers" and "The Means and the End." In "Three Brothers," Fry solves a perplexing murder mystery and in "The Means and the End" he flushes a notorious outlaw out of hiding by staging the public hanging of the outlaw's wife.

Among the better Case episodes is "The Last Gunfight," in which McCord handles a tragic confrontation with great insight. Two young gunslingers are each seeking a showdown with a retired fast gun who has settled in Silver City. After the man refuses to meet either of them, the two quarrel over which will goad him into a shoot-out. As the two face off in the middle of the street, the ex-gunman steps between them and is killed. McCord, after examining the body, tells them that only one of the shots has found its mark, and adds that since it is impossible to determine which one fired the fatal shot, neither one will be able to claim that he killed the notorious fast gun. Actually both bullets did hit the man—and either one would have been fatal. Fry, arriving on the scene to receive McCord's final report of the shooting, is pleased at the way McCord has handled the situation. The cause of death will be officially listed as a single bullet from an unknown assailant. Fry observes, as the story ends,

> Funny thing, you'd expect a fast draw like Clay McCord to handle a gunslinger's problem with his gun. Instead of which he used his head and his heart and I ain't seen the day when a gun could do as well.

The Deputy would have been renewed for a third season, but Fonda wished to pursue movie commitments and rather than continue to feature him in little more than cameo spots, NBC decided to drop the series. Case went on to a much more forgettable Western television series, *The Legend of Jesse James*, while Fonda later tried his hand at family drama in television's *The Smith Family*. The fact that Fonda was never a big success on television did nothing to diminish his status as superstar in the film world. Some students of the genre rank *The Deputy* as one of the better Westerns on television at the time. Castleman and Podrazik claim that

> This oater is out of the ordinary and well worth seeing. And even without Fonda on screen in every episode, the themes and mixture are perfectly suited to his personal approach to the Old West.[50]

Still another "law and order" Western of some durability was ABC's *Tombstone Territory*. The series focused on the efforts of fictional sheriff Clay Hollister in keeping law and order in "the town too tough to die." The sheriff's only friend and ally was Harris Claibourne, the equally fictional editor of the town's famous newspaper, *The Tombstone Epitaph*, who also served as narrator of the stories. It seems the business interests of Tombstone wanted the town left wide open for the drovers and miners who came there to spend their wages. Sheriff Hollister, dressed somewhat like Wyatt Earp, minus the fancy vest and jacket, was a no-nonsense lawman who wore two guns and knew how to use them. Claibourne was a staunch advocate of using whatever force was necessary to clean up the town's lawless and corrupt elements.

Producers Frank Pittman and Andy White claimed that *Tombstone Territory* was "produced with the full cooperation of Clayton A. Smith, editor of *The Tombstone Epitaph*, and D'Estell Iszard, Historian." At the opening of each show, Claibourne's voice intoned that this was "an actual account from the pages of my newspaper, *The Tombstone Epitaph*. This is the way it happened..." Sheriff Hollister appears to have been based on Earp, while Claibourne was clearly modeled after John P. Clum, founder, editor and publisher of the *Epitaph* and active in community affairs. The stories occasionally included historical figures of the era like Doc Holliday, Geronimo and Curley Bill Brocius, but usually refrained from depicting actual historical events.

Cast in the role of Clay Hollister was Pat Conway, son of the famous MGM director Jack Conway and grandson (on his mother's side) of the silent screen matinee idol

Francis X. Bushman. A native of Beverly Hills, California, Conway grew up on his father's 125 acre ranch in Pacific Palisades and was an excellent rider and roper by the time he was ten. He studied at the Pasadena Playhouse and trained with London's Old Vic before being given several small roles in some of his father's films. Conway's screen debut came with a bit part in William Wellman's *Westward the Women* in 1951. It was his role in *Tombstone Territory* that gave Conway any claim to stardom, however.

Richard Eastham, a Louisiana native, was cast as the editor and narrator, and during the first season Gil Rankin appeared as Hollister's deputy Riggs. The series premiered on October 16, 1957, for ABC with a somewhat offbeat story, "The Gunslinger from Galeyville." Goaded by one of the town's leading businessmen, Sheriff Hollister leaves Tombstone to collect taxes from outlaws living in the surrounding hills. In order to accomplish this, he appoints the leading outlaw, Curley Bill Brocius, as his special deputy, who cheerfully takes the lawman to various hideouts and helps him collect the taxes. In the end, after Hollister has gunned down a particularly mean gunman, Brocius allows him to leave with the tax money intact. *Variety* (October 18, 1957) stated that "the best audience for this kind of nonsense is in Alcatraz." Its highly critical review began:

> And still they come. Latest oater series "Tombstone Territory," stacks up as routinish fare. Story in the first stanza is a far-fetched and ridiculous yarn with a weird sense of morals. In the niche following Disneyland, "Tombstone" will have to do much better to chalk up any following.

Still the series drew respectable ratings, and remained on ABC for two full seasons. Then, in an unusual move, new episodes were produced (for a full year after the program was canceled) for sale in syndication.

Some of the episodes were quite interesting and employed some of the better actors and actresses of the fifties, including Angie Dickinson (in "Geronimo"), Diane Brewster (in "The Lady Gambler"), Lon Chaney (in "The Black Marshal from Deadwood"), John Carradine with Michael Landon (in "The Man from Brewster"), Lee Van Cleef (in "Gun Hostage"), Harold Perry, radio's "Great Gildersleeve," effective in a completely offbeat role as a cold blooded killer (in "Heat Wave Killer"), and William Conrad, radio's Matt Dillon, who also directed several episodes (in "The Heliograph").

One of the better episodes, "The Black Marshal of Deadwood" relates the story of retired Marshal Daggett of Deadwood, a man so tough and brutal in his methods of law enforcement that he is called the "black marshal." He claims he has come to Tombstone to settle down and raise chickens. A gunman, who has lost his eye as a result of the "black marshal," and his pal are trailing Daggett, bent on revenge. Daggett's right hand has been crippled by a wound which did not heal properly. In the end, Daggett bests the two (with a little help from Hollister) in a wild fistfight and decides to put away his gun forever. Although the story is typical of several used on other shows, Lon Chaney chews up the scenery in a riveting performance as Daggett. The character he plays is reminiscent of his role in *High Noon* (1952), although his reaction to his disability is completely different.

Tombstone Territory was an effective show when the scripts and cast were at their best. Attesting to its continuing popularity is the fact that it is still widely seen in syndication on various local stations throughout the country. At the time of its initial release, however, the most popular syndicated show in the country was said to be the contemporary Western police drama, *The Sheriff of Cochise*.

In the tradition of *Highway Patrol* and *State Trooper*, *The Sheriff of Cochise* employed all of the modern methods of law enforcement, including car radios, fingerprint analysis, helicopters and roadblocks. Set in Cochise County, Arizona, the series was actually

Pat Conway was resolute as Sheriff Clay Hollister in *Tombstone Territory*.

filmed in the county seat Bisbee, and related the efforts of Frank Morgan to maintain law and order in Southeastern Arizona. Gunplay was usually replaced by high-speed chases and fistfights. The first two seasons (1956–1958), Sheriff Morgan was aided in his efforts by Deputy Olson. In 1958, Morgan was promoted and the title of the show was changed to *U.S. Marshal*. His jurisdiction now covered the entire state. At the same time two new deputies, Blake (1958-59) and Ferguson (1959-60) replaced Olson.

The series was created by Stan Jones, who also played Deputy Olson. Jones, who was born and raised in Cochise County, was descended from one of the three families who actually founded the county. Among his other talents, Jones was an accomplished songwriter who wrote such hits as *Ghost Riders in the Sky* and theme songs for many of Walt Disney's films. In order to achieve the highest degree of accuracy possible, the producers of *The Sheriff of Cochise* had Jack Howard, the then-current sheriff of Cochise County, review each script before filming began.

Sheriff Morgan was played by John Bromfield, a native of South Bend, Indiana. When he was in high school, he emphatically rejected his buddies' suggestions that he try out for a school play. Years later, however, when a professional scout suggested an acting career, he was more receptive. Before making that decision, Bromfield was Pacific Coast Golden Gloves boxing champion while a student at St. Mary's College in Oakland, California, a navy seaman and a tuna fisherman. Fittingly, he made his film debut in a film called *Harpoon* (1952) in which he actually harpooned two whales while on location.

One critic noted that the only thing that distinguished Sheriff Morgan of Cochise from other contemporary video lawmen was that he was not above playing a game of poker with his cronies for money. Maybe this was legal in Cochise County or maybe the sheriff was not about to arrest himself and his friends for having a little harmless fun. In any case it was a humanizing touch. Otherwise Morgan and his deputies did pretty much the routine tasks associated with enforcing the law in stories that seldom rose above the level of stereotype. Bromfield was quite competent in the role, however, and he was frequently aided in his efforts by young actors on the rise like Doug McClure, Gavin MacLeod, David Janssen, Stacy Keach, Charles Bronson, Jack Lord, Ross Martin, Martin Milner, and Michael Landon. Neil Summers reports that at its peak, *The Sheriff of Cochise* was seen in as many as 61 markets across the United States and Canada.[51] In all, 156 episodes were made under the two titles during its original four year syndication. In rerun syndication, all of the episodes were combined under the title *Man from Cochise*.

Another contemporary Western police drama, *State Trooper*, made its appearance on the home screen at approximately the same time as *The Sheriff of Cochise*. Supposedly based on actual case histories of the Nevada State Police, *State Trooper* related the activities of Rod Blake while investigating such diverse cases as murders, bombings and kidnappings. In his role of state trooper, Blake used modern means of transportation like police cars, as well as the old reliable horse, in tracking villains to such Nevada sites as Las Vegas, Reno, and Lake Tahoe. Sometimes it would be necessary for Blake to don a disguise and work undercover to apprehend his man. Filmed on location in Virginia City, Nevada, *State Trooper* had an aura of authenticity about it, blending the traditional Western with both the mystery and adventure genres.

State Trooper starred veteran film actor Rod Cameron in his second television series. The son of a Presbyterian minister, Cameron was born in Calgary, Canada. He had wanted to be a lawman in the Canadian Royal Mounted Police as a boy, but his family moved to Brooklyn when he was 11. During the first six years following his graduation from high school, he held 33 different jobs including construction worker, truck driver, skin diver, file clerk, surveyor, cashier in a gambling house and sandhog in the New York subway system. After extensive traveling, Cameron ended up in Hollywood in the late thirties. There, England's Earl of Warwich helped him get a screen test. His first film job was as Fred MacMurray's stand-in. From then on, Cameron was seen in numerous action films, especially Westerns, first as a stuntman and later as a lead. In 1953 he landed his first starring role on television as detective lieutenant Bart Grant on *City Detective* (1953-55).

When that series was canceled, Cameron was cast in the part of Trooper Rod Blake. The pilot ran as an episode of NBC's *Star Stage* dramatic anthology series in February 1956. It did not make the network schedule, but was sold through syndication to local stations; 104 episodes were produced between 1956 and 1959. The series provided plenty of standard police action set in the modern West, but was distinguished only by Rod Cameron's presence. (Later Cameron starred in yet another police series, *Coronado 9* in 1959, while making numerous guest appearances on such Westerns as *Bonanza*, *Laramie* and *Alias Smith and Jones*.)

Touted as both a cop show and a Western, *Cade's County* represented an almost perfect melding of the two genres. Especially designed to lure veteran film actor Glenn Ford to the television screen, *Cade's County* was a slickly produced, big budget contemporary Western police drama broadcast over CBS on Sunday evenings during the 1971-72 season.

CBS-television President Robert Wood and the network's director of programming, Fred Silverman, had long been searching for the proper vehicle in which to star Ford.

Another successful film actor, Glenn Ford, moved into television as Sheriff Sam Cade in the contemporary Western *Cade's County*.

After attending a Glenn Ford film festival, both men decided he would be most comfortable in a Western format. Executive producer David Gerber and head writer Cliff Gould studied Ford's best Westerns, *The Fastest Gun Alive* (1956), *3:10 to Yuma* (1957), *The Sheepman* (1958), *Cowboy* (1958), and *Cimarron* (1961). From these films they developed a "Ford profile," a composite of traits which they wrote into the *Cade* series:

> From *Fastest Gun Alive*: Doesn't draw his gun unless he's going to shoot—he hits the target dead center. Does not believe that there is bravery in gun play of any kind.
> From *3:10 to Yuma*: Ford's speeches are consistently short and to the point. . . . He's one good listener.
> From *The Sheepman*: Very dry sense of humor . . . often delivering lines of a serious nature with a twinkle in his eyes. Not by nature violent, yet is capable of greeting impending violence with hard-nosed bluntness. . . . A maverick who'll bend the rules to get the job done.
> From *Cimarron*: A gentleman . . . not afraid that his manhood might be challenged by showing that quality . . . does his own stunts.[52]

These qualities, which were incorporated into the character of Sheriff Sam Cade, were not unlike Ford's own personal profile. Ford had always loved the West, once explaining in an interview:

> The Western is a man's world, and I love it. If I could do whatever I wanted to do for the rest of my life, I wouldn't do anything but Westerns. The Western in my opinion, is very straightforward and uncomplicated. Simple stories about big emotions. That's one reason

they appeal to people in foreign nations so much. . . . You literally don't have to speak English to understand the story.[53]

Ford was born in Quebec, Canada, in 1916. When he was 12, his parents moved to Los Angeles because his father accepted a job with a firm based there. Educated in Los Angeles public schools, Ford entered the acting profession as a stage manager for a local production of *Golden Boy*. Since the stage manager had to understudy all the male characters in the play, Ford ended up acting a lot. When he discovered that acting paid more than stage managing, Ford concentrated his energies on acting.

In the late thirties and early forties, Ford was given roles in both Westerns and dramatic films. (His first Western film was *Texas* in 1941.) He demonstrated considerable potential for drama, so many of his early roles were of this type. During World War II, Ford served in the Marine Corps. Following the war, he returned to Hollywood and got work in Western and detective films. He also made a few comedies and romantic films and finally in the fifties returned again to his first love, Westerns. (He recalls *The Rounders* made with Henry Fonda in 1965 as his favorite.) By 1971 he was ready, at the age of 55, to star in his own contemporary Western series, *Cade's County*.

Sheriff Sam Cade was based in the fictional town of Madrid in sprawling Madrid County, located somewhere in the Southwest. Three different sources list Madrid County as being located in California,[54] but two factors make the author skeptical of this location: first, Madrid is near a Chiricahua Apache Indian Reservation which would imply an Arizona location; second, in several episodes (e.g., "Slay Ride") evidence is sent to "Austin" for further analysis, implying a Texas local. Cade was a tough lawman of few words who ran Madrid County as his own domain. He drove a jeep instead of riding a horse and carried a police special instead of a Colt .45, but he was every inch the same classic cowboy hero he had portrayed in his big screen Westerns.

Cade was assisted in his duties by veteran Deputy J.J. Jackson (Edgar Buchanan in his last regular series role) and three younger deputies, Arlo Pritchard (Taylor Lacher), Rudy Davillo (Victor Campos) and Pete (played by Glenn's real-life son, Peter). Other regulars included dispatcher Joannie Little Bird (Sandra Ego), who was subsequently replaced by Betty Ann Sundown (Betty Ann Carr). Both actresses were Native Americans playing Native American characters and together they tackled a wide range of cases though often focusing on the sensitive relationship between Native Americans and whites.

The stories dealt with subjects which ranged from modern to traditional. One week Cade would try to prevent an unstable demolitions expert from destroying a nuclear missile base ("The Armageddon Contract"), the next week he would investigate a crime ring involved in the illegal sale of wild horses ("The Mustangers"). In another episode he was called upon to capture a gunslinging escaped convict who thinks he is Billy the Kid ("A Gun for Billy"). Kidnapping ("Ragged Edge"), gold smuggling ("Shakedown") and art theft ("The Fake") were other crimes Cade had to deal with.

Guest stars turned in strong performances in a number of episodes. Chief Dan George was outstanding as an Indian philosopher in "The Witness." Bobby Darin was chilling as a deranged killer in "A Gun for Billy" and Martin Sheen was coldly calculating as a kidnapper in "Safe Deposit." *Variety* (September 22, 1971) was optimistic when the series premiered:

> Ford fits the role of sheriff Sam Cade quite handily, it being a good contemporary con-
> tinuation of his basic movie image. . . . Despite the preponderance of law-and-order entries
> this season, "Cade's County's" mix of modern crime-fighting midst classic western scenery
> could be distinctive enough to catch on, buttressed no end by Ford's substantial presence as
> the lead.

Variety's opinion notwithstanding, the series was canceled after only 23 episodes. According to a survey taken after the series went off the air, *Cade* never achieved high ratings because of competition from big-budget movies scheduled against it, scripts that were badly plotted or plots that were clumsily "upgraded." It deserved a better fate. Perhaps the best assessment of *Cade's County* has been done by David Martindale who says:

> "Cade's County" was a curious cross between a TV Western and a contempory cop show. The community was populated by modern-day cowboys and Indians, but they rode in Jeeps and in pickups instead of on horseback. Bad guys still carried guns, too, but nowadays they were concealed weapons, not openly holstered to their hips. And unlike a great many TV westerns, "Cade's County" treated Native Americans with the utmost reverence. These weren't two-dimensional red-skinned villains. They were flesh-and-blood people, often subjected to the same prejudices and injustices as big-city blacks and Hispanics.[55]

(Another quality Western cop show, *Nakia*, will be considered with other series featuring Native American characters in Chapter IX.)

Lawman and lawyers usually go together, but law "by the book" was slow in reaching the real West. It was even slower in reaching the video West. Only three of television's Western heroes packed law books in their saddle bags and all three were more proficient with their guns and fists than they were with legal advice. However, Tom Brewster of *Sugarfoot*, Henry Clay Culhane of *Black Saddle* and *Temple Houston* all preferred to settle disputes through legal rather than violent persuasion.

Tom Brewster was first called "sugarfoot" by the daughter of the dead sheriff whose boots he tried to fill in the pilot episode of the Warner Bros. Western. She explained that a sugarfoot was one step *below* a tenderfoot. The town roughnecks and trail-hardened cowpokes quickly applied this nickname to the peaceful, quiet cowboy who, because he was rather idealistic and preferred talking to fighting, was considered a gullible coward. Some of his adventures had a humorous side while others were more serious.

A law school correspondence student, Brewster was a gentle fellow with a mild sense of humor and a strong sense of justice who preferred to study his law books as he drifted from town to town. Never looking for trouble, he always somehow seemed to find it. Every week he met someone who needed the services of a lawyer or at least a friend to help him out of a scrape. Along the way he also would usually find a pretty girl. In the course of defending her honor or helping his new friend, Brewster would get pushed around, beaten up and generally humiliated. Although he struggled mightily to avoid gunplay and violence, he did not run from a fight if justice required it. In the end he always won out either with his fists and guns (with which he was remarkably adept, considering his demeanor) or with words of wisdom. There was more than a little of Max Brand's "Destry" in *Sugarfoot*. Among his more memorable homilies:

> When a man lets a gun do his talkin' for 'em, he loses the one thing that makes 'em a man—his good sense and power to reason.
>
> I guess there's no way for a man to prove he's honest 'cept by just bein' that way.
>
> Places are decent when folks make 'em that way.
>
> Ever see ants workin'? One of 'em don't amount to very much, but a bunch of 'em can tote off somethin' ten times their size.... Folks are the same way.

The son of a dentist, Will Hutchins, who played Tom "Sugarfoot" Brewster, was born Marshall Lowell Hutchason in 1932 in Los Angeles. As a child, he had his heart set on becoming an actor. He began his career in show business, by presenting little magic shows in his garage. Later, while attending John Marshall High School, he won a

Will Hutchins traded his six-guns for lawbooks as the title character on *Sugarfoot*.

Shakespearean festival best actor award in a competition with college students. From 1948 to 1952, Hutchins studied drama at Pomona College. The comprehensive curriculum he took included shouting Greek plays "at the top of his lungs," declaiming Elizabethan prose, and singing and dancing in modern musicals. He also found time for track and basketball. Before earning his BA in drama, Hutchins starred in college productions of *Ah Wilderness, All My Sons, Of Thee I Sing, What Every Woman Knows* and *Liliom*. After graduating in 1952, he produced and starred in *Run for Cover*, a musical revue at the Ivar Theatre in Hollywood.

Before he could continue his career, Hutchins was drafted and served two years in the Army as a cryptographer stationed in Paris. In 1954 he returned to college pursuing a master's degree in film production at UCLA. There Hutchins studied cinematography, direction, editing, and set design. One of his projects was a 20 minute film which he wrote, produced, photographed and edited. To support himself, while waiting for the acting opportunity he knew would come, Hutchins engaged in such prosaic jobs as golf caddy, special delivery messenger, bus boy, grocery clerk, and handbill distributor. Finally

Albert McCleery, the producer of *Matinee Theatre*, selected Hutchins from among some sixty collegiate thespians for the lead in an experimental, all-student production of the series. In "The Wisp End," which aired on December 14, 1956, Hutchins played a young man who accidently kills a girl, stuffs her body in a closet and then tries to "run away from himself." McCleery later recalled that

> He was outstanding. The show became alive because of his personality. He has two of the most important things that an actor can wish for: a voice that's peculiarly his own, and charm.[56]

In addition to rave reviews, Hutchins got a new name from this experience. Marshall Lowell Hutchason became Will Hutchins. After executives at Warner Bros. saw the show, they, along with two other major studios, bid for Hutchins to test for a contract. He selected Warners because he wanted to work on an episode of their dramatic anthology series *Conflict*, called "The Magic Brew." Producers William T. Orr and Roy Huggins decided that Hutchins had definite potential, as Orr explained: "We saw immediately that he was quite different from any actor around today. He is completely natural. People of all ages take him to their hearts."[57] Hutchins subsequently appeared in two additional *Conflict* shows, "Stranger in the Road" and "Capital Punishment."

When ABC asked Warners for another Western to alternate with the popular *Cheyenne* series, the studio proposed three possibilities: *Maverick*, *Colt .45* and *Sugarfoot*. After some consideration, it was decided that *Sugarfoot* would work as a biweekly substitute for *Cheyenne* (and the other two shows were assigned to different time slots). The pilot episode of *Sugarfoot* was adapted from a short story by Michael Fessier which had originally been published in *The Saturday Evening Post*. The story related the misadventures of a misfit cowboy who bungled his way through the West but always managed to come through when the chips were down. Tom Brewster's shy, fumbling Destry-like cowpoke—a peace loving law student lost among belligerent gun-toting cowboys—provided a pleasant contrast to the somber *Cheyenne* played by Clint Walker.

The initial episode, "Brannigan's Boots," relates the story of Tom Brewster's arrival in a small Western town where he is appointed sheriff (because of his apparent lack of expertise with guns) by the crooked mayor. Brewster, however, decides to investigate the murder of his predecessor, encouraged by the late sheriff's beautiful young daughter. Then the mayor brings his cousin, Billy the Kid (played to frustrated perfection by young Dennis Hopper), to town to stop Brewster's snooping. Ultimately, Brewster sends for his father's guns (his mother encloses a note with the advice that in using guns "it is better to give than to receive") with which he proves to be remarkably proficient. In the final showdown, Brewster talks Billy out of a gunfight and instead nails the crooked mayor (who it turns out was responsible for the murder of the sheriff) with his trusty shooting iron. Thus "Sugarfoot" proves himself worthy of his predecessor's (Brannigan's) boots. The show ends with Brewster riding off into the sunset to await his next adventure. All of this folksy humor and low key romance did not impress reviewers. *Variety* (September 19, 1957) wrote:

> ... it's mostly talk, talk, talk, with little action, and adds up as a routinish western which may be trampled to death in this bountiful season of hoss operas.

The critic does concede that "Hutchins fits into the sub-tenderfoot role easily," but adds that he "is helpless against the weak material given him." Despite such criticism, *Sugarfoot* was to ride the video range for four seasons and 69 episodes, alternating with *Cheyenne* for two seasons, then with *Bronco* for another year before finishing its final

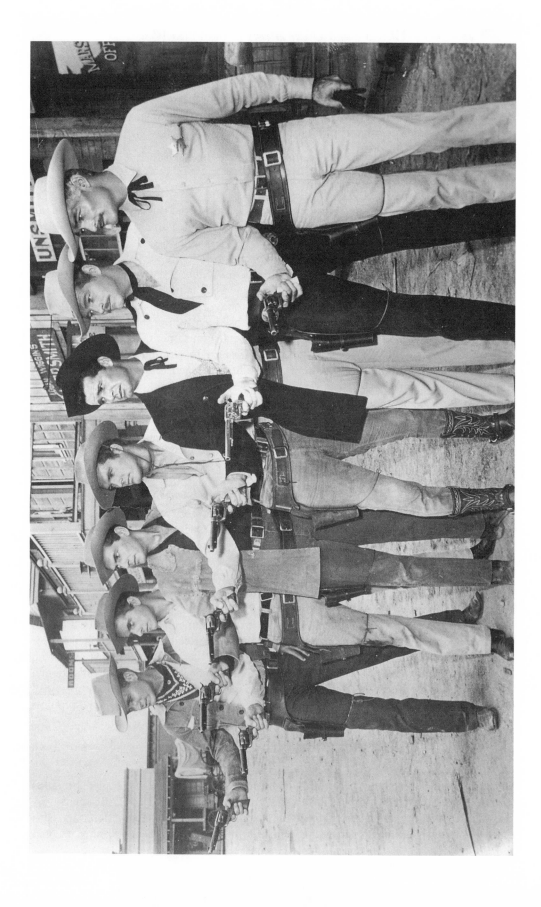

season by alternating with both. The factor that seemed most responsible for *Sugarfoot*'s success was the warmth with which viewers accepted Hutchins' boyish charm.

Tom Brewster functioned only intermittently as a lawyer: in "Misfire," he proves that an accused murderer's gun would not fire; in "The Hunted," he defends an army deserter who turns out to be a psychotic killer; in "Yumpa Crossing," he helps establish the paternity of a man so he can collect his rightful inheritance; in "Wolf," he defends a shiftless but likeable old loafer who is being hounded by a vicious rancher; in "The Trial of the Canary Kid," he defends his own lookalike cousin who is wrongly accused of murder; in "A Noose for Nora," he represents a beautiful young woman who has shot and killed a ruthless land company president; and in "Trouble at Sand Springs," he defends two brothers accused of killing the local banker.

During *Sugarfoot*'s second season, the producers came up with a way to give Will Hutchins more to do and take him out of his pat, shy and reticent character who is roused to action only when he is pushed. They created "The Canary Kid," a ruthless desperado who looks exactly like Tom Brewster. The Kid is the complete antithesis of "Sugarfoot." He is arrogant, cynical, worldly, over-bearing, rough, crude, quick to use his fists, and his guns and has no respect whatsoever for the law. (Their only similarity, other than appearance, is their *skill* at fisticuffs and gunplay.) In his first appearance, the Kid kidnaps Tom so that he can assume his identity as part of a scheme to rob the local bank. The Kid, however, falls for the judge's daughter and decides to keep Tom's identity. To do this he must eliminate Tom. He plans to kill him, but when his plans are thwarted by his outlaw girlfriend, he tries to convince the authorities that he is Tom and Tom is the Kid. The judge foils his scheme, however, by asking a legal question that only the real Tom Brewster could answer. Hutchins appears to have a fine time playing both roles and handles the duality with competence. So successful was this gimmick that the Kid was featured in three more episodes during the next two seasons: "Return of the Canary Kid," "The Trial of the Canary Kid" and "Canary Kid, Inc." They are easily among the best the series had to offer.

Another gimmick effectively used on *Sugarfoot* (indeed, on all the Warner Bros. Westerns) was cameo visits by the stars of Warners' other series—in their original roles: Donald May (as Sam Colt, Jr.) in "The Canary Kid," and "Journey to Provision," Wayde Preston (as Chris Colt) in "Return of the Canary Kid" and "The Trial of the Canary Kid"; James Garner (as Bret Maverick) in "Misfire," Ty Hardin as Bronco Layne in "The Trial of the Canary Kid" and "Angel," and Peter Brown (as Johnny McKay) in "The Trial of the Canary Kid." Other notable guest stars (many also under contract to Warners) included Pernell Roberts and Connie Stevens in "Misfire," Dan Blocker in "Deadlock," Charles Bronson in "Man Wanted" and "The Bullet and The Cross," Ruta Lee in "The Dead Hills," Efrem Zimbalist, Jr., in "The Wizard," Martin Landau in "The Ghost," Roger Smith in "Yampa Crossing," Dorothy Provine in "The Giant Killer" and "The Avengers," Richard Long in "The Vultures," Troy Donahue in "The Wild Bunch," and James Coburn in "Blackwater Swamp."

During the fourth and final season, *Sugarfoot* added a new character, "Toothy Thompson." In his initial appearance, Toothy is charged with the attempted murder of a man running for governor and would have been lynched had it not been for Tom Brewster, who is serving as acting deputy. Simple-minded and lacking in ethical principles,

Opposite: **Warner Bros. television Westerns starred such actors as (from left) Will Hutchins, Peter Brown, Jack Kelly, Ty Hardin, James Garner, Wayde Preston and John Russell.**

Toothy attaches himself to Sugarfoot after the incident, and is constantly trying to protect and please him. Later, he even kidnaps the crooked governor's wife in a misguided scheme to make Tom Brewster governor. All is forgiven in the end and the two ride off together seeking new adventures.

In the final episode of the series, "Angel," Toothy becomes a deputy and falls in love with a deaf-mute. The show ends with Toothy and the girl planning to get married. Toothy was played by Jack Elam, in one of his "lighter" roles. Elam has been described by one movie critic as "the roughest, meanest, dirtiest heavy ever to cast a shadow across a movie-lot cowtown."[58] Elam, a native of Arizona, began his career in show business as an accountant and bookkeeper in the forties. In return for his services, he negotiated a deal to appear in *The Sundowners* in 1950 as a villain. This launched a long and lucrative screen career for the tall, tough-looking Elam. Although he frequently appeared in television Westerns, Toothy Thompson was his first continuing role.

A number of historical characters were also occasionally woven into the plots of *Sugarfoot*. In addition to Billy the Kid, Tom Brewster had occasion to meet the notorious Frank James in "Hideout," Polish pianist Frederick Pulaski in "The Mysterious Stranger," Judge Roy Bean in "Vinegarroon," and future President Teddy Roosevelt, whom he befriends in one of the more lighthearted episodes, "Man from Medora." (Peter Breck turns in a "smashing" performance as the 23 year old Roosevelt. He reprises the role on *Bronco* the following season in "Yankee Tornado." Brewster shows up in this story too. Both scripts were finely crafted by Warren Douglas.)

Another *Sugarfoot* asset, typical of most Warner Bros. television Westerns, was a catchy theme song with music by Ray Heindorf, and Max Steiner, and words by Paul Francis Webster. *Sugarfoot* had clever lyrics and an easy to hum melody.

After *Sugarfoot* was canceled, Will Hutchins was given an opportunity to try his hand at straight comedy. Unfortunately for Hutchins, each of the two sitcoms in which he starred, *Hey Landlord* (1966) and a remake of *Blondie* (1968), was canceled after only one season. He did manage to keep quite busy as a guest star on such popular series as *Gunsmoke, Alfred Hitchcock Presents, Perry Mason* and *Love, American Style*. His most successful role, however, remains that of Tom Brewster, the shy, would-be lawyer of *Sugarfoot*.

Leaving a considerably less lasting impression was gunfighter-turned-lawyer, Henry Clay Culhane, of *Black Saddle*. After both of his brothers were killed in a shootout, Clay (as he was known to his friends) decided that the practice of law was a better way of settling frontier disputes. (The story of Clay's transformation is related in a second season episode entitled "The Saddle.") Riding circuit throughout post–Civil War New Mexico Territory offering help to those needing legal assistance, Culhane always carried his law books in the saddlebags attached to his beautiful black saddle.

In the opening episode, "Client: Travers," Culhane rides into Latigo, a town taken over by a rancher bent on revenge for the earlier killing of his son. He and his gang have bought up all the land in town except one parcel, which a young widow will not sell. The vengeful rancher drives everyone else out of town and prevents anyone from entering. Culhane, representing the widow, uses his guns rather than his lawbooks to single-handedly smash the gang and save what is left of the town.

The widow, Nora Travers, is owner of the town's hotel where Culhane decides to stay and set up an office. Also introduced in the episode is the town marshal, Gib Scott, who is concerned about Culhane's returning to his violent and often lawless ways. The citizens of Latigo seem to have more faith in his guns than his lawbooks, but Culhane always tries valiantly to avoid gunplay.

Clay Culhane was played by Peter Breck, a native of Rochester, New York. The son of a bandleader and a former chorus girl, Breck had begun his show business career as a singer, but wound up in stock. He had appeared in 140 plays before he was "discovered" by Robert Mitchum and signed for a role in *Thunder Road* in 1958. (He would later have much greater success in *The Big Valley*.)

Veteran actor Russell Johnson (who subsequently became famous as the professor on *Gilligan's Island*) was cast as the marshal and Anna Lisa played Nora Travers, the manager of the Marathon Hotel and sometime confidante of Culhane. *Black Saddle* was produced by Dick Powell's Four Star Productions and premiered on NBC, January 10, 1959. *Variety* (January 12, 1959) viewed the series as just another typical television Western:

> Here's what television needs—another western. What with the saturation of hoss operas on TV, the newest entry "Black Saddle," has a fair-to-middlin' chance to make the grade. On the plus side there are some fine actors in the oater, and overall production is another asset, showing skill and know-how. On the debit side, there's the familiarity of the series' premise—a retired gunslinger.

Culhane's clientele as circuit lawyer was diverse. In one episode ("Client: Meade"), he represents a young man who has been forced to kill a ruffian in self-defense. (The catch is that the only witness to the crime is afraid to testify because of threats made against his family by the dead man's brothers.) In another ("Client: McQueen") he helps an elderly rancher regain possession of the land his scheming daughter and son-in-law have stolen from him. (The catch is that the transaction appears to be legal.) In yet another story ("Client: Frome"), Culhane takes the case of a man thought to have been killed in the war who unexpectedly returns home to claim his estate and now remarried wife. (The catch here is that the wife is legally entitled to his estate and to remarry.) In another episode ("Client: Jessup"), Culhane represents a man who offers to make restitution for money he had stolen many years earlier. (Here the catch is that his wife, fearful of losing her estate, kills him before he can repay the money.) In another ("Client: Tagger"), Culhane refuses to represent a man who has served time in prison for killing a man who was not in fact dead. (The catch this time is that he intends to kill the man for whose murder he was imprisoned and then hide behind the "double jeopardy" provision of the law.) Culhane might one week represent a bounty hunter ("Blood Money") and another week, a bounty hunter's prey ("Client: Neal Adams").

The stories varied in quality, but Breck turned in a consistently fine performance. What probably killed off the series, which received respectable if not high ratings, was being shuffled around the schedule from NBC on Saturdays to ABC on Fridays. Forty-four episodes had been made when the series was canceled in September 1960. Still, Clay Culhane as a lawyer who is invariably forced to use guns rather than the law to see that justice is achieved, reaffirmed violence as a key ingredient of the television Western.

Temple Houston, the only other series of note to feature a lawyer, was very loosely based on the exploits of the son of Texas hero Sam Houston. Houston, like Clay Culhane, was a circuit lawyer who roamed the Southwest in the 1880s taking clients wherever he could find them. Although he was as adept at using his fists and guns as he was arguing the law, Houston was probably the best lawyer who rode the video range. He was both a skilled speaker and an elegant dresser. Houston was accompanied on his travels by a rough, slovenly, over-the-hill gunfighter and sometime lawman named George Taggart. The two men were as unlikely a pair as one could find in the television West and were often at odds with each other. (In the opening episode, they engaged in a furious knock-down, drag-out fight for little apparent reason.) Taggert sometimes was called upon to serve as lawman for a local town and might side with the very men Houston was trying to convict.

Handsome young movie star Jeffrey Hunter played Temple Houston, while veteran bad guy Jack Elam was cast as George Taggert. Born in New Orleans, Louisiana in 1925, Hunter had extensive film credits including his memorable role as the fiancé of John Wayne's niece in the John Ford classic *The Searchers* (1956). Touted as the next Tyrone Power by 20th Century–Fox Studios, Hunter appeared in more Westerns than any other film genre during the fifties, among them *Three Young Texans* (1954), *The Great Locomotive Chase* (1956), *Gun for a Coward* (1957), *The Story of Jesse James* (1957), and *Sergeant Rutledge*, (1960) also directed by John Ford.

The pilot for *Temple Houston*, called *The Man from Galveston*, was considerably different from the series. Directed by actor William Conrad, it related the story of circuit lawyer Timothy Higgins (played by Hunter), who comes to a small Texas town to defend a woman accused of murder. The first series episode (broadcast on September 19, 1963) was produced by veteran television actor and producer Jack Webb and appeared to be a mixture of courtroom drama (*Perry Mason*) and action Western (*Zane Grey Theatre*). Entitled, "The Twisted Rope," the story relates how Houston discovers who has killed the town marshal. The surprise ending has the murderer turning out to be a highly disturbed woman who bore a grudge against her two wild, weak and unfeeling stepbrothers. Despite the twists and turns in the script, *Variety* (September 25, 1963) was unimpressed:

> Preem episode of NBC-TV's "Temple Houston" tried to mix many elements in the old oater form, but came out with neither a fast-paced actioner, nor an absorbing, if slowly developed character study . . . it was a ho-hum outing.

It was not a very auspicious beginning for a series that was to last through one full season of 26 episodes. Some of the stories were certainly unusual. In "The Law and Big Annie" a militant women's group fighting for the more humane treatment of a circus elephant named "Big Annie" is befriended by Houston. In "Ten Rounds for Babs," he represents a woman prizefighter.

Perhaps the most interesting episode in the series was entitled "Sam's Boy." Three elderly men with a martyr complex (two of whom rode with Sam Houston), lead a "demonstration" armed with toy guns. Houston, who defends them in court, argues that these men are more to be pitied than persecuted. "Dreaming empty dreams and mouthing mocking memories of days long gone and dead," they should not be prosecuted, he explains. Rather, they should be looked on as "ancient warriors whose day of glory is long past. Remember what these men once were and shed a tear for that memory," he concludes. It is a moving story of the changing of the West and the men who helped to found it. Hunter is at his best and Douglas Fowley, Kenneth Tobey and William Fawcett are quite effective as the three old men.

Before the series was canceled (on April 2, 1964), Houston uses a ruse from the pages of history to thwart a gunslinger out to kill him. In "Do Unto Others, Then Gallop," he convinces the gunman that he has a gun under his blanket by cracking a peanut shell — which simulates the sound of a gun being cocked. Jim Bishop, author of the script, claimed that this deception was based on an actual incident.

With *Temple Houston*'s cancellation, Jeffrey Hunter went directly into the original (failed) pilot for *Star Trek* ("The Cage") where he played Captain Christopher Pike of the starship U.S.S. *Enterprise*. Unfortunately, Hunter died in 1969 at the age of 43 after a serious fall, never reaching the potential he had demonstrated in *The Searchers*.

Not counting such lightweight and short-lived heroes as *Dundee and the Culhane*, *Judge Roy Bean* and *Steve Donovan, Western Marshal*, these were the men who brought law and order to the video frontier. Wyatt, Bat and Dan Troop rode head and shoulders above the others, but each attracted his share of viewers. They were the television representatives of America's Cold War era popular culture. Demonstrating that might makes right and that the best solution to a problem is simple direct action, they dominated the video range for nearly a decade.

There was one other type of Western hero who roamed the television West of the fifties and sixties. Challenging the lawmen, by sheer weight of numbers, were the "loners." They too were concerned that justice be done on the video frontier, but unlike the lawmen they often functioned outside the established institutions of law and order.

V. *Alone Against the Wild West*
OR, HOW CHEYENNE BODIE, JIM HARDIE
AND JOHNNY YUMA LEFT THEIR MARK
ON THE TELEVISION WESTERN

They roamed the video range by the score in the early years of the adult Western. They were wanderers without ties or permanent attachments. Some were veterans of the Civil War, others were former lawmen, still others, reformed outlaws. Some were looking for a place to settle down, others, just a short term job that would give them three square meals a day. One week they might be driving cattle, another, scouting for the army, and still another, serving as a temporary lawman. A few had steady jobs which required extensive travel, like working as a secret agent for the government or troubleshooting for a large company like Wells Fargo. At least one was trying to clear his name of an unjust charge of cowardice, while another, suffering from amnesia, was trying to discover his identity.

As different as the purposes of these men were in wandering the West, they all had certain common characteristics. Each was a loner. Each had an acute sense of right and wrong and could not stand idly by while an injustice was done. Each was relatively young, strong, handsome in a rugged way; attracted to women in general (but to no one woman in particular for more than a short time); an expert in the ways of survival on the frontier; brave to a fault; a man of few words (but when he did speak, he commanded respect); adept with his fists and highly skilled in the use of a gun. And each had an unerring way of finding himself in a situation in which he was called upon to right some wrong each week.

The first and most successful of these loners was Warners' Cheyenne. Referred to by one writer as "a composite of the American westerner in all his possible roles,"[1] *Cheyenne* depicted the exploits of Cheyenne Bodie, a wandering frontier scout as learned in the ways of the Indian as in those of the white man. Cheyenne's parents had been killed when the wagon train in which they were traveling was massacred by the Cheyenne Indians while he was still a baby. Discovered alive in the ruins by Chief White Cloud, Cheyenne was raised as if he were the chief's own son. Given the name Grey Fox because "he looked so wise," he lived with White Cloud's tribe until he was 12. There he learned their language, customs, and reverence for nature, which he retained for the rest of his life. (This story is related in "Legacy of the Lost.")

At the age of 12 he left the Cheyenne and went to live with the white family of Jeff and Mary Pierce, which included a boy, Randy, and a daughter, Fay, who were several years younger than Cheyenne (as he was now called). For the next three years, he lived happily with the Pierces where he learned to read, write and speak English while becoming familiar with the ways of the white man. (Mary Pierce taught at the local High Point school.) Cheyenne had known the best of both worlds, but now he was to learn the worst. One night a band of whites wearing masks arrived at the Pierce ranch and accused Jeff Pierce of stealing cattle and killing their owner. Although he protested that the cattle were strays and that he had shot the man in self-defense, he was strung up while his horrified wife, young son and daughter—and 15 year old Cheyenne —looked on. The sheriff of High Point had been conveniently "out of town." Feeling she could no longer remain in such a hostile environment, Mary Pierce packed her belongings on a wagon and left town with her son and daughter. Cheyenne could have gone with them, but he chose to go his own separate way. (This story is depicted through flashbacks in "The Long Rope.")

Thus did Cheyenne Bodie become a wanderer. As he grew older and stronger, he remembered how he had been raised by the Pierces to respect law and order and fight injustice in its many guises. Nor did he forget the reverence for all living things that he had learned from his Red brothers. Roaming the West, Cheyenne was always ready to help the oppressed, the mistreated, the disadvantaged—with a fast gun and a heavy fist. One week he might be a scout for a wagon train, another, foreman of a ranch and still another, a deputy sheriff. Tall, handsome, deep-voiced, but soft-spoken, tough as nails, Cheyenne was a Western hero with genuine screen charisma.

To play this charismatic hero Warner Bros. chose an unknown actor named Clint Walker, who in real life bore many characteristics of the fictional Cheyenne Bodie. Walker was born Norman Eugene Walker (along with a twin sister) on May 20, 1927, in Hartford, Illinois. Clint's father, Paul, was restless and liked to keep on the move, so the family traveled up and down the Mississippi while he worked at a variety of jobs including professional wrestler, bartender, coach and musician. Clint, conditioned to this restless existence, began his own wandering when he quit school, where he had been an outstanding football player and the state wrestling champion at the age of 16 after his sophomore year. For the next two years, Walker worked on river boats and harvested farm crops. When he was 18, he joined the merchant marine, spending three years at various seaports in the United States and abroad.

Returning to Alton, Illinois, Walker held a series of jobs ranging from busboy, caddy, playground director, baker, lumberjack, steeplejack, carpenter, house painter, truck driver, to insurance agent and automobile and vacuum cleaner salesman. In 1948 at the age of 21, he married his high school sweetheart. Two years later, after the birth of a daughter, the Walkers packed all their belongings into a Model A Ford and headed for Texas. Here, Clint barely made ends meet while working on construction jobs, prospecting for oil and hazing cattle. Walker's next move was to California where he found employment as a guard at a shipyard, a private detective and a bouncer in nightclubs. The wanderlust struck again and this time Clint moved his family to Las Vegas where he had heard there were plenty of opportunities to make good money. He homesteaded two and a half acres about ten miles out of town while living in a trailer. Then Clint got a job as a deputy sheriff charged with keeping the peace at the new Sands and Desert Inn hotels. Several visiting celebrities, including film star Van Johnson, suggested he give acting in Hollywood a try. So, once again, Walker moved his family.

In Hollywood, Clint took acting lessons while supporting his family as a nightclub bouncer. About six months later, Walker got his first big break. He was spotted by Fred

Clint Walker made a name for himself as loner Cheyenne Bodie in *Cheyenne*.

Somers, a veteran Hollywood stunt man and character actor, while in the Universal-International commissary. Somers later described their meeting in *TV Guide*:

> . . . I saw this newcomer. . . . He seemed to combine power and gentleness in one impressive package. I went up to him and said hello. During our conversation I learned he was looking for work in pictures but everybody had been telling him he was too tall and no leading man would want him in the same picture.[2]

Somers contacted Cecil B. DeMille who gave Walker a screen test, which led to a six month contract and a small role in DeMille's Biblical epic *The Ten Commandments*. Walter tested for the role of Joshua, but he ended up playing a bodyguard to the pharaoh with one line of dialogue. Unfortunately that line and most of Walker's appearance was cut from the final print of the film. DeMille later told Walker that it was because of his height— "You looked like a tree among a bunch of stumps. No one could see our leading men."[3] Walker's first speaking film role was perfect for the six-foot, six-inch, 235 pound actor. He was cast as Tarzan in *The Bowery Boys Go to Africa* (1955). Later Walker commented publicly on the disadvantages of being big:

Being big is kind of unhandy. Part of me is out of camera range sometimes. I have to do these tight shots and stand abnormally close. It restricts your motions and actions. You have to take a short step where you would naturally take a long one and stoop when you want to stand straight.

And I can't fight one man unless he is at least as big as I am. I don't let it happen. If they give me a little man, I'll insist they balance it up. Either put me at a disadvantage or balance it up some other way. That's why I've probably taken more beatings than any other star in the business. They light into me and knock me out. I have to take a pretty good licking so I'm justified in giving them a good licking.[4]

According to author Robert G. Strange, Jr., Walker's height also cost Walker a number of on-screen kisses:

... most of his kisses ended up on the cutting room floor because the difference between his height and that of his leading ladies was often so great that even with the lady on a stool or box the kiss would not look as natural as it should.[5]

Walker's contract option was not renewed and in order to stay close to any acting opportunities that might come up, he found a job at the Warner Bros. studio as a guard. After several tests for movie roles, the studio considered him for the role of Cheyenne Bodie. Producer Arthur Silver later recalled:

All of a sudden I see this monster coming at me in blue jeans and a white polo shirt, with a physique that was so frightening. But he was the most beautiful man I've ever seen.[6]

Later when the screen tests were being shown to boss Jack Warner, he looked briefly at the Walker segment and said "This is your boy. I don't want to see anybody else."[7]

It was Jack L. Warner who had made the decision for his company to take the plunge into producing films for television. To develop these shows Warner established a television division and appointed his stepdaughter's husband, William T. Orr, as executive producer. The first show to be developed was appropriately called *Warner Bros. Presents* and would be telecast over ABC. Actually, the program was made up of three alternating shows: *Casablanca*, *King's Row* and *Cheyenne*. *Casablanca* starred Charles McGraw as Ric Jason in a television version of Humphrey Bogart's hit film. *King's Row* was a medical drama again based on a successful Warner Bros. film of the same name. It starred Jack Kelly as a young psychiatrist dealing with the problems of people living in a small town in the early 1900s. The third show, *Cheyenne*, was also taken from a Warner Bros. film, but used only the title, there was no resemblance whatever in terms of characters or plot.

Cheyenne, debuting on September 13, 1955, three days after *Gunsmoke* and one week after *The Life and Legend of Wyatt Earp*, became the third adult Western series to be broadcast on television. It was the first to be one hour in length and was unique in another way—no pilot episode was filmed in order to get ABC's approval. It was also Warners' longest running series, lasting for eight seasons. The show gradually rose in the Nielsen ratings and from 1957 through 1960 it finished in the top 20. By the second season Clint Walker was getting nearly 6000 fan letters a week. Although *Cheyenne* is considered by practically all critics and historians today as having been one of the most representative adult Westerns on television, this was not the opinion of the *Variety* (September 28, 1955) critic:

... This is almost strictly kideo fare, squared by the 7:30 starting niche.... No "adult westerns" for WB's video entry....

... Opening story is standard desperado Injun fighting—virtue triumphant fodder, but nicely plotted and dialoged....

> ... Walker is the strong and per alfalfa tradition not overly loquacious type; in manner
> and especially speech of the Gregory Peck school with some Gary Cooperisms.

John Crosby, the *New York Herald Tribune* television and radio critic, writing in January 1957, interpreted the series quite differently:

> The other night the bad guy's sister on "Cheyenne" was sobbing: "You know why he's a murderer! Because his mother told him killing was wrong and twice he saw his father kill men." The fact that his father was sheriff and that these killings were in line of duty didn't help at all; the trauma set in anyway and the boy grew up to be a killer....
> Cheyenne is the name of a tall, spare hero—none of these cowboy heroes look as if they have had a square meal in years—who roams about the far West righting wrong on the slightest pretext. As played by Clint Walker, he talks slowly in a dreary monotone as if conversation hurt him. Almost always he brushes against a girl who yearns for him but he can't have her for various reasons. Sometimes, she is already married, and while from the light in her eyes she clearly prefers Cheyenne to her husband, we can't have any hanky-panky of that nature in westerns.

Still, even Crosby sees some characteristics of the old B Westerns in *Cheyenne*:

> If you collect western dialogue, you'll find not all the old styles have changed. You'll find some real dillies in the neurotic westerns. Here are a couple from "Cheyenne": "The sky's black all over when you're looking up a rope." "If you ever show your face around here agin, I'll kill you on sight." "Saddle yourself a horse. I'll swear you in with the others." "No posse is hanging me out to dry."[8]

Walker felt that *Cheyenne* should appeal to both adults and children. Disgusted by the fact that the new so-called adult Westerns so heavily emphasized talk, reason and character analysis, he believed it was time to "get the hero off the couch and back on the horse." To Walker it seemed clear that what viewers looked for in Westerns was action. In a 1957 interview with Dave Gelman of the *New York Post*, he explained:

> I insist on action because I think that's what people like.... I feel action is what I owe the public and that's what I look for in Westerns. If you ask me, the reason the others talk so much is it's a lot cheaper to sit around and talk than it is to fight. Instead of sittin' around yakkin' why don't they do it with action?
> When I see a hero yak-yak-yakkin' I lose all interest. A guy that does a lot of talkin', as a rule he doesn't have much confidence in himself. When it's time, I just like to see him walk up and belt the old boy in the beak, and have it over with.[9]

Nor did Walker feel that the new emphasis on adult Westerns should detract in any way from the image of the cowboy personified in the earlier juvenile Westerns. The cowboy still represented a hero that everyone, young and old alike, could look up to, as he explained in a 1955 fan magazine:

> We are a nation of hero-worshippers and the cowboy can be anybody's hero. Now being a nation of hero-worshippers isn't bad, it's good. This is a big country and a hundred years ago when our people were pushing across the plains and over the Great Divide, every citizen had to have some of the good stuff cowboys are made of—if he wanted to survive....
> It's the kind of heroism that makes it possible for a man to live alone and at peace with himself, or to do what seems right whether it comes easy or comes hard, to stand up for what he believes in, even if it's going to be the last time he stands up. Well, from the time we Americans are little shavers sitting on grandfather's knee until the time when we're grandfathers ourselves, there's always the special need to have somebody kind of important to look up to. The problem is finding a hero everybody can agree on.... Yet there seems to be one good place where such men are still bred ... the storied West. And part and parcel of the invincibility of the West is the figure of the cowboy who inhabits it ... as long as he and the West retain their heroic proportions, he and the Western drama won't go out of style.[10]

Producer Silver later summed up *Cheyenne* in very similar terms: "'Cheyenne' is the personification of a type of man that roamed the West in a period of our history. He is many heroes rolled into one."[11] Another reason for the show's appeal was the physical attraction of Walker himself. A conscientious body-builder, Walker possessed broad shoulders and bulging muscles. Not unmindful that a significant segment of the audience was teenage girls, the producers managed to have Walker stripped to the waist for at least one scene in almost every show.

Cheyenne evolved in several ways over the eight-year, 108 episode, run of the series. During the first season, especially, the program was more like a juvenile Western than the other so-called adult Westerns being broadcast at the time. For example, during the first five episodes, Cheyenne had a sidekick named Smitty who provided occasional comic relief in much the same way that Edgar Buchanan complemented Hopalong Cassidy and Pat Buttram played off Gene Autry. Smitty, a government mapmaker, was played by L.Q. Jones. The first season also featured a number of routine stories based on the classic cowboy versus Indians confrontation with the U.S. Cavalry coming to the rescue at the last minute as was true in so many of the B Westerns of the forties. (The pilot episode, "Mountain Fortress," and "Decision," "West of the River" and "Quicksand" all featured variations on this theme.) Generally, the Indians in these episodes are depicted as bloodthirsty savages with few redeeming qualities.

By the second season this stereotype was replaced by that of the noble Redman who has been wronged by greedy whites and is defending his land in the only way he knows how. In "War Party," for example, Cheyenne comes to the aid of a young couple who have discovered gold on land given by treaty to the Indians. If news of this discovery leaks out, the Indians' land will be overrun by whites eager for gold. The situation is further complicated by three outlaws who are intent on stealing the gold. After the Indians have killed two of the outlaws, the chief allows Cheyenne and the couple to leave the area unharmed, after receiving their promise to keep the discovery of the gold a secret. The remaining outlaw is later killed (in self-defense) as Cheyenne leads the couple to safety, and the gold nuggets are poured back into the stream. This episode shows the Indian in a much more favorable light and makes clear that, while Cheyenne was raised by Indians, is blood brother to the Cheyenne, and has great respect for their way of life, he is totally white. (James Garner turns in a noteworthy performance, complete with mustache, as the leader of the outlaws, and Angie Dickinson is quite appealing as the prospector's wife.) Two of the best episodes dealing with this theme were presented during *Cheyenne*'s final season. In "Indian Gold" Cheyenne defends the honor of an Indian chief who is wrongly accused of stealing gold, and in "Johnny Brassbuttons" he helps one of his Indian blood brothers prove he did not arrange the ambush of a wagon train. (Tony Young is quite effective in the title role.)

Although many of the stories on *Cheyenne* deal with such standard Western topics as cattle drives ("The Long Winter," "Winchester Quarantine"), range wars involving cattle ranchers and sheepmen ("Showdown at Oxbend"), the building of the railroad ("Pocketful of Stars") and—by far the most frequently presented subject—law enforcement in the old West (including "Star in the Dust," "The Law Man," "Born Bad," "Town of Fear" and "The Bad Penny"), contemporary issues are also considered. The psychological problems of men who have become killers are treated in "The Brand" and "The Idol." The clash of different cultures is effectively depicted in "White Warrior" (Indian vs. white) and "Apache Blood" (Indian and Mexican vs. white). In "Home Is the Brave," the problem of racial discrimination is maturely handled. (The body of an army hero is returned by Cheyenne to his hometown for burial. The townspeople refuse to allow the burial to take place because the young man was part Indian. The matter is finally resolved when the Army accepts the body for burial in Arlington, Virginia, the final resting place of military heroes.) And in one of the most unusual stories, "The Vanishing Breed," Cheyenne accepts the unexpired term of a recently deceased state senator in order to promote the enactment of a law prohibiting the wanton slaughter of buffalo.

Although, in general, actual historical figures are not featured in *Cheyenne* stories, two outstanding episodes deal in a factual way with one of the most significant and well-known events in the conquest of the American West, the massacre of Custer's Seventh Cavalry at the Little Big Horn. In "Gold, Glory and Custer—Prelude," background events leading up to the military confrontation are depicted through the eyes of Cheyenne Bodie who becomes one of Custer's civilian scouts. As the narrator explains in the opening:

> . . . what actually took place is still shrouded in mystery. United States Army records bear the notation: "casualties: 225 officers and enlisted men; no survivors!" But the dead were scarcely in their graves when there appeared on the Western scene various men who claimed to have survived the massacre. Nearly every one of their stories has been exposed as a hoax or a lie, but there remains a few that have never been disproved. This is one of those stories. . . .
>
> And so the curtain rose on one of the world's strangest dramas, an American tragedy that would forever emblazon the names of its heroic cast of actors across the pages of history. One such was a civilian army scout attached to the Second Cavalry at Fort Laramie, but now under orders to join the Seventh at Fort Abraham Lincoln. In this story he shall be called Cheyenne Bodie.

Part two of the story, "Gold, Glory and Custer—Requiem," which is even more interesting, is based on the army's investigation of Mayor Reno's conduct in the debacle. Bodie gives testimony, at the risk of his own court martial, which clears Reno of dereliction of duty and cowardice charges. (Lorne Greene, in a pre-*Bonanza* television appearance, gives a commanding performance as Colonel Bell, the army's chief investigating officer.)

To fans of Warner Bros. Westerns, however, the most interesting episode of the series is undoubtedly "Duel at Judas Basin," broadcast during the 1960-61 season. This is the only episode in which all three of the then rotating stars appear. Bronco Layne is a deputy U.S. marshal secretly working for the Army to expose a corrupt trader who is selling rifles to the Sioux. Tom Brewster (Sugarfoot) becomes involved when he is framed by the trader for murder. Cheyenne helps prove Sugarfoot innocent and rescues Bronco when he falls into the hands of the trader and his gang. The episode was exciting with plenty of action and an opportunity for each hero to show his courage and resourcefulness.

Cheyenne also featured one of those great Warner Bros. theme songs with music by William Lava and words by Stan Jones that conjured up the image of a lonely man destined to wander from place to place carefree as the wind.

One of the more unusual aspects of *Cheyenne*'s eight year broadcast history is the scheduling changes brought about by the failure of several other shows and Clint Walker's contract disputes with Warner Bros. By the time the second season rolled around, both of the other two original alternating series, *Casablanca* and *King's Row*, had been canceled. Now *Cheyenne* was broadcast on alternate weeks with a new Warner show called *Conflict*. This was a dramatic anthology dealing with stories of people in conflict and served as a training ground for such future Warner Bros. series stars as Will Hutchins, James Garner, and Efrem Zimbalist, Jr. By the 1957-58 season, Will Hutchins had been given his own series, *Sugarfoot*, which alternated with *Cheyenne*.

In 1958, Walker walked off the set and demanded a new contract. In addition to more money, he wanted the freedom to do features and more time off. (He wanted to do 13 episodes a year instead of 20.) Walker also felt he should be paid more for reruns—$500 instead of the $45 he was then making. Finally, he wanted a better deal for personal appearances. (Under his existing contract, Walker had to give half of everything he earned for such appearances to the studio.) According to Bob Anderson, Clint Walker's biographer, Walker was also upset over the studio's merchandising campaign:

> ..."Cheyenne" comics [Dell], gloves and chaps, pistols and Ricochet rifles, sheet music, coloring books, puzzles, arcade or exhibit cards, "Cheyenne" theme songs on 45 rpm & 78 rpm records, "Cheyenne" board games and on and on! WB didn't miss a single opportunity to capitalize on their star's success. The merchandising angle really got to Clint when Warner's circulated ads for one of the show's sponsors Chesterfield cigarettes, which had a color photo of Walker in the left-hand corner, as if he's endorsing their product! Clint didn't smoke and resented the ad's implication that he did. "I didn't want fans of the series, especially children and teenagers, thinking that if cigarettes were all right for Cheyenne Bodie, they were all right for them, too!" He confronted the WB's brass about the ad, but their only reply was, "We have to re-coup our investment in you!" [and] the ad stood![12]

Proclaiming that he felt "like a caged animal,"[13] Walker remained off the show for a year and vowed he would stay away until his contract expired in May 1962, if necessary. He returned in 1959 after Warners agreed to make some concessions, but he remained afraid the *Cheyenne* role would forever typecast him and he yearned to be free of it. (Warner Bros. did allow Walker to star in two motion pictures in addition to his work on *Cheyenne*: *Yellowstone Kelly* in 1959, and *Gold of the Seven Saints* in 1961.) While Walker was "on strike," the studio brought in a new actor, Ty Hardin, to play a character very similar to Cheyenne Bodie named Bronco Lyne. The program alternated with *Sugarfoot*, but the name of the series remained *The Cheyenne Show*. *Bronco* eventually did get its own theme song. According to Robert G. Strange, Jr., in 1959-60, after Walker had returned to the role of Cheyenne Bodie, *Bronco* and *Sugarfoot* split off from *Cheyenne* to alternate on the *Bronco-Sugarfoot Hour*, and *Cheyenne* was preempted every third week by *Shirley Temple Specials*. For the 1960-61 season (the last for *Sugarfoot*) the three shows combined to make *The Cheyenne Show*. The following year, 1961-62 (the last for *Bronco*), *Bronco* and *Cheyenne* alternated on *The Cheyenne Show* and in 1962-63, the last 13 episodes of *Cheyenne* were broadcast.[14]

Walker continued to make films, averaging one a year, and also earned top money for his rodeo appearances. In 1964 he was cast as Doris Day's old college sweetheart in *Send Me No Flowers*. Then Frank Sinatra gave him a key role in the war film, *None But the Brave*, in 1965. Playing a rancher who tracks down and kills a huge grizzly bear that has been terrorizing the countryside, Walker returned to a Western setting for *Night of the Grizzly* in 1966. The script was based on a story idea developed by Walker. Even more successful at the box office was *The Dirty Dozen* with Lee Marvin released in 1967 in which Walker played Samson Posey, a Sioux Indian who was part of a special commando unit of ex-cons sent to operate behind German lines during the war.

In 1968, Walker again returned to the genre he knew best in *Sam Whiskey* with Burt Reynolds, followed by a Western spoof, *The Great Bank Robbery* in 1969 with Zero Mostel and Kim Novak in which he played a hilariously "square" Texas Ranger. Between 1971 and 1974, Walker returned to television in a series of five 90 minute films for ABC: *Yuma* (1971), *Hardcase* (1972), *The Bounty Man* (1972), *Scream of the Wolf* (1974) and *Killdozer* (1974). This led to his second television series *Kodiak*, broadcast over ABC during the 1974-75 season.

Kodiak was a contemporary outdoor action-adventure series in which Walker played Cal "Kodiak" McKay, a member of the Alaskan State Patrol which was responsible for maintaining law and order and providing emergency assistance in a rugged, wilderness area of some 50,000 square miles. *Kodiak* was a giant of a man who got his nickname from the local Indians because of his resemblance to the huge bears that roamed the territory he patrolled. Instead of the horse he rode on *Cheyenne*, Walker now used a four-wheel-drive truck, a snowmobile and even skis or snowshoes to move from place to place. The show was filmed in Oregon, Washington, and Canada because the air was cleaner and the sky bluer than on a back lot in Hollywood. It was also more accessible than filming on location in Alaska itself. Walker not only starred in *Kodiak*, but he also owned a half interest in it and was even responsible for the title. Unfortunately, although 13 thirty-minute, color episodes were filmed, only five were ever aired. (Low ratings brought swift cancellation in 1974.) Walker's attitude toward the character for which he will always be remembered, Cheyenne Bodie, was perhaps best expressed in an interview with Bob Thomas of the Associated Press shortly before the series left the air:

> It's what I want to do on my last day at Warner Brothers. I'd like to go out on the back lot and dig a hole, about 6 feet long and 3 feet wide. I'd lay this outfit in it, hat, gun and all. Then I'd cover it over and put a sign above it saying: "Here lies Cheyenne Bodie. Let him lie in peace."[15]

Fortunately for *Cheyenne* fans Walker mellowed over the years and he once again donned that familiar buckskin jacket in 1991 for Kenny Rogers' star-studded reunion Western, *The Gambler Returns: The Luck of the Draw*. Reprising the role of Cheyenne Bodie, he came to the aid of Kenny Rogers (playing a character named Brady Hawkes) and his pals with his trusty rifle, as he had done for so many others in those golden years of Warner Bros. television Westerns. In February 1993 Walker was cast as a former Western film star who thinks that someone is trying to kill him on the CBS late night detective series *Sweating Bullets*. Astride his trusty steed and attired in the familiar fringed buckskin jacket, Walker evoked memories of his glory years as Cheyenne Bodie.

If imitation is the sincerest form of flattery, then *Cheyenne* must have been the most flattered Western on television. Of the nearly twenty *Cheyenne* clones which rode the video range during the late fifties and sixties, none more resembled the prototype than *Bronco*. That series was, of course, designed to replace *Cheyenne* permanently if the contract differences with Clint Walker could not be resolved. Bronco Layne (nicknamed by the Indians because "there wasn't a horse that he couldn't tame") is an ex–Confederate captain who, after the Civil War, returns home to Texas to find himself stripped of honor and his home confiscated (as related in "The Long Ride Back"). Roaming the Southwest in search of adventure, Bronco, like Cheyenne, is a loner who prefers to avoid trouble, but who refuses to stand by while an injustice is done to others. Like Cheyenne, Bronco also works at many different jobs during his wanderings including secret government agent ("Trail to Taos"), drover on a cattle drive ("Prairie Skipper"), miner ("Silent Witness"), guard on a stage ("The Belles of Silver Flat"), deputy sheriff ("Backfire"), instructor at a boys' military school ("School for Cowards"), pilot on a river boat ("Red Water North"), and guide for a wagon train ("Then the Mountains"). During his exploits, Bronco encounters such interesting characters as John Wesley Hardin ("The Turning Point"), Billy the Kid ("The Soft Answer"), Jesse James ("Shadow of Jesse James"), Pat Garrett (when he tries to prevent the killing of Billy the Kid in "Death of an Outlaw"), Teddy Roosevelt ("Yankee Tornado"), Shakespearean actor Edwin Booth ("Prince of Darkness"), and Wild Bill Hickok ("One Evening in Abilene").

Newcomer Ty Hardin found fame as Bronco Lane in *Bronco*.

Ty Hardin, star of *Bronco*, was born Orison Whipple Hungerford, Jr., on New Year's Day, 1930, in New York City. His father, an acoustical engineer attached to the U.S. Army, moved his family to Austin, Texas, six months later. Ty (as he was called from his nickname, "Typhoon"), attended schools in Austin and later Houston. Ty's size coupled with his scholastic record earned him a football scholarship to Blinn College in Brenham, Texas. In 1950 he dropped out of school to enlist in the army where he spent four years. Discharged in May 1954, Ty entered Texas A&M University, on an athletic scholarship. He planned on a career as a professional football player until a severe leg injury took him off the gridiron and gave him the time to try acting. His first role was in a college production of *Ah, Wilderness!* by Eugene O'Neill. In 1957, one semester short of a degree in electrical engineering, Ty left Texas for California.

In California, Ty was soon hired by the research and development division of Douglass Aircraft. While at Douglass, he decided to attend a Halloween party as an authentic cowboy and went to the prop department at Paramount Studios to rent some real guns. By accident he wandered into talent scout Milton Lewis' office and was signed for a screen test. This was the first acting Ty had done since college, but a couple of days later he was offered a stock contract that more than doubled his salary as an engineer (which had been $100 a week). Credited as Ty Hungerford, his early film appearances in *The Space Children* (1958), *As Young As We Are* (1958), *The Buccaneer* (1958), and *I Married a Monster from Outer Space* (1958) were far from memorable. He was, however, given some brief television exposure. On *Queen for a Day*, Ty appeared as an anonymous male fashion model and he had three brief scenes in a *Playhouse 90* drama.

It was May 1958, when Ty's second break came. He was spotted by William T. Orr at Warner Bros., who promptly took over his contract from Paramount, gave him a new last name, Hardin, and cast him in the role of Bronco Layne. Another advantage Ty had was his ability to perform all his own riding and fighting stunts (skills he had learned growing up in Texas). The first episode of *Bronco* was broadcast on *The Cheyenne Show* on September 23, 1958. In a story entitled, "The Besieged," Bronco helps a band of Quakers who are being attacked by three desperadoes. They are after the gold that is on the land on which the Quakers are about to settle. The episode gave Hardin a chance to look both handsome and tough and drew some reasonably good reviews. *Variety* (October 1, 1958) said:

> What the viewers saw was a boyish-looking worthy, with the appearance of fuzz on his face rather than adult stubble. He was eased into his heroic role without the usual gunplay and dueling....
> It's too early to tell how Hardin will react to the gunslingin' and rough-and-tumble ways of the Old West, but there was plenty of evidence in his favor. He has the looks and build and knows how to time and punch a line.

The fans were not as enthusiastic at first as the critics. The vast majority of the letters he received during his first season were quite critical of Hardin for trying to replace Walker. The ratings, however, began to improve and by the second season, *Bronco* was considered to be a hit and was even given its own theme song, written by Jerry Livingston and Mack David, which did not, however, measure up to *Cheyenne*'s. *Variety* (September 30, 1959) gave another positive review after the second season's opening *Bronco* episode ("Game at the Beacon Club") aired:

> Good can come out of bad, and for Warner Bros. that's precisely how the studio came to have its cake and eat it too. "Bronco" was born out of the necessity of finding someone to replace Clint Walker in "Cheyenne" during his walkout against the studio. Today, WB has Walker back in "Cheyenne" as a once-a-week hour and still has Ty Hardin as a solid entry in "Bronco"....
> "Bronco" is neither the best nor the worst of the Warner western catalogue. Put it somewhere in the middle.

Still, all good things must eventually come to an end, and *Bronco* was canceled after 68 episodes in 1962. Hardin spent the next two years making theatrical films for Warner Bros. Among the most successful were *Merrill's Marauders* (1962), a war film; *The Chapman Report* (1962), a potboiler about a Kinsey-like sex study; *PT 109* (1963), based on John F. Kennedy's exploits in the Pacific during World War II; and *Palm Springs Weekend* (1963), about a group of teenagers having a wild time in the resort town.

In 1965 Hardin went to Spain to appear in *The Battle of the Bulge*. He played the part of a Nazi soldier disguised as an American MP guarding the bridge at the River Ur so that he could mislead the American forces when they came by. Deciding to stay in Europe, he made some 40 films, most of which were never seen in the United States. Several that were released in the United States included *Custer of the West*, with Robert Shaw (1968), *Berserk*, with Joan Crawford (1967), and *The Last Rebel*, with football star Joe Namath

(1971). Hardin, however, passed up what might have been another big break when he turned down an offer to appear in the Italian Western *A Fistful of Dollars* and recommended Clint Eastwood for the part.

Hardin also found time for some stage work in Britain, performing in *A Streetcar Named Desire* with Veronica Lake in 1969 and *Party to Murder* in 1973. In 1969 he went to Australia to make a syndicated television series called *Riptide* in which he played a charter boat captain named Moss Andrews. (This series has not been shown in the United States.)

Finally returning to the states in 1976, Hardin appeared as guest star in an episode of *The Quest* entitled "Prairie Woman." This led to a role in the television film *Fire* the following year. Later Hardin made appearances in the pilot episode of *Trapper John, M.D.* with Pernell Roberts in 1979, a 1981 episode of *The Love Boat* entitled "First Voyage, Last Voyage," and more appropriately was given a cameo role in the television remake of *Red River* in 1988 starring James Arness. He will best be remembered, however, as the lone adventurer who roamed the post–Civil War West, Bronco Layne.

Christopher Colt, another Warner invention differed in one distinctive way from Bronco Layne and Cheyenne Bodie. Although he could be found each week wandering through the West, Colt at least had a steady job. Ostensibly he was a salesman for the Colt Firearms Company. (His uncle, Sam, had been responsible for developing the famous Colt .45.) In reality, however, he was an undercover agent working for the United States government. This rather loose premise permitted writers a great deal of latitude in the scripts they wrote. One week, Colt might be searching for raiders in Mexico ("One Good Turn"); another week, he might pose as an outlaw to learn information for the army ("The $3,000 Bullet"); and on another occasion he would impersonate an infamous gunman who has been hired to assassinate a senator ("Dead Reckoning").

As in the case of Warners' other Western loners, Chris Colt came in contact with many famous figures of the era—Edwin Booth ("The Man Who Loved Lincoln"), Judge Roy Bean ("Law West of the Pecos"), Doc Holliday ("The Devil's Godson"), Buffalo Bill Cody ("A Legend of Buffalo Bill"), Billy the Kid and Pat Garrett ("Amnesty") to name a few. The characters were the same, only the stories were changed to protect the writers.

Colt .45 was the brainchild of Warner Bros. producer Hugh Benson who was responding to a request from a national beer company that wanted to sponsor a new Western. The idea came from a film the studio had made in 1950 starring Randolph Scott. Entitled *Colt .45*, it related the story of a gun salesman (Scott) whose gun samples are stolen by an outlaw. To clear his name, he sets out to capture the outlaw. The film had been popular and the title was short, to the point and easy to remember. Warners contacted ABC with the format for *Colt .45* and they obtained the approval of the beer company. All that was needed was an actor to play Christopher Colt. Rugged, good-looking Wayde Preston was given the role even though he was unknown and had practically no previous acting experience.

He was born William Preston (the studio changed his first name to Wayde) in Laramie, Wyoming, son of a high school teacher. As a young man, he became an expert marksman with a rifle and skilled in riding and breaking horses. For a while he was a park ranger in Grand Teton National Park and occasionally traveled the rodeo circuits as a bareback bronc rider. Later Preston entered the University of Wyoming where he earned a degree in pharmacy. In addition to athletics, he took an interest in music, playing bass fiddle and vibraharp with a jazz quartet, and began developing his acting talent by appearing in school plays. After a hitch in the Army and a job as an electronics technician at a guided missile plant, Preston decided to try acting. After a routine screen test by Solly Baiano, talent executive for Warner Bros., Preston was considered for the role of Chris Colt and given a contract by executive producer William T. Orr. The initial episode of *Colt .45*, "Judgement Day," aired on October 18, 1957, to generally favorable reviews. *Variety* (October 22, 1957) said:

> Warners introduces a new western character in this series, Christopher Colt, an undercover Army officer who poses as a traveling salesman for the new Colt .45. It's a peg that will permit use of a varied western background and the opener gives promise the show will effectively fill its niche. [The] series doesn't compete with the so-called "adult" western, but is a solid entry for general appeal in the sagebrush sweepstakes.
> Wayde Preston is Colt and he handles himself easily.

It is certainly debatable whether *Colt .45* should properly be called an adult Western. The plots were generally routine, filled with a maximum of action. In comparison with Warners' other Westerns, *Colt .45* probably featured more dialogue than *Cheyenne*, *Bronco*, or *Lawman* but less than *Sugarfoot* or *Maverick*. In general, the stories were on a par with *Lawman*, Warners' only other 30 minute Western. There were a few interesting plot twists. In "Mirage," Colt prevents a Mexican village from being taken over by a band of renegade Army officers with the help of a U.S. Cavalry unit that is not really there. (It is a mirage—but the renegades think it is real.) "Rebellion" concerns the efforts of a group of ex-Confederates called "The Brotherhood of the Black Cross" to seize control of New Mexico Territory and proclaim it an independent country. "Last Chance" is actually a murder mystery with a surprise ending. The early use of photography is a key element in "The Magic Box."

Still, the most compelling feature of *Colt .45* was Preston himself. Dashing in his tight, dark riding breeches, light colored shirt, white Stetson, shiny boots and two pearl-handled Colts strapped to his waist, Preston opened the first season's episodes by confidently striding directly toward the camera. With a lightning quick draw, he fired six shots in rapid succession as the letters in the title C-O-L-T-.4-5., simultaneously appeared on the screen.

The accompanying theme song was also one of Warners' best. With music by Hal Hopper and lyrics by Douglas Heyes, it certainly captured the spirit and mood of the series about the "gun that won the West."

Colt .45 seemed destined for success and a long run, but that was not to be. Events which occurred behind the scenes were to cut short the series in its prime. As Robert W. Malsbary explains:

> "Colt .45" was, at the very least, a unique show. It was sold before being created and contained a plethora of action—most of it not on the screen. With all of the strange things that happened on Warners TV shows, probably no other show was as bizarre as this one. In its three seasons on the air, "Colt .45" was a hodgepodge of uncertain sponsorship, a walkout, many repeat episodes, and an abrupt change in the starring role with no explanation.[16]

After the 26 first season episodes had aired, ABC announced that the series had been canceled. The sponsor had abruptly dropped the show. Preston, who had just returned from a cross-country tour to promote the series, was very angry. He believed that the reason that the sponsor refused to renew was because the Colt Company got a fortune in free advertising while the actual sponsor had to pay all the bills. The sponsor denied Preston's accusations and ABC finally did renew the series for a second season. The new *Colt .45* episodes did not begin until April 1959, however, and only 13 were made; the rest were reruns. Somehow the series survived and was given a third season by ABC.

Wayde Preston played Chris Colt, gun salesman and sometime undercover operative for the government, in *Colt .45.*

Further problems arose, however, during what turned out to be *Colt .45*'s final season. Preston, after refusing to perform what he considered to be a particularly dangerous stunt, quit. He indicated that he might not be cut out for the television business. A replacement had to be found quickly. Producers selected Donald May, a Warner contract player who had appeared on an earlier *Colt .45* episode as Chris's cousin, Sam Colt, Jr., son of the inventor. While filming switched over to the Sam Colt episodes, ABC ran some of the unaired Chris Colt stories.

One of the most confusing aspects of the transition is that no explanation was made in the story line as to why Cousin Sam had taken over the same undercover job that had been held by his cousin — or, indeed, what had happened to Chris. Instead, the first eight episodes of the third season (October 4–November 22, 1959) featured Chris. Sam was introduced in "Alias Mr. Howard" on December 6, 1959; his character is looking for a mail robber who is hiding on a farm owned by Jesse and Zee James. The Jameses have changed their names and are trying to be law-abiding citizens until the mail robber, who rode with Jesse earlier, shows up to complicate matters.

Chris returned the following week. Then Sam returned. The two appeared together in only one episode, "Phantom Trail," broadcast March 13, 1960, in which they team up to discover why herds of cattle being shipped to an Indian reservation have disappeared with their crews. Then Chris was featured in six more episodes (March 27–May 3, 1960), with Sam finishing the season (May 10–June 21, 1960). The stories do not vary in quality, with either character being appropriate to carry the plotline, but the sequence of episodes made little sense to the viewers.[17]

Preston was clearly the stronger lead and most closely identified with the series, appearing in 55 of the 67 episodes. In the later episodes his macho qualities were emphasized, Preston having discarded his dandified clothes for more rugged attire and having added a small moustache to his appearance.

Preston made several guest appearances on other Warner Bros. Westerns during *Colt .45*'s second and third seasons on the air. Seeming to be at his best when playing opposite a somewhat comical character, Preston appeared in three of the four "Canary Kid" episodes of *Sugarfoot* ("Return of the Canary Kid," "The Trial of the Canary Kid," and "Canary Kid, Inc.") as Chris Colt. And in one of the best episodes of the *Maverick* series, he played Waco Williams, a fearless gunman who befriends Bret Maverick, in "The Saga of Waco Williams" opposite James Garner. Ultimately Preston gave up acting, moved to Australia and became a pilot. It is a shame that he never fulfilled the obvious potential he demonstrated in *Colt .45*.

Donald May, who was selected to play Sam Colt, had considerable previous acting experience before coming to *Colt .45*. Born February 22, 1929, he lived in Houston and later Cleveland while he was growing up. In 1949 he graduated from the University of Oklahoma. Then May attended Yale, where he studied drama, and spent a season in summer stock in New York City. He eventually landed a role in *Yellow Jack* in Albany, New York. During the Korean War he served as a gunnery officer on board a destroyer. After his stint in the Navy, May returned to New York where he eventually appeared in over 250 Broadway and Off Broadway plays. Then in mid-1959, he left for Hollywood. His first continuing television role was that of cadet Charles C. Thompson in CBS's *The West Point Story*, appearing in the first 20 episodes. Before being cast in *Colt .45*, he played a heavy on an episode of *Sugarfoot* ("Journey to Provision").

After the cancellation of *Colt .45* in 1960, Warner Bros. starred May as reporter Pat Garrison in *The Roaring 20's* with Dorothy Provine and Rex Reason. Similar in many ways to the much more popular series *The Untouchables*, *The Roaring 20's* was canceled after two seasons. In 1967 May shifted his acting career to daytime television. For ten years he played attorney Adam Drake on *The Edge of Night*. He has also had continuing roles on *As the World Turns* and *Falcon Crest*. His meager contribution to the development of the television Western have long since been forgotten.

A more familiar face to fans of television Westerns is that of Dale Robertson. His role as Jim Hardie, trouble shooter for the Wells Fargo Company in *Tales of Wells Fargo*, was of far greater significance in the early evolution of the television Western. Like Christopher and Sam Colt, Jr., Jim Hardie had steady employment. He worked as a trouble shooter and detective for Wells Fargo. In this capacity he covered a lot of territory and met many unusual people, some good, some bad. Much of his work was routine, but some of it was anything but routine. It was this aspect of Hardie's job upon which *Tales of Wells Fargo* focused.

In 1955 a film producer named Nat Holt began to kick around the idea for a series

Donald May replaced Preston as his cousin, Sam Colt, Jr., during the final season of *Colt .45*.

based on such an agent. He believed that Wells, Fargo & Co. would be an excellent subject for a television Western series. The company had been established as a joint stock association in New York during March 1852 by a group of experienced Eastern expressmen, among them Henry Wells and William G. Fargo, to take advantage of the express, freight and banking opportunities in California. Within two months the company was shipping mail, newspapers, packages and freight of all descriptions from the Eastern seaboard to San Francisco and from there to and from the mining camps in California. By 1860, the company had attained a monopoly of the express business.

Stagecoaches were utilized by the company in conveying gold dust, business papers

Dale Robertson was Wells Fargo special agent Jim Hardie for five seasons on *Tales of Wells Fargo*.

and other freight. Sometimes riders on horseback were sent by Wells Fargo to deliver or pick up an important message, treasure or package. Soon the company was operating branch stage lines between the terminals of the Central Pacific Railroad in California and western Nevada and those of the Union Pacific railroad in eastern Nevada and Utah territory. After all sections of the two railroads were completed in 1869, Wells Fargo set up branch lines to carry mail, express and passengers to and from the railroad into the mining towns of Idaho, Montana, and Colorado as well as Utah and Nevada. Wells Fargo also engaged in banking services. All of these activities of course, made it a tempting target for outlaws and bandits.[18] In the pilot episode of the series, which was broadcast December 14, 1956, on the *Schlitz Playhouse of Stars*, entitled "A Tale of Wells Fargo," Hardie's supervisor explained:

SUPERVISOR:	First, it was our offices, then the stagecoaches, now it's the trains. It's got to stop. We've got to teach these outlaws that it isn't healthy to rob Wells Fargo.
HARDIE:	We've also got to teach them that it's unhealthy to kill a Wells Fargo man.
SUPERVISOR:	Wells Fargo is more than just an express company. It's an institution we built solidly. The name of our company has come to mean something: safety, security. We've got to safeguard that reputation and the law too.
HARDIE:	Trouble of it is, there isn't any law in half the places we operate, except the law of the gun. Mind you I've got a good healthy respect for the law. I'll fight for it and defend it whenever it's possible. When it isn't, we've got to use our rules and our laws.
SUPERVISOR:	The company's behind you, Jim. Whatever it costs, you've got to bring in these outlaws or make sure they never rob another Wells Fargo strongbox, anywhere.

Thus was the stage set for Jim Hardie's first Western adventure. In the episode, adapted from a story by Zane Grey, Hardie breaks up a gang of train robbers and recovers a stolen Wells Fargo shipment of gold.

In the first regular series episode, "The Thin Rope," which aired on NBC, March 18, 1957, Hardie's narration opens the story:

> The firm of Wells Fargo played an important part in the settling and development of our American West. As the frontier moved toward the Pacific Ocean, Wells Fargo moved with it. Hundred of towns sprang up in that great wilderness with roads over which their stages and freight wagons traveled. Wells Fargo's business was transportation and security It's motto was to safeguard and deliver the goods, whether it was human or freight cargo or a consignment of that precious yellow metal that men call gold. The West was a lawless place in those days and a man who worked for Wells Fargo had to be long on courage to hold down his job. My name is Jim Hardie, special agent and sort of a traveling detective for Wells Fargo.

It was a solid premise for a Western adventure series. All that was needed to make *Tales of Wells Fargo* a success was an actor who could bring alive the larger than life character of Jim Hardie. Such an actor was Dale Robertson. Robertson, the youngest of three sons, was born on July 14, 1923, in Harah, Oklahoma, and attended public schools there. Following high school, he attended Oklahoma Military College where he won 28 letters in eight sports and studied law. He spent his summer vacations working as a cowboy and training polo ponies. A wrangler from Texas once called Robertson a "cowboy's cowboy" which was high praise because rarely does a Texan take his hat off to an Oklahoma cowboy. Later Robertson tried professional boxing in Oklahoma and Kansas, winning 38 of 40 professional bouts.

In 1942, Robertson enlisted in the U.S. Army. He became a first lieutenant of engineers with General George Patton's Third Army, building the roadways for the assault tanks' advance into Germany. Wounded in the right knee by German mortar fire, he was honorably discharged in 1945. Unable to return to boxing, Robertson began to consider another career. While on furlough to Hollywood from Camp San Luis Obispo, California, before he was shipped overseas, he had had his picture taken. The photographer had put a copy in his store window and several agents who saw it inquired where they could reach the soldier. So after the war, Robertson returned to Hollywood and contacted several agents. Now, however, they were not interested; Hollywood was full of handsome young actors.

Because he had no previous acting experience, Robertson decided to learn every aspect of the business. Borrowing $20,000 from relatives in Oklahoma, he enrolled in the drama program at the University of Southern California. He spent the next three years studying film editing, stage design, and writing. During this period, Robertson bribed studio employees for advance peeks at shooting scripts then being duplicated. He hired an agent to ask producers to give him speaking bits in scripts that had not yet been given to the casting departments.

In 1949, Robertson's persistence paid off. He uncovered a two-scene gem in Frank Guber's screenplay for a Nat Holt picture entitled *Fighting Man of the Plains*. The role he wanted was that of Jesse James and when he asked his agent Ned Marin about the film, Robertson discovered that the director was his agent's brother, Ed. He got a screen test and the role. When the picture was previewed, Robertson was named "best actor" by 183 of the 190 who turned in cards—even though veteran actor Randolph Scott was the star of the film. As result of his success in *Man of the Plains*, Robertson was signed to a seven-year contract by 20th Century–Fox where he soon became a box-office star. In all, he starred in 42 films for Fox, and challenged John Wayne for the number one spot as top-drawing actor in the early fifties. Among his films were musicals such as *Call Me Mister* (1951), with Betty Grable and Dan Dailey; *Golden Girl* (1951), with Mitzi Gaynor and Dennis Day; *The Farmer Takes a Wife* (1953), in which Robertson costarred with Grable; and his preferred genre, Westerns, with supporting roles in *The Caribou Trail* (1950), *Two Flags West* (1950), and starring roles in *The Outcasts of Poker Flat* (1952), *Return of the Texan* (1952), *The Silver Whip* (1953), *City of Bad Men* (1953), *The Gambler from Natchez* (1954), *Sitting Bull* (1954), *Dakota Incident* (1956), and *A Day of Fury* (1956).

In June of 1956, Robertson was approached by producer Nat Holt (with whom he had worked on *Man of the Plains* and *The Caribou Trail*) and popular Western writer Frank Gruber (who had written the scripts for those same films) with a *Wells Fargo* script. However, Robertson, busy with his film carer, turned it down. He later explained:

> I thought there were going to be too many Westerns on TV. I knew of about a hundred unsold test films for Western series and I had my sights on something else. I was up for "Perry Mason," but they didn't want to make Mason the kind of a character I talk like. Another fella had an aviation series I was hot on.[19]

These projects fell through, but Robertson did make appearances on several television series including *Climax!* and *The Schlitz Playhouse of Stars*. Several months later Holt and Gruber returned with their proposal for a Western based on the exploits of a Wells Fargo agent. In addition to his film experience, Gruber was an established author of pulp Westerns. In 1942 his novel *Peace Marshal* was filmed under the title *The Kansan*, starring Richard Dix. He had also written the script for *Silver City* (1951), and was working on film adaptations of two of his other novels, *Tension at Table Rock* (released in 1956 by RKO) and *Town Tamer* (1957). (Gruber was to create three highly successful series for television, *Tales of Wells Fargo*, *The Texan* and *Shotgun Slade*. In addition to serving as story editor on these shows and writing many of their scripts himself, he was instrumental in bringing in many of his fellow members of the Western Writers of America as script-writers.)[20] Out of respect for such impressive credentials and on the hunch that opportunity might just be knocking twice, Robertson decided to make the pilot for the *Schlitz Playhouse*. When the series was launched three months later, Robertson was given half ownership. Enthusiastically promoting the series, Robertson proclaimed:

> It is not a run-of-the-mill Western in any sense of the word. People don't realize that Wells Fargo was the biggest banking and express agency in the West. They had offices all over the world and still have. If the Western craze begins to wear a little thin, all we have to do is send Jim Hardie packing off to Rome and we have practically a brand new show going for us. But where can Wyatt Earp go?

Furthermore, Jim Hardie has a family—parents and a sister and a brother and a couple of other relatives. We're trying to make a human being out of him. When he gets hurt, he hollers just like anybody would. He doesn't stand there taking 40 solid punches on the jaw, any one of which would have crumpled Joe Louis.[21]

In a later interview, Robertson related the story of his appearance on *The Steve Allen Show*. Showing Allen the pistol his sponsor had given him, he was asked, "Is that a Colt .45?" "No," drawled Robertson, "it's a Nielsen .38."[22] He was making an indirect reference to the fact that *Wells Fargo* had beaten the mighty *Arthur Godfrey's Talent Scouts* by two Nielsen points on its first broadcast. Critical reviews of the series, however, were mixed. *Variety* (March 20, 1957) wrote:

> . . . This Revue [MCA] series is strictly formula, with none of the characterization or human values that have embellished the better class of TV westerns to date.

On the other hand, the *TV Guide* reviewer liked the series, for some of the same reasons that *Variety* did not:

> . . . The show represents a backward step so far as TV Westerns go because it's not one of these new-fangled adult types. It's an old fashioned cowboy show with not a single psychological overtone. Maybe that's what makes it a darned good series.
>   The bad guys (and there are plenty of them) are killers not because they suffered some traumatic experience as children but simply because the plot calls for them to be mean and ornery. And the good guys win out all the time because they draw faster and shoot straighter and because the good guys in Western shows by tradition are all-conquering heroes . . . [and] the action is fast and furious.

Robertson believed that the key to *Tales of Wells Fargo*'s success lay in the fact that it was not an adult Western—or a kids' Western either, for that matter. He promoted the series as a "family" show and criticized practically all of the so-called adult Westerns then on the air. In an interview published in the *L.A. Journal* on September 11, 1959, he told columnist Atra Baer:

> Adult Westerns are dishonest in approach. They are a cheap, underhanded way of making up for lack of a good story. Most people think you have to be downbeat and depressing to be "adult". . . . What counts is a good story. Lots of people making Westerns for TV aren't qualified to make them. Some actors think if you put on a Western suit and adopt a Western accent that makes you believable. It just isn't so. . . . [Most of the fault] lies in the unrealistic attitudes found in the scripts. TV should take those textbooks by Freud and those guys and throw 'em out before Westerns are completely killed.

As far as other television Westerns were concerned, Robertson went on record as endorsing *Gunsmoke* and *Maverick*. He said he liked *Cheyenne* when it starred Clint Walker and felt Richard Boone was a "pretty fair actor," but the character he portrayed, Paladin, was "ridiculous" with "an air of unbelievability about the show" as if it was "straining to be different."[23]

Probably the most important reason for *Tales of Wells Fargo*'s popularity was Dale Robertson himself. He was in many ways a cross between Gary Cooper and Clark Gable. Built like Cooper, Robertson spoke with a rich, deep twang that led some critics to accuse him of trying to mimic Gable. Actually, he was raised only about a hundred miles away from where Gable grew up and his accent was as natural as that of Gable. Producers took advantage of Robertson's resonate voice by including considerable voice-over narration for Jim Hardie in both the opening and closing segments of *Tales of Wells Fargo*. Another appealing aspect of Robertson's television persona was his decision to make Jim Hardie a left-handed gunman. Although he was naturally righthanded, he observed early in his Western films career that whenever a man was writing, shaking hands or lighting a cigarette he was vulnerable "because his gun hand was all tied up." So Robertson practiced drawing and shooting with his left hand until he became as proficient as he was with his right.[24]

Robertson's horsemanship was genuine too. Network executives compared him when riding into action with cowboy superstar Ken Maynard. Wranglers admitted that while Robertson was not quite up to Tom Mix (called the finest horseman ever to appear before a camera) or Joel McCrea (considered the best of Robertson's contemporaries), he was a horseman of considerable ability.[25] Raised around horses, Robertson well knew that riding was one of the tools of his trade. In fact, he would prefer to be remembered not as the star of a television show, but as a breeder of thoroughbreds on a scale that would rival the fabulous King Ranch. His Haymaker Farm, an Oklahoma horse ranch managed by his brother and partner Chet, consisted of nearly 400 acres and over fifty head of some of the finest blue ribbon breeding stock in the state. Perhaps, what viewers appreciated most was Robertson's naturalness. He was happy and comfortable playing Jim Hardie and it showed. He once explained:

> A fellow should stick to what he knows best. Playing a cowboy is what I know best. I've been around horses all my life. Raised and trained them once. So I'm doing what I like, and people like the sort of thing I do....
>
> Westerns deal with the most popular era in American history. They're fun, exciting—they make people forget the cares of everyday living.... In Westerns, the problems are simple—black and white.[26]

As played by Robertson, Jim Hardie was a likable Western hero with an interesting past. The opening episode of the fourth season, "Young Jim Hardie," relates the story of how Wells Fargo "found" Jim Hardie. Hired by a gang of outlaws to blow up a bridge and assist in the hanging of a judge, young Hardie finds that his morals are too strong for this kind of lawless violence. He turns the tables on the would-be hangmen and is hired on the spot by Wells Fargo. Thus do viewers discover that Jim Hardie is actually a reformed bandit. Several of Hardie's idiosyncrasies are revealed in "The Thin Rope." Hardie's pistol has a hair trigger and he keeps only five chambers loaded, so that the hammer rests on an empty chamber. Furthermore, the barrel is inscribed: "Be not afraid of any man that walks beneath the skies. Though you be weak and he be strong, I will equalize." Hardie's horse was named Jubilee.

During his many action-packed adventures, Hardie became involved with apparent good men who turn out to be bad (like "Button" in the pilot episode, played with toughness and charm by Chuck Connors in a pre–*Rifleman* role, and Major Carl Orleans, played with convincing duplicity by Bruce Gordon in "Return to Red Bluff") and apparent bad men who turn out to be good (like saloon owner Bill Bolliver in "The Inscrutable Man," written by *Stagecoach* author Ernest Haycox, Doc in "Doc Holliday"; and Nathan Chance, played with charisma by veteran Rod Cameron in "Assignment in Gloribee.")

There was even occasional humor in the stories. In "Lady Trouble," Agatha Webster (delightfully played by character actress Faith Domergue) provides chuckles as a wealthy, Eastern society matron who owns a large mining company that is considering a major contract with Wells Fargo to transport its ore and payrolls. Taken in by a slick con artist out to steal her gold shipment, the crusty old woman is won over by Hardie after he exposes the conman and saves her gold.

After four successful seasons as a 30 minute series (ranking third in the Nielsens in 1957-58 and seventh the following year), both the length and regular cast were expanded in 1961. Although still a Wells Fargo agent, Hardie was now also the owner of a ranch located in Gloribee, just outside of San Francisco. He was also given a young assistant named Beau McCloud (Jack Ging) and a ranch foreman named Jeb Gaine (William Demarest). For possible romance, Hardie had only to look to the ranch next door, owned by Widow Ovie (Virginia Christine) who had two attractive daughters, Mary Gee (Mary Jane Saunders) and Tina (Lory Patrick). Ovie was after Jeb, but the daughters were attracted to Jim.

Most of the stories, now an hour in length, during this final season took place on the Hardie ranch or in San Francisco, although he was occasionally sent on special assignment somewhere else in the West. Even with "name" guest stars, the new format did not catch on and *Tales of Wells Fargo* was canceled at the end of the 1961-62 season, after 167 episodes had been filmed (32 during the final season). Still, the series had firmly established Dale Robertson as one of television's top Western stars and with the program in syndication, his financial future seemed secure as well. Furthermore, Robertson became so interested in the subject matter of the stories that long after the series disappeared, he authored a book, *Wells Fargo, The Legend* (1975), that included true stories of "the Concord stage, Black Bart, the intrepid stage drivers and shotgun messengers, the California gold rush, and Nevada silver strike."

Within four years, Robertson was starring in another television Western, *Iron Horse*. The series began as one of the first made-for-television films. Entitled *Scalplock*, it first aired over ABC on April 10, 1966. In addition to Robertson, several of the film's stars continued on the series including Bob Random and Roger Torrey. Gary Collins replaced Todd Armstrong in the other major continuing role. Robertson played Ben Calhoun, a gambler and Western businessman who won a railroad in a card game (with four queens beating an aces-over-tens full house). The only problem was that the line he won (the Buffalo Pass, Scalplock, and Defiance) was only half built and on the brink of bankruptcy. Realizing that the future of the country was in the West, Calhoun decided to complete the line and rounded up a loyal crew to help him: Dave Tarrant (Gary Collins), a young construction engineer; Barnabas Rogers (Bob Random), a young orphan who idolized Calhoun served as his clerk and had a pet raccoon named Ulysses; a huge Swedish giant (over 300 pounds) of a man, Nils Torvold (Roger Torrey), as leader of the construction crew; and (the second season) lovely young Julie Parsons (Ellen McRae, now Ellen Burstyn) as freight station operator and proprietor of the General Store.

Thus did Dale Robertson go from playing a wandering loner to a wealthy rancher to a railroad magnate on the home screen in just under ten years—a success story that would make Horatio Alger wince. As Calhoun, Robertson was flamboyant and colorful, dressing well and smoking the best cigars. There was plenty of action (three brutal fist fights in the pilot episode alone) with crooked businessmen, rampaging Indians and all kinds of assorted outlaws along the way. Calhoun was dedicated to completing his railroad and would not stand for any interference from man or nature (if he could help it). Filmed in color on location in Sonora, California, using a vintage train, *Iron Horse*, which premiered on September 12, 1966, drew some favorable response from critics. Cleveland Amory wrote in *TV Guide* (January 24, 1967):

> There are two kinds of Westerns—good 'uns and bad 'uns, and this 'un is basically, well, not too bad.... When you've got a train for a hero, you don't horse around, and to say this horse opera in on the heavy side is to put it—well, lightly ... if ... you enjoy Westerns where men are men and the women aren't bad either, then this may be your brand.

Nevertheless, *Iron Horse* was canceled by NBC in January 1968 after 47 episodes leaving Robertson free to pursue his many other interests. From 1965 to 1970, he served as host and occasionally guest-starred in episodes of *Death Valley Days*. He spent seven years studying motion picture editing with Elmo Williams, and an equal period of time studying motion picture scoring with Lionel and Alfred Newman. Then he worked with Leon Shamroy and Paul Vogel for two years each, learning the art of color and black and white cinematography. He later served as president of United Screen Arts, which financed and distributed motion pictures throughout the world.[27] In 1965 all of these skills were brought into play when Robertson wrote, produced and recorded the lead voice for *The Man from Button Willow*. This completely animated cartoon Western related the story of America's first undercover agent in 1869 who prevents outlaws from forcing settlers to sell their land.

Robertson was also instrumental in developing *The American Sportsman* for television and often filmed and narrated his hunting expeditions all over North America and throughout the world. He also had an interest in *Wild Kingdom*. A country and Western music enthusiast, Robertson recorded an album for Artco Records in 1973. In addition, he remained in demand for personal appearances in the United States, Britain, and Australia at fairs and rodeos.

After a few guest appearances on television shows as *The Love Boat*, Robertson attempted one more television series, *J.J. Starbuck*, in 1987. Once again Robertson played a flamboyant character who solved crimes using a downhome approach, plenty of charm and, when all else failed, his vast personal wealth and connections. J.J. Starbuck drove around the country in a 1961 Lincoln convertible with steer horns on the hood and a horn that blared "The Eyes of Texas." Since he was a Texas millionaire, he never had to charge for his services and usually aided those who had been framed or abandoned by the system. A tour de force for Robertson, the show was full of homey aphorisms. Unfortunately the series never achieved respectable ratings, even after producer Stephen J. Cannell tried to add interest by introducing a character from one of his previous shows, Ben Vereen as E.L. Turner of *Tenspeed and Brownshoe*. A total of only 14 episodes were broadcast by NBC. Robertson, having left his mark indelibly on the television Western as Wells Fargo agent Jim Hardie might yet make a television comeback as some new eccentric knight errant.

Described by one television historian as "the genre's definitive malcontent,"[28] Vint Bonner of *The Restless Gun* was a sympathetic, working cowpoke who never stayed in one place very long, spending six months in one town, eight in another. Usually a quiet, easy-going individual, he preferred not to fight if there was some other acceptable way out of a confrontation. Unfortunately his idealism often forced him into potentially violent situations. Alone he wandered the post–Civil War West getting involved in other people's problems each week.

Unlike many of his television contemporaries, Bonner made no attempt to pass himself off as a young Western hero. To avoid gunplay with another mature gunfighter, Bonner might exclaim, "We're both too old for this kind of foolishness on such a nice summer day."[29] Although he was known as a "fast gun," Bonner was no gunfighter, and he tried to play down this skill as much as possible. John Payne, creator and star of *The Restless Gun*, once described his character this way:

> ... I can be a fast draw when the script calls for it, but we don't concentrate on it. People sort of naturally gravitate toward Bonner when they've got problems, and Bonner tries to solve them as best he can. If there is such a thing as a next-door neighbor in a Western, that's Vint Bonner.[30]

John Payne (right) played Vint Bonner on *The Restless Gun*.

Payne went on to explain that he had deliberately stayed away from making Bonner a sheriff or a marshal because he did not want to tie him down to any one locale "in the vast reaches of television's West." Furthermore, he didn't want to give him any more authority than the average man could command through "the force of his own personality and reputation."

Starring in his first television series, the 46 year old Payne brought 26 years of show business experience to the video range. Born in 1912 in Roanoke, Virginia, he wanted to be an aeronautical engineer as a boy. Then one day he tried to fly a home-built glider and crash-landed on his nose. That ended those plans. He was a star swimmer when he attended Mercersberg (Pennsylvania) Academy, a band singer while at Roanoke College, and a pulp magazine writer while working his way through the Juilliard School of Music and Columbia University. He also earned $25 a match as a professional wrestler. After some experience singing on the radio, Payne landed a job as a $35 a week actor with the Shubert's summer stock company. In 1935, he appeared as a soloist and quartette member in *At Home Abroad*, a Broadway musical which starred Eleanor Powell, Beatrice Lillie and Ethel Waters.

One year later, Payne went to Hollywood where he appeared in his first film, *Dodsworth* for United Artists. Many of his early movies were musicals: *College Swing* (1938), with Martha Ray, Bob Hope and Betty Grable; *The Great American Broadcast* (1941), with Alice Faye; *Sun Valley Serenade* (1941), with Glenn Miller and Sonja Henie; *Springtime in the Rockies* (1942), with Grable again; and *Hello Frisco, Hello* (1943) with Faye again. Among Payne's more notable films was the Christmas classic, *The Miracle on 34th Street* (1947).

Only about a half dozen of Payne's nearly 80 films were Westerns, the first being *El Paso* in 1949. Others included *The Eagle and the Hawk* (1950), *Passage West* (1951), and *The Vanquished* (1953). In addition to acting in *The Restless Gun*, Payne served as executive producer and occasionally wrote scripts for the series. He also owned 50 percent of the show through Window Glen Productions which he established to produce the series. Young David Dortort (who would eventually hit the big time with *Bonanza* and *High Chaparral*) was coproducer on the series. *The Restless Gun* premiered on NBC, September 23, 1957, to reasonably good reviews and ratings. *Variety* (September 29, 1957) said:

> This [Western] has John Payne, a vet performer, who does right well with his role, a fast man with a gun on the side of the angels who in his own words—"ain't a killin' man."

That opening episode, "Duel at Lockwood," had a psychological twist that provided insight into the character of a mean, young would-be gunfighter (played to nasty perfection by young Vic Morrow). He was so ornery that he shot the clothespins out of the hands of his grayhaired grandmother while she was hanging out the family wash. Of course, he wanted to outshoot the fastest gun in town, Vint Bonner (who was working on a nearby ranch). At the end of the story, Bonner is reluctantly forced to gun the kid down in a typical Western face-off.

The stories on *The Restless Gun* varied greatly in both content and mood. Most of them involved some variation on the sharpshooter rivalry theme. Occasionally, one would attempt to dramatize some social issue like women's suffrage ("The Suffragette" with Ellen Corby) or child abuse ("Multiply One Boy") or even vegetarianism (the humorous "The Sweet Sisters" with Jeanette Nolan). In the latter, two kindly, old ladies (named Sweet) were rustling cattle and hiding them in a canyon at night to prevent them from being slaughtered for meat. Bonner, realizing they were harmless, if a bit eccentric, convinced the sheriff to let him cover for them. When the ladies realized that homesteaders would be blamed for their activities, they agreed to leave the area ("there's lots of cows in California"). The sheriff then convinced the ranchers that he had killed the rustler (Bonner in disguise). This all may sound pretty silly, but Payne and his supporting cast were able to effectively present an entertaining and unusual Western drama.

In order to introduce fresh story ideas into the series, David Dortort persuaded several members of the theretofore standoff Western Writers of America to write for *The Restless Gun*. He convinced three, Thomas Thompson, Hal Evarts and Frank Bonham, to do screenplays of their own stories. All three had written for books and pulp magazines, but only Thomas had any previous Hollywood script experience (having written one episode of *Wagon Train*).

In its first season on the air, *The Restless Gun* ranked eighth in the Nielsens. So pleased was NBC, that network executives tried to get Payne to expand the show to an hour for the following season. He, however, was unwilling to alter the successful pattern of the show, stressing quality over length. Nevertheless, the show plummeted in the ratings during its second season, as Westerns saturated the airwaves, and the series was canceled after a total of 77 episodes had been made. Ironically ABC bought the rights to the series and ran reruns weekdays from October 1959 to September 1960 (and Saturday mornings from November 1959 to March 1960). Like many of Payne's films, *The Restless Gun* was good entertainment at the time and made a lot of money, but is little remembered today. Payne limited his later career to guest appearances on such shows as *The Name of the Game, Cade's County* and *Columbo.*

Big Bill Longley was a Civil War vet—a captain (on which side is never mentioned) who wanders through Texas like (as one reviewer described it) Ulysses. The title of the show in which he is featured was called simply *The Texan.* That was the title of a Paramount film made back in 1930 which starred Gary Cooper and was based on O. Henry's short story "Double-Dyed Deceiver." But if the title did come from the film, that was the only thing writer Frank Gruber borrowed. He described Longley as "the Robin Hood of Texas."

There actually was a famous Texas gunman named William Longley who killed several men before he was 20. He was in no way heroic, however. Tall and quick-tempered, he generally murdered in response to some supposed insult. The authorities forced him to leave Texas for a while, and although there are conflicting reports of his wanderings, it is evident that a pattern of violence occurred wherever he went. He was hanged for murder on October 28, 1878, in Galveston, Texas, at the age of 27[31] (certainly too young to have been a captain in the Civil War).

The official version of *The Texan*'s origin makes no mention of either Longley or the film. Film producer Victor Orsati and actor Rory Calhoun had met while Calhoun was working on the film *Flight to Hong Kong* in 1956. The two men decided to go into business together as Rorvic Productions to produce a television series. Their initial proposal involved a sea story, but when they approached producer and actor Desi Arnaz, he told them that people wanted more Westerns. Calhoun, who felt right at home in the Old West agreed:

> No matter what they say, Westerns will always be made and enjoyed. They're part of our American heritage.[32]

Orsatti later claimed that *The Texan* was not really a Western at all but a "drama with a Western background." The premise upon which the series was based, however, certainly fit the Western mold. Longley was a roving gunman who did not really like to shoot people, although he could when he had to, of course. According to the soundtrack he tried to use his gun "as little as possible. When I do, it's for things and people I believe in—fair things; good people." Each week *The Texan* finds something "to believe in." In the first town he hits, he saves an old Civil War buddy's life and prevents a lynching ("Law of the Gun"). Then he moves on and settles a homesteaders versus ranchers dispute ("The Troubled Town"), prevents a young man from becoming a gunslinger ("The First Notch") and shoots his way out of a murder rap ("Jail for the Innocents"). *Variety*'s assessment (September 9, 1959) of the series praised the acting while dismissing the scripts:

> ... if the premium here isn't on logical scripts, it is more than compensated for by a little sex, a few rough-tough fights, a showdown or two, a weak sheriff, and a bunch of unscrupulous heavies.
>
> Calhoun leaves little to be desired as the hero of this network domain. He delivers a sound, convincing performance, and does all that is required of the TV western hero.

Rory Calhoun (Francis Timothy Durgin) had been born and raised in Los Angeles. From a poor background, he was often in trouble with the law. He served time in prison

Rory Calhoun brought to life Big Bill Longley, *The Texan*.

until a caring chaplain set him straight. During World War II, he worked in Santa Cruz as a lumberjack. Calhoun also found employment as a cowhand, gas station attendant, a miner and a dump truck driver. One day while riding in the Hollywood Hills, he met movie star Alan Ladd, who introduced Calhoun to his agent wife, Sue Carol. She signed him to a film contract. After several bit parts, Calhoun finally scored big in *The Red House* (1947) with Edward G. Robinson and within a few years he was one of the most popular actors in town. Calhoun had good looks, a pleasantly wry personality and an easy manner—and he photographed especially well astride a horse. Thus, his career concentrated heavily on Western roles. Although he made dozens of Westerns, only Otto Preminger's *River of No Return* (1954), in which he costarred with Marilyn Monroe and Robert Mitchum, is well remembered today.

During the fifties Calhoun made many appearances on television, often in roles similar to those he played on the big screen. He was seen on such shows as *Ford Theatre* and *Screen Director's Playhouse*. When asked why he gave up his still-flourishing movie career for the weekly grind of series television, Calhoun replied, "Where else can twenty-eight million people see me in one night?"[33]

Although ending its first season (1958–59) at number 15 in the Nielsen ratings, *The Texan* was canceled the following year after 78 episodes had been made. Calhoun continued his television career, however, with frequent guest appearances on Westerns like *Wagon Train*, *Death Valley Days* and *Gunsmoke*, and later on crime dramas and television movies. In 1982 he joined the cast of the new daytime serial *Capitol* as Judson Taylor, patriarch of the McCandless family. He also appeared that year in the miniseries *The Blue and the Gray* as General George Meade. In retrospect the best thing that can be said of *The Texan* is that it starred Rory Calhoun.

Shotgun Slade was an unusual mixture of *Peter Gunn*, *Tales of Wells Fargo* and *Wanted: Dead or Alive* combining the detective and Western genres. Slade got his name from the unique weapon he carried, a two-piece shotgun that could be used as a conventional shotgun or without the barrel extension in much the way Josh Randall used his "Mare's Leg" on *Wanted: Dead or Alive*. Slade was a detective who roamed the Old West in search of clients. One week he might work for Wells Fargo, another week, an insurance company, and still another, a bank. Any individual who wanted a crime solved could become his client, for the right price.

Shotgun Slade resembled *Peter Gunn* not only in the occupation of its star but also in its frequent use of jazzy background music (by Gerald Fried). Slade, however, was one up on Gunn—he had his own theme song sung under the credits (and in one story) by vocalist Monica Lewis. The music was pulsating and the lyrics stressed the romantic appeal of Slade. The opening of a typical episode ("Mayor Trouble") included Slade's voice-over narration to set the scene:

> My name's Slade. I'm a detective for hire. The client's letter had said come to Palamar. Straighten things out and I'll consider that you've earned this. Two thousand dollars was enclosed, but no signature. Somebody in Palamar was plenty worried about something, even if they wouldn't say what it was.

Slade also always summed up each story at the conclusion:

> Well, at least some good came out of all that bad. The town of Palamar was out from under its one man rule and another man had earned the right to the badge he wore and to the woman who believed in him. Knowing these things makes my kind of job a little bit easier and a little less lonely.

The pilot for *Shotgun Slade*, which was created by the *Tales of Wells Fargo* team of writer Frank Gruber and producer Nat Holt, aired on March 27, 1959, as an episode of *The Schlitz Playhouse* entitled "The Salted Mine." This same episode was broadcast as the first show when the syndicated series was released in November 1959. In an unusual casting move, the famous television comedian Ernie Kovacs guest-starred effectively as a bewhiskered villain. There was plenty of action. In the pilot episode alone, there was an ambush, a mine explosion, a knock-down, drag-out fight in a saloon, a hanging and numerous gun shots filling the air. It did not make a lot of sense, but certainly kept Western adventure addicts fully entertained.

Motion picture star Scot Brady was cast as Slade. Brady had been born in Brooklyn in 1924. In his youth he had worked as a lumberjack and was a lightweight boxing champion during his service in the Navy. After leaving the service in the late forties, he became an actor, often playing tough guys, frequently in Westerns. Brady's credits included *The Gal Who Took the West* (1949), *Bronco Buster* (1952), *A Perilous Journey* (1953), *The Law vs. Billy the Kid* (1954), *The Vanishing American* (1955), *The Restless Breed* (1957), *The Storm Rider* (1957), and *Ambush at Cimarron Pass* (1958). The best known Westerns in which Brady appeared were *Johnny Guitar* (1954), with Joan Crawford, and *The Maverick Queen* (1956), with Barbara Stanwyck. Brady was also frequently seen on television during the fifties, being practically a regular on *Ford Theatre* and *The Schlitz Playhouse of Stars*. *Variety* (November 11, 1959) lauded the action in the premier episode of *Shotgun Slade*:

> ... what redeemed the episode for the beer drinking crowd was the action. What a pile up of action! ...
>
> Scot Brady registered okay as the gun-for-hire lead, ... one of those kissing cowboys who prefers women over horses.

Perhaps the oddest aspect of the series was its frequent use of offbeat casting in supporting roles. In addition to Kovacs' appearance as a desert rat, other unlikely actors included football star Elroy "Crazylegs" Hirsch as a saloonkeeper, World War II ace Gregory "Pappy" Boyington as a wealthy rancher, recording stars Johnny Cash, Tex Ritter and Jimmy Wakely as sheriffs and golfer Paul Hahn, baseball players Chuck Essegian and Wally Moon, and heavyweight boxer Lou Nova in other roles.[34] Unfortunately the show never cracked the Neilsen top 25 rankings and *Shotgun Slade* role off into the sunset for the last time in 1961 after 78 episodes. Its unique music and casting certainly placed it a step above such better known "loner" Westerns as *The Restless Gun* and *The Texan*.

Much more solemn and cerebral than *Shotgun Slade* was *The Rebel*. Johnny Yuma was a veteran of the Civil War who had been greatly affected by the South's bitter defeat. An angry young man, Yuma roamed the West in search of inner peace. One television historian has described *The Rebel* as "historically noteworthy" because "it was the only one of nearly fifty television Westerns to show Reconstruction as a period of hurt and great soul-searching," rather than as a marketplace for the military talents of Civil War veterans.[35] Nick Adams had created, in his subtly understated portrayal of Johnny Yuma, "television's first truly tragic hero." Johnny Cash intoned the series' popular theme song beneath the credits about a "fightin' mad," "rebel lad" whose quick draw and tough fists were a match for any adversary. The words and music of Richard Markowitz and A. J. Fenady certainly captured the mood of the series and resulted in a hit single for Cash.

As he tried to find a place for himself in the turbulent West, Yuma would meet people in need of his help. A man of high moral principles, Yuma would apply his own brand of justice while assisting those in trouble. Being a proud man, he still wore the remnants of his rebel uniform and was often forced to defend himself against slurs directed at him and the fallen South. Using both his fists and a sawed-off shotgun he wore strapped to his leg, he exhibited an intensity that belied his slender build.

Nicholas Aloysius Adamshock was born in Nanticoke, Pennsylvania. His father was a coal miner who decided to change occupations after Nick's uncle lost his life in a mine cave-in. Moving to Jersey City, New Jersey, he became an apartmenthouse superintendent. Nick attended Snyder High where he won letters in baseball, basketball, football and track. While a senior, Nick learned from a book dealer that auditions were being held for an Off Broadway production of Sean O'Casey's *The Silver Tassie*. While waiting his turn, he struck up a conversation with Jack Palance, who also hailed from the coal-mining region near Nanticoke. Palance took a liking to him and when Nick did not get the part in *The Silver Tassie*, urged him to audition for a role in the Junior Theater's production of *Tom Sawyer*. This time he got the part—Muff Potter. Other roles followed as Nick gained acting experience.

Finally Nick decided to hitchhike to California where he might find work in films. Nick made the rounds of the Hollywood casting offices and got himself an agent. To support himself, Nick worked at a variety of odd jobs—truck driver, fry cook, gas jockey, usher, relief doorman and general maintenance man at the Beverly Hills Theater. He was fired from the theater job for putting his name up on the marquee one night. (Later his name actually would appear on the same marquee when he costarred with Andy Griffith in *No Time for Sergeants*.)

Beginning in 1952, Nick served three years in the Coast Guard. This led directly to a role as a sailor in Mervyn Le Roy's film production of *Mr. Roberts* with Henry Fonda and James Cagney. He supplemented his early film work by joining Elvis Presley's troupe, where he sang and did comic impersonations of Grant, Brando, Cagney and Bogart. His film credits included *Strange Lady in Town* (1955), *Our Miss Brooks* (1956), *Rebel Without a Cause* (1955), with James Dean, *I Died a Thousand Times* (1955), with Jack Palance, and *Teacher's Pet* (1958), with Clark Gable and Doris Day. His best role came in Mervyn Le Roy's *No Time for Sergeants* (1958), which made him famous, but led to his being typed as a comic Southerner. Meanwhile, Nick had begun to appear on television in *Playhouse 90*, *Wagon Train*, *Richard Diamond*, and *Zane Grey Theatre* productions.

On New Year's Eve, 1958, while a guest at the home of movie producer Andrew J. Fenady, Nick made a pitch for a weekly series in which he would star. Fenady, a 31 year old actor turned writer and producer (he later wrote and produced television's *Branded* and *Hondo*, as well as the John Wayne film *Chisum*) and his friend and partner Irwin Kershner, a 35 year old former photography instructor turned director assisted Adams in outlining a pilot episode of a series they planned to call *Young Johnny Yuma*. The three agreed to become equal partners in the series, which would relate the wanderings of a former Confederate soldier in the West after the Civil War. Then they sold Dick Powell on the idea of premiering the series as an episode of the *Zane Grey Theater*.

However, a better offer came along. Fenady and Kershner convinced the vice president of the Goodson-Todman agency to finance the series in return for half ownership. Thus, October 4, 1959, firm-lipped, steel-jawed, flinty-eyed Adams made his first appearance on ABC as Johnny Yuma in a series called *The Rebel*. (The date happened to be Fenady's birthday and Kershner's wedding anniversary.) More recently, Fenady explained in an interview in *The TV Collector*:

> ... my conception of "The Rebel" was Jack London in the West. It was fashioned after Jack London's life. Jack London was young, he was robust, he was rebellious, he was adventurous, he wanted to be a writer—but he couldn't write it unless he lived it.
>
> And that's exactly what the rebel did. And that's what set him apart from all the other pistolleros, the Wyatt Earps, who were sheriffs and marshals and detectives. They were all the same thing. The rebel was a breed apart. He was a young, inquiring, movable young man who sought adventure and wanted to write about it.[36]

The pilot episode, simply entitled "Johnny Yuma," was a variation on the highly successful *High Noon* scenario. Young Yuma returns to his hometown following the Civil War only to find that his father, the sheriff, has been killed and the rest of the population, including his aunt and uncle, have been terrorized by a tyrant and his gang. After enduring their taunts and finding that no one will back him, Yuma takes matters into his own hands and dispatches the outlaws with a well thrown grenade. Then he rides off to find himself. The story was suspenseful, the action taut and the acting uniformly good. (Appearing in support of Adams were Dan Blocker as the chief heavy, John Carradine as the newspaper editor and Jeanette Nolan as the aunt.) The early reviews were quite positive. *Variety* said:

> "The Rebel" is one new series that has something new about it.... Fenady and Kershner gave the story vitality and freshness.... Adams is a rugged-looking young actor who played his part in appealing style ... [and] fits both action and mood nicely.[37]

Los Angeles Times television critic Cecil Smith was even more enthusiastic in his praise:

> Among the new shows that have been added to the already overpopulated West, there seems to me to be great merit in a half-hour effort called "The Rebel".... I think it stands apart because it does not seem to be essentially a western but to have a timeless quality, as true to one era of man's existence as any other. It could have been set in ancient Greece or medieval Europe—or our own time—as well as in the post–Civil War frontier....
>
> "The Rebel" is a study in the fundamental restlessness and rebellion of youth.... Johnny Yuma ... [is] seeking some unknown destiny, some meaning, some reason for his existence.
>
> ... I can find parallels for Johnny Yuma's search for meaning in the slum kid heading

Nick Adams gained great popularity as Johnny Yuma, better known as *The Rebel*.

out into the streets of the city, aimlessly walking, seeking, or in Young David with his slingshot walking toward Goliath.

Speaking practically, the format of the series . . . is ideal—limitless in scope. But as an impracticable person, it is the romantic idea of the young man on the move that appeals to me. I wish I were young enough to join him.[38]

Although it consistently depicted the harsher aspects of survival on the Western frontier and frequently dealt with the baser side of human nature, *The Rebel* benefited from interesting and unusually well-written scripts. In "Yellow Hair," Yuma chances upon a fort whose military force has been slaughtered by the Kiowa Indians. There is only one white survivor, a soldier who hid and later feigned insanity because the Indians would not harm a crazy man. A truly tragic figure, the man must remain dead to his family or reveal himself to be the coward that he is. Yuma is captured and about to be burned alive, when a young white woman who has been raised by the Indians since her parents perished on a wagon train intervenes. She tells him that he may challenge a brave to "run for the knife." If he survives, he will be set free. Not only does Yuma survive, he is made a blood brother by the chief. The plot here is simple but moving and the acting is effective with Royal Dano as the cowardly survivor, Carol Nugent (Adams' real-life wife) as the young white woman, and Rodolpho Acosta as the chief. In this episode, we discover that Yuma is writing a book based on his experiences.

Another interesting episode, "Johnny Yuma at Appomattox," focuses on General Grant's sympathetic approach to General Lee's surrender. Using a story within a story device, Yuma tries to squelch some of the bitterness felt by a rebel boy whose father had been killed during the war "by those bluebellies." In a flashback, Yuma relates how he planned to kill Grant at Appomattox when he accepted Lee's surrender. Hidden behind a vent in the attic of the court house, the young rebel attempted to draw a pistol bead on the bluecoated general during the negotiations. Finally, however, he realized, after observing Grant's statesmanship and respectful attitude toward Lee, what a tragic mistake a successful assassination would be. Yuma is particularly moved by Grant's willingness to allow Southern soldiers to keep their horses and mules and his refusal of Lee's sword.

The meeting of the generals was excellently played out by William Bryant as Grant and George MacReady as Lee. Producer Andrew J. Fenady not only wrote the script, but he also played General Phil Sheridan with considerable poise. In this episode, as in many of the others, there is a moral interwoven into the story and heroism is displayed without the usual need for violence.

"The Hunted" begins by revealing the more ignoble instincts of man. A friend of Yuma's, who had been wrongly convicted of murder, flees to escape hanging. Later, another man confesses to the crime. The posse, unaware of this development, is in close pursuit of the man who has escaped. Yuma tries to find his friend and the posse before a tragic wrong is perpetrated. Meanwhile, Johnny discovers that the man's closest friends have turned against him and he has resorted to stealing a horse and money. Inadvertently, he has caused a trapper to suffer a broken leg and burned down the cabin of two homesteaders. Johnny finally catches up with his friend and takes him back to stand trail—not for murder, but for the harm he has inflicted on those who had gotten in the way of his mad dash for freedom. In the end, however, the men injured by Johnny's friend drop the charges against him and he agrees to make restitution. It is a rare upbeat ending for a series which usually depicted the more negative aspects of man's nature. (Leonard Nimoy turns in an excellent pre–*Star Trek* performance as Yuma's hunted friend.)

The emphasis in *The Rebel* was on characterization and many of the stories were more cerebral than those on most other television Westerns of that era. Fenady recently described the advantages of this approach:

> ... I can make a plot out of any damn thing, but give me an interesting character and that will pave the way toward the plot. If there's somebody who has something he wants to do or avoid doing or has some kind of a problem, is facing some kind of an issue, then you've got an interesting character and the situation will come out of the person. And that's what we did.
>
> We did a show about a kid that wanted to assassinate the President of the United States, long before Kennedy was shot. We did [a show] about a kid whose father was a famous bull fighter but the kid was afraid of bulls ... [about] a sheriff who was afraid, when a gunfighter was gonna come back [after being released] from prison, that he would lose his nerve and not be able to stand up to him....
>
> What happened was when the gunfighter came back ... he was a broken old man (and) there was nothing to be afraid of.
>
> In almost all the episodes I snuck in a little bit of philosophy, a little poetry, something from the classics.[39]

Notwithstanding these distinctive characteristics, *The Rebel* was canceled in June 1961 after 76 episodes had been filmed. The ratings had never lived up to expectations. (The following summer, however, NBC aired reruns of the ABC series.)

Unfortunately, Nick Adams never quite achieved the stardom he so ardently craved. He was given another series, *Saints and Sinners* (1962-63), in which he portrayed a crusading young newspaper reporter, but the show lasted only four months. In 1963, Adams was nominated for a Best Supporting Actor Oscar for his role as a murder suspect in the theatrical film *Twilight of Honor*, which starred Richard Chamberlain, Claude Rains, and Joey Heatherton. From that point, his career went downhill with roles in monster movies and scattered appearances on television action shows. Nick Adams died of a drug overdose in 1968 at the age of 37. Like the character he had created for the video West, Adams never found whatever it was in life for which he was searching.

One of the most critically acclaimed television Westerns ever made, *The Westerner*, related the adventures of Dave Blassingame, who wandered the Old West with only his faithful mongrel dog, Brown, for company. Subsequently hailed by critics and fans as "a splendid little exercise in superior television"[40]; "a Western with a high degree of realism ... [and] obviously a superior product"[41]; ". . . a compelling, offbeat Western. . ."[42]; and "probably the most underrated and overlooked western in the history of television,"[43] *The Westerner* was canceled after only 13 weeks on NBC (September 30–December 30, 1960).

The series was the brainchild of Sam Peckinpah, who would later direct some of the most unusual—and violent—theatrical Westerns ever made (for instance, *Ride the High Country*, 1962; *The Wild Bunch*, 1967; and *Pat Garrett and Billy the Kid*, 1973). It was Peckinpah's experience in writing and directing television shows, primarily Westerns, that first brought him to the public's attention and paved the way for his work in feature films. After writing scripts for *Gunsmoke, Broken Arrow, Tales of Wells Fargo, Trackdown, Tombstone Territory, Man Without a Gun, The Rifleman,* and *Have Gun, Will Travel,* Peckinpah was approached by Dick Powell early in 1959 to write and direct the pilot for a 30 minute Western. If the show was well received on Powell's *Zane Grey Theatre,* it would be marketed as a series under the title *Winchester.* Given a free hand, Peckinpah began to work on a script.

Peckinpah conceived the main character as a self-reliant drifter, named David after Peckinpah's father and Blassingame after a ranching family he knew from his youth. Blassingame rode an Appaloosa, was followed about by a large mixed-breed dog named Brown, and to justify the title, carried a specially made Winchester rifle equipped with an eight-power, cross hair sight and bored to fire a larger than average grain bullet. His avowed aim was to settle down on his own ranch and breed quarter horses, but he never seemed to stay out of trouble long enough. The pilot was entitled "Trouble at Tres Cruces."

To play the pivotal role of Dave Blassingame, Peckinpah selected craggy Brian Keith, a capable actor who looked completely at home in Westerns. Born in Bayonne, New Jersey, in 1921, Keith was the son of character actor Robert Keith and actress Helena Shysman. His parents brought him on stage at the age of one month and got him his first film role at 3. After serving as a machine gunner for the Marines in World War II, Keith decided to pursue a career as a stage actor—without much success, until his father got him a bit part in *Mr. Roberts* in which the elder Keith was starring as "Doc." Brian later appeared on stage in *The Moon Is Blue.*

Television, however, seemed to offer more potential for the struggling actor, and Brian made his debut on the home screen in 1952 on *The Campbell Sound Stage.* This appearance was followed by roles on many of the live drama anthologies of the fifties: *Studio 57, Ford Theatre,* and *Lux Video Theatre.* Meanwhile, Keith was pursuing a film career. His first theatrical screen appearance was in *Arrowhead,* starring Charlton Heston and Jack

Palance, in 1953. He followed this with three films in 1954, *Alaska Seas*, *The Bamboo Prison*, and *The Violent Men*, which starred Barbara Stanwyck, Glenn Ford and Edward G. Robinson and in which Keith effectively played a villain. In 1955, Keith was given his first starring role in a television series. He was cast in *Crusader* as Matt Anders, a freelance writer who devoted most of his time to helping people living under Communist oppression escape to free countries. The show was broadcast for slightly more than a season over CBS. After *Crusader* was canceled, Keith returned to theatrical films in *Storm Center* (1956), with Bette Davis, *Run of the Arrow* (1957), with Rod Steiger, *Fort Dobbs* (1958), with Clint Walker, and *Villa!* (1958), with Cesar Romero. He also made frequent guest appearances on such television dramas as *Alfred Hitchcock Presents*. By 1960 Brian Keith was more than ready for his own Western series.

"Trouble at Tres Cruces" was telecast on the *Zane Grey Theater* on March 26, 1959. Dave Blassingame rides into the Mexican town of Tres Cruces only to discover that his uncle has been killed and the peasants bullied into submission by a self-styled dictator (played to evil perfection by veteran bad guy Neville Brand). After a rough-and-tumble, no-holds-barred fistfight, (which Blassingame loses!) the stage is set for a bloody confrontation between the two men. Refusing to gun down his opponent with his superior rifle from a safe distance (true to the code of cowboy heroes), Blassingame faces off against him in an open field. Blassingame survives because his Winchester is able to penetrate the fallen log his enemy has jumped behind, fatally wounding him. There were no immediate offers to sponsor the proposed series although the episode received generally favorable reviews. *Variety* (March 30, 1959) said:

> Keith is realistic and quietly overpowering in the role . . . and the solid outdoor production values stamp this as an ambitious, if not altogether successful attempt.

As it turned out, Four Star did not have the rights to the name *Winchester* so the name of the proposed series was changed to *The Westerner*. David Levy, the current head of NBC-TV, liked the concept, found a sponsor and added the show to his fall 1960 schedule. By the date set for its premier, September 30, 1960, ten episodes had been completed. As producer of the series it was Peckinpah's responsibility to select the episode that would act as the series opener. He decided on an episode entitled "Jeff" which he had directed and cowritten with writer Robert Heverly. Because of the extremely adult nature of the story, "Jeff" caused quite a stir. Peckinpah recalled later:

> Some "Westerners" were pretty rough for that time. In fact, some of the network affiliates didn't want to telecast the first show we had. It was about a guy who goes to take this young whore, who he knew as a kid, home. They just absolutely refused to air it. At least until David Levy and Dick Powell got to them and worked it out.[44]

Dave Blassingame is introduced as a rather violent and gloomy character who is determined to take home a saloon girl ("Jeff") he has known since she was a child. Her "pimp," an ex-boxer, objects, and there is a bloody fight (Blassingame wins this time!) and Blassingame is about to take Jeff away from her squalid, sordid life, when she has a change of heart and decides to stay after all. The plot, though somewhat simple, is filled with nuances, innuendo, tension—and violence—as every critic noted. *Variety* (October 3, 1960) commented:

> The code of the industry against violence went out the window when the gate opened on this brawler and bruiser. Nothing seemed to matter other than who swung hardest or shot straightest. It has one redeeming feature, however, in the character etched by Brian Keith, as rough and tough an hombre as ever roamed the back lot. . . . He may yet salvage it but

it's going to take better writing and some semblance of a plot line to give him something to go on over the long haul.

James Powers of *The Hollywood Reporter*, who reviewed "Jeff" the Monday following its telecast, was considerably more impressed:

> "The Westerner" is made by people who know that time has nothing to do with breathless theater; a half-hour is just as good in the right hands as three hours. It is made by people more interested in telling a story than aping a formula in the naive hope that guiltless plagiary will make them rich. It shows again that TV's whine of "no time" is just another way of saying "no talent." "The Westerner" is a great show, a stand-out series, and its strongest competition in the weeks ahead will be its own standards.
>
> The opening show had Brian Keith, the running character, concerned with prostitution, sadism and pimping. One man in the show came right out and said "damn." It was, you may be surprised to know, a moving poetic drama . . . written with expert economy and directed and acted the same. Characterizations were complex but they were explored and analyzed as if there was all the time in the world. The half-hour had only one flaw, a couple of descents into violence that didn't help the story at all. They seemed like second thoughts, as if someone said "nothing's going on here, liven it up." Plenty went on and it was memorable.
>
> Keith is fine, getting to be a better actor all the time, thoughtful and electric.[45]

As favorable as Powers' review of "Jeff" was, it is interesting to note that he faults it for "descents into violence," a charge that was frequently leveled against most of Peckinpah's work. However, when this episode was shown later at a San Francisco Film Festival featuring his work, the audience actually applauded this violence—expressing another opinion of Peckinpah's use of violence, no less valid than that of Powers. Throughout the series, controlled violence is employed by Peckinpah, usually to depict realistic situations in the West as it existed during the period following the Civil War. In "Mrs. Kennedy," Blassingame is forced to kill the husband of a woman who has been flirting with him when the man comes after him with a pitchfork. The attempted murder is caused by jealousy while Blassingame must kill in self-defense. Blassingame's refusal to take the woman away with him when he leaves is proof of his "honorable intentions."

"Hand on the Gun" is more "Western" in its subject matter. A young punk (played by Ben Cooper) thinks that being fast is all that really matters in gunfighting. Michael Ansara portrays an aging Mexican gunslinger who tries to dissuade the kid from needless gunplay. He shows him an old bullet wound—a small round scar in his stomach where a bullet entered and an ugly sprawling scar where the bullet came through his back, tearing his flesh away with it. Later, when the punk refuses to learn his lesson and insists on calling the old Mexican out, Ansara walks resignedly into the street where the kid is waiting. The kid quick-draws and gets off the first two shots, which miss. The Mexican, however, calmly aims and kills his adversary. Without the violent gunfight, the story would have lost its impact.

Not many viewers realized that of the five *Westerner* episodes which Peckinpah directed, three were comedies. These three, "Brown," "The Courting of Libby" and "The Painting," were all written by Bruce Geller, an extremely talented man (who later became the creative force behind *Mission: Impossible*). They reveal a side of Peckinpah's directorial ability seldom considered by his critics. Still, they feature, especially "Brown," his distinctive use of violence.

In "Brown," we are introduced to a humorous character named Burgundy Smith (played by the veteran radio and film actor John Dehner), who also appears in the other two Geller Scripts. Smith has been described as "an eloquent rustler out to take the West for what he could get in a charming, roguish sort of way."[46] Smith takes a fancy to

Blassingame's dog (played by the dog featured in Walt Disney's movie, *Old Yeller*) and attempts to buy him. When Blassingame refuses to sell the dog, for any price, Smith tries to cheat him out of the dog, again unsuccessfully. At the end of the episode, the two men part as friends, but along the way they engage in a brutal fistfight and brawl employing virtually every slapstick and sight gag ever seen on film. To prevent Blassingame from winning a race he is in, Smith hires a man to knock him down—into a quagmire of mud which covers him from head to foot. Later the two men get fall-down drunk together and tumble around the dance floor with two pretty chorus girls. In a fit of mock anger, Smith shoots the legs off a piano so the piano player will stop playing the same tune. When Blassingame passes out, Smith has him arrested and thrown in jail—for a crime which never took place. When Blassingame wakes up in jail, he finds a bag of coins and a signed receipt for the sale of Brown.

Dave convinces the sheriff to release him in time to see Smith making off with his dog. Catching up to him before he can get away, Dave grabs Smith and the two engage in one of the funniest fistfights ever depicted in a "serious" adult Western. After crashing through railings and over tables, the climax comes when the two burst through the bedroom window of a woman who has been sleeping. The two men leave by the door, with Smith tipping his hat to the lady in apology. It is a comedy tour de force that would please Mack Sennett or Hal Roach.

However, despite the high quality and variety found in *The Westerner*, it was canceled after only 13 shows. This was at least partially due to the controversial subject matter of some of the stories which caused resistance, especially among affiliates serving rural areas. Peckinpah believed that the show's "tough-minded realism" brought about its downfall. "The show," he told *TV Guide*, "is evidently too adult. Advertisers are afraid of it. These [were] the determining factors."[47] Another factor was its time-slot competition— *The Flintstones* on ABC, which turned out to be a surprise hit, and *Route 66* on CBS, which was just beginning a successful four year run. Furthermore, *The Westerner* was given a temporary time slot, which had been reserved for *The Nanette Fabray Show*, scheduled to begin on January 6, 1961. This was also the season that found the American viewing audience showing a decided preference for hour-long shows over half-hour ones (12 of *Four Star*'s 14 thirty-minute prime time shows were canceled that season). Brian Keith (who has starred in six additional television series as of 1994) later explained in an interview with *Los Angeles Times* television critic Cecil Smith that

> So much fuss was raised when we went off the air that CBS came running with an offer to put "The Westerner" back on. Then we found out they wanted us to stretch it to an hour and put it on at 7 o'clock at night, which meant that we'd have to cut the realism, make it for kids—in other words, cut everything out of it that made it good. We told 'em to go fly a kite.[48]

Keith also expressed interest in making a theatrical film with Peckinpah using the Blassingame and Smith characters, but nothing ever came of it. Making *The Westerner* was clearly an enjoyable experience for Keith:

> Playing Dave was the most satisfying job I ever had. The greatest satisfaction is in cowtowns where guys come out of doorways and grab me to tell me how good the series was. One drunk swore up and down I was one of the Tyree brothers from Deming. Said he knew 'em well and I had to be one. Later, when he found out he'd seen me on the series, he said old Dave was just like one of the Tyrees on a brannigan.[49]

Peckinpah did, however, film another version of *The Westerner* for *The Dick Powell Theater* (which was broadcast January 15, 1963) using an entirely different cast, but the same characters. Written by Geller and entitled "The Losers," it set Dave Blassingame and Burgundy Smith, along with Brown, in the West of 1963. Again it was a comedy, with Lee Marvin cast as Blassingame and Keenan Wynn as Smith. The characters were virtually unchanged — "two hard-drinking, girl-chasing, card-cheating drifters." The show had little violence, however, and featured vocalist Rosemary Clooney as a singer with a disfiguring birthmark and Mike Magurki as a rough horse trader that Blassingame and Smith have cheated at poker. A blind Mexican-American Gospel singer and his young orphaned helper completed the cast of characters. The story ended with an uncharacteristically (for Peckinpah) happy ending as the two singers and the orphan are brought together into a ready-made family by Dave and Burgundy. Unfortunately, Dick Powell fell seriously ill and died of cancer in January of 1963, before seeing "The Losers." Although Peckinpah had hoped to use the episode as a pilot for a series, Powell's successor at Four Star was not interested.

Meanwhile Brian Keith went on to star in his most popular series to date, *Family Affair* (1966–1971) opposite a stuffy English butler (Sebastian Cabot) and three adorable children. This was followed by *The Brian Keith Show* (1972–1974), another family comedy, *Arch* (1975), a detective show, *The Zoo Gang* (1975), a European adventure series, *Hardcastle and McCormick* (1983–1986), an action-adventure show and, more recently, another sitcom, *Walter and Emily* (1991-92). Still, Keith, in only 13 half-hour episodes, has with Peckinpah's assistance left his indelible mark on the television Western as the laconic loner Dave Blassingame. (Fans enjoyed seeing him once again as Blassingame doing a humorous cameo with Dub Taylor in Kenny Rogers' television miniseries *The Gambler Returns: Luck of the Draw* in 1991.)

Branded, which made its debut over NBC on January 24, 1965, seemed to have all the prerequisites for success — a unique plot, a novel weapon and a proven star in the lead. Created by Larry Cohen, a 29 year old former NBC page turned writer, *Branded* depicted the adventures of Jason McCord, a West Point graduate and cavalry officer (with the rank of captain), who was wrongly cashiered out of the service as a coward. McCord's disgrace was simply and concisely presented at the opening of each episode. The drums rolled ominously as the blue uniformed soldiers marched across the parade grounds of the frontier fort. Over the tatoo of the drums the series' theme song (music by Dominic Frontiere, lyrics by Alan Alch) musically explained the premise, the events at "Bitter Creek," upon which the show was based.

Because he was the only one to survive a massacre, McCord was branded a coward. Actually, viewers learn in a flashback during the second episode, "The Vindicators," that McCord was trying to protect the reputation of a much respected general, General Reed, who, in trying to promote peace between the Indians and whites, is caught unprepared. Just before the massacre, the general becomes mentally deranged and orders his men to fight until all the Indians are killed although they are hopelessly outnumbered. Shortly thereafter McCord is knocked unconscious and inadvertently spared, leaving the army brass to think that he ran and hid or maybe worse during the battle. McCord will not allow the publication of letters written from another officer to his wife explaining the growing mental breakdown of General Reed since it would destroy the deceased general's good name (even though it would clear the name of the very much alive McCord).

Week after week McCord is called upon to prove his courage to various individuals with whom he comes in contact as he wanders the West. His half sword (broken at the time he was drummed out of the service), now sharpened to a gleaming point, is his favorite weapon, although he is quite proficient with both a six-gun and a rifle. He is, however, often forced to defend himself with his fists. His previous military experience as an engineer, geologist and cartographer enable McCord to find assorted, interesting jobs. Six-foot, five-inch Chuck Connors, popular star of *The Rifleman* (see Chapter VIII) was cast as the hero of *Branded*. Series creator Cohen explained:

> My intellectual concept of the show is that it's like a Shakespearean tragedy. You must have a great man to experience true tragedy. That's why I like Chuck Connors so much in this part. He's so big—he's the tallest underdog in the West.[50]

Cohen described Jason McCord as "a man mistakenly, unfairly hated and persecuted—a man who must fight to destroy the image of dishonor that follows him."[51] Connors was pleased to be back in a Western. *Branded* was the first half-hour Western since *Have Gun, Will Travel* left the air in 1963. In Connor's opinion:

> There'll always be a place for Westerns on television, because they're Americana and you can't take America out of America. The Western is the American fairy tale.[52]

Connors tried to make Jason McCord different from his *Rifleman* character. He cut his hair short and let his sideburns grow. He wanted it to look military since McCord was a West Point graduate. He also lost weight. Reviews of *Branded* were mixed. *Variety* called attention to the fact that the series was beginning at mid-season:

> Midseason series are jinxed, the records show, although there have been exceptions.... That's why production companies usually avoid a first-of-the-year starter.[53]

Cleveland Amory of *TV Guide* was more critical:

> This show is NBC's all-too-obvious Western switcheroo on ABC's "The Fugitive." Instead of the unjustly accused murderer, we have the unjustly accused coward. "Branded" stars, as ex–Capt Jason McCord, Chuck Connors, who, we will admit at the onset, is not our idea of a man to carry a show by himself—if for no other reason than because, despite his 6-foot-5-inch height, he is regularly being beaten up by men who don't come up to his elbows.[54]

In retrospect, this seems like a grossly unfair assessment when the show is compared to other television Westerns of that period. Castleman and Podrazik writing some 24 years later state that "the stories are slightly above average Western fodder, with the first dozen or so the best of the lot."[55] Connors was surrounded by some fine guest stars including Michael Rennie ("Salute the Soldier Briefly"), Pat O'Brien ("The Greatest Coward on Earth"), Gary Merrill ("Romany Roundup"), Marilyn Maxwell ("Price of a Name"), Claude Akins ("The Vindicators"), Ben Johnson ("McCord's Way"), and Burgess Meredith ("Headed for Doomsday"). Johnny Crawford, Connor's costar from *The Rifleman*, appeared in "Coward Step Aside." *Gunsmoke*'s Burt Reynolds was in "Now Join the Human Race," *Black Saddle*'s Peter Breck in "The Mission" and *Rawhide*'s John Ireland in "Cowards Die Many Times." In somewhat unusual casting choices, singer Tommy Sands appears in "That the Brave Endure" and disc jockey Dick Clark in "The Greatest Coward on Earth."

Guest stars turned in some of the best performances on *Branded*. Martin Landau is spellbinding as Edwin Booth, John Wilkes Booth's actor brother in "This Stage of Fools." McCord is hired as Booth's bodyguard while he is touring the West with his one man dramatic show. Booth is actually searching for the guard who got drunk and left his post outside President Lincoln's box in Ford theater the night he was killed by John Wilkes. Edwin holds him responsible for the shame brought on the Booth name by the assassination and plans to kill him. McCord discovers his objective in time and saves the man's life while convincing Edwin that the only way he can exorcise the ghosts of his past is by returning to his stage career in the East. The story is both interesting and well-acted.

William Bryan, who played President Ulysses S. Grant in several *Branded* episodes, turns in a riveting performance in "A Destiny Which Made Us Brothers." The story, told as a flashback, depicts McCord's first chance meeting with General Grant during the Civil War. Grant is having doubts about his ability as a military leader as the war drags on with the increasing loss of life on both sides. Not only does McCord help save Grant's life, he helps him find the self-confidence to go on to a great Union victory at Vicksburg. This may explain why Grant, as President, did not really believe that McCord was a coward and frequently sent him on special secret missions for the federal government. In "The Mission" (a two-part story), Grant sends McCord into Mexico to infiltrate a band of banditos who are making raids across the border on American garrisons. This, of course, provides McCord with another opportunity to prove his courage.

In "Call to Glory," the only three-part story in the series, Grant sends McCord to check up on George Armstrong Custer, with whom he had become friends at West Point. According to the script, McCord helps Custer put his political ambitions into proper perspective and avert an Indian war (for the time being). Robert Lansing is quite effective in the role of Custer and the story allows for greater character development than the usual 30 minute format. McCord, always a loner, rides off before Custer faces his debacle at the Little Big Horn.

Occasionally, the writers permitted McCord to become romantically involved with a woman. Only once, however, does the relationship appear to have any future. In "Mightier Than the Sword," McCord is attracted to the beautiful (and brave) editor of a small town newspaper (appealingly played by Lola Albright). She returns (or rather McCord returns to her) in "Cowards Die Many Times," the next to last episode in the series. There is a strong implication that McCord will settle down and make a fresh start with this woman. However the series was canceled a week later and, of course, a married McCord would have changed the entire focus of *Branded*. In the 48 episodes produced for the series can be found some of the better quality "loner" stories. In this sub-genre of the television Western, *Branded* must rank near the top.

> In the aftermath of the blood-letting called the Civil War, thousands of rootless, restless, searching men traveled West. Such a man is William Colton. Like the others, he carried a blanket-roll, a proficient gun and a dedication to a new chapter in American history—the opening of the West.

Thus began Rod Serling's fascinating Western series, *The Loner*. Serling, best known as the creator and host of *The Twilight Zone*, had come up with the idea for a one-hour pilot about a former Civil War officer heading West "to get the cannon smoke" out of his eyes, the noise out of his ears and "maybe some of the pictures" out of his head while *Zone* was still running on CBS. After that ground-breaking series was canceled in 1964, Serling decided to pursue the Western concept. William Dozier, production head of Screen Gems, liked the idea, but suggested that the story be trimmed to a half-hour. His first choice for the lead was Lloyd Bridges, who had achieved television stardom in *Sea Hunt*. Bridges agreed to do the show:

> Rod Serling was the main reason. With him doing 75 percent of the scripts and Bill Dozier producing, I knew I'd be in a quality show.[56]

When Dozier approached CBS President Jim Aubrey, all he had was the concept. There was no pilot film, not even a written presentation—just the names of Serling, Bridges and Dozier. CBS bought it solely on the reputation of these men.

The Loner turned out to be a series of weekly 30 minute dramatic vignettes set against

Lloyd Bridges starred as William Colton in Rod Serling's offbeat Western, *The Loner*.

a Western background. One week the show might present a love story; the next week, a comedy; another, a tense confrontation. All that the stories had in common was a solitary, disillusioned Union cavalry officer searching for something to give his life meaning. He tries to understand and relate to the various kinds of people he encounters along the way. This kind of legitimate, human drama was, in many respects, ahead of its time. Castleman and Podrazik point out:

> Such a low-key, introspective format is very unusual for a TV series and it foreshadows the national cultural introspection just around the corner in the late 1960s (keyed off by the Vietnam War)....
>
> It is not too farfetched to postulate that the character of Colton is a bit of a surrogate for Serling. Having gained wealth and fame from his days of writing hit TV drama scripts and creating "The Twilight Zone," Serling was always highly frustrated by the shackles put on his creative powers due to the corporate structure of film and TV production.[57]

In addition to Serling's writing, *The Loner* benefited from the presence of Lloyd Bridges. That Bridges was able to transcend a role that would have typecast many other actors—that of underwater diver Mike Nelson in *Sea Hunt* (1957–1961)—was a credit to his acting ability. Born in 1913 in southern California, Bridges gained experience on the stage during the thirties and broke into movies in 1941. Thereafter, he played supporting roles in many action films. One of his best performances came in the Western classic *High Noon* (1952) as the ambitious, calculating deputy.

Bridges was also one of the first established film actors to try television, appearing in many live dramatic anthologies during the fifties. In 1956, he earned a Best Actor Emmy nomination for his outstanding performance in the Sidney Lumet production of Reginald Rose's "Tragedy in a Temporary Town" on *The Alcoa Hour* (February 19, 1956). After *Sea Hunt*, Bridges got even better roles and made guest appearances on such shows as the *Zane Grey Theater* and *The Eleventh Hour*. His own anthology series, *The Lloyd Bridges Show* (1962-63), however, was canceled after only one season. The show had an interesting premise, with Bridges playing journalist Adam Shepherd *and* a second character which he created in each story. (One of the best episodes was the Civil War Story, "A Pair of Boots," which featured Bridges's son Beau. Bridges also provided acting opportunities on the series for his daughter, Cindy and his other son, Jeff.)

Receiving almost universal acclaim from the critics, Bridges did some of his finest work on *The Loner*. Cleveland Amory wrote in *TV Guide* (January 15, 1966): "Lloyd Bridges ... is convincing in every department of an exceedingly demanding role ..."; *Variety* (September 22, 1965) said: "The oater is a fresh video environment for star Bridges and he fits it well...."

In the series opener, "An Echo of Bugles," which debuted on September 18, 1965, Colton runs up against a young tough spoiling for a fight. The climax of the story comes when the two face off in a shootout forced upon Colton by the kid. As Colton waits for the inevitable gunfight, the viewer sees through flashbacks, the final moments of the Civil War when Colton is forced to kill a young Rebel soldier in self-defense. In revulsion at the needless carnage of young men on both sides, Colton resigns from the Army and heads West. In the shoot-out, Colton only wounds the kid, and hopes that he will learn from the experience. Then Colton continues his journey West. The *Variety* assessment (September 22, 1965) was largely positive:

> Rod Serling has switched his symbols, from sci fi to the sagebrush arena. His yen to engage some human issues, cosmic and lesser, seems to have segued intact.... "Loner" could prove a provocative entertainment and it just might survive the rating scramble.

Unfortunately the Nielsen ratings were disappointing. Cleveland Amory tried to determine why viewers were not attracted to the series in significantly larger numbers:

> Unfortunately, what Mr. Serling obviously intended to be a realistic, adult Western turned out, judging from ratings, to be either too real for a public grown used to the unreal Western or too adult for juvenile Easterners.... This is a pity because there are fine episodes here.[58]

Among the more notable episodes is "The Homecoming of Lemuel Stove," in which guest star Brock Peters gives an outstanding performance as a Negro Union soldier who returns to his home town looking for his father. He discovers that his father has been lynched the night before by a group of pre–Ku Klux Klan bigots. The story makes a strong statement about the racial violence then sweeping across the country.

In "The Oath," Barry Sullivan turns in an equally strong performance as a surgeon who has lost his right hand. In order to save the life of a gunfighter who has ruptured his appendix, he directs Colton to perform the operation. This was another powerful episode with a realistic ending (the man dies despite the best efforts of Colton and the doctor).

The Loner was canceled in March 1966 after filming 26 episodes. The reason given by Michael H. Dann, vice president in charge of programming for CBS, was that the show lacked "action—movement, chases, running gun battles, runaway stagecoaches, etc."[59] As in the case of *The Westerner* and *Branded*, *The Loner* was another quality Western which people simply did not care to watch. Interest in the genre was obviously declining.

This was also the fate of another interesting "loner" Western which debuted in September 1965: *A Man Called Shenandoah*. The series starred Robert Horton, who had risen to stardom on another popular television Western, *Wagon Train* (see Chapter VII). When he left that series, Horton had vowed never to do another Western, but three years without steady work changed his mind.

Created by producer E. Jack Neumann, *A Man Called Shenandoah* related the adventures of a man suffering from amnesia who wandered the West in search of clues that would lead him to his real identity. In the opening episode, "The Onslaught," two buffalo hunters stumble upon a stranger who has been shot in a gunfight and left out on the prairie to die. Assuming that he may have been an outlaw with a price on his head, they drag the nearly dead man into the closest town. Unfortunately for them, they find out he is not wanted for any crime, and even more unfortunately for the stranger, he cannot remember who he is or why he has been shot. *Variety* (September 15, 1965) was not impressed:

> The mixture of fast, straight action and psychological voodoo just didn't jell. Sigmund Freud in the Territory of Arizona was out of his element.
> Horton . . . was fine in the action sequences. He bogged down when playing the amnesia victim, however, wearing a one tone frown to show his disturbance.

Actually most of the stories were interesting and well done. The lyrics of the series theme song were written and sung by Horton to the tune of the familiar folksong "Shenandoah." They evoked the melancholy and longing that lay beneath the surface of each episode. Horton even wrote special verses to end some of the episodes, for instance "Obion—1866," "Requiem for the Second" and "Incident at Dry Creek."

Some episodes dealt directly with Shenandoah's search. In "The Fort," he locates a man who had responded to an ad he ran in a Denver newspaper. Claiming that the two men were patients together in a Civil War hospital, he tells Shenandoah that, although he does not know Shenandoah's real name, his wife, who was their nurse, will. Then the man is executed for desertion by a firing squad. In "The Caller," Shenandoah tracks down a lawyer with whom he did business before losing his memory, only to arrive at the moment the man is being murdered. The lawyer's wife has died and his daughter, while she remembers Shenandoah's visit, does not remember his name or occupation.

Shenandoah chases a man who recognizes him in "Obion—1866." When he catches up to the man, he learns only that he lived in a town called Obion in 1866 and faced down a gunslinger who had murdered a young man. The man he was chasing had been the cowardly sheriff who ran away instead of facing up to his responsibilities as a lawman. He did not, however, remember Shenandoah's name—only his face. When Shenandoah returns to the town, he finds it deserted. There is a grave on Boot Hill, however, where the gunman is buried.

In "Requiem for the Second," Shenandoah comes face to face with a man who knew him when they both served in the Second Cavalry unit of the U.S. Army. The man, however, is a deserter and is executed before Shenandoah can learn the truth about his own identity. Such were the frustrations Shenandoah faced in his futile search to discover who he really is.

Robert Horton was given his own series when he played the title role in *A Man Called Shenandoah*.

Some episodes do not deal directly with the issue of Shenandoah's amnesia—e.g., "Town on Fire" and "Incident at Dry Creek." Still, Shenandoah continues his wandering search at the end of each show. It seems unrealistic to expect that someone in similar circumstances would be able to discover the truth of his identity. But this fact did not eliminate the sense of frustration regular viewers must have felt when the series was canceled after 34 episodes without a resolution of Shenandoah's search.

At first glance *Hondo* appears to fall into the category of "loner" Westerns. The legendary Western character was a literary creation of best selling Western author Louis L'Amour, whose novel *Hondo* was first published in 1953. Warner Bros. produced a version of the novel based on a screenplay written by John Edward Grant. Originally filmed in 3-D, *Hondo* starred John Wayne as the tough, wily cavalry scout Hondo Lane. Hondo is an embittered loner. He had once been a captain in the confederate cavalry and had lived for a while with the Apaches. Chief Vittoro's daughter, his Indian mate, had been killed in a massacre by the U.S. Army. Now he wanders the West with a dog named Sam, trying to avert further violence between the Indians and whites. Hondo discovers a woman and her young son living alone in the desert. After rescuing them from an impending Apache uprising, Hondo is later forced to kill the woman's greedy, treacherous husband. Eventually Hondo heads West with the woman and her son to begin a new life in California. Hondo is alone no longer. The theatrical film was critically acclaimed and popular at the box office, which undoubtedly led to its adaptation for television.

Hondo the television series premiered on ABC September 8, 1967, and ran for only 17 episodes. The first two ("Hondo and the Eagle Claw" and "The War Cry") related the same basic story presented in the film. Additional subplots and characters were added, however. In addition to Angie Dow (Angie Lowe in the film) and her son Johnny (played by Kathie Browne and Buddy Foster), other continuing roles included Buffalo Baker (Noah Beery, Jr.), a colorful scout; Captain Richards (Gary Clarke), the arrogant commander of Fort Lowell; and Michael Pate, reprising his role in the film, as the Apache Chief Vittoro.

Thus surrounded by a host of supporting characters and employed as a U.S. Cavalry scout operating out of Fort Lowell in Arizona Territory, television's Hondo Lane hardly typifies the traditional Western "loner." Although filmed in color on location (in the Mojave Desert), *Hondo* suffered from routine and predictable plots (e.g., stringing the first telegraph, in "Hondo and the Singing Wire"; opening a silver mine in "Hondo and the Sudden Town"; capturing bandits in "Hondo and the Commancheros"; fighting renegade Indians in "Hondo and the War Cry"; combating vigilante justice in "Hondo and the Hanging Town") as well as stereotyped characters. On the plus side were appearances by a distinguished group of guest stars including Robert Taylor ("Hondo and the Eagle Claw"), Rod Cameron ("Hondo and the Sudden Town"), Jack Elam ("The Rebel Hat"), Fernando Lamas ("Hondo and the Commancheros") and Dan O'Herlihy ("Hondo and the Hanging Town").

There was also plenty of action. What was lacking was a dynamic star to play Hondo Lane. Any actor would undoubtedly have suffered from comparison with John Wayne, but the actor selected, Ralph Taeger, seemed especially unsuited for the role. Although tall and handsome, Taeger lacked charisma. Laconic and soft-spoken, Taeger had previously starred in two short-lived television adventure series: *Klondike* (1960-61), set in Alaska during the famous gold rush of 1898, and *Acapulco* (1961), set in sunny Mexico in the present. Taeger largely retired from acting after the cancellation of *Hondo* in 1968.

A chapter on loners would not be complete without considering television's quintessential mountain man, Grizzly Adams. True, he did not *ride* the video range, but he did wander the frontier on foot during the late 1800s communing with nature in all its many splendid guises. The series, entitled *The Life and Times of Grizzly Adams*, came about after a film of the same name scored a surprisingly high rating when it was shown on NBC in 1976. *Grizzly Adams* was loosely based on the life of James Capen Adams, who committed a crime in 1853 and then fled into the Rockies where he became friends with all the animals. The real Adams had been born in Massachusetts in 1812, and later moved to the Sierra Nevada after going bankrupt as the result of a series of unfortunate business deals.

In *The Life and Times of Grizzly Adams*, Adams has been accused of a crime he did not commit and, after seeking refuge in the wilderness, he discovers he likes living there better than the "civilized" life of the city. Animals are attracted to Adams, even though their natural instincts would make them suspicious and fearful of man. He rescues a grizzly bear cub from a ledge and names him Benjamin Franklin because he is so smart; the bear becomes his constant companion. (Hence the nickname "Grizzly.") By training Ben from the time he is a small cub, Adams wins his life-long trust, even though the bear eventually grows into a 600 pound animal.

Later, Adams saves the life of a young Indian brave who falls over a cliff after being attacked by a mountain lion. Grizzly nurses the Indian (whose name is Nakuma) back to health and they become blood brothers. (Nakuma later has an opportunity to save Grizzly's life.) The only other regular human characters in the series are a garrulous old trapper called Mad Jack, and Robbie Cartman, the son of a farmer who lives nearby and occasionally visits Grizzly's camp to listen to his tall tales.

In addition to the human characters, *Grizzly Adams* is filled with raccoons, deer, beaver, rabbits, skunks, foxes, bobcats, owls, mountain lions, porcupines, otter, coyotes, badgers and ferrets. Most of the stories involve Adams' experiences in coping with nature, the elements and the few strangers that pass through his territory. (A typical episode, "The Adventure of Grizzly Adams at Beaver Dam," concerns the efforts of the mountain man at dissuading a family of beavers from building a dam which he fears will flood his valley home.) Filled with beautiful sunrises and sunsets, waterfalls, streams and mountain ranges, the series is visually stunning. It also benefits from the music of Thom Pace, which helps to create the proper mood. The persona of the actor playing Grizzly Adams, Dan Haggerty, is also a real asset. With no previous acting experience, Haggerty nonetheless comes across as a man with a genuine love of animals.

That was primarily because until a couple of years before *Grizzly Adams* went on the air, Haggerty had been perfectly contented to work solely with animals. He had trained more than 30 African lions and assorted wolverines, eagles, elephants, chimpanzees, hawks, bears, wild boars and Siberian tigers. Haggerty had been working with wild creatures since he was 18 when he acquired his first pet, a two week old lion cub named Simba. At the time, he had been out of school for only a year, was married, had a small child, and another on the way. He also owned a half-dog, half-fox named Lady and lived in a decrepit cabin in the mountains north of Malibu. Buying the lion cub seemed crazy at the time. They had to hock their livingroom sofa to get the money. But Haggerty had been raised in military schools because his parents were separated. Not being allowed to possess a dog or cat like most other children, he fell in love with the lions he saw at the zoo and in circuses.[60]

Haggerty bought Simba at an animal park called Jungle Land in Thousand Oaks, California, with only a vague idea on how he could earn a living with the pet. While buying food for the lion, however, he met an English animal trainer named Stewart Raffill who owned an elephant, lion, bear, leopard and six chimpanzees that were used in television shows and movies. Impressed with the natural affection between Haggerty and Simba, Raffill asked the young man to join with him in supplying trained animals for the motion picture industry.

Raffill moved all his animals to Haggerty's mountain retreat and gave his new partner advanced instruction on the techniques of animal training. Soon the two were hired by Walt Disney to work their menagerie in such films as *Lt. Robin Crusoe, USN* (1966), with Dick Van Dyke, and *Monkeys, Go Home!* (1967), starring Yvette Mimieux. Raffill and Haggerty continued their successful collaboration through the sixties and into the seventies, working their animals in such films as *The Christmas Tree* (1969), starring William Holden, which featured nine wolves raised from cubs by Haggerty, and the Ron Ely *Tarzan* (1966-69) television series (made in Brazil with the entire menagerie).

Haggerty's acting talent lay dormant until 1974, when he was handling the tigers for a film called *Where the North Wind Blows*. (Raffill was the director and Haggerty's wife,

Diane, was the script supervisor.) Haggerty had to do a bit part in the film because the tigers would not listen to anyone else. Pat Frawley, the Schick razor millionaire who owned Sunn Classic Pictures, realized that Haggerty had that elusive quality called "screen presence" and decided to make a movie in which Haggerty would star. That film was *The Life and Times of Grizzly Adams.*

Haggerty played Adams with the tender loving care that had become his distinguishing characteristic as an animal trainer. His acting was strictly amateur, but it did not matter because he cavorted naturally with the animals, especially with Bozo, the grizzly bear who played Ben. Who could forget the memorable scene in which Bozo awakened Haggerty by pulling the blanket from his bed, chased him playfully through a meadow, then allowed Haggerty to chase her (Bozo was a female), equally playfully, finally rolling over on her back in the grass to allow Haggerty to scratch her belly. None of this was in the script. It just happened. This sequence was especially remarkable when one realizes that the grizzly bear is one of the most ferocious and unstable of animals. Even Bozo's four bear doubles could be utilized only when their movements were restrained by electrically charged wires. No previous grizzly had ever been tame enough to work without restraint in films or elsewhere. (Gentle Ben in the television series of that same name was a much more domesticatible black bear.)

Bozo was owned by Lloyd Beebe, a famous animal impresario in the state of Washington, who found her working in a circus. She was ten years old and had obviously been raised from a cub as someone's pet. In any case, the chemistry between Haggerty was such that Frawley's film, which cost a mere $140,000 to make, ended up earning over $65 million at the box office. Its Nielsen rating on television led to the weekly series of 37 hour-long episodes shown between February of 1977 and July of 1978. A two hour sequel, *The Capture of Grizzly Adams* was broadcast in 1982. Haggerty attributed the popularity of the show to the fact that

> People can relate to it and watch it 'cause it's so "comfortable." The show is so damn normal it's a change for viewers who are sick of screaming brakes, cars exploding and fight scenes. Pretty scenery and a couple of guys traipsing through the woods is a relief.[61]

Another fascinating aspect of *The Life and Times of Grizzly Adams* is that the simple characters and plots of the series were the products of a highly sophisticated data processing system. Charles E. Sellier, Jr., the articulate, young, Mormon producer of the series, used a complicated testing process to determine what the audience wanted. Operating on the verified assumption that *Grizzly Adams* was a "bimodal" show (appealing primarily to the young and the old), these were the two groups of viewers tested. (Testing the age group in the middle would not be the "real world" for that series.)[62] Sellier tested every element in the production and acquired a basic foundation of conclusions beginning with the bear:

> We tested a variety of bears, but our audiences preferred the awesome grizzly, with the big claws and the silver-tipped look. They had no fear of the grizzly because Grizzly Adams had no fear . . . the audience [also] delights in otters, chipmunks, beavers, skunks, but horses, surprisingly, test poorly—so instead of a horse, we use a burro in the series. [Furthermore], our audience dislikes animals being violent to humans and to other animals, and humans being violent to animals and other humans. They dislike hunting, either for sport or food— Grizzly can fish but he doesn't hunt and he doesn't eat meat. He's portrayed as one of the first vegetarians. He wears only homespun clothes, never any animal skins. It's not whim, it's all tested.[63]

When NBC instructed Sellier to put women into an episode (prompted, Sellier contended, by women executives at the network), he "tested" the idea and got a sharply negative reaction. *Grizzly*'s audience did not want any women in the wilderness. (An Indian and a 12 year old boy were used in the episode instead of women.) Visual aspects of the show also fell under Sellier's close scrutiny:

> Our audience likes waterfalls, pretty vistas and high mountain ridges, preferably with actors and animals as part of the scene. They dislike snow, except at Christmas. What they like is eternal summer in the primeval, womanless wilderness.[64]

Dan Haggerty, however, differed sharply with Sellier's methods, as well as his conclusions:

> People change, the testing doesn't always hold up. I'd like more growth, more pizazz. Isn't it logical that Adams would fall in love with something other than that damned bear? What would be more logical for a mountain man than to love an Indian woman? But they say it wouldn't test.[65]

Most of the filming for *Grizzly Adams* was done at Park City, Utah, a popular ski resort about thirty miles from Salt Lake City, although some location work was done at Payson, Arizona. Critics seemed most impressed with this setting. Robert MacKenzie wrote in *TV Guide* (May 28, 1977):

> ... it might touch a wistful spot in harassed grownups who yearn for a simpler life. It's good family viewing with an almost total absence of violence and not many situations that would frighten a child.

Furthermore, each episode contained a pretty valid moral lesson. In one, Grizzly pointed out, "If yuh live with nature and not against her, she'll do an awful lot for yuh." In another, a jittery traveling salesman (well-played by *F Troop*'s Ken Berry) who had stolen a sack of money was taught by Grizzly's wholesome example that the best things in life are free.

For the record, the real Grizzly Adams was considerably less altruistic than his television counterpart. Having deserted his wife and children, he spent much of his time hunting and killing animals and capturing others for zoos. The real Ben died in a zoo that Adams himself had opened in San Francisco in the 1850s. Adams died while on tour with P.T. Barnum in 1860.[66]

From Cheyenne Bodie to Grizzly Adams, they roamed the video range alone, the most popular type of Western television hero. Indeed, at one time there were so many of them that one wonders why they did not keep bumping into each other. There is, of course, something basically heroic about one man standing alone against all manner of adversaries—nature, the elements, villainy—that appeals to young and old alike.

Several loners of some popularity and significance have not been included in this discussion. Kwai Chang Caine of *Kung Fu* merits a chapter of his own (see Chapter XIV) and Paladin of *Have Gun, Will Travel* and Josh Randall of *Wanted: Dead or Alive* were prototypes of a new kind of Western figure—the antihero.

VI. Bounty Hunters, Gamblers and Hired Guns

THE ANTIHERO IN
THE TELEVISION WESTERN

By the fall of 1957 the television Western craze was in full swing with 18 "horse operas" scheduled during prime time viewing hours. Virtually every show featured a stalwart hero who possessed exceptional courage, rugged individualism, lofty moral principles, expert marksmanship, unflinching honesty and commendable generosity. In addition, he usually wore a white hat and more often than not rode a trusty white steed.

Two of the Westerns that debuted that season broke the mold of the traditional cowboy hero, introducing central characters who were guided more by their own self-interest than by any "mythical code of the West." The *Maverick* brothers, who would rather run than fight, were professional con-men and gamblers. Paladin, whose business cards read "*Have Gun Will Travel*," was a professional gunfighter who sold his services to the highest bidder. Joining them at the top of the Nielsen ratings one season later was bounty hunter Josh Randall, who in *Wanted: Dead or Alive* seemed to be less interested in upholding the law than in collecting a sizable reward for his efforts. Thus did the antihero come to television's make-believe West—in the guise of gamblers, hired guns and bounty hunters.

The Maverick brothers, Bret and Bart, were everything traditional heroes were not. They were sneaky, lazy, interested more in money than in honor, and exceedingly slow with a six-gun. In Bart's words, "I've got a brother who can outdraw me anytime he wants to, and he's known as the second-slowest gun in the West" ("A Tale of Three Cities"). The name of the show (and the family name of the leading characters) was taken from a term used by cowhands to describe an unbranded steer, which in turn came from a rugged cattleman named S.A. Maverick who lived from 1803 to 1872, refused to brand his steers and was famous for his outspoken independence. Series creator and producer Roy Huggins later explained:

> What we set out to do was create a character that deliberately broke all the rules of the traditional Western hero. He's a little bit of a coward, he's not solemn, he's greedy, and not above cheating a little. He's indifferent to the problems of other people. He's something of a gentle grafter.[1]

233

Bret Maverick was a self-professed coward. In one episode he declined the office of sheriff by proclaiming, "I'm unreliable. I'm a terrible shot. And I mean this most sincerely.... I have been, for as long as I can remember, a coward" ("The Sheriff of Duck 'n' Shoot"). And he was decidedly unsettled if someone implied that deep down he was a man with moral principles. "Maverick, I guess you're about the only man in the world who'd be insulted if somebody called you a good man," says Waco. "Not insulted— embarrassed," replies Bret ("The Saga of Waco Williams"). It was, in fact, a family tradition to avoid even the appearance of heroism. When Cousin Beau accidentally becomes a hero in the Civil War, Pappy exiles the "white sheep" of the family to England until he mends his ways. Five years later Beau returns to America and is met by Bart, who demands an explanation of his war record ("The Bundle from Britain").

Beau explains that he was in the habit of slipping through the Union lines to play poker with a certain Yankee general who was a much better strategist on the battlefield than at the poker table. One night the general lost all his money and threw down his cards in exasperation, exclaiming, "I give up!" Unfortunately at that very moment the general's tent was being surrounded by Confederate troops who had taken the camp by surprise, and the officer who overheard the general's words declared Beau a hero. Believing it to be more sensible to accept a medal than tell the truth and risk a court-martial, Beau took the medal. Bart is satisfied with this explanation and Beau is accepted back into the family.[2]

In every episode the viewer could be certain that when it came time for a showdown, the Mavericks would try to "talk" their way out of a jam, and, failing in that, they would slip quietly out of town—thus following another of their Pappy's famous axioms, "He who fights and runs away, lives to run away another day" ("Greenbacks Unlimited"). They also possessed other vices. Although they were usually honest in poker, they loved to "cheat a cheater." As Bret would say, "No one is easier to win from than a cardshark, if you know his twist." They had learned from their father, a retired Mississippi River gambler, a hatred for cheaters and a respect for honesty in gambling. They were not, however, above cheating each other, as in "Maverick and Juliet," where Bret and Bart are pitted against each other in a poker game to decide an ongoing feud between two families. To complicate matters, each brother is threatened with death if he loses.

Revenge, long a common motive for Western heroes, is another aspect of the traditional code that is disdained by the Mavericks. In an early episode called "A Fellow's Brother" (originally entitled "The Code" by the author Herman Epstein), Bret is challenged to a gunfight by a man who claims Bret killed his brother. "Man's brother gets gunned, he's got to do something about it...." Bret throws him off his trail by claiming that it must have been Bart that shot his brother.

When Bret later receives a telegram saying that his brother has been killed, everyone in town expects him to seek vengeance. "Man's got to avenge his brother's death! It's the brotherly thing to do." Bret knows the report is a mistake since Bart was nowhere near the town in which he was supposed to have been killed. Still, the alleged gunman arrives in town and tries to kill Bret in "self-defense." At that exact moment a mysterious stranger shows up and shoots the first gunman for killing *his* brother. When Bart is brought in for another crime and locked in jail, Bret makes his getaway. So much for brotherly love and "the code" of Western heroes on *Maverick*. Marion Hargrove, who wrote several *Maverick* scripts, described the series as "the sassiest and most freewheeling horse opera on the air":

> As Western heroes go, Maverick is singularly unheroic. He abhors gunplay.... On the
> rare occasions when he is forced to stand up and shoot it out with the villain, he survives only

through skulduggery or dumb luck. In the face of danger, Maverick quite sensibly tries to sneak away. There are only five things that can persuade him to come to the aid of a damsel in distress: greed, libido, curiosity, anger or self-preservation. There are times he has said "when a man must rise above principle..."

Maverick is not only no braver than the average man in his audience; he is quite often no smarter. He can be bamboozled or robbed by his best friend or his own brother or almost any passing female...

Disappointment and even indignity are commonplace in Maverick's life. He is the one Western hero who never knows at the beginning of the picture how it is going to turn out in the end. Actually there are two Maverick brothers ... [who usually] end up deflated, derided, dead-broke or perhaps tied hand and foot in the middle of nowhere.[3]

Bret and Bart supported their gambling habits and expensive tastes with clever schemes and con games. Rather than devoting their energies to helping their fellow man like most other respectable Western heroes, the Mavericks would rather fleece them. They occasionally worked to perfection as a team. In "A Shady Deal at Sunny Acres," Bret wins a large sum of money. He goes to the bank after it has closed, sees a light on, and knocks on the window. The banker, Honest John Bates (played by John Dehner), allows him to come in and make the deposit. The following morning when Bret goes to the bank to pick up his money, Honest John pretends never to have met him before. It is clearly a swindle. So brother Bart is invited in and with the help of a group of likable scoundrels from previous episodes, including Dandy Jim Buckley (Efrem Zimbalist, Jr.), Gentleman Jack Darby (Richard Long), Big Mike McComb (Leo Gordon), and Samantha Crawford (Diane Brewster), carries out a successful "sting" on the banker to get back Bret's money. Throughout most of the episode Bret sits on the front veranda of the hotel simply whittling on a stick and proclaiming to all who inquire that he is "working" on a way to get his money back from Honest John (who has already been taken in by Bart).

One of the most important distinctions of *Maverick*, and the major contribution of the series to a genre that was rapidly becoming overcrowded, was its humor, a quality notably absent in most Westerns. *Maverick* refused to take itself too seriously and its efforts at tongue-in-cheek comedy proved to be, in the words of one critic, "a breath of fresh air in an increasingly self-righteous environment."[4] Creator Huggins developed a set of instructions to prospective script writers entitled "A Ten-Point Guide to Happiness While Writing or Directing a *Maverick*" which emphasized this aspect of the show.

Describing Maverick as the "original *dis*organization man," whose "primary motivation" is that "ancient and most noble of motives: the profit motive," Huggins urges writers and directors to shun the "comfort and security" of clichés and "live dangerously." He also points out that Maverick's schemes are "seldom grandiose" because of his "essential indolence." Furthermore, the "heavies" on Maverick are usually likable rogues because they are "always beloved to someone."

Although Maverick's travels sometimes *appear* to be aimless, they never are because "he always has an objective in view: his pockets and yours"—unless, of course, he is "merely fleeing from some heroic enterprise." Huggins further explains that Maverick is "cautious" rather than "cowardly" ("certainly a more kindly" description), and not really a "gambler" because "in his hands poker is not a game of chance." Finally, the guiding principle of all writers should be Huggins' belief that:

> In the traditional Western story the situation is always serious but never hopeless. In a "Maverick" story the situation is always hopeless but never serious.[5]

Several of the funniest and best remembered episodes of the series were actually spoofs of other popular television shows, especially Westerns like *Gunsmoke*. In an

James Garner began a long and successful career as television's Bret Maverick.

episode entitled "Gunshy," Bret outwits Marshal Mort Dooley; his lame deputy, Clyde Deffendorfer; his dancehall girlfriend, Amy; and Doc Stukey. In a wild parody of *Bonanza* called "Three Queens Full" the leading characters are Joe Wheelwright and his three sons, Moose, Henry and Small Paul, owners of the vast Subrosa Ranch. There were also satires of other popular television shows such as *Dragnet*, in which Bret turns in a Joe Friday–like deadpan narration, and *The Untouchables*, where Lancelot Vest comes west to battle Frank Nifty, Captain Scarface, Slugs Moran and Jake Gooseneck. It is easy to concur with the conclusion of television historian John Javna that because *Maverick* taught the television establishment that America had a sense of the ridiculous about its heroes, "its influence is still visible thirty years later."[6]

Actually for the first few episodes, *Maverick* was a fairly straight series about a dapper cardshark and his adventures in the West. Then a bored scriptwriter decided that James Garner had "beady eyes" and wrote into a script "Maverick looks at him with beady little eyes." Garner thought it was hilarious and played the whole scene for laughs. It worked and soon the entire series had become satirical in nature. In fact, brother Bart (Jack Kelly) was added to the cast in November 1957 (two months into the season), to keep the stories from straying too far from the traditional Western mold.[7]

Another unique aspect of *Maverick* was its determined effort to avoid the usual Western plots, sometimes even adapting stories from literary classics. Huggins, a phi beta kappa, found ideas for stories in some pretty unlikely places: episodes were based on Shakespeare's *Othello*, *The Wrecker* by Robert Louis Stevenson, Euripedes's *Alcestis*, Aristophanes's *Lysistrata*, *A Tale of Two Cities* by Charles Dickens, Guy de Maupassant's "Boule de Suif" and Perceval Christopher Wren's *Beau Geste*.[8] (One episode was even based on Walter Brennan's hit record "Dutchman's Gold.") Generally, however, a "formula" was followed: "A dishonest person or crook tries to use Maverick for an illegitimate purpose only to be outwitted and see justice done in the end. The Mavericks will readily use the con-man devices they know so well, whether in handling cards or verbal trickery, to serve a worthy cause...."[9] Most stories involved an interesting swindle, scheme or method of cheating.

Land scandals, fleecings over railroad rights and mining frauds were used. For instance, penny mining stocks were popular at the time and were sold all over the world through large exchanges in Denver, Reno, Carson City, San Francisco and every other major city of the West. Swindles were apparently so common that at one point the federal government enacted a special prohibition against fraud by mail. Racetrack stories were also popular with *Maverick* writers. Great racetracks existed during the 1870s from Missouri and Kansas west to Montana and Colorado. Quarter horses were at the height of their popularity. One of the most common methods of cheating in quarter horse races was to disguise a thoroughbred as a quarter horse and enter him in a race. There were also fabulous real characters from out of the pages of American history that could be used as the focal point for a racetrack episode like Pittsburgh Phil, Yellow Kid Weil, Henry Fink, Bet-a-Million Gates, Colonel Bradley and a dozen or so others. It was this kind of material that made *Maverick* unique—and memorable.

Another key ingredient of the series was its star, James Garner. Garner, although appearing to possess the characteristics of the standard hero (he was six feet, three inches tall with a determined gaze, youthful vigor and good looks), was actually typecast. "I'm playing me," the actor admitted. "Bret Maverick is lazy: I'm lazy. And I *like* being lazy."[10] James Garner was born James Baumgarner in Norman, Oklahoma, on April 7, 1928. When he was a teenager, his family moved to Hollywood where Jim dropped out of school at 16. He worked for a while at odd jobs including gas station attendant, oil field worker, swimwear model and carpet layer (for his dad's business). Then he was inducted into the army and saw 14 months of combat as an infantryman in Korea.

After his discharge in 1952 a friend got him a nonspeaking role (as one of the judges) in the stage production of *The Caine Mutiny Court Martial*. This led to small parts on television and ultimately a contract with Warner Bros. after being spotted by Richard Bare, a Warner director, in a restaurant bar. The studio was just getting into television production and although they cast him in small roles in such minor films as *Toward the Unknown* (1956) and *Shoot-out at Medicine Bend* (1957), it was in television that Garner was given his first real opportunity to act. He appeared as a cavalry lieutenant in the premier episode of *Cheyenne* ("Mountain Fortress") and again the next season as a memorable villain in "War Party." He also made several appearances on Warners' dramatic anthology series *Conflict* ("The Man from 1997," "Girl on a Subway").

By 1957 (the same year Garner made his first quality film as Marlon Brando's officer buddy in *Sayonara*), Warner Bros. were ready to star him in their new Western, *Maverick*. One of Garner's qualifications for the role, he later said, came from the fact that his closest pal during the Korean War had been a Reno blackjack dealer. "He taught me quite a few things—and now I don't need a stand-in to do card tricks on *Maverick*. I do my own."[11]

The series became a hit and Garner became a major star. However, Garner (like Clint Walker and others) was unhappy with what he considered to be a very one-sided contract, which he had signed years before when he was a virtual unknown. After lengthy behind the scenes bickering he walked off the series in 1960 at the end of the third season. (One original Garner-Kelly episode, "The Maverick Line," was broadcast during the fourth season and several episodes were repeated during the final season.) Later, producer-writer Roy Huggins explained:

> Up to 1960 he was locked into a contract which paid him only $500 a week to start and a top salary of $1,250 (after the show was an established hit).... "Maverick" brought in over $8 million. He wanted out ... he outfoxed their lawyers and won his freedom.[12]

Garner elaborated in a subsequent interview:

> ... before I escaped "Maverick" and what I call the "Warners' Penitentiary" ... I was offered $7,500 to appear on Pat Boone's show. But Warners wouldn't allow it. They owned me then. I never forgot what they did to me.[13]

While an official of the Actors Guild, Garner later discovered that actors were getting little or no pay for television residuals:

> ... and soon we had legislation that changed all of that, and about thirty-five Warners players collected a bundle.... We [also] took care of the matter of WB contractees being forced to appear at rodeos, telethons, and peanut-pushing contests for free. Now the price went up to more than $500 per performer.[14]

During the sixties Garner tried to parlay his television success into movie stardom. Although he appeared in several excellent films (including *The Great Escape*, 1963, and *The Americanization of Emily*, 1964), his charisma was not as well suited to the large screen. In 1971 he returned to television in a role that was quite similar to that of Bret Maverick—the title character in *Nichols*. *Nichols* is reportedly Garner's favorite television series to date. Set in Nichols, Arizona, in 1914, a town founded by Nichols' ancestors, Garner plays an army veteran who is pressured into becoming sheriff. Now Nichols' real aim in life is to get rich with as little work as possible (shades of Maverick!) and he dreams up all kinds of schemes to achieve that end. He hates violence and does not even carry a gun, but sometimes he has to trash a bad guy or two. The series had an interesting early twentieth century Western setting and Nichols utilized a motorcycle and an automobile rather than a horse for his transportation. Unfortunately, although the series was well received by most critics, it did not catch on with the public and was canceled after only one season (26 episodes). (Among the more interesting episodes are "Peanuts and Crackerjacks" about a baseball game, and "Fight of the Century," featuring a boxing match.)

In 1974, Garner finally made it big on the home screen with *The Rockford Files*, as a Maverick-like contemporary detective, Jim Rockford. The series ran for six seasons. This role earned Garner his first Emmy as "Best Actor in a Drama Series" (1977). Besides his appearances as Bret Maverick in the *Young Maverick* pilot (1978) and *Bret Maverick* (1981), Garner starred in a sit-com, *Man of the People* (1991) as a Maverick-type local politician. Meanwhile he was featured in a number of successful theatrical films, including *Murphy's Romance* (1985), which won him a Best Actor Oscar nomination, and several television films, including *Decoration Day* (1991), which earned him another Best Actor Emmy nomination. He also set up his own production company, Cherokee Productions (named, no doubt, because although Garner is mostly of German ancestry, he is proud of his part Native American Cherokee heritage). Cherokee Productions was responsible for two of Garner's most popular films, *Support Your Local Sheriff* (1969)

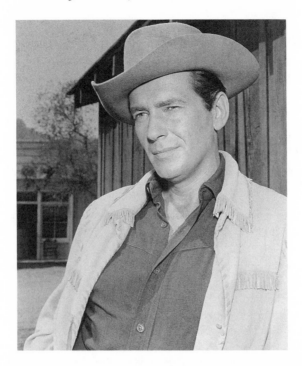

Jack Kelly was soon added to *Maverick*'s cast to play Bart, brother of Bret.

and *Support Your Local Gunfighter* (1971), both delightful send-ups of his Maverick character.

Jack Kelly, although a late addition to *Maverick*, fit in perfectly and many viewers seemed to think he and Garner really were brothers. They appeared together in several episodes before Bart was given his solo debut in "The Jeweled Gun." Bart, always willing to assist a beautiful woman, accepts the job of escorting Daisy Harris through the Badlands, unaware that she and her lover have already killed her real husband and plan to get rid of Bart next. Later, in "The Naked Gallows," Bart attempts to clear the name of a friend who had escaped from jail after being falsely accused of murder. These and the rest of Bart's solo appearances during the first season were introduced by brother Bret as narrator.

Women seemed to enjoy Kelly's sexy nature and he got many of the more romantic stories. Kelly protested that he too could handle comedic stories and eventually (especially after Garner's departure) he got more humorous storylines. Indeed, one of the funniest episodes of the entire series was the *Bonanza* spoof, featuring Bart, broadcast during the final season. Jack Kelly brought more show business experience to television than Garner. Born of actor parents and brother of the Oscar nominated Nancy Kelly (for *The Bad Seed*), he had stage and radio experience as a child in the thirties. (As a baby he had modeled for an Ivory Soap ad.) He made his film debut in B features during the late forties after returning from overseas military service. With the rise of television, Kelly appeared on several live dramatic anthologies, including *Studio One, Kraft Theatre, Philco Playhouse* and *Pepsi-Cola Playhouse* in the early fifties.

In 1955 he got a big break by landing the romantic lead in Warners' prime time soap, *King's Row*, which was based on the popular 1942 film. Kelly played Dr. Paris Mitchell, a hometown boy who returns to the small Midwestern town of King's Row at the turn of the century to set up a psychiatric practice. Unfortunately for Kelly the series, which alternated every third week with two other Warner Bros. series based on films, *Casablanca* and *Cheyenne*, was canceled after only seven episodes. At about the same time he played another physician on the syndicated *Dr. Hudson's Secret Journal*, but here his role was subordinate to that of John Howard. Although 78 episodes were filmed, the series did little to further Kelly's acting career.

Then Roy Huggins, who had produced *King's Row*, realized that *Maverick* needed "another good-looking, chicken-livered gambler" to meet the production schedule and remembered Kelly. Several other actors had been screened as possible costars with Garner, but Kelly seemed to fit the role much better than anyone else. According to executive producer William Or:

> We never made a whole test of Jack Kelly. We took him down, had him stand with Jim and improvise: chat back and forth and do a kind of improvisational scene. From that we cast him.[15]

After three seasons of playing second fiddle to Garner, Kelly's patience and conscientiousness paid off and he was given top billing. Kelly later took pride in his work as Bart Maverick and claimed that he "wouldn't have minded playing the role forever."[16] When the series ended he continued in television only as an occasional guest star on shows like *Bob Hope's Chrysler Theater*, *Batman*, *The Lucy Show*, *The Name of the Game*, *Alias Smith and Jones*, *Ironside*, and *Quincy*. He also made brief appearances in the *Young Maverick* pilot and the final episode of *Bret Maverick* ("The Hidalgo Thing"). During the seventies, he served a short stint as host of the daytime game show *Sale of the Century*. He also reprised the role of Bart Maverick in the memorable gambling sequence of Kenny Rogers' *The Gambler Returns: The Luck of the Draw* in 1991.

As far as character traits are concerned, Bret and Bart were virtually indistinguishable, both overtly claiming to be devout cowards and materialists who on various occasions might win, lose, spend, use, enjoy or even lust after money. They would spend their winnings as ostentatiously as possible on well-tailored suits and ruffled shirts, suites at the best hotels, and arrangements for elaborate confidence games.

Still, hidden away in a Maverick brother's heart was a small strain of altruism and courage. Although he would not engage in gratuitous bravery or obvious unselfishness, he could rise to the occasion and help a friend—when absolutely necessary. Indeed the Mavericks did occasionally display the stalwart qualities common to other heroes of the genre. In fact Huggins in his first draft description of the proposed series made clear that "the brothers would use their fists or even resort to a gun when words fail," to serve a *worthy* cause, and were "unable to resist a challenge, particularly a challenge to right a wrong."[17]

In the pilot episode, "War of the Silver Kings," Bret not only ends up leading independent miners against the deceitful and conniving Phineas King, a powerful silver magnate, but helps to rehabilitate an ex-judge turned alcoholic in the process. He also initiates a brutal fistfight against Big Mike McComb who has been hired to kill him. This was certainly not the stuff cowards are made of.

In another episode, "Stampede," Bret takes the place of a hillbilly boxer, Noah Perkins, on whom he has wagered a sizable bet, when Perkins backs out of his bout with the mighty Battling Kruger at the last minute. A week earlier the Maverick brothers had demonstrated a bit of uncharacteristic chivalry when they risked their lives to rescue the kidnapped daughter of an aristocrat. Their real motive was to gain an invitation from the aristocrat to travel on an elegant new steamship, which is loaded with wealthy, second-

The Maverick brothers—in a rare development—rush into action (James Garner leaps over Jack Kelly).

rate poker players. Thus, in each instance, the Maverick's "heroic" behavior is "excused" by making it appear that they were motivated solely by monetary considerations.

Beau, like his American cousins, could also exhibit non–"Maverick" behavior. In "The Town That Wasn't There," he passes up an opportunity to make $10,000 by selling a piece of land to the railroad. He explains, "My old uncle used to say there are things more important than money, but he'd never found one.... I guess for once Uncle Beau was wrong." It seems that Beau placed a higher priority on what is best for a town full of new friends he has made than on his personal self-interest. Later he reflects, "Ten thousand dollars. . . . If Uncle Beau knew about this he'd send me back to England for sure!"

Perhaps the motives of *Maverick* are best examined in "The Saga of Waco Williams," an episode that was, in effect, a wonderful spoof of the entire series. Not only does Bret save the life of a famous gunslinger (Waco Williams) in the opening scene, he watches over him during the entire story, even coming to his rescue when Waco is outnumbered seven to one by gunmen out to kill him. (This is the act of a real coward?) Bret is supposedly motivated by a desire for the $2500 reward money on the head of Waco's outlaw friend Blackie Dolan. At one point in the story Bret advises Waco as he prepares for a showdown with a notorious outlaw: "Your whole philosophy of life is wrong. Don't go out there. Come out the back with me." Later at the end of the story as he rides out of town, Bret turns to the camera and muses: "Now he did everything a man shouldn't do. But he's still alive. Looks like he'll be elected sheriff. I know he'll end up with the biggest ranch in the territory. I'm broke. Nobody even knows I'm leaving—or cares. Could I be wrong?"

When *Maverick* first appeared on ABC, September 22, 1957, it was only one of some 32 Westerns on television, and it was brashly pitted against the toughest competition on the air: Jack Benny, Ed Sullivan and Steve Allen. In a few weeks it had beaten all three in the ratings and by the second season had won over most critics. The *Variety* critic wrote (September 16, 1959):

> The essential elements of comedy and drama that made this Sunday night Western entry a success continue to be present. The fast-talking, slow-drawing brothers are the focal point of the various adventures that unfold in the usual tongue-in-cheek manner.

Maverick won an Emmy that year (1959) as Best Western Series.

When Garner left the series after the third season, Warner Bros. decided to replace him with the British-educated cousin Beauregard (namesake of his "Uncle Pappy"). To play Beau, Warner brought in one of their contract players, Roger Moore, from *The Alaskans*, which had just been canceled. London-born Moore had started acting at the Royal Academy of Arts while a student. He also had experience in plays like *Circle of Chalk* and *The Italian Strawhat* with the London Arts Theatre. After a stint in the British Army as an officer in the Guards Armored Division, Moore joined a repertory group and toured with *Miss Mabel*. This, in turn, let to his first film role, a bit part in *Trittie True*. His subsequent stage credits included *The Little Hut* and *Mr. Roberts*.

After gaining some experience in radio and television with the BBC, Moore moved to the United States, where he was given a small role in *Robert Montgomery Presents* just four days after his arrival. In 1954 he went to Hollywood and spent the next couple of years appearing in such films as *The Last Time I Saw Paris* (1954), *Interrupted Melody* (1955) and *The King's Thief* (1955). In 1957-58 he returned to Britain to star in *Ivanhoe* for Screen Gems. He made 39 episodes and then worked in two Warner Bros. pictures, *The Miracle* (1959) and *Rachel Cade* (1960). Soon thereafter Moore appeared in an episode of *Maverick* with Garner and Kelly entitled "The Rivals." One of the more amusing episodes in the series (and based on Sheridan's classic *Rivals*), it provided Moore with a major television role as a handsome young millionaire, Jack Vandergelt, who exchanges identities with Bret so that he can win the hand of a young lady who despises wealthy young men. The chemistry between Moore and Garner was excellent and it would have been fun to see Moore and Garner paired together in more episodes. Instead, Moore was offered one of the leads in Warners' new series, *The Alaskans*.

At first Moore refused, but meanwhile he watched an *Alfred Hitchcock Presents*

In *Maverick*'s final season Robert Colbert (far right) appeared (in two episodes) as brother Brent, while Roger Moore (center) continued as cousin Beau and Jack Kelly as brother Bart.

episode entitled "The Avon Emeralds" which he had filmed earlier. After seeing the show, which he felt was "unbelievably bad," he changed his mind about doing *The Alaskans*. He felt he should be under the protection of a major studio and signed a seven year contract with Warner Bros. and accepted the role of Silky Harris on *The Alaskans*. Silky was a smooth-talking confidence man who lived by his wits "talking himself into and out of trouble with equal ease." He felt there was a better way to get gold than digging for it. Still he was basically a decent sort underneath this rather sleazy exterior and upon occasion was known to actually risk his own life to save that of others. (Just the perfect sort of chap to play a Maverick.)

Unfortunately Beau and Bart are rarely teamed up, although the episode that launched *Maverick*'s fourth season, "The Bundle from Britain," and Beau's first episode, which includes a brief, but hilarious, send-up of *My Fair Lady*, and "Last Wire from Stop Gap," about a scheme to divert all the money in town into a very special safe, are exceptions. Moore does demonstrate his flair for Maverick-style comedy in several very funny episodes: "The Town That Wasn't There," where Beau convinces the townspeople of Silver Hill to literally move their town to a sheep ranch and back again in order to make an unprincipled railroad agent pay them a fair price for their land; "Bolt from the Blue," where Beau is almost lynched by an angry mob that mistakes him for a horse thief, and shot by the sister of a woman she thinks he left standing at the altar (Will Hutchins is featured as a Sugarfoot-type lawyer); and "Family Pride," where Beau is swindled by two con-artists and a pretty woman (whose grandmother turns out to have been a Maverick).

Beau lasted one season. His character was both believable and entertaining, but the show was sliding in the ratings and Moore was replaced by an unknown actor in a new role. For the next couple of years Moore played guest shots on other Warner Bros. shows like *77 Sunset Strip* ("Tiger by the Tail") and *The Roaring Twenties* ("Right Off the Boat"). In 1963 Moore took on his best remembered television role, that of Simon Templar in *The Saint* for five seasons and 114 episodes. This was followed by *The Persuaders* (1971–1977), in which Moore costarred with Tony Curtis in a short-lived action-adventure series. It was undoubtedly as James Bond that Roger Moore made his most lasting mark on American popular culture. Succeeding Sean Connery as agent 007 in the highly successful film series, he appeared in seven Bond films from *Live and Let Die* (1973) to *A View to a Kill* (1985). Moore chose to walk away from the role but it is possible that he (like Connery before him) might decide to return at some future date.

For *Maverick*'s final season (1961-62) the studio created yet another Maverick (younger brother—Brent—who had never before been mentioned). He just arrives on a stage pulling into the town of Sunburst ("The Forbidden City"). He physically looks somewhat like Garner and is dressed almost exactly as Bret dressed. The dialogue even sounds the same, but Robert Colbert, who was cast in the part, just did not have Garner's charisma and only appeared in two episodes. (Colbert later got a steady job playing Stuart Brooks on the popular daytime soap, *The Young and Restless*, from 1973 to 1983.)

There were two attempts to revive the *Maverick* formula long after Bart and his cronies had ridden off into the sunset on the last broadcast of the original series. The first, *Young Maverick* (1979-80), was introduced by a well-received made-for-television film, *The New Maverick*, which starred James Garner as Bret. The film, about some stolen government guns, captures the old Maverick style perfectly and is lots of fun. Charles Frank is featured as cousin Beau's son Ben and Jack Kelly makes a brief appearance as Bart in the last ten minutes. Frank is likable enough as Ben and exhibits those traditional Maverick traits of gambling as a profession, fleeing in preference to fighting and taking advantage of any honorable situation, but the film belongs to Garner.

However, Ben is the only Maverick appearing in the series and although there is an attempt to duplicate the con-game competition so characteristic of the original series, it just does not come off. Frank's real-life wife, Susan Blanchard, was cast as Neil McGarrahan, who is just as cunning and clever as Ben and is always trying to outwit him for financial gain (much like Samantha Crawford on the original *Maverick*). She is a strong, independent woman who challenges Ben as an equal and often gets the better of him. There is also an annoying marshal (played by veteran actor John Dehner) who is constantly harassing them, convinced that they are con-artists and determined to catch them in the act.

Charles Frank seemed right for the role of Ben, having grown up in the West. He learned to ride as a small boy and won his first horse show ribbon when he was only 4. He went East for his schooling and theatrical experience, but returned to the West Coast to appear in *Riding High* (1977), the pilot for a series based on the film *Hearts of the Golden West*, and *The Chisholms* (miniseries, 1979). The critics liked Frank as *Young Maverick*. Cleveland Amory wrote in *TV Guide*, "Charles is not as funny as Garner but funnier than Kelly and better looking than either." Still, the series was canceled before it had a chance to prove itself (after only eight episodes), because of poor ratings.

In October 1981, NBC-TV caught everyone by surprise by announcing that James Garner would return to NBC in an updated *Maverick* series. Young Brandon Tartikoff,

An older James Garner returned to the video range in 1981 as Bret Maverick in an attempt to revive that popular character.

president of NBC Entertainment, defended the network's decision to revive the series that had been so popular (on ABC) twenty years earlier by stating that

> "Maverick" was not a Western in the usual sense because it always maintained a contemporary attitude in its approach to comedy and drama. Besides, we're buying a known quantity—and Garner is the ultimate TV actor. We're not scared about Westerns. Western movies have done well for us.[18]

Actually the idea to revive *Maverick* was largely Garner's himself. He explained in an interview later:

> I started thinking what Bret would be like twenty years later and what the series would look like updated from the 1860s to the 1880s.... I couldn't find anything I wanted to do more and I realized that there were two generations who'd grown up never having seen me in the role, so I thought, why not? Let's do it ... and the minute I voiced that, everybody seemed to say "Hooray! Wonderful!" and we soon couldn't get our minds on anything but "Maverick."[19]

Garner had but one stipulation. He could not carry the entire show himself. The new version would need plenty of other characters. He simply was not physically able to be on screen one hour every week after six grueling years on *The Rockford Files*. So seven regular major characters were incorporated into the pilot.

The series debuted on December 1, 1981, with a two hour film entitled *The Lazy Ace*. It opens with Bret arriving in the sleepy town of Sweetwater, Arizona, to participate in the biggest poker game of his life (along with old pal Doc Holliday and other assorted, notorious card sharks). By the time the game is over, Bret has won over $100,000 in cash and one-half interest in the Red Ox saloon. He decides to use half of his winnings to buy a small ranch outside of town and settle down. Of course, complications arise when the bank is robbed and Bret has to track the thieves with the help of a self-styled Indian guide named Philo Sandine (played by *Rockford Files* alumnus Stuart Margolin, who also directed the pilto film), who was really just another con-artist; the sheriff Tom Guthrie (Ed Bruce), who was even then being voted out of office; the emancipated feisty newspaper editor Mary Lou Springer (Darleen Carr); and her young, well-meaning assistant Rodney Catlow (David Knell). Other regulars in the series included cranky, irascible Cy Whittaker, foreman of the Lazy Ace; newly-elected Sheriff, Mitchell Dowd (John Shearin) who struggled to bring "civilization" to Sweetwater with the help of his stupid deputy; and Elijah Crowe (Ramon Bieri), the opportunistic and manipulative banker. Minor roles included Jack the bartender (played by Garner's real-life brother, Jack) and the dishonest house dealer at the Red Ox, Shifty Delgado (played by longtime Garner pal Luis Delgado).

The series had an appropriate new theme song that is "sung" over the credits in the pilot by Garner himself and in the remaining episodes by colyricist Ed Bruce. It melodically relates the story of a wandering gambler who has tired of his lonely life style and has decided to settle down. Brooks and Marsh assess the series as presenting

> . . . a more mature, less adventure-some Bret Maverick than the one who had wandered from town to town in search of poker games and excitement. The sense of humor and friendliness were still there, but Bret had become a solid citizen and fulltime resident of a community trying to shed its untamed rural image.[20]

Castleman and Podrazik see the series as working, for the most part, "very well":

> . . . Garner is relaxed and comfortable as ever in the role, and he has a good supporting cast and some excellent writing to see him through. . . .
> Perhaps the only major flaw with the series is that the writers deal Bret Maverick too good a hand. He always seems to be working on some con game (in contrast to the original series, when he pulled such stunts only when necessary). The man obviously has too much time on his hands and no one to keep him in line.[21]

Still, Bret is willing to lend a helping hand to others in need when the occasion arises (even Billy the Kid) because he knows that "things are not always what they seem" (according to "The Ballad of Bret Maverick"). Reviews of the series were mixed. Robert Mackenzie wrote in the January 23, 1982, issue of *TV Guide*:

> . . . The character he plays is pretty much the same . . . an easy-natured, slightly insolent charmer with a wry sense of humor and a sensible aversion to violence who reluctantly shoulders somebody else's troubles, grumbling and griping all the while . . .
> . . . The role becomes the man . . . Garner is heavier these days and slower on his feet. But his delivery of a line is as dryly chipper as ever.

On the other hand, less than a month later Cecil Smith of the *Los Angeles Times* said:

> "Bret Maverick" . . . seems like just a nice, easy amusing show, something to kill an hour with if there's nothing better on—pleasant and forgettable. We thought the old "Maverick" was hell on wheels . . . were we so naive?[22]

Jack Kelly was asked to appear in what turned out to be the final episode of *Bret Maverick* ("The Hidalgo Thing"). It was strictly an "eighteen second" cameo and Kelly did it only at the personal urging of Garner. "We've written ourselves into a tunnel," he explained in a phone call, "and Brother Bart is the only way out." Kelly was later highly critical of the show:

> ... There were only about three lines in the entire scene—it was mostly reaction. We
> looked at each other, recognized each other. I was in a carpetbagger's outfit and he was play-
> ing some kind of phony CPA on a swindle. I didn't like the play because it wasn't the essence
> of "Maverick." He was a ... thief. He was providing scams to make a living out of scams.
> The real Maverick *never* did that![23]

About this time Roy Huggins, *Maverick*'s original producer, was approached to
come and help revise (and, it was hoped, save) the series. Huggins' response to his agent
helps explain what went wrong with *Bret Maverick*:

> ... First of all they're not doing "Maverick" ... the series is located in one town. All
> in one place ... I don't see how I could save that show. I'd have to go back to the original
> concept. "Maverick" was a wanderer and I don't know how to say this, because I don't want
> to hurt Jim's feelings.[24]

Huggins never had to talk to Garner about the show because to almost everyone's
surprise, it was canceled three days later. Alan Shayne, president of Warner Bros. television who was "shocked" and "crushed," declared that *Bret Maverick* was NBC's seventh highest ranked show and that Garner was the eighth (out of 490) most popular star
in the country.[25] Perhaps, as Castleman and Podrazik believe, it was a "borderline" case
that would probably have been renewed a decade later "or just slid to some cable network."[26]

Had Maverick played his last confidence game, won his last big poker pot, pulled
his last boot or shirt-sleeve derringer and ambled (or ridden) off into the setting sun of
the video range? Garner, Kelly and the others certainly could be content with the
knowledge that they had helped to make television history with their fresh approach to
the Western genre. They had introduced a Western hero who did not take himself (or
anyone else, for that matter) too seriously—the television West's first and most likable
antihero. Anyway as old Pappy would undoubtedly have said, "No use crying over spilled
milk; it could have been whiskey."

However, in 1994 a theatrical film version of *Maverick* was released by Warner Bros.
starring the popular Australian actor Mel Gibson as Bret and James Garner as U.S. Marshal Zane Cooper. (A delightful twist ending in which Cooper is revealed to be Bret's
Pappy pleased series fans.) Two time Academy Award winner Jodie Foster costarred as
Annabelle Bransford (written in the mold of feminine con-artist Samatha Crawford) and
a host of Western movie and television stars had cameo roles including Doug McClure,
Robert Fuller, Bill Williams, Will Hutchins, William Smith and Paul Brinegar. The film
did well at the box office and there was talk of a sequel—maybe *Maverick* had not played
his last card yet. In any case, as Ed Robertson says in his excellent study, *Maverick, Legend
of the West*:

> "Maverick" has burned itself indelibly into the hearts and minds of its followers in a way
> few television series can. "Maverick" wasn't just a popular TV show about "the legend of the
> West," as the theme song proclaimed. "Maverick" becomes a legend unto itself.[27]

Another popular Western figure rode onto the television screen in the fall of 1957.
He, like Maverick, was part hero, part antihero. Unlike *Maverick*, however, there was very
little humor in *Have Gun, Will Travel*. A professional gunman, Paladin was a mercenary
who sold his services to almost anyone who could afford them, but he was far from your
average illiterate, unrefined gunslinger. This Western soldier of fortune was decidedly
different. Paladin was definitely a good guy, but defying Western custom, he dressed all
in black. Rather than being a crusader for justice, Paladin performed many of his "good
deeds" because he got paid for them. He was a gentleman of culture, refinement and

impeccable taste who resided in elegance in a fine San Francisco hotel. He preferred gourmet food to chuck wagon vittles and frequently quoted from the classics, not homespun homilies. This may have been because he was college-educated, having attended West Point in pursuit of a military career.

In addition to his black outfit, Paladin had two other distinguishing trademarks: a black leather holster that bore the symbol of a white chess knight (also known as a paladin), and a calling card that read, "Have Gun, Will Travel. Wire Paladin, San Francisco." Paladin clearly functioned within the Western genre, but managed to break the genre's stereotypes and he quickly became television's most interesting nonconformist. Nobody "owned" him. In fact Paladin often displayed open contempt for the rich people who invariably hired him. Another unique characteristic Paladin exhibited was patience. He was one of the few Western types who took the time to think things over before taking action.

Have Gun, Will Travel was endowed with action and interesting plots by such distinguished writers as Sam Peckinpah. Paladin was called upon to do an astonishing variety of things in pursuit of justice—from dashing across the desert on a camel to bargaining with an Armenian vintner for his daughter's dowry on behalf of a bashful Texan. A camel, cast off by the U.S. Army after they have attempted unsuccessfully to adapt them for use in the American West, figures prominently in "The Great Mojave Chase." In "High Wire," Paladin helps a former high wire artist, who has become an alcoholic, find the courage to walk a wire across a deep ravine. He tutors a shy, uneducated cowboy (played by young Charles Bronson) in the social graces so that he may woo and win a beautiful and cultured young woman with whom he has fallen in love, in "The Gentleman."

Even the music on *Have Gun, Will Travel* was first class. The producers, wishing to avoid the twangy guitars and catchy ballads of other television cowboys, hired award winning composer Bernard Herrmann to write the main title theme and the score for the pilot. Typically Herrmann delivered the unexpected. Suddenly, Paladin appears on the screen to the accompaniment of a series of violent four note bursts of brass and percussion.[28] Herrmann's music for the pilot was reused for scoring many episodes of the series until its last new broadcast in 1963. The opening refrain used over the establishing shots of the swank Carlton Hotel in San Francisco was Herrmann's, as was the strain (a variation on the main theme) used for the inevitable appearance of Paladin's business card. Herrmann's end title music was only played the first year.

The decision was made to put a conventional theme song, one that could be merchandized, over the credits at the end of the program. The "Ballad of Paladin" was written by Johnny Western, Sam Rolfe and Boone himself and sung by Western. It became a hit single in the early sixties and certainly conveyed the proper image for the show— that of a wandering "soldier of fortune" in a "savage land."

Richard Boone, a distant relative of Daniel Boone, was an appropriate choice for the role of Paladin. At six feet, two inches, Boone was a former ordinance man in the U.S. Navy who was right at home working with Paladin's belt derringer, six-shooter, saddle rifle, and self-styled machine gun. He played the role with relish, explaining that "he's an intriguing sort of a guy with an air of mystery about him . . . he's no mere observer. He's a participant who lives like a king with a need to make the most of every moment, whether he's drinking a glass of wine or hunting somebody down."[29] Richard Gehman wrote in *TV Guide* that "few actors are so perfectly cast for their roles. Paladin . . . is a cultured, sophisticated and sensitive man who also is a man of action and so is Boone."[30]

Opposite: **Richard Boone riding the video range as Paladin in** *Have Gun, Will Travel.*

Time Magazine (March 30, 1959) called Boone "perhaps the only television gunslinger who is worth his whiskey as an all-around actor...."

Born in Los Angeles in 1917, the second of three children, Boone had come from a family noted for its eccentricities. His grandfather, who owned 27 race horses and bore the improbable name of Bower Boone, was a San Francisco gold miner who began the family tradition of flamboyance. (He was said to have bought a silk shirt in the morning and thrown it away at night.)[31] Boone's father Kirk, was a lawyer, however, who had worked his way up the corporate ladder to become chief counsel of the General Petroleum Company in Los Angeles. Richard grew up to be an intense, sensitive youth, with an extraordinarily impulsive streak. He managed to embroil himself in enough trouble to get thrown out of Stanford University where he was enrolled in the liberal arts program majoring in drama. While a student, Boone held the amateur light-heavyweight boxing championship for two years (1936 and 1937). Then he went through a long period of soul-searching while earning a living as a roustabout and truck driver in the Southern California oil fields. He pursued dramatic studies at night at the Art Students League in Los Angeles. After an impulsive marriage, Boone helped make ends meet by working, in turn, as a bouncer, an adobe bricklayer and a bartender.

When World War II came along, Boone joined the Navy, serving three and a half years, most of it as a gunner aboard an aircraft carrier in the South Pacific. After returning in 1946, Boone enrolled under the GI Bill at New York City's Neighborhood Playhouse, a drama school which was then directed by Hollywood coach Sandy Meisner and it was here that he first realized that he wanted to be an actor. He emerged from the Playhouse as one of its most competent actors *and* one of its most pugnacious.

While playing Yank in the road-company of *Hasty Heart*, Boone got into an argument with the producer and quit. After a disagreement with Michael Redgrave, Boone was fired from the Shakespearean Company to which they both belonged. Later Boone tried professional dancing and ad libbing television sports announcements. A part in *The Man*, a play starring Dorothy Gish, resulted in a movie contract at 20th Century–Fox. When he was cast as Pontius Pilate by Fox in Hollywood's first Cinemascope production, *The Robe* (1953), he promptly got into another hassle that shut down production. Boone had appeared two years earlier in *Halls of Montezuma* (1951), where he met radio and television actor-producer Jack Webb. This led to about a half dozen appearances on the *Dragnet* radio show. Meanwhile, Boone's other screen credits included *Beneath the Twelve Mile Reef* (1953) and *Kangaroo* (1953), shot on location in Australia.

After making 13 films for Fox, Boone was approached by one of *Dragnet*'s writers, Jim Moser, to star in a new medical show he was writing called *The Doctor*. Boone was so enthusiastic that he attempted to break his seven-year contract with 20th Century-Fox, which had four years to go. Boone was subsequently released from his obligation. (He later claimed it was because he was so difficult.) Moser's television show became *Medic*. It premiered in 1955 on NBC and remained on the air two seasons (60 episodes). Boone played Dr. Konrad Styner, both the narrator and a character in the stories, with scripts based on actual case histories. The show was highly praised by critics and earned Boone two Best Actor Emmy nominations—and established him as a major television personality.

Have Gun, Will Travel was the brainchild of two imaginative former radio writers named Sam Rolfe and Herb Meadow. Boone reportedly was given a crack at the role of Paladin because Randolph Scott, the creators' first choice, was unavailable. Besides, they were impressed with Boone's performance on *Medic*. The series was one of the most popular Westerns of its day (third, behind only *Gunsmoke* and *Wagon Train*) and was

Richard Boone shared billing with a camel on one episode of *Have Gun, Will Travel*.

an overnight hit with viewers and critics alike. The critic in *Variety* (September 18, 1957) wrote:

> ... it's strictly an actioner. There's no overlying psychological motif—it's strictly business...
>
> ... a well-done action series ... Under the production aegis of Julian Claman and the direction of Andrew McLaglen, "Have Gun" was a taut and vigorous exercise in the hard-boiled category of western...
>
> ... Boone is authoritative and commanding in his role.

At the peak of *Have Gun, Will Travel*'s popularity, Richard Schickel assessed what made the series superior to other television Westerns of that period:

> ... it is more carefully rehearsed than most of its competitors.... Even the camera setups seem more adroit than they do on competing programs.
>   More importantly, "Have Gun" casts good actors and buys good scripts. It also prospers through careful attention to detail. On one recent day, Boone handed down the thesis that all his actors look as if they had just stepped out of a painting by Frederick Remington. He devoted most of his time to fussing over such items as bandannas, chaps, and spurs...
>   "'Have Gun' is one of the few shows that offer an honest professional challenge to creative people," says Frank Pierson, its producer ... "People will work for us for less than their usual fees because of this."[32]

It was said that Boone drew the largest and most loyal feminine fan mail of any Western television star—4,000 letters a month. After watching a segment in which Paladin philosophized on Pliny and Aristotle, San Diego columnist Donald Freeman remarked, "Where else can you see a gun fight and absorb a classical education at the same time?" And a high school teacher wrote Boone, "Yours is the only Western I recommend to my students. You speak English."[33] Many years later Castleman and Podrazik wrote:

> *Have Gun, Will Travel* is one of the purest, most imaginative examples of the golden age of TV Westerns. It presents the underlying concept in all TV Westerns, the battle of good versus evil, in a setting we can easily understand. Its quality comes from its restraint, its style, and its ability to transcend its sparse setting ...
>   Richard Boone turns in an acting gem in this show, presenting Paladin as a tower of strength.[34]

Boone's success as Paladin brought him a number of other starring roles, several on *Playhouse 90* (including the title role in William Faulkner's "The Old Man," which resulted in the highest audience rating in that program's history) and *The United States Steel Hour*. He also received critical acclaim for his 1959 performance as Abe Lincoln in *The Rivalry*, a Broadway play based on the Lincoln-Douglas debates. Although he could have gotten as much as $15,000 for a personal appearance, he refused to do rodeo performances, insisting that Paladin was not a cowboy. Like Paladin on the screen, Boone was totally in control on the set. No script was bought until he approved, no actor cast until he gave his OK. Boone even supervised the costumes. He directed 27 out of the 225 episodes. Television critic Schickel once analyzed Boone's desire to always be in control:

> One school of thought believes that our inability to make things happen is the cause of all contemporary anxiety. If that is true, then the appeal of Paladin as a character and Boone as a man is obvious. Both want to control their lives completely and both get very prickly when that ambition is thwarted.[35]

By 1962 Boone was ready to leave the show, having tired of the Western formula. He explained in a *Newsweek* interview: "Every time you go to the well, it's a little further down. The show has carried one or two seasons too long." The series was canceled by CBS at Boone's request one year later. Boone followed *Have Gun, Will Travel* with another more serious effort—a dramatic anthology that he hosted, often starred in, and sometimes directed called *The Richard Boone Show*. After one season, he left television to live in Hawaii for the next seven years in order to spend more time with his young son.

Boone occasionally appeared in a theatrical film at the request of his friend John Wayne, for whom he had played Sam Houston in *The Alamo* (1960). Among his better big screen performances were *Big Jake* (1971) and *The Shootist* (1976), both for Wayne.

Boone did return to television in 1972 as the cowboy detective *Hec Ramsey* (see Chapter X). He died of cancer in 1981. Despite his many notable achievements, it is as Paladin that Boone will longest be remembered.

It was not until the beginning of the final season of *Have Gun, Will Travel* that viewers learned the unusual story behind Paladin's name, dress and behavior. In an episode entitled "Genesis" (in which Richard Boone plays a dual role), the story of his origin is related through a series of flashbacks. Young Paladin had been raised in a happy and prosperous home in St. Louis, a home that had been rudely shattered by the outbreak of the Civil War. He had never known poverty, since his father was a partner in the wealthy fur trading firm of Chonteau and Company. He had been very close to his father, who had taken him on many business trips to New York. Once they had even gone to Europe. He had liked that, but he had enjoyed the trips to the West more, for he instinctively loved the outdoors. There he had learned to ride and to shoot.

Paladin's home life had been surrounded by luxury. His mother had been an Atlanta belle of quality and culture. However, the War Between the States had been fast approaching and the sympathies of his parents had been divided. His New York father was strongly for the Union, while his mother was deeply and intensely loyal to the South. Because Missouri was a border state, they had both hoped that it would not be drawn into the struggle. Paladin had been given an appointment to West Point through the influence of a Missouri senator and he had been there when hostilities broke out.

Paladin's own sympathies had been with the Union. He had talked it over with his father, and they had agreed that it would be fatal to his mother if she knew he would be fighting against her beloved South. Yet he had known that he could not keep out of it. It had taken some influence, but Paladin had been appointed to secret military duty as a spy. He was sent to join the Confederate Command of General Sterling Price in the Missouri district. His father had been able to tell his mother, with genuine sorrow, that her son was serving in the Confederate army.

Within a few weeks lines of communication had been set up by which he could report the movements of General Price's army back to General Buell, the Union commander. Though Paladin had not liked it, his father's office in St. Louis had been a clearinghouse for his messages. Unfortunately, a counterspy had discovered Paladin's true identity and murdered his father. Paladin himself barely escaped with his life. Later disguised as a hillbilly farmer, he joined Quantrill's raiders. He rode with them for three months, but sickened and repulsed by their brutal tactics, he finally deserted the band of guerrillas, warned the small settlement they were about to attack, and helped the settlers defend themselves in the ensuing battle.

Gradually Paladin had worked his way back to St. Louis only to learn that his mother had never recovered from the shock of her husband's death and had followed him to the grave within a week. He had finished out the war in the cavalry guarding the mail route against Indian attacks and when it was over he had returned to St. Louis. There was not much left of his father's business, though his Uncle Ben was striving to make a go of it. Unable to settle down in the business, Paladin had gone West again, and had finally established himself at the Carleton Hotel. His uncle sent him a monthly remittance. This was Paladin's situation when he got involved in a card game (using the name Smith) with one of San Francisco's most notorious and successful gamblers—a big, bulky man with nimble fingers named Norge (played to sinister perfection by William Conrad). When Paladin, after losing $15,000 to Norge, agrees to challenge a gunman named Smoke to a duel, Norge destroys the IOU. Smoke has driven Norge out of an isolated, but valuable valley, and taken control of it for himself. Norge wants revenge.

At their first meeting Paladin finds Smoke (also played by Boone) to be both intelligent and fair. Dressed all in black, Smoke is lightning fast with a gun, quotes Samuel Johnson and suffers from painful coughing spells. Paladin finds himself drawn to this unique man and it is Smoke who gives him the name he will use for the rest of his life:

> SMOKE: So Norge sent a gentleman this time. What do you call yourself?
> PALADIN: A gentleman. The name doesn't matter Smoke. That's no ordinary cough you have there.
> SMOKE: Excuse it. It'll be the death of me some day. Death won't come from the likes of you.
> PALADIN: I wouldn't be too sure of that. I didn't come here to bushwhack you, but to challenge you to a duel. You didn't kill me last night when you had the opportunity, so I take it you also consider yourself a gentleman. Shall we settle it like gentlemen?
> SMOKE: In the books there's a name for your kind. Yes, a paladin—a knight in shining armor, armed with a righteous cause and a lance.

In the subsequent gunfight Smoke draws and fires first, but a spasm of coughing spoils his aim and he is mortally wounded by Paladin. Smoke's dying words ring in Paladin's ears, "Your armor does shine brightly, and your arm is strong. Don't you see, noble Paladin, you've slain the dragon but turned the leopard loose. There's always a leopard loose somewhere. How long man must sometimes search before he finds himself." Paladin understands that Smoke was a frustrated philosopher who had made a study of his fellow man. He was well-read, stood far above his fellows in intelligence and disdained being a common working man. So he had become an outlaw. . . . Yet there had been good underneath the mask of evil that the man chose to wear. Smoke was a man Paladin would never forget. It is then out of respect for his vanquished foe that Paladin decides to take up Smoke's challenge. Dressed all in black, astride Smoke's horse, with Smoke's gun thrust in his belt, Paladin sets forth to slay the "leopards" of the world.[36]

Paladin, was a man with his own code of ethics not unlike those of more traditional Western heroes. Although he was usually commissioned by "good" people who were unable to defend themselves, if he discovered that his employer was taking unfair advantage of someone, Paladin would confront his employer and sacrifice his payment. He would never change sides in a dispute simply for more money but only as a matter of principle. Nor would he take another job before he had finished the one on which he was working.

In one episode Paladin switches sides when his cattleman employer insists on trying to kill two trespassing homesteaders (a man and his wife) who have not left his land by a deadline he has set. Paladin kills the rancher and one of his hired gunmen in a shoot-out, but then he insists that the homesteaders leave because the land did legally belong to the rancher. In a number of episodes, Paladin captures a wanted man and turns him over to the law, only to discover that he is innocent. He then sets out to find the real criminal in order to free the man he has apprehended.

In "A Matter of Ethics," Paladin refuses to help a murderer (who has hired Paladin to prevent a mob from lynching him) escape from jail. Advising the townspeople who would resort to mob violence that "you don't buy law and order, you fight for it," he fulfills his agreement with an obviously evil man while at the same time seeing to it that justice is done.

In another episode Paladin not only defends the right of an Indian family to own land against the efforts of white racists to force them out, he presents his mercenary fee of $2000 to the Indian and his pregnant wife with an apology for "this imperfect world" and expresses his "hopes for a better one in his [child's] lifetime." Is this the act of a man without principles?

Further insight into Paladin's values may be found in "The Five Books of Owen Deaver." Deaver is a sheriff's son who has just returned from the East, where he has been studying law to take his father's job in Three Winds. He brings with him five books containing the code of Philadelphia to use as a guide for the law in his town. Paladin argues that to apply this code to a raw Western town like Three Winds is absurd. For Paladin, written law is unnecessary, "just a loose set of morals based mostly on Thou Shalt Not." He goes on to recite these: "Thou shalt not kill a man unless he's armed and facing you; thou shalt not steal a man's house; thou shalt not rob at gun point." Deaver, however, is not convinced that an admittedly "loose" set of morals is sufficient. Who is to decide whether acts like drunkenness or disturbing the peace are crimes? Paladin responds that the sheriff should decide what a crime is in any given area. Deaver retorts, "What if the sheriff gets up on the wrong side of the bed one morning and everything is a crime?" To Paladin the answer is simple, get another sheriff. But what happens when the sheriff prevents you from replacing him? Clearly for Paladin there is a code—but it is found in the morals of the lawman himself, not in any set of books.

Paladin could be a ruthless fighter, not above taking advantage of an enemy in order to survive. This was especially true when Harry Julian Fink wrote the script. Fink began writing for *Have Gun, Will Travel* during its first season and by the second season was one of the main writers. In one of these episodes, Paladin is challenged to a duel by a particularly evil killer who has taken over a town. Paladin very practically walks into the nearest general store, borrows a shotgun, returns to the street, and shoots the villain dead. (Fink also frequently had Paladin use the concealed Derringer he always carried in addition to his usual revolver and rifle.[37])

Paladin was not a conventional kind of hero, but he *was* heroic in thought and deed. He was truly unique. As a devout Jewish father whom Paladin has helped, in "The Fatalist," observes, "In what other country could you find a hired killer who could quote you the words of the holy Torah?" With the last broadcast of *Have Gun, Will Travel* in May 1963, *Los Angeles Times* columnist Jack Smith wrote this fitting tribute to Paladin:

> Paladin, they say, has gone. Slung his gun for the last time and rode forever out of television's wasteland. He'll be ridin' back, I suppose, on a weary horse called Residuals. But it won't be the same.
>
> Someday sociologists may note that a whole generation of American boys grew up on Saturday night doses of Paladin, for better or for worse.
>
> ...I was a Paladin man. I was fond of this sardonic, flinty, compassionate knight. He was bigger than life, mystic, lusty, erudite, and not quite mortal.
>
> My own boys for six years absorbed those weekly Paladin sermons. For that's what they were. Paladin played no less a role than redeemer. He risked his skin to deliver the weak and punish the wicked.
>
> Perhaps Paladin served this generation no less nobly than Ivanhoe, Frank Merriwell and the Rover boys served mine.
>
> Who was Paladin, anyway, but Ivanhoe, riding off to unhorse the tyrannical and rescue the chaste....
>
> Whenever he did have to kill somebody, Paladin came up with some nice quotation from Shakespeare, Milton, Baudelaire or the Holy Bible. It made everything all right....
>
> Maybe the main reason I admired Paladin was his devotion to duty. The way he would get on his horse, with a shrug, as if to say, "Que sera, sera," and ride out into the brutal wilderness to redress wrong, turning his back on some steamy seductress, and a table set with champagne and Alaskan king crab....
>
> Now that he's hung up his spurs, I like to think that Paladin is back in that San Francisco hotel room, his last errand done, and a sign outside the door:
>
> "Do Not Disturb—reading Wm. Shakespeare."[38]

An unusual and somewhat sad footnote to the story of television's Paladin is related by Stephen W. and Diane L. Albert in the November–December 1991, issue of *The TV Collector*. They reported that an 83 year old Rhode Islander named Victor de Costa had just won a lawsuit against Viacom (syndicators of *Have Gun, Will Travel*). De Costa had been making personal appearances at rodeos and in parades since the 1930s. Dressed all in black and using a calling card (complete with a chess piece logo) which read "Have Gun, Will Travel," he was riding his horse in a parade one day in 1946 when an old Italian shouted at de Costa, "Paladino!" meaning "champion of knights."

When the television series later premiered, de Costa was shocked to see the character he had created played by a man who looked just like him. De Costa was accused of being an imposter, and his children were taunted at school, so he went to court and sued. The case dragged on for over thirty years. However, in September 1992, a federal jury awarded de Costa $3.5 million and key tradework rights to the show. In order to continue marketing the series, Viacom was required to delete all references to the calling card and logo from each episode and acknowledge de Costa as the character's creator. Unable financially to accept these restrictions, Viacom officially withdrew ("possibly forever") *Have Gun, Will Travel* from syndication on October 4, 1991.

Josh Randall, the central character of *Wanted: Dead or Alive*, was by profession a bounty hunter. He checked the wanted posters wherever he happened to be, tracked down and captured the culprit, and returned to claim the reward. At first glance he appeared to be more interested in collecting a sizable reward than upholding law and order. As played by Steve McQueen, he showed little emotion and was a man of few words who was adept at using his gun—a cross between a handgun and a rifle. This was one of the most unique aspects of the series. The producers of the show took a Model 92 Winchester lever-action rifle and turned it into a belt gun by sawing off most of the barrel and fitting it with a special stock. This gave it some of the power and accuracy of a rifle with the mobility and easy handling of a revolver. In the Old West they called a gun a hog's leg, but McQueen dubbed this one a "mare's laig," because "she kicked a lot harder than a hog." In order to reduce the recoil, they had to switch from full to quarter-power blanks.

There were a number of shortened rifles and shotguns used in the early West. Doc Holliday carried a sawed-off, double-barreled shotgun into the famous gunfight at Tombstone's O.K. Corral. Sawed-off rifles and shotguns enjoyed such popularity among gangsters during the Prohibition era that Congress passed the National Firearms Act, subjecting any rifle or shotgun with a barrel length under 18 inches, as well as machine guns, to severe restrictions and limitations. This led to an additional expense for series producer John Robinson. Before he could use a hacksaw and file on a Winchester, he had to pay the government $500 for a manufacturer's permit, plus $200 licensing fees for each of the three rifles altered. The spares were necessary to prevent a broken gun from disrupting shooting schedules. The total cost of each gun came to nearly $1100.[39]

In the beginning when McQueen took the mare's laig on location, he had a uniformed officer ever at his elbow to assure that the gun was not misused. Later he obtained special permission to take out the gun without supervision. In addition to a stubbier stock, McQueen's gun had the loop of the cocking lever enlarged and rounded to enable him to spin the gun and cock it one-handed. The weapon which, was originally designed to be fired with two hands, could now be used with one. The holster and gun were both given a rustic appearance to give the impression that Josh Randall had made them himself. To

Opposite: **Steve McQueen got the big break he had been waiting for as Josh Randall in** *Wanted: Dead or Alive*; **it made him a superstar.**

heighten the fearful appearance of the weapon, the cartridge belt was looped with a string of huge, old .45-.70 cartridges. They couldn't be fired in the .44-.40 Winchester, but they looked extremely dangerous.[40]

Since bounty hunters were common in the West during the last half of the nineteenth century, the stories had some historical basis. The opportunity for bloodshed and violence in the plots was great because it did not matter if the criminals were captured alive. This, coupled with the rugged, unflappable charisma of McQueen, proved to be a winning formula.

Steve McQueen was born March 23, 1930, in Slater, Missouri. He ran away from home when he was 15 and did a lot of "wrong things." ("Hunger has no conscience," he later said.) He tried his hand at many jobs in order to survive. He served a hitch on an oil tanker; he was a carnival pitchman; he was a lumberjack; he drove a mail truck; he even tried prize-fighting. As soon as he was old enough, he enlisted in the U.S. Marines and became a qualified tank driver and mechanic before his honorable discharge in 1950. Soon afterwards, this jack-of-all-trades headed for New York City. He took a job as a television repairman while waiting to attend school under the G.I. Bill of Rights. A chance meeting with Sandy Meisner, well known dramatic coach, led to an audition at New York's famous Neighborhood Playhouse. McQueen was one of 72 young men and women selected from over 3,000 aspiring thespians.

After graduating from the Playhouse in 1952, McQueen got his first part in the summer stock company of *Peg O' My Heart*, starring Margaret O'Brien. Roles in *Member of the Wedding*, with Ethel Waters, and *Time Out for Ginger*, with Melvin Douglas, won critical praise and offers of television work. In his fourth television appearance, he starred in the *Studio One* production of "The Chivington Raid." He also played choice roles to good reviews in "Bring Me a Dream" on *The U.S. Steel Hour* and "The Defenders" on *Studio One*. McQueen was one of five actors chosen from an audition group of 2,000 by the famous Actors Studio. His biggest stage break came when he replaced Ben Gazzara as the lead, Johnny Pope, in *Hatful of Rain*. His first film role was a bit part in *Somebody Up There Likes Me*, starring Paul Newman (1956), which led to leads in the successful *Never Love a Stranger* (1958) and cult hit *The Blob* (1958).

About this time McQueen learned that producer Vince Fennelly was looking for an actor to play a bounty hunter in *Trackdown*, a CBS Western he was doing about the Texas Rangers starring Robert Culp. Although skeptical at first ("No more Old West crap for me. No darn ten-gallon hats. No guns. No horses!"), McQueen relented and agreed to talk to Fennelly. Fennelly found in McQueen the special quality for which he had been searching: vulnerability. He later explained why he had selected McQueen for the role of Josh Randall:

> A bounty hunter, by nature, is a sort of underdog. Everybody's against him—lawmen, bandits, townsfolk. They don't like what he does for a living—hunting down fugitives and being paid a bounty for either capturing or killing them. So if he's some big, aggressive football type, your audience will turn against him. I need a kind of "little guy" who looks tough enough to get the job done, but with a kind of boyish appeal behind the toughness. He had to be *vulnerable*, so the audience would root for him against the bad guys. McQueen was just what I had in mind. I knew he was my man the minute he walked through the door.[41]

McQueen, in turn, himself an individualistic nonconformist, felt right at home in the role:

> Josh was real to me. I felt that I *knew* him. Lived inside his skin for years. You do a character that long and you begin to *be* that character. It's like *I* was living in the Old West

chasing bad guys. I'd look in the mirror and see Randall. For a while I thought I'd never be anybody else.... I wanted to play him for real—as a guy trying to do a dangerous, unglamourous job with a minimum of fuss.[42]

"The Bounty Hunter" aired on *Trackdown* on March 7, 1958, as the narrator intoned:

> Big Bend, Texas wasn't much of a town—a wide spot on a road where cattlemen and ranchers met and lived. The wealth that ran underground hadn't been discovered yet and most people still believed that the only way to live good was to work hard. One man who didn't go along with this thought was Josh Randall. Josh had ridden a long trail. He'd came half way across Texas, but he had a special reason to be in Big Bend.

Later Josh explains to Ranger Hoby Gilman why he is a bounty hunter:

JOSH:	... we both got the same kind of job. Sure, we're both on the same side of the fence. The only difference is you bring 'em in for the law and I do it for the reward.
HOBY:	There's one other difference.
JOSH:	How's That?
HOBY:	I don't enjoy it.
NARRATOR:	Sometimes he ran into people like that. They had the wrong idea, but it didn't pay to try and put them straight. Bounty hunting wasn't too bad a way to live. You got to see a lot of the country. You met a lot of people and it was better than digging in the dirt or standing on his feet all day back of a bank counter. It was a living and now and then a good one! His income came from finding lost brothers and runaway husbands. Josh liked the life and it seemed to like him.

CBS network executives liked what they saw and ordered the series. McQueen would be paid $750 a week to play Josh Randall in *Wanted: Dead or Alive* for Four Star Productions. The half-hour show was launched on September 6, 1958, and McQueen's offbeat qualities attracted audiences from the opening episode. In an episode called "Never the Twain," Josh's occupation as bounty hunter is questioned. A newspaperman, Arthur Pierce Madison, determined to chronicle the methods of a bounty hunter, follows Randall and presses him:

MADISON:	... Do you like your work?
JOSH:	Well, I'm doin' it.
MADISON:	That's not what I asked ya, Josh. Do ya like it?
JOSH:	Well, let's put it this way pal. It's all I know.
MADISON:	Is it all you want?
JOSH:	(pause) Almost. Not quite.
MADISON:	It seems to me everything you've got is on that horse over there.
JOSH:	Yeah, suppose so. But it kinda leaves me free, ya know.
MADISON:	We're all free.
JOSH:	Well, somebody sent ya down here, didn't they?
MADISON:	That's right, my editor.
JOSH:	Told ya what to write.
MADISON:	He gave me my assignment... With you it's one assignment after another isn't it?
JOSH:	Most of th' time.
MADISON:	Month after month, year after year?
JOSH:	Uh huh.
MADISON:	A rolling stone gathers no moss, huh, Josh? One day you'll be too old for this kind of life. Haven't you ever thought of a home, a place you can call your own?
JOSH:	Yeah, I thought of it.

Josh Randall, man of few words, obviously liked his lifestyle, but realized that there was something more to life too.

A typical episode, "The Bounty" by Samuel A. Pebles, an authority on Western lore, was a simple but classic morality tale. Both Randall and another bounty hunter named Daimler (played with ominous intensity by veteran supporting actor Mort Mills) are both preparing to bring back an accused murderer named Vasquez, who has a $500 bounty on his head. Daimler indicates that he intends to kill Vasquez on the assumption that this would be the simplest way to collect the reward, while Randall makes it equally clear that he will try to bring him out alive to stand trial. Either way Vasquez is worth $500 to the bounty hunter who is able to return him to the authorities.

Later Randall creeps up on Daimler's camp, gets the drop on him with his "mare's laig," and warns him not to kill Vasquez in cold blood. In the course of their confrontation Daimler reveals a large callus on his right thumb. It is the gunslinger's trademark, the result of long hours of practicing thumbing the hammer of his single-action Colt. This enables him to fire several shots in rapid succession. Suddenly Charlie Two Hawk, a bare-chested savage, appears, fires a shot and orders the two intruders to throw down their weapons. Then he lowers his rifle and rides off into the darkness without further explanation. Daimler suddenly jumps Randall, knocks him unconscious and steals his "mare's laig." Randall soon recovers and follows Daimler into the canyon.

A day later Vasquez, a frail, white-haired old man, is seen talking in his home in the canyon to Charlie Two Hawk. Charlie is warning him of the two bounty hunters coming to get him. For fifteen years, Vasquez has lived as a fugitive under an assumed name, dreading such a day, but preparing for it. When Daimler arrives, Vasquez explains that he had killed a man who had stolen his wife and caused her death. But he agrees to go willingly with the bounty hunter.

Randall arrives just as Daimler and Vasquez start to leave. When Vasquez's daughter tries to prevent her father from being struck by Daimler, he uses it as an excuse to gun the old man down. Randall prevents him from firing again, but the damage has been done. Vasquez has been mortally wounded.

"This is what you wanted," the old man tells Daimler. "A body to take back for the reward... You think the game is over and you have won. But you are wrong. You see, I thought of this. I, too, have posted a bounty...." Charlie Two Hawk and his Apaches watch from a distance as Daimler picks up the frail old body and slings it like a bed roll across the back of this horse. As Daimler begins the long ride back through the canyon, the Indians, led by Charlie follow. Randall, still weaponless, follows at a distance.

The ride out of the canyon takes two days. During this time the Apaches harass Daimler with rifle shots and animal cries, but never show themselves. They cause Daimler to lose his canteen, his food, and Vasquez's body. He empties his gun at the shadows and collapses exhausted. When Randall rides up, he expects to find Daimler dead. But he is alive—astride his horse, in a state of deep pain and shock, unable to tell what has happened. Seeing Charlie Two Hawk silhouetted on a nearby hill, Randall shouts, "What was the bounty?" The Apache shouts back, "The thumb from his right hand." It was a punishment Daimler far worse than death. In this way, good does not merely triumph over evil; nor is evil destroyed. Evil is punished in such a way that it is a living warning to others.

By the end of the first season, McQueen was already unhappy with his contract. It was not, however, more money that he wanted. It was script approval. He claimed that too many of the situations in *Wanted* were not compatible with the type of character he was playing. In an interview with Los Angeles *Mirror News* columnist Hal Humphrey, McQueen later explained:

> I remember one script which had three big guys in a saloon telling me to get out of town. Believe me, if you had seen these guys, you'd know there was only one thing for me to do—go! But in this script I knocked all three of 'em down. Is that silly![43]

In the same interview he discussed his concern for authentic wearing apparel for Josh. "CBS was really frightened when they saw the beat-up hat and coat I was wearing. Too old and musty-looking, they told me—but I refused to change them."

One of the most interesting and unusual stories was broadcast during the third season. An episode called "To the Victor" was actually an updated version of Greek dramatist Aristophanes' classic *Lysistrata*, cleverly scripted by Ed Adamson. (The central characters were named Liz and Mike Strata to alert educated viewers.) It was played tongue-in-cheek by McQueen and avoided any suggestion of the biological sex drive around which the original story had been built. The approach taken by Adamson was to have the wives walk out on their mates until they put up their guns. What the men missed most was the home cooking (in *this* version). The women holed up in the town hall, dressed like men and rejected all peace offers by the hungry menfolks. McQueen took the job of reconciling the families and tricked the women into calling off their strike by having a pair of friendly "bandits" raid the bank only to be repulsed by the guns of the town males. That did it: the women conceded that guns were necessary to keep the peace of the community and returned to their husbands' arms. The story was farfetched, but amusing and effective. It also revealed the more human side of Josh Randall.

For all the hard indifference he projected on the surface, deep down Josh Randall was really a caring person with a "heart of gold." In story after story, he would go to the aid of the weak, the oppressed, the unfortunate, the underdog. Especially where children were concerned—and they popped up in many episodes—Randall was a real "soft touch."

In "Drop to Drink," Randall donates the $1000 reward he has received for apprehending a bandit to a church whose "holy water" kept him alive on his trek through the desert. Randall will not reveal the identity of a reformed bank robber who is now leading a respectable life under a different name as a sheriff in another town, even though he has been offered a large fee for capturing him in "Give Away Gun." In "Eager Man" he gives the reward money he earned when he was forced to kill a wanted outlaw to the outlaw's needy widow. Randall even helps restore a little boy's faith in Santa Claus when the lad offers him the total of his savings, eight cents, for finding and bringing old St. Nick to his poverty stricken ranch in a poignant Christmas story entitled "Eight Cent Reward." These are certainly not the actions of a man with no emotions or values.

In "Montana Kid," Randall encounters a 12 year old boy who has been taught how to deal "three card monte" (which is like the old hidden pea game) in order to fleece unsuspecting marks. The kid (with his dog) lands in jail, but Randall takes him under his wing. To repay him for his kindness, the pooch barks at just the right moment to get Josh out of a tight spot. Then the kid deals him a hand of cards that cleans out his wicked mentor (shades of Dickens' Fagan) and wins for Randall a sizable bundle of cash. Did the kid cheat to help his pal? What do you think? Who cares, as long as the ends of justice have been served? Josh Randall's sense of justice is, in fact, different from that of the conventional cowboy hero. In "Rope Law" he helps prevent the lynching of a man for a murder Randall knows he did not commit even though he is certain that the man is guilty of an earlier murder.

In "Rawhide Breed," Randall guides an unpleasant Eastern tenderfoot named Klingsmith through miles of desert badlands on foot, protecting him from Indians and outlaws along the way. As the two finally approach civilization, Klingsmith turns to

Randall and asks, "You want money for bringing men in. How much do I owe you?" Randall responds, at last revealing the principles by which he has lived:

> I expect nothin' from you mister, but if you ever talk to me like that again, I'm gonna walk all over you. I dunno, maybe it's because you don't know any better, so I'm gonna tell you something, just once. Most towns have got sheriffs and marshals. We're a long way between towns out here. There's not much law. Men like Hod Krieger are free to do what they like—pushin' people around, killing. Somebody's gotta stop 'em.

These sentiments could have been voiced by a Roy Rogers, a Ben Cartwright, or a Gil Favor.

The critics were very tough on *Wanted: Dead or Alive* when it made its first appearance. The *Variety* (September 10, 1958) review read:

> "Wanted," the story of a bounty hunter, was almost stuffy in its allegiance to the breed—the rugged, silent, cynical yet big hearted hero. Steve McQueen could ... do little else than preserve a wax-like countenance and say the few words ... he had to say.
>
> Acting is okay. It's obvious what the half-hour needs is scripting and perhaps some cleaner direction.

Only the fans liked the show, which reached sixteenth in the Nielsen ratings during its first season and was ninth at the end of the second. Even *Variety* had changed its tune by the second season (September 8, 1959):

> What is said about most westerns is applicable ... Just sit back and enjoy it; no Freudian problems to unknot ... Steve McQueen ... wears easy and should finish strong.

During the third season, however, the series disappeared from the top 20 and was canceled. Steve McQueen, although he enjoyed the role, shed no tears. Ahead for him was cinematic superstardom in such films as *The Magnificent Seven* (1960), *The Great Escape* (1963), *The Sand Pebbles* (1966), *Bullitt* (1968), and *Papillon* (1973). He died of cancer in 1980 at the age of 50.

Gamblers, hired guns and bounty hunters had their moment of glory and left their mark on the television Western. *Maverick, Have Gun, Will Travel* and *Wanted: Dead or Alive* each have their cult of followers today. The first two were unquestionably among the finest Westerns ever produced for television. By 1960 the antihero had been firmly established as a popular figure in the genre and endowed on the home screen with a sense of humanity not readily found in the theatrical Western.

VII. Wagon Trains and Cattle Drives
TREKKING WESTWARD TELEVISION STYLE

Two classic ingredients in the oft-told story of the development of the early American West are the wagon train and the cattle drive. The subject of countless books and films, each was successfully brought to the television screen in the late fifties, in *Wagon Train* and *Rawhide*, respectively. Two of the most popular television series on the air, these shows are alike in many ways in their depiction of the westward movement.

Both series deal with a group of individuals who have a common goal: the wagon-master and his crew are dedicated to seeing that everyone on the wagon train gets safely to where they want to go (which is west to California); the trail boss and his crew are dedicated to moving cattle safely to the railhead. The wagonmaster (Seth Adams and later Christopher Hale), who has the authority of a ship's captain and the honorary title of major, is assisted by one or more scouts, a cook and an assistant wagonmaster. The trail boss (Gil Favor and later Rowdy Yates), with similar authority, is assisted by a ramrod, a cook and a varying number of drovers (determined by the size of the herd).

Each crew is a community unto itself (although in the case of *Wagon Train* the people in the train are themselves part of that community). As television historian Ralph Brauer points out, each crew "is held together by a common purpose . . . and a common set of rules. These rules . . . define what the crew can and cannot do."[1] In each case the leader (wagonmaster or trail boss) is the final authority and has the final say in all matters relating to the welfare of the train or herd. They may consult with the members of their crew and may sometimes even heed their advice, but they are always responsible for making the final decision. The trail boss has been employed by a rancher (or ranchers) to move his cattle and must delegate all authority to him until the cattle have reached their destination. The individuals and families who make up the wagon train not only participate in the selection of their wagonmaster, they become part of the community moving west and must abide by whatever rules he has set down (no gambling, no liquor, etc.). If they break these rules, they must face the consequences.

The basic difference in the two series can be found in the focus of each weekly episode. *Wagon Train* episodes focus on people and are entitled "The Willy Moran Story" or "The Colter Craven Story" or whoever happens to be the featured member of the train for that week, while *Rawhide* episodes, although also employing guest stars, are usually about places or things encountered on the trail and are entitled "Incident of the Tumbleweed Wagon" or "Incident at Barker Springs."

Many of the shows dwell on conflicts—internal conflicts between members of the crew (or of the train and crew) and external conflicts against Indians, outlaws and natural forces. In each case the mission of the community is placed in jeopardy. Invariably the conflict, insofar as it reflects a clash between the interests of the few and the interests of the many, is resolved in favor of the many (the community).[2] Both shows successfully combined the elements of a dramatic anthology series with a stable cast of regulars. Each week a new group of characters (portrayed by guest stars) join the train or drive or are encountered on the trail. Some are settlers or drovers, others adventurers and still others scoundrels. The regulars in the casts are seen in costarring or sometimes (more often on *Wagon Train*) even supporting roles.

Wagon Train debuted on NBC September 18, 1957. It had been inspired by John Ford's epic film *Wagonmaster* (1950). Ford had become attached to the Mormons when they were serving as his cavalry in *She Wore a Yellow Ribbon*. He came to admire the way they arose at 6 a.m. and worked with pride until sundown. So he decided to make a film explaining how such people came west.[3] Shot without stars or fanfare, *Wagonmaster* relates the story of a group of people traveling toward a promised land through a series of dangers. It is about a community in adversity. The wagons tie the film together, just as they bound the people together. The screen is filled with lines of wagons that climb it or strain down it or criss-cross over it. Critics have described the film as "lyrical, poetic and beautiful."[4]

Although Ben Johnson is cast in the title role of Travis Blue, the real hero of the film is Elder Wiggs, a man with great faith in God and himself, played by veteran actor Ward Bond. Wiggs is wise, courageous, purposeful, sly and dedicated. Major Seth Adams is much like Elder Wiggs and Bond was the perfect choice to portray him.

Ford was so pleased with *Wagon Train* that he agreed to direct an episode in 1960. Entitled "The Colter Craven Story," it relates the story of an alcoholic doctor who is unable to give up the bottle after witnessing the horrors of war at the Battle of Shiloh. Major Adams inspires Craven to sober up enough to perform a serious operation by telling him the story of how General Ulysses S. Grant (depicted as a close friend of Adams) was dismissed from the U.S. Army for alcoholism, but was later reinstated, allowing him to lead the Union forces to victory. This, of course, helps propel him into the White House. Ford presents this "great American story" in a way that makes Grant's disgrace an inspiration and his weakness the cowardly doctor's opportunity for redemption. This episode has a much larger cast than usual and is populated with John Ford regulars like Ken Curtis, Cliff Lyons, Chuck Roberson, Hank Warden, Willis Bouchey, Mae March, Jack Pennick and Chuck Hayward. There is much more attention to detail and the action sequences appear to have been filmed "on location." Most surprising of all is the appearance of John Wayne in a cameo role as General William Sherman although he is billed in the screen credits as Michael Morris. (Wayne's real name was Marion Michael Morrison.) It is Wayne's only dramatic appearance on television. Wayne later indicated that he did it "for a lark" to surprise Ward Bond on his birthday. Ironically, Bond died of a heart attack three weeks before the episode was aired.[5] In any case, the Colter Craven episode is one of the finest in the series.

The show was given authenticity by the supervision of Western historian and novelist Dwight B. Newton. Produced at the then staggering cost of $100,000 per episode, the list of guests who appeared on the series included such Hollywood stars as Mickey Rooney,

Ward Bond (left) starred as Major Seth Adams, wagonmaster, on *Wagon Train*, while Robert Horton played scout Flint McCullough.

Barbara Stanwyck, Ernest Borgnine, Ricardo Montalban, Shelley Winters, Eddie Albert, Ronald Reagan, Cliff Robertson, Jane Wyman, Peter Lorre, Charles Laughton, Mercedes McCambridge and Lou Costello (in his only serious dramatic role on television).

Bette Davis made several appearances as different characters traveling west. In one episode she plays Elizabeth McQueeny, a cultured and refined Eastern lady who is taking nine beautiful young women schooled in music, dance and the theater to Nevada, ostensibly to start a girls' finishing school. The pioneer women on the train, however, doubt her intentions. They see the women as a threat to "lead their menfolk astray." Later

Madame McQueeny reveals privately to Adams that she is a female impresario who plans to establish a "place of entertainment" in the West. When an epidemic of spotted fever hits the wagon train she and "her girls" demonstrate great strength of character by unselfishly and tirelessly tending the sick and dying. Major Adams himself falls victim to the fever and is nursed back to health by Madame McQueeny. Intended as a pilot for a series starring Ms. Davis, the episode failed to generate sufficient network interest, although it provides one of the more interesting character studies on *Wagon Train*. Such stories contributed to the series' popularity, but its enduring success rested largely on the capable shoulders of its cast members. Ward Bond during the first three and one-half seasons (and John McIntire during the remaining four and one-half), created strong, believable and intensely likable characters.

Bond, born in 1903 in Nebraska and raised in Colorado, began his film career in 1929 after he shoved his way onto a bus full of John Wayne's friends from the University of Southern California being recruited as extras for John Ford's *Salute*. Ford singled Bond out by ordering, "Send in the big one with the ugly mug!"[6] Although he graduated from USC two years later with a degree in engineering, Bond turned to acting full time in order to earn more money. Beginning with small supporting roles, Ford gave him progressively juicier parts, usually as a rugged, warm-hearted pal of the leading man. Bond was as fearless in his personal life as the characters he portrayed on the screen. In 1944, after being hit by a car, his left leg had to be surgically reconstructed and needed continued medical care. Four years later Bond plunged into the McCarthy-Communist controversy by launching an attack on actor José Ferrer accusing him of subversive associations.

Appearing in some 200 films, 150 of which were Westerns (with about half of these involving wagon trains), Bond saw the role of Major Seth Adams as a fitting reward for his long years of yeoman service in the acting profession. A week after the show placed number one in the Nielsen ratings (reaching 22,736,000 homes—the highest number of television sets tuned to one program up to that time), Bond said in a *Newsweek* interview, "I was happy playing the hero's best friend in movies, but here I am. I lived this show when it started and I got this damned ulcer. . . . I'd rather not be a star, but you can't let go of a good thing."[7] Bond put much of himself into the character, took great interest in the show and had considerable influence over its production. He once rejected a script in which a woman was murdered for no apparent reason. Bond felt the killer would be portrayed as a psychopath and flatly stated that "nobody is going to make me play in a story with a degenerate in it on a television show children are watching."[8] Production was held up for two days on another occasion while Bond and the show's staff rewrote 63 pages of a 70 page script that he found offensive.

The humanity and compassion of Seth Adams was demonstrated from the very first episode. In "The Willy Moran Story," Adams rescues an old friend, with whom he had served at Gettysburg during the Civil War, from a street brawl and gives him a job on the wagon train despite his obvious addiction to alcohol. Adams' faith later proves justified when Willy risks his life to save the train from an assault by Quantrill's raiders.

Adams is continually helping those in need, like a young man who has lost his horse ("The Rutledge Monroe Story"), a man who has been beaten and left on the trail for dead ("The Joshua Gilliam Story"), and a fatherless crippled boy ("The Dick Jarvis Story"). During *Wagon Train*'s first season, Adams' own past is explored in the two part, "The Major Adams Story." Related through flashbacks, the story of Seth's tragic love affair with Ranie Martin unfolds. Bill Hawks and Seth are running a lumber mill in Galena, Illinois, when the Civil War breaks out. Adams organizes a regiment of volunteers and prepares to go off to war. He asks Ranie to marry him before he leaves, but she is unwilling to wait while he is away fighting and turns him down. Seth is seriously wounded and spends months recovering his strength in an army hospital. He returns, unopened, the letters Ranie sends him.

Following the war, Seth, Bill and Charlie Wooster sign on with a wagon train heading from St. Louis to Sacramento. Finding the work to their liking, they continue trekking across the plains, guiding groups of settlers moving west. Several years later, Seth by accident discovers that Ranie, thinking Seth had been killed in the war, has married another. Now that Ranie is a widow, Adams wants to renew their romance, only to find that Ranie is seriously ill. Tragically, she dies in his arms. That Adams never fully recovers from this loss is made abundantly clear in an episode aired during the fourth season entitled "The Beth Pearson Story." Shaken by the resemblance to Ranie of a widow traveling with her son on the wagon train, Seth finds himself falling in love again. The widow, Beth Pearson, wants him to be certain it is she, and not the memory of the dead woman, that he is in love with. After a tragic accident in which Mrs. Pearson breaks her neck and almost dies. Adams realizes that he *is* still in love with Ranie's ghost and he cannot marry Beth. (Virginia Grey, who had played Ranie Webster in the earlier episodes, is cast as Beth Pearson.) This episode was the last one Ward Bond filmed and was in fact broadcast almost four months after his death. A decision had been made not to explain the disappearance of Seth Adams from the series, but loyal fans could rationalize his absence by assuming that after his ghostly experience with love, he was so emotionally drained that he suddenly decided to leave the train and take life easy, or perhaps, even search out Mrs. Pearson, whom perhaps he has decided he really did love after all.

Bond's close friend John Wayne offered to star in three episodes at no fee, but other obligations prevented him from doing any.[9] A number of stories that had been written for Bond were adapted for Robert Horton, who had been playing scout Flint McCullough, second lead on the series. Horton, who was itching to leave the show, regretted agreeing to the switch, feeling that the plots were tailored for the older character and that the end result was ludicrous.

The producers realized, however, that they would have to replace the role of wagonmaster, and after considering several actors, selected John McIntire to play the newly created character Christopher Hale. McIntire accepted the part after being assured that it would not interfere with family life on his Montana ranch. Although it took viewers a while to accept a replacement for their beloved Major Adams, the actor was immediately welcomed by the *Wagon Train* cast and crew. Part of the success of the transition from Bond to McIntire lay in the similarity of the two actors. McIntire was only four years younger than his predecessor, had also been born and raised in the West (Montana rather than Colorado) and was, in fact, the son of a frontier lawyer who had served many years as Commissioner of Indian Affairs. McIntire had spent two years at Bond's alma mater (the University of Southern California) majoring in speech. After touring the world as a seaman on a cargo ship, he returned to the states and became a radio actor-announcer. He later worked extensively in films (in supporting roles) and television, appearing as a regular on the popular police drama *Naked City* in 1958-59. (He had writers kill off his character because he did not like the role.)

McIntire had made one guest appearance on *Wagon Train* prior to his signing on as wagonmaster. During the series' second season he was cast as a preacher who wanders into the desert after accidently shooting one of his parishioners in "The Andrew Hale Story." It is never explained how Hale acquires a new first name and a new profession, but the new character is introduced on March 15, 1961, as a retired wagonmaster who is overcome with grief after his family has been massacred by Indians. It seems that the

After Bond died, John McIntire (second from left) replaced him as wagonmaster Chris Hale, shown here with (far left) Terry Wilson as Bill Hawks, Frank McGrath as Charlie Wooster and Scott Miller (right) as Duke Shannon on the *Wagon Train* set.

owners of the train have already hired a new wagonmaster who arrives with his four armed "associates." How Hale wins the job away from the corrupt Muerto and his men is told in the exciting "Christopher Hale Story" (Lee Marvin is featured as one of the gunslingers in this episode).

Hale exhibits many of the same character traits as Seth Adams. He too is strong, wise, resourceful and compassionate. He gives a blind man a chance to prove he can care for his sister and his son ("The Saul Bevins Story"), saves an orphan boy's life after he has been badly injured in a wagon accident ("The Davey Baxter Story"), and hires an aging pioneer as scout out of respect for his former exploits ("The Zebedee Titus Story"). Major Adams could not have done more. Chris Hale is even permitted to fall in love in "The Heather Mahoney Story," although his romance is as ill-fated as those of Major Adams. In "The Kate Crawley Story" a tough-mannered freight line operator (played by Barbara Stanwyck) falls in love with Hale, and his friends fear that the independent woman will take over leadership of the train. They need not have worried, however, for an Indian war party interrupts their wedding plans permanently.

Hale has another fleeting romantic involvement in "The Chottsie Gubenheimer Story," in which his sweetheart is played by McIntire's real-life wife Jeanette Nolan. Earlier in the series (during the fourth season), Nolan had appeared in "The Janet Hale Story," playing Hale's wife. Flashbacks in this episode relate the story of how Hale's duties as wagonmaster kept him away from his prairie home. A truce with the Indians had reassured him that his wife and children would be safe during his absences, but renegade Indians break the truce and massacre his family.

In other interesting casting assignments, McIntire's real life daughter, Holly, was given a role in "The Sarah Proctor Story" and John was given the opportunity of playing a dual role, adding that of Chris Hale's older brother in "The Levi Hale Story." Similar in appearance to his brother, Levi is an ailing convict who is being paroled in Chris' custody on the condition that he never return to Wyoming territory.

The second lead for the first five years of *Wagon Train* was Robert Horton, who fashioned his character, Flint McCullough, the train's scout, as an educated and refined cowboy. Unlike most of the rough and wild film cowboys, McCullough's behavior implies that most of the real cowhands of the 1870s were from England or the East. McCullough, like the other continuing characters on the series, was featured in his share of the stories, especially during the second and third seasons.

In "The Cliff Grundy Story," Flint stays behind when a man is trampled in a buffalo stampede and becomes embroiled in the search for a lost gold mine. Some of McCullough's past life is revealed in "The Flint McCullough Story," when he unexpectedly encounters an old enemy. Flint escorts three nuns to Nevada where they plan to establish a mission school for the Indians in "The Sister Rita Story." He is first accused of being a renegade and then asked for help in rescuing her fiancé by the daughter of an army commander in "The Martha Barham Story." In "The Larry Hanify Story," Flint agrees to care for the delinquent son of a dying thief. He is captured by slave traders and leads his fellow prisoners in an escape attempt in "The Amos Gibbon Story." A countess tempts Flint to desert the train and lead her on a quicker route to Alaska in "The Countess Baramov Story." While in temporary charge of the wagon train in "The Jim Bridger Story," Flint meets his foster father, who demands that he take the train into hostile Ute territory in order to rescue a trapped cavalry garrison. And in "The Artie Mathewson Story," Flint discovers that his opportunistic foster brother, who has been elected mayor of a boom town, is part of a plot to swindle the townspeople. These are among Horton's best episodes.

Horton's contract expired on May 15, 1962, and unhappy, with the way his character was being written into scripts, he opted to leave the show. He remarked to *TV Guide*, "Too often Flint is a traffic cop directing guest stars through the show."[10] He criticized the show for becoming badly written, badly staged and badly edited. As the series had progressed, the producers had stopped filming on location. (During the first several seasons most episodes had been shot on two California locations, either Rancho Guadalasco or Conejo Flats, both rich in wide open spaces, prairie and water holes with a Mexican atmosphere.) By the fifth season most of the shows were being filmed on an indoor soundstage at Universal Studios, with location shots edited in from stock footage of previous episodes, an obvious cost cutting move.

Completing the original cast regulars, and staying with the series for its entire run were comical Frank McGrath, who brought great warmth and humor to his part of the cook, Charlie Wooster, and veteran movie stunt man Terry Wilson, who served quite capably as the able assistant wagonmaster and lead wagon driver, Bill Hawks.

Charlie carries the story in several of the better episodes. In "Chuck Wooster, Wagonmaster," Wooster must lead the train to safety through a raging blizzard after Adams and Flint mysteriously disappear. Charlie falls in love with a female con-artist (palmist, astrologer, medicine peddler and phrenologist) who has been snubbed by the other passengers, in "The Madame Sagittarius Story." A female outlaw and her two sons mistakenly kidnap Charlie in "Charlie Wooster-Outlaw." And Charlie reminisces about his younger days in Pierce's Bend in "The Jarbo Pierce Story," the last episode of the series.

Hawks is the central character in "The Jose Morales Story," where he is captured by a gang of Mexican bandits determined to steal the wagons. In "The Lisa Raincloud Story," Hawks is wounded and captured by Indians. Although he has been marked for death, during his recovery he falls in love with an Indian princess. Hawks develops a strong affection for a 13 year old boy who has come west alone to find his sister in "The Barnaby West Story." And he comes to the aid of an Indian girl who has killed the chief's son in "The Indian Girl Story." These episodes give Wilson a chance to act, as well as perform several difficult physical stunts.

In preparation for Horton's departure, Scott (Denny) Miller was hired to play a new scout, Duke Shannon. After being introduced on April 26, 1961, in the "Duke Shannon Story," Duke is featured in a number of interesting episodes. In "The Hobie Redman Story," Duke's limited experience is put to the test when he leads a group of newcomers across the desert to join the train. A mutiny breaks out when one man refuses to follow the same trail on which his family died earlier. While escorting a group away from the train on foot in "The Charley Shutup Story," Duke breaks his ankle and is left behind in a snowbound cabin with a wounded Indian. In "The Frank Carter Story," Duke discovers he is a dead ringer for a gambler that someone is trying to kill. He assumes the man's identity in order to help the man's panic-stricken mother. Duke in persuaded to give up his job as scout to become the administrator of a welfare program for Indians in "The Hiram Winthrop Story." In "The Johnny Masters Story," Duke saves an Indian who has become a soldier from the hostility of his comrades, who detest him for his Indian ancestry. And Duke faces the vengeance of a dictatorial town boss after he accidently kills one of his gunmen in self-defense in "The Emmett Lawton Story." Miller fills the lead role well in these episodes.

By the time *Wagon Train* entered its seventh season it had begun to slip in the ratings. To generate interest, the show was expanded to 90 minutes and filmed in color for the first time. New blood was also added to the cast with the entrance of scout Cooper ("Coop") Smith, played by Robert Fuller, fresh from starring in *Laramie*. And young Michael Burns, who had previously appeared as various characters in several episodes, became Barnaby West, a 13 year old boy searching the West alone for his sister, in the final episode of the sixth season.

Each new character took his place in the rotation of featured regulars. Coop's best episodes include "The Widow O'Rourk Story" where he unwittingly stumbles onto the vast, hidden agricultural empire of an empress. Because of his resemblance to her late husband (a dual role in flashbacks for Robert Fuller), she offers to adopt him, provide him with a bride and bequeath him all her riches. Coop appears to be callous and unfeeling when he apparently toys with the affections of the daughter of a singer who is touring the West with her troupe in "The Sandra Cummings Story." In another romantic plot, "The Alice Whitetree Story," Coop is attracted to a halfbreed girl he finds wandering in the wilderness. Coop's boyhood blood brother, now blind, joins the train in order to kill him in "The Richard Bloodgood Story." And Coop finds himself recruited to pose as the husband of his old girlfriend's twin sister in "The Betsy Blee Smith Story." Through such lead appearances, Fuller makes a solid contribution to the show.

Barnaby has a key role in "The Sam Spicer Story" when he is taken hostage by two fleeing bank robbers. He causes a distraught Hawks to make a disastrous error in judgment, when he runs away after a spanking in "The Whipping." In "The Hide Hunters," Barnaby is taunted by a group of buffalo skinners, and in "The Katy Piper Story," he kills a masked bandit who turns out to be a boy his own age. Burns turns in a credible performance in each of these episodes.

One of the most unusual episodes of *Wagon Train*, "The Horace Best Story," featured comedian George Gobel as Major Adams' mother's cousin ("twice removed") and includes an original song written especially for the show. Horace, an Easterner who has never been west, is trying to become a wagonmaster like his "cousin Major." After he recruits virtually all of the suppliers and crew members in St. Louis who have previously worked for Seth, Horace holds a big parade in order to entice settlers going west to join his train. Although the episode is a delightful tour de force for Gobel and includes a hilarious cameo by Ken Curtis as "Pappy" Lightfoot, it contains a serious and meaningful message about the responsibilities and rigors of being a wagonmaster. When Horace informs Seth that he has recruited 100 wagons for the trek west, the following conversation transpires:

> SETH: A hundred wagons ... that means that you've accepted responsibility for better than three hundred lives and you'd better not let 'em down either.
>
> HORACE: I'll do my best!
>
> SETH: That's all any man can ask of you. But you know so many times the best is just not good enough ... when you think of all the people—seventy-five or a hundred of 'em who are gonna die when the cholera hits your camp without you knowin' it's comin' ... and that Indian war party that comes down off the high hills. Their screams splinter the night and their arrows set fire to it ... you say, well, I did my best. That's what you say to all those silent dead. I did my best ... you know your heart begins to falter a little bit and you begin to wonder with all those people lookin' to ya, dependin' on your judgement, willin' to follow you into the wilderness... Then you come to the mountains... Of course, the mountains are usually covered with rock and shale and the wagons wheels slip and slide back and they break and yer wagon itself lurches backwards and the horse collars cut into the bleeding shoulders of yer horses... Yes sir, those barren hillsides where ya know there was gonna be grass, but there wasn't any grass and then ya come on a dry creek bed where you was sure there was gonna be water, but there isn't any water. Yer people are thirsty. All those moments of decision Horace, those are the tough moments. You have to decide whether to cross the river at night or whether yer gonna wait till dawn ... whether ya want to take the uncharted short cut or the long mountain trail that's safe... And all the time you feel that those people are lookin' at ya and waitin'. They're yer people Horace, yer people... So finally ya have to make a decision to move on and at that minute Horace you pray that Almighty God is close to your hand when you make that decision.

This is as touching and poignant a description of the awesome burdens and responsibilities of a wagonmaster as can be found anywhere in the lore of the American West.

Most episodes of *Wagon Train* are mini-morality plays, with the moral often being that people are basically good and the evil in them—that would threaten the well-being of the community—comes from their environment. Usually these misguided people who endanger the train are capable of being converted. Ralph Brauer in his book, *The Horse, the Gun and the Piece of Property* uses two episodes to illustrate this thesis, "The Nancy Palmer Story" and "The Sam Paulaski Story."[11] Nancy Palmer (played by Audrey Meadows) and her husband are a wealthy couple who have lost everything and bitterly resent others on the wagon train who have more than they. ("They're nobodies and their families are nobodies. How could they know what loss is? They never had anything to lose.") Nancy, however, is friendly with the children on the train and when most of the adults go into a nearby town she is given the responsibility of watching them. This serves as an opportunity for her and her husband to rob the train and run away. Pursued by the crew, Nancy's husband abandons her in the desert and dies in his attempt to escape alone.

She is rescued, however, and gives back the money. The story tries to show that it was Nancy's elitist upbringing that led to her wrongdoing, causing her to believe she was better than other people rather than one of them.

On the other hand, Sam Pulaski (played by Ross Martin) is a small time crook from the Bowery in New York who dreams of better pickings in the West. So he goes off to California with his mother, sister and gang on the wagon train. Along the way the gang decides to "shake down" the train and is caught in the act. Sam Pulaski's problem is just the reverse of Nancy Palmer's—he's never had enough. In the tough environment of the Bowery he had to turn to crime in order to support his mother and sister. Furthermore, law and order on the Bowery have broken down to the point that even the cops are "on the take." When one of Sam's gang tries to pay off the wagon crew, he learns that not all communities function like the Bowery. It is then that Sam realizes his mistake and is redeemed like Nancy. And "that's the way it happened moving west," at least on *Wagon Train*.

The series, initially at least, was not acclaimed by critics. *Variety* (September 25, 1957) gave *Wagon Train*'s pilot broadcast a less than glowing review:

> Perhaps an hour's worth of western cliches could hold an audience; perhaps sticking to principles with adult treatment could do the same; but it's probable that a bad combination of the two won't succeed in holding anybody—the adult treatment will lose the kiddies and the potboiler aspects will lose the adults....
>
> Production and casting credits are top flight throughout, except for the script's inadequacies. Bond is authoritative and believable as the tough ex–Army major wagon master.... Only problem for NBC appears to be that of making up its mind just what kind of show it wants to do and then doing it.

Time, however, proved the *Variety* critic wrong. The show took a year to catch on with viewers but was rated number two by Nielsen during the next three seasons. *Wagon Train* finally replaced *Gunsmoke* as America's most popular television series in 1961-62. The show dropped to twenty-fifth the following year, however, and although it remained on the air until 1965, it never reached its former popularity.

The dichotomy described in *Variety* (if one did, indeed, exist) was resolved in favor of an adult approach. Children, however, did have their own version of *Wagon Train* to watch during the 1963-64 season: *The Travels of Jaimie McPheeters*. The series featured stories about a 12 year old boy (played by Kurt Russell making his first regular television appearance) on a wagon train bound for California in 1849. He was accompanied by his eccentric father, an irresponsible doctor (broadly played by veteran actor Dan O'Herlily).

Based on Robert Lewis Taylor's 1958 Pulitzer Prize–winning novel of the same name, *Travels* followed the *Wagon Train* format. Jaimie would get into some harrowing adventure each week involving some of the colorful supporting characters also heading west or ne'er-do-well or troubled souls (played by various guest stars) that the train met along its journey. Youngsters could readily identify with Jaimie, Jenny, a 17 year old orphan, and the Kissel brothers (Micah, Leviticus, Deuteronomy and Lamentations) played by the Osmond Brothers (who also sang the show's catchy theme song). Charles Bronson made his final television series appearance as wagonmaster Linc Murdock before becoming a superstar in films. Unfortunately, the series was canceled after only one season (26 episodes).

It is significant to note that *Wagon Train* only reached its final destination three times: at the end of the first season ("The Sacramento Story"), when some of the characters who had been introduced in earlier episodes were on hand; the end of the fifth season ("The Heather Mahoney Story"), when Hale falls for a pretty widow and almost leaves the train; and at the end of the seventh season ("The Last Circle Up"), in a story filled with all the emotions one might experience at the end of the trail—sorrow, joy, love, hate, as well as birth and death. For most of its run, however, the focus of *Wagon Train* was on making the journey, not arriving at the final destination.

And so it was with the cattle drives on *Rawhide*. Only the first two drives are shown reaching their destination. The first drive is from San Antonio to Sedalia, Missouri, and the second from San Antonio to Abilene, Kansas. An episode focuses on the end of each drive. In "Incident of the Promised Land," when Gil Favor and his men arrive in Sedalia (during the third season) the herd finally reaches the end of the trail (where they are faced with a selling panic which has driven cattle prices to an all-time low). At the end of the fourth season, in "Abilene," the second drive ends. (This time one of the drovers contracts smallpox and all of them are quarantined for four days in a hotel room. Although Favor threatens to retire, buy some land and settle down, he and his men return for another long drive the next season.)

Rawhide has been dismissed by some critics as "the cattleman's answer to *Wagon Train*,"[12] but it probably was the closest television has come to creating a "sweat and blood" Western. The series, which premiered on January 9, 1959, as a mid-season replacement, made no attempt to embellish the basic format of man-against-the West and thus achieved a rugged documentary realism that concentrated on the harsher aspects of life on the frontier.

Rawhide was the creation of veteran Hollywood writer-director Charles Marquis Warren, who had been instrumental in developing the television version of *Gunsmoke* and had recently finished directing the film *Cattle Empire* (1958). The program owes much in style and integrity, however, to the classic Howard Hawks film *Red River* (1948), which in turn had been inspired by Borden Chase's novel *The Chisholm Trail*. Trail boss Gil Favor was presented as a father-figure, John Wayne's film role, and young Rowdy Yates was a character comparable to that played by Montgomery Clift. Originally entitled *Cattle Drive* but later changed to *Rawhide*, Warren's creation (like Hawks') set out to depict the "working West" of the Cattle Kingdom and the men and women who inhabited it.

In the first episode Favor introduces himself to the audience with an opening monologue that is to become one of the series' trademarks:

> It's not the roundin' up and the ropin' and the brandin' of the cattle that's the big problem for the ranchers. It's gettin' um to market—fifteen hundred bone weary miles from the southern tip of Texas to the railhead at Sedalia. That's where I come in. Gil Favor's my name—trail boss.

Another episode from that first season opens:

> Ridin' herd over a long trail may be a headache, but I can tell you that it's never boresome even when it's goin' smooth. When there's plenty of sweet grass, blue skies, clear spring water, you can ride lazy thinkin' of what you left behind, dreamin' of what's ahead. But ridin' easy doesn't come often on a drive when you're pushin' 3,000 head and twenty hands. There's always something about ta happen. Whatever it is and whenever it comes up, I got ta meet it. That's my job. I'm Gil Favor, trail boss.

Seeking authenticity, Warren based much of his detail for the series on a diary written by George Duffield, who had served as a drover on a real cattle drive from San Antonio to Sedalia in 1867. From Duffield's diary came the unique terminology that gave the series much of its realism. Terms such as "beeves" (a collection of cattle), "drover" (a working member of the crew), "trail boss" (supervisor of the drive with total authority over the men), "ramrod" (second in command on a drive), "drag" (member of the crew

Eric Fleming starred for six seasons as *Rawhide*'s trail boss, Gil Favor.

whose job was to ride behind the herd and "eat dust"), and "point" (member of the crew who rode ahead of the herd scouting the terrain) were used extensively in the stories.[13]

Warren sometimes even invented terminology to cover aspects of the drive not defined in Duffield's diary, such as "swing" to describe the drovers who rode along the sides of the herd rounding up strays. He also authored the lines used to close each episode, "Head 'em up! Move 'em out!" Later a cattleman told Warren that that was what cowhands had been saying for years.[14] It was Warren's intention to make *Rawhide* unique from other Western series. In an interview he explained:

> With us, the herd is primary. We're always up against the elements, and we never leave them entirely behind. For instance, the "Wagon Train" people come across their exploits and suddenly the wagon train disappears while they tell their story.... With the acute beef shortage and a nation starving after the Civil War, if it came to a choice between men and beeves, the beeves won.[15]

When Warren cast the series, he chose relatively unknown actors for the leading roles. To play trail boss Gil Favor, "a tough man of action who possessed good judgment, compassion and an iron will," he selected Eric Fleming. Fleming, with his height and deep voice, proved an excellent choice although his prior acting experience was quite limited. In fact, Fleming had surpassed great obstacles to become an actor. He never knew exactly when or where he was born. His father said it was Santa Paula, California, but he was never able to find any record of his birth anywhere. Various sources list the year of his birth as 1925, 1924, or 1926.

Fleming's childhood was so cruel and hard that it marked him for life. He later related in an interview in Britain for *Weekend* magazine that his father beat him periodically, and even refused to spend the money to pay for an operation he needed for osteomyelitis, a life-threatening illness. When his mother agreed to pay the cost out of her meager wages his father did not visit him once during the six months he was hospitalized. When he finally returned home Fleming's father continued the beatings (even while Eric was still on crutches), justifying them on the grounds that the hospital had made a "baby" out of him and he needed "toughening up." Eric later tried to shoot his father, but the gun misfired and Fleming ran away.

Eric was nearly 11 and big for his age when he became a runaway. He had no money so he hopped freight trains, befriended hoboes, begged and stole the food he needed to survive and was arrested twice in Los Angeles. Returned home by the police, he ran away again going as far as Chicago and New York. He worked as a newsboy, errand boy, soda jerk, swept floors and did odd jobs for the madam in a house of prostitution. As he grew older he found work as a hod-carrier, short order cook and merchant marine seaman.

During World War II, Fleming spent four and a half years with a Navy Seabee unit constructing bases throughout the South Pacific. One night he bet his fellow sailors $10 that he could lift a 200 pound iron block over his head. The weight slipped and the iron block fell, crushing and mutilating his face. He survived and Navy plastic surgeons rebuilt his nose, jaw and forehead so well that his pals urged him to pursue a career in Hollywood.[16] After studying for two years, Fleming got his first acting job in the road company productions of *Happy Birthday* starring Miriam Hopkins. He toured with the show for a couple of months on the West coast and earned his "passport" to the Broadway stage.

Still it was a long hard struggle for the aspiring actor. For years he could only get a day or two of work at a time. During one of his best years, he earned a total of $1,980 before the cameras. In 1951 Fleming got his first crack at television in *Major Dell Conway of the Flying Tigers* for Dumont, in which he played the lead role. The action series, which was shot on a shoestring, featured the adventures of a heroic pilot who served with the Flying tigers squadron in China during World War II. Unfortunately, Fleming was replaced after only a few episodes and the series was soon canceled. Then he was cast in a series of low-budget science fiction and horror films like *Conquest of Space* (1955), *The Queen of Outer Space* (1958) and *Curse of the Undead* (1959—filmed just before *Rawhide* went on the air). *Rawhide* was Fleming's first (and only) break, but by then he had become by his own account "a bitter, twisted man who trusted no one" and who suffered from so much insecurity and inner turmoil that he was afraid to marry and "take on the responsibilities of a family."[17]

Fleming was also intensely superstitious, suffering from a recurring nightmare that he would suffer an early and violent death. He once confided grimly to an actress he had been dating, "Mine is going to be a short life. I don't know when it's going to happen or where. But I know the time isn't far off."[18] In September 1966 he went to Peru to film an episode of M-G-M television's new ABC series for children, *Off to See the Wizard*, called "High Jungle." In one sequence he was required to paddle a canoe across the furious flow of the Huallaga River. The canoe capsized and his Peruvian costar Nico Minardos swam to safety. Twenty men working on the film made a desperate effort to rescue him, but the mountain current was too violent. His body was recovered four days later. Fortunately his six seasons on *Rawhide* remain as testimony to his ability as an actor to capture the essence of the rugged, lonely taciturn trail boss.

Fleming's Favor was not a hero cast in the traditional Western mold. He made mistakes for which he usually had to pay the consequences. In "Incident of the Long Shakedown," Favor decides it is time he started to drive his men to find out if the long layoff between drives and the aging process has caused them to slow down. After veteran drover Jim Quince falls asleep from the pressure, he is fired by Favor. Rowdy tries to get his boss to slow down, but finally quits after they have a heated argument. Joe Scarlett and most of the other experienced hands join Rowdy and Favor names one of his newly hired hands, Jess Clayton, ramrod. Undermanned, overworked and inexperienced, the new drovers are unable to prevent a stampede when one of them takes a shot at a wildcat. All the cattle are lost and Favor is forced to let his entire crew go. Only the cook, Wishbone, and his assistant, Mushy, remain loyal to their boss. However, Rowdy and the other veterans have remained nearby and are able to round up the herd once again. Favor realizing how wrong he was in doubting his older hands, hires them back and all is forgiven and forgotten. Favor is now a wiser and more confident trail boss.

In "The Lost Herd," Favor tries to beat another trail boss and his herd to the nearest railhead because of a shortage of cattle cars. He decides to gamble by taking the herd over dangerous ground through a treacherous mountain pass, but a storm stampedes all but nine steers over a cliff. Both the Cattleman's Association and his own men, even Rowdy, question his judgment. The Association's local representative would like to see Favor discredited and barred from the trail and a hearing is called to look at all the facts. Favor's career hangs in the balance as the Association prepares to set up a new, even bigger herd, for another drive. There are three candidates for the position of trail boss: Favor, a rival trail boss and Rowdy. In his interview, Rowdy is asked whether Favor's decision to take the lost herd through risky country was right. He answers, "I'm just his ramrod, I'm not supposed to judge whether he was right or wrong."

Favor is given the job because of his honesty in accepting responsibility for his mistake and his ability to attract good men. A trail boss must be able to lead a team, develop them into a close-knit unit and keep them together through difficult situations. A good trail boss is one who selects the best man for each job. Rowdy's answer has demonstrated that he is loyal to Favor and knows his place on the team. He is a good ramrod, perhaps the best, but he is not a trail boss. Favor's gamble failed this time, but he has been right many more times than he has been wrong and every long drive is a gamble in the cattle business.

In an episode that is a decided "change of pace" from most stories, another side of Favor's character is shown. "Incident of the Fish Out of Water" finds Favor traveling to Philadelphia to visit his two young daughters, Gillian and Maggi, who are being raised

Clint Eastwood costarred on *Rawhide* as ramrod Rowdy Yates.

by his sister-in-law, Eleanor Bradley. Once there, he is faced with deciding whether to be "a real father" or one who "just brings presents." He discovers that because they have not seen him for two years, they are afraid of him, but he gradually wins them over. Much to the disapproval of their aunt, who is raising them to be proper young ladies, he teaches them how to ride and shoot a bow and arrow.

After hearing that Favor has decided to retire from droving to bring up his daughters, Wishbone and Pete Nolan come to the city to talk Gil into going back with them. Once there, they discover that a Pawnee chief is being held prisoner by a carnival owner who has been exhibiting the Indian in a sideshow. When the three drovers free the chief, Favor realizes that he belongs on the trail and that his daughters are better off being raised by their aunt. The girls, however, are left much the better from his visit. (The girls appear in a later episode of the series, "Boss's Daughters," when Aunt Eleanor brings them west while considering a marriage offer from a prosperous rancher.)

While Gil Favor was the real "star" of the show, ramrod Rowdy Yates was featured prominently in many of the stories. Clint Eastwood, another unknown, was selected for the role—a break that launched him on a career that made him one of Hollywood's true superstars. Born in 1930 in San Francisco, Eastwood had also experienced a tough childhood and had worked as a laborer before settling down to an acting career. His television work had hardly been noticed, although he was known to have appeared in small roles in such series as *Navy Log*, *West Point* and *Maverick* ("Duel at Sundown").

Eastwood had been able to land bit parts in such forgettable films as *Revenge of the Creature* (1955), *Francis in the Navy* (1955), and *The First Traveling Saleslady* (1956). The closest he had come to a starring role was as second male lead in *Ambush at Cimarron Pass* (1958), a film that Eastwood later called "the worst Western ever made," although it was a screening of that film that convinced Warren to cast him as Rowdy Yates.

In addition to benefiting from the show in terms of salary, Eastwood was given great exposure to American audiences and learned a great deal about filmmaking techniques through working with such directors as Ted Post. Even today Eastwood claims that working on *Rawhide* was one of the most valuable acting experiences he has ever had, and he credits this experience with expanding his acting technique:

> Having the security of being in a series week in, week out gives you great flexibility; you can experiment with yourself, try a different scene different ways. If you make a mistake one week, you can look at it and say, "Well, I won't do that again," and you're still on the air next week.[19]

Not only did *Rawhide* enable the young actor to sharpen his skills as a performer, it sparked in him the urge to direct an episode himself. He planned one such show but at the last moment was unable to shoot it because higher-ups declared that episodes of other series directed by actors had been flops.[20] Rowdy Yates was a very different type of role for Eastwood from that which would later make him famous. Cast as a good-natured young cowhand, in a series devoid of sex with limited violence, Eastwood found himself in a world where the bad guys were unmistakably evil and he represented the "clean-cut" good guy in the classical Western tradition established on the big screen by Gary Cooper and John Wayne. Furthermore, the character he played often let his emotions get him into trouble, especially when a pretty girl was involved.

Eastwood as Yates is made a fool of by a woman ("Incident of the Widowed Dove"); becomes the victim of a killer epidemic ("Incident of the Town in Terror"); gets involved in a fight he can not hope to win ("Incident of the Misplaced Indians"); is unwittingly persuaded to break a killer stallion ("Incident of the Day of the Dead"); is arrested for murder ("Incident of the Big Blowout"); and is even handcuffed to a dead man while trying to warn an army outpost of an impending attack ("Incident of the Running Man").

In one of the most interesting plots featuring Rowdy ("The Race"), he quits the drive after an argument with Favor. A cattleman named Lockwood hires Rowdy to boss his drive. After hiring a ramrod named Weed and luring Wishbone and Mushy away from Favor, he boasts to Lockwood that he will beat Favor to the railhead even though Favor's crew has a two-day headstart. Taking his herd over a shorter, but more dangerous route, Rowdy passes Gil, but escapes disaster from a prairie fire only because of a fortunate rainstorm. Then he brags to his men that he had telegraphed ahead and knew a storm was coming. It is not until the race is over and he has won that he learns how lucky he actually was. His herd would not have been saved had the storm not veered off course. So, even though he is offered another herd, Rowdy decides to go back to work for Favor.

Eastwood was proud of *Rawhide* and its classic approach. In a *TV Guide* interview he proclaimed, "We did honest stories, pretty much the way they happened. Now and then we may have rearranged things to heighten the drama, but in general, we respected historical truth."[21] Eastwood wanted to believe the legend of the classic Western hero and consequently cultivated his own image as an all-around nice guy.

Rowdy Yates' father was not such a nice guy, however, and in "Incident at Rio Salado" viewers were introduced to Jake Yates, a good for nothing alcoholic who had deserted Rowdy and his mother years earlier. After insulting some of Favor's drovers in a Mexican cantina, Jake is recognized by Rowdy. Later Jake presents a proposition to his son — that together they ambush and kill a Robin Hood–style Mexican bandit for the reward money. Rowdy refuses to help, but is tricked into it when Jake beats up the bandit's elderly father and frames Rowdy for it. When Rowdy and the Mexican bandit later face off in a gun duel, Jakes shoots the bandit in the back. Rejecting any part of the reward money, Rowdy forces his father to leave town. Outside of town, followers of the slain bandit kill Jake and steal the money. Rowdy reveals a depth of character rarely shown in the series as he tries to explain to Favor his feelings about his dead father:

> He wasn't always the kind of man you saw today. He lived kind of a rough hard life. He was quite a man once. All those stories . . . they weren't lies, at least I don't think they were. . . . Ya know when I was a kid, I used to really worship him. All the kids around did. He taught us how to hunt and fish and defend ourselves. . . I owed him a lot. . . Then he went away and left Ma and me. I got ta hatin' him for that. I guess for what he did ta Ma. I dunno. . . Maybe I was bein' selfish about the whole thing. . . He wasn't as bad as you think. . . If you'd known him like he was when I was little.

Feelings about his father seemed to haunt Rowdy. In the last episode of the series, "Crossing at White Feather," Rowdy tells a young boy who has lost faith in his drunken father, "There's something that I've been keeping tight inside of me for a long time too. . . My Pa . . . he never went to school a day in his life, never carried more than he could throw on his back, and never stayed in one place longer 'n he could help it. . . Then one day, I told him I hated him and ran off, just like you're doin' today. . . ."

Later, at the close of the episode, in comments that conflict with the events depicted in the "Rio Salado" episode, Rowdy responds to the boy's question of what became of his father, "I don't rightly know. . . I think about him. I try to forget the past, but once in a while you find yourself wondering where he is, what he's doin'. Ya know, I don't even know if he's alive. That's when ya know you're alone. . . But ya try not to think about it too much. . . ."

By the time *Rawhide* was in its fourth season, Eastwood had become a pro and pretty well realized that an actor reaches a certain saturation point on television. He had set his sights on the big screen and decided to take his chances in Spain working from February to June 1964 during a break in *Rawhide*'s production schedule. There he made the first of three so-called "spaghetti Westerns," *A Fistful of Dollars*, directed by Sergio Leone, in which he played a macho cynic — lawless and without fixed principles or creed — an image which Eastwood would later find harder to shake than his nice-guy Rowdy Yates screen persona.

Eastwood played the poncho-clad, cheroot-puffing "Man with No Name" who defied the code of the conventional Western hero twice more for Leone in *For a Few Dollars More* (1965) and *The Good, the Bad and the Ugly* (1966). He would follow these with a Hollywood Western in the same tradition, *Hang 'Em High* (1968).

Eastwood's later Westerns, which he produced himself, were also nonconformist films. In *High Plains Drifter* (1973), he plays a vengeful ghost. *The Outlaw Josey Wales* (1976) resists the war-is-hell clichés and insists that war is just plain absurd. *Pale Rider* (1985) finds Eastwood's "preacher" representing Death. These are not Westerns about good versus evil. They are Westerns that pose the deeper question, what is good and what is evil? It was, however, his role as a contemporary police detective named Harry Callahan, who bent the rules to effect his own definition of justice in *Dirty Harry* (1971) and four sequels, that brought Eastwood celluloid immortality.

Meanwhile, prior to *Rawhide*'s final season, CBS and Eric Fleming parted company over a variety of contractual differences and Eastwood was elevated to the starring role.

Rowdy Yates is "promoted" to trail boss. Other changes were also made in the cast, including the addition of Jed Colby, played by veteran screen actor John Ireland, as Yates' second-in-command; Ian Cabot played by David Watson, as an English remittance man and Simon Blake, played by Raymond St. Jacques, who becomes the first black star to have a major continuing role in a television Western.

Actually, although *Rawhide* had won four Western Heritage Awards from the National Cowboy Hall of Fame in Oklahoma City as the most outstanding program of its genre, its ratings had been slipping. The show was sixth in its second season, thirteenth the third year, twenty-second the next year and forty-fourth the fifth and sixth seasons. Changes in the cast and format seemed to be needed and when Fleming opted to leave the series to pursue a film career, changes at the management and production level led to additional changes in cast. Sheb Wooley, James Murdock and Robert Cobal were all axed.

To fill in the gaps CBS hired a black Shakespearean actor (St. Jacques) who had never been in a Western saddle before but had impressive acting credits (films: *The Pawnbroker*, *Black Like Me*, and *Mister Moses*; television: *Slattery's People*, *The Defenders*, and *Dr. Kildare*). Executive producer Ben Brady denied, in a *TV Guide* interview, that St. Jacques had been hired to cash in on a trend:

> St. Jacques is not being brought in because it is sociologically opportune to have a Negro in a sympathetic role, or to placate civil rights groups. St. Jacques will be a drover, exactly the same as any white drover, except he's colored. There will be no reference to race.[22]

Since there were many black cowboys in the West, authenticity did not suffer. Still in one episode Blake expresses understanding for a pale-faced Chiricahua Apache who is three-fourths white, one-fourth Indian. "Let's say I got a skin that itches for him," Blake says. "And I'm better off than him, see? When you're all one color you know where you stand." Thus was the issue of race "avoided" on the revamped *Rawhide*.

The second addition, Watson , however, looked in the opinion of one critic, "about as much at home on the range as Dean Martin would at a WCTU convention."[23] A spindly youth of 24 who appeared 18, he had just one prior film to his credit, *King Rat*, and his scene in that had ended on the cutting-room floor. Remittance men from England had lived in the West on money sent then from home. Furthermore, the wealthy-lad-from-England figure was a fixture of Western novels written at the turn of the century but had been mercifully omitted from more contemporary rangeland adventures. A Western novelist, when told of *Rawhide*'s revival of the remittance man, is supposed to have said: "My gawd! The old bow and Harrow set!" In any case, Cabot, who was to provide "a new perspective and sense of humor" in the show, was given such ridiculous lines to utter as "How's the paterfamilias?" and "smashing food order" and "rather splendid day."

The addition of John Ireland was made after a screening of the new season's first three episodes revealed the need for a mature, established, "name" actor. Ireland, who had appeared in countless classic Western films like *My Darling Clementine* and *Red River* and nearly every major television Western from *Gunsmoke* to *Bonanza*, filled the need nicely and was given second billing, just below Eastwood.

Eastwood, when asked his reaction to his elevation from ramrod to trail boss, commented, "I used to carry half the shows. Now I carry them all for the same money."[24] The effects of Rowdy's promotion, however, could be seen in the stories themselves. With Rowdy Yates as trail boss, the emphasis of the show changed. Favor had been a father-figure leader who treated his crew as his "boys." He was a rigid disciplinarian who ran the whole show and permitted no dissension. Rowdy, however, because as ramrod he had often functioned as a spokesman for the entire crew, could not very well become a Favor-type trail boss. As leader he functioned, not as a benevolent despot, but as a consensus taker whose decisions were made democratically. This style of leadership is evident in an episode entitled "Brush War at Buford," when a meeting of the entire crew is held to make a decision. There is open discussion revealing some conflict of opinion among the drovers. At one point one says, "The only reason I took to droving in the first place was I figured it was the only place left where a man could ride the way he wanted to." As Ralph Brauer points out, that speech would never have been acceptable to Favor, but under Yates "it becomes the credo of the whole crew which with its own law and morality roams through the limitless space of the West."[25]

Directly below Favor and Yates in the chain of command was Pete Nolan. Sheb Wooley brought several years of experience in Western film character roles to the part (for instance, as one of the three gunslingers waiting for the train to arrive in Hadleyville in *High Noon*) and was an accomplished singer and songwriter as well. Serving as scout, Pete rode ahead of the herd looking for water, river crossings, good grazing land and campsites. Nolan was featured in his share of *Rawhide* stories. In "Incident of the Dust Flower," Pete "stands in" as the fiancé of a spinster heading west who can not stand the embarrassment of telling her family that she is not really engaged. In "Incident of His Brother's Keeper," Pete agrees to accompany the attractive young wife of an invalid to a square dance only to find out later that he has fallen into a romantic triangle when her brother-in-law shows up. In "Incident of the Blackstorms," Pete is given the job of taking the body of a notorious killer who has been shot by one of the drovers into town for burial and falls victim to a kidnapping scheme. In "Incident of the Lost Tribe," Pete is forced to lead a band of renegade Cheyennes safely across the border (where it is revealed that Pete was once married to a Cheyenne maiden). In "The Reunion," Pete is given the responsibility of working out a treaty with the Pawnees who will give the tribe 500 head of cattle to keep the peace.

Another leading character in the series was the cook, Wishbone. The comical role was a tour de force for veteran character actor Paul Brinegar, who had played a similar role in Warren's *Cattle Empire*. A cantankerous character who got fed up with the men when they bellyached about his grub, he invariably got mixed up in everybody else's business. In "Incident of the Thirteenth Man," Wishbone goes to town to get his aching tooth pulled. There he is "drafted," along with Rowdy, for jury duty on a local murder trial. In "Incident of the Tinker's Dam," Wishbone is captured by Indians who mistake him for his brother T.J. (who has learned that renegades are holding an Indian chief prisoner to prevent him from signing a peace treaty). In a hilarious episode entitled "Incident of the Deserter," Wishbone leaves the drive in disgust over the drovers' always making fun of his cooking, and gets mixed up with a widow who takes an immediate liking to him and tries to convince him to settle down and open a restaurant (much to the dismay of a local merchant who has his eyes on the widow's money). In "Incident at Superstition Prairie," the viewer sees the humane and caring soul that lies beneath the crusty front Wishbone always puts up. Wishbone, finding an old Indian who has been left to die by his tribe, nurses him back to health and incurs the wrath of the Comanches who do not like outsiders meddling in their tribal customs. In "Incident of the Prairie Elephant," another humorous episode, Wishbone gets mixed up in a domestic quarrel involving a clown and an acrobat who work in a traveling circus.

Wishbone's assistant, and the other humorous character on the show, was Mushy Mushgrove played by James Murdock. Although he was slow-witted and the constant object of the drovers' good-natured kidding, Mushy was loyal and especially devoted to his friend and tutor, "Mr. Wishbone." Occasionally, Mushy too, had his moment in the *Rawhide* "spotlight." In "Incident of the Captive," Mushy's mother catches up with him

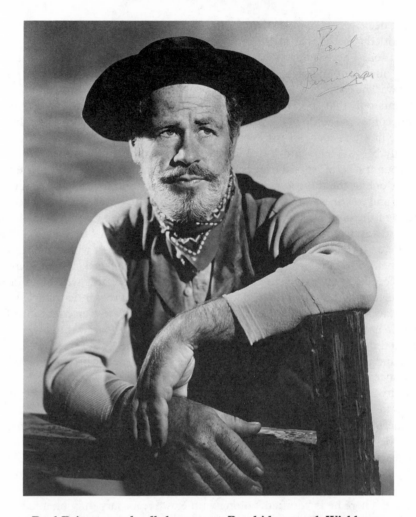

Paul Brinegar rode all the way on *Rawhide* as cook Wishbone.

after a long search. She has come out West to take her son home with her to run his recently deceased father's barber shop. Since Mushy prefers to remain with the cattle drive, he devises a plan to get his mother to let him stay out West by having her kidnapped so he can rescue her. In "The Child-Woman," Mushy runs into his two cousins, Laverne and Posie, who are working as singers in a saloon and gets beaten up by some thugs when he tries to rescue the younger from the evils of barroom life.

Other regulars on *Rawhide* included drover Jim Quince (played by Steve Raines) and wrangler Hey Soos Patines (played by Robert Cabal). Raines had appeared in *Cattle Empire* with Brinegar. His role on the series was, however, more prominent, with several episodes focusing on some aspect of Quince's life. In "Incident at Poco Tiempo," Quince and Rowdy are accused of killing a priest, arrested and put on a stage headed for the closest jail. In "Incident of the Running Iron," Quince is out chasing a cattle rustler when a posse arrives and mistakes Quince for the rustler. He is taken to the nearest town where he is sentenced to hang. Rowdy and Favor arrive in the nick of time, just as a lynch mob has placed a noose around Quince's neck. Several members of Quince's family are introduced in "Judgment at Hondo Seco." Quince learns that his niece is in trouble. Her father,

Judge Quince, Jim's estranged brother, sends a posse out looking for her fiancé, a gambler who has killed a man in self-defense. When he is captured, Quince helps him escape and is sentenced by his brother to hang.

Although appearing in numerous episodes, Hey Soos (probably a phonetic spelling of Jesús) had a smaller role than most of the other regulars, usually appearing in stories dealing with the horses belonging to the cattle drive. He was clearly the superstitious member of the crew and enjoyed telling his fellow drovers' fortunes with a deck of cards. By the end of the fourth season, Hey Soos' role had been enlarged. In "Incident of the Blue Fire," he spreads eerie tales of death caused by prairie storms. He explains that whenever a steer's horns begin to glow blue (an electrical phenomenon resulting from lightning storms) someone is supposed to die. Shortly thereafter Hey Soos' prophecy appears to have come true when one of the drovers is killed. In "Incident of the 100 Amulets," Hey Soos goes into town where his mother lives to buy her some groceries. The local residents believe she is a witch and he is a warlock. Favor and Rowdy go to their aid when an angry, superstitious mob begins to stone them.

Guest stars also played a prominent role in many of *Rawhide*'s episodes, although they were not featured at the expense of the series regulars as was often the case on *Wagon Train*. Such established and capable stars as Dan Duryea, Margaret O'Brien, Mercedes McCambridge, Kim Hunter, Gary Merrill, Brian Keith, Cesar Romero, Peter Lorre, Frankie Laine (who warbled the show's theme song every week), Ed Wynn, Burgess Meredith, Barbara Stanwyck, Walter Pidgeon, James Whitmore, Keenan Wynn, Neville Brand and Mickey Rooney all made one or more noteworthy appearances on the series. Each became caught up in some way with the drive, providing ample opportunity for both character development and physical action.

Although beginning slowly, the show was quite popular with viewers during its first five seasons, being ranked as high as sixth in 1960-61. The critics also grew to like it, although *Variety* wrote this of the opening episode on January 12, 1959:

> Both Fleming and Eastwood show promise as opposite types, the former levelheaded and straightforward, the latter colorful and enthusiastic. More footage should be devoted to each in future episodes. . . . It's going to take more than on-the-spot footage of cattle, a whip-lashing theme song . . . and an effective "canned" score to rack up ratings here, although just being a Western should insure the series a good share of the audience.

By the beginning of its second season in September 1959, *Variety* was saying:

> "Rawhide" was one of the big surprises of last season . . . it was an immediate click and is now sold out. From the looks of the opener, it should continue as an important factor for CBS on Friday nights.

Even the show's theme song was a classic. Who does not remember Frankie Laine's macho rendition to the accompaniment of cracking whips as hundreds of longhorns kept "rollin', rollin'" across the screen?

Nevertheless, when *Rawhide*'s slide in the ratings could not be halted despite the massive cast changes, the series was canceled. It might have run longer if CBS had not refused to film the series in color. (*Rawhide* was the last remaining network show to be filmed exclusively in black and white.)

And so within a span of four months both *Wagon Train* (September 1965) and *Rawhide* (January 1966) came to an end. Gil Favor and Rowdy Yates had worked their last cattle drive; Seth Adams and Chris Hale had led their last wagon train. Only three Westerns remained on the home screen longer, *Gunsmoke*, *Bonanza* and *The Virginian*. Broadcast for eight seasons (although *Rawhide* began and ended in the middle of a season), these two Westerns together accounted for a total of 501 episodes (284 for *Wagon Train*, 217 for *Rawhide*) of adult Western action and adventure. Deeply coloring the average American's perception of our Westward movement, these programs reinforced the mythic image of brave men on horseback leading with honor, integrity and determination fearless pioneers through all manner of danger to "the promised land." Television has not seen their like since.

VIII. Single Parent Families on the Video Frontier
OR, HOW "THE RIFLEMAN" FOUND A "BONANZA" IN "THE BIG VALLEY"

As we have seen, early television Westerns focused primarily on the exploits of roving loners or lawmen attempting to bring justice and order to the early frontier. The late fifties and early sixties, however, saw the emergence of a new breed of adult Western—the "domestic" or "family" Western. Several of these series were quite successful, lasting four or more seasons—*The Rifleman* (first of this format), *Bonanza* (second in longevity only to *Gunsmoke*), *The Virginian* (television's first 90 minute Western), *The Big Valley* (featuring a matriarchal, rather than a patriarchal, family), and *The High Chaparral* (a slightly modified imitation of *Bonanza*). *Lancer*, which ran only two seasons, also fit this format. As if to emphasize the rigors of life in the old West, each of these television families was headed by a widower (or in the case of *The Big Valley*, a widow). Several of these patriarchs had been widowed more than once. In fact, Ben Cartwright (*Bonanza*) had suffered the loss of three wives! Only Big John Cannon (*The High Chaparral*) was married at the time the stories took place.

The first successful family Western, *The Rifleman*, debuted on September 30, 1958. At first glance this series appeared to be another gimmick-gun Western, emphasizing the hero's use of a rifle instead of the traditional six-shooter. What made this program unique, however, was the warm relationship between Lucas McCain, a widowed homesteader struggling to make a living off his ranch, and Mark, his young son.

Because of its title and the opening which focused on McCain's skill with a rifle, this series might be considered as marking a transition between the gun-oriented Westerns of the early fifties and the later family-oriented Westerns. McCain was referred to as "the rifleman" because of the specially designed .44 Winchester which he always carried. He was deadly accurate even when firing eight shots in less than five seconds (according to one storyline). His rifle had the ring placed so that he could cock it with a twirl. The action could trip the trigger by means of a screw on the trigger guard. Thus, he needed to only recock the gun to fire eight shots without pulling the trigger.[1] Despite this, the shooting was played down and Lucas' attempt to make a man of Mark gave the hero more credibility than many other Western heroes. In every episode of *The Rifleman*, Mark learned something about life, either from his father or his own observations, making the series an adult Western with genuine family appeal.

The stories were set in North Fork, New Mexico, during the 1880s where Lucas was continually being called upon to help the marshal bring the countless bullies, drunks, rustlers, and killers that popped up in most episodes to justice. The series was the brain-child of aspiring writer-director Sam Peckinpah. Peckinpah, who was virtually unknown at the time, was to subsequently become one of the silver screen's most acclaimed Western directors.

In 1958 Peckinpah wrote a script for *Gunsmoke* which the producer turned down. After reworking it, he submitted it to Dick Powell, head of Four Star Films, which was producing several popular Western series (*Trackdown, Zane Grey Theatre*). Powell liked the script and it was broadcast as "The Sharpshooter" on the *Zane Grey Theatre* Western anthology series March 7, 1958.[2] In the story, Lucas McCain, who had already gained a reputation as a fast and accurate "rifleman" and his 10 year old son, Mark, arrive in North Fork, a growing New Mexico town. Lucas attempts to win enough money in a shooting contest being held there to make the down payment on a ranch. The crooked town boss, Jim Lewis, has bet considerable money on another fast gun named Vernon (well-played by young Dennis Hopper) and threatens to harm Mark unless Lucas "throws" the contest. Lucas deliberately misses his last shot and bitterly prepares to leave North Fork with Mark. Before leaving, however, he teams up with Vernon to rid the town of Lewis and his cronies and is invited to settle down and make North Fork his permanent home.

Chuck Connors, a six-foot, five-inch former major league baseball player (Brooklyn Dodgers and Chicago Cubs) was selected to play Lucas, while young ex–Mouseketeer, Johnny Crawford, became his son, Mark. The producers of the show, Arthur Gardner and Jules Levy, who were, along with director Arnold Laven, to become producers of the new series, persuaded Powell to develop *The Rifleman*. Because of the popular response it received, a sponsor was quickly found and the series was placed on the fall 1958 ABC schedule. Among the contract stipulations was one that guaranteed Sam Peckinpah a chance to direct.[3]

One of the keys to the success of *The Rifleman*, was the casting of Connors, Crawford, and Paul Fix. Connors' introduction to the acting profession came quite by accident. A year after the Dodgers traded the burly first baseman to the Cubs, he was sent to Chicago's minor league team in Los Angeles. In L.A., Chuck batted a substantial .321, hit 23 home runs and conducted an interview show on television between games. It was there that he was spotted by a movie talent scout who got him a job playing a state policeman in a movie called *Pat and Mike* starring Katherine Hepburn and Spencer Tracy. Earning $500 a day, Chuck decided to forsake baseball for the more lucrative profession of acting.

Connors hung around Hollywood for several years playing parts that called for a man nearly six and a half feet tall. After a while he got a role as a heavy opposite James Arness in *Gunsmoke* and he became typed as a Western badguy. Then he heard they were casting the lead in a new series called *The Rifleman* and went to see the producer. When they heaved a rifle across the room at him, he grabbed it with authority, remarking that "it felt just like a Louisville Slugger."[4] He was hired on the spot and that is how "the rifle-man" became an actor.

Johnny Crawford came to *The Rifleman* with more than 60 television shows under his young belt, including 15 *Matinee Theaters*, the memorable title role in the *Lux Video Theatre*'s 1956 version of "Little Boy Lost," and a six-month stint as a Mouseketeer. The 12 year old Crawford was also a veteran of the stage, having first appeared in a play at

The Rifleman, the first of the single parent Westerns, featured Chuck Connors as Lucas McCain with Johnny Crawford as his son Mark.

the age of 5. Furthermore, he was an expert fencer, an amateur cook and a guitar student (which he would later put to good use in the series). Johnny, an avid baseball fan, and Chuck got along marvelously from the start.[5]

Paul Fix, who became marshal of North Fork in the series' fourth episode, was a brewer's son from New York. He had been a playwright and director before trying his hand at acting in the early thirties. Becoming a close friend of John Wayne, he appeared in over 25 films with the Duke between 1931 and 1973, as well as serving as his unofficial vocal and acting coach. His prolific screen career evolved from sinister cowardly villains to dependable upholders of law and order in the mold of Marshal Micah Torrence in *The Rifleman.*[6]

During the first season, Peckinpah directed four episodes of *The Rifleman* including "The Marshal" which introduced Micah Torrance, "The Boarding House," "The Money Gun" and "The Baby Sitter." He also scripted the second episode of the series "Home Ranch." Peckinpah left the show after the first year as the result of differences with the show's producers, whom he claimed "refused to let it be the story of a boy who grows to manhood learning what it's all about."[7] Yet in many ways the series turned out to be exactly what Peckinpah hoped it would be. In "Home Ranch" Mark gets an early lesson in the law of survival on the frontier and has his faith in God put to the test. A powerful cattle baron named Jackman tries to force the McCains off the ranch they have just purchased. Lucas is dragged by a horse, his prized rifle is stolen and their ranch house is burned to the ground. Mark, in despair, questions God's will:

> Pa, it's just not fair! We ride half way across the country looking for the right place and when we finally got it—well, look what happens! Looks to me like the Lord's dead set against us havin' our own place!

In response, Lucas relates to Mark, in his own homespun way, the biblical story of Job and how his faith was tested by the Lord, concluding:

> Mark, Job was as miserable as a man could be ... but he knew he'd been good and righteous ... and he'd not lost faith with the Lord... The Lord was so proud of Job that he restored all the old man's children, and his house and his camels and sheep and gave him over twice as many cattle as before and Job lived over one hundred and forty years as happy as a birddog.

Mark concludes that Job's suffering makes their troubles "kind of piddlin!" His faith thus restored, Mark agrees to stay and guard the ruins of the ranch. Lucas sets out to regain his rifle and convince Jackman that he will not be driven off his land. He not only succeeds, but convinces Jackman to provide the men and materials to rebuild their home.

Mark learns another kind of lesson in "End of a Young Gun." A young outlaw, Will Fulton (played by Michael Landon with the same enthusiasm he was later to display as Little Joe in *Bonanza*), who has been seriously wounded, is given refuge with the McCains while he recovers. He and Mark immediately became friends. Will has become embittered toward the world because his parents were cheated out of the property they had struggled so hard to acquire. At the urging of his older brother, he has turned to a life of crime. Mark remarks that he once read a book about outlaws and "it sure sounded like an awful lot of fun." Will responds:

> It's seemed like a lot of things to me in the last couple of years, but it never seemed like fun. What's fun about being chased all the time, never staying in one place long enough to know anybody, never knowing where your next meal is coming from, never having anybody trust you or being able to trust anybody else? Like right now we're playing checkers and all the time I have to keep my eye on that door... It's not fun... It's not fun at all.

Later Lucas perceptively points out to Will that "You've had a taste of regular life and ya like it. You met a girl ya might be in love with. And you've probably even got a notion about settlin' down." Thus it is not surprising that when his brother returns for him, Will decides to go straight. He will turn himself and the stolen money in to the marshal and begin a new life. When Lucas is forced to kill his brother, Will realizes he has made the right choice—and so does Mark.

Experienced, durable Paul Fix played *The Rifleman*'s marshal, Micah Torrance.

Many episodes close with Lucas patiently explaining to Mark the importance of some lesson to be learned from their most recent adventure. A frequent theme, especially during the first several seasons, stresses toleration and understanding of people who are in some way different: an Argentine gaucho in "The Gaucho," a Chinese merchant and his son who wear pigtails in "The Queue," an older youth who has not learned to read and write in "Three Legged Terror," even a mentally disturbed old man who thinks he is Abe Lincoln in "Honest Abe."

Mark learns a lesson of a quite different sort in "None So Blind" when he befriends a blind banjo player. The banjo player is seeking revenge on the man responsible for his blindness and the loss of his sweetheart. Mark believes that the man he is looking for is the government inspector who has just forced Lucas to kill his entire herd of diseased cattle. So he helps the blind man locate him and then watches in horrified disbelief as the he mistakenly attacks Lucas. A shaken Mark explains to his injured father that he was only trying to "get even" with the man who had brought them so much grief. Lucas quickly explains that "vengeance is mine, sayth the Lord" to his remorseful son.

Mark also learns much from the compassionate example set by his father. In "The Fourflasher," Mark sacrifices an opportunity to race his own horse, Blueboy, in order to ride the horse of an injured farmer who has staked virtually everything he owns on the race. Mark, of course, wins the race and finds that the warm feeling of having helped someone else outweighs the disappointment of not being able to prove the superiority of his own horse. Later, in "The Quiet Fear," Mark takes it upon himself to teach the fundamentals of reading and writing to a young deaf and mute woman with equally gratifying results.

Many individuals who are befriended by Lucas and Mark, find that their lives are profoundly changed for the better. Through their involvement with the McCains, they often learn some new insight into human nature and societal values. Lucas (with support from Micah) helps the basically good citizens of North Fork overcome their blinding, unreasonable fear of a yellow fever epidemic in "Panic." A young man regarded by many in the community as a coward conquers his fear with Lucas' encouragement in "The Hero." Lucas teaches a runaway princess the responsibilities that come with the status into which one is born in "The Princess." Another young man, whose vocal cords have been severed by the Indians, making him unable to speak, learns the true meaning of friendship, forgiveness and patience from Mark and Lucas in "The Silent Knife," one of the most moving episodes in the series.

Even Mark Twain comes under the benevolent influence of the McCains when he visits North Fork shortly after the death of his only son. Blaming himself for his son's death, Twain has decided never to write again. However, thanks to Mark and Lucas' faith in him, he regains the will to continue writing ("The Shattered Idol"). Who would have believed that without the rifleman, *The Adventures of Huckleberry Finn* might never have been written?

Another recipient of McCain friendship is a Harvard-educated Apache named Sam Buckhart, who discovers, with Lucas' help, that he has much to learn about how to function as a Native American law officer in a white frontier community. The episode is entitled simply "The Indian." This episode served as a pilot for another Four Star Western series, *Law of the Plainsman*, starring Michael Ansara as Deputy U.S. Marshal Sam Buckhart (1959-60 on NBC). Marshal Buckhart also appears in another episode of *The Rifleman*, "The Raid," when he returns to North Fork to help Lucas rescue Mark who has been kidnapped by renegade Apaches.

However, no one received more assistance from *The Rifleman* than the kindly, but ineffectual, marshal of North Fork, Micah Torrance. In the fourth episode, "The Marshal," Micah is introduced into the series as an alcoholic deadbeat, who is literally picked up out of the gutter by Lucas. Sometime in the distant past, it is explained, Torrance, then a lawman to be reckoned with, had earned the respect of law-abiding citizen and outlaw alike. But alcohol (for 22 years, by his own admission, he never drank "less than a quart of whiskey a day") and age have taken their toll and now Micah is a man without courage or self-respect. Furthermore, he has lost the use of his right arm from a sort of mental paralysis. Lucas gives Micah a job on his ranch, where he struggles to kick the bottle. When two gunmen, whom Micah had brought to justice many years earlier, arrive in North Fork bent on revenge, Lucas takes his trusty rifle to town. The gunmen, who have killed the marshal, lie in wait for the rifleman who is being led into an ambush by one of their confederates. Meanwhile, Micah is able to find the courage to come to Lucas' aid with his shotgun. When he arrives, he finds that Lucas has killed one of the gunmen, but has been seriously wounded. Micah with unflinching courage kills the other two gunmen in a face to face shoot-out and becomes marshal of North Fork.

Although Micah becomes almost a father figure to Lucas (and a grandfather to Mark), consistently exhibiting such admirable qualities as loyalty, honesty, and kindness, he is surely one of the least competent lawmen in the video West. Lucas must repeatedly come to his assistance with his Winchester (e.g., "The Prisoner"), and on one occasion must again rescue him from the demon rum ("Closer Than a Brother"). Indeed, when Micah is out of town for any reason, Lucas usually becomes acting marshal.

One of the more interesting episodes in the series, "Guilty Conscience," features Paul Fix in a dual role. A woman named Leota shows up one day in North Fork with her son claiming that Micah is her long lost husband, Norman Ambrose Carroway. Lucas soon discovers that the real Carroway (also known as "Charmin' Billy") is a wanted two-bit outlaw, Walt Hacklock (delightfully played by Fix with a brogue and wig), whom he apprehends and brings to North Fork. Meanwhile, Micah has begun to like the idea that he might actually have married and fathered a son 16 years earlier. The life of a husband and father appeals to the old marshal. Nevertheless, Carroway reluctantly accepts his family responsibilities and leaves North Fork (and a wistful Micah) with his wife and son.

Chuck Connors is also given the opportunity of playing a dual role in "Deadly Image." With the aid of a bushy mustache and a wicked scar, Connors becomes the mean, vicious outlaw Earl Bautry who kills for the sheer pleasure of it. Mistaken for McCain by several townspeople, he is accidently killed by Lucas in a bloody climatic struggle. This role gives Connors an opportunity to demonstrate a much broader dramatic range than he normally uses, which he does with obvious relish.

The Rifleman, like many other Westerns of its day, received considerable criticism for what some felt was excessive violence. In the pilot episode there are, for example, five on-screen killings, with six more plus a bloody fistfight in the next three shows. Furthermore, in the second episode, Lucas is brutally dragged behind a horse by a gunman. Violence, was in fact, common on the program throughout its five year run. In "The Man from Salinas," broadcast during the fourth season, the story begins and ends with Lucas killing a man—the first, a gunman in the act of robbing the North Fork bank, and the last, a bounty hunter out to steal the gunman's body so he can claim the reward.

Often the violence, however, is integral to the story and critical to the building of the tension and suspense that many viewers had come to expect in a good Western. Two of the series' more exciting episodes serve to illustrate this. Lucas is accidently blinded in an explosion in "Dark Days at North Fork." When a gunman seeking revenge shows up in North Fork, the rifleman arduously practices shooting at objects in relation to the location of their sound. Then, when the gunman appears, Lucas is able to put four bullets into him by firing in the direction of his voice. Without the final, bloody shootout, this story would have made little sense. In "And the Devil Makes Five," a rattlesnake crawls into Lucas' bedroll. In order to save him, Micah who has a broken arm, must set free a gunman he has in custody. Ultimately Micah is forced to shoot his prisoner, when he flings the rattler at Micah and grabs Mark's rifle in an attempt to escape. Again, the killing seems natural and justified within the context of the story.

Connors, and others associated with the series, steadfastly defended the use of violence as necessary, while pointing out that killings occurred in only about half of the shows. In fact one of the reasons cited for the declining popularity of the series during the last two seasons was the decreasing use of gunplay. The emphasis was, however, always on moral values with the stories' focusing on the reasons the violence was necessary in a climatic scene involving Mark and Lucas. Indeed, the real appeal of this series, which helped to bring it five seasons on the home screen, was the father-son relationship between Lucas and Mark. Whenever Mark was in danger, as he frequently was, Lucas displayed concern, courage and ingenuity. His parental outrage seemed genuine and woe be unto any villain whom he caught harming a hair on the youngster's head. In the afore-mentioned episode, "The Raid," Lucas fought like an army regiment in rescuing Mark from the Apaches who had kidnapped him.

And Mark's concern for his father was no less sincere when Lucas was in jeopardy. In "Stand-In," Lucas is kidnapped by an unscrupulous prison guard to replace an escaped convict in a tumbleweed wagon. Mark frantically summons Micah and together they suc-cessfully search for the rifleman. In "Skull," Mark escapes from an outlaw's sanctuary, where he and Lucas have been held captive and gets help in freeing his father. Moreover, the love that the two feel for each other is openly expressed—sometimes by a look or a touch, but often by a hug or even a kiss. When Lucas is forced by financial considerations to take a job assisting a lawman in Wyoming, he must leave Mark behind in the series' first two-part story, "The Wyoming Story I and II." As the days drag into weeks, Mark becomes more and more worried about the safe return of his father. When Lucas finally does return to North Fork, his reconciliation with his son is a genuinely heartwarming one. In another memorable episode depicting Mark's devotion to his father, "First Wages," Lucas chastises Mark for getting a parttime job at the local livery stable and subsequently neglecting his chores at home. In the episode's final moving scene, viewers, along with Lucas, learn the purpose of Mark's job—he has used the money he earned to purchase a saddle for his father's birthday.

As a single parent trying to raise a young boy on the early Western frontier, Lucas found little time for romance. However, occasionally after the first season, he did become involved with the opposite sex. In "Eddie's Daughter," an attractive young woman of questionable virtue literally throws herself at the rifleman. However, Lucas is quick to realize that she is only trying to trick him into helping her thwart two men who are after some money she has stolen. Although she reforms in time to save her father's life and returns the stolen money, it is clear that the high principled Lucas McCain would never really be interested in "that kind" of woman. A more serious romantic encounter occurs when Ann Dodd comes to North fork to visit her uncle, in "The Visitor." Ann and her family were close friends with Lucas and his wife many years earlier. In fact her son and husband died in the same epidemic which took Lucas' wife. Ann and Lucas share a com-mon bond of past joys and sorrows and she is obviously a woman who would make an exemplary wife and mother. The two are mutually attracted to each other, but the romance is not allowed to flourish. Although Lucas does save Ann's life at the end of the episode, he is not sure Ann could take the place of his dead wife and Ann shares that doubt. She leaves North Fork, hinting that she may return simply because "good friends visit each other." Interestingly, the script for this show was based on a storyline suggested by Chuck Connors himself. Maybe things were getting a little lonesome for the rifleman out there on the masculine frontier.

Thus, it is not surprising that a continuing female character, Miss Milly Scott (sedately played by Joan Taylor), is introduced into the series early in the third season as a potential love interest for Lucas (in "Miss Milly"). The demure and ladylike Miss Milly becomes the storekeeper in North Fork, and although she appears, at least briefly, in most episodes during the next two seasons, nothing ever comes of their relationship. (She does look after Mark for Lucas when he is away and offers the rifleman comfort and encouragement in times of crisis.)

As ratings for the popular series begin to slip, a more dynamic female is brought to North Fork in the fall of 1962 (in "Lou Mallory"). Lou Mallory, played with feisty good humor by Patricia Blair, is an aggressive woman who might be described as a kind of "con-artist-with-a-heart-of-gold." In her first appearance on *The Rifleman*, she breezes into town, flaps her "baby blues" at the male citizenry, and begins buying up property around town because she has learned that a railroad is soon going to be built there. Lucas, with Micah's help, ends up rescuing her from a ne'er-do-well and his three half-witted sons. They do not much like the idea of being out-smarted by a woman, and have kidnapped her, hoping to convince her to marry one of the sons. Lou Mallory is a high-spirited, self-made woman whose parents were poor Irish immigrants. She has struggled all her life and finds it difficult to say even "thank you." Seemingly a perfect match for the equally stubborn and independent Lucas McCain, Lou, nevertheless, is unable to tie the matrimonial knot around him.

Other changes were made in the last several seasons of *The Rifleman*. Mark, who by this time has become a teenager, begins to experience the problems associated with adolescence. In "A Young Man's Fancy," Mark discovers girls—or rather one particular young lady, Sally, the beautiful teenage niece of Miss Milly who has come to North Fork for a visit. Although Sally is several years older and much more interested in another young man nearer her own age, Mark is smitten. In this episode Johnny Crawford gets to demonstrate his vocal ability by singing Sally a love ballad while accompanying himself on the guitar. He also exposes Sally's boyfriend as a hot-tempered bully, although to accomplish this he has to endure a brutal beating. All is well that ends well, however, as Mark receives not one, but two, farewell kisses from Sally as she leaves North Fork. In the series' last episode, "Old Tony," girls discover Mark when a particular young lady, Lorrie, develops a "crush" on the handsome 15 year old McCain. Again Johnny Crawford gets to demonstrate his musical abilities with a beautiful rendition of "Greensleeves."

Comedy was also utilized in some episodes in an effort to stimulate ratings. Guest star Agnes Moorehead turns in a delightful performance as an eccentric old lady bent on collecting the reward on a wanted gunman so she can move into an exclusive old folks' home, in "Miss Bertie." Veteran character actor Jack Elam heads a superb cast in "Knight Errant," the hilarious tale of two old friends who have spent most of their lives tying to beat each other at chess with the aid of their two unscrupulous manservants. In an outright departure to slapstick, black sheep Neb Jackson and his three dull sons return (they initially appeared in "Lou Mallory") as bumbling, but surprisingly effective, lawmen, in "Which Way Did They Go?" That this is clearly a last gasp for the series is evident when Lucas and Mark appear only briefly, as virtual bystanders, in the opening and closing of the show. The producers had apparently run out of ideas and the show disappeared from the schedule two weeks later after 168 episodes. Initially, the series had drawn considerable praise from critics. *Variety* (October 8, 1958) had proclaimed:

> Looks as if Jules Levy, Arthur Gardner and Four Star have a winner in "The Rifleman". It's a Western, all right, but it combines an offbeat type of character with a plausible and delicately handled family relationship and crisp, well-defined action in a pattern that arrests and retains attention.
>
> ... [Chuck] Connors registers strongly in the parental aspects of his role, and young [Johnny] Crawford is appealing without the stereotyped good looks and is exceptionally convincing in his adoration of Connors.

Thus *The Rifleman* had debuted with great promise, being the most popular new series of the 1958-59 season and ranking fourth in the overall seasonal Nielsens. By the second season, it had slipped to thirteenth and in the third it dropped out of the top 25. Scheduling certainly hurt *The Rifleman*, coming up against the long-running hit family comedy *Father Knows Best* in the 1960-61 season. The ratings improved a little in 1961-62, but *The Lucy Show* delivered the final blow the following season.

Nevertheless, *The Rifleman*, had made a significant contribution to the development of the television Western. This had been a series in which the personality of the hero had outweighed his expertise in firearms. Here was a widower who displayed a fatherly, protective love for his young son, while at the same time exhibiting a concerned involvement in the frontier community in which they made their home. Here, too, was a man who did not just talk about the principles a man should live by, but who actually lived by those principles. *The Rifleman* will indeed be remembered as the heart-warming story of a man of moral fiber, conscientiously raising his son to honorable manhood. Most viewers would undoubtedly agree with Connors' own assessment: "Our show was good for family life in America."[8]

While the McCains represented lower class homesteaders struggling to eke out a living from the land, the Cartwrights were representatives of the upper class struggling to defend their vast property holdings. Set in the vicinity of Virginia City, Nevada, during the Civil War period soon after the discovery of the fabulous Comstock Silver Lode, *Bonanza* was the story of a prosperous family of ranchers. Widower Ben Cartwright, patriarch of the all male clan and owner of the 1000 square mile Ponderosa ranch (so named for its abundance of Ponderosa pines), had three sons by three different wives. Adam, the oldest of the half-brothers, was the most serious, thoughtful, and balanced, and the likely successor to his father as manager of the sprawling Cartwright holdings. Hoss, the middle son, was a giant of a man who was as gentle as he was strong, sensitive and, at times, naïve. Little Joe was the youngest, most impulsive, and most romantic of the Cartwrights.

Bonanza differed from the majority of television Westerns in that it emphasized the bonds of affection between four strong men, as well as their affinity for the land. Although constantly engaging in family scrapes, father and sons clung together to protect the family name and the family property from corrupt and thieving outsiders. Indeed, the producers of the show referred to the land itself as the fifth member of their cast, and reruns of the series were, for a while, retitled *Ponderosa*. Television historian Ralph Bauer considers *Bonanza* as the prototype of a new breed of Westerns which he calls "property Westerns," pointing out the prominence of the property symbol in the opening of each episode which begins with a map of the Ponderosa and Nevada territory burning away to reveal the Cartwright family riding across their land.[9] The importance of the land to the Cartwrights is revealed in the dialogue of the opening scene of the very first episode ("A Rose for Lotta"):

BEN: Feast thine eyes on a sight that approacheth heaven itself.
ADAM: You been to a lotta places and you seen a lotta things, Pa, but you never seen or been to heaven.
BEN: Well, Maybe I never been to heaven . . . but heaven is gonna have to go some to beat the thousand square miles of the Ponderosa.
ADAM: As long as it's ours, as long as we keep it in Cartwright hands. . .
BEN: Know anyone that could take it away from us, son?

Later in an episode entitled "The Courtship," Hoss explains to a woman who has never seen so much beautiful land:

I reckon the Ponderosa holds about as much claim to us as we do to her. It's more like a partnership. Like we're all sort o beholdin' to one another. What I mean to say is that Pa won't let us cut a tree down unless there's another tree growin' ta take its place, er take a cup of water outta the lake if it makes the lake go down that much. The Ponderosa's got a mighty lot ta give. Like Pa says, we ain't to take one ounce out of her that she can't grow back.

The Cartwright attitude toward the Ponderosa is almost paranoid. Frequently, during the show's early years, they spend their time and energy chasing away squatters and others who covet the "bonanza" of wealth that the land can bring. (After all, one of the dictionary meanings of "bonanza" is "a rich source of profits.") In "Enter Mark Twain," one squatter caught trespassing explains he was only "just passing through." Little Joe responds, "Well, next time you go around, you hear?" Later another squatter says, "It's kind of hard to figure where your property ends and the world begins" in view of the enormous size of the Ponderosa. Joe answers, "Well, if you have any trouble . . . we'll be happy to show you. . . . The next time you want to know where the rest of the world begins, you might try asking."

There is never any doubt that the Cartwrights will fight together to the death to protect their land. At the conclusion of the pilot episode, the four ride off laughing and singing the words of the show's theme song, to the effect that anyone fights with a Cartwright has taken on all four of them. This occurs after they have thwarted the attempt of a group of unscrupulous Virginia City businessmen to acquire an unlimited supply of Ponderosa timber by kidnapping Little Joe.

In the third episode, "The Newcomers," Ben declares to a group of miners who have "slaughtered Cartwright beef, cut and burned Cartwright timber and dug holes in the best Cartwright pastureland," that "nobody's going to destroy the Ponderosa," adding that he will kill any man who tries, "if he has to." Yet there were limits to how far Ben would go to protect his land. In "The Truckee Strip," Little Joe falls in love with the daughter of a neighboring rancher who is feuding with the Cartwrights over a timber-rich strip of land that both families claim. When Joe tells his father that he plans to marry the girl no matter what he says or does, Ben admits that the land is not worth jeopardizing the mutual respect and love of a father and son. (Although the dispute is peacefully settled in the end, the girl is tragically killed.)

Still, the battle between the Cartwrights and those who would take from them what is rightfully theirs continued season after season. A phony Spanish countess with a falsified land grant ("The Spanish Grant"), sheepherders ("Blood on the Land"), cattle rustlers ("The Rescue" and "The Jackknife"), and a power-hungry businessman ("To Own the World") all posed early threats to the Ponderosa.

According to series creator and producer, David Dortort, the characters on *Bonanza* were consciously calculated to appeal to all segments of the audience: "the patriarchal Ben Cartwright to older Americans; the earnest number one son Adam, to young married couples; the hot blood and cutup, Little Joe, to teenagers; and the jolly giant, Hoss, to children of all ages." To spice things up, Dortort made the Cartwrights into the Virginia City equivalent of the "three musketeers." The Cartwrights did not just ride home, they rode home to a feudal barony. "The Ponderosa," explained Dortort in an early interview, "is not just a dusty, down-at-the-heels ranch. There's power, wealth and permanence there, and as such, it is the most important single home in television. The great house is like the castles of old, its occupants, kings, princes, knights. . . . We are against the phoney West. Our men swear allegiance not to the silver but to the land."[10]

However, while stressing his "realistic" treatment of the West he admitted that the show constituted a return to old fashion romanticism. "Entertainment must not be entirely a mirror of life," he said. "Our westerners are not just drinking, fighting, carousing, shiftless cowboys. They have other values of faith, hope, and morality. . . . We are not afraid to show our feelings. A father grieves for an injured son; brothers are happy at being united; a son is grateful to an understanding father. We have made more people cry than anybody in the business."[11] In a later interview, Dortort elaborated on the same theme:

> We don't need gimmicks or strange plot twists because our scripts delve into character, deal with human relationships, which is where the best stories are. And we try to teach meaning about human values like love and hope, so in a sense you could say that most *Bonanza* scripts are morality plays....
>
> [Furthermore], this show has guts, which is one reason why people stay with it. We deal with contemporary issues—racial prejudice, mercy killing, problems of conscience from dozens of angles. We also do tender love stories and comedies that show the lighter side of the Old West.[12]

As J. Fred MacDonald points out in *Who Shot the Sheriff?*, the sense of family love and struggle for the common good was well described in the publicity kit that accompanied the syndicated *Bonanza* programs:

> The sight of the Cartwrights charging down a hillside on horseback—Old Ben with his great mane of hair whipping behind him like a Biblical prophet; Adam, with the deadly eyes of a swooping hawk; Hoss, so huge of chest and shoulder that the giant bay under him looked puny by comparison; and Little Joe, a wild rebel yell on his lips—was enough to cow the coolest man. And this close-knit family of men stood between the silver barons and the most extensive stretch of timberland in the Comstock Lode area.
>
> The Cartwrights controlled the vast Ponderosa, a ranch that extended from the lush shores of Lake Tahoe down the snow-capped slopes of the Sierras and east to the desert-like environs of Virginia City. Over part of its thousand square miles roamed 10,000 head of cattle, grazing in the grassy lowlands; the rest of the acreage was covered with thickly wooded hills, studded with magnificent evergreens.
>
> The job of patrolling and protecting their holdings, of guarding the treasured territory against cattle rustlers and timber raiders, was a task calling for the utmost vigilance and bravery, the sharpest eyes and the surest aim. The Cartwrights possessed these qualities and more. Woe to the stranger who set foot on their land.[13]

The central concept linking the four Cartwrights together (after Adam left, three) was the life and times of the family unit—all stories centered about the Cartwright personality and involved the Cartwright family, individually or as a group. This, in fact, was one of the prime requirements for writers of *Bonanza* scripts:

> Stories must *always* deeply involve the Cartwrights. We do not want the Cartwrights "looking in" on the problems of someone else. At times we have used, and will continue to use, guest stars of considerable stature, but when we do the problem is still to be a Cartwright problem and the solution a Cartwright solution.... What we do want is western action and western adventure, concerning a worthy and dramatic problem for the Cartwrights, and strong opponents. We want human drama built around a specific local and specific period in the country's history; simple basic stories as seen through the eyes of Ben, Hoss, and Little Joe Cartwright.[14]

In a 1964 *Look* interview Lorne Greene explained:

> ... A big reason for this show's popularity is the strength and warmth of the family. The father-son relationship is the strongest there is. It's been the basis of drama all the way back to the Bible. Notice, Abraham wasn't told to sacrifice a *daughter*.[15]

Again in a 1972 interview Green explained the success of *Bonanza* this way: "One of the reasons is love. The Cartwrights happen to be a family that other families want to be like. Nobody wants to be a son-of-a-bitch. He wants to be a nice guy. He wants to love and be loved. The Cartwrights love each other."[16] It is also clear that the "togetherness" of three sons with their father had a potent appeal during the sixties to a nation obsessed with security (even though the very term "togetherness" nettled certain members of the cast). Even the show's Jay Livingston–Roy Evans theme song (whose words were sung only once—at the end of the pilot episode as the Cartwrights ride out of town) stressed the family members' support for each other.

More than any other Western series with continuing characters, except *The Life and Legend of Wyatt Earp*, *Bonanza* relied on historical events and characters to develop its storylines. Especially during the first several seasons, references to the Civil War, statehood for Nevada and the discovery of the Comstock Lode were common. Appearances by such historical figures as entertainer Lotta Crabtree ("A Rose for Lotta"), author Mark Twain ("Enter Mark Twain" and "The 26th Grave"), Virginia City madam Julia Bulette ("The Julia Bulette Story"), German mining engineer Philip Diedesheimer ("The Philip Diedesheimer Story"), Apache Indian leader Cochise ("The Honor of Cochise"), Nobel prize-winning scientist Albert Michelson ("Look to the Stars"), British spy Bill Stewart ("The War Comes to Washoe"), British author Charles Dickens ("A Passion for Justice"), notorious outlaws Doc Holliday and Calamity Jane Canary ("Calamity Over the Comstock"), and actress Adah Isaacs Menken ("Magnificent Adah") occurred frequently.

The problem with this device was that many of these events could not have taken place within the purported time frame of the stories. For example, the map, which hung behind Ben's desk in the huge ranch house and appeared in every opening sequence, depicted grossly distorted distances as well as locations which had not yet been named. (The town of Reno was not named until May 1868, yet many of the incidents occurring in the stories took place considerably before that date. Thus Ben's map showed a nonexistent town.)

In several flashback episodes, *Bonanza* traced the migration of Ben to Nevada. Adam had been born in Boston in the early 1840s and Hoss a few years later in Missouri. Ben finally settled in the Tahoe area of Nevada, sometime before the silver boom. Herein lies *Bonanza*'s major historical distortion, its time compression, for the area on which the Cartwrights established the Pondorosa did not come under settlement until the 1850s. Thus the earliest Ben could have settled in the area was 1851. Yet, many times in the series he refers to events that happened fifteen to twenty years previously. Furthermore, Virginia City is implied to have had the same life span yet was not settled until November 1859, nor officially incorporated until three years later. Moreover, during the community's early years, the town was quite crude in appearance, with few permanent buildings and only about 400 inhabitants. Television historian Richard K. Tharp points out this inconsistency in the series quite bluntly:

> Where was the boisterous mining town, the center of a mining industry that produced 40 million dollars worth of bullion between the years 1860 and 1864? For that matter, where were the miners? For a series supposedly based on the Comstock Lode, there was a dearth of miners ... and all of this was watched over by one lonely sheriff, with a deputy or two.[17]

When Sheriff Roy Coffee is in danger of being replaced by a younger man (in "No Less a Man"), he claims to have been sheriff of Virginia City for over "twenty years" and could still handle the job. The absence of a railroad in the town indicates that the story must have occurred prior to its construction in 1869. Therefore, Coffee could not have been sheriff for more than ten years because Virginia City did not exist before that. To most viewers these historical inaccuracies apparently mattered little, but are certainly indicative of the sloppy history that permeated many television Westerns.

Producer Dortort was also concerned about the damage television had been doing to the image of the American father, who was being portrayed as a "buffoon" and "an incompetent." Dortort wanted to reinstate him as the head of the American household in his depiction of the patriarch of the Cartwright family. Ben Cartwright was not only a father his sons could respect, but a stern, though gentle, role model for fathers across the land. By strengthening the image of the father figure, *Bonanza* became sort of a virile,

Westernized version of *Father Knows Best*. Even more than this, however, Dortort took pride in the fact that there were no moms built into the show—nor for that matter any continuing woman characters whatsoever.

In keeping with his philosophy that television creates its own stars, Dortort chose relatively unknown actors to portray the four major characters. In the pivotal role of Ben, Dortort cast Canadian actor Lorne Greene. In retrospect one can hardly imagine a more perfect choice. Greene had a most distinguished career long before *Bonanza* was ever conceived. As a young man, he had studied chemical engineering but became interested in acting. While attending Queen's University in Kingston, Ontario, from 1932 to 1937, Greene was active in the Drama Guild—trying his hand at acting, directing and producing. After graduation, he accepted a fellowship at the Neighborhood Playhouse School of the Theatre in New York City and also trained in stage movement at the Martha Graham School of Contemporary Dance. Finding that acting jobs were scarce, Greene sought a career in broadcasting. Within a short time he had risen to become the chief announcer for the Canadian Broadcasting Corporation. He soon became known as the "voice of Canada," reassuring his countrymen with a deep, commanding voice during the darkest days of World War II. Greene also did many Voice of America broadcasts beamed into Nazi-occupied nations, in cooperation with the National Broadcasting Company in the United States.

After a short wartime stint as an aviator in the RCAF, Greene returned to Canadian radio. His interest in acting, however, persisted and led him to become a cofounder of the Jupiter Theater in Toronto and to establish the Academy of Radio Arts, both of which were to serve as training grounds for young Canadian talent. Then, on a trip to New York in the early fifties to demonstrate a special stop watch he had invented which ran backward enabling a radio director to know how much time was left, he had a chance meeting with a producer friend, Fletcher Markle. This led to his appearance as a dynamic symphony orchestra conductor in Markle's *Studio One* production of "Rendezvous." Later, he was featured in the same series as Big Brother in a dramatization of George Orwell's *1984*. He went on to appear in a variety of outstanding television shows, including guest appearances on *Climax, Star Stage, You Are There*, and *Alfred Hitchcock Presents*. He also starred as a freighter captain in the Canadian-produced adventure series *Sailor of Fortune*. While in New York, Greene also starred in three Broadway plays, *The Prescott Proposals, Speaking of Murder*, and *Edwin Booth*. Returning briefly to Canada, he starred in several productions of the Stratford Shakespeare Festival.

By this time his versatile career had come to the attention of several motion picture producers and he went to Hollywood for appearances in a series of films, beginning with *The Silver Chalice* in 1954. Other films included *Peyton Place* in 1957 and *The Buccaneer* in 1958.[18] However, it was his appearance in an episode of *Wagon Train* entitled "The Vivian Carter Story" that brought him to the attention of Dortort. At this point in his career, he had never been on a horse—except once, as a boy on a Percheron. Greene was, nevertheless, just the actor that Dortort was looking for. He saw in him "some of the old fashion attitudes and old-world charm and courtesy" that Ben Cartwright was to possess. Although the role was conceived by Dortort (whose own father's name was Ben), the character was largely shaped by Greene himself. In fact, if Ben Cartwright had a model, that model was Greene's father, Daniel. "My father was not a big man," he explained in an early interview, "but he gave the impression of bigness. He didn't have to punish; all he had to do was look. He had almost perfect control, never got excited, period. Like Ben he *thought* things through."[19]

Lorne Greene did not realize it at the time but the role of Ben Cartwright was to

***Bonanza* made Lorne Greene an international star.**

occupy him for the next 14 years to the exclusion of almost everything else. It was also to win him awards for most popular television star (*Radio-TV Mirror*) and best performance by an actor (Foreign Press Association), as well as an invitation to preside over the hour-long nationally televised memorial tribute to President John F. Kennedy following his assassination.

Bonanza was also to lead Greene into another career direction—the recording field. Taking advantage of *Bonanza*'s popularity, RCA issued several cast albums: *Bonanza—TV's Original Cast* and *Bonanza—Christmas on the Ponderosa*. These proved so successful that in 1964 Greene was given a complete LP all to himself entitled *Welcome to the Ponderosa—An Evening of Songs and Stories*. Included was the only recorded vocal version of the show's theme song (written by J. Livingston and R. Evans) and a special ballad detailing the odyssey of Ben Cartwright entitled "Saga of the Ponderosa" (written by Ken Darby, who had performed a similar service for Hugh O'Brian on *The Life and Legend of Wyatt Earp*). The liner notes on the album were presented in the form of a letter from Ben to his three sons and dated April 1860:

> My Three Sons:
> I trust, now that you are men, that these songs will be passed on by you to your children with the same fondness, pride and love as I now feel. For these are the songs and stories which tote up to a sum of riches, the greatest wealth possible—the remembrance of human experience. This memory is the champagne of the history of the American West, and all those years were vintage ones.
> Long after we are all gone—maybe a hundred years from now—if we could return just once to re-hear these songs and stories, I am hopeful that they would be told in this form. And quite possibly some feller named LORNE GREENE, who looks like me, could re-tell and re-sing these things to three fellers who look like you.

Not only did the album climb onto the best seller charts and remain there for weeks, but Greene's single version of another selection from the album *Ringo* went over a million sales and earned him a gold record. Demonstrating his versatility, Greene also narrated *Peter and the Wolf* for RCA and recorded several contemporary numbers in Nashville, including "Daddy, I'm Proud to Be Your Son," "I Love a Rainbow," and "The First Word." Other successful albums included *Young at Heart, Portrait of the West* and *Lorne Greene's American West.*

The story of Ben Cartwright's early life is skillfully told through a series of flashback episodes, all written by Anthony Lawrence and scattered throughout the first four seasons. Ben had grown up in New England where he had served in the merchant marine. His travels had taken him to many areas of the world; for instance, he had once served as a soldier of fortune in Nicaragua ("The Colonel"). Ben is serving as first mate on board *The Wanderer* when the ship's captain, Abel Morgan Stoddard, is forced to retire because of his age. Ben meets and falls in love with Stoddard's daughter, Elizabeth, and decides to settle down and open a business as a ship's chandler in Boston. After the wedding, Elizabeth becomes pregnant and gives birth to a son. Ben and Elizabeth name him Adam after reading Milton's *Paradise Lost.* Shortly after Adam's birth, Elizabeth dies. Saddened, but not disillusioned, Ben decides to sell his business and head west with his infant son ("Elizabeth, My Love").

Ben eventually reaches Galesburg, Illinois, where he finds work and meets Inger Borgstrom a beautiful, young Swedish immigrant who operates a general store with her brother Gunnar. Although Ben does not get along with Gunnar, he falls in love with Inger and proposes to her. Inger, who has fallen in love with both Ben and 6 year old Adam, accepts and the new Cartwright family heads west once again ("Inger, My Love"). The Cartwright family reaches St. Joseph, Missouri, where Ben begins a trading business. Before long, however, Ben, still in pursuit of his dream of owning his own land in the West, helps to organize a wagon train to California. On the way, Ben's second son is born and named Eric after Inger's deceased father, and given the nickname Hoss, which was her brother's nickname. Tragedy, however, befalls the wagon train just outside of Denver. They are attacked by Indians and Inger is killed ("Journey Remembered").

Ben continues his trek westward with his two young sons, eventually arriving on the eastern shore of Lake Tahoe in Nevada territory. There he establishes a ranch which he names the Ponderosa after the towering pine trees. Later when one of his ranch hands is killed in an accident while saving Ben's life, Ben decides to visit New Orleans to inform the man's widow, Marie DeMarigny. When Ben meets the lovely Marie, he discovers that she is bitter toward her deceased husband for abandoning her and the child she carried. The child was taken from her by her mother-in-law shortly after birth and Marie was later falsely told he had died of the fever. Ben, however, soon learns that Marie's husband left because he believed his wife to be unfaithful. Discovering that the rumors of her unfaithfulness are untrue, Ben decides to clear Marie's name and, in the process, falls in love with her. He marries Marie and takes her back to the Ponderosa, where she gives birth to Ben's third son, Little Joe. After a few years of happiness, Marie is fatally injured in a tragic fall from a horse, and Ben buries her on the Ponderosa near the magnificent Lake Tahoe she loved ("Marie, My Love"). *Bonanza* is the continuing story of how Ben struggles to raise three motherless sons while building, with their love and help, a paradise in the wilderness during an era of violence and lawlessness.

No episode illustrates Ben's success better than one entitled "The Legacy." Ben is shot and wounded while on the trail of a poacher. His horse, with blood on its saddle, wanders into the camp of three ex-convicts. Believing they will be blamed for the death of a man they have never met, each one flees in a different direction. One of them takes the rifle Ben always carried on his saddle. When their father fails to return, Adam, Hoss, and Joe go after him and find only the horse. Each thinks his father was murdered and each of the three brothers follows the trail of one of the ex-cons. Meanwhile, a peddler has found Ben and cleaned and dressed his wounds. Ben knows that his sons will be out for blood and hopes that the values he has taught them will prevent them from taking the law into their own hands. While he waits for news of their return, the following dialogue occurs between Ben and the peddler:

> JACOB DOHRMAN (the peddler): If it was me I'd feel pretty good knowin' I had three boys ready to kill anyone who did me in.
> BEN: No, they've been taught the exact opposite.
> DOHRMAN: Then why're ya worried?
> BEN: Why does any father worry? It's like when ya plant seed blind. You don't know whether they're gonna grow and keep growin' long after you're past knowing and gone.
> DOHRMAN: From what ya tell me about your two oldest boys, it don't seem likely they're too apt to go against what they've been taught. You didn't tell me much about the third boy.
> BEN: He's quick tempered. Sometimes I see an anger in him . . . Three wives and three sons, all of them so different.
> DOHRMAN: So ya got doubts about what he'll do?
> BEN: No, no I guess I got doubts about me . . . About whether I was able to make them understand.

Ben need not have worried, for after each of the Cartwright brothers successfully tracks down his prey, he realizes, as he has been taught by his father, that vengeance is wrong and it is up to the law to determine a man's guilt or innocence. Even the quick-tempered Little Joe, who has cornered the guilty man, turns him over to the sheriff for proper punishment.

The image of *Bonanza*'s father figure grows during the 14 seasons from that of an iron-handed disciplinarian into an older, more sophisticated advisor who plays the role of mediator rather than parent to his grown sons. Ben's relationship with the town likewise undergoes a transformation over the years. During the early episodes many of the leading citizens of Virginia City seem to resent the Cartwright wealth. This is sometimes manifested in attempts to gain some of that wealth for themselves (in the opening episode, for example) and at other times in their refusal to help the Cartwrights when they are in danger.

In one such episode, entitled "Vendetta," Ben foils a bank robbery by killing a member of the notorious Morgan gang. However, Ben is himself seriously wounded. When the posse, which is sent to capture the rest of the Morgan gang, is ambushed and killed to a man, the townsmen who had earlier been so grateful for Ben's heroic action, now refuse to help protect him. It seems the remaining brothers of the dead outlaw have vowed to ride into town at sundown and take vengeance on Ben and anyone who stands with him.

In a story that parallels in many respects the classic Western film *High Noon*, Ben finds himself nearly alone in a fight against the gang with only the town drunk, an un-armed doctor and Hoss willing to help him. Various shots of clocks are used to show the time of confrontation growing ever closer (in a manner similar to that used in the film). Everyone Hoss approaches has an excuse why he cannot come to Ben's assistance. The bottom line is, of course, fear. In the end the outlaws are killed, at the cost of the life of the town drunk. Then, a wounded Ben must face the gang leader in a shoot-out. After the smoke clears, the townspeople guiltily return from their hiding places to shamefully acknowledge Ben's courage.

Ben's prominence in the community, however, is made clear during a first season episode called "The Stranger," in which Ben campaigns for the governorship of Nevada. Although he must withdraw his candidacy before the election for personal reasons (which become clear in the story), Ben is obviously a man whom people would support for governor.

In "No Less a Man," Ben, as well as Adam, are presented as members of the Virginia City town council. Ben Cartwright has clearly become—if not *the* leading citizen of the town—one of them. He is the preeminent joiner—going to meetings of some chamber of commerce type group called The Nevada Club. Speaking of Ben in a episode entitled "Ride in the Sun," one outlaw says, "He's a joiner. Belongs to lodges. Never misses a meeting."

Furthermore, being the area's major land owner, an upstanding citizen and member of the town's most important club, Ben frequently finds himself called upon to assist the town's law enforcement officer when peace and order are in jeopardy. In "The Night Virginia City Died," an arsonist is terrorizing the town. Sheriff Coffee asks Ben for help: "I've been wearing this badge for a lot of years now and I can handle robberies and rustling and a lot of other things, but... When it comes to firebugs, I'm... I'm just in trouble Ben. I could use your help." And, of course, Ben comes to his assistance. Actually Roy has asked for Ben's help on a number of other occasions. Television historian Ralph Brauer has noted that "on those occasions when Ben and the sheriff ride together, they are usually shown side by side or with Ben in front. Once in a while the sheriff leads, but Ben is never far behind."[20] It is clear that Ben will not only do his utmost to protect his own property but, like the model good citizen he is, will come to the aid of his community when its security is threatened.

Ben becomes the "paternal old sage" of not only the Ponderosa, but the town as well. He is the one everyone turns to for help and leadership in times of crisis. In a moving Easter episode entitled "Blessed Are They," Ben is called upon to make peace between two warring families. When he is forced to decide custody of orphaned twins whose mother came from one family and whose father came from the other, Ben turns to the Bible for help. He finds "the wisdom of Solomon" in II Samuel and awards the boy to one family and the girl to the other. When the two families realize how distraught the children are at being separated, they put aside their differences for the well-being of the twins, as Ben sensed they would. The community's trust in Ben has not been misplaced.

In "One Ace Too Many," Greene is given the opportunity of playing a dual role: Ben's lookalike double is a roguish conman with an outlandish scheme to liquidate the Ponderosa during Ben's absence. Greene handles himself well in the unaccustomed role of a villain, albeit a likable one. One other aspect of Ben's character should be mentioned. The void in his life left by the loss of three women, each of whom he deeply loved, is never filled. He is, however, allowed an occasional romance as, for example, in "My Son, My Son," where he courts an attractive widow. Inevitably, his marriage plans are thwarted by some unforeseen and insurmountable obstacle (in this case, the widow's troubled son).

Dortort was equally fortunate in casting the role of the eldest Cartwright son, Adam. Pernell Roberts, after flunking out of college on three different occasions, was bitten by the acting bug. In 1950 he joined the Arena Stage in Washington, D.C., where he won a part in *The Firebrand*. He remained a permanent member of that group for two years, receiving valuable dramatic experience. From there he went on to New York, where he performed in a variety of plays, including *Doctor Faust*. In 1954 he became part of New York's Shakespearewrights Repertory Company and performed in a number of Shakespearean productions, including *Macbeth*, which won him the Drama Desk Award for best

Off Broadway actor in 1955. His appearance in the Broadway production of *The Lovers* with Joanne Woodward brought him to the attention of moviemakers and Paramount signed him in April 1957 for *Desire Under the Elms*. He later also won a part in M-G-M's *The Sheepman*. Moving into television, Roberts had done several small roles on *Gunsmoke* at the time he was discovered by Dortort.[21] Dortort's conception of Adam can be found in this early studio publicity release:

> Adam possesses the hard-headed, tight fisted qualities of his New England ancestors. There is a gruffness about him, at times even a bitterness, savage and sharp as a northeast wind. . . . Cold and fearless with a normally narrow-eyed tight-lipped expression, he is known throughout the territory for his deadliness with a six-shooter or a rifle, and for his iron-willed determination to serve his father.[22]

Actually the quality that best describes Adam within the context of the series is level-headed, certainly in comparison with his more impetuous younger brothers. He might also be described as solid, reliable, stubborn and, at times, even dull. After all, these are desirable qualities in an oldest son who will be expected to carry most of the responsibility for managing vast property holdings. Adam never knew his mother since she had died shortly after he was born. He had, however, participated in his father's long and tragic trek westward and experienced the loss of two step-mothers, which must have had a sobering effect on his personality. Later he had traveled east to study architecture. Returning to the Ponderosa, Adam became his father's chief assistant. Unlike his younger brothers, Adam had actual duties rather than "chores" and often handled business transactions for his father.

Though Adam did not seek them out, adventure and romance often found him. In "The Last Trophy," Adam finds himself the target of a married English woman's affection. In "The Hopefuls," Adam is attracted to a beautiful young Quaker woman traveling west with her father on a wagon train. In "The Dark Gate," Adam finds himself wrongly accused by an insanely jealous husband of having an affair with his wife. In "The Way of Erin," a young Jewish girl is attracted to Adam and involves him in a family dispute.

Adam also frequently finds himself drawn into dangerous situations not of his making. In "The Crucible," Pernell Roberts turns in one of his finest performances. Adam is waylaid by a couple of crooks who rob him of money he has received for selling Cartwright cattle. They also steal his horse and leave him in the middle of the desert with no water or food. Adam stumbles into the camp of a deranged prospector (superbly played by Lee Marvin), who tries to see if he can turn Adam into an animal through cruelty. He forces Adam to work in his mine by depriving him of food and water. When Adam tries to escape, the crazed prospector shoots the only pack mule. The madman is trying to force Adam to give in to his animal instincts and murder his tormenter. However, Adam refuses to yield, and after he overpowers the prospector, he drags him down the mountain on a travois, where days later in a dazed and incoherent state he is rescued by Ben, Hoss and Little Joe. Ironically, the man he had refused to kill, even to save himself, has died along the way and Adam has been dragging a corpse. In "The Lawmaker," Adam is beaten and nearly killed by a ruthless sheriff and is saved from death only by the timely intervention of his father. In "The Long Night," Adam is waylaid by a escaped convict who steals his horse and clothes. Later he is mistaken by a posse for the wanted killer and nearly lynched.

Although Adam often appears as rather cold and aloof, his compassionate nature is portrayed in a number of moving episodes. In "Broken Ballad," Adam tries to help a reformed gunfighter settle down and begin a new life on his family's land. In this episode,

Pernell Roberts reveals another side of his talent when he sings first a duet and then in a trio with guest star Robert Culp. (This led Roberts to record an album, *Come All Ye Fair and Tender Ladies*, in 1963.) In "The Jackknife," Adam helps a rustler (played by John Archer) live up to the expectations of his loving son by turning himself in to the law. In "The Way Station," Adam prevents an impressionable, headstrong young girl from running away with a doomed outlaw. And in "Song in the Dark," Adam helps a young man wrongfully accused of murder clear his name.

Adam was, of course, being a Cartwright, a man of strong convictions. In "The Ride," Adam persists in proving a man guilty of robbery and murder despite the fact that no one will believe him and all the evidence indicates that he is mistaken. Viewers are shown a different side of Adam's character in "My Brother's Keeper." While out hunting a wolf, he accidently shoots his brother Joe. After he has taken his injured brother back to the Ponderosa he learns that his father is away and he will have to take charge of the situation himself. Sending Hoss for a doctor, he manages to extract the bullet. The accident seems to crystalize Adam's dislike of life on the frontier and when Hoss returns without a doctor he is just about convinced that he should return to civilization where a man can live like a man and not some animal struggling for survival. This might have provided the unhappy Pernell Roberts with a storyline excuse for leaving the series, but Adam is to remain on the Ponderosa two more seasons.

From the very beginning, Roberts had taken a dim view of Dortort's tendency to do stories written for all four actors. "I felt," said Roberts in an early interview, "as if I'm playing one-fourth of a character. We need time to develop individuality in the given situation. As far as I'm concerned, the only question is: is an actor good or isn't he? After all, it's *his* face hanging out there."[23] This frustration led Pernell Roberts to declare that he intended to leave the series at the end of the 1963-64 season, and writers began to devise a way of gracefully removing him from the story. After it became clear that Adam would be "married off," Roberts made a "bombshell" suggestion on how this should be handled. He wrote NBC:

> Let the network cast the role of my bride as an Indian girl, and get a Negro to play the part.... Recent events in the South have done tremendous damage to our national prestige and have clearly indicated the grievous wrong that has been perpetrated upon American Negroes. I have found this tremendously distressing, embarrassing and humiliating as a man, as an American, and as a Southerner (birthplace: Waycross, Ga.).... It seems to me that the forthcoming addition to the format of *Bonanza*, the impending marriage of Adam Cartwright, offers an unparalleled opportunity which might help toward, the rebuilding or our national image and integrity.... [This] would be one of the most progressive and constructive statements in television drama, as both the Negro and the American Indian have consistently been exploited "second class citizens."[24]

NBC's reply to Roberts simply thanked him for his suggestion and indicated that the part would be cast "in consideration of the requirements necessary for the role." Dortort claimed that the suggestion came too late to be implemented even if the network had been receptive to the idea, but when pressed, the producer maintained that while the suggestion was "well-meaning," it was "confused." To ask a Negro to play an Indian would be only an "empty gesture toward civil rights."[25]

It was eventually decided that Kathie Browne (a Caucasian) would play a young

Opposite: **The original cast of** *Bonanza* **(from the left): Lorne Greene as Ben Cartwright, and his sons, Pernell Roberts as Adam, Dan Blocker as Hoss, and Michael Landon as Little Joe.**

widow named Laura Dayton whom Adam would meet, court and marry. This story was developed over four episodes spaced throughout the season. In "The Waiting Game," Adam meets Laura, whose husband has been accidently killed, leaving her with a young daughter to bring up. Adam is attracted to the troubled woman who cannot seem to tell her daughter about her father's death. Adam eventually discovers that Laura secretly despised her husband and is afraid that if her daughter ever finds out, she will hate her mother. Adam, of course helps her to find the strength to do what she must. Two months later in "The Cheating Game," Adam helps prevent Laura from being bilked out of her inheritance by some con-men and is further attracted to the young widow and her daughter.

On March 22, 1964, in "Return to Honor" a new character is introduced, Ben's nephew Will Cartwright, with the expectation that he will replace Adam as a permanent continuing character. Will (played by Guy Williams, who had gained fame as Walt Disney's *Zorro*) is a drifter who has a habit of getting mixed up with the wrong people. Ben takes the young man under his wing and invites him to settle down on the Ponderosa. The stage is thus set for Adam's graceful departure. Meanwhile, the network decides that they will not let Roberts out of his contract. He will have to remain with the show until the end of the 1964-65 season.[26] Once again the storyline has to be altered. In "The Pressure Game," Laura is introduced to Will. When business keeps Adam from seeing as much of Laura as she would like, they quarrel, and although Adam does finally propose marriage to Laura, she turns him down, thinking that he does not really love her. Enter Laura's Aunt Lil (played to perfection by Joan Blondell), a born matchmaker, who decides to use Will to make Adam jealous. Will goes along with the plan and it works. Adam is aroused enough to convince Laura that he really does love her and she accepts his proposal. The only problem is that by now Will has also fallen in love with Laura. In the following episode, "Triangle," Adam and Laura make plans for their wedding. Adam, however, begins seeing less and less of Laura because he is secretly building them a home so they will not have to live at the Ponderosa. As a result of Adam's absence Laura begins to spend more time with his cousin Will. At the engagement party—which Adam misses—Will tells Laura of his feelings for her. Laura realizes that she loves Will, not Adam, and although matters are complicated for a time, when Adam is seriously injured in a fall, the conflict is eventually resolved with Will getting Laura and the two of them leaving the Ponderosa (and the show).

At the end of the following season, Roberts does leave the series. His oft-mentioned complaints of scripts that were banal and inconsistent, his feeling that he was stagnating as an actor in limited characterizations and restricted rehearsal conditions, and his opinion that he was only playing "one-fourth of a part" are given as reasons for his departure. Author Melany Shapiro gives this explanation in her recent book, *Bonanza: The Unofficial Story of the Ponderosa*:

> "I feel like I'm an aristocrat in my field of endeavor," Pernell Roberts said in a 1965 interview, just after completing the last season of *Bonanza*. "My part of *Bonanza* was like Isaac Stern sitting in with Lawrence Welk."
>
> Pernell Roberts hated *Bonanza* almost from the beginning. He felt the scripts appealed to an elementary school mentality and accused NBC of producing mediocrity while shying away from controversy. Starring on *Bonanza* he also said, was hard on his conscience. Dubbing the show "a reprehensible lie" he was infuriated at how *Bonanza* gloried the wealthy at a time when poverty was so widespread. He also disliked the objectifying of women, pandering to women's fantasies of being carried off by a Cartwright....
>
> [In addition] the antagonism between him and his co-stars was no secret, especially his problems with Michael Landon. "You can imagine how it is for an actor to be delivering his

lines and get nothing but a blank stare from the person he is talking to," Landon said. " . . . Pernell said he only gave 10 percent of his creative effort to the show. Well, maybe 20 percent, would have helped us a little more."

. . . Roberts [later] acknowledged that the tension between him and Landon was caused by a misunderstanding and was partially his fault. "When he asked why I wanted to leave the show, I told him," Roberts said. "I pointed out that there was not an equity of competence among the actors. That he himself was untrained, that he was perpetuating bad acting habits. I meant all this constructively. I was trying to convey that he was not getting the fullest potential from his talent. I was attempting to say that he wasn't developing himself. Somehow he took it as a personal attack. He never forgot. I'm sorry."[27]

Thus does Pernell Roberts earn a place for himself in television history as an actor who walked out on a hit series without having a contract dispute (along with *M.A.S.H.*'s McLean Stevenson). On those rare occasions when Adam was mentioned in the stories it was explained that he had gone to California, back east or to Europe to study advanced design and architecture, or to the sea. (In an episode broadcast during the seventh season entitled "Home from the Sea," Adam's character becomes a focal point of the story when the Cartwrights receive a visit from a young man named Gilly Maples, a friend and former shipmate of Adam. Actually he is not really Maples at all, but a shipmate of Maples and Adam, who is planning to steal some gold from the unsuspecting Cartwrights. He and his accomplice have stolen some letters from Adam, in which Ben explains how he is going to buy a huge herd of cattle from a man who insists on payment in gold.)

Perhaps Dortort's most fortunate casting selection was his choice of six-foot, four-inch, 300 pound Dan Blocker to play the role of Hoss. In retrospect it seems that the role of Hoss was written especially for Blocker. Blocker was a mountain of a man who, at birth, was said to have been the largest baby ever born in Bowie County, Texas, at 14 pounds. When he entered Texas Military Institute at age 12 he was six feet tall and 200 pounds and by the time he reached college, six feet, four inches and 275 pounds. (According to Blocker, his dad once said that Dan was "the only man in Texas that wears a No. 14 plus shoe and a size 3 hat. He's too big to ride and too little to hitch to a wagon—no good for a damned thing."[28]) Fortunately, Dan stopped growing then, in time to be pursued by every football coach in the Southwest. He ended up at Sul Ross State College in Alpine, Texas, where he participated in 33 football games (of which his team won 31 and tied the other two).

Something of far more lasting significance, however, happened to Blocker while at Sul Ross. He discovered that he loved the theater. The college drama club needed somebody strong enough to carry the bodies out of the basement in *Arsenic and Old Lace*. Since Blocker was then dating a young lady drama student, she was able to talk him into taking the part. Much to his surprise he had a ball and went back for more. Soon he had the whole football team involved and at one point he directed a production of *Mister Roberts* with a cast made up of every member of the football team. Blocker became so interested that he changed his major from physical education to drama. His special interest was the Elizabethan Theater and with heavy makeup he was cast as Othello. His most notable achievement in college drama, however, was his performance as De Lawd in *Green Pastures*, a production which won him an award for the best college acting in 1949.

In 1950 he tried stock and Broadway (where he appeared in *King Lear*) but soon decided that the theater was too tough for him. Shortly thereafter he was drafted, and after returning from the Korean War in 1952, married his college sweetheart and settled down to teaching school while continuing to work on his master's degree in drama at Sul Ross. By 1956 he had decided to work on his Ph.D. at UCLA. Since finances were a

Dan Blocker as Hoss (shown here with guest star Julie Harris) was given a number of opportunities at romance on *Bonanza*.

problem, he decided to fall back on his training as an actor by seeking work in television. Most of his early work consisted of small roles as bad guys on television Westerns such as *Gunsmoke*. However, when he played a character named Hog Nose Hughes in a *Maverick* episode, critics called him the "new Wallace Beery." Hog Nose was a loveable souse that no jail could hold and although he appeared only briefly in the opening sequence of the show, it was a memorable role. This led to Blocker's portrayal of Tiny Budinger on an episode of *Cimarron City* which was so successful that the character was added permanently to the show. Tiny was a good-natured local citizen who often helped the sheriff in the cause of law and order.

It was shortly after *Cimarron City* was canceled that Blocker was discovered by Dortort, who was producing *The Restless Gun*. Dortort did not see why the big man should be confined to playing dim-witted heavies as other producers had invariably seen fit to cast him. Dortort's decision to put him in a sympathetic role—the lead in a sentimental story about a hulking deafmute—encouraged Blocker to continue his career as an actor. Dortort felt that "the man had range" with "great tenderness and sensibilities."[29] To Dortort it was only natural, then, that Blocker move into the role of Hoss. Hoss quickly became the most popular character in the series, blending great physical strength with great gentleness. Western movie and television critic Rita Parks describes Hoss' character in this way:

> Hoss became a symbol of values dear to the heart of a democracy that had become sophisticated to the point of boredom—or desperation. Hoss—and, curiously enough, Blocker himself—came to represent the pure and homespun qualities of the uneducated man whose simple, wide eyed, and eternally optimistic approach to life could be experienced only in fantasy by the ... disillusioned and near-paranoid individual struggling to survive the complexities of contemporary American life. Audiences could also empathize with the hurt Hoss often experienced when other characters—friends or enemies—took advantage of his simplicity and good nature. Yet another aspect of his character, related to his physical size and direct approach to life, was his awesome stature as an opponent when roused.[30]

Viewers are given some insight into Hoss' character in an episode entitled "The Last Viking," when he accidently meets his mother's brother, Gunnar Borgstrom, whom he has idolized all his life. Unfortunately for Hoss, Gunnar is not the simple, devil-may-care vagabond he would like the Cartwrights to believe he is. In actuality, he is the leader of a group of Comancheros who have been raiding the area. While Gunnar is visiting at the Ponderosa, his men raid a nearby ranch and take as hostages Little Joe and his girlfriend. Heartbroken, Hoss sets out to track them down. Believing Gunnar has killed Little Joe, Hoss is determined to gain revenge. It turns out that Gunnar has actually helped Little Joe and his girlfriend escape from the Comancheros and ultimately sacrifices his life to save Hoss in a tragic closing scene. Thus Hoss come to realize that while Gunnar was not the hero that he had imagined him to be, there was much good in this man.

Most of the episodes featuring Hoss were heavy on comedy. However in the third episode of the first season, entitled "The Newcomers," Hoss is involved in a tender love story. He falls in love with a beautiful but frail young lady dying of tuberculosis. Realizing that she has only a month to live, she tells Hoss she must travel to San Francisco but that she will return in the spring. When Hoss learns the truth, that she could not bear to have him watch her suffer and die, he is grief-stricken. In this episode, Dan Blocker proves himself capable of playing a role that calls for great warmth and tenderness as well as strength and humor.

Hoss falls for an attractive young widow in "The Courtship." While bringing her from Sacramento to the Ponderosa after the death of her husband, Hoss proposes to her and she accepts. Later, however, Hoss discovers that she is a compulsive gambler and although he does not want to believe it, he is finally faced with the fact that she has only been using him to get his money. In still another love story, "Knight Errant," a beautiful young mail-order bride whom Hoss is bringing back to Virginia City for a close friend, falls in love with him. She mistakes Hoss' kindness and consideration for love. Later, Hoss finds his life in jeopardy when the friend, believing Hoss is stealing his girl, offers a reward to anyone who will kill him. Eventually, however, Hoss is able to convince the girl that she has misunderstood his true feelings toward her, and the friendship is restored. As Blocker's ability to handle romantic stories became established, more frequent love interest plots were developed for Hoss. In "Fallen Woman," an affair of the heart has Hoss risking his life to protect a lovely actress involved in a killing.

Some of the most entertaining episodes featuring Hoss, of course, were comedies. Dan Blocker, along with Michael Landon, gets to play a dual role in an episode entitled

"The Gunmen." In addition to appearing in their regular roles, they also appear as two wanted killers, Big Jake Slade and his brother Shorty Jim Slade. How Hoss and Little Joe are mistaken for the two gunmen and arrested and their subsequent escape makes for a most amusing story and gives both actors a chance to demonstrate a wide range of dramatic skill. Hoss's gullibility is demonstrated in an episode entitled "The Infernal Machine." When inventor Daniel Pettibone comes to Virginia City with his latest invention, a horseless carriage model which he calls a "power wagon," everyone but Hoss laughs at him. He, however, believes in Pettibone and is willing to put money into the further development of his invention. Later, an unscrupulous con-man arrives and convinces citizens to invest money in the inventor's project. When he skips town with the funds, Hoss feels partly responsible and helps to apprehend the con-artist in a hilarious scene bordering on slapstick. Meanwhile, the inventor has been thrown in jail to protect him from the irate mob of investors, where the frail man dies of a heart attack. Hoss is crushed to discover the fate of the inventor, but persists in his belief that the man was a true genius who was "ahead of his time."

Hoss' "blind faith" is put to the test again in another delightfully humorous episode entitled "The Ponderosa Birdman," starring the great funnyman Ed Wynn. In fact, Hoss nearly sacrifices his life to prove that Wynn's invention will actually enable man to fly. It is only the timely intervention of the other Cartwrights that saves Hoss from certain disaster. This story is another fine example of Hoss' basic belief in the honesty and decency of his fellow man.

Another hilarious Hoss comedy is "Maestro Hoss," which features guest star Zsa Zsa Gabor as a gypsy fortune teller named Madame Marova. She convinces the gullible Hoss that he is a musical prodigy, sells him an old fiddle claiming it is a rare and valuable Stradivarius and tells him he will give his first concert within a week. When Ben and Joe try to convince Hoss that he has been conned, he gets very defensive:

> Hoss: This ain't no fiddle, it's a Stradivarius.
> Joe: What in the world is a Stradivarius?
> Hoss: Well, there was a violin maker named Stradi and he made various violins and this is one of 'em.

Hoss practices day and night, much to the dismay of Joe and Ben (to whom his playing sounds like the cries of a wounded animal), and even when it is apparent that Madame Marova has swindled many other people in town, Hoss refuses to give up his dream of musical greatness. Ben decides that by hiring a legitimate music teacher for Hoss, he can put an end to the matter, believing that she will tell Hoss that he has no talent. The plan backfires, however, when the teacher takes one look at Hoss and falls in love with him. It is a delightful story, well-played by the cast and the incomparable Zsa Zsa.

"Hoss and the Leprechauns," has come to be considered by fans and critics alike as the "classic" Hoss episode. While fishing, Hoss spies five little men dressed all in green, carrying a strong-box full of gold. Frightened by the giant-sized Hoss, the little men run away, leaving him with the gold. Of course, when Hoss tells his story no one believes him. Later, however, when the little men break into the house and reclaim the gold, Ben finds himself defending Hoss' story to Sheriff Coffee. One person in town does believe Hoss—a certain Professor McCarthy. Fresh from Ireland, he tells one and all that the little men are none other than Leprechauns. Not only that, but he claims that whoever catches one of the wee people can keep the gold in exchange for letting the little man go. Soon, the Ponderosa is inundated with Leprechaun seekers, all looking for the pot of gold. Actually, it turns out that the little men are in fact midgets who work for McCarthy in a traveling carnival and have been prospecting for gold on the Ponderosa. Not realizing that they were trespassing, they are willing to return the gold to the Cartwrights. Professor McCarthy tries to steal the gold but, with the help of the little men, he is captured. In the end, it turns out that the little men merely want to settle down and raise their families in the beautiful Tahoe area, and what began as a whimsical story ends with an impassioned plea for toleration of people who are different by Hoss:

> Folks, I know that none of you would, purposely or mean to, hurt anybody's feelings. But, Timothy here, and the others, feel like they ain't welcome here. They think you're makin' fun of 'em cause you don't want 'em around. Now, of course, you've noticed that they're different from you—they're a whole lot littler. Well, it's a funny thing... See, I notice the same thing about you. [laughter] Now, these fellers are here for the same reason most of us are... That's to help settle our town, make it grow... raise their families. They're plannin' on buildin' their homes here, workin' their crops, bein' good neighbors. Now in the past, we've always welcomed folks like that, and I don't see no reason we should treat these fellers any different... You, Mr. Lucas, you're the banker, you ought to be happy to see new investors in the town. Their money is just as big as mine. An you, Daryl Gillespie, it ought to tickle you t' death to find prospective buyers for that bottom land you've been tryin' to sell. And that ain't all... They're gonna need tools to work that land and ta build their homes. We got five brand new families here in Virginia City that's gonna raise their young'uns, they're gonna buy clothes and buy food and get haircuts and get their teeth fixed and buy seeds and support a church. I figure every one of us is gonna benefit from their bein' here. I think we oughta give 'em a great big Virginia City welcome.

The townspeople are moved to welcome the little people with open arms and presumedly they "all live happily ever after." (However, we never see any of the little people around Virginia City during *Bonanza*'s succeeding nine seasons!)

Hoss' most endearing quality is his willingness to help those in trouble. Many of *Bonanza*'s most moving stories relate Hoss' efforts to assist the lonely, discouraged, unfortunate, disadvantaged people with whom he comes in contact. In "Feet of Clay," Hoss is the only one who can break through to a lonely boy whose father is an escaped convict. In "The Mission," Hoss helps the town drunk who was once an expert army scout regain his self-respect. In "The Ape," Hoss befriends a lonely, slow-witted, hot-tempered giant of a man who wants only to be left alone so that he can settle down on a farm of his own. After being taunted and taken advantage of, he commits two murders. Unfortunately, in the end, even Hoss is unable to prevent him from being shot down by a posse.

In "Gift of Water," Hoss overcomes enormous obstacles in helping some lowland farmers who have been stricken by a disastrous drought to find water by constructing a windmill-powered well. In "Gallagher's Sons," Hoss assumes the responsibility for two young orphaned girls who have been stranded in the middle of the desert, and returns them to civilization. Hoss plays matchmaker to a discouraged immigrant farmer and a widow with a young daughter in "The Good Samaritan." Even after they have married and settled down they are faced by one catastrophe after another: first they are swindled out of their cattle; then a serious drought threatens to destroy their crops. Hoss persists in helping them until they finally convince him that they need to stand on their own two feet. In "A Dream to Dream," Hoss intercedes in a family dispute and rescues a woman and her two children from an abusive, alcoholic husband.

As with his brothers, Hoss often finds himself in jeopardy. A case in point is related in "Hot Day for a Hanging," when Hoss is mistakenly accused of robbing a bank. Thrown in jail by an ambitious and unscrupulous sheriff, Hoss is in danger of being lynched by an angry mob when Ben arrives in the nick of time to save his son.

Like the other Cartwrights, Hoss is a man of principle and when he believes he is right, he too is capable of great stubbornness. In "The Jury," Hoss is the only member of a jury who believes that there is a "reasonable doubt" that a derelict accused of murder and robbery is guilty. Ultimately, with Adam's help, Hoss' stubbornness is vindicated when the real murderer is apprehended and it becomes clear that Hoss has kept an innocent man from being hanged.

After the thirteenth season was finished, on May 13, 1972, Dan Blocker died from complications following gall bladder surgery. Michael Landon, who played Hoss' younger brother Little Joe, had written a script called "Forever" in which Hoss was to be married. With some changes, this becomes the two-hour story which opens the 1972-73 season. It is now Little Joe who takes a bride but she, unfortunately, dies before the end of the show. "What I wanted to do with it," explained Landon in an interview, "was to try to make it a catharsis for everyone—not just the audience but for us, too—to try to incorporate a sense of loss. We mention Hoss' death very simply in passing, the way it happens in real life, there's no discussion of how or when because everyone knows how and when. It might not please everybody. I'm sure that some people would rather have a whole hour memorial to Dan, but we just couldn't do that. We tried to do what we thought he would have wanted us to do."[31]

In one scene of "Forever" that was filmed on the Sonora River, Little Joe says to his bride, "My big brother and I used to call this the happy place." And she replies, "You must have loved him very much." Later in the episode Ben says to another character, "I know what it means to lose a son." Thus does Hoss Cartwright disappear from *Bonanza*. But for 13 years there was the massive vital presence of a warm and caring person named Dan Blocker, and it is clearly no coincidence that only those 13 seasons of *Bonanza* were originally put into syndication.

Michael Landon, although the youngest of the four principle stars on *Bonanza*, had the most prior television and motion picture experience. When Dortort cast Landon in the role of the impetuous and romantic 17 year old Little Joe, Landon had not yet reached his twenty-second birthday. Landon was, however, both intelligent and talented and fit comfortably into the role that he was to play for some 14 years. Landon was born Eugene Maurice Orowitz and raised in Collingswood, New Jersey, the son of an East Coast movie studio publicist. Landon later claimed that his father hated the theater business and spent his life trying unsuccessfully to get out of it. Describing him, as "a wonderful guy who always missed the boat," Landon says his father failed first in radio and later in publishing movie fan magazines, which made him pretty frustrated most of his life. His mother had been in musical comedy under the familiar show-business name of Peggy O'Neill and gave up her career to marry Emo. When Emo's career failed to pan, it created what one close acquaintance described as a "confused" family relationship. The effect on son Eugene, hungry for security, was almost immediate. Eugene seemed to find the world unfriendly and perverse. Then he made an interesting discovery: he was comfortable on a stage. It gave him a good feeling, but he also found that it left him vulnerable and made him reluctant to care too much about anything.[32]

Landon as a child was in the near genius category with an IQ approaching 150. He got straight A's through the sixth grade. Then in the seventh grade he decided, for reasons known only to himself, that studying was a "square" activity and achieved the dubious distinction of being the only near-genius to graduate from high school 299th in a class of 301.[33] Landon's first acting experience came with the Haddonfield Players near Collingswood. At 13 he played the Japanese houseboy in an ancient melodrama, *The Bat*. "For the first time I knew the excitement of fooling an audience," he later said in an interview. "Ha! They all thought I was Japanese." Unfortunately the social mores of the teenage set

Michael Landon, initially as "Little" Joe, attracted younger viewers to *Bonanza*.

he ran with would not allow him to follow up his initial enthusiasm. "Being a movie star was OK," explained Landon. "But the itty-bitty theater—it wasn't cool. I was afraid they'd laugh at me."[34]

Consequently Landon dropped play acting and turned to sports, becoming an expert in throwing the javelin. He won the state championship and was offered a scholarship to the University of Southern California. After making up some scholastic deficiencies at a junior college, Landon entered USC in February of 1955. He lasted three weeks, long enough to compete in one meet, winning the freshman javelin throw with a toss of 183 feet. When he tore a ligament, USC lost interest in him. Bitterly disappointed, he left college after his freshman year and worked at a variety of jobs in order to survive. He was briefly a process server, a blanket salesman, a car-washer, and a glue-melter in a ribbon factory.

When the acting urge struck, he decided to call himself Mike Lane. Unfortunately there was already an actor named Mike Lane and since he was six feet, nine inches tall, Eugene decided not to try to take his name away from him. Instead he plucked "Michael Landon" from the phone book. His first Hollywood acting experience came shortly thereafter in a little theater production of *Tea and Sympathy*.

One day while visiting a friend who happened to be testing at Warner Bros., Landon caught the eye of a talent scout, who arranged a test for him, and his television career began. His big break came in an episode of *Telephone Time*, an anthology series, in a story called "The Mystery of Caspar Hauser." In it he was featured as a teenaged boy who had been imprisoned in solitary darkness all his life. The ripple of critical acclaim caused by this show led to other live dramatic appearances and Landon did a couple of *Playhouse 90*s and then began to branch off in Westerns like *The Texan, Wanted: Dead or Alive, The Rifleman, Gunsmoke* and *Tales of Wells Fargo*. Meanwhile, Landon earned the starring role in what has become a camp classic—*I Was a Teenage Werewolf*. It was, however, his role as a heavy in the pilot telecast of *The Restless Gun* in early 1957 which caught the eye of producer Dortort, and directly led to his being cast as Little Joe. Dortort saw in Landon "the most highly intuitive set of natural acting responses I've ever seen in a young actor."[35] Television historian Rita Parks describes Little Joe's initial character as being

> . . . a combination of the rascal and the foolish but loveable youth. As a teenager he represented a facet of the heroic persona that can act immaturely and impulsively and still be acceptable because of his basic goodness. . . . During the life of the series, however, Joe not only lost the "Little" from his name, he also matured into a responsible and stalwart son. . . . Possessing some of the qualities originally assigned to Adam, the older Joe had an advantage that Adam never had—a residual personality. The audience knew him when and had fondly watched him grow.[36]

Like his two older brothers, Little Joe lost his mother while very young and never really had a chance to know her. Still his love for her was strong, leading him to identify with the South, her birthplace. In the several episodes which deal with the Civil War, Little Joe is consistently drawn to support the Confederacy ("A House Divided," "The War Comes to Washoe"). When a stranger from New Orleans shows up in Virginia City and tells stories of his mother's checkered past, an unbelieving Little Joe becomes enraged. (It should be noted here that apparently the writers decided after the series began to change Little Joe's mother's first name. In the pilot episode Joe tells actress Lotta Crabtree that his mother's name was Felicia, but later, in an episode entitled "Marie, My Love," Little Joe's mother is identified as Marie. Ironically, the actress chosen to play Marie in the episode, which was broadcast on February 10, 1963, was Felicia Farr.)

In the first episode of the fourth season, "The First Born," Little Joe discovers that he has another half-brother, Clay Stafford. Clay is a drifter hired by Ben to work on the Ponderosa who becomes friends with Little Joe. Later Joe learns that two years before his mother married Ben, she gave birth to Clay. Marie was told that the baby had died and Clay was raised by his grandparents. When Clay is forced to shoot a man in self-defense, Little Joe comes to his aid and is badly beaten. Ben, upon learning Clay's true identity, invites the young man to settle down on the Ponderosa and become part of the family. Clay, however, realizes that his presence will bring trouble to Little Joe and his family and convinces them that the only life that he knows is that of a drifter. Clay bids Little Joe farewell, although it is clear that he is reluctant to leave his newfound family and friends.

Because of his youthful good looks, many stories featuring Little Joe involve him in romantic situations. In the pilot episode he is attracted to the beautiful entertainer Lotta Crabtree. In the initial season's sixth episode, "The Julia Bulette Story," the script requires Landon to play a highly charged death scene with actress Jane Geer that would have been a severe test for any actor. Geer plays Julia Bulette, the owner of Julia's Palace, one of Virginia City's leading saloons and brothels. Despite an attack by a citizens committee determined to put her out of business, Julia continues to prosper. Little Joe is soon attracted to the young woman of French stock from New Orleans partly because his mother came from the same background. Little Joe's father and brothers object to the romance but Joe is stubborn. When an epidemic from the mines hits the town, Julia is one of the few people willing to nurse the sick. This leads the Cartwrights to change their minds about the woman. Julia, however, decides that it is in Joe's best interest to stay away from her and urges him to leave her alone. The episode culminates in Julia's murder, which is based on an actual historical Virginia City incident. Little Joe discovers the dying Julia. In this scene every emotion in Landon's acting repertoire is utilized as genuine tears begin rolling down his face. His audience—which included his producer, costars Dan Blocker and Lorne Greene, and representatives of the press—were too shaken to speak. Dortort later commented: "Mike didn't play that scene, he lived it."[37] Unfortunately, many of Little Joe's sweethearts were killed off by the end of the episode in which they appeared. For example in "The Truckee Strip," the young lady is accidently killed by Little Joe's rival, a corrupt foreman. In "The Storm," Little Joe's intended bride dies of an incurable disease. Of course, in the opening episode of the final season, "Forever," Little Joe actually gets to marry his sweetheart, Alice, but by the end of the show she too has been killed off.

Sometimes, as in "Bullet for a Bride," another solution is devised by script writers to prevent Little Joe from marrying and settling down. In this episode Joe accidently wounds a young lady while hunting a mountain lion and the resulting injury causes the girl to go blind. Distraught and feeling guilty, Joe spends every free moment helping her rebuild her life. Meanwhile, the girl's father sees his chance to gain a piece of the Cartwright fortune. Joe, out of pity, and the lady, out of dependence, appear to be falling in love. Joe proposes and, at the insistence of her father, the young lady accepts. When an accidental fall causes her to regain her sight, she withholds the truth from Joe. The wedding is about to take place when she realizes that what the two feel for each other is not genuine love and she confesses her deception to Joe. They depart warm friends, with Little Joe's bachelorhood still intact. (Television viewers did not get to see Michael Landon as an established family man until his new series, *Little House on the Prairie*, appeared in 1974; see Chapter XV.)

Like the other Cartwrights, Little Joe has inherited a genuine interest in and compassion for others. In "The Friendship," Little Joe helps a convict who has saved his life receive a parole. Then when he has a rough time adjusting to life outside of prison, he stands by him until his faith in the young man is ultimately justified. In "Day of the Dragon," Little Joe assumes the responsibility for a Chinese slave girl he has won in a poker game until he is able to safely return her to her people. In "The Mountain Girl," Little Joe accepts the custody of a young mountain girl from her dying grandfather, agreeing to contact her only living relatives, an aristocratic family in California. Then he tries to make a proper lady out of her before they arrive to claim her. Like the other members of his family, Little Joe is always there when someone needs his help.

Little Joe also possesses the Cartwright sense of responsibility. In "The Tin Badge," Little Joe is tricked into agreeing to become sheriff of a small mining town by an unscrupulous mayor and a mine owner who plan to commit an elaborate murder. By the time Joe realizes that something is wrong, he is in so deep that his sense of responsibility will not let him quit. In the end, of course, Joe is able to deal with the situation and apprehends the killers. Little Joe plays a key role in helping to free his father and brothers who have been framed for robbery and murder in "The Gamble," an episode written by Landon himself.

"The Last Haircut" presents the character with a most intriguing dilemma. While Little Joe watches in horror, a brutal gunslinger shoots and kills a man just because he was in the barber's chair when the gunman wanted a haircut. Joe had no chance to stop the killing, but still feels responsible for the now fatherless son of the murdered man. The gunman is soon apprehended and held for trial in Carson City, but his fast-talking lawyer gets him off. Joe is livid, and both he and the dead man's son want to kill the gunman. Ben persuades Joe that, according to the "good book," vengeance is the Lord's. After accepting his father's advice, he must explain to the young man, Paco, why they must not seek revenge on the killer:

> JOE: Let me try to explain something to you. When a fella grows up like I have, he sometimes says things when he's angry and he forgets some of the truths he learned when he was a boy.
> PACO: What truths?
> JOE: Where does a man go when he dies, Paco . . . a good man?
> PACO: To heaven?
> JOE: And where does a bad man go, when he dies?
> PACO: To hell?
> JOE: Yes, that's where he goes. 'Cause nobody goes unpunished, Paco.
> PACO: The man who killed my father—he must be punished now.
> JOE: The court said he's innocent even though we know he's guilty. And that's because the courts are not perfect, Paco. But God is.
> PACO: Yes, but?
> JOE: You believe in God, don't you?
> PACO: Yes.
> JOE: All right, then you must believe that God will punish Duke Miller. . . Look, I know it's hard—it's hard for you and it's hard for me. But son, if you believe in God, then you must believe that.
> PACO: You want me to go to my grandparents in Juarez and leave vengeance to God?
> JOE: Yes, that's what I want.
> PACO: I don't want to, but, if you go with me, Little Joe, I'm ready.

Before they leave, however, they run into the killer. Once again he is in a barber shop, and Joe is determined to see justice done. After a bloody fistfight, Joe shaves the vain killer's head completely bald and drags him cowering before the townspeople. It is a fitting way for the story to end, although most viewers, undoubtedly, expected some kind of climactic shootout.

All of the Cartwright sons maintained a strong relationship with their father, but Little Joe's was closer, perhaps, because he was the youngest. In "The Quality of Mercy," Little Joe turns to his father for advice after discovering that one of his close friends has killed his prospective father-in-law when he found him with a broken back in a mine cave-in. The friend claims that the man begged to be put out of his misery, but Joe is deeply troubled and asks his father's advice on whether it is morally right ever to take another human life. His father assures him that killing is wrong under any circumstance and only the Lord has the right to take a person's life. Later, it turns out that Joe's friend had actually committed a cold-blooded murder so that he, through his impending marriage, can inherit the dead man's property.

An episode entitled "The Quest" best illustrates the changing role of Little Joe in the Cartwright family structure. Joe is tired of being the baby of the family and having Adam and Hoss watching over everything he does. Ben sympathizes with his youngest son and allows Joe to bid on a contract to supply timber for a mining company's construction project. Joe wins the bidding but finds that he is in for more trouble than has imagined. His competitor in the bidding is determined to see that Joe does not complete the job. His henchman obtains the job of Joe's foreman. Before Joe can finish the job of getting the timber to the miners, the saboteur blows up part of the flume Joe's men were using to float the logs off the mountain. Joe realizes that without help he will never finish the job on time. When his father and brothers pitch in to help him, Joe learns that while standing on one's own may be a worthy goal, it is equally important to have a family one can depend on.

Bonanza was to provide additional opportunities for the development of Landon's many latent talents. It was here that he got his first opportunity to both write and direct. Landon, who had never written a script before, set about writing his first one to fill an unexpected void during the 1962-63 season. His turn at the typewriter came naturally and instinctively. "One Friday night when we finished work," Landon later recalled in an interview, "we were all told to take the next week off. Some nonsense about not having a suitable script. Driving home, I kept mulling an idea I had about the Cartwrights' being blamed for a bank robbery in another town." Scrawling out his efforts in pencil on a lined tablet, Landon finished a 60 page script, complete with camera angles, by Sunday night. The next morning an astonished Dortort read the script and on Tuesday filming began on "The Gamble."[38]

Several years later Landon was also given an opportunity to direct. His first directorial effort was also of a script he had written entitled "To Die in Darkness." Televised on May 5, 1968, it dramatized the story of a man who has been sent to prison for a crime he did not commit, in part because of Ben Cartwright's testimony. He returns a bitter man and traps Ben and Candy (a ranch hand) in the pit of an old mine—to show Ben what prison was really like. In the end, Ben is rescued when the man admits what he has done. The moral of the story clearly is that in some cases, at least, individuals who turn to crime are plainly victims of their environment.

Eventually, Landon joined the Screenwriters Guild and began turning out scripts with some regularity. He was also given more frequent opportunities to direct. Landon's favorite episode, which he both wrote and directed, was called "The Wish," and featured guest star Ossie Davis. In the story, Hoss assists a neighboring black family but unwittingly becomes a fumbling and insensitive, if well intentioned, liberal—in part, the target of Landon's script. Landon explained later, "I wanted to get across the idea to whites just why black people are angry and frustrated and I wanted to help cool some of the backlash. One black writer saw the show and he said to me you've gotten so close to what it's like to be black, I could hardly believe it was written by a white man. For me that was my Emmy."[39] All of this writing and directorial experience, of course, proved invaluable several years later when Landon launched his own series, *Little House on the Prairie*, in which he not only starred but frequently wrote and directed.

There were other additions to the *Bonanza* cast through the years. Eventually Dortort felt the need to replace Pernell Roberts and at the start of the 1967-68 season, a wanderer named Candy was hired as a ranch hand for the Cartwrights. Candy was played by a rugged 30 year old actor named David Canary who claimed to be a descendent of one of the old West's most notorious hell-raisers, Calamity Jane (real name: Martha Jane Canary). The son of a J.C. Penney store manager, Canary started out to become a singer, but was diverted by football in the football happy town of Massillon, Ohio, where he was raised. Later he escaped to the University of Cincinnati, supposedly to study voice. He broke his nose in his sophomore year at Cincinnati, but nevertheless was drafted in his senior year by the Denver Broncos of the American Football League—possibly the smallest (170 pounds, five feet, eleven and a half inches tall) end ever drafted by a professional football team. He turned the offer down and walked out, never to play football again. After graduation, he went to New York where he landed a chorus job Off Broadway. Soon, he was working up from bits in shows like *The Happiest Girl in the World* with Cyril Richard to the lead in the long-running Off Broadway musical *The Fantasticks*. It was while appearing in a road show of that production in San Francisco in December 1964 that he was discovered by Universal Studios. In no time he was doing movies like *Saint Valentine's Day Massacre* and making frequent television appearances in series like *Peyton*

Place, Gunsmoke and *Cimarron Strip*. Dortort spotted him playing the bully in the saloon scene in a Paul Newman Western, *Hombre*, which happened to be shooting next door to another Dortort show, *The High Chaparral*, and quickly cast him as Candy.[40]

Candy was created by Dortort to provide some contrast to the "goodie-goodie" Cartwrights. He is illegitimate and has spent most of his life as a loner, a stray. He is also capable of actions a little more underhanded than the Cartwrights would commit, and this makes him, in some respects, more human. Soon, however, Candy is accepted as part of the Cartwright family. In "To Die in Darkness," Candy explains his feelings at being a part of the Cartwright household:

> When I first met you all I couldn't believe it. The way you are, the way you care about each other. I guess I just wasn't used to it. You know the way I was always sayin' I wouldn't stay in the same spot very long. I was makin' out like I was gettin' ready to leave. I just never meant it, that's all.

Candy, after being integrated into the cast, was featured in his share of stories. In "Trouble Town," he is held without bail in a town paralyzed by fear of a corrupt sheriff. In "The Stalker," Candy becomes romantically involved with a woman whose husband he is forced to kill in self-defense while being stalked by a mysterious gunman. In "The Silence at Stillwater," Candy is again thrown in jail—this time by a small town sheriff who will not tell him why. Each episode shows Candy as a character who could get away with some of the rougher, nastier things for which members of the Cartwright family might be criticized. David Canary left the show at the end of the 1969-70 season to try his hand at writing and directing his own films. Two years later, however, he jumped at the chance to return, when Dortort decided to bring Candy back to the series, after the death of Dan Blocker.

In 1970, Dortort felt that "the warmth of the show was in danger of being weakened by the absence of the father-son relationship." So Dortort decided to add another younger, permanent cast member. By this time Little Joe had reached his early thirties and the idea of Ben Cartwright dispensing fatherly wisdom to a man this age did not seem realistic. And Hoss was beyond needing much fatherly advice. Thus Jamie Hunter, a stray kid who is given refuge by the Cartwrights, becomes a new audience in need of Ben's parental guidance. To play the new character, Dortort selected five-foot, four-inch, 14 year old, red-headed Mitch Vogel. At the age of 10, Vogel had been given the choice of taking guitar or acting lessons. Choosing acting, he was enrolled in the Orange County Performing Arts Foundation and soon found himself doing leads in *Tom Sawyer*, *Heidi* and *The Wizard of Oz* with such proficiency that a Hollywood agent was inspired to get him a professional audition. This led to a small part in the movie *Yours, Mine and Ours*, starring Henry Fonda and Lucille Ball. He got major recognition in *The Reivers* with Steve McQueen and was selected to appear in two adventure films for *The Wonderful World of Disney*: *Menace on the Mountain* and *Bayou Boy*. This is where he was spotted by Dortort.[41]

Jamie Hunter is introduced into the series at the beginning of the 1970-71 season as the orphaned teenaged son of a rainmaker who has been killed. Eventually he is adopted by Ben and appears as the featured character in a number of *Bonanza* episodes during the final three seasons. In "A Home for Jamie," Ben gives young Jamie a tour of the Ponderosa, showing him everything from the beautiful timber country to the rolling cattle ranges. Along the way Jamie learns a lesson about handling responsibility. In "The Bucket Dog," the story focuses on Jamie's new bird dog, a beautiful Irish setter whose very life depends on winning a grueling three hour field trial. Thus Jamie's adventures become an integral part of the Cartwright saga.

To help fill the void created by Dan Blocker's loss, Dortort added a new character, Griff King, shortly before shooting began for the 1972-73 season. Cast in the role as an ex-convict who comes to work on the Ponderosa against his will is Tim Matheson. Matheson got his start in acting while in grade school, when one of his friends introduced him to his producer-father, Mike Stokey. Young Tim was soon hooked on show business and landed his first regular role within a year on the Robert Young show, *Window on Main Street*. He then worked fairly steadily in episodes of series such as *The Twilight Zone*, *My Three Sons*, *The Farmer's Daughter*, and *Leave It to Beaver*. In addition, he provided voices for numerous Hanna-Barbera cartoons playing Jonny Quest, Young Samson, Sinbad, Jr., and others. Matheson caught Dortort's attention during the 1969-70 season of *The Virginian*, in which he played Jim Horn.[42] The casting of Matheson was part of Dortort's shifting emphasis on youth. Griff is a young man who helps save Ben Cartwright's life in a prison riot and is paroled in his custody to the Ponderosa ("Riot!"). Griff is not too pleased at being restricted to the ranch and tries to do everything he can to break loose ("New Man").

Other continuing characters of importance on *Bonanza* included the Cartwrights' Chinese cook, Hop Sing. Played by veteran Chinese actor Victor Sen Yung, Hop Sing appeared in the very first episode and every season thereafter in from 14 to 18 episodes a year. Given lines like "Missa Cartlight, you betta come home tonight because Missa Hoss, he eat too much. He not feel good. He come in kitchen, I cut off his hand!" Yung could hardly expect viewers to believe that he held a degree in economics from the University of California at Berkeley and had pursued graduate studies at UCLA and the University of Southern California. Furthermore, he had served as a USAF intelligence captain in World War II. Despite his seemingly one-dimensional comic role on *Bonanza*, however, Yung had come to the series with extensive acting experience. His early career included 25 appearances as "number two son" in Charlie Chan movies and other roles in more than 300 motion pictures and television shows. His roles had included Chinese bankers, doctors, bartenders, and spies on *Hawaiian Eye*, *The Islanders* , *I Spy*, *The FBI*, and *Hawaii Five-O*. Furthermore, for several years while he was making *Bonanza* appearances he also played "cousin Charlie," the fast talking con-artist who kept *Bachelor Father*'s houseboy in hot water for five years.[43]

Roy Coffee was added to the series at the beginning of the second season and remained through 1970-71. He was played by veteran actor Ray Teal, a solidly built fatherly man with a thick mustache who indeed looked like a town sheriff. Teal had appeared in scores of movies from the thirties to the seventies. In most of his films the lawman he portrayed was usually corrupt, but television made a honest man out of him as the sheriff on *Bonanza*.[44]

In addition to the excellent cast of characters, generally well-written scripts, and frequent appearances by well-known guest stars, *Bonanza* had yet another important distinction. It was the first network Western to be televised in color. The great expanse of gorgeous outdoor scenery utilized in the show was probably the most significant single factor in stimulating the early sale of color television sets. Although *Bonanza* was one of the most popular and successful shows in television history, initially it was considered a flop. *New York Times* television critic Jack Gould called it "disastrous ... early–Autry at its most advanced ... a terrible waste of cash and color."[45] The *Variety* (September 16, 1959) review was even more negative:

> Another western is just what Saturday night television needs least, and that's what "Bonanza" appears to be — just another western. For all its pretensions, with a large cast, name

> guest, color and an hour's length, [it] proves to be little more than a patchwork of stock oater ideas without a fresh twist to distinguish it....
>
> At the heart of the matter is the patent insincerity with which the show has been conceived. To all appearances, it's gunning to be several things at once, an adult and a juvenile western in a single ball of wax. For instance, there are four principal characters, each with his presumed appeal to a different level of audience....
>
> The show received capable performances from its regulars, Lorne Greene, Pernell Roberts, Dan Blocker and [Michael] Landon, but they play stock roles and there's little opportunity to do a standout job.

Worst of all, it was competing with the highly popular *Perry Mason* on CBS. The early ratings were weak. Still NBC held its ground, giving the new show a chance to develop a following. In 1961, *Bonanza* was moved from Saturday to Sunday evening and the ratings began to climb. *Bonanza* was to become the most watched television program of any genre during the sixties. It reached seventeenth in the Nielsen ratings during its second season, zoomed to second during the third year, and held the number one position from 1964 to 1967. The show was never out of the top 20 until its final season.

At the peak of it popularity, *Bonanza*'s producers were getting 5000 letters a week from everyone from school children to college professors eager to explain the show's great popularity. Architects were pondering requests for plans of the Ponderosa ranch house—and the studio was seriously considering making them available. Librarians reported a marked increase of interest in the history of the Comstock Lode. Members of over 450 *Bonanza* booster clubs were glued to their television sets every Sunday night. Such loyalty helped the show to win the *TV Guide* Award for favorite dramatic series. Even the opposition was taking its hats off to the success of *Bonanza*. Charles Marquis Warren, creator of *Gunsmoke, Rawhide* and *The Virginian*, admitted, "Let's face it, *Bonanza* is pretty good." And James Arness, the hero of *Gunsmoke*, exclaimed privately to his producer, "Damn it, I like those fellows!"[46] By the sixth season even *Variety* (September 15, 1965) had changed its mind:

> Television's No. 1 Nielsen rater galloped back to the home tribe corral last Sunday to begin its sixth season. The familiar ingredients that have made this show so popular were all in evidence on the preem episode. Fearless father Lorne Greene is still the "mature" interest, and ... turned in his usual competent job.
>
> ... If past seasons are any guide. Blocker as the enormous "Hoss" will provide the necessary muscle and chuckles while Landon as the youngest offspring can be counted on to get himself in plenty of trouble for the rest of the family to solve.

(What a difference success makes!)

At the beginning of the fourteenth season, however, the series, in addition to cast and character changes, was moved out of its traditional niche on Sunday night. It was placed on the Tuesday evening schedule, in the process losing its long time sponsor, Chevrolet. The death of Dan Blocker, of course, hurt the show more than any other single change. Lorne Greene admitted in an interview shortly after the fourteenth, and what was to be the final, season began:

> That's it, it's finished.... I know Michael felt the same way. But that's the way it is in any family when a death occurs. The family feels that something so radical has happened that life can't go on, that everything has changed. Nevertheless, you do go on. Things are changed, but not as much as you first thought. You don't go out and hire somebody else to take the place of the member who died. What happens is that the character of the family unit changes to include other people.[47]

For once, however, Ben Cartwright was wrong. *Bonanza* could not survive the loss of its most popular and beloved character. All of the changes could not compensate for that disaster and the series was cancelled midway through the season, broadcasting its last new episode on January 16, 1973. It had been a long and fruitful ride—only *Gunsmoke* with 20 successful seasons could boast a longer run over the video range. And the series left a rich legacy behind. With 430 color episodes continually in syndication, broadcast in eight foreign countries in five languages, reaching over 800 million viewers, *Bonanza* would not soon be forgotten. In June 1993, over twenty years after *Bonanza* had galloped off into the video sunset, the series was voted the "All-Time Best television Western" in a *TV Guide* poll. Nearly one-third of the 65,000 readers who took part in the poll chose the saga of the Cartwrights over all other television Westerns including *Gunsmoke*, which had been ranked number one by the magazine's editors. (The editors had selected *Bonanza* as the "Best Western" of the sixties and "champ of the ranch-type Western.")[48]

Lorne Greene went on to a number of less successful television projects (*Griff*, *Lorne Greene's Last of the Wild*, *Battlestar Galactica* and *Code Red*), but he would always be remembered as Ben Cartwright. Michael Landon was, of course, to achieve even greater success on the home screen with *Little House on the Prairie* and *Highway to Heaven*. Castleman and Podrazik's final assessment of *Bonanza* as a four star Western classic is a valid one:

> ... "Bonanza" earned its following as the definitive family western, a tag that serves it well today....
> One reason "Bonanza" works so well is that each of the central characters has such a distinctive personality.... As a result, the series can shift among the characters sometimes focusing on the entire family, in other cases showcasing just one or two members. So it's like having a half-dozen different series leads under one title, offering a wide range of characters interacting not only among themselves but with the weekly guest stars as well.
> That same variety applies to the stories, too.... "Bonanza" isn't tied down to one formula.[49]

Early in 1987 plans were made to revive the series with a two hour syndicated television movie called *Bonanza: The Next Generation*. Until his untimely death in September of that year, Lorne Greene had been slated to return as the patriarch of the Ponderosa. Broadcast in March 1988, the pilot was set in 1905, some forty to fifty years after the original series took place. Aaron Cartwright, a sea captain and artist, who had spent most of his life "drinking and chasing women all over the South Pacific," has come to Virginia City to take over management of the Ponderosa following the death of his brother, Ben. Little Joe has been "missing in action" since the Spanish-American War and Hoss is dead. (Adam's status is, of course, never mentioned.) Living on the ranch with Aaron is Little Joe's wife Annabelle ("Annie"), the cook Mr. Mack (who had at some point in the past replaced Hop Sing) and Charlie Pike (who had been rescued from a lynch mob by Ben years earlier and raised as if he were another son). Soon, Little Joe's son Benj (obviously named after his grandfather) arrives home from the East in a brand new automobile with a medal for his father from President Teddy Roosevelt for "heroism above and beyond the call of duty" as a member of the rough Riders at San Juan Hill.

Then a young man claiming to be Hoss' illegitimate son Josh appears, set on killing his father for deserting his mother, who has just died. When he produces a photo of Hoss and his mother, the family realizes that Josh's mother was a young lady whom Hoss had saved from drowning. Hoss had proposed to her, but she had turned him down and left without telling him she was expecting his child. Aaron takes Josh to his father's grave overlooking beautiful Lake Tahoe situated between Little Joe's mother and Ben's grave. Viewers cannot help but feel the pangs of nostalgia in reading the inscription on his tombstone "ERIC HOSS CARTWRIGHT—A Gentle Giant (1848–1881)." Josh decides to stay and become a part of the Cartwright family to which he belongs.

Once the characters are introduced, the story settles into a familiar pattern. A mining company is "raping" the land adjacent to the Ponderosa with hydraulic equipment. Aaron had given them permission to cross Cartwright property to the mining site for the purpose of making some sample excavations. The company had promised to employ some 200 workers and this would give a badly needed boost to the declining Virginia City economy. After Aaron discovers the methods being utilized by the mining company, he forbids the miners from crossing the Ponderosa. In retaliation, the unscrupulous company foreman tries to stir up the townspeople against the Cartwrights. In the end, however, the foreman is killed and the president of the mining company promises to "clean up" his mining operations so that the environment will not be ruined.

More noteworthy than the plot is the casting and some scenic touches. Little Joe's son is played by Michael Landon's 23 year old son, Michael Landon, Jr., and Lorne Greene's 19 year old daughter Gillian is cast as Jennie Sills, a beautiful young neighbor who has more than a passing interest in Benj and Josh. Veterans are cast in most of the other key roles: John Ireland (a regular during *Rawhide*'s final season and featured guest star in countless television Westerns) plays Aaron; Robert Fuller (Jess Harper in *Laramie* and Cooper Smith on *Wagon Train*) is Charlie Poke; Barbara Anderson (Eve Whitfield on *Ironside*) is Annabelle, and John Amos (whose television credits include *The Mary Tyler Moore Show*, *Good Times*, and *Roots*) is Mr. Mack. Newcomer Brian A. Smith is good as Josh (although one wonders why Dan Blocker's son Dirk was not given the role).

The scenery is both familiar and beautiful since it was filmed in the same area and on the same sets *Bonanza* used (Incline Village and Spooner Lake State Park in Nevada). There are also some fascinating shots of antique hydraulic mining equipment and several vintage automobiles from that period.

The interplay between the Cartwrights seems natural (Benj and Josh get into a fistfight—shades of Little Joe and Hoss!). And overlooking the entire proceedings is a magnificent life-sized portrait of Ben hanging in the Ponderosa ranch house. (Aaron even talks to it in one scene.) In fact his presence in the show is very strong, both by reference and inference. It was also rumored that if the new show had become a successful series, Little Joe would make an appearance (based on Michael Landon, Sr.'s interest in the project). All in all, there seemed enough of the old *Bonanza* in the new one to offer renewed hope to viewers longing for a revival of Westerns in general and of one of the most popular in particular. Unfortunately, the ratings did not justify a series and, with the death of Michael Landon in 1991, all of the original *Bonanza* cast members (except Pernell Roberts) were dead.

Dortort, however, reasoning that the show, which had in its prime attracted an average of 41,000,000 Americans each week plus another 309,000,000 viewers abroad, deserved at least one more chance at revival. In the spring of 1993 filming began on *Bonanza: The Return* which was scheduled for broadcast by NBC in November of that year. This two-hour movie was also shot on the show's original Lake Tahoe location in Nevada (which had been turned into a *Bonanza* theme park that attracts a quarter of a million visitors annually). Produced by Dortort, Tom Sarnoff (son of the NBC and RCA patriarch, General David Sarnoff) and Tom Brinson, the film followed a storyline quite similar to that of *Bonanza: The Next Generation*: the Ponderosa is being threatened by an unscrupulous businessman (played with appropriate menace by Dean Stockwell, alumnus of *Quantum Leap*) bent on strip-mining the surrounding countryside.

Standing on the side of family values against these forces of evil are Little Joe's son (again played by Michael Landon, Jr.), Hoss' son (this time portrayed by hefty Brian Leckner, whose resemblance to Dan Blocker earned him the nickname Hoss when he played high school football in the eighties), Little Joe's daughter (played by "spunky" Emily Warfield), and Adam's son (played by English Actor Alistair MacDougall, presumably because he was born and raised in England while Adam was studying architecture there). Aiding them in the conflict are a newspaper reporter (reportedly inspired by the one in Clint Eastwood's *Unforgiven* and played by Dan Blocker's son Dirk, thought by Dortort to be too old to play Hoss' son), the new Ponderosa manager (a tour de force for veteran Western actor Ben Johnson), a loyal black ranch hand (burly Richard Roundtree of *Shaft* fame) and a local saloon owner (an interesting role for Linda Gray, formerly of *Dallas*). In addition, the production employed many crewmen who had worked on the original series. The producers felt that the time was right for a *Bonanza* revival, as associate producer Dan Sarnoff (son of Tom) explained in an interview for *Entertainment Weekly*:

> There are 30,000 letters a year on the Prodigy computer network about the old shows. Westerns are huge—"Unforgiven"; "City Slickers"; "Dr. Quinn, Medicine Woman."[50]

Leckner added:

> People say "Bonanza" is square, but its almost like coming home—and you can *always* go home. These grunge rockers, when they're at home cracking an Old Milwaukee and lighting up a Lucky Strike, they're probably watching "Bonanza."[51]

Broadcast on Sunday, November 28, 1993, in *Bonanza*'s old 9 P.M. timeslot, *Bonanza: The Return* was preceded at 7 P.M. by a special tribute to the series, *Back to Bonanza*. Ads proclaimed, "Revisit the Ponderosa for a nostalgic look at the family that started it all, and the hundreds of guest stars who rode through. . . . At 7 P.M. share the magic of the original. . . . Then at 9 P.M. meet the next generation!" It featured excerpts from a number of early episodes. Pernell Roberts turned down Dortort's invitation to host the special so Michael Landon, Jr., and Dirk Blocker shared those responsibilities.

Both the special and the new film pulled high ratings with the later making Nielsen's top ten. Critics were less supportive, however. *TV Guide*'s Jeff Jarvis wrote (November 27, 1994):

> . . . time, costumes and the story advance to 1905 but the political sensibility fast-forwards to the ecocrazed 1990s. . . . When they're not saving the planet, they mostly explain how old Cartwrights died and make up the plot as they go. A well-intentioned but pale sequel. My score:4.

Even more critical was Ken Tucker who wrote in the November 26, 1993 issue of *Entertainment Weekly* that *Bonanza: The Return*

> . . . only *looks* like a deadpan parody of the classic 1959-73 Old West TV series. . . . "The Return" is so poky, poorly written, and awkwardly acted that it's difficult to sit through. The only character to be fully enjoyed is this updating's replacement for the Ponderosa's cook, Hop Sing. The kitchen chief is now Buckshot Patterson, a grumpy eccentric played by the great, gravelly-voiced character actor Jack Elam.

Despite such negative reaction, Dortort talked about continuing the new series with three or four movies a year (in the same fashion as the successful *Perry Mason* revival). There was also show biz talk about a Broadway musical version of *Bonanza*. Only time would tell if this new generation of Cartwrights would be able to effectively carry on the tradition of television's ultimate family Western.

On initial viewing, *The Big Valley* might appear to be but a slightly more elaborate version of *Bonanza*. The series does focus on the trials and tribulations of a single parent

family, the Barkleys as they strive to manage a 30,000 acre ranch in California's San Joaquin Valley during the 1870s. Even the show's opening is somewhat similar, stressing the
vastness of the land with scenic views of the rivers, forests and mountains, presumably
belonging to the Barkleys, before cutting to close-ups of the individual family members.

There are, however, several significant differences. The Barkley holdings, while not
nearly as large as the Cartwrights', are more diversified, including a mine, a vineyard and
an orange grove, as well as extensive open range for cattle. (This permitted a wide variety
of plotlines.) Furthermore, the house itself is markedly more sophisticated. The Barkley
home is a white-pillared structure that resembles an antebellum Southern mansion. In
addition to its Victorian furnishings and the best in wine, books and china, the Barkley
mansion includes a uniformed black servant named Silas. Guests are served brandy in
glasses made of beautiful delicate crystal. Most important of all, the family is a matriarchy
headed by the recently widowed Victoria Barkley. It should be noted that at the time *The
Big Valley* was being telecast (1965–1969) women were being treated by television producers as domestic consumers who were vital members of the viewing audience. Successful television Westerns like *Wagon Train, Rawhide, Bonanza* and *The Virginian* all had
featured female guest stars on a regular basis for some time.

What made *The Big Valley* unique is that Victoria Barkley is a *continuing* character
who is featured in many episodes. Furthermore, she runs the family empire with a strong
hand and in a crisis is more than a match for any man. Unlike the Cartwrights, however,
family decisions are made democratically rather that autocratically. Victoria solicits input
from the four male Barkleys—Jarrod, the level-headed eldest son; Nick, the hot tempered
middle son; Heath, the feisty step-son, and Eugene (until he disappears—"away at
school"—in the middle of the first season), the shy and sensitive youngest son. Beautiful
daughter Audra completes the Barkley clan.

The Barkley ranch is located near the thriving town of Stockton, which has become
the center of a growing agricultural paradise with strong commercial ties to the San Francisco Bay area. While not directly involving historical events and personalities of a national character like *Bonanza*, the stories do occasionally deal with local issues and
concerns. The Barkleys, like the Cartwrights, possess a strong sense of social and civic
responsibility and often offer their assistance to less fortunate, but deserving, individuals
and groups. The fact that Jarrod is a lawyer, as well as the oldest male member of a
wealthy and powerful family, provides additional opportunities for public service.

In "Heritage," Heath stands up for the rights of oppressed miners. In "Pursuit," Victoria risks her life to help an Indian who has measles which might wipe out his entire tribe.
In "Wagonload of Dreams," the entire family take on powerful and greedy railroad officials (and their corrupt political allies) who are charging exorbitant fees to a Greek farmer.
He is trying to get his fruit to market before it spoils. In "A Flock of Trouble," the
Barkleys befriend a troubled sheepherder over the opposition of much of the predomi-
nantly cattle-oriented community. In "Cage of Eagles," the Barkleys protect a wanted
Irish rebel from extradition. In "Rimfire," Jarrod defends a Chinese family from being
forcibly evicted by an unscrupulous mine owner. In "Run of the Savage," Nick helps a
misguided young man who is well on the way to becoming an outlaw. In "Lightfoot,"
Jarrod supports the efforts of a college educated Indian to gain equality and respect for
his people.

The Big Valley deals in a constructive way with many contemporary problems. For
example, Negro cowboys, who played a significant role in the development of the real
West but were largely ignored in television Westerns, are seen in many episodes and
featured in several ("The Buffalo Man" and "Joshua Watson"). Other minorities are also

The cast of *The Big Valley*: the Barkley siblings Audra (Linda Evans), Heath (Lee Majors, left), Nick (Peter Breck), Jarrod (Richard Long), with matriarch actress Barbara Stanwyck.

presented in a sympathetic way—the Chinese in "Rimfire" and "The Emperor of Rice" and the Mormons in "Passage of Saints." Problems like aging, in "The Stallion" and prison reform, in "Alias Nellie Handley" are considered in intelligent and thought-provoking stories. Comedy is even effectively employed upon occasion (especially during the last season). Comedian Marty Allen plays a ne'er-do-well who seems to be perpetually jinxed in "The Jonah." In "The Battle for Mineral Springs," Jarrod and Victoria assist the residents of a forgotten town in developing their own stage and freight line. The efforts of a rival town to drive them out of business provide some humorous situations.

The Big Valley also featured more "name" guest stars than either *The Rifleman* or *Bonanza*, although each episode intricately involved at least one member of the Barkley family. Established actors like Lew Ayres ("Presumed Dead"), James Whitmore ("The Death Merchant" and "Shadow of a Giant"), James Gregory ("Pursuit" and "Ambush!"), Milton Berle (outstanding in a straight role as the sheepman in "A Flock of Trouble"), Buddy Hackett (also in a straight role in "The Lost Treasure"), Fritz Weaver ("Four Days to Furnace Hill"), Dan O'Herlihy ("Image of Yesterday"), and Robert Walker ("My Son, My Son") frequently appeared. New talent was also developed: 19 year old Richard Dreyfuss ("Boy into Man"), young Katherine Ross ("Winner Lose All"), Charles Bronson before he became a superstar ("Earthquake"), Ronny Howard on leave from *The Andy Griffith Show* ("Night of the Wolf"), William Shatner, before *Star Trek* ("A Time to Kill"), Bruce Dern ("A Noose Is Waiting"), and Cloris Leachman, before *The Mary Tyler Moore Show* ("Plunder"). Even Pernell Roberts, who was still looking for more "serious" roles after leaving *Bonanza*, appeared twice on *The Big Valley* (as the Irish rebel in "Cage of Eagles" and as a professional hunter in "Run of the Cat"). Nor did the producers of *The Rifleman* forget two former stars from that popular series: Johnny Crawford appeared as a young deputy in "Shadow of a Giant" and Paul Fix as a lawyer in "The Murdered Party" and an aging bronc buster in "The Stallion."

The "cement" that held the show together, that gave it character and quality, was *Miss* (as she was always billed) Barbara Stanwyck. Stanwyck, a "legend" at 58 when the series began, not only played the iron-willed matriarch of the Barkley clan, she influenced practically every aspect of the series. According to *TV Guide* writer Dwight Whitney, she "ruled everything and everyone. . . . She ruled the grips, the gaffer, the guest stars, her co-stars, the directors, the camera operators, the wardrobe people, the soundmen."[52] She had final approval of scripts, guest cast and directors.

Stanwyck was born Ruby Stevens, the orphaned child of a ne'er-do-well Brooklyn bricklayer. The feisty aspiring Irish actress made it the hard way—up from the chorus line to superstar status. Called "the best actress never to win an Oscar," she had a long and distinguished career in films (1927–1968) before assuming the lead in *The Big Valley*. She had given some of her best performances in Westerns (*Annie Oakley*, 1935; *Union Pacific*, 1939; *California*, 1947; *Cattle Queen of Montana*, 1955; *The Maverick Queen*, 1956; *Forty Guns*, 1957). Stanwyck's first appearance on television was as a guest on *The Jack Benny Show* in 1954. This was followed by two appearances as guest hostess on *The Loretta Young Show* in late 1955, during Young's recovery from surgery. During the 1958-59 season she made four appearances on *Dick Powell's Zane Grey Theater* and in early 1959 she was the star of Jack Benny's famous takeoff on the film *Gaslight*, entitled "Antolite." According to biographer, Al DiOrio:

> Throughout the fifties Barbara's agents received numerous offers from each of the networks asking her to star in her own series but none was willing to give Barbara what she desperately wanted, a Western series of her own. Again and again they told her the same story, Westerns were beneath her, she deserved something classier, something prettier.[53]

One of Stanwyck's appearances on *The Zane Grey Theater* was in an episode entitled "The Freighter," in which she played the proprietor of a freight company which sent Conestoga wagons across the prairies. Powell had intended the show to serve as the pilot for a series, but the Madison Avenue advertising moguls backed away. They apparently felt that the public would not accept a Western starring a woman. She also wanted to do a series based on James D. Horan's book *Desperate Women*, about the rugged pioneer women of the Western frontier, but the networks also nixed the proposal.

In January of 1960 Stanwyck and NBC-TV finally agreed to an anthology format similar to that used by Loretta Young which would broadcast Monday evenings at 10:00.

Four Western scripts were to be included to satisfy Stanwyck's preference for Westerns. Of the 39 episodes of *The Barbara Stanwyck Show*, Stanwyck was featured in all but four. One was to be the pilot for a continuing series in which she was to star as an American adventuress in Hong Kong, but the concept was turned down because of difficulties connected with its Hong Kong locale. For the most part, the show received good reviews and drew good ratings. It earned Stanwyck her first Emmy Award from the Television Academy of Arts and Sciences for Outstanding Actress in a Series. Still, surprisingly, NBC did not renew the show for a second season.

The early sixties led to more guest appearances for Stanwyck including two memorable roles on *The Untouchables* and four on *Wagon Train* (her favorite television show). Twice she played the same character, Kate Crawley, a woman not unlike Victoria Barkley in many respects. In the meantime, Lou Edelwon, producer of *The Barbara Stanwyck Show*, had developed a Western for Stanwyck tentatively called *The Big Valley*. Unable to interest the networks in the idea, he sold the property to Jules V. Levy, Arthur Gardner and Arnold Laven, the team responsible for producing *The Rifleman*. In January 1965, ABC announced that *The Big Valley*, in which Stanwyck was to star as the widowed owner of a big California ranch in the 1870s, would be on its fall schedule. Before agreeing to star in the series, Stanwyck made sure the producers understood certain conditions involved in her acceptance of the role:

> I'm a tough old broad from Brooklyn. Don't try to make me into something I'm not. If you want someone to tiptoe down the Barkley staircase in crinoline and politely ask where the cattle went, get another gal. That's not me.[54]

Later in an interview in the *New York Journal-American*, Stanwyck explained why she wanted to play the "blood and guts" matriarch of a Western series:

> When I was a little girl nothing fascinated me more than the history of our West. I loved the cowboy and Indian stories, but more than that, I marveled at the pioneers. The real people who went into the wilderness with little other than their courage. I still love everything about the West—the people, the land, everything.
>
> Some producers think women did nothing in those days except keep house and have children. But, if you read your history, they did a lot more than that. They were in cattle drives. They were *there*.
>
> I try to make Victoria Barkley as human as possible. She doesn't came waltzing down the staircase in calico to inquire as to the progress of the cattle. She's an old broad who combines elegance with guts.[55]

In its four-year run, *The Big Valley* produced 112 episodes. Stanwyck appeared in all but seven—through an arrangement which had her either carrying a story completely, sharing it with a guest star or other member of the family, or appearing briefly when someone else carried it. Stanwyck's stamina amazed everyone and she insisted on doing most of her own stunts. In one case the script called for her to be dragged through the street on the end of a rope tied to a horse. Director Virgil Vogel cleared a path 50 feet long and instructed Stanwyck to let go at the end of the clearing. Not Stanwyck. She held on for 150 feet with two cameras on her and it produced a terrific shot.

Stanwyck's status on the set of *The Big Valley* was undisputed. She was the "Queen" but she never interfered with the director's responsibilities. She was a professional and those who worked with her knew it. Consequently, when she spoke, everyone listened. During the run of the series, any comment that referred to the show as a female version of *Bonanza* or called Stanwyck "a Lorne Greene with skirts" aroused her anger. In its review of the premier episode, *Variety* (September 22, 1965) had stated,

"The Big Valley" registers on the home screen as "Bonanza" in drag. It's a direct variation of the proven theme only with a femme at the head of the clan, a daughter included in
the offspring, and of course, the name is changed to Barkley.

The reviewer did go on to point out that

The acting is strong, the cast attractive, and the production coffers opened wide, at least
on the preem.

These positive comments, however, did nothing to pacify Stanwyck who was thoroughly
incensed by the comparison:

Fine, let them compare us to "Bonanza." You've got to be compared to something, so
why not "Bonanza"? I'll tell you, though, . . . Lorne Greene is the Loretta Young of the West.
That's not for me. . .

. . . What I mean is that I feel he is far too pontifical. When he passes judgement—that's
that! When Lorne Greene has an opinion, it has to be right. Well, damn it all! I've had my
own ranches. I am a horsewoman. I ran ranches and herds and bred livestock years before
Lorne Greene even knew what a saddle looked like. And you don't run ranches anywhere
by being pontifical about any bit of it. Nobody on any ranch can ever tell what's going to
happen next. You just can't afford to become too opinionated or too conceited. If you do,
you portray the West badly, and you do the West an injustice. The West was tough, hell-
country, full of fights and wrongs and hardness. Pontifical wiseacres did not survive long out
there![56]

Later she expanded on these thoughts:

Our family is much tougher. My sons are strong. They're real men. This is not one of
those "Mother Knows Best" things. Hell, I wouldn't play one. Our family behaves like any
normal family. We fight, argue, discuss things. We're not like some of the TV family today.
I don't know where the hell those people are. I never see anybody like them in real life. The
woman I'm playing has plenty of battles with her boys. She's a very vital person. So are her
sons. They all have minds of their own.[57]

Stanwyck was also able to demonstrate her great versatility as an actress in the series.
There were humorous episodes like "The Great Safe Robbery," moving ones like "Boots
with My Father's Name," "Teacher of Outlaws," and "The Disappearance"; terrific
fights such as those in "The Challenge" and "The Emperor of Rice"; and perils to rival
any of those experienced by Pearl White in "Four Days to Furnace Hill," "Alias Nellie
Handley," "Earthquake," "The Long Ride" and "Ambush." *The Big Valley* brought
Stanwyck more recognition and greater honors than she had received in years.

In 1966, *Photoplay* magazine presented Stanwyck with its Editors' Award. In 1967
and 1968 Photoplay's readers voted her "Most Popular Female Star" and *TV Radio Mirror*'s Television Critics Poll honored her in 1966 as the "Best Dramatic Actress in Television." The National Academy of Television Arts and Sciences awarded her a second
Emmy in 1966 as "Outstanding Actress in a Dramatic Series" and nominated her again
in 1967 and 1968. Biographer Ella Smith assesses her work on the series:

Heading things with a firm and vivid portrayal, Stanwyck was very much in her glory.
She was playing a woman she could admire, she understood her thoroughly and she
developed a character that will remain as strongly associated with Stanwyck as any she has
ever created. Not because she played her for as long, but because she played her so well.[58]

Victoria Barkley was described in an "authorized" novel as "close to fifty" yet she

. . . carried herself with the spark and vitality of a much younger person. She had silver-
grey hair that was like a halo around her smooth, unlined face. Her features had been faintly
touched by the sun, giving her skin a golden glow. . . . It was difficult to believe that she had

only recently been widowed. . . . Yet her courageous spirit helped her bear her portion of the responsibilities of running the many enterprises that her husband had founded.[59]

The character of Victoria Barkley functions as part of a team, rather than the all-wise sage and pillar of the community role assigned to Ben Cartwright. Instead of seeking advice from their mother, the Barkley children, especially the males, are often in the position of giving her advice. In "Run of the Savage," when Nick is kidnapped, Victoria is inclined to pay the ransom to insure his safety. Jarrod and Heath urge her to call in the sheriff and she finally agrees. In a number of episodes, Victoria finds her life in great jeopardy and it is her children who must come to her rescue, quite the reverse situation usually presented on *Bonanza*. In the semicomic episode "The Great Safe Robbery," Victoria and Audra are kidnapped by three inept bank robbers and although Nick and Heath arrive with the sheriff at the end of the episode to free them, Victoria has already outwitted her captors.

In "Earthquake," Victoria is trapped under an old mission with a pregnant Indian woman and a bitter alcoholic malcontent after an earthquake. Before she is once again rescued by her children, she displays great physical and mental courage. First, in delivering the baby, and later in standing up to the alcoholic (played with appropriate menace by Charles Bronson), who had been fired earlier by Nick. When he tries to force her to drink with him, she grabs the bottle, breaks it and declares: "I've broken trails, hunted and ridden shotgun with my husband. I've kicked, clawed and gouged my way with him. So don't you ever dare touch me again!" In "Teacher of Outlaws," Victoria is kidnapped by a gang of outlaws in order to teach their illiterate leader, Sam Beldon, how to read and write. She later discovers his real reason for wanting to learn is the desire to personally write an inscription on his dead wife's tombstone. Again rescued by her sons, Victoria feels compassion for her captor. Beldon helps save her life when one of his confederates tries to use Victoria as a shield after they have been surrounded by a posse. After Beldon is killed in the subsequent shoot-out, Victoria places her textbook over his grave.

In "Pursuit," Victoria meets a shabbily dressed, heavy-drinking buffalo hunter named Simon Carter who has lost all self-respect. Together they track down an Indian who has the measles. He must be reached before he infects his entire tribe. First, Carter saves Victoria from dying of thirst. Later Victoria nurses Carter, who has been seriously wounded by the Indian, back to health. Carter finds that there are some things you cannot put a price on. He regains his self-respect as together they accomplish their mission. Proof of his reformation comes when he appears the following season in "Ambush!" Now he is clean-shaven, wears clean clothes and a white hat, and boasts that he has not had a drink in the year since he last saw Victoria.

Victoria renews acquaintances with an old friend who has become a professional gunman in "Image of Yesterday." He and his men have been hired to protect the local ranchers from a murderous band of outlaws who have been terrorizing the countryside. They end up looting and destroying the community. When confronted by Victoria, who accuses him of being as evil as the marauders, the gunman replies, "We prefer to think of ourselves as protectors, just like soldiers." Victoria responds, "It's not the same; soldiers fight for what they believe in." The gunmen obviously do not believe in anything but money and, therefore cannot be trusted. Victoria would rather be killed by the marauders than by "the enemy within" their community. Ultimately the gunman decides he still believes in "causes" and drives off the other hired guns with the help of Victoria.

In "Presumed Dead," Victoria discovers an entirely different kind of lifestyle when she is seriously injured in a stage wreck and loses her memory. Rescued by the leader of a small band of rustlers whose wife has recently died, Victoria is deliberately misled into believing she is his wife. He is gentle and kind to her and she becomes very fond of him. Later, after she regains her memory, Victoria leads a posse to the rustler's hideout and he is killed. Although glad to regain her true identity and return home to her family, Victoria comes to realize what her life might have been like under different circumstances.

In a number of episodes, Victoria's life is placed in great jeopardy. In "Four Days to Furnace Hill," while on her way to a mining company stockholder's meeting, she is kidnapped by ruthless prison guards to serve as a hostage in place of a prisoner they have murdered. Victoria stays to help a wounded outlaw when she could have escaped. Later her faith in human nature proves justified when he sacrifices his life for her before help arrives with Jarrod and Heath. In "The Emperor of Rice," Victoria is imprisoned and brutally tortured by a man and his scheming wife who are trying to force her into selling them two shiploads of rice so they can corner the rice market. The episode is a dramatic tour de force for Stanwyck before her character finally escapes. In "Alias Nellie Handley," Victoria changes her identity, and commits a robbery in order to get arrested and sent to the state prison. A member of the Prison Reform Board, she is trying to discover what conditions are really like for women behind prison walls. Using an Irish brogue, Stanwyck turns in another outstanding performance in the dual role.

Victoria is also capable of great courage when any of her children's lives are threatened, especially the beautiful, but seemingly helpless, Audra. In "The Disappearance," Victoria and Audra stop to spend the night in a bustling "cattle town" on their way home to Stockton. While Victoria is sleeping, Audra and all of her belongings disappear and all of the townspeople with whom Victoria comes in contact claim the girl was never there. Driven nearly crazy with worry and fear, Victoria, with the aid of a cowardly sheriff, finally discovers what happened to her daughter. Audra had become sick and the doctor had diagnosed the illnesses as anthrax. She was then drugged and hidden away by the unscrupulous town boss, so that cattle buyers would not find out there was anthrax in the area. Not only did Victoria's courage and stubbornness save Audra's life, it helped the sheriff find his self-respect.

In "The Long Ride," Audra, while hiding in the attic, witnesses the brutal robbery and murder of a family she is visiting. When Victoria arrives to take her home, she finds that Audrea has retreated into a mute trance to blot out the memory of the massacre. On the stage ride home, they discover that the murderers are following them—in order to eliminate the only witness to their heinous crime. One by one, the other passengers and driver are killed or frightened off so that only Victoria, unarmed, on foot, stands between the killers and their prey. Running, falling, running again, through the rock hills, Victoria uses every bit of her strength and cunning to stop the two desperados. A rock slide and burning tumbleweed stop one and enable Victoria to seize his rifle with which she kills the other, thus jarring Audra back to reality.

Even the male Barkleys need their mother's help occasionally. In "By Force and Violence," Victoria must search for help when Heath is pinned under their wagon following an accident. Her only hope is an escaped convict who is being chased by two unscrupulous bounty hunters. Victoria convinces him to help her. She, in return, believing him to be innocent, later helps him escape from the bounty hunters.

Victoria Barkley was indeed unique among television's Western heroines. She possessed feminine characteristics and yet had the inner strength typical of only men in Westerns. While most men deferred to her charm, virtually all men came to respect her courage and integrity. These qualities she instilled in her children—but unlike the Cartwright brood—they rarely came running to her for either advice or help.

The Big Valley producers selected a totally unknown, inexperienced young actor named Lee Majors to play the key role of Heath, the illegitimate half–Indian son of Victoria's late husband. In winning the coveted role, he beat out several dozen other young actors, including Burt Reynolds. The tall 24 year old, blond, blue-eyed kid from Kentucky was soon dubbed by critics as "the new James Dean." Things had not always gone well for the young actor, however. His childhood was far from ideal. Orphaned at 2 when his mother died (his father had died before he was born), he was brought up by an aunt and uncle in Kentucky. He attended Eastern Kentucky State College on an athletic scholarship, and earned a degree there in physical education. Turning down an offer to try out for the St. Louis Cardinals, he headed for Hollywood. His first job was as an assistant playground director for the parks department. Several actors that he met while working there encouraged him to try his hand in the more lucrative acting profession.

So Majors enrolled in the M-G-M acting school and hired himself a dramatic coach and an agent (the same agent who had worked for James Dean). In early 1965, a little over a year later, he was signed for his first major television appearances on episodes of *Gunsmoke* and *The Alfred Hitchcock Hour* (on which he starred as a doomed racecar driver). *The Big Valley* offered him a chance at stardom.[60] On the set Barbara Stanwyck found his "magnetism" irresistible. She took him under her wing and tried to help him get over the jitters that beset him during the early shooting. (It was no secret among the cast that Majors was receiving the most attention and publicity and his fan mail was nearly twice as much as any of his costars. This particularly upset Peter Breck, who had starred in his own series before coming to *The Big Valley*.)[61] The early episodes did focus on Heath, described as

> . . . a tough-grained man in his middle twenties. His blond hair, worn long, was shielded by a battered gray Stetson. He had a tightly muscled body, flaring widely in the chest, but narrowing sharply in the hips. His skin had a tanned, weathered look from constant exposure to sun and wind.[62]

The pilot episode, "Palms of Glory," relates the story of Heath's arrival at the Barkley ranch. Heath has been a drifter, moving from place to place, wrangling horses and punching cattle. His mother's sudden death has brought him back to Strawberry, the nearly deserted mining town where he was born, to handle the funeral arrangements. While he is going through her personal effects, a newspaper clipping falls out of her Bible. It relates the story of Tom Barkley's death in an ambush. Heath, of course, had heard of Barkley and the vast California empire he had built, but he was amazed to discover other papers clearly indicating that Barkley had been his father.

The wealth of the Barkleys means little to him, but Heath longs to become part of a family group. With his mother's death, Heath is alone. The Barkleys are now the only people whom he can call family—even though he has never laid eyes on them. The newspaper account of his father's murder had mentioned a widow, three sons and a daughter. Naturally Heath's arrival at the Barkley spread, together with his announcement that his is Tom's son, comes as a distinct shock and the Barkley children (especially Nick) are reluctant to believe his story. Heath's only proof is some letters written to his mother in Tom Barkley's sprawling handwriting. However, Heath takes a stand with the other Barkleys against the corrupt and powerful railroad that is attempting to drive neighboring farmers out of their homes. It is this display of courage that earns Heath acceptance into the family. Although Nick continues to remain skeptical, Heath soon demonstrates his willingness to step in and do his share of the work in running the vast Barkley enterprises.

In the second episode, "Boots with My Father's Name," Victoria travels to Heath's birthplace to learn all that she can about Heath's mother and her relationship with Victoria's late husband. Victoria discovers that Leah (Heath's mother) had found Tom Barkley half beaten to death in an alley, brought him home and nursed him back to health. Heath's nanny gives Victoria a letter that Tom wrote to Leah expressing his love for his wife and family and urging Leah to find a man worthy of her, get married and raise a family. It is clear to Victoria and Heath that Tom Barkley never knew about the son Leah bore him.

The third episode, "Forty Rifles," continues the story of Heath's attempt to fit in and be accepted as a Barkley by the other ranch hands. He wins the respect of some with his fists, of others through his courage in standing up to an ex–Union general, a man idolized by Nick. The general has become a mercenary, selling his services to the highest bidder. He joins the Barkley's cattle drive. After Nick is badly wounded, Heath is put in charge. The general, however, tries to turn the men against Heath, who is still considered an outsider by the drovers. He convinces them to join his band of renegades. Later Heath is able to expose him as a deranged, power-hungry tyrant in a courageous confrontation alone against the turncoat general. Heath finishes the drive and is accepted by the men as a genuine Barkley.

Heath must live down his illegitimacy once again in "Winner Lose All" when he falls in love with the daughter of a Spanish nobleman. Her father disapproves of the romance because of Heath's mixed blood and in the end his daughter is forced to chose family honor over love. It is not the last time that the uncertainty of Heath's birth returns to haunt him. In "The Lost Treasure," a man shows up at the Barkley ranch claiming to be his real father. Heath ultimately discovers that the man is not really his father, although he had been married to Heath's mother. On his deathbed the man admits that he deserted her over two years before Heath was born, thus reaffirming the contention that Tom Barkley was actually Heath's father. "Into the Widow's Web" brings a childhood sweetheart from Strawberry back into Heath's life when she appears in Stockton as a singer with a traveling carnival. Later, she murders her husband and tries to frame Heath for it. It is only by matching the bullets from the dead man and Heath's gun that Jarrod is able to prove that Heath is innocent. He was being "used" by the girl who thought Heath would never go to trial because of his family's influence. Like all the other Barkley offspring, Heath is unlucky at love.

Heath is also framed for murder in "Fall of a Hero," and again Jarrod defends him. Two witnesses claim they saw Heath kill a man he had threatened earlier. Heath, who was hit over the head, cannot remember what happened. However, there was another witness to the crime who had been hiding in the barn where the murder was committed. He does not want to testify, but Jarrod forces him to describe what he saw. The murder was actually an accident and the fault of a friend of the man who was killed. He had decided to put the blame on Heath rather than risk an investigation into his own unsavory past. Heath's life is placed in jeopardy in quite a different way in "Journey into Violence," when he is kidnapped by the fanatical relatives of a man he was forced to shoot years earlier. Imprisoned in a cage and forced to work like a slave, Heath's only chance for escape is to persuade the widow of the man he killed to help him. She finds herself attracted to Heath because he is "a real man, not an animal" like the other men she has known in her life. With the understanding that he will take her with him, she releases him from his cage but is shot before they can make good their escape. As she dies, Nick and Jarrod arrive to rescue Heath.

In "Hell Hath No Fury," Heath becomes romantically involved with a beautiful young woman who is actually the leader of a ruthless band of outlaws. She literally throws herself at Heath, but when he begins to suspect who she really is, he rejects her advances. Even when she promises to reform, Heath tells her that he simply does not love her. Out of hurt, anger and spite she takes Heath prisoner, while she and her gang make plans to rob the local bank. When she is unable to resist one last kiss, Heath grabs her and frees himself. Later when the gang invades the Barkley ranch and sets the barn on fire, she wounds Heath, but is unable to bring herself to kill him. She is trampled to death by the horses as they flee the burning barn. Such was invariably the fate of women who became romantically involved with Barkley men—especially Heath. More of the stories focused on Heath than any other character in the series thus giving Lee Majors a showcase for his considerable talent. He did not disappoint his growing number of fans and gained valuable experience for his subsequent starring roles as *The Six Million Dollar Man* and *The Fall Guy*.

A bit part in an old movie with Barbara Stanwyck (*All I Desire*, 1953) helped Richard Long land the part of eldest son Jarrod on *The Big Valley*. Long was one of six children born in Chicago to a commercial artist and his wife. During the war the Long family moved to Hollywood, where Richard attended Hollywood High. According to one story, Long was "discovered" by casting director Jack Murton one day when he gave a ride to two high school coeds who had missed their bus during a rainstorm. In casual conversation they told him of their crush on Dick Long, who had the lead in the school play. Murton gave them his card, and they in turn gave it to Long, who called Murton at Universal Studios. This landed him a role in *Tomorrow Is Forever*, starring Orson Welles and Claudette Colbert. Later, Long explained in an interview, "I had no intention of becoming an actor. I took the senior drama class because it was a snap course, and I needed the credit for my English requirement."[63]

Long spent 11 years at Universal International, appearing in over twenty films, including the popular Ma and Pa Kettle series where he played the eldest (and most level-headed) son. At U-I, Long was part of an up-and-coming group of stars and starlets that included Clint Eastwood, David Janssen, Barbara Rush and Rock Hudson. It was here, too, that Long met his first wife, a spirited young actress named Suzan Ball, who was diagnosed shortly thereafter as having cancer. The following year she died and was buried in her wedding gown. It took Long a while to get over his grief.[64]

After Suzan's death, Long decided to try television. His video debut came in *Climax* with Mary Aster, followed by appearances on *Reader's Digest*, *Lux Video Theatre*, *Schlitz Playhouse* and *The Millionaire*. Occasionally, he appeared as the lovable scoundrel Gentleman Jack Darby on *Maverick* (1957–1959). Then, Long landed a starring role in the Warner Bros. series *Bourbon Street Beat* as private detective Rex Randolph. Unfortunately, the series was canceled after a year, but Long's character was moved over to the established Warners show *77 Sunset Strip*, where he remained for one more season (1960-61). By the time Long was cast as Jarrod, he had gained enough experience in television to be given an opportunity to direct several episodes ("Plunder!" and "The 25 Graves of Midas"). Long wanted to play Jarrod Barkley in somewhat the same tongue-in-cheek manner he had used on *Maverick*, but the management was not interested in roguishness. It wanted nobleness and nobleness is what Long gave them.[65] Jarrod also could be described as calm, collected, steady and dependable. After all, he was a lawyer who had many business dealings in San Francisco. Physically,

> ... His eyes were dark brown and strikingly sharp. His mouth and chin were firm, his black hair neatly barbered. His six-foot frame showed the solid weight of muscle and sinew. He [usually] wore grey trousers, low-heeled boots, a white shirt ... with a black string tie.[66]

Since Jarrod is a lawyer, some interesting storylines could be developed involving courtroom scenes. Unlike Perry Mason, however, Jarrod's clients do not always turn out to be innocent. In "The Murdered Party," Jarrod defends a man accused of murder whom he believes to be innocent. In order to win the case, he must discredit the testimony of Heath, who saw the murderer leaving the scene of the crime. Although Jarrod is successful in doing this, there was another witness to the crime whose testimony convicts his obviously guilty client. What is noble about Jarrod's actions in this case is the fact that he put that ancient legal principle, that every accused person is entitled to the best defense possible, above even loyalty to his family.

In the final episode of the last season, "Point and Counterpoint," Jarrod defends another accused killer whom the sheriff saw leaving the scene of the crime. This jeopardizes Jarrod's chance at being nominated for the office of state attorney general. Because his client has a twin brother, he is able to come up with an alibi and Jarrod wins the case. However, he later discovers that he has helped free a murderer. Justice is ultimately served, however, as Jarrod is forced to kill both brothers when they attack his mother. Again nobility triumphs over expediency as Jarrod turns down the nomination to political office.

Loyalty to a friend is involved in another interesting episode featuring Jarrod called "A Time to Kill." An old law school friend of Jarrod's pretends to be interested in permanently settling in Stockton. Actually, he is visiting the Barkleys so that he can "case" the local bank. In the end, however, he finds it impossible to go through with the betrayal of his friends. He helps Jarrod apprehend his two cronies and recover the money they have stolen. Jarrod's trust in his friend has not been misplaced. Jarrod often feels the need to right wrongs. In "Deathtown," Jarrod investigates the lynching of three Mexican brothers and discovers that they were framed by the husband of the woman they were supposed to have raped and murdered. In "They Call Her Delilah," Jarrod defends a woman he once loved of murder charges. The woman has been framed because she was once a spy for the Confederacy. (Singer Julie London turns in an outstanding performance as the featured guest star.)

Even when he is unaware of the fact that he is a Barkley, Jarrod feels compelled to come to the aid of the weak and oppressed. In "The Man from Nowhere," Jarrod is ambushed and loses his memory. He is taken in by a woman whose husband has deserted her. She is struggling to take care of her son and elderly mother. Powerful ranchers are trying to force her off her land. Jarrod stays to help her even while seeking to discover his own identity. This unusual episode concludes with Jarrod engaging in a gunfight with Nick and Heath before he finally regains his memory. Once again the story is greatly enhanced by the solid acting of Long.

Peter Breck, an established television actor, was chosen to play the tempestuous middle son, Nick. Born and raised in Rochester, New York, Breck had done professional singing while still in high school. Upon graduation, he got jobs as a singer, dancer and comic in Buffalo area night clubs. After a stint in the Navy, Breck enrolled at the University of Houston, where he majored in drama and minored in psychology. He apprenticed at Houston's famous Alley Theatre and later, at Margot Jones's Theater in Dallas, where he played parts from modern romantic leads to Shakespeare and Shaw.

Moving to New York City, Breck was soon acting in road productions touring the United States and Canada. Robert Mitchum saw him in a play, *Man of Destiny*, in Washington, D.C., and offered him a part in his new film, *Thunder Road* (1958). While in Hollywood, he was signed for an episode of *Have Gun, Will Travel*, where he played the part of a deaf mute. After over thirty appearances in various television shows, including *Cheyenne*, *Tombstone Territory*, *Sugarfoot* (as Teddy Roosevelt), *77 Sunset Strip* and

Perry Mason. Breck was offered the lead in the television Western *Black Saddle* (see Chapter IV). After *Black Saddle* was canceled, Breck was given the role of Doc Holliday in the established Warner Bros. Western *Maverick*. He appeared in six episodes with Jack Kelly (Bart) in 1961 and 1962. During this period Breck was also active in films: *Portrait of a Mobster* (1961), *Lad: A Dog* (1961), *The Couch* (1962), *Shock Corridor* (1963, for which he won a "Best Actor" award at the Cannes Film Festival) and *Black Gold* (1963).[67] He thus came well prepared for his role on *The Big Valley*. Nick Barkley was characterized as

> Four years younger than Jarrod's thirty-two, he brimmed with untamed energy and power. He was a rangy, wide-shouldered individual with tough-hew features that just missed being rugged. He had hazel eyes and a generous mouth that hinted at humor, but actually he was quite serious and intense. He was hardy and impatient, quick to anger, handy with horses, cattle, and guns.[68]

In "Night of the Wolf," Breck turns in one of the best performances of his career—one, in fact, which earned him a nomination for a "Best Actor" Emmy. Nick is bitten by a rabid wolf. This, of course, is before the development of a serum to treat the disease. All the doctor can tell him is that if he is alive in 60 days, he will probably survive. He decides he must make his last days, if so they be, "count for something." So, without telling anyone but Heath of his condition, he leaves the Barkley ranch for Willow Springs to look for a girl he once knew. He discovers that she has died in a typhoid epidemic, but is taken in by a woman and her son who live in the house once occupied by the dead girl's family. Since the boy was illegitimate and the boy's father was hanged when he was only a year old, the woman asks Nick to marry her and give her son a proper family name. The woman is mortally wounded when two men try to rob Nick. On the sixtieth day Nick marries her shortly before she dies so that her son will have a legitimate name. After burying her, Nick leaves to take his new step-son to Massachusetts to live with his grandparents. It is a moving and well-acted story.

Another exciting episode featuring Nick is "Barbary Red." Nick and several of his men are shanghaied on his birthday. Jarrod plays up to Barbary Red, who is an accomplice to the crimp responsible, and Heath allows himself to be shanghaied so that he can be followed. In a blazing finale the men are rescued and the crimp killed. In "Lady Killer," Nick is attracted to the daughter of a family of thieving murderers. The daughter has been flirting with men who stop at an isolated way-station until her father and brother can bash their heads in, rob them and throw their bodies into the river. When they decide to kill and rob Nick, she cannot bring herself to go through with it. After her father and brother are killed, she begs Nick to help her escape. He must, however, turn her over to the law. This is just another example of Nick's misfortune in affairs of the heart.

Nick falls in love with a beautiful but hot-tempered Mexican revolutionary in "Miranda." She is trying to steal a valuable necklace entrusted to the Barkleys to help finance a revolution. When Nick convinces her to stay with him instead of returning to Mexico, the other rebels take her hostage and demand the necklace. They release Miranda, but seize Nick, when he brings the necklace. Nick is able to turn the tables on his captors, but Miranda returns to Mexico. She is unwilling to desert her people, even though she loves Nick—another lost love for the impetuous middle Barkley brother.

Breck turns in another sterling acting performance in "Run of the Cat." When Nick is mauled by a cougar, scars are inflicted on not only his body, but his mind, as well. He suffers from nightmares and hallucinations in which the big cat is attacking him. Jarrod hires a professional hunter (well played by Pernell Roberts) to track down and kill the cougar, but Nick insists on going along. Although he is neither physically or emotionally well, Nick believes that the only way he can overcome his irrational fear of the animal is to kill it himself. How he finally accomplishes this makes for an exciting story.

Another aspect of Nick's character is brought out in "Run of the Savage." He shows great understanding and compassion for a 14 year old boy whose mother has rejected him and whose father was an Indian. The boy has become a cocky thief and kidnaps Nick when he follows him to get back stolen Barkley property. Holding him for ransom in an old mining shaft, the boy is seriously injured in a cave-in. Nick not only rescues him, but helps set him on the road to becoming a responsible young man. Nick shows more patience and understanding than usual in this story, demonstrating that Nick is far from a one dimensional character.

Linda Evans, who played the only Barkley daughter, Audra, was born Linda Evanstad in Hartford, Connecticut. Her parents brought her to Los Angeles when she was two months old. They were dancers, but after Linda and her two sisters came along, Mrs. Evanstad retired from dancing and Mr. Evanstad became a successful interior decorator. When Linda began acting, she was so young that her mother had to go along with her on calls. It was pure chance that got her into television. She went along with a Hollywood High classmate who was auditioning for a part in a Canada Dry commercial. The company liked Linda's looks so much that they hired her too. After doing only three commercials, she landed a role in *Bachelor Father* in an October 1960 episode entitle "A Crush on Bentley." (Ironically, the role of Bentley Gregg was played by John Forsythe, the middle-aged star of the series, who would later become Blake Carrington, Linda's distinguished husband on *Dynasty*.) For the next several years, Linda continued to play supporting roles on such shows as *Ozzie and Harriet*, *The Untouchables*, *The Eleventh Hour* and *My Favorite Martian*.

Linda's movie career began with a small role in *Twilight of Honor* starring Richard Chamberlain, followed by a featured role in Walt Disney's *Those Calloways*. The biggest break of her career, however, was winning the role of Audra on *The Big Valley*.[69] Audra, the beautiful, young heroine,

> ... had elf like features, ... at twenty-one, she had clearly inherited her mother's smooth, softly textured skin, warm generous mouth, and vibrant, electric spirit. Her soft golden hair was worn low against her neck. Her green, flashing eyes were deep wells of color beneath finely arched brows.[70]

Unfortunately Audra was usually relegated to damsel-in-distress or young-maiden-in-love stories. In her first featured episode, "The Young Marauders," she falls in love with a handsome, young man who unbeknown to her is the leader of a band of outlaws who prey on small farmers extorting from them "protection" money. While "courting" Audra in order to gain information about the Barkleys he finds himself genuinely attracted to her. When his identity is discovered by Nick, Jarrod and Heath, Audra does not believe them and follows him to his hideout. His gang turns on him and decides to hold Audra for ransom. After the ransom is paid the young outlaw sacrifices his life so that she can escape.

In "My Son, My Son," the ne'er-do-well son of a neighboring rancher attempts to force his unwelcome attentions upon Audra. Even a couple of beatings by Heath fail to deter him and finally Victoria is forced to shoot him in order to save Audra's life. In defending his mother, Jarrod reveals that the boy had a long record of trouble-making: arson, assault, attempted murder. His parents had felt compelled to cover up for him. As Victoria points out to Audra, "He was their son. When your child is in trouble you defend him without question, without reservation—the way I had to defend you when that moment came. There are times when there isn't any other choice."

Audra had a habit of falling for the wrong man. In "The Midas Man," the object of her affections is an unscrupulous land speculator. He is young, handsome, well-traveled, wealthy and utterly ruthless when it comes to turning a profit out of the misfortunes of others. When he invites Audra to travel to Europe with him as his mistress, she sees him for what he really is. Nevertheless, she is willing to accept his offer if he will grant extensions on the notes he holds on the property of neighboring drought-stricken ranchers. He sees that she will actually go through with her offer despite her obvious aversion to everything he represents. At this point, he decides, out of respect for her courage, to grant the extensions without holding her to her part of the bargain. This episode contains one of Linda Evans's best performances in the series.

In "Joaquín," Audra is attracted to a mysterious Mexican wrangler who calls himself Juan Molena, but who some suspect is the legendary Joaquín Murietta. When Juan is forced to kill a man in self-defense, he asks Audra to provide him with an alibi. When she refuses, he tells her that he is indeed Joaquín. Meanwhile, Heath beats an admission out of the dead man's accomplice that the shooting was in self-defense. Not knowing this, Juan leads a raid on the Barkley ranch and Heath is forced to kill him. It is clear that Juan was not Joaquín, but another would-be suitor for Audra has bitten the dust.

Audra finds her life in jeopardy from a deranged doctor out to gain revenge against the Barkleys, whom he holds responsible for the death of his father many years earlier in "A Noose Is Waiting." The doctor (superbly portrayed by Bradford Dillman) entices Audra into taking a buggy ride into the country with him and stopping at "an old ranch house" (which in reality is his old family homestead). He plans to kill her so that her mother will suffer as his did after the suicide of his father. Jarrod and the sheriff save Audra in the nick of time and the doctor topples into an old well. Audra's life is threatened in quite a different way in "Last Train to the Fair," when she is stricken with an attack of appendicitis and has to have emergency surgery while on a train. Moreover, the doctor performing the operation is being hunted by men out to kill him. A former outlaw who learned medicine while in prison, the doctor saves Audra's life and the Barkleys, in turn, help save his. Linda Evans was capable of doing more than looking beautiful and helpless. Unfortunately, she was given little opportunity to do so in *The Big Valley*.

The final Barkley, Eugene (played by Charles Briles), appeared only sporadically during the first season. The youngest, at 18, he was described as having

> ... light-brown hair, a broad mouth, and wide-set, gray-green eyes. Not as tall as his three other brothers, his slenderness gave him an appearance of greater height than he actually owned. There was a quality of sensitivity about his features.[71]

Only in "The Way to Kill a Killer" does Eugene play a significant part in the storyline. Here, as a student home from agricultural college, he explains how a vaccine has been developed to protect cattle against anthrax. He asks one of his professors to come to the ranch and inject the Barkley prize bull with the serum before it is used on the entire herd of cattle belonging to a poor Mexican friend of Nick's. When the vaccine works, the cattle are saved and possible bloodshed is avoided. Eugene disappeared completely by the second season — presumably he had returned to college and remained there. In any case, the producers must have decided that the show already had enough major characters.

The Big Valley never achieved high Nielsen figures and was canceled after the fourth season. Probably the low ratings were the result of poor scheduling (Mondays at 10 P.M. opposite the popular *Carol Burnett Show*). However, according to biographer Ella Smith,

> ... syndication kept *The Big Valley* on the home screen with a popularity that astounds even its producers who "knew it was a good show." At the end of 1972, *Variety* reported that

the series was being recycled for another syndication run because "it is consistently at the top of the list of *all* the off-network hour shows in syndication."[72]

The series was responsible for bringing to the home screen the first (and only) Western to be built around a heroic female lead. Furthermore, the lush theme music by George Duning was superior to that of any other television Western. There were several other single parent television Westerns of note. *The Virginian* which fit this basic mold will be covered in a separate chapter, but *Empire, The High Chaparral* (although it does not strictly fit this category) and *Lancer* should be included here.

Superficially, at least, *Empire* was the story of a single parent family managing vast property holdings, but set in the contemporary (1962-63) rather than the historical West. The Garret family, which owned this vast "empire," consisted of Lucia (played by Anne Seymour), widow of Frank Garret, who had carved his ranch four years earlier out of the New Mexico wilderness, her son, Tal (played by Ryan O'Neal), and daughter, Constance (played by Terry Moore). The Garret holdings covered half a million acres and included cattle, sheep, horses, crops, lumber, mining and oil and was worth millions of dollars. Here, however, the similarity to *Bonanza* and *The Big Valley* ends for the focus of the series was neither Lucia, titular head of the family, nor her children, but rather the foreman, Jim Redigo (played to macho perfection by six foot, 200 pound Richard Egan). Redigo was an iron-willed loner who refused to compromise with his bosses, hired hands, or any outsiders who happened to cross his path. In fact, the Redigo character was so much more popular than the others that their roles practically disappeared midway through the season. Charles Bronson, who had played a ranch hand named Paul Moreno in the pilot episode, was brought back as a regular and the series became even more male-centered. Anne Seymour and Terry Moore, although initially given costar billing, like Barbara Stanwyck and Linda Evans on *The Big Valley*, never had more than incidental roles in the stories.

The series was interesting, featuring episodes about drilling for oil ("Ballard Number One"), logging ("The Tall Shadow"), fighting oil fires ("The Fire Dancer") and assorted big business take-overs ("Ride to a Fall"). Nevertheless, it never really caught on with viewers and was completely revamped for the second season. Shortened to half an hour and retitled *Redigo*, Egan's character now owned his own spread and the rest of the *Empire* cast was eliminated. Perhaps this was only fitting since, until the addition of Bronson, Egan had been a sort of one-man, modern-day *Bonanza*. Not as old as Ben Cartwright, as romantic as Adam or as big as Hoss, he had to combine characteristics of all of them as he carried almost the whole show on his own shoulders. Even with these changes, however, the series was canceled after just one more season.

The High Chaparral took its name from the ranch which was owned and operated by the Cannon family in Arizona during the 1870s. The stories depicted the efforts of the family, their ranch hands and their friends to establish a flourishing cattle empire in the Indian-infested territory. Chaparral is the generic label for all moisture-hungry vegetation that grows in the foothills bordering Southwestern desert valleys. Chaps, a word derived from chaparral, are the open-backed leather overalls worn by wranglers as protection against cacti, horse bites and thickets of stiff or thorny shrubs.[73] In the opening episode both the ranch and the series are named. As explained in the script:

> We see the two horseback images of AnnaLee and Big John against the big sky and great spread of open country as they watch the magnificent sight of a cattle herd on the move, with the cowhands shifting and turning and riding in the dust, edging the massed ranks of cows along through the flowing grass.

(Close-up)—Big John and AnnaLee
> They appraise each other—husband and wife; then Big John turns to look at his herd...
> She looks out over the wide vista of country.
> ANNALEE: Isn't it beautiful, John? It should have a name.
> BIG JOHN: You name it.
> ANNALEE (eyes bright; looking at the country): What is that bush called—that green one?
> BIG JOHN: Chaparral.
> ANNALEE: That's it—Chaparral. (She looks happily from her husband to the wide country)
> I christen thee—The High Chaparral, the greatest cattle ranch in the whole
> territory—the whole world.[74]

Actually, according to story editor Tim Kelly, another name had been selected for the series: *Saguaro*. As he explained in an article for *Arizona Highways*,

> The Giant Saguaro cactus often reaches a height of fifty feet and can weight up to seven tons. Pima and Papago Indians gather its fruit for food and, with amazing skill, fashion water vessels from its thick stem. Its evening glory, a creamy waxy, magnolia-like bloom, is the official state flower.
>
> About seventeen miles east of Tucson, along the Old Spanish Trail, lies the Saguaro National Monument, a sprawling cacti forest dedicated to the preservation of this fluted "tree cactus." Here, Spaniards, Americans, Mexicans and Apaches fought a century or more ago. "Saguaro" for a title was a natural.
>
> [However], not many people unacquainted with its pronunciation could sound "Saguaro" correctly. The word appeared to be an oddity, in terms of the general public.
> "Chaparral" was easier all the way around.[75]

Created by the successful producer of *Bonanza*, David Dortort, *The High Chaparral*, purported to be one of the more authentic television Westerns. Most of the filming for the Southwestern saga was completed in the adobe pueblo of Old Tucson, located amidst 30,000 acres of natural desert growth and mesa land. (The handsome rancho of Don Sebastian was, in actuality, the Mission of San Xavier del Bac, "the White Dove of the Desert," which was built in the 1780s nine miles southwest of present-day Tucson.) A century earlier, this was the land where Apache leaders like Diablo, Geronimo, Naqiuno, and Cochise fought Spaniards, Mexicans, American settlers and troops of the First U.S. Cavalry. It is an area rich with legends of sourdough miners and Indian scalp hunters. Tim Kelly later explained:

> The years following the Civil War were a time when Chiricahuas lived in competition with the coyote, when blueclad cavalry troopers and infantrymen in brown canvas sweat for their $13 a month, when irregular soldiers of a distracted Mexico, lancers, rode back and forth from the Santa Cruz River valley to Sonora hunting Indian scalps, when the Santa Rita Mountains sheltered a burly community of sourdough miners, when Tucson was pictured as "a paradise for devils" and the hamlet of Tubac printed its own money and performed marriages that later proved null and void.[76]

In order to make the series as close to history as possible, Dortort methodically poured through archives at the Huntington and UCLA libraries in California, as well as dusty old diaries, letters and military reports on file at the Department of the Interior in Washington. Dortort became convinced that the story of the Apache nation's struggle for survival would make exciting television fare and *The High Chaparral* was constructed around the story of 3000 Apaches who, against overwhelming odds, attempted to protect their homeland against land grabbers, banditos, and corrupt government bureaucrats. Still, Dortort stressed in an interview,

> *Chaparral*'s greatest asset is the thrilling scenery of Arizona itself. We're out to capture this. We'll be filming in color with expert crews and the newest and best camera equipment

available. Each week the viewer will see a realistic drama set in the natural beauty of Arizona.[77]

Big John Cannon, head of the fictional Cannon family, was based on General George F. Crook, a grizzled cattle-rancher "imbued with the dream that Apaches, American settlers and Mexicans could live in atmosphere of harmony, rather than extermination."[78] Dortort also decided to portray the positive aspects of both Apache and Mexican society—in contrast to the view usually presented in big-screen Westerns. The Mexicans had, after all, predated other white settlers in the American Southwest by some 400 years bringing with them a highly developed civilization. (Dortort also broke with custom insisting that, insofar as possible, Indians should be cast as Indians.) Dortort elaborated on this theme:

> I think it's important that the setting of Southern Arizona be considered from a number of viewpoints. Take the Apache—certainly he could and did fight like a demon, but he had reason to. He was fighting for *his* homeland. Ruthless, granted. But we mustn't forget his courage and honor, nor the many outrages perpetrated against him that contributed to his anger.
>
> Too often the Mexican in a western is presented as a sullen character useful as background color, or as a foil to manufacture some questionable humor. What about his emotions, his commitment to the land, his dreams?
>
> The newcomer, the rancher, the miner, the cattleman—each had his own way of seeing things. Often it was a mixture of the good and the bad. But it was a new land and a new challenge. And it had its own share of heroism, often in impressive degree.
>
> "The High Chaparral" is not one story—it's many, a chronicle that belongs to all the people who loved the land and fought for a place on it.[79]

In this setting Dortort developed the saga of the patriarchal Cannon family—a family suffering from a common malady of the 1960s, the generation gap. It presented a forceful father (Big John) and his shy, sensitive son (Billy Blue), who had difficulty communicating. As described by Dortort in the pilot script, Big John Cannon is:

> About fifty, tall, powerfully built man whose fierce, flashing eyes have seen a half-century of struggling for survival in the American West. His hair is grey now, but his body is still strong, the shape of his own inner strength which is indomitable. He is a man who can not surrender. A man who knows what he is, who he is, and where he is going. He is a grizzled patriot who will find his destiny in the Arizona territory. A kind of a [man] you can pit against mountains and desert, thirst, hunger and savagery, unbearable hardships and fierce storms, or who will enter a room and be the most awesome presence in it. He is 4 inches over 6 feet tall, big shouldered with strong arms and great, powerful hands. He will cast a long shadow on the ground.[80]

Billy Blue Cannon is:

> ... twenty, a good looking young man who has a strange combination of ruggedness and refinement that is the combination of his father and mother. He is a tentative seeking youth who questions everything and as more often as not left to find his own answers by his father. He is almost 6 feet tall, slender and quick. A first rate horseman and a quick tempered, fighting man who has a lot to learn, but often makes up for his lack of experience with his quick reflexes and ingrained spirit. He is a vivid young man, in whom sensitivity and life's force commingle explosively.

Decision-making on *The High Chaparral* is far from democratic. Indeed, Big John subscribes to the old axiom that "a man's home is his castle," stating on more than one occasion, "The Chaparral is my kingdom and I'll make all the decisions for the best of everyone." Located in a primitive area, the land is divided between a powerful Mexican family—the Montoyas—and the Cannons. What they do not control is ruled by the Apaches, with whom Big John has signed an uneasy peace treaty. (Cannon signs treaties and enforces his own laws).

High Chaparral **was not a conventional single parent family Western, but Big John Cannon (played by Leif Erickson, center rear) ran his family with an iron hand. Others shown, front, Mark Slade as Billy Blue Cannon, Cameron Mitchell (left) as Buck, Linda Cristal as Victoria, and Henry Darrow as Manolito Montoya.**

In the first episode of the series, Billy Blue's mother, AnnaLee, is killed by an Apache arrow, thus presenting the Cannons—ever so briefly—as a single parent family. Before the episode is over, however, Big John has arranged a marriage with Don Sebastian Montoya's daughter, Victoria, thereby uniting the two kingdoms like some feudal European alliance. Both Cannon and Montoya run their kingdoms like feudal monarchs, commanding absolute obedience from family as well as ranch hands. Victoria is described by Dortort as follows:

> ... twenty-five, a serene and beautiful Spanish woman in whose blood flows an ancestry that is as illustrious as a Queen's. She is proud, silent, yet compassionate and understanding,

both gentle and fierce tempered, so that when she speaks she does so with an aristocratic authority that cannot be ignored. She becomes the wife of John Cannon by the political alliance between her father and the Cannons, in the fashion of the ancient courts of Europe, which decree that alliances and pledges of mutual defense [be secured] by bond of marriage to assure their lasting compact. But, she was beyond the age young girls of aristocratic families usually marry and the appearance of John Cannon into her life was not an altogether unpleasant one, so that she accepted the decree of marriage issued by her father without reluctance and brought to John Cannon's home all of the grace, beauty and dignity that was her station.

Her father Don Sebastian Montoya is said to be

> fifty-five—ruler of an empire in Mexico. A proud defiant bold man, full of life who controls an area which he calls his ranchero, greater than some kingdoms of Europe. He is a Feudal Lord, Commander of a personal army that has successfully beaten off both Apache and government intrusion. A politician and a sly old fox who recognizes in John Cannon a kindred soul.

In addition to Big John, Billy Blue and Victoria, the Cannon family consisted of Big John's younger brother Buck and Victoria's brother Manolito. Buck is described as

> seven years younger than his brother John. He is a carousing, hard voiced, big fisted roar of a man who leads himself a roaring life and loves it. He can out drink, out work and out fight any man in the world except his older brother. He does not have his brother's dedication or determination, but contains within his compact powerful frame, every ounce of fighting spirit that nature can give a man.

Victoria's older brother is described as "a Spanish counterpart to Buck":

> thirty, the brother of Victoria and the son of Don Sebastian Montoya. The black sheep of the great Montoya family. A fighting man who has no fear and a horseman who looks like he was born in the saddle ... and even dissipated, drunk, [and] wild, maintains his dignity of person that is his breeding. He was bred from a long line of noble families and shows it. He is 5 feet 10 inches slender with bright, vivid eyes and dark hair.

Ranch hands included Sam Butler, the foreman, and Reno, Pedro and Joe. The last season Wind, a half-breed youth who helped Big John avoid a major disaster during a roundup, was added to the household. Also during that season Victoria's father passed away, and that character was dropped from the series while his brother Don Domingo de Montoya was added.

The cast of *The High Chaparral* was consistently outstanding. Veteran actor Leif Erickson was perfect as Big John. He was born William Wycliffe Anderson on October 27, 1911, in Alameda, California. Erickson's father was a sea captain on the Alaskan Packer Corp.'s square-rigger bark that sailed out of San Francisco. (Later in life, he invented a push-button turn-on for furnaces and became an executive of Magic-Way Furnace Co. in Los Angeles.) Young Bill Anderson became a singer in spite of his father and while singing in a posh speak-easy on the Sunset Strip in 1931 he was "discovered" by bandleader Ted Fio Rito. It was Fio Rito who changed his name to Leif Erickson. A screen test led Erickson to his first role in *A Midsummer Night's Dream*, with young Mickey Rooney and Olivia de Havilland. In 1935 he signed a contract with Paramount where he played supporting roles in more than one hundred films. He married Frances Farmer, one of the brightest (and later tragic) stars of the era. He even tried method acting with the Group Theatre in New York in an attempt to refine the rough edges.

As Dwight Whitney explains it, Erickson "fell into the limbo reserved for nearstars ... who were too good-looking to be believable. To make matters worse, someone was always rediscovering him; his career would take a spurt, then peter out again."[81] He even appeared on Broadway in 1953 with Deborah Kerr in *Tea and Sympathy*. In the fifties and sixties Erickson was seen on television mostly in Westerns, including the *Zane Grey Theater, The Virginian, Bonanza, Rawhide* and in macabre tales on *The Alfred Hitchcock Hour*. David Dortort first noticed him in a 1961 *Bonanza* episode entitled "The Rescue" in which he played a stern Jeremiah-like hermit who was mistaken for God by a little boy who sought help for his sick father. Erickson's fame seemed assured when Dortort cast him as the blue-eyed, stone-visaged father and Indian fighter on *The High Chaparral*.

Argentine-born Linda Cristal played Victoria. Cameron Mitchell did some of his finest acting as Buck. Young Mark Slade was Billy Blue. Henry Darrow became extremely popular as Manolito. Frank Silvera finished a distinguished acting career as Don Sebastian Montoya and Gilbert Roland added another fine Latin portrayal to his list of credits as Don Domingo. Joan Caulfield played Big John's first wife AnnaLee, in the opening episode.

Family relationships were often confused on the show, but there was always present an underlying bond of love. In an episode entitled "No Bugles, No Drums," a little girl asks Buck, "Is John Cannon your daddy?" Buck good-naturedly responds, "Sometimes he's my daddy, but most of the time he's my big brother." In common with the other domestic Westerns considered in this chapter, *The High Chaparral* also stressed moral values. In an episode entitled "Spokes," Buck protects a wounded trapper from the wrath of a town and the town boss.

> BOGGS: China Pierce is a vindictive man, a violent man, a mad man and his son was killed...
> BUCK: His son was cheatin'! He pulled a gun when he was called on it. And he was fair killed.
> BOGGS: I don't care about that. I care about this town, Cannon. One person is not as important as many persons. You must move him, Cannon.
> BUCK: Well, Boggs, I talked to quite a bit of your town and my answer to them is the same as ta you. Jones here, or whoever he is, stays because he's hurt and deservin'. And on top of it all, stinkin' and low-life as you might find him, it's him and his type, engine ta honesty, who made this land so such as you could build your carbuncle to nowhere.
> BOGGS: I warn you there will be measures taken.
> BUCK: Stays, Boggs, stays.
> BOGGS: But you will die, Cannon! Jones will die if Pierce takes a notion, which he most probably will...
> BUCK: He lives or he dies, but he just plain ain't movin; not for somethin' he didn't do. Pierce will have to kill me ta do it and this year I take some killin'. Tell your town that a man's gonna get a man's needs and the devil take the hindmost ...

The man, of course, stays and survives, as does Buck.

In "The Last Hundred Miles," a general, skeptical of the intentions of the Apache says to John Cannon, after discovering that it is the duplicity of unscrupulous white men that have almost cost them their lives: "The good Lord must have known what he was doing to direct a man like you to this desolate land." Viewers seem to have agreed, at least for four seasons. The critics were mixed in their reviews of the series. *Variety* (September 6, 1967) wrote of the two-hour pilot:

> A whole season of primetime action drama was packed into this simple two-hour grind. It had every cliche of violence since Hoot Gibson, every tear and smile of meller-drama since "East Lynne," and virtually every two-bit, blue-sky, apple-pie, hair-shirt notion of morality and manhood in the redneck manual.
>
> It will be a hit. The Nielsen sample has imbibed at this trough since Tex Ritter soup-bones were doing three-a-day on the New York independents....
>
> Erickson is a sufficiently strong lead in producer David Dortort's big-daddy "Bonanza" tradition.

> Production values are solid, if not yet as slick as "Bonanza." "High Chaparral" should
> out run the Chevy truck models blurbed in the opening hour.

However, *Variety* was wrong. *Chaparral* was never a big hit. In 1971 the Cannons and *The High Chaparral* left the airwaves, never having made the Nielsen top 25.

Lancer was a single-parent Western that lasted only two seasons (1968-1970). Bearing a strong resemblance to *Bonanza*, it related the story of a rancher, Murdock Lancer and his two sons struggling to protect their 100,000 acre cattle and timber ranch. The show was set in *Big Valley* country, the San Joaquin Valley in the 1870s. Murdock (played by veteran actor Andrew Duggan) had not seen his sons since they were boys. One, Scott (Wayne Maunder), had been born of an Irish lass, while on a visit back East to escape the rigors of a range war. He had been raised and educated in Boston and was somewhat of a "dandy." The other son Johnny (James Stacy), was born of a Mexican señorita and had spent most of the early years of his life as a drifter wandering through the border towns of the Southwest.

Plagued by land pirates, Murdock had located his sons through the Pinkerton Detective Agency and offered to give them each one-third of his sprawling ranch if they would help him manage it. Completing the "family" was Teresa O'Brien (Elizabeth Baur), Murdock's ward and the daughter of his late foreman. During the second season, *Rawhide* veteran Paul Brinegar was added to the cast to play the new foreman, Jelly Hoskins. The two half-brothers were strangers to each other, as well as to their father, and this made for some interesting situations. Scott, who surprisingly made the transition to Western life more easily than Johnny, was able to adjust to the responsibilities of being tied down to one place. In an early episode, the following exchange took place between Johnny and his father, after Johnny had run off to catch some wild horses, instead of finishing the task of stringing fence.

> JOHNNY: Look there's only a small section left. If it makes ya happy, I'll go finish it right
> now.
> MURDOCK: Now is too late. About fifty head of cattle strayed through that little hole in that
> section you didn't finish. What's left of them is now at the bottom of the south
> gully. That's what your time off cost.
> JOHNNY: How was I ta know that was gonna happen?
> MURDOCK: Maybe ya never will know. Maybe it takes twenty years of just living with this
> kind of land. Maybe it's not for you, Johnny.
> JOHNNY: Look, all right, I... I'm sorry about the cattle ya lost.
> MURDOCK: *We* lost Johnny—not *you*—*we*. And all of the responsibilities that go with it.
> JOHNNY: I'd do fine—if only ya wouldn't push so hard.
> MURDOCK: I wish I had a chance to break you in easily, but I don't. You've got to make up
> your mind who you are and where you belong ... and if it's not going to be here
> I want to know it now.

Ultimately, Johnny did decide to settle down on the Lancer spread, but not before he put his father through some rather harrowing experiences. Such situations were, of course, common on single parent family Westerns.

These family oriented Westerns were generally popular and among the longest running Westerns which populated the video range. Of course, as historian Rita Parks has pointed out, dramatic programs which focused on family life have always been "a staple in mass media story telling."[82] Even the seemingly realistic touch of heading these families with a single parent, was common in other genre. Situation comedies of this era from *Bachelor Father* to *My Three Sons*, for example, successfully utilized this format. Nevertheless, programs like *The Rifleman, Bonanza* and *The Big Valley* can rightfully be considered landmarks in the evolution of the television Western.

IX. Meanwhile Back on the Reservation
"GOOD" AND "BAD" INDIANS IN TELEVISION WESTERNS

One of the most dramatic chapters in the story of the westward movement involves the confrontation between the white man and the Indian. Long a popular subject in novels and films, stories depicting this conflict were frequently utilized in television Westerns. Embodied in these programs can be found all the same problems of stereotyping and oversimplification found in both print and celluloid versions.

Usually the Native American is placed in one of two general categories, both equally one dimensional: that of savage sinner or redskinned redeemer. The Indian as savage sinner is presented as strange, exotic, dangerous and deceptive. In this role he may appear as a bloodthirsty enemy of progress and a vengeful retaliator, whose primary occupation is plunder, whose principle recreation is rape and whose greatest pleasure is the torture and seduction of the innocent, particularly women and children. This is the image of the "bad" Indian, so often the primary villain of juvenile and B Westerns.

At the other end of the spectrum comes his alter ego, the "good" Indian, the redskinned redeemer. In this role he may appear as a good and generous helper (descended from the corn-bearing redmen in American grade school Thanksgiving pageants), serving his white master in the preordained task of Westward expansion—a noble savage giving up his way of life to make a better world for all. Here the Native American is often depicted as stoic and unemotional. In this guise he may also be presented as the first conservationist. All are positive images, to be sure, but equally one-dimensional.

There is yet a third role that Native Americans have occasionally been given in the saga of Western expansion, that of tragic but inevitable victim. This time the Indian appears as a mysterious subspecies whose way of life is doomed to extinction. He may become, in this scenario, an educated half-breed, unable to live in either white or Indian worlds, or an oil-rich illiterate. Sometimes the Indian as victim is seen merely as lazy, fat, shiftless and drunk. Here again the Indian is a one-dimensional figure.

If there is one constant in the screen portrayal of the Indian, according to Dr. Rennard Strickland, dean of the Southern Illinois University Law School, "it is that rarely was the Indian an Indian." In a lecture he presented at the Smithsonian Institution in October 1988 entitled "A Funny Thing Happened to Tonto," Dr. Strickland concluded:

> It is an endless parade in which we have "good" Indians and "bad" Indians.... In the thousands of individual films and millions of frames in those films, we have few if any, real Indians—Indians who are more than cardboard cutouts, Indians who have individuality or humanity. Almost five hundred Indian tribes, bands and villages are reduced to one homogenized Hollywood Indian.

Other film historians agree with this assessment. Wayne Michael Sarf writes in *God Bless You, Buffalo Bill: A Layman's Guide to History and the Western Film*:

> Badly handled in Westerns generally, physical detail becomes especially suspect where real or alleged Indians are concerned. The usual attitude taken consciously or not, has it that all Indians are pretty much the same despite whatever vast tribal differences may actually exist. The Hollywood concept of the well-dressed redskin, like the popular stereotype, resembles in the case of the man a painted warrior from one of the nomadic, buffalo-hunting Plains tribes such as the Sioux, Cheyenne, or Crow—beaded, buckskinned and befeathered ... Less amusing than the outfits of movie Indians are the misuse and desecration of Indian customs, traditions, and ceremonies.[1]

Although Strickland and Sarf are primarily concerned with film Westerns, other writers have been equally as critical of television. J. Fred MacDonald claims in *Who Shot the Sheriff?*

> ... Native Americans were generally portrayed in one of three ways: noble anachronisms in the way of white expansion; hostile savages harassing the innocent and disrupting the march of history; or less frequently, assimilated and often fighting in the name of white social dominance.[2]

Ralph Brauer in *The Horse, The Gun and the Piece of Property: Changing Images of the TV Western* takes the view that the white stereotyping of Indians stemmed from a fear of them rooted in "a deep belief that Indians are so different that we cannot possibly understand them." Brauer also saw Indians stereotyped in two categories:

> The "good" Indian acts like a white man, with "rationality" and "decorum" while the "bad" Indian acts in some way that seems irrational or childish.... Behind this paranoia is the belief that Indians—at least TV Indians—are primitive people whose lack of sophistication and so-called civilized virtues makes them savages who are apt to commit the most heinous crimes or participate in the most irrational kind of actions.
> ... The good Indian may dress like an Indian, pound on a drum now and then, sing a few songs and smoke a peace pipe, but he judges his whites as individuals.... The standards the good Indian uses to judge his whites are white standards ... and the Indians who are good Indians are not unlike good whites in their dress (which may be buckskins, beads and a warbonnet, but which is worn with decorum) and social status (notice how most good Indians wear warbonnets and ride fancy horses). All of this ignores Indian cultures, which have different standards of measuring good and bad individuals than ours....
> ... the good Indian uses the same standards as the show and its stars which enables the stars to be fast friends with the good Indians. The good Indian ultimately reinforces our own image of ourselves and our values enabling us to have a clear conscience about them.[3]

Michael Hilger, in his excellent study *The American Indian in Film*, has observed that Indians are usually portrayed in film as "either too good or too bad" and "as such they are often the most extreme fictions in the western, a genre which seldom comes very close to reality."[4] Elaborating on this thesis, Hilger offers this comprehensive explanation:

> ... Associated with the image of the bloodthirsty savage is the theme of the Indian as enemy of the white's progress in westward expansion and as adversary used by the western hero to prove himself....

Associated with the image of the noble savage in western films in the theme that the Indians are doomed because, as primitive children of nature, they ultimately have no power to resist manifest destiny and thus will be inevitable victims of the superior white race. Indians portrayed as children of nature frequently become objects of paternalism who need to be helped by heroes since they can be so easily manipulated by villains, be they outlaws or Indian agents....

Generally, film-stereotyped Indian men and women have childlike, primitive emotions: if treated well they are capable of powerful love, loyalty and gratitude; if treated badly, of tenacious, fierce vengeance. Their goodness or badness is always measured by their reaction to whites, never by their intrinsic nature as American Indians .... For example, the cinematic Indian woman, usually a dark, beautiful young maiden ... has a special ability to recognize the superiority of the white man and will often fall in love with one rather than an Indian....

The male Indian character is also good if he is a friend and loyal companion to the white man.... In these friendships the white man is dominant, but the two learn from each other and do share a deep affection. Another basis for friendship is education; Indian men educated in white colleges often show their loyalty and affection for whites in addition to using their knowledge to help their tribes. Such young Indian men are also the most appealing to white woman....

Older Indian men usually have friendships with whites as surrogate fathers.... Such fathers are often kind and wise old chiefs, a character type that is probably the strongest representation of the good Indian male.

The Indian man is portrayed as bad if he is an enemy of whites or a threat to white women. Half-breeds or leaders of hostile bands are the Indians most often presented as devious, unscrupulous, and fierce enemies who will use ambush and other guerrilla tactics. Such Indian men are also threats to society because their rebelliousness and vengeance sometimes leads them to rape and kidnap white women.[5]

This chapter will demonstrate how completely Hilger's thesis of the "good" and "bad" Indian stereotype in films applies to most Native American characters in television Westerns. From Tonto in *The Lone Ranger* to John Taylor in *Paradise*, television's treatment of the Indian has differed little from that of motion pictures. Indian stereotyping was given the greatest public attention during the 1973 Academy Awards ceremony when Marlon Brando, rather than accept the Oscar he had won for *The Godfather*, sent in his place one "Sasheen Littlefeather," otherwise known as Maria Cruze. She appeared in colorful tribal regalia to read Brando's written statement, which explained that he had refused his award in protest against "the treatment of Indians by the film industry, on television and in movie reruns."[6] The audience response, however, was not enthusiastic.

Native Americans had been trying to arouse public awareness of this issue since 1960. In the spring of that year, a meeting of delegates from 11 Indian tribes was held at Fort Gibson, Oklahoma. The delegates appointed a committee to draw up and submit a petition to President Eisenhower protesting portrayals of Indians on the television screen as ruthless savages intent only on plunder and atrocity. They felt that these false portrayals might give viewers, particularly impressionable children, a distorted and harmful picture of frontier life and the historical role of Indians.

One Indian spokesman, Harry J. W. Belvin, principal chief of the Choctaw Nation, explained that there was "no excuse for television producers to ignore the harm" that could be done to American children "by repetitious distortion of historical facts pertaining to the way of life of any race or creed, including the American Indian."[7] Most of the Indian leaders involved in the protest made it clear that they did not want television to rewrite frontier history, but merely to show what really happened—including the fact that the Indians were fighting to defend their homes against what they considered to be invasions by the white man. The tribal action was endorsed by the Public Education Committee of the Association on American Indian Affairs (A.A.I.A.). The committee hoped to change the state of television Westerns through public information programs. Chairing the committee was the assistant to the general manager of the *New York Times* (and later its publisher), Arthur Ochs Sulzberger. The unit also offered its services on a consulting basis to television and motion-picture producers. The executive director of the A.A.I.A., LaVerne Madigen, stated in a *Times* interview (June 26, 1960) that

> Accurate portrayal of frontier history and Indian wars does not require that the white man be presented as a ruthless invader; he was that—and yet he was more, because he built a democracy when he could have built a tyranny. Accurate portrayal, however, does require that the American Indian be presented as a brave defender of his homeland and a way of life as good and free and reverent as the life dreamed of by the immigrants who swarmed to these shores.[8]

Not all television Westerns incurred the ire of Native Americans. Several were singled out by the association for their "outstanding portrayals of frontier life" including *The Lone Ranger, Law of the Plainsman, Gunsmoke* and *Have Gun, Will Travel*. On the other hand, the A.A.I.A. found *Wagon Train, Riverboat* and *The Overland Trail* to be particularly objectionable. This chapter will examine the images of Indians presented in a number of the more popular and significant television Westerns from the fifties to the eighties. Several made-for-television films like *I Will Fight No More Forever, The Legend of Walks Far Woman, The Mystic Warrior* and *Son of the Morning Star* will also be explored.

Any consideration of Native Americans in television Westerns must begin with Tonto, the Lone Ranger's faithful Indian companion. He was not only the first continuing Indian character to appear on television (in 1949), but the first on radio as well (dating to 1933). One would assume that Tonto, who was actually played by a real Indian (Jay Silverheels) and who saved the life of "the masked rider of the plains" on numerous occasions, would be universally acclaimed as presenting a positive image of the Native American. Not so. The A.A.I.A. did applaud Tonto's "co-hero status" in the series back in 1960, but the character has more recently come under considerable criticism and Silverheels himself even expressed reservations about the role in later years. (Dr. Strickland describes Tonto as "smarter than Step 'n' Fetchit, and almost as clever as Charlie Chan without being inclined to spout ancient wisdom....") The popular mythology of *The Lone Ranger* radio program has always said simply that Tonto was created to give the Ranger someone to talk to. According to writer Dave Holland, who has done the most exhaustive research to date on the subject, Tonto was the creation of series writer Fran Striker:

> ... the early Lone Ranger was off-stage quite a bit, if not too much. The powers-that-be wanted to cut to the title character more than they were. Now, when that happened, so the audience could share in the anticipation of the action, the Ranger needed to talk about what he was going to do. That was why he needed someone to talk to.[9]

It is in the twelfth script (broadcast February 25, 1933) that Tonto makes his first appearance: Two miners set off a blast and then hear a faint voice calling for help. Buried in the landslide is the half-breed Tonto! One of the miners wants to kill him, but the Lone Ranger appears suddenly and forces them at gunpoint to spare his life. Thus initially, Tonto was not young and tall (as in the Silverheels image), but short and old—and only half Indian. Not until 1936 is the term half-breed dropped from the scripts (without any explanation—as if any could be devised). For the first 16 years (i.e., the radio years) Tonto is a man without a past. He is merely a man alone—isolated from his people for (again) unexplained reasons.

Eventually the "official" ambush story evolves from a comment made in a 1938 script ("some say ... Tonto saved his life one time when he and all his partners were shot up by outlaws ... and the Lone Ranger was the only one that survived") to a full-blown episode aired on the fifteenth anniversary broadcast in 1948. This is the version that was presented in the premier television broadcast, "Enter the Lone Ranger," on September 15, 1949: Six Texas Rangers are led into an ambush by a treacherous guide, who is secretly working for the notorious Butch Cavendish gang. Only one of the Rangers survives (John Reid). Tonto, an Indian, finds the seriously wounded Ranger and nurses him back to health. It seems that when the two were boys, young John saved Tonto from a band of renegade Indians and the two had become blood brothers. (This story appears in much greater detail in *The Life of Tonto*, a Merita Bread giveaway printed in 1940. Probably written by Fran Striker, the 11 chapter account provides Tonto with a detailed past.)

What kind of Indian was Tonto? Speculation would lead one to the conclusion that he would be a Comanche or an Apache, the nation's most prevalent in west Texas, the probable site of the ambush. "Officially," however, Tonto was a Potawatamie. Why? Because, according to Holland, many of the Indians who lived in Michigan were Potawatomies; "ergo, that was the first Indian name that came to the Detroit creators when pressed." (Some Potawatomies did migrate to Western Iowa and there were a few Potawatomies on reservations in Oklahoma—but how a Potawatomie named Tonto made it all the way out to western Texas was never explained on radio or television.)

Television's Tonto, Jay Silverheels, was born on September 26, 1913, on the Six Nations Indian Reservation in Ontario, Canada. His legal name was Harold J. Smith, but an elder of the Mohawk tribe gave him the name Silverheels, which became the name by which he was publicly recognized. (He did not legally change his name until 1971.) Before his fame as Tonto, Silverheels made a reputation for himself as an athlete, arriving in Hollywood in the early thirties as a professional lacrosse and hockey player. He became acquainted with sports enthusiast and comedian Joe E. Brown at whose suggestion he became an extra in films. His first notable role was Coatl in *Captain from Castille* (1947). It was *Key Largo* (1948), which starred such Hollywood greats as Humphrey Bogart, Edward G. Robinson and Lionel Barrymore, that gave him his most important early role as one of the Osceola brothers.

In 1949 Silverheels began playing the role for which he will forever be identified, a role that he felt brought him both "opportunity" and "bondage." First opposite Clayton Moore, then John Hart (for 52 episodes) and finally Moore again, Silverheels appeared as Tonto in all 221 television episodes and two theatrical films, *The Lone Ranger* (1956) and *The Lone Ranger and the Lost City of Gold* (1958). The series was originally broadcast by ABC, but was later rerun on both CBS and NBC and is still widely syndicated. James C. Jewell writes that

> Although the character of Tonto was beloved by the viewing public, Silverheels once confessed that he never felt truly comfortable playing the Lone Ranger's sidekick. Silverheels felt that it was contradictory that Indians in films were habitually outsmarted by being trapped and tricked from behind even though the Indians' sense of hearing has long been known to be extremely acute.... The films, according to Silverheels, consistently portrayed Tonto as subservient to the Lone Ranger, who would rescue his Indian cohort from being outsmarted by mutual foes. Silverheels always viewed his work as Tonto realistically, however, recognizing that he had to play the role as written and directed to gain recognition as an actor. This, in turn, would allow him to bring about favorable changes in Indian portrayals.[10]

Silverheels firmly believed that Indian roles should be played by real Indians so that the false stereotypes that had been created by filmmakers could be corrected. To that end, he established the Indian Actors Workshop in 1967 which was designed to provide Native Americans with the training necessary for becoming successful actors, writers and dancers. Championing Indian rights, especially in drama and the other performing arts, became Silverheel's greatest cause. He believed that producers and directors had a limited knowledge of Indian life and were primarily motivated by what could be sold to the public. He also castigated films and television for failing to reflect the fact that the contemporary American Indian may be found productively employed in every endeavor including such professions as medicine, the law, dentistry, psychiatry, and business executive.

Silverheels denounced producers and directors for failing to treat professional Indian actors the same as others. Aside from criticizing the usual practice of not casting Indians to portray Indians, he also claimed there was a widespread practice of refusing to utilize makeup to the same degree it was used to broaden the employment versatility of white actors. In an interview with Will Tusher of *The Hollywood Reporter* (March 23, 1972), Silverheels complained:

> Indians trying to make a living in this industry are not considered. If they want an Indian 60 years old he's got to look 60 years old. There's no such thing as makeup with Indians. They write stories in which every Indian cast almost has to be 16. [But] they'd take a non-Indian and make him look 100 years old like they did with Dustin Hoffman in "Little Big Man."

The scornful Silverheels also had little use for the Hollywood superstar who, after becoming a big name, suddenly discovers that he is part Indian and goes on a publicity and talk-show binge exploiting the claim:

> A full-blood Indian wonders why he should be represented by someone who claims to be $1/16$ or $1/32$ Indian. But they're not known as an Indian until they get up there and then divulge the secret that they are part Indian. There's no respect for that kind of thing.

However, Silverheels could see little hope that aggrieved Indian performers could change this distorted television and film image of Indians through the kind of militancy that spurred dramatic gains for blacks. In the same *Hollywood Reporter* interview he explained:

> I don't think we're really going to attain anything by militancy. You take the blacks — they are an economic entity. Indians are so few in number that they are not an economic entity. If they were to boycott a picture they wouldn't even dent the box office. But the blacks can use that as a lever to make themselves heard. And more power to them.

Silverheels saw that the hope of the Indian for some measure of job parity and image improvement lay in making common cause with other minority groups. To this end he supported and became a member of the Screen Actors Guild ethnic minority committee:

> What we're going to do with the minority group committee is band together minorities from all ethnic groups and support each other to see that each group is properly treated, and that the images in the media are made more acceptable. In that way, even though the Indians are small in number, they would have the backing of all the ethnic groups, whether Mexican-American, Oriental, or black . . .
> . . . We are trying to appeal to the producer and the director in an intelligent way so that they will realize that the things we want are just.

In recognition of this advocacy, as well as his achievements in acting, Silverheels became, on July 20, 1979, the first North American Indian to be honored with a star on the Hollywood Walk of Fame.

Jay Silverheels (right), the Lone Ranger's faithful companion, Tonto, was television's first Native American star. (Clayton Moore is at left.)

Keith Larson in full regalia as Cheyenne Chief Brave Eagle.

As far as the character of Tonto is concerned, while it must be admitted that he did often have to be rescued by his masked companion, he was also frequently called upon to save the Lone Ranger from some life-threatening situation. They rode together, fought together and were equally committed to promoting peace and brotherhood. And stilted dialogue notwithstanding, Tonto always displayed those qualities of character—honesty, integrity, courage, honor, pride, loyalty and kindness—that made him a positive role model for any race. His devotion to justice, his respect for law and order and his reverence for human life were in no way inferior to those of his white cohero. Certainly, Tonto never experienced the degrading status of many sidekicks in B and juvenile Westerns who were little better than buffoons injected into the stories to provide comedy relief and make the hero appear braver and more intelligent by comparison. In fact, Indians in general were never reduced to this status in television Westerns except in comedies like *F Troop* where virtually every character, white as well as red, was held up to ridicule.

Brave Eagle, which aired on CBS during the 1955-56 season, represented a radical departure from most previous Westerns in its depiction of the Native American. An intelligent and well made series produced by Roy Rogers' Frontier Productions, *Brave Eagle* presented the story of the Western movement from the point of view of the Indian. Set in the American Southwest during the 1860s or 1870s, the series related the adventures of the young chief (Brave Eagle) of a peaceful tribe of Cheyenne; his young foster son, Keena; his sweetheart, Morning Star, and a half-breed named Smokey Joe. Although most of the cast was typically white actors portraying Indians (including the title role, which was played by Keith Larson), Keena was portrayed by a real 13 year old Indian named Kenna Noomkeena.

One television historian has characterized the series as being "remarkably free of stereotypes," with the Indians depicted as "the possessors of a great and ancient culture."[11] The white man was sometimes shown as a greedy aggressor who perpetrated great wrongs on the redman, sometimes as a courageous pioneer who sought only to live in peace with his red brothers. Disputes between the two fractions were settled as often by reason as by violence.

Just as there were "good" and "bad" whites who populated the early West of *Brave Eagle*, so were there "good" and "bad" Indians. One program opened, "The evil deeds of a few men can bring whole nations into ill repute and the man whose evil deeds left the widest trail of blood was a Piegan chief named Wolf Head." The episode went on to relate the story of how Brave Eagle and his warriors, working in cooperation with enlightened members of the United States Army, brought Wolf Head and his band of renegades to justice.

In another episode, a white settler who feared the Indians put up a fence to prevent Brave Eagle's tribe from crossing his land to get to their cornfields. Later when Morning Star helped deliver his wife's baby in the absence of a white doctor, the redman and the white became friends. "So we harvested our corn at peace with our neighbors, for Bill Hardy learned that firm friends spring forth in the hour of need and that in mutual help lies individual fulfillment." Not only did *Brave Eagle* present the Native American in a positive and realistic light, each week the Cheyenne chief taught his young ward a lesson about charity or justice that was, of course, equally appropriate for a white child. One week, for example, Noomkeena might learn that "one can make a mistake and still redeem himself with honesty, determination and courage."

Apparently *Brave Eagle* was too tame for the juvenile audience for which it was intended and after one season it disappeared from the video range. This was unfortunate for even though the characters in the stories lacked depth, the series did present a positive view of the Native American, stressing appreciation for differences and toleration through understanding.

Lasting one season longer than *Brave Eagle* with an Indian character as true cohero was *Broken Arrow* (1956-58) which featured the exploits of Apache Chief Cochise and Indian agent Tom Jeffords. Together they fought the injustice perpetrated by corrupt, greedy "White Eyes" and treacherous, renegade Indians in the West of the 1870s. The series was based on the 1950 film of the same title which in turn had been adapted from Elliott Arnold's novel *Blood Brother* (1947). The novel relates the purportedly true story of the unusual friendship between Cochise and Jeffords and Jeffords' love for and marriage to the Apache maiden Sonseeahray. The author asserts that the main events in the book are entirely true—specifically, that Cochise broke with Magas Coloradas and made peace for the Chiricahua tribe, lived it honorably, was arrested treacherously and then started a war. Thomas Jeffords ran the mail, went alone to meet Cochise, became his friend and later his blood brother, and then led General Howard to Cochise's camp to negotiate the final peace. Even most of the smaller details are true, although woven into the fictitious episodes of the story. Nowhere in the book, Elliott states, "is there anything that is in any way contrary to the large historical truth. Many of the conversations in the book are the actual conversations as reported by participants in later years."

Cochise was, of course, one of the most renowned figures in American Indian history, but in spite of his status as an American folk hero, surprisingly little is known of the facts of his life. It is true that in 1872 President Grant dispatched General Oliver O. Howard to Arizona to secure a permanent armistice with Cochise. Working through Thomas Jeffords, who had become a close friend of Cochise, Howard was able to meet with the Apache chief in the Dragoon Mountains in southeastern Arizona. He promised the Indian leader a reservation of his own choosing and the result was the huge Chiricahua reservation, set aside by executive order in October 1872, which included most of the southeastern corner of the territory. Jeffords was made the reservation's special Indian agent.

Perhaps because he had been the victim of unjust actions taken earlier by white men and because of his peaceful capitulation, Cochise was destined to become "a latter-day 'noble savage,' one enshrined by historians of the West, writers, and filmmakers as the symbol of the 'good Indian,' an Apache whose hostility was understandable and even justified." Arnold was one of those writers who romanticized Cochise, but his novel features one of the few sympathetic portraits of the Apaches to appear since the days of Edgar Rice Burroughs and Will Levington Comfort, in definite contrast to the stereotyped blood-thirsty savages so typical of formula Western fiction.

The 20th Century–Fox film starred the popular James Stewart as Tom Jeffords. Jeff Chandler was nominated for an Oscar as best supporting actor for his portrayal of Cochise. (Cochise's grandson Nana Cochise had tried out for the part and had been dismissed as not being "the type.") The film represented one of Hollywood's first large scale attempts to present a sympathetic picture of the American Indian and how he was mistreated by his white conquerors. *Newsweek* termed the film, "undoubtedly one of the most emotionally satisfying Westerns since *Stagecoach* (1939) and *The Virginian* (1929)." Jack Spears, in his book *Hollywood: The Golden Era* (1971), states:

> *Broken Arrow* further stimulated the flood of pro-Indian films and the oppressed but valiant redmen, usually personified by a dignified chief, became as much of a stereotype as the villainous savage had been. All the injustices to his race were charged to greedy, brutal and unsensitive whites—and to an impersonal government that ignored its responsibilities to the Indians.[12]

In the television series, John Lupton was cast as Jeffords, while Michael Ansara played Cochise. Ansara was a swarthy actor of Lebanese descent who became known for his Indian portrayals. (He played an Apache chief in his first film, *Only the Valiant*, in 1951.) The six-foot, three-inch actor claimed to be a student of history and indicated in a 1957 interview in *TV Guide* that he learned more about the American Indian through his television role than from books:

> Quite a few real Indians are cast in the *Broken Arrow* episodes and I'm always pumping them for information, not only to help me in my portrayal of Cochise, but because I've always enjoyed history.

Ansara first appeared in films during the early fifties earning plaudits for his brief portrayal of Judas in *The Robe* (1953). Most of his roles, however, were as Indians and when asked if this might typecast him, he replied at the time, "It will give us all a chance to find

Michael Ansara was an effective Cochise to John Lupton's Tom Jeffords in *Broken Arrow*.

out."[13] Although he had no Indian blood, he was still playing an Indian twenty years later (e.g., an Arapaho chief in the miniseries *Centennial*, 1978-79). He later explained, "I guess it's my size [6'3"] and dark complexion that makes me suitable for the Indian role."[14]

With the exception of the fictional love story, the first three episodes of *Broken Arrow* follow the film and novel closely. Jeffords is given the assignment of getting the United States mail safely through Apache territory in Arizona by the army. Jeffords makes friends with Cochise and secures the safe passage of the mail riders in the first episode ("The Mail Rider"). The second episode focuses on the events surrounding the "Battle at Apache Pass" and by the end of the third episode, "Indian Agent," Jeffords has agreed to serve as Indian agent on the Chiricahua Reservation.

Five months earlier, on May 2, 1956, an hour long *Broken Arrow* pilot had been presented as a segment of *The Twentieth Century Fox Hour* with Lupton as Jeffords, Ricardo Montalban as Cochise and Rita Moreno as Sonseeahray. The tragic romance between Jeffords and Sonseeahray was dramatized along with the other elements of the novel. *Variety* (October 3, 1956) was skeptical of the series' plausibility after its initial episode, but willing to suspend judgment based on future episodes:

> ... as TV Westerns go, it's a well-made, intelligently paced entry that holds juve and some adult appeal. ...
> ... Director Alvin Garger held dialogue to the necessary minimum and turned out a tight show with some outdoor shots that held a fair degree of realism.
> Lupton is a personable newcomer who somehow seems young for the role but handles it very well. Michael Ansara as Cochise brings restrained authority to the part.

The series depicted Jeffords' long struggle against the blind prejudice that many whites felt against Apaches and more episodes dealt with "bad" whites than "bad" Indians. The episode "Massacre" related the story of a U.S. Cavalry captain's blind hatred of Indians and his subsequent slaughter of a band of peaceful Apaches being led by Cochise's friend Nana. "Attack on Fort Grant" on the other hand, dealt with the misguided treachery of the Apache renegade Geronimo. The plight of the Apaches who were faced with starvation when game was scarce and government supplies did not arrive during the winter months is sympathetically depicted in "Ghost Face." An apparently indifferent Army officer agrees to expedite delivery of the needed supplies when the honesty of Cochise is dramatically demonstrated by Jeffords, who has purchased cattle for the Indians with his own money.

The series consistently focused on the plight of the Indian to a much greater extent than any other television Western before or since. There were a minimum number of violent cavalry charges and bloody shootouts with an emphasis on the human condition of the redman. Stories dealt with smallpox epidemics, struggles with corrupt officials who were stealing reservation-bound supplies, the right of a white boy raised by the Indians to remain with them, Apache wedding and funeral customs, and the soul searching of Indians who found themselves torn between their heritage and the opportunities offered by the world of the "White Eyes." All in all, *Broken Arrow* was an intelligent show which dealt realistically with the problems caused by the interaction of white and red cultures. Even so, there were some detractors, if mild, like Jason Betzinez, a former Apache warrior and U.S. Army scout who describes a meeting with Ansara on the Fort Sill reservation:

> At the post I found that an actor was there, who takes the part of Cochise on a television program. They wanted me to pose for a picture with him. ... I was glad to do so, though I told this young man, "You are a good actor, and you take the part of Cochise almost as well as if you were an Apache. But there are a few incidents in the film that are not entirely the way things happened."

In any case Ansara moved easily into his next television Indian role, that of Sam Buckhart in *Law of the Plainsman*. The character had been introduced on an episode of *The Rifleman* ("The Indian"). Buckhart was unusual because he was a Harvard educated Apache Indian who had become a deputy U.S. marshal stationed in Santa Fe. He had gained his education because of the generosity of a cavalry captain whom Buckhart had befriended and nursed back to health after he had been wounded in an Indian ambush. When the Captain died, he left money for Buckhart to attend a private school and later Harvard University.

After learning respect for the white man's law, Buckhart decides to become a United

States marshal. To achieve that goal he returns to New Mexico where he served under Marshal Andy Anderson. In his initial appearance he faces racial derision and threats on his life from otherwise law-abiding settlers because he is an Apache Indian who is trying to arrest a white man accused of murder. Lucas McCain helps the courageous Apache carry out his duty through the use of "reverse psychology." The most significant moment in the script (otherwise well written by Cyril Hume, but here using with very little change the words of Shakespeare in *Merchant of Venice*) comes when Buckhart tries to explain the basic equality of the races to an Indian-hating white:

> Has not an Indian eyes, hands, organs, senses, affections, fed with the same food, hurt with the same weapons, warmed and cooled by the same winter and summer as a white man? If you prick him, does he not bleed? If you tickle him, does he not laugh? And if you wrong him will he not revenge?

Even though Buckhart was ridiculed by most of the whites he encountered, as a "civilized redskin" he demonstrated a strong aversion for those Indians who operated outside the laws of the white community. He makes this clear in "The Raid," his second appearance on *The Rifleman*. While following Apaches who have kidnapped McCain's son Mark, Buckhart explains to his white friend the nature of those he is tracking:

> . . . I know the Apache. I know what must be done. I know that if their senses warn them that something is wrong, you've got to stop breathing, stop living, stop being for the moment. . . And don't sweat because they can smell it and it'll kill you. You don't attack by day, but lie quiet, wait and crawl. Crawl so they will not see you. You must kill them in the darkness, Lucas. Even the Apache must sleep. That's when you must take them, Lucas, when they sleep. . . The Apache does not give back prisoners.

There is obvious bitterness and pent up anger in these words.

Buckhart's appearances on *The Rifleman* garnered such strong ratings that NBC decided to give him his own series. *Law of the Plainsman* premiered on October 1, 1959, and lasted through 34 episodes. Although the series did not earn high ratings, it had its loyal viewers and received good reviews from the critics. One referred to it as a "tough, frequently penetrating Western tale"[15]; another, "an interesting western that aims for a more moderate view of the cowboy-Indian struggle"[16]; and a third, "a cut above average for television Westerns [which] added greatly to the so-called adult Western trend [and] dealt intelligently and realistically with the problems an Indian marshal might face in a mostly hostile [white] community. . . ."[17]

In his struggle against white prejudice, while attempting to maintain law and order on the wild New Mexico frontier, Buckhart displayed courage, restraint, compassion, strength of character and above all, dignity. In some episodes little note was even made of his race as he brought to justice murderers, thieves, land grabbers, con-artists and other lawless elements. Here was a multidimensional Indian character and role model. The Native American was now being accorded genuine equality in an adult Western that might have been depicting the exploits of a white peace officer. Although Michael Ansara brought authority to the part, one wishes that the producers could have found a Native American actor of stature to play the role.

Yet another television Western with a continuing Indian character was *Yancy Derringer* (1958-59). In this case the Indian, Pahoo-Ka-Ta-Wah (Wolf Who Stands in Water), chief of the Pawnees, was secondary to the title role (suavely played by Jock Mahoney) in much the same way that Tonto supported *The Lone Ranger*. Together they have been described as forming a team that was part police, part detective and part secret agent.[18] Set in New Orleans in the years following the Civil War, *Yancy Derringer* depicted the exploits of a former Confederate soldier turned cardsharp and adventurer working as a special agent for the civil administrator of the city. His job was to prevent crimes whenever possible, and capture the criminals when it was not. Pahoo was his constant friend and companion. There was one gimmick: Pahoo and Yancey communicated only in sign language. Pahoo never uttered one work in the entire 34 episodes of the series.

Cast in the role of the Pawnee chief was an actor named X Brands who claimed to be part Indian. According to his official studio biography X was "his name and not an initial." His great-grandfather and grandfather both had identical first, middle and last names, and so an X was used to differentiate between them. This persisted until X became a full-fledged name and was bestowed upon the youngest Brands. Born in 1927 in Kansas City, Missouri, the actor had, in addition to American Indian blood, more recent German, Irish and English strains. After serving in the Navy during World War II, Brands decided to try his luck at acting. Since he had some difficulty securing roles as a fledgling actor, he also became a bareback rider and toured the rodeo circuit as a bronco buster. Then he began to land roles in Westerns, playing an Indian in films like *Hondo* (1953). Brands also did stunt work in *The Wild One* (1954) and *The Conqueror* (1956).

In April 1958, he was picked from some 300 applicants for the part of Pahoo. The only new craft he had to learn was sign language, which Brands claimed was real. He explained in a *TV Guide* interview:

> It makes me practically the only actor in Hollywood who writes all of his own dialogue. Scripts simply say, "Pahoo makes signs." So, I make signs.[19]

The role, however, called for a minimum of acting skill, and X Brands was largely confined to waving his hands and arms, looking stern, throwing an occasional knife with accuracy, crashing through windows, walking through fire and plunging off balconies. It did little to enhance the image of the Native American on television. In fact, Pahoo was undoubtedly a step backward from the image of Cochise and Sam Buckhart. In the opinion of author Raymond William Stedman:

> Television carried the taciturnity device to an extreme with the Pawnee Pahoo (played by X. Brands), a mute Tonto of the *Yancy Derringer* series. With his opulent pointing, Pahoo could have put to shame Charles Dickens's silently cogent Ghost of Christmas Yet to Come.[20]

Whereas Pahoo spoke not one word of English, Mingo, *Daniel Boone*'s faithful Indian companion spoke perfect English without the trace of an accent. This was explained by the fact that Mingo had been born in England and educated at Oxford.

Daniel Boone debuted over NBC on September 24, 1964, dramatizing the fictionalized adventures of one of America's greatest folk heroes. The stories depicted his hunting and fighting exploits in the American Southeast before and during the American Revolution. The emphasis was on his exploring expeditions which inevitably led to run-ins with the Indians. Among his friends was a brave and enlightened Cherokee named Mingo — the quintessential example of the "good" and noble savage. Mingo could fight, run and climb as well, or better, than any white man and was adept at such Indian specialties as the use of the bow and arrow, the throwing of a knife and (a unique TV-Indian skill) the flicking of a buckskin whip. After being rescued from a tribe of hostile Indians (who apparently did not like educated Cherokees) by Dan'l in the pilot episode ("Ken-tuck-E") not once, but twice, Mingo became Boone's friend for life (or at least for the first four of the six seasons the show was broadcast). Mingo learned from Boone how to expertly fire a long rifle, while imparting his skill with a whip to his white mentor. In subsequent

Ed Ames as Mingo in *Daniel Boone*.

episodes the two blood brothers were virtually inseparable and could be seen every week running from or after presumably uneducated savages who did not appreciate the coming of the white man's civilization.

Cast opposite Fess Parker's Daniel Boone (still dressed in Davy Crockett's coonskin cap) was Edmund Dantes Urick (better known as Ed Ames) in the role of Mingo. Ames was the former lead baritone with the Ames Brothers. He had grown up in Malden, Massachusetts, where he and three older brothers had formed a singing group which they called the Urick Brothers. They had entertained World War II troops in Boston, and by 1955 had become America's top vocal combo with such hits as "Rag Mop," "Sentimental Me" and "The Naughty Lady of Shady Lane." In 1960, Ed split off from the group to study acting and took a $40 a week role in an Off Broadway revival of Arthur Miller's *The Crucible*. Later he played the lead in national companies of *The Fantasticks* and *Carnival*.

Next came a stint on Broadway as Chief Bromden, the schizophrenic Indian in *One Flew Over the Cuckoo's Nest*. The show lasted only long enough for Ames's agent to get a call for glossy photo of Ames in swimming trunks from the producers of the upcoming *Daniel Boone* series. So successful was his portrayal of Mingo that by the third season, Ames was receiving more fan mail than Fess Parker. Still, he decided to leave the show after the fourth season (1967-68), feeling that he was becoming too closely identified with the role.

Nevertheless, Ames, who reached the pinnacle of his career during the years he played Mingo, will probably be remembered most for an appearance he made in 1965 on Johnny Carson's *Tonight* show. A natural athlete who could hit a bull's-eye from twenty paces with a bowie knife, Ames went on the program as a guest in his role as Mingo. According to the script, he was to fling a tomahawk at an eight-foot-high cardboard cutout of a cowboy; during the rehearsal, he hit the target in the heart 19 times straight. On the air, with a home audience of at least ten million watching, Mingo took aim, let fly and ripped the cutout right in the crotch. Carson, his crew and the audience broke into waves of hysterical laughter that lasted for three minutes and 45 seconds on the tape—certainly one of the longest laughs in television history. While it hardly damaged Ames' career, it was not the finest hour for Mingo, who was identified as an Indian by millions of Americans.

Although the image of Mingo on the *Daniel Boone* series was that of a dignified, intelligent, and educated Native American who possessed unusual physical skills in addition to bravery, he was nonetheless a one-dimensional character. It was, however, the portrayal of most other Indians on the show that provoked the most controversy. Dressed in full warpaint, with blood-curling war whoops and evil leers, they spent most of their time trying to drive the whites out of Kentucky. Utilizing every familiar stereotype, the Indians were shown dancing around whites who were tied to a stake, attacking settlers' homes, sneaking up on military outposts—burning, pillaging, looting, kidnapping and generally wreaking havoc on the white community. It was the brutal savage, the "bad" Indian at his worst.

Unfortunately, this more than offset the positive aspects of the series for most Native Americans: Parker's charm, Ames' acting ability, the high production quality and the emphasis on traditional family values. As late as 1971, for example, the Boston Indian Council protested syndicated reruns of *Daniel Boone* as being "little more than white racist indoctrination especially detrimental to Native American children." The courts permitted a special Indian Committee to preview the *Boone* episodes and eventually 37 of the 165 programs were excluded from broadcast because they depicted "Indians scalping settlers, burning, dragging women, being called savages, red devils, painted devils, [and] red monsters."[21]

During *Daniel Boone*'s initial run (1964–1970) for NBC, another Western that was to provoke the ire of Indian organizations debuted on ABC. Based on the career of George Armstrong Custer during the period between 1868 and 1875 (the year before his death in the Battle of the Little Big Horn), *Custer* featured depictions of frequent and bloody battles between the Seventh Cavalry and the Indians. Again, the only continuing Indian character of note, Crazy Horse, was played by a non–Native American, Michael Dante. (Dante had some limited experience in playing the stereotyped role of a "bloodthirsty savage" as when he essayed the part of the Apache Chief Red Hawk in *Apache Rifles*, 1964.)

Even before its pilot telecast (September 6, 1967) Native American organizations began to assail *Custer* as "detrimental to Indians." First the Sioux in South Dakota and then the Chippewa in Minnesota criticized *Custer*, alleging, in the words of a spokesman, that "the series will stir up old animosities and revive Indian and Cowboy fallacies we have been trying to live down."[22] Following the premier show, the National Congress of American Indians demanded equal time to reply to the misrepresentations it detected. In the opinion of J. Fred MacDonald:

> The series offered an outdated image of the Old West. The depiction of savage Indians slaughtering white men was offensive to civil rights groups, and especially to Native Americans. The brutality of the stories—from knife fights to scalping to old-fashioned cavalry charges—violated the sensibilities of many critical of TV violence. A bear-hunting expedition offended those sensitive to ecological issues....
>
> The distortions of frontier history in "Custer" were also pronounced. Those seeking historical reconstruction or even accuracy were discouraged. The stress on military glory ran counter to a growing public debate by 1967 over the military role of the United States in the Vietnam War.[23]

Custer did pay occasional lip service to promoting understanding between the two races, as in this exchange between Custer and Crazy Horse in the pilot episode:

CUSTER: We don't want to enslave your people.

CRAZY HORSE: I've heard those same words spoken by your Indian commissioners. And they lied. They try to take from us everything that we have known. And try to make us over in the image of themselves. Is your way of life so fine, so great, that no other should exist?

CUSTER: If I were a philosopher, I might have an answer for you. But I haven't. But this I do know. Our country will be great some day, but only if it has a chance to grow. Time always brings changes. No people can stand still. Without progress, they die as many ancient civilizations have died before us.

CRAZY HORSE: You may speak truth, Yellow Hair, but it does not make the love of our people for their way of life any lesser. You really do not understand us. You cannot see the beauty, we see. You cannot feel the emotions we have.

CUSTER: We're all human and we can learn to live together in peace.

Such scenes were, however, few and far between, since most of the stories dealt with the efforts of whites and Indians to exterminate each other. Dante made a valiant attempt to bring dignity to the role of Crazy Horse, but in the face of such scripts, his efforts proved futile. In any case, the impact of the series was minimal, since viewers in sufficient numbers failed to watch the show and *Custer* was canceled in midseason after only 17 episodes.

By 1974, television was again ready to try a Western series with a lead character who was Native American. Unfortunately, they were either unable or unwilling to find an Indian to play the role.

Nakia was a contemporary Western police drama about a Navajo Indian named Nakia Parker who worked as a deputy in the Davis County, New Mexico, Sheriff's Department. Because of his Indian heritage, he frequently found himself torn between his duty as a police officer to enforce the law and his allegiance to his Native American brothers. Instead of the standard police car, Nakia used both a pickup truck and a horse for transportation and mixed modern crime solving methods with tried-and-true Indian customs. Although the Indians did not always trust Nakia, feeling that he had sold out to the whiteman, he consistently fought to see that the Indians in his jurisdiction were treated fairly by the law. Nakia's boss was Sheriff Sam Jerico (Arthur Kennedy) and they often disagreed, but Sam was an honest man and the two lawmen respected each other. A rugged individualist, Nakia did things his way, and reached his decisions based on the evidence he had at hand.

David Gerber, who headed Columbia's television operations, sold the concept of

Nakia to ABC, and hired writer Sy Salkowitz to flesh out the idea. (Salkowitz was later listed as creator.) Gerber was also responsible for selecting a non-Indian, Robert Forester, to play Nakia Parker. Born in 1941, Forester was educated at the University of Rochester, Alfred University (in New York) and Heidelberg College (in Ohio). Intent on pursuing a career in acting, Forester moved to the west coast and was soon being cast in leading roles in such films as *Reflections in a Golden Eye* (1967), with Elizabeth Taylor and Marlon Brando, *The Stalking Moon* (1968), with Gregory Peck, *Medium Cool* (1969), and *The Don Is Dead* (1973). In several of his better films, Forester played an Indian: Nick Tara, Indian friend of the hero in *The Stalking Moon*; Frank, an alcoholic and rebellious Sioux Vietnam veteran in *Journey Through Rosebud* (1972); and Tom Black Bull, a Ute who becomes a champion bronc rider in *When Legends Die* (1972).

In 1972 Forester was given his own television series on NBC in which he was cast as the title character, *Banyon*, a forties detective. It lasted only five months, however, and Forester returned to films and guest star roles on television. The pilot film for *Nakia*, which lured Forester back to television, was filmed on location in Albuquerque, New Mexico. ABC broadcast the 90 minute pilot film on April 17, 1974: When a ruthless land developer tries to buy a tract of city land—and destroy the sacred mission built upon it—Nakia finds himself torn between his duty as a policeman and his Indian heritage. A crisis develops when what began as a peaceful demonstration by the Indians threatens to turn violent. Stephen McNally is effective as the unscrupulous businessman and Chief Dan George (an actual Native American actor!) is excellent in the role of the tribal chief.

The ratings for the film were significantly high enough to convince ABC to launch a *Nakia* series during the 1974-75 season. Charles Larson was brought on board by Gerber to serve as executive producer. Larson was an experienced script writer whose credits included *Sky King*, *The Lone Ranger*, and *Rawhide*. Later he was associate producer on *Twelve O'Clock High* and producer of *The FBI*, *The Interns* and *Cade's County*. Recently Larson discussed the emphasis that was placed on authenticity in *Nakia*:

> ... We loved the Albuquerque look ... the mountains, the tram, the Hopi and Navajo backgrounds ...
> ... Everything about "Nakia" was as authentic as we could make it, but maybe this authenticity wasn't as attractive to the audience as it was to us.... In the beginning, we also had to contend with a number of threatened lawsuits from actor Tom Laughlin, who felt that "Nakia" infringed on his film "Billy Jack." The only connection that anyone could see was that both heroes were Indian lawmen and eventually the furor died down.[24]

The series premiered over ABC on September 21, 1974. The opening episode story focuses on a young Indian named George Two Horses (played by A Martinez) who is charged with the murder of the owner of a stereo shop. The actual assailant is a burglar who was caught by the owner in the act of stealing a radio. The evidence against George is convincing, although circumstantial. George has dark skin and squeaky rubber soles (both characteristics of the assailant) and on the afternoon of the burglary, he had an argument with the storekeeper who had refused to extend him credit to buy that same radio. When the police show up to question him, he runs away. Furthermore, dried blood is found on his shirt at the time of his capture. So damning is the evidence that his chief, Ben Red Earth (played with dignity by veteran actor Victor Jory), casts him out of the tribe. Not convinced that George is guilty, Nakia tries to solve the crime while keeping the Indian youth from destroying himself. Using the basic methods of detection along with his knowledge of the traditions of his people, Nakia is able to find the real killer and help George regain his status within his tribe. (Along the way there is a chase and rough-

and-tumble fight within an Indian museum.) Reviews were mixed; *Variety* (September 25, 1974) said:

> The potentially viable concept of a contemporary Indian hero reconciling white laws with Indian morals got a mixed workout in the premiere episode of "Nakia." Its strength is Robert Forester in the title role. He convincingly blends both worlds into his characterization of a New Mexico deputy sheriff....
> If the Indian values were an asset to the series, the basic crime plot was not.

The best episodes were those in which Native American themes and traditions played a prominent role in the solution to a crime: In "The Quarry," Nakia applied an old Indian custom to better understand the man he was tracking; in "Pete," he called upon his native acumen to capture a couple on a crime spree; in "The Dream," he utilized his knowledge of Indian folklore to interpret a mysterious vision; and in "The Fire Dancer," he called on an old medicine man to help him when an Indian chief came out second best in a fight with a bear.

Unfortunately most of the episodes dealt with more routine problems, like a bank robbery ("The Hostage"), a gang of hired assassins ("No Place to Hide"), organized crime ("The Driver"), an attempted murder ("The Moving Target"), and the illicit drug trade ("A Matter of Choice"). In any case, the homilies that Nakia spouted every week, like "the bear steals the honey, then complains to the Great Spirit because the bee is unkind," undoubtedly reduced the authenticity that the producer was trying so hard to achieve. Contemporary opinion as to *Nakia*'s effectiveness has been largely negative. Castleman and Podrazik have nothing positive to say about the series:

> "Nakia" is preachy, strident, obvious, and outdated in its fervent condescension....
> "Nakia" tries real hard to be significant and deep. All it winds up doing is being superficial, trivializing the real efforts of Indians in the modern age.[25]

On the other hand, David Martindale is more neutral in his assessment:

> It's not easy straddling the fence between widely differing ideologies—but Nakia Parker tried his damnedest.... He was a man in the middle. How Nakia dealt with that inner conflict, in fact was just as important as how he solved crimes.[26]

The show never won its time period, and was canceled December 28, 1974, after only 13 episodes. Still it did have a cadre of fervent viewers. Producer Larson explains:

> ... "Nakia" is the only series I was ever connected with that drew letters to me personally regretting its demise. Stars, certainly, always get such letters, but Executive Producers?[27]

While *Nakia*, in common with most of its predecessors, employed very few Native American actors, this was *not* true of the short-lived imaginative *Born to the Wind*. This NBC summer series broadcast only four episodes (August 19 through September 5, 1982), but had a most unusual setting—the village of a small Indian tribe located somewhere in North America around 1800, prior to the arrival of white settlers. All of the characters were, of course, Native Americans: Painted Bear, the leader (but not designated chief), who made most of the major decisions; Prairie Woman, his squaw; Star Fire, his daughter; Two Hawks, his teenage son; One Feather, the village medicine man; and Low Wolf and White Bull, two other prominently featured braves. Three of these roles were played by Native Americans: Will Sampson was cast as Painted Bear, Linda Redfearn portrayed Prairie Woman, and Dehl Berti made a convincing One Feather.

Will Sampson was born in Okmulgee, Oklahoma, in 1934, a full-blooded Muscogee-Creek Indian who was named Kos-Kuna, meaning left-handed. He grew up in Indian

Territory and began painting as a child, boasting that he had sold his first picture at age 3. He was an established artist before he turned to acting. He continued to paint and his work—primarily of cowboys, Western landscapes and Indian scenes—were exhibited at the Smithsonian. Before he took up painting and sculpting, he worked as an artist's model. He supported himself as a hunting guide, trapper, fisherman, lumberjack, black-smith and rodeo rider. He mastered every major rodeo event, after dropping out of school at age 13. Along the way he acquired three wives, six children and a 17 acre ranch in Oklahoma. Sampson got into acting by accident. A rodeo announcer recommended him to Michael Douglas, coproducer of the film version of *One Flew Over the Cuckoo's Nest*, who was looking for someone to play Chief Bromden, the psycho ward inmate who suc-cessfully defied the system by pretending to be deaf and dumb. Writing in *The New York Times* in 1976, Grace Lichtenstein explained Sampson's impact:

> ... The high cheekbones, impassive stare, the impression of dignity tinged with men-ace were straight out of the paintings of George Catlin or the photographs of Edward S. Curtis.[28]

On the basis of his performance in *Cuckoo's Nest*, Sampson was signed to featured roles in three Westerns: as William Halsey, Sitting Bull's eloquent, seemingly incorruptible in-terpreter, in Robert Altman's *Buffalo Bill and the Indians* (1976); as Ten Bears in Clint Eastwood's *The Outlaw Josey Wales* (1976), and as the Sioux medicine man, Crazy Horse, in J. Lee Thompson's *The White Buffalo* (1977). Sampson's other film credits—all playing majestic Native Americans—included *Orca, the Killer Whale* (1977) and *Fish Hawk* (1978). In 1976 *Newsweek*, describing Sampson's potential, said:

> ... Will Sampson has become that most belated of Hollywood discoveries—a full-blooded American Indian who has all the makings of a full-blooded American movie star....
> Hollywood's usual way with Indians has been to turn them into one of three stereotypes: the old sage (Chief Dan George), the white man's loyal friend (Tonto, Jay Silverheels) or the Big Bad Brave (numerous bit players). Sampson, a Creek Indian who is 43 and 6 feet 5, is something else again—a towering figure of genuine mystery who not only has the white man's number but is working on one of his own.[29]

The same year *The New York Times* proclaimed:

> In the space of two years Sampson has become the film world's foremost native American. He came along just in time, because in this age of ethnic awareness Hollywood can no longer get away with smearing brown makeup on a Jeff Chandler or a Burt Lancaster, sticking a feather in his hair and calling him an Apache.[30]

Naturally, Sampson soon moved into television playing Indian roles in made-for-television films like *Relentless* (1977), *Standing Tall* (1978), and *Alcatraz: The Whole Shocking Story* (1980), but also non–Native American characters in *The Hunted Lady* (1977) and *From Here to Eternity* (1979). He was also given a recurring role as Dan Tanna's (Robert Urich's) Indian friend, Chief Harlon Two Leaf, in *Vega$* (1978-1981). Feeling that Hollywood had tended to treat Indians like "livestock" in the past, Sampson was concerned about improving the Indian's self image. He once told an interviewer:

> All the Indians' heroes are long dead. We don't have today's heroes, like white people. Indians are a proud people, but we can't say Crazy Horse is going to win the World Series. There are a lot of good minds going to waste on those reservations. I'd like to be able to be someone that Indian children can look up to and relate to.[31]

In keeping with this attitude, Sampson narrated the television documentary series *Images of Indians* in 1980 and founded and chaired a nonprofit organization called the American

Indian Registry for the Performing Arts. His finest television achievement, however was undoubtedly his work on the short-lived *Born to the Wind*.

Linda Redfearn had previously appeared in the 1975 television film *I Will Fight No More Forever*. Dehl Berti's earlier film work included roles in such diverse films as *Apache Warrior* (1957) as an aged Apache Chief and *The Wolfen* (1981) where he played an old Indian. The stories on *Born to the Wind* dealt with "the Indian's attempts to cope with an often hostile environment, relationships with each other and the strong moral and ethical code by which they lived."[32] One wishes that this series had been given sufficient time to prove itself with viewers instead of being shifted around on the schedule over its brief run.

One of the Native American actors on *Born to the Wind*, Dehl Berti, was given a regular role as an Indian hermit named John Taylor, in the more recent CBS Western series, *Paradise* (1988–1991). John Taylor lived in the woods near the mining town of Paradise, California. Befriended by retired gunfighter Ethan Cord and his young wards, especially Ben and George, John Taylor becomes practically a member of the family. A shaman who is well versed in the lore of his people as well as the ways of nature, Taylor is sometimes called upon to apply his native healing skills since there is no regular doctor living in Paradise. On more than one occasion he is responsible for saving the life of Ethan or someone near and dear to Ethan (including Ethan's special ladyfriend and the town's only banker, Amelia Lawson, in an episode entitled "Stray Bullet").

Prejudice against Indians is effectively dealt with in an episode called "The Ghost Dance." John Taylor is accused of killing a white man who had insulted and bullied him earlier. After the townspeople have been whipped into a frenzy by the real murderer and a few other Indian-hating whites, a mob is ready to hang Taylor. The inept marshal of Paradise, worried about his political career, refuses to intervene until Ethan and his young sons are able to convince the mob to disperse. The object of the townspeople's fear is a small group of Indians, mostly women and old men, who have been performing an Indian ritual known as "the ghost dance" a few miles outside of town. They believe that they can bring back to life the spirits of their departed ancestors. Young George thinks that by participating in this ceremony he can bring back his dead mother. The subject is handled with seriousness and dignity and Dehl Berti is quietly effective as the stoic John Taylor, prepared to die, however unjustly, if that is to be his destiny.

In "The Last Warrior," John Taylor plays a less passive role when a large lumber company comes to Paradise to strip the nearby mountains of their rich timber. Claiming that the land still belongs to his tribe, of which he is the last surviving member, Taylor tries to prevent the destruction of his mountain. All of his ancestors are buried on this mountain, and Taylor is willing to sacrifice his own life to save the forest. Wiring himself with dynamite, Taylor threatens to blow up the workers unless they leave his mountain. Ethan intervenes (over John Taylor's vigorous objections) and tries first persuasion and compromise and, when that fails, legal means to prevent violence and bloodshed. The circuit judge invokes the Dawes Act, which provides an allotment of 80 acres of land to each living adult Indian. John Taylor cleverly takes claim to the 80 acres which controls the only road up the mountain, thus thwarting the efforts of the lumber company.

Again Dehl Berti turns in a powerful, if low key, performance as "the last warrior" willing to die to preserve his heritage. Fiercely independent he rejects any effort by his friends to help him, but he is just as powerless to prevent their assistance as he is to stop the efforts of big business to despoil his mountain. In this episode, ecological and environmental issues are dealt with, as well as the status and treatment of Native Americans. Ethan is able to prevent the massacre of a small band of Indians by a ruthless, Indian-

Native American actor Dehl Berti was featured as Indian John Taylor in CBS's *Paradise*.

hating cavalry commander in "Burial Ground." In this episode the children ask John Taylor (since he is the only Indian they know) why the Indians have returned (to the hills near Paradise):

JOHN TAYLOR:	Because it's their home, Ben. They were here long before Christopher Columbus learned to swim.
BEN:	Why did they leave?
JOHN TAYLOR:	That's a long story.
GEORGE:	As long as "Jack and the Beanstalk?"
JOHN TAYLOR:	Oh, longer.
BEN:	We have lots of time.
JOHN TAYLOR:	Well, Indian people left their home because the white man wanted their land and made them move.
GEORGE:	That's not nice.
JOHN TAYLOR:	The Indians didn't think so either, so they decided to fight.
BEN:	But they lost.
JOHN TAYLOR:	You know the white man's a lot like your giant in "Jack and the Beanstalk." He just takes whatever he wants...
GEORGE:	If the Indians attack, will you join them?
JOHN TAYLOR:	No... I'm not a part of that world any more.
BEN:	Will you fight with the army?
JOHN TAYLOR:	I never was a part of that one.
GEORGE:	He's a hermit, remember!

Later, John Taylor is captured by the cavalry and dragged through town. The commander threatens to kill him unless he reveals the location of the Indian's camp. Ethan's oldest nephew, Joseph, risks his life to save John Taylor.

In these episodes of *Paradise*, John Taylor served many purposes: he was the wise sage, skilled in the folklore of his people; he was the brave warrior, standing against overwhelming odds to preserve his heritage and environment; and he was the victim of the prejudice and ignorance of most of the townspeople of Paradise. In each instance, John Taylor was powerless to affect the outcome of the story without the help of Ethan and his friends. Thus, while *Paradise* presents a multidimensional portrait of the Native American in the person of John Taylor, he is still stereotypically wise, brave and weak.

One of the most recent television Westerns, *The Young Riders* (1989–1992) also included among its cast of regulars a "token" Indian character. Buck Cross, one of the Pony Express riders, is half Kiowa Indian (his mother) and half white (his father). An orphan, Buck is quietly brave and often turns to his Native American spiritual nature for inner strength. Buck was played by Gregg Rainwater, who was part Cherokee Indian himself.

In one episode of *The Young Riders*, the Kiowas go on the warpath led by Buck's half-brother, Red Bear. Buck is forced to make a choice between his loyalty to his friends, the Pony Express riders, and his blood ties to his tribe. In this episode, Teaspoon sets forth the "contemporary explanation" of the conflict between the Indians and the whites,

> JIMMY: We ain't takin' their land, we're just ridin' on it, right Buck?
> TEASPOON: Indians is fightin' for their way of life, the right to live the way they did before we got here. Just like our kin fought the British almost a hundred years ago, 'cept the Indians is called savages. Our kin was called patriots, because they won.

Buck later returns to his tribe in order to gain the release of one of the other Pony Express riders who had been captured. Then he participates in a ceremony where his white nature is expelled from his being so that he may become completely Kiowa. A line is painted down the center of his body—white on one side, red on the other to symbolize his two natures. In the end, Buck chooses to return to the white world that he has known for most of his life. Although a half-breed, the character of Buck Cross is frequently utilized in *Young Riders* episodes as if he were entirely Native American (e.g., the animosity of the townspeople against Indians is focused on Buck). Buck, thus, becomes a "traditional" Indian character in stories with a decidedly "contemporary" orientation.

In the CBS series, *Walker, Texas Ranger* (1993–) one of the continuing characters, Cordell Walker's Uncle Raymond, is played by another veteran of Kevin Costner's hit film *Dances with Wolves*, Floyd Red Crow Westerman. Westerman (like Graham Greene and Rodney A. Grant) was to find work in various television and film roles which called for a Native American actor. In the tradition of Chief Dan George, Westerman brought a certain stateliness, dignity, and believability to wise elderly Indian sages. (On *Northern Exposure*, for example, he was cast as Ed's invisible spirit guide, One-Who-Waits, in several episodes.)

The Indian versus white man theme was frequently employed by most of the best and most popular television Westerns—sometimes with excellent results, sometimes with not such excellent results—even on the same series. Take *Gunsmoke*, for example. By considering four episodes spread over the period from 1958 to 1973, one can see both perceptive and thoughtless portrayals of the Native American on one of the highest quality television Westerns. (In *each* case, however, *Gunsmoke*'s producers cast non–Indians in Native American roles.)

In "Sunday Supplement," written by John Meston, two New York writers come to

Dodge City in search of a story that will thrill their Eastern readers. Disappointed by the lack of dramatic gunfights or bloody Indian massacres, they decide to stir things up themselves. They disturb a Pawnee burial ground and steal a sacred totem, causing an Indian uprising that is brutally suppressed by the cavalry. The sacred customs of the Indians are treated here with sensitivity and respect, while the white man's ignorance and lack of compassion is shown in stark contrast.

A 1965 episode entitled "Chief Joseph" deals with an actual historic figure, the much revered leader of the Nez Percé Indians. Chief Joseph stops in Dodge while on route to a peace conference with President Ulysses S. Grant. Joseph is suffering from pneumonia and must stay at the Dodge House for medical treatment and rest. There he encounters the hostility of many town residents who have lost relatives in the Indian wars. They threaten violence if Chief Joseph is allowed to remain in Dodge. Matt Dillon vows to protect the Chief from harm. Meanwhile, thousands of Indians are secretly arming themselves, while they await the outcome of Chief Joseph's negotiations, which could lead to either peace or another war. The crisis is peaceably resolved when Chief Joseph recovers and leaves Dodge City with a better understanding of the feelings of the whites (and they of his). Veteran character actor Victor Jory plays Chief Joseph with dignity and the script by Clyde Ware is both respectful and believable.

In "The First People," John Eagle Wing, grandson of the chief of the Wichita Indians, White Buffalo, gets into a dispute with a tyrannical Indian agent. After examining the merits of the controversy, Matt supports young Eagle Wing. Matt is then framed for a murder on the reservation by the treacherous Indian policeman Mako and suspended as U.S. marshal. It is only through the intervention of a representative of the United States Attorney General's office that Matt is cleared and peace is again restored to the Wichita Reservation with John Eagle Wing as the new chief. Although, once again, all of the Indian characters (with the exception of one small role of an Indian policeman) are played by white actors, both "good" (Eagle Wing, White Buffalo) and "bad" (Mako) Indians are depicted. Furthermore, the story, by award-winning Western author Calvin Clements stresses the dignity of the Native Americans. These words are spoken by Eagle Wing as he pleads for respect for the ways of his people:

> We stand on ground of Kira Kirish—the first people ... I, Eagle Wing, am Kira Kirish. Before me was nothing. After me come all other men. Since there was time, this is so. One day my people, Kira Kirish, will cease to be. One day they will be nothing but a memory and yet another day even that memory will die.... All I ask is dignity for the passing of Kira Kirish.

Unfortunately not all episodes of *Gunsmoke* presented such a sympathetic picture of Native Americans. In "Woman for Sale," a two hour story televised over two weeks at the beginning of the fall 1973 season, the central character, a Comanche renegade named Blue Jacket (played with greedy, sadistic nastiness by white actor Gregory Sierra) kidnaps white women and children for the purpose of selling them to a white slaver. *Variety* "decried" the episode as loaded with "mean, drunken, Indian rapists."[33]

One might expect that *Cheyenne*, the title character having been raised by Indians, would present Native Americans in a favorable light. Not necessarily so. In many episodes, from the premier broadcast of "Mountain Fortress" through "Lone Patrol" and "Massacre at Gunsight Pass" during the fifth season, most Indians are depicted as one-dimensional, stereotypical, bloodthirsty redskins, killing, pillaging, raping and scalping whites. Only occasionally, as in "The Long Search" (a third season episode), the two-part "Gold, Glory and Custer" (fourth season episodes), "Legacy of the Lost" (a sixth season

Native American actor Floyd Red Crow Westerman (left) plays Uncle Raymond to *Walker, Texas Ranger* (played by Chuck Norris).

episode) and "Indian Gold" (a seventh season episode) are Native Americans depicted with dignity and compassion as an honorable and wronged people.

On *Wagon Train*, one of the series singled out by the A.A.I.A. for its biased portrayal of Indians "as drunken, cowardly outlaws ... usually attacking wagon trains,"[34] one is hard-pressed to find an episode which treats Native Americans sympathetically. On one such episode, "The St. Nicholas Story" (broadcast during the 1959 Christmas season), a young boy wanders away from the wagon train to look for St. Nicholas. He meets an Indian boy and the two become friends. The qualities basic to all human beings are stressed and the possibilities for peace and understanding between the two races are considered. All too often, however, *Wagon Train* presents the Indians not only as a threat to the westward expansion of whites, but as a people without any redeeming human qualities.

The drovers on *Rawhide* had less frequent contact with Indians than the settlers who traveled with Major Adams and Chris Hale, but there were some notable episodes dealing with Native Americans. In "Incident of the Haunted Hills," both "good" and "bad" Indians affect the destiny of Gil Favor's cattle drive. An outcast (but "good") Indian named Tasunka attempts to find water for the thirsty cattle and leads a three man scouting party into hostile Indian territory. There they are captured by "bad" Indians and Tasunka tries to bargain for the lives of his white friends. Both Indian stereotypes are also represented in "Incident at Superstition Prairie," when Wishbone ignores Indian tribal customs and nurses back to health an old Indian left by his people to die, thus incurring the wrath of the Comanches. The Indians seem more "bad" than "good" in "Incident of the Lost Tribe," when drover Pete Nolan is forced to lead a band of Cheyenne Indians across the border into Mexico.

"The Reunion," perhaps the most interesting *Rawhide* episode featuring Native American characters, focuses on two generational disputes between fathers and sons — one set who are white, the other, Indian. In each instance the father and son disagree on whether or not to observe the terms of a treaty that has been negotiated between the Army and the Indians to keep the peace. There are heroes and villains on both sides of the dispute, with neither age nor race being a determining factor. On the other hand there appear to be only "bad" Indians in "Incident of White Eyes" where the Jicarillo Apaches are depicted as bloodthirsty savages. It should be noted, however, that a "bad" white has provoked their anger. Indian religious beliefs are again the cause of trouble in "Incident at Ten Trees," when a mentally disturbed white woman is believed to be a witch by the Cheyenne. *Rawhide* never incurred the condemnation of the A.A.I.A., but neither was it ever lauded by that group. As in the case of most other television Westerns, the most disappointing aspect of *Rawhide*'s depiction of Native Americans was the use of white actors to portray them (such as John Drew Barrymore in "Incident of the Haunted Hills" and, with more effective results, such experienced Indian impersonators as Michael Ansara and Michael Pate in several episodes).

Bonanza, America's favorite family Western, is also not above criticism when it comes to utilizing stories about Indians. For example, a Native American religious movement is distorted in an episode entitled "A Sense of Duty" (1967). The Ghost Dancers, represented by a fictional Indian "holy man" named Wabuska (the actual Ghost Dancers were led by a Paiute medicine man named Wovoka), is portrayed as a fanatic who believes that bullets cannot hurt him, because "fire, air, wind, and water are the friends of Wabuska." After Ben Cartwright's militia detachment has lost several men trying to escort Wabuska to jail for inciting the Indians, Ben exposes this fraud by pointing a pistol at him and threatening to pull the trigger, while proclaiming, "He's a man, a man like you and me." Ralph Brauer takes *Bonanza* to task for trying

> . . . to assert that underneath Indians are just like whites. In order to do this they have to demonstrate that something that makes them Indians, their religion, is absurd; so they pick the wildest and most distorted example they can think of. . . .
> . . . The Wabuska episode seems to follow the belief that Indians were primitive and irrational and the only way you motivated Indians to futilely attack a few whites was to convince the Indians they were invincible.[35]

A 1968 *Bonanza* episode, "Burning Sky," deals with a white-Indian marriage by contrasting the attitudes of prejudiced whites (portrayed as unshaven "riff-raff" who wear sloppy clothes, and speak poor English — the leading agitator even owns a still) with those of good whites like the Cartwrights. The story concerns Indians and whites of the same high social strata. As the white husband puts it, "My wife's father, grandfather, and great-grandfather were Sioux chiefs and my great-grandfather served under George Washington." Brauer explains:

> . . . What we have here is the union of two established families, but the question is never faced about what to do with those Indians who aren't chiefs. . . . Apparently good Indians are not unlike the good whites in that they are "quality people" rather than "riff-raff." Just to make sure we know they're quality people, these chiefs and their offspring are played by whites.[36]

Another historical figure is portrayed in a *Bonanza* episode entitled "The Honor of Cochise." The incident depicted, the apprehension of an Army captain who poisoned some of the Apache chief's warriors while they were attending peace talks, is, however, entirely fictitious. The story focuses on Ben Cartwright's attempts to persuade Cochise to release the captain and come with him to confront the captain's superior officer who gave the orders to kill the Apaches. The point of the story is that the redman's word is as good as (or, in this case, better than) that of the white man. (Cochise is solemnly played by Jeff Morrow.)

All of the "good"-"bad" and white–Indian stereotypes are featured in a two-part, two-hour story about the founding of the Pony Express entitled "Ride the Wind." The climax of the story centers on the differences of opinion between two factions as to how to solve the problem of Paiute raids against the Pony Express—by negotiating a treaty or waging an all-out war against the Indians. When the son of the Paiute chief is captured and scheduled to be hanged, the Paiutes seize Little Joe. Ben, over considerable opposition from the politically ambitious owner of the Pony Express, prevents the hanging and obtains the exchange of the chief's son for Little Joe. Peace between the Paiutes and whites is thereby secured. Grievances on both sides of the controversy are presented, but "right" clearly appears to be on the side of the Indians in this particular episode.

On balance, *Bonanza* is no worse or better at depicting the Native American than *Gunsmoke* or *Rawhide*. (The same old stereotypes are presented, but the emphasis is decidedly on the "good" Indian.) Even *The High Chaparral*, despite producer David Dortort's claims about the show's realistic portrayal of Indians, was guilty of misrepresenting the Native American from time to time. One episode shows Indians riding horses with blankets over what are obviously saddles, and uses (Asian) Indian sitar music as a background theme for the (American) Indians, one of whom is plainly wearing a gold wedding ring. According to the story, the Ghost Dancers are a bunch of renegade Indians who go about wantonly butchering white men's cattle and scalping people. Ralph Brauer comments:

> ... As TV land would have it, the Ghost Dancers did a good deal of raiding, but not too much dancing. How they got their name seems to be a mystery to the TV writers, even though the real Ghost Dancers were a pacifist movement that did a good deal of dancing and no raiding.[37]

Other shows criticized by the A.A.I.A. for their distortions of Native Americans included *Laramie* (1959–1963), where Indians were depicted "holding white girls captive, in addition to other brutal actions," and *The Overland Trail* (1960), where they were shown as "unbelievably stupid savages, believing in the most ridiculous witchcraft."[38]

A decade and a half later saw little improvement in the status of the Indian as portrayed in the few television Westerns still on the air. A series called *The Oregon Trail* (1977) provided an old scout with such a line as, "Well, sometimes an Indian bein' friendly means just stealin' your stock instead of cuttin' your throat." Later in the same episode, a passing reference to "Indians" leads a child in the wagon train to assume that someone is about to be scalped. And in response to an unintended desecration of a burial ground by the hero's son, a band of Indians steals the caravan's extra horses, kills the guard and murders the old scout who had ridden out to negotiate with them. [39]

The Chisholms (1979-80) continued the practice of using menacing music when a few Indian riders are shown outside of Fort Laramie. This accompanied such lines as, "Smells like trouble's comin'!" The Sioux spoke in superimposed subtitles, "Let no whites leave the fort!" Raymond William Stedman explains in his excellent study *Shadows of the Indians: Stereotypes in American Culture*:

> Recurrent scenes of sneak raids by various parties of warriors produced so vicious a tone that the occasional good deeds of Santee Sioux—returning prisoners taken by bad Indians

or curing a white man's tomahawked "squaw"—hardly balanced matters, nor did the incessant attribution of Indian misdeeds to "them renegades."[40]

Stedman also takes *How the West Was Won* (1978-80) to task for "dressing a 'renegade Sioux' unaccountably in Apache costume." Furthermore, Stedman explains:

> ... the "whole Sioux nation" was ready for war because a boorish Russian nobleman had celebrated his ransoming from brief captivity by whacking proud-chief Ricardo Montalban on the cheek with a riding crop. As ever, the critical provocation—in this instance the decimation of the buffalo herds—is smothered by histrionics and by the enticing fantasy of an armed confrontation of Romanovs and Dakotas in the Black Hills.[41]

This is despite the fact that the pilot episode opened with a clear and objective description of the relationship which existed between whites and Indians in the post–Civil War West:

> Generations of Americans have viewed the Indian as either the noble redman, a pure and innocent child of nature as uncomplicated as the wilderness in which he lived, or as a half naked and barbaric savage whose cruelty knew no bounds. Neither context is true. The Indian, like any man or nation, was a mixture of many qualities. Before his lands were usurped and his people decimated, he was a loyal friend to the white man. The Pilgrims survived the winter of starvation thanks to the kindness of the Indian and Lewis and Clark were rescued by the Nez Perce. But just as the white man dealt in deceit with the Indian, so not every overture of apparent friendship by the Indian toward the settler could be taken at face value.

During the two-season course of the series, hero Jeb Macahan came in contact with both "good" and "bad" Indians as well as "good" and "bad" whites. Still, no Native American actors were cast in Indian roles and *How the West Was Won* failed to distinguish itself in its portrayal of the conflict between whites and the redman.

During the fifties, the trials of Native Americans were occasionally the subject of stories on such outstanding dramatic anthologies as *Playhouse 90*. The interesting, if controversial, "Massacre at Sand Creek" was presented on that series December 27, 1956. Written and produced by William Sackheim, "Massacre" contained the following disclaimer in its opening credits:

> The characters and incidents portrayed ... are fictitious and any similarity to actual persons or events is entirely accidental and unintentional.

Although the names of the characters were changed, the story was clearly based on an actual event which occurred on the Sand Creek Indian Reservation in Colorado Territory on November 29, 1864. This event, known in history as the Sand Creek Massacre, involved the slaughter of over 200 Cheyenne, mostly women and children, by the Third Colorado Volunteers under the command of Colonel John Chivington. The Indians believed themselves to be in custody and under the protection of the army, but Chivington had ordered the surprise attack and given instructions that no prisoners were to be taken. As a result the troopers slaughtered the living and mutilated the dead, soon displaying the scalps and severed genitals of the Indians they had killed before cheering crowds in Denver. News of the massacre and the mutilation of men, women and children caused a wave of public indignation, and investigations were conducted by the Committee on the Conduct of the War, a joint congressional committee, and the military. Although Chivington escaped punishment because he had left the army, his actions were condemned by the investigating bodies.

In the *Playhouse 90* production the Chivington character was named Templeton (forcefully played by Everett Sloan) and Black Kettle, chief of the Cheyenne, was called Little River (unbilled in the credits). A purely fictitious character called Lieutenant Norman

Tucker (effectively portrayed by John Derek) attempts to halt the senseless slaughter and is court-martialed by Templeton. In his subsequent trial (which serves as the closing focus of the drama) much of the testimony from the actual investigation is incorporated into the dialogue by Sackheim:

> TEMPLETON: When you've been out here as long as I have, you'll learn that there is no such thing as a peaceful Indian ...
>
> DEFENSE COUNSEL: Now Colonel, the dictionary defines a battle as an engagement between two opposing hostile forces. Do you concur in this definition?
>
> TEMPLETON: I do.
>
> DEFENSE COUNSEL: Would you then define a village of Indians, men, women and children, sleeping peacefully under the protection of a treaty, as an opposing hostile force?
>
> PROSECUTOR: Objection, the defense is badgering the witness.
>
> DEFENSE: Defense has based its case on the contention that a state of war did not exist; that the accused could not possibly have given aid and comfort to the enemy because there was no enemy; that what has been described as a condition of battle was in reality, no battle at all, but a purposeful, successfully executed mass murder!

In the *Playhouse 90* version of history, the influence of Colonel Templeton is such that, despite overwhelming evidence to the contrary, Lieutenant Tucker is found guilty. He is, however, given the opportunity to appeal. On the way to his appeal hearing he is fatally wounded, but before he dies he gives a copy of the transcript of his court-martial to his "blood brother" Cheyenne (son of the dead Chief, Little River, who was gunned down by the soldiers while waving a white flag). From there, with the Indian's help, the transcript makes its way into the hands of the authorities in Washington, an investigation is ordered and Templeton is stripped of his rank. (All the loose ends are neatly tied up, although the hero does have to die!)

The most glaring inaccuracy in *Playhouse 90*'s "Massacre" comes in a scene in which the surviving Indian leaders are discussing what action to take in revenge for Sand Creek. Sackheim puts these words into the mouth of one of the Cheyenne chiefs:

> I am tired of fighting. All our chiefs are killed. Our old men are dead. My people have fled to the hills. They are without blankets, without food. I must go seek my children to see how many of them are left. Perhaps I shall only find them among the dead. Now hear me! I am tired. My heart is sick and sad and from where the sun now stands I shall fight no more.

Noble sentiments, but as any high school student of American history knows, they were expressed not in 1864 by a Cheyenne chief, but some thirteen years later by the great leader of the Nez Percé, Chief Joseph. It is not surprising that the moving story of the flight of the Nez Percé which preceded Joseph's immortal speech should also be the subject of a made-for-television movie—and that it should also misrepresent what actually occurred.

On Monday evening, April 14, 1975, the American Broadcasting Company presented a two hour dramatic production entitled *I Will Fight No More Forever*. The screenplay by Jeb Rosebrook and Theodore Strauss claimed to offer the "true story" of Chief Joseph, leader of the Nez Percé tribe. In 1877, the tribe became a target of the United States government's policy of "forced containment" against American Indians. Contrary to provisions of a treaty signed in 1863, the Nez Percé were ordered to relocate on a reservation. Chief Joseph eventually found himself leading a retreat over 1600 miles of land in the area where the states of Washington, Idaho and Oregon now meet. That event was the central focus of the film.

In addition to providing viewers with entertainment, the film was touted by its sponsor, the Xerox Corporation, as an accurate historical recreation of one of the last significant events of this country's Indian Wars. A press release proclaimed that director Richard Heffron had amassed "more than one thousand pounds" of written material during his research. The production was accompanied by a 12 page classroom study guide published by Glenn and Company and freely distributed to schools across the country by Xerox. The guide did indeed contain useful information on the history of the Nez Percé, but (as *New York Times* television critic John J. O'Connor pointed out) "at no place does it even hint that, in several respects, the television drama strays distressingly far from historical truth."[42]

The beginning of the story, at least, broadly corresponds with the historical facts. In June 1877, two Nez Percé braves are shown hunting an eagle on a ridge above the Wallowa Valley in northeastern Oregon. The Indians are soon surprised by two surly white settlers who unjustly accuse them of stealing several horses. One of the settlers shoots the older Indian in a particularly cowardly and sadistic fashion. When the surviving Nez Percé returns to his camp, many of the younger warriors are eager for revenge, but Chief Joseph, the 37 year old chief (portrayed with genuine dignity by non-Indian actor Ned Romero) restrains them. This sequence of events sets the stage for a meeting that takes place between Joseph and his Nez Percé and Major General Oliver Otis Howard, the commander of the Department of the Columbia and an Indian agent named John Monteith. General Howard (played in gruff-but-kindly manner by James Whitmore) is a 46 year old veteran of the Civil War, in which he lost an arm and earned a reputation for humaneness and decency in his treatment of the freed slaves. As presented here, the general is clearly sympathetic to the Nez Percé position and a personal friend of Chief Joseph. After an exchange of pleasant amenities between Howard and Chief Joseph the Indian agent reads an order from the Secretary of the Interior which, by authority of President Grant, commands the Nez Percé to "give up their land and settle on the reservation within thirty days of this notice."

Up to this point there are two major errors of fact in the film. The shooting of the Indian depicted as occurring just before the meeting between Howard and Joseph, actually took place some two years earlier in 1875. More significant is the false impression presented of General Howard as a friend of the Nez Percé who is simply carrying out his orders, unpleasant as they may be. In reality, it was Howard who forced the issue of moving the Nez Percé to a reservation. As Alvin M. Josephy explained in his excellent history *The Nez Percé Indians and the Opening of Northwest*:

> Soon afterward [in 1876], Howard's thinking had become settled on matters. Taking the position . . . that the whites could no longer be ousted, he had decided that the government should end the conflict . . . by extinguishing the Indians' rights to all off-reservation lands through a just and fair purchase of those claims. . . . Howard, by his future actions, showed that he had totally abandoned his [earlier] position . . . that it would be a mistake to take the Wallowa from the Indians. Now he would take it, by negotiation and payment if possible, but by force if necessary. Moreover, by having the government accept and promptly execute his policy, he would make inevitable an injustice that might have been avoided.[43]

In the television account, the night of the Nez Percé meeting with Howard, three young braves (including the son of the murdered Indian) ride into a nearby settlement, where they find the white man in a saloon. They kill him (when he goes for his gun), but graciously leave the other settlers in the saloon unharmed ("Woman, your white man is not worth killing") and return to camp.

Although this is true to the "spirit" of what really happened, certain details were altered or omitted. The son of the slain man with two reluctant companions rode into a nearby settlement to avenge the murder—but two years had elapsed and the killer had since left the territory. The Nez Percé trio came upon various other settlers and killed four and wounded another. In the next few days, other Indians joined the three and massacred approximately fifteen white settlers in the area of White Bird Canyon. From his headquarters, General Howard notified Washington that another Indian war had broken out.

Thus began the great saga of the Nez Percé retreat of more than 1600 miles—pursued at various times by ten different detachments of the United States Army—from Oregon through the Idaho Territory, across the Bitterroot Mountains, into the Montana Territory, across the Continental Divide, through Yellowstone Park, and, eventually, into Wyoming Territory toward Canada. In most respects the television account appears faithful to the broad outline of the Nez Percé odyssey, but there are some relatively minor changes in detail. (This might have been due to ignorance or the application of literary license.) Michael J. Arlen, television critic for *The New Yorker*, concluded after extensive research that

> ... [while] this "true" film account of the Nez Percé is generally faithful to the situation as a whole, and achieves a commendable accuracy in matters of costume and war paint and the like, its value to the audience is more likely to be that of entertainment (as in a good historical novel) than that of a filmed historical record—or truth ....
>
> Overall, probably the most important alterations in detail and texture are in the films similification of the two key roles. General Howard and Chief Joseph. James Whitmore's Howard is a dramatic portrait that has been painted with some praiseworthy realism, but in the end it remains that of a conventional actor-hero, and takes into account neither that Howard had a considerable role in provoking the Nez Percé war through his own reservation policies nor that by the end of the campaign he was not the nobly authoritative figure depicted as receiving Joseph's surrender.
>
> Ned Romero's portrayal of Joseph, for its part, seems on the surface to be adequately faithful to the dignity and common sense of the notable Indian, but here, too, the television version created distortions in its simplifications—in this case, of Chief Joseph's actual position among the Nez Percé and in the Nez Percé war....
>
> The facts seem to be that though Joseph's sagacity and diplomacy eventually came to carry dominant influence in Nez Percé councils ... during most of the fighting period on the long march Joseph had been but one of several chiefs and by no means the most militarily adept among them.[44]

Still, despite its shortcomings, Arlen finds *I Will Fight No More Forever* to be a laudable undertaking and worthwhile viewing:

> ... It is certainly an entertaining and interesting rendering of an exceptional saga, and it has been transformed into telefilm with a greater concern for the Indian position than has been shown by most filmmakers in the past. All the same, it raises questions of accuracy and truth which I suspect may become more common as the public's penchant for reality, or dramatized reality, becomes more widespread....
>
> ... "This story is true," says the prologue to the television film about the Nez Percé war. Alas, it is not quite true. It is nearly true; and much of the trouble certainly lies in our restless, modern tampering with reality in the guise of providing attractive "information," or even of righting past wrongs: thus if Indians were once mis-shown as savages, we will now presumably assist the Indian by mis-showing the settlers as brutes....
>
> ... [But] if it happens that there are imperfections in this historical entertainment, with details of fact or character not fully portrayed, or else distorted, perhaps it will also happen that "I Will Fight No More Forever" may encourage some in its audience to pursue the story further, into history and the considerable literature on the subject—and that itself would be no small achievement.[45]

John J. O'Connor, the *New York Times* critic, did not agree with Arlen—either as to the entertainment value of the television film or as to the presentation of "imperfect truths":

> ... Purely as drama, as entertainment, the production turned out to be a disappoint-
> ment. Laudably attempting to avoid the old Hollywood cliches about American Indians, the
> script backed into another batch of cliches. Chief Joseph ... rarely got beyond the type of
> nobility projected by the Indian in the famous public-service commercial against pollution,
> the one with the tear running down his nose. And, on the other side, the white settlers were
> uniformly sadistic and unpleasant....
> ... Excuses are made for productions that are "almost true" or "nearly true." But
> something cannot be almost true. Falling short of the mark, it is quite simply false. Keeping
> the distinction clear is crucial for at least the semblance of social sanity.[46]

Other reviewers were less critical, but most found some fault with the epic film. The
Variety (April 23, 1975) critic wrote:

> Employing a variation of the documentary approach, the struggle of the last band of In-
> dians who resisted confinement to a reservation emerged on the tube as flat when it should
> have been moving and dramatic.
> ... [T]he Wolper production concentrated too much on the sheer logistics of the trek
> at the expense of the humane aspects....
> The tribal hierarchy was composed of real Indians playing Indians (and doing it well)
> with occasional scraps of folklore registering effectively.... But overall the show lacked the
> wallop the detail seemed to dictate.

Note the reference to "real Indians playing Indians." Actually, although many Native
Americans were used as extras, the only Indians with significant speaking parts were
Linda Redfearn, who portrayed Joseph's wife, Toma, and Vincent St. Cyr, who was a
competent Chief Looking Glass. *New York Daily News* critic Kay Gardella had similar
mixed feelings about the television film (April 14, 1975):

> Provided you can put out of your mind all the great Hollywood movies about America's
> expansion to the West and the plight of the American Indian and accept tonight's ABC
> drama, "I Will Fight No More Forever" about Chief Joseph's 1877 surrender, on the level
> of a television special, the drama will have its moving moments. But it's not as stirring as one
> would expect, considering the subject....
> The photography is good, and the shots of the Mexican countryside where it was filmed
> are lovely, but throughout the presentation one is haunted by the feeling that the actors are
> walking through their parts.
> What the drama suffers from strangely enough, is its noble aim. Instead of setting out
> to tell an exciting story, and using a slice of history as its peg, the obvious intention of the
> producer, Stan Marquilies, was to soften the stereotypes of American Indians and, in a way,
> apologize to them for the past offenses of white men. What we get then is a drama with a soft
> underbelly....
> The battle scenes are more believable than other segments in this so-so Xerox special.

Two years later when the film was released for sale and rental to schools (after winning the 1977 American Film Festival Blue Ribbon—first place—for films on "U.S. History and Culture, Feature Length"), James Manilla wrote in *Film News* (volume 34,
number 5, 1977):

> "I Will Fight No More Forever" is a colorful film and has the full production values of
> a Hollywood feature, plus the awesome grandeur of the Big Sky Country chromatically
> photographed by Jorge Stahl....
> Some moments are dramatically gripping, some scenes are genuinely moving. Perhaps
> by reason of its television origin, the story is slowpaced and somewhat overlong, and the play-
> ing of the secondary parts—both white man and Indian—is not on as expert a level as those
> of its principals....
> ... [However] this film, for both school and adult viewers, with a teacher's guide rich
> in background information, is a vivid lesson.
> Its chief value lies in its accent on human values, family relationships, the proper concern

of a leader for his people, the courage of that leader ... who spoke with his chiefs like the poet he was in his final declaration to them: "From where the sun now stands I will fight no more forever."

Raymond William Stedman, using *I Will Fight No More Forever* as an example, concludes:

> ... For its own purposes television tended to lean toward patronization or historical adjustment in its occasional efforts to uplift the first American.... At several points James Whitmore (as the ubiquitous "Bible-reading" Howard) and a junior officer (Sam Elliott) become so orally entangled in the moral aspects of relentlessly dogging a valiant foe that the courageous Nez Percé families were almost lost sight of by the writers.[47]

Stedman also takes the producers of the film to task for certain "sins of omission":

> ... of the long pursuit's only atrocity—the exhumation and mutilation of Nez Percé casualties by the army's Bannock Indian Scouts. However inconvenient to the Noble Savage message, that outrage happened, some Indians perpetrated it and the moralizing General Howard approved it. It was no worse than many other barbarous actions by whites against Indians through the years. And no reasonable person will condemn an entire race for some dramatized outburst of violence by a single group, when the presentation is balanced. But to conceal or disguise any action that stands in the face of the philosophical message and then to boast of the honesty of your presentation ... is either dishonesty or misguided charity. The Nez Percé, like all other Indians have had enough of both.[48]

Still on balance, *I Will Fight No More Forever* must be considered a milestone in the evolution of the made-for-television Western as it relates to the depiction of Indian-white relations. Viewers must keep in mind, however, that it is a somewhat flawed milestone because of its historical distortions and omissions. One cannot, on the other hand, be so generous in an evaluation of another made-for-television film, *The Legend of Walks Far Woman*.

When actress Raquel Welch was sent the script for *Walks Far Woman* (by a New York agent she did not even know), she was convinced that it was the sort of project she had been waiting for all her professional life. Raquel had always been considered a sex symbol and now she thought she had an opportunity to be taken as a serious actress. Furthermore, as she later explained, this was "a chance to do a serious, sensitive story with some universality, treating Indians as human beings."[49] Director Mel Damski agreed. He described the script (by Evan Hunter) as "sensational," and felt that "This film was a chance to demythologize the American Indian."[50] Great emphasis was placed on the authenticity of the film. A half-Crow who taught Indian studies at a nearby college was brought in as the technical adviser. Furthermore, Welch refused to play her character as a stereotypical Indian stoic, believing the Indians to be "a passionate people." So the Indians in the film do a great deal of smiling and laughing—some of which seemed rather forced.

Shot on location near Billings, Montana, during the summer of 1979, the film was beset with problems from the beginning. Raquel twice landed in the hospital—once for food poisoning and once for a knee injury. When she did not like the first rushes on the film, she had the cinematographer fired. His camera crew then quit. Then she tried to have Damski fired, but the producers, EMI Television, refused. Her leading man, her production manager, her secretary, her makeup man and her hairdresser all quit. Meanwhile, Raquel was working "twelve to fourteen hours a day, six days a week, for almost six weeks, in dusty, broiling, ninety-degree heat—often with mosquitoes so thick that she wore more insect repellent than makeup."[51]

Although *The Legend of Walks Far Woman* was completed in 1979 and shown soon after on British and French television, it remained on the shelf at NBC for almost three years. This was partly due to several changes in the top-level administration of the NBC movie division and the fact that none of the executives who were originally involved in the production pushed to have it shown. They were especially reluctant to schedule the film during a crucial "sweeps" period. Finally, after the three hour film had been cut by 30 minutes, it was decided to air the epic on May 30, 1982, one week after the May sweeps in a carefully selected time slot opposite the tape-delayed Indianapolis 500 auto race.

Raquel, with darkened skin and a long black wig, portrays a Pikuni Blackfoot tribeswomen forced to leave her tribe when she avenges the death of her husband by killing the two braves who had murdered him. She stumbles into an old Sioux and is taken prisoner when he takes her to his village. Treated as an outcast at first, she is accepted into the tribe as a sister after she saves one of the tribesman, Many Scalps, from drowning. She then catches the eye of a friendly half-breed trader named Singer who runs the local trading post and although he proposes marriage after making love to her, she declines. Instead she becomes the wife of Horse's Ghost, a Sioux brave, and bears him a child. Things go badly for Walks Far Woman after the Battle at the Little Big Horn. Her child is killed and when her husband goes insane she is forced to kill him in self-defense. Leaving the Sioux tribe, she at last settles down with Singer. In the final scene she looks back over her eventful life at the age of 102.

Unfortunately, the story sounds better in summary than it looks played out in a 150 minute film, although Raquel does her best. Even Damski was forced to admit that some of her emotional scenes were very good. (In fact, when the filming was completed on the scene in which she gives birth, the crew burst into applause.) She even did most of her own stunts—riding a bucking bronco, sliding downhill, jumping into a river, running a fast race. She often appears far from glamorous—muddied, bloodied and bruised, with her lips cracked and blistered. (At the end of the film, when she is 102, she is wrinkled, trembling, tight-lipped and has stringy gray hair.) Alas, it was all of little consequence in the end. As *TV Guide* writer David Shaw explained:

> . . . what can you say about a "serious" movie that includes such lines as "His spirit may leave his body from time to time." And: "It's getting chilly out. Let's wrap ourselves in your blanket, and you can tell me about yourself."[52]

The critics justifiably crucified the film. Judith Crist, writing in *TV Guide* (May 20, 1982), said:

> Raquel Welch paints a portrait of a proud squaw in "The Legend of Walks Far Woman," based on Colin Stuart's novel, but the pedantic teleplay by Evan Hunter, directed at a snail's pace by Mel Damski, never quite tells us what made the heroine worthy of legend. . . . The action is sparse and the excitement sparser.

Kay Gardella writing in the *New York Daily News*, is even more brutal in her review of May 28, 1982:

> If you can believe Raquel Welch as an Indian, then you're just the person the commercial networks want glued to your TV set nightly. As legend has it, . . . "Legend of Walks Far Woman" has been on the network's shelf for a long time. It's unfortunate that it wasn't left there. It's so bad it's funny . . .
>   . . . I can't pretend to know what Indian women talk about when they're sitting around in a circle, but in this film they get a little bawdy. It's too bad they weren't speaking in an Indian dialect, sparing us a cheap tale.
>   The dialogue in this Montana drama set in 1875 is as flat as the Western plains. It's ridiculous, for instance, to include a line in which Singer asks Walks Far if she can speak

Raquel Welch as the title character in *The Legend of Walks Far Woman*.

English when all the time she's speaking perfect English, which we're expected to believe is Sioux.

"The Legend of Walks Far Woman" is very light drama. So light that it doesn't rate one feather.

A final assessment of *Walks Far Woman* is mixed at best. In terms of its portrayal of Native Americans one can point to the use of a number of Native American actors in supporting roles: George Clutesi is particularly effective in the role of the Old Sioux Grandfather who first befriends Walks Far, and the ever reliable Dehl Berti makes an all too brief appearance as Sitting Bull's envoy. Most of the others (e.g., Gerald Red Elk, Winona Plenty Hoops, Marie Pretty Paint) are relegated to very minor parts. Indeed, the majority of the Indian characters are played by Mexican-Americans.

With respect to the lead character, in spite of her efforts to prevent it, Welch lets too much of her "Hollywood image" come through. Certainly the commercial aspects of her sex symbol status were not lost on the producers. The cover of the video-cassette of *The Legend of Walks Far Woman* marketed by Interglobal Home Video contains an artist's rendition of the upper torso of the film's star, nude from the waist up, with her ample breasts only partially covered by the credits and a few strands of hair! As to the film's entertainment value, the *New York Times* critic, perhaps, said it best: "It's just that the entire story is boring as it trudges through clichés about Indian nobility and the stupid ways of the white man, who does not even know enough to live in portable houses."[53] Alas, Welch, Walks Far Woman, is tangible proof that good intentions and hard work are not always enough.

The controversy and delay surrounding *The Legend of Walks Far Woman* was considerably less than that which erupted over *The Mystic Warrior*. Conceived and produced by David L. Wolper and Stan Margulies, who had been responsible for developing *I Will Fight No More Forever* and the phenomenally successful 12 hour miniseries *Roots*, *Mystic Warrior* had begun as a straight adaptation of an 834 page bestselling novel called *Hanta Yo*. Written by a 65 year old white woman named Ruth Beebe Hill, *Hanta Yo* was a fictional narrative based upon the chronicle kept on tanned hide by a member of the Mahto band of the Teton Sioux. Hill's story followed the tribe from 1794 to 1835 in its seasonal moves across the plains. She related the tale of two families, and in particular, the close friendship between Ahbleza and Tonweya, the son of a warrior-leader and the son of a hunter. Ahbleza, reflective and strong-willed, would not accept unquestioningly the rituals handed down to him, and could not comprehend his father's single-minded pursuit of the warrior ideal. He believed that he must discover for himself, through a vision-quest with Tonweya and his own solitary participation in the most rigorous of the tribe's purification ceremonies, the meaning of his life and how he should serve his people. While relating the story of the trials and suffering Ahbleza must endure to become leader of his tribe, the book provided detailed descriptions of Indian rituals, intertribal warfare, family relationships and the mystical religious experiences of the Sioux.

Author Hill's fascination with Indians dated back to her childhood in Cleveland, Ohio. Her first published story was about Indians and won an essay contest sponsored by *The Cleveland Plain Dealer* when she was 9 years old. She began researching *Hanta Yo* (a Sioux term meaning "clear the way") in 1949, by interviewing Indians during a cross-country trip. Later, she spent nearly three years reading everything she could find about Indians in the UCLA library. During the summers she did field research wandering among buffaloes on a range in Montana and observing grizzlies in Alaska.

In 1963, Hill met Chunksa Yuha, a full-blooded Sioux who had been looking for a writer to help him record the stories he had been told about his ancestors. Hill showed Yuha a 2000 page manuscript based on her interpretation of the surviving records of a band of Teton Sioux, depicting each year's most outstanding event on tanned hide. Yuha persuaded her that she could not convey a true sense of Indian consciousness unless she learned the Sioux language. First they translated Hill's manuscript into the Sioux dialects in use around 1800, then they translated the Sioux back into English based on Webster's 1806 dictionary. Some non–Indian concepts (for which their were no Sioux equivalents) had to be deleted from the narrative. In addition, natural phenomena like "snow" was replaced by descriptive phrases—"falling softly as the owl flies."[54] Hill claimed in a *Newsweek* interview that she did not set out to write a popular, easily readable story. On the contrary, she explained,

> I worked hard to make sure that the book was so dry, so repetitious that it would be totally alien to the jet world. This is a book written in Indian time. The white man is controlled by watches. With the Indian, time is as wide as the day. The book is not "Ruth Hill's view." It is an *Indian* story.[55]

When the book was first published by Doubleday in 1979, it drew both rave accolades and damning criticism. Among the most favorable reviews was one written by Dorothy Wickendeen for *The New Republic* (February 17, 1979):

> "Hanta Yo" is not a book to read quickly and forget. To make your way through this remarkable historical narrative you need the kind of patience, wonder and respect that Ruth Beebe Hill brought to its construction . . . the result is a narrative whose language is surprisingly direct, vital and evocative. . . .
>
> Possessing an artist's eye for detail, Hill delicately depicts the centrality of gesture, symbolism and ritual in this culture. . . . Implicitly, the unassuming dignity of the Dakota begins to emerge.
>
> In writing a book of this sort, one risks lapsing into a romantic vision of the displaced culture. . . . To a large extent Hill avoids this trap. To be sure, her white traders are presented as coarse, exploitative antagonists, mindless oafs in comparison to the lithe, spiritually intense and soft-spoken Dakota. And the trader's insidious influence comes to a climax in the final tragic scenes, when they bring chaos to the Mahto by introducing them to firearms and liquor. Still, the whiteman is not solely responsible for the growing internal disputes among the Mahto, nor are the Indians simply noble savages. The band has its own share of power-hungry individuals, its own petty disputes and rivalries, and a deeply ingrained warrior ethic that condones theft and bloodshed as a means of gaining predominance over other tribes. Hill is not reluctant to confront these issues or to deal realistically with their moral consequences. . . .
>
> . . . [T]he overall effect is moving and the picture of this people authentic and carefully rendered.

Writing in *The Nation* (April 28, 1979), Raymond J. DeMallie looked at the novel from a very different perspective:

> . . . Ruth Beebe Hill has invented this Lakota world with the aid of a mysterious Sioux collaborator named Chunksa Yuha . . . she chooses to fabricate an Indian existence as she would like it to have been—a primitive emotional paradise in which every character's individuality shines undiminished by the restraints of society.
>
> Historians, anthropologists and linguists can find hundreds of specific points with which to quarrel. . . . [e.g.] the misleading implications that the Dakota suddenly moved westward from the Mississippi valley in 1750, invented ceremonies involving oral sex and sodomy between men, both of which are contrary to Lakota ethnography; the unfounded assertion that war captives were sodomized by their captors; . . . the indefensible statement that words such as admit, assume, because, believe, end, forget, forgive and many others have no comparable concepts in the Dakota language. To correct the errors of "Hanta Yo" would amount to writing a full-scale historical ethnography of the Sioux. . . .
>
> But the truly fraudulent aspect of the novel is the false and pernicious sense of historical accuracy it imparts to the unknowing reader . . . [Furthermore] the book is surely no compliment to Native Americans. . . .
>
> . . . Far from bringing the reader close to the Lakota sense of the world, the convoluted linguistic tricks and the overuse of Lakota terms are reminiscent of the sing-song verse in "The Song of Hiawatha."
>
> Beyond the nearly impenetrable style , the message of "Hanta Yo" is a damaging one for Native Americans. Greed, envy, lust, love, sex, hate, murder, torture—every imaginable passion of the unfettered, childlike and noble savages runs wild in the rambling narrative. . . .
>
> . . . Hill uses Indian materials to comment on America. She characterizes the fierce individualism that her book glorifies as "the spiritual source of not only the American Indian but of America itself." She ignores the strongly cooperative, integrative aspects of traditional tribal life and glorifies instead the individuality of the warrior and hunter. Her characters are all societal misfits, forsaking sex, life, marriage, happiness, religion or life itself in an incessant mystical quest after individual self-expression.

A book that could produce this much controversy was bound to provoke those opposed to what they considered to be Hill's heretical ideas when adapted for a television miniseries. After all, it might well be seen by millions more people than read the book.

Still, optimism was high at ABC when, on February 27, 1979, they threw a big, fancy party to announce that the same team that produced the miniseries *Roots*, which had broken every ratings record (displacing *Gone with the Wind* as television's all-time biggest draw) and then broken those records with the 14 hour *Roots* sequel had acquired the rights to *Hanta Yo*. Wolper and Margulies believed that they had "lucked into a new piece of material so rich, so relevant, so long-neglected, and yet so germane to the American experience that it made Alex Haley's contribution seem modest by comparison." Wolper regarded *Hanta Yo* as "a masterpiece." "This epic book," he later wrote, "makes every other book about Indians seem shallow and out of date."[56] Wolper hired Sterling Silliphant, the well known screenwriter, to prepare the "bible" (an exhaustive catalogue of characters and background details from which all subsequent scripts are to be written) for the series.

Then came a storm of protest from Indian academicians, anthropologists, activists, and intellectuals, including spokespersons for the Black Hills Treaty Council, the Pine Ridge Sioux Tribal Council, the National Advisory Council on Indian Education, and the American Indian Historical Society. The Lakota Studies Department of Sinte Gleska College in Rosebud, South Dakota, prepared a long commentary challenging the novel on numerous factual points. A group of Indians led by Jo-Allen Archambault, an Oakland anthropologist, and Lois Red Elk, a Los Angeles activist, formed "The Ad Hoc Committee to Stop Hanta Yo." Claiming that the book was "demeaning, insulting and offensive" to the Indian people, the group demanded that the proposed miniseries be killed. Archambault, a former member of the Standing Rock Sioux Tribe in North Dakota, explained:

> Sioux people who are knowledgeable about their culture and language find the book's portrayal to be insulting, offensive, pornographic, and occasionally pathetic. Other tribal members are outraged by passages in the story referring to the savagery of the Sioux. No one's objecting to what did happen—we tortured, we ate dogs. What we're objecting to is what didn't happen.[57]

A $2 million class-action suit was filed and pickets followed author Hill around the university lecture circuit carrying signs saying "Hill Has a Tonto Complex" and "Hill Speaks with Forked Tongue." The litigation sought to block production of any television show based on *Hanta Yo*. Sioux activists also tried to force the book out of bookstores and libraries. Archie Lame Deer, the chief and spiritual leader of one of the Lakota Sioux tribes, claimed that the book was 90 to 95 percent inaccurate. What particularly disturbed Lame Deer were the homosexual scenes and an incident where a mother gave birth and then ate part of the placenta. A *Hanta Yo* television series, he charged "would set us back ten years and encourage the false idea that we are savages."[58] Among those helping the Sioux argue their case was Max Gail, a non–Indian who starred as the cop Wojo in ABC's *Barney Miller* series.

Vine Deloria, Jr., the Native American author of *Custer Died for Your Sins*, said *Hanta Yo* "did not deserve to be called a book," but was rather little more than "a pile of typing." Adding that Hill was ethnologically illiterate, Deloria said in his review for *The Native People* (May 23, 1980):

> She thinks there were no Indians after 1830 .... [Her novel] is so preposterous in its presuppositions that no competent scholar would dream it possible that the monstrosity would see the light of day.[59]

Hill answered the attacks on her work by asserting that she

> ... was in touch with 700 Indians—Sioux, Kiowa, Omaha, Cheyenne, even Navaho, you name it—and I showed many what I had written.[60]

Most of the material, she insisted, was verified by at least four sources. In fact some Native American scholars, including Barbara Adams, an Oglala Sioux who taught Indian Studies at Skagit Valley College in Mount Vernon, Washington, defended the book.

Hill's critics also charged that Chunksa Yuha was a fraud—that he was in fact an Episcopal deacon's son named Lorenzo Blacksmith, who had lived most of his life off the reservation in places like Seattle and the San Fernando Valley. Hill admitted that Chunksa's name was Blacksmith but contended that it was imposed on her collaborator's father by the Bureau of Indian Affairs and that Chunksa had spent all of his formative years being steeped in tribal history. Probably what angered Native Americans most about Hill's work was the fact that not only were people taking her seriously, they were viewing her as an expert. Thus she was placed in the awkward position of seeming to explain the Indians to themselves.

Meanwhile, ABC quietly shelved the project while it considered what to do. Wolper wanted to go ahead, but he also wanted his film to be accurate, so he and Margulies sought the cooperation of the Oglala Lakota tribe. At first the Tribal Council at the Pine Ridge Indian Reservation in South Dakota refused to even read the first draft of the screenplay which had been written by Jeb Rosebrook. Lois Red Elk informed the wire services that the Indians would "pursue every avenue of protest, including going out to the film locations and trying to stop the filming."[61] To placate such opposition, Wolper agreed to hire numerous Sioux consultants, crew members and actors for the miniseries. He even held out the possibility of filming on tribal land for a fat location fee. Furthermore, he promised that he would submit all scripts to the Lakota Council for advance approval before filming.

In 1982 ABC agreed to revive the project and coproducer Margulies hired Tim Giago, publisher and editor of *The Lakota Times* in South Dakota, to serve as liaison between the filmmakers and the tribe to insure as much accuracy as possible. Giago in turn consulted regularly with the tribal elders and historians. (For his services, Giago reportedly received $5000.[62]) Wolper in effect disowned the novel *Hanta Yo*. Henceforth the film would be known as *The Mystic Warrior* and the book upon which he had once lavished praise would now be just one of the sources from which the film would be taken. (When she objected, Ruth Beebe Hill was barred from the set.) This gave the producer the license to include (or exclude) anything he wanted. The nine hour running time was reduced to five (the three generations of the Mahto band that gave the novel its "epic" quality now became one) and the location filming was moved from beautiful Alberta, Canada, to the much less expensive (and less scenic) New Mexico. (The filming was eventually done just an hour from the studio in Thousand Oaks, California.) In casting the film, Wolper and Margulies rejected Hollywood's miniseries "regulars" in favor of relatively unknown actors, most of whom bore at least some Indian blood.

Margulies said that of the 50 principal actors, only two had no Indian blood. The two leads, Ahbleza and Heyatawin, were both played by Native Americans, Robert Beltran and Devon Ericson, and Will Sampson made a cameo appearance as Wambli. Sonny Skyhawk was Heyatawin's father. The experienced Nick Ramus (who had played a continuing Indian role in *The Chisholms*) was given the key part of Ahbleza's father, Chief Olepi. Ramus was of part Blackfoot Indian descent. Victoria Racimo, who was also part Native American (and a veteran of *The Chisholms*), was cast as Ahbleza's mother, Napewaste. Paul Freeman was assigned the day-to-day production chores and Richard T. Heffron was hired to direct. By October 1982, the filming of *The Mystic Warrior* was at last underway. In shaping his final screenplay, Rosebrook followed the basic plot of Hill's novel, but under pressure from the Sioux he altered some details. Margulies later explained:

> In doing our research, we learned certain things. For instance, we found out about a very
> elaborate procedure for banishing someone from the tribe. We were fascinated by it and
> added it to the story.[63]

Giago also exerted some influence in shaping the script. Concerning the Indian practice of polygamy, Giago pointed out:

> When the chief, Olepi, takes a second wife, it was originally written that his first wife
> was livid with jealousy. I told them they were way off base because this was a very common
> practice among the Sioux. They would not give up the jealousy entirely, but they rewrote it
> that the first wife was angry because the second wife was not doing her share of the work.
> It was a compromise.[64]

In general, the producers did their best to make certain that the film was accurate
in its depiction of Indian customs, wardrobe, settings and makeup. George Amiott from
the Lakota tribe and George American Horse, who had worked on other Hollywood films
about Indians, acted as technical advisers on location. Finally the project was finished and
ABC, showing renewed confidence, scheduled *The Mystic Warrior* for the May sweeps.
Wolper and Margulies made no apologies for their creation.[65] A public screening was held
in Rapid City, South Dakota, for the Oglala Lakota Sioux tribe several weeks before the
film was to be broadcast. Most of the 100 Lakotas who attended praised its authenticity.
Speaking for the majority, Robert Fast Horse, director of national resources for the tribe,
said:

> I was definitely pleased. The film presented the Lakotas in a non-stereotypic way. Usually
> Indians are shown either as drunken, lazy, stupid figures or as noble savages.[66]

Giago was also happy with the outcome:

> There were slight things that were wrong with the film, but at the end of the screening
> . . . my own tribe stood up and applauded. That was the acid test. I felt vindicated for having
> hung in there all those years.[67]

Anthropologist Archambault, however, was not satisfied:

> It's still a bunch of Hollywood pap. They're still having us speak Hiawatha English, as
> if we really walked around saying "Many horses have I."[68]

And what did the television critics think of *The Mystic Warrior*? Most of the reviews
included both positive and negative comments. For example, *Variety* (May 23, 1984)
said:

> . . . The depiction of Indian life as more complex than usually portrayed was an in-
> teresting plus, but the tale of Ahbleza confronting his ultimate destiny was strangely devoid
> of dramatic intensity. . . .
> . . . The Sunday episode moved painstakingly slow. . . . The mystical visions and the
> methods of their inducement provided the miniseries' most provocative moments. . . .
> The trouble was not in the performing but seemingly in a script that was more anxious
> to make a case for the Indian way of life than in dramatic tension. The tragic finale, when
> it came, seemed decidedly limp, considering what the viewer had been subjected to in the
> prolonged buildup to that moment. . . .
> What was missing was the wallop that moved the audience to comprehension of the
> potential import of Ahbleza's quest.

Harry F. Waters wrote in *Newsweek* (May 21, 1984):

> . . . "The Mystic Warrior" resembles, by disconcerting turn, nothing ever before
> presented on television and something decidedly familiar. To begin with the bad news, the

epic . . . suffers from a language blight approaching sheer camp. . . . When not trafficking in the cute, the Sioux-speak heard here lists toward obtusity. . . . Some of the acting doesn't help. Robert Beltran manages only a fitfully interesting evocation of the warrior-protagonist, while Devon Ericson, as his favorite maiden, looks like Ali McGraw but emotes like Tug McGraw.

Happily . . . director Richard Heffron has imbued the film with a hauntingly mystical aura: silent love scenes unfold like soft-focus poetry and violent action sequences take on a startlingly eerie beauty. In the most entrancing passage, a pair of Sioux youths puff the forbidden "sacred pipe" and soar off on a hallucinogenic flight across the evening sky's constellations, which assume through animation the deer, horse and bear shapes of Indian legend. In short, "The Mystic Warrior" transports us to a place we've never imagined, a dreamy panorama of strife and solitude viewed as if through a shaman's vision. Gerald Fried's dazzling musical score, with its suggestions of Indian, Oriental and Gregorian chants, also helps atone for the words that fail.

Writing on May 18, 1984, John J. O'Connor of the *New York Times* was also critical:

> . . . "The Mystic Warrior" is nothing if not careful and almost obsequiously reverent. However, unlike the 1975 television biography of Chief Joseph of the Nez Percé Indians in "I Will Fight No More Forever," . . . the new film does not gloss over key historical facts that might prove embarrassing to American Indians, such as raids in which innocent whites were killed. A preface solemnly explains: "This is the story of an original people, the Mahto band of the Teton Sioux. They live as one with the land as their grandfathers have for centuries, finding beauty and mystery in sky, earth and all creatures."
>
> . . . The sociological ambitions are admirable, but dramatic tensions too often go distressingly slack.
>
> Even the vaunted authenticity occasionally becomes suspect. The language sounds pompously formal, evidently somebody's idea of dignified. . . . And some of the casting is unconvincing, notably Devon Ericson as the hero's wife. Miss Ericson looks like Ali MacGraw with a tan.
>
> The shame of it all is that "Hanta Yo" was a promising candidate for dramatization. Now with "The Mystic Warrior," the American Indian is likely to remain the truly invisible man of television for at least another decade.

Jennifer Regan, writing in the *New York Post* (May 18, 1984), was most favorably impressed by the miniseries:

> "The Mystic Warrior," ABC's last miniseries of the season, is one more version of how our native son, the American Indian, lived proud and free before the white man drove him off his lands and into the sunset.
>
> . . . [It] has a slow dreamy quality that at first risks being boring. Sticking close to the rich details of ritual and ceremonies the Mahto tribe lived by, there is so little plotline that, with its scant dialogue and musical accompaniment of chants, howls and chorales [besides the usual tom-toms], it could almost qualify as an oratorio.
>
> There's a National Geographic appearance to the stark settings that make it seem more educational than entertaining. . . . Besides the painstaking care to be authentic, there's a lot of weird magic going on. . . .
>
> In one scene, the magic goes a bit too far towards Star Wars fantasy when young braves soar in the galaxies among objects as unrelated as U.F.O.'s and Bambi. . . .
>
> But real-life events—deaths and battles, tests of loyalty and faith (all accompanied by the consistently inventive score)—heighten the drama, culminating in the inevitable arrival of the white trader with the barrel of fire water. . . .
>
> This is serious stuff, treated in an original manner. You have to let it cast its spell to appreciate the care with which this production was put together. . . .
>
> . . . [T]he actors keep the spirit of authenticity alive. Beautiful and surprising are many of the details from Indian life. . . .
>
> You might think you've seen all there is to see about life in the teepee and home on the range, but this pre-white man Indian passion play is a moving documentary-cum-personality of a lost civilization at the peak of its achievement and pride.

The Mystic Warrior earned an Emmy Award for Dino Ganziano for hair styling and Emmy nominations for Gerald Fried for his magnificent score and for the costume designers and makeup artists. In the more significant categories of acting, directing, and cinematography, however, the series was completely overlooked. Despite the controversy it provoked, *The Mystic Warrior* was clearly a landmark presentation in the depiction of Native American culture. With all its shortcomings, the series was unique in involving Indian input in nearly every stage of its production. The producers, albeit under considerable pressure from the Indian community, made a genuine effort to involve Native Americans in the technical as well as cultural aspects of its development. Furthermore, no other film, before or since, has captured so well the ethereal, mystical nature of the Native American religious experience.

That *The Mystic Warrior* is largely based on the work of a white woman who traces her ancestors back to the Mayflower should not detract from its significance. The five hour miniseries represents a considerable step forward in television's portrayal of Indians from the days of *Wagon Train, Daniel Boone* and *Custer*. Here more than in any other television production, Native Americans are depicted as human beings—with a wide range of subtle shadings in character and emotion that separate them from traditional stereotypical film Indians.

Native Americans were to play yet another key role in a made-for-television miniseries. *Son of the Morning Star*, based on Evan S. Connell's best-selling biography, was adapted for television by Academy Award–winning screenwriter Melissa Mathison (*ET: The Extraterrestrial*, 1982). The four-hour, two-part film traced the military career of George Armstrong Custer (who was given the name "Son of the Morning Star who Attacks at Dawn" by his Indian Scouts) in the West and his crucial role in the U.S. government's brutal war of attrition against the Indians. The Sioux Indians had already been displaced by settlers moving west and had made a treaty with the government, giving them the rights to the Black Hills in South Dakota. However, after gold was discovered in the Black Hills, President Ulysses S. Grant chose to ignore the treaty. He permitted white miners to stampede into the region and ordered that the Indians be moved out. Custer, having been recently court-martialed, saw the removal of the rebellious Indians as an opportunity to redeem himself (and possibly promote his candidacy for the Democratic presidential nomination).

On June 25, 1876, under a sweltering sky on a grassy ridge near the Little Big Horn River (or the Greasy Grass River, as the Indians called it) in Montana Territory, Custer and 265 officers and men of the Seventh Cavalry perished in one of the most famous disasters in U.S. military history. Custer's forces had ridden into the midst of one of the largest-ever Indian gatherings, perhaps several thousand, convened under the leadership of Chief Sitting Bull, Crazy Horse and Gall. Custer's Indian scouts had suggested their number, but he had refused to believe them. Although the Indian forces won on the battlefield, their victory, when placed in the greater context of their struggle to retain their land and culture in the face of white westward expansion, was a great disaster. That confrontation was followed by death, exile, humiliation, relentless pursuit, and betrayal.

Up until the civil rights movement of the sixties, Custer's last stand was presented in history textbooks as a great moment in American history, part of "the then-standard scenario of military heroes battling perfidious 'savages'." Then, as Native Americans became caught up in the movement for equal rights, that view began to change. Connell's extensively researched book published in 1984 represents a culmination of that revisionist view of American history. As summed up by one Indian observer, "It was no massacre.

Them soldiers were stupid. They rode to their deaths."[69] As *New York Times* television critic John J. O'Connor put it:

> ... Quite dramatically, the terrorizing "savages" of the relatively recent past, familiar villains of Hollywood's old cowboy movies, have become today's "Native Americans," whose continuing grievances seem on the verge of becoming the most fashionable social cause of the 1990's.
>
> Kevin Costner's acclaimed film "Dances With Wolves" certainly won't hurt the American Indian cause. Neither will television's "Son of the Morning Star," which leaves Crazy Horse looking far more noble than not only Custer but also President Ulysses S. Grant and his close advisers.[70]

A statement precedes the opening credits verifying that "Tonight's film is a dramatization of Evan S. Connell's book 'Son of the Morning Star' and other historical accounts." It is clear that the film was far more faithful to Connell's highly acclaimed book than *The Mystic Warrior* was to *Hanta Yo*. It must be noted, however, that *Son of the Morning Star* when first published in 1984 had generated little controversy. Indeed lavish praise had been heaped upon Connell's study of Custer at the Little Bighorn:

> Connell has produced a new American classic. — *Time Magazine*
>
> In a masterly display of literary structure, Connell has drawn from hundreds of pertinent historical accounts and created the modern equivalent of a biblical work of witness although "Son of the Morning Star" is, in fact, a work of many witnesses. — *The Los Angeles Times*
>
> Mr. Connell, who has exceptional skill in presenting characters, action, and visual detail, brings all these long-gone people excitingly back to life for the instruction and entertainment of the reader. — *The Atlantic Monthly*
>
> This is — a masterpiece.... The superiority of "Son of the Morning Star" is in the telling; the book is great because of the way it is written, not just what it includes. — *The Dallas Morning News*

In keeping with the book's emphasis, the film presents official policies toward the Indians as being, almost without exception, reprehensible. For example, a proposal to make Indians citizens is rejected by President Grant because "you want to hold them collectively, not individually" accountable. Later, a top government official is heard saying, "We've been killing Indians for hundreds of years—let's get it over with."

The film focuses attention on the two chief protagonists of the confrontation at the Little Bighorn—Custer and Crazy Horse, military leader of the Oglala subdivision of the Teton Sioux. Perhaps in deference to the title of the production, much more of the film is devoted to Custer (Gary Cole) than to his native American enemies. He is depicted as a controversial commander, a notoriously tough soldier, and a devoted husband. He is both contemptuous of the Indians and curious about their way of life. In O'Connor's words he was "a fairly representative creature of his times."[71] Crazy Horse, meanwhile, is shown in flashbacks as a 14 year old youth. After his family is attacked by soldiers while he watched helplessly, the boy has a vision of a warrior riding out of a lake "impervious to weapons and nature." By 1866, he is already a leader, battling white men who believe that, as one observer explains, "No Indians have any rights that a white man need respect." Ironically, the two adversaries, only a year apart in age, each behave as if they are invincible and immortal.

The first two hours of *Son of the Morning Star*, broadcast over ABC on Sunday, February 3, 1991, present in some detail the background events which led with apparent inevitability to the bloody battle at the Little Bighorn. The second two hours, broadcast the following evening, first depict, in elaborate detail, preparations for the battle—from both the soldiers' and Indians' point of view—and then the battle itself, filling nearly half

Rodney Grant—here depicted as Wind in His Hair in the theatrical release *Dances with Wolves*—played Crazy Horse in *Son of the Morning Star*.

of the two hours and re-enacted with vivid realism and great attention to detail. Filming was done on location less than forty miles from the actual site of the battle near Montana's Little Bighorn. A casting search was conducted on seven reservations to find Native Americans to play the Plains Indians.

Fresh from his acclaimed performance as Wind in His Hair in Kevin Costner's Academy Award-winning film, *Dances with Wolves* (1990), Rodney A. Grant was selected for the key role of Crazy Horse. Grant grew up on an Omaha Indian reservation in northeastern Nebraska. As a young man, Grant was not immune to the lure of drugs and alcohol—two of the most serious problems facing youth living on reservations. At 20, he broke into a liquor store and as a result spent two days in the Nebraska jail. Later he spent time in an alcoholic rehabilitation center and now speaks to Indian groups about alcohol and drug abuse. Grant decided to become an actor in the late eighties while watching a Western on television, an obscure movie called *Eagle Wing*. He later explained:

> Sam Waterson played an Indian guy. I really liked him in "The Killing Fields," but here he was, riding in a tattered breechcloth. It blew my mind. I thought, "What is this? . . . I'm going to Los Angeles."[72]

He promptly quit his job as a meatpacker in Macy, Nebraska, and went to Hollywood. His first job was a small role in *War Party* (1988) followed by some stunt work in *Powwow Highway* (1989). Then the roles dried up. Grant heard all the typical excuses:

> There are no Native Americans who can act. Mainstream audiences don't want to see movies about Native American life. People won't relate to Native American characters unless they're played by big, white Hollywood stars wearing makeup.[73]

Then came *Dances with Wolves*.

Although Grant was pleased with the outcome of Costner's film (which he credits to the director's "vision and commitment"), he was less satisfied with his work in *Son of the Morning Star*. Noting that Crazy Horse got considerably less screen time than Custer, Grant asserted:

> It's just a glorification of Custer. The Indians are there just to make background noise.[74]
> In the long run, [Crazy Horse] is not going to be seen favorably enough. They don't show enough of his homelife . . . his family. You see Custer with his wife, but there's no time to show that for Crazy Horse.
> In general, how Indians are portrayed in the movies often depends on the editing. And "Son of the Morning Star" seems to be no exception. Whenever a cut has been made, it's the Indians who seem to have lost their lines and Custer who emerges dominant. I've been getting these script updates dealing with Custer and the fight, and it's: "Omit scene this-or-that"—all to do with the Indians.[75]

David Schildt, a 37-year-old Native American actor and rodeo rider, cast as one of Custer's Indian scouts, also struggled with alcohol problems on the reservation. He recalls spending years trying to get away from the reservation mentality that he believes was the end result of Custer's mission to eradicate the Indians. He elaborated in an interview in *TV Guide*:

> My father used to come home drunk all the time. Later I found myself following in [his] footsteps. Alcohol and drug abuse affects 100 percent of the reservations.[76]

Schildt's solution was to leave home, get himself a good education and eventually give up drinking. When asked if he would ever return to the reservation, he responded, "Never!" Schildt believes that Hollywood's depiction of Indians "is a lot better now than it ever was," but he resents the fact that such recent films as *War Party* still used whites to play some Native Americans.

Other Native Americans given speaking roles in *Son of the Morning Star* include Floyd Red Crow Westerman as Sitting Bull, George American Horse as Stone Forehead, and Sheldon Wolfchild as Bloody Knife. A number of the people who had worked on *Dances with Wolves* were also involved in the production of *Son of the Morning Star*. Doris Leader Charge served as the Sioux language and cultural adviser and with teacher Albert White Hat translated the script into Lakota, the language of the Sioux. They also taught some of the Indian actors to speak in the tongues of the four major tribes involved in the battle (Arikara, Cheyenne, Crow and Sioux).

Cathy Smith, a 19th century Plains Indian expert and renowned Indian beading and quilt artist, also worked on both films. Until *Dances with Wolves* she had spent her entire life restoring Indian artifacts for galleries, museums, and private collections. The films gave Smith and her fellow consultant Larry Belitz the chance to reveal the beauty of

Sioux culture to a mass audience. Smith also checked the costumes and sets for historical accuracy. Smith operates a restoration and reproduction business out of her Santa Fe home and had never before worked on a film. She was referred to *Dances'* costume designer, Elsa Zamparelli, by word of mouth. In making the costumes, Smith used traditional Lakota skills, including brain tanning (in which buffalo brains are rubbed on skins to soften them), beading (using antique beads from Venice made by the original manufacturers of glass "tradebeads" like those that the 19th century Indians traded for), and affixing porcupine quills to costumes. In addition, she advised the makeup artist on Sioux war paint, like that worn by Rodney Grant.[77]

In a significant departure from Connell's book, the screenplay utilizes two narrators, which gives the production stylistic originality and provides greater insight into the Native American's perspective of these events (one of the narrators is an Indian woman named Kate Bighead—and the other is Custer's wife Libby). Libby explains the unfolding drama from the viewpoint of a white officer's wife, while Kate presents the opposing attitude of a Native American likewise caught up in events beyond her power to control. Each woman's (Rosanna Arquette as Libby and folksinger Buffy Sainte-Marie as the voice of Kate) narration complements—and often contradicts—the other's. As television critic Ken Tucker described it, "The pain in their voices dramatizes the agony of this period in our history as effectively as everything on the screen."[78]

Kate Bighead appears only briefly in the final chapter of the book. She is described as "a Northern Cheyenne women" who explained in sign language her experiences when living as a young woman with "the southern branch of the tribe in Oklahoma." Present at the Washita Massacre, Kate saw Custer attack the village of Black Kettle. Later, she saw her cousin, Me-o-tzi, occasionally go riding with Custer. Me-o-tzi claimed that Custer was her husband and "had promised to come back for her."[79] Kate had also visited the Little Bighorn site shortly after the battle had ended. All of her comments were recorded by a Dr. Thomas Marquis, who had learned sign language while working as a government doctor on the Cheyenne reservation. These accounts were later published and studied by Connell while researching his book. Scriptwriter Mathison imaginatively put some of the most moving and descriptive narration into the mouth of Kate Bighead's off-screen voice:

> I was very young the first time I saw him. He sat on his horse. He had a large nose, deep set blue eyes and light hair that was long and wavy. I admired him. All of the Cheyenne women talked of him as being a fine looking man.... Through almost forty years, many a time I thought of that handsome man I first saw in the South. We Cheyenne called him ... "Yellow Hair." The Arikara called him "Creeping Panther Who Comes in the Night." The Crow called him "Son of the Morning Star Who Attacks at Dawn." I remember him as something bad....
>
> ... [Crazy Horse] felt destined to protect his people from the white man. The white people had been moving west for years—cutting roads, pushing the Indians before them. By 1866 barely an Indian nation in America was living on the land it was born to. The Indians did not intend to move further....
>
> The Indian people began to long for a separate America. The reservation system was a terrible sadness. I remember that the men drank; the women cried; the children went to school. As Crazy Horse and Sitting Bull resisted, so did many others. The number of hostiles grew.
>
> I was a young woman that winter [1875-76]. I had come to the camp with Crazy Horse after my village had been attacked and burned. Crazy Horse took us with him. Together we traveled North to join Sitting Bull. The tribal nations grew larger and larger while we traveled from place to place.... The white man brought us together....
>
> Sitting Bull gathered the old people and the women and the children. He cried to his

warriors—"Take courage. It is a good day to die!" The bluecoats attacked the Hunkpapa circle at the end of the village, a good two miles from our Cheyenne camp. In all the camps there was great excitement. Warriors kept going, going, going! I wanted to go too. Anger was our best weapon that day. . . .

[Later, when Kate visited the battlefield] we recognized him, even though his hair was short and his face dirty. A Lakota warrior came to cut him. The Cheyenne women pleaded for Custer. They said he was a relative—the husband of Me-o-tzi. The warrior only took a fingertip. The women punctured his ears with their sewing awls. They did this so that he would hear better. He had promised never again to make war on the Cheyennes. And we had promised his death if he did. He forgot his promise. He did not remember our words. In the next life he should hear us better. . . .

My people traveled with Crazy Horse. We were pushed into the Big Horn Mountains and then down into the Powder River Country. We froze. We starved. The white man kept coming. . . .

They called it Custer's last stand, but it was not his—it was ours.

In a kind of "postscript," *Son of the Morning Star* concludes with the surrender of Crazy Horse six months later to the United States authorities. He is shown being bayonetted by a soldier while his arms are held by a jealous rival warrior. Neither Crazy Horse nor Custer had been invincible or immortal, after all.

Despite all the efforts taken by director Mike Robe to accurately depict Native American culture, many of the Indians working on the film were unhappy with the overall result. As reporter Stephen Galloway described the situation for *TV Guide*:

> . . . little by little, the Native Americans on the set have come to resent the intrusion of "Custer's" presence among them. "Custer's still the hero," one of the Indians complains in a quiet, private moment. "Things don't change."
> . . . [A]s they see it, they're playing second fiddles in a story whose hero they detest. For these actors, the legacy of Custer is felt to this day—and their resentment of him can be detected, simmering right under the surface at all times during the shoot.[80]

Still, some Native Americans after viewing *Son of the Morning Star*, were favorably impressed. Faith Smith, a Northern Wisconsin Chippewa and president of the Native American Educational Services in Chicago, together with a group of her colleagues, was given a sneak preview of the film several days before it was broadcast. She later told Kenneth R. Clark of *The Chicago Tribune* that she was pleasantly surprised. "We were really prepared to hate it, but the people liked it," she said. "They felt it dealt with the issues and that it was fair. There was nothing that was particularly jarring."

Most of the critics also liked *Son of the Morning Star*. Judith Crist, writing for *TV Guide* (February 2, 1991), called it "a big, brawny, but flawed accounting of a man who continues to fascinate and explain America." She gave the film three stars primarily on the strength of the second segment, which "delves into the politics of the Indian wars and the ways and symbolism of the Plains people." In the same issue, of *TV Guide*, Paul Andrew Hutton, author of *The Custer Reader* (published by the University of Nebraska Press), after tracing the fascination of the film industry for Custer's last stand, said:

> ABC's "Son of the Morning Star," based on Evan S. Connell's 1984 bestseller, should restore this compelling figure to his proper place in history as a brave but driven soldier marked by compelling contradictions. . . .
> Rodney A. Grant is resplendent as Crazy Horse. The TV-movie, for the most part, is rigidly faithful to history and quite sensitive to the plight of the Indians. The Battle of the Little Bighorn, produced here on an epic scale, is by far the most accurate version ever filmed—though it undoubtedly will not be the last.[81]

Ken Tucker (*Entertainment Weekly*) gave the film an "A–" rating and explained:

> ABC's "Son of the Morning Star" is a big, chancy, expensive miniseries, the kind of first-rate film-making for TV that hasn't been done since—well, since "Lonesome Dove" first aired in February 1989....
> ... [T]his version ... attempts to do right by the Indians. We learn a lot more about the plight of Native Americans in the late 19th century than we have in any other telling of the Custer legend.[82]

Matt Roush, *USA Today*'s resident television critic, was likewise impressed:

> "Son of the Morning Star" is an epic of irony, an anti-epic, an impressive cinematic clash of myth-making and legend-deflating.
> Anytime you begin to feel manipulated by Mike Robe's stirring direction or Craig Safan's mournful score, Melissa Mathison's intriguingly double-edged script gives you pause....
> Arquette's tear-swollen account of her husband's heroism is juxtaposed with Buffy Sainte Marie's plaintive readings from an Indian woman's point of view. It's a provocative way of viewing valor as vain glory....
> ... What makes "Morning Star" so effective is the way it cuts through the haze of history, and dares not to make simplistic conclusions.

Son of the Morning Star clearly continues the progress initiated in *The Mystic Warrior*—of involving Native Americans not only in key acting roles, but as technical consultants and extras. That the production was sympathetic to the plight of the Indians is not in dispute. A legitimate case that the Indians were short-changed in screen time might be made, however. For example, although he was one of the principal protagonists in the battle of the Little Bighorn, Gall, chief of the Hunkpapa Sioux, is barely mentioned. This is not only a glaring historical omission, it also could be viewed as an insult to the Indian people, since Gall was considered "to be one of the greatest men of his nation."[83] After the treaty of 1868 that created the reservation system for certain Sioux tribes in the Black Hills and Montana, Gall allied himself with the hostile element that refused to remain on the reservations. When Sitting Bull became holy man and political leader, Gall became his military chief. While Gall fought battles against army troops on the Yellowstone River in 1872 and 1873, his exact role at the Little Bighorn is still a matter of controversy. He did, however, lead the forces that routed Major Marcus Reno and then cooperated with Crazy Horse in surrounding and annihilating Custer. Gall's omission from the film must be considered an oversight since Connell gives his role ample attention.

On the other hand, Sitting Bull's participation is accurately depicted, including his fasting and his vision of dead soldiers "falling like rain" into the Indian camp. (During the subsequent battles, Sitting Bull took no active part in the fighting.) Certainly the family life of the Indians is shown only briefly. The production relies heavily (perhaps too heavily) on the narration of Kate Bighead to convey the cultural disruption produced by the coming of the white man. Most significantly, however, the stereotypical "good" and "bad" film Indian is nowhere to be found in *Son of the Morning Star*.

How valid then are the charges which have been made by critics regarding the stereotyping of Native Americans in television Westerns? Clearly, as we have seen, some programs were guilty of this oversimplification and many specific examples can be cited. Some series indulged in this practice more than others, but even some of the programs which frequently depicted the Indian at his simplistic worst (like *Wagon Train*) occasionally presented the Native American at his noble best. These one dimensional portrayals of "good" and "bad" Indians abounded on the video range, but probably to no greater degree than those of other minorities, especially blacks, Mexican-Americans and Orientals. Furthermore, the role of whites in precipitating the violent conflicts between the races has been frequently dramatized (e.g., in many episodes of *Broken Arrow* and in several outstanding *Gunsmoke* stories).

In some programs Native Americans have been presented with depth and perception and a few have reached an heroic stature equal to that of any white hero (Cochise, Brave Eagle, Sam Buckhart, Nakia, Chief Joseph, Crazy Horse). Until recently the major problem has been that few Indians on television have been portrayed by Indians. This has been partly due to the lack of trained and available Native American actors. The situation is changing, however, in large measure because of the success of *Dances with Wolves* and the emergence of such outstanding Indian actors as Rodney S. Grant and Graham Greene, who received a Best Supporting Actor nomination for his work as Kicking Bird in *Dances* (the first Native American to be nominated for an acting Oscar since Chief Dan George played opposite Dustin Hoffman in 1970's *Little Big Man*).

Elisabeth Leustig, the film's casting director, discovered Greene, a Canadian-born Oneida Indian, working in Canadian regional theater. Greene had been acting professionally for 17 years in such Canadian films as *Captain Power* and *Lost in the Barrens*. American film audiences might have recognized him from *Revolution* (1985), when he played a Huron Indian opposite Al Pacino, *Pow Wow Highway* (1989), and more recently *Thunderheart* (1992). His television debut came as a Native American attorney in a 1991-92 episode of *L.A. Law*. In 1992 Greene turned in an outstanding performance as Ishi, the sole survivor of the Yahi tribe, in the HBO television film *The Last of His Tribe*. He has also appeared in a recurring role on the popular CBS series *Northern Exposure* as the Indian healer and sculptor, Leonard. Still, as Leustig discovered when casting *Dances*, the pool of Indian actors is very small. The first thing she did was to "watch as many television shows and movies starring Indians as I could find." Then she contacted Indian Theater companies throughout the United States and Canada to let them know she was shopping for talent. Next she went to South Dakota, where she held auditions at two Indian reservations. She explained later in *Entertainment Weekly*:

> We saw about 2,000 Indian actors. Most had no experience whatsoever. Moreover, even those who did were often very wary. Indians aren't always portrayed positively in movies. We had to convince them that this wasn't going to be just another shoot-'em-up Western.[84]

According to Dr. Strickland this problem is now being addressed by Native Americans:

> The American Indian is making a concentrated assault on films and film-making. Today talented and aggressive Native American film makers are producing films and videos which portray Indians in real life situations using real Indians to play real Indian parts. The news is that the Indian is very much alive in the film industry. The Native American film registry in Los Angeles has published a new directory of professional Indians, as well as, a handbook for non-Indian producers to help them find Indian people so they can get it right. The crisis is that last year there were only two major motion pictures about Indians—a far cry from the hundreds produced in the earlier years. Today Indians must create their own film opportunities. Film workshops are being held to help tribes become involved in filmmaking.... Indians are beginning to seize the opportunity to reshape their cinematic image.
>
> The good news is that Indian-made films are excellent entertainment. The bad news is that few people have a chance to see them.

Raymond William Stedman would also "respectfully offer a few candles that one might reach for whenever an 'Indian' is called into the circle of popular culture"[85] to shed light on possible distortions and misrepresentations (whether it be in novels, movies or television programs). In *Shadows on the Land*, he presents a series of questions one should ask when Native American characters are depicted or referred to in our popular culture:

"Is the vocabulary demeaning?" As examples, Stedman cites commonly used expressions such as "another redskin bit the dust," "buck," "heap big," "Indian giver," "Lo, the poor Indian," "Ugh!," "war whoop," and "wild Indian," among others.

"Do the Indians belong to the feather-bonnet tribe?" Here, he cites the Hollywood habit of treating all Indians as if they belonged to the same tribe and, therefore, dressing and acting alike.

"Are comic interludes built upon firewater and stupidity?" That is, are Native Americans depicted as either "drunken fools or sober dolts"?

"Are the Indians portrayed as an extinct species?" Are they referred to in the past tense? Stedman reminds us that there are "more than 1.3 million Indians living varied lives today within the boundaries of the United States."

"Are the Indians either noble or savage?" This oversimplified stereotyping persists, he notes, despite all efforts to eliminate it.

"Is the tone patronizing?" and "Is Indian humanness recognized?" That is, are they treated as individuals with strengths and weaknesses like those of any other race or nation?

These criteria can, of course, certainly be applied to Native Americans as portrayed in television Westerns. Perhaps, final eradication of the stereotyping and patronizing will come only when television Westerns are *produced* and *directed*, as well as acted, by Native Americans.

Until that time arrives, Native Americans will have to rely on documentaries like the highly acclaimed *How the West Was Lost* to tell their story. This ambitious six part series was originally broadcast on the Discovery cable channel in the spring of 1993. Providing a vivid and compelling look at the epic struggle for the American West as viewed through the eyes of the Indians themselves it depicts the Navajo, Nez Percé, Apache, Cheyenne and Lakota fighting to preserve their way of life from the encroachment of white settlers. Poignant interviews with Indian descendants are interspersed with spectacular views of the landscape and archival photographs. The narrative is taken from historical documents that provide a thought-provoking new perspective on the "conquest" of the American West. Perhaps, someday these same sources will be utilized to present, in dramatized form, the definitive Native American television Western.

X. The Video Range Gets Bigger

"THE VIRGINIAN" INITIATES THE WESTERN MOVIE SERIES

In March of 1962, the National Broadcasting Company announced plans that would forever enlarge the scope of the television Western. Owen Wister's classic novel of the American West, *The Virginian*, was going to be transformed into a television series that would be "the most ambitious and costly programming enterprise in network television history—one that will present television features with motion picture dimensions each week. This, "the network publicity release continued, "will be achieved not only by the ninety-minute length—which allows for full character development and expanded story-telling opportunities—but by color photography, location shooting, outstanding scripts and original musical scores."[1]

The Virginian was to be the first 90 minute long weekly network dramatic series since the days of CBS' *Playhouse 90*. Unlike those live productions, however, *The Virginian* was to be filmed, and rather than being an anthology drama with changing guest stars, it would present a continuing story with continuing characters. "Name" guest stars would also be featured and each episode would be complete with a beginning and ending plotline. Furthermore, at least one member of the regular cast would be intricately involved in the weekly story. It was not by chance that to launch its blockbuster project NBC had chosen "the granddaddy of all cowboy yarns," *The Virginian*. The American public had long been fascinated by Owen Wister's epic story.

Wister had been born in Germantown, Pennsylvania, the son of a successful physician. His family was wealthy and active in the cultural activities of their community. As a child, Wister had attended boarding schools in Switzerland and England. Later he graduated from Harvard *summa cum laude*. It was there that he began a lifelong friendship with the future president, Theodore Roosevelt. (Wister, in fact, dedicated *The Virginian* to his famous friend and later wrote an intimate portrait of the man in *Roosevelt: The Story of a Friendship*.[2])

After college Wister decided upon a musical career and went to Paris to study composition, but failing health forced him to return to the United States. In 1885, on the advice of his doctor, he followed Roosevelt to the West. He spent the summer of 1885 on a ranch near Buffalo, Wyoming—a location that was to reappear constantly in his Western stories. By autumn his health was sufficiently improved so that he could enter Harvard Law School, from which he graduated in 1888. For a number of years thereafter, he spent his summers in Wyoming, where he stored up impressions, anecdotes and character profiles that he was to use later in his novels and short stories.

Following graduation, Wister became a member of the Philadelphia Bar Association, affiliating himself with attorney Francis Rawle's office. In 1891, having returned to Wyoming for the fifth summer, Wister wrote his first two Western stories, "Hanks's Woman" and "How Lin McLean Went East," both of which were published the following year in *Harper's* magazine. The stories proved so popular with readers that the editor of *Harper's* worked out a contract with Wister where the magazine would finance him on a trip throughout the West, promote his stories and hire the well-known Western artist, Frederic Remington to do the illustrations. It was through this collaboration with Remington that a friendship developed between the two men that was to have a major impact on the way the West was perceived by the Eastern establishment.[3]

Wister's first Western "novel" was *Lin McLean*, published in 1897, which actually consisted of six short stories that he strung together about the same central character. *The Virginian*, which was published in 1902 by Macmillan, became an immediate bestseller and has never been out of print since. At the time NBC launched the television series, hardcover copies had grossed in excess of $1,600,000. Grosset and Dunlap also published a hardcover edition, as well as two paperback editions. The Pocket Book edition alone sold over 400,000 copies between 1957 and 1962, proving the novel's continuing popularity.[4]

The Encyclopedia Americana credits *The Virginian* with "doing as much to shape the romantic concept of the cowboy West as any other single factor." Wister's daughter, Fanny Kemble Wister (named for his actress grandmother), wrote that his novel was "the master design on which thousands of Westerns would be molded."[5] The Virginian's remark to Trampas, the villain of the story—"When you call me that, smile!"—is probably the best-known line in all Western fiction, and the lingering notoriety of this remark points up the immense influence of *The Virginian*. Literary historian James K. Folsom, flatly states that

> the novel firmly established the form for later fictional studies of the American West.... Wister's hero is the first and ... best visualized cowboy hero, a figure later to become a ubiquitous literary character in Western fiction.... [T]he strength of *The Virginian* is not that it gives an accurate description of the facts of Western life, which it obviously does not, but that it gives stature to the theme of the dude who goes West and learns to come to terms with the totally different life he finds on the frontier. Hence, ... [the novel] is true to a larger American attitude about the presence of the West itself and to its importance to the country at large.[6]

The plot of *The Virginian* relates the Virginian's courtship of Molly Stark, an Eastern visitor to the West and, of course, features the laconic tall-story–telling hero and, most significantly, what became a staple ingredient of virtually all subsequent Western fiction and films—the shootout between the hero and villain. The *New York Herald Tribune*'s John K. Hutchens later wrote that "the legend of the romantic cowboy was consciously designed by Wister as the latter-day counterpart of a Round Table knight and the prototype of those close-mouthed gunslingers who at this very moment are heading 'em off at Eagle Pass on more television programs than you'd wish on the ugliest varmint skulking around the ranch."[7]

Prior to the NBC television series, *The Virginian* had been produced as a film under its original title on four separate occasions adapted by the author and Kirk La Shelle for the stage and considered for television as both a dramatic special and a 30 minute black and white pilot. The first two film versions were silent. Renowned producer-director Cecil B. DeMille first brought the classic novel to the screen in 1914 as a five-reeler for Paramount. Dustin Farnum played the title role in a film that was praised by critics for its "drama, comedy and photographic spectacle" (*New York Dramatic-Mirror*) and "splendid horsemanship" and "rugged mountain scenery which ... add greatly to the charm of the picture" (*Los Angeles Daily Times*).[8] In 1923 Preferred Pictures presented the second film version based on the stage play which made its debut that same year. Expanded to eight reels, this version had Kenneth Harlan as the Virginian and was called by *Photoplay* magazine "an exceptionally good Western."[9]

The best-known screen version was released by Paramount in 1929 and was both the first talkie edition of the Wister story and the first sound film of Gary Cooper (who played the lead). Victor Fleming, assisted by Henry Hathaway, directed the 90 minute film, which was shot on location near Sonora in the high Sierras. Soon-to-be Western star and native Virginian Randolph Scott served as Cooper's special dialogue coach for the box-office hit, which was so successful that it was reissued in 1935. Eager to duplicate its past success, Paramount made yet another version of the novel in 1946, adding Technicolor as a bonus attraction. The popular and competent actor Joel McCrea was cast in the lead and the film was directed by Stuart Gilmore. By this time, however, the storyline was too familiar and even the addition of color failed to attract large numbers of patrons.[10]

Surprisingly television, which had earlier "established the Western as America's favorite spectator pastime" did not consider the Wister classic for one of its "oaters" until 1958. The first known effort to put the sixty year old classic on television was part of a proposal by Robert Saudek, producer of such series as *Omnibus*, to do a number of dramatic specials which would have been entitled *The Great Westerns*. He planned to include *The Virginian* which would have been filmed on location in Arizona starring Tony Perkins. Apparently copyright problems "got in the way" of clearing the novel for television. In any case, the series was never aired.[11]

Later in 1958, however, a 30 minute pilot film, *The Virginian*, was made and shown as part of the NBC summer-replacement series *Decision* on July 6. (All of the programs on *Decision* were pilot films for proposed 1958-59 network series.) The program related the story of a mysterious stranger, known only as the Virginian, who comes to work as the foreman of a ranch owned by a retired judge. The Virginian's task is to discover the cause of a series of mysterious accidents that are jeopardizing the judge's efforts to build a railroad spur to his ranch. The story and characters were more faithful to the novel than the later 90 minute series would be. The Virginian is portrayed as a Western dandy complete with shiny hunting boots, skintight pants, a checkered shirt with frilly cuffs and a tiny pistol. Furthermore, he is a man of peace rather that violence. When the judge tells him that his first job is to find out who is causing all the trouble and "stop him dead," he replies:

> VIRGINIAN: That's not the job you put in the letter, Judge. You said bookkeeping, new stock handling methods, disease study. [Later in the story the Virginian reveals that he studied veterinary medicine back East.]
> JUDGE: You fought in the war?
> VIRGINIAN: Jeb Stuart's Cavalry.
> JUDGE: Your pa said you could shoot before you could talk.
> VIRGINIAN: Well, I grew up since then, Judge. Now I try to talk first.
> JUDGE: I need your help, son. You help me push this railhead through, then you can get

> to work on your new methods. You help men run the ranch, and we'll build up a township.
>
> VIRGINIAN (thoughtfully and with obvious interest): I never built a town before.

Although the pilot did not sell, it received good reviews; *Variety* (July 9, 1958) wrote:

> It was a good Western done in real pro fashion, building suspense nicely.... [I]t delivered slick entertainment in the horse-opera genre.... [T]he script by Leslie Stevens ... showed a feel for characterizations.

The unknown actor who had been cast in the title role also received plaudits:

> James Drury, a young, handsome actor registered well as the Virginian. He was adept at the usual fisticuffs and shooting, and what's more evidenced good acting ability in his relationships with the other players.

Perhaps that is why NBC decided to again feature Drury when they launched their "blockbuster" version of the Wister novel in the fall of 1962. Drury was to be joined by five other regulars: the distinguished Lee J. Cobb as Judge Henry Garth (in the novel the Judge's *last* name was Henry), owner of the Shiloh Ranch; Doug McClure as Trampas, a wild, fun-loving cowpoke (now a good guy, he had been a baddie in Wister's story); Gary Clark as Steve, his fun-loving, but hard-working sidekick (Steve had been a friend of the title character who got mixed up with rustlers and was hanged in the novel); Pippa Scott as Molly Wood, a crusading newspaper publisher and sometime sweetheart of the Virginian (she had been Molly Stark, a prissy schoolmarm from the East in Wister's version), and Roberta Shore as Betsy, the judge's teenage daughter (a new character created especially for the television series).

As filming began for the first episode, network brass were optimistic that this series would do for television Westerns what *High Noon* had done for movie Westerns. After all, *The Virginian* was not only the longest cowboy series ever broadcast, it was also the first to boast two separately functioning production units (because the shooting schedule per episode was eight to ten days) and the first to use a helicopter to shuttle its cast to and from the ranch locations (thirty-five miles from the studio). To accomplish all this, each episode was budgeted at a whopping quarter of a million dollars (as compared to *Wagon Train*'s $100,000 budget) In fact, everything about *The Virginian* was big—for one sequence, 80 extras were employed. Not large by DeMille standards, but still expensive for a medium where frugality had always been the sacred standard.[12]

It was this large-scale approach to the Western that had lured Charles Marquis Warren and Roy Huggins away from other lucrative projects to produce the series. Warren had been responsible for launching the television version of *Gunsmoke* in 1955 and four years later developed *Rawhide*, certainly two of television's highest quality and most popular sagebrush sagas. He drew up the blueprints for the series, selected the initial cast and produced the first 13 episodes. Then he turned over the reins to Huggins, creator and producer of the highly successful *Maverick* series. As Warren conceived the show, *The Virginian* would be different, not only in length, but also in setting. From the 1870s where Wister set his novel, Warren advanced the time to 1896, when the locale, Medicine Bow, Wyoming, had a thriving population of 3400 hearty souls and was graced with paved streets, gaslights and other reasonable touches of civilization.

A recurring theme of the early episodes was the encroachment on the West of turn-of-the-century ideas and values of the urban East. As Warren later explained it, "Aside from being virgin territory, dramatically, setting the scene in 1896 eliminates a few well-entrenched clichés—to wit, the embittered Civil War veteran heads West; also 'Hurry,

Marshal, the Injuns are attacking the fort.' Summed up, *The Virginian* takes place after the Indian but before the automobile."[13] Despite all the planning, money and talent that went into *The Virginian*, the series debuted on September 19, 1962, to terrible reviews. Ben Gross, radio-television critic for the *New York Daily News* (September 20, 1962) wrote:

> ...the premiere of this expensive series ... was both a dramatic and an entertainment disaster. One wondered how the producers Reval and NBC could have fathered it ... But the story was a completely hackneyed one ... [which] could have been told in 30 minutes or in an hour at the most. But it was padded to produce seemingly interminable boredom.

The New York Times (September 20, 1962) review was scarcely better:

> The program's chief method of filling an hour and a half when 60 minutes would have been ample is to have the actors talk more slowly and the horses run longer.

Variety (September 26, 1962) said:

> *The Virginian* is not a Western. It's a soapy oater fashioned after *Wagon Train*. It is almost not a question of whether it is better or worse than *Wagon Train* since the two programs are now competing. Judging by the first episode ... it is no better—and no worse ... it is almost the same ... the only substantive differences in execution being that the new program is in color and 30 minutes longer.

The acting of the regulars was compared to "wooden soldiers" who "had little to do which was fortunate considering how uniformly poorly they acted." Cobb and Drury were especially singled out. If Cobb "chose to act out his bland lines with more vigor he could aid in improving the show." As for Drury the review said that "if he didn't hurt, he certainly didn't help." About the only favorable comment on the show was about the scenery. Ben Gross wrote "the color itself was enchanting and the background scenery more beautiful than any I have ever seen in a Western. If *The Virginian* depended solely on these, it would be a smash hit."

The story, entitled "The Executioners," was written by Mort Fine and David Friedkin (who also directed). It featured guest stars Hugh O'Brian, Colleen Dewhurst and John Larch. O'Brian played the son of a man just lynched by bloodthirsty townspeople who discovers that his father was innocent. Larch played the sheriff who failed to prevent the hanging. It seems that the father had spent the night in question with the local schoolmarm (Dewhurst), who let him hang rather than confess to her relationship with him. The Virginian's involvement in the story consists primarily of engaging in a fistfight with O'Brian near the end of the show. It was not an auspicious beginning for the Western film series.

Some episodes were, of course, better than others, but this was due mainly to the presence of such distinguished and capable guest stars as George C. Scott, Charles Bronson, Lee Marvin, Charles Bickford, James Gregory, Bette Davis and a young Robert Redford. For the most part, the regulars still had little to do. In "The Brazen Bell," one of the better (if not the best) of the Warren episodes, Scott turns in a superior performance as a cowardly schoolteacher who risks his life to save the lives of six children being held hostage in the town schoolhouse by a couple of escaped convicts. The teacher, Arthur Lilley, who was opposed to violence and afraid of guns, had earlier run away from a fire in which several children had perished. His wife Sarah, who had both encouraged his fear, and protected him is killed by the convicts when she panics and attempts to run away. It is then that Lilley finds the inner strength to stand up to the killers. Discovering that Molder, the leader, is fond of poetry, Lilley distracts him by reading one of Oscar Wilde's

James Drury was *The Virginian*.

poems about prison life (from which comes the title of the story). Then he grabs Molder's gun long enough for Judge Garth to kill him, but is himself mortally wounded by "Dog," the other thug (who is in turn killed by the Virginian). Thus in death Lilley gains the respect of his students and their parents—a respect he was never able to attain in life.

What keeps this story from being both routine and maudlin is the fine, sensitive acting of Scott and an excellent supporting cast, especially Anne Meacham as the overprotective wife, John Davis Chandler as the mentally defective "Dog" and Royal Dano (who has added stature to many a television Western) as the disturbed, crafty Molder. The regulars, although being in for the "kill" at the end, are extraneous and do little but stand around and wait for much of the story. (This is one episode, however, in which Pippa Scott has a few meaningful lines—early in the show.) Another notable early episode is "It Tolls for Thee," written and directed by Samuel Fuller, which tells the story of a psychopathic killer (played with his usual competence by Lee Marvin) out to gain revenge against Judge Garth for sending him to a hellhole prison when he was a sitting judge.

When Roy Huggins took over as executive producer after the first 13 weeks, he vowed to make two basic changes in the foundering show: first, to tell "full-length features" with "no padding," and second, "not to do any stories which give the whole play to guest stars."[14] Some subsequent episodes do involve one or two of the central characters more fully (e.g. Trampas and the Virginian in "Say Goodbye to All That" and Steve in "A Distant Fury"), but most of them follow the pattern established by Warren. For example, in "The Money Cage" Steve Forrest guest-stars as a confidence man planning to swindle the local bank (and Judge Garth) out of $150,000. Most of the episode focuses on Forrest unintentionally falling in love with the banker's daughter (played by Bethel Leslie) and deciding to cross up his confederates by returning the money. The Virginian is virtually never seen in this story and Trampas and Steve have maybe ten lines between them. (Judge Garth does get to play in a couple of important scenes.) Again, the acting is good but not good enough to transcend the familiar and rather banal plot. There is not even much scenery to redeem this episode either.

James Drury, the ostensible star of *The Virginian*, was a strange, but fascinating actor. During the series' fourth season, *TV Guide* writer Peter Bogdanovich characterized him thusly:

> James Drury is temperamental. He refused to be photographed or interviewed for any magazine article on the series unless the piece was only about him and the cover photo of him alone. On location, he sits impassively in his chair, dark sunglasses hiding his eyes.[15]

Drury was born in New York City, one of three children. His younger brother, Jon, was an actor who once appeared in John Houseman's UCLA theater group. His sister, Joan, was a housewife. His father was a respected member of the faculty at New York University where he taught marketing and advertising and was the coauthor of a widely used textbook, *Outlines of Marketing*. His mother, whose ancestors were of rugged Oregon pioneer stock, was at various points in her life a cattle rancher (on the family ranch near Salem, Oregon), a toy manufacturer, a real-estate broker and an editor (of *The Dairy-Men's League News*).

Young James spent his youth shuttling between New York and Oregon, while his father taught at New York University and his mother alternated managing the ranch with her other enterprises. When he was 8, he was introduced to the theater via a children's play at the Greenwich Village settlement house where he played King Herod and wore a beard. At 10, he contracted polio and spent his time endlessly reading stories—and then acting them out. In time Drury became obsessed with becoming an actor. His father later recalled in an interview:

> At NYU he got straight A's in drama and incompletes in everything else. He really went theater crazy. I remember once he and a pal of his hauled a sofa by subway all the way from Kew Gardens in Queens just to use on a set.[16]

In 1954, Drury visited Los Angeles with his parents where, armed with a letter from Dudley Wilkerson, chief M-G-M talent scout in New York, he was signed by the studio. He made his screen debut in *The Blackboard Jungle* (1955) as a one-day, one-line actor. His career, however, while modestly successful, never really got off the ground. So the following year he approached 20th Century–Fox and accepted a couple of good roles as second leads in Elvis Presley (*Love Me Tender*, 1956) and Pat Boone (*Bernadine*, 1957) films. Then he was suspended by the studio for refusing several parts they assigned him. For a few months, he was forced to take a job selling insurance, in which he was so successful that he won an award for best salesman of the month.

It was Walt Disney who gave Drury his first big break when he cast him as the dishonest sheriff in an episode of *The Nine Lives of Elfego Baca* in 1959. Disney followed this up by giving him major roles in three films (all released in 1960): *Toby Tyler*, *Pollyanna* and *Ten Who Dared*. In between films he worked as a mechanic on a used-car lot. Occasionally Drury appeared on television. One of his choicest early roles was in the *Playhouse 90* production "Bitter Heritage," in which he played Jesse James' son. He also appeared, usually as a heavy, on such television Westerns as *The Rifleman*, *The Rebel* and *Gunsmoke*. It was on the latter series that he was spotted by Charles Marquis Warren. Drury played featured roles in four of the 30 minute *Gunsmoke* episodes between December 1955 and March 1961. Particularly noteworthy was his portrayal of the title character "Johnny Red," a hardened criminal that Matt Dillon must force to leave Dodge City. Another break came for Drury when he was given a small but memorable role in Sam Peckinpah's *Ride the High Country* (1962). This film, which starred the aging Western superstars Joel McCrea and Randolph Scott, has come to be considered a near-classic Western.

Although Drury seemed at last to be on the verge of stardom, few early episodes of *The Virginian* actually featured the title character. In several stories his actions are crucial to the plot, however. In "It Tolls for Thee," he tracks down Judge Garth's kidnappers and saves his boss' life. In "Devil's Children" he brings a young, unbalanced murderer to justice. In "50 Days to Moose Jaw," he overcomes numerous obstacles in leading a successful cattle drive to Saskatchewan, Canada. In "The Accomplice," he tries to clear Trampas of a charge of bank robbery by appealing to the conscience of an eyewitness who is deliberately lying. Nevertheless, in each of these episodes the plot revolves around the actions of a character portrayed by a guest star (Lee Marvin, Charles Bickford, James Gregory and Bette Davis, respectively).

In fact, in the first 13 episodes, the most interesting aspect of the series may have been the clever manner in which the most famous line from the novel is worked into a story. In the book, the scene is a poker game. One of the players is Trampas, described as "a cow-puncher, bronco-buster, tinhorn, most anything." It was the Virginian's turn to bet "and he did not speak at once." So Trampas spoke: "You bet, you son-of-a____." Wister goes on, "The Virginian's pistol came out, and his hand lay on the table, holding it unaimed. And with a voice that sounded almost like a caress, but drawing a very little more than usual, so that there was almost a space between each word, he issued his orders to the man Trampas: 'When you call me that, *smile!*' And he looked at Trampas across the table." It is not recorded that Trampas smiled—but he did not "draw his steel," Wister says. "So I perceived a new example of the old truth, that the letter means nothing until the spirit gives it life." Thus ended Chapter II.

In "The Accomplice," as Trampas and the Virginian are riding out of town, Trampas holds up his hand as they pass the bank, turns to his companion and says, "Considerin' all the trouble this town give us, maybe we should rob that bank. You'd make a good bank robber." The Virginian slowly turns in this saddle and says with mock seriousness (but with a twinkle in his eye), "When you call me that, *smile!*" Thus ends the thirteenth episode of NBC's blockbuster television Western.

As time progressed, Drury got juicier stories—and better reviews. In "Big Image, Little Man," the Virginian helps transform a spoiled, conceited, arrogant, young millionaire railroad owner into a responsible, hard-working team member on a cattle drive after he has been pushed from a train and left to die on the desert. In the words of Leland (the young magnate): "When I look at you, I'm looking at a man that took another man and worked him like a dog and wore him down and scraped away his self-esteem and made him realize that no matter how bad things got he could still survive and do a job . . . and earn a dollar a day on a cattle drive." This episode as much as any deals with one of the basic continuing themes of the series—that a century-old way of life on the Western frontier was being slowly eroded by the "civilizing" encroachment of the East. The change was not easily accepted by the rough pioneers of the prairie and *The Virginian* realistically depicted these clashing cultures. Only the Virginian himself refused to be broken or moved by this conflict, becoming, in fact, a kind of antihero, a man more interested in preserving the past than in submitting to inevitable change.

In "Big Image," the dialogue which defends the traditional frontier way of life comes not from the Virginian himself (the eternal man of few words—in the Cooper mold), but from a supporting character called "Hoagy" (superbly played by Slim Pickens), when he explains to Leland,

> I got me a way of life that just suits me to a "T." There ain't no place else that I'd want ta be. An' do you know what it cost me? Just the years that I've put into it and the few that I've got left ta put out. That ain't much of a price ta pay considerin' what I got back in return. An' let me tell you somethin' mister. Here's where I belong an' you couldn't buy me one thing if you spent every last million that you own.

Later Leland learns another important lesson from Hoagy, about loyalty to one's friends:

> LELAND: Why are you guys pushin' yourselves so hard?
> HOAGY: 'Cause there's a need for it that's why. You think I took this job just for th' dollar a day? No Sir! See them cattle yonder: Them cows all belong to some people that I call friends. It's been a tough year in the cattle business an' if we don't get this herd to Seattle before them California cattle hit the market, there's a lot of them people that's gonna go under. That's why men and time is so important!
> LELAND: Yeah. Well, you're killin' yourself. A friend can't be worth that!
> HOAGY: Well Now, how would you know? Did you ever have one?

And that is how moral lessons were learned on the video range of *The Virginian.*

In "Legend for a Lawman," the Virginian displays both loyalty and courage when he helps prove young Randy Benton innocent of robbery and murder while helping an aging sheriff regain his self-confidence as the two bring the real outlaws to justice.

By the fifth season Drury was winning some well-deserved critical plaudits, while the series was also gaining stature. The *Variety* critic wrote on September 28, 1966, in a review of "Ride to Delphi":

> As evidenced by this episode, *The Virginian* can be said to be providing on sponsored TV what pay TV promises to deliver—a full length feature that would carry its own weight

in a theater, at least for Western fans. It represents some of the best oater scripting around, the regular cast is excellent, and the guest stars were first rate. The color photography and editing is topnotch.

It is also surprising that, in his fifth season, James Drury has not attained greater video eminence. He is not only consistently believable as the ranch ramrod, but adds some nice stylistic touches of his own.

Despite Drury's obvious romantic appeal, there are remarkably few stories involving the Virginian with a love interest. In "No Tears for Savannah," an old flame from the Virginian's past shows up as the girlfriend of a swindler he is trailing. Circumstances, however, prevent the old romance from being effectively rekindled. During *The Virginian*'s final season (before becoming *The Men from Shiloh*), Drury's character is permitted by the script to fall in love and express his plans for the future in an episode entitled "A Love to Remember." This exchange takes place between the Virginian and the object of his affections:

LISA: Tell me more about it—that place you're going to build some day.
THE VIRGINIAN: It's in Wyoming country. The river runs through there, called the Sweet-
               water—snows some in the winter. But in the spring the whole valley comes
               up green. Man could get a couple sections pretty cheap. Start a herd—even
               a family, maybe.
LISA: In that order?
THE VIRGINIAN: Well, that all depends. You start a herd all by yourself. My understanding's
               that a family takes a certain amount of cooperation.
LISA: Seems to me I've heard that myself.
THE VIRGINIAN: Tell you this though—be a fine place to watch a bunch of kids grow up.

Love has come at last to the Virginian—and he has even found the words to express it—well, sort of.

Even though the Virginian (and James Drury) was getting more and better stories and dialogue, there were a number of other appealing characters in the show. There had to be. As *TV Guide* critic Cleveland Amory put it, "shooting a 90-minute show each week may 'allow for full character development' all right, but it also must be allowed that the character gets to be so fully developed that he can survive physically only if he has a chance to rest every other week and appear in only about half the shows."[17] So if you did not care for the Virginian, you could always wait until next week and catch an episode featuring his side-kick Trampas (or Sheriff Ryker, or Judge Garth, etc.).

Besides Drury only Doug McClure, who played Trampas, remained with the series for nine years through its transformation to *The Men from Shiloh*. Writer Peter Bogdanovich made this assessment of McClure after visiting the set during the fourth season of *The Virginian*:

Doug McClure likes physical contact; on the set, he can usually be found tumbling about with a fellow actor or rolling on the grass with a willing ingenue. Just like Trampas, by gosh. Doug doesn't like it when magazines publish stories about his private life. . . . Taller and thinner than he appears to be on television, Doug has more white teeth than Burt Lancaster—but then he doesn't like references to his looks. "I'm a good actor!"[18]

Born in Glendale, California, McClure grew up in Pacific Palisades; the youngest son of an accountant and a newspaper woman. By the time he was 8, he was riding his own horse with a skill that won him several top awards in Nevada rodeos years later. Active in both athletics and drama during high school (where the yearbook immortalized him as "the boy with the cutest nose"), McClure attended Santa Monica Junior College and UCLA, studying to become a speech and drama teacher. It was there he began his

Other regulars on *The Virginian* included Doug McClure (center) as Trampas and Gary Clarke (right) as Steve, here shown with James Drury.

professional career in television commercials. His first break came as the result of a commercial when he was seen and selected to play the role of a midshipman in the syndicated series *Men of Annapolis* (1957). He then landed a featured role in an episode of *Jim Bowie* by performing a saddle fall (a stunt man's specialty he had learned while still in high school). Before long he was playing parts in feature films like *The Enemy Below* (1957), *Gidget* (1959), *The Unforgiven* (1960) and *Because They're Young* (1960). He also began to appear regularly on various television shows like *The Court of Last Resort*, *The Gale Storm Show* and *Schlitz Playhouse*.

It was as the result of an appearance on *Schlitz Playhouse* in a comedy starring William Bendix in 1958 that McClure landed his first continuing television role. Bendix in 1958 played a retired Marine sergeant returning to college on the GI Bill with McClure cast as a young student who made it rough for him on campus. A year later, when Revue Studios was casting *The Overland Trail*, Bendix remembered McClure and suggested him for the role of Frank "Flip" Flippen. Bendix played Frederick Thomas Kelly, a crusty former civil engineer and Union Army guerrilla, who had helped open the Overland Trail, one of the major stage routes to the West. Kelly was the manager of the line who hired Flippen to be his assistant. "Flip" had been brought up by Indians and was full of an adventurous enthusiasm that complemented Kelly's more curious nature. Although the series was canceled after only one season, McClure gained valuable television experience and exposure. He starred in the third episode (with Bendix appearing only briefly) and "carried" about half of the shows thereafter.

When *The Overland Trail* was canceled, McClure immediately moved into another television series, *Checkmate*, in which he was given equal billing with Anthony George and

Sebastian Cabot. He was cast as Jed Sills, a recent-college-graduate criminologist who teamed with George and Cabot to prevent crimes before they happened. Even though McClure later protested that he "was cast as the cute kid with the grin,"[19] the series lasted two years (1960–1962) and led to McClure's selection as Trampas on *The Virginian*. There his role was given considerably more substance and he became a bona fide star.

Although Trampas probably appeared in more episodes than any other character (with the possible exception of the Virginian himself) he was only occasionally given the lead role. In "Say Goodbye to All That," Trampas is forced into a gunfight with neighboring rancher Big John Belden (guest star Charles McGraw) and wounds him, causing permanent paralysis. The old man tries to goad his son, Martin (well played by rock singer Fabian), into seeking revenge. Trampas is able to avoid a showdown with the younger and less experienced Martin until he, at last, comes to realize that he must be himself and not try to become a copy of his aggressive, bullying father. Even Big John Belden finally is able to accept this. This human conflict is set against the colorful backdrop of a cattle round-up and the quest for a huge, vicious bear named Old Moses. McClure handles himself well, but, because of the emphasis on the maturation and growth of Martin, the episode really "belongs" to Fabian.

The opening episode of the second season provides viewers with some insight into Trampas' background and family when his gambler father is introduced. The story focuses on Trampas' attempts to avenge the killing of his father (played by Sonny Tuffs in an interesting piece of casting) by Judge Garth. It turns out, of course, that the Judge was forced to shoot the old man in self-defense. McClure handles the challenge of his expanded role well.

One of the best Trampas stories is, however, "Man of Violence," also from the second season. The episode deals with Trampas' quest for the men who killed and robbed his Uncle Josh of the nearly $1500 (his inheritance from his father) that Trampas had entrusted to him. Along the way he joins forces with an alcoholic doctor who is seeking to live up to his dead father's expectations (superbly played by *Star Trek*'s De Forrest Kelly), the wife of one of the killers who feels she failed her husband when he needed her, and a murderer searching for a gold mine. When they arrive at the killer's camp, Trampas finds he cannot shoot the man in cold blood and tries to take him back for trial. In self-defense, however, Trampas is forced to seriously wound him. In order to return to civilization the party must cross through dangerous Apache territory. One by one, they are killed by the Indians until only Trampas and the doctor are left. The two men stagger across the hot desert. When Trampas falls, the doctor drags him to water and civilization thus saving Trampas' life (and proving to himself that he is indeed a man).

Trampas is the only series regular appearing in the episode and McClure proves that he can handle the challenge of a story demanding a wide range of emotions and almost constant on-screen time. Furthermore, Trampas' usual "happy-go-lucky" personality has been effectively replaced by a serious, single-minded, purposeful "man-with-a-mission." In "A Matter of Destiny," a wealthy, self-confident Eastern businessman (slickly played by future *Mission: Impossible* star Peter Graves) steals Trampas' girl. When Trampas later accidently uncovers a plot by one of his friends to murder the man (a business rival in the East is paying to have him killed), he is forced to shoot his friend in order to save his rival's life. But, of course, that is the kind of man Trampas is.

Yet another aspect of Trampas' character is revealed in "The Old Cowboy." Although as usual guest stars (in this case veteran movie actor Franchot Tone as "Gramps" and soon-to-be *Lost in Space* star Billy Mumy as Willie) are prominently featured, this story reveals Trampas' warm and caring nature. Feeling sorry for an itinerant, down-on-his luck, old cowhand and his grandson, Trampas finds jobs for them at Shiloh. The boy begins to idealize Trampas—as the father he never knew. "Gramps" however, who is still reliving memories of his past accomplishments (when he was one of the wranglers on the Chisholm Trail) fouls up every task he is assigned. He brands the wrong cattle, angering one of Judge Garth's neighbors, gets thrown from a horse causing a stampede and accidently ignites a fire when he starts a fight with Trampas (because he is jealous of the younger man's skill and strength). Kind-hearted Trampas decides to give Gramps one more chance when he takes him along on a cattle drive to winter grazing land. When Trampas becomes deathly ill from his infected burns, Gramps successfully completes the crucial drive single-handedly in a blizzard. Because of Trampas' faith and humanity, the old man has been able to prove himself. It is a very satisfying story made more believable by the fine acting of McClure.

Another interesting story featuring Trampas is "The Challenge." Badly injured and half conscious, Trampas staggers to a nearby farm—where his loss of memory makes him a prime suspect in a recent murder and stage robbery. How Trampas regains his memory and is cleared of the crime make for one of the series' more engrossing episodes. Occasionally, Trampas is given a romantic plotline. In "A Touch of Hands" he falls in love with a girl from his childhood (perceptively portrayed by Belinda Montgomery). Trampas is willing to settle down and assume a large debt, but her father's opposition to their marriage and subsequent sudden death end any chance for Trampas and the girl to achieve marital happiness.

Star power and dramatic respectability was given *The Virginian* by casting the experienced and well-known actor Lee J. Cobb as Judge Henry Garth. Still Cobb constantly grumbled about the quality of the series. As late as February 1966, Peter Bogdanovich wrote in *TV Guide*:

> Lee J. Cobb doesn't like *The Virginian*. [He] feels he is slumming; he looks at you with tired, glazed eyes and says, "I'm ashamed of it." He has been ashamed of it for three years and, it seems, he is going to keep right on being ashamed of it and keep right on takin' all that money.[20]

Actually Cobb left the show at the end of the 1965-66 season.

Cobb, however, was well-known for his outspokenness and had expressed himself vigorously and frequently on a variety of subjects about which actors were usually silent and preferred other actors to be likewise. For instance:

Concerning critics:	"Who the hell are they to criticize?"
Concerning television:	"The theater is the actor's medium. Movies are the director's medium. Television is nobody's medium."
Concerning ratings:	"They are a fraud."
Concerning *The Virginian*:	"It is a good show, but only in a relative sense. It's a hit-or-miss proposition."[21]

Cobb was born Leo Jacob on December 9, 1911, in New York City and went to Hollywood after completing high school. His parents financed the trip with the understanding that if he could not make a living in the movies by the end of the summer, he would come home and go to college. He had never acted in his life and was able to get only one screen test in three months—and that was of the back of his head. That fall, he enrolled at City College of New York. He wanted to major in aeronautical engineering, but his mother urged him to do something he could earn a living with—so he took accounting. He helped pay his way by selling sporting goods after classes. At night he worked with the Curtain Club, the college dramatic society, and there his acting ambitions were revived—

encouraged, without his mother's knowledge, by his father. It was Leo's father, a compositor on a newspaper, who suggested that he change his name to Lee J. Cobb.[22] That name first began to attract attention in the mid-thirties, when Cobb became a member of the famous Group Theater in New York. He had already spent two years at CCNY, then three at the Pasadena Playhouse in California, acting and directing. When he returned to New York once more, he found that he was able to get roles written for men far older, because by the time he was 21, he was nearly bald. His Broadway debut in 1935 was a lineless bit as a hobbling old man in *Crime and Punishment*. His first solid role was as Papa Bonaparte in *Golden Boy*, which he played on the stage and later in the film in 1939. (He was only 27 at the time, while William Holden, who played his son, was 21.)

More plays and films followed (including two Hopalong Cassidy pictures). During World War II, Cobb served in the Army Air Corps and appeared in *Winged Victory*, an Air Corps show. The greatest triumph of his career came in *Death of a Salesman* which opened at the Morosco Theater in New York on February 10, 1949. Cobb's performance as Willy Loman was almost universally acclaimed and he received the Donaldson Award for his performance. (In the film version, made in 1952, the role went to the better known Fredric March, but Cobb reprised the role for television in 1966.)

After 11 months, and 330 performances, Cobb returned to Hollywood so exhausted that he turned down an offer to do *King Lear*. In 1954, however, he was cast as the tough, union boss in the highly praised *On the Waterfront* with Marlon Brando. For his performance, he was nominated for an Oscar for Best Performance by a Supporting Actor. Cobb had also appeared in a number of prestigious television productions during the fifties like *Playhouse 90* and *The Dupont Show of the Month*. By such dramatic standards, it is not difficult to see why Cobb at age 50 may have regarded *The Virginian* as anticlimactic.

Cobb had few stories that he could really sink his teeth into on *The Virginian*. One such episode came midway through the second season. In "A Time Remembered," viewers both learn more about Judge Garth's past and have an opportunity to see him practice law. The Judge's old sweetheart, Helen Halderman, now billing herself as "Elena," an operatic soloist (played by the beautiful Yvonne DeCarlo), comes to Medicine Bow to give a concert. Deciding to renew a friendship that began many years earlier when Garth was a struggling young lawyer in Fayesville (no state is ever mentioned), he invites Elena to Shiloh ranch. The Judge, who has been a widower for many years, has nearly decided to ask Elena to marry him when she becomes involved in a murder. Elena has shot a man she claims was attacking her. It appears to have been in simple self-defense, but soon holes begin cropping up in her story. The man was not a stranger but Elena's business manager—and perhaps, even her husband. Other lies in her initial account of what happened lead to a charge of murder being placed against her. Garth, still having faith in her innocence, agrees to defend her—even though he has not practiced law in many years. Ultimately the true story is revealed by Elena. She was trying to prevent her daughter (traveling with Elena as her personal secretary) from running away with the man, who was a con artist and crook. She did, indeed, kill him in self-defense and is acquitted. Unfortunately for the Judge, Elena feels she must leave Medicine Bow and begin life anew with her daughter somewhere else and the episode ends with a fond farewell at the railroad station.

This episode does give the Judge a prominent and integral role in the story and Cobb seems to involve himself in the character more fully than in most previous episodes where he had been accused by critics of "somnambulating the full course of his role."[23] Furthermore, the plot is more interesting. Incorporating both a genuine mystery and dramatic

During *The Virginian*'s first four seasons, Academy Award winning actor Lee J. Cobb was featured as Judge Henry Garth, owner of the Shiloh ranch, with Roberta Shore as his daughter, Betsy.

courtroom scenes, one might even describe this story as "Perry Mason on the Western Frontier."

Another Garth-centered episode is "A Man of the People." Here an Eastern politician (effectively portrayed by veteran character actor James Dunn), who is an old friend of the Judge, shows up in Medicine Bow with a large group of his constituents, set upon buying homesteads on the Wyoming range. Garth knows that the land is unsuitable for farming and thinks the senator is just trying to win votes back home with a fraudulent scheme. It turns out, however, that the senator's private secretary was behind the swindle all along (in order to steal the homesteaders' money) and the senator had been duped along with the others. In the end, the real culprit is apprehended, the senator and Judge Garth cooperate to find suitable homes and jobs for the new settlers, and everyone lives "happily ever after." Although Garth is featured, the story is rather tenuous and banal—unfortunately typical of most of Cobb's featured episodes.

Pippa Scott, whose only previous series exposure as a regular was as Magie Shank-Rutherford in the short lived mystery-adventure series *Mr. Lucky* (1959–60), was cast as

Molly Wood. In Wister's novel, Molly (Stark) was a "priss-face, whipped-cream" school teacher. In the television series, she became a "feisty, half-female, half-feminist" crusading newspaper editor. While Molly ended up in the arms of the Virginian in the original story, she only provided an occasional romantic interest for him on the television show. In fact, she was given so little to do that the character was entirely dropped after the first season.

Gary Clarke, who played Trampas' sidekick Steve Hill, lasted somewhat longer and was given a few interesting story leads and considerably more screen time. Clarke's only previous television series experience had been as Dick Hamilton, the younger brother of detective Michael Shane's girlfriend-secretary Lucy, on *Michael Shane* (1960-61). In "A Distant Fury," the story is built around Steve's love for the beautiful daughter (played by the voluptuous Joey Heatherton) of a scheming, ambitious widow (a tour de force for Ida Lupino). Steve had helped send a robber (played by Lupino's real-life husband, Howard Duff) to prison several years earlier. When the man unexpectedly returns to Medicine Bow, Steve believes he is out for revenge. They fight in public and later when the man is found shot in the back, Steve is blamed for his murder. Actually the man had been killed by the widow, who was his accomplice in the robbery. She wants the money so she can take her daughter back East and turn her into a real lady. Steve, with the help of the daughter, is ultimately able to clear himself. The story, while certainly not original, does give Clarke the opportunity to prove his acting ability and television appeal.

An even better episode featuring Steve is "Run Quiet." In this episode, Steve befriends a deaf-mute named Jud (a superior performance by Clu Gulager), gives him a job at Shiloh and tries to help him adjust to his new friends. All his life he has been made fun of and the butt of practical jokes. Now he must learn to trust people and it is a difficult process. Later when a gambler is robbed and murdered, Jud is blamed. He had actually tried to help the man, but because he is unable to explain what happened, everyone thinks he is guilty—everyone that is, but Steve. Jud, panics, however, and runs away. A posse goes after him, but Steve finds him first. He has been thrown from his horse and taken in by a lonely, bitter woman. Steve, with Jud's help, captures the real killers and, as the story ends, Jud prepares to begin a new relationship (and life) with the woman. This is a moving and well-written story, with all of the actors believable in their roles. Steve is quite likable and Clarke endows him with real warmth and humanity.

Early in the third season, Steve is featured in another story, "The Girl from Yesterday." In this episode, Steve is asked by a United States marshal to renew his relationship with a childhood sweetheart from Kansas City, Jane (Ruta Lee), who is now working in Medicine Bow as a saloon singer. Jane is suspected of being part of the notorious Jack Wade gang and this will enable Steve to spy on them and "feed" the information to the marshal. Steve agrees reluctantly, but later has reason to regret his actions. Jane still cares for Steve and urges him to run away with her. Steve, however, must go along with the gang to learn their plans for stealing a gold shipment. When Wade discovers that Steve is a spy and tries to kill him, Jane saves his life. When the gang is captured, Steve reluctantly turns her over to the authorities knowing that because of her cooperation she will receive a lighter sentence. Although the story is rather routine and drawn out, the acting is good and once again Clarke turns in a solid performance. For some unexplained reason, the character of Steve disappears midway through the third season. (Perhaps, Jane has been pardoned and he has gone off to make a new life with her!)

Although she was only 19 when *The Virginian* first aired, Roberta Shore, who played Judge Garth's daughter, Betsy, had had considerable previous television experience. A talented child star who could sing as well as act, she had appeared for a season (1958-59) in the popular *Father Knows Best* and later as Hank Gogerty, the teenage daughter of the owner of the airstrip where Bob Cummings kept his planes, on *The Bob Cummings Show* (1961-62). Hank, a tomboy, who rode a motor scooter to the airstrip every day, spent much of her time flirting with Bob and trying to get him to take her on assignments.

As Betsy, Shore added a refreshing charm to the stories in which she appeared and on occasion she got to sing. When Randy Boone was added to the cast during the second season, the two frequently sang duets—usually in some kind of ranch party setting (shades of the old B musical Westerns). Betsy's function in the series was occasionally to provide the female love interest. For example, in "A Man of the People" there is a secondary plot dealing with a young cavalry lieutenant's romantic interest in Betsy. (He was the nephew of the Eastern senator who was the focal point of the story.) At the end of the third season, Roberta Shore was dropped from the cast (without any explanation). The producers, however, decided to bring her back as a featured guest star in a fourth season episode entitled "The Awakening," where she falls in love with a young, widowed, itinerant minister named David Henderson (competently portrayed by Glenn Corbett).

When Henderson is injured in a vain attempt to save a miner's life, Betsy nurses him back to health. He soon becomes a spokesman for the miners who are fighting to improve the terribly dangerous conditions in which they must work. Henderson engineers a peaceful compromise between the owners and the workers and accepts and assignment in a small Pennsylvania mining community. (He is motivated by the fact that his father had been killed in a mine cave-in years earlier and his wife had died because proper medical care was not available in the backward, isolated mining community where they had lived.) Henderson asks Betsy to marry him. Although she is reluctant to leave her father and Shiloh, she knows she will be happy wherever she is as long as it is with him. The episode ends with the wedding. Then David and Betsy ride off into the sunset in a little fringe-covered surrey dragging old cans and high-button shoes along behind them. It is a satisfying (if unimaginative) way of writing Betsy out of the series. (Shore is "replaced" by Diane Roter, who is brought in to play Judge Garth's teenage niece Jennifer, during his final season, 1965-66, as owner of Shiloh.)

Handsome Randy Boone became part of the regular cast of *The Virginian* during the second season (1963-64) as the young orphan, Randy Benton, who is taken in and given a home at Shiloh. Boone had previously appeared in the comedy series *It's a Man's World* (1962-63) as Vern Hodges, a footloose guitarist who lived with three other guys on a houseboat in a small Midwestern college town. (The show was canceled after only four months.) Randy could sing and play the guitar and he was frequently given the opportunity to display those talents on *The Virginian*. Peter Bogdanovich had this to say about Boone:

> Randy Boone is an anachronism. In the ultramodern Universal commissary, he eats lunch at the counter, his guitar in his lap; in the nervous streamlined world of television he says the sort of "homey" things press agents get paid a fortune to dream up for their clients.[24]

In the final episode of the second season, "A Man Called Kane," viewers learn that Randy has a half-brother named Johnny whom he has not seen since he was 6. Because Johnny is wanted for bank robbery and murder (although he tells Randy he "didn't kill anybody"), he is keeping his identity a secret and uses the name "Kane." (Jeremy Slate is quite effective in the role.) Johnny is actually planning to steal a quarter of a million dollars in coins and negotiable British bank notes that have been buried by a Confederate government official many years earlier on the Shiloh ranch. Johnny is a cold-blooded killer who shoots the man in the back who has dug up the treasure. Randy discovers that

Johnny is preparing to leave Shiloh and begs him to let him come along. Johnny is the only "blood" relative Randy has left and he is strangely drawn to him (not knowing the kind of man Johnny is). When the Virginian discovers them about to leave, he urges Randy to stay at Shiloh. When Johnny tries to kill the Virginian (who has been tied and gagged), Randy intervenes, now realizing how evil Johnny is. Johnny cannot bring himself to kill his only blood relative and during that moment of hesitation Steve rides up and shoots him. As Randy bids farewell to the dead half-brother, he comes to the realization that his real home is Shiloh and his real family consists of the friends he has made there. It is a painful revelation and Boone is quite believable in the role, thus proving that he can act as well as sing and "horse around."

At the beginning of the third season another new character was added to the cast (just before Steve is phased out), in an episode entitled "Ryker." Emmett Ryker, a tough gunfighter who is hired to kill a rancher but has a change of heart and backs out, is played by Clu Gulager. Gulager, a native of Oklahoma, was a baby-faced, former marine who made his early reputation on television as "Mad Dog" Coll on *The Untouchables* in 1959 and then starred for two seasons as Billy the Kid on *The Tall Man* (1960-62). He made a strong impression on the producers of *The Virginian* when he turned in an outstanding performance as the deaf-mute a year earlier in "Run Quiet."

Ryker remained on the show after his initial appearance as a reformed gunfighter who became deputy sheriff of Medicine Bow. (There is some confusion regarding this: in some episodes, Ryker appears to be the actual sheriff and in others he appears to be "reporting" to a superior, i.e., to the sheriff.) Ryker is occasionally featured in the storyline as in "Shadows of the Past." In this episode, Ryker tries to help an old friend, John Conway, who is a storekeeper in Medicine Bow (engagingly portrayed by Jack Warden). Conway has proposed to a woman, Rita Bolin, who took care of him while he was seriously ill, unaware of the fact that the woman is an alcoholic trying to escape the memory of the tragic death of her husband and two children who drowned in a storm. Meanwhile, Ryker teaches Conway how to defend himself with a gun. When two gunmen Ryker earlier sent to prison come gunning for him, it is Conway that helps save his life. In the emotionally satisfying conclusion of the episode, the gunmen are captured and Rita and John discover they really do care for each other and are able to honestly face up to her drinking problem. Love, it appears, really does overcome all obstacles.

Clu Galager obviously came from the "method school" of acting and sometimes appeared to be mumbling his lines. He was a likable screen personality, however, and provided a significant contrast to the other lead characters in the series. Ryker appeared from 1964 to 1966, left for a season, and returned for the sixth season, 1967-68.

By the beginning of the fifth season (1966-67) only James Drury and Doug McClure remained from the original cast. Charles Bickford, in the role of John Grainger, has purchased the Shiloh ranch from Judge Garth, and although his role was only pivotal in occasional shows, Grainger projected the same sort of moral responsibility so well depicted by his predecessor.

Bickford was a rugged, intense, principled actor who had appeared in a number of fine Western films (*The Plainsman*, 1936; *Duel in the Sun*, 1946; *The Big Country*, 1958; *The Unforgiven*, 1960). He became quite active in television during the fifties with frequent appearances on dramatic anthologies like *Playhouse 90* and *Ford Theater*. His guest appearance as the stubborn father of two malevolent children in "The Devil's Children" episode of *The Virginian* during the first season had been memorable and he was an excellent choice to succeed Lee J. Cobb as the patriarchal figure in the series. Unfortunately Bickford suddenly died early in the sixth season (November 7, 1967) and the producers had to make another search to find a suitable actor to serve that function in the series.

The steady and reliable John McIntire, who had so capably replaced Ward Bond as the wagonmaster on *Wagon Train* for four seasons, was introduced as John Grainger's brother Clay. He brought with him his wife, Holly (played by the real-life Mrs. McIntire, Jeanette Nolan). They joined with John's grandson, Stacy (played by Don Quine), and John's niece, Elizabeth (played by Sara Lane), both of whom had been added to the cast with Bickford, to form the new Shiloh "family."

During *The Virginian*'s final three seasons, further changes were made in the cast. In 1968-69 a new continuing character was introduced. In the opening episode of the season, "The Saddlewarmer," a drifter named David Sutton is hired to work at Shiloh. Sutton has dropped out of medical school because he was unable to prevent the death of his coal miner father from silicosis. He gets into a scrape with Trampas, who breaks his leg chasing Sutton downstairs. Subsequently, Sutton applies for work at the ranch to fill in for the injured Trampas and has a difficult time mastering the skills involved and overcoming the prejudice resulting from his previous profession and the bitterness caused by Trampas' accident.

Cast in the role of Sutton was a promising young actor under contract to Universal Studios named David Hartman. Hartman had been a star athlete who was more interested in the theater than professional sports. His earliest roles were singing and dancing in Off Broadway and Broadway musicals, his best role being Rudolph, the singing waiter in the original production of *Hello Dolly* in 1964. He had also toured with the Henry Belafonte Singers and with the road company of *My Fair Lady* in the mid-sixties. His straight acting led him into television movies and series, which resulted in a guest appearance on *The Virginian*. (After being a regular for one season, Hartman went on to bigger and better things: four years on *The New Doctors*, 1969–1973; star of his own series, *Lucas Tanner*, in 1974-75, and finally host of *Good Morning America*, 1975–1987.)[25]

Sutton disappeared after one season (when Hartman left the series for a juicier role as Dr. Paul Hunter on *The Bold Ones*) and yet a new character entered the story—James Joseph Horn. Horn, played by another young television veteran, Tim Matheson, was described by the Universal Studios press department as an

> . . . exuberant and inexhaustible young newcomer to *The Virginian*'s staff of cowboys . . . with the background and experience of a boy who has seen and done many things as the sidekick of an itinerant trail bum. His experience on the road gives him the skill and maturity of a man but his adventurous nature and sharp sense of humor show he's not at all short on boyish spirit. He lacked a family from a very early age, so his life on the trail was only infrequently happy. But that life ends and a new one begins upon his acquaintance with the Grainger family which results in immediate affinity and mutual adoption.

Obviously Horn was to serve the same function in the series as Randy Boone had in the early years and Don Quine later. Horn was introduced in the season opener, "Long Ride Home" with Leslie Nielsen guest-starring as the itinerant trail bum. Despite his young age, Matheson, who played Horn, had appeared in many popular television shows of the sixties, including *A Window on Main Street*, *Twilight Zone*, *The Farmer's Daughter*, *Leave It to Beaver* and *Adam-12*. After one season Matheson left and later was given a bigger role on *Bonanza*.

The stories took on a more contemporary orientation during the eighth season with subjects like prison reform (with an emphasis on rehabilitation), women's suffrage, political corruption, the plight of the Indians, the generation gap, and environmental pollution and waste all being treated in dramatic ways. There was also more emphasis

In the fifth season Charles Bickford (right) took over as John Granger, the new owner of the Shiloh, with Don Quine (left) and Sara Lane as his son and daughter, Stacy and Elizabeth; here with James Drury.

on romance as several of the leading characters, including the Virginian himself, as well as Trampas and young Jim Horn, experienced unfulfilled love affairs.

Despite these changes *The Virginian* began to slip noticeably in the ratings. The series had climbed into Nielsen's top 25 during its second year on the air and remained there through 1968. It rose as high as eleventh in 1966-67, but thereafter it gradually began to fall until it dropped off the list entirely in 1969-70. In 1970 the decision was made to completely overhaul *The Virginian* in a final attempt to revitalize the series. It was even given a new name— *The Men from Shiloh*. The NBC publicity brochures proclaimed the improvement; "an increased budget! . . . three separate production units each with its own executive producer! . . . a new owner of the Shiloh Ranch! . . . . multi-star guest casts! . . . featuring powerful dramas of the West of the 1890's with relevance for today!"

The new owner of Shiloh was retired British colonel Adam MacKenzie. He came to Wyoming seeking "a new beginning" after the death of his wife and the end of a long military career with the British army. The release went on to explain that "in a strange and unsentimental way, Colonel Mackenzie perhaps has a purer notion of 'the American Dream' than many native-born Americans. And when he sees some of the same signs of corruption that affected the Old World, he feels impelled to fight." British-born Stewart Granger, who was cast in the role of Colonel Mackenzie, had little previous experience in television although he had a long list of respectable film credits including *King*

Solomon's Mines (1950), *Scaramouche* (1952) and *The Prisoner of Zenda* (1952). *Variety* (September 23, 1970) said of his debut in the initial broadcast of the new series:

> Granger, grey-haired and charming, ran the gamut well from courtly gentleman, through gentle-with-kids sentimentality to very-handy-with-a-gun outdoorsman ... with romantic appeal for the Wyoming ladies, plus a rebellious belief in causes that plays to the younger demographic element.

The second major change involved the addition of Lee Majors as a wrangler named Roy Tate. "Tate," said the release, "has made his own way as long as he can remember, asking neither questions nor favor. Very much of a man of today, he quietly does his own thing—and lets others do theirs." Majors, who was fresh from his success in *The Big Valley* and the memorable film *The Liberation of L.B. Jones* (1970), was featured in approximately every third episode along with a host of guest stars (e.g., "The Best Man," with James Farentino, Katy Jurado and Desi Arnaz.)

One of the basic changes in the new show was a de-emphasis on the family aspect of the earlier series. It was now a kind of "Western of the Week" with no regular female leads (guest stars filled this void). Television historian Ralph Brauer described the difference between *The Men from Shiloh* and its predecessor this way: "where *The Virginian* was more about Shiloh than the Virginian, *The Men from Shiloh* is more about the men than Shiloh. Each episode features someone in the cast, who is usually involved in a situation having nothing to do with Shiloh and rarely taking place on the ranch."[26]

What had not changed was the length (it was still the only 90 minute television Western), the high quality production values, its familiar Wednesday night time-slot (7:30 P.M. EST) and, of course, the two central male stars, James Drury and Doug McClure. The critics and public still generally liked the series and it finished the season at a respectable eighteenth, easily winning its time period. Still with production costs soaring and sponsors difficult to find, NBC decided to cancel *The Men from Shiloh* and on September 8, 1971, after 249 episodes and 373 ½ hours of prime time programming, the Virginian rode into the sunset for the last time.

Perhaps the most important legacy of *The Virginian* was in proving that the public would accept a feature length television show. The next step, a two-hour made-for-television film, was practically inevitable. As a result of *The Virginian*'s success, NBC contracted with Universal in 1964 to begin producing feature length films that were not part of a series but meant to stand on their own in the regular network movie slots, by-passing any traditional theatrical release. Although they failed at first to generate much viewer or critical enthusiasm, higher budgets and more elaborate publicity were to turn the made-for-television film into a popular television staple by the late sixties.

Many outstanding directors worked on *The Virginian*, among them Leo Penn, David Friedkin, Andrew V. McLaglen, William Witney, Bernard McEveety, Harry Harris, Ted Post, Sam Fuller, Don McDougall and even Gene Coon (before his involvement with *Star Trek*). The music on *The Virginian* was also superior to that on most television Westerns. Percy Faith was responsible for the distinctive theme and Leonard Rosenman, Hans Salter and Leo Shuken contributed background orchestrations.

The Virginian also spawned another moderately popular Western, *Laredo*. An episode entitled "We've Lost a Train," featuring guest star Neville Brand, about four Texas Rangers who become involved with bandits while on their way to Mexico to get a prize bull served as the pilot for that series. The episode was later released theatrically as *Backtrack* (1969).

A number of episodes of *The Virginian* eventually found their way into general theatrical release, primarily in Europe, including *The Brazen Bell* (1963), featuring George C. Scott; *The Devil's Children* (1963), with Charles Bickford; *The Final Hour* (1963), guest-starring Jacques Aubuchon; and two films that were edited "compilations" of several episodes: *The Meanest Men in the West* (1967), with Charles Bronson and Lee Marvin (from "It Tolls for Thee," and "The Reckoning,") and *The Bull of the West* (1965), with Charles Bronson and Brian Keith (from "Duel at Shiloh" and "Nobility of Kings"). Here was a rare case of television furnishing films for theatrical release rather than the common situation of theatrical films being released to television.

Meanwhile, there were several other Westerns that attempted to ride the 90 minute video trail broken by *The Virginian*: *Wagon Train* (1963-1964), *Cimarron Strip* (1967-1968) and *Hec Ramsey* (1972–1974). As discussed in an earlier chapter, the 90 minute version of *Wagon Train* lasted only one season. Then ABC returned the series to the hour format (and, in an ill-advised move to save money, reverted from color back to black and white). *Cimarron Strip* represented CBS's attempt at duplicating NBC's success with *The Virginian* and was the network's most costly show of the season. Like the NBC series, *Cimarron Strip* focused mainly on characters played by guest stars, but despite using many of the same writers and directors, the show was definitely inferior.

The show was set in the thousand-square-mile border region between Kansas and the Indian Territories during the 1880s against the backdrop of a range war festering between the cattlemen and the homesteaders. Patrolling this vast area was the responsibility of U.S. Marshal Jim Crown, who was based in Cimarron City. (*Cimarron Strip* should not be confused with *Cimarron City*, set in the same local about a decade later starring George Montgomery and broadcast on NBC in 1958-59). Crown had no full-time deputies but he often availed himself of the assistance of an itinerant Scot named Mac Gregor and Francis Wilde, a young photographer. The other series regular was Dulcey Coopersmith, a young woman from the East who had moved to the frontier to take over an inn that had been run by her late father.

Cast in the lead role of Marshal Crown was Stuart Whitman, a rugged Hollywood veteran who appeared in many action films but never quite made it to the top. The major studios overlooked Whitman, until they had difficulties with recalcitrant top-echelon stars. When Charleton Heston bowed out of *Darby's Rangers* (1958), Whitman replaced him. He also substituted for Robert Wagner in *The Sound and the Fury* (1959), Stephen Boyd in *The Story of Ruth* (1960) and David Janssen in *An American Dream* (1966). A former boxer, Whitman was seen frequently in television Westerns during the fifties and early sixties, before getting the lead in *Cimarron Strip*. He was given a lucrative one-third partnership with Philip Leacock (former executive producer of *Gunsmoke*) and the creator and supervising producer, Christopher Knopf. Whitman insisted in an interview that

> My character has got more range than what we've seen in the past. Jim Arness limits himself to kissing a girl or getting wounded. Crown has no limitations. He is a policeman with a heart, a Western hero who hasn't been seen for a long time. I hope to live with him for many years.[27]

Whitman's expectations were to be unfulfilled even though many of television's top directors took their turn at directing one of the series' 26 episodes, including Bernard McEveety, Lamont Johnson and Don Medford.

Most critics panned the show. *TV Guide*'s Cleveland Amory wrote (October 7, 1967):

> The only difference between this show and the 4048 other Westerns you have seen over the past 44 years is that it lasts an hour and a half, and by the end of the first episode they have killed everything in sight except (a) the hero and (b) the time.

Although the production values were generally quite good, the show suffered most from poor scripts—a problem that had often plagued *The Virginian* (at least during the first few seasons)—and indifferent acting. (Amory noted that Whitman "had a weird, husky way of speaking" and that the supporting cast, Randy Boone as Francis, Percy Herbert as Mac Gregor and Jill Townsend as Dulcey, had "so little to do, and what they did do is so irritating, that if it was left just to them [and Whitman] there would be no show at all.") The public must have agreed because *Cimarron Strip* was consistently outrated by ABC's *Batman, The Flying Nun* and *Bewitched* and *Daniel Boone* and the first half of *Ironside* on NBC and the show was canceled after only one season.

Hec Ramsey was a considerably higher quality series. Shown once a month as part of the rotating *NBC Sunday Mystery Movie*, only ten 90 minute episodes (plus a two-hour pilot) were produced. The series was created and produced by long-time Jack Webb associate Harold Jack Bloom as one of Webb's Mark VII Productions. *Have Gun, Will Travel* star Richard Boone played the title role. Ramsey was a grizzled old gunfighter with a philosophical turn of mind, living at the turn of the century, who had become interested in the "newfangled" science of criminology and spent years learning all he could about it. At one time (so the theme song went) Hec "drew first and asked questions later," but it seemed that there were too many gunslingers trying him out but he was always just a bit quicker.

As the series began, Ramsey arrived in the small Western town of New Prospect, Oklahoma, to take a job as deputy chief of police. The chief, Oliver B. Stamp (well played by television newcomer Rick Lenz), was young and inexperienced (he had been a schoolteacher), and he often liked to push the more rugged Hec around in order to flaunt his authority. (Stamp had convinced the reluctant town council to establish a police department, but they had insisted he hire the experienced Ramsey as his deputy.) Eventually Stamp came to appreciate Hec's innovative methods—chemical analysis, fingerprinting (and even hoofprinting) and ballistics. In his jerry-built laboratory, Hec utilized such scientific paraphernalia as magnifying glasses, scales and microscopes to solve crimes and track down culprits. Modern devices such as the electric chair ("Hangman's Wages") were also carefully woven into the storylines.

Hec Ramsey was clearly not your standard Western hero—he was a detective who operated in a Western setting at the time when law enforcement methods were changing from reliance on gunpower to greater utilization of brainpower—just as the horse was giving way to the automobile. Or as Cleveland Amory put it, he was a "Sherlock at home on the range." All of this would not have worked had it not been for the outstanding characterizations. Hec was a labor of love for the veteran Boone:

> I'm doing this because, dammit, I like this Hec Ramsey. He's dead honest. He walks right through the ridiculous standards of victorian America. He's Paladin, from *Have Gun, Will Travel*, grown older. If Paladin had lived all those years, he would have run out of patience with the idiots and would've gotten as grumpy as Hec. He would have said to the dame, "Lady, you're not in distress. You're just stupid."[28]

Despite this assessment, in actuality, Ramsey was polite and courteous to the ladies. (In one episode, he carries a woman across a large mudpuddle, explaining, "I would have put down my coat, but cleaning costs twenty cents while a shoe shine is only a dime.") Furthermore, he was a man of integrity. In "Hangman's Wages," a former outlaw crony, Wes Durham (superbly played by Steve Forrest), awaiting public execution in a new-fangled electric chair, appeals to Hec for help in escaping:

WES: This a pretty good job?
HEC: Spirits, bacon an' beans ... steak twice a week.

***Have Gun, Will Travel*'s Richard Boone starred in the title role of the 90 minute mystery Western series *Hec Ramsey*.**

> Wes: Hangman's wages. You ain't gettin' no younger. What happens when the miseries curl up your fingers?
> Hec: (Pause) I'll steal fewer drinks
> Wes: What if some young punk calls you out and yer packin' about a pound of slugs in ya?
> Hec: Well, I can always burst inta tears.
> Wes: And then give him a mealy mouth grin so's he'll buy you a drink.
> Hec: Hey Wes, maybe they gonna put me out ta stud.
> Wes: Hec ... there's five thousand dollars in gold to bust me outa here.
> Hec: You offerin' me a livin' legend fer five thousand dollars?
> Wes: What er ya askin'?
> Hec: I'm not askin' nothin'.
> Wes: Six thousand.
> Hec: No.
> Wes: I won't offer it ag'in.
> Hec: I guess I just got this talent for poverty, Wes.

Other regulars on the series included one of television's most versatile character actors, Harry Morgan as Amos C. Coogan, M.D., who doubled as town barber and doctor and, on occasion, assisted Hec (in his scientific research) as coroner. Another newcomer, Dennis Rucker, rounded out the cast as one of the department's young policemen. Most critics liked *Hec Ramsey*. Amory wrote:

> Richard Boone has always seemed to us to be an actor who is awfully good at what he does ... an actor playing action parts. He has always been determined, however, to add new dimensions to such parts. The writers have done it for him here with a fine light—heavyweight characterization.[29]

Why, then, did what was assuredly the best 90 minute Western on television fail after only ten episodes spread over two seasons? Boone later offered this explanation:

It should have, by all signs, been a booming success—except for one factor: violence. To me violence played an integral part in taming the West and I wanted violence in scripts where it was called for. But we ran afoul of antiviolent Milquetoasts who put so many damned restraints on what we could and could not include in scripts I couldn't live with it and do a good job and told them so in no uncertain language. Jack [Webb] sided with me too, but even though he produced the show there were powers higher than he—advertisers—and they won in the end.

The scripts we'd laboriously planned ahead for old Hec meant nothing with the new restraints and cutting to them, and so our series died a quick death, befitting that of a typical Western shootout scene. Oh, we've got thousands of letters from loyal fans who loved old Hec and what I was trying to build into him and who bitterly complained about our show being canceled....

I've since talked to my good buddy Jim Arness and learned his longest-running series on TV met the same inevitable fate mine did. Big-money advertisers would simply not sponsor any or all segments of our shows with violence in them. In other words, you'd have both Hec and Matt Dillon trying to be Western-type Columbos talking their way in and out of battles but never drawing a gun. I dunno. So help me, sometimes I think the whole country's going effeminate—conned into it by antiviolence Milquetoasts, be they viewers, producers, or advertisers![30]

However, the video range was destined to get a whole lot bigger with the coming of *Centennial* in 1978. It was, perhaps, only fitting that the longest television Western ever made should have been an adaptation of James Michener's mammoth 909 page novel about the American West, *Centennial*. The 1974 bestseller could be described as part history, part soap opera, part editorial (on environmental issues), but always moving and exciting. A meticulous researcher, Michener filled his novel with accurate information about everything from the formation of the earth's crust and the fashioning of arrowheads and the ventilating of tepees by the Indians, to the manufacture of scrapple by the settlers.

Random House, Inc., the book's publisher proclaimed *Centennial* to be "an enthralling celebration of our country—a stunning panorama of the West brimming with the glory and the greatness of the American past ... the story of the land and its people ... trappers, traders, homesteaders, gold seekers, ranchers, hunters—all caught up in the dramatic events and violent conflicts that shaped the destiny of our legendary West." Michener's novel was hailed by the critics and press. *Newsday* called it "much more than a novel." *The Pittsburgh Press* said:

> If you're a Michener fan, this book is a must. And if you're not, a Michener fan, *Centennial* will make you one.

The *Cleveland Plain Dealer* proclaimed it to be:

> ... An engrossing book, an imaginative and intricate one, a book teeming with people and giving a marvelous sense of the land.

And the *Los Angeles Times* added:

> While he fascinates and engrosses, Michener also educates as he has done in the 18 books which preceded *Centennial*.

The story's scope was as broad as that of *Roots*. Beginning in the late 1700s with the coming of the white man—in this case a French-Canadian fur trader named Pasquinel—upon the domain of the Plains Indians, the novel depicts (through the eyes of his many descendants) all the cataclysmic events which shaped our Western frontier: an Indian massacre, a cattle drive, the clashes between ranchers and sheepmen and railroaders, the gold rush, the speculation in land, the Dust Bowl drought and the gradual erosion and destruction of the natural environment. The emphasis was on the growth of Colorado from 1776 to the present (1974).

From the beginning, the filming of Michener's epic novel was the most ambitious project ever attempted by television. It was initially budgeted by Universal Studios at one million dollars per hour (or $26 million total for the entire series—more than four times the cost of *Roots*). The final cost, however, was in excess of $30 million dollars. The cast literally included thousands, all shooting was done "on location" and an entire town was constructed near the South Platte River on the site of Orchard, Colorado.

To understand the enormous expenses involved, one need only consider the problems which beset the cast and crew during the filming of the first two segments—the opening three hours, ("Only the Rocks Live Forever") and the two hours which followed ("The Yellow Apron"). They were supposed to take 39 days to film, but took 64 days instead and cost $3 million over budget. During this period, the original director was fired, the executive producer caught hepatitis, the president of Universal's television division left to supervise feature films and most of the 110 man production crew had to be rescued off the Continental Divide.[31] Richard Chamberlain, who portrayed Scottish trapper Alexander McKeag, later explained in an interview:

> It was quite miraculous how totally against us nature was in Colorado. If it wasn't blowing 80 miles an hour and tipping all the tepees over, it was raining. Or if we wanted snow, it would suddenly get hot and the snow would disappear. Then when we didn't want snow, suddenly we'd be in a foot of it.[32]

In addition to the weather, there was the problem of logistics. Poudre Canyon, for example, was the only place wild enough to simulate the American West of the late eighteenth century and it was located over ninety miles from the company's home base in Greeley, Colorado. Augusta, Kentucky, a small agricultural community on the banks of the Ohio River, was chosen as a facsimile for St. Louis circa 1800. This was fifty miles away from location headquarters near Cincinnati. A special unit was sent to Del Rio, Texas, to film the Longhorn cattle drive from Texas to Colorado and an Amish community near New Philadelphia, Ohio, provided the setting for the scenes in Lampeter. Other sequences were filmed in such far-flung locations as Arizona, New Mexico, Utah and California. One of the most unusual locations utilized was the lobby of the Ramada Inn in Greeley. The hotel allowed the crew to put down two layers of plywood, topped with several inches of dirt. An Indian tepee was then set up for interior shots. In this way the problems caused by excessive rain were solved.

Another problem involved the casting of Indians. An attempt was made to cast real Indians to play the Indians in the story. The trouble was most of the Indians available lived near Denver, which was a two hour bus ride to the nearest location. After the Native American extras arrived, they had to spend another hour or so getting into makeup. Then they stood around most of the day in freezing temperatures. For this they got paid $25 a day plus expenses. It was no surprise that by the third day, no one showed up for the bus. Consequently, the producer ended up using a number of Mexicans (who were part Indian) from the Greeley area which was closer.

Despite all the problems, however, *Centennial*, was a labor of love for executive producer John Wilder, whose own ancestors had migrated West along the Oregon Trail. When NBC asked the 42 year old director of *The Streets of San Francisco* to produce the series, he told the network:

> I'll do this as long as you understand that I only mean to please one man—James Michener. If you can't live with that, get someone else."[33]

Wilder knew the project would take time—he felt the picture should be filmed where the story took place because it was about "man's relationship to the land." He suggested that the series be held until midseason, but NBC insisted that it be ready for broadcast in the fall of 1978. *Centennial* was to be aired in blocks, on two or three consecutive Sunday nights, followed by a production gap, and then two or three more Sundays until completed. Thus while the first three episodes were being broadcast, episodes eight, nine and ten were still being filmed.

The first three episodes rated well, but then the plan began to fall apart. Someone in the programming department noticed that a rival network was showing the popular movie *The Sting* on the Sunday night that *Centennial* was to make its first return. So it was rescheduled for a Saturday night. The next episode was also shown on a Saturday, but episode six was broadcast on a Sunday. Wilder complained that viewers "needed a map to find *Centennial*." Fans of the series became confused. Ratings began to drop. Then NBC told Wilder it wanted a rush job on the last two episodes (the two hour eleventh episode, "The Winds of Death" and the three hour twelfth episode, "The Scream of Eagles"). They wanted to move up the finale from February 11 (1979) to February 4 (so that it would not be scheduled against CBS' *Gone with the Wind*.) Instead it ended up being aired opposite *Rocky*.

In addition to serving as executive producer, John Wilder adapted much of the script from Michener's novel. He wrote the first two "chapters" (as the episodes were called), Chapter 6 ("The Longhorns"), and the final three hour chapter. Jerry Ziegman wrote three chapters and Charles Larson adapted the other five. The directors included Virgil W. Vogel, a veteran director of television Westerns (90 episodes of *Wagon Train*) who directed six of the episodes (accounting for 14 of the 26 hours).

Wilder assembled a cast of epic proportions to breathe life into seven generations of Michener characters. Dominating the story during the early episodes were Robert Conrad (of *The Wild Wild West*—see Chapter XII) and Richard Chamberlain (star of *Dr. Kildare*). At the age of 43, Conrad had landed what he considered "the role of a lifetime" as the French-Canadian trapper Pasquinel. Runner up to Warren Beatty for the lead in *Splendor in the Grass* (1961), to Richard Beymer in *West Side Story* (1961), to Troy Donahue in *A Summer Place* (1959) and *Parrish* (1961), and to Gene Hackman in *The French Connection* (1971), Conrad was not the first choice for *Centennial*. James Caan, Robert Blake, and Charles Bronson all turned the role down before Conrad was offered the part. Conrad later explained in an interview:

> You don't know what it does to an actor to be runner-up for 21 years. Finally, I've played the biggest, most important role of my life. The first thing I've done with no apologies for my acting.[34]

Stardom still, did not come easily to Conrad. The filming took four months of laborious work, including 12 hours a day with a tape recorder perfecting the French-Canadian dialect. (He had to sing five songs in French.) To add 20 pounds to his normal 175 pound weight, Conrad drank copious quantities of beer. The part required a beard that took an hour and a half to apply every morning. On locations in Kentucky, Ohio and Colorado he took terrific physical punishment: packing 200 pounds of animal pelts on his back, being knocked through a window, being bitten by a spider which caused his eyes to swell shut, being thrown into 26 degree water which was polluted. (He wound up with a 105 degree fever and dysentery.) Would Conrad do it again? To this day he considers Pasquinel his most significant role.[35]

Also central to the early episodes of *Centennial* was red-bearded Alexander McKeag—

a tall, shy, rather elegant mountain man whom Pasquinel rescues from the Cheyenne and who becomes his partner. Chamberlain (subsequently to star in numerous television miniseries) turned in a fine performance utilizing a thick Scottish burr.

Other notable actors and actresses had their moments on the screen and then passed from the scene as age and the shifting storyline moved forward. Among the more important were Barbara Carrera as the lovely Indian maiden, Clay Basket, who would become the mother of Pasquinel's three children and later would become McKeag's wife; Raymond Burr as St. Louis silversmith Hermann Bockweiss, who would finance the early trapping expeditions of Pasquinel and McKeag; Sally Kellerman as his lovely daughter Lise, who would marry Pasquinel, but never tame him; Gregory Harrison as Mennonite Levi Zandt, who would found the town of Centennial; Alex Karras as his good friend, German immigrant Hans Brumbaugh, who would be the first to realize the agricultural possibilities of the land; Chad Everett as Maxwell Mercy, the young army officer who would help guide the early immigrants west; Richard Crenna (in an outstanding performance) as Colonel Frank Skimmerhorn, the militia leader who hated the redman for killing his family and would inflict his own form of vengeance; Dennis Weaver as R.J. Poteet, who would organize and lead the first cattle drive north to Colorado; Timothy Dalton as the wealthy Englishman Oliver Seccombe, who would realize his vision of vast herds of cattle grazing the land; Lynn Redgrave as Charlotte Buckland, who would marry Seccombe and eventually inherit his huge empire; William Atherton, as Jim Lloyd, the poor cowboy who would finally marry the widow Seccombe and manage her extensive holdings; Anthony Zerbe, as Mervin Wendell, who would stop at nothing—even murder— to gain wealth and power; Lois Nettleton as Maude Wendell, his equally venal wife; Brian Keith as Axel Dumire, who would bring law and order to Centennial and ultimately pay for it with his life; and David Janssen (who also narrated the series) as rancher Paul Garrett, whose family line could be traced all the way back to Pasquinel, and who would fight to prevent the senseless exploitation of the land by the ruthless Wendell descendant, Morgan (played to lip-curling perfection by Robert Vaughn).

Even those in lesser roles read like a who's who of television: Clint Walker, Pernell Roberts, Mark Harmon, Andy Griffith, Sharon Gless, Henry Darrow, Morgan Woodward, Richard Jaeckel, Geoffrey Lewis, Nick Ramus (in an Indian role, of course), Michael Ansara (likewise), Cliff De Young, James Best, Greg Mullavey, Dana Elcar, Julie Sommars, Stephanie Zimbalist, A. Martinez, Stephen McHattie and dozens of others.

James Michener himself appeared at the beginning of the first episode which aired on Sunday October 1, 1978, to explain his reasons for writing the book and (by implication) the reasons why viewers should watch the television adaptation. He also made a plea for environmental conservation:

> ... I suppose my primary reason for writing the book *Centennial* was to ask us—you and me—if we're aware of what's happening right now to this land we love, this earth we depend upon for life....
>
> It's a novel, of course, its characters and scenes are imaginary, but there were French trappers from Canada like the man who calls himself Pasquinel, there were mountain men from Scotland like the man named Alexander McKeag; there was a silversmith at St. Louis like Herman Bockweiss; an army officer like Maxwell Mercy; a militia commander like Frank Skimmerhorn; a Texas trail boss like R.J. Poteet.
>
> And certain background incidents and characters are real: in the 1820s and 1830s the mountain men did hold an annual rendezvous in the Rockies; in 1851 there was a great convocation at Fort Laramie that saw ten thousand Indians gather to approve a treaty with our government; in 1864 there was a massacre that is to this day one of our nation's greatest tragedies; and the same decade did see the great longhorn trail drives north from Texas.

> The cattle would bring the need for a town—a town like the one I call Centennial. This is the story of that town. But the big story is about the people who helped make the country what it is and the land that makes the people what they are. And its a story about time—not just as a record, but also a reminder—a reminder that during the few years allotted to each of us, we are the guardians of the earth. We are at once the custodians of our heritage and the caretakers of our future. Stay with us for the great adventure of the American West!

Although the ratings were respectable several of the critics tore *Centennial* apart. Kay Gardella of the *City News* (October 1, 1978) called it a "gigantic bomb" whose "one saving grace" was its scenery. James Wolcott writing in *The Village Voice* (October 16, 1978) proclaimed that "verbless dialog and Monty Python accents turn this epic into disastrous camp." The *New York Post* television critic Frank Swertlow entitled his review (October 11, 1978) "How the West Was Lost (Again)" offering the opinion that the miniseries should be thus named and that "producers have turned Michener's best-seller into a comic book filled with some of the funniest, or rather the worst, acting ever...." He is particularly critical of Conrad and Chamberlain. However, the most unkind observations were made by Harry F. Waters writing in the October 9, 1978, issue of *Newsweek*:

> ... NBC masters platoons of characters, yet all too many of them are stereotypes. Much of the acting is equally pedestrian.... The saga's center is Pasquinel but as vacuously played by Robert Conrad, the center simply doesn't hold.... Some unintentional humor is provided by the star's tenuous grip on their ethnic accents, most of which sound like something heard at a reunion of Berlitz dropouts.

However, Sam Papa of the *New York Daily Press* (October 2, 1978) had mixed reactions to the initial episode. While critical of the dialects, he lauds Conrad's performance which, he believes, "saves whatever there is to savor" in the production in a role in which he is "perfectly cast." *Variety* (October 4, 1978) was more favorable in its assessment, stating that "Conrad easily dominated the opening stanza with a macho interpretation of a determined, self-reliant outdoorsman." Overall the *Variety* reviewer felt that the production "achieved a nice feel of the land along with engaging the interest in the main characters on screen." The *Los Angeles Times'* Cecil Smith agreed with *Variety* and went even further in the praise he lavished on the series. Writing on October 1, 1978, he raved:

> "Centennial" is a movie to match its mountains. It is big and brawny and as beautiful as the awesome Colorado Rockies it celebrates ... it's a movie that matches James Michener's magnificent novel.... John Wilder's dramatization not only captures the grandeur of Michener's theme but the narrative power of the great storyteller and, to an extent, even his literary style. More than any of its predecessors, this is truly a "television novel." ...
>
> Robert Conrad [gives] the best performance I have seen him give in all his years on television....
>
> But the actors, for all their stature, are virtually dwarfed by the immensity of the Colorado wilderness, the soaring mountains, the rocky cliffs, the placid river, the forests and plains, the Indian camps."

Viewers must have wondered if Smith saw the same program as Gardella, Wolcott, Swertlow and Waters.

In any case the bottom line was ratings. The series peaked in the opening episode with a rating of 23.4 but unfortunately never again reached that level in the Nielsens. John McMahon, vice president of programming at NBC later admitted that if the series had remained on Sunday nights it probably would have retained its audience and fared much better in the ratings. The final average for the entire twelve episodes was 19.5, placing it 33rd out of the 112 ranked series for the 1978-79 season.[36] This would have been considered a reasonable rating for most programs, but *Centennial* was decidedly not "most" programs. At a cost of $1,150,000 per hour, it was the most expensive series produced to that date. NBC was able to re-broadcast *Centennial* during the fall of 1980, when an actor's strike delayed the availability of new programs. Subsequently it has been rerun several times on cable channels, most recently on the Family Channel during the summer of 1994. *Centennial*'s final place in the history of the television Western is difficult to assess. It certainly was a landmark in the expansion of the video range—in both length and cost. It would be over a decade before a Western miniseries achieved both the critical and popular success that had been expected of *Centennial*.

The made-for-television Western film, however, never completely disappeared from the video range. In addition to *Centennial*, other miniseries carried on the tradition established by *The Virginian* including *The Macahans* (1976), *The Sacketts* (1979), Kenny Rogers' *Gambler* series (1980, 1983, 1987, 1991 and 1994), as well as highly rated remakes of such classic Westerns as *Stagecoach* (1986) and *Red River* (1988). The most successful were, of course, the critically acclaimed ratings phenomenon *Lonesome Dove* (1989), and its sequel *Return to Lonesome Dove* (1993). (See Chapter XVI.) In fact, for a while it appeared that this was the only type of Western program deemed sufficiently profitable by the networks to broadcast on the home screen.

To some extent, these made-for-television Western films all benefited from the success of *The Virginian*. In blazing that first 90 minute trail, *The Virginian* forever enlarged the video range.

XI. Spoofing the Television Western

OR, HOW THE "F TROOP" FOUND "PISTOLS 'N' PETTICOATS" ON "DUSTY'S TRAIL"

Humor has been a part of the Western film scene since sidekicks were introduced in the B Westerns of the thirties. This format was carried over into juvenile Westerns on radio and television in the forties and early fifties. Notable adult Western satires, from *Destry Rides Again* in 1939 to Mel Brooks' *Blazing Saddles* in 1974, have been box office hits. Furthermore, humor could often be found in many of the more successful adult television Westerns like *Maverick, Sugarfoot, Laredo* and *The Wild Wild West*. Even the more serious Westerns like *Gunsmoke, The Rifleman, Bonanza* and *The Big Valley* contained humorous elements and occasionally presented entire episodes of a comedic nature.

Comedy Westerns on television, however, have been few and their success has been quite limited. If one defines this genre as involving either a spoof, parody, burlesque or satire of the traditional Western, the number broadcast can be placed at nine or ten; only one of which, *F Troop*, lasted more than a single season. It should be pointed out that not all historians of the television Western would accept *F Troop* as a bona fide Western. Ralph Brauer, for example, claims that "*F Troop* is merely a television situation comedy in a pseudo Western setting" having more in common with *Sergeant Bilko* and *McHale's Navy* than with the Western. His "test" is whether or not it attempts "to treat or examine the Western myth and its components."[1]

Long-time *TV Guide* critic Cleveland Amory once flatly stated that if it is labeled a "comedy Western ... you can probably be certain it's going to work at it too hard."[2] Michael Shane, critic for the *New York Post*, later wrote that "the last gasp of any form is spoof and parody.... So it seems the hackneyed American Western could only be presented to a jaded 1981 viewership as a spoof—a reach-for-the-sky-pardner parody."[3]

On the other hand, Harry Castleman and Walter J. Podrazik in their monumental history of television broadcasting, *Watching TV—Four Decades of American Television*, state that *F Troop* turned "the traditional John Wayne Western on its head ... and demonstrated that fresh comedy could still be found in the perennial television staple of the old West."[4] And British critic Ronald Searle pointed out (with tongue planted firmly in cheek) that "many a reputation has been destroyed by the excessively romanticized misrepresentation of historical events. We can afford to laugh at some of the naivetes of the Indian wars for we know perfectly well that it was Debbie Reynolds who won the West.... F Troop is an example of this."[5]

In any case, for the purposes of the present work the comedy Western will be considered a legitimate part of the television Western genre. Naturally, one should begin with the most successful example of this format, F Troop, which survived two seasons (1965-67) and experienced a long "after-life" through syndication. Besides, a program which produced such memorable aphorisms as "swallow who fly high in sky cannot build dam with tail of beaver" and "when field mouse see shadow, time to string beads" must certainly have some socially redeeming significance.

F Troop made its ABC debut on September 14, 1965, to good reviews and reasonably good ratings. The pilot episode begins with the story of how Captain Wilton Parmenter became commander of Fort Courage, told through brief flashbacks narrated by the (uncredited) off-screen voice of William Conrad. It seems that in an unidentified Union camp during the closing months of the Civil War, Wilton Parmenter, a private in charge of officers' laundry, inhaling an excess of pollen, suddenly sneezes, blurting out what sounds like "Charge!" Standby troopers are thus jolted into an attack that foils Confederate plans and leads to a complete Union victory. In a special ceremony, in which his distinguished relatives (including his father, General Thor Axe Parmenter, and various uncles and cousins of military rank) take part, Wilton is promoted to captain, and awarded the Medal of Honor. (When the medal is pinned on, Wilton is stuck by the pin and subsequently also awarded the Purple Heart—the first soldier ever "to get a medal for getting a medal.")

Wilton (now known as "The Scourge of Appomattox") is assigned to command F Troop, a group of army misfits stationed at Fort Courage (named for its hero-founder General Sam Courage) in Kansas. Arriving and assuming command, Parmenter meets his men: Sergeant Morgan O'Rourke, head of the illegal O'Rourke Enterprises, a business dealing in Indian souvenirs made by the friendly Hekawi Indians (he has an "exclusive" franchise to sell all their handmade goods to the tourists); Corporal Randolph Agarn, O'Rourke's vice president, chief aide and assistant schemer; Private Hannibal Shirley Dobbs, the inept company bugler (who blows reveille at ten o'clock because "there's a three-hour time difference"); Trooper Duffy, a survivor (?) of the Alamo ("There I was standing shoulder to shoulder with Davy Crockett and Jim Bowie, cannon balls to the right of us, cannon balls to the left of us..."); Trooper Vanderbilt, the lookout, who wears thick glasses and is almost blind; and a host of other incompetents. The mail is delivered by the beautiful sharpshooter Wrangler Jane (Jane Angelica Thrift), who is the proprietress of the general store, as well as postmistress of the local post office. She is also in the market for a husband (and quickly sets her sights on Captain Parmenter).

The episodes relate the misadventures of Parmenter (dubbed by O'Rourke "The Scourge of the West") and his men, as they struggle to maintain peace and order on the wild frontier. Complicating matters are O'Rourke and Agarn, who are constantly devising schemes to conceal or expand their illegal enterprises; Wrangler Jane, who is constantly devising schemes to get Wilton to the altar, and the peaceful, but devious, Hekawi led by their chief Wild Eagle, his aide Crazy Cat and the Medicine Man, Roaring Chicken. (The Hekawis who "invented" the peace pipe, are "lovers, not fighters" and have even forgotten how to do a war dance. Roaring Chicken remembers, "It like rain dance, only drier." Agarn has to teach it to them in the pilot episode.)

F Troop, **television's most successful Western spoof, featured (left to right), Larry Storch, Forrest Tucker and Ken Berry as Corporal Randolph Agarn, Sergeant Morgan O'Rourke and Captain Wilton Parmenter.**

The show presents a completely egalitarian view of the frontier—the troopers and the Indians alike are equally bumbling and inept and both are far more interested in drinking, sleeping, gambling, and turning a profit than in fighting each other. The only real threats to the happy and profitable life of F Troop and the Hekawis come from outsiders—either visiting military brass that insist the men at the fort go "by the book" (drills! exercise! reveille!) or undomesticated Indian tribes, who have never made peace with the white man, like the ferocious Shugs.

The series was a total farce with a heavy emphasis on physical humor, well-written scripts and marvelous characterizations. The physical humor was of the old burlesque slapstick school. Take, for example, the fort's lookout tower, an important gimmick in virtually every episode of the show. Whenever the cannon is fired, it always fails to go off until kicked by Corporal Agarn. This dislodges the right wheel and lowers the trajectory of the shot so that it knocks down the thirty-foot platform. (The tower was especially constructed with the legs hinged on one side. When the shot went off the legs were yanked and a stunt man, permanently employed to play the sentry, was catapulted from his perch.) Another sight gag used almost every week was much simpler. Invariably, Parmenter or Agarn would drop something down the fort's well. When they failed to hear a splash, they would bend over the edge to see what had happened and, of course, be deluged with a sheet of water. Then there was the time Dobbs tried to remove a freshly laid egg from his bugle with the anticipated consequences.

The script was usually based on a humorous premise with plenty of funny one-liners. Consider these examples: In "Dirge for the Scourge," Sam Erp, the fastest gun in the West, comes gunning for "the Scourge of the West." Wrangler Jane tries to impart some of her sharpshooting skills to Parmenter, but there is no way he is going to out-draw Erp. After futilely trying to injure his shooting hand, O'Rourke and Agarn devise a Rube Goldberg–like device which leads to Erp's capture and makes everyone think the Captain was faster than Erp. The shoot-out at the end is quite hilarious.

In "The Girl from Philadelphia," Parmenter's high society fiancée, Lucy, arrives at Fort Courage from Philadelphia and attempts to pry him away from F Troop and Wrangler Jane. Lucy's best weapon is "fainting spells," while Jane fights back first by demonstrating her considerable skill with a gun and a rope (shades of *Annie Get Your Gun*) and later by dressing and acting like a lady (shades of *Pygmalion*). Lucy is finally persuaded to return East (without Wilton) when O'Rourke and Agarn get a Hekawi Indian squaw to pretend that the Captain is the father of her papoose. It is a clever and funny episode.

In "A Gift from the Chief," Captain Parmenter accidently saves Chief Wild Eagle from a falling boulder. According to Hekawi tradition Parmenter must accept a gift from the chief—which turns out to be an Indian papoose. In order not to offend the Indians, O'Rourke and Agarn must learn how to change and amuse the baby, while trying to figure out a tactful way to return him. One way would be by letting the Chief save Parmenter's life, but Parmenter ends up saving the Chief's life again and being given the first baby's brother as his reward. Wrangler Jane finally figures out a way to return the babies without offending the Hekawis.

In "Iron Horse Go Home," the Hekawis sell their land to the government to make room for a railroad. ("Funny country. Once only buffalo live here. Injun come. Then paleface come. Now paleface give three hundred dollar for land Indian take away from buffalo. Could only happen in America.") In order to get the Indians to sell their land the Captain tells them they can live anywhere—and they move into the fort. ("This first peace treaty with room and board.") All F Troop's efforts to drive them out fail. The Hekawis finally leave because the squaws have become too much like white women—spending all day shopping and spending wampum, while the men must cook, clean and take care of the papooses. In "The Phantom Major," we meet Major Bentley Royce, a man who has lived for a month on curried cartridge belts. He is not a man to be trifled with—at least when it comes to the art of camouflage. The Major attempts to make phantoms out of F Troop by disguising them as tree stumps, horses, even buffaloes, and the result, as one might expect, is hilarious.

Other amusing stories focus on O'Rouke's attempts to set up a business in mail order brides ("Old Iron Pants"), F Troop's being chosen to test a bulletproof vest which a spy is after ("Spy, Counterspy, Counter Counterspy"), O'Rourke's attempts to play cupid for Jane and the Captain ("The Courtship of Wrangler Jane"), Agarn leaving the army to become an Indian brave ("Heap Big Injun"), Parmenter trying to trick the men of F Troop into enlisting when they discover they never legally enlisted in the first place ("Captain Parmenter—One-Man Army"), and a visit from Parmenter's bossy mother, who tries to take over Fort Courage and run things her way ("A Fort's Best Friend Is Not a Mother").

New story ideas apparently ran thin during the second season and more unusual plotlines were developed, involving gypsies ("Play Gypsy, Play"), a Japanese samurai warrior and his sweetheart ("From Karate with Love"), an Italian suitor being challenged by the Blackfoot Indians ("La Dolce Courage"), the appearance of a Dracula-like count ("V Is for Vampire"), and even a vaudeville routine involving all the cast regulars

("That's Show-Biz!"). Often the script writers resorted to song parodies in their constant search for humor. For example in "Indian Fever," when O'Rourke asks if a Hekawi brave might have been sleepwalking, Agarn responds, "Did you ever see a dream walking?" In "How to Be F Troop Without Really Trying," a young officer, hoping to be given command of Fort Courage, says to Jane, "Jeepers creepers, where'd you get those peepers—where'd you get those eyes?" Of course, there is also a continual play on words. When an Indian peers into the barracks window, Agarn exclaims, "It's a peeping tomahawk!" Then, there are the ever present, "Wild Eagle-isms." The writers have made Chief Wild Eagle a master of "the droll comment, the sententious retort, the trenchant grunt." Consider these "point-of-the-moment maxims":

> You can no make fur coat from feathers of goose.
> Old Apache saying: "merashi gogum monogoogoo!" Would give translation, but I not understand Apache.
> You show me squirrel with acorn, and I show you happy moose.

F Troop also benefited from excellent casting. In the pivotal role of Sergeant O'Rourke, Western con man par excellence, the producer cast veteran character actor Forrest Tucker, fresh from 2,008 performances as the greatest con man of the musical theater, Professor Harold Hill, *The Music Man*. Tucker had begun his career in show business at the age of 15 in a burlesque theater in Washington, D.C. He grew up during the Depression and after the death of his father when he was 4, the family moved from place to place, as his mother, a radio singer, sought work anywhere she could find it. (Forrest attended 17 different schools.)

One summer when the burlesque theater was closed (because there was no air conditioning), Tucker went to Hollywood "to look around" and ended up with a small part in *The Westerner* with Gary Cooper. After that, Hollywood became his home as he made 91 films, mostly Westerns, "with a couple of years off for World War II," Tucker later recalled in an interview. "I never really made it in pictures—I was always the other guy, the one that didn't get the girl."[6] After meeting with little success in series television (he did make several notable guest appearances on shows like *Gunsmoke*), he got his big break by being cast as Beauregard in *Auntie Mame*. Morton DeCosta, who directed *Auntie Mame*, was also directing the national road company of *The Music Man*, the show that led him directly into *F Troop*.

Ironically, Tucker as a boy had spent some time in the cavalry which gave him some firsthand experience as to "how orders were given." It was, however, the role of Professor Hill that best prepared him to play O'Rourke. "Like Professor Hill, I'm a con man. I've negotiated a private peace treaty with the Indians, who are bigger con men than I am."[7]

In one particularly memorable episode, "Did Your Father Come from Ireland?," Tucker gets to play a dual role—that of O'Rourke *and* O'Rourke's Irish father, who arrives at Fort Courage while O'Rourke is out of town. While waiting for his son to return, he tries to turn the fort into another version of Ireland by planting shamrock seeds, teaching Wrangler Jane to cook Irish stew and sing Irish love songs (to help her land the Captain), and by organizing both the troopers and the Indians into fire brigades (with near disastrous results). It is an acting tour de force for Tucker with muttonchop whiskers and a near perfect Irish brogue.

Night club comic Larry Storch auditioned for the role of O'Rourke, but even though that role was given to Tucker, executive producer Hy Averback was so impressed with Storch that he created a new role especially for him—the nutty corporal, Agarn (a hypochondriac who has no use for white doctors—he goes to the Hekawi medicine man

Forrest Tucker (left) and Larry Storch in a typical scene from *F Troop*.

for treatment). "He's our gravy comedian," Averback later said.[8] Like Tucker, Storch was a product of the Depression, his childhood haunted by memories of his cab-driver father trying to budget 65 cents a day to feed a family of four. Storch hated school and spent all the time he could holed up in cheap all-day movie houses. Pretty soon he was entertaining his friends with impressions of the actors he saw (Guy Kibee, Charlie Grapewin). At 13, he won a $2 amateur contest and shortly thereafter became a working pro.

After a stint in the Army during World War II, he landed a job on the *Kraft Music Hall* because he could imitate the voice of star Frank Morgan so well that he could substitute for him while Morgan was elsewhere. This interesting talent landed him in the Copacabana in New York and Ciro's in Hollywood, which in turn led to a season as Jackie Gleason's summer replacement on television (1953) and a few small film roles. Still Storch's career did not seem to be going anywhere until actor friend Tony Curtis helped him land the part of a Russian in his film *Who Was That Lady?* (1960). (Storch had played the same role in the Broadway stage version some years earlier.) Five years later, he landed the role he is still best remembered for, on *F Troop*.

Storch was given a chance to show off his knack for dialects in the role. In one episode he played Agarn's lookalike French-Canadian fur-trapping cousin ("The Singing Mountie"); in another, his lookalike Russian Cossack cousin ("Only One Russian Is Coming! Only One Russian Is Coming!"); and in still another his lookalike Mexican bandit cousin ("El Diablo"). He also played characters ranging from old ladies to General Grant.

Ken Berry, who became the bumbling Captain Parmenter, had been around show business for about fifteen years before he hit the big time in the sixties. As a teenager in the forties he toured the country for more than a year with Horace Heidt's Youth Opportunity caravan. He made his television debut on Arlene Francis' *Talent Patrol* in the mid-fifties, and that was followed by a spot on *The Ed Sullivan Show*. Soon, he began to land small roles in television comedies before he became a regular on *The Ann Sothern Show* (1960-61) and *The Bob Newhart Show* (1962).

Of his role on *F Troop*, Berry later said, "I loved the show and I loved the guys. It was like two years of recess."[9] As Captain Parmenter, Berry got to don funny disguises too. In one particularly amusing show ("Go for Broke"), he becomes the dashing Southern gambler Beauregard Clayton, complete with handlebar mustache and charming Southern drawl. Berry also got a chance to show off his talent for slapstick because Captain Parmenter "fell down a lot."

The other regular cast members of *F Troop* also contributed significantly to the show's success. Veteran character actor Edward Everett Horton capped an outstanding career as the old Hekawi medicine man Roaring Chicken. Cowboy star Bob Steele is said to have appeared in more than 400 films in a career that spanned fifty years before becoming Trooper Duffy. Don Diamond was right at home as Crazy Cat after playing Kit Carson's sidekick El Toro (1951–1955) and Zorro's nemesis Corporal Reyes (1957–1959). Television newcomer James Hampton brought an earnest freshness to the role of the inept bugler Hannibal Dobbs. Melody Paterson was not only beautiful, but spunky as the Calamity Jane take-off, Wrangler Jane.

Last, but certainly not least, were the brilliant performances of various popular comedians who were featured in one-time special appearances: Don Rickles as the renegade Indian who tries to go straight in "The Return of Bald Eagle"; George Gobel as Henry Terkel, Jane's inventor cousin (e.g., the "talk-a-box," oatmeal boxes strung together that people can talk over; the "hear-a-box" that will play music that has been carried from miles away through sound waves; an "extra" folding table, for use only when needed; and a wagon-mobile—in which *F Troop* invests its entire pension fund—that unfortunately does not work) in "Go for Broke"; Henry Gibson as a jinxed cavalry trooper in "Wrongo Starr and the Lady in Black" and again in "The Return of Wrongo Starr"; Milton Berle as Wise Owl, a phony Indian detective who has been stealing from the troop and trying to blame it on Agarn, in "The Great Troop Robbery"; Pat Harrington, Jr., as Maxwell Smart–clone B. Wise, spy of many disguises and concealed weapons in "Spy, Counterspy, Counter Counterspy"; Paul Lynd as Sergeant Ramsden, a singing Mountie in "The Singing Mountie"; Harvey Korman as a Prussian balloonist in "Bye, Bye, Balloon"; Phil Harris as Flaming Arrow, a 147-year-old Indian warrior who wants to take over all of America, in "Where Were You at the Last Massacre?"; screen baddie Jack Elam as the sharpshooting outlaw Sam Erp in "Dirge for Scourge" and Vincent Price as (what else?) a Dracula-like count in "V Is for Vampire." For once the critics liked a comedy Western. The usually critical Cleveland Amory said:

> If you don't mind your humor stretched far and wide and then some, you could do far worse this season than make a ... date with *F Troop*—which is not only the spoof to end all spoofs on Indian warfare but also tells you in no uncertain terms, how the West was lost.[10]

The British critic Ronald Searle wrote, "Gentlemen of *F Troop*, we salute you! *F Troop* is one of the funniest ideas to have hit television in years."[11]

Television historians Castleman and Podrazik, pointing out that *F Troop* was in the best tradition of *Sergeant Bilko*, stated that, "*F Troop* was a Western Bilko ripoff that worked ... even the men of F Troop maintained the Bilko tradition resembling a collection of refugees from the bowery rather than Civil War veterans" and "each carried the

Bilko banner of deception, double-dealing, and self-interest proudly."[12] *Variety*'s reviewer had this to say (September 13, 1965):

> Imagine the comedic team of Wayne & Schuster doing a spoof of a John Wayne cavalry picture. That's the premise, and in the first few minutes of the preem, the fast sight gags and gay cinematography grasped the mood. Even the lines rolled merrily.
>
> The spirit of fun and farce were all there but, alas, pratfall after pratfall took over, until the whole idea looked overworked and tired.

After singling out Tucker, Storch, Berry, Paterson and de Kova for praise, the reviewer observes that "repetition took the fun away." He concludes:

> Warner Bros. had all the oater props and not a dollar seemed to be stinted on production values. If only the premise had been realized!

Of course, it was the public who had the final word. The show was popular enough the first season to be renewed for a second. This time filmed in color, the show was in some ways now more visually pleasing. However, the writers seemed to run out of plausible ideas about halfway through the season, the rating dropped markedly and the series presented its last new episode in August 1967. Through the marvel of syndication the series still remains popular in some areas today. Sixty-five original episodes were produced (the equivalent of three seasons of a weekly show by today's production standards), enough for 13 weeks of Monday through Friday viewing. *F Troop*, however, remains the sole example of a successful (if modestly so), comedy Western.

After *F Troop*, the longest running comedy Western was *Guestward Ho!* True, one might have to stretch the definition a bit more to include this show in the present work, but consider this: it is set on a contemporary ranch (albeit a *dude* ranch) in New Mexico and features an Indian chief who is constantly "on the warpath" trying to win America back for the Indians. These factors seem to more than offset the fact that the stories relate the trials and tribulations of a city family trying to adjust to rural life.

The show was based on a bestselling book of the same title written by Patrick Dennis and Barbara Hooten relating the experiences of a Mrs. Hooten. Fed up with the hustle and bustle of life in New York City, Bill Hooten, a New York advertising executive, decides to purchase a dude ranch (called Guestward Ho) in New Mexico, sight unseen. When Bill, his wife Babs and son Brook arrive they find, to their surprise, that the ranch is not what they expected. It is badly run-down and in need of repairs. Furthermore, the only source of supplies for miles around is a trading post run by an Indian named Hawkeye. Hawkeye reads the *Wall Street Journal*, sells Indian trinkets that have actually been made in Japan and is determined to find a way to return the country to its rightful owners (*his* people). He is not really militant—but he *is* sly and conniving and his attempts to outsmart the white folks provide the basis for some highly amusing stories. Other continuing characters in the show include Lonesome, the Hootens' foreman, and Pink Cloud, Hawkeye's assistant at the trading post.

Many (although not all) of the humorous situations grow out of the Western setting and the continual competition between Indian and white man. In one episode ("The Matchmakers"), the Hootens hire a young Indian wrangler in order to make their lovesick cook happy. Hawkeye, however, does not believe in intertribal dating, so he tries to break up the budding romance. In "Injun Bill," Hawkeye tries to get the Hootens to rent him the ranch so he can use it as the site of the Corn Festival Celebration. Bill is named Great White Eagle in "The Honorary Indian" and is accepted as the first "immigrant member of the local Indian council." In "The Hootens' Statue," Hawkeye becomes upset when the town votes to erect a statue of Bill's pioneer grandfather instead of a statue of himself. Hawkeye arranges a wrestling match between Bill and an Indian in an episode appropriately called "The Wrestler." In "The Wild West Show" Hawkeye decides to make Babs the queen of the rodeo because the Hootens have allowed him to hold his annual rodeo at the dude ranch.

The cast of *Guestward Ho!*, like that of *F Troop*, was a mix of experienced and novice actors. In the lead role of Hawkeye was one of Hollywood's most versatile character actors and dialecticians, J. Carrol Naish. Naish was equally convincing as the naïve Italian immigrant Luigi Basco (on radio and television's *Life with Luigi*) or the wise, aphorism-sprouting Chinese detective Charlie Chan. Actually of Irish descent, Naish rarely portrayed that nationality because of his swarthy complexion. Over the years he played virtually every sort of foreigner in films and later on television.

Babs was played by the veteran screen actress Joanne Dru. A film star in the forties and early fifties, Dru did a good deal of television "theater" work in the fifties before joining the cast of *Guestward Ho!* in 1960. Rounding out the cast were newcomer Mark Miller as Bill, juvenile actor Flip Mark as Brook, Earle Hodgins as Lonesome and *Zorro* veteran Jolene Brand as Pink Cloud. However, even the occasional presence of such experienced character actors as Jackie Coogan, Richard Deacon, Jeanette Nolan, and ZaSu Pitts in featured roles was not enough to save the series from cancellation. *Guestward Ho!*, which predated *F Troop* by five years, aired 38 episodes in 1960-61. Failing to dent the ratings, it disappeared after only one season.

Following *F Troop*'s modest success, several comedy Westerns were developed for the 1966-67 season—*Pistols 'n' Petticoats*, *The Rounders* and *Rango* (a mid-season "replacement"). Of these three, *Pistols 'n' Petticoats*, produced the most episodes (26) and remained on the air the longest (September 17, 1966, to August 19, 1967). Set in and around the town of Wretched, Colorado, in the 1870s, *Pistols 'n' Petticoats* told the story of the Hanks family—Grandma and Grandpa, widowed daughter Henrietta ("Hank") and granddaughter Lucy. All except Lucy (who had spent most of her life at a finishing school in Philadelphia) were experts in the use of firearms. They could outdraw and outshoot any hotheaded gunslinger or renegade Indian who crossed them. It certainly must have been embarrassing for a reputedly dangerous outlaw to be subdued by a woman and her two elderly parents, but that was a common occurrence in and around Wretched. It was a good thing the Hanks family was able to do their part in maintaining law and order in Wretched since the sheriff (Harold Sikes) was so bumbling and inept. (He carried two guns which he either forgot to wear or was constantly tripping over.) Still, Lucy was sweet on him.

In one typical episode entitled (for no particular reason) "Quit Shootin' Folks, Grandma," Henrietta and Grandma foil a bank robbery by shooting two of the desperados with pistols concealed in their purses, while Grandpa plugs the other four (there were actually only two—Grandpa sees double without his spectacles, which he is always misplacing) with a shotgun. But what can you expect from a family so tough that they keep a mountain lion and a wolf (named Bowzer) for pets?

Later in the story, the same three sharpshooters head off an Indian attack by visiting the camp of the hostiles ("not to hurt um, but just to teach um some manners"). One example of the type of humor employed on the show comes when Grandma is asked if she understands what one of the Indians is saying. "Of course," she replies, "but he has a dreadful accent." Grandpa has some funny lines too: when he is passed a finger bowl he responds, "What in blazes is a finger bowl? I ain't plannin' to eat no fingers." In the same episode there is slapstick—the town drunk is hit on the head with a horseshoe—and sight gags galore—Grandma plays "musical bowls" with drugged firewater so the chief's son will not be able to lead the attack on the town (and yet will not "lose face" with the tribe).

The cast was certainly competent. Ann Sheridan, the pretty, fun-loving "Oomph Girl" of Hollywood in the forties, played Henrietta. Sheridan had appeared on a number of television's dramatic anthologies (*Ford Theater, Lux Video Theater*) in the fifties. Later she had become a regular on the daytime soap *Another World* before taking what was to be her last role on *Pistols 'n' Petticoats*. (She died of cancer before the season ended.) The marvelous character actress Ruth McDevitt, whose television experience dated to the early fifties when she played Wally Cox's mother on *Mr. Peepers*, played Grandma. Douglas Fowley, who had gained television fame in two different roles on *The Life and Legend of Wyatt Earp* (as Doc Fabrique in 1955-56 and as Doc Holliday from 1957 to 1961) was perfect as Grandpa.

The beautiful Carole Wells, who played Lucy, appeared to be on her way to a long and successful acting carer. She already had two years' experience as the spoiled big sister, Edwina Brown, on *National Velvet* (1960–1962). (After *Pistols 'n' Petticoats*, however, she virtually retired from the screen. Being married to one of California's wealthiest men, Edward Lawrence Doheny IV, was apparently a full time job in itself.) Gary Vinsor, who was cast as the bumbling Sheriff Sikes, had moved directly into the role after four successful seasons as Christy on *McHale's Navy* (1962–1966).

Rounding out the cast of regulars was screen veteran Lon Chaney, Jr., as Eagle Shadow, chief of the Kiowas. Chaney had played many monsters in films, following in the footsteps of his father, "the man of a thousand faces." A big, hulking brute of a man, he made a number of television appearances in the fifties and early sixties, mostly on dramatic anthologies and Westerns. He also did several memorable guest roles on *Route 66*. Chief Eagle Shadow, however, turned out to be his last major role.

With all this talent, where did *Pistols 'n' Petticoats* go wrong? As was the case in most of television's comedy Westerns, the writing left much to be desired. There were too few gags spread too thin to make a consistently quality show week after week. As *TV Guide* critic Cleveland Amory explained in his review of *Pistols 'n' Petticoats*:

> The big trouble is it evidently started out to be a satire of other Westerns and then ended up a satire—well, of itself. Satire, they say is something that closes on Saturday night. As for satire of satire—well, our only suggestion is to send it to finishing school.[13]

Pistols 'n' Petticoats did have one distinction, however. It was one of the first CBS shows regularly broadcast in color. That of course, did not save it from cancellation after only one season.

The Rounders was based on a successful novel of the same name by Western writer Max Evans. In 1965 the novel had been made into a feature film starring Glenn Ford, Henry Fonda and Chill Wills. Wills reprised his film role as Jim Ed Love, owner of the J. L. Ranch, in the television version, which also boasted John Wayne's son, Patrick, as Howdy Lewis. A robust comedy, set in the contemporary West, *The Rounders* tells the story of Ben Jones and Howdy Lewis, two rowdy, fun-loving, but dim-witted cowboys, who work as hired hands for the unscrupulous Jim Ed Love, the second richest man in Texas. (Andy Devine makes a guest appearance as Honest John Denton, the richest man.) Love is a fast talking wheeler-dealer who wears custom tailored white cowboy suits and rides the range in a souped-up station wagon. Ben and Howdy are so in debt that they have to put up with Love's constant shenanigans. (He makes them ride a mean old roan named Old Fooler.) Ben and Howdy have some fun every Saturday night, however, when they bust up the Longhorn Cafe in the nearby town of Hi Lo with the assistance of their girlfriends, Ada and Sally.

Chill Wills (he was named "Chill" because he was born on the hottest day of the year in Seagoville, Texas) was an easygoing supporting actor with a gravelly voice who had appeared in scores of Hollywood Westerns in the thirties and forties. He had also gained some notice as the voice of Francis the Talking Mule in a series of films starring Donald O'Connor. On television, Wills had been seen in many Westerns before coming to *The Rounders*. Wayne, who was to become a respected producer and director, as well as actor, was appearing in his first continuing series role. Ron Hayes' only previous television appearance was, before taking the part of Ben, in the forgettable crime series, *The Everglades* (1961-62).

Of the others in the cast only J. Pat O'Malley, who played Love's right-hand man, Vince, had any significant prior acting experience. The English-born O'Malley, a beaming, elderly "Irishman" made frequent television appearances from the sixties through the early eighties and had played Mr. Harry Burns on *My Favorite Martian* prior to joining the cast of *The Rounders*. Again, however, competent acting and promising premise were no substitute for consistently good stories. Even the presence of the "Wayne" name and an actor of Wills' proven ability could not save *The Rounders* from being canceled on January 3, 1967, after only 17 episodes.

Although some critics thought *Rango* was superior to *Pistols 'n' Petticoats* and *The Rounders*, it had an even shorter run, debuting on January 13, 1967, as part of ABC's "second season" and lasting 13 episodes. Rango is an inept, bumbling Texas Ranger who has been assigned to the Deep Wells Ranger Station, the quietest post in the state, in an attempt to keep him out of trouble. The pilot episode "Rango the Outlaw" relates the efforts of the rangers to get Rango out of the way so they can trap a dangerous band of outlaws.

Rango's assistant in the post supply room is Pink Cloud, a "civilized" Indian who has discovered that the white man's ways are much to his liking. (He would rather lie in a comfortable bed reading an interesting book than go skulking around the dusty plains.) He is also given some of the show's funniest lines: "Rango say him return when sun high over tepee. By that, I presume he meant he would be back at noon." Rango's nemesis is Captain Horton, the post commander, who would love to have him transferred, but cannot because Rango's uncle happens to be head of the Texas Rangers.

A look at some of the plotlines reveals the level of humor found in the show. In "Gunfight at the K.O. Saloon," Rango impersonates a classy thief in order to find his hidden loot. Rango tries playing detective to find a gang that is running guns to the Indians in "The Spy Who Was Out Cold." In "What's a Nice Girl Like You Doing Holding Up a Place Like This?," Rango mistakes a female bank robber for the governor's daughter, so he helps her case the bank.

"My Teepee Runneth Over" finds Rango disguising himself as a pots and pans salesman in order to rescue Pink Cloud, who has been captured by unfriendly Indians. Rango mistakes a disguised Captain Horton as a gang member of the female prisoner he is transporting in "The Not So Great Train Robbery." In "It Ain't the Principle, It's the Money," Rango and Pink Cloud pretend to be infamous outlaws so they can break up a gang of crooks. Rango and Pink Cloud visit the peaceful town of Rockhill which has not had a crime in twenty years in "If You Can't Take It with You, Don't Go." They soon discover a couple of bandits using a jail cell to tunnel through to the assay office next door. Rango dresses up as an Indian in order to capture Chief Angry Bear and finds that the Chief's daughter wants to marry him in "You Can't Scalp a Bald Indian."

Rango was played by veteran television comedian Tim Conway, fresh from four years as Ensign Charles Parker on *McHale's Navy*. He had been discovered by comedienne Rose Marie on a local television station in Cleveland and was given his first network exposure on *The Steve Allen Show* in 1961. *Rango* was only the first of several unsuccessful series starring Conway. It was not until later on *The Carol Burnett Show* (1975–1979) that he was to achieve his greatest popularity.

Guy Marks, a veteran of *The Joey Bishop Show* (1962) and *The John Forsythe Show* (1965–66), played Pink Cloud. Character actor Norman Alden, who had played Pulaski in Jackie Cooper's comedy series *Hennesey* (1960–1962) appeared as Captain Horton. The show's theme song was sung by Frankie Laine (who had performed a similar function for the successful *Rawhide* series).

The critics were divided in their appraisal of *Rango*. *New York Times* critic George Gent referred to *Rango* as a "hack in the saddle" in a January 14, 1967, review and claimed that the series was "grossly misrepresented as a spoof of television Westerns." Regarding Conway's acting he stated, "Not even Alec Guinness could be funny with such lines as 'If you Indians are so smart, how come you lost the West?' and Mr. Conway is no Sir Alec." His only "positive" comment pertained to Guy Marks' portrayal of Pink Cloud who "affected a disdainful air.... It was a winning touch. Mr. Marks has the makings of a critic."

TV Guide's resident critic Cleveland Amory called *Rango* "a carbon copy of about eight other shows" that has managed "to combine the faults of half a hundred shows. Think for a moment of some irritating little thing you don't like about some show.... All right, no matter what you've thought of, take our word for it, this one has it too."[14]

There were some critics who liked the show, however. In an unsigned (maybe this should tell us something) review in *Variety* (January 18, 1967), *Rango* was referred to as "a little gem in a bucket of lodestones." The reviewer went on to praise the series:

> This pleasant surprise begins with ... some laughable punch lines and a couple of unpredictable sight gags. Then there is lead Tim Conway ... who seems to know how to play farce for farce's sake.... Then there is some crisp editing which delivers the sight gags with some kick.

Finally, Joel Eisner and David Krinsky, in their highly regarded episode guide to *Television Comedy Series*, describe *Rango* as "one of the funniest spoofs ever produced."[15] In any case, the public did not respond to the show, and the last original episode aired on June 25, 1967.

It was six years before another attempt at a comedy Western was made. Sherwood Schwartz, producer of the successful *Gilligan's Island* (1964–1967), developed *Dusty's Trail* as a new starring vehicle for Bob Denver who had achieved considerable popularity as Gilligan. The series was syndicated to individual stations in the fall of 1973 as a package of 26 episodes. *Dusty's Trail* is set in the 1880s as a wagon train begins a long and hazardous journey to California. Through the efforts of a dim-witted scout (Dusty), a stage and wagon are separated from the main body of the train and lost. The stories relate to the efforts of the wagonmaster to deliver his passengers safely to their destination. A good case has been made by television historians Tim Brooks and Earle Marsh that *Dusty's Trail* was "almost an exact copy, character for character, of *Gilligan's Island*" — only set in the West:

> Bumbling their way across the prairie in a wagon train were Dusty (Gilligan), wagonmaster Callahan (the Skipper), the rich socialites the Brookhavens (the Thurston Howells), two sexy gals, sassy Lulu (Ginger) and sweet young Betsy (Mary Ann), and the nice young man, Andy (the professor). The simple-minded knockabout humor was also the same.[16]

The cast was certainly experienced—in the situation comedy genre. Denver had begun his carer as Dobie Gillis' beatnik buddy Maynard G. Krebs in *The Many Loves of Dobie Gillis* (1959–1963) before graduating to *Gilligan's Island*. The wagonmaster was played by Forrest Tucker of *F Troop* fame. The gals Lulu and Betsy were played by two alumnae of *Petticoat Junction* (1963–1970), Jeannine Riley and Lori Saunders. Only Ivor Francis and Lynn Wood as Mr. and Mrs. Brookhaven and Bill Cort as Andy could qualify as bona fide newcomers to the home screen. The show was panned from its initial episode. The *Variety* critic said (September 21, 1973):

> *Dusty's Trail* is plain dreadful, a silly packaging of Bob Denver in a new setting.... Denver and Tucker did pure cornball shtick with an occasional sassy line from dancehall type Jeannine Riley, with other regulars mostly standing around wondering what they were supposed to do. Nary a chuckle was to be found in the unimaginative script.

As, indeed, it was. *Dusty's Trail* disappeared in the spring of 1974 and to this writer's knowledge has not been seen since.

Eight years would pass before another comedy Western made its network appearance. In September 1981, *Best of the West* debuted on ABC. The premise for this show is clever, if not original: a "straight-arrow" Philadelphian brings his pampered family to the Wild West to fulfill his dime novel fantasies of drunken gunslingers and upright lawmen.

It seems that Sam Best, a widower and father of a 10 year old son (Daniel), had met Elvira Deveraux, a beautiful Southern belle, while he and his fellow Union soldiers were burning down her father's plantation during the closing days of the Civil War. They fall in love and marry. Following the war, the Bests settle in Philadelphia, but soon afterward Sam decides to forsake city life for the simple life of a shopkeeper out West. Misguided and naïve, Sam settles in the rough-and-tumble town of Cooper Creek, Montana.

Needless to say, the flighty Elvira (her vocabulary ranges from "my, my" to "oh my") and the smart-mouthed Daniel are not exactly happy in the rugged mining town. Elvira does try to keep a clean cabin for Sam though. Dabbing daintily at the floor with a broom, she sighs, "I just can't seem to get the dirt off this floor"—to which Sam replies, "Honey, it's a dirt floor." Meanwhile, Daniel, homesick for Philadelphia, tells his father, "I want you to understand, I'm never going outside."

Sam has more serious problems, however. The town is owned and operated by Parker Tillman, the insidious proprietor of the Square Deal Saloon. (When his construction company put up the new jail, it collapsed; when the townspeople had to fight a flood, he rented them shovels.) Then there is the vicious but incompetent gunfighter who is terrorizing the town, The Calico Kid. ("You can call me Calico or you can call me Kid, I'm easy.") When fate intervenes and Sam accidently drives him off, the grateful citizens elect him their town marshal. (The Kid, who has been a gunfighter since he was 15, realizes that one day, "I was gonna get my butt shot off" and gives up gunfighting to be cook in the saloon.)

The stories deal with Sam's misadventures as a general store owner and town marshal and the problems his ill-equipped family face as they attempt to adapt to life on the wild frontier. In the third episode a little warmth is added with the appearance of Elvira's father (played with a folksy touch by guest star Andy Griffith). Lamont Deveraux adamantly says that Elvira is no longer his daughter for having married a Yankee. He refuses to even enter their home, until Sam cons him into doing it by explaining that he will be visiting Mrs. Best, rather than his daughter. As father and daughter talk, it begins to thunder and Elvira jumps, frightened, into her dad's arms. He repeats what he used to say to her as a child: "It's only God cracking walnuts." This note of sentiment was welcome in an otherwise pretty silly show.

Virtually the entire cast were newcomers to television. Joel Higgins, who plays Sam, was seen only briefly in Andy Griffith's ill-fated series *Salvage 1* (1979). (Later Higgins did find a successful comedy series when he became the wealthy father, Edward Stratton III, on *Silver Spoons.*) Carlene Watkins (Elvira) had been seen for only a few weeks on *The Secret Empire* segment of *Cliffhanger* (1979). Before playing Daniel, Meeno Peluce's only prior television exposure came in *The Bad News Bears* (1979-80). Leonard Frey was debuting as the evil Parker Tillman. Two other cast members should be singled out, however. Veteran screen actor Tom Ewell (who costarred opposite Marilyn Monroe in *The Seven Year Itch*, 1955) added genuine humor as the town drunk, Doc Jerome Kullens, and Christopher Lloyd (The Calico Kid) who had already attained some fame as "Reverend Jim" Ignatowski in television's *Taxi* (1979–1983), would later achieve super-stardom on the big screen as the crazy inventor in the *Back to the Future* series.

Once again the critics agreed with public opinion and it was "thumbs down" for *Best of the West*. Kay Gardella, noting in the *New York Daily News* (September 10, 1981) that the series had been created by Earl Pomeranty and produced by Stan Daniels and Ed Weinberger who had so successfully collaborated on *Taxi* and earlier on *The Mary Tyler Moore Show*, then commented:

> The only reason I can assume they turned in the direction of the Old West is that it's clean fun, the kind the moral majority and other TV watchdog groups can't attack. It's also the kind of comedy over which youngsters in the family will be slapping their thighs. If you're over 10, however, the laughter begins to peter out. . . .
>
> The saloon gunfight and all of the other Western cliches are the targets for the series' satire. But the problem is, we've seen them so many times they've lost their potency. They provide only limp laughs, pale reminders of things we once considered worthy of satirical treatment. Time unfortunately, has run out. A Western has become a satire on itself. And *The Best of the West* has already reached the bottom of the barrel.

In a condemnation of all attempts at comedy Westerns, Gardella seems to be "writing" off the genre completely. Michael Shain of the *New York Post* (September 10, 1981) is hardly more optimistic:

> . . . it seems the hackneyed American Western could only be presented to a jaded 1981 viewership as a spoof. . . . It's remarkable how few good jokes can be milked from the dim-bulbs that populate Cooper Creek and from sex-role reversals. The female fur trapper and the lady blacksmith show bad comedy instincts beyond shame. . . . *Best* is a silly fabrication in search of a soul.

And it bit the dust on August 23, 1982.

So, it was back to the drawing boards for a Western spoof that worked. Given their track record in the field of general comedy, it is not surprising that the last two attempts at comedy Westerns to date were products of the Disney Studios: *Gun Shy* and *Zorro and Son*. That they both premiered on CBS less than three weeks apart (*Gun Shy* on March 15, 1983, and *Zorro and Son* on April 4, 1983) is, however, surprising. They both met the same fate—only four episodes of *Gun Shy* were ever broadcast and only six of *Zorro and Son*. Both series were also based on earlier Disney triumphs: *Gun Shy* on the Apple Dumpling Gang films (*The Apple Dumpling Gang*, 1975, and *The Apple Dumpling Gang Strikes Again*, 1979) and *Zorro and Son* on the original *Zorro* television series starring Guy Williams, which had been broadcast more than twenty-five years earlier. *Zorro and Son* even utilized footage from the opening of the earlier series, as well as the theme song, in its own opening.

Gun Shy is set in the small California town of Quake City in 1869 and depicts the misadventures of Russell Donovan, a good-natured gambler and the two precocious children (Clovis and Celia) he won in a poker game. The other major continuing characters are Theodore and Amos, two bumbling, self-styled outlaws vainly trying to establish reputations as feared desperados; Homer McCoy, Quake City's barber, sheriff and justice of the peace; Homer's ex-wife Nettie, who runs the Quake City Hotel, and Colonel Mound, the owner of the Quake City Overland Stage. The stories deal with Russell's attempts to bring up the children and the unpredictable antics of Theodore and Amos.

A pilot for the series was aired on January 16, 1982 and called *Tales of the Apple Dumpling Gang*. The show related the story of how Donovan won his wards in a card game and is forced to settle down and care for them. Meanwhile, Amos and Theodore, two hopeless outlaws, team up with the two children to form the Apple Dumpling Gang—a gang that performs good deeds. The Gang ends up saving Donovan from two bounty hunters who are seeking the $5000 reward posted on him for cheating at cards.

The cast for the series was considerably different from the one in the initial pilot, retaining only Henry Jones as Homer McCoy. It took over a year to get the program on the air and thus it became necessary to assemble a new cast. Barry Van Dyke, the son of actor Dick Van Dyke, was selected to play Russell Donovan. Barry had made his acting debut at age 9 on his father's show and later played bit parts in *The New Dick Van Dyke Show* (1971-1974) before striking out on his own. (Bill Bixby had played the role of Donovan in the original film version.)

Tim Thomerson, a veteran of five canceled situation comedies (*Cos*, *Quark*, *Angie*, *The Associates* and *The Two of Us*), became Theodore. (Comedian Don Knotts portrayed Theodore in the two Disney films.) Geoffrey Lewis, with only one previous television role (on the short-lived *Flo*), was cast as Amos. (Tim Conway was Amos in the films.)

Henry Jones, a character actor said to have appeared in more than 400 television dramas like *Kraft Theater*, *Alfred Hitchcock Presents*, *Thriller*, *Bonanza*, *Gunsmoke* and *Night Gallery* over the years, continued in the role of Sheriff McCoy, which he had created in the earlier pilot. The vivacious red-haired star of dozens of film musicals and comedies, Janis Paige, became Nettie McCoy. At one time she had starred in her own television series, *It's Always Jan* (1955-56), as a widowed show-biz mom with a cute kid. She had also appeared as a regular on *Lanigan's Rabbi* (1977) as Art Carney's wife. In between series she kept busy with guest spots on shows like *Schlitz Playhouse*, *Wagon Train* and *The Fugitive*.

Once again all the ingredients seemed to be present for a successful comedy Western— a proven concept, an experienced cast and competent writers—backed this time by one of the most successful studios in Hollywood. The failure of *Gun Shy* was a surprise to most observers, but even before that show had been canceled, Disney producer William Robert Yates had launched what was believed to be a sure winner, *Zorro and Son*. *Zorro and Son* updates the legend of Zorro, twenty-five years after the masked defender of the people had first made his name in old California. Walt Disney Productions had decided to put a contemporary satirical flavor to their venerable property.

The basic premise is that Don Diego (Zorro) is getting old and is no longer quite nimble enough to keep up his "Zorroing." When Zorro falls from a chandelier while trying to live up to his reputation, his faithful manservant decides that "the old gray fox isn't what he used to be" and sends to Spain for young Don Carlos, Diego's son. When Don Carlos arrives in California and discovers that the new commandante, Paco Pico, is unjustly oppressing the local citizens, he is filled with a desire to help them. Seeing this, Don Diego reveals to his son his other identity (the son never knew his father was Zorro) and launches a training program to prepare his son to become the new Zorro, defender of the people.

Don Carlos is impressed with his father's deeds, but he is not convinced that the masked caballero guise is the way to get the job done anymore. At the same time the elder Zorro has great difficulty adjusting to his son's use of guns, gas bombs, and other modern weapons, instead of a simple sword. The stories depict the comical adventures of Zorro and his son as they struggle to protect the oppressed. In addition to father, son, faithful servant and evil commandante, other regulars in the cast include Sergeant Sepulveda, Pico's wishy-washy assistant; Corporal Cassette, a "human recording machine capable of rapidly repeating an entire conversation verbatim over and over. . ."; Señorita Anita, a beautiful young woman who is "sweet" on Zorro and Brother Napa, a local Franciscan monk—who is arrested by Pico in the pilot episode for "selling a wine before its time."

The humor on the show can be found in send-ups of everything from commercials (e.g., Orson Welles' wine commercial) and popular music (e.g., in one episode when Zorro, Jr. is sent on a mission to the North, he responds, "Yes, father, I know the way to San Jose"), to superheroes (e.g., Zorro, Jr., proclaims in the opening episode that he is fighting for "truth, justice and the American way," which, of course, was Superman's motto) and contemporary politics (e.g., when El Excellente fires Pico he laments, "The people won't have Paco Pico to kick them around any more").

Then there is Commandante Pico's idea of torture: "forcing a man with a hangover to listen to a mariachi band." And Bernardo's description of the bald "Butcher of Barcelona": "his hair left on purpose because it wanted to live on a nicer person." Sight gags like Zorro, Jr., dressed in a ridiculous Zorro costume made from flowered drapes (because the genuine Zorro outfits have been seized by Pico), also abound.

Plotlines for the stories include protecting an escaped flamenco dancer who is actually a Mexican revolutionary (if you listen carefully you can hear her—she never moves without clicking her castanets), tracking down the Zorro imposter (Pico) who is robbing the poor to ruin Zorro's reputation and smoke out his real identity, preventing Bernardo from being hanged as Zorro (since he was captured while doing Zorro's laundry), and saving Pico from being fired from his post by his superiors ("to prevent a greater evil"— i.e., a more competent commandante might replace the bumbling, ineffective Pico).

Again, little fault can be found with the cast. Don Diego is played with the proper degree of dash and energy by *High Chaparral* alumnus Henry Darrow. Paul Regina brings an appealing "street-wise quality" to Don Carlos. Gregory Sierra (with plenty of previous television exposure in *Sanford and Son*, *Barney Miller* and *Soap*) effectively combines arrogance and pomposity into his comic portrayal of Pico. Bill Dana, the star of such popular comedy shows as *The Steve Allen Show*, *The Spike Jones Show* and his own show (as the lovable José Jímenez), is delightful as Bernardo. And John Moschitta (well-known for his rapid fire Federal Express commercials) has his funny moments as Corporal Cassette.

Nevertheless, *Variety* (April 13, 1983) wrote that the show was only "mildly" successful and badly needed "a stronger satirical cutting edge to amuse adults along with the target kid audiences." Alas, the viewers again agreed with the critics and another genuinely clever concept failed to generate sufficient ratings to avoid cancellation.

Thus the track record of comedy Westerns is dismal—especially in light of the general popularity of both situation comedies and Westerns (at least through the mid-sixties). The most successful use of satire in Westerns occurred when popular, established series like *Maverick*, *Gunsmoke* and *Bonanza* used comedy to poke fun at various aspects of the Western myth. Still, the serious student of television Westerns cannot ignore the continuing attempts by the networks to discover an effective comedy Western formula.

XII. James Bond Goes West
A VISIT TO "THE WILD WILD WEST"

James T. West was the James Bond of Western heroes. Exciting as well as humorous, the show in which he starred borrowed from such successful series as *The Man from U.N.C.L.E.* and *Maverick*. Representing an almost perfect blend of espionage thrills, fantasy, science fiction adventure and cowboy action, it was called *The Wild Wild West*, in a play on both the hero's name and the geography. West was a superspy who battled super villains with super weapons. There was only one significant difference from all the other secret agents filling the home and movie screens of the 1960s — West lived in the 1870s, and his boss was President Ulysses S. Grant. His assignment was to defeat assorted lunatics who were out to take over this country (or in some cases, the entire world) usually with the aid of some kind of futuristic doomsday machine.

The series was the brainchild of Michael Garrison. In 1955 Garrison and his partner, Gregory Ratoff, discovered a novel by a little-known author named Ian Fleming called *Casino Royale*. It introduced a British secret agent named James Bond. Feeling that a "great" movie could be made from this story, Garrison and Ratoff bought the screen rights and tried to convince 20th Century–Fox to finance a film. There was, however, no interest at the time. When Ratoff died, his widow needed money, so she and Garrison sold the film rights. By 1965, James Bond movies were breaking box office records.

Garrison now began to work on a concept for a new television series involving secret agents and spies, but in an early Western setting. He later candidly admitted in an interview, "We combined some trends. We knew the Western was good and we knew the Bond trend was good.... I see nothing wrong with television following the Bond or any other trend. It's necessary. Television reflects what people are thinking. [But] I don't think you can really transpose Bond to a 7:30 PM time slot, because of all the sex...."[1] The new series incorporated much of the gadgetry associated with the spy craze in an embryonic form. Garrison resorted to primitive explosives and hidden weapons and borrowed heavily from Jules Verne's cadre of "mad scientists."

By the time the show reached viewers in the fall of 1965, it had undergone several changes. When CBS first announced plans for the series, veteran Western actor Rory Calhoun (*The Texan*) had been slated for the lead. When the pilot went into production, however, young Robert Conrad was cast as James T. West. As Conrad's costar, a versatile character actor named Ross Martin was signed to play West's partner, Artemus Gordon.

The music for the series also underwent revision. Initially, film composer Dimitri Tiomkin and lyricist Paul Francis Webster were contracted to write a theme song for the series. However, Garrison thought their work was too tame for the show and hired Richard Markowitz (composer of "The Ballad of Johnny Yuma" theme for *The Rebel*) to compose a livelier tune.[2] Even the name of the series underwent a slight revision. The title on the pilot film was simply *The Wild West*, but by the time it reached the airwaves it had gotten a little wilder. Furthermore, that opening episode originally entitled "The Cannonball Eightball" had now become "The Night of the Inferno," a pattern that all future episodes were to use.

Another remarkable and ingenious feature of the series was the opening and commercial break format. The screen was divided into five panels. Each panel was animated. In the center is a man (clearly James T. West). The bottom left shows a robber backing out of a bank with a bag of loot. West knocks the robber down. Then, a card falls out of the boot of the gambler depicted in the upper right corner. West draws a gun on the card cheat. Then the figure in the top left corner draws on West. West drops his gun and slowly raises his hands, in the process shooting the man with a derringer he had up his sleeve. In the bottom right corner, a beautiful woman approaches and hits West with a parasol. West grabs and embraces her and she tries to stab him. In the first season, he then pushes her away, picks up his hat and walks off into the distance. In subsequent seasons, he slugs her, then picks up his hat and walks away. All of this is accomplished in nonstop, slam bang action to the springy strains of the show's opening theme.

Each commercial break was preceded by the same five panel frame. The scene would invariably end in a "cliffhanger" situation with a freeze frame of the action dissolving into either a drawing (the first year) or a tinted picture which replaces one of the four corners from the opening sequence. At the end of the show, the train (home base of James and Artie) would fill the center frame and chug off into the distance. This unique animated sequence was supervised by Albert Heschong, the art director for the series.[3]

As is so often the case, in retrospect the two stars of *The Wild Wild West* seem perfectly suited to their roles. Robert Conrad, a surprise last minute replacement for the more experienced Calhoun, was young and handsome. What probably got him the role, however, was his ability to do his own stunts. Conrad was not only capable of performing the difficult feats of physical prowess demanded by the show, he gloried in it. He once told a *TV Guide* interviewer, "It's an emotional, psychological, physical release for me. It's exciting."[4] (Conrad did, however, suffer serious injuries on one occasion when in "The Night of the Fugitives," West was supposed to sail off a balcony, grab a chandelier and land on a villain below. His timing was off and he landed on his neck and head instead.)

Born Conrad Robert Falk in 1935, he had been interested in performing for most of his young life. By the time he was in high school, he had appeared on stage and came up with a new name, reversing his first and middle names and dropping his last name. In 1957, Conrad found himself supporting a wife and two young daughters by driving a milk truck during the day and singing in a small Chicago nightclub at night. A self-described "young man in a hurry," he got his first break when he met actor Nick Adams. Adams suggested that Conrad give acting a try and promised he would "try to help" if Conrad ever came to Hollywood.

Conrad immediately enrolled as a parttime student at Northwestern University in speech and drama. After only a year of study and with a little encouragement from a Columbia Studios scout he met during one of the perennial university talent searches, Conrad set out for Hollywood. Adams, who became Conrad's best friend, did introduce him

The stars of *The Wild Wild West*:Ross Martin (left) as Artemus Gordon and Robert Conrad as James T. West.

around and helped him obtain a Screen Actors Guild card and an agent. After only a few bit parts in B movies and television shows (*Sea Hunt, Highway Patrol,* and *Bat Masterson*), he was signed by Warner Bros. and appeared on *Lawman, Maverick* and *77 Sunset Strip* before becoming Tom Lopaka in *Hawaiian Eye*. This series, which lasted four years (1959–1963), gave Conrad the opportunity to doff his shirt and display his awesome muscular development (which he kept in shape with daily workouts).

After the cancellation of *Hawaiian Eye*, Conrad bided his time waiting for just the right vehicle to come along, refusing to "compromise" his career by taking minor roles or single guest starring shots on someone else's show. Instead, he made a film in Spain, toured Australia with a night club act, did a special on Mexican television and a stint in a Mexico night club. His patience paid off when he landed the lead in *The Wild Wild West*.

The one aspect of Conrad's role of James T. West which bothered him was his height. Even in the three-inch heels which he always wore, he barely looked to be the five-foot-ten attributed to him in CBS publicity releases. The casting office had orders not to hire any women over five-foot-six and although men could be of any height, the producers were careful never to surround him with groups of tall actors.[5] Nevertheless, Conrad was a master of self-defense and weaponry and a regular feature of each episode came when Jim West was attacked by at least five thugs, all of whom he dispatched in impeccable style.

James T. West had been born in July 1842 and enlisted in the army at an early age. By the 1870s, the period that the series depicts, he had ten years' military experience and had risen to the rank of captain. He was also skilled at karate and various forms of judo and was an expert with small arms (e.g., derringers, revolvers). In fact, in "The Night of the Surreal McCoy," he is acknowledged as "the fastest gun alive" in dispatching Lightnin' McCoy, one of the top fast-draw artists in the West. He was also a master in the use of samurai swords, as viewers discovered in "The Night of the Samurai."

West had a way with the ladies too. In fact, it was often his power over members of the fairer sex that kept him alive. Even women who were supposedly strong and independent typically became putty in his hands when he turned on his boyish charm. A certain Sergeant Musk finds this out to her dismay in "The Night of the Red-Eyed Madman." In fact the only vulnerability of West's archnemesis, Dr. Miguelito Loveless, came from the women he kept around him. They invariably succumbed to West's charms and turned on Loveless when the chips were down (e.g., characters Greta Lundquist in "The Night That Terror Stalked the Town" and Kitten Twitty in "The Night of the Murderous Spring").

The homebase for the agents was a three car train complete with dining, sleeping and recreational facilities. A hidden wardrobe provided ample changes of clothes for the two (although Jim seemed to favor one of two blue suits with Spanish-cut jackets and tight, tight pants). Jim also would frequently pull down a concealed arsenal of weapons. Certain pool balls were bombs, one cue stick contained a rapier and the other a derringer. Furthermore, the car was equipped with materials to concoct all sorts of bizarre weapons and devices with which to foil their adversaries. There was a telegraph transmitter key located inside fake books on a desk near the first coach's rear door. The agents also utilized carrier pigeons located near the rear of the second coach.

West used many concealed weapons and devices: a derringer on a spring-loaded track strapped to his right arm; the butt and barrel of a broken-down derringer in his hollow boot heels; a throwing knife just below the collar in the lining of his coat. His vest buttons were hand bombs. His belt buckle often hid the wire and grappling hook he used with a pulley to traverse seemingly uncrossable chasms. He also kept a key-like device under his left lapel for unlocking all sorts of locks.

Ross Martin was born Martin Rosenblat in Poland. He did not speak English until he was 4 and he was raised amid gang wars on New York's East Side and in the Bronx. Still, his favorite pastime as a child was playing the violin. At 10, Martin tied for first place in an amateur contest with a boy who later became known as Red Buttons. About that same time he was playing the violin in the symphony orchestra at Columbia University's Teachers College. When he was 15 he received a scar between his eyes from falling into a quarry during a gang fight. Later he referred to it as a "scowl line" and claimed it gave his face character.[6]

While in college Martin teamed up with Bernie West (later a very successful television comedy producer) in a stand-up comedy act called Ross and West. The two of them did funny impersonations of the popular stars of the day (e.g., Nelson Eddy bellowing

Ross Martin excelled in impersonations, with a variety of disguises and dialects on *The Wild Wild West*.

a love song into the ear of a bravely smiling Jeanette MacDonald) as part of a Major Bowes (*Original Amateur Hour*) traveling unit. Other roles played by Martin in this act included FDR, Hitler, Ronald Colman and even the RKO-Pathé rooster. In college, Martin studied business administration, education and later, law. In 1940 he graduated with honors from the College of the City of New York. Among the many jobs he held in order to pay his tuition, were sheet metal worker (like his father), department store buyer, government economist and public relations agent. But it was acting that had fascinated Martin all along.

During the late forties he played three parts on the radio soap opera *Janice Grey* and later appeared in *Hazel Flagg* on Broadway. Guest appearances on early television dramatic anthologies like *Philco Playhouse* and *Studio One* followed. He also turned up often on *Lights Out* (1949–1952) and was seen on such series as *Treasury Men in Action*, *The Court of Last Resort*, *Alcoa Presents* and *Peter Gunn*. Motion pictures beckoned and Martin appeared as an intrepid astronaut in *Conquest of Space* (1955), the psychopathic, asthmatic killer in *Experiment in Terror* (1962), and as a swashbuckling swordsman in *The Great Race* (1965). His first continuing role on a television series was as John Vivyan's helper, Andamo, in *Mr. Lucky* (1959-60).

Mostly, Martin was noted for his portrayal of villains—often those marked by unusual traits of appearance, like one-fourth of the split personalities locked in the body of one small, mean man in *The Twilight Zone*'s famous episode, "The Four of Us Are Dying." He also later claimed he gained valuable experience on the charades game show, *Stump the Stars*. The role of Artemus Gordon in *The Wild Wild West* suited Martin to a T, giving him a chance to play many different character roles as Artie donned frequent disguises. It was, he later admitted, "A show-off's showcase!"[7] Ross Martin accomplished these many character changes with the aid of a special eight-piece plastic nose that he designed himself. This changed his facial appearance and by also altering his voice and body mannerisms, Artie was able to successfully pass as numerous different characters.

Martin had a unique approach to each *Wild Wild West* role. First he read the script and did a pen and ink drawing of the character he was going to play, down to the last detail including glasses, mustache, clothes, posture, shoes, and so on. Then he took the sketch to make-up artist Don Schoenfeld, and together they molded his face until it looked like the drawing. "As the face emerges," Martin said in an interview, "I begin to really feel the character. By the time we're through, I'm beginning to behave like that character."[8]

The character Artemus Gordon was born in 1835 and experienced a relatively normal childhood until high school. Remembered as always being in need of a haircut, Artie became a "silver-tongued speaker." Later he tried his hand at acting and was, in his own words, "on the boards" for a time ("The Night of the Big Blast"). Before joining the Secret Service, Gordon must have had some higher education; he was an accomplished chemist, devising many of the ingenious explosives that West and he used. (For example, in "The Night of the Glowing Corpse," Artie invents an oxygen mask and putty that will support a man's weight for ten seconds, which later saves Jim's life.) He also seemed to understand the scientific principles involved in many of the strange weapons they encountered. (In "The Night of the Falcon," Artie figures out the secret of a weapon of incredible force, by analyzing fragments of a shell casing.)

In spite of Artie's great analytical powers, his real strength lay in the "creative arts." He was a gourmet cook and sometimes used that skill as a cover ("The Night of the Infernal Machine" and "The Night of the Big Blackmail"). He also could play a wide variety of musical instruments ("The Night of the Returning Dead"). Of course, it was as a make-up artist and character actor that Artemus really excelled. The character also could speak numerous foreign languages and could shift from a Spanish dialect to a Russian, Italian, French or German one with ease.

Among Artie's more interesting disguises were those of a Mexican peasant ("The Night of the Deadly Bed"), a circus clown ("The Night of Sudden Death"), a Shakespearean actor ("The Night of the Casual Killer"), an Irish delivery man ("The Night of the Glowing Corpse"), a German military expert ("The Night of the Red-Eyed Madman"), President Ulysses S. Grant ("The Night of the Bottomless Pit"), a fastidious tailor ("The Night of the Vicious Valentine"), a blind, crippled beggar ("The Night of the Deadly Bubble"), Lightnin' McCoy, "the fastest gun in the West" ("The Night of the Surreal McCoy"), a sophisticated French artist and a grizzled old prospector ("The Night of the Bogus Bandits"), a French doctor ("The Night Dr. Loveless Died"), a Bosnian count with an iron hand ("The Night of the Iron Fist"), an Indian chief ("The Night of the Arrow'), a salty old seaman ("The Night of the Headless Woman"), an Eastern newspaperman ("The Night of the Vipers"), a wealthy Texan ("The Night of the Juggernaut"), a Portuguese fisherman ("The Night of the Kraken"), and General Robert E. Lee ("The Night of Fire and Brimstone").

(Author Lorraine Beaty has compiled an extensive episode-by-episode list of Artie's impersonations and cites more than 120 different disguises donned by Ross Martin in his four seasons on *The Wild Wild West*. The annotated list is included in James Van Hise's book on the series. A detailed and fascinating discussion of the artistry of make-up technician Don Schoenfeld, complete with extensive photos and drawings, is presented in Susan E. Kesler's *The Wild Wild West: The Series*, the definitive work to date on the show).[9] Gordon also performed many of his own stunts and received his share of cuts and bruises. In "The Night of the Juggernaut," Artie is seen only from the waist up because early in the filming he had broken his leg. During the final season (1968-69), a more serious calamity befell Gordon. He suffered a heart attack and was forced to take a leave of absence for nine episodes. In these episodes Artie was said to be on "special assignment" in Washington. Meanwhile, West carried on either alone (in "The Night of Bleak Island" and "The Night of the Tycoons") or with another agent.

For four episodes Jeremy Pike (played by veteran actor Charles Aidman) was West's new partner ("The Night of the Camera," "The Night of Miguelito's Revenge," "The Night of the Pelican," and "The Night of the Janus"). Pike also demonstrated quite a flair for disguises, donning no fewer than three, including that of an English gambler, in his very first episode. Ned Brown was West's assistant in "The Night of the Sabatini Death." Brown was played by Alan Hale, who had recently gained fame as "the Skipper" on *Gilligan's Island*. As a sort of inside joke, when Brown tells West that he plans on taking a vacation on a desert island in the Pacific, the strains of the theme to *Gilligan's Island* are heard in the background. The remaining two episodes without Artie featured William Schallert (who had played a villain in "The Night of the Bubbling Death," and an escaped criminal in "The Night of the Gruesome Games") as agent Frank Harper. This was the only two part story in the series ("The Night of the Winged Terror"). Harper, following in the tradition of West's other partners, appears in the disguise of a German scientist.

Mention also should be made of the appearance of popular comedian Pat Paulsen as neophyte agent Bosley Cranston in "The Night of the Camera." Cranston has only one special talent, a photographic memory. Bosley's job is to get a look at an opium smuggler's code book and memorize it. Not only does he accomplish his task admirably (despite breaking his spectacles) but in the end he proves to be quite handy with his fists and quite a charmer with the ladies (much to the amazement of West and Pike). Paulsen does quite well in what is essentially a "straight role."

One of the most appealing aspects of *The Wild Wild West* was its host of fascinating, but generally quite insane, villains usually played by some "name" guest star. By far the most popular of these was the dwarf Dr. Miguelito Loveless, delightfully portrayed by Michael Dunn. Dr. Loveless clashed with West a total of ten times, four times during each of the first two seasons and once during each of the final two.

Michael Dunn's real name was Gary Neil Miller, and he was born in Shattuck, Oklahoma, of Irish, Scotch and Indian ancestry. He did not develop normally; both of his hips were dislocated, making walking a constant source of pain throughout his life. By the time he was 4 he knew he would be a dwarf, growing to a height of only three feet, ten inches, and when he was 5 the disease was diagnosed. It was a rare form of nonhereditary dwarfism believed to be caused by a chemical imbalance during gestation.

Dunn was exceptionally bright and talented. He enrolled as a student at the University

of Michigan and later transferred to the University of Miami when his illness required
a warmer climate. At Miami he became editor of the college newspaper, acted in plays,
became a cheerleader and sang in a local nightclub (his voice was booming and resonant
despite his size) in order to pay part of his tuition. He knew by the time he graduated that
he wanted to become a professional actor. "Frankly," he told a reporter, "I knew there
wouldn't be too much competition for roles. There are a great many professional midgets,
but there aren't too many dwarfs who can act."[10]

While waiting for his big break, he found temporary employment as a sports writer,
a hotel detective and a missionary. Soon he got some small parts as jesters, fools, and the
like in Off Broadway productions. Then he landed a role as the "insides" of a robot in
the Broadway production of *How to Make a Man*. In 1963 he was cast as Cousin Lyman
in the Edward Albee adaptation of Carson McCullers' *The Ballad of the Sad Cafe*, for
which he was critically acclaimed and nominated for a Tony Award. This performance
changed Dunn's luck for good and opened the door to fame in the theater, movies and
television. In addition to the Tony nomination, in 1965 he received an Academy Award
nomination and the Laurel Award as the best supporting actor in *Ship of Fools*, in which
he played Karl Glocken, an evil dwarfed hunchback, who also narrated the film. He later
earned Emmy nominations for guest appearances on television in *Bonanza* and in his
most famous home screen role as Dr. Loveless on *The Wild Wild West*.

Still Dunn was frustrated by the lack of variety in the parts he was offered. "'Here's
a midget part,' producers say," he complained, "'Mike's available.' Then they soft-soap
me about what a great actor I am. I don't want to play Charlton Heston parts, but there
are a lot of roles I can do."[11] Nevertheless, Dunn's appearance in *The Inner Journey*, a
tragedy that was performed at the Lincoln Center in New York City in 1969, brought the
following comments from *The New York Times* drama critic Clive Barnes:

> Michael Dunn as the dwarf is so good that the play may be worth seeing merely for him.
> Controlled, with his heart turned inward, his mind a pattern of pain, Mr. Dunn's Antaeus
> deserves all the praise it can be given.[12]

After Dunn's death (of an apparent suicide at the age of 39 while filming on location
in London in 1973), Robert Conrad commented in an interview in *Starlog* that his contributions to *The Wild Wild West* helped the program tremendously. "Dunn never felt like
he was being made a joke of; that is not what we set out to do with his character. In fact,
he loved the role so much that he really came to think he *was* Dr. Loveless."[13]

From his ten appearances on *The Wild Wild West* and the appearance of his son
Miguelito, Jr. (played by another actor), in *The Wild Wild West Revisited*, Dr. Loveless'
background can be described. He was born in 1848 somewhere in southern California
of Spanish ancestry. He died in 1880 of, according to his son, ulcers brought on by worry-
ing about the meddling of West and Gordon in his affairs. It is not clear whether or not
the "doctor" was an earned or honorary title, but it is a fact that Loveless was a brilliant
scientist who was vastly ahead of his time in the fields of science and technology.

Among Loveless' discoveries and inventions were "a device that can project and
receive voices and music through the air," a medicine made "from ordinary bread mold,
so potent that with it one can begin to conquer all illness," a machine "that one day will
travel over roads by its own power," a machine "that will fly through the air," an explosive
"that can move mountains, change the course of rivers, blast channels for the waters of
life to flow into dry deserts" and a device that could "send pictures through the air and
catch them in a glass tube." And these devices were only those Dr. Loveless presented
in his first appearance in "The Night the Wizard Shook the Earth." Declaring that he

Michael Dunn was brilliant as West's archenemy Dr. Miguelito Loveless in a number of *The Wild Wild West* **episodes.**

could "make a world without blemish, where children can grow up in beauty," Loveless proclaimed his hatred for "any twisted thing."

There was, unfortunately, another side to Dr. Loveless. His family had once been granted nearly half of present-day California by the Spanish crown. Loveless was willing to kill 5000 people unless the governor of California agreed to return the demented doctor's ancestral lands to him. Loveless also obviously had an inferiority complex based on his size and had dedicated his life to getting even with all those who felt superior to him because of their taller stature—which, of course, included most of the population. In one episode, "The Night of the Raven," he comes up with the perfect revenge—a device which can shrink human beings down to a size of six inches without harming them.

Dr. Loveless' other nefarious plans included creating an exact duplicate of West through plastic surgery so that he can infiltrate the Secret Service ("The Night That Terror

Stalked the Town"), ruining the economy of California by killing each financier who has invested in the state with exploding toys ("The Night of the Whirring Death"), poisoning the water supply with an LSD-type drug that turns its drinkers into murderers through hallucinations ("The Night of the Murderous Spring"), inventing a pesticide that will eliminate bugs and cause a famine in the Indian Territory so that he can use the Indians as slaves in his new utopia, Sherwood Forest ("The Night of the Green Terror"), projecting gunmen into another dimension inside paintings which are then hung in banks, so that after hours the gunmen can jump out and rob the banks ("The Night of the Surreal McCoy"), and breaking simultaneously into the federal penitentiary, the federal arsenal, and the federal mint ("The Night of the Bogus Bandits").

"The Night Dr. Loveless Died" provided Dunn with the opportunity of playing a dual role—Dr. Loveless and Loveless' uncle, Dr. Werner Leibknicht, complete with spectacles, grey locks and beard. In this episode Loveless tricks West into believing he is dead and not even the world's greatest secret agent suspects that Leibknicht is really Loveless. The ruse is necessary because Loveless needs West's help in disposing of a troublesome rival named Deuce. Once this has been accomplished, Loveless plans to perform brain surgery on him but Artie comes to the rescue in the nick of time. It is a typical slam-bang Loveless adventure, with Dunn outstanding, as usual.

Dunn's final appearance on *The Wild Wild West* occurred during the final season ("The Night of Miguelito's Revenge") and involved a new plan to get rid of Jim and have some fun at the same time. Several prominent people have disappeared recently, and Jim and Jeremy have only one clue to go on: a message that "Tuesday's child has far to go." Loveless is using a circus as a cover while he kidnaps people according to the nursery rhyme. Six people are missing, one for each day of the week (except Sunday), and each is slated for death. According to the doctor, each of the seven has committed some heinous offense against him in the past. Number seven, Sunday's child, is of course, James T. West. How West and Pike escape Loveless' clutches makes for an entertaining adventure.

Unfortunately some of the clever touches the writers added to the Loveless stories during the first season are missing from later episodes. For example, in the first four episodes the diminutive doctor is accompanied by his towering bodyguard Voltaire, masterfully underplayed by the seven-foot, two-inch Richard Kiel (who was later to earn screen immortality as James Bond's nemesis "Jaws" in two of the *007* films). At first, it appears that the giant is mute, but in "The Night of the Whirring Death," Voltaire does speak. Voltaire's loyalty to Loveless, unlike many of the doctor's feminine companions, is total. Additionally, during the first six Loveless episodes one of his most devoted companions is Antoinette (portrayed by Phoebe Dorin), who invariably sings a duet with the doctor, often while playing the harpsichord. This provides Dunn with an opportunity to demonstrate his vocal ability and adds another dimension to the show as they harmonize beautiful folk songs like "False-Hearted Lover," "Sloop John B" or "Bring a Little Water, Sylvie."

Another popular villain who returns after his initial encounter with Jim and Artie, is the evil magician Count Carlos Mario Vincenzo Robespierre Manzeppi, adventurer, poet and "lover of all that is corrupt, forbidden and blasphemous." Played by the superb character actor Victor Buono, the Count bedevils our intrepid heroes twice during the second season, in "The Night of the Eccentrics" and "The Night of the Feathered Fury." Buono also had the distinction of appearing in both the pilot episode (in the dual role of the fiendish Wing Fat and Juan Manola) and in the final film sequel, *More Wild Wild West* as Dr. Henry Messenger, United States secretary of state (in a delightful parody of Dr. Henry Kissinger).

Along with the amazing gadgets and weapons introduced into each story, it was the diabolical criminal types that West and Gordon battled each week that stimulated viewer interest. Some of the more outlandish would fit nicely into practically any of the better James Bond films. There is, for example, Ironfoot (Charles Howath) in "The Night of the Glowing Corpse," a human lethal weapon with six-inch blocks of iron in each shoe. Topping him, Iron Man Torres (John Dehner), an ex–Union officer, has had the injured parts of his body replaced with steel, making him virtually invulnerable in "The Night of the Steel Assassin."

Asmodeus, the magician, provides a different kind of challenge to West and Gordon, in "The Night of the Druid's Blood." Played straight with fiendish cunning by comedian Don Rickles, Asmodeus could, among other things, make himself disappear. He turns out to be a front man for an insane doctor who had discovered a way of keeping the brains of murdered scientists alive. Other memorable villains in the series include the Prince (played by Conrad's old friend Nick Adams), in "The Night of the Two-Legged Buffalo," Maharajah Singh (portrayed by the screen's most famous "mad scientist," Boris Karloff), in "The Night of the Golden Cobra," and the grotesquely deformed Tycho (Christopher Cary), in "The Night of the Winged Terror."

In a turnabout from usual casting practices, the criminal masterminds are women in several interesting episodes. Veteran screen actress Ida Lupino plays Dr. Faustina, a brilliant female scientist who plans to gain revenge on U.S. Cabinet members for refusing to grant her funds for research, in "The Night of the Big Blast." "The Night of the Vicious Valentine" provides another established stage and film actress, Agnes Moorehead, with the juicy role of Emma Valentine, who has invented a computer dating machine that systematically matches the wealthiest men in the United States with her cadre of trained beauties. After each marriage, the groom is murdered and his wealth becomes part of the corrupt Valentine empire. When West is captured by Emma the following exchange takes place:

> EMMA: Yes, Mr. West. I regard myself, not as a criminal, but as savior of all womankind.
> WEST: Interesting ... and what do women have to be saved from?
> EMMA: From domination of the spirit, economic exploitation, annihilation of the mind, in brief, all the injustices wrought by men.... Your ideal mate Mr. West (after she extracts the information from the computer) ... is a combination of Aphrodite, Helen of Troy and Lola Montez. Oh, Mr. West I'm afraid it can't be done.
> WEST: Well, frankly I like to do my own shopping anyway.

Emma Valentine was not only a computer genius, but a feminist-liberationist, far ahead of her time!

Other notable villains were played by Burgess Meredith as the deranged geologist Professor Orkney Cadwallader, in "The Night of the Human Trigger," Sammy Davis, Jr., as the mysterious stableman Jeremiah, in "The Night of the Returning Dead," Carroll O'Connor, as the undertaker Fabian Lavendor, faking the deaths of wanted criminals by using lookalike corpses in "The Night of the Ready-Made Corpse," Ricardo Montalban as the insane ex–Confederate officer Vaultrain in "The Night of the Lord of Limbo," Joseph Campanella as the "wolf man" Talamantes in "The Night of the Wolf," Robert Duvall as powermad Dr. Horace Humphries, the Falcon, in "The Night of the Falcon," Mark Lenard, Count Draja, in "The Night of the Iron Fist," Edward Asner as sadistic killer Furman Crotty in "The Night of the Amnesiac," Harvey Korman as the diabolical German Baron Hinterstoisser, in "The Night of the Big Blackmail" and Khigh Dhiegh as the notorious criminal Din Chang in "The Night of the Pelican."

In addition to the fascinating villains, viewers of *The Wild Wild West* also delighted in the far-out gadgetry converted into weapons and arrayed against the good guys by those terribly cunning and evil bad guys. Again the Bond influence is quite apparent. Most of these strange death-dealers were conceived in conference, but the leading light behind many was a man named Henry Sharp, a one-time ad designer, one-time cartoonist, one-time script writer who had been made chief story consultant for *The Wild Wild West*. Sharp would sketch a preliminary design. The concept and sketch would then be given to the writer and he would write a story around it. This unorthodox procedure was described by one writer "as a bit like thinking up a baby and then building a family—mother, father, grandparents and siblings—around the infant."[14]

Over the course of four seasons Jim or Artie or both, and often populations of entire cities as well, faced death at the hands of the following ingenious devices: a canopy bed whose top consisted of daggers descending to skewer its unfortunate occupant ("The Night of the Deadly Bed"), a highly radioactive and potentially explosive substance called Franconium, an obvious type of plutonium ("The Night of the Glowing Corpse"), an army of life-size puppets ("The Night of the Puppeteer"), the X-2 rifle, a revolutionary weapon that fires explosive bullets, along with the prototype of a modern tank ("The Night of the Freebooters"), a remote-controlled torpedo that will be used to control the world's shipping lanes ("The Night of the Watery Death"), a time machine that projects Jim and Artie back into the midst of the Civil War ("The Night of the Lord of Limbo"), a glass roof of a wedding chapel designed to shatter when a certain chord is played on the organ, hurling the agents to their death ("The Night of the Vicious Valentine"), a tidal wave machine built to inundate the population centers along the East Coast, thus "punishing" mankind for polluting the oceans ("The Night of the Deadly Bubble"), a moat filled with highly corrosive acid ("The Night of the Bubbling Death"), a cannon so powerful that it can level a whole town with a single projectile ("The Night of the Falcon"), a flame-throwing machine that destroys everything in his path ("The Night of the Juggernaut"), a fire-belching submarine ("The Night of the Kraken"), and even a giant tuning fork that can level buildings as it vibrates ("The Night of the Avaricious Actuary").

In "The Night of the Man-Eating House," a supernaturally oriented episode, the agents face death at the hands of an old mansion controlled by the ghost of the mother of a prisoner in Jim and Artie's custody. (Interestingly, this entire episode is depicted as it is dreamed by Artie. When he wakes, however, the events in his dream actually begin to happen, leaving the viewer with the impression that the agents are going to experience everything in Artie's dream.)

Other more "mundane" life-threatening dangers also were often faced by our intrepid heroes. In "The Night of Sudden Death," for example, West and Gorden narrowly avoided death from poison, a crocodile, a tiger, arrows, and a suit of wet skins that would crush its victims as they dry. In "The Night of the Dancing Death," Jim must dispatch adversary Prince Gio in hand-to-hand combat.

The agents' assignments were varied and interesting but almost always involved some plan to take over the country (or the world). Jim must convince a band of cold-blooded killers that he had killed Artie in a fit of rage in order to gain membership into an exclusive cult of assassins, in "The Night of the Skulls." West's assignment was to destroy the organization which had been created by a ruthless and ambitious United States senator, who planned on circumventing the usual path to the White House by having his men kill the high-ranking officials above him. He would then step into the leadership void and take control of the country.

Frequently West and Gordon were called upon to protect their boss (President

Grant) from some madman bent on either revenge or power ("The Night of the Steel Assassin," "The Night of the Colonel's Ghost," "The Night of the Arrow," "The Night of the Big Blackmail," and "The Night of the Winged Terror"). Happily, they were always successful in their mission.

All of the violence depicted in *The Wild Wild West* produced a great deal of criticism from various PTA and educational groups.[15] However, these protests had little effect on the popular series and in any case, most of the violence was of the comic-book variety, with little blood or gore ever actually shown. Ironically, according to Conrad, there was always a lot more violence put into each show than they really wanted. "The men from Program Practices [the censors] would say: 'We're going to take out two punches ... two of this ... three of that....' So when they finished, we were still left with what we really wanted anyway...."[16] The network censors may, however, have had the last laugh after all. The year after the series left the air (which was in 1970), CBS brought back the series as a summer replacement. In these selected reruns, the networks saw fit to edit out some of the more violent scenes and situations.

The final Bondian ingredient in *The Wild Wild West* was lots and lots of beautiful women, both good and evil, most of whom inevitably succumbed to the charms of agent West. Among the lovely guest stars in such featured roles were Suzanne Pleshette ("The Night of the Inferno"), Leslie Parrish ("The Night the Wizard Shook the Earth"), Katherine Ross ("The Night of the Double-Edged Knife"), Dana Wynter ("The Night of the Two-Legged Buffalo"), Madlyn Rhue ("The Night of the Bubbling Death"), Lana Wood, Natalie's sister ("The Night of the Firebrand"), Susan Oliver ("The Night Dr. Loveless Died"), and Joanie Sommers ("The Night of the Tycoons"). They certainly did not need to take a back seat to any of James Bond's beauties.

From the beginning most critics liked the series. *Variety*'s television reviewer saw the potential for its success in the very first episode, writing on September 22, 1965:

> Although it is straight comic book fiction, "Wild, Wild West" is produced with such a slick hand it seems to belong to a slightly higher species. Director Richard Sarafian has masked all the inconsistences and implausibilities admirably in the opener.... If it doesn't lapse, the CBS entry has a first-class chance....
>
> It's strictly hokum, and okay as long as the viewer is kept lulled and unaware....
>
> As for the regulars, [Robert] Conrad is stock, but suited to the flamboyant role. [Ross] Martin is pretty good at disguises.... [But] the real hero of the piece is director Sarafian, who keeps it moving and has a way of disguising all sins.

Although *The Wild Wild West* reached Nielsen's top 25 only once (placing twenty-third during its initial year), it did attract sufficient viewers to remain a CBS Friday night fixture for four seasons. Furthermore, it was popular enough to be successfully rerun in syndication for many years. In fact, its continuing popularity prompted the network to attempt a revival of the show via a series of made-for-television movies. The first of these specials was broadcast as a two hour film on May 9, 1978. In the story, ten years have elapsed since West and Gordon retired from the Secret Service. Jim is living in Mexico with four wives ("for some men, four women is barely enough"). Artie is touring the Southwest as part of "The Deadwood Shakespearean Strolling Players with assorted jugglers, fire-eaters, and three, count 'em, three beautiful live girls!" The former agents are called out of retirement for an important mission—to thwart the diabolical plans of Dr. Loveless' son, Miguelito, Jr., to blackmail the major world powers with a prototype atomic bomb. As part of this scheme, the rulers of the United States, Great Britain, Spain and Russia have supposedly been kidnapped and robotic impostors put in their places.

Our heroes discover that Dr. Loveless (who has been dead for five years) had two

In the 1979 television movie, *The Wild Wild West Revisited*, singer Paul Williams played the son of the now deceased Dr. Loveless.

children by different wives—"Junior" (well-played by singer-composer Paul Williams), a slightly larger version of his father, and Carmelita, a normal-sized and very beautiful young woman. In addition to a desire for world domination, they are determined to gain revenge on West and Gordon for causing their father's death through constant "meddling in his affairs." (After capturing the two American agents, Junior gets great satisfaction from showing them a huge monument to the evil doctor built high on a hill. Located at the bottom of that hill, so that Miguelito, Sr., can look down on them, are two small tombstones for Jim and Artie). To carry out his plan, Junior has developed a pair of unique weapons worthy of this father's admiration—a $600 ("actually 609 dollar") version each of the "six million dollar man" and woman—quadruple amputees fitted with super-powerful artificial limbs.

The new head of the Secret Service, Robert T. "Skinny" Malone (delightfully played by *M.A.S.H.*'s Harry Morgan), decides that Jim and Artie are the only agents capable of thwarting Junior's nefarious scheme. The British and Russian governments have also both sent special agents after Junior. (Artie even gets to carry on a romance with the beautiful British agent Penelope, which includes a kissing scene worthy of his partner. Of course, Jim has his own passionate kissing scene with Carmelita, who is trying to deceive our stalwart hero.) The following exchange between West and Junior takes place after the agents have been taken to Miguelito's underground lair—reminiscent of the humor of earlier series:

> WEST: Junior, you're crazier than your father ever was.
> JUNIOR: Did it ever occur to you that my father was, and I am, completely sane and the two of you and the rest of the world are mentally deficient?
> WEST: No, that never occurred to me... Did it ever occur to you, Artie?
> GORDON: Never.
> JUNIOR: Did it ever occur to you that my father was normal sized and the two of you might be throw-backs to cave-men types?
> GORDON: Now *that* occurred to me.

The movie contains all the ingredients that made the original series so successful—diabolical villains, beautiful women, and bizarre, anachronistic scientific devices. (In addition to the mini–atom bomb, with its mushroom cloud, and the two robots developed by the bad guys, it seems the British have developed "noise suppressors" for their revolvers and the Russians have invented shatter-proof glass.) Furthermore, Artie gets his chance to don a marvelous disguise as a dance hall girl. In the end, of course, Jim and Artie outwit Junior, save the world, and return to the relative peace and quiet of their retirement. (Or have they saved the world? A doubt is placed in the viewer's mind at the end when Jim says to Artie, "How can we be sure these are the real leaders? Maybe they are the robots and we're playing into Junior's hands by replacing the real leaders with robots? ... In fact, how can I be certain you're the real Artie and how can you be certain I'm the real Jim?")

The movie was one of CBS' most highly-rated special presentations of the year, and naturally led to another *Wild Wild West* film entitled *More Wild Wild West*, which was broadcast in two one hour segments on October 7 and 8, 1980. Malone again calls the agents out of retirement. This time they must stop the diabolical (again!) archcriminal Albert Paradine II (cleverly portrayed by comedian Jonathan Winters) from using a superbomb (again!) to sabotage a world peace conference and provoke a world war. ("I think I'll call it World War I and the one after that World War II to keep them straight," he tells Jim and Artie).

Once again the widely watched film had the basic Bond-type ingredients to provide plenty of action, as well as laughs: our heroes battling a couple of incredibly strong men and hanging by their heels in a tiger's cage, Artie in a marvelous disguise, this time as a dark-faced snake charmer, and lots of beautiful women, along with some new gadgets including a dirigible propelled by peddling a bicycle and a wonderfully humorous send-up of Henry Kissinger (by the aforementioned Victor Buono). There is also a funny bit by comedian Avery Schrieber as the Russian ambassador and cameos by Dr. Joyce Brothers and Jack La Lane.

The major criticism leveled mainly by fans of the series was that the emphasis in these film sequels was "on slapstick comedy rather than action and adventure while in the original episodes, the reverse was true with tongue-in-cheek humor clearly secondary to action."[17] Conrad took issue with this charge: "We still play it seriously. It all comes down to how we play the script, not how they write it; we play it *real*. What results may be slapstick, maybe a little bizarre, but we play everything with some degree of authenticity.

You never make a laugh, because if you do there's something wrong. When Ross and I play the roles we don't say, 'Hey this is a laugh-line.' It's not done that way at all."[18]

Undoubtedly there would have been more *Wild Wild West* films had Ross Martin not died of a heart attack on July 3, 1981. By gently spoofing both Westerns and spy shows, *The Wild Wild West* presented consistently off-beat and intriguing stories and in many ways expanded the creative limits of the television Western as no other program has before or since.

XIII. Two by Two into the West
MEMORABLE PAIRS OF
ADULT WESTERN HEROES

As we have seen, most of the adult Western heroes on television rode alone. Some joined wagon trains or cattle drives and a few had families. Most of the juvenile cowboy heroes, on the other hand, had sidekicks or "faithful companions." There were several pairs of heroes, however, who rode the video range during the waning years of the adult Western. A couple are worthy of consideration. They include a grandfather and his grandson, two bounty hunters (one white, one black), two "reformed" outlaws, two brothers searching for their long-lost sister, and twin brothers (one a doctor, the other a gunslinger), both played by the same actor.

The basic premise for *The Guns of Will Sonnett* (1967–1969) was concisely and poetically explained in the opening sequence of each episode. Silhouetted against the sky, two men on horseback, one old, one young, moved slowly up a hill as the voice of a grizzled old man intoned a song about a search for a man. This unusual Western, set in the 1870s, dramatized the search by an old ex–cavalry scout, Will Sonnett, and his grandson, Jeff, for the boy's father, James Sonnett, a man the boy had never known. Some 19 years earlier Jeff had been born in Sacramento, California. The boy's mother had died at birth and James had sent the infant east to Bent's Fort in the care of a sergeant's wife with instructions for his father, Will, who was stationed there. She explained James' request, "Not many of us gets a second chance." With the bag of gold James had sent along, Will took the baby to Wyoming and raised him as his own son.

Now grown to manhood, Jeff Sonnett was determined to find his father. With the help of his grandpa, he set out on this quest. James, in the meantime, had become a famous gunfighter, who, in order to survive, had become extremely adept at covering his trail. Will and Jeff were not the only ones tracking the elusive gunman. There were bounty hunters, men seeking to make their reputation by besting Jim Sonnett in a gunfight, and countless others whose paths he had crossed. Some, with bitterness and hatred, sought revenge; others, with gratitude and respect, sought to repay his kindness to them.

This interesting premise was the creation of Aaron Spelling, who also produced the series, but the key to the series' appeal was the veteran character actor Spelling landed to play Will Sonnett—Walter Brennan. Brennan, with fifty years' experience in the acting profession, had accomplished a feat never before achieved in the business. In his comparative youth he had won three Oscars for Best Supporting Actor for his roles in *Come and Get It* (1936), as a self-made empire builder's simple Swedish pal; in *Kentucky* (1938), as a lovable horsetrainer; and in *The Westerner* (1940), as the unforgettable Judge Roy Bean.

Brennan had perfected the role of a toothless old codger while he was still in his thirties (after losing his own teeth in a riding accident). His long career in Hollywood had begun in the silent films of the twenties. During the thirties, forties, and well into the fifties, Brennan turned in many memorable performances in Westerns: *Law and Order* (1932), *The Texans* (1938), *Northwest Passage* (1940), *Red River* (1948), *The Far Country* (1955) and *The Proud Ones* (1956). However, aside from *The Westerner*, his most notable Western roles were the evil Old Man Clanton, obsessively protecting his brood of murderous sons in John Ford's classic *My Darling Clementine* (1946), and the lame, grumpy old jail-keeper in Howard Hawks' *Rio Bravo* (1959).

Brennan also did a good deal of television work during the fifties playing a string of wheezy, gosh-darned oldtimers. He was the grandfather of Richard Crenna on *The Real McCoys* (1957–1963) and of Pat McNulty in *The Tycoon* (1964–1965) before becoming Dack Rambo's grandpa in *The Guns of Will Sonnett*. In a 1968 interview, Brennan admitted that the series "isn't much, maybe, but it has a good moral, it teaches young people."[1] Carolyn See's description in *TV Guide* of Brennan at the time he was playing Will Sonnett was that of a man happy with his career, and his life:

> In a country where money is everything and youth the supreme adventure, fate has been kind to Walter Brennan. He is by now practically a corporation. His grown son Andy currently works as his associate producer; he owns acres out in the San Fernando Valley and quantities of land in Oregon, he has two other children—non-professionals—15 grandchildren and one great grandchild. He is a rich man, but most important, . . . Walter Brennan at 73 is *making* television, working all day long, chuckling around with his cronies, sitting in a chair with his name on the back.[2]

What becomes clear from See's 1968 interview with Brennan was that here was a man who personified all the characteristics—both good and bad—on the "parental" side of the Vietnam era generation gap: "an American, first, last and always," who proudly "served in the trenches" during World War I; a patriot who strongly believed that there was a "leftist plot" run by Communists to take over the country; a conservative who blamed the country's racial troubles "on just a few Negroes"; an informed citizen who got all his information from *Human Events* and the Liberty Lobby newsletter; and a paradoxical family man who loved to help his children, but refused assistance from his own parents.[3]

Costar Dack Rambo, who played Brennan's grandson, Jeff, and was born almost fifty years after Brennan, certainly typified the other side of the generation gap. In 1962, at the age of 20, while visiting an aunt with his twin brother, Dack was seen by actress Loretta Young at St. Victor's Church in West Hollywood. After Mass one Sunday, Young approached the boys and asked if they would like to appear in her then-projected new television series. The Rambo brothers, who had never acted in their lives, were delighted.

The New Loretta Young Show (1962–1963), starred the ageless actress as the widowed mother of a large brood. (Dack and brother Dirk played two of her children.) It did not last long, but it opened up a whole new career for the Rambo twins, as well as providing them with new names. Born Orman and Norman Rambo, they were rechristened by a legendary Hollywood agent named Henry Willson (who was also responsible for tagging such earlier clients as Tab Hunter, Rock Hudson and Touch Connors).

Walter Brennan as the eponymous grandfather in *The Guns of Will Sonnett*, with newcomer Dack Rambo playing Will's grandson Jeff.

When the show was canceled, the brothers returned to their family's farm in Earlimart, California, the twins' birthplace in the fertile San Joaquin Valley. After a stint in the National Guard, they eventually returned to Hollywood, where Dack got a job in the lipstick department at Max Factor's and Dirk parked cars. Finally, both Rambo brothers auditioned for an ABC soap opera, *Never Too Young*, and Dack got the part. (Soon afterwards, Dirk, who had just been put under contract by Universal, was killed in an automobile accident.)

A self-proclaimed outdoorsman, who was interested in ecology and preserving the environment, Dack became a loner living in a small rented home above the Sunset Strip at the top of one of the Hollywood Hills. He took guitar and singing lessons and built a solid if unexceptional career in soap operas while waiting for his big break. *The Guns of Will Sonnet* appeared to be that break. Ratings lagged, however, and reviews of the series were not favorable. *Variety* (October 2, 1968) said:

> Economy back-lot sets, an improbable and uninteresting script, and actors for whom it seemed almost too much trouble to read their lines added up to a genuinely unpleasant premiere half hour....

> Brennan is more than enough actor for any season, and Rambo has demonstrated competence on other occasions, but they're going to have to come alive to sustain this show even until January.

Cleveland Amory, writing in *TV Guide* (December 28, 1968) was even more brutal in his condemnation of the series:

> To give the devil his due, Walter Brennan, as grandfather Will Sonnett is his usual competent, believable self.... The trouble comes primarily with grandson Jeff. He finds himself in an impossible role that one minute demands he outdraw a murderous badman and the next minute blubber into his Dr. Pepper that his father never really loved him. This is bad enough, but, besides, most of the episodes are stereotyped plots involving a (a) boy-meets-fight, (b) boy-wins-fight and (c) boy-regrets-fight. If this sounds thin, it is.... We've also seen ... episodes in which the only thing you had to root for was the end.

Castleman and Podrazik are more generous in their assessment, attributing the show's failure to weak scripts:

> It's a workable premise, ... but the individual stories never break from typical western formulas.[4]

Actually the quality of the stories varies greatly. By far the best are those which feature Will's son Jim, played with an effective air of mystery by Jason Evers. Evers had previously starred in his own short-lived Western, *The Wrangler* (1960), and in *Channing* (1963–1964) as a college English professor. Jim made his first appearance in the sixth episode, "Message at Noon." Will and his grandson learn that Jim will be visiting a friend in a nearby town and they wait for him there. Unfortunately, a young gunman, who has been trailing Jim, catches up to him in another town first. The kid forces a showdown and Jim is compelled to kill him (and his crony) in self-defense. Then he rides off to lose himself in the vast spaces of the West—just *before* a telegraph message from Will arrives to tell Jim that his father and son are on their way to meet him. It is a simple story, but there is action, suspense, tension and a marvelous performance by character actor Strother Martin as a bartender who befriends Jim before the shootout. Twice more during the show's first season (in "End of a Rope" and "Alone") Jim appears in the story, but each time circumstances prevent Will and Jeff from catching up to him. Each time, however, they learn a little more about their mysterious son/father. And each time they press on in their search with renewed vigor.

During the second season of *The Guns of Will Sonnett*, Jim is used in seven episodes ("Reunion," "Joby," "Meeting in a Small Town," "A Town in Terror Part II," "Jim Sonnett's Lady," "The Trail," and the final episode, "Reconciliation"). In the second part of the two part story, "A Town in Terror," Jeff actually comes face to face with his father. After being told that a notorious professional gunman has murdered his father, Jeff rushes into a saloon to confront his father's killer. As the man slowly turns to face Jeff, the startled young man suddenly realizes that the gunman is actually his father. Before Jeff has time to react, however, Jim knocks him cold and disappears. Later in the story Will and Jeff come to Jim's rescue, when he is trapped in a barn by a gang of gunmen who have been hired by the cattlemen to drive out a group of sheepherders. They see Jim from a distance, but have no opportunity to speak to him. Jim makes his escape and Will and Jeff's search continues.

Most of the stories, however, are mundane, as Will and Jeff come into contact with various individuals who have, for one reason or another, an interest in Jim Sonnett. Usually they are bounty hunters out for the reward on Jim's head (e.g., in "Chapter and Verse") or someone who has been wounded by Jim (e.g., in the pilot episode, it is a gunman who has lost his left arm) or someone whose brother (or son or father) has been killed by Jim (e.g., in "Jim Sonnett's Lady"). In one story ("The Sins of the Father") a woman claims Jim Sonnett is the father of her baby (but it is all a trick to get Jeff to take her to the real father of her child).

In one of the lighter episodes, "What's in a Name?" Will and Jeff run into a man claiming to be Will Sonnett (well played by Edward Andrews). He is a trick-shot artist like the real Will Sonnett, but not nearly as quick on the draw. Will forgives him in the end.

> He didn't mean no harm back there,
> Jus' lookin' for someone to be.
> But I'm mighty content right now...
> That there's just one of me.

Unlike many another series based on a similar premise, *The Guns of Will Sonnett* concludes its second (and last) season with the successful resolution of the major characters' search. Will and Jeff Sonnett finally catch up with Jim just outside the town of Samson. Will ends up being appointed sheriff of Samson with Jim and Jeff as his deputies. Standing shoulder to shoulder, the three dispatch five bounty hunters in a blazing shoot-out on the town's main street. As the smoke clears, this meaningful exchange takes place:

> JIM: How do you feel, son?
> JEFF: A little sick.
> JIM: Pa?
> WILL: I wish I hadn't et.
> JIM: Yeah, it's like that with me—always.

There was not any generation gap in the Old West. None of the Sonnetts enjoyed killing—even though they were forced to do so on occasion. The three decide to settle down and begin a new life in Samson, and the episode closes with grandfather, son and grandson striding down the darkened street, side by side. As was the practice in each episode, Walter Brennan closes the story with a voice-over prayer:

> Dear Lord, our lives are in Your hands.
> You brought us together at last.
> Help us now to defend the right
> Let vengeance forget the past.

For those who enjoyed Brennan's hit recordings, like "Dutchman's Gold," the prayer was moving and folksy at the same time, just as *The Guns of Will Sonnett* tried to be. "No brag, just fact"—as each of the three Sonnetts was heard to exclaim from time to time: it was Walter Brennan's show from beginning to end.

Perhaps the most unusual pair to ride the video range were two bounty hunters, Earl Corey and Jemal David, of *The Outcasts*. Corey, a former Confederate officer, was an aristocratic Southern white planter who had owned slaves before the Civil War. David, who had been a Union soldier, was a former slave who had escaped three years before the war began. The uneasy alliance of these two outcasts was born of necessity (both were in need of money). Their contrasting backgrounds and points of view set the stage for some explosive conflicts. Although at first they did not trust each other, as time passed, each came to realize that he could depend on the other in a crisis. Both were quick on the draw and proficient at the business of tracking down and capturing men with a prices on their heads.

The Outcasts made its weekly hour long debut on September 23, 1968, over ABC. The network was apparently encouraged by the three year success of the popular inter-racial adventure series, *I Spy* (1965–1968) on NBC, which starred Robert Culp and Bill Cosby. Cast in the pivotal role of Jemal David was the relatively obscure Otis Young. Young had been born in 1932 in Providence, Rhode Island and with his twin brother was the oldest of 14 children, including three other sets of twins. He dropped out of high school to help support his family and at 17 joined the Marines, later serving in Korea. After his discharge, he headed for New York. Working there for a while as a Garment Center messenger, Young decided to attend college on the GI Bill. Enrolling in the Education School at New York University, he earned a B.S. degree. (Young had the distinction of being admitted to college without finishing high school. He later claimed that while working for a publisher he "read a book a day" and "had the best vocabulary" in his class even though he "couldn't pronounce the words."[5])

It was while he was a student at NYU that Young became interested in acting. From there he enrolled in the Neighborhood Playhouse in 1957 and studied theater with Frank Silvera. He also joined the Second City Troupe, gaining valuable backstage experience as stage manager of *Call Me By My Rightful Name* (1961) and *In the Counting House* (1962) and as production assistant for *The Days and Nights of Beebe Fenstermaker* (1962). In 1962, Young joined the Actors Studio Broadway production of *Blues for Mister Charlie* as stage manager and lead understudy. Two years later he heard through the underground that a Los Angeles production of it was being planned and he set out to land the leading role. This was Young's first major stage role. Meanwhile, Young was gaining experience in television with small roles in such distinguished dramatic anthologies as *The U.S. Steel Hour* (in "A Bride for Oona") and *The Hallmark Hall of Fame* (in "The Green Pastures"). He also appeared with George C. Scott in an episode of *East Side, West Side* in 1963. Young's big screen debut came in 1968 when he landed a part in *Don't Just Stand There*, which starred Robert Wagner and Mary Tyler Moore. When Young was first approached to play the role of Jemal David in *The Outcasts*, he was elated because, as his costar Don Murray later explained in an interview in *The New York Post*:

> It took a classic American hero, a total Western hero, the one thing that's thoroughly American, and made him black. And for the first time in a TV show we see a black man shoot down a white man.[6]

Furthermore, as Dick Hobson wrote in *TV Guide* (March 1, 1969):

> ... for the first time in American television they didn't deny that when a black man rode into Western towns he was going to run into trouble and they didn't deny that the white men he ran into might be bigots.
> ... [Consequently], Young threw himself into the role [and] played it for all it was worth, drawing upon a lifetime of anger, resentment, and deep hostility engendered by racial prejudice.[7]

Don Murray, who played Earl Corey, was born in Hollywood, California, in 1929. The son of Dennis Murray, a dancer, dance director and long-time stage manager of Olsen & Johnson revues and of former Ziegfeld girl Ethel Cook, Don attended the American Academy of Dramatic Arts. He began his stage career on Broadway in a revival of *Insect Comedy* and then played the young sailor in *The Rose Tattoo*. Next came another Broadway revival *The Skin of Our Teeth*. During the Korean War, Murray was a conscientious objector (as a member of the antiwar Church of the Brethren) and served a brief term in jail until he was assigned to a special service unit in Germany and Italy. After the war Murray decided to try his luck in films back in Hollywood.

Murray was nominated for a best supporting actor Oscar for his first film role in 1956—that of the galoot of a cowboy who falls in love with an untalented nightclub singer while both are waiting for a bus—in Joshua Logan's film version of the William Inge play, *Bus Stop*. Murray's performance almost overshadowed that of his costar Marilyn Monroe. Most of Murray's subsequent portrayals were critically acclaimed in such outstanding films as *The Bachelor Party* (1957), *A Hatful of Rain* (1957), *Shake Hands with the Devil* (1959), *The Hoodlum Priest* (1961), *The Hustler* (1961), *Advise and Consent* (1962) and *Baby, the Rain Must Fall* (1965).

While turning out a string of successful films, Murray did a few guest spots on television shows. Then in 1968 Screen Gems offered him his choice of three series, one of which was *The Outcasts*. Why did he select that particular one? Well, several of his films had been Westerns, including *From Hell to Texas* (1958) and *One Foot in Hell* (1960). Furthermore, his most recent film had been *Sweet Love, Bitter* (1967) which explored an interracial friendship. It was based on the life of black jazz musician Charlie "Bird" Parker and costarred Dick Gregory. In addition, Murray believed that *The Outcasts* "offered viewers an important message without glorifying violence."[8] He explained to *TV Guide* writer Carolyn See:

> I picked "The Outcasts" because I thought it was sociologically important because it gave a Negro a chance for good exposure on TV [and] because the abrasive relationship between the two men was the closest thing to realism that television had given us so far. Also I thought it was artistically important, so I did it.[9]

The series premiered on September 23, 1968, over ABC, as the narrator intoned:

> In the decade following the Civil War, people of all creeds and colors were part of the West. This is the story of two of these people.

And *The Outcasts* was underway. Jemal and Corey meet while competing with each other in a shooting match for a $50 prize. The sparks fly immediately:

> COREY: Where'd you learn to shoot like that, boy?
> JEMAL: Different times, different places, mostly 'minding people I wasn't their boy.

The two tie and split the prize money. Later Jemal asks Corey how many slaves he owned. "I don't rightly know," he replies, "it wasn't me that looked after the inventory." After the two team up as bounty hunters in order to bring in a wanted criminal who is posing as a cook with a Seventh Cavalry wagon train, this exchange takes place:

> JEMAL: With or without you, I'm going down there tonight in the dark.
> COREY: Well, you do have a natural advantage in the dark, don't you, boy—unless, of course, you smile.

Despite this initial friction, the two successfully bag their quarry and decide to stick together. The clear impression is given, however, that this partnership is temporary and may be terminated by either one at any time. The viewer is also left with the impression that the two bounty hunters have crossed paths before. In a paperback novel written by Steve Frazee that was based on the series, their initial meeting is described is some detail:

> Two—no, it was three now—weeks before, they had met on the Smoky Hill Trail. Corey had been guiding two titled Englishmen on a buffalo hunt ... things had worked out pretty well until a small band of determined Cheyennes broke into the scene....
> [The Englishmen and Corey soon found themselves] lying behind their dead horses on an open prairie, with seven Indians trying to overrun them....

It was then that Jemal David came out of the sand hills behind the Indians. He rode like a wild man. He got one with his pistol as he broke through the group, and he sure as hell confused the others....

Straight up to the dead-horse barricade he came, dismounting in a flying lead. He whipped a rifle from his boot and began to fire at the two Cheyennes who had been heading toward them. They gave up the idea and went back to the main group.

With the odds in their favor greatly reduced, the Cheyennes decided it was a bad gamble ... and rode away.[10]

Corey found it difficult to believe that a Negro could shoot and ride like that. Two days later the four men joined a wagon train. During that time Corey got Jemal's story of how he was born in slavery and had run away after one week as a field hand, three years before the war. When one of the Englishman commented that "Mr. Lincoln's Proclamation must have relieved your mind a great deal," Jemal quietly responded, "He didn't free me. I figure I was born free." According to the novel, the two then parted, running into each other several weeks later in the saloon of a small, dusty Western town.

Regardless of how the two first met, there was considerable difference of opinion among critics as to the merits (or lack thereof) of *The Outcasts*. Cleveland Amory, in *TV Guide*, was enthusiastic in his support, *Variety* was skeptical, and most others were downright hostile toward the new Western. Amory wrote (November 30, 1968):

> ... the fact that "The Outcasts" tells it like it was—at a time when it wasn't like it is—really presents problems. But there's no hedging—the show gives us the two most opposite opposites possible. Jemal David [Otis Young] is a former slave, his partner, Earl Corey [Don Murray], is a former Virginia plantation owner....
>
> There was good writing [and] both Young and Murray proved themselves star-quality series actors....
>
> It was basically believable because of fine performances and good writing. Even if you don't like Westerns, this show is worth a look.[11]

Earlier (September 25, 1968) the *Variety* critic had written:

> Marked by routine competence, its only visible assets are a couple of strong black & white leads in Don Murray and Otis Young, an odd-couple faintly reminiscent of the "Defiant Ones" movie pairing, who team up as bounty hunters....
>
> ... The pair-off produced some good irony, and over all the impression of workable chemistry. This could thin out fast, however, if not bolstered by subsequent storylines.

The New York Times (September 24, 1968) television critic George Gent labeled *The Outcasts* "a routine oatburner":

> Except for the novelty of seeing racial hostility made explicit in a television program, the American Broadcasting company's new Western series, "The Outcasts," is little more than a routine oatburner out of the old Republic studio mold....
>
> To be more accurate, the series does have two other assets—superior performances by Don Murray and Otis Young, the co-stars....
>
> What drama exists in this cliché-filled saddle saga results from the sparks engendered by these two strong-minded men as they test each other's mettle.
>
> Mr. Young, particularly, brings a strength and humor to his role of the wiley bounty hunter that is a pleasure to watch. Mr. Murray is good but is inclined to overact, particularly when he is called upon to snarl at Mr Young.
>
> ... The men's mutual respect is established early and grows with each encounter. They are equally matched in everything and superior to everyone else around. If they are not precisely friends at the fadeout they're not exactly enemies either.
>
> This may not be the Robert Culp–Bill Cosby camaraderie of "I Spy," but the essence of their relationship is not too different. This is Sociology I, era 1870. Take away the name calling, and it's just another Western.

Kay Gardella, writing in *The New York Daily News* (September 25, 1968), did not like the show any better:

> Unfortunately, this is the season when the racial question will be the dramatic force in a good many television scripts, and for blacks as well as whites, the going could get a little heavy before the season ends....
>
> Stress in the script was on the fact that the two Southern outcasts are evenly matched in everything—physical prowess, shooting, and we might add, acting. Neither Murray, with his Southern accent, and Young without one (can't figure that one out), sent us running for an Emmy. But one cannot place the blame on the performers, since the series is a contrived, trumped-up excuse for such dialogue as "I growed up with that look.... Color don't rub off."

In a column entitled "'Outcasts' Aims High, Misses," syndicated television writer Barbara Delatiner was even more critical of *The Outcasts*:

> A series of social significance? Okay, how's this? We'll take this black man and this white southerner and let them join forces just this side of the law. Only, to avoid controversy, we'll drop them back into history, 100 years back on the post–Civil War frontier, whee, an announcer can assure us, "all creeds and colors were part of the West." And then we'll have "The Outcasts." ...
>
> It fails on several counts. First, the very relationship doesn't hold water. Then, the dialogue, reminiscent of the present scene, is as phony as a $3 bill, or a TV series with social significance. Says the Virginian to a one-time field hand: "That's mighty white of you." The black man scowls. The white man, acknowledging his sensitivity, adds, "as the saying goes."
>
> ... [The opening episode] promised little besides ... a lot of self-conscious, superficial prattling about equality.

Contemporary critical assessment notwithstanding, racial themes were prevalent in nearly every episode of *The Outcasts*. For example, in "Take Your Lover in the Ring," the concept of blacks as property is utilized as the capstone of a clever and, at times, amusing story. A gambler (played to stuffy perfection by the venerable John Dehner) ostensibly loses his black ward (attractive newcomer Gloria Foster) to Corey in a poker game. Corey gives her to Jemal, more or less as a joke, for a Christmas present. The joke is on Corey, however, when the girl turns out to be part of a con game. She steals the money Corey won from the gambler and gives it back to the man. Corey, of course, is furious, especially when he discovers that Jemal, who rejected the girl on Christmas Eve, realizes he is in love with her on Christmas Day. "She is," Jemal explains, "a black sheep in a world of wolves." Nevertheless, all ends well, when the girl repents and shoots the gambler. Still, Jemal's love goes unrequited as the girl rides off into the sunset at the episode's close.

In what is perhaps the best written episode, "The Heady Wine" by George Eckstein, Jemal finds out what it is like to have power when he becomes sheriff of a small town near the Mexican border. Furthermore, early in the episode the reasons for Corey and Jemal's partnership are explored in this meaningful exchange of dialogue:

JEMAL: A few years ago that man [Corey] was master of one of the biggest plantations in Virginia. He owned over a hundred slaves. Crystal ... horses ... white linen on the table every meal.

SHERIFF: Why, you came down just as long a road—six years ago you was a slave, couldn't read, couldn't write. You told me once you was a stake at a poker game—more'n once.

JEMAL: Guess we both came a long road—up or down.

SHERIFF: Funny how you two hooked up and three months later you're still ridin' with him. Ever ask yourself why?

JEMAL: Yeah.

SHERIFF: WHY?

JEMAL: No reason. No reason a'tall ... except...

SHERIFF: What? You work good together?
JEMAL: Well, if you need a reason, that's as good as any.

When the sheriff is fatally wounded shortly thereafter, he appoints Jemal his successor with his dying breath. Jemal does not want the job, but Corey goads him into accepting it for the money. He agrees to serve as sheriff for ten days and appoints Corey as his deputy.

Soon, it appears clear that the power and prestige of the office have gone to Jemal's head. When he arrests a bigoted redneck for the sheriff's murder primarily because of his dislike for the man, Corey tries to persuade Jemal to resign and leave town with him:

CUREY: Come on, let's ride outta here! It's not our town—it's not our work!
JEMAL: You're forgettin' about Sheriff Rayburn. He was my friend.
COREY: Oh so that's why you're doin' it? For good old Sheriff Rayburn, heh, heh. Who you think you're foolin' with that kind of talk?
JEMAL: All right, when he was shot it cost me five hundred dollars. That makes it my work!
COREY: And I'm still sayin' that's not all of it. I'm sayin' that you're beginnin' to like the view from up there. From up there wherever you think that badge puts ya! And now you're bound to hang an innocent man just 'cause he don't like the color of your skin!

Later, however, when the townspeople try to get Corey to take Jemal's place as sheriff, Corey defends his partner,

MERCHANT: We gave him that badge in good faith. And it's all right to ask for it back if we think we made a mistake.
COREY: The only mistake you gentlemen made is not givin' him a chance. Now I know he has his faults—as we all do. I know he's quick tempered and he's hard-headed, but he is fair! What's happenin' to him could happen to any man. All he needs is a little time.

When the chips are down Corey and Jemal stand side by side to hold off a band of Mexican bandits who invade the town. The redneck is released from custody by Jemal, who has become convinced of his innocence and he even fights alongside them, saving Jemal's life at the cost of his own. It is an effective lesson in race relations, 1870s style.

Another excellent episode dealing with a similar theme is "The Night Riders" by Richard Bluel. Corey and Jemal return to Virginia in response to a plea from Ben, one of Corey's trusted former servants. When they arrive they find Ben's farm has been taken over by a band of black-hooded night riders, one of whom seriously wounds Jemal. The leader of the band is Corey's former overseer, Jeb Collins (Steve Ihnot), who asks Corey to join them and recruit other former planters. Their avowed objective is to restore the South to its former splendor and drive out the Yankee carpetbaggers. When the military governor of Virginia (Larry Gates) stops at the farm to get out of a storm, he is taken hostage along with his wife, her servant, and all of his ill-gotten booty. The military governor subsequently tries to bribe Corey into helping him escape, and Corey is forced to make a decision as to which side he will join:

JEMAL: That's a bad man out there, your friend Jeb. He's got you so blinded by stories of the old days at Willow Hill and Yankee Carpetbaggers that you can't see nothin'.
COREY: Only a Southerner would understand.
JEMAL: You're forgettin', it's my South too. You think just 'cause I left it, I don't love it no mo'.
COREY: How could ya love somethin' that brought ya such misery?
JEMAL: Maybe 'cause I had so little, I loved it more.

Opposite: Otis Young (left) and Don Murray teamed up as bounty hunters Jemal David and Earl Corey in the underrated series *The Outcasts*.

Corey removes the bullet from Jemal, but decides to join the night riders because, "I've been asleep too long without dreams. Maybe, I've turned my back for too long on what I should have been a part of." Jemal tells him, "I'm worried about my neck, Captain, 'cause from where I'm layin' there doesn't seem to be any place in your plans for me." When Corey discovers the dead body of Ben hidden in the barn and learns that Jeb's men have brutally murdered three Union soldiers, he changes his mind about the motives and tactics of the night riders. In the ensuing gunfight Corey is forced to kill Jeb in order to save Jemal's life.

In "Three Ways to Die," by Edward J. Laski, Jemal faces bigotry and discrimination from a ruthless lawman (chillingly portrayed by James Gregory) who hates bounty hunters even more than he hates blacks:

> SHERIFF: You are a bounty hunter?
> JEMAL: That's right. You put your finger on it, sir...
> SHERIFF: And that's how ya bought the fine horse and saddle and the rest of that fancy rig?
> JEMAL: Over the years.
> SHERIFF: Must pay pretty well, bushwhackin' wanted men.
> JEMAL: Mister, I don't bushwhack.
> SHERIFF: All the years I've been a lawman, I've known killers I'd trust better'n I would a bounty hunter. A killer don't say somethin' else. He don't hide behind the law. He is what he is.

Imprisoned for a fight in a bath house, Jemal is framed for murder by the demented sheriff. Corey subsequently breaks him out of jail before he can be lynched by the angry townspeople. While crossing the desert, Corey is bitten by a rattlesnake. Jemal cuts and cleans the wound and nurses Corey back to health. Eventually they succeed in turning the tables on the sheriff and he reveals his duplicity in front of the posse. In this episode each man is called upon to save the other's life and it becomes clear that despite their differences and bickering, a bond of mutual respect and affection exists between the two men. This is a common occurrence on *The Outcasts*. Corey clearly demonstrates his feeling toward Jemal in "They Shall Rise Up" when Jemal is arrested on trumped-up charges and sentenced to six months of hard labor in a goldmine. There the prisoners are treated like animals by a sadistic deputy (superbly played by William Bramley). Corey gets a job as a guard at the mine and helps Jemal and the others to escape. Later he prevents Jemal from beating the cruel deputy to death. In this way Corey becomes a wanted man himself with a price on his head.

Occasionally, episodes deal with both the racial and social differences that threaten to destroy the partnership of the two. One such episode is "The Thin Edge." When Corey shoots a young girl (albeit in self-defense), he begins to doubt his nerve and to question the kind of work they are in:

> COREY: See, that's just it. You don't even remember him, do ya? He was a bounty we took down by the border...
> JEMAL: All right, I remember. What about him?
> COREY: Later we found out his wife was pregnant.
> JEMAL: I don't wanna hear it!
> COREY: We took him in dead!
> JEMAL: He had a shotgun on us. Why don't you remember that instead of his widow!
> COREY: It was us that made her a widow! ... All those faceless people, all those people without names...
> JEMAL: Outlaws, killers, wanted men!
> COREY: How many widows? How many fatherless children?
> JEMAL: I don't wanna know about them. I don't wanna hear nothing about what they was

before the bounty posters went up on them. Guilty or innocent? We can't decide that. We ain't judge, we ain't jury and we sure in Hell ain't God!

COREY: Yes we are! When we pull that trigger, we are GOD!!!

JEMAL: You're in it, same as me.

COREY: Yes, I'm in it, but I sure as hell am not proud of it! I remember that much of my background!

JEMAL: And I remember mine! And if I'm proud of where I am, it's because I remember where I was and who I was a few years ago. If they don't want me in their town because I hunt bounty, that's fine with me. But when I leave it's on my own horse, with my own saddle and blanket under me, my wrists and my ankles free.... I'm a bounty hunter—make of it what you want—callin' or dirty job! But up to now, Corey, you ain't showed me you're any different with all your manners, your learnin', and your once-upon-a-time, one-hundred-slave plantation. But if you think you're too quality for it, now's the time ta say it. Before we ride another mile...

In the end, of course, Corey and Jemal remain together. The common bonds of mutual respect and trust prove greater than the divisive forces of race and social status. Although the racial (as well as social) differences of the two men are made obvious in each episode, a number of the stories did not deal overtly with this theme. In "The Heroes," the bounty hunters almost become role models for a young man who thinks he wants to be a gunfighter when Corey and Jemal are caught up in a range war.

The issues of pacifism and the brutality of war are dealt with in "The Man from Bennington," when Corey exposes a former Union officer (Fritz Weaver in a sterling performance) who killed ten innocent men while searching for a wounded Confederate soldier. (Corey was that wounded soldier.) The "butcher" has been posing as a crippled school teacher who has "adopted" the young son of one of the men he killed. Complicating the situation is the fact that the man once befriended Jemal when he was destitute and needed a job.

On the other hand "Give Me Tomorrow" is a love story. Corey contracts to guide an aristocratic Southern family to Arizona where they plan to recover a fortune in buried gold and re-establish their ancestral home. On the way Corey falls in love with their beautiful daughter. The situation is complicated by the fact that she is the fiancée of the man who has financed the expedition.

Meanwhile trouble was brewing on the set of *The Outcasts*. Otis Young refused to say a line written for Jemal in the twelfth episode ("They Shall Rise Up"). The line was, "Ain't nothin' like darkies for prayin'."[12] Young later explained to *TV Guide* reporter Dick Hobson:

> ... The reason I refused to do this particular line was that it was just the beginning. If this line went through, the next thing they'd have up there is Stepin' Fetchit. If I compromised myself on this script, it would be a little easier next time and in three or four years I'd wake up one morning and be a wealthy Negro who forgot who he was.[13]

Later when the network assigned a black publicist to the series and a black writer to a script, Young became even more upset. The black writer made his villain black and had Corey shoot the badman dead. According to Young:

> The network wouldn't let a white hero shoot a black villain because it might upset Black America. They ordered a rewrite so that I could shoot him.... When they asked me how I felt about it, I said I thought it was more valid for Donald to shoot him because the villain had been Donald's personal pickaninny as a child.... The network thinks it's all right for me to shoot white men every week, but they don't want Don Murray shooting any Negroes on ABC.[14]

The identity of the executioner subsequently went through so many changes that Young forgot who ended up shooting the badman. (This kind of problem certainly never bothered the networks—or stars—back in the days of the Warner Bros. Westerns.) Young was critical of other aspects of sixties television as well. He did not like the depiction of the Negro on shows like *I Spy* and *Julia*:

> Bill Cosby does not play the nuances that a Negro would feel. His lines are interchangeable with Robert Culp's ... [and Diahann Carroll's "Julia"] shows that you must be an extremely beautiful woman according to white standards before you can wear clothes from the highest fashion people in Hollywood.... Negroes should be portrayed as Negroes, not as appropriations of white people.[15]

Otis Young had not always been critical or militant. However, *The Outcasts* had made him an instant television personality and he took the responsibility that came with this new fame seriously:

> I feel I have been given a forum. I want all of Black America to identify with Otis Young and Jemal David. It is my job as a Negro actor to make sure that I do not alienate the Negroes who watch this program. I owe them more than just riding it out, taking the benefits and slipping away.[16]

How did Young's costar feel about his criticism of the show and his newly adopted militancy? Actually Murray and Young got along very well. According to *New York Post* writer Roberta Brandes Gratz, "Off-screen Murray and Young are an ebullient, fun-loving team who are having the time of their lives at the network's expense parading around the country publicizing the show...."[17]

When pressed for an opinion by writer Dick Hobson, Murray's response was, "I think Otis is usually right. I tell the executives they're lucky to have someone who speaks up...."[18] Several months later, however, in an interview with Carolyn See, Murray denied that Young was a militant at all, insisting that Young just "had a bad day" (when Hobson interviewed him):

> Otis isn't like that at all.... Generally he's one of the most delightful, charming men in the world. He's open. He's funny. He's good to work with.... He's more optimistic about a lot of the American scene than I am.

See added, "He is right. To be the white man on a black-and-white show is to be in second place."[19] Young's attitude, however, seemed to have little relevance to the fact that *The Outcasts* was not enthusiastically received by viewers. Consequently ABC canceled the series after one season of 26 episodes. In retrospect, television historians have been divided in their opinion as to the significance of *The Outcasts*. Jeff Rovin wrote in 1977:

> ... "The Outcasts" [was] another courageous attempt by television to bring unwanted realism into American homes.... Unfortunately, viewers did not ... want to know that there really were black cowboys and that they were treated with even less respect than the beleaguered Indian. As a result, the angerfilled but promising "Outcasts" was cast out.... It had too much sinew for the average viewer.[20]

A year later, television chronicler Larry James Gianakos described *The Outcasts* as "interesting, poignant and (for its time) novel."[21] Neil Summers referred to *The Outcasts* as an "excellent television western that unfortunately failed to catch on.... Both men played off of each other very well, and 'The Outcasts' was an exceptionally well acted and well written show."[22] On the other hand, Castleman and Podrazik were not impressed: "It's pretty stilted.... Gee, ain't brotherhood great? They learn to get along and live together. If only we could learn that lesson. Hmm. Actually there is a lot of moralizing going on here...."[23]

Actually the series was ahead of its time. It was only the second Western to costar a black actor. (*Rawhide* during its final brief season in 1965-66 had featured Raymond St. Jacques in a continuing lead role.) Much of the writing was superior to that found on most other contemporary television Westerns and the acting, especially that of the leads, was effective and believable. Some of the episodes dealt with the issue of racial prejudice in a mature and thoughtful manner. And the music by Hugo Montenegro was rousing and invigorating—perhaps exceeded in quality only by George Duning's score for *The Big Valley*.

Still, *The Outcasts* was not as good as it might have been and the viewers, in any case, turned to their television sets for escapism, not realism, as the turbulent sixties drew to a close. Realism would not return to favor until the Vietnam War ended in the mid-seventies and yet another duo rode the video range.

Unlike *The Guns of Will Sonnett*, which used a rhyming verse to explain the series premise at the beginning of each show, *Alias Smith and Jones* employed a montage of scenes from the two hour pilot plus a voice-over narrative to open each episode:

> Hannibal Heyes and Kid Curry, the two most successful outlaws in the history of the West, and in all the trains and banks they robbed, they never shot anyone. This made our two latter-day Robin Hoods very popular—with everyone but the railroads and the banks.
> (Heyes and Curry are shown being chased by a posse)
> KID: There's one thing we gotta get, Heyes
> HEYES: What's that?
> KID: Outta this business!
> (Heyes and Curry are shown listening to)
> SHERIFF TOM TREVORS: The Governor can't come flat out and give you amnesty now. First, ya gotta prove ya deserve it!
> HEYES: So all we've gotta do is stay outta trouble until the governor figures we deserve amnesty.
> CURRY: But, in the meantime we'll still be wanted?
> SHERIFF: Well, that's true. Till then, only you, me, and the governor'll know about it. It'll be our secret.
> HEYES: That's a good deal?
> (Another shot of Hayes and Curry being chased by a posse is shown)
> HEYES: I sure wish the governor'd let a few more people in on our secret.

The series, created by Glen A. Larson and produced by Roy Huggins, was obviously inspired by the popular 1969 film *Butch Cassidy and the Sundance Kid*, which starred Paul Newman and Robert Redford. The movie romanticized the lives of two actual bandits who robbed trains and banks at the turn of the century. Directed by George Roy Hill from a screenplay by William Goldman, *Butch Cassidy and the Sundance Kid* did well at the box office and with critics. *Newsweek*'s Paul D. Zimmerman wrote:

> The Western, that Hollywood archetype, has outlived its usefulness as a straight dramatic device in which good, dressed in white, guns down evil, dressed in black. Instead Goldman and Hill have turned out an anti Western ... [in which] the railroads are the villainous symbols of an increasingly impersonal, industrialized and mercantile society.... The century and frontier life are both ending, but Butch Cassidy and the Sundance Kid refuse to surrender to this changing America, holding up trains and banks as though the sheriff and the local posse were their only adversaries.[24]

Years later noted film critic Leonard Maltin gave the film four stars and described it as a "delightful seriocomic character study masquerading as a Western."[25] *Alias Smith* and Jones emphasizes the lighthearted comic side of its two main characters, Kid Curry and Hannibal Heyes (alias Thaddeus Jones and Joshua Smith), but can hardly be considered an "anti–Western." Heyes and Curry are depicted as two charming and courageous outlaws (formerly of the Devil's Hole Gang) trying to go straight. There is a considerable price on the head of each man ($10,000 "dead or alive") and practically every marshal, sheriff and bounty hunter they run into would like to collect that reward.

Like Butch Cassidy and the Sundance Kid, who really existed, Kid Curry was based on an actual historical character. (There is no record of a "Hannibal Heyes.") The real "Kid," however, bore little resemblance to the television version. Born Harvey Logan in Dodson, Missouri, in 1865, he was the eldest of four boys who were orphaned in the early seventies and sent to live with an aunt. At the age of 19, Harvey set out with two of his younger brothers who planned on becoming cowboys. They fell in with a gang of rustlers in Wyoming, however. The leader of the gang was an ugly man with a distinctive swagger and an even more distinctive name—Big Nose George Curry. Harvey was fascinated by the man and from then on adopted the name Kid Curry.

In appearance, the Kid was much shorter than the actor who played him on television (Ben Murphy). He stood five foot, seven and a half and weighed 150 pounds. His eyes were dark brown and a heavy, "ratty looking" moustache grew under his prominent nose. Despite his appearance, the Kid was reputed to have had a fair share of success with women, perhaps because he was polite and always acted like a gentleman. In fact it was because of a girl, a pretty young miner's daughter called Elfie, that Kid Curry shot and killed his first man—Pike Landusky, her stepfather. Fifty-five year old Landusky had long been critical of the Kid's association with his step-daughter, and there was a terrible tension every time the two men came near each other. Finally Curry found Landuskey half drunk in a bar and goaded him into going for his gun, whereupon the Kid shot him down. He would kill at least seven more men before his own death.

Joining up with Butch Cassidy and the Wild Bunch, Curry participated in several train robberies as well as a prison break. Whereas Butch Cassidy was a genuinely likable man, Kid Curry was not. He was cold and ruthless, spoke little and drank a lot. By the autumn of 1901, with train robbing played out and with Butch and the Sundance Kid about to leave for South America, Kid Curry was one of the West's most hunted men. He had killed two lawmen and two cowboys the year before, and with bounty hunters, Pinkerton Agents and sheriffs following his trail of stolen bank notes he became even more vicious.

The Kid tried to reach Butch Cassidy in South America, but the heat was on and he fled across the West from Montana to Colorado. He shaved off his moustache and formed his own gang. After robbing a train on July 7, 1903, a huge posse cornered the Kid and his gang in a small canyon. There, he was wounded, and before the law could reach him, he shot himself in the temple. Drawn, haggard, in ragged clothes and a battered hat, nobody recognized him as Kid Curry. In fact Lowell Spence, a Pinkerton Agent who had been hunting the Kid, had to go to Colorado and dig up the body before an official identification could be made. Kid Curry's life had been a far cry from that of the amiable and gallant hero of television's *Alias Smith and Jones.*

Ben Murphy, who played television's Kid Curry, was born Benjamin Edward Murphy, in Jonesboro, Arkansas. However, his father, who ran a wholesale business, moved twice while Ben was still young and he did his growing up in Memphis and Chicago. Working summers driving a pie truck in Chicago, he earned $150 a week toward his college expenses. It was a hard and dangerous job—drivers frequently got mugged during the 60 stop route and Ben's supervisor dropped dead of a heart attack, but Ben persevered.[26]

Peter Deuel (left; later simplified to Duel) as Hannibal Heyes and Ben Murphy as Jed "Kid" Curry starred in the original version of *Alias Smith and Jones*.

Murphy's first theatrical experience came as a spear carrier in a University of Illinois production of Shakespeare's *Julius Caesar* and he later played the "Young Man" in Edward Albee's *The American Dream*. Then he left college and drove to California. There, while appearing at the Pasadena Playhouse in *Life with Father*, Murphy was "discovered" and signed by agent Jack Donaldson. This led to a one-line role in the Mike Nichols film, *The Graduate* (1967), where Ben uttered the words, "Save me a piece" (of wedding cake). He was paid $125 for one day's work and had to borrow money from his mother to pay his Screen Actors Guild dues. Murphy was, however, soon signed to a contract by Universal Studios and began appearing in episodes of several of their television series, including *The Virginian*, *It Takes a Thief*, and a couple of their made-for-television movies. On *The Name of the Game* (1968–1971) he was given the part of a young reporter named Joe Sample and appeared intermittently for three seasons. Then at an NBC cocktail party, a producer apologized for not using Ben more often on the show. "That's all right," Murphy replied. "I'm using my free time to look for film jobs"—and he was promptly fired.[27] As Kid Curry on *Alias Smith and Jones*, Murphy was often compared to Paul Newman in the Butch Cassidy film. When reporters suggested that was why he got the role, he would bristle. Series creator Larson and executive producer Huggins were both impressed with Murphy. Huggins said in an interview with *TV Guide*:

> He's beautifully willing not to be the typical Western hero. He's even willing to be the butt of the jokes. [But the role] is better played straight than silly and sometimes Ben goes too broad.[28]

Peter Deuel was cast as Kid Curry's pal Hannibal Heyes. A loner who liked to walk in the woods while growing up in Penfield, a small one-stoplight farming community outside of Rochester, New York, Deuel was the son of the town's general practitioner and nurse. Pete was interested in acting as early as kindergarten, but did not contemplate a professional career until he was in college. He was a poor student at St. Lawrence University, but when his father saw him in the school production of *The Rose Tattoo*, he told Pete, "If you want to go to school, why don't you go to drama school instead of wasting my money here?"[29]

Pete was accepted into the American Theater Wing school in New York City and buckled down to serious study. After graduation he appeared in a Family Service Society play about syphilis. Then he earned his Equity card as a member of a Shakespearean company and appeared in his first film, *Wounded in Action*. This was followed by a stint as Tom Ewell's understudy in the road company of *Take Her, She's Mine*. When the show reached Los Angeles, Deuel decided to try his luck in a television series and then to return to Broadway after five years. His plan worked well, with Pete landing the role of John Cooper, Sally Field's brother-in-law on *Gidget* (1965–1966), after guest spots on such popular shows as *Combat*, *Twelve O'Clock High*, *The Fugitive* and *The Big Valley*. At the end of the five years, however, Deuel was offered the lead in the well-received, though short-lived, situation comedy *Love on a Rooftop* (1966–1967) as the newly married struggling apprentice architect David Willis, opposite Judy Carne (who would later become famous on *Laugh-In*). Deuel later explained why he dropped his personal five year plan to accept the role:

> . . . It was a fine series. It was sentimental without being maudlin, although every once in a while it got a bit sticky. I don't usually like to watch gooey sentimentality myself, but sometimes it's a release. It allows you to sit and cry, and you may be crying for a lot of other things.[30]

When *Love on a Rooftop* was canceled after only one season, Deuel turned to films. He appeared in the two hour pilot of Robert Young's hit series *Marcus Welby, MD* (1969) and with Walter Brennan as a footloose young gambler named Honest John Smith who was searching for the owner of a mysterious fortune (shades of his role in *Alias Smith and Jones* right down to the character's last name) in the made-for-television film *The Young Country* (1970). He also was given his first major big screen film role as pregnant Kim Darby's husband in *Generation* (1969). Deuel's most satisfying and stimulating roles came as a junkie in the pilot episode of Universal's *The Psychiatrist* ("God Bless the Children") in 1970 and as a patient who desperately needs a kidney in *The Interns* ("The Price of Life"), also in 1970. Deuel claimed that "these roles made everything else seem dull by comparison."[31] Despite Deuel's preference for serious parts, he seemed comfortable as the wide-eyed safecracker Hannibal Heyes, trying to go straight in the dying days of the Old West in the comedy-adventure series, *Alias Smith and Jones*:

> I was footloose and fancy free at Universal before this came along. Still, if I have to make a TV series I prefer being in the great outdoors and around horses than playing a lawyer, say, in a courtroom.[32]

However, comparisons that the press made with *Butch Cassidy and the Sundance Kid* annoyed Deuel:

> I frankly resented the constant needling by the press every time I did an interview. It was always the first question asked, and in my opinion a moot point.[33]

What made the interviews even more difficult for Deuel (and Murphy, as well), was the fact that Universal wanted to divorce the series from the movie. They tried to play down the similarity which, Deuel claimed, began and ended with the fact that "it was no longer profitable for two guys to continue as outlaws." Deuel later mused,

> It would be funny if the series runs a couple of years, then the film is rereleased, and the new audience that hasn't seen the movie will say "Butch Cassidy and the Sundance Kid" resembles "Alias Smith and Jones."[34]

Alias Smith and Jones debuted with a two hour film on January 5, 1971. Written and produced by former singer Glen A. Larson (who would later produce such hit series as *Switch*, 1975–1978; *B.J. and the Bear*, 1979–1981; and *The Fall Guy*, 1981–1986), the pilot film laid the plot groundwork for the series. As the opening narration (written by Glen Larson and Matthew Howard) explains:

> Nobody can really pinpoint just when that period called the West ended. Maybe it was when the last outlaws were captured or put out of business. If so, this story is about the end of the West.
> This was America's frontier at the turn of the century . . . indoor plumbing and telephones, automobiles and nickelodeons.
> The West was getting to be downright comfortable for everyone. Well, everyone but outlaws. . . .
> (Shot of Heyes and Curry riding hard.)
> These two gentleman had gained great notoriety for their crusade to keep the banks of the West open around the clock. They were terribly successful. Something had to be done . . . the days of the outlaw were numbered. But they hadn't given up yet.

Hannibal Heyes and Jed "Kid" Curry, a pair of notorious outlaws, are offered amnesty by the governor of Wyoming Territory if they will bring in a vicious desperado and his gang. They later discover, however, that their amnesty (offered through a lawman friend, Sheriff Tom Trevors) has several other strings attached. They must change their names and stay out of trouble for a year (with only Trevors and the governor aware of the agreement). As the concluding narration explains:

> So . . . for the following year, the West's two most-wanted men would lead model lives . . . lives of temperance—moderation—and tranquility. Hannibal Heyes and Kid Curry would cease to exist.
> In their places would ride two men of peace. . . . Alias Smith and Jones.

In addition to Deuel and Murphy the film featured former *Virginian* James Drury as Trevors, *F-Troop* alumnus Forrest Tucker as a deputy, Susan Saint James as the romantic interest, and veteran Western performers Jeanette Nolan, Earl Holliman and John Russell in supporting roles.

On January 21, 1971, the weekly hour-long version premiered with an episode entitled "The McCreedy Bust." The show, which drew a respectable viewing audience, relates the efforts of Smith and Jones to recover a bust of Julius Caesar stolen from a wealthy rancher (McCreedy) by a Mexican grandee. The pair are successful and paid a $10,000 fee, only to lose it back to McCreedy in a clever poker ruse. It seems that according to Hoyle, a straight does not beat two of a kind in draw poker unless specifically agreed to by the players in advance. (*Hoyle's Book of Games* was usually followed in the latter part of the nineteenth century. This ploy had been used years earlier on *Maverick* when Samantha Crawford used a pair of nines to beat Bret's straight in "According to Hoyle.")

The duo do ultimately get the last laugh, however. Heyes (alias Smith), an expert poker player, bets McCreedy $20,000 that he can take any 25 cards dealt to him at random and make five pat poker hands out of them. After he wins the bet, he explains to McCreedy that it works nine out of every ten times. Then, to add insult to injury, the Mexican grandee and his men show up and steal all the money as well as the bust of Caesar. Burl Ives was delightfully robust as McCreedy, Cesar Romero was fine as the Mexican grandee, and Edward Andrews turned in a typically solid performance as a bemused banker friend of McCreedy's. Most critics applauded the show. Respected critic Ben Gross of the *New York Daily News* (January 22, 1971) wrote:

> A rarity came to TV last night . . . a new Western series, "Alias Smith and Jones," over ABC. . . . As oatburners go, it's a pretty good one, certain to please the aficionados and—who knows?—because it is invested with a light touch and a sense of humor, it may even snare a sophisticate or two. . . .
>
> The new show . . . has all the expected conventional elements: the raw frontier town, the lawmen and the outlaws, the gamblers, the stage coach, the saloon with its garish girls, etc. etc. In other words, present are all of the atmosphere, the settings and the props that one associates with this escapist form of entertainment. . . .
>
> . . . Pete Duel and Ben Murphy give picturesque performances as the two former badmen now trying to go straight. . . . What I especially liked about the opening installment was its vein of comedy buried beneath the obvious melodrama of the action.

Tom Mackin of the Newark, New Jersey, *Evening News* (January 22, 1971) echoed Gross' sentiments:

> There was a lot to like about "Alias Smith and Jones" the light-hearted western brought in by ABC last night. It teetered precariously on slapstick throughout the hour, but it managed to stay honest, retain its sense of humor and even come up with a new plot twist or two.
>
> . . . It was a droll, fast-moving episode, well acted by a particularly adept cast.

Cleveland Amory was not as lavish with his praise in *TV Guide*, but did have to admit he liked the show in his March 6, 1971, review:

> One thing you'll have to grant this show. It doesn't promise very much . . . but it's got a terrific premise. . . .
>
> Another thing you'll have to grant is that the two principals are fine actors. . . . [The show] also has a plethora of guest stars. . . .
>
> . . . But that is about all we can say.

At the beginning of the third season, *Variety* (September 20, 1972) was still singing the show's praises:

> The operative word for "Smith and Jones" is amiable. While they usually carry guns, they rarely fire them. . . . While their frontier world is largely populated by the usual assortment of toughs and macho types, the whole thing is played for laughs.

Between the first episode of January 1971, and episode number 38, which marked the opening of the series' third season, however, tragedy had befallen the show. Pete Duel (he had changed the spelling for simplicity) had embarked upon a television career with high expectations. The longer he remained in Hollywood, however, the more frustrated he became. He thought most of the scripts he was required to do were garbage and he had developed a reputation for fighting with directors. Duel had attempted to change the system by running for office in the Screen Actors Guild, but lost. As biographer Tim Brooks explains:

> Usually clad in jeans, [Duel] was a political activist working for McCarthy in '68 and caring about ecology—he was a true child of the '60s. Thousands of young hopefuls would have given their eyeteeth for his success, but Duel always wanted more, both as an actor and as a person.[35]

Still, Duel's apparent suicide came as a shock. It was New Year's Eve, 1971. He had been filming an episode of *Alias Smith and Jones* earlier in the day. That evening he read the script for the next show and watched a completed episode of the series. Duel was with his girlfriend, who later said nothing seemed wrong, although he had been drinking and said that he hated the show he had watched. Late that night, she heard a gunshot from the next room, and ran to find him sprawled on the floor. Despite all the evidence to the contrary, many friends, as well as fans, felt that it must have been a terrible accident— or murder. Police ruled Duel's death a "probable suicide" and closed the case. It was an ending unlike any ever contemplated for the popular lighthearted series of which he was a star.

With four more episodes needed to complete the season, the role of Joshua Smith had to be quickly recast. Roger Davis, who had been doing the show's opening and closing narration, was chosen, and a partially completed episode, "The Biggest Game in the West," was finished with Davis redoing scenes that had already been filmed by Duel. No explanation was made in the storyline, with Davis taking over the role as if he had been playing it for the entire run of the show (in much the same way that Dick Sargent had taken over for Dick York in *Bewitched* in 1969).

Davis, a native of Louisville, Kentucky, made his television acting debut in 1962 as Private Roger Gibson, a callow young driver, on ABC's World War II drama *The Gallant Men*. Later he appeared in ABC's daytime serial *Dark Shadows* as Peter Bradford (Maggie's love interest when she is transported to the past). The opportunity for his involvement with *Alias Smith and Jones* undoubtedly dates to his selection as the amiable conman Stephen Foster Moody, in *The Young Country*. That 1970 made-for-television film was written, directed and produced by *Alias Smith and Jones* producer Roy Huggins. Aaron Spelling also used Davis in the 1971 beach-bum "buddy" picture *River of Gold* (with *Guns of Will Sonnett*'s Dack Rambo).

In addition to his work as narrator, Huggins also gave Davis a guest-starring role as the title villain in an earlier episode of *Alias Smith and Jones* called "Smiler with a Gun." During that episode, Davis, as gambler, con-artist and ladies man Danny Billson, teams up with Duel and Murphy to help an old prospector (Will Geer) mine gold. The night before they are set to return to civilization with the fruits of their joint labor, Billson sneaks off with the gold and leaves the other three with no horses and little water.

The Kid and Heyes survive the trek across the desert, but the old prospector dies and the two vow revenge on their former crony. They finally find Billson running a saloon. After refusing to turn over the proceeds from the sale of the gold to Heyes and Curry, Billson goads Curry into a showdown gunfight. In front of the town sheriff's eyes, Curry

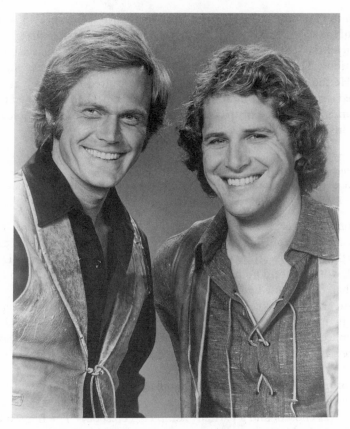

Roger Davis (left) and Ben Murphy finish the series as *Alias Smith and Jones*, from 1972 on.

is forced to kill Billson in self-defense. (This is one of the few instances in the 49 episode series that Curry, who usually has his gun out and leveled before his opponent can even clear his holster, actually kills anyone.) The repartee among the three worked well, especially during the first half of the story when all are pals. This, as well as Davis' physical stature and easy-going manner, obviously impressed Huggins. Perennial television game show host Ralph Story replaced Davis as narrator and several new segments were filmed for the opening montage showing Davis as Hannibal Heyes.

The quality of the series did not suffer noticeably when Davis took over for Duel, but this was as much the result of good scripts and supporting casts as it was the efforts of its two stars. The series bore the indelible mark of executive producer Huggins, who wrote most of the stories under the pseudonym John Thomas James. Huggins, who was one of the creators of *Maverick* in 1957 and would serve as producer and occasional writer for the first three seasons, loved clever stories about con games, poker, gambling, switches, land swindles and frauds, horse racing and the like, incorporated such plot devices into many of the episodes of *Alias Smith and Jones*. "The McCreedy Bust," "Exit from Wickenberg," "The Night of the Red Dog (in which a variation on poker called Montana Red Dog plays a significant role in the story), "The Men That Corrupted Hadleyburg," "The Biggest Game in the West," "Which Way to the O.K. Corral?" "Don't Get Mad, Get Even," and "What's in It for Mia?" all feature poker or some other card game like blackjack. (Heyes had a real knack for exposing cheating of all kinds—especially marked

Walter Brennan (left), in another of his patented character roles, appeared with Murphy (center) and Deuel in several episodes of *Alias Smith and Jones*.

cards.) Jewel switches are central to the plots of "A Fistful of Diamonds" and "Never Trust an Honest Man," and money is cleverly switched in "Jailbreak at Junction City," "The Men Who Broke the Bank at Red Gap," "Don't Get Mad, Get Even," "The Girl in Boxcar Number Three," and "What's in It for Mia?" while gambling on horse races is essential to the story of "The Great Shell Game." A land swindle is employed in "Dreadful Sorry, Clementine" and "The Root of It All" concerns a search for buried treasure.

Huggins, who was also involved in the production of such hit series as *The Fugitive* (1963–1967), *Run for Your Life* (1965–1968) and *The Lawyers* segments of *The Bold Ones* (1969–1972) and would later produce Jim Garner's television series *The Rockford Files* (1974–1980), especially favored stories where a crook was beaten at his own game. Notable among episodes with such a theme were "Dreadful Sorry, Clementine," "The Wrong Train to Brimstone," "The Great Shell Game," "A Fistful of Diamonds," "The Man Who Broke the Bank at Red Gap," "The Men That Corrupted Hadleyburg," "Which Way to the O.K. Corral?" "Don't Get Mad, Get Even," and "What's in It for Mia?"

Another *Maverick*-type Huggins touch was the inclusion of likable and interesting con-artists who would be used in several episodes. Among such characters were Silky O'Sullivan, a lovable retired con-artist (a tour de force for Walter Brennan), in "The Day They Hanged Kid Curry" (in which Brennan also appears in drag as Curry's grandmother), "Twenty-One Days to Tenstrike" and "Don't Get Mad, Get Even"; "Mac" McCreedy, a cagey, stingy rancher (Burl Ives at his droll best), in "The McCreedy Bust," "The McCreedy Bust — Going, Going, Gone" and "The McCreedy Feud" (each episode also featured Cesar Romero as Señor Alvarez, a charming and crafty Mexican grandee—each episode being a continuation of the earlier stories); "Soapy" Sylvester, a distinguished and suave former confidence man, much like Silky Sullivan only considerably more polished (a witty role for *Ben Casey* alumnus, Sam Jaffe), in "The Great Shell Game" and "A Fistful of Diamonds"; Winfield Fletcher, a tightfisted, seedy, scheming banker (a superb characterization by Rudy Vallee), in "Dreadful Sorry, Clementine" and "The Man Who Broke the Bank at Red Gap"; and the persistent, obnoxious and slightly dishonest detective Harry Briscol of the Bannerman Detective Agency (J.D. Cannon giving a slick and professional performance), in "The Wrong Train to Brimstone," "The Legacy of Charlie O'Rourke," "The Reformation of Harry Briscol" (in which Briscol actually steals $50,000 but is convinced by Heyes and Curry to return it) and "The Long Chase."

Women con-artists were plentiful too—à la Samantha Crawford, Melanie Blake, and Modesty Blaine of *Maverick*. The best remembered is Clementine Hale (a delightful portrayal by future Emmy and Academy Award winning actress, Sally Field, fresh from three years as television's *Flying Nun*), although she appeared in only two episodes, "Dreadful Sorry, Clementine" and "The Clementine Incident." (Clementine had the only photo in existence of Curry and Heyes and used it to get them to help her with various schemes.) Appearing more often was Georgette "George" Sinclaire, another beautiful schemer who doubled occasionally as a saloon singer (a showcase for the multitalented Michele Lee), in "Which Way to the O.K. Corral?," "Don't Get Mad, Get Even," and "Bad Night in Big Butte."

Another recurring character was the Mexican bandit El Clavo, who was featured in two episodes, "Journey from San Juan" and "Miracle at Santa Marta." Nico Minardos was cast as the bandito in the first El Clavo episode, which set off a controversy involving "reverse discrimination" in the entertainment world that was to have consequences far beyond the series itself. The ethnic minorities advocacy group Justicia voiced their strong objections to ABC regarding their selection of Minardos, stating that a Mexican American should have been cast in the role. The company, however, stood its ground and Minardos played the role. The series' producers felt the episode was so well done and the character of El Clavo so interesting that a sequel was written for the following season. They intended to have Minardos repeat his role.

However, the producers were notified by ABC that they preferred that the casting be revised, and, in compliance with this request, Minardos was dropped from consideration and another actor, one of Latin origin, was engaged for the role originally intended for Minardos. Minardos complained to both ABC and the Screen Actors Guild. The associate national executive secretary of SAG wrote a strongly worded letter to ABC executives objecting to their treatment of Minardos and charging them with reverse discrimination. The landmark statement read in part:

> It is a vital principle involving actors which concerns us—that is the right of all actors to compete and play roles for which they have the training, background and experience. The essence of minority hiring lies within that statement also. All actors should have the right to compete for roles. If the premise is not correct, minority groups of actors are doomed to portray only their ethnic minority roles....
>
> The concept that Italians play Italians, Mexicans play Mexicans, Greeks play Greeks and they all play nothing else is not what "fair employment"; was intended to achieve. The inconsistency of such a hiring practice with both the goals of fair employment and the essence of the actor's craft is painfully clear.[36]

What the Guild was saying was that under such a narrow interpretation of minority rights, Yul Brynner could not have portrayed the King of Siam nor Anthony Quinn, Zorba.

It was wrong, in effect, to penalize one minority to help another. The ultimate result was that Minardos was reinstated in the role, a precedent was established and viewers were treated to another entertaining episode of *Alias Smith and Jones*.

Another recurring character was Sheriff Tom Trevors who appeared in the two hour pilot, and in the episodes "Shootout at Diablo Station," "The Day the Amnesty Came Through," and "Witness to a Lynching." *Lawman*'s John Russell played Trevors in all of the episodes except "Shootout." Inexplicably, Mike Road was Trevors in that episode, while Russell appeared in a bit role as a deputy marshal in "Which Way to the O.K. Corral?" Russell was perfect as the stern-faced lawman who knew Smith and Jones' real identities as well as the governor's conditional offer of amnesty. (Road also had prior experience playing a lawman—as Marshal Tom Sellers in *Buckskin*.)

During their adventures, Joshua and Thaddeus encounter more than their share of beautiful women. Some are vulnerable, like Heather Menzies in "The Girl in Boxcar Number Three"; some are treacherous, like Diana Muldaur in "The Great Shell Game"; some are greedy, like Judy Carne in "The Root of It All"; some are motherly, like Vera Miles in "The Posse That Wouldn't Quit"; some are ambitious, like Jane Merrow in "The Reformation of Harry Briscoe"; some are sexy, like Sheree North in "The Men That Corrupted Hadleyburg"; some are schemers, like Ida Lupino in "What's in It for Mia?"; some are pawns of men they love, like Shirley Knight in "The Ten Days That Shook Kid Curry"; some are devoted to their fathers, like Brenda Scott in "Witness to a Lynching"; some are dominated by an older brother, like Laurette Spang in "Only Three to a Bed"; and some are husband hunters, like Jo Ann Pflug in the same episode.

Three of the most interesting and diverse women appear in "Six Strangers at Apache Springs": Carmen Mathews plays a spunky widow who hires Smith and Jones to dig up the gold she and her husband hid from marauding Indians; Patricia Harty is the spoiled wife of an Indian agent who neither likes the West nor appreciates her husband's courage and dedication to duty; and Sian Barbara Allen portrays a quiet but devoted evangelist who has been duped by a crooked gambler. The lives of each are changed for the better by Smith and Jones.

In their attempts to "go straight," Curry and Heyes engage in a variety of occupations, although each episode usually involves them in some sort of gambling or con game. Some of their jobs are as mundane as prospecting for gold in "Smiler with a Gun" and "The Night of the Red Dog," herding cattle (or rounding up strays) in "The Reformation of Harry Briscoe," "Journey from San Juan" and "Bushwhack!" or capturing and breaking wild horses in "Three to a Bed." On other occasions they engage in more dangerous work, like transporting money for a lawyer in "The Girl in Boxcar Number Three" and protecting two government witnesses in "Witness to a Lynching." In "Something to Get Hung About," they start out playing Cupid and end up solving a murder and saving an innocent man from the gallows. But Curry and Heyes always try to stay on the "right" side of the law. As they explain to a would-be counterfeiter and his daughter in "What's in It for Mia?":

> CURRY: We try to avoid violence at all times, not to mention anything illegal.
> HEYES: Sometimes shady maybe, but never illegal.

Another enjoyable feature of *Alias Smith and Jones* is the use in many guest and supporting roles of the stars of previously canceled television Westerns. It is a real pleasure to see such veterans of the video range as Neville Brand of *Laredo* (in "Shootout at Diablo Station" and "Which Way to the O.K. Corral?"), Peter Breck of *Black Saddle* and *The Big Valley* (in "The Great Shell Game"), the aforementioned Walter Brennan, Pat Buttram of *The Gene Autry Show* (in "Bad Night in Big Butte"), Rory Calhoun of *The Texan* (in "The Night of the Red Dog"), Rod Cameron of *State Trooper* (in "The Biggest Game in the West" and "High Lonesome Country"), David Canary of *Bonanza* (in "The Strange Fate of Conrad Meyer Zulick"), Robert Colbert of *Maverick* (in "Twenty-One Days to Tenstrike"), Jackie Coogan of *Cowboy G-Men* (in "Which Way to the O.K. Corral?" "McGriffin" and "Dreadful Sorry, Clementine"), Glenn Corbett of *The Road West* (in "Twenty-One Days to Tenstrike" and "Bushwhack!"), Andy Devine of *Wild Bill Hickok* (in "The Men That Corrupted Hadleyburg"), James Drury of *The Virginian* (in "The Long Chase"), Buddy Ebsen of *Davy Crockett* and *Northwest Passage* (in "What's in It for Mia?" and "High Lonesome Country"), Jack Elam of *The Dakotas* and *Temple Houston* (in "Bad Night in Big Butte"), Paul Fix of *The Rifleman* (in "The Night of the Red Dog" and "Only Three to a Bed"), Earl Holliman of *Hotel de Paree* in ("The Day They Hanged Kid Curry"), Jack Kelly of *Maverick* in ("The Night of the Red Dog"), Lee Majors of *The Big Valley* (in "The McCreedy Bust—Going, Going, Gone"), Cameron Mitchell of *High Chaparral* (as Wyatt Earp in "Which Way to the O.K. Corral?"), George Montgomery of *Cimarron City* (in "Jailbreak at Junction City"), Slim Pickens of *The Outlaws* and *Custer* (in "Exit from Wickenberg," "The Man Who Murdered Himself," and "The Strange Fate of Conrad Meyer Zulick"), Pernell Roberts of *Bonanza* (in "Exit from Wickenberg" and "Twenty-One Days to Tenstrike"), the aforementioned John Russell and William Smith of *Laredo* (in "What Happened at the XST?") and Chill Wills of *The Rounders* (in "The Biggest Game in the West").

Roy Huggins kept many otherwise unemployed television actors and actresses busy. In addition to the Western stars and others already mentioned there were Jack Albertson of *The Thin Man* (in "Jailbreak at Junction City"), Jim Backus of *I Married Joan* and *Gilligan's Island* (in "The Biggest Game in the West"), John Banner of *Hogan's Heroes* (in "Don't Get Mad, Get Even"), Joseph Campanella of *Mannix* (in "The Fifth Victim"), Judy Carne, Duel's former costar in *Love on a Rooftop*, and Tom Ewell of *The Tom Ewell Show* (both in "The Root of It All"), Jack Cassidy of *He and She* (in "How to Rob a Bank in One Hard Lesson"), Wally Cox of *Mr. Peepers* (in "The Men that Corrupted Hadleyburg"), Howard Duff of *Felony Squad* (in "Shootout at Diablo Station"), Joe Flynn of *McHale's Navy* (in "The Night of the Red Dog"), Alan Hale of *Gillian's Island* (in "The Girl in Boxcar Number Three"), Diana Hyland of *Peyton Place* in "Return to Devil's Hole"), Dean Jagger of *Mr. Novak* and John Kerr of *Peyton Place* (both in "Only Three to a Bed"), Mark Lenard of *Star Trek* (in "Exit from Wickenberg"), Patrick Macnee of *The Avengers* and Juliet Mills of *Nanny and the Professor* (both in "The Man Who Murdered Himself"), John McGiver of *The Patty Duke Show* (in "Witness to a Lynching"), Robert Morse of *That's Life* (in "The Day They Hanged Kid Curry"), Diana Muldaur of *McCloud* (in "The Great Shell Game"), Arthur O'Connell of *Mr. Peepers* (in "Bad Night at Big Butte"), Ann Sothern of *Private Secretary* and *The Ann Sothern Show* (in "Everything Else You Can Steal"), Craig Stevens of *Peter Gunn* (in "Miracle at Santa Marta"), William Windom of *The Farmer's Daughter* (in "The Wrong Train to Brimstone"), and Jane Wyatt of *Father Knows Best* (in "The Reformation of Harry Briscoe"). All in all, *Alias Smith and Jones* provided viewers with a veritable "who's who" in television land.

An analysis of one of the more meaningful and interesting adventures is in order. "The Bounty Hunter" features guest star Louis Gossett as Joe Sims, "bounty hunter—professional." Sims captures Curry and Heyes on the trail and though they try to talk him out of it, he declares his intention of turning them over to the nearest sheriff for the reward:

SIMS: Any description on any outlaw worth more than two thousand dollars, I got locked up in my head down to the last button on his shirt. And I don't just go by one description on a man. I compare different ones, talk to people, ask questions. Yeah, I'm workin' all the time. That's how I was able to spot you two right off. . . . I ain't got nothin' against you personally, but like I said, I'm a bounty hunter—professional. But for twenty thousand dollars for the two of you, gonna be the biggest score I ever made . . .

HEYES: How'd you get in this line of business, Joe?

SIMS: Well, I'll tell ya. Ain't much a black man can do these days. Before the war, I was a slave. Then, afterwards, I just drifted West and the further I went, the further I got away from the way things used to be back home. Sometimes, that's good. Sometimes, that's bad. Depends on the kind of people you run into. Nobody pay a black man more'n room and board and that's if he can get work. In the old days, if ya got sick, why the master, he'd have to take care of ya. Now days if you get sick, you just out of luck. That's why I became a bounty hunter, for the money. Black man ain't gonna be out of luck if he got money.

Curry and Heyes are able to escape when a rattlesnake spooks Sims' horse. In the chase that follows, Sims accidently shoots and kills the horse of a white cowboy and he and his white cronies prepare to string Sims up. After saving Sims' life, by chasing off the would-be lynchers with a volley of gunfire, Curry and Heyes continue on their way, content that they have done the right thing. Shortly thereafter, Sims ambushes Curry and Heyes and again takes them prisoner. When questioned about his lack of gratitude, Sims explains he did it for the money.

HEYES: Joe, I hate to say this but I don't think you're showin' the proper gratitude.

SIMS: What's that?

CURRY: Don't you know why we did this?

SIMS: Tell ya the truth, that's what's been puzzlin' me. Seems kinda stupid ta me.

HEYES: Stupid!?!

SIMS: Yeah sir! Don't know why ya wanna save my skin, when ya could have saved your own skins instead, especially since I'm dead set on taken ya in. Now, don't that sound kind of stupid ta you?

A little farther along the trail, three white drifters stop Sims and take his prisoners from him so that they and not he can collect the reward. Meanwhile, Sims walks to the nearest ranch, buys another horse and gun and is able to recapture his prisoners along with two of the three men. The third one, however, sneaks back to their camp that night and is about to kill Sims. Curry, who has gotten loose from his ropes, shoots the drifter and again saves Joe's life. Still, Joe is set on turning Curry and Heyes in for the reward:

CURRY: You know what you are? You are a miserable ingrate! You know that? He was gonna kill you. We have now saved your life twice. Now, how can you do this ta us?

SIMS: Well, don't think it's so easy! You're takin' all the pleasure I'm ever gonna get outta spendin' that twenty thousand dollars. Every time I think of the way you saved my life, ain't gonna be no fun spendin' that money, no fun at all. In fact, I may just invest it instead.

Later, the story becomes more serious:

HEYES: Just tell me one thing. Why are you so all fired ornery?

SIMS: Nothin' I can do about that. Some black folks, ya know, figure they owe white folks a lotta harm for all what they done. I don't feel that way. I don't feel I owe 'em any harm. I don't feel I owe 'em anything else either. I guess that's why I don't know nothin' 'bout gratitude. It been taken outta me a long time ago.

HEYES: That's sad, Joe. That's a sad way ta be.

SIMS: I guess . . .

Another group of whites come upon them. Since their leader feels that it is not the place of a black man to arrest white folks, he orders two of his men to take Curry and Heyes into town to check their identities and shoots Sims in the back as he rides away. Curry and Heyes escape, but arrive too late to save Joe, who dies in their arms. They bury him, but decide to report Joe's murder to the nearest sheriff, even at the risk of their own safety. They had become fond of Joe and feel it is the least that they can do for him now, although they know in their hearts that, had he lived, Joe would have turned them both in for the reward money. This excellent story by John Thomas James (Huggins) contains both humor and tragedy. It is both a comment on the plight of the black man at the end of the Civil War and on his contemporary problems. It represents *Alias Smith and Jones* at its best.

In the final episode, "Only Three to a Bed," it appears that our two heroes are at last going to find themselves wives and settle down. Alas, as in each of the preceding 48 episodes, they escape the clutches of respectability at the last minute. Still, they had managed, with great difficulty, to trod the "straight and narrow" for nearly three seasons. Smith and Jones deserved a better fate than cancellation before their amnesty came through. The producers should resurrect this fine series for a special television film (à la *Gunsmoke*) and finally resolve this problem once and for all. (Of course, then they would not be "Smith" and "Jones" anymore.) One can heartily recommend this series in its syndicated reruns.

Inspiration for *The Quest* began one day late in 1975, when David Gerber, a vice president of Columbia Pictures Television, decided that the time was right to try a new television Western. It must have seemed like a strange decision to some, for the heyday of the television Western had passed and during the previous season there had not been one Western on prime time network television for the first time in over twenty years. All that viewers appeared to want were tough cop shows. Gerber, however, believed that the Western was not dead—all that was needed was a new approach. He thought he knew what that approach might be—an emphasis on realism. His new series would depict the West as it really was, raw, seamy and hard—full of violence, bloodshed, brawls, gunfights, rapes, gambling, saloons and brothels.

The next step was to find a writer. Gerber appeared to hit the jackpot when he selected Tracy Keenan Wynn, who had already won two Emmys for previous scripts. Wynn came from a theatrical family which had celebrated over a hundred years in show business. His great-grandfather, Frank Keenan, was an Irish stage actor born in 1876 who appeared in Shakespearean roles before heading for California to make silent films. (John Barrymore took over one of his roles after he died.) Ed Wynn, the beloved American comedian, married Frank Keenan's daughter and enjoyed a long and active career which spanned vaudeville, films and television. Frank Keenan Wynn, Tracy's father, was a respected serious actor who had appeared in dozens of films and television productions. (He would play a cameo role in the pilot film for *The Quest*.)

Tracy tried acting, but did not like it. "An actor," he later explained, "has little creative freedom."[37] Graduating from the University of California—Los Angeles with a degree in fine arts, Tracy set out to become a script writer. In 1970 he wrote a television movie with Marin Schwartz called *Tribes*. That first script won him an Emmy and an award from the Writer's Guild of America. He was nominated for another Emmy for his second script, *The Glass House* (1972), but the award went to someone else. Eventually, he did pick up a second Emmy, as well as several other awards, for *The Autobiography of Miss Jane Pittman* (1974). His theatrical film credits included *The Longest Yard* (1974) for Burt Reynolds and *The Drowning Pool* (1976) for Paul Newman and Joanne Woodward,

The Quest **featured Kurt Russell (left) and Tim Matheson as the Beaudine brothers, Morgan and Quentin, searching for their sister who had been kidnapped by Indians eight years earlier.**

and he had begun to work on a screen adaptation of Peter Benchley's *The Deep*. Wynn was excited about doing a Western. He told *New York Daily News* columnist Kay Gardella:

> I'm frankly getting weary of the same old formula. I'd like to see a series based on American history. The 1880s in the West was a colorful time. It had flamboyant, larger-than-life characters and business families like the Goulds and Vanderbilts to add spice.[38]

The writer vowed that the series would have some social significance and would show both sides of such controversial subjects as the struggle between Indians and whites:

> Indians died at the hands of other Indians, not just whites....
> We're getting a clearer picture of history today. Everything was highly romanticized in the past. Cowboys, for instance, were always made to appear bigger than they really were. Even the gunfights were never quite the way they were depicted in films like "High Noon." The famous gunfight at the OK Corral was actually a business battle between the Earps and Clantons over the house of prostitution in town. It had nothing to do with good guys versus bad guys.[39]

The secret of Wynn's success as a writer lay in the long hours of research he did before he ever put a single word on paper. For *The Quest*, he spent weeks researching the Old West, digging about in old bookshops, picking up out-of-print volumes of cowboy lore, immersing himself in everything there was to know about the American frontier of the 1880s. The result was a collection of characters who came across on the screen as real people—which was not too surprising since many of them were based, at least in part, on actual people who lived and died during that era. The part of Morgan "Two Persons" Beaudine, for example, had historical precedents. There really was a Cheyenne chief who was half white. (Unfortunately for *The Quest*, Wynn wrote a script only for the two hour pilot film.)

The next step in getting *The Quest* on the home screen was to find two young actors to play the Beaudine brothers who roam the Old West in search of their younger sister, who was kidnapped by the Cheyenne eight years earlier. Handsome, young Kurt Russell was chosen for the role of Morgan "Two Persons" Beaudine, who had been raised by the Cheyenne. Born in Springfield, Massachusetts, in 1951, Russell had begun his career as a juvenile performer, appearing both on television and in films. The blond, square-jawed actor's father, Bing Russell, was a former baseball player who had turned actor. (He played the role of the deputy sheriff intermittently for years on *Bonanza*.)

An actor since the age of 10, Kurt began his career with guest spots on series like *Our Man Higgins* and *The Fugitive*. Young Russell got his first big break at the age of 12 in 1963, playing the lead in the television series *The Travels of Jaimie McPheeters*. He also made several appearances on *Daniel Boone*. Russell's theatrical film debut also came in 1963, when he was cast as a kid who kicked Elvis in the shin, in Presley's 1963 film *It Happened at the World's Fair*. It was Walt Disney, however, who gave Russell his biggest boost to stardom by featuring him in a series of family comedies in the sixties and early seventies, including *Follow Me, Boys!* (1966), *The One and Only Genuine Original Family Band* (1968), *The Horse in the Gray Flannel Suit* (1968), *The Computer Wore Tennis Shoes* (1970), *Now You See Him, Now You Don't* (1972), *Charlie and the Angel* (1973), *Superdad* (1974), and *The Strongest Man in the World* (1975). Russell also continued to gain television experience with guest roles in series like *Police Story* and *Harry-O* and made-for-television films like *Search for the Gods* (1975). He attracted considerable attention for his portrayal of deranged student and mass murderer Charles Whitman in the television docudrama *The Deadly Tower* in 1975. With his long blond locks and buckskin garb, Russell seemed perfect for the role of Morgan Beaudine in *The Quest*.

Cast as Quentin Beaudine, who was raised in San Francisco and trained to be a doctor, was Tim Matheson. Matheson was no stranger to television or to Westerns, having appeared as Jim Horn on *The Virginian* (1969–1970) and as Griff King on *Bonanza* (1972-73). Matheson had also entered show business at an early age. He began at age 12 with small roles in episodes of *Leave It to Beaver*, *My Three Sons* and *The Twilight Zone*. His big screen debut came in Dick Van Dyke's *Divorce, American Style* in 1967 and he had juvenile roles in two successful Bob Hope films, *Yours, Mine and Ours* (1968) and *How to Commit Marriage* (1969). Working steadily in television, Matheson's credits included such diverse shows as *Window on Main Street*, *Owen Marshall*, *The Farmer's Daughter*, *Medical Center*, *Police Story* and *Jigsaw John*. He also had a featured role in Clint Eastwood's second "Dirty Harry" film, *Magnum Force*, in 1973. Matheson believed that the Western was due for a revival in popularity. He later explained in an interview:

> One of the problems with Westerns, and possibly a reason for their demise, is that the reality of the time didn't contain any relevance for today. In this respect, the West [as depicted] in "The Quest" will be modernized....
> ... [T]he series will be more realistic in terms of today's television audience and today's values.[40]

Tracy Keenan Wynn's script was beautifully filmed in Old Tucson and Wise Woman Mesa, Arizona, by Robert Morrison, with stirring theme music provided by Richard Shores. Under the taut direction of Lee H. Katzin, an outstanding cast of guest stars turned in powerful performances. The film was scheduled for broadcast on May 13, 1976, by NBC.

The story, which was obviously inspired by the John Ford–John Wayne classic 1956 Western, *The Searchers*, set the premise for the series that was to follow. Morgan Beaudine was abducted by Indians and raised as a Cheyenne. His brother Quentin escaped and was brought up by an aunt in San Francisco where he became a medical student. Eight years later, after Morgan has been rescued by the cavalry (who in the process killed his Indian wife), he is reunited with his brother. They join together in a common goal—the quest for their younger sister, Patricia (now called White Antelope) who was also captured by the Cheyenne and is believed to be still living with them.

The focus of the pilot film is the relationship which evolves between the Beaudine brothers and Tank Logan, a reprobate who is driving a herd of mostly stolen cattle to market when he and his men are ambushed by rustlers. The Beaudines drive off the rustlers and are attracted to the colorful and gregarious Logan, who has in his time operated on both sides of the law. Paralyzed from the waist down as the result of an Apache knife wound, Logan can still defend himself with the help of his trusty guns and the bulletproof vest he always wears—as a young bounty hunter finds out in the final moment of his life.

The role is a tour de force for Brian Keith in what is perhaps his best part since *The Westerner* was canceled. Eventually the law catches up with Tank for his past transgressions. Whether he is being hanged for a crime he actually committed is not clear, but Tank obviously believes that sooner or later the hangman was bound to mete out what passed for justice in the Old West. Just before the noose tightens around his neck, Tank reads his own epitaph:

> This might seem a little flowery to ya, I wrote it myself. I want it to be my epitaph: Now that my soul seeks rest beyond that great divide, they planted me here in this lonely stretch that's sunny, free and wide. Let the cattle rub my tombstone down and coyotes mourn my kin; let the horses paw and tromp this mound; but pard, don't fence me in!

Other stand-outs in the cast include *Sugarfoot*'s Will Hutchins as Tank's devoted, young, but not too bright, helper Earl; *Laredo*'s Neville Brand as a cocaine-smoking cutthroat; *The High Chaparral*'s Cameron Mitchell as the marshal who eventually captures Tank, Shadrack Peltzer; veteran Western actor Morgan Woodward as the town sheriff; author Wynn's father Keenan as the flamboyant showman, H.H. Small, who engineers an unusual and colorful race between a camel and a horse; lovely newcomer Irene Yeh-Ling Sun as the beautiful prostitute with a heart of gold, China, with whom Morgan falls in love; and the venerable Iron Eyes Cody in a bit part as an Old Indian. While ratings for the pilot film were good, the reviews were mixed. Most favorable was John J. O'Connor of *The New York Times* (May 13, 1976):

> "The Quest" has an exceptionally good script by Tracy Keenan Wynn, several solid performances and some very attractive scenery.... The format retains the usual barroom brawls and other bric-a-brac of the western form, but it attempts to go farther, particularly in its portraits of American Indians....
>
> This pilot for the series is obviously an expensive production with a good share of the nicely unexpected.... [It's] an adventure yarn, spiked with a jarring routine about a camel, but fleshed out nicely with unusually factual details. The standard "dancing girls" are portrayed bluntly as prostitutes. Chinese ghettos are introduced into the western scene. And, in the prevailing spirit of fairness, Morgan is even allowed to fall in love with a Chinese prostitute....
>
> Given the same care and budget considerations, the series could add up to respectable television.

There were two different reviews in *Variety*. On May 13, one reviewer wrote:

> . . . Concept is valid enough, and Wynn's attention to character development works well. . . .
>
> Wynn provides a wide gallery of Western characters. . . . Christopher Morgan's production, filmed completely in Arizona at Old Tucson and at Wise Woman Mesa, shines with color and spirit.
>
> [T]he brothers have plenty of room for development. . . . But the quest as developed in the series should furnish mucho adventure material, particularly if future scripts stick to Wynn's idea of letting the reds, whites and yellows act like frontier humans who behave and misbehave no matter what the color.

The following day another review appeared in *Variety*, written by a different reviewer:

> Still the movie had its pleasures, if nothing else than watching Brian Keith, Keenan Wynn, Will Hutchins, Neville Brand and Cameron Mitchell chew up the scenery in mostly secondary roles. . . .
>
> The stars of the forthcoming series, Matheson and Russell, were largely obscured by the astute works of the veteran character actors. Russell appears to be the key to the series and he is interesting in a sturdy, blond and boyish kind of way. . . .
>
> Tracy Keenan Wynn's script was picaresque, densely-packed and generally engrossing.

However, Bob Williams of the *New York Post* (May 12, 1976) was mostly negative in his comments:

> NBC will respond with a Western of no consequence, as you'll see tomorrow in the two-hour pilot film. . . . Basically, it's the story of two brothers who get out the guns, knives, languish with frontier prostitutes, get into a senseless camel-horse race, and go nowhere in search of a sister who's a captive of the Cheyennes in Wyoming, who killed their parents.
>
> Be forewarned that it's a lowbrow Western in the initial breakaway by a TV network from the crime-show scourge which brought the wrath of Washington down on the heads of the networks.
>
> NBC's conscience in scheduling "Quest" escaped us in the screening room. . . . There are reminders, of course, amid the blood and guts, of how awful it was in the Winning of the West.

Despite such critical reviews, *The Quest* was scheduled as a weekly series by NBC for fall 1976. On September 22, 1976, the first regular episode, "The Captive," was broadcast. Ninety minutes in length, the script was written by Mark Rodgers and featured guest stars Susan Dey (a decade before her starring stint on *L.A. Law*) as Charlotte Ross, a white woman who was captured years earlier by the Cheyenne when her wagon train was raided. She is now the widow of an Indian warrior and has a small son, Little Eagle.

The opening (as was to be the case in every episode) set the stage by explaining events which had occurred earlier through a montage of scenes from the pilot film accompanied by the following narration:

> The legend of the Beaudine brothers has etched itself into frontier history in the last quarter of the nineteenth century. Morgan "Two Persons" Beaudine, captured by the Cheyenne and freed eight years later by the army; Quentin Beaudine, a young doctor from San Francisco. Across thousands of miles from the Missouri breaks to the Canadian River, from the Rockies to the high plains, both joined together in a search for their sister, Patricia, still a captive of the Cheyenne. The legend of the Beaudine brothers—this is their story. This is "The Quest."

The Beaudine brothers join a cavalry raid on a Cheyenne encampment, hoping to find their long-missing sister. Instead they find Charlotte and when the soldiers kill the Indians and destroy their encampment, take the white woman and her Indian son with them to the army town of Fort George. Sharing a house with the two brothers, Charlotte finds it increasingly difficult to return to and be accepted in a white man's world.

Moreover, the townspeople are hostile and bitter toward a white woman with an Indian son. Little Eagle is regarded with hatred and treated cruelly by the local children. Worst of all, Charlotte realizes that she can never return to the Cheyenne after having lived with the whites.

Charlotte's unhappiness is made more terrible when one of the former troopers in the outfit that rescued her sneaks into the house and rapes her—in full view of her young son. Quentin and a young officer named Callendar (who has become increasingly interested in Charlotte) ride up just in time to hear her screams. Enraged beyond control, Quentin throws the man out the window, breaking his neck. Now totally disillusioned, Charlotte takes a job at a brothel hoping to earn enough to give her son a good education. Quentin and Morgan finally convince her that she has chosen the wrong path to help her son, and she agrees to leave Fort George with them as they continue their search for their sister. Just as they are about to leave, Callendar rides up and proposes to Charlotte. Knowing that he will be a good husband and father to her son, Charlotte accepts and, at last, the future appears to brighten for the lonely, embittered woman.

The episode was well acted by the leads, as well as guest stars Richard Egan (of *Empire* and *Redigo*) as the commander of the Cavalry, Christopher Connelly (of *Paper Moon*) as Callendar, Russ Tamblyn (of *Seven Brides for Seven Brothers*) as the rapist, and Dennis Cole (of *Barbary Coast*) as the brothel owner; but the emphasis on violence and brutality detracted from the show's other good qualities. Virtually every reviewer commented on the show's violence. Even *TV Guide* in its Fall Preview issue (September 18, 1976) pointed out:

> ... This series is explicitly not intended for Family Viewing Time. Its producers and writers seem intent on reminding viewers that the years of westward expansion were a violent and sometimes sordid period of American history.

Variety (September 29, 1976) was even more blunt:

> When the antiviolence vigilantes get around to the licensing of networks, "Quest" will be cited as the prime example of the net's total inability to exercise self-restraint. This grossly violent, poorly written, ineptly directed and badly acted premiere does more mayhem to the medium than it does to the fictive characters—beaten, stomped, killed and raped in the show.
> ... [T]he premiere was essentially a repeat of the pilot, only bloodier.
> The real crime was just not its offense to reason, judgment and taste, but the fact that it paves the way for the proponents of blandness on television.

Even John J. O'Connor of the *New York Times*, who wrote such a favorable review of the two-hour pilot, could not find one praiseworthy quality in the first episode. He wrote in an article published the day the series premiered (September 22, 1976):

> With "The Quest" which begins this evening at 9:30 in a special 90-minute production, NBC appears to be exploring further possibilities for expansion on the violence frontier....
> The Indian village is decimated by soldiers. Dead bodies cover the camera foreground. The Army Captain shoots one of his own men in a "mercy killing." The Army's wounded volunteer for suicide duty. The woman's half-breed son is assaulted by other kids. She is brutally raped by an Army man, whose neck is broken when he is thrown through a window. And she, under the influence of the town pimp, goes to work in the local brothel.
> For the moment, the most charitable comment on this cynical exercise in exploitation is that, at least, NBC didn't try to slip "The Quest" into the family hour.

Several days later (September 26), O'Connor, in another article deploring the increase in violence depicted on television, again chastised *The Quest* for its excessive brutality:

> ...According to one insider on the project, the first five scripts are so violent that even Columbia Pictures TV, which is producing the series with David Gerber Productions and NBC, couldn't believe the network allowed acceptance.

New York Daily News columnist Kay Gardella was willing to take a "wait and see" attitude, writing in her column of September 22:

> Ever since "Gunsmoke" was put out to pasture by CBS, the networks have tried unsuccessfully to restore the Western to its rightful place on the tube. Where the channels were once overrun by this TV form, there is now one, token Western making its bid for recognition. It's on NBC tonight at 9:30—the David Gerber—produced series "The Quest."
> The question is: can this series pioneer a new, youth-oriented following that falls comfortably within the heavy-buying-audience range of 18 to 49? Appeal to older viewers, has been the one big complaint against the TV Western and is the key reason it bit the dust. But Gerber, wise in the way of salesmanship, has loaded the cast with young people and contemporary problems....
> ... This is the kind of series that will depend from week to week on the scripts.

Unfortunately the series' second episode, "The Buffalo Hunters," was almost as violent as the first. Written by *Gunsmoke* veteran Paul Savage, the story is filled with torture and sadism as the Beaudines encounter a loathsome pair of buffalo hunters who steal their horses. On the trail of the thieves, they encounter three men who work for the buffalo hunters in the process of slaughtering a herd of buffalo. To prevent this massacre, the Beaudines stampede the herd.

During the night, the brothers' camp is raided and they are taken captive by the three men. The buffalo hunters claim that the Beaudines owe them compensation for stampeding the valuable animals and they will be forced to work for them to pay it off. Morgan and Quentin are separated and told that should either escape the other will be tortured and killed. Another prisoner is a beautiful young Cheyenne squaw. She tells Morgan that her warrior husband will kill all the white men in order to rescue her. As, one by one, the men meet terrible deaths, fear grows in the camp. When the brave comes to rescue his squaw, only Morgan's knowledge of the Cheyenne language saves Quentin from being killed with the other white men. Husband and wife are reunited and the brothers continue their quest for their sister. This episode is most memorable for the slaughter it depicts of both men and animals. Alex Cord turns in a chilling performance as the leader of the buffalo hunters, McWhorley, and Linda Moon Redfearn (a Native American actress) is effective as the Cheyenne squaw.

The third series episode, "Shanklin," is a tour de force for pro-football-star-turned-actor Don Meredith in the title role. While searching for their sister along the Texas border, Quentin and Morgan encounter Captain Victor Shanklin, the no-nonsense commander of Texas Rangers operating in that area. Shanklin administers his rangers under a simple black and white code:

> There're two kinds of people: outlaws and law-abiding. Your first order is to respect all law-abiding. I don't care about size, language or color. You respect law-abiding. Each of you has a copy of "The Outlaw Book." Get to know it. The men named there have burned, plundered, raped, and killed and they think they're bigger than the law. Our job is to prove that they're not.

The Beaudines learn that Shanklin is recruiting men to ride south against a notorious Mexican bandit. Eager to continue their search, the Beaudines are reluctant to join Shanklin's band, but do agree to accompany him part of the way. When Shanklin learns that the bandit has crossed the Rio Grande River into Mexico, he must make a grave decision. He asks his men to accompany him across the border in order to bring the bandit to justice. The Beaudines, having witnessed the aftermath of the bandit gang's brutal murder, rape and plunder of a white homesteader and his family, decide to accompany Shanklin and his rangers. The Rangers locate the bandits in a Mexican bar and in the ensuing gunbattle, the leader and many of his men are killed. Returning to Texas, Shanklin learns that he has been dismissed from the Rangers for making an unlawful excursion into Mexico. The ever-dignified Shanklin accepts the news calmly, satisfied in knowing that he brought law where none had existed before.

"Shanklin" is another episode filled with violence, but as before the violence seems essential to the story. It does not appear to be gratuitously added for shock value, but rather was an attempt to depict the lawless and turbulent West as it really was.

"Day of Outrage," the series' fourth episode, is based on an actual historical incident. Written by Frank Telford, the story relates the Beaudines' encounter with "the only woman in the annals of American history ever hanged for cattle rustling." Amanda Blake, fresh from 19 years on *Gunsmoke*, is cast as Miss Sally, the colorful and notorious madame of a brothel, who speaks out against the powerful and ruthless cattle barons who are trying to destroy the smaller landowners. It is a moving performance by the first lady of television Westerns. Seeking refuge from a severe wind storm, the Beaudine brothers stop at a bordello run by Miss Sally. She offers to pay them for helping with the chores and for Quentin to assist her in writing journals and columns for the local newspaper. The brothers accept the offer. While rounding up Sally's cattle, the Beaudines are informed by wealthy rancher R.L. Gorham that Sally employs rustlers to steal other people's cattle. Gorham then threatens newspaper editor Sam Grant for printing Sally's columns, which often denounce wealthy cattle barons like himself and stir up controversy.

Later, a local man is murdered by some of Gorham's men when he tries to organize a protective association against ranchers like Gorham. Furious, Sally rallies the townspeople and tries to convince them to unite against the murderous cattle barons. She expresses these sentiments in Grant's paper. This infuriates Gorham, who orders some of his men to ransack Sally's house to find her journals, which contain incriminating names and facts. Failing to discover them, the men take Sally and Quentin to a nearby clearing and prepare to hang them. Morgan arrives in time to save his brother, but not Miss Sally, who has already been hanged. Grant then arrives on the scene with a group of angry townsmen. He tells Gorham, now in possession of Sally's journals, that he will continue her crusade for justice against the greedy cattle barons. Unable to be of any further assistance, the Beaudines ride off to continue their search for their sister. This episode contains considerably less violence (except for the incredible sight of a woman hanging from a tree!). The story is, however, except for the involvement of the fictitious Beaudines, remarkably close to the actual facts of the incident.

"Prairie Woman," by Earl W. Wallace, also emphasizes historical realism. Here the viewer is exposed to the harsh realities of life on the frontier from the viewpoint of a woman. The story is "framed" by the Beaudine brothers' search for an escaped killer, Tom Kurd, who claims to know the location of their missing sister. Seeking Kurd, they stop at an isolated prairie house and find young Seba Alcott alone tending her sick baby. Seba, only 23, has been prematurely aged by her hard, lonely life on the windswept prairie. Not wanting to leave the woman alone, Quentin reluctantly sends Morgan off to continue the search for Kurd. Despite Quentin's medical assistance, Seba's child dies. The woman nearly loses her sanity, for this is the second child she has seen die on the prairie. Quentin helps her overcome her depression and she begins to feel more optimistic about the future. Meanwhile, Morgan has tracked Kurd down—in time to see him shot by the marshal. Before Morgan can learn the whereabouts of his sister, Kurd dies. Back at Seba's house, the Beaudine brothers are reunited. Seba's husband Samuel has returned home from his travels, and they too are reunited, saddened by the loss of their child, but hopeful about their future.

Three stars of earlier television Westerns are featured in "Prairie Woman." Ty Hardin (*Bronco*), in a complete change of character, plays the evil Tom Kurd; Jim Davis (*Tales of the Century*) is cast as the marshal and Paul Brinegar (*Rawhide, Lancer*) has a cameo as a grizzled cellmate of Kurd. Acting honors in the episode, however, belong to Laraine Stephens for her heartfelt portrayal of the long suffering Seba Alcott. This is another episode of *The Quest* in which the violence in minimized, except for that which is essential to the story. Character development and the difficulties of life on the Western frontier are stressed, with great attention again being given to historical reality.

In "Welcome to America, Jade Snow," author Anthony Lawrence presents a story dealing with the exploitation of Chinese workers in the West. In Rock Springs, Wyoming, Quentin and Morgan come upon an angry group of miners striking against the American Pacific Railroad. The miners are enraged by the arrival of Chinese laborers, who they fear will be used to break the strike. When a fight breaks out and a Chinese man is injured, the Beaudines help the local sheriff take him to the Chinatown section for medical treatment. There Quentin takes a position with the Chinese doctor—to earn money for supplies and so that he may learn from the unique practice of Oriental medicine. Meanwhile, Morgan discovers that "China," a former prostitute with whom he had once been involved (in the two hour pilot), is living there with her merchant husband, Jim Fo, and her baby daughter, Jade Snow. Miners, aroused by hatred and prejudice, and fearful of losing their jobs, smash Jim Fo's store to pieces. Feeling that the situation is unbearable, Jim Fo tells China they must return to their homeland. Not wishing to leave America, China plans to run away with her child. Mining director, H.P. Pierson, continues to import Chinese workers—for him they are but a cheap source of labor. As he explains:

> I don't want to just bring those strikers to their knees by using the Chinese against them, I want to eliminate them altogether—because we're going to import more Chinese. John Chinaman is a marvelous discovery. . . . He comes here from a foreign country with generally little or no knowledge of English and no need to be taught any; He works long hours at back breaking labor, for less than anyone human and he can be fed for less than the camp dogs; he keeps to himself, doesn't bother white women, is frugal, and unless pushed to the edge of death, offers little resistance. He's an almost inexhaustible work supply and the best part of it is when there's a severe economic depression and no one to blame, we can charge him with causing it, burn his house down, cut off his queue, and if it's in the interests of the general good, hang him.

It would be difficult to find a more cogent explanation of the attitude with which the American businessman viewed the Chinese worker during the opening of the American West.

Despite the efforts of the sheriff, the miners go on a rampage of destruction, razing most of Chinatown and killing and wounding many Chinese. Although the miners are ordered to leave the state, the sheriff resigns his office in protest. China decides to remain with her husband and the Beaudine brothers ride off to continue the search for their sister. Again, actual incidents are taken from the pages of American history and used effectively to present a realistic picture of the Western frontier. The cast includes Richard Loo as the Chinese doctor, Frank Aletter as Pierson, Gary Collins as the sheriff and Irene Yeh-Ling Sun recreating her role as China.

Other episodes of *The Quest* involve the Beaudines on a cattle drive ("The Longest Drive," the only two part story), in the problems of maintaining law and order in a cow town ("Seventy-Two Hours"), with a 16 year old gunman, whom Quentin is forced to kill ("Portrait of a Gunfighter") and on a mission to rescue a government road expedition that has been stranded 300 miles from the nearest town ("The Freight Train Rescue"). In this episode the brothers discover that those who have survived did so by eating the remains of those who did not (similar to the situation faced in real life by the Donner party). The men who have been saved must live with the disapproval of society as well as their own feelings of guilt and memories of horror.

One of the most interesting episodes, "The Seminole Negro Indian Scouts," was never broadcast by NBC, but only seen later in syndication on cable television's the Family Channel (one of four such episodes). In the story, written by Dick Nelson, the Beaudine brothers witness firsthand the bigotry and injustice faced by a group of fine black soldiers in a white town. Quentin and Morgan are rescued by four black Army scouts from Comancheros who are selling guns and whiskey to the Indians. The ancestors of the blacks had fled slavery and joined the Seminole Indians living in Florida. Later they moved to Mexico, where they had been recruited six years before the time of the episode by the U.S. Army with promises of land and seed. The Army, however, has never lived up to its promises to the blacks and the town is prejudiced against them—the merchant refuses to sell them food and the doctor will not treat them. Their commanding officer tries in vain to improve matters.

Later, the scouts, with the help of the Beaudines, lead a raid on the Comancheros' camp and kill their leader. One of the four scouts is also killed, however. On their return, they learn that Washington has officially refused to honor the Army contract with the blacks. Quentin and Morgan decide to help them return to Mexico. That night, they raid the local store for food, hardware and seed, leaving a note to bill the U.S. Army. They then set out for Mexico. Near the border they are overtaken by Army troops and pursuing townsmen. The commander, however, orders his troops to line up between the fleeing blacks and the angry townsmen. As the scouts cross the border to a better life, the Beaudines are advised to leave the area quickly. They have greatly antagonized the local townsfolk by aiding the blacks. In this episode, while much violence is implied, little is actually shown on the screen. A cast of competent, if not well-known, actors, including Henry Brown, Ted Gehring, Kurt Grayson and Bill Williams, bring life to an important chapter in the history of the American West. Unfortunately the series had already been canceled as a result of low ratings by the time this episode was scheduled to air. (According to *Variety*, *The Quest* was ranked ninety-first out of 101 shows at the time of its cancellation.[41] It was scheduled opposite the popular *Charlie's Angels*.)

Shortly after *The Quest* was canceled, the National Citizens Committee for Broadcasting issued a report that NBC-television led all the networks in prime time violence during the fall season and that *The Quest* was the most violent program on the air. NBC, in obvious reference to the series, took issue with the conclusions of the survey, because it provided

> no information on who commits the violent act, under what circumstances, with what consequences for either perpetrator or victim and with what audio visual treatment. The result is that depicting violence in a way calculated to discourage it gets counted equal to a depiction that glorifies violence.[42]

It is difficult to assess the significance of *The Quest* in the development of the television Western since only 11 episodes were broadcast. However, most television historians and critics who have commented on the series have emphasized its violent aspects. J. Fred MacDonald is quite negative in his assessment:

... In its desire to be relevant, this series in the fall of 1976 offered an alluring mix of violence, youthful initiative, sympathy for racial minorities, and antimilitarism.... "The Quest" employed violence to picture the West as a brutal, sinister, and unhappy domain.... Stark meanness permeated "The Quest" ... this was a brutish series that attempted to interpret American frontier history in terms of the conflicting political passions that followed U.S. humiliation in the Vietnam War.[43]

Neil Summers views *The Quest* much more favorably:

"The Quest" was an above average television Western and the producers tried to be authentic in most of their details. It is a shame that the network did not move the show around on their schedule. I am sure that if a little care was shown for "The Quest," it would have eventually found an audience, and thus been renewed.[44]

Castleman and Podrazik consider the importance of the series mainly in terms of its stars:

A late model western ... with strong leads and a workable premise ... It's as good an excuse as any to wander the Old West, giving Morgan and Quentin the chance to get involved with both Indians and settlers. Definitely worth catching for the leads, even if its only the pilot film.[45]

Perhaps *TV Guide* critic Robert MacKenzie placed *The Quest* in its proper perspective when he wrote in a 1976 review:

Every generation remakes the Western in its own image; here it is the setting for the mean streets and starved spirits of modern urban life.

Still, looking at *The Quest* from the perspective of the 1990s, one can see yet another interpretation. With its emphasis on the harsh realities of life in the early American West, *The Quest* presents the frontier as a brawling, bawdy outpost of civilization, where the only law was survival of the fittest. In the West of *The Quest*, there is good *and* bad, sacrifice *and* freedom, courage *and* cowardice, growth *and* destruction, men *and* women, whites *and* racial and ethnic minorities.

By more than a decade *The Quest* foreshadowed the so-called "new Western history" of such historians as Patricia Nelson Limerick, Richard White and Donald Worster. Writing in 1991, Clyde A. Milner II, Charles E. Rankin and Limerick came up with this definition for a new approach to the interpretation of the westward movement:

... the New Western History offers a more balanced view of the western past. It includes failure as well as success; defeat as well as victory; sympathy, grace villainy, and despair as well as danger, courage, and heroism; women as well as men; varied ethnic groups and their differing perspectives as well as white Anglo-Saxon Protestants; an environment that is limiting, interactive, and sometimes ruined as well as mastered and made to bloom.[46]

This description could also fit that view of the Western frontier depicted in most episodes of *The Quest*—if one disregards the happy endings frequently tacked on to the stories in an apparent effort to make them more commercially palatable. Consider such unromantic and nontraditional topics as atrocities committed by whites against Native Americans (in "The Buffalo Hunters"), the hardships imposed by the frontier on women (in "Prairie Woman"), the treatment of ethnic minorities (the Chinese in "Welcome to America, Jade Snow" and Negroes in "The Seminole Negro Indian Scouts"), such necessities of survival as cannibalism ("The Freight Train Rescue"), and the lynching of women ("Day of Outrage") and one can readily see that the darker aspects of life on the American frontier were not neglected or glossed over on *The Quest*. Perhaps, although the Beaudine brothers never did find their sister, they nonetheless fulfilled a useful function as they rode the video range on their quest.

No discussion of two character television Westerns would be complete without a consideration of *Two Faces West*. Although it was syndicated (by Screen Gems, the television subsidiary of Columbia Pictures) and lasted only one season (1960-61), it was unique in that it related the adventures of two young men who were identical twins played by the same actor—Charles Bateman. The two January brothers discover each other after a separation of 25 years. They had been parted as babies during a savage Indian raid on the Western village where they were born. One, Ben, had become a doctor, educated at an Eastern college. Rick, on the other hand, had grown up on the frontier and was a rough, happy-go-lucky drifter, quick with his guns and his fists.

Unaware of his brother's existence, and separated by thousands of miles, Ben feels a sympathetic and painful twinge in his shoulder when Rick is shot in the same spot during a saloon brawl. Medical books convince him that such an occurrence actually has happened in the case histories of identical twins. Setting out to find the brother he now believes exists, Ben comes face to face with Rick on the dusty streets of the frontier town of Gunnison, Colorado. There, they both fall in love with Julie Greer, the proprietress of the town's only hotel, and become involved with the town's sheriff, Roy Maddox, the other regular character in the series.

Two Faces West was the creation of two veteran television producers, Donald Gold and Jonas Seinfeld. They conceived of the twins' being played with entirely different mannerisms, alike only in physical appearance. Obviously the actor playing these roles would be required to be seen on screen in double, talking with himself and perhaps even fighting with himself. The use of a split screen to achieve this effect had occasionally been employed in movies (e.g., *The Corsican Brothers*) and even on television. However, *Two Faces West* marked the first time such a technique was utilized for an entire series.

In selecting a star to assume the split-screen assignment, Screen Gems' executive producer Robert Sparks and producer Matthew Rapf spent months testing actors for the difficult requirements necessary to project the dual roles for the cameras. They discovered their leading man right in their own organization: Charles Bateman, who had been seen regularly during the past year as Detective George Peters, Victor Jory's assistant, in Screen Gems' *Manhunt* series. Bateman, while far from achieving star status, was a versatile actor who had numerous motion picture and television credits, having appeared in Westerns and detective stories as well as straight dramatic roles.

A native of San Diego, California, Bateman became interested in acting while a student at San Diego Junior College, when a classmate suggested that he try out for a part in a college play. After that theatrical initiation, he began to seek a dramatic career in earnest. He even turned down a lucrative offer to work in his father's industrial chemical manufacturing firm, shunning the business world for a career in the theater. Enrolling at the Carnegie Institute's School of Drama in Pittsburgh, Bateman graduated with a fine arts degree and considerable acting experience in college productions. Returning to San Diego, he joined the San Diego National Shakespeare Company and the Starlight Opera. Later he appeared at the La Jolla Playhouse and with numerous stock companies both on the West Coast and in the Midwest.

When Bateman finally tried Hollywood, he discovered there were no acting roles awaiting him. Undaunted, he took a job as floor assistant at the CBS television studios. Slowly, but steadily, he moved into other phases of telecasting and became production coordinator of the popular West Coast CBS-TV show, *Panorama Pacific*. Within two years (1958) he was lured into returning to acting with the offer of a juicy role on the

Charles Bateman played two roles in *Two Faces West*: mild-mannered Dr. Ben January and his twin brother, gunslinger Rick January (left).

Maverick series (in "Black Fire"). This was followed by appearances on *Rawhide*, *M Squad*, *State Trooper*, and *Yancy Derringer*. He also had a small role in *The F.B.I. Story* (1959), a film which starred James Stewart and Vera Miles. It was, however, his featured part on *Manhunt* (based on the files of the San Diego Police Department) which won for him the dual starring roles in *Two Faces West*.

Both brothers were attracted to the beautiful young Julie Greer, but each, of course, expressed his affection for her in a different way. This was one of the most difficult aspects of the role according to a press release issued by *Screen Gems*. Bateman explained:

> As Dr. Ben January, I have to be tender and politely affectionate. After all, Ben is a well-raised Boston gentleman, circa 1880, and would never offend a lady. Rick, on the other hand, is the come-and-get-it type of lover to whom the problem of catching his lady is not unlike the job of lassoing a stray calf.
>
> The big problem is to remember which part I'm playing at any particular moment. It wouldn't look very well if, as Doctor Ben, I grabbed June roughly. But as Rick that's right in character.[47]

Copper-haired, green-eyed June Blair was the pretty young leading lady chosen to play the proprietress of Hotel Gunnison who entrances and captivates the twin January brothers. Born in San Francisco, the actress' grandfather was Spanish, her grandmother, Cherokee and her father, Irish. Orphaned as a baby, Blair was shuttled from family to family, had to work as a child and never had much time for recreation with children her own age. When she was 16, Blair was spotted by a commercial photographer, and thus began her modeling career. When she finished high school, she went to Hollywood to work as an extra in films and decided that she would pursue a career in acting.

The break that all aspiring actresses dream about came when an executive at Warner Bros. studio saw Blair's picture on a magazine cover and she was signed by the studio and sent to acting school. Her first screen credit came in the Howard Koch film *Hellbound* and she won a small role on television's *Our Miss Brooks*. In 1957 she landed a contract with 20th Century–Fox, who gave her featured roles in *Lone Texan* (1959) and Jerry Wald's *Rabbit Trap* (1959) starring Ernest Borgnine. More television roles followed and Blair appeared in episodes of *Sea Hunt, Bat Masterson, Lock Up* and *Hawaiian Eye*. Julie Greer was Blair's first major role, but she was soon to land the continuing role of June Nelson, David Nelson's wife on the popular family sitcom, *The Adventures of Ozzie and Harriet* (1961–1966). (This was a role she would later play in real life.)

Cast as Roy Maddox, sheriff of Gunnison, was veteran character actor Francis De Sales. Born in Philadelphia, where he attended public schools, De Sales' first ambition was to become a screenwriter. After completing two scenarios, at the age of 18, he bought a Model-T Ford and worked his way to California — first at a bathtub foundry in Uniontown, Pennsylvania, then on a ranch in Kansas. After three and a half months, he finally arrived in Hollywood. When his scenarios were rejected by studio after studio, he survived by working odd jobs. Finally, he decided to return to Philadelphia.

There De Sales attended a private dramatic school to study the art of theatrical writing. Although he never was a success in that phase of dramatics, he did learn a little about acting. This prompted him to go to New York where he took more advanced courses in dramatics. This, in turn, led to De Sales' first stage role, as "Baby Face Martin," a gangster in the famous Broadway production of *Dead End*. There followed prominent roles in 14 New York plays (as Ilka Chase's leading man in several) and an impressive career in radio drama (where he eventually appeared in more than 6,000 shows). About this time an enthusiastic agent brought De Sales back to the West Coast for a role in a Warner Bros. film opposite Bette Davis. However, the results of his screen test ("No personality, no sex, and too forceful an actor") convinced De Sales to return to Broadway.

Five years later, in 1951, after more Broadway plays and summer stock appearances, interspersed with a few live television dramas (e.g., *Studio One*), De Sales finally made it back to Hollywood to stay. His film credits included *It Started with a Kiss* (1959), with Glenn Ford and Debbie Reynolds, as a Navy officer in Cary Grant's *Operation Petticoat* (1959), and with James Garner in *Up Periscope* (1959). De Sales' television career was even more impressive. He was best known for his continuing roles as Lieutenant Bill Weigand on *Mr. and Mrs. North* (1952–1954) and as Harry Dobson, the attorney, on *The Adventures of Ozzie and Harriet* during the fifties. He was also featured in episodes of *Cheyenne, Sugarfoot, Maverick, 77 Sunset Strip, Whirlybirds*, and *Navy Log*.

Two Faces West was more than just another action Western with a gimmick. The gimmick, two identical twin brothers who are reunited in a violent Western town after a lapse of 25 years, provided Charles Bateman with the opportunity of being a belligerent, swaggering, trigger-happy cowboy, with the instincts and emotions of a killer, one minute, and a well-bred, Eastern college educated medical man, slow to anger and trained in the ethics of his profession, the next — in fact sometimes in the same scene. Bateman was able to successfully accomplish this feat with the help of a stand-in named Paul Pepper (who actually plays a separate role in one episode), used in over-the-shoulder shots. Julie Greer was drawn to both men, but felt more affection for Ben than Rick. She was afraid of Rick's quick temper and tendency to solve all problems with a gun. Rick, however, was careful never to break the law as he was usually being closely watched by Sheriff Maddox. The show was a notch above most other television Westerns because of the leads (especially Bateman), competent supporting players (like DeForest Kelley, James Griffith, Walter

Dr. Ben January at work removing a bullet, in *Two Faces West*, as June Blair, featured as love interest Julie Greer, assists.

Coy, Robert Faulk, Ron Soble, Walter Burke, Lou Krugman, Dabbs Greer, L.Q. Jones, Denver Pyle, Gary Walberg, Victor French, Kenneth Tobey, and Leonard Nimoy) and generally well-written stories. At the height of its popularity, *Two Faces West* was seen on more than 150 stations in the United States and Canada.

In an unusual episode, "Performance Under Fire," Ben and Julie decide to travel to Stagg City to see a performance by the great Sarah Bernhardt, stopping on the way to spend the night at the Baker ranch. Here they meet two gunmen whom Ben and Rick once bested in a fight. The two men claim they are waiting for Mr. Baker to return from Stagg City with medicine for the ailing Mrs. Baker. Ben finds that Mrs. Baker must have her appendix removed. While Ben and Julie are tending to Mrs. Baker, the two gunmen discover that Mr. Baker has hidden a large quantity of gold on the farm. When the two men attack Ben in order to obtain the gold and exact revenge on Ben, the doctor uses one of them as a shield. After the other cold-bloodedly shoots his partner, Julie tells him where the gold is hidden. While he is engrossed in grabbing the gold, Julie throws dirt in his eyes, thus giving Ben a chance to shoot the killer. In this episode Ben, a man usually concerned with saving lives, is forced to take one.

A more typical episode, "The Witness," finds Ben saving the life of a gypsy who has been shot by two men before he can testify against their brother at his murder trial. After beating Rick unconscious, the two men follow Ben to the gypsy camp and attempt to prevent him from saving the wounded gypsy. Just as they are about to shoot Ben, Rick appears. He kills one and beats the other senseless. In this story Ben fulfills his expected role as a preserver of life, while Rick is the brother who must resort to violence. In "The Proud Man," Dr. Ben January becomes involved in a range war between a cattleman and a homesteader. With the help of his brother, he is able to bring about an end to the feud, but not before Rick has been forced to kill a man.

Several of the stories are built around the natural premise of one twin brother being mistaken for the other. In "The Operation," a gang of robbers needs a doctor to tend one of its wounded members and discovers it has kidnapped Rick instead of Ben. In "The Dead Ringer" Ben must save Rick from a gang's vengeance after Rick has tricked the outlaws into mistaking him for his twin brother. Unfortunately there were only so many possible variations on the mistaken identity theme and most of the stories were more routine. (For example, in "The Hanging," Ben is held hostage to insure the release of a killer who has been condemned to death; in "The Trigger," Rick and Ben try to stop a crazed man from blowing up the town of Gunnison; and in "The Last Man," a blood-thirsty bounty hunter rides into Gunnison to claim the reward on a friend of Rick's.)

Two Faces West ran one season, producing 39 episodes before it was canceled. Charles Bateman can still be seen on television, occasionally appearing as a guest star on such shows as *Hunter*, but *Two Faces West* seems to have disappeared since it left the air in the fall of 1961. It was an interesting Western series with an unusual premise: two contrasting characters standing side by side to uphold truth and justice on the early frontier, with both portrayed by the same actor.

Outside of juvenile Westerns, where the hero nearly always had a sidekick, there were few duos who rode the video range — and those that did invade the realm of the adult Western, like the Sonnetts, Earl Corey and Jemal David, Hannibal Heyes and Kid Curry, and the Beaudine and January brothers did not remain on the home screen very long. Still, several of these shows were of superior quality and deserved a better fate than early cancellation.

XIV. *When East Met West*
WALKING THE VIDEO RANGE
WITH KWAI CHANG CAINE

As the television Western approached the twilight of its popularity in the early seventies, the most unlikely of heroes came trekking across the video range. Kwai Chang Caine, searching for his long-lost brother, was half Chinese and half American. He was being pursued by agents of the Chinese government as well as American bounty hunters. It was as if Confucius had come to rescue the Western from oblivion. *Kung Fu*, a philosophical Chinese Western, appeared to prolong the life of the apparently moribund genre. A former Shaolin monk preaching pacifism, but practicing the mysterious fighting arts of China, became, almost overnight, the newest American cult hero.

Since kung fu was rooted in humility, patience, and reverence for life, Caine was an unusually pacifistic hero. He had been taught as a young Shaolin disciple in China:

> Learn ways to preserve rather than destroy. Avoid rather than check, check rather than hurt, hurt rather than maim and maim rather than kill—for all life is precious nor can any of life, even that of the meanest creature, be replaced.

Still Caine could defend himself and others in jeopardy when the need arose, since kung fu had been originally devised as a means of keeping the peace and was actually a multisystemed science of self-defense. It required the cultivation of the *chi*, the "inner strength" which belongs to the essence of being, and a surgeon's knowledge of the human nerve system. Its effectiveness was based on speed of sight and movement. Kung fu masters could maim or kill at a touch and break pine boards without apparent effort by striking them with the palms of their hands. Such experts were masters of stealth, camouflage, and deception.

Kung fu actually covers numerous (perhaps, as many as a hundred) different schools of martial arts, each with its own distinct style of attack and defense. The history of these is shrouded in mystery, but most Chinese trace its origins back to the Shaolin Temple in the Horan province of central China. It might have been brought from India by Buddhist monks who came to China in the third or fourth centuries A.D. According to one legend, Bodhidharma, an Indian monk known in China as Ta Mo, established at his temple not only Zen Buddhism (*ch'an*) but certain exercises and breathing techniques that became fundamental to the fighting arts. Even more important, he taught the concept of *wu-te* (or martial virtue) wherein the fighter seeks his own spiritual growth rather than mere victory over other men.[1] Some scholars, however, believe that it began at Shaolin. After many hours of sitting in one place, meditating, the monks needed some form of exercise, and the basic kung fu movements were designed for this purpose. Initially, however, the physical exercises were extensions of the spiritual ones, and the emphasis was mainly on perfecting the movements rather than using them for actual fighting. (In the pilot film, Master Kan tells young Caine, "the development of the mind can be achieved only when the body has been disciplined.")

The Shaolin temple was destroyed several times during its long history due to various persecutions of the Buddhist faith by imperial troops. On one such occasion, in A.D. 574, the monks were scattered. Because times were troubled and acts of violence were common the monks taught their method of fighting to the people, so they could protect themselves against the attacks of bandits and corrupt officials. At the time, ordinary citizens were forbidden to carry weapons. From this beginning, Shaolin Temple Boxing (as it was then called) spread through China, modified with the passing of time into the various different schools which exist today.

These schools of kung fu can be roughly divided into two types, the "soft" and the "hard." The "soft" systems are probably the closest to the original concept of the Shaolin monks, with their emphasis on exercising for health, flexibility and peace of mind. One such school, *tai chi* ("the supreme ultimate"), performs all its exercises in "slow motion." The "soft" systems can also be used in combat, but for purposes of self-defense rather than attack. Like Japanese judo, the strength of the attacker is used against him with throws and subtle counterattacks.

The "hard" systems are better known in the West, being the type of kung fu usually seen in films and is similar to Japanese karate, which developed much later also from Shaolin Temple Boxing. Here, however, the emphasis is on violently expressed outer strength. There are more noticeable differences among the various "hard" systems than among the "soft," although all emphasize the use of both hands and feet to strike the opponent a variety of devastating blows. Some of the "hard" schools are named after animals, birds and insects, with the practitioners taking on the characteristics of the particular creatures. (The pilot film's Master Kan explains, "To accomplish the discipline of the body, the ancients have taught us to imitate God's creatures.") The young Caine received training in five such schools:

> From the crane we learn grace and self control.
> From the snake we learn suppleness and rhythmic endurance.
> The praying mantis teaches us speed and patience, the epitome of defense.
> The way of the tiger is the most aggressive and closest to the natural, instinctive
>   form of combat.
> And from the dragon, we learn to ride the wind.

The style which is probably the most deadly system of close-range fighting ever devised, *wing chun*, dispenses with the elaborate poses of the animal styles. On the principle that attack is the best form of defense, once a fight has started, the *wing chun* practitioner never takes a backward step. Unbalancing his opponent by continually advancing, he unleashes a flurry of specially developed punches to the face and body. A *wing chun* master can deliver a punch faster than the eye can see.

Over the years, many new styles of kung fu have been developed, some differing very little from the others, some being distinctive enough to take their place among the more established schools. As kung fu spread out from China, it altered and adapted to local conditions, becoming karate and judo in Japan, tae kwon do in Korea, and Thai boxing in Southeast Asia. Pure kung fu, however, remains a fighting art, unlike karate, which has become largely a sport with points being awarded for style while the blows never actually land.

Films depicting the fighting arts of kung fu had been popular in Asia for several years before invading the United States. For a long time, the film industries of Hong Kong and Taiwan were almost unknown to the West, in spite of turning out about 200 films a year. These films were made with a specifically Chinese audience in mind, and although they had a vast market in the overseas Chinese communities scattered around the world, there was little to interest the Western movie-goer. The main objective of these filmmakers (until about 1970) was to produce an unending stream of immensely bloodthirsty sword-fighting movies. These were usually very cheaply made, with plots so complicated that most Westerners found them impossible to unravel.

Then Eastern audiences seemed to tire of the sword-fighting films and the producers were forced to hunt for a new style. The answer was, of course, kung fu, and they began turning out hundreds of kung fu movies annually. The credit for establishing the trend seems to belong to an actor called Wang Yu, one of the most popular Chinese stars, although he was not well known in the United States. He wrote, directed, and starred in a film called *The Chinese Boxer* for the gigantic Shaw Brothers organization, and the film proved so successful that both Shaw's and other companies started turning out kung fu films at a high rate.

In 1971, Golden Harvest, a film company formed about the same time the sword-fighting pictures were declining in popularity, pulled off a major coup. They signed Bruce Lee (Hsiao Lung), who would become the greatest kung fu star of all. Lee was born in San Francisco, although he spent most of his childhood in Hong Kong. After appearing in several Chinese films as a child, he started studying *wing chun* kung fu at the age of 13. He later returned to the States to attend college and then founded three schools to teach his own style of kung fu called *jeet kune do*. Among his "students" were such well-known stars as Steve McQueen and James Coburn. This paved the way for Lee's appearances in several American television series, including the costarring role as Kato in *The Green Hornet* (1966–1967) and the recurring role of James Franciscus' self-defense instructor in *Longstreet* (1971–1972). As Asia's biggest superstar, he became known as "the fastest fist in the East" and his salary per film rose from $10,000 to $250,000.

Bruce Lee appeared in the first American-produced kung fu movie, *Enter the Dragon* (1973), an enormously popular film. Unfortunately, Lee died in July 1973 and a gigantic funeral was held in Hong Kong demonstrating how much he was respected and admired by his Chinese audience. One of the things which Lee brought to kung fu films during his short and meteoric career was a sense of authenticity. Though they were cheaply made, and sometimes poorly plotted, the Chinese kung fu movies did have one thing in their favor. With their authentically staged fights and fast-paced action, they brought to the screen a very exciting and popular form of film. These movies contained an improbable blend of camp and violence and their appeal spread across class lines. Part of the audience was attracted to the fun, part to the gore, part to both. Each film had a hero (or, on occasion, a heroine) who was a master in the martial arts. (He, or she, usually employed all of the Eastern forms including karate, jujitsu, aikido, keno, tae kwon do or kap ki do.) The hero was always an underdog and the highlights of each film were beautifully choreographed battles pitting him (or her) against four, six, ten or twelve enemies. After having won these contests, the hero would then face the villain, who was also a great master of kung fu, and triumph here too. Of course, the hero—except in the direst of emergencies—used no weapons (although the villains always had knives or clubs).

One spinoff effect of these kung fu films was a growing interest in martial arts classes. Several schools already in existence exhibited a marked increase in attendance and new schools began appearing in virtually every major U.S. city. In addition to traditional judo and karate, these schools offered training in the ancient Chinese exercise of kung fu. In Los Angeles, sales of books about kung fu rose over 50 percent between January and May of 1973 and merchants reported doing a "brisk business" in kung fu uniforms. Steve Gerhardt, manager of the Joe Lewis Judo-Karate School in Hollywood explained to *Newsweek*:

> Everyone wants kung fu although they don't know the difference between it and karate. Businessmen want to keep in shape. Students say it helps them study better, and the girls like the way it looks. . . . Most schools still don't teach the meditative side of kung fu, but an increasing number of customers, especially young people, are asking for it.[2]

In the same article Wellington Lee, a United Nations interpreter and *tai chai* master, told *Newsweek*'s Phyllis Malamud:

> It is believed that mental concentration can mobilize an energy current called chi which in turn guides the physical movements. Thus, the movements are no longer the result of a conscious, physical effort, but rather of mental concentration.

It was this interest in kung fu that helped launch the *Kung Fu* television series. As producer Jerry Thorpe explained to the *New York Times* (October 22, 1972):

> "Kung Fu" seems to have touched something in the temper of the times, a rejection of violence, a thrust toward brotherhood, a feeling for the universal principle of nature, perhaps.

It was, however, the lucrative overseas film market that led Warner Bros. to purchase a kung fu script from a writer named Ed Spielman in early 1971. The studio intended to produce this movie only for Asian distribution, but when business for Warner Bros. went into a slump, the Spielman script was put on the shelf. About a year later it was rediscovered by a writer-producer named Jerry Thorpe. Thorpe conceived the idea of eliminating most of the violence, emphasizing the philosophy and making it into a television film. After getting the approval of the head of Warners' television division, Gerald Leider, Thorpe set about the difficult task of casting Kwai Chang Caine. Leider remembered David Carradine's stunning and balletlike performance as the Inca god-king in the Broadway play *The Royal Hunt of the Sun* and he recommended the young actor to Thorpe. According to Thorpe, Carradine arrived for his interview

> Seething with rebellion and accompanied by his part Great Dane, part Labrador dog, Buffalo. . . . David didn't say two words in that first interview. There were six of us on one side of the room and David and Buffalo on the other side of the room and no communication between us whatsoever.
> Finally David left and I got the idea that he was putting us on—sort of a slap at the Establishment. So I called his agent and asked if David and Buffalo would come back and see me alone. They did and this time man and dog were totally co-operative. We made the deal for him to do the movie, little realizing then that it would become the pilot for a series.[3]

Carradine's recollection of that first meeting was somewhat different:

> Man, I read the pilot script and flipped! But I *never* believed it'd really get on TV. I mean a *Chinese Western*, about a half–Chinese, half–American Buddhist Monk who wanders the Gold Rush country but doesn't care about gold, and defends the oppressed but won't carry a gun, and won't even step on an ant because he values all life, and hardly ever *speaks*? No way! But I went to Warners to see Jerry Thorpe, the producer. I took one look at him and man, I thought I saw *the Devil*. He was driving a new brown Continental, and his clothes and briefcase were all matching brown, and I said to myself, "This man is Satan!"[4]

By an odd coincidence, Carradine had already shaved his head before he knew that the producers were looking for an actor to play the part of a bald-headed priest. In order to play an Indian in a film, Carradine had had his hair dyed black. Deciding that there was no other way to regain his natural color, he shaved it all off and started again. (As the series progressed, he merely let his hair grow out again at its natural rate.)

After Carradine began work on *Kung Fu*, he and Thorpe became good friends. As he later explained, "The work made us brothers."[5]

Like the character he portrayed on the home screen, David Carradine's early life had been anything but typical. He was the second son of famous film star John Carradine, born to his second wife, Ardanelle Abigail McCool in Hollywood on October 8, 1936. The boy attended no fewer than six schools on both coasts and was expelled from each of them. After spending time in a reform school, he was provided with a private tutor. During this period he got a look at life backstage while traveling with his father on tour, but neither travel nor acting interested the teenager. At 15 he worked on a dairy farm in Vermont, and at the time thought he would like to become a farmer.

After graduating from Oakland (California) High School, David took some courses at Oakland Junior College, but was soon drafted. While serving his army hitch, his strain of rebelliousness surfaced again when he was court-martialled three times for relatively minor offenses. After leaving the military, Carradine enrolled as a music major at San Francisco State College, for now music had become his passion. Still, he seldom attended classes, preferring to associate with drama rather than music students. For fun, he accompanied a group of them to auditions at the Theater of the Golden Hind in Berkeley and ended up playing roles in four or five productions.

Carradine thought of himself as strictly an amateur, but liked acting so much that he dropped out of college to stage a production of *Othello* with a friend in a small San Francisco theater. David played Iago, but the production went bust. He found work for a while in a little theater in Vallejo and then returned to Berkeley to play in the Arthur Miller version of Ibsen's *An Enemy of the People*. While appearing there in *Time Limit*, he learned how to act (and play chess) from director Robert Ross. This led the young actor to join a professional Shakespeare repertory company in San Francisco where he played Malcolm in *Macbeth*, Claudio in *Much Ado About Nothing* and Sebastian in *The Tempest*. In between acting jobs, Carradine supported himself working as a photographer and selling sewing machines and encyclopedias.

At the same time, Carradine became a coffee-house poet and one of the first "beatniks." This was a term coined by San Francisco columnist Herb Caen to describe Eric Nord and his disciples, of whom David was one. (Carradine later claimed that there were only "about fifty" real "beatniks." The rest were "hangers-on and completely phoney."[6]) It was in New York that Carradine did his most notable stage work. In addition to playing the Inca god-king in *Royal Hunt of the Sun*, he also appeared in the Broadway production of *The Deputy* as the rebel Jesuit. He regarded his performance as a hippie representing himself as the Christ in an Off Broadway production of *The Transgressor Rides Again* as the best work he had ever done, though the critics did not agree with him. Carradine also tried Hollywood films during the sixties and appeared in supporting roles in *Taggart*, a Western which starred Dan Duryea and Tony Young in 1964, *Bus Riley's Back in Town*, with Ann-Margret and Michael Parks in 1965, and *Heaven with a Gun*, a Glenn Ford Western in 1969. For a while, Carradine could only get work in second-rate Westerns like *The Violent Ones* (1967), *Young Billy Young* (1969), and *The Good Guys and the Bad Guys* (1969). (His best film role came later in Martin Scorsese's highly acclaimed *Boxcar Bertha* in 1972.[7])

In the meantime, Carradine was gaining experience on television. He appeared on an episode of the highly rated *Wagon Train* (in "The Eli Bancroft Story") in 1963 and on one of the last episodes of *The Alfred Hitchcock Hour* in 1965 (as a strangler in "Thou Still Unravished Bride") and later as several different characters on episodes of *Ironside*. His first real chance at stardom, however, appeared to be his selection to play the title role in the television version of *Shane* in 1966. The series was based on the 1953 hit theatrical Western which starred Alan Ladd as the silent, brooding gunfighter who rides onto the homestead of the Starrett family. At first the family is wary of Shane, but once he removes his guns and begins to help with the farm chores, Joey, the young son, starts to idolize him. Shane wants to lead a peaceful existence but he always seems to get drawn into the violence of the range wars. When the cattle barons try to force the Starretts and other homesteaders off their land, Shane again takes up his gun to defend his new friends. In a bloody shoot-out, Shane confronts and kills the cattlemen's hired guns and despite (or perhaps, because of) his fondness for Joey and his growing affection for Mrs. Starrett, he knows it is time to leave. He rides off into the twilight, refusing to heed the boy's cries of "Shane, come back!"

Produced and directed by George Stevens, *Shane* has been acclaimed as a superior film and possibly one of the best Westerns ever made.[8] For this reason any attempt to convert the story into a television series was bound to be difficult. To make possible a continuing storyline in which a romance between Shane and Mrs. Starrett could be developed, producer Herb Brodkin (*The Defenders, Studio One*), depicted Marian Starrett as a recent widow trying to farm her husband's homestead with her young son Joey and her father-in-law, Tom Starrett. Shane rode onto the scene just as brutal cattleman Rufe Ryker and his paid gunmen were trying to terrorize the homesteaders into leaving. For 17 episodes, Shane aided the Starretts in their struggle while Marian tried not to let herself or her son become too attached to the mysterious gunfighter, knowing he might be killed or decide to move on at any time.

Although the cast was competent with the lovely film actress Jill Ireland playing Marian, veterans Tom Tully as Tom Starrett and Bert Freed as Ryker, and young Christopher Shea (who had provided the original voice for Linus in the early *Peanuts* television specials) in the role of Joey, the series failed to catch on with viewers. Perhaps it was because most of the scenes, although filmed in color, were obviously played out on a soundstage; or because most of the scripts were routine involving much used plot-lines — or it could have been that Carradine was a bit too young to play Shane. In any case, ABC canceled the series on December 31, 1966.

Once David Carradine had been cast as Caine, *Kung Fu* producers began filling the supporting roles. Since all of the roles in the flash-back sequences (depicting Caine's training in China by Shaolin monks) as well as several key characters in the railroad building segments, were Chinese, veteran Oriental film actors were selected. Richard Loo, Philip Ahn and Keye Luke were cast as Caine's three Shaolin teachers, Master Sun, Master Kan and Master Po, respectively. Han Fei, who befriends Caine and gets him a job working on the railroad construction gang, was played by Benson Fong. Victor Sen Yung, who had been Hop Sing, the cook, on *Bonanza* for 14 years, portrayed Chuen, one of the railroad coolies. The most outspoken young worker, Fong, was played by Robert Ito (who was only a few years away from a major continuing role on the popular *Quincy, M.E.* series as Jack Klugman's assistant, Sam Fujiyama).

David Chow, who also provided "technical advice" (on the art of kung fu), was an excellent villain: Little Monk, an agent of the Chinese Imperial House and former Shaolin monk sent to bring Caine back, "dead or alive." Chow, a self-made millionaire,

David Carradine (right) as the young Caine, learns from blind Master Po (Keye Luke), shown in frequent flashbacks on *Kung Fu*.

originally from Shanghai, was the only member of this group who lacked previous acting experience. He had learned the art of kung fu as a child after being beaten up by Japanese occupation forces. One of the meanings of kung fu is "hard work"; the knowledge had proven useful to Chow in building up his vast financial empire.

Ahn and Luke would become regulars on the series. As masters Kan and Po, they were frequently shown in flashbacks providing instruction to the young Caine. Ahn, who was of Korean extraction, was probably most noted for his portrayals of villainous Japanese in World War II movies. His father, Chang Ho Ahn, was one of the founding fathers of the Republic of Korea. A park and a street in Seoul have been named for him.

Philip Ahn was "deadly serious" about the roles he played during the war, explaining in an interview: "The Japanese were not only our enemies, they were responsible for my father's death in a Japanese prison."[9]

Ahn was initially deferred in the draft because he was considered of greater value to the war effort for the movies he made. Finally, however, he was asked to play one Japanese soldier too many. He wanted to play a Korean colonel in one such film, but was cast as yet another villainous Japanese officer. When Ahn refused the part, he was promptly inducted into the U.S. Army. (The camp newspaper headline read, "Japanese General Becomes GI Private."[10]) Born in Los Angeles, Ahn was working his way through the University of Southern California in 1936 when he decided to augment his income by becoming an extra in movies. His first role was in *Anything Goes* (1936) with Bing Crosby and Ethel Merman. By the time he was selected to appear in *Kung Fu*, he had appeared in over 100 films, some of which he did not remember when they turned up years later on the late show on television. He also appeared on the home screen in early episodes of *Hawaii Five-O*. In 1969, Ahn was run down by a car in a crosswalk and was still walking with a cane when he was approached to play Master Kan in *Kung Fu*. At the time, he was also the proprietor of a popular Chinese restaurant.

Keye Luke's parents brought him to Seattle from Canton, China, at the age of 3. After working there as an artist for a theater, Luke came to Hollywood in 1927 and got a job painting posters for Grauman's Chinese Theatre. After a friend suggested him for a role in *The Painted Veil* with Greta Garbo, he was signed to a contract by M-G-M. He appeared first in some Leon Earl–Edgar Kennedy comedies. Then, in 1935, a few months after *The Painted Veil* was released, he became "No. 1 son" to Warner Oland's Charlie Chan. Luke never worked with Sidney Toler, the second Chan, but returned in 1949 to play the same role with Roland Winters. Luke had some 150 movies to his credit by 1972, including such notable films as *Oil for the Lamps of China* (1935) and *The Good Earth* (1937). He also appeared as a young intern in the "Dr. Kildare" series during the forties with Lew Ayres and Lionel Barrymore. On the stage Luke played Wang Chi Yang in the Rodgers and Hammerstein Broadway musical *Flower Drum Song*.

As one of Hollywood's leading Chinese-American actors, Luke made appearances on the home screen in shows ranging from *Fireside Theater* to *Star Trek*. He also had continuing roles on *Kentucky Jones* (1964–1965) as Thomas Wong and as the Kralahome in the short-lived *Anna and the King* in 1972. At the time *Kung Fu* was being filmed, Luke was also doing the voice of Charlie Chan for the weekend cartoon series *The Amazing Chan and the Chan Clan* (broadcast from 1972 to 1974). After playing brisk, often comic, usually stereotyped Orientals, Luke enjoyed portraying Master Po: "I've never played a part that so caught the real spirit of Chinese philosophy. I *like* the things they give me to say."[11] Luke was still, at 69, so young looking that it took make-up men over two hours to apply the make-up he wore as Master Po.

Spielman's 90 minute film was broadcast by ABC on February 22, 1972. In addition to Carradine and the Orientals, *Kung Fu* featured veterans Barry Sullivan as the unscrupulous railroad executive, and Albert Salmi as his ruthless foreman, and newcomers Wayne Maunder as the railroad engineer trying to do his job in spite of the greed and corruption of his bosses, and Radames Pera as the boy Caine in most of the flashbacks.

Caine, a fugitive with a price on his head for killing the Chinese emperor's nephew, joins a coolie gang working on the first transcontinental railroad. He tries to blend in, but cannot hide his philosophy or feelings when he sees how the Chinese workers are being abused. Coming to their aid when they are forced to use explosives to build a tunnel, even though the engineer has warned of the danger of cave-ins, Caine finds his life in immediate jeopardy. Not only do the railroad bosses want him out of the way, but a paid Chinese assassin has arrived to claim his quarry. Caine must resort to hand-to-hand combat with the former Shaolin monk, who is as adept as he at the deadly art of kung fu.

The film drew unexpectedly high ratings and a flood of mail from viewers. In fact, the pilot was so successful that it was rebroadcast during the summer, again winning its time period. Reviewers, like Craig Fisher of *The Hollywood Reporter* (February 24, 1972) were, however, less impressed:

> ... "Kung Fu" without the gloss of authenticity would have been the same—high-class hokum. ... What depth it had came not from any spiritual truths, but from a well-delineated performance in the lead role by David Carradine.
>
> [Director] Thorpe was wise to have chosen Carradine—one of the few young actors who knows how to use his body, as well as face and voice, in building a characterization—to star as the young Chinese-American. ...
>
> With the aid of cinematographer Richard Rawling—who shot the flashback sequences in softer tones—and art director Eugene Lourie—who created a mood mostly by the simple expedient of using lots of candles—Thorpe was able to sustain interest despite the script's rather skimpy texture.
>
> ... [Technical advisor] Chow and Carradine worked diligently to create realism, and in their climactic battle, their work paid off. ... The music, by Jim Helms, was effective, but couldn't avoid sounding cliché Oriental.

Warily, ABC ordered three more segments and scheduled them, one a month, in what was then called television's "Death Row," the Saturday night spot opposite CBS's hit comedy series *All in the Family*. (The show alternated with three episodes of *Alias Smith and Jones*.) However, the ratings were sufficiently high by November that the network contracted for 12 more episodes, and gave the series its own weekly slot, Thursday evenings at nine. The weekly episodes debuted on January 18, 1973.

In the first hour segment, "King of the Mountain," Caine befriends a young man whose father has been killed by Indians and his mother taken captive. They stay with a woman ranch owner until Caine must leave to confront a bounty hunter. On the way he is forced to defend himself from three frontier bullies. Later with his legs in irons, Caine manages to disarm the bounty hunter of his rifle and knife and pitch him over a cliff. *Variety* (October 18, 1972) did not share the public's enthusiasm for the show and predicted a short future for the series:

> This potboiler in its preem looked like "The Fugitive" out of "Shane." ...
>
> David Carradine gives an imposing performance as Caine ... [but] nothing has changed in loony oater fantasy since Hoot Gibson except the style of combat.
>
> This heroic rubbish was made passable by some good acting, especially from Carradine. ...
>
> Small matter, any of this. The series will be wiped out in the Nielsens by CBS's Saturday night comedy block.

This, of course, did not happen. In the second episode, "Dark Angel," viewers learn more about Caine's American roots. Caine arrives in Lordsville looking for information about the father he never knew. His grandfather (played by Dean Jagger), who is a stone mason, lives there, but wants nothing to do with his grandson. He has never forgiven Caine's father for marrying the Chinese girl who became Caine's mother. His wife (Caine's grandmother) was taken ill shortly after Caine's father and mother left Lordsville. She never recovered from this illness and Caine's grandfather blames Caine's father for her death. Caine's presence only stirs up bitter memories for his grandfather. But who really was responsible for this unfortunate chain of events? When Caine returns to meditate at his grandmother's grave, a blind preacher (played by David's father John

Carradine) named Serenity Johnson, whom Caine has befriended, confronts Caine's grandfather:

SERENITY: Get down on your knees before your avenging angel. I claim your immortal soul, Henry Raffield Caine, for crimes rendered, for your grandson whom you curse, for your son whom you drove from your house, for your wife whom you drove into the grave. I know you Henry Raffield Caine. Drunk, you drove your son out of your house because it shriveled your soul to see his Chinese wife. Drunk, you closed your ears to your wife, when she pleaded to let them stay. Bigot . . . all these years you've blamed someone else. . . . Your son, your grandson, because you didn't have courage enough to look at yourself!

HENRY CAINE: That's a lie!

SERENITY: It's the God's truth. I've seen you drunk. I've dried you out and sent you back into the world. It was you that killed her, old man, when she saw what you were.

HENRY: You're blind!

SERENITY: Which one of us Henry Raffield Caine is blind?

Finally, the old man walks slowly over to his wife's grave, where Caine is sitting in silent meditation:

HENRY: Stand up. . . . You have your father in you. I've nothing to give you.

CAINE: Through you I have a father, a grandfather, a great-grandfather, stretching back to the roots of time.

HENRY: You have a brother. These letters from him, I never answered. [He offers Caine a packet of letters.] Take them. Find him. This, was my father's . . . . [He gives Caine a beautiful pocket watch.] This, was your father's. [He gives Caine a beautiful ring.] That's all I have.

This *Kung Fu* episode, which also features David's brother Robert, as the preacher's mute assistant, effectively employs the use of the split screen. The screen is divided into quarters to depict various stages in the construction of a church. Serenity is building a church for Lordsville with the money he has saved. Caine had given him the courage to fulfill his dreams. As the episode ends, Caine trudges off in search of a step-brother he never knew he had, a search which is not completed until the next to last episode of the series. (John Carradine reprises his role as Serenity Johnson once in each of the two succeeding seasons: in "The Nature of Evil" during the second, and "Ambush" during the third.)

In "Chains," Caine is chained to a man who has been imprisoned for murder. The man, a miner named Huntoon, worked with Caine's step-brother, Danny. Seeking information about Danny's whereabouts, Caine is recognized by the sheriff as a man being sought for killing the nephew of the Chinese emperor. Huntoon promises to take Caine to Danny if he will help him escape from jail. Caine agrees and the two escape, chained together, wrist to wrist. Actually, although Huntoon worked a claim with Danny and two other men, he does not know where Danny is now. After helping Huntoon clear his name of a murder he did not commit, as well as adjust to living in society as a free man, Caine must continue his search alone.

In order to give the series consistency and cohesion the story department at Warner Bros. Television developed a "*Kung Fu* Writers Guide." It was divided into two parts, the first dealing with "FORM" and the second with "CONTENT."[12] Among the guidelines was the requirement that each story consist of four equal length acts plus a brief epilogue. Dialogue was to be kept "as sparse as possible" with "particular attention being given to character interaction." Writers were urged to include at least one "flashback" per act. Caine was to be given a chance at least once in each episode "to reveal his physical skill in kung fu." He was, however, "to resort to physical action only when there is no other alternative for him to pursue." Furthermore, although he would always triumph, he would never kill or maim an opponent.

With respect to content, the story should always stress the triumph of good over evil with an emphasis on the precepts of Confucianism, Taoism and Zen. Since the Chinese did not believe in celibacy, there was no "obstacle" to "Caine's having relationships with women" (other than the fact that he was a fugitive and therefore constantly on the move). All stories should avoid "the cloying and the cliché" although it was important that they be "spiritually uplifting rather than downbeat or tragic." Finally, writers were admonished to avoid stories about Indians, since "it is virtually impossible to reproduce the culture of the American Indian with any sense of reality." Stories about single Indian characters "seen apart from" their own civilizations were permitted, however.

After *Kung Fu* was installed as a weekly Thursday night series, its ratings continued to climb. Eventually it tied the popular *Mary Tyler Moore Show* in the Nielsens and the series was renewed for another season. As Carradine later explained in a *New York Times* interview: "People, especially youth, responded right away to the lead character, his philosophy of non-violence. Kwai Chang Caine is a very contemporary man...."[13] Cleveland Amory, of *TV Guide* soon hopped on the show's bandwagon:

> This show is a combination of "The Fugitive," "Run for Your Life" and President Nixon's trip to China....
>
> If you come in cold on this show or late after the tease you're going to think you've been had. It may seem silly—particularly a lot of the proverbs which seem to have been borrowed form a fortune-cookie factory. But if you'll give it a chance, come in at the beginning and stay with it, you'll find that David Carradine has such an "accomplished technique" of his own in playing Caine that he may well make a believer out of you.[14]

Other television critics were soon singing the praises of television's newest Western. Cecil Smith of the *Los Angeles Times* wrote:

> ABC-TV's "Kung Fu" is the hit of the second season.... The wonder of "Kung Fu" is not that it's a hit—its philosophies are very much of these times—but that it's on.... "Kung Fu" is nothing like television has done before.

John J. O'Connor of the *New York Times* said:

> There is ... another new element in TV programming this season ... of attempting to deal with human values...."Kung Fu" ... unexpectedly successful ... is attempting a new direction, away from the "eye-for-an-eye" brand of confrontation.

The UPI's Rick duBrow observed:

> "Kung Fu" ... is by far the most interesting of these [mid-season] series ... a western, all right, but highly contemporary in the outlook of its hero played extremely well by Carradine.... "Kung Fu" seems to have struck a public chord.

Jerry Buck of the Associated Press proclaimed:

> ... A new hero, steeped in oriental philosophy, and eschewing such age-old trappings as machismo and retribution, Caine, the mystical hero of ABC's "Kung Fu," seems to be striking a responsive chord among young people.

Freelance critic Margrieta Clarkson expressed mixed feelings about the series:

> ... The very best moments are when he performs one of his incredible leaps [once from the top of a fort]—again in slow motion. You see him gather and then expel the surge of power that lifts him to incredible heights and across incredible distances....

[However] when Caine descends to the level of common folk (i.e., when he's bewitched by a fancy lady doing the dance of the veils), "Kung Fu" becomes a soap opera about a half caste struggling along in the West. Then the moral wrapped in the phrases of a parable and played out each week comes across as pure corn, and the effort to underplay any violence appears to be a tactic to suggest to parents that it's really a kiddies show.

And an anonymous critic known as "Cyclops" blasted *Kung Fu* in *Newsweek* (February 12, 1973):

"Kung Fu" features David Carradine as an Oriental monk . . . [full] of night school notions about Buddha, Confucius and Lao-Tse. . . .

There is no excuse for any of this. It is as though the producers had been caught, naked, in a retirement home for old clichés when the fire alarm went off, and as they ran toward the exit, they grabbed whatever came to hand whether it fit or not: non-violence, Eastern wisdom, Old West, Charlie-Chan-meet-Jimmy Stewart-meet-Paladin-meet-Gandhi. What will it be next season—a black homosexual dwarf ex-cop, adept in voo-doo, with a liberated female mongoose as his side-kick?

Perfectly respectable actors and a lot of money have been wasted on "Kung Fu."

Kung Fu, like most other Westerns, did not please everyone.

And some of those who were not pleased were Chinese, like playwright Frank Chin, author of *The Chicken-Coop Chinaman*. Chin wrote a scathing attack on *Kung Fu* for its stereotyping of Orientals in the Sunday edition of the *New York Times* on March 24, 1974. It read, in part:

The progress that Asians of all yellows have made in the movies and on television is pitiful compared to the great strides in self determination made by apes. . . .

In 40 years, apes went from a naked gigantic, hairy King Kong, with nitwit sex fantasies about little human women, to a talking chimpanzee leading his fellow apes in a battle to take over the planet. *We've* progressed from Fu Manchu, the male Dragon Lady of silent movies, to Charlie Chan and then to "Kung Fu" on TV.

Judging from the way everyone—the critics, the stars, the producers—talks about "Kung Fu" being one of the more "human" shows on the air and a sort of Chinese Western, it seems they don't know that Chinese have been a part of the Old West for seven generations.

The Chinese were never slaves in this country. But on "Kung Fu" the only Chinaman who can do anything other than display cultured stupidity, cowardice or deceit is a man of some white blood. The full-blood yellows are helpless fools. . . .

Pick up an Asian-American magazine or newspaper. A debate is raging. The yellows who are against "Kung Fu" are advised to sit down and be grateful that Charlie Chan reruns and the "Kung Fu" series are making us sympathetic in the white man's mind. And the majority . . . are so grateful to "Kung Fu" for making us likable that they look on its insults and inaccuracies as merely the price of acceptance in America.

The *New York Times* allotted series creator Ed Spielman equal time to respond three weeks later (April 14, 1974). Spielman's response was an impassioned and cogent defense of the series, reading, in part:

If one is to believe the countless letters of thanks which I have received from Oriental-Americans for my creation of ABC-TV's "Kung Fu," it would seem that Mr. Chin's radical opinions are very much in the minority. . . . While his objection to any racial stereotyping is well-founded, his view can only be termed "misguided!"

Mr. Chin's objections to "Kung Fu" are a mass of contradictions. He asserts that "on Kung Fu the only Chinaman who can do anything other than display cultured stupidity, cowardice, or deceit is a man of some white blood." Baloney! Has he ever watched the show?

In what way are Orientals portrayed as "passive," "docile" or "timid," when the drama deals with a student of the Shaolin Temple who is schooled in the martial arts for 15 years?

It would appear that Mr. Chin has a preconceived notion of how Orientals have been maligned in the past, and projected this upon a creation which seems to have accomplished just the opposite. No one ever formed a negative opinion of a Chinese from having watched "Kung Fu." It is the main stream of public opinion which indicates that "Kung Fu" changed the negative Oriental stereotype to an image of sensitivity and dignity.

Perhaps, the most controversial aspect of *Kung Fu* was the off-camera behavior of its star, David Carradine. Disdaining the plush Hollywood life, Carradine lived in a tiny clapboard house consisting of little more than one room in Laurel Canyon while earning $10,000 a week for his work on *Kung Fu*. To reach the house he had to climb 78 wooden steps. Once inside there were but a few rickety chairs and a Japanese mat for a bed. He had adopted the simple life and, on his days off, he could be found twanging his guitar or growing apricots. Although he drove a Lancia sports car, it was hardly a status symbol, having no radiator grill and no glass in the side lights and the license plate was tied on with string.

Carradine's hostility toward the establishment included television. He claimed that he never watched his own show and refused to tolerate a television set in his home. His idiosyncrasies extended to his eating habits. He would live on a rigid diet of watermelons and wild greens for months on end. He also engaged in experimentation with hallucinatory drugs, trying everything from LSD and peyote to a certain, sometimes lethal, Hawaiian mushroom.[15] Rebelling also from Hollywood's dress standards, Carradine would show up at formal industry affairs barefoot and in ragged jeans. He also liked to give the impression that he was frequently stoned on marijuana. Still, he worked out with weights for an hour or two every day at a nearby gym to keep in shape. Carradine's political views were also unorthodox:

> ... I feel it doesn't matter who gets elected any more. The government only relates to industrialists and property owners anyhow. The simple person is unaffected by government. His life goes on exactly as it did before.
> I'd turn down any politician who asked for my support just as I'd turn down any religious leader or karate school or advertiser or movie-maker. I'd say "NO!" to almost everything and everybody because I want my life to be personally expressive rather than expressive for somebody else.[16]

For a while, Carradine lived with actress Barbara Hershey, who changed her name to Barbara Seagull after she inadvertently killed a seagull while filming *Last Summer* (1969) and felt its spirit enter her. She and David met in 1969 when they both appeared in *Heaven with a Gun*. Three years later they made another movie together, the aforementioned *Boxcar Bertha*. Out of this relationship was born a baby boy whom they named Free. (Later, after the two had split up, Barbara resumed her acting career using the name Hershey again.)

Carradine was also serious about the art of filmmaking. Sinking virtually all of his own financial resources into the project, he made three independent films while on hiatus from *Kung Fu*. Two, *The Round* and *A Country Mile*, were filmed in the wilds of Kansas. The other, *You and Me*, was shot in Oregon. These represented Carradine's first attempts at directing. *You and Me* was "part motorcycle picture, part Walt Disney and part its own thing."[17] Caring little whether the films were a commercial success, Carradine made them for the sheer pleasure of it—like a painter paints a picture. The subject matter, in one, a former soldier who works as a fairgrounds roustabout and in another a man who sits in a shack all day composing songs while everyone else is going off to fight in World War II, were hardly designed for financial success. It was not surprising that each lost money.

So involved with the character of Caine did Carradine become that he zealously guarded him from any tampering by the writers, directors, or producers:

> It's important that the show be subordinated to the philosophical precepts of Kung Fu
> . . . In other words there can be no circumstances in which Caine can fight unless someone
> is trying to kill him. . . .
>
> The very essence of Kung Fu is not to fight under any circumstance. The whole idea
> of Kung Fu is to magically make things work so a confrontation can be avoided.[18]

Furthermore, Carradine influenced the growth and development of Caine's personality:

> . . . Caine's character has really grown. Like, just physically, I let my hair grow out as
> we went along, as Caine's would—I use a skullcap now, for the flashbacks—and I took off
> the boots that wardrobe had me wearing, and left them off. Caine doesn't *need* shoes! I wanted
> him to have, besides that sense of dignity and peace, a sense of humor, and he got one, though
> it's very low key. . . . I wanted him to be affected by America, the new-culture changes him
> very subtly. . . .
>
> . . . I wanted to develop a whole style of playing him that would be very quietly stylized,
> satirical, a sort of formal way of moving, the deadpan reading of those far-out lines of his.
> I mean, I dig Caine, I respect him, I believe in what he does, but I wanted to comment on
> him when I acted him.[19]

In spite of the influence, however, that Buddhism had on Carradine's philosophy of life, he never became a true practitioner of the martial arts. When asked (as he repeatedly was) whether or not he could actually split bricks with his bare fists, he would smile incredulously:

> Who *me*? Man I don't know Kung Fu combat, no way! When we started the series, we
> asked some Kung Fu experts to help us, and they wouldn't.
>
> They're very serious about the art of Kung Fu. They thought we were just some commercial rip-off bull. All the fights in the show are faked, choreographed. I'm not a fighting man,
> I'm a dancer.[20]

Unquestionably, *Kung Fu* bore the imprint of Carradine's "stylized" acting as well as his "choreographed" martial arts performance.

In 1973, *Kung Fu* received the recognition that many critics and fans felt it deserved when it received six Emmy nominations:

Outstanding Drama Series—Continuing.......	(Jerry Thorpe, Producer)
Outstanding New Series....................	(Jerry Thorpe, Producer)
Outstanding Continued Performance by an Actor in a Leading Role..................	(David Carradine)
Outstanding Directional Achievement in Drama.................................	(Jerry Thorpe for "Eye for an Eye" episode)
Outstanding Achievement in Makeup........	(Frank C. Westmore in "Chains" episode)
Outstanding Achievement in Cinematography for Entertainment Program...............	(Jack Woolf for "Eye for an Eye" episode)

Although it won only in the two latter technical categories, *Kung Fu* had obviously earned the respect of the members of the Academy of Television Arts and Sciences.

Most critics consider *Kung Fu* a combination of the martial arts film and the Western. John Gourlie, professor of mass communications at Quinnipiac College in Hamden, Connecticut, on the other hand, views it as "a meaningful extension of the Western genre":

> . . . I would like to argue that the protagonist, Kwai Chang Caine, illuminates the nature
> of the cowboy hero even as he departs significantly from it. In addition, the western is enriched
> as a genre by being flexible enough to contain a variation as radical as "Kung Fu." . . .
>
> We have only to compare episodes of "Kung Fu" with a typical western to be impressed
> by the philosophy of peace existing within Caine's total but restrained command of violence.

For as a Shaolin priest, Caine is preeminently a man of peace. . . . But the wild American frontier of the 1870s thrusts Caine repeatedly into violent encounters and unjust situations maintained by unscrupulous force. Like many a western hero, Caine is compelled to do battle when peaceful remedies fail. Like certain of the cowboy heroes, Caine is himself a fugitive, having killed the Royal Nephew. . . . Except for the Chinese background, the portrait of the good man unjustly hunted and turned into a drifting fighter is hardly unfamiliar in the western. . . .

This blending of Eastern mysticism and Western action creates an inner dimension of the spirit rarely incorporated in the conventional cowboy drama. Caine typically remembers experiences from his youthful training under the Shaolin Masters, and through these memories, he gains the insight necessary to resolve his present crisis. The memories are, of course, rendered by flashback. The overall effect clarifies and vindicates our traditional assumption that the cowboy hero's actions derive their force from some inner strength of character and not from mere physical Prowess. . . .

. . . "Kung Fu" makes it clear that the triumph of the western hero we so much admire and celebrate is essentially one of the spirit. By setting aside many of the surface conventions of the western, "Kung Fu" also makes clear that the hero—who commands fighting skills—is not dependent upon or limited to such skills. Instead, it is the character—or spirit—of the hero which conquers.[21]

Most other television critics and historians have been much more negative in their assessment of *Kung Fu*. Brooks and Marsh dismiss it as a "philosophical Western" which "attracted quite a bit of notoriety and a cult following."[22] Castleman and Podrazik describe it as "a pretentious, heavy-handed effort" with "lots of stylized violence" reeking of "early 1970s relevance." While admitting the show "may seem to have its heart in the right place, espousing peace and tranquility," they point out that "the amount of butt-kicking violence Caine both dishes out and receives makes one think that perhaps the show protests too much." They also note that "the mysticism of 'Kung Fu' went out with lava lamps."[23]

J. Fred MacDonald is most critical of the racial implications of the series. After deploring the stereotyping of Asiatics in the video West as cooks and launderers (in the Hey Boy, Hop Sing mold), he asserts:

Not until 1972 and the appearance of Kwai Chang Caine . . . did the TV Western offer an Asian character who was . . . recognizably human. Nonetheless, even this character had his familiar limitations: he was depicted with "inscrutable" Oriental mystery, he was prone to Charlie Chan-styled aphorisms, he was half Caucasian, and he was portrayed by a non-Asian actor.[24]

At the same time, MacDonald claims that Bruce Lee was rejected for the leading role on *Kung Fu* "because the producers felt a Chinese actor could not be accepted as a hero by the American television audience."[25] No corroboration of this assertion could be found, however, and, at the time *Kung Fu* was being developed Lee was appearing on a regular basis as Mike Longstreet's self-defense instructor on *Longstreet*.

An analysis of several typical *Kung Fu* episodes will shed light on the merits of the series. In "The Way of Violence Has No Mind," Caine encounters Captain Lee and his band of bandits. Lee (played by Ron Soble) is a sort of Oriental Robin Hood who robs wealthy whites to help poor Chinese. As he explains to Caine:

LEE: . . . they took all our gold. I figured the only way to live in this country of white devils is to learn their ways, use guns like they do, and take back our gold. . . . We keep what we need and spread the rest around amongst our people. . . .

CAINE: Your way—the way of violence can only end in sorrow.

LEE: You're Chinese, whether all or part makes no difference to these white devils. If you were smart you'd join with us. . . .

Caine rejects Lee's invitation, preferring to make his own way alone. One of Lee's men (a young Chinese played by Robert Ito) asks what he thinks of Caine's words. Lee responds, "I heard them many times before, from laundrymen just like him." "But," the young man persists, "he had a way of making everything he said sound important." Lee's answer: "Just his style, boy. Talks, slow, quiet, and fancy like some missionary...." By the end of this episode, Caine is able to persuade Lee to lay down his arms and surrender to the authorities. Before this occurs however, a friendly farmer (Gary Merrill) is nearly killed and Caine bests Lee in a martial arts contest. Once again pacifism triumphs—after considerable violence has taken place.

"Crossties" deals with much the same theme. Caine becomes involved in a war between a group of farmers and representatives of the railroad over land the railroad is after. He must outrun horses to warn the farmers of duplicity by the Pinkertons, who have been hired by the railroad to drive the farmers off their land. The railroad is willing to offer amnesty to all who have been involved in the violence, but the Pinkertons (especially their leader, played to deceitful and indignant perfection by Barry Sullivan) hope to prevent this and prolong the war. A battle ensues until Caine is able to convince the farmers to agree to the railroad's terms while discrediting the leader of the Pinkertons. Peace and justice again defeat violence. (A young Harrison Ford is effective in a small role as spokesman for the railroad.)

In "The Spirit Helper," an Indian boy named Nashiba, who has been fasting in the wilderness, meets Caine and thinks that he has been sent by the Great Spirit to teach Nashiba how to be a man. Refusing to believe that Caine is not his "Spirit Helper," Nashiba asks him to help rescue his mother who has been kidnapped by Commancheros after they killed his father. Caine and Nashiba follow the Commancheros to their hideout and ultimately rescue Nashiba's mother—after Caine has defeated their leader (a burly Irishman well-played by Bo Swenson) in brutal hand to hand combat. Nashiba has become a man and Caine continues on his quest for his step-brother.

The meaning of justice is also a common theme in *Kung Fu* stories. In "The Stone" two immigrants, one a black Brazilian whose father was a slave who worked in the diamond mines, and the other an Armenian who hopes to one day return to his homeland and fight injustice, learn what justice is in America—with a little help from Caine. The black, Isaac Montoya, has come to America with a diamond he has stolen hoping to earn the respect he believes his talents and abilities entitle him to. The Armenian, Zolly, is an itinerant piano player who has rejected the love of a widow and her three little boys, because he is afraid of losing his independence.

Montoya, upon arriving in a dusty Western town, is set upon by three black-hating rednecks. Although Montoya handles himself well in the fight, Caine saves his life when one of the rednecks tries to shoot him. In the scuffle, however, Montoya loses his diamond, which is found by one of the little boys. In his subsequent search for the missing stone Montoya accidently kills the sheriff and becomes a hunted man. Caine again saves Montoya's life when he attempts to rescue one of the boys from quicksand. Montoya, however, believes that Caine has stolen his diamond and pursues him when he accompanies Zolly to return the three runaway boys to their mother.

Montoya threatens to kill Caine if he will not return the diamond. Caine cannot understand why the stone is so important to Montoya. Montoya explains:

> Until that piece of stone, there was nothing. Do you think I started out intending to steal a diamond, or to kill another human being? All I wished was the opportunity to do all that my mind and body were capable of doing. Only then I discovered that that was not the way for the son of a slave to think even after he had educated himself beyond his masters. The

stone changed everything. It lay there on the ground and as I held it in my hand, I thought of my father and my grandfather and generations of my people working that same mine, all slaves. I took it. I can not go back.

Caine subsequently subdues Montoya, but when the rednecks show up to kill him, Caine, Zolly and the boy's mother place their lives in jeopardy to save the life of Montoya. Montoya then surrenders himself to the U.S. marshal, having learned the meaning of justice in America. Zolly, meanwhile, has discovered that "to fight injustice anywhere is to fight injustice everywhere" and decides to marry the woman he loves and remain in America. As in most stories, Caine has simply been a facilitator, helping others to see what has been there all the time. In "The Stone" Moses Gunn turns in a dignified and restrained performance as Montoya while Gregory Sierra is equally effective with a more flamboyant characterization of Zolly.

In "The Ancient Warrior," a Native American is the object of prejudice and injustice. On the way to Santa Fe, Caine helps rescue an elderly Indian (the Ancient Warrior) from three young hellions who are bent on pouring a bottle of whiskey down his throat. The Ancient Warrior has been searching for a doctor to tend to his gravely ill son. It is too late, however, for the Indian brave lies dead on the travois. Caine assists the old Indian in building a funeral pyre, but when he asks him if he mourns his son's death, the Ancient Warrior responds:

> His death, yes. I regret he had to go the way of smoke.... I would have preferred that he be buried ... [but he could not] because he did not die on the land on which he was born. We have places designated at birth. To die and be buried there is to save our souls the journey of a thousand moons in their voyage toward completeness. I, myself, was on the way to that sacred, final resting place, when Hawk of Peace became sick.

CAINE: Then he ... was taking *you*.

ANCIENT WARRIOR: Yes ... No more than a moon ago, I felt death circling, like a sick owl, outside my tepee. Instead, death swooped down to take my son first ...

CAINE: Will you return to your people now?

ANCIENT WARRIOR: My people? ... *I* am my people. There is no one else left.

CAINE: You mean you are alone?

ANCIENT WARRIOR: I mean my people are all dead. I am the last.

CAINE: What will you do?

ANCIENT WARRIOR: My way is clear, but not simple. I must go back to the land where I was born—to find my burial place, so that I can die.

CAINE: The journey will not be possible for you alone.

ANCIENT WARRIOR: I know that my friend. I am willing to pay you to come with me.... I have a paper here with white man's words that my son told me had great value.... I also have three pouches full of gold.... You may have it all after I am buried in my ordained burial place.

CAINE: You are very generous, But I do not seek wealth ... and my way lies in another direction.

ANCIENT WARRIOR: If you will not accompany me out of greed, do so then out of friendship.

Unwilling to reject the old Indian's offer of friendship, Caine decides to go with the Ancient Warrior to the town of Purgatory, a journey of two days' duration. The difficulties that lie ahead for Caine and the Ancient Warrior are foreshadowed by a large sign fastened to a building on the outskirts of town reading:

Opposite: **Caine had to resort to the use of martial arts to vanquish villains in every episode of *Kung Fu* (here: "The Chalice," October 11, 1973).**

Warning! You are now
entering *PURGATORY*.
Drifters, claim jumpers,
strangers of any kind—
not welcome.

Sheriff Aldon Pool

The Ancient Warrior finds that the spot where he must be buried is located under a large tree in the middle of the town's main street.

Caine soon discovers that Indians are hated in Purgatory because of the massacre of fourteen white men and boys which occurred there eight years earlier. The Ancient Warrior, however, holds a legal deed to the entire valley in which the town is located. He is willing to exchange that deed for permission to be buried in his appointed final resting place. With the assistance of the town's judge, Judge Marcus, the matter is brought to the town council for a vote. Here the bitter feelings of the town toward Indians are expressed and Sheriff Pool threatens to resign if the transaction is approved. The Ancient Warrior responds:

> White history sees only with the white of its eye. Why did it not record the fourteen men of my tribe who were killed first? Why did it not record the two hundred seventeen men, women and children of my tribe who were slaughtered by the white soldiers one week later? Why can you not try to forget—and discover the sweet solace of forgiveness as I have?

Caine then discredits the sheriff by revealing that he witnessed a man shot from ambush on a rooftop by one of Pool's men while facing off against the sheriff in a supposedly fair gunfight.

When the vote is taken, the Ancient Warrior wins by a vote of four to three. He can be buried in his designated burial place. Surprisingly, however, the Ancient Warrior refuses:

> It is a hollow victory. This place is filled with hatred. The Great Mystery no longer touches its soil with fertile sweetness. If the hatred is not removed its barrenness will grow deeper, until neither blossoms nor souls will care to touch it ever again.

Caine and the Ancient Warrior leave Purgatory and after he dies, Caine builds a funeral pyre on which the elderly Indian's remains are burned. In the episode's closing scene, Caine returns to Purgatory to spread the Ancient Warrior's ashes over the town's main street, explaining to Judge Marcus that "it is better to cover the land with love than to allow it to cover you with hatred...." Judge Marcus nods his understanding, "An act of forgiveness. Do you think people will understand?" Caine shrugs, replying, "Not everyone will. For those who do not—the story of the Ancient Warrior will always be told." It is a moving episode, well written by A. Martin Zweiback with an outstanding cast, including Chief Dan George as the Ancient Warrior, Will Geer as Judge Marcus and Victor French as Sheriff Pool turning in powerful performances.

"Empty Pages from a Dead Book" relates the story of Caine's encounter with a Texas Ranger named McNally. The ranger is carrying on the work of his dead father who had the reputation of being one of the toughest law enforcement officers that ever lived. His father had kept a book listing anyone who had ever committed a crime in Texas. All had been apprehended or killed except for the four Fishers. Caine is a witness to the wounding of Bart Fisher by McNally while he was attempting his arrest. The man is later freed by the local judge, who claims that McNally has no jurisdiction outside of Texas and takes away his badge. Subsequently the four Fishers goad McNally into a fight.

Seeing that the ranger is outnumbered, Caine intervenes in his behalf. When one of the Fishers is accidently killed in a fall (while attempting to reach a gun on a balcony railing), McNally and Caine are arrested and tried for murder. The judge hears testimony from both sides and then renders his verdict:

> The rendering of a sentence is never a simple task for a magistrate who is human and, therefore, realizes he could be wrong. And yet there is an over-riding demand of law to demand that there will be law and that it will be enforced. Now a man is dead, and I must believe someone about how it happened. Now the Fishers here, to a man have never stepped out of line, never once since they settled here is Dos Leos, never once. Unfortunately I can not say the same for you, McNally. You started it all by shooting Bart Fisher with a highly doubtful cause and without proper warning and then even after I took your badge from you, you made it quite clear that you still intended to carry out your father's work. All things considered, I can only believe that you and your partner took advantage of Joe Billy's anger and changed what should have been a simple fistfight into an act of deliberate murder. And that is exactly what your father would have done! It is therefore, the judgment of this court that at midday tomorrow you will both be taken to a place of execution and hanged by the neck until you are dead. And may God have the mercy upon you that I, by the law, am not entitled to show.

Later as McNally contemplates his death in a jail cell with Caine, his devotion to the law is shaken:

> I always thought the law was the most important thing. Now it's goin' to kill me for something I didn't even do. And it's legal. The trial was legal. The judge did what he thought was right. Altogether it's the law. I lived by it, I sure don't wanna die by it.

Caine helps NcNally break out of jail, but in their escape the sheriff is seriously injured. If they do not get him to a doctor, he will die and they will be murderers. Caine convinces McNally to do the right thing and the sheriff's life is saved. The judge is so impressed with their willingness to sacrifice their lives for that of the sheriff, that he reverses his initial decision and sets the two men free. McNally turns over his father's book to the judge, having learned that the letter of the law must, from time to time, be tempered with reason and mercy. Upholding the spirit of the law more often serves the interests of justice. "Empty Pages of a Dead Book" presents another excellent story enhanced by a superior cast. Especially noteworthy are Robert Foxworth as McNally, Nate Esformes as the judge and Slim Pickens as Bart Fisher.

"In Uncertain Bondage" deals with both greed and resentment. A former Confederate officer named Tate kidnaps the daughter of a wealthy Southern planter in order to extort $50,000 from the Burnam family. His two black accomplices, Jenny and Seth, are motivated not only by the money they will receive for their assistance in the kidnapping, but also by resentment at the way they have been treated by their former masters, the Burnams. Jenny, who grew up with Dora Burnam and later became her maid, is especially angry at the way she was always "used" by her owners. Shortly after the kidnappers reveal their intentions, this exchange takes place:

> DORA: Jenny, I just don't understand what's gotten into you. Haven't I always been good to you? Haven't I always given you things?
> JENNY: Things? Things you didn't want no mo!
> DORA: But Jenny, we played together when we were babies.
> JENNY: When I was five years old, they put me up on a box so I could iron your birthday dress.
> DORA: Why, I always remembered you on your birthday. I always made sure you had your own cake.
> JENNY: I eat it out back after I was through cleanin' up the kitchen. You got to go ta school an' learn! Did I? When you were sick and ailin' the ol' doctor came. Who came when

I was sick? Did I sew your dress or was you a sewin' mine? Did I draw your bath water or was it th' other way around?

DORA: But you never complained. Even after the war, Jenny. You were free. You could have left any time you wanted to.

JENNY: Where was I goin' and with what? I'd a been fetchin' and doin' for you the rest of my days . . . if it wasn't fer Seth. When he told me what Mr. Tate was a hatchin' up, I knew it was my chance . . . only one I'd ever get.

When Dora refuses to write a ransom note to her father, she is thrown into a deep pit with Caine. (Caine had inadvertently become involved when he stopped to help the planter's daughter while she was experiencing a fainting spell.) It is while she and Caine are alone in the pit that Dora comes to realize what true friendship means. As Caine explains in order to *be* served, one must first learn how to serve others. She nurses Caine back to health after he has been wounded trying to escape and he tends to her needs when she becomes deathly ill after having a bucket of ice water dumped on her.

When she realizes that Tate intends to kill Miss Burnam, Jenny refuses to cooperate and she too is thrown into the pit. By this time, Dora has come to understand Jenny's pent-up resentment toward her. Dora explains, "I never realized what I was doin' to you. I never even thought about your life. I was wrong." The two reconcile and, after Caine has dispatched Tate in hand to hand combat, leave for what will hopefully be a better life for both. Again, *Kung Fu* has presented an interesting and well acted episode. Lynda Day George and Warren Vanders are outstanding as Dora and Tate, but Judy Pace "steals the show" as Jenny.

Two of the more memorable episodes of *Kung Fu* deal with the Tong, a Mafia-like Chinese organization which extorts protection money from Chinese merchants through the use of terror and violence. In "The Tong," Caine becomes involved while working as a clerk and soon becomes the champion of the shopkeepers. Caine bests the Tong thugs in a series of hand to hand encounters but, although the merchants are grateful, they demonstrate little will to resist the Tong on their own. They know that when Caine, with his superior martial arts skills leaves, they will again be powerless to resist the Tong's intimidation. They thus conclude that resisting now will only incur the Tong's wrath later.

Caine realizes that he must change the attitude of the merchants. He must put aside his fighting skills and assume the role of teacher rather than warrior. He must set a moral example and demonstrate a kind of heroism that transcends combat and force. After meditation and ritual purification, Caine stations himself in the center of a barn and awaits the Tong assassins. He is shot in the back with an arrow, but is, nevertheless, still able to rise and face his attackers. They flee in panic. When the merchants come out of hiding to learn how Caine has managed to survive, he pulls the arrow from his back and staggers off to heal himself. Caine was, in this way, able to overcome the merchants' fear of the Tong by instilling in their enemy a greater fear. Once the Tong could no longer use terror to coerce the merchants into obeying them, they were powerless, and fled. Richard Loo, Diana Douglas and Carey Wong all contribute to the effectiveness of the episode with powerful performances.

In "Arrogant Dragon," Richard Loo is again featured in a moving story about the Tong. In a small Western town, Wu Chang, the elderly head of the Tong is being forcibly removed from his position of leadership by an ambitious and ruthless young Chinese thug (played with understated evil by Clyde Kusatsu) so that he, himself, can run the local Tong. First by deception (with a drug that produces the appearance of death), and then in combat, Caine thwarts the sinister plot to eliminate Wu. Finally, Wu and his daughter are permitted to leave the town without interference from the Tong. Once again pacifism has won the day—but not without considerable assistance from violence.

Much of the uniqueness of the series resulted from the flashbacks to Caine's life as a young man in training to become a Shaolin priest. These always involved exchanges with Caine's teachers, especially Master Po and Master Kan. They invariably presented some graphic moral lesson. For example, in "The Ancient Warrior" this exchange takes place during one such flashback:

> YOUNG CAINE: Master, what is the best way to meet the loss of one we love:
> MASTER KAN: By knowing that when we truly love, it is never lost.... It is only after death that the depth of the bond is truly felt, and our loved one becomes more a part of us than was possible in life.
> YOUNG CAINE: Are we only able to feel this toward those whom we have known and loved a long time?
> MASTER KAN: Sometimes a stranger, known to us for moments, can spark our souls to kinship for eternity.

During the third (and what turned out to be the final) season, *Kung Fu*'s popularity began to decline, despite Warner Bros.' efforts to keep the craze alive. In 1974, a record was issued called *Kung Fu* with excerpts of wisdom backed by music from the soundtrack of the television series. Warner Paperback Library published four novelizations of *Kung Fu* television scripts and a hardcover book suitable for libraries entitled *The Saying of Kung Fu* was assembled. Furthermore, magazines like *Black Belt* and *Karate Illustrated* doubled and tripled their circulations. And everywhere enrollment in some 2000 martial-arts schools was flourishing.

It is difficult to pinpoint exactly what caused *Kung Fu*'s demise. The series continued to feature big name guest stars like Patricia Neal, Eddie Albert, William Shatner, Lew Ayres, Leslie Nielsen, Rhonda Fleming and Carol Lawrence during the 1974-75 season. (Barbara Hershey Seagull was featured in a two-part episode in November, 1974.) In the opening two hour episode "Blood of the Dragon," Caine's cousin, Margit McLean (played by Season Hubley) was introduced, but she was seen only infrequently thereafter.

Some viewers might have felt the stories were becoming too abstract, with a greater reliance on drugs, hallucinations and outright magic woven into the plotlines. Caine's credibility was constantly being stretched to the breaking point. Maybe the Kung Fu craze had simply run its course. In a much later interview for *USA Today* (January 23, 1993), Carradine claimed that *Kung Fu* was not canceled. "I just walked off," he said. "I saw the scripts were falling down and ... I wanted a movie career." (Carradine went on to make *The Long Riders* in 1980, write a book, *The Spirit of Shaolin*, and produce two home videos, *David Carradine's Kung Fu Workout* and *David Carradine's Tai Chi Workout*.) In any case, the last original episode of *Kung Fu* was aired on April 19, 1975. In all, 62 shows had been broadcast over the three season course of the series.

Fans of the series were undoubtedly pleased that Caine's three year search for his half-brother Danny came to a successful conclusion in the third episode of the four-part storyline that ended the third season. All four episodes were written by the husband and wife team of Stephen and Elinor Karpf. In the first, "Barbary House," Caine learns that he has a nephew, Danny's son, Zeke (appealingly portrayed by John Blyth Barrymore). He also meets Zeke's mother, Delonia (a substantial role for Lois Nettleton) who is reunited with her estranged son. The three set off together to find Danny who is hiding from a gangster named Corbino (Leslie Nielsen as a villain) who has been trying to kill him. "Flight to Orion" continues the story of their search. Delonia dies after being bitten by a rattlesnake while protecting Zeke.

David Carradine (left), with Chris Potter as Caine's contemporary son Peter, in *Kung-Fu: The Legend Continues* (1993).

In "The Brothers Caine," Zeke agrees to live with his rich grandfather (his mother's ruthless father) in order to obtain enough money from him to learn the hiding place of his father. When Caine, following Zeke's directions, reaches Danny, he must convince his half-brother of who he is and that he means him no harm. While Kwai Chang exhibits his usual reserve, it is clear how much Danny means to him. Danny, on the other hand, gradually comes to respect and love his half-brother.

Kwai Chang and Danny set off in the final episode, "Full Circle," to find Zeke while at the same time being pursued by Corbino and his men. For the first (and only) time in the series Kwai Chang actually rides a horse—after apologizing to the animal for any suffering he may cause it! All of the plotlines are resolved as Danny is reunited with his son but is forced it kill Corbino in self-defense. Kwai Chang is pleased that his quest for his brother has been completed, but he feels that he must move on. He literally "bows out" of the series—that is, as he bows a farewell to his newly found family, the screen fades to black. It is a fitting way for the series to end, although one might wonder why Caine does not stay with his brother. David Carradine later offered author Herbie J. Pilato this possible explanation:

> The basic principle of the Taoist teachings is that goals don't matter. You climb the mountain and you never get to the top of it. If you got to the top of it, what are you going to do? You can sit on it, I suppose and drink tea and meditate. Or you have to walk down the other side.[26]

In February 1986, *Kung Fu: The Movie*, a two hour television film, was broadcast on CBS, giving David Carradine a chance to reprise the role of Kwai Chang Caine. Only Carradine and Keye Luke (as Master Po) appear from the series, although a number of the flashbacks are identical to those employed in the original episodes and feature Radames Pera (as Young Caine) and Keye Luke as Master Po. Master Kan (with Philip Ahn then long dead) frequently appears to Caine as a transparent spirit offering his customary sage advise and posing perplexing questions.

Neither the story, nor the cast is up to the high standards of the series at its best. (Even Carradine looks tired most of the time.) The plot concerns an illicit opium trade which Caine uncovers while investigating the murder of an American minister who has just returned from China. While assisting the missionary's widow, Sarah Perkins (Kerrie Keane), in finding the murderer of her husband, Caine discovers that opium is being sent from the United States to China inside the coffins of dead Chinese who are being returned to China for burial. The opium is being paid for with ingots of gold being smuggled back to the States in coffins of American missionaries who have died in China and are being returned to the United States for burial. This clever and lucrative operation is being financed by Sarah's father-in-law (Martin Landau), who ordered that his own son be killed after the latter had learned what was happening. A crooked deputy sheriff (William Lucking) is also involved in the scheme and frames Caine for murder.

Adding to Caine's problems is an evil Manchu (Mako), the father of the young man whom Caine killed many years earlier in China. The man is, of course, seeking revenge, and his secret weapon is Caine's son (a son Caine never knew he had) who has been mesmerized by the vengeful Manchu. (Caine's son is played by Brandon Lee, Bruce Lee's son, making his acting debut.) It all gets pretty muddled; Sarah falls in love with Caine (they actually partake of two prolonged screen kisses) but is finally killed by the crooked deputy. Caine kills the deputy, but then must face his own son in a hand to hand fight to the death. Ultimately, Caine is able to break the Manchu's spell and turn it against him. The villain dies in a flash of fire and steel. Caine and his son are reconciled and wander off together as the closing credits roll.

Some of the dialogue is vintage *Kung Fu*. When Sarah, surprised to learn that Caine has a son, asks him, "Is it common for priests to have children?" Caine responds, "Should it not be? Is not love in harmony with nature?" Later when asked who he is, Caine replies, "a man, a warehouse laborer, a humble Shaolin priest." However, if the television film was to be a trial balloon for a new series, it was a failure. The ratings were not spectacular and the critics booed the movie. *Variety* (February 12, 1986) said:

> Caine's ability to levitate, pass through walls, drop from high buildings, stands him in good stead even if it isn't much of a tale from which he rises, through which he slips and into which he drops.
> ... [I]t's blatant exploitation of martial arts and loaded with pseudo–Oriental thinking.
> ... The Chinese may find themselves offended by the silliness .... They need not, since not many people will stick around to watch it.

Still, the *Kung Fu* concept was not dead. In 1987, an attempt to revive the series, but setting it in the modern era, resulted in a new 60 minute pilot, *Kung Fu: The Next Generation*. David Darlow plays the great-grandson of the original Caine, who is trying to bring his wayward son (Brandon Lee) back into "the family business," which is fighting injustice. The young man has left home and is involved in the illegal activities of a crime lord (Miguel Ferrer). He is caught and returned to his father's supervision. There is considerable animosity between father and son before Lee has his showdown with Ferrer (with Darlow secretly accompanying him, hidden in the back of a pickup truck). Father and son successfully dispatch the villains and all is well again between them. Once again *Variety* (June 24, 1987) turned thumbs down:

> ... The original series had a fascinating mysticism about it that is missing from the contemporary version, with only one scene ... suggesting the grace and discipline of the martial arts. Otherwise, the pilot ... is little more than routine action-adventure....

In any case *The Next Generation* could certainly not be classified as a Western.

Another attempt at reviving the series was made in January 1993. Called *Kung Fu: The Legend Continues*, the show was broadcast only over the newly formed Warner Bros. Prime Time Entertainment Network and consequently was not available in many of the smaller markets. Apparently the ratings were considered to be sufficiently high enough for the series was renewed for a second season.

In this modern-day version, David Carradine plays Kwai Chang Caine, the grandson of the original character. He displays the same knack for cryptic quotes and still fights for the underdog. As Carradine described it in an interview, he was still playing the same character as he had in the Western series:

> I'm 146 years old—that's how I can play the same role. We give lip service to my being the grandson but I'm the same guy. Only the face is older. There's the story of a Kung Fu master who lived to be 253 years old. Who knows? I may still be doing the series in 2080.[27]

Carradine went on to explain that he had rejected past ideas to revive the series because "he didn't want to do 'Kung Fu' with car crashes." Furthermore, he added, "It's hard to define to somebody that what is spiritual television is also an action/adventure series."

In *The Legend Continues*, television newcomer Chris Potter costars as Caine's contemporary son, Peter, who is a police detective. In the two-hour pilot film, father and son are reunited while trying to bring down a Chinatown crime lord. (Each had thought the other was killed when the Shaolin Temple in which Caine was a teacher and Peter a student had burned down fifteen years earlier.)

At nearly 57, Carradine was still practicing *tai chi* and the martial arts, but the actor let the part of the son handle much of the more demanding physical stunts on the series. Claiming that the primary message of the show was love, rather than violence, Carradine explained that both Caine and he had "learned so much more that I try not to kick people. I don't like to kick people.... It's love first, truth second, then wisdom."[28] (Still, as in the old series, practically every episode of *The Legend Continues* provided Caine/Carradine with an opportunity to display his martial arts skill in dispatching some evildoer.) Carradine's observations on the new series further illuminate his attitude toward the old:

> I think the show's appeal lies in a mystery that's kind of unsolved. Caine manages to be heroic without being macho or even seeming to notice it. He's a man who has a real knowledge of the nature of the universe and doesn't use tricks.
>
> When the show first began, Richard Nixon shook hands with Mao in China. There was a desire to see East meet West. I think that had a lot to do with the thirst. Now we're living

in a world where everyone studies martial arts and Oriental philosophy. The ideas we present are no longer radical.

I think Caine's innocence had a lot to do with it, too. Prejudice was incomprehensible to him. He was a man who helped others.[29]

And, he might have added, continues to do so—only now instead of this occuring in the American West of the 1870s, the setting is contemporary urban America. In both cases, *Kung Fu* provides viewers with an unusual blend of pacifistic philosophy and violent action.

At its best, the original *Kung Fu* was a unique and thought-provoking action Western with interesting plots, plausible situations, and excellent acting. At its worst, it was a strange mixture of mysticism and violence presenting cardboard stereotypes in unbelievable situations spouting "fortune cookie aphorisms." The television Western has certainly never seen its like.

XV. The Saga of "Little House on the Prairie"

WESTERN SOAP OPERA OR FARMING ON THE FRONTIER?

The farmers' frontier, the last of Frederick Jackson Turner's four frontiers, has received considerably less attention from television than any other aspect of the historic American West. Perhaps, it is because their story has been considered less exciting and less violent than those of the trappers, miners, and ranchers. Certainly, it was none the less heroic. These pioneer farmers made no compromise with nature—their objective was not to adapt but to conquer. They viewed the forests or grasslands of the continent as obstacles to overcome. Millions of acres of prairie sod were turned under by their plows. Most of them hated the Indians with a fervor born of firsthand experience with massacres. They cursed those traders who supplied the Indians with firewater and firearms, and wanted to see the natives exterminated.

Although many of the pioneer farmers were perennial movers who shifted with the frontier, their goal was to transform the Western wilds into replicas of eastern communities. In the words of noted Western historian Ray Allen Billington, "theirs was a romantic, if arduous existence."[1] They were first into each new area, alone or with a handful of kindred spirits. They made the first clearings, built the first rough dwellings and mapped out the first passable trails through the forests or across the plains. With courage, ingenuity, and independence, the farmers brought fences, windmills, farm machinery—and civilization to the Western frontier.

The waning years of the nineteenth century saw the greatest westward movement of peoples in American history. Millions of farmers held back for a generation by the forbidding features of the Great Plains surged onto them between 1870 and 1880. They filled Kansas and Nebraska, engulfed the level grasslands of the Dakotas and eventually spilled over into the rolling foothills of Wyoming and Montana. Among these settlers was the family of Charles Ingalls, who migrated from Wisconsin to Missouri and then on to Kansas, ending up in Minnesota. It was through the experiences of this family that the farmers' frontier first came to television.

Laura Ingalls Wilder, the second of four Ingalls daughters, wrote a series of nine books for children that detailed the life of pioneer farmers. Born in 1867 in a log cabin at Lake Pepin, Wisconsin, Laura had traveled with her family as they moved from place to place until settling permanently in DeSmet, Dakota Territory. In 1885, after teaching school for a short time, Laura married Almanzo Wilder. Wilder was a homesteader who lived in the DeSmet area. Nine years later the Wilders established their permanent home that Laura called Rocky Ridge Farm in the Ozarks region of Missouri. Later Laura began her writing career for the local newspaper in Mansfield, Missouri, with a column entitled "As a Farm Woman Thinks."[2]

Nostalgic after the deaths of her parents and older sister, Wilder wrote her first book, *The Little House in the Big Woods*, which detailed her early family life in Wisconsin in 1932. Its success led to seven more books: *Farmer Boy* (1935) which related her husband's boyhood in upstate New York; *The Little House on the Prairie* (1935), which continued the autobiographical accounts she had begun in her first novel and is set in Kansas from 1869 to 1871; *On the Banks of Plum Creek* (1937), which told the story of the Ingalls family in the wheat region of Minnesota; *By the Shores of Silver Lake* (1939), which covered the joys and tribulations of homesteading in the Dakota Territory; *The Long Winter* (1940), which dealt with the severe hardships the family encountered during the winter of 1880-81; *Little Town on the Prairie* (1941), which narrated Laura's efforts to put her blind sister Mary through college by teaching school in the DeSmet area; and *Those Happy Golden Years* (1943), which included the events leading up to her marriage to Almanzo Wilder.

A ninth volume was published after Wilder's death by her daughter Rose Wilder Lane. Lane had discovered the manuscript, written in pencil on a school tablet (as were all of Wilder's manuscripts) among her mother's belongings. The posthumous novel, *The First Four Years* (1971), covered the early years of the Wilders' marriage, beginning the story where *Those Happy Golden Years* left off. Taken collectively, these books serve as a celebration of the pioneering spirit of yesterday and provide us with useful documents in our understanding of what everyday life was like, especially for farm women. Ironically, Laura Ingalls Wilder once said, "I had no idea I was writing history." However, her biographer, Donald Zochert, accurately proclaimed that "more people have learned of the frontier in America through the writings of Laura Ingalls Wilder than ever heard of Frederick Jackson Turner, the great historian of the frontier."[3] Wilder probably did not think of her work as history because she lived the experiences related in her books.

Although the novels had been popular, inspiring and fascinating generations of readers for more than forty years, no one had seen their dramatic potential. By the standards of the seventies, the stories seemed too tame. A former network vice president and co-producer of the *Laugh-In* series, Ed Friendly, nevertheless, purchased the dramatic rights to the series. There was a movement underway to bring more family oriented shows to television. The networks were becoming more sensitive to concerned groups, who charged that children were being shortchanged by producers more interested in advertising revenues than program content. It was decided that the early prime-time hour was to be set aside for family entertainment.

One would expect that the *Little House* stories would have fit perfectly into the family hour concept, but when Friendly shopped his series around he could find no takers. Apparently because there were no special effects or gimmicks, everyone passed it over. Friendly's next step was to try to tie the series to a major star. Star power, he thought, would sell the show. At some point Michael Landon's name came up, and Friendly found he could envision him in the role of Charles Ingalls. Besides, Landon had considerable influence with NBC, where he had successfully costarred for so many years on *Bonanza*.

Although Landon was attracted to the concept and the material because it would provide him with the opportunity of promoting moral values in a family setting, he did

Michael Landon, as Charles Ingalls, with Karen Grassle as his wife Caroline, sought a new home in the West in _Little House on the Prairie_.

not want to commit himself too fast. He would be putting his career on the line and he did not want to fail. So he took the idea home to discuss with his wife Lynn. In a _TV Guide_ interview, Landon later explained:

> I couldn't make up my mind until I came home and found my 12-year-old daughter Leslie Ann devouring the Laura Ingalls Wilder books. Then I discovered that my wife had devoured them too when she was a girl, and was reading them again. I thought "How wonderful if parents and children can watch this series together—and maybe it would start the kids reading the books after seeing the episodes on television. Imagine a TV show that would make kids read. So I went to NBC and told them _Little House_ was it."[4]

Though they were not as enthusiastic about the series as Landon, NBC gave him a contract because they believed he had the ability to spot what would appeal to television audiences. Even though network executives saw only an uneventful, quiet, dull program, they put their trust in Landon's intuition. Landon disagreed entirely with their interpretation of the *Little House* novels. He believed that the real heart of the series was its realism. "Whether a hundred years ago or today, some things never change, like jealousies in the home, or adolescent love. These are among the adversities that make life what it is—what it really is," he said. Finally NBC agreed to finance a two-hour pilot, and, if ratings warranted, to place it on their fall series lineup.

Landon put a great deal of effort into casting the central characters. Forty-seven actresses auditioned to play Ingalls' wife, Caroline, before Karen Grassle. He knew instantly that Karen would be perfect because she "looked like a pioneer woman." *TV Guide* writer Leslie Raddatz wrote, "In *Little House on the Prairie* Karen Grassle breaks new ground . . . as the pioneering wife and mother, Caroline Ingalls: she is not cast in the glamorous Hollywood image."[5] Raddatz went on to point out that most legendary American pioneer women "are usually described as resolute, dauntless and indomitable" but wind up being portrayed by such glamorous Hollywood beauties as Irene Dunn (*Cimarron*, 1931), Jean Arthur (*Shane*, 1953) and Debbie Reynolds (*How the West Was Won*, 1963). Grassle's prior experience was limited. A graduate of the University of California at Berkeley, she had studied under a Fulbright Scholarship at the Royal Academy of Dramatic Art in London, and then spent several years with various regional repertory theaters in the United States (Memphis, Cincinnati, Boston, Atlanta and finally New York). She also appeared in several daytime television serials and even an episode of *Gunsmoke*. Despite her lack of television credits, she was perfect for the role of Caroline Ingalls.

The hardest task for Landon was casting the children. He had seen enough child actresses in the business to know what he did not want: "professional daughters with stage mothers." He searched for real little girls, and finally settled on Melissa Sue Anderson as Mary, the Ingalls' oldest daughter, and Melissa Gilbert as Laura, the sensitive middle girl and future author. Anderson had been barely 11 years old when she made her first television appearances on episodes of *The Brady Bunch* and *Shaft*. Less than a year later she was cast as one of the leads on *Little House*. Gilbert, on the other hand, had appeared in a commercial at age 3 and later appeared in episodes of *Gunsmoke*, *Emergency*, and *Tenafly*. She was a winsome 9 year old when she won the part of Laura. Carrie, the Ingalls' baby, had to be portrayed by twins. Hollywood's strict work rules for small children made it impossible to get by with just one baby, so identical twin girls (only their parents could tell them apart), Lindsay and Sidney Greenbush landed the role.

Friendly and Landon agreed that the series should have an authentic look. Disagreement arose, however, over the appearance of the children and their father. Many men, among them Ingalls, had full beards in the late 1800s and Friendly was convinced Landon should grow one to look more like Ingalls. He also wanted the children to wear tattered clothes and go barefoot, as they did in the books. After all, the Ingalls were very poor. Landon refused both requests. That was carrying things too far. Landon felt his fans would not accept a beard. He also thought that it would be too dangerous to allow the youngsters to run around barefoot (due to snakes, broken glass, the weather, and so on).[6]

The *Little House on the Prairie* pilot movie premiered on March 30, 1974. The film opened with the voice of Laura telling viewers "how it was when we left our little house in the big woods to go west to Indian Territory" as one of the enduring classics of American literature began to unfold. Due to poor harvests and the harsh Wisconsin climate, Laura and her family travel to the plains of Kansas in search of a new life. Everything they own is on their wagon with them. The country they travel through is lonely and

Mr. and Mrs. Charles Ingalls (Michael Landon and Karen Grassle) with their family. From the top: Laura (Melissa Gilbert), Carrie (Lindsay or Sidney Greenbush), and Mary (Melissa Sue Anderson), in *Little House on the Prairie,* **year one.**

dangerous and the Ingalls clan is forced time after time to rely on their wit, ingenuity and the sheer good luck that often makes the difference in survival. After a long struggle to establish their homestead on the Kansas prairie, they are struck by a new disaster. This time their enemy is civilization. Political interests have redrawn the district lines in their state and the Ingalls must move on.

In addition to starring as Laura's father, Landon codirected and coscripted the two hour pilot and served as executive producer. The film also benefited from the fine photography of Ted Voigtlander, who provided a vivid glimpse of the landscape that faced prairie homesteaders more than a century ago. *The New York Times* television critic John J. O'Connor had mixed feeling about the film. He wrote.

> ... If "The Little House on the Prairie," shown on the National Broadcasting Company network a couple of Saturdays ago, had been presented as a 90-minute afterschool special for young people, the program and the network might have been praised for doing something good in an area begging for something good. Instead, the production was stretched to two hours and run in the adult prime-time slot of 9 to 11 P.M., demanding a different evaluation and considerably less praise.
>
> ... [T]he script contained enough family warmth and struggle to make "The Waltons" look like a pack of pampered snobs ...
>
> ... There was much, however, of purely historical value; the building of the small windowless log cabin; the threat of wild wolf packs and prairie fires; the hunting for fox, muskrat and beaver; the diet of rabbit stew and biscuits.... And then there were the Indians despised and feared by Ma although they were the ones being driven off the land being settled. Pa was more tolerant. And, of course, little Laura was positively radical chic, observing that "it's not fair—they were here first." ...
>
> ... In the end, Mr. Ingalls made his peace with the Indians, neatly blowing the historical fact that the plains of Kansas had been generously seeded with the bodies of murdered Indians.[7]

In conclusion, O'Connor, after noting that the film was a pilot for a possible weekly series, admits that "the idea does have some promise." "The pilot, though," he concludes, "never rose much above the level of those American commercials for 'natural' cereals which insist that they contain no artificial ingredients." Still, those cereals, he points out, are "chock full of sugar" and "the kids will love it."

The people at NBC were elated when the film easily beat its competition by winning a 26.2 rating, which represented 45 percent of all television sets in operation at the time. The series was scheduled into the fall line-up for 8 P.M. Wednesdays. Only Friendly was unhappy and he bowed out over what were called "creative differences." Friendly wanted to stick faithfully to the original storylines of the Wilder books; Landon wanted simply to take incidents from the books and build fictional stories around them. Landon explained:

> ... It would be impossible to follow the books completely. We did the original two-hour pilot and it ate up a whole book. At that rate, it would mean at the end of nine shows we'd have gone through nine books and that would be it. We'll remain faithful to the characters but we have to make at least 22 hours of episodic TV [a year] and every one of those shows will have to carry itself.[8]

It was also more important to Landon that the Ingalls' courage be emphasized rather than the family's weaknesses. An absolutely accurate portrait of Charles Ingalls might not be too flattering, since, in the books, Landon explained, Ingalls was the type of man who could lose a crop and sing a song. Nothing ever bothered him. He was a dreamer. He always wanted to do well but he never had a knack for it. He sometimes moved five times in a year. Landon wanted to play Charles Ingalls as a man beset by adversities, which he overcame because he was strong, wise and concerned about his family. Ingalls would face his difficulties and never accept defeat. This Landon felt, was a more positive message for children than of a man running away from his problems. Not that Landon wanted Charles Ingalls to lose his vulnerability. On the contrary, he saw the series as providing an opportunity to show that a grown man could be emotional. He thought that it was "important for young boys growing up to see a man cry and know that it's not a sign of weakness."[9] Perhaps, that was one of the more important lessons offered by *Little House on the Prairie*.

There were some problems with the network as well: NBC turned down Landon's two hour Thanksgiving Day script about the death, at nine months, of the Ingalls' only son. Too depressing, they said. Nevertheless, with only a few changes it was aired a few weeks later (December 18, 1974) as "The Lord Is My Shepherd," with an upbeat ending. Laura's faith in God is restored. (She had blamed herself for the baby's death, having wished the baby dead because her father appeared to care more for him than for her.) Landon also won a dispute about a proposed story in which Charles Ingalls is suspected of having killed a girl found in his barn because he had made her pregnant. "Over my dead body!" raged Landon. "The story is totally out of character with the nature of Ingalls and the nature of the show."[10] Landon was, of course, right.

In addition to writing, directing and starring, Landon even got personally involved in the *look* of the series. Together with the art director, Trevor Williams, he reviewed more than fifty books on frontier life in Minnesota in the 1870s. They looked at every old photograph they could find. As a result (as John J. O'Connor, among others, had noted), "the show was probably the most authentic, visually, of any ever made about the Old West." Every building was a replica of one that actually existed. Landon later pointed out that even the flapjacks were "big and fat like a discus— the way they were made in those days—instead of the skinny modern ones."

The interior shots were made on two sound stages at Paramount—each about eight stories high and big enough for a football field. Outdoor shots were made mainly in the Simi Valley, about forty miles north and west of Hollywood. The community of Plum Creek was constructed in the arid, khaki-colored desert land of Ventura County. Only the setting was green, watered by several miles of underground pipes that helped to convert California into Minnesota.

With Landon, wearing all his creative hats, at the helm, *Little House* made its fall debut on September 11, 1974. Most critics seemed reluctant to give it unequivocally good notices. As Landon's biographer, Marsha Daly, explained it, "It was as if they resented its simple, sweet characters, and preferred the trash-with-flash type show then making inroads on television."[11] Among the more severe critics was Cleveland Amory of *TV Guide* who wrote:

> ... the show apparently wants to have it both ways—it wants to be both an adult show and a children's show. It isn't bad as either, or, for that matter, as both. But if it had decided to be just one or the other, it would have been a whole lot better. For one thing, it's pretty quiet.... [Y]ou have to be awfully interested in the cast to stay with it.[12]

Later, at the end of the season, Amory somewhat modified his views on the series: "The review that drew the most disagreeable—excuse us, most disagreeing—mail was our critique of *Little House on the Prairie*. Most of the writers put their fingers on the same point—i.e., that it is a good family show.... Anyway we went back and watched it again, and now agree that maybe we were too hard on it."[13]

Kay Gardella wrote in the *Daily News*, "This could easily out–Walton the Waltons

Laura Ingalls (Melissa Gilbert, with Michael Landon) prepares to race her horse against a neighbor's in the episode "The Race," on *Little House on the Prairie*.

and take the polish off the Apples," while admitting, "Landon is likeable, the cast is good, and all of the warm family values are there...."[14] Richard Schidel of *Time* claimed that "Star-Producer Michael Landon looks as if he just stepped out of a unisex beauty salon on the Strip rather than 430 episodes of *Bonanza*," but he too had to admit that the show "genuinely seems to be striving for a simple, straightforward style, minimizing both melodramatic and sentimental excesses."[15]

The most critical review was found in *Variety*, "that jaded bastion of show business information," which labeled the new series "a saccharine imitation of *The Waltons*" and " a victim of superficial characters." Landon was dismissed with the comment that "he directs himself in the lead with plastic sentimentality."[16] On the other hand Arthur Unger writing for the *Christian Science Monitor* was one of *Little House*'s most enthusiastic supporters:

> Gather round the hearth tonight (a flickering TV set will do) and spend an hour with a family so wholesome they make the Waltons look like juvenile delinquents.
>
> Yes, goodness, honesty . . . and joy premiered last Wednesday night on NBC and, one hopes, will find a permanent home there for years to come. *Little House* has confounded those pre-season scoffers (myself included) who predicted merely a syrupy sweetness-and-light variation of *The Waltons*, sort of a *Waltons Go West*. Well, certainly *Little House* is sweet—but it also sounds a gong of integrity which resounds loud and clear throughout every moment of the hour.
>
> . . . *Little House* is neither pure fantasy nor pure reality . . . [rather it] somehow combines the two into a unique child-adult, real-unreal world reflecting a purity and truthfulness all its own. Plum Creek, Minn., represents a sort of moral Shangri La: the way things ought to be once more. If by chance things were never actually quite like that—well, they should have been.
>
> . . . [T]o watch *Little House on the Prairie* is to fall in love with a time, a place, a way of life, a particular family, an astounding skillful production . . . magically, instead of oozing out as cloying cliché, it triumphs as heartwarming honesty . . .
>
> To make a series as marvelously unsophisticated as this one requires the ultimate in sophistication. Real sophistication—not that superficial reliance on trend and fad which too often passes for worldliness today. But a deep understanding of the nature of people in their places. . . .
>
> *Little House* evokes an ambivalent response of mixed joy and sorrow in the viewer. The sweet sadness of innocence? . . . or is it that we weep for the loss of innocence . . . in ourselves and in society?[17]

Landon could certainly not have written a better review himself.

As for the constant comparisons with *The Waltons*, Landon was flattered to be in such company. Responding to an interviewer's query, he explained:

> Any show that doesn't promise murder and mayhem is now accused of being a *Walton* copy. All I can do is make a show that I like, that I have pride in. I don't want the Ingalls family to become a sweetsy how-wonderful-we-are kind of family. I'd like them to come through as a family held together by enough love so that everybody understands that nobody is perfect, that we all make mistakes, that if we just talk to each other we can figure out what to do about the mistakes.[18]

The first episode, "A Harvest of Friends" begins where the two-hour pilot left off: the Ingalls move to Plum Creek; they build a house with their own hands; the children go off to school in homespun clothing; and they make friends with the residents of the nearby eight house town of Walnut Grove. Father Charles has to moonlight at the town mill to pay for a plough and seed. When he is injured, his neighbors come to his assistance.

In the second episode, "Country Girls," the older girls run into prejudice, a spoiled brat, a playground bully and ultimately love and understanding when they attend the little Walnut Grove one-room school. In subsequent episodes, the Ingalls crop is destroyed by a hailstorm and Charles must find work far from home. After "The 100 Mile Walk," he works as a blaster in a mine until he can save enough to return to farming. Later stories range from such lighthearted subjects as bachelor neighbor, Mr. Edwards, babysitting the three Ingalls girls ("Ma's Holiday") and log splitting contests ("Founder's Day") to the more serious problems of love ("Doctor's Lady"), illness ("Plague") and death ("The Lord Is My Shepherd").

Compared to the pilot's showing, *Little House*'s initial ratings were low. The network, NBC, was concerned, but it was struggling with most of its offerings and Landon's series was considered one of its better bets. Although not as high as expected, the ratings were steady, which indicated that *Little House* was holding on to its viewers. Furthermore, NBC was not about to "pull the plug" on a program that had received high praise from parent and teacher groups all across the country. Fortunately NBC realized that quality shows often take time to build an audience and its loyalty ultimately paid off. By the end of the season, *Little House* had climbed into the top 20 (finishing at number 13) and it became one of NBC's most popular prime time series. (For four years, 1977–1981, it was NBC's highest rated show, reaching seventh on the Nielsen chart in 1977-78.) After the show had been on the air for four years, Landon commented on its success:

> I think the show is successful because it's what real families are all about. Despite what you see in the movies and on many TV screens, loving families do exist. They don't spend hours screaming and yelling at each other. What's wrong with a show that depicts family love: I feel sorry for people who think "Little House" is too sweet to be true. That's baloney.[19]

During the first several seasons *Little House* relied on a judicious combination of series regulars and competent guest stars. Academy Award winners like Ernest Borgnine ("The Lord Is My Shepherd"), Red Buttons ("The Circus Man") and Patricia Neal ("Remember Me") were used along with established performers such as Forrest Tucker ("Founder's Day"), Richard Basehart ("Troublemaker"), Theodore Bikel ("Centennial"), Johnny Cash ("The Collection"), Burl Ives ("The Hunters"), John Ireland ("Little Girl Lost"), Ray Bolger ("As Long As We're Together" and "Come Dance with Me"), Arthur Hill (as Charles' father in "Journey in the Spring") and Barry Sullivan (as Caroline's father in "Author, Author").

Other guests gave the series a second generation flavor: Dirk Blocker ("School Mom"), son of the late Dan Blocker, *Bonanza*'s "Hoss"; Anne Archer ("Doctor's Lady"), daughter of *Make Room for Daddy*'s Marjorie Lord and film actor John Archer; Julie Cobb ("Money Crop"), daughter of actor Lee J. Cobb of *The Virginian*. Landon's friend, actor-director Victor French, appeared in the pilot film and came back for several appearances as Mr. Edwards, eventually becoming a series regular (1974-1977 and 1982-83). He also directed several episodes. Mostly, the series stuck to stories about the farmer, his family and his close friends.

Among the most important early regulars in the cast were Karl Swenson as Lars Hanson (founder of Walnut Grove and owner of the town mill); Richard Bull as the decent, hard-working store owner Nels Oleson; Katherine MacGregor as Oleson's snobbish and prejudiced (but humorous) wife Harriet; and Alison Arngrim as their spoiled daughter Nellie; Jonathan Gilbert as their bratty son Willie; Kevin Hagen as the dedicated town doctor, Dr. Baker (several of the series' finest episodes featured this character—"Doctor's Lady," "Plague," "To Run and Hide," and " A Child with No Name" to list a few); and Dabbs Greer as the kindly Reverend Alden.

There is considerable difference of opinion as to whether or not *Little House on the Prairie* should be considered a Western—and further, whether it should be classified as a "soap opera." Writers and critics tend to be split on the first question. In *Harry and Wally's Favorite TV Shows*, authors Harry Castleman and Walter J. Podrazik describe the series as "not so much a western as a prairie soap opera."[20] J. Fred MacDonald simply ignores the show in *Who Shot the Sheriff?* Richard West, author of the brief (and largely inaccurate) *Television Westerns*, classifies the series as a "schmaltzy" sitcom.[21] Tim Brooks and Earle Marsh, in their authoritative *Complete Directory to Prime Time TV Shows*, point out that *Little House* was "not a Western in the usual sense."[22] On the other hand, Douglas Brode, writing in the *Television Quarterly*, described the series this way:

Perhaps it first hit the national consciousness that the cowboy hero was a thing of the past when NBC premiered *Little House on the Prairie* in 1974. A decade and a half earlier, farmers were relegated to secondary roles in westerns as the unromantic hardworking characters a roaming cowboy hero must help out of a jam. Now, our national vision and collective sensibility had shifted drastically enough that the routine existence of farmers could touch us in a way that an idealized image of cowboys as rugged individualists could not.[23]

Edward Buscombe, in his comprehensive *BFT Companion to the Western*, lists the series as a "domestic Western" structured in the same fashion as other pioneering family-on-the-move dramas such as *The Chisholms*.[24] *Little House* is also listed by Buck Rainey in *The Shoot-'Em-Ups Ride Again* as one of ten in the "second echelon of television rangeland series"; he stresses that "the stories were more frontier than Western and more about farmers and domestic problems than about cowboys and Indians."[25] Most television critics and reviewers have classified the program as a "pioneer drama" or a "family Western." Indeed, what are the essential criteria of a Western but time and place. Nearly every other television series which is set west of the Mississippi in the nineteenth century is classified as a Western. Just because there are few cowboys or Indians, little gunplay and a scarcity of saloons does not divorce the show from the genre. In fact a number of examples of the aforementioned ingredients can be readily cited by any regular viewer of the series.

The Ingalls come in contact with both cowboys and Indians in the two-hour pilot. Later in "Freedom Flight" (fourth season) an ailing Sioux chief is brought to Dr. Baker by his son, Little Crow. The Ingalls give the Indians refuge and subsequently help them escape when a group of hostile townspeople attempt to kill them. (Ironically, this episode is at variance with historical fact. Little Crow, who was chief of the Kapozha band of the Mdewakanton Sioux, led an uprising near New Ulm, Minnesota, in 1862 and was later killed on July 3, 1863. The *Little House* episode which takes place about 1878 presents Little Crow sympathetically as a man of reason and peace seeking only to lead his tribe to sanctuary in Canada.)

Several episodes deal with the gunmen and violence so common to the Western genre. During the fourth season, the legendary James brothers appear in Walnut Grove. They are seeking refuge under assumed names and the guise of respectability after their abortive bank robbery in Northfield, Minnesota. This incident actually occurred in 1876, close to the time of the story, and is at least historically plausible. Mary Ingalls befriends the brothers and is then taken hostage by the two, only to be rescued by her father in exchange for helping them escape. There is considerable gunplay as a band of bounty hunters show up and fill an empty farmhouse full of lead in the mistaken assumption that the James brothers are hiding there.

The episode, however, which best captures the flavor of the classic Western is the first part of a two-part story entitled "He Was Only Twelve" (broadcast at the end of the eighth season). In the episode James (adopted son of the Ingalls) is seriously wounded in a bank robbery. Charles and Isaiah Edwards track the robbers down. Isaiah is forced to shoot one while Charles almost strangles the other. It is a classic Western story in every respect.

Gunplay is also featured during the final season of *Little House: A New Beginning* in an episode about a band of bank robbers known as the Younger Brothers, humorously entitled "The Older Brothers." This is a delightful spoof of the traditional shoot-'em-up Western. A saloon also plays a prominent role in the episodes set in Winoka. Thus, while violence, gunfights, Indians, and other typical elements of standard Western fare were not common to the series, they were occasionally employed. After all, the stories were set in the American West of the 1870s and 80s.

The entire Ingalls family during the sixth season of *Little House on the Prairie*: from left, Matthew Laborteaux as Albert; Melissa Gilbert, Michael Landon, Dean Butler as Almanzo Wilder, Melissa Sue Anderson, Linwood Boomer as Adam Kendall; with Karen Grassle and one of the Greenbush twins in front.

As to whether *Little House* should be classified as a "soap opera," the evidence is far less clear. Harry Castleman and Walter J. Podrazik categorically describe the show as "a prairie soap opera" and "like all soaps," they continue, "if you get involved with the characters you can overlook many minor flaws and weaknesses in the show."[26] Tim Brooks and Earle Marsh revert to comparing the series to *The Waltons* "in a different setting . . . the story of a loving family in trying times." As time went on, they assert, "the program became more and more like a serial."[27] Certainly, by following the hardships and triumphs of one family and their friends, the series did come to resemble the traditional "soap opera." Early episodes relate the efforts of Charles, his wife and their three daughters to adjust to life in the young and growing frontier community of Walnut Grove. Stories dramatize the experiences of the family in their constant struggle against the forces of nature and their relationships with other members of the town.

Many of the events that were dramatized on the series were taken directly from Laura's books or from the actual lives of the Ingalls family (through not necessarily in chronological order). Although often embellished with fictional details and subplots, such actual events as the birth (and death nine months later) of the only Ingalls son, Charles Frederick Ingalls (in the two part "The Lord Is My Shepherd"); the great blizzard of 1880 (in "Blizzard"); the birth of a fourth daughter, Grace (in "A Most Precious Gift"); oldest daughter Mary's loss of sight (Melissa Sue Anderson was nominated for an Emmy for her performance) and her subsequent attendance at a school for the blind (in the two part "I'll Be Waving as You Drive Away"); the family's move from Walnut Grove to Winoka, Dakota Territory (actually the family moved earlier to Burr Oak, Iowa), to work in a hotel (in the two part "As Long As We're Together"); their subsequent return to Walnut Grove (in the two part "There's No Place Like Home"); Laura's becoming a teacher (depicted in various episodes); the engagement and marriage of Laura to Almanzo Wilder (in the two part "Laura Ingalls Wilder"); the birth of a daughter, Rose, to the young couple (in "I Do, Again"); and the birth of a baby boy to the Wilders and his death twelve days later (in "A Child With No Name") are all included.

As one might expect many of the stories were pure fabrications—most written by Michael Landon himself (it is presumed with the assistance of Blanche Hanalis who "developed" the books "for television"). Each, of course, was true to the spirit of the book stories. For example, when Victor French was given his own series, *Carter Country*, Mr. Edwards leaves Walnut Grove. His character is replaced by Jonathan Garvey (played by former Los Angeles Rams star Merlin Olsen). Garvey comes to town with a wife named Alice and a young son, Andy (in "Castoffs"). Another new fictional character is added when Mary falls in love with her instructor at the school for the blind, Adam Kendall (played by Linwood Boomer). The couple marries in Winoka, where they both teach in a school for the blind (in "The Wedding"). When Walnut Grove falls on hard times and the whole family moves to Winoka, another cast member is added—Albert, a young orphan they later adopt, played by Matthew Laborteaux (in the two part " As Long As We're Together").

Eventually everyone, including Mary and Adam, moves back to Walnut Grove, where Mary has a baby boy who is tragically killed (along with Alice Garvey) in a fire that burns down the school for the blind they had established (in the two part "May We Make Them Proud"). Jonathan Garvey, now a widower, moves to Sleepy Eye to manage a warehouse, and convinces Charles to set up a freight business between there and Walnut Grove (in "A New Beginning"). Soon thereafter, Adam regains his sight as the result of a freak accident and is accepted into law school (in the two part "To See the Light"). Later Adam's father offers him a position in his law firm in New York and the couple leaves Walnut Grove forever.

In stories focusing on other series characters, Nellie Oleson marries a promising young Jewish accountant named Percival Dalton played by Steve Tracy (in "He Loves Me, He Loves Me Not"). When Nellie becomes pregnant, a conflict arises over how the child will be raised. Since Nellie has twins, the dispute is resolved by deciding to raise the son as a Jew and the daughter as a Christian (in "Come Let Us Reason Together").

Dean Butler and Melissa Gilbert played Mr. and Mrs. Almanzo Wilder on *Little House on the Prairie.*

There are several more cast changes before the series is given a new name. The parents of James Cooper (James Bateman) and his sister Cassandra (Missy Francis) lose their lives when their wagon overturns, leaving the children homeless. They are adopted by Charles and Caroline in the last episode of the seventh season (part two of "The Lost Ones"). The eighth season opens with the Olesons taking in an orphan named Nancy (Allison Balson) who bears a striking resemblance to the departed Nellie in both appearance and personality (in "The Reincarnation of Nellie"). And Isaiah Edwards, whose problems with drinking had resulted in a failed marriage, returns to Walnut Grove the following spring ("A Promise To Keep").

The most radical changes result from Michael Landon's decision to leave the series in the fall of 1982. The title is changed to *Little House: A New Beginning* and focuses on the lives of Laura and her husband Almanzo. Economic problems have forced Charles to sell "the little house" and move to Burr Oak, Iowa, where he has found a new job. Moving into the Ingalls' home is John (Stan Ivar) and Sarah Carter (Pamela Roylance) who run the town newspaper and their sons Jeb (Lindsay Kennedy) and Jason (David Friedman) and some of the episodes feature these characters.

Laura gives up her teaching job to raise her daughter Rose and her niece Jenny (Shannon Doherty), who is orphaned when her father (Almanzo's brother) dies (in the two part "Times Are Changing"). (The new schoolteacher, Etta Plum, is played by Michael Landon's daughter Leslie.) Laura even tries her hand at publishing a novel based on her childhood experiences, but is unwilling to make changes in the story to satisfy the publisher (in "Once Upon a Time"). It is, of course, too early for Laura Ingalls Wilder's stories to be published. (In reality, Laura was 65 years old when the first *Little House* book was published.)

Only 21 episodes of *Little House: A New Beginning* were broadcast and the series came to an end during its tenth season on the air with three two-hour "special" films. In "The Last Farewell," Walnut Grove is actually blown up by the townspeople to prevent it from falling into the hands of a ruthless land baron. Ten years earlier, when NBC leased the large parcel of land on which the series was filmed from the Getty Oil Company and the Newhall Land and Development Corporation, they agreed that when they were through with the location, they would restore it to its original state. So when the network and Michael Landon decided to cancel the show, they knew the elaborate sets would have to be destroyed. It was Landon's idea to incorporate that contractual obligation into the story and dismantle the sets on camera. The plot he concocted has an unscrupulous businessman legally buying up title to the town—and the only protest the residents can make is to destroy their own property rather than see it taken over by him. Landon later explained in a *New York Times* interview:

> I think it makes for a good strong pioneer ending. It was also a nice catharsis for the cast and crew. There were lots of tears when we finally blew up the town. The actors had all become very attached to their own buildings, so it was all very emotional.[28]

After a few tests to see that no one would get hurt, the destruction of the town "went like clockwork" in one day. Only the original "little house," occupied for eight of the series' ten years by the Ingalls family, was left standing. Landon felt its demolition might be too traumatic an experience for the television audience, especially the younger viewers. Ironically, Walnut Grove appeared (intact) one last time, thanks to the capriciousness of the television programmers. A Christmas episode filmed earlier was broadcast several months after "The Last Farewell" when NBC decided, at the last minute, to reverse the order in which the shows were to be shown. A voice-over was used to explain that the events dramatized in "Bless All the Dear Children" occurred a few weeks before the destruction of the town.

Why was the long running saga of life on the agrarian frontier terminated? Landon felt it had run its course, partly because ratings were declining in the last season and also because Laura (or rather, Melissa Gilbert) had grown from a young girl to a woman. "I didn't think a married woman should still be coming to her father for advice," Landon explained. "But when we started this show, we never imagined it would last this long."[29] Thus while many of the characteristics of a soap opera may be found in *Little House on the Prairie*, the series ranks far above contemporary daytime soaps in authenticity, plausibility, sincerity and quality of production values. Even the popular and long-running contemporary Western soap *Dallas* (1978 to 1991) cannot compare with *Little House* in its attempts to depict honestly a time, a place and a family's way of life. (The only other Western series that might correctly be classified as a soap is *The Yellow Rose*, broadcast during the 1983-84 season, which starred David Soul, Edward Albert, Cybill Shepherd and Sam Elliott.)

Furthermore, many of the *Little House* episodes deal with social issues. For example, prejudice of various kinds is frequently held up to ridicule or scorn with that perennial representative of "opinion formed in disregard of facts," Harriet Oleson, inevitably being taught the error of her ways. "Dark Sage" deals with racial prejudice against a black doctor; in "Whisper Country" it is prejudice of a more insidious kind, against new ideas (as expressed through education); "Come, Let Us Reason Together" concerns a form of antisemitism; and "Injun Kid" focuses on white resentment toward Indians (or in this case a half–Indian boy). Perhaps, the most powerful example of prejudice can be found in "Little Lou," which was broadcast during the last season of *Little House: A New Beginning*. This episode, like so many of the better ones, was written by Michael Landon and concerns prejudice (and subsequent discrimination) against "little people" (midgets). Lou Bates (superbly portrayed by Billy Barty), whose wife has died in childbirth, tries to get a job as a bank teller in Walnut Grove so he can support his infant daughter and mother. He is thwarted at every turn by Mrs. Oleson. Here is found one of the clearest descriptions of prejudice ever written. When John Carter asks Harriet Oleson why she is so against Lou Bates settling in Walnut Grove, she responds:

> I don't want *his kind* here in Walnut Grove... He's deformed. *He's not like us.* He's a troll, that's what he is... He's spent his entire life in a sideshow... Let him earn a living somewhere else... Because, *he's not like us.* I don't trust him with the children. He's... *He's different!*

Of course, when Lou rescues little Nancy Oleson, who has fallen down a well, Harriet realizes the error in her judgment. In a quite moving scene, she apologizes to Lou. (It is interesting to note the similarity between this story and a *Bonanza* episode entitled "It's a Small World," also written by Landon, dealing with discrimination against a midget played by Michael Dunn.)

The subject of aging is also treated with compassion and tolerance in several episodes of the series. During the first season, the episode "Founder's Day" deals with the pride of a man who has long been the best at his trade. However, he refuses to accept the fact that age is taking its toll and he is slowing down. In the fourth season, "Castoffs" presents the harmless fantasies of an elderly woman and how she is perceived by her fellow townspeople (as seen through Laura's eyes). "Come Dance with Me" brings back the delightful Ray Bolger in the role of the aging Toby Noe (a role he originated in part one of "There's No Place Like Home" earlier in the fifth season). Romance between "senior citizens" is the story's subject.

The related issue of death is treated with reverence and respect in several of the most moving episodes of the series. From "The Lord Is My Shepherd" during the first season to "Times Are Changing" during the final full season, death is a continuing reality with which Laura and her family must repeatedly deal. The two part "May We Make Them Proud" in which both a child (Mary's son) and a parent (Jonathan's wife) are killed in a tragic fire is probably the most emotional story of the entire series. The two hour special "Look Back to Yesterday," in which Albert and his family come to realize that he is dying from an incurable blood disease, also handles this subject in a mature and intelligent manner. (Ironically in an earlier episode, Laura tells viewers that Albert grows up to become "a doctor of great service to Walnut Grove." This contradiction is never explained.)

More contemporary and controversial problems like drug addiction, child abuse, premarital sex, rape and even menopause are also considered in various episodes of the series. In the fourth season (in "Be My Friend," a 90 minute episode), a young girl (Lenora May) has a child out of wedlock, hiding it from her disapproving father (Donald Moffat). She puts notes (asking simply, "Be my friend") in a series of bottles that she drops in a stream. They are found by Laura who convinces her father to help her find the sender. Instead they find her apparently abandoned baby. Later they succeed in

reuniting the baby's father (a blacksmith's son) and mother and saving the child's grandfather from a fire he has set to destroy his "sinful" daughter. The moral here is not clear:
apparently premarital sex is okay as long as the two young people involved really love each
other. (One wonders what the various PTA organizations thought about that particular
episode.)

Even more confusing is the position taken by the series on rape. In the controversial
two part story "Sylvia," a 14 year old motherless girl (Olivia Bavash) is raped by a man
in a mask (who later turns out to be the village blacksmith) while on her way home from
school. Her father (Royal Dano) blames her for somehow inviting the attack and takes
her out of school, planning to move away where no one will know of her shame. Sylvia
tries to run away with Albert, who has fallen in love with her, but she is attacked again
by the rapist (Richard Jaeckel) and falls to her death while trying to escape. This story
provoked considerable reaction, including a letter from one Mary R. Morgan of New
York City, a parttime teacher, writer and mother of several young children, which was
published in the August 1981 issue of *Channels of Communication*. She wrote:

> At twelve years old, my daughter was both frightened by the subject matter and in-
> credulous that *Little House* should put on such a show . . . and, on the other hand, she felt
> maybe something like that could actually happen.
> I was shocked because the educationally harmful and sexually exploitative message given
> by these two programs must have left many young viewers in a state of fear and confusion. . . .
> I feel the girl's death at the end of the program produces an added destructive twist: She is
> mistreated, rejected as unclean, and then somehow must die. What is *Little House* saying?
> That victims of rape are punishable by death?
> Perhaps the most serious implication of these two shows is that there is no longer any
> family programming that parents can trust.[30]

This was an obvious overreaction to the show. Warnings were made in both the
newspaper and magazine television listings and before each episode was broadcast, that
it might contain "material too intense for young children." Nonetheless, the distressing
conclusion to the story was not in keeping with the series' usual upbeat (or uplifting)
endings.

Almost as surprising was Landon's treatment of the subject of menopause in "I Do,
Again." Although handled in a realistic and positive way by Caroline, it was still an
unusual topic for the series to tackle. In the final season, *Little House: A New Beginning*
presented the story of a mistreated deaf boy ("The Wild Boy") in two episodes and considered the issue of drug abuse (in the two hour "Home Again"). In the latter episode
Charles Ingalls returns to Walnut Grove in an attempt to rehabilitate Albert, who has
become addicted to morphine. Both of these problems are treated with the good taste fans
of the series had come to expect.

Virtually every episode of the series included some religious or moral lesson. Landon, who wrote most of the scripts was at a loss later to explain exactly how this happened:

> I sit down with the Ingalls family characters in mind and it begins to flow, and what goes
> on those pages is like a miracle. While I'm writing I lose all sense of myself, where I am and
> what I'm doing. I don't even know what day it is. I write a whole show straight through in
> one sitting. Then when I read it, what's on those pages is incredible to me. The content of
> each script always has something to do with faith and God, subjects that have never been big
> in my conversations. It's as though God is the one writing those scripts, using my mind and
> my hands. . . . Maybe, I am a religious man and don't even know it.[31]

So where does *Little House* fit into the history of television Westerns? It was certainly
a step above the traditional "soap opera" and considerably more than a "domestic Western."

Unquestionably, it was one of the best-loved television programs of all time. A 1975 poll of *Scholastic Newstime*, a publication for elementary students, named the show their national favorite by a wide margin and it was almost always found in the Nielsen top 25.[32] As recently as June 1993, nearly ten years after the last original episode of *Little House* was broadcast, some 65,000 readers polled by *TV Guide* named the series the "All-Time Best Family Show" by a considerable margin. The editors commented:

> [Readers] voted for "Little House on the Prairie" followed by "The Waltons." It's hard to argue with these preferences—they're both warmhearted period pieces that hark back to a kind of simple, close-knit family life that seems all but extinct. and "Little House's" victory may also be testament to the enduring popularity of the late Michael Landon.[33]

Meanwhile, Ed Friendly had tried his hand at producing a program based on a book by Laura Ingalls Wilder's daughter, Rose Wilder Lane. The series focused on a couple of teenage newlyweds from Iowa, Molly and David Beaton, who had settled on the inhospitable Dakota frontier. Starring Linda Purl and Roger Kern, *The Young Pioneers* was completely faithful to the book. Reviewing the two-hour pilot, *New York Times* critic John J. O'Connor proclaimed it "excellent" and further noted that it was the work of the same team (producer Friendly and writer Blanche Hanalis) that had created *Little House on the Prairie* "which was subsequently turned into insubstantial cotton candy by Michael Landon...."[34] Friendly also produced a two-hour sequel, *The Young Pioneers' Christmas*. However, when ABC bought the show, Lorimar Productions took over. They hired *The Waltons'* Earl Hammer and Lee Rick to produce the new series, but it was canceled after only three episodes.

In 1981 Landon himself decided to do a new series for NBC which would closely resemble *Little House on the Prairie*. This time, however, he would work strictly behind the scenes. Called *Father Murphy* after the lead character, it relates the adventures of John Michael Murphy, a gold prospector of the 1870s who impersonates a priest to save a group of orphans from the workhouse.

Delivering a cartload of goods to a small town in the Dakota Territory, Murphy discovers that the entire town is owned and controlled by a nasty boss. Seeking to rally the local prospectors, he teams up with a black drifter named Moses Gage. The boss and his henchmen retaliate by blowing up the miners' camp, thereby orphaning some two dozen children. Murphy decides to establish and run (with the help of a schoolteacher named Mae Woodward) the Gold Hill School for these parentless children. (The very first scene had established Murphy as an orphan himself, who had been sent out on his own after his father had been killed.) To make the orphanage appear legitimate, the bearded prospector poses as a priest ("Father" Murphy). While Murphy and Mae try to teach and care for the children, they are threatened at every turn by two pompous representatives of the Dakota Territory Authority, Howard Rodman and Miss Tuttle, who seek to have the children sent to the territorial workhouse at Claymore. Finally (in a show broadcast in the spring of 1982), when Murphy's deception is exposed, he and Mae get married, adopt all the children and endeavor to keep the family together.

For the crucial lead role, Landon had selected one of his buddies from *Little House*, Merlin Olsen. Olsen, a former professional football star, was cut from the same mold as Dan Blocker—big, soft-spoken and lovable. He was also a devout family man and Mormon, and in the words of John J. O'Connor, "radiated an uncommonly pleasant kind of personality."[35] Moses Gunn (as Moses Gage) and Katherine Cannon (as Mae Woodward) were also excellent choices for the two key supporting roles. There were lots of appealing youngsters around too, led by Timothy Gibbs as Will Adams.

It was disappointing to Landon that the series was canceled after only two seasons. It was *Little House on the Prairie* that would stand as Landon's most important and lasting contribution to the television Western.

Based on one of the most successful series of children's books of all time, *Little House on the Prairie* focused in Landon's words, "on the little things nobody seems to care about today—the simple needs of people and how difficult it was in those days out West to supply them."[36] *Little House* presented unusually realistic stories of life on the farmers' frontier in a warm and caring manner.

XVI. Which Way Did They Go?

OR, HAS THE TELEVISION WESTERN RIDDEN OFF INTO THE SUNSET FOR THE LAST TIME?

What has become of the television Western? How could the American public so embrace a genre and then so completely cast it aside? Is there a future for Westerns on television? Critics have been wrestling with these questions for twenty years—ever since *Gunsmoke* rode off for the last time into the video sunset. The observations of Associated Press writer Lee Margulies, writing in 1976, shed some light on this perplexing subject:

> What killed the television Western was demographics. There were too many series and the plots became too familiar.... [T]he biggest problem was that the cowboys were discovered to be lacking in appeal to the right audience, the 18- to 49-year old city-dwellers who are the primary target of most TV advertisers.[1]

Former NBC programming chief Larry White concluded that "the traditional Western fulfilled certain fantasies for people who grew up in the twenties, thirties, and forties— independence, rugged determination, romance, the pioneer spirit. But the form, at least in its traditional, usually simplistic depiction of good guys versus bad guys, is not meaningful in that way to younger people. Audience appetites are more sophisticated ... they want a closer approach to reality...."[2] Michael Isner, then head of prime time production at ABC, added: "It's a different country today than it was 25 years ago, and television in a way reflects the attitudes of the country. People have moved out of rural America and into the big metropolises. They've replaced their shotgun with a Saturday Night Special...."[3]

More recently William A. Henry III, the Pulitzer-Prize winning media critic and associate editor of *Time Magazine*, wrote a perceptive analysis for the December 1989-January 1990 issue of *Memories*. It is his view that the mythical "simplicity and purity," which was so essential to the Western's popularity in the fifties, "made it wrong for the 60's, and painfully out of sync with the 70's." The political turbulence of the sixties with the explosion of the civil rights movement and the rise of the feminist movement, coupled with growing opposition to the war in Vietnam and an increasing revulsion toward violence in general resulting from a sickening series of assassinations, made the Western less and less relevant. The American people were rejecting "rugged individualism" in favor of "collective action." According to Henry,

> As blacks and other minorities grew more assertive of their rights, they grew less tolerant of entertainments, no matter how accurate historically, that showed them being put down. At the same time, the nation as a whole slipped from jingoistic pride in wars of conquest against American Indian tribes to a distinct sense of shame.... [Furthermore], the women's movement changed the consciousness of the nation's wives and mothers, and of their husbands and sons. As a result of the new value placed on male sensitivity rather than stoicism, the nation's male archetype shifted from John Wayne to Alan Alda.[4]

There were, of course, significant changes in American foreign affairs as well. The cold war was replaced by détente, which later gave way to "glasnost" and ultimately to the collapse of Communism in the Soviet Union. Furthermore, Henry contends that "trends within the television industry" also hurt the Western:

> The shows were expensive to make and required at least some costly and inconvenient on-location shooting (to convey the sense of sweeping vistas), and increasing concern as union and other wages rapidly escalated.[5]

All of this was occurring in a genre that appealed primarily to children, senior citizens and poor, unsophisticated rural viewers—widely regarded by advertisers as the least susceptible "to pitches for impulse-purchase of consumer goods."

Henry believes that the most significant factor in explaining the passing of the Western was "the passing of the West itself, both as physical reality and as personal memory."[6] The frontier, with its brave sheriff standing up to the land barons and corrupt political bosses, had been part of the "dominant image of the American past" from the turn of the century through the fifties. Today, however, he argues, "the quintessential American image is the immigrant melting pot of Ellis Island" and "the struggle to break free of urban ghettos ... seems a lot more meaningful than those great voyages across the windswept plains." Moreover, while people are still moving west in significant numbers, this West is a "New West" of skyscraper cities and neatly regulated suburbs. "No [television] cowpoke could be comfortable for long," he concludes, "in a country where Mustang refers to an automobile and Colt .45 is just a pop-top can of brew."[7]

Does this mean that the television Western is dead, as television historian J. Fred MacDonald contends in his widely acclaimed study, *Who Shot the Sheriff?* With various aspects of the genre "co-opted by space adventures, urban police dramas, seductive prime-time soap operas and even situation comedies," MacDonald sees little reason to expect its resurrection. In fact he predicts "the possibility of its extinction by the twenty-first century."[8] Have other genres "co-opted" essential elements of the Western? One school of thought finds them thriving in space epics like *Star Wars*, which makes some sense at first glance: Luke Skywalker who must grow up fast after his family has been wiped out; Han Solo as the outlaw hero; Chewbacca as his humorous sidekick; Princess Leia as the spunky heroine; and Darth Vader as the irredeemably evil villain are "all archetypal Western forms."[9] This school holds the view that the only element missing from the "modern" Western is that there is no longer a West—the only unexplored frontier today is space, the "last frontier." The only problem with this explanation is that Hollywood has been making space epics almost as long as Westerns. Flash Gordon and Hopalong Cassidy appeared side by side on the home screen from almost the dawn of television. Moreover, with the exception of the *Star Trek* phenomenon, there have been few successful space epics recently either.

It is even more difficult to make a case for cop drama "Westerns." Those who hold this view liken 80-mile-an-hour car chases to 20-mile-an-hour horse chases, see the "new" frontier as the urban ghetto, complete with roving outlaw gangs, and proclaim *The A-Team* to be the modern reincarnation of *Bonanza*, Michael Knight of *Knight Rider* to be television's newest version of Paladin, and *Hill Street Blues*, an urbanized form of *Gunsmoke*. This analogy lacks as much credibility as the space epic theory. *Dragnet* battled *Gunsmoke* for number one in the ratings during its first years on the tube; later *Hawaii-Five-O* challenged *Gunsmoke*'s popularity. For years *The F.B.I.* provided strong Sunday night competition for *Bonanza*. In fact cops and robbers shows have coexisted with Westerns from the earliest days of network television.

According to Knight-Ridder News Service columnist Bill Cosford, "the closest parallel we find in today's films to formula Westerns is Sylvester Stallone's *Rambo* series,"[10] with a lone hero (shades of Paladin) fighting the Asiatic hoards (replacing the Indian as villain). There does not, however, appear to be any comparable series, as yet, on the home screen.

In order to more carefully assess the present state of the television Western, a careful analysis of television Westerns in all guises during the past decade is needed. With the exception of the 1989 miniseries *Lonesome Dove*, the two hour second season opening episode of *Paradise* (1989), the two hour pilot of *Dr. Quinn, Medicine Woman* (1993), and the opening segment of *Return to Lonesome Dove* (1993), none has cracked the Nielsen top ten.

In the spring of 1985 ABC made a half-hearted attempt to revive the moribund genre with a promising series called *Wildside*. The major problem was with scheduling. It was slotted at 8 p.m. Eastern time on Thursdays opposite two of the most popular shows on the air—*The Cosby Show* (NBC) and *Magnum P.I.* (CBS). To no one's surprise it lasted only six weeks (March 21–April 25). This was unfortunate since the series showed signs of promise. The show was produced by the newly formed Touchstone Division of Walt Disney Productions and was their most ambitious television effort since the long-running Disney anthology.

Critics gave the series mixed reviews, describing it as a Western version of *Mission Impossible* and *The A-Team* while comparing it to *The Wild Wild West*. Actually the series had more in common with that classic film *The Magnificent Seven*. The stories were built around five prominent citizens who resided in the frontier town of Wildside, California, during the decade following the Civil War. When trouble threatened their community, they banded together to dispense their own brand of law enforcement, or as the narrator intoned during the opening credits: "Into a lawless land they brought their own style of justice—five men, one mission . . . the Chamber of Commerce of Wildside." A journalist in one of the episodes described them a little more poetically:

> On the surface they display the calm exterior of a mountain range. Underneath they are chaos in a bottle of pandemonium. Woe to that outlaw or renegade who dares to open the bottle or attempts to dilute its contents.

The characters were well-drawn. Their unofficial leader seemed to be rancher Brodie Hollister ("fastest gun in the West"). The only one who could match his skill with a six-gun was his son, Sutton. The black owner-manager of the community's general store, Bannister Sparks, was also an expert with explosives. The proprietor of the local gunshop was actually a transplanted Argentinean Gaucho, Vargas De La Cosa, who was a master in the use of the knife and the bola. Completing the quintet was the gentle giant, Prometheus Jones, a veterinarian with unrivaled skill in the use of a lariat.

With the possible exception of William Smith (Brodie), who had played Ranger Joe Riley in *Laredo* (in the mid-sixties) and more recently appeared in the popular prime time soaper *Rich Man, Poor Man*, and Howard E. Rollins, Jr. (Bannister), who was memorable on the large screen in *Ragtime* and *A Soldier's Story*, there were no established "stars" in the series. All were, however, competent and likable. Handsome J. Eddie Peck was Sutton, suave John DiAquino played Varges and huge Terry Frank was alternately lovable and threatening as Prometheus. The supporting cast also included several newcomers who were soon to make their mark: Meg Ryan (who played the only continuing female role—Cally Oaks, editor of the Wildside newspaper) would later star in films with Sean Connery, Mark Harmon, Billy Crystal and Tom Hanks; Jason Hervey (who played Zeke) would soon costar as the older brother, Wayne, in ABC's hit comedy *The Wonder Years*.

The plots were imaginative. In the pilot, "Well-Known Secret" (written by series creator Tom Greene), a band of renegade rebels under the leadership of a psychotic general is tearing up small towns searching for a hidden cache of Union gold when the Wildside Chamber of Commerce comes to the rescue. In another, "Delinquency of a Miner," young Zeke is lured to a gold mine by an ad promising quick riches, but the mother lode turns out to be coal and unsuspecting fortune hunters become the slave labor to mine it. Again our vigilante force provides a quick and dramatic liberation.

In "Buffalo Who?" a man posing as Buffalo Bill Cody brings a phony Wild West Show to Wildside so that he can kill the Spanish ambassador (responsible for his imprisonment in Cuba) who is visiting Bannister. A blind man proves his undoing (with the help, of course, of the Wildside Chamber). A British cavalry unit left over from the Crimean War provides the protagonists for the Chamber in "Crimea of the Century." In "Until the Fat Lady Sings," the five comrades are lured into a trap in a ghost town by an old nemesis who is anxious to get even with Brodie for shooting off his trigger finger years earlier.

The cinematography creatively utilized close-up, slow motion and stop-action techniques under the skillful direction of Ozzie Smith—the like of which had not been seen since the heyday of the spaghetti Western of Sergio Leone. The spectacular stunts were expertly coordinated by Wayne Van Horn. The music of Jack Elliott was invigorating and featured a catchy martial theme whenever the five heroes strode shoulder to shoulder into battle. All-in-all *Wildside* provided highly enjoyable "light" Western adventure.

The next network attempt at a continuing Western series was *Outlaws*, broadcast by CBS between December 1986 and May 1987. Actually this show combined elements of the detective drama and the fantasy adventure along with the action Western in producing a unique and unusual series. In a *USA Today* (December 26, 1986) review written by Monica Collins the program is described as "have gun, will time-travel" (in an obvious reference to the popular Richard Boone series). While pointing out the difficulty the show would have in its scheduled Saturday 8 to 9 P.M. time slot against popular comedies like *Facts of Life*, Collins was favorably impressed:

> Here you are asked not only to suspend your belief but to abandon it entirely. And, if you manage the feat, you might be oddly pleased and delighted with the efforts.... [T]he show's promise is its outlandish premise.[11]

The pilot opens (and this sequence is reprised at the beginning of each succeeding episode) in the Texas of 1899. Sheriff John Grail (played by veteran actor Rod Taylor)

Opposite: Wildside **featured (from left) William Smith, John DiAquino, Howard E. Rollins, Jr., J. Eddie Peck, and Terry Funk as the Wildside, California, "Chamber of Commerce."**

is leading a posse in hot pursuit of a gang of bank robbers (Charles Napier, Richard Roundtree and Patrick Houser) led by Harland Pike (William Lucking)—a gang the sheriff had been a member of before going straight and becoming a peace officer. In the middle of a climactic showdown in an Indian burial grounds during a freak electrical storm, Grail and the gang are catapulted through time by a bolt of lightning. They awake just outside contemporary Houston—to an amazing world filled with airplanes, television, showers and horseless carriages.

So knowledgeable and self-reliant in the world they left behind, they now find themselves as innocent as babes in this alien concrete jungle. Not only must they cope with the changes wrought by technology, they must deal with their own personal differences in order to survive. Four of the men are used to living outside the law while the sheriff is accustomed to keeping the peace. Now that they have become dependent on each other, the five must learn how to compromise, far away from their home on the old range. Realizing what has happened, though having no idea how, they reconcile their differences and use the gold coins obtained in the robbery to buy a ranch (which they name the Double Eagle) and attempt to adjust to the modern world. At Grail's suggestion they open the Double Eagle Detective Agency in an effort to bring old fashioned justice to Houston.

They don new outfits that are styled like those they had worn at the turn of the century and continue to carry their dated weapons. Thus do they do battle against a wide variety of modern perpetrators of lawlessness and violence—organized crime, street gangs, white-collar crooks and the like. An attractive female police officer (played by Christine Beford) befriends them and tries to keep them out of trouble, while providing romantic interest for Grail. In addition to the setting and appearance of the heroes, the series displayed several additional characteristics of the Western genre. The five frequently strode into danger, guns drawn, spouting dialogue straight out of a dime novel:

> McADAMS: Well, Gentlemen, let's do it!
> WOLF: Amen, brother.
> GRAIL: Slow and easy.
> HARLAND: But all the way.
> BILLY: To the hilt!

Flashbacks to the earlier period were also occasionally employed—filmed in sepia tones for effect. (For example, in "Tintype" Harland falls in love with a woman who looks exactly like his sweetheart Jenny who had died of cholera nearly a hundred years earlier.) None of these devices proved effective enough to capture and hold a sufficiently large audience, however, and the series was canceled after only five months.

CBS launched another quasi-Western in January of 1988 with *High Mountain Rangers*. This series was a straightforward contemporary outdoor action drama filmed on location in the beautiful Sierra Nevada mountains near Lake Tahoe. In fact the best thing about *High Mountain Rangers* was its scenery. The series was the brainchild of Robert Conrad (*The Wild Wild West*) and was almost totally a family affair. Conrad played semiretired ranger Jesse Hawkes and his two real-life sons, Christian and Shane, played his two ranger sons, Matt and Cody, on the show. Furthermore, his daughter Joan was the executive producer and her husband, Timothy Erwin, had a featured role.

The stories, which usually involved the rangers in the rescue of some lost camper, explorer or visitor, or the apprehension of some criminal trying to escape the law by heading

Opposite, photograph on left: Howard E. Rollins, Jr., was explosives expert Bannister Sparks. *Photograph on right* (left to right): John DiAquino, Howard E. Rollins, Jr., William Smith, J. Eddie Peck, and Terry Funk (front), on *Wildside*.

for the high country, were pretty cut and dry. Emphasis was on the use of the latest high-tech equipment, along with the rangers' knowledge of mountaineering and survival techniques, with plenty of references to protecting the ecology. Despite the beautiful scenery the series only lasted 14 episodes. Meanwhile, during the 1987-88 season, there were a number of abortive pilots for prospective Western series aired and an occasional made-for-television Western film. Among the failures were *Independence* (1987), *The Gunfighters* (1987), *Longarm* (1988), and *Bonanza: The Next Generation* (1988).

Independence was intended as the pilot for a new NBC Western series. The film had several assets. Handsome, rugged John Bennett Perry, whose previous television experience included leading roles in *240—Robert* (1979–1981), *Paper Dolls* (1984) and *Falcon Crest* (1985-86), played Sheriff Sam Hatch trying to bring peace and civilization to the frontier town of Independence. Anthony Zerbe (with prior credits in *How the West Was Won* and *Centennial*) was cast in the role of the murderous cutthroat General Oral Gray, and Paul Brinegar (from *Wyatt Earp*, *Rawhide* and *Lancer*) had a small supporting part.

Among the "offbeat touches were overlapping dialogue, fastpaced intercutting and melding of comedy and drama,"[12] elements that characterized creative consultant Michael Kozoll's earlier television series *Hill Street Blues*. The story was presented from the woman's point of view with voice-over narration in Irish brogue provided by Sam's lady love (Isabella Hoffman). However, the story is difficult to follow and the film did not pull ratings deemed sufficient to merit a regular weekly spot on the NBC schedule.

Among the other failed pilots was *The Gunfighters*, filmed in Canada and released in syndication. The only bona fide "star" in the film was George Kennedy, chewing up the scenery as a ruthless empire building rancher. The leads were three cousins (one English, two American) struggling to survive in the cattle business: played by Art Hindle (who had a brief stint on *Dallas*) and newcomers Tony Addabbo and Reiner Schoene. The most interesting aspect of this lackluster oater is a barroom fight between the English hero and one of the baddies, in which both use bullwhips. The film did feature a rousing martial score by composer Domenic Troiano. The story, by veteran television Western scripter Jim Byrnes (*Gunsmoke*), was routine and certainly not one of his best.

Early in 1988 ABC broadcast *Longarm*, starring "a brooding young Clint Eastwood-like actor," John Terlesky, as the title character from Tabor Evans' lengthy (over 100 titles to date) and popular series of books. Veteran Western writer David J. Chisholm wrote the occasionally humorous script. Terlesky's only previous television experience was in the forgettable seven episode long detective series, *Legmen* (1984). The only recognizable faces in the film were longtime screen villain Malachi Throne and veteran supporting actor Rene Auberjonois (in a cameo as Governor Lew Wallace). Richard J. Lindheim, studio executive vice president, described *Longarm* as "a comedy-western with sex . . . about an amorous Marlboro man of a U.S. marshal often caught with his pants down." The film featured a beer-drinking dog, a man-hating horse, and an obstreperous orphan. It also employed trendy cinematic techniques like slow-motion violence. To date there have been no sequels.

Also released in syndication about the same time was David Dortort's attempt to revive *Bonanza* (*Bonanza: The Next Generation*). Although, as noted earlier, the film boasted an experienced cast (John Ireland, Robert Fuller, Barbara Anderson and John Amos) along with Michael Landon's real-life son Michael, Jr., as Little Joe's son and Lorne Greene's daughter Gillian as a "love interest," and was directed by veteran *Bonanza* director William F. Claxton, the proposed series did not catch on. (One wonders how successful it might have been had Lorne Green, who passed away shortly before filming began, lived to recreate his old role.)

The only "successful" Western pilot to be aired during this period was *Desperado* (April 1987). While not generating a conventional weekly series as had been hoped, the film did prove successful enough to spawn four subsequent two hour television films and an order for five additional ones. Described as a cross between a Western-style *Columbo*, a horse-opera version of *The Fugitive* and a dime-novel shoot-'em-up, *Desperado* relates the story of Duell McCall, a lone Western rider who comes into a company mining town owned and run by unscrupulous men. They want land occupied by a decent settler and his daughter and resort to downright unpleasant methods to get it until the hero comes to their rescue. The father is killed and the hero framed and jailed, then released so the heavies can knock him off. Duell outwits them and guns down the baddies in a predictable shootout. But the hero must leave the woman he loves and ride off into the sunset looking for the one man still alive who can exonerate him of the murder charge.

The screenplay was written by the popular novelist Elmore Leonard. Although the pilot pulled decent enough ratings, it earned mixed reviews from the critics. The *Variety* (May 6, 1987) reviewer wrote:

> *Desperado* is a rather pathetic mediocre attempt to revive Westerns.... It's peopled with black-and-white characters and shot with cliches—a miss all the way. Long stretches of boredom are interspersed with senseless violence.... [The] screenplay is a miserable collection of familiar shticks, seemingly written from memory.

However, *TV Guide* called it "nice looking and agreeably unpretentious..." and Matt Roush, writing later in *USA Today* (May 24, 1988), declared, "Those desperate for new Westerns could do worse than ... *Desperado*."

The critics were unanimous, however, in their approval of Alex McArthur in the role of Duell McCall: *TV Guide* called him "amiable," *Variety* labeled him "okay" and *USA Today* flatly stated that Duell "has what it takes to be a cowboy for the 1980s. The look: shaggy hair, intense blue eyes, a disarming grin. The attitude: laconic, mostly mute, with a solid moral code...." Lise Cutter as the hero's sweetheart (a role which recurs in several of the sequels) also drew favorable comment, but Virgil Vogel, who had directed many earlier television Westerns, was accused by *Variety* of being "more attentive to stunts than to his characters."

Among the heavies were veteran actors David Warner, Yaphet Kotto and Robert Vaughn. Pernell Roberts (*Bonanza*'s Adam) and Dirk Blocker (Dan's son) contributed nicely to the Western ambiance in much smaller roles.

Universal Studios, producer of *Desperado*, decided that while the ratings were solid, the show did not merit weekly status. Furthermore, as Richard Lindheim pointed out, the two hour film format would make possible "better production values, because you have more time and money to shoot it, and you can attract better 'marquee' names to act and direct." This approach was also favored by McArthur, who felt that it would "give his character greater room to grow" and would not tie him down like a weekly series. Thus the recently successful *Perry Mason* format was launched with the second film, *The Return of Desperado*, which aired on February 15, 1988.

The problem with the first *Desperado* sequel, according to *Variety* (February 24, 1988), was that it was "creatively undernourished—contrived, cliché-ridden" with "a premise as old as the hills." The hero rides into a town run by a slick con-man (Robert Foxworth) who has victimized the gullible citizens and is trying to seize the land of some black homesteaders (led by Billy Dee Williams). In the process, he has framed a black man for murder. By the end of the film, Duell had rid the town of the bad guys, kissed the girl good-bye and ridden off into the sunset to continue his search for the man who can clear him of murder charges. *Variety* thought the characters "shallow" but did comment on the beautiful photography by Robert Jessup. The ratings were again respectable.

The second sequel, *Desperado: Avalanche at Devil's Ridge* (May 24, 1988) got better reviews. Matt Roush of *USA Today* called Duell McCall the best "recurring Western hero on television" and *Variety*'s critic (June 8, 1988) described the film as "an improvement over past efforts ... executed with a certain flair [and] a good deal of style intermingled with humor." He also called attention to the standout performances of Lise Cutter as Duell's sweetheart, Alice Adair as the woman Duell rescues from kidnappers, Rod Steiger as the pompous, sadistic villain, and Hoyt Axton as the sheriff. Even director Richard Compton and composer Michel Columbier are lauded for their contributions.

In this film, McCall is caught posing as a lawman and jailed on a bogus murder charge. Then the local town boss' daughter is kidnapped and Duell offers to get her back in return for his freedom. As he leads a posse up a mountain after the crazed kidnapper, a series of dynamite explosions are set off with spectacular results. By the finale, Duell has rescued the girl, who turns out not to be the town boss' daughter, but his slave. Hero and evil tycoon meet in a showdown, which McCall wins. However, the "daughter" decides to stick around and inherit the slain baddie's estate since everyone thinks she is his only kinfolk, so Duell returns to his girlfriend.

The fourth Desperado film (*Desperado: The Outlaw Wars*) was aired on October 10, 1988, with only 48 hours notice when the San Francisco earthquake caused a postponement of the scheduled World Series game. A standout in the cast was Richard Farnsworth as a sheriff who promises Duell a pardon if he will help the lawman gain revenge on the gang of cutthroats responsible for his wife's death. This time the baddie is played by Geoffrey Lewis. Lise Cutter returns as Duell's sweetheart and Buck Taylor (*Gunsmoke*'s Newly O'Brien) has a featured role.

After two hours of nonstop action featuring some of the best stunts in the series, McCall is ultimately successful in bringing the villains to justice. The sheriff is killed in the process, however, and Duell must once again leave his sweetheart and infant daughter as he continues his quest for the man who can clear him. Despite the lack of advance promotion which television films usually receive, *The Outlaw Wars* finished second in the ratings for its time period. The fifth film *Desperado: Badlands Justice* was aired in mid-December 1989.

The final Desperado film featured a wicked English land baron (John Rhys-Davies), sinister Arizona Territory townfolk, Mexican revolutionaries, murdered miners and a missing little girl. It was called "nice looking (with 1000 square miles of handsome location scenery) and agreeably unpretentious" by *TV Guide*. Of course, just before the closing credits roll, Duell McCall again rides off into the sunset to continue the quest to clear his name.

During this period of failed two-hour pilots, a number of additional made-for-television Western films were broadcast. In 1986 singers Willie Nelson, Johnny Cash, and Waylon Jennings joined with Kris Kristofferson and John Schneider in a remake of John Ford's classic *Stagecoach*. Most critics felt it to be decidedly inferior to the original but it rated moderately well with viewers.

The Alamo: 13 Days to Glory was presented to commemorate the one hundred and fiftieth anniversary of the valiant stand by the doomed Texans at the mission-fortress utilizing the same set built in 1959 for John Wayne's epic *The Alamo* (in Brackettville, Texas). Such familiar faces as James Arness from *Gunsmoke* (as Jim Bowie), Brian Keith from *The Westerner* (as Davy Crockett) and Lorne Greene from *Bonanza* (in a cameo as Sam Houston) joined Raul Julia and Alec Baldwin. Notable aspects of the film included the robust battle scenes and Julia's flamboyant performance as Santa Anna. Although it may have been more accurate historically (based on J. Lon Tinkle's book), it could not surpass John Wayne's theatrical film for sheer spectacle. This is but another example of television's futility in trying to improve upon an earlier screen success.

Gunsmoke: Return to Dodge (1987) with Arness, Amanda Blake, Buck Taylor and Fran Ryan from the original series proved to be an enjoyable visit with old friends. Steve Forrest was a formidable villain for Arness and it was nice to see Matt and Kitty together again. Although Chester, Doc and Festus were missed, the film did very well in the Nielsens.

Kenny Rogers scored big in the ratings with his third television Western film special, *Kenny Rogers as The Gambler, Part III—The Legend Continues* (1987) in two parts. This time his fictional character got involved with such real-life personalities as Sitting Bull and Buffalo Bill. Popular stars like Bruce Boxleitner, Linda Gray, George Kennedy and Charles Durning contributed to this colorful spectacle. This followed Roger's first two successful Gambler films of 1980 and 1983 all featuring the character from the hit song. (The first one, in fact, held the record—briefly—as the most-watched television movie ever!)

Elizabeth Taylor even got into the television Western scene with the lighthearted *Poker Alice* in 1987. It is played strictly for chuckles as Liz wins a brothel at the poker table. George Hamilton helps her run it while bounty-hunter Tom Skerritt provides the love interest. The veteran Western author James Lee Barrett wrote the script but the film only pulled so-so ratings.

Westerns entered the cable television market in 1987 with *The Quick and the Dead* produced for Home Box Office. The script (written by James Lee Barrett) was based on a Louis L'Amour story of the *Shane* school involving a homesteading couple (Tom Conti and Kate Capshaw), their young son and a mysterious stranger (Sam Elliott) who rides to their rescue when they come under the attack of a ruthless gang of cutthroats. Critics rated the film well above average and Leonard Maltin lauded the efforts of British cinematographer Dick Bush for craftily capturing the flavor of the old movie West on film.

Another HBO film, *The Tracker* (1988), which was British director John Guillerman's first Western, did not earn such high plaudits. It depicted the story of a retired Old West tracker (Kris Kristofferson) who joins with his estranged college-educated son (Mark Moses) in hunting down a wild-eyed religious fanatic on a murder spree.

The next network Western was another remake—this time (1988) of Howard Hawks' classic *Red River* (1948). The only thing going for it was James Arness in the role originated by John Wayne. The original screenplay of Borden Chase and Charles Schnee was adapted for the television version by Richard Fielder. Bruce Boxleitner (who had worked with Arness in *How the West Was Won*) was featured along with Gregory Harrison, Ray Walston and Laura Johnson (but they were not up to the original cast of Montgomery Clift, John Ireland, Walter Brennan and Joanne Dru). One of the most interesting aspects of the film was the use of veteran television cowboys from the fifties in cameo roles (Ty Hardin of *Bronco*, Robert Horton of *Wagon Train*, John Upton of *Broken Arrow* and Guy Madison of *Wild Bill Hickok*). It was also well filmed in color and drew respectable ratings.

The humorous *Once Upon a Texas Train* (1988) was a Willie Nelson contribution to television Westerns that lightheartedly spoofed the genre and boasted such television veterans as Stuart Whitman (*Cimarron Strip*), Chuck Connors (*The Rifleman*), Ken Curtis (*Gunsmoke*), Jack Elam (*The Dakotas*), and Dub Taylor, Gene Evans and Harry Carey, Jr. (each with scores of supporting Western roles to their credit). Shaun Cassidy played a young rebel out to sabotage the plans of ex-con Nelson and his over the hill gang to rob a train. Also out to stop him is his old adversary Richard Widmark and his posse of old-timer lawmen. The well-received effort was both written and directed by old Western hand Burt Kennedy.

Later that year, the same team (Willie Nelson and Burt Kennedy) was responsible for another television oater, with considerably less enjoyable results. *Where the Hell's That Gold?!!* featured eye-rolling Jack Elam, buxom Delta Burke, Gerald McRaney and Gregory Sierra in addition to Nelson, and related the sometimes funny story of a search for a cache of stolen gold. As film critic Leonard Maltin wrote, this "flaccid comedy-Western" was produced, directed and written by Kennedy, "who ought to have a posse on his tail. Below average."[13]

Several made-for-television Westerns have been shown on cable television's TNT Network. On May 10, 1989, *Gore Vidal's Billy the Kid* was telecast, featuring Val Kilmer as Billy and Duncan Regehr as Pat Garrett. The film was Vidal's attempt to rectify the distorted version of Bonney contained in the 1958 film *The Left Handed Gun* starring Paul Newman, which had been based on a teleplay by Vidal. Vidal had been squeezed out as producer of the film and was upset by the changes that had been made in his story. (Actually, Billy could shoot with either hand.)

Vidal's television film was immensely sympathetic, depicting Bonney as a likable but misunderstood teenager who happened to get caught up in a range war, became embittered and went bad. Others in the cast included Wilford Brimley as New Mexico's territorial governor Lew Wallace, Julie Carmen as Billy's love interest and Michael Parks as a corrupt prosecuting attorney. Rene Auberjonois had an offbeat role as a poet-drunkard who showed up occasionally to comment directly to viewers on the tragedy of Billy's life. *New York Times* (May 10, 1989) critic Walter Goodman described the film as "an OK low-key show that brings the smiles and yawns of familiarity." The director, William A. Graham, is credited with managing "to churn up a good deal of dust without breaking any new ground," while Kilmer turned in "an easygoing, nicely contained performance."

The modern West is brought to life in *Montana*, telecast over TNT on February 19, 1990. The story was by *Lonesome Dove* author Larry McMurtry and was directed by William A. Graham largely on location in Bozeman. As John J. O'Connor comments in a *New York Times* (February 18, 1990) review, the film "is filled with some splendid vistas of Big Sky country," but "McMurtry's script goes off in so many directions at once that it gets lost." The story concerns Bess and Hoyce Guthrie (Gena Rowlands and Richard Crenna), who find it increasingly difficult to pay their bills. When a strip-mining coal company makes them a handsome offer for their land, Hoyce and their high-living son agree to sell. Bess is adamantly against the sale, supported in her stand by their environmentalist daughter.

More interesting that the plot is the view of life in today's West. As O'Connor commented: "The Wild West, it seems, is alive and kicking and is cussedly unbending as ever.... [W]ith few exceptions, ranchers and Indians still glower at each other suspiciously. Violence explodes with depressing regularity, battering wayward wives and turning gun-toting thugs into killers...." One certainly cannot accuse McMurtry of romanticizing the contemporary rural West.

Another indication that the television Western was not dead came from a most unlikely source: soap opera land. A full page ad in *TV Guide* for the ABC daytime serial *One Life to Live* proclaimed: "February 8, 1988, was just another hot dusty day in Buchanan City 'til a stranger came to town. He called himself Clint Buchanan and said he came from the future." Clint (one of the lead characters, played by Clint Richie), after being blind for several months, decides to return to his Arizona ranch. Determined to take a horseback ride (because "he knew his horse and his horse knew the land"), he is thrown from the horse, regains his sight and wanders for days in the desert. Eventually, he sees a sign that reads Buchanan City, 2 miles. There, the Wild West story unfolds (via a time warp) and viewers are treated to a full-blown Western town, complete with stage coaches and gunfighters.

The Old West sequences were actually filmed on three Western locations: Old Tucson, a movie set used from the early 1940s through the present for many Western movies and television series; Gates Pass in Tucson Mountain Park, a protected natural environment which includes thousands of wild cactus; and Mescale, another old movie location where the film *Monte Walsh* was shot. The outdoor scenes were spectacularly beautiful in what was truly a first for network soap opera. To bring this fantasy to life required the efforts of hundreds of people, including writers, directors, scene designers, production personnel, technicians and 75 extras, fitted out as everything from dance hall girls to a mortician—plus dozens of horses. Several of the regular cast members played dual roles, including *Laredo*'s Phil Carey, who normally portrayed Asa Buchanan, but who appeared in the Old West segments as Asa's grandfather, Buck Buchanan. For weeks the parallel storyline between past and present continued involving Clint's confrontations with gunfighters, a "widder-woman" and her son, and a dance hall queen, while members of his family and friends continued their vain search for him in the present. Although, Clint was eventually permitted to return to the present, the ratings for *One Life to Live* were measurably affected for the better during this period. Was it curiosity or genuine interest in the Old West—who can say?

In the fall of 1988, the Disney Studio tried once again to breathe new life into the Western genre with a revival of their "Davy Crockett" series. The original plan was to present a new Crockett episode every three or four weeks as part of *The Magical World of Disney* on NBC. (Davy would rotate with two series based on successful Disney movies, *The Absent-Minded Professor* and *The Parent Trap*, and a new action-adventure program.)

The format was to have an older Crockett (about 50—just before he left for the Alamo) introduce stories which would be dramatized as flashback adventures when Davy was much younger. (Actually, this approach was used only in the two-hour pilot film.) Fess Parker (the original Crockett) was approached to play the older Davy and act as host and narrator. His reply to the offer was reportedly: "I don't do piecework!"[14] Instead the role went to country music star Johnny Cash.

Tim Dunigan was selected from among the nearly 1000 actors auditioned to play the young Davy Crockett. At six-foot-five and 33 years old, Dunigan was taller and older than Parker had been when he created the role, but he had extensive acting credits. Discovered in the theater in Bridgeport, Connecticut, he had recurring roles on television's *Mr. Smith* and *Wizards and Warriors* and had made guest appearances on *Cheers*, *The Fall Guy* and *The Paper Chase*. (He also played the character "Faceman" in the pilot episode of *The A-Team*, but was dropped when the show was sold for being "too tall and too young.") Dunigan had grown up in Missouri and was able to recapture the twang he had so carefully eliminated while studying theater.

Gary Grubbs, who was cast as Georgie Russell, also had some prior television experience. He had appeared in two short-lived dramas, as Captain Stephen Wiecek in *For Love and Honor* and as Detective Hamill in *Half Nelson*. While Dunigan seemed "born" for the role of Davy, Grubbs seemed ill at ease and out of place on the video frontier.

The show was heavily promoted by NBC. The network trotted out several well-known entertainers including rock-and-roller Little Richard, comics Shecky Greene and Don Novello (better known as Father Guido Sanducci) and a papal lookalike to sing, hum and shake their way through the 20 and 30 second promos for the show (each, of course, attired in the familiar coonskin cap). Trying to recapture the magic of the original series, the pilot episode was introduced by the highest ranking executive at the studio in his best Walt Disney manner (albeit on horseback, something Walt had never attempted on camera):

> Hello, I'm Michael Eisner. Tonight, we celebrate the return of the all new adventures of Davy Crockett. Davy Crockett lived in a time when our country was new. Indians inhabited the land. Settlers moved West only to find an uncertain future in the unexplored wilderness. It was during these difficult times that Davy Crockett joined with General Andrew Jackson to fight the Creek Indians. Always a fair man, it was Crockett who years later as a U.S. congressman stood up and opposed President Andrew Jackson when his old general tried to deprive the Indians of certain governmental rights. Let's take a journey back into history and join Davy Crockett on the American frontier.

The episode, entitled "Rainbow in the Thunder," dramatized a fictional version of Crockett's 1813 campaign against the Creeks. Although the story implied that the Americans were victorious, in large measure because of Crockett's cleverness, in actuality the struggle with the natives was uneven, and Davy took little pleasure in it. "We shot them like dogs,"[15] the real Crockett noted with disgust after Jackson's slaughter of the Creeks at Tallussahatchee in November 1813.

The Disney Studio even inserted the old Davy Crockett theme song into the story (as sung by Georgie Russell), complete with a brand new verse. However, other than generating a brief spurt in the sale of coonskin caps (Orvis, the Vermont mail order house, reportedly sold out its inventory of $95 hats), the series did not generate much public interest. Four hour-long episodes were filmed, but only two ("A Natural Man": while out hunting a grizzly that mauled Georgie, Davy meets up with his uncle, now an old mountain man who has somehow survived for twenty years living among the Creeks; and "Guardian Spirit," in which Davy saves a young Creek boy from a wolf during his rites of manhood and becomes his guardian spirit) were ever aired by the network.

In explaining why the new series failed, Castleman and Podrazik point out that "these stories didn't have quite the same impact or innocence as the originals."[16] (Undoubtedly, the American experience in Vietnam had destroyed that "innocence.") Furthermore, Tim Dunigan was no Fess Parker (the charisma simply was not there) and Michael Eisner was no Walt Disney (despite his proven executive ability, he lacked Walt's on-screen charm).

In January 1989, the Family Channel (formerly CBN) began airing its own 30 minute Western series (joining the many golden oldies like *Gunsmoke*, *Bonanza* and *The Big Valley* already being broadcast over that cable network). A joint Canadian-French production, *Bordertown* was filmed in British Columbia by Canada's Global TV. Sixty-five carpenters worked five and a half weeks to construct a complete Western town on a ranch located east of Vancouver. The set, which cost half a million dollars to build, included a cluster of buildings complete inside and out. Every shelf and drawer of the general store was stocked—the lace drawer contained lace, the saloon included antique bottles, the livery stable was equipped with period tack and hundred year old saddles.

All of the filming (both interior and exterior) was done in the town with no studio work necessary. The streets were just naturally muddy in the winter and dusty in the summer. Glen Wonnacott, who worked as an extra in over fifty *Bordertown* episodes, explained the historical premise on which the series was based in a fascinating article in *The Westerner* magazine:

The brass plate on the marker post on the west side of the dirt road across from the mountie and marshal's office reads "International Boundary 49 degree North 114 degree West of Greenwich, was established 1857-1861, surveyed and marked 1872-1876, convention of 1818, Treaty of 1846."

Dig out an Atlas and pinpoint that spot on a map and it lines up pretty close to the Waterton Lakes on the Canada-U.S. Border about 150 miles north of Missoula, Montana and about 35 miles south-west of Standoff, Alberta, where Charles Russell wintered in 1887-88 with the Blood Indians learning sign language and studying Indian ways.

The time setting is the early 1880's when this area was still the graze of the last of the northern buffalo herd. In Canada, the Canadian Pacific railroad was being built westward across the prairie. Regina, on Pile of Bones Creek, was chosen as capital of the Northwest Territories by Lieutenant Governor and Indian Commissioner, the Honorable Edgar Dewdney. Sitting Bull had left the land of the white grandmother, crossed the medicine line and surrendered at Fort Buford on July 20, 1881....

"Bordertown" grew from a settlement on an old north-south Indian trail. When the international boundary line was established, it bisected the town, necessitating the presence of both a United States Deputy Marshal and a Northwest Mounted Police Constable.[17]

Canadian corporal Clive Bennett (of the Royal Canadian Mounted Police) shared an office with U.S. marshal Jack Craddock (a former Texas Ranger). The two law enforcement officers worked together when necessary to preserve law and order along the forty-ninth parallel, but were highly competitive not only during but after working hours. They both had romantic designs on the town's only doctor, the beautiful Marie Dumont. Richard Comar, a native of Edmonton, Alberta, was cast as Craddock; John Brennan, born in Montreal, played Clive Bennett; and French actress Sophie Barjac costarred as the town doctor, Marie Dumont.

The contrasting styles of the two lawmen were emphasized. Craddock was a gunfighter-turned-marshal, a disorganized pack rat who once had belonged to the Texas Rangers. He usually needed a shave, was sloppy in his dress, often drank to excess and frequently cursed. After his wife and daughter had been murdered by a Mexican rancher who claimed they had been illegally squatting on his land, Craddock had gone to Bordertown to ease the pain and to partially retire. Bennett, on the other hand, was a spit-and-polish officer, who spoke perfect English, drank only off-duty and in moderation, was organized to a fault and functioned strictly by the book. (In an AP press release, Comar compared Craddock to a New York street cop and Bennett to a London bobby.) A number of episodes stressed the complex relationship between the two men and the differences in their character. None was better written or acted than "Devil's Right Hand," by Peter Mitchell, in which this exchange took place between the two after Craddock has learned that his dead father was a ruthless, cold-blooded killer.

CRADDOCK: Quite the bloodline, ain't it? Son of a thief and a murderer...
BENNETT: Put it behind ya. Come home.
CRADDOCK: Sure, just wipe my hands clean of it, like it never happened. You can still make peace with your father. I got to see mine for what he really was.
BENNETT: You're not the first man that something bad's happened to ... and you're not your father's son.
CRADDOCK: Yeah, then what am I?
BENNETT: Who raised ya?
CRADDOCK: Well, my ma and me, we helped each other.
BENNETT: Then she's the one ya owe yourself to, not him.
CRADDOCK: Yer a preacher's son and I'm a killer's. There ain't no gettin' away from that!
BENNETT: Ya already have.

More about Craddock's background is learned in "In Cold Blood," when he comes face to face with the man who murdered his wife and young daughter. Bennett, however, is forced to kill the Mexican nobleman in self-defense before Craddock has an opportunity to gain the revenge he craves.

In "Straight from the Heart," viewers discover that Bennett's estranged father is a clergyman who expected Clive to follow in his footsteps to the pulpit. When the Reverend Harrison Bennett pays a surprise visit to Bordertown, the two put aside their differences. The Rev. Bennett is reconciled to the fact that his son *is* doing the Lord's work (although in a different way) at this frontier outpost where the citizens rely on him to uphold the law and maintain order.

Another interesting episode focusing on Bennett is called "Sight Unseen": Bennett is temporarily blinded when his pistol backfires and is rescued from two cutthroat killers by a woman from his past whom he once helped.

Marie Dumont (played by Sophie Barjac) is also featured in several episodes. In "Skirmishes," her right to practice medicine in Canada is challenged by a young French doctor who has come to Bordertown to replace her. As a nurse, Dumont learned medicine from her late husband, who was a doctor. She never, however, obtained a license. When she skillfully performs an operation which saves a man's leg, the young doctor realizes that she is providing the best possible medical expertise for the town's residents. In "White Feather," an Indian brave becomes infatuated with Dumont after saving her life. In this episode the brave, "White Feather," is played by a Canadian-born Native American actor named Byron Chief Moon. (Most Native American roles in the series are played by real Indians.)

Actual historical events and characters are often woven into the storylines on *Bordertown*. A young Teddy Roosevelt is the title character in "Four Eyes." Bat Masterson (a superb portrayal by the talented Canadian actor Stephen Makaj) makes two appearances in *Bordertown* (in "Hunter's Moon," before he grew his mustache, and a slightly older Bat in "Nebraska Lightnin'"). The Pony Express comes to Bordertown in "The Pony Riders," and they violate the sanctity of a nearby Indian burial ground (although why the Pony Express was operating over a thousand miles north of its actual route is never explained).

The most exciting history-based story is "Killer with a Smile," which dramatizes a fictionalized attempt to assassinate President James A. Garfield as he passes through Bordertown, ostensibly while on the political campaign circuit. The plot to kill him during a "pyrotechnics" (fireworks) display is thwarted with the help of Craddock and Marie. Prior to the closing credits, viewers are informed that Garfield *was* assassinated less than six months later. (One interesting concession to the passage of time is made on the show: during the first season, a large photo of Garfield hangs behind Craddock's desk; during later episodes that photo is replaced by one of Chester A. Arthur, the man who succeeded Garfield as president in 1881.)

Some stories even include a fair amount of comedy. In "Let There Be Light" (in another concession by writers to changing times) electricity comes to Bordertown and electric lights are installed—as is a burglar alarm (which produces several humorous situations). In "Sons of Thunder," Craddock befriends a half-breed accused of stealing horses and the two take turns in saving the other's life. Although the basic plot may not seem funny, the halfbreed is broadly played and his girlfriend is also a comic character. (She boldly walks in on an embarrassed Craddock while he is taking a bath!)

Although new episodes of the series were broadcast for nearly three full seasons (1989-1992), critical appraisal of *Bordertown* was "mixed." The Canadian publication *Chatelaine*'s reviewer Donna S. Miller took the writers and producers to task for perpetuating Canadian versus American clichés:

***Bordertown*'s Marshal Craddock (Richard Comar, left), Clive Bennett (John Brennan) and Dr. Marie Dumont (Sophie Barjac).**

> . . . Because it's written by Canadians and filmed in B.C. the show provides the perfect opportunity to explode clichés about the differences between the two nations. Instead, it panders to them. The American, drinks, swears and needs a shave; he even calls the bad guys "hombres." The Canadian always acts responsibly and keeps his boots shiny. All the other clichés are there too: the two men trade jibes but are loyal as burrs to each other underneath their crusty/squeaky clean exteriors. . . . The plots are pleasant enough—and that's the problem. The wild West was never so bland.[18]

With American critics Castleman and Podrazik, *Bordertown* rated only slightly better, earning a two star (acceptable or average) evaluation and the comment that "all that cheaper-to-film-up-there-than-here footage from 'up North' makes sense."[19] The most favorable review came from *TV Guide*'s Robert MacKenzie (February 9, 1991):

> If you remember when the half-hour Western was a popular TV-series form, don't tell anyone. . . . But there is a living example of the 30-minute Western. "Bordertown" is now in its third season on cable's Family Channel. . . .

I can see why "Bordertown" has gathered fans, particularly—among the generation that doesn't remember cowboy movies. It's a back-to-basics Western with shootouts and bad guys, poker games and saloon brawls, and pretty women arriving by stagecoach. And it's agreeably succinct.

Bordertown earned the highest ratings of any new original program on the Family Channel and was one of the most popular drama series on the CTV Network during the first two years it was broadcast. In 1990 it earned a silver medal in the action-adventure series category at the 33rd International Film and Television Festival in New York.[20] Its success was sufficient to justify the filming of 78 episodes over three seasons. Actually, once past the clichés (and what Western does not have its share of them?), *Bordertown* represents a noble effort to breathe new life into the television Western. The production values were high (largely due to the on-site filming), the stories interesting and the acting credible (and in several cases, outstanding). Fans of the television Western might well hope that more episodes of *Bordertown* would be made in the future and that all episodes might be made more readily accessible to the television viewer.

Undoubtedly buoyed by the public response to *Bordertown*, the Family Channel began production almost immediately on a new version of Disney's hit series *Zorro*. According to Zorro historian, Bill Yenne, "In what was to become another milestone in the history of Zorro's depiction, Gary Goodman and Barry Rosen of New World Television ... undertook in 1989 to produce what was to be the most thoroughly planned and executed Zorro project ever."[21] Also responsible for the highly rated, Emmy Award-nominated series *The Wonder Years* and the popular daytime soap *Santa Barbara*, Goodman and Rosen hired Robert McCullough as supervising producer. McCullough came to the *Zorro* project with a wealth of television production experience, which included writing and directing such hit television shows as *BJ and the Bear*, *Sheriff Lobo*, *Battlestar Galactica*, *The Six Million Dollar Man*, and *Falcon Crest*, and he was currently serving at Paramount as supervising producer of *Star Trek: The Next Generation*.

For story editor, Phillip John Taylor was selected. A graduate of the Royal Academy of Dramatic Art in London, Taylor had spent two years as associate director at the American Shakespeare Theater in Stratford, Connecticut. Among Taylor's writing credits were episodes of *All in the Family*, *Mork and Mindy*, *The Incredible Hulk*, *Knight Rider* and *The Fall Guy*. (Taylor was to personally author over a quarter of the scripts with McCullough responsible for another third.) Many of the finest directors working in television during the eighties were chosen to direct episodes of the new series including Ron Satloff (whose credits included *Love Boat*, *Perry Mason*, *Hunter* and *Dynasty*), Michael Vejar (*Jesse Hawks*, *Magnum P.I.*, *Cagney and Lacey* and *Star Trek: The Next Generation*), and Ray Austin (*Hawaii Five-0*, *Sword of Justice* and *The Avengers*).

Perhaps the best stunt coordinator in the business, Peter Diamond, was added to the production team to supervise all fight and action sequences. Diamond had staged the laser-light sword fights for all three of George Lucas' *Star Wars* films and had choreographed the swashbuckling swordplay in Rob Reiner's *The Princess Bride*. His other experience included training Bob Hoskins for his grueling role in *Who Framed Roger Rabbit?* and staging the sword fights in remakes of *The Master of Ballantrae*, *The Man in the Iron Mask*, *Ivanhoe*, *The Three Musketeers* and *Treasure Island*. An accomplished fencing master and stunt double, Diamond also had choreographed stage dueling for the Royal London Opera House, the Old Vic, the National Theater and eight West End Productions in London.[22]

The experienced Canadian actor Duncan Regehr was selected to play the demanding lead role. Regehr had played numerous Shakespearean roles on both stage and film

Duncan Regehr as *Zorro*, on trusty Tornado.

and starred as Errol Flynn in the CBS miniseries on Flynn's life, *My Wicked, Wicked Ways*. (Ironically, Flynn had been Darryl F. Zanuck's first choice to play Zorro in the 1940 20th Century–Fox film—the role that went to Tyrone Power.) Other television credits included starring roles as Prince Dirk Blackpool in *Wizards and Warriors*, and Pat Garrett in *Gore Vidal's Billy the Kid* (on the TNT network), and featured parts in *The Blue and the Gray*, *The Last Days of Pompeii*, *Goliath Awaits*, *V*, and *Earth Star Voyager* (for Disney). Furthermore, Regehr was an Olympic boxing contender, a champion figure skater and a trained fencer. He seemed ideally suited for the role and when attired in

Zorro's black costume, complete with pencil-thin mustache, he could easily have been mistaken for Guy Williams who had earlier created the "ultimate" Zorro for Disney. In a later interview Regehr commented on playing the role of folklore's "original caped crusader":

> Zorro is so much fun to play. It is truly a childhood fantasy come true. . . .
> When I play Zorro, I play him the way I want to. I try to play him in a different format to anyone else who has played him before . . . tongue-in-cheek. . . . I [also] like to do as much of my stunt work as I can, because I feel that's how it should be.[23]

As a kid in Canada, Regehr admitted to having "caught a few" episodes of the original *Zorro* on television, but while preparing for the new series "purposely didn't watch the old series" because (as he told *USA Today*'s Peter Johnson in January 1990), "If you're going to do Hamlet, you don't want to do somebody else's Hamlet. You want it to be new and different."

For the key role of Don Alejandro, Zorro's father, Goodman and Rosen chose Efrem Zimbalist, Jr., best known to most television viewers for playing FBI inspector Lew Erskin on *The FBI* broadcast over ABC from 1965 through 1974. Prior to that, Zimbalist had starred for six years on *77 Sunset Strip* (1958–1964) as Stuart Bailey, and his film credits included *House of Strangers*, *By Love Possessed*, *The Chapman Report*, *Harlow*, *Wait Until Dark*, and *Airport 1975*. Although Zimbalist seemed comfortable in the role and was featured in several episodes, he was replaced the second season by Henry Darrow. Darrow was familiar to fans of television Westerns for his work as Manolito Montoya on *The High Chaparral*, but he had also played Zorro himself in the short-lived spoof *Zorro and Son* in 1983 and was the *voice* of Zorro in the 1981 Filmation animated series. Darrow thus became the first actor to appear in a leading role in three different Zorro productions.

To play Zorro's romantic interest (and owner of the local inn), Victoria Escalante, the producers selected young Patrice Camhi, a native of New Mexico who had appeared with Steve Martin and Chevy Chase in the comedy *The Three Amigos* in 1986 under her stage name Patrice Martinez. She also had the distinction of guest-starring twice as Tom Selleck's love interest on *Magnum PI*. Camhi (Martinez) had worked with the repertory company La Compania de Teatro de Albuquerque and later attended the Royal Academy of Dramatic Arts on a scholarship.

Sergeant Garcia, a character created to provide comedy relief by Walt Disney, does not appear in the New World production of *Zorro*. Instead, Hispanic character actor James Victor was cast as the bungling, humorous Sergeant Mendoza. Born in the Dominican Republic, Victor had emigrated with his family to New York City when he was a child. There he came under the influence of Miriam Colon's bilingual theater company, where he received his early training. His screen credits included *Rolling Thunder* and *Stand and Deliver* and he had made guest appearances on television's *Falcon Crest* and *Remington Steele*.

Michael Tylo, a veteran of the ABC daytime drama *General Hospital*, was selected to play the *alcalde* (mayor) of Los Angeles. With degrees in acting and directing, Tylo had considerable experience in live theater, but received his greatest television exposure in the role of Dee Boot on the highly acclaimed miniseries *Lonesome Dove* in 1989. For some reason, Tylo (who was excellent in the role) was replaced during the second season by unknown John Hertzler, who continued to play Zorro's chief nemesis thru the next two seasons. The old deafmute valet Bernardo (who was featured in the Disney series) does not appear in the new *Zorro*. In this version, Zorro's manservant is a young man (also deaf and mute) named Felipe. He is effectively played by Juan Diego Botta, a young

Zorro (Duncan Regehr) shown with (from left) the Alcalde (John Hertzler), Sergeant Garcia (James Victor), Victoria (Patrice Camhi), Felipe (Juan Diego Botta) and Don Alejandro (Harry Darrow).

Spanish actor who does not speak a word of English. (Actually, neither Felipe the present character nor Disney's Bernardo was really deaf. Their feigned deafness was used as a ploy to gain valuable information for Zorro.)

An international coproduction of Zorro Productions, New World Television, the Family Channel in the United States, RAI in Italy and Ellipse Programme-Canal Plus of France, *Zorro* was filmed entirely on location in Spain and (during the third and fourth seasons) southern France. Bill Yenne, in his authoritative study, explains:

> Technical accuracy was placed in higher stead than it had ever been in a "Zorro" production. Since California was originally a Spanish colony, researchers from the Spanish National

Archives and the California Historical Society provided the production with volumes of material, which included wardrobe sketches, photographs, manuscripts on manners and customs, military uniforms and weapons of the period. Clothing had to be assembled to dress the extras as citizens of the pueblo, and uniforms for a full military garrison had to be created, so costume designers went about producing a full wardrobe for the principal actors, as well as for guest players....

Many of the props and decorative items on the set were faithful reproductions of the original items that Spanish and French craftsmen had made in the early eighteenth century. Certain irreplaceable one-of-a-kind items ... were given on loan to the production by various historical societies and museums....

Art directors constructed two sets. The first was an elaborate interior set the size of several basketball floors, which were built on a sound stage in Madrid. The second was a detailed recreation of the pueblo of Los Angeles, circa 1820, based on the original plans ... on a 34-acre lot just 30 miles north of Madrid.... [It was] complete with church plaza, military garrison, rancho haciendas, adobe structures, cantina and main street.[24]

The "new" *Zorro* premiered on the Family Channel in January 1990 complete with a new theme song written by Jay Asher and Dennis Spiegel, which was not quite up to the Disney version, but it came close, depicting Zorro as courageous, "larger than life" and a "friend" to all.

The series opened with a two hour film (later shown in four half hour episodes) entitled "The Legend Begins," in which the story of Zorro's origins is dramatized via flashbacks as Zorro lies seriously injured at the foot of a cliff. The script, written by Robert McCullough, follows the basic plot of the earlier stories with several added unique twists: the use of a hang glider to aid Zorro in his first surprise appearance (before he has captured and tamed his trusty steed Tornado) and a display of fireworks to convince the Alcolde that Zorro had a large army outside the gates of the pueblo waiting to do battle with his outnumbered forces.

The inaugural broadcast of the new *Zorro* series was accompanied by a massive worldwide advertising campaign to promote the sale of Zorro related items including a Marvel comic book (using the new cast as models), toys, books and clothes. It was a marketing approach that rivaled those of Hopalong Cassidy, Roy Rogers and Disney's *Zorro* during the heyday of the juvenile Western on television.

Many of the episodes of the new *Zorro* featured stories not unlike those developed for the Disney series (e.g., in "Double Entendre," a famous swordsman is hired by the Alcalde to impersonate Zorro in order to discredit him; in "Honor Thy Father," Don Diego reveals his true identity to his father, although Don Alejandro lay in a coma at the time and later thought he had dreamed the revelation; and in "The Deceptive Heart," a young woman and her lover try to take advantage of Don Alejandro by murdering the woman with whom he has been corresponding—object: matrimony.)

The villainy of the Alcalde is stressed in such episodes as "Water," when, during a drought, he discovers an unknown water source and sells the water to the desperate peasants at exorbitant prices. In "Symbol of Hope," the evil mayor uses a little boy who is dying of an unknown illness as bait to trap Zorro.

The romantic attraction of Victoria and Zorro is implied in virtually every episode, but in "An Affair to Remember," the unthinkable happens: Zorro takes an injured Victoria to his secret cave and almost reveals his true identity to her. He *does* give her a ring and proposes to her, promising that they will marry at some future date when the evil in the world has dissipated to the extent that he can reveal his identity.

Among the more interesting and original stories are "An Explosive Situation," by Philip John Taylor (first season), "The Wizard," by Robert McCullough (second season), and "Like Father, Like Son," by Tim Minear (fourth season). In "An Explosive

Situation," Don Diego, Don Alejandro, Victoria, the Alcalde and Sergeant Mendoza are all bound and gagged and left to die in an explosion set by a man seeking revenge. As they await what appears to be certain death, the Alcalde, Sergeant Mendoza and Victoria each fantasize their greatest wishes: the Alcalde, that he has captured Zorro *and* won the hand of the fair Victoria; Sergeant Mendoza, that he is mayor of Los Angeles and is being honored at a dinner featuring his favorite imported beans; and Victoria, that she is rescued by Zorro and carried off on Tornado.

"The Wizard" features Adam West, television's original Batman, as an eccentric inventor named Dr. Henry Wayne (in an obvious reference to Bruce Wayne, Batman's alter ego). Played in the same campy style that proved so effective on Batman, Wayne arrives in Los Angeles with his wagonload of gadgets and potions—including the world's first "vacuum cleaner," "mechanical bread mixer" and "patented automatic hair drier." At first employed by the Alcalde to invent a device that will facilitate Zorro's capture, Wayne is later convinced by Zorro himself that he should use his talents to promote good and thwart evil. The irony of Wayne visiting Zorro's secret cave laboratory is certainly not lost on longtime *Batman* fans. (After all, did Bob Kane not admit to having created his "caped crusader" in Zorro's image, right down to the black mask and cape?) This exchange between Zorro and Wayne is truly inspired.

> WAYNE: Incredible! A secret cave—how splendid!
> ZORRO: I thought you might appreciate it.
> WAYNE: Oh, I do, I do. . . . Is that a laboratory I see?
> ZORRO: Exactly. I have great respect for scientific endeavor, Dr. Wayne, so long as it is used for progress and not suppression. You do have a certain inventive genius.
> WAYNE: You really think so?
> ZORRO: The only proof of it will be what good you can do with it. Any fool can wreak havoc.

"Like Father, Like Son" presents a clever variation on the Don Quixote story. Don Alejandro is accidently hit on the head while reading Cervantes' classic novel. When he comes to, he finds he has fallen into Zorro's secret cave and believes that *he* must be Zorro. Off he goes to tilt at windmills and rescue the fair Dulcinea (actually Victoria) from the evil clutches of the Alcalde. In so doing he is captured, exposed and sentenced to hang. The real Zorro, of course, rescues his father in the nick of time. In making his escape, Don Alejandro receives another blow to the head and wakes up as his old self. The episode contains elements of humor, action and romance—all in all, one of the more entertaining and satisfying episodes of the new *Zorro*.

During the fourth season a new character is added for several consecutive episodes. Following the pattern established in the fifties by Disney, each episode contains a complete story, but the continuing threat to Zorro remains over the duration of the series.

In "The Arrival" viewers learn that Don Diego has a twin brother who was stolen from his mother at birth by a treacherous midwife. In fact none of the de la Vegas are aware of his existence. He arrives in Los Angeles ostensibly as a special envoy of the Spanish king, sent to the colonies to raise money for Spain's war against France. Actually, he has an ulterior motive. Goaded on by letters from the woman he believes to be his mother, his real mission is to ruin the de la Vega family. In the process he takes over the local government, threatens the Alcade with execution, seizes the property of the church and, of course, comes into direct conflict with Zorro who ultimately brings about his downfall. (Ironically, he is shot in the back by the Alcalde, just as he is about to reveal Zorro's true identity.) It is an interesting storyline and provides a new protagonist for Zorro other than the Alcalde. (In fact, Zorro actually saves the Alcalde's life when he is about to be shot by a firing squad.)

Critics, however were not very kind in their assessment of the New-World *Zorro*. Writing for *USA Today*, Peter Johnson said:

> With the new "Zorro" series, ... The Family Channel continues its puzzling habit of shelling out bucks to produce something that looks and sounds just like the primitive reruns that fill the schedule....
>
> Duncan Regehr ... plays the hero with enough eye makeup to resemble the silent Zorro, Douglas Fairbanks....
>
> Everything else about the new "Zorro" appears similarly ancient: the phonily staged action sequences (what few there are), the stock action of the supporting players.

Ken Tucker's review for *Entertainment Weekly* (February 23, 1990) was more favorable, but claimed there was too much talk and too little action:

> This new version of "Zorro" features a masterful casting job: physically, Duncan Regehr is a perfect new Zorro; he look like a youthful version of the Zorro from the '50s, Guy Williams, right down to the little mustache that resembles a black French fry. And Regehr plays the part well, capturing this masked swordsman's playfulness and romanticism. At the same time, Regehr is careful to keep his interpretation from slacking off into a winking, campy character. That said, however, I'm obliged, to report that this new "Zorro" is dull and humorless, its stories tiresomely didactic.... This is a peaceful Zorro; an earnest Zorro; a Zorro who spends more time lecturing his enemies than crossing swords with them. They should have called it Z-Z-Z-Zorro (Rating: C-).

Another problem arose when shortly after the new *Zorro* was launched it came under fire from an antidiscrimination group called United Hispanics of America. In a full-page ad in *Variety*, the coalition pointed out that "the legendary Spanish hero is being played by a non–Hispanic actor as are the characters Don Alejandro and the Alcalde." (There was a similar protest over casting a Hispanic role in an *Alias Smith and Jones* episode: see Chapter XIII.) Although the ad's sponsors, who included actor Edward James Olmos, did not call for a boycott of the show, they stated that they would address later what the ad termed "injustices in the discriminatory hiring practices in the motion picture industry." When the Family Channel was asked about the protest, a spokesperson responded that a Hispanic actress played Zorro's love interest and other Hispanics were cast in key roles, adding that "A number of Hispanics did try out for the lead role, but no one ... matched Duncan Regehr's fencing skills or acting ability. We don't want to resort to tokenism."[25] Apparently nothing more came of the protest.

A total of 88 episodes of the New World *Zorro* were filmed (25 each of the first 3 seasons, 13 during the fourth). With production values vastly superior to those of Disney (even though his episodes have now been colorized), competent (if not superior) acting and a number of interesting storylines, this version may stand for some time as the "definitive" screen version of Johnston McCulley's acclaimed caped crusader—that is, until someone like Stephen Spielberg or George Lucas decides to develop a version of that wise, brave, charming, cunning and romantic Western hero.

Meanwhile, as the Family Channel was doing its part to revive the television Western via the 30 minute format, CBS, home of the granddaddy of all television Westerns, *Gunsmoke*, was making plans to launch a new 60 minute oater of its own. The last successful network Western had been NBC's *Little House on the Prairie*, which had gone off the air in 1984, and CBS had not attempted one since the forgettable *Chisholms* in 1979.

David Jacobs, the writer-producer who had changed the face of television back in 1978 when he created *Dallas*, the first successful nighttime soap opera, was once again ready to challenge established wisdom at the networks. In October of 1988, CBS broadcast the pilot episode of Jacobs' newest brainchild, *Paradise*, on which he acted as executive producer, cowriter and director. *Paradise* dramatized the adventures of a reformed gunfighter who lived in a rugged California mining town just before the turn of the century and must take charge of his sister's four young children (three boys and a girl) after she dies. Patric Faulstich, the CBS vice president who approved Jacobs' new series, explained to the *New York Times* correspondent Stephen Farber:

> We had been working with an embargo on the Western. So had the other networks. I read that Brandon Tartikoff said recently that one requirement for NBC programs was that there be no horses. We don't go quite that far. We also have "Lonesome Dove," a Western mini-series, this season. We've done well with our Kenny Rogers movies, which were westerns. We did well with a "Gunsmoke" revival movie. We think the genre might be viable again.[26]

Nevertheless, Faulstick admitted that there were some major obstacles to the success of any television Western series:

> The younger contemporary audience is separated from the entertainment tradition of the western. The older audience that caught Saturday matinees in the 1950's or the Sam Peckinpah and Sergio Leone westerns of the 1960's and early 70's may have some affection for the genre. But we know we'll have a hard time attracting younger viewers.[27]

One way that CBS countered this so-called prejudice against Westerns was by promoting *Paradise* as a family drama rather than as a straight Western. Jacobs and his cowriter Robert Porter had suggested a Western miniseries to CBS a few years earlier (about a gunslinger-turned-salesman who cannot escape his sharpshooting past) but the network turned their project down. Then Jacobs read a magazine story about couples who were choosing not to have children because it would interfere with their careers. His wife pointed out that many of them probably would make good parents if they chose to take on the responsibility. This inspired Jacobs to propose a series about a childless man who has several children thrust upon him unexpectedly.

At the suggestion of Kim Le Masters, president of CBS Entertainment, he decided to place these characters in a Western setting. In order to convince the networks that Westerns were not dead, Jacobs was attempting to revive the "domestic" or "family" Western that had worked so well during the fifties and sixties when single parent families on *Bonanza*, *The Rifleman*, *The Big Valley* and *High Chaparral* rode the video range.

One of the major difficulties in doing Westerns in the eighties and nineties, cost, was circumvented to some extent by using an existing set at the Disney ranch (which had been constructed for *Roots, the Second Generation*). Each episode usually took five days for location shooting plus an additional two to four days in the studio for interior scenes.

To play the lead character, Ethan Allen Cord, a popular and experienced actor was selected: Lee Horsley of *Matt Houston* fame. For Horsley the role seemed to be a perfect match since he had always wanted to be a cowboy. Born in Muleshoe, Texas, in 1955, he had grown up on his grandfather's cotton farm near Plains. Then his family had moved to Colorado.

In high school, Horsley was attracted to both the stage and the gridiron. His first significant role was Cornelius in *Hello Dolly*. He studied acting at the University of Northern Colorado, dropping out after his second year. Obtaining his union card, he began traveling in stock theater appearing in such productions as *West Side Story*, *Oklahoma* and *1776*. His first break through in films came with a small part in the television miniseries *The Gangster Chronicles*. This was followed by the second lead in *Nero Wolfe*. (Horsley was Archie, assistant to William Conrad's Nero Wolfe.) A year later (1982), he landed the lead in the theatrical release, *The Sword and the Sorcerer*.

Lee Horsley as Ethan Allen Cord and Sigrid Thornton as love interest Amelia Lawson, on *Paradise*.

Shortly thereafter, Horsley was cast as a super-rich Texas oilman who would leave his ranch each week to pursue detective work as a hobby. *Matt Houston* ran for three seasons (1982–1985) and moved Horsley to star status. Because of his macho build, mustache and dark hair, he was often compared to Tom Selleck. (*TV Guide* ran a story on him in its November 27, 1982, issue entitled "Presenting Tom Selleck ... Oops, Lee Horsley." While preferring to be judged on his own merits, Horsley politely insisted that he was "flattered" that people saw the "resemblance.") In March 1990, Horsley told a *Washington Post* columnist that he was elated to do *Paradise*:

> The western has always been a morality play, and I think people want to see that. There is a right ... It's well defined. I think they're back to stay.... I grew up on them. I missed them. I liked the code of the west.... That's why I care so much about this show and what I'm doing now.[28]

(Horsley's work on *Paradise* earned him induction into the Newhall, California, Walk of Western Stars on March 24, 1990.)

Australian actress Sigrid Thornton was cast as Amelia Lawson, owner of the Paradise Bank, who has been deserted by her husband. She is waiting to save enough money so she can leave the dreary mining town. It is from Amelia that Ethan rents his farmhouse. Later she becomes his love interest. A native of Canberra, Australia, Thornton had been acting since she was 7. She had joined the Unicorn Theatre Club in London, which was designed to stimulate the interest of young children in the theater. Her father, who lectured on philosophy at Queensland University, had taken his family to England for two years while he was on sabbatical. When she returned to Brisbane with her family, she joined the Twelfth Night Theatre, mixing school with acting for six years.

Eventually Thornton was discovered by Crawford Productions and cast in the Australian television series *Homicide*. Additional television experience came in *Division 4* and *Prisoner*, two other popular television shows. Her first role on the large screen was in the highly acclaimed *The Getting of Wisdom*, released in 1980. Her other film credits included the "outback sagas"—*The Man from Snowy River* (1982) and *Return to Snowy River* (1988)—and the HBO Premiere Films miniseries *All the Rivers Run* (1983). An "outback" saga was not unlike an American Western and provided Thornton with just the experience she would need to make the character of Amelia in *Paradise* believable. (The original script called for an educated Englishwoman, but after watching a tape of Thornton, Jacobs and Porter knew they had the perfect Amelia and the role was modified to that of an outback-born, socially ambitious young woman.)

The four Carroll children are not only attractive to look at, but credible actors as well. Their mother, Lucy Cord Carroll, is Ethan's sister, who sings in a musical revue in St. Louis. When she realizes she is dying, she sends them to live with their uncle because she believes that he is a respectable hardware store owner. Claire (13) is played by Jenny Beck, Joseph (11) by Matthew Newark, Ben (9) by Brian Lando and George (5) by Michael Patrick Carter.

The other major character in the series is John Taylor, an Indian shaman who becomes Ethan's closest friend and develops a special relationship with young Ben. Taylor has lived alone since his family was killed years earlier by white soldiers. Dehl Berti plays the role with dignity, gentleness, and a subtle sense of humor.

Despite an excellent cast and the best efforts and plans of CBS, Jacobs, and others, most reviewers were, however, critical. After but one episode they were ready to write off the series as a failure which would not last out the season. *Variety* (October 31, 1991) said:

> There's trouble in "Paradise," new with familiar ingredients clumsily meshed together. There really isn't much that is appealing in this threadbare script by David Jacobs and Robert Porter, who also created the vehicle, directed routinely by Jacobs. It is a tedious tale that takes forever to reach its predictable finale.
>
> Horsley is convincing as the gunman, not so as the new pop. Sigrid Thornton turns in a nice performance in support.

John J. O'Connor writing in the *New York Times* (October 27, 1991) dismissed the new television Western as "about as authentic as a Gene Autry movie, and not nearly as entertaining.... Bring back Autry and let him sing 'Back in the Saddle Again.' Authenticity has its limits." Kay Gardella of the *New York Daily News* concurred:

> ... This predictable and tired-looking western is standard B-movie fare. What a waste of such a handsome actor! I must admit, the kids *are* cute, all four of them. They're allowed to act like normal youngsters and not given any of those dumb, cute lines to say....
>
> What we have here is the old struggle: Cord tries to go straight for the kid's sake but can't shake his past reputation. One can almost write the scenario.

Respected New York critic David Friedman was, however, more circumspect in his evaluation describing *Paradise* as a "laid-back Western":

> Where "Paradise" succeeds best is in bringing back some of the staples of the form—scenes in which fine men on horseback ride across a mountain stream, for instance. Clearly, this is a well-produced, even beautiful-to-watch, show. Trouble is, the series brings back too many of the *other* staples of the western form, the ones we call clichés. Things like incredibly violent gunfights. I swear I saw 12 people die in 12 seconds in one memorable bit encounter. Compared to Ethan Allen Cord, Matt Dillon was downright lazy.

Robert MacKenzie, writing in *TV Guide* (May 13, 1989) at the *end* of the first season, presented by far the most favorable and analytical review of *Paradise*:

> "Paradise" looks to revive the TV Western in a pure and respectful form.... [I]t has some fine scenery and a convincing period look, and its stories are about the things that Western are supposed to be about: self-reliance and manly honor and all that....
>
> Horsley is not too clever or too pretty in the role. We can believe his Ethan is hotheaded and stubborn but rueful and good for his word. His love interest Amelia (the clean-lined and dignified Sigrid Thornton), would have been the upright schoolmarm 20 years ago, here she's the upright banker, who loathes all this gunplay and macho posturing. The children ... are likable youngsters when the writers can refrain from giving them wiser-than-their years dialogue.... And the series has what good Westerns must have: simplicity....
>
> If the old-movie West is largely baloney, it is good baloney, and this series earnestly serves it up, free of spoofery.[29]

With a preponderance of negative reviews, however (MacKenzie notwithstanding), and miserable ratings, it was a miracle that *Paradise* lasted through its first year. Moreover, in one of the biggest programming surprises of the 1989-90 season, the show was renewed by CBS for a full second season (22 episodes). There were, of course, some sound business reasons for the renewal. Despite the fact that *Paradise* finished its first year on the air at a woeful 68 among all the shows broadcast during the 1988-89 season, it was CBS's highest rated new one hour drama. Furthermore, although it had by far the lowest "awareness level" of any hour series, its "Q rating" (a marketing survey that charts viewer satisfaction) was third highest of all network programs. Network executives were also impressed by the loyalty of *Paradise*'s fans, who were older, rural and largely women (traditionally CBS's strongest bases of support).

Europe also offered a lucrative market for Westerns and with only one season of *Paradise* filmed, there were not enough episodes to sell the show abroad. In addition,

Jacobs promised to make the show "a lot looser" during its second season, aiming especially for "a feisty, Maureen O'Hara–John Wayne sort of relationship" between Ethan and Amelia and a lot more action.[30] In keeping with the second part of his pledge, Jacobs literally "shot the works" in the two hour, second season premiere of *Paradise* featuring along with the regular series characters, Bat Masterson, Wyatt Earp, young Maverick, the Rifleman's son and numerous other television Western stars of the past. Gene Barry reprised his portrayal of *Bat Masterson* for the first time in nearly thirty years; likewise, Hugh O'Brian returned to the home screen as Wyatt Earp (it was the first time the two had ever appeared on the video range together, since each had worked on a different network). Charles Frank (who starred in *The Chisholms* for CBS in 1979 and *Young Maverick* also for CBS in 1979-80) again appeared as Amelia's estranged husband, Pierce Lawson; Johnny Crawford (Mark McCain on ABC's *The Rifleman* from 1958 to 1963) played a small role; Jack Elam (of ABC's *The Dakotas* in 1963 and NBC's *Temple Houston* in 1963-64) was cast as a likable prison convict; and Charles Napier (from NBC's *The Oregon Trail* in 1977 and CBS' *The Outlaws* in 1986-87) was featured as a ruthless lawman who kidnaps Ethan and throws him into a prison fortress hoping to extract from him the location of a cache of buried Confederate gold.

The cast of "A Gathering of Guns" was clearly a who's who of the video range. Two popular non–Western television stars were thrown in for good measure: Ray Walston of *My Favorite Martian* (1963–1966 on CBS) as a carnival pitchman and John Schneider from *The Dukes of Hazard* (1979–1985 on CBS) playing Sheriff Pat Garrett, the man who killed Billy the Kid. This "over the hill gang" comes to rescue Ethan from an impregnable prison. All of the regular cast members are also featured in a story that involves action, violence, humor, romance—and a hot air balloon! It was a show with something for almost every viewer and *Paradise* leaped from near the bottom of the Nielsen ratings to ninth place for the week. The biggest unanswered question was could the series sustain this kind of following when it returned to its regular hour format. Most of the critics still were not impressed; *Variety* (October 4, 1989) again blasted the show:

> ... it's not the same show. Just what it is remains a mystery....
> "Paradise" has borrowed liberally from "Gunfight at the O.K. Corral" and "High Noon." Everything but originality has occurred to those who put all this together. There's lots of gab but little action in this directionless series.
> "Paradise" is a waste of time and talent.

It was a harsh and undeserved appraisal of the series. Actually the story ("Home Again") cleverly involves a newspaper reporter named Frank who follows Ethan and Wyatt back to Paradise (from the prison) in search of a story. In the end it is revealed that Frank is L. Frank Baum, who authored *The Wizard of Oz*, and in a bit of fanciful fiction, viewers are led to believe that Claire was the model for Dorothy, and the scarecrow, hot air balloon, pail of water and other plot devices from the series opener helped inspire that children's classic. Whatever else might be said, it certainly seems grossly unfair to cite the story for a lack of originality.

Nevertheless, the series slipped still further in the ratings during its second season, ending the year at 79. CBS told Jacobs that there was little hope the show would return in the fall. Still, while rarely winning its time slot, it was a steady second. After 44 episodes, *Paradise* actually bit the dust briefly during the spring of 1990. Jacobs rushed east at the news and begged and cajoled CBS executives to keep the show alive (landing in the hospital with pneumonia) and did win a reprieve for the series. It was scheduled to become a midseason replacement beginning in January 1991. CBS senior vice president

Paradise: clockwise from top: Lee Horsley as Ethan Allen Cord, Sigrid Thornton as Amelia Lawson, Matthew Newmark as Joseph Carroll, Dehl Berti as John Taylor, Jenny Beck as Claire Carroll, Michael Patrick Carter as George Carroll, and Brian Lando as Ben Carroll.

Peter Tortorici later explained, "This wasn't a case where we canceled the show only to change our minds later. We just wanted to put on a lot of half-hour comedies and didn't have the right slot for 'Paradise'."[31]

Tortorici went on to say that CBS stuck with the show because of Jacobs' passion for the series and strong viewer mail. Jacobs bent over backwards to makes changes that would broaden *Paradise*'s appeal to viewers. First, he changed its name to *Guns of Paradise* (so it would not be confused with shows about Hawaii). Then he added more shoot-'em-up sequences and another younger character to attract more teenage viewers. The new character was a young gambler called Dakota, played by handsome, 29 year old John Terlesky. Terlesky was a native of Wyoming, Ohio, who played fullback and linebacker for the 1977 state championship Wyoming High School Cowboys' football team. He also ran track and wrestled for the Cowboys. The son of two doctors, Terlesky entered college as a pre-med major, but realized that acting was his true love. After three years of college, he was accepted by the American Conservatory Theater (ACT) in San Francisco.

Terlesky's prior television experience included NBC's *Legmen*, where he played a college kid named David Taylor who worked for a seedy private eye (Claude Akins). The series was canceled, however, after nine weeks. He also starred in several television pilots which never made it to the home screen and made guest appearances on such shows as *Empty Nest*, *The Famous Teddy Z*, and *Facts of Life*. In addition, Terlesky appeared in two feature films, *The Allnighter* (1987) and *Damned River* (1989) in addition to the aforementioned *Longarm* (1988).

Dakota was a gunslinging gambler who goes West to avenge his father's murder and is befriended by Ethan. When he discovers that it was Ethan who killed his father, there is a confrontation between the two men (in "Valley of Death"). After Ethan convinces Dakota that he was forced to kill his father in self-defense, the friendship is reaffirmed and on several occasions, Dakota saves Ethan's life.

During the show's third season, 13 additional episodes were filmed. Sigrid Thornton, unfortunately, left after the first eight episodes (in the story, she leaves Paradise because she can no longer face the daily possibility that Ethan may be killed) and is seen again in the final episode only via flashbacks. During that final season (January–May 1991), the mining town strikes it rich again with the discovery of a rich vein of copper. Ethan reluctantly agrees to become town marshal and plans are again made (and broken) for Amelia and Ethan to wed. Jacobs and Porter tried to give the show a harder edge by including more action and violence without losing the family appeal. *Paradise* might resemble *Little House on the Prairie* one week and *Gunsmoke* the next.

In fact, all of the 57 episodes of *Paradise* can be roughly divided into two categories: those that are more or less action-oriented, traditional shoot-'em-ups and those that focus on a problem or issue like the treatment of Indians or the destruction of the environment. In the first group were such exciting episodes as "Matter of Honor," a two part story featuring Chuck Connors (*The Rifleman*) as Ethan's old saddle pal, Gideon McKay, a notorious gunman. Hired by a powerful rancher who has started a range war over water rights, McKay has become a falling-down drunk. After being sobered up by Ethan, McKay turns against him to lead the escalating war against the small ranchers. There is plenty of action and nostalgia as Ethan and Gideon "stage" a showdown on the streets of Paradise to bring an end to the killing and violence. It is all very slick—and very entertaining.

Another action-packed episode, "A House Divided," featured Don Stroud (who played Captain Pat Chambers in *Mickey Spillane's Mike Hammer*) as the leader of a murderous gang of outlaws who seize the Paradise hotel and hold a group of townspeople (including Amelia Claire and George) hostage. Stroud will kill the hostages if his seriously wounded brother does not receive medical attention. John Taylor does succeed in saving the man's life, but ironically must kill him in the bloody shoot-out which brings the story to its dramatic conclusion.

In "The Common Good," another superior example of this type of episode, the gang of vicious outlaw, Johnny Ryan, is about to break their leader out of the Paradise jail and Deputy Charlie appears unwilling or unable to stop them. The townspeople turn to Ethan and pressure him into accepting the job of marshal. When the gang threatens to shoot

Ethan (Lee Horsley) saves John Taylor (played by Dehl Berti) from a lynching, in an early episode of *Paradise*.

up the town, the merchants overrule Ethan and release Ryan, but not before Ethan has humiliated him. Ryan vows revenge as he rides out of town. Ethan in disgust throws his badge onto the dusty street (shades of *High Noon*).

Several episodes (weeks) later Johnny Ryan does return to *Paradise*. In "Revenge of Johnny Ryan," the vicious outlaw escapes from a cage in which he is being transported and returns to Paradise to get even with Ethan. Using Amelia and the children as bait, Ryan lures Ethan into a trap. Ethan, however, is able to outsmart Ryan and finally kills him in a violent, action-packed gunfight. (Actor Craig Bierko turns in a thought-provoking performance as the ruthless outlaw, giving the character depth and believability.)

"Devil's Escort" is another superior action adventure story involving both the complex relationship between two men on opposite sides of the law (Ethan and his black prisoner, Don Bishop) and the attempts of a gang of men (led by the brother of one of the men Bishop has killed) to achieve their own brand of vigilante justice. Ethan and Bishop gradually come to respect each other as they cooperate to thwart the efforts of the vigilantes.

Several episodes—shown over three seasons—involve attempts to take Ethan back to Texas to stand trial for a killing Ethan claims was committed in self-defense. Actually, a bounty has been placed on Ethan's head by the family of the man Ethan killed and most of the men who try to capture Ethan are bounty hunters who plan to string him up along the way and collect the reward. A Texas ranger named Matthew Grady (a recurring role for John Beck, a veteran of *Nichols* and *Dallas*) saves Ethan's life in the first of these stories, "Hard Decisions," and allows Ethan to return home to his family in Paradise. (Ethan returns the favor in "Squaring Off" when he rescues Grady from the hangman—and incurs the wrath of the corrupt police chief who framed the ranger.)

During *Paradise*'s final season, Ethan voluntarily returns to Texas to stand trial for murder after he has been left for dead, hanging from a tree, by a gang of bounty hunters. (Dakota arrives in time to cut him down and thereby save his life.) In a rigged trial Ethan is convicted of murder and sentenced to hang. When it looks as if Ethan is about to escape, the dead boy's mother threatens to kill Joseph to gain revenge against Ethan. Even when her husband reveals that he witnessed the shooting of their son by Ethan and admits that it was done in self-defense, she refuses to accept the truth. As he attempts to prevent her from shooting Joseph, the gun goes off and the woman is killed. (Barbara Rush is excellent in the role of the embittered and hateful woman.)

One of the most enjoyable action-oriented episodes, "Crossfire," reunited one of television's most venerable on-screen father-son teams, Chuck Connors and Johnny Crawford. It was the first time the two actors had appeared together in over two decades and their first as on-screen father and son since *The Rifleman*. Doug McKay, the son of Ethan's pal Gideon, has volunteered them as hired guns in a range war that Ethan wants no part of. (Interestingly, both Connors and Crawford were reprising roles they had previously played on *Paradise*: Connors in "Matter of Honor" and Crawford in "A Gathering of Guns.") It was great fun for fans to see the two together again with Connors and Horsley playing off each other nicely.

A number of *Paradise*'s best episodes, however, deal with social issues or problems, which, while set in the Old West of 1890s, had considerable relevance to modern America in the 1990s: "Childhood's End" dramatically deals with child prostitution when Claire befriends a girl her age, whose stories of a glamorous life hide a steamier existence with her mother's traveling "social club"—Ethan intervenes when the girl is forced to have sex with a wealthy businessman; prejudice against Native Americans is handled effectively in a first season episode entitled "The Ghost Dance," and discrimination against the Chinese is presented in another first season episode called "A Private War," when an unscrupulous mine manager sets out to recapture two young Chinese indentured servants while ruthlessly taking over the business of a Chinese merchant; the problem of juvenile delinquency is movingly dealt with in "Crossroads," a story in which Joseph gets involved with a gang of fugitive teenagers after breaking the window of Mr. Axelrod's grocery store. Other timely social problems considered on *Paradise* during its first season include destruction of the environment (by a greedy lumber company) in "The Last Warrior" and gun control in "Stray Bullet" when Ethan accidently wounds Amelia while trying to subdue a rampaging drunk who is firing indiscriminately into a crowd of townspeople.

During *Paradise*'s second season, the series becomes even more explicitly political: an adoption scheme is thwarted by Ethan in "Orphan Train"; the use of illicit drugs comes under fire in "Dangerous Cargo," when Ethan puts an end to the opium trade which is being employed by mine owners to more easily control their immigrant Chinese miners; the fear of and prejudice against mentally disabled persons is effectively dramatized in "Shadow of a Doubt," when a young man is almost executed for a murder he did not commit solely because of his handicap; wife abuse is the subject of "Till Death Do Us Part," in which Ethan exposes a respected liberal judge as a wife-beater; when a smallpox epidemic hits Paradise in "The Plague," the reaction of the panic-stricken townspeople might be compared to the attitude many otherwise reasonable, intelligent citizens feel today toward victims of AIDS; in "Avenging Angel," the show's creators seem to be making a clear statement with regard to televangelists when a charismatic killer-turned-preacher cons and manipulates the town's faithful Christian believers while plotting revenge against Ethan and his family.[32] Even the reading disorder dyslexia is treated with concern in "The Bounty," when George is shown experiencing the effects of that problem.

Undoubtedly the most unusual episode of the entire series is "The Gates of Paradise," an allegorical drama, broadcast in January 1990. As the end of the year approaches, a mysterious black-clad horseman (Joseph Campanella) spooks Ethan's horse on a mountain trail, causing Ethan to fall into a deep abandoned mine shaft. The stranger coldly observes the accident, winds his pocket watch and rides off, leaving Ethan trapped in the mine. Ethan is discovered by Jerome, a mentally disabled young man, who leads him to safety. Ethan takes Jerome to Paradise, where he is recruited by Claire to help fix up the church. (Effectively played by Patrick Laborteaux, Jerome becomes a semiregular cast member.)

Meanwhile, the mysterious horseman arrives in Paradise and is surprised to find Ethan alive. John Taylor guesses who he is and the grim mission he is on when the stranger explains to him that he still has two appointments to keep before the New Year begins. Clearly the stranger represents Death—the Pale Horseman, the Grim Reaper— although why Ethan's life has been spared (or even, for that matter, why he was marked for death in the first place) is never made clear. Nevertheless, it is a most interesting and out-of-the-ordinary story.

Some of the most entertaining episodes are those that focus on the continuing characters and their relationships with each other. In "Long Lost Lawson," the final episode of the first season, Amelia's estranged husband Pierce returns to Paradise. Badly in need of money and on the run from a man he has swindled in a fraudulent land deal, Pierce sells Amelia's bank and then steals the papers that would give her the divorce she so desperately wants. During the second season, Amelia regains the favor of Paradise's residents when she loans out her own savings in order to help townfolk who have lost everything when a new gold strike (on Ethan's ranch) turns out to be a bust ("fool's gold") in an episode entitled "Boom Town." (The following week, when banker Henderson is shot by Johnny Ryan, Amelia regains her former position as *Paradise*'s banker.)

In the final episode of the second season, "Dust on the Wind," Amelia and Ethan finalize plans to tie the knot, but the closure of the mine (after a disastrous explosion and cave-in) ruins not only their plans but the town of *Paradise* as well. With no jobs and no money, residents begin a mass exodus. Ethan plans to leave with the children for a better paying desk job in Denver, but Amelia decides to stay and tough it out. Finally, in what Jacobs probably believed would be the last scene in the series, Ethan returns with his family to the welcoming arms of Amelia and to the happy relief of John Taylor and their other friends in Paradise.

Regular series fans also must have enjoyed meeting the children's father, Robert Carrol (well played by Edward Albert), a charming, handsome con-man who had (unbeknownst to them) abandoned their mother years before she died. Ethan must face the possibility of losing the children to their rightful father in "Birthright." However, seeing the depth of the children's love for Ethan and his affection for them (after he has seriously wounded Ethan), Carroll decides to leave Paradise without revealing his real identity to them. (The younger children still believe that their real father died a hero, although Claire and Joseph suspect the truth.) All's well that ends well, but "Birthright" does include one development that certainly made devoted fans unhappy: it is Amelia's last episode, as she too leaves Paradise—presumably forever.

The final episode of the series, "Unfinished Business," provides a fitting close to an outstanding series. Ethan sends the children away with Dakota before facing the gunman who once left him for dead and has returned to finish the job. While waiting for the showdown, Ethan reflects on his years with the children and the other friends he has made in Paradise. Flashbacks from earlier episodes are effectively used to illustrate his feelings.

In a moving scene with John Taylor, Ethan articulates the "code" by which he has lived—and by which he may now die. It has been the code of nearly every Western hero who rode the video range from Hopalong Cassidy to Matt Dillon:

> JOHN TAYLOR: It's not the only choice, letting him kill you.
> ETHAN: No?
> JOHN TAYLOR: No. Ethan, tomorrow morning you be standing at that window. I'll be across the street at a window with a buffalo rifle. When Bridges steps out onto the street, we fire!
> ETHAN: I can't do that.
> JOHN TAYLOR: Why not? You're not a hero out of a dime novel, you're a man defending his family... A man defending his family doesn't worry about rules. He wins any way he can. Lies, cheats, steals...
> ETHAN: Listen, John Taylor...
> JOHN TAYLOR: And he doesn't worry about chivalry. Whatever he does is fair because he's a man protecting his family.
> ETHAN: I said no! Now listen, I have lived my life a certain way. It may not make any sense to you, but I cannot go against that now. If I did, if I changed the rules just to stay alive, what would be left? I wouldn't be any good to the children. I wouldn't be any good to myself. And it wouldn't be all that much different than dyin'. You don't think so?
> JOHN TAYLOR: It doesn't matter what I think Ethan. If you think so, then it's so.

Happily, with more to live for than his adversary, Ethan "wills" himself to beat him—even though the killer is faster—and Ethan stands triumphant as his family returns to show him their love and concern. The camera pulls back as Ethan embraces the four children in the dusty main street of Paradise. He is a man who has remained true to his principles *and* his family. It is a vivid depiction of the quintessential moment in any family Western.

One of the most comprehensive reviews of *Paradise* was written following the first season for *The Westerner* by Michelle M. Sundin who had recently visited the set. Among other things, she observed that:

> ... Executive story consultant and co-creator Robert Porter has put together a concept that differs significantly from the formula western....
>
> The hero does not wear a white hat or a marshall's star.... Ethan Cord is aware of his many faults and failings, but his strength is his humanity, ... his stubborn willingness to do what he feels is right....
>
> The children aren't the smart mouthed brats from the sitcoms. They come from a very closed environment and their arrival in "Paradise" lands them in a world of wonder, excitement and modern day problems.... The relationships that develop and grow are the glue that holds the show together.... "Paradise" isn't vulgar, cutesy, or a stale rehash of tired stories set in Cowpie Gulch. It is a thoughtful, sensitive program that combines powerful writing and excellent casting into an hour you won't sleep through.[33]

Castle and Podrazik were not quite as enthusiastic in their assessment but did state that *Paradise* "is an admirable late 1980s attempt to revive the nearly moribund western format."[34] This writer would go much further and state unequivocally that *Paradise* was the best network Western to be broadcast in over a decade.

A casual meeting early in 1985 between author Larry McMurtry and Suzanne de Passe, head of production for Motown Productions, at a health spa in Tucson was to have

Robert Duvall as Augustus "Gus" McCrea, in *Lonesome Dove*.

far reaching consequences for the future of the Western on television. The two became friends and de Passe asked if McMurtry had anything she could buy the rights to. He sent her a copy of the manuscript for his latest novel, *Lonesome Dove*—about 1000 typewritten pages. De Passe paid McMurtry $50,000 for the television rights, later discovering that all three networks had already rejected an opportunity to purchase those rights.

When *Lonesome Dove* won the 1985 Pulitzer Prize for literature, de Passe realized she had a hot property on her hands. Always a strong supporter of the television Western, CBS was then persuaded to provide the largest portion of the money needed to finance the production of the miniseries. (The novel was considered to be too long and complex to fit the usual two hour television film format.) The novel had won wide critical acclaim and had become an almost instant bestseller with 300,000 hardcover and 1.2 million paperback sales. Among the long list of plaudits it received were these:

> Everything about "Lonesome Dove" feels true.... These are real people, and they are still larger than life" [*The New York Times*].
> A marvelous novel ... "Lonesome Dove" has all the action anyone could possibly imagine ... a wealth of tales, an extravagance of good talk and an abundance of energetic humor appearing on most every page ... superb [*Chicago Tribune*].
> If you read only one western novel in your life, read "Lonesome Dove"[*USA Today*].
> "Lonesome Dove" is Larry McMurtry's loftiest novel, a wondrous work, drowned in love, melancholy, and yet, ultimately, exultant [*Los Angeles Times*].

Stephen Harrigan, writing in *Texas Monthly*, said that

> Though the novel borrows elegantly from a variety of sources—trail drive memories, the works of J. Frank Dobie, the historical friendship of Charles Goodnight and Oliver Loving, even old movies—its own singular vision is never in question. Overlong, slow-to-start, "Lonesome Dove" is nonetheless an irresistible book, a ragged classic fueled by McMurtry's passionate regard for his outsized characters and by his poignant reckoning of their limitations.[35]

Larry McMurtry is a self-avowed critic of the myth of the cowboy. In an interview with Mervyn Rothstein of *The New York Times* (November 1, 1988), he explained, "I don't feel that it's a myth that pertains, and since it's a part of my heritage I feel it's a legitimate task to criticize it."[36] *Lonesome Dove* focuses on the differences between the mythic West of pulp fiction and the much less romantic reality of day-to-day life on the frontier (in this case specifically an 1870's cattle drive). As one reviewer, Nicholas Lemann put it, "the lonely ignorant, violent West."[37] According to McMurtry, his criticism of these Western myths has sometimes been misunderstood and has often met with considerable resistance:

> Sometimes the resistance is total. Some people read "Lonesome Dove" as a reinforcement of the myth. They want to believe that these are very good men. They are clinging to an idealization, to the pastoral way of life as being essentially less corrupt than the urban way. And thinking otherwise threatens them, threatens the little comfort they've had.
> The worst effect of clinging to these myths is simplification, or rather oversimplification, not merely of the cowboy, but of human experience itself, as lived in the American West or any other place....
> It occurred to me in "Lonesome Dove" that the men who drove the cattle up the trail were in the process of killing the very thing they loved. They knew it, and that knowledge lent poignancy to what they were doing, and their memories of it. And the point at which a certain way of life begins to die, and begins to be transformed into a very crude myth, is interesting.[38]

It was clear that the film version of *Lonesome Dove* would not be an ordinary movie. Logistics alone precluded that from happening: eight hours of air time (less commercials), a budget of nearly $20 million, a big-name cast, and a devastating 16 week shooting schedule involving massive location shifts, dozens of sets, 89 speaking parts, 1000 extras, 90 production people, 1400 head of cattle, 100 horses and 30 wranglers. Though it was being produced for the home screen, the film's scale was a vast throwback to the bygone days of such large screen epics as *The Alamo* and *How the West Was Won*. (To place the logistical task confronting Motown Productions in perspective: they would be filming the equivalent of one feature-length movie every 30 days for 120 days.)

The "guardian angel" of the project—the man responsible for faithfully adapting this literary classic to the screen—was Bill Wittliff, a veteran writer-producer-director whose credits included such films as *The Black Stallion* (1979), *Barbarosa* (1982) and *Red-Headed*

Stranger (1986). In the opinion of Stephen Harrigan, "Most of his films reflected, in one way or another, a preoccupation with the myths and lingering values of the Texas frontier."[39] Like his friend Larry McMurtry, he grew up in rural Texas in the forties and fifties, when it was still possible to observe firsthand the fading spectacle of the open range. In an interview, Wittliff explained: "I think I was the perfect screenwriter for this. I really do. The people in the book are all Larry's people, but I knew them too. I never got jammed even for a second wondering who these people were or what was at their core."[40] As Harrigan observed,

> . . . Wittliff was obviously more than "Lonesome Dove"'s screenwriter or its executive producer. He was its custodian. I stayed up for three nights with his script and found that in its 373 pages it managed to accommodate all the book's vital particulars while discreetly pruning its shaggy story line.[41]

The man selected to direct *Lonesome Dove* was a 44 year old Australian director named Simon Wincer. Wincer had recently gained prominence with two Australian films, *Pharr Lapp* (1984) and *The Light Horseman* (1988). In these films he had demonstrated a stylish way of handling narrative and a talent for moving around large groups of animals.

Why was an Australian chosen to direct what was a profoundly American story? Wittliff, whose screenplay *Barbarosa* was directed by Australian Fred Schepisi, believes "that Australian moviemakers share important perceptions with Western Americans. They have a good sense of frontier and landscape and epic scale. Simon has demonstrated that he can capture the epic scale in film."[42] Wincer who has a cattle ranch in Australia, commented in an interview: "I'm used to large-scale projects. And this one is as epic as they come. When I came to Texas I realized it was like remaking the Bible."[43]

Wincer was blessed with a superb cast of veteran actors in the lead roles. The incomparable Augustus McCrae was played by the Academy Award-winning (for *Tender Mercies* in 1983) actor Robert Duvall. In the course of the story, Gus rescues a beautiful whore from the clutches of an appallingly villainous half-breed, slams a surly bartender's head onto the bar of a saloon, engages in two desperate battles with Indians and dies a heartbreaking, unforgettable death in Montana.

Actually, Duvall had been originally approached to play the other lead, Captain Woodrow F. Call, but Duvall preferred to play Gus. As he later explained in an interview with *TV Guide*:

> Great character. A lot of people thought I should play Call, but my ex-wife, who's very sharp—she's an actress—said, "Bobby, you should play Gus." When I do theater, Gus is the kind of part I would play. In films, Call is the kind of part I usually get. Both parts are terrific, but I just wanted to try something different.[44]

Later, he explained how the book influenced his portrayal of Gus:

> . . . The book was my guide for this character. I'm not an authority, but to me, it was wonderful literature. As I read it and let it dictate what was there to me, I found that McMurtry gave me what I needed to know as a guideline. The script was great, but the book was the catalyst. It was a part I really looked forward to doing, because it was something different for me, something new for me to do.[45]

Tommy Lee Jones seemed equally perfect for the role of Captain Woodrow F. Call. Jones, who had won an Emmy for playing the ruthless killer Gary Gilmore in *Executioner's Song* (1982), is a Harvard educated native Texan who raises cattle and horses on his ranch in San Saba, Texas. An avid rider and polo player as well, Jones insisted on doing his own riding stunts (which included subduing a bucking bronc) for *Lonesome Dove*. Jones told

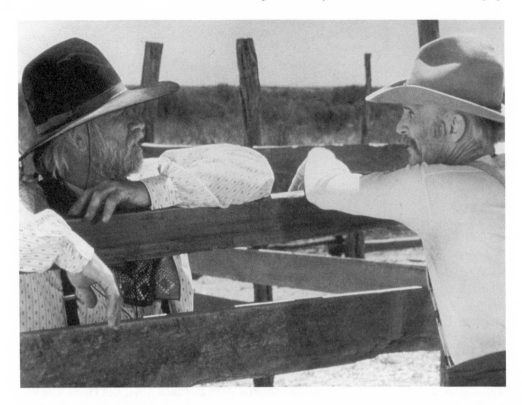

Tommy Lee Jones (left) as Captain Woodrow F. Call and Robert Duvall as Augustus McCrae (Gus), in *Lonesome Dove.*

writer Stephen Harrigan that he based his interpretation of Call—"a man so interior and taciturn that he cannot even bring himself to acknowledge his own son"—partly on his own two grandfathers, as well as Charles Goodnight. Harrigan, who personally visited one of the location shoots, described Jones' portrayal of the larger than life Call:

> ... on a horse, he was spectacularly convincing. There was about him a certain unstated pride—a reveling—in the fact that he was a Texan, that the character he was playing came to him not just through research but as a kind of legacy, through his own bones.[46]

Duvall and Jones played off each other well. Their characters were almost opposite in their personalities: Call is the quintessential introvert, quite, sullen, and taciturn, while Gus is an extrovert, gregarious, charming and philosophical. Although they have spent nearly all of their lives together, Gus and Woodrow remain vastly different people. A man who believes "any job worth doing is worth putting off indefinitely," Gus wiles away the day sitting on his porch, drinking whiskey, swapping lies and moseying into town around sundown to enjoy the comforts of the sweet Lorena, who never charges him too much and actually seems to enjoy having sex with him.

Call, on the other hand, is a rigidly proper man of few words and even fewer vices, who seems content with a lackluster existence that offers him few pleasures beyond riding across the river occasionally to steal some cattle from a Mexican bandit who stole the cows from Texas ranchers. "You like money even less than you like fun," Gus loves to remind him.

The central female character in *Lonesome Dove* is Lorena Wood, the town prostitute

The women of *Lonesome Dove*: Anjelica Huston (left) as Clara Allen and Diane Lane as Lorena.

at the Dry Bean Saloon. Lorena joins Call and McCrae's cattle drive to Montana and is subsequently kidnapped by a renegade half-breed and his gang of cutthroats. After being sold to a band of traders, she is rescued by Gus. Selected to play this demanding role, Diane Lane's extensive experience belies her youthful appearance. Lane first appeared on stage when she was only 6 years old and at 13 played opposite Laurence Oliver in *A Little Romance*. The daughter of a theater workshop director and a model and singer, Lane has starred in *Cattle Annie and Little Britches* (1980), *The Outsiders* (1983), *Rumblefish* (1983), *The Cotton Club* (1984), *Streets of Fire* (1984) and *The Big Town* (1987). Lane expressed her feelings about landing the role of Lorena in an interview promoting the miniseries:

> Lorena is the true cliché whore with a heart of gold. She's not a conniving person. She wishes she was because everyone else is.... [She is] a very introverted character and that can be difficult to play on a TV schedule. I thought it would be a great challenge.
>
> Lorena loves Gus but she's not in love with him. Sex has been such a bitter experience for her. She loves him like a father figure. But it's more than that. He loves her completely. He knows her better than she knows herself. She's powerless to resist his love. She could win a fight with a dragon, but there's no point in fighting Gus.[47]

The role of Clara Allen, Gus' long lost love, was given to *Prizzi's Honor* (1985) Oscar winner Anjelica Huston. Huston, daughter of the late and much revered actor and director John Huston, is a respected actress with such outstanding films as *The Dead* (1987), *A Handful of Dust* (1988), and *Crimes and Misdemeanors* (1989) to her credit. Citing the quality of the cast and the book as dual incentives for joining the project, Huston later explained:

> It's a fascinating book and I was very hard-pressed to put it down. It was one of those books where the closer you get to the end, the more upset you are . . . but you can't resist going on. . . . The part [of Clara] provided me with the opportunity to play a Western woman who wasn't necessarily just a sort of prototype.[48]

Danny Glover was cast as Joshua Deets, the black cowboy tracker and longtime friend of Gus and Call. Deets is the Hat Creek Outfit's most dependable cowhand and sets a high moral tone for the story. Glover, who gained his greatest fame as Mel Gibson's partner in the *Lethal Weapon* film series, was the recipient of a cable-television ACE Award for playing the title role in the HBO drama *Mandela*. He played a role similar to that of Deets in the 1985 large screen Western epic *Silverado*. To prepare for this role, Glover studied his historical notes on the earlier movie:

> A lot of blacks fled the South to the Southwest during Reconstruction. Many of them worked as cowboys. That was the first equal employment opportunity that people had. The black cowboy was skillful. And who knew more about horses than those who had been taking care of the master's horses during slavery? They became great cowboys in the West.[49]

Robert Urich, best know for his heroic television roles like Spenser in *Spenser for Hire* and Dan Tanna in *Vega$*, was cast against type as Jake Spoon, a suave but unreliable cowpoke who falls in with a gang of rustlers and ends up dangling from the end of a noose. After playing a series of good guys in urban settings, Urich was intrigued by the opportunity to play a womanizing drunkard in an historical period the actor confessed he knew little about:

> I realized my whole notion of the West and cowboys was fashioned by Hopalong Cassidy. I've also spent most of my career playing good guys who always got it right, who always made the proper moral choice. And that's boring. I thought it was time to grow up and play a real grownup character who had different textures and failings.[50]

A surprisingly mature Rick Schroder was chosen to play Newt, a young cowpoke and the illegitimate son of Call, who refuses to recognize him as his son because the boy's mother was a prostitute like Lorena. Despite his age (18), Schroder had both film (*The Champ*, 1979) and television (*Silver Spoons*) experience, although he had never appeared in a Western. "I didn't even know how to ride a horse," he later announced. "They took me out to Texas three weeks early. I learned how to rope, bulldog, tie and run."[51]

Other key roles in *Lonesome Dove* went to D.B. Sweeney (as Dish Boggett, a young cowboy infatuated with Lorena); Chris Cooper (as Sheriff July Johnson, who is encouraged to hunt down and arrest Jake for a shooting incident); William Sanderson (as saloon piano player Lippy Jones, who decides to leave Lonesome Dove with the cattle drive); and Frederic Forrest (as Blue Duck, the renegade half-breed who has long been the avowed enemy of the two former Texas Rangers).

The final casting choice (Forrest) greatly upset Duvall. After considering a number of actors for the role, the producers gave it to Forrest. Duvall was displeased because a Comanche Indian whom he had recruited to take a screen test for the role was rejected. Duvall's choice, who was not a professional actor, was given a lesser role in the film. Duvall later complained: "They wanted a name. Somebody suggested Rudolf Nureyev; somebody else wanted Klaus Kinski. I mean, it was ridiculous. Now Freddy did all right in the part, but Freddy was not right for the part and he knew it."[52] Duvall attributed the error to last-minute casting decisions that he believes are typical for television.

Wittliff took the 900 page novel with its 102 untitled chapters and divided it into four appropriately titled two-hour sections: "Leaving," "On the Trail," "The Plains" and "Return." The haunting themes of Basil Poledouris provided the perfect background

music. In addition to being the story of fascinating relationships between and among unforgettable characters, *Lonesome Dove* is the exciting story of a hazardous cattle drive from
Texas to Montana dramatized in the second and third parts. Jake Spoon, on the lam from
the law in Arkansas where he accidently killed the town dentist, spins a romantic yarn
about his travels to Montana, a land so lush and beautiful it would be the ideal spot for
a cattle ranch. For Call this is an opportunity for one last adventure, one last test of manhood. For Gus, the drive will provide a chance to see once more the only true love of his
life—Clara Allen, a woman who rejected him to marry a more stable and reliable horse
trader in Ogallala, Nebraska. And so, against Gus's better judgment, he reluctantly agrees
to Call and Spoon's plan for a cattle drive to Montana.

Lonesome Dove, while paying tribute to the courage and fortitude of the drovers, also
symbolizes the passing of an era. "They're people makin' towns everywhere," observes
Gus. "It's our fault too. We chased out the Indians ... hung all the good bandits ...
killed off most of the people that made this country interesting to begin with." But Montana offers them one last opportunity "to see the country before the bankers and lawyers
get it all." Still, as *Time*'s Richard Zoglin observes, *Lonesome Dove* "is surprisingly non-
revisionist in its picture of the West. The good guys still perform stunning heroics with
six-shooters, and Indians are faceless villains who whoop when they ride.... This may
be the most vividly rendered Old West in television history."[53]

Since the action of McMurtry's novel takes place on a wide variety of locations from
southern Texas to Arkansas to Nebraska and finally Montana—which would be pro-
hibitively expensive—alternate sites had to be located. While New Mexico was used to
film many of the Northern scenes, Wittliff insisted that the Texas scenes be shot in Texas.
The production company set up shop on a 56,000 acre ranch outside Del Rio. Within
its fences were landscapes that could credibly represent anything from desert to brushland
to a Hill Country glade. Some filming—including the San Antonio scenes were filmed
at Alamo Village near Brackettville.

One of the most difficult scenes to film was the stampede. Ideally, longhorn cattle
would have been used, but, as head wrangler Jimmy Medearis explained to Stephen Harrigan, longhorns—particularly cows with calves—were not "maneuverable." For the sake
of historical accuracy, Mexican Corrientes were the next best thing. They were framey,
wild-looking beasts with substantial horns, with a few in the herd that looked as shaggy
and humpbacked as buffalo.[54] Roy Reed of the *New York Times*, who was on hand to
observe the filming of this climactic scene, described it for his readers:

> To create a convincing sandstorm and stampede, you start with 300 head of bony,
> Mexican-bred Corriente cattle, the kind they use for roping at rodeos. The animals are graz-
> ing 200 yards away. Beside the camera are three huge fans and about a ton of sand in paper
> bags. As the wranglers urge the cattle toward the camera, the fans start and the sand is thrown
> in front of the blades. The sand mixes with the dust on the ground, and in seconds there is
> a cloud whirling and darkening. The wranglers, out of camera range, shout and try to frighten
> the cattle. The animals surge forward into the storm. The cameras roll....
>
> They head past the camera in a frenzy, and whooping cowboys plunge beside them on
> speeding horses, firing guns. Mr. Wincer waits until he sees the whites of their eyes. Then
> he commands, "Action!" and the camera rolls ... there is happiness all around. This was
> a stampede.[55]

Stephen Harrigan, who also observed one of the more difficult scenes being filmed
firsthand, could attest to its gritty realism:

> A group of horsemen came riding from one end of the street toward the deep wash that
> led down to the river. They were seated on antique highbacked saddles and armed with horse

pistols and Henry repeating rifles and Green River skinning knives. The horses looked lanky and weathered as the men who rode them, and the spectacle of them wading into the tranquil river in the charged evening light was exhilarating.[56]

Happily, for once all the money, time, effort and care put into a television Western paid off. This time critics and viewers alike were in agreement about the merits of a television Western. *Lonesome Dove* received lavish praise from media reviewers, as well as high Nielsen ratings. The critic for *Variety* (February 9, 1989) proclaimed that:

> ... "Lonesome Dove" not only revitalizes the traditional Western but gives new life to longform TV period pieces, gallantry adventure and romance, as well as just straight ol' story-telling. Starting with a compelling, vigorous first hour, the 8-hour, $20-million telefilm just keeps getting better.... The camaraderie, the bickering between stern Call and the irrepressible Gus, and the collected energy of all the gathering cowhands light up the TV set.
>
> Scripter Bill Wittliff's extraordinary teleplay bursts with energy.... Douglas Milsome's gorgeous camerawork tracks a furious woman down Fort Smith's boardwalk, arches lightning igniting the horns of the charging cattle in a sudden storm, pulls in tight on men's faces caught in oppressive heat, or, in magnificent long shots, captures the solitude and beauty of the Western frontier....
>
> The richness and sense of period authenticity have been fashioned by production designer Cary White, [and] costumer Van Broughton Ramsey.... Basil Poledouris' supportive score reflects the intimacy and grandeur of the work.

Martha Bayles writing in *The Wall Street Journal* (February 6, 1989) pointed out in her admittedly "rave review":

> ... A word about wit. If breathtaking scenery, gritty realism, funky characters and heart-stopping adventure aren't enough for you, then add salty dialogue. It's a relief, after seasons of TV miniseries that spend gobs of money on everything except a decent script, to relish Mr. McMurtry's colorful language (adapted by Bill Wittliff). You may not guffaw, but you will grin for eight solid hours—that is, when you're not misting up at the sad parts, which also are delivered with Texas eloquence instead of Hollywood [insipidity]....
>
> [T]he miniseries pulls off the rare feat of updating a myth without also outdating it. As a uniquely American image of honor, the Western hero still packs an emotional wallop—when he is done right. And in "Lonesome Dove," he definitely is done right.

Richard Zoglin, *Time Magazine*'s resident television critic, wrote (February 6, 1989):

> ... "Lonesome Dove" rides rings around the overstuffed soap operas that usually pass for "epics" along Broadcast Row. Larry McMurtry's fat novel has been brought to TV—by writer Bill Wittliff and director Simon Wincer—with sweep, intelligence and sheer storytelling drive....
>
> "Lonesome Dove" is surprisingly nonrevisionist in its picture of the West. The good guys still perform stunning heroics with six-shooters, and Indians are faceless villains who whoop when they ride. Yet in its everyday details—the dust and the spit, the casual conversations about whoring, the pain of a man getting a mesquite thorn removed from his thumb—this may be the most vividly rendered old West in TV history.

Tom Shales of *The Washington Post* (February 3, 1989) was enthusiastic:

> "Lonesome Dove" is enough to give one new respect for the mini-series, new respect for Texas, new respect for CBS and even new respect for television. There is almost never anything this good on network TV.

The only "discouraging words" about *Lonesome Dove* were written by David Braun, Texas director of the Nature Conservancy, for *The Washington Post* (February 9, 1989). Braun took issue with what he labeled "old wives' tales and distortions about nature that are truly misinformed and harmful." Braun also objected to the "man against nature"

theme of McMurtry's book (and the subsequent miniseries) in which the heroes were sub-
jected to "a fantastic series of natural disasters: floods, dust storms, lightning, hailstorms,
snake bites, and a grasshopper invasion." In Braun's opinion "any one of these oversized
events might happen once in a decade, but not all in one year on one trail drive." Other
errors cited by Braun in the book and television production included the effects of a cen-
tipede bite, an attack by a swarm of water moccasins, the aridity depicted in south Texas
and the "casual" presence of an armadillo:

> ... most centipede bites are no more harmful than a bee sting. While the venom can
> cause pain and swelling, even the largest Texas centipede would not have caused Lonesome
> Dove's barber, Dillard Brawley, to lose his leg. By far the worst inaccuracy in the book (and
> the mini-series) is the fatal attack on the young Irish immigrant by a swarm of water moc-
> casins as he crosses the Nueces River. ... To begin with, water moccasins do not live as far
> south as the Nueces River. Moreover, they do not go around in poisonous swarms attacking
> humans and horses. ...
>
> [The] town of Lonesome Dove is said to be in south Texas less than 100 miles from the
> mouth of the Rio Grande River, but it is described as dry and dusty as if it were in a west
> Texas desert.... South Texas of the time was covered with a humid sub-tropical forest of
> amazing natural diversity.
>
> There are also historical inaccuracies. At one point in the story. Gus kicks an armadillo
> out of his path without remark. But a real Texan of the time would have been astonished,
> since the armadillo had only recently wandered into Texas from South America.

While earning almost universal critical acclaim, *Lonesome Dove* was also a huge commercial success by nearly every criteria. It scored the biggest miniseries ratings triumph
in five television seasons and made money for the network from its first airing alone, a
rare phenomenon for a miniseries. *Lonesome Dove* scored a four-night rating of 26.1 with
a 39 percent share of the audience. The first two-hour segment was the most watched
program of the week (January 30–February 5), drawing over 44 million viewers, a 28.5
rating and a 42 percent share. Part four ranked first for the following week (February
6–February 12) with comparable figures: 41.5 million viewers, 27.3 rating and a 41 percent share. Parts two and three ranked eighth and fourth for the week respectively, with
only slightly less impressive figures.

The series almost singlehandedly turned around a season and a half of dismal ratings
and helped CBS escape a second consecutive year in the Nielsen basement. In total,
Lonesome Dove generated more than $30 million in advertising revenue for an investment
by CBS of less than $20 million. The numbers were also impressive for the companies
which controlled the rights to subsidiary sales. Qintex Entertainment, the company in
charge of rights distribution of the series, and its partner, Motown Productions, shared
in almost $20 million from the sale of foreign, cable, video and syndication rights (from
an initial output of $4 million by Qintex and $50,000 by Motown).

A Western on television had not generated such critical acclaim and financial
rewards since the golden age of television Westerns during the late fifties and early sixties.
There was immediate talk of not only one, but two network reruns, discussion of a "prequel" featuring McCrae and Call in their younger days, and even the possibility of a
regular weekly series based on *Lonesome Dove*. The series was repeated once on CBS and
then sold to Ted Turner for use on his TBS or TNT cable channels.

Given the ratings (*Lonesome Dove* was the highest rated miniseries of the 1988-89
season) and the critical acclaim (it won seven Emmys and a Peabody Award), a sequel
was inevitable. In fact, television's *Return to Lonesome Dove* was in development long
before Larry McMurtry's own published sequel, *Streets of Laredo*, was written. Scripted
by screenwriter John Wilder (of *Centennial* fame) with McMurtry only a consultant,

Return picks up the story of Captain Woodrow Call immediately after he has buried his beloved partner Gus at the conclusion of *Lonesome Dove*. Its plot follows Call's return from Texas to Montana with a herd of wild mustangs, and while it retains many of the surviving characters from the original series, it also introduces a number of new ones.

There are also a number of significant cast changes. Among the leads, only Rick Schroder reprises his original role as Call's illegitimate son Newt. Two of the major characters, Captain Call and Clara Allen, had to be recast because of Tommy Lee Jones' and Anjelica Huston's unwillingness to return. Oscar-winner Jon Voight now assumed the role of Call and Barbara Hershey became Clara.

Voight had given outstanding performances in such landmark films as *Midnight Cowboy* (1969) and *Coming Home* (which earned him an Academy Award in 1978) and had appeared in such cable movies as *Chernobyl: The Final Warning* (1991) and *The Last of His Tribe* (1992). Giving full credit to Jones' initial screen interpretation of Call, Voight later explained to *Chicago Tribune* writer Jay Buffin (November 14, 1993), "If I ignore it, I do so at my own peril. His portrait [of Call] was so moving and so perfect to me that in some sense, I almost didn't want to do this." Schroder had suggested Voight to the producers after Jones had turned down the sequel. Schroder and Voight had worked together in Schroder's first film, *The Champ* (1979).

Barbara Hershey had appeared in several *Kung Fu* episodes with David Carradine. Her recent film work included such diverse theatrical films as *The Right Stuff* (1983), *The Natural* (1984), *Hoosiers* (1986), *Hannah and Her Sisters* (1986), *The Last Temptation of Christ* (1988) and *Beaches* (1988) and such highly acclaimed made for television movies as *Killing in a Small Town* (which earned her an Emmy nomination in 1990) and *Paris Trout* (1991). Hershey's Clara Allen was so completely different from Huston's that she quickly made the role her own. Her biggest problem was that physically she was too slight and had to project her strength internally.

Other major roles in *Return to Lonesome Dove* were played by film veterans Lou Gossett, Jr. as Isom Pickett, an old pal of Call and McCrae who helps drive the mustang herd to Montana, and William Petersen as Gideon Walker, a former Texas ranger buddy, who becomes involved in a discreet romance with Clara. Newcomers Reese Witherspoon, as a married young woman who becomes romantically involved with Newt, and Nia Peeples, as McCrae's illegitimate daughter, were also featured.

Virtually stealing the film from an acting standpoint, however, were the villains. England's Oliver Reed as George Dunnegan, a scheming Scotch cattle baron who wants Call's land and son, brought to life every scene that he was in. Dennis Haysbert (who drew favorable attention in the Alex Haley miniseries *Queen*, a season earlier) as the sinister Cherokee Jack, a murderous half-breed, made his every moment on the screen memorable.

A number of important supporting characters were reprised by the actors who played them in *Lonesome Dove*. Tim Scott as Pea Eye Parker, Chris Cooper as July Johnson, Barry Tubb as Jasper and William Sanderson as Lippy helped provide continuity with the original. In addition to Wilder, there were other changes in key production personnel. Mike Robe (whose previous credits included *Murder Ordained* in 1987) replaced Simon Wincer as director and Douglas Milsome, *Lonesome Dove*'s director of photography, was promoted to second-unit director.

Horses replaced cattle as the key nonhuman participants. The head wrangler on *Return* was Corky Randall, whose late father had been a horse trainer for Roy Rogers and Gene Autry. His experience working with horses dated to *Duel in the Sun* (1946) and included *The Searchers* (1956) and *The Misfits* (1961). For *Return to Lonesome Dove*, Randall had to obtain 250 horses including 150 that were unbroken to play the wild mustangs.

The horses were leased from the Sombrero Ranch in Boulder, Colorado. He also had 30 horses brought in from Hollywood that were trained to work in front of the camera. (These animals cost $250 a week, plus feed, shoeing, and veterinary care.) At least one wrangler was on call to feed livestock 24 hours a day. Another problem inherent in such an operation was logistics. There was a continual shifting of animals and equipment between locations, with much of the filming done in Montana near Butte and in various parts of Texas.

Although a considerable portion of the film is spent on dialogue in which characters digress at length about what happened to them in the earlier series, there are plenty of exciting moments. Among these are a massive roundup of wild horses, a raging brush fire, and a climatic range war.

Return to Lonesome Dove was aired in three segments, Part I—"The Vision" on Sunday, November 14 (9–11 P.M.), Part II—"The Force" on Tuesday, November 16 (9–11 P.M.), and Part III—"The Legacy" on Thursday, November 18 (8–11 P.M.), 1993. Despite the fact that *Return* earned the highest ratings of any CBS Sunday movie that season to date (*A Walton Thanksgiving Reunion* surpassed this the following week), it was not considered a rousing success by network executives. It had lost 8.5 million viewers from its lead-in, the top-rated *60 Minutes—25 Years*, and drew less than two-thirds as many viewers as the first installment of the original *Dove* in 1989. Parts two and three slipped even more. Three million less viewers watched part two and 300,000 less turned in for the concluding segment which finished eleventh and sixteenth respectively in the week's Nielsen's.

Reviews of *Return to Lonesome Dove* were mixed and none of the critics could escape making a comparison with the original. *Entertainment Weekly*'s Ken Tucker called it (November 12, 1993), "an honest and often entertaining piece of work" which "serves primarily to mar our memories of the original." Yet he urged viewers to:

> Stick around for seven hours and you'll find that this is a perfectly decent Western, you might even shed a tear or two. But you'll also know that, when it's finished, a grand piece of TV mythmaking has been reduced to a horse opera. C+.

USA Today's Matt Roush (November 12, 1993) made a similar comparison:

> ... *Return to Lonesome Dove* is an honorable and often effective attempt to recapture the original's stirring, poignant magic.
>
> Breathtaking to look at, with sequences of action that thrill or horrify, *Return* unfolds deliberately, slowly staking its own epic claim on the surviving characters and inventing several of its own.... While short of a classic, this remains tall in the saddle.

His evaluation of Voight, however, was not as favorable. In Roush's opinion while "Voight tries hard," he "lacks Jones' grizzled inscrutability" and thus his Call "is not as forbidding, remote or tragic."

John J. O'Connor of the *New York Times* (November 12, 1993) also had mixed reactions to *Return*, "There are the same long shots of majestic plains and dramatic skies. There is also something else: a naggingly pervasive dullness." On the other hand, O'Connor went on to say:

> Exceptionally patient viewers will be rewarded. There are a few riproarin' scenes. Sunday's episode ends with Call, in his long johns, flinging himself from a cliff into a river to escape the diabolical Cherokee Jack. Thursday's closes with a raging fire destroying Allen's ranch. And Thursday's final hour is the high point as Dunnegan and Call finally have their showdown. Good stuff, but three hours would have been more than sufficient to contain the bulk of it.

Time and *Newsweek*, however, saw little of merit in the series. Martha Smilgis and William Tyman writing for *Time* (November 15, 1993) saw *Return to Lonesome Dove* "as less a sequel than a lazy recycling of scraps from older, blander westerns.... In place of the hardscrabble poetry of the original is a meandering frontier soap opera, which lopes at a pace that could put tumbleweed to sleep."

Newsweek's David Gelman stressed the fact that *Return* was "not based on McMurtry's own praised sequel but rather a script by John Wilder in which the clichés sometimes thunder as loud as the hooves. ('Sounds like a hard man, this captain.' 'Yes sir, but he's fair.' 'And you're loyal—I like that.')" Surprisingly, Gelman was the only critic who liked Schroder's performance, calling it "the best" in the film while he claimed Gossett was "just along for the ride," Hershey seemed "to have wandered West from the Upper West Side," and Reed was a "hammably hissable villain." He concluded that "the sudsy plot complications ... mostly get in the way of the scenery. And that, at least, is worth tuning in."

The producers, of course, knew "up front" that a sequel to such a universally recognized classic as *Lonesome Dove* would not please everybody and would probably antagonize some, but they felt it needed to be done. As executive producer Suzanne de Passe later explained to *USA Today*'s Matt Roush (November 12, 1993):

> ... there was a tremendous appetite for it, and it occurred to me I had an obligation as well. *Lonesome Dove* defined my career as a producer. I did love it, and I wondered if I could be content to go off and watch others make it. Once I jumped in, like everyone else from cast to crew I did it wholeheartedly and didn't hold back.

De Passe and co-executive producer Robert Halmi, Jr., also secured rights to *Streets of Laredo* for future CBS broadcast (with no announcement of who would play Call, Jones or Voight). And plans were made for a syndicated series based on *Lonesome Dove* that would premier in the fall of 1994. *Variety* proclaimed, "*Lonesome Dove: The Series* is the most anticipated television series since *Star Trek: The Next Generation*." Released in syndication in September of 1994, the series opened with a three-part story.

The episode begins in the den of a modest frame house. The time is 1925. An old wooden sign reading HAT CREEK CATTLE COMPANY AND LIVERY EMPORIUM hangs on the wall. A 70 year old man (obviously Newt Call—his face is never shown), pulls out a book from his collection entitled *Lonesome Dove, Tales of the Plains* by Newt Call and begins speaking:

> It would surely confound them that knew me as a young fella to learn that I'd ever made a dollar as a book writer. Ain't nobody more surprised than myself. Ya see folks just assumed that I could scarcely read and write back then. I was so busy soakin' it all up, I'm sure they took me for shy or plain dumb. Truth be told, it was a bit of both. My father, Captain Woodrow Call of the Texas Rangers, had given me a good horse by the time he finally owned up to bein' my paw. He gave me his name and I rode off from him to make good of it. I wanted my own dream, I just didn't know right off what that was....

Thus did *Lonesome Dove: The Series* begin relating the adventures of Newt Call via flashbacks. According to the offiicial studio synopsis:

> It's been three years since Augustus McCrae and Captain Woodrow Call left the dusty chaparral of Southwest Texas on a cattle drive that would change their lives, and the shape of an entire frontier, forever. Although he couldn't have known it at the time, the events that began on that epic journey would also forge the character of the shy, hard-working boy they brought along, then known as Newt Dobbs. Now, with his father's name, and a strength borne of unforgettable adventures, heartbreaking losses and quiet joys, Newt Call bids the Captain goodbye and rides off into the vast, rugged plains of late 1870s Montana, ready to make his own way.[57]

Early in the course of his travels, Newt encounters none other than Buffalo Bill Cody. After rescuing a cultured black woman named Ida Grayson on her way to join her husband who is an army scout at a nearby fort from an attack by outlaws, Newt and Bill arrive in a picturesque little town known as Curtis Wells. It is here that Newt meets the lovely Hannah Peale, a bright, sophisticated and willful young woman with whom he immediately falls in love. Hannah's father, Josiah, is the liberal, enterprising, Eastern-educated publisher of the *Montana Statesman*, who runs his business and his family with a stern but fair hand.

After a whirlwind courtship, Newt and Hannah overcome the resistance of her father to marry and build a life together. Newt had won Hannah from another equally ardent suitor—Clay Mosby, a dashing Southern gentleman and former Confederate Colonel. (It seems Hannah bears an uncanny resemblance to Mosby's late wife, Mary.) Meanwhile Ida Grayson, who has recently become a widow when her husband was killed by renegade Indians, decides to buy the local hotel using Newt as her "front" man.

The joyous occasion of Newt and Hannah's wedding is shattered by an attempted bank robbery. Mosby's gang of cutthroats are stealing a gold shipment that is to be used to finance construction of a railroad through Curtis Wells. The wedding resumes after Newt and Buffalo Bill thwart the robbery (although Mosby himself escapes) and Ida, as a wedding present, rechristens the hotel, "THE LONESOME DOVE."

The old man closes his book, and the first tale is finished. But there are many more stories to be told as Newt and Hannah set out to build a life together. As the producers explain:

> Newt devotes himself to starting a ranch, constructing a cabin, gathering horses and clearing the land. To that end, he accepts employment and has numerous adventures whenever his skills as a scout or horseman are called for. When these adventures end, however, it is always to the task of putting down roots that Newt returns, willing to work hard, assuming that life will be as constant as he.
>
> Hannah wants to start a family. We'll see her learn to build, ride, shoot, and master all the skills necessary to eke out a life amidst the frontier's harsh vicissitudes. But she also yearns to travel, to experience firsthand the rich lore of the West. Not fully aware of it yet, Hannah is a restless soul who isn't ready to be tied down.[58]

Relative newcomer Scott Bairstow was selected from hundreds of candidates in the United States and Canada to play Newt after an extensive audition process. The 24-year-old Bairstow, who had been born in Manitoba, Canada, had just landed the starring role in his feature film debut, Walt Disney's *White Fang 2: Myth of the White Wolf*. His previous television experience consisted of a costarring role opposite Cybill Shepherd in the highly rated CBS movie *There Was a Little Boy* and a guest star spot as a faith healer in an episode of *The X Files* on Fox.

Christianne Hirt was signed to play Hannah. A veteran of more than fifteen films and movies of the week, Hirt had appeared in such television series as *The Commish*, *Bordertown*, *MacGyver*, and *21 Jump Street*. Her role as a 15-year-old figure skater in *Skate* earned her a Gemini Award nomination (Canada's equivalent of the Emmy) in 1988. She also appeared in the *Summer of '45*, an eight-part CBC miniseries spanning World War II, where she aged from 25 to 60 years old.

Other continuing characters on *Lonesome Dove: The Series* included Paul LeMat as Josiah Peale, Diahann Carroll as Ida Grayson and Eric McCormack as Clay Mosby. Many well-known actors were featured in guest roles including *Gunsmoke*'s Dennis Weaver in a delightful portrayal of hard-drinking, straight-shooting, fun-loving, Buffalo Bill (as a sort of "Wild Bill Hiccup," according to one reviewer); *Trackdown*'s Robert Culp

Scott Bairstow stars as Newt Call in *Lonesome Dove: The Series* (Chris Large/Canadian Dove Productions).

smoothly playing an unscrupulous businessman; Billy Dee Williams as Army scout Aaron Grayson; George Kennedy as a hanging judge; Jack Elam (veteran of many a television and film Western) as a roving cowhand; and two experienced Native American actors Graham Greene (of *Dances with Wolves*) as Red Hawk, a would-be educator, and Gordon Tootoosis as Indian John, a would-be doctor (who was actually far more competent than the town's only white physician). *Lonesome Dove: The Series* certainly did not lack star power.

Considerable expense and effort also went into providing an appropriate setting for the series. Located in the majestic rolling foothills of the Rocky Mountains, about 45 minutes from Calgary, Alberta, Canada, two full Western sets were constructed. The town of Curtis Wells occupied some 100 acres, while the other set for the town of Sweetwater comprised about 350 acres. At a cost of nearly a million dollars, it took 70 workmen three months to construct the two towns. Decorating each town in period antiques cost an additional quarter million dollars and included 20 cast iron stoves, enough tables and chairs to seat 100 people in the saloons at one time, hundreds of yards of period wallpaper, 10 beds, a complete functioning blacksmith shop, a fully outfitted newspaper with a working period press and 50–60 period oil lamps.

In the story, Curtis Wells is located in Montana Territory ("in the middle of fine cattle country"), where the stagecoach stops and cowboys, frontiersmen, gunfighters, and pioneers mingle freely on the main street. The town is, according to the writers, "new and full of promise." Sweetwater, on the other hand, is situated in the Black Hills of Dakota Territory. It is built in a low gulch with hills surrounding it. Modeled after the actual town of Deadwood, it is dusty when it is dry and muddy when it is wet with lots of "atmosphere" which is found in saloons, brothels, a Chinatown, gunsmith, dancehall, wash house and an opera house. Described by writers as having "a forlorn look and feel about it with endless possibilities for misadventure," Sweetwater has a sheriff's office which is always busy and an undertaker with the most successful business in town.

In addition to beautiful scenery and big stars, *Lonesome Dove: The Series* is blessed with an outstanding musical score by Terry Frewer (based on themes by Basil Poledouris in the original). Most reviews of the series were favorable. Paul Droesch of *TV Guide* (October 1–7, 1994) said:

> It looks terrific ... stars Scott Bairstow and Christianne Hirt are likeable . . . [and] director Sidney Fune keeps things moving and knows when to point the camera at the scenery. My score (0 to 10): 7.

Under the expert and loving guidance of executive producers Suzanne de Passe and Robert Halmi, Jr., *Lonesome Dove: The Series* should succeed despite the absence of Robert Duvall, Tommy Lee Jones, Ricky Schroder, Jon Voight, et al. The unknown quantity is the writing. "Based in part on characters created by Larry McMurtry in *Lonesome Dove*," the series seems to be totally devoid of any continuing input from McMurtry. It is hoped that this handicap will not prove fatal. Fans of the original series as well as viewers who enjoy good Westerns may still hope for a series based on the early exploits of Texas Rangers Gus and Woodrow.

Meanwhile, no doubt buoyed by the success of *Lonesome Dove*, executives at ABC prepared to launch their own weekly Western series, *The Young Riders*, in the fall of 1989. The two men most responsible were Josh Kane, executive producer of the program, and partner in Ogiens-Kane Productions under whose aegis *The Young Riders* was being made, and the main writer for the series Ed Spielman (who was responsible for creating *Kung Fu*). For Spielman it was the culmination of a six year dream, which had begun in 1983 in Fargo, North Dakota, when he had spotted a 120 year old "help wanted" circular asking for men of good moral character to deliver the mail.

The Young Riders related the story of the Pony Express, young men who faced marauding bandits, hostile Indians, wild animals and the harsh elements of nature to deliver the mail along a rugged 2000 mile route that stretched from St. Joseph, Missouri, to Sacramento, California. The work was considered to be so dangerous that the Pony Express hired only orphans who would not leave any family behind in the event they were killed. Their survival often depended on teamwork, and that was the basis for *The Young Riders*.

Surprisingly, only one previous television Western dealt with the exciting adventures of the Pony Express riders. In 1959-60, thirty-nine black and white episodes of a syndicated series called *Pony Express* were made starring Grant Sullivan as a trouble-shooter for the Pony Express with Bill Cord and Don Dorell in featured roles. Castleman and Podrazik called it "basic Western fodder" and advised, "let it ride by undisturbed."[59] Kane explained that one of the goals of *The Young Riders* was to introduce the Western to a new generation of television viewers:

> There is an audience that has grown up pretty much without a Western tradition, television or films. Part of our job and part of what I think ABC wants to do is bridge that gap, perhaps bring a new audience to the Western form.[60]

To launch the series, two of the cast members of *The Young Riders* joined a memorial ride along the eight-state route of the actual Pony Express. This was part of a campaign to make the trail part of the National Trails System.

Initially the series focused on a group of six Pony Express riders plus their trainer, their cook and the local marshal. They were an unlikely mixture of races, sexes and famous-names-to-be: "The Kid," a handsome, soft-spoken young man who is so poor he has to earn money in a boxing match (last three rounds with a professional fighter) to buy a horse; Jimmy Hickok (who will become known as "Wild Bill" of Deadwood fame), a youth with a considerable reputation as a gunman; Billy Cody (who will make his fortune later as "Buffalo Bill"), hot-tempered and cocky and always eager to prove his superiority; bald, mute Ike (who lost his voice and hair in a childhood bout of scarlet fever), the handicapped representative; the minority rider, Buck, who is half Kiowa Indian; and Lou, a girl who masquerades as a boy so she can get a job as a rider to earn the money she needs to pay the orphanage that is boarding her younger brother and sister. Their mentor and the stationmaster at the Sweetwater way station is grizzled, old Teaspoon Hunter, who provides experience as well as understanding when necessary. On hand to cook and act as surrogate housemother is Emma Shannon (during the first season), who has been deserted by her husband. Emma is sweet on the town marshal, Sam Cain, who tries to keep the young riders from getting into too much trouble (also during the first season only). With two exceptions, the cast members were relative newcomers to television.

Ty Miller, who began acting to earn spending money while he was in college, played "The Kid." Commenting on the character at a press conference, Miller explained: "The Kid is a pretty simple person. He takes information in, doesn't say much, but is morally honest, and if something needs to be done, he does it."[61]

Josh Brolin, son of actor James Brolin, was cast as Hickok. Brolin claimed to have been fascinated by Westerns during his childhood while growing up in Paso Robles, California.

Stephen Baldwin, youngest brother of Alec Baldwin, was signed to portray Cody. The 23 year old Baldwin (who had been featured in such films as *Married to the Mob*, *Beetlejuice* and *Working Girl*) actually had considerable previous acting experience. After appearing Off Broadway with Daryl Hannah in *Out in America*, he won a succession of film and television roles. His movie debut came in *The Beast* (1988) and was followed by a role in *Homeboy* (1989). He also guest-starred in television episodes of *China Beach*, *Family Ties*, and *Kate and Allie*. On PBS, he portrayed Gutter Pup in *The Prodigious Hickey*. (His later screen credits included such acclaimed films as *Born on the Fourth of July*, 1989; *Last Exit to Brooklyn*, 1989; and the black Western *Posse*, 1993.) In a telephone interview Baldwin later said:

> When I heard about the show, I tried to avoid it. I thought it was going to be one of those typical, phony-baloney TV Westerns ... [but] at the audition, I changed my mind because Cody is a nice guy, but tough.... [The show] is a lot more than good triumphing over evil. It gives you an idea of who each person is individually.[62]

The role of Ike McSwain was the first regular series role for Travis Fine. He said he, "welcomed the challenge of playing a young person afflicted, yet still living a life of adventure and being productive due to his inner strength."[63]

Gregg Rainwater, whose grandfather was a Cherokee and Osage Indian, seemed ideally cast as the halfbreed Buck Cross. Rainwater said of his role:

> ... there is a responsibility on me to give a positive role model, basically. That's something I'm hoping for, and I know that through the writing that'll come about. [I will try] not to just do Buck as an Indian, but as a person. Hopefully, then, someone who sees the show, who may have racial prejudices, will think he's pretty okay and carry the attitude into his daily life.
> The important thing about him, is his spiritual quality everyone can relate to. He's level-headed and clear, and his thinking is inspired. He's the sensible one of the young Pony Express riders.
> Too, he's faced with the problem of adjusting to a white world, and still retains ties to his Indian background.[64]

Yvonne Suhor, who played Lou McCloud, was pleased to be cast as "one of the guys, offering me something most actresses don't have: a chance to ride, shoot and play a real character."[65] Unfortunately Suhor's disguise (especially with her glasses off) would not have fooled anyone—certainly not five healthy young men who worked every day with her and slept every night in the same bunkhouse.

The pivotal role of Teaspoon was given to veteran character actor Anthony Zerbe, whom *TV Guide* once described as having been "born with an actor's face, lean, saturnine, half-starved, villainous."[66] After a few starving years onstage in New York, he began to earn a good living on television from the mid-sixties on with roles in such action shows as *Mission: Impossible, Gunsmoke* (in "The Noon Day Devil," Zerbe, in a genuine tour de force, portrayed twins—one a missionary padre, the other a gunslinger) and *Mannix*. Zerbe's first big break came in 1975 when he was cast as Lieutenant K.C. Trench opposite David Janssen's *Harry-O* (Harry Orwell). Although the series only lasted one season, it won for Zerbe a Best Supporting Actor Emmy. The role of Teaspoon was tailor-made for Zerbe. The raw-onion-chomping, tobacco-spitting Teaspoon was so tough that he took baths in a horse watering trough, where he rubbed on bear grease for soap and instead of drying off with a towel, used a horse's tail! (You could watch this scene repeated every week in the opening credits.)

Melissa Leo, who played Emma, was much younger than the middle-aged character she portrayed—a tribute to her acting skill. Discussing the role with Norman Zollinger of *The New York Times*, she said:

> I'm excited about this series. It isn't bound by convention in picturing the Old West. In Buck we have a part–Indian character without the stereotype, and Gregg Rainwater, who plays him, is, of course, of native American heritage himself. I think we're telling a good story about real people.[67]

Rounding out the regular cast for the initial season was Brett Cullen as Sweetwater's intrepid marshal, Sam Cain. Born in Houston, Cullen had appeared in the television Western series *The Chisholms* as Gideon Chisholm and in the highly-rated miniseries, *The Thorn Birds*.

It was no easy task to star in *The Young Riders*. The members of the production

Opposite: The Young Riders **featured Pony Express riders (from left) Yvonne Suhor as Lou McCloud, Gregg Rainwater as Buck Cross, Josh Brolin as James Butler Hickok, Ty Miller as The Kid, Stephen Baldwin as William Cody, and Travis Fine as Ike McSwain.**

company, cast (except for Zerbe and Cullen), technicians, crew (except, of course, the wranglers, who were genuine cowboys), were all newcomers to the West. They hailed from New York and California and a few points in between, and had never been exposed to the real West. All of the young leads and many of the crew members were sent to something called a cowboy camp in Arizona prior to shooting the pilot, where they learned how to ride, shoot, rope, etc.—at least "well enough to fake it." All of the exterior scenes and much of the interior work was shot at Mescal, Arizona, one of the two movie towns operated by the Old Tucson Company, a private promotional firm that stages gunfights and historical minidramas for tourists to the Southwest.

Set high in the Sonoran desert and mountain country thirty miles Southwest of Tucson, Mescal, with its mesa of sage, yucca and ocotillo and the Santa Catalina Mountains and Rincon Peak in the background, was as convincing as it was picturesque. The Western buildings that served as the set for Sweetwater and various other frontier towns were not just falsefronts, but complete with interiors which eliminated the necessity of frequent trips back to Hollywood. Cast members, however, often had to work in 120 degree heat dressed in buckskins and flannels. In the winter the temperature often dropped to 30 degrees and 16 to 18 hour work days were not uncommon. Scheduled at 9 P.M. Thursday evenings, ABC launched the series with a pilot episode on Wednesday, September 20, 1989. That day many newspapers carried the following uncredited AP review:

> "The Young Riders" is so mundane and cliché-ridden that teen-agers who see it may say, "So this is how the West was wan." . . .
> Our young riders . . . are a varied lot. One swaggers, is tough and eager to use his pistol. Another is a halfbreed; he wears an earring. Another can hear but can't speak due to a childhood disease that left him bald. . . .
> There's even a William Cody, who . . . he is so cocky that Teaspoon, the grizzled old plainsman who is teaching survival skills to the new riders, is moved to ask, "You think you're pretty hot stuff, don't you?" "Yup," young Cody says. Teaspoon fixes him with a steady gaze. "Cowpies," he sneers. . . .
> This retort indicates a minor flaw in the show, such as an awful script. And an awful script sometimes means there will be more of the same.

Most of the other reviews were nearly as critical. *Variety* (September 27, 1989) said:

> Judging from its opening episode, the makers of "The Young Riders" have little to offer fans of "Bonanza" or "Gunsmoke." The Western genre is strictly a backdrop to showcase a stable of prospective teen idols in a series revolving around a group of youthful Pony Express riders.

Matt Roush, writing in *USA Today* (Sept 20, 1989) offered this "mixed" opinion of *The Young Riders*:

> "The Young Riders" probably won't make TV history—unless it's a hit, in which unlikely case it would be real news. But it succeeds as a lovingly produced and craftily targeted stab at making the Western appealing to teeny-boppers. . . . "Riders" nicely captures the exhilaration of the ride, with glossy photography and bouncy music, taking sudden detours for often violent encounters. As TV Westerns go, this one breaks no new ground, but sure does earn its keep.

The NY *Daily News* (September 20, 1989) television critic, Kay Gardella, offered a cautious assessment:

> If you like action-adventure series, with a touch of history, and the accent on youth, "The Young Riders" may appeal to you. But it needs a better script than tonight's to shoot it out in the ratings battle.

The Young Riders got only one star from David Bianculli in the New York *Post* (September 20, 1989):

> A saga about the formation of the Pony Express is a great idea if it's handled properly, but "Young Riders" handles it all wrong, which makes the idea a grating one.
>
> Instead of Dodge, this series runs its heroes right through Cliché City. There's a gunfight that sheds no blood (and makes no sense), a young girl disguised as a boy (in a disguise about an impenetrable as Clark Kent's glasses), and a lot of other nonsense, including a musical theme that reappears at the drop of a hat—or a hoof.
>
> The only saving grace is the unusually pretty photography, credited to director Rob Lieberman and John Toll, director of photography.... Even so, "The Young Riders" is a far cry from "Lonesome Dove." It's even a far cry from "Paradise."

Newsday's (September 20, 1989) Bill Kaufman was more negative than positive in his comments:

> Judging from the preview episode, "The Young Riders" might please some die-hard western fans who aren't too picky, since the show seems to be a hell-for-leather pastiche of every oat-burning cliché ever written....
>
> How saloon scenes will be handled remains to be determined, since ostensibly most of the Pony Express boys are underage. But the sunsets are all spoken for, with at least a handful of postcard-like scenes, where mount and rider slowly disappear over the horizon.

As if mediocre reviews were not problem enough for *The Young Riders*, on September 14, 1989—before the first episode had even been broadcast—Morgan Creek Productions filed a lawsuit against ABC and MGM/UA TV and the Ogiens-Kane production company, claiming that the title of the series was "a patent ripoff" of its 1988 theatrical film *Young Guns* and that the series also appeared to be copying the film in its story and advertising. Morgan Creek sought "damages in excess of 1.1 million dollars," and "an injunction against further infringement," and "impoundment of any infringing products."

The representatives of MCP, who admitted that they had yet to view an episode of the series, asserted that *The Young Riders* was designed to trade on the success of *Young Guns*—a tale of six corruption-fighting youths known as "The Regulators." Series creator Ed Spielman claimed that the concept for the show predated the film by "over sixteen years" and was based on his 1971 short story "On the Plains." He said he later developed this as a pilot teleplay that aroused the interest of Kane and Ogiens in 1982.

Patricia Glaser, one of the attorneys representing ABC and MGM/UA TV, told *Variety* (September 17, 1989) that the film and the series were "totally unrelated" and said that the only similarity was that they were both Westerns: "It's the good guys and the bad guys, and people get shot." However during the third season, ABC ran disclaimers at the beginning of each episode and over the preview promos for the next week's episode stating that *The Young Riders* was: "A production of MGM Worldwide Television Group. Not based on Morgan Creek's films *Young Guns* and *Young Guns II*."

Every continuing character in *The Young Riders* is featured in at least one episode and most of the Pony Express riders in several. Hickok (Jimmy, as his friends called him) is the focus of more stories than any other character. Because he is a young man who has already earned a considerable reputation with a gun, he has sought the relative peace, tranquility and obscurity of the Pony Express. Yet his past is always catching up with him—in the person of a bullying hired gun who has tracked him down in order to challenge him, or a boastful impersonator who is committing bank robberies in Hickok's name, sending a bounty hunter on his trail poised to kill him for the reward that has been put on his head (in "Dead Ringer").[68] Sometimes Hickok uses his special talents in a noble cause—as when he defends a pacifist religious group against a hostile town (in "The

Peacemakers"). When Hickok accidently kills a young woman during a gunfight, he takes on the job of sheriff in a lawless town hoping to meet death quickly as his just retribution (in "Bad Company"). During the third season, he becomes involved with a band of vigilante abolitionists led by a religious fanatic who is wanted for murder, because Jimmy's sister and her husband have joined "the cause." In another episode, Hickok searches for a new rider who has disappeared in a town overrun with outlaws. All of the Hickok-centered stories are action-packed with traditional gunfights and violence.

The Kid (most assuredly not Billy the Kid—who did not move West until the early 1870s, over a decade after the demise of the Pony Express) is involved in many of the stories—both action and romance oriented. From the opening episode, when the Kid learns that Lou is really a woman while tending to a wound she has received, there is a growing romantic attraction between the two that ultimately culminates in their marriage. During the first season, the Kid meets up with his older brother, Jed, who seems to have found a place for himself in the Army. Actually Jed is leading a gang that is posing as a cavalry unit in order to steal gold for the budding Confederacy. In an exciting two-part story, the Kid infiltrates a band of Southern guerrillas led by a charismatic Southern Robin Hood in order to expose them for the Army. Meanwhile, the Kid's romance with Lou falters from time to time as he becomes involved with a schoolteacher (in "Color Blind"), his childhood girlfriend, and even a beautiful and charming Southern spy.

Cody is, of course, young Buffalo Bill, whose Wild West Show featured a Pony Express rider as one of its attractions and helped keep it from passing into obscurity. Even as a young man Cody was noted for his enormous ego and flair for exaggeration and self-promotion. In one episode he writes a story about the Pony Express which is published by an Eastern magazine. The other riders resent the way he has built up his own role and minimized, slanted or otherwise distorted their contributions. In another Cody story, he unknowingly becomes involved in a plot to assassinate U.S. General John C. Fremont when he almost joins a theatrical troupe (in "The Play's the Thing"). Finally, Cody helps three wealthy, retired Eastern businessmen experience the real West *and* conceives the idea for a Wild West Show. (Stacy Keach, Sr., son of director James Keach and father of actor Stacy Keach, Jr., plays one of the Eastern tycoons with great gusto.) At the close of the story, Cody suggests to another Eastern entrepreneur:

> CODY: Instead of bringing people to the West, take the West back to your people in the East.
> MR. MARSH: I don't quite follow you.
> CODY: I've been thinkin' about this, Mr. Marsh, ever since I met you. Now imagine this—if you got yourself together a couple of real fancy shooters an' a couple of dozen horses and maybe some wild animals or somethin' like that, like buffalo or somethin'. Put that all together, bring it back to New York and start to put on some shows.

Buck, who is uncomfortable in both the Indian's world, which he has sensed is doomed, and the white man's world, which rejects him because he is a half-breed, is the focus of some of the series' most moving and meaningful stories. In one episode a young woman, who has just arrived in Sweetwater, takes a fancy to Buck, but he is caught in the crossfire between her, her tyrannical father and a cruel suitor. In another ("Pride and Prejudice"), Buck finds storekeeper Tompkins' long-lost wife and daughter. The problem is that they have assimilated the culture of the Sioux tribe that had taken them in and are no longer "acceptable" to the other white townspeople.

Ike can communicate only through sign language and becomes very frustrated when others are unable to understand him. In one early episode, Ike witnesses a stagecoach robbery and massacre. He identifies the leader of the gang responsible, but the robber's men set out to permanently silence Ike. During the second season, viewers learn (in "Old Scores") that Ike's family was murdered by a gang of cutthroats while Ike was a little boy. Hiding in the barn, Ike gets a good look at one of the men. Now years later, Ike spots the man traveling in a wagon train. The problem is that the man has reformed and now has his own wife and son. Ike ends up saving the man and his family from a vengeful gang whose loot he once stole and donated to a church. In the best Ike-centered story, "The Littlest Cowboy," Ike, bitter after being beaten by men who took advantage of his handicap, befriends a terminally ill little boy and learns a lesson about courage.

Lou (Louise) has been forced to disguise herself as a man in order to get the job of Pony Express rider. Complications arise when her female instincts and romantic impulses threaten to interfere with her work. She is constantly being torn between the traditional desires of a woman and those attitudes that have come to dominate the modern woman. Still Lou could shoot as well as most of the men and had no peers in the way she could handle a horse. Several of the episodes that focus on Lou relate via flashbacks the tragic story of her earlier life. Abandoned by her father, who was a gunrunner, Lou took her younger brother and sister to a church orphanage after the death of her mother. Several years later, Lou set out to earn enough money so that the three of them could live together. She got a job doing laundry at a bordello and did not discover until later what the women who resided there did for a living. After being raped by the pimp who ran the house, she runs away with the help of one of the other prostitutes (a woman named Charlotte). It is then that Lou cuts her hair short, purchases thick eyeglasses and dons the pants, shirt and hat of a man.

In one first season episode Lou, decides to return to the orphanage to retrieve her brother and sister, but her estranged father gets there first and kidnaps them. With the help of the other young riders, Lou rescues them from the isolated fortress where he has taken them. In the ensuing gun battle, the Kid has to kill her father.

During the final season, Charlotte arrives in Rock Creek, with money she has stolen from the pimp, to start life over running a dress shop. Unfortunately, the pimp tracks her down and, rather than go back to her old life as a prostitute, Charlotte kills herself. The pimp discovers Lou's identity and tries to kidnap her, but she turns the tables on him. When he tries to escape, the Kid has to kill him. Thus Lou's secret earlier life is safe—but she decides to share it with the Kid, with whom she has fallen in love. Before the first season is over the other young riders have all discovered Lou's real identity—it took Teaspoon a little longer (and a dip in the old swimmin' hole). Of course, it did not matter that Lou was a woman, and she continued to ride for the Pony Express and share in their adventures until the final episode.

The most entertaining episodes of *The Young Riders* featured stories about Teaspoon. In "Then There Was One," Teaspoon, who had been sent for reinforcements shortly before the fall of the Alamo and thus survived the bloody massacre which followed, sets out for Texas with one of his fellow survivors. A serial killer is on the loose, eliminating all the couriers who survived the Alamo tragedy twenty-five years earlier. The final confrontation between Teaspoon and the killer (another courier who has gone insane) takes place inside the Alamo mission lighted only by candles in the middle of a raging storm. When it is over, only Teaspoon remains as the sole Alamo survivor.

Teaspoon faces off against an old enemy in "Ghosts," when a loathsome murderer known only as "The Buzzard Eater" appears in Sweetwater. Teaspoon proves faster and more accurate than the villain, menacingly played by *Kung Fu*'s David Carradine (in a dramatically different kind of role for the usually "heroic" actor). "The Exchange" was a two hour episode which ended the second season. When Teaspoon arranges for a bank robber to be hanged, the man's brother kidnaps a young woman who has been "like a daughter" to Teaspoon. He wants to exchange her for his brother or he will kill her. This precipitates a massive and explosive shoot-out involving all of the young riders who have rallied to Teaspoon's assistance.

Teaspoon demonstrates that he is not too old for romance in several moving stories. A beautiful woman posing as a French piano teacher distracts Teaspoon while a gang she is involved with plots a bank robbery in one episode. After discovering her real identity, Hickok allows her to leave Rock Creek without breaking Teaspoon's heart with the truth. She is arrested outside of town—at the same moment that Teaspoon ponders the rose on her piano which has withered and died. It is a poignant moment. In another episode, Teaspoon's favorite former wife (number three), Polly, comes to town to open a saloon and falls prey to a killer seeking vengeance against Teaspoon. Teaspoon discovers he still has strong feelings for her.

Even Emma and Sam are featured in episodes. After surviving a massacre of wealthy settlers near Salt Lake, Emma's estranged husband arrives in Sweetwater looking for shelter from Emma. In another story, Sam finds his dedication to the law sorely tested when the man responsible for his wife's murder comes to Sweetwater.

Changes in *The Young Riders* occurred at the end of each of the first two seasons. At the end of the first season, Sam Cain is promoted to territorial marshal and leaves Sweetwater with Emma. In the first episode of the second season, Teaspoon becomes the new peace officer for Sweetwater and a new rider is added to the cast. Noah Dixon, an educated freeborn black who is active in the abolitionist cause, passes through town and decides to stay and join the Pony Express. By the season's second episode a replacement has been found for Emma, when Rachel Dunn is hired as the way station's cook and general housekeeper.

Don Franklin, a veteran of two short-lived cop shows (*Knightwatch*, 1988-1989 and *Nasty Boys*, 1990), is cast in the role of Noah and is featured in several episodes involving slavery. In "Kansas," he is enslaved when he tries to free his former teacher. In another episode Noah winds up in a race riot when he tries to see a woman with whom he has fallen in love and is accused of murdering an army recruiter.

The beautiful Clare Wren makes her television debut as Rachel, a woman haunted by her past. She has killed one of the men who murdered her husband, and his father and brothers are out for revenge ("Ghosts"). In another episode, "Daisy," Rachel's former lover leaves his 9 year old daughter in Rachel's care while he flees from a riverboat gambler he has cheated. Rachel, who intuitively discovers Lou's secret the first time they meet, forms a special bond with the young female Pony Express rider, and they frequently have "woman-to-woman" talks.

At the beginning of the third season the setting is switched from Sweetwater, Wyoming, to Rock Creek, a larger town in Nebraska Territory, lying on the line between slave and free soil. Teaspoon sends the Kid and Hickok to rebuild a way station near Rock Creek which has been destroyed by a gang of ruthless gunrunners seeking to take advantage of the abolitionism-slavery controversy. Teaspoon later joins them and decides to stay, when Rock Creek's marshal (an old friend) is murdered. Teaspoon becomes marshal in the new town and the entire crew is relocated to Rock Creek.

In the season's second episode another new cast member is added when the riders befriend a young man whose guardian has been killed by a band of outlaws. The teenager turns out to be Jesse James. Later, in another episode, his older brother Frank shows up. (He has been captured by Hickok after participating in a bank robbery gone wrong.)

Frank tries to get Jesse to return to Missouri with him and join a band of renegades preparing to do battle against abolitionists and Union sympathizers, but Jesse declines — for the time being. He has become part of Teaspoon's extended adopted family. But Frank is to return in a later episode with different results. (Young Christopher Pettiet with his innocent, yet brooding, face is fine as Jesse, and Jamie Walters, a dead ringer for Robert Blake, is perfect as the misguided Frank.)

Early in the third season, Ike is killed off. Ike, who was always shy around girls because of his handicap, meets and falls in love with a young woman named Emily. When her father is murdered by an unscrupulous gambler, Emily seeks revenge. Ike intervenes to protect her and is fatally shot by the gambler. Buck, who was closest to Ike ("Ike would look at me and I could hear the words"), feels the loss most and it is not until he saves a young expectant mother from a gang of outlaws that he is able to put his grief behind him. After he assists with the birth of her baby, the grateful woman offers to name the child after him. "I'd be honored," he replies, "but I'd be more honored if you'd name him Ike." In this way The Young Riders' handicapped representative is written out of the series.

When The Young Riders was finally canceled due to low ratings during the third season, two one-hour episodes were scheduled back to back on July 23, 1992, which fittingly brought the series to a close and tied up several loose ends in the story. Lou and the Kid are finally married by Teaspoon as their love story comes to a fitting and inevitable conclusion (although only Teaspoon learns what the Kid's real name is). Frank appears on the scene again and this time Jesse decides to return to Missouri with his older brother (but not before he has performed on final act of loyalty to the group). Cody enlists in the U.S. Army and becomes a scout. And in the most jarring note of the final episode, Noah is killed in a battle between a gang of Southern renegades and a regiment of Union soldiers. Each individual must now decide on which side he will make his or her stand as the Union begins to dissolve. Noah's funeral, attended by all the remaining young riders, provides a moving setting for the series' final scene.

Despite surviving for three seasons, The Young Riders could by no means be considered a hit. Its renewal for a second and third season had been problematical at best. Although it was usually second in its time period, the show steadily declined in the ratings, finishing no better than 73 during the second season. Among the positives, The Young Riders can be cited for its competent cast of fresh young actors, the superb photography (of Earl L. Clark), stirring musical scores (by John Debney), a few memorable performances by guest stars like Della Reese (in "Born to Hang"), Brian Keith and Pernell Roberts (in "Star Light, Star Bright"), David Carradine, and of course the always invigorating presence of Anthony Zerbe. On the negative side there were too many episodes dealing with the impending Civil War and innumerable clashes between abolitionists and pro-slavery renegades. The stories, with a few notable exceptions, were not equal in quality to those of Paradise. Of what, if any, significance, does The Young Riders have in the development of the television Western? Brooks and Marsh have labeled the series "revisionist":

> The Pony Express rode again in this revisionist view of the Old West, which strove mightily to make Westerns palatable to the socially sensitive 1990s....
> The riders did deliver some mail from time to time in their "mochila" pouch, but spent most of their time receiving escaped slaves, protecting the innocent, and being nice to the Indians. Rumblings of the imminent Civil War allowed some moralizing on that subject. In the third season the entire crew moved to the larger town of Rock Creek, on the Nebraska-Kansas-Missouri border, to allow for the introduction of more "urban" concerns. Perhaps AIDS or a crack epidemic?[69]

Obviously, "rescuing escaped slaves, protecting the innocent, and being nice to the Indians" does not alone make *The Young Riders* a revisionist Western. Plenty of examples of the last two activities can be found in episodes of most adult Westerns from *Gunsmoke* to *Bonanza* and if Matt Dillon and Ben Cartwright did not rescue any escaped slaves, it is only because *Gunsmoke* was set in the post–Civil War West and few escaped slaves found their way to the Nevada site of *Bonanza*. (In fact, it is difficult to think of any television Western hero who did not or would not have pursued these objectives if he had had the chance.)

John Donahue, in an unpublished paper presented at the 1992 annual convention of the Popular Culture Association, more effectively made the revisionist case by pointing out that the characters on *The Young Riders* worked as "a team" and that while episodes tended to feature one at a time, there were no episodes that failed "to involve the group, a clear break with the rugged individualism familiar to most Western buffs." His paper went on to explain:

> Thematically, the show voices modern concerns—the power structures of oppression against Indians, half-breeds, blacks, women, the handicapped, religious minorities. It explores the power of self-image or illusions to entrap and enslave the individual, inhibiting self-realization and growth. It studies attempts to shrug off or escape responsibility or accountability for actions. And often this is done with surprising flair, sensitivity and insight. As well, it looks at the Western myth-making process with perceptiveness and humor, commenting on how truth is often built to serve our needs.[70]

The revisionist view of Western history represents a rejection of the traditionally accepted Turner thesis that the West was a rough-hewn egalitarian democracy, where every man had a piece of land and the promise of prosperity. Led by University of Colorado history professor Patricia Nelson Limerick, author of the most comprehensive summary of the new view, *The Legacy of Conquest,* the revisionists claim that the West became quickly dominated by big money and big government and instead of a place of success, happiness and progress, it became a region rife with tragedy, conflict, destruction and failure. They contend that in "winning the West" pioneers were motivated by economic greed, resulting in the plunder of the environment, dislocation of Native Americans and exploitation of women and minorities.

These historians see the legacy of the West as depleted natural resources, fragmented families, racial strife and vast disparities between the rich and poor. For decades, claim Limerick and her colleagues, Western history was not only male, but white. The Indian was either a savage to be conquered or a noble primitive waiting to be civilized. The Hispanic was the enemy (remember the Alamo). Blacks and Chinese were simply left out. Their goal is to set the record straight and dismantle the myth that has been perpetuated in factual as well as fictional accounts of the Old West for the better part of a century.

How does *The Young Riders* fit into the great debate now raging among scholars regarding the nature of the real West? Perhaps, a second season episode entitled "Requiem for a Hero" sums up the series' point of view best and tips the scales in favor of the revisionists. In this story, penned by Bruce Reisman, Cody meets his boyhood idol, Western author and frontiersman Hezekiah Horn (played to perfection by Pernell Roberts in what must be his finest Western role since he left the Ponderosa). Horn, however has become disillusioned by what he sees as the exploitation of the West in the name of progress and has disowned all his earlier romantic writings and visions of the West. When Cody, puzzled and disappointed, presses Horn for an explanation, this exchange takes place:

CODY: I always got a special feeling when I read that book.

HORN: Forget it, son ... the words, how I felt when I wrote this ... dead. (He tosses Cody's copy of his first book into the fire.)

CODY: What'd did you do that for?

HORN: Cause it's over.

CODY: What is over?

HORN: Everything ... the West ... there's nothing left but a lot of debts no one is willing to pay.

CODY: You're wrong! The West is just gettin' stronger. Cities are growin'. Progress is...

HORN: Progress? ... Let me tell you about progress, boy. When the telegraph gets here, you and a lot of other folks are gonna be out of work. Progress! See what we've done to the Mexican, the Indian—how we're on the verge of a Civil War because of what we did to the African... In California, they're doin' the same to the Chinese. Is that progress? This rifle can kill people faster than any other! You call that progress? Come on boy, can't you see where it's leadin'?

CODY: No, I guess not.

HORN: Ashes ... my book ... this rifle ... my body ... ashes.

It is difficult to conceive of a clearer or more concise statement of the revisionist attitude regarding the development of the American West. Although there are many examples to be found in *The Young Riders* of the traditional, romantic vision of the Westward movement, Hezekiah Horn's assessment certainly reflects the opinion of Limerick and her followers.

Meanwhile, during the early nineties, made-for-television Western films continued to be shown intermittently on network television (primarily on CBS, that patron of the television Western) and the Turner cable network (TNT). Some were largely forgettable like *Brotherhood of the Gun* (1991), which relates the story of a young Confederate sharpshooter (overplayed by Brian Bloom) with a shady past who is out to get revenge on the psychopathic outlaw leader who killed his younger brother. David Carradine has an interesting role as a land baron, with a hook for a right hand, who vacillates in his feelings toward Bloom. While saving his life during the final gun battle, he still vows that the two will "always be enemies." Meanwhile, the villain gallops off into the sunset with a tomahawk protruding from his chest—compliments of Bloom. There is also a likable Hispanic lawman (played with Cisco-like humor by Jorge Cevera, Jr.), a spoiled young rich boy, lots of long-haired, unshaven, beady-eyed baddies and—best of all, beautiful newcomer Jamie Rose as the love interest. Although never specifically stated, it would appear, since so many plotlines are left unresolved, that this is a pilot for a possible series. All things considered, *Brotherhood* probably deserved the low ratings it received.

Blood River (also 1991), on the other hand, beautifully filmed on location in British Columbia and featuring *Lonesome Dove*'s Rick Schroder and Wilford Brimley (star of *Cocoon*, television's *Our House* and a barrel of oatmeal commercials) fared better. Schroder plays a young man who kills the three gunfighters who had murdered his parents and burned down their homestead. Overnight he is forced to become a fugitive when the range boss (played with appropriate menace by John P. Ryan), who ordered the killings, sets his army of gunmen on Schroder's trail. Running for his life, he stumbles into the camp of an old trapper named Culler (Brimley), who helps Schroder elude the bad guys. Brimley is a lovable old codger in a Gabby Hayes type role and he gets to sing, play the harmonica and piano, and even pound out a few measures on a pipe organ before the movie is over. *Blood River* pulled respectable Nielsen's, largely on the strength of its stars, despite being panned by critics like Knight-Ridder Newspapers' Ron Miller:

> The blame goes to the awful script by John Carpenter, whose actress wife, Adrienne Barbeau, plays a frontier madam in the second half. ... It asks us to believe that Schroder

is really a decent kid who hates killing, even after drilling three guys and sending a couple of tons of hot lead in the general direction of hundreds more. It also wants us to think he's too dumb to figure out that Brimley's old codger is something more than an itinerant trapper.[71]

What the reviewer does not mention is that in spite of all the shooting, very few people get killed—or even wounded. Even though dozens of rounds of bullets are fired at Schroder he never gets so much as nicked—nor does Brimley. Of course, they are the good guys. In fact Brimley turns out to be a federal marshal using Shroder as bait to get the goods on Ryan. (Brimley is so good that he knocks out one of the baddies with just a gentle tap on the head.) The ending, however, is different and worth mentioning: it involves a fight to the finish between Brimley and Ryan in a church bell tower!

Most interesting of the early 1990s made-for-television Westerns is TNT's *Conagher* (1991). It is based on Louis L'Amour's lonely hearts tale of the Old West about a restless cowboy and a love-starved pioneer widow who writes sheets of poetry that she then ties to tumbleweeds. The script was written by the film's two stars, Sam Elliott and his wife Katharine Ross, along with Jeffrey M. Meyer (who not only served as Elliott's stand-in, but was a wrangler and played a small role as a stagecoach shotgun guard in the film). Elliott and Ross were handpicked by L'Amour for the roles nearly eleven years before his death. Elliott had become friends with the Western author after appearing in the 1979 miniseries *The Sacketts*. Three years later he costarred in the miniseries version of L'Amour's *The Shadow Riders* (which also starred Ross). Elliott later appeared in a third L'Amour film, *The Quick and the Dead*, shown on HBO in 1987. It was Elliott's friendship with L'Amour that strengthened his faith in the Western. This was bolstered by the huge ratings generated by *Lonesome Dove*. Elliott told television critics in Los Angeles:

> In the 25 years that I've been in this business, I've heard continually, year after year, that one of the reasons that Westerns aren't made is that there is no longer a viable market out there.
> And I've always fully disagreed with that.... I happened to have bought this book from Louis L'Amour the year that he passed away, and it's something that he brought to my attention and to Katharine's attention about 11 years ago.
> He said that he had this story that he thought we'd both do well with. And it was one of those long-term projects that finally landed where it landed.

Conagher tells two separate stories that occasionally cross and finally merge at the end. One follows Evie Teale (played by Ross) who is left to face the open prairie with her two children when her husband is killed on a cattle-buying trip. She turns her cabin into a temporary rest stop for a stagecoach line. One guest is Conn Conagher (portrayed by Elliott), a wandering cowboy who becomes involved in a range war. He continues to drift in and out of Evie's lonely life.

The supporting cast includes such familiar Western faces as *Gunsmoke*'s Ken Curtis and Buck Taylor and Buck's dad, Dub. Barry Corbin is the stage driver and Cody Braun and Anndi McAfee are the children. Louis' daughter Angelique L'Amour makes a cameo appearance. Even though admitting that the production "bends over backward to be true to the author's vision," *USA Today* (July 1, 1991) critic Steven Jones had mixed reactions to the film:

> ... Elliott does breathe life into the stoic, principled Conagher ("When I take a man's money, I ride for the brand"), especially when he corners some back-shooting rustlers around their campfire. But it is Ross who is the movie's saving grace.
> She is determined, yet vulnerable as Teale, an Easterner whose dang-fool husband drags

her and two children into the wilderness only to ride off and get crushed by his horse. She's gritty when standing down Indians, compassionate when consoling her grieving daughter and lilting when serving weary stagecoach riders....

Ultimately, though, "Conagher" shoots blanks when it's time for action. By sticking to the book, the movie is long on talk. But the book was also fraught with tension and desperation. Much of this movie is as dry as Evie's tumbleweeds.

In addition to turning out the star-studded fourth entry in his highly popular and successful *Gambler* series, Kenny Rogers made an unusual television Western movie entitled *Rio Diablo* (shown during the spring of 1993). Rogers plays Quentin Leech, a bounty hunter who is trying to come to grips with his troubled past, while on the trail of a gang of bandits who kidnapped a young bride as they fled from a bank robbery. Leech's creed is: "There's no such thing as an innocent man—some are just less guilty."

Billed by *TV Guide* as "an Old West saga with a psychological edge," *Rio Diablo* drew a large audience. It is of particular interest to country and Western music fans for the acting debuts of Travis Tritt as the groom (labeled "a stiff" by *USA Today*'s Matt Roush) and Naomi Judd as a madame with a heart of gold (whom he calls "surprisingly flat"). Stacy Keach, Jr., puts in an appearance near the end of the story as a rival bounty hunter. The "sturdy" Rogers, however, carries the film as the fatalistic bounty hunter.

If there is some doubt as to whether or not *The Young Riders* was a revisionist Western, no such doubt should exist as to the status of *Dr. Quinn, Medicine Woman*. Focusing on a woman is a role traditionally performed by a man (that of physician), *Dr. Quinn* is unquestionably the most revisionist television Western yet to be broadcast.

The closest television had come to *Dr. Quinn, Medicine Woman* was a short-lived series called *Sara* which debuted on February 13, 1976. Set in the frontier town of Independence, Colorado, during the 1870s, *Sara* related the story of a strong willed schoolteacher named Sara Yarnell who had given up a dull and predictable existence in the East to face the challenges of the West. Like Dr. Quinn, Sara battled ignorance and prejudice instead of the usual outlaws and Indians found in most Westerns. While her profession was more acceptable to her contemporaries than that of Dr. Quinn, her views were not and the more conservative townspeople, expecting a more passive schoolmarm for their children, were shocked. Some of the schoolboard members wanted her removed although the editor of the local newspaper backed her and most of her students enthusiastically approved of her unconventional methods.

Clearly the first feminist Western, *Sara* was canceled after only 13 episodes. Neil Summers describes the show as a "talkfest which did not get much attention in the ratings."[72] As in the case of *Dr. Quinn*'s Jane Seymour, *Sara*'s star, Brenda Vaccaro was its greatest asset. Prior to playing Sara, Vaccaro had a busy stage career winning Tony nominations for her work in *Cactus Flower, How Now Dow Jones* and *The Goodbye People*. In the early seventies she became more active on television with appearances on shows like *The Name of the Game, Marcus Welby, M.D.* and *McCloud*. In 1974 she won a Best Supporting Actress Emmy for *The Shape of Things*. The public, however, was not ready in 1976 for a Western which was built around a liberal-minded female character. Attitudes had changed by 1993 and *Dr. Quinn* was the beneficiary of this new mood.

Created by Beth Sullivan, a former production executive at Fox television and the co-creator of the admittedly feminist *The Trials of Rosie O'Neill*, *Dr. Quinn* was inspired by the huge success two seasons earlier of a CBS television movie called *Sarah, Plain and Tall* about a woman who answers an ad in the early 1900s to become a farmer's wife. Andy Hill, executive vice president of CBS Entertainment Production, made a script deal with Sullivan, whom he considered to be a promising young writer. CBS suggested that she develop a series similar to *Sara* and to "give it a franchise."[73] In television terms, a franchise usually means a show about a doctor, lawyer or police officer. Sullivan, who was once a medical student herself, decided to make the central character a young woman doctor. Through her research, she found that a few female doctors went West after the Civil War from the two medical colleges that then existed for women. Testing the concept on her own family first, Sullivan later explained:

> I have a huge, huge working class family on my mother's side. At a Fourth of July gathering, after we'd eaten and the kids were rolling around..., I said, "I'm doing this thing, let me run it by you and see what you think."
> ... They gave me a lot of feedback, and said "That's what's missing," and "I like this" and the girls had some suggestions, and a couple of my uncles said a few things.[74]

It proved much harder to sell network heads on the idea, however. For one thing, Sullivan asked for Saturday nights, a time usually considered a graveyard for television dramas. She believed that baby boomers were staying home with their children and would provide the nucleus for an audience. Furthermore, Sullivan's show was bucking a trend toward targeting narrow segments of the audience. She hoped her series would appeal to everyone: "I said we need a family show, something that can hold the interest of adults and appeal to children."[75]

Sullivan had to deal with the fact that although many women coproduce television shows, there was little precedent for a woman creating and executive producing a show by herself:

> I had to push. There's no question that had my name been Bob Sullivan or Bill Sullivan, I wouldn't have had to give them [the network] that song and dance. It wasn't a war but I did have to stand up and make the point.[76]

Finally, CBS committed itself to producing and testing a two-hour pilot. The problem was they could not find a suitably big star for the lead role. Hill later explained:

> We were 48 hours from the start of shooting. Then we [CBS] got enormously lucky; Jane Seymour's agent called.... Jane Seymour is very significant. She's a big-name television star. Everyone knew her from all the miniseries she'd been in.[77]

Seymour later said she was taken with the show from the moment she read the script for the pilot:

> When I got to the end, I wept. It really struck a chord with me.... This is my first series and I'm stunned by the reaction. Especially by women who are so thrilled that there is a role model they can respect on TV.[78]

One of the reasons Seymour fell in love with the role may be the parallels between her own life and that of Dr. Quinn. Born Joyce Penelope Wilhelmina Frankenberg, in Wimbledon, England, Seymour is the daughter of a physician, as is Michaela Quinn, and both fathers believed devoutly in their daughters. As Seymour explains: "My father never put any limitations on me as to what I could do with my life. Neither did Michaela's."[79] Seymour, like Dr. Quinn left home for a better life elsewhere.

Seymour was originally trained as a dancer. She performed with England's Royal Festival Ballet at the age of 13, but a knee injury ended her dancing career three years later. It was then that she turned to acting and appeared both in films and on television. She came to the United States in the seventies, where she was soon playing lead roles in a number of big, glossy, romantic television productions. When *The Onedin Line*, a BBC dramatic series was first shown on American television in 1974, Seymour began to attract

Dr. Quinn (Jane Seymour) and her young wards: Erika Flores as Colleen, Chad Allen (top) as Matthew and Shawn Toovey as Brian.

a following in this country. This nineteenth-century saga of the sea followed the private and professional exploits of the Onedin family who owned one of Liverpool's biggest shipping companies. Seymour was striking as Emma Fogarty.

Seymour had already appeared in several British-made theatrical films: *Young Winston* (1972) in a small supporting role and as the spectacularly sexy Solataire in Roger Moore's first Bond film *Live and Let Die* (1973). Seymour's first American miniseries was *Captains and the Kings* (1976). She stood out in the role of Marjorie Chisholm Armagh in the adaptation of Taylor Caldwell's novel that was loosely based on the rise of the

Kennedy family. She also appeared in *Seventh Avenue* (1977), Norman Bogner's potboiler about the New York garment district. *The Awakening Land* (1978) gave Seymour her first taste of life on the frontier in the miniseries based on Conrad Richter's novel set in Ohio around the beginning of the nineteenth century. A guest appearance on television's imitation of *Star Wars, Battlestar Galactica* (1978) followed, as well as 1979's forgettable *Dallas Cowboy Cheerleaders*. (Seymour takes acting honors as a reporter writing an exposé on the cheerleaders.)

In the eighties, Seymour's career shifted into high gear with such theatrical releases as *Somewhere in Time* (1980), costarring Christopher Reeve (*Superman*), and *Lassiter* (1984), which costarred Tom Selleck (*Magnum, P.I.*). On the home screen she had featured roles in *Phantom of the Opera* (1983), *The Sun Also Rises* (1985) and *The Woman He Loved* (1988). Her acting also dominated such miniseries as *East of Eden* (1981), *Onassis: The Richest Man in the World* (1988) and the landmark 29½ hour ABC miniseries *War and Remembrance* (1988-89) in which she replaced Ali MacGraw as Natalie Jastrow. (Seymour was far more believable than MacGraw, who had played the same character in the prequel series, *The Winds of War* in 1983.) Seymour received an Emmy in 1988 for her portrayal of Jackie Kennedy Onassis in *Richest Man in the World*, for "Outstanding Supporting Actress in a Miniseries or Special." Thus in Jane Seymour CBS had a proven, bankable star.

To hold down costs, CBS decided to produce *Dr. Quinn* in-house. As David F. Poltrack, senior vice president of research, explained it, Saturday night had so little revenue potential, they had to think of ways to avoid losing money on the night.[80] As owner of the show, CBS could later sell the international rights to defray the expected losses. Sullivan wrote and produced a two-hour pilot film that CBS tested in the spring of 1992. It scored the "most favorable test rating in the network's history."[81] Still, CBS was reluctant. They considered the show to be so old-fashioned that it was revolutionary.

The response to the pilot among sponsors was extremely cool. CBS executives were fearful that *Dr. Quinn* was "a likable show that would never make it." The ad agencies felt that the show was "too soft—too much a throwback to another television era, with its homespun charm."[82] Furthermore, they strongly objected to scheduling the series on Saturday since the combined network viewership on that night had been steadily declining for several years. (Potential viewers had abandoned network television on that night in favor of outside activities, rented videos, or movie offerings on cable channels and it was feared they would never come back to network television.)

With the concerns of the advertisers added to those of the network, CBS decided to pull *Dr. Quinn* from its fall 1992 schedule. However, true to form, CBS's other Saturday night shows bombed, and the network decided to give *Dr. Quinn* a chance in January 1993. The network made what proved to be a shrewd choice—to broadcast the two-hour pilot on New Year's Day, a Friday, against two college football bowl games. Football haters— especially those without cable—had a powerful incentive to tune in. A lot of them did—it ranked in the Nielsen top ten—and came back for the second episode the very next night. It was CBS's first hit series on Saturday night in more than ten years.

Seymour's opening voice-over narrative (well written by Sullivan) carefully set the scene and explained the premise on which the series was based. It began:

> I was born on February 15, 1833, in Boston, Massachusetts the last of five children—the four before me all girls. My father, being a man of science, firmly believed that the odds were to finally dictate the birth of a long awaited son. He would be named Michael. . . . I was named Michaela.
>
> I was determined to attend medical school, but none would admit women! I finally

received my M.D. from the Women's Medical College of Pennsylvania. To my mother's dismay, my father made me a partner in his practice and for seven years we worked side by side....

When he died, ... our practice virtually disappeared. I was afraid my life as a doctor was over, but I'd promised him to carry on....

I found an advertisement in "The Globe," for a town doctor in Colorado Territory. I sent a telegram detailing my experience, and in less than a week, I received a reply offering me the position. It was the frontier, a place where people made new beginnings, a place where my services would be needed, where my skills would be appreciated, where I would finally be accepted as a doctor....

When the townspeople of Colorado Springs realize that Dr. Quinn is a woman (it seems the telegraph operator thought the "a" at the end of her first name was actually a middle initial and dropped it), they do not welcome her with open arms. On the contrary, even the preacher, who placed the advertisement, urges Dr. Quinn to leave:

REV. JOHNSON: ... I want to apologize for the inconvenience, but we will, of course, pay your way back to Boston.
DR. QUINN: That won't be necessary, thank you. Colorado Springs needs a doctor, and I happen to be one.
REV. JOHNSON: You don't understand. No one around here has ever heard of a lady doctor.
DR. QUINN: There's always a first time.
REV. JOHNSON: But, Miss, there are no respectable single women in Colorado Springs.
DR. QUINN: That's a shame, Reverend. Every town should have at least one.

Only the widow Charlotte, who runs the town's sole rooming house, will accept Dr. Quinn. As she unpacks, Dr. Quinn ponders her future: "My expectations of a warm reception were vastly disappointed. Apparently the prevailing opinion of women doctors was no better in Colorado Springs then it had been in Boston...." And thus, a mere ten minutes into the story, the stage is set for the trials and tribulations of *Dr. Quinn, Medicine Woman*. To prove that she can take as much pain as any man, she has the town's accepted medical authority—the barber—pull out one of her teeth with pliers, in full view of the assembled townsfolk. But it is only after she has successfully fought off an influenza epidemic single-handedly (in the first hour episode) that she is able to convince them (or at least most of them) of her competence as a doctor.

In a rather contrived plot device, Dr. Quinn is provided with a ready-made family of three children when her friend Charlotte dies suddenly. The pilot ends with Dr. Quinn (or Dr. Mike, as she becomes known to her friends) and her three adopted children bravely singing Christmas carols. Viewers know that the series qualifies as wholesome family fare when the youngest boy asks, "Do you think Maw would mind if I called you 'Maw' too?" And Dr. Mike responds, "For Christmas I received the greatest gift of all—the gift of love."

The other continuing roles in the series were well cast, although most had very little previous television experience. The youngsters are especially appealing. Matthew, the eldest son, is played by Chad Allen, daughter Colleen by Erika Flores and young Brian, by Shawn Toovey, who steals almost every scene he is in. Only Allen had appeared on television before—in *Webster* (1985-1986), *Our House* (1986-1988) and *My Two Dads* (1989-1990).

Dark and handsome newcomer Joe Lando is featured as Sully. When Sully's young wife died, he became a recluse—a loner who lives among the Indians, develops a deep and abiding respect for the wonders of nature, and has only a wolf for a companion. Sully can throw a tomahawk with unerring accuracy, but has to be taught how to ride a horse by Dr. Mike. He finds himself inexplicably drawn to the beautiful medicine women as

Jane Seymour shown with romantic interest, frontier loner Byron Sully (played by Joe Lando), on ***Dr. Quinn, Medicine Woman***.

their friendship slowly blossoms into romance. (He kisses her for the first time on her birthday!) Whenever Dr. Mike is in trouble, Sully has a habit of turning up to help her, whether it is to provide an Indian remedy when she is ill, rescue her from a falling tree or find her runaway son, he is there when she needs him. In the opinion of one critic, Connie Passalacqua, who can speak for the women's point of view: "Joe's a most savvy creation—perhaps the ultimate fantasy of the 1990s woman who's too busy with kids and career for romance. Sully's completely hassle-free...."[83]

Orson Bean, a character actor and comedian from television's early years, joins the cast on the first hour episode as the crotchity storekeeper, Loren Bray. Bean was familiar to most older viewers as a television game show panelist on programs like *I've Got a Secret*, *To Tell the Truth*, *Keep Talking*, and *Pantomine Quiz*. In later years, he would occasionally turn up on dramatic shows like *Ellery Queen* and *Mary Hartman, Mary Hartman*.

Loren's sister Olive was played by Gail Strickland. Strickland's television credits included brief stints on *The Insiders*, *What a Country*, and *Heartbeat*. Geoffrey Lower, who had appeared in Sullivan's *Rosie O'Neill*, was cast as The Reverend Johnson. Jake, the barber, was nicely portrayed by Jim Knobeloch. The telegraph operator, Horace, a slow-witted, but kind, honest and brave young man, who falls in love with one of the town's "sportin' ladies," is sensitively played by Frank Collison. Myra, the soiled, but sweet, object of his affections is Helene Lidy's first major television role. The town's long-haired bully and all-around resident nasty, Hank, who runs the local saloon and "manages" the town's prostitutes is played with the proper amount of menace by William Shockley. The town's blacksmith and resident black, Robert E., is effectively played by Henry G. Sanders.

There are also a number of other recurring roles in *Dr. Quinn* involving immigrant homesteaders, Indians from the surrounding area and soldiers from the nearby fort. This makes for a large cast, but contributes significantly to the show's realistic quality. (One legitimate criticism here might be, however, that few of the Indians are played by Native American actors.)

Occasionally guest stars from television's golden age of Westerns are featured on *Dr. Quinn*. Robert Culp (*Trackdown*) turns up in one episode as a medicine show con-man, who is really a famous surgeon who has lost his nerve. In another interesting episode, Ben Murphy (of *Alias Smith and Jones*) is cast as the children's long-lost father. He is unable to give up his shady ways, however, and is prevented from stealing the money the townspeople have raised for charity only by the timely intervention of Sully (who allows him to leave town minus the money, but with his reputation undamaged—for the sake of the children).

Johnny Cash plays a retired gunslinger looking for a quiet town in which to retire. After he intervenes to prevent a young Swedish immigrant from being lynched for cattle rustling, however, he decides to move on. Other prominent guest stars include Jane Wyman as Dr. Mike's estranged mother, Elizabeth, who shows up one day, unexpectedly from Boston. (During the second season veteran soap star Peggy McCay (*Love of Life*, *General Hospital*, *Days of Our Lives*, *Trials of Rosie O'Neill*) replaces her in the role. And in the first season's final episode Kenny Rogers turns in an outstanding performance in one of the series' best stories as a former Civil War photographer who is losing his sight to a severe case of diabetes.

During the first month, *Dr. Quinn* averaged four points better than any other Saturday night offering and more than three points above the network prime time average. About 14 million households were watching it. CBS was especially pleased because the show, although originally targeted for older women, was attracting younger viewers—notably young women and children and teenagers (thought not to be watching television on Saturday nights) and was even doing reasonably well with younger men. David F. Poltrack, CBS's senior vice president of research, saw the show as "perfect for most television advertisers" because "it had no problems with offensive content" and "appealed to the whole family." Advertisers were "pushing to get into it."[84] Sullivan was, of course, pleased by the high ratings:

> I said to all involved, "Don't be surprised. This is going to look like something from outer space to these guys. It's not going to be trendy. It's the farthest thing from hip that you could find. . . . It's going to look soft to people," and I used the word, "It's going to be corny to some people."[85]

The critics, however, had a field day attacking *Dr. Quinn* from all sides: *Time Magazine* called it "treacle"; *TV Guide* labeled the show "sometimes silly, often sappy" and ridiculed its "gooey-hearted, doctrinaire dialogue." At a television press conference held in Los Angeles, the show's creator and stars were accused by reporters of being "overly politically correct" and "an historical anachronism."[86] The *New York Times'* John J. O'Connor was relentless in his criticism (February 4, 1993):

> One recipe for a successful series: take a contrived concept, sprinkle with homespun truisms updated for political correctness and mix well with tired plot devices. Process and serve. And out comes "Dr. Quinn, Medicine Woman," CBS's new hit on Saturdays at 8 P.M. Possible subtitle: "Little Shtick on the Prairie," and very little, at that. . . .
>
> Developed by Beth Sullivan with CBS Entertainment, "Dr. Quinn" is a television construct, its every nuance calculated out of lowest-common-denominator concerns. Art, or even craft, decidedly takes a back seat to commerce. . . .

Jeff Jarvis liked nothing about *Dr. Quinn*, except its star. Writing in the February 20, 1993, issue of *TV Guide*:

> "Dr. Quinn" has everything a Western should have: dust, horses, gunfire, saloons, good guys who are 99.44 percent good, and bad guys who are 99.44 percent bad. But this isn't every Western.... This is the Politically Correct Western, where justice is defined by the good Dr. Quinn. She defends the environment against plunder (curing a Bambi of a gunshot wound, then setting it free). She practically endorses gun control. She is a living argument for sexual equality. She tirelessly preaches tolerance toward immigrants, blacks, Indians, and ladies of ill repute. I wouldn't be surprised if this becomes the first Western to call Indians "Native Americans" and cowboys "cowpersons." ... Yet "Dr. Quinn" is a success—as a Saturday ratings hit ... and as a show. Give Jane Seymour all the credit.... She can act in anything, even in a sometimes silly, often sappy Western.

Tony Scott of *Variety* (December 21, 1992) was able to find some merit in the series, and was guardedly optimistic about its chances for success:

> Seymour adds finesse to her characterization in the first episode of the one-hour series, [but] this pilot, jammed with strained vignettes, tries too hard.... The film also drums up Western clichés and femme-doctor struggles, but for youthful audiences it could all be brand spanking new.... Tech credits are acceptable, with Agoura's Paramount Ranch offering its customary good Western town flavor. ... "Dr. Quinn" could work into a workable family Saturday evening practice.

The unkindest cut came in a special *TV Guide* (March 6, 1993) column written by Harry Stein entitled "'Dr. Quinn' Should Shrink from New Age Nonsense." After admitting that "it is hard these days for parents to find shows for kids that even try to be wholesome and uplifting" and that *Dr. Quinn* "never trades in pointless violence or smirky sexual innuendo," he attacks the show for its "slavish devotion to the dictates of political correctness." Stein finds the series "objectionable" for "casually distorting our common past":

> ... Sorry, but environmentalism, ... was just *not* a big deal on the frontier. Yet in a recent episode we find Dr. Quinn ... nailing a big, bad mid-19th-century polluter for fouling local water. This is a time and place when, according to Time Life's "The Pioneers," medical practice was so primitive that these were common remedies: "warm manure for snakebites ... a roasted mouse (well done) ingested to cure measles, nine pellets from a shotgun shell swallowed for boils...." Which is to say, even as it serves up pap, "Dr. Quinn" ignores genuine history that is truly riveting....
>
> [T]he missed opportunity is no joke. There is endless talk just now about the disappearance of heroes and an absence of role models. Not long ago, that was a void westerns helped to fill. Yet how can it happen again if even the creators of such shows don't get it?

Sullivan was irked by critics who challenged the show's accuracy. While admitting that "our plots are appropriate today," she insists that the show is historically correct:

> Everything is absolutely accurate right down to the 1867 medical syringe. Our medical adviser is from the Smithsonian.... There were two medical schools that admitted women then. In those days it was hard for a woman to do more than lower-echelon things like working in almshouses. To set up her own practice, a likely place for a woman to go was the frontier.[87]

Are Dr. Quinn's liberal political views an anachronism? She is

> ... a strong feminist and humanitarian who favors the underdog. She's allied herself with Native Americans, blacks, recent immigrants, even the town prostitute. In past episodes she's taken on big business and environmental polluters; she favors gun control and the rights of animals to remain in the wild.[88]

In response to those who label the show "politically correct," Sullivan responds:

> People don't know their history, the ones who pronounced it so politically correct as to be out of place ... don't know what they're talking about. I do my research, believe me.[89]
>
> The post–Civil War years were a very progressive era, kind of like the 1960s. There were a lot of interesting ideas flying around. Michaela is from a family of Boston abolitionists who talked politics constantly. You have to remember women had been the backbone of the abolitionist movement. After the Civil War, women's rights was very much on people's minds. In a way, it was a more volatile time than it is right now.[90]

Dr. Quinn is clearly a show that women can relate to. Not since Gail Davis' *Annie Oakley* in the fifties and Barbara Stanwyck's Victoria Barkley in the sixties has there been such a dominant female role model in a television Western. Even male viewers have come to the defense of *Dr. Quinn*. Writing in the "Letters" column of *USA Today* (March 8, 1993), Robert J. Tamasy of Hixson, Tennessee, defines the show's appeal to many Americans:

> A huge mass of viewers still hold dear to long-revered values of integrity, kindness and compassion. For them, this show offers relief from series soaked in gratuitous sex, pointlessly graphic violence and a hodgepodge of perversions.
>
> TV executives are concerned about a decline in regular viewers. If they build programs which celebrate humankind's virtues instead of its vices, the viewers will come back. Contrary to prevailing opinion, traditional values did not go out with the stagecoach.

Clearly, the modest revival of the television Western is due as much to the success of *Dr. Quinn, Medicine Woman* as it is to that of *Lonesome Dove, Dances with Wolves* or *Unforgiven*. In attempting to understand the reasons for this success, one needs to see beyond the show's relevance to women, and the fine work of its star Jane Seymour. In the epilogue to his excellent study of the television Western, historian J. Fred MacDonald sets down a list of requirements—"social and intellectual specifications"—that he believes necessary if there is ever to be a "renaissance" of the Western on television.[91] *Dr. Quinn* scores high on several, if not most, of these specifications.

For example MacDonald stresses that each ethnic group which has played a role in the development of the Old West must be portrayed with proper "dignity" and accuracy. The contributions of Native Americans, Asians, Hispanics, African Americans and other non–Caucasians were "substantial" and their contemporary constituencies "will not tolerate" a misrepresentation or exclusion of these achievements. Furthermore, MacDonald believes that the destructive aspects of racism, "where it existed" should be highlighted, showing it as one of the darker sides of life on the frontier.

Several episodes of *Dr. Quinn* deal with the mistreatment of Native Americans—the ruthless extermination of the buffalo which is destroying their way of life; the exploitation of an Indian and his young son in a traveling medicine show. Respect for the culture of Native Americans is frequently shown—the use of Indian "medicine" saves Dr. Mike's life when she is stricken with influenza. The brutal treatment of blacks is dramatized in an episode featuring the local blacksmith, Robert E. Another, deals with prejudice against Scandinavian immigrants who are "different."

MacDonald also believes that women must be depicted as "coequals with men," working and suffering together to build the frontier. Their role in the development of the West must be accorded the attention and respect it deserves.

Dr. Quinn, herself, is the most obvious example: she is discriminated against as a doctor—even by other physicians; in buying property—when she tries to purchase a building to use as a clinic. There are also several episodes dealing with the problems of women in general—prostitution and battered wives and such rights as the right to hold public office or even ride with men in a horse race.

MacDonald is further concerned that characters in television Westerns be shown to be aware of the physical world around them and of their dependency on their natural environment. There must be demonstrated "respect between people" and "their social and natural ecologies." One story deals with Dr. Quinn's attempts to prevent the pollution of the water by a gold mining company; another, with Sully's efforts to end the needless slaughter of the buffalo herds.

It is MacDonald's contention that the neo–Western should serve an "informational" function by providing fresh perspectives on the Old West and "demonstrating interesting techniques and physical skills." It can thereby entertain as well as "impart understanding" to its viewers. Several episodes of *Dr. Quinn* consider early superstitions and fears about medical progress—many of the townspeople are reluctant to be vaccinated against smallpox; they turn to their barber for medical expertise. Another episode focuses attention on people's unreasonable fear of a "developmentally disabled" boy.

Television producers and writers, according to MacDonald, must become aware of today's growing audience of young people. Most younger viewers have had little or no exposure to the Western. Without lowering standards to the teenage mentality, the new television Western must be made to stimulate the interest of contemporary youth. *Dr. Quinn*'s inclusion of three children of various ages—and their problems in growing up—provides considerable appeal to young viewers. One story, for example, deals with teenager Matthew's first social involvement with girls and his subsequent love affair with a young immigrant girl; in another, Colleen struggles with her exclusion from the social life of her peers when she is not invited to a party.

The final episode of *Dr. Quinn*'s first season is one of the best. Superbly written by Josef Anderson, it movingly brings to life the theme stressed most often in earlier stories—that of toleration for all people. A photographer dying of diabetes (and going blind) arrives in Colorado Springs. He is trying to capture on film as much of the beauty and wonder of the Old West as possible in the time he has left to live.

When the photographer (played by Kenny Rogers in, perhaps, the best dramatic performance of his career), Watkins, decides to take a picture of the residents of Colorado Springs, all the barely suppressed animosity and resentment the various groups have held toward each other boils to the surface. The white elite (Loren Bray, his sister Olive, Jake, Hank and others) want to exclude "blacks, Indians, immigrants and saloon girls" from the photograph. Others, like Dr. Mike, feel that all inhabitants of the community should be included. (Horace wants to include Myra; Matthew, his immigrant girlfriend, Ingrid.)

During the story Watkins captures the inner essence of each of the program's major characters in brilliant freeze-frame portraits (that fade from color to black and white). The fact that these photographs linger hauntingly in the viewer's memory is ample proof of their impact.

In the final scene all the townspeople put aside their differences and come together for the huge group photograph. The white community leaders, the less affluent blacks and their families, the immigrant homesteaders, and even the Indians are all included as they have all individually and collectively contributed to the well-being of their community. And in the forefront stand Dr. Quinn, her three "wards"—and Sully. While dramatically proving the old cliché that one picture is worth a thousand words, it provides a vivid visual lesson in brotherhood, the likes of which have not been seen since the old Coca Cola commercials of the seventies.

If one doubts that Dr. Quinn presents a revisionist view of the changing West consider this exchange which takes place between Watkins and Sully as they prepare to photograph the scenic landscape:

> WATKINS: It is beautiful...
> SULLY: The Cheyenne say this is the place where heaven and earth come to talk each day.
> WATKINS: What do they talk about?
> SULLY: Lately, they talk about how everything's changing.
> WATKINS: Ya can't stop progress, Mr. Sully.
> SULLY: Progress?... All I see is a bunch of selfish folks doin' anything for greed. Killin' off the Indians... Killin' the animals... Beaver, buffalo, elk... Even killin' each other for an acre of land and an ounce of gold.

While *Dr. Quinn* dealt with the Old West in ways compatible with the revisionist interpretation of the Westward movement, a number of other 1990s television Westerns did not.

Walker, Texas Ranger, which premiered on CBS in April 1993, was a traditional action Western set in the contemporary West with some deference to modern trends. Cordell Walker is a 1990s lawman, a karate-chopping crimebuster whose methods are rooted in the Old West. (Walker sometimes bends the law, but seldom actually breaks it.) The series is full of contrasts between the "new" and the "old" West. Although based in the urban Fort Worth-Dallas area, Walker lives on a ranch out in the country. He usually chases down criminals in a pick-up truck, but he can ride a horse as well as any nineteenth century cowboy (and he even rides steers in rodeos during his spare time). While he lives with his full-blooded Cherokee Uncle Ray (Walker is half Cherokee himself), his partner is a college-educated black from an urban ghetto and his sometime romantic interest and law enforcement associate is a "liberated" feminist prosecuting attorney for the district attorney's office.

Tailored to fit martial arts expert Chuck Norris by series creators Albert S. Ruddy, Leslie Grief, Paul Haggis, and Christopher Canaan, *Walker, Texas Ranger* brought the popular film actor his first weekly television show. Norris later explained his reasons for moving into the medium he had shunned for years:

> I swore I'd never do a TV series because I still get a lot of movie offers. But, when this came along, I realized it was the kind of character I could play week after week and be comfortable. Episodic TV is a whole different animal than making movies.... You're doing an eight-week movie in just three weeks.[92]
>
> TV is a gamble. The question was, do I do it now or later? Ten years ago, I would have been scared to do it. If you did TV, you were dead, movie-wise. Now, you can jump back and forth.[93]

Born Carlos Ray Norris in Oklahoma, Chuck, the oldest of three boys, moved with his family to California when he was 12. As a child, he was "shy, insecure and decidedly nonathletic." His father, part Cherokee, was an alcoholic, who drank all the time and would disappear for months. Chuck admits his self-esteem was zero. To bolster his confidence, Norris became interested in martial arts. Norris took up karate after losing a fistfight with a burly sergeant at a noncommissioned officers club in Gila Bend, Arizona. He established a set of goals for himself—white belt, then red, brown and black: "Suddenly, my life was focused. Martial arts was the turning point. Earning my black belt was the first time in my life I'd accomplished something difficult on my own."[94]

Norris had established a chain of karate schools in the Los Angeles area. It was Steve McQueen, one of his students, who persuaded the young Norris, who had never even appeared in a high school play, to pursue a career in acting. (Norris had played bit parts in *The Wrecking Crew,* 1969, and *Return of the Dragon,* 1973, with Bruce Lee. But these roles did not call for much acting, just a lot of "kicking and chopping.") McQueen's suggestion started Norris thinking:

> Bruce Lee was dead by then, and I thought, "Maybe I could do what Bruce did." The image of men on the screen in the early 1970s was antiheroic. I thought, "There's always room for a strong, positive hero."[95]

It took three "long lean years" before Norris was able to find investors willing to back him with the million dollars necessary to make *Good Guys Wear Black*, the first film in which he starred. Released in 1978, it earned $18 million, largely due to the flashy action sequences. (Anne Archer, James Franciscus, and Dana Andrews also appeared in the story about conspirators trying to take over America.) Next came *A Force of One* in 1979 on a similarly meager budget, with Jennifer O'Neill and Clu Gulager, and Norris was on his way to becoming a major movie star. Nearly all of the 17 films made by Norris from *Good Guys* through 1993 have earned money, with *Missing in Action* (1984), *Invasion U.S.A.* (1985) and *Delta Force* (1986) qualifying as bona fide box office hits.

The background of Texas Ranger Cordell Walker is not unlike that of Norris. As Walker explains to a young girl who has been brutally raped in the two hour pilot of *Walker, Texas Ranger* written by Louise McCarn:

> I remember when I was about twelve years old, a carnival came to this town we were living in. I'd never been to a carnival before and I wanted to go in the worst way. . . . It was a terrific evening—watching my mom and dad laugh. . . . We were walkin' back to the car. . . . My dad had one arm around my mom and was holding my hand with the other. As we approached the car, these three guys walked up to us. They were big guys, filthy clothes and smelled of alcohol. They started saying these crude things to my mom—like how could she be with a "dirty rotten Indian" and bring a half-breed into this world. My dad was a very proud man and he confronted these guys and a fight started. They must have figured three on one would be no contest, but they didn't know my dad. My dad was whopping-up on them pretty good when I saw a knife appear in one of the guys' hands and I saw him stab my dad right in the back. And he stabbed and he stabbed—like my dad was a sack of grain that he was trying to open. My mom screamed and ran in to try and stop him. He spinned around on my mom and I saw the shocked look on her face and I saw blood all over the front of her dress. She looked down at her stomach and slowly fell to the ground next to my dad. . . . My dad died where he fell. My mom died two days later at the hospital. . . .

Walker has both feet firmly planted in the Old West and as one of his fellow Rangers points out, "Nobody expects you to come smilin' into the twenty-first century." Consequently, Walker is given a partner who carries around a lap-top computer, uses electronic equipment to enhance his effectiveness and always prepares a plan before he acts. When asked by Walker how a black kid from a Baltimore ghetto became interested in becoming a Texas Ranger, this interesting exchange takes place:

> TRIVETTE: . . . When I was a kid, every Saturday morning I used to get up and sneak into the living room and watch my favorite TV show about the most famous Texas Ranger of all time, the last surviving member of a squad ambushed by bandits. Nursed back from death by an Indian, he became. . .
>
> WALKER: Don't tell me. . .
>
> TRIVETTE: That's right, man! The Lone Ranger!

The television Western had come full cycle in less than 50 years—from *The Lone Ranger* to *Walker, Texas Ranger*, from the nineteenth to the twenty-first century, from a hero on a white horse with an Indian sidekick to a hero in a black pickup truck with a black sidekick.

Clarence Gilyard, Jr., played the likable but tough Trivette (accent on the last syllable).

Gilyard had appeared in several series, including *CHIPs* as Officer Webster (1982-1983) and *The Duck Factory* as Roland Culp (1984), but his biggest break came when Andy Griffith cast him as private detective Conrad McMaster at the beginning of the fourth season of the successful *Matlock* series, a role Gilyard played for three years. Rounding out the cast of regulars in *Walker, Texas Ranger* were Native American actor Floyd Red Crow Westerman as Uncle Ray (see Chapter IX) and Sheree J. Wilson (formerly of *Dallas*) as the vivacious, self-reliant prosecuting attorney Alex Cahill.

There are some positive aspects to the show—the sincerity projected by Norris, the charisma of Gilyard, and the gentle humor of Westerman (in one episode he even does a stand-up comedy routine). The ethnicity of Walker's character is also interesting. The fact that he is half Cherokee permits writers to include situations which explore his Native American origins (e.g., the feather ceremony he performs at the grave of a dead Texas Ranger in the opening episode). It was also good to see James Drury back on the video range once again. (He plays Walker's supervisor in the first three episodes.)

The biggest problem facing the producers of *Walker, Texas Ranger* is the amount of violence in the show. This is a program in which the hero dispatches four men in a bloody karate and fistfight, in the pilot episode, before the credits have stopped rolling. Walker has followed these no-goodniks across the border into Mexico and one of the baddies cries, "You have no right down here." An instant later Walker smashes him with a right cross, commenting, "I think that's a pretty good right." Obviously winking at the law, Walker throws the subdued lowlife into the back of his truck and tells the border authorities that he has a load of "dirty laundry." The officer then permits Walker to take his human cargo back into the United States

In this same episode the body count piles up as a Texas Ranger is shot down and explosions, gunfights and truck and car chases abound—all energetically choreographed by veteran director Virgil W. Vogel. There is no let-up of the violence in subsequent episodes: in one, a sadistic ex-con stalks Alex seeking revenge by brutally killing her favorite horse; in another a corrupt politician is chopped to pieces (albeit off-camera) with a samurai sword by a Japanese mafioso seeking vengeance for his father's murder; and in the first episode of the second season, "Bounty," another sadist brutally beats up a woman (again off-camera) to extract information about the location of some stolen money.

All this mayhem comes at a time when television violence is under sharp attack from critics who claim that staged carnage on television often leads to similar brutality in real life. In defending the show, Norris told *TV Guide* writer Frank Swertlow:

> Kids can differentiate between defensive and offensive violence. They are not stupid. I do not think this is detrimental to youth. If my movies are so violent, why are they shown every night on TV at times when kids can see them?[96]

Later Norris commented to columnist James Brady:

> In the first two-hour episode, I take on four guys and kick butt. There's a lot of action right through the series but done kind of humorously. And there are scenes I've never done before, in which I open myself up.... He's vulnerable, my Walker character. His friends take advantage of him.[97]

As Swertlow pointed out, Norris may be "bucking the tide on this point." When the first episode of *Walker, Texas Ranger* was screened, journalists and industry people in Los Angeles hissed the hero's brutal beating of the bad guys. Although CBS, apparently satisfied with the ratings, placed the series on the fall 1993 schedule, most of the critics did

Film star Chuck Norris tries television as the title character in the contemporary Western, *Walker, Texas Ranger*.

their own bashing of the show. *Variety*'s (April 21, 1993) critic Todd Everett said the show was

> marred by problems (studio's financing failed and production halted at completion of four hours of CBS's 13-hour order). Overinflated two-hour pilot shows promise on a simple minded action film level. "The A-Team" did the same thing with much more wit, though, and in a timeslot more consistent with its greatest potential audience—kids.... According to credits, it took several people to "create" these time-honored characters and relationships— perhaps no one of them could remember every single cliche of action films.

Meanwhile, Norris made *Walker, Texas Ranger* a family affair, utilizing his son Eric as stunt coordinator on the series. His other son, Mike, an actor, appears in one episode as a prison guard taken hostage by a group of escaped convicts. Norris himself seemed content to continue the series as long as CBS would air it. He was able to spend most of his free time at home—a 650 acre ranch located between Dallas and Houston where he raises 200 head of Brangus cattle—since the show was being filmed near Dallas. His place in the history of films is secure. Only time will determine his place in the history of television Westerns.

If *Dr. Quinn, Medicine Woman* was the most revisionist of the new breed of Westerns roaming the video range in the 1990s and *Walker, Texas Ranger* was the most violent, then *Ned Blessing: The Story of My Life and Times* was the most unusual. Created and produced by genre veteran Bill Wittliff (who had also adapted *Lonesome Dove* for television), the limited run series first aired as a two hour television movie in April 1992 and then returned as a five week summer series in August 1993. Wittliff claimed that if it was not picked up as an ongoing television program, he would publish it as a book. It started as a series of short stories written by Wittliff in 1982. After he fell in love with the character, he decided to develop it for television. *Ned Blessing* is rich in the ethnic traditions of the Old West. As Wittliff later explained:

> Because it's set in Texas and in the Southwest, by the very nature of that region, there's a very heavy ethnic influence, and a Mexican one in particular. I mean, Crecencio's got a gourd, and he looks into the gourd and talks to three old grandfathers. Other than a few questions about it, between Crecencio and One Horse, that's just accepted as part of the reality. I'm not making this stuff up, because I lived down on the border for a time and in the Hill Country later, and it's very much a part of the fabric of everyday life there.[98]

The first film, entitled *Ned Blessing: The True Story of My Life*, relates the early adventures of Ned as a boy and later as sheriff of a lawless Texas town called Plum Creek. The story is narrated by Ned, now a crusty, cranky old man with one arm waiting in jail to be hanged. Because he is fed up with the distortions of newspaper "scribblers" who have written about his escapades, Blessing decides to write his own life story in the short time he has left. The grizzled codger wets the tip of the pen with his tongue and begins:

> Chapter 1—Tors Buckner Robs Me of My Past and Future
> Ned Blessing—You've probably heard of me by now—newspapers, magazines, the Police Gazette and such. The scribblers have been comin' in here on a daily basis, pushin' and shovin' to get the story of my life. That's all right with me. I wouldn't let Sheriff James T. Neemeier and his mob of lice-scratchers catch me in the first place if I wasn't lookin' for attention. I want everybody to know I'm locked up in this tight little cell. I especially want Tors Buckner ta know. . . . They got me sayin' I want ta apologize, that I'm sorry for my life. I never said it or anything like it! My life's been Hell with the lid off, yes. More thunder and lightnin' than poetry and lace, that's true too. . . . The only thing I'm sorry for is that it's not Torance C. Buckner sitting here in my place for the foul murder of my father and sixteen others. That was many long years ago. . . .

After Blessing explains that maybe he has got "a little surprise waiting" at his hanging, the story flashes back to when Ned was a boy crossing the Great Plains with his father, Anthony. Young Ned is kidnapped by a brutal gang of comancheros and, placed in the keeping of the cook, a Mexican-Indian mystic named Crecencio. This wily sage teaches the boy how to survive—by lying and stealing—so that later, when he has escaped the clutches of the bandit chieftain, he becomes known as "the Boy Bandit of Texas."

Young Ned eventually finds his father, who was severely wounded and left for dead by the bandits, being cared for by a beautiful and talented girl his own age named Jilly Blue. She sings ditties like "Beautiful Dreamer" in the local saloon in order to earn enough to support herself and Ned's father. Young Ned must leave town to get medicine for his father and while he is gone Jilly is kidnapped by her piano player.

Twenty years pass. Ned has become the respected sheriff of Plum Creek, his now healthy father is a successful music teacher and all is peaceful—"there hasn't been so much as a fistfight" in town since he took office. Then Jilly returns as an international singing star. While Ned goes off to renew his romance with her, a gang of robbers led by the ruthless Tors Buckner ravages the town, killing Ned's father and 16 other citizens. Racing to get back to Plum Creek in time to avert the disaster that Crecencio has envisioned, Ned leaves a message (which she never receives) for Jilly, whom he plans to marry. Ned arrives too late and the film ends with this narrative by old Ned:

> We buried seventeen men the next day at sunset including my father. The town blamed me. So did I.... I sent a telegram to Jilly telling her what had happened. Years later I learned the sly ol' Marquis had never given her my note and she thought I had jilted her. Heart-broken, she had married the Marquis and returned with him to Europe.... I resigned as sheriff ... then, swearing terrible vengeance, and taking only my pistol and my brass-mounted Henry .44, I rode off from there in search of Tors Buckner....

Here the pilot ends. Never answered are such questions as did Ned ever gain his revenge on Tors Buckner? Why did Buckner ravage Plum Creek and kill Ned's father? How were Jilly and Ned finally reunited? Why was Ned waiting in jail to be hanged? How did he lose his left arm?

Daniel Baldwin, brother of Alec and Stephen, turns in a credible performance as Ned. (Later, Daniel appeared in the critically acclaimed *Homicide: Life on the Street*.) Veteran Hispanic actor Luis Avalos is delightful as Crecencio. Avalos, well-known to kids as Dr. Doolots and Pedro (among others) on the PBS series *The Electric Company*, on which he appeared for ten years, had played Hispanic characters on such brief series as *Highcliffe Manor* (1979), *Condo* (1983), *E/R* (1984-85) and *I Had Three Wives* (1985). Unfortunately the first two-hour film did not immediately lead to a weekly series although it did win decent ratings and favorable comments from critics like the *New York Times'* John J. O'Connor (April 14, 1993):

> ... Part gory realism, part tall tale, part solid adventure, part goofy humor, part—but that's the problem. "Ned Blessing" has so many parts that getting them to mesh convincingly is a chore. Still, there's promise Mr. Wittliff has a good bead on his subject. And Mr. Baldwin, really just getting warmed up in this pilot, looks as if he could keep Ned Blessing walking tall and furious. Hearst Entertainment would seem to be facing a very close call.

Sixteen months later, however, with a new lead, a mostly new cast and a new title— *Ned Blessing: The Story of My Life and Times*—Ned Blessing returned to CBS, on August 13, 1993. Brad Johnson was now featured in the title role. A veteran of such hit films as *Always* (1989) and *Flight of the Intruder* (1991), Johnson, like Wittliff, lives in Texas. In an interview with the *Chicago Tribune's* Jay Bobbin, Johnson elaborated on his view of Blessing as a classic American hero:

> If there was a message that Ned could convey, it is that you are responsible for your actions, plain and simple. It's not that there's honor in shooting somebody (as happens in the show), but there is honor in a face-to-face confrontation and in saying, "This is what you did, this is the chance you took when you did this action, and now you're going to have to pay the consequences." The first time I read this, I got a lot of the same feelings as the first time I read the script for "Lonesome Dove." I read for various parts (in that drama) and didn't get any of them, but I couldn't get on the phone soon enough to try to find out how I could be a part of this, and I think that's because there's such a closeness between the way that Bill writes and the way that I think. We're like cousins who were raised and never met, because I know a lot of the same things that he knows. The way he describes how people wear their hats, or how they speak or gesture, are all things that strike true to me.[99]

The only cast members carried over from the original two hour film were Avalos and Tim Scott as Deputy "Sticks" Packwood. (Scott also appeared in *Wildside* and *Lonesome Dove*.) New characters included a soft-hearted whore known as "The Wren," who reforms after falling in love with Ned (played by lovely Brenda Bakke of *Hot Shots! Part Deux*); an eccentric (and humorous) Indian named One Horse, who carries around a sack that holds some unknown and mysterious contents (played by Native American actor Wes Studi, who won acclaim as the evil Maqua in the 1992 remake of *The Last of the Mohicans*); ruthless villain Verlon Borgers, who abuses his three sons and probably murdered his wife (portrayed by Bill McKinney, a veteran of such television Westerns as *The Family Holvak* and film Westerns as *The Outlaw Josey Wales*, 1976); Big Emma, Borgers' partner in crime and proprietress of Plum Creek's only saloon (a tour de force for Rusty Schwimmer); and alcoholic Judge Longley (played by Richard Riehle, whose previous television experience included four months as *Ferris Bueller*'s pompous principal, Ed Rooney).

The second two-hour pilot relates the story of how Ned became sheriff of Plum Creek (thus occurring sometime during the twenty year period from when he left to get medicine for his father and the Buckner massacre). The same flashback format is used, with an elderly Ned Blessing writing down the earlier adventures of his youth.

In the story that follows (entitled "A Ghost Story"), Ned and Crecencio get some supernatural assistance from the hereafter when Ned's Mexican adversary, General Pelo Blanco, lines up against him. In perhaps the most unusual episode of a television Western ever broadcast, the body of the town's former sheriff returns from the grave to reclaim his head (which Borgers has kept in a pickle jar on the bar of the Plum Creek saloon). In the process he strikes Borgers deaf, dumb and blind, transforming him into a zombie with vacant starring eyes. Big Emma pleads to take care of Borgers, hoping that at some point he will return to normal. In the final scene, Ned digs up the sheriff's coffin and finds that the corpse is now complete with its head! The rest of the stories relate Ned's adventures (or misadventures) as sheriff of Plum Creek. As old Ned explains:

> Now I've had some joyous times in my life, as many as the next man, I reckon. But becomin' sheriff of Plum Creek, Texas, wasn't one of um. The trouble with holdin' public office, I soon found out, was havin' ta deal with the public.

The third episode, "The Smink Brothers," skillfully blends humor and gunplay. When two notorious killers ride into Plum Creek and harass One Horse, Ned arrests them. He is unaware that Big Emma (with the help of her two sisters who are married to the Sminks) have hired the brothers to kill Ned. Although there are several very funny exchanges (notably between Big Emma and her sister Eda, played by Sage Allen), a blazing gunfight between Ned and the brothers provides plenty of action and suspense.

In "Oscar," Bill Wittliff creates a minor masterpiece. "Oscar" is the Irish-born author Oscar Wilde, who was well on his way to becoming one of Britain's finest writers. When he arrives in Plum Creek (unbeknownst to Ned, he is looking for "the Boy Bandit of Texas" for Jilly Blue), he is immediately attracted to the Wren. After Oscar invites her to travel to Europe with him, Ned must decide the depth of his feelings for her. Oscar, realizing the deep attraction the two have toward each other, sends the Wren a gift from Ned and, in the dramatic climatic scene, risks his life to save Ned from a vicious gunman. At the end of the story Ned sympathizes with Oscar's problems—his foppish apparel, his controversial lifestyle—while holding him in high regard: "I've known my share of indecent men, and Oscar Wilde wasn't one of um."

The two hour pilot of *Ned Blessing* received surprisingly high ratings, tying for eighth place with 17.1 million viewers. The following week, however, it dropped to forty-third. The reviews ranged from good to fair.

Matt Roush writing in *USA Today* (August 18, 1993) liked the second version better than the first and gave it two and a half stars (out of four):

> "Ned Blessing" is a twice-told tale, playing quite a bit better the second time around. ... At least this has a story. And the new Ned, Brad Johnson, is a more iconic Marlboro Man—stoic macho, with subtle glimmers of irony....
>
> There's much to savor in these first two hours, despite a deliberately slow pace and enough archetypal clichés to choke a mule, from glowering villains to a winsome noble town whore (here called "the Wren"). Wittliff takes these conventions seriously and drops in eccentric, novelistic details along the way, portrayed convincingly by a generally terrific cast....
>
> If you've a taste for wild oats, "Ned Blessing" is as good a place as any to sow them.

This time Walter Goodman reviewed *Ned Blessing* for the *New York Times* (August 18, 1993):

> Ned Blessing is a western hero for the 90's. In a few minutes, he proves himself to be no racist, sexist, ageist, ethnicist or speciesist. Having subdued a rattlesnake, he tosses it back to its natural habitat, and he stands up for the speech impaired....
>
> Whether Bill Wittliff, the writer and executive producer, intends his upscale series to be a shoot-'em-up with an up-to-the-minute sensibility or a sendup of the latest television conventions, I cannot be sure. But it's more fun if you think of it as a deadpan Deadwood gag.

Jeff Jarvis of *TV Guide* (August 14, 1993) was more critical:

> ... I had hoped this summer series would turn into a parody of Westerns. But it's not. It's just another Western, a "Lonesome Dove" wanna-be, all dark and dusty with glum townfolk, crackling bad guys, half-wit flunkies, plucky whores, and one good guy.... It has its moments, but it is a Western and you have to like Westerns to like "Ned Blessing." My score: 6

The most negative review is found in *Entertainment Weekly* (August 27–September 3, 1993) whose reviewer, Ken Tucker, called it "vapid" and referred to it as "Westward Woe":

> In attempting to present an earnest, elegiac, eloquent vision of the Old West, "Ned Blessing: The Story of My Life & Times" instead comes off as sappy, silly, and staid.... CBS' programmers were probably hoping for a male version of their hit Western "Dr. Quinn, Medicine Woman"; they've ended up with a slow-pokin' string of clichés. D+

Another (fifth) episode of *Ned Blessing* was scheduled for broadcast on September 15, but was withdrawn too late for publication in *TV Guide* or any of the weekly television listings. (The two hour pilot episode of *Dr. Quinn, Medicine Woman* was substituted.) According to the synopsis in *TV Guide* (September 11–17, 1993) the episode would have provided answers to many of the series' unresolved questions. The reason for the cancellation of the episode given by the Program Department at CBS was that *Ned Blessing* was being considered as a January (1994) replacement. Consequently, the story was left open so that additional episodes might be written extending the plot. Unfortunately no new episodes have been made and the September 15th episode was never shown.

A Western as unique as *Ned Blessing* certainly deserved another chance at success. From the gritty realism of the settings and the melancholy, lilting music of Basil Poledouris (first pilot) and David Bell to the intriguing, quirky characters and bold, unique plotlines, *Ned Blessing* was a worthy successor to the spirit of *Lonesome Dove* and a memorable achievement for Bill Wittliff.

The two television Westerns which premiered in the fall of 1993 both aimed for laughs. There was obviously room in the "new" West for humor and *The Adventures of Brisco County, Jr.* and *Harts of the West* represented a modest revival of the comedy Western. The primary difference between the two was that while *Harts of the West* was set in the contemporary West, *Brisco County* was a period series. It is difficult to describe *Brisco County* because its creators have borrowed so liberally from so many sources for their ideas. Start with the basic elements of the "B" Western, add a cliffhanger device, mix in some gadgets and inventions from a later era, plus equal amounts of sight gags, slapstick and word humor and, if you are series creators Jeffrey Boam and Carlton Cuse you will end up with *The Adventures of Brisco County, Jr.*

The series has good guys and bad guys, chases on horses and chases in trains, gunfights and fistfights plus a little kung fu, explosions and drownings, a mad (or at least eccentric) scientist, and the prettiest saloon girl this side of Kitty Russell. *Brisco County, Jr.* has been compared to *Maverick*, *Raiders of the Lost Ark*, and *The Wild Wild West*. Furthermore, guest stars from such old oaters as *The Virginian* (James Drury), *Cimarron Strip* (Stuart Whitman), *Rawhide* (Paul Brinegar), and *Laramie* (Robert Fuller) are frequently featured. There is even a strong element of science fiction present. This mix is not quite so surprising when one looks at the credits of its creators. Boam coauthored such film scripts as *Lethal Weapon 2* and *3* and *Indiana Jones and the Last Crusade*; Cuse, such television series as *Crime Story* and *Elvis & Me*. Fox asked them to develop a contemporary cliffhanger, and they came back with a Western. "With a Western, your imagination can run wild," said Cuse. "It can allow us to have big action events."[100]

The basic concept underlying all this fun and mayhem is simple: Brisco County, Jr. ("It's not a place. It's who I am") is a bounty hunter who is hired by five business tycoons who each control a different facet of the economy (banks, mines, cattle, railroads and shipping) to track down the 13 most notorious outlaws in the West. County's father had been the West's most famous and successful marshal until he was killed by members of the John Bly (number one on the list of bad guys) gang. Brisco is a graduate of Harvard where he majored in English and minored in theater (and flunked Greek philosophy twice). However, he can "outshoot, outspit, outfight and outthink" John Bly or any member of his gang!

Brisco is played, tongue-in-cheek, with a mischievous twinkle in his eye, by Bruce Campbell, a veteran of such popular cult films as *Army of Darkness* (1992), *The Evil Dead* (1983), and *Evil Dead II* (1987). At a press conference held to promote the show, Campbell did a bone-crunching back flip to show off his prowess at the physical stunts he performs in the series. When asked the inevitable question about all the violence in *Brisco County, Jr.*, Campbell noted that he had two children, ages 9 and 6:

> ... I made a lot of movies that I wouldn't show them until they understood how movies and TV are different from reality.... [But] "Brisco" is a quantum leap from an NC-17 rating ... [and] despite the graphic roughhousing the hero tries to get out of his scrapes with a minimum of gunplay.[101]

Fox is banking on Campbell's appeal to bring the series respectable ratings. According to Fox Entertainment chief Sandy Grushow: "If Bruce Campbell isn't the next big television star, I'll eat my desk.... [He's] just too good. He's going to happen."[102]

Other characters include Brisco's assistant and the representative of his employers (actually, he is more of a comedy sidekick) Socrates Poole, played with gentle restraint by Christian Clemenson (who had appeared in the short-lived *Capital News*). A tall black rival bounty hunter named Lord Bowler is constantly trying to beat Brisco to his quarry—

for the reward, of course. Still, they usually end up working together to help each other out of "difficult" situations. Bowler is nicely played with just the proper amount of hostility by Julius Carry (best known for his role as the network boss on *Murphy Brown*).

Stealing most of the scenes he is in, John Astin is cast as the absent-minded rocket scientist and inventor, Professor Albert Wickwire. Astin's extensive experience in television comedy roles, including his classic portrayal of Gomez Addams on *The Addams Family*, is put to excellent use in *Brisco County, Jr.* As one might expect, the villains on the show are wildly drawn and broadly played. Appearing occasionally as John Bly, the neurotic outlaw mastermind, is newcomer Billy Drago (described by one reviewer as "a flamboyantly repellent cross between Martin Short and Willem Dafoe"). English actor John Pyper-Ferguson is even better as one of Bly's henchmen, Pete Huttor.

Best of all perhaps is Kelly Rutherford as sexy, blond, Western dance hall singer, Dixie Cousins. The 24 year old Rutherford, daughter of a professional model, left California for New York at 17 to pursue a career in acting. After working is such soaps as *Loving* and *Generations*, she landed the plum role of the smoldering bartender Judy Owen on ABC's prime time drama *Homefront*. This led to the even sexier *Brisco* part. When asked by *TV Guide*'s Rick Marin if this was typecasting, she replied:

> It's so funny because I was pretty much a tomboy when I was growing up. My acting teacher always said, "We need to work on your sexuality." She had me do every love scene known to man.[103]

When asked about the character Dixie, Rutherford expressed admiration for "the girl who went out and hustled and wanted to be where the excitement was, while other girls just stayed home." Furthermore, the role has enabled her to finally "live out her fantasy of being Madeline Kahn in 'Blazing Saddles'."[104] Attired in some of the bawdiest clothes ever seen in a television Western—lace bodices, red lingerie, black garter belts and stockings—and with a husky drawl that could melt the heart of the toughest cowpoke, Rutherford delivers some of the funniest lines on the show:

> DIXIE: (as she prepares to seduce Brisco) Ya like the bed? It comes from France.
> BRISCO: (eyeing the antique bed) Louis XIV?
> DIXIE: No. I think Louie was the ninth or tenth, but then a lady never counts.

Another humorous exchange between Dixie and Brisco takes place as the stagecoach in which they are riding careens out of control:

> DIXIE: What are we gonna do?
> BRISCO: Well, I could swing out an' get a good foothold and climb up to the top of the stage. Then if I'm real careful and, God is on my side, I could leap on to the back of the rear horse and work my way out to the lead team, taking care not to fall beneath their thundering hooves. Then reach out, grab the bridle of the lead horse, and rein him in to a safe and steady stop.
> DIXIE: Oh, my!
> BRISCO: Or—we could jump! (and they jump—with Brisco landing on top of Dixie—at the feet of Dixie's boyfriend.)
> BRISCO: (as he tries to rise) Your dress is caught in my fly.
> DIXIE: (as she moves her hand toward the spot) I'll get it.
> BRISCO: (pushes her hand away) No, I'd better get it.
> (This scene plays even funnier than it reads!)

The series is filled with references to the old "B" Westerns and Saturday matinee serials. In addition to a sidekick, Brisco has a horse that gets featured billing. As the credits roll we see a horse rearing on its hind legs in best Champion (or Trigger) fashion and the words "with Comet" appear. True to his movie equine heritage, Comet occasionally rescues his master and provides someone for him to talk to out on the lonely plains. (Once, in a sendup of *Mr. Ed*, it actually appears that Comet, "who doesn't know he's a horse," actually talks back—but it is just a trick employed by Lord Bowler.)

Furthermore, each episode is divided into chapters, most with catchy or humorous titles. At the end of each chapter, the hero's life is threatened by some perilous predicament that is resolved after the commercials. There were seven chapters in the two hour pilot, with such titles as "The Blast Supper" (which ends as a bundle of dynamite sticks sit on a restaurant table with the fuse burning down); "Hot Flames, Two Dames and Loose Reins" (ends with an out-of-control stage about to go over a cliff); and "Yell to Your Horse" (ends with Brisco and Lord Bowler tied to the tracks as a train bears down on them). Other episodes feature "Our Ace in a Hole" (Brisco is dropped down a well); "No Man's Land" (Brisco arrives in a town inhabited only by women); "Get the Drop, Tie 'Em Up, Shoot 'Em Dead, Rawhide" (which not only describes the precarious situation Brisco finds himself in at the end of the chapter, but is a play on the dialogue used at the close of every episode of *Rawhide*); "Guns or Hutter" (when Mexican revolutionaries must deal with outlaw Pete Hutter to obtain badly needed guns); and "Rushin' Roulette" (in which Brisco finds himself tied to a huge spinning wheel as hatchets are thrown at him). There is not much real suspense in these situations—viewers know Brisco will somehow escape each time. The fun comes in watching *how* he eludes the traps of the evildoers.

Another clever device employed by creators Boam and Cuse is the newspaper headlines which flash by in the opening title sequence of each episode. They briefly and concisely explain the basic series premise: "Federal Marshal Brisco County Murdered"; "John Bly Gang Escapes"; "Tycoons Hire Bounty Hunter Brisco County, Jr.," and "Rival Manhunter on Bly's Trail." A colorful animated map is also used whenever Brisco travels any distance. Futuristic weapons and devices like a fire-belching rocket, a deep-sea diving suit and a tread-drive tank ("mobile battle wagon") with a 70mm cannon and eight-inch steel-plated armor lead to comparisons with *The Wild Wild West*. But the devices in *Brisco County, Jr.* are played much more for laughs.

Boam and Cuse also poke fun in one episode at the popular CBS Western, *Dr. Quinn, Medicine Woman*, by naming the doctor in "No Man's Land" Dr. Quintano, Medicine Woman. They also enjoy rhyming words and names—e.g., "the Swill Brothers—Will, Bill, Phil and Gil—a good reason why inbreeding is a bad idea." Still another clever example of their humor comes when Brisco injures his thumb. Holding it straight up as he walks along the road, Brisco becomes the West's first hitchhiker when an old man in a wagon stops to give him a ride.

Examples of slapstick also abound: A huge rock is painted to look like the landscape, so a train will crash into it. Four outlaws are killed in the crossfire when Brisco, who is facing off against one of John Bly's gang, decides to simply fall flat on his face. (The man in front and the back-shooter kill each other and the men on the right and left of Brisco shoot each other.)

In another episode, Socrates flips Comet to see who gets to sleep in the stall. When Comet hits Socrates in the face with his tail, it is obvious that the horse has called "tails." The coin does come up "heads," however, and Comet stalks off in a huff. Still, it is the verbal comedy that elevates the humor of the show. A gang of Oriental thugs show up unexpectedly at Brisco's hotel room to kill him and Brisco says (with a straight face), "There must be some mistake, I didn't order Chinese." In another episode Brisco rescues a little girl from being blown up by sweeping her up onto his horse. Her response, "I have to go to the bathroom." Brisco replies: "I know what ya mean." Some of the humor has a remarkably contemporary slant. Pete says to Dixie as he is about to shoot Brisco: "I'm a stickler for gun safety. Could you move a little to the left?" In another episode:

> BRISCO: Correct me if I'm wrong, Pete. Weren't you killed in a gunfight?
> PETE: I was only gut-shot. I healed. I'm stronger now with less appetite.
> BRISCO: You could be a pioneer in the field of weight loss.
> PETE: Weight loss? Why would anyone want to lose weight?

As Jeffrey Boam liked to point out: "We're not approaching this show as if we were doing a period piece. We see it as a contemporary program. Our characters just happen to be in the West with 1990s sensibilities...."[105]

There's even a touch of the supernatural in *Brisco County, Jr.* When one of the tycoons (gleefully played by Stuart Whitman) tampers with the power of the orb (called an Unearthed Foreign Object—U.F.O.—by the government authorities), he rapidly ages, his face shrivels up and his body turns to dust. It reminds one of the fate awaiting all vampires when exposed to the rays of the sun.

Most reviewers gave *Brisco County, Jr.* high praise. Matt Roush, *USA Today*'s television critic, gave the pilot episode three out of four stars and wrote (August 27, 1993):

> [Bruce Campbell is] the season's savviest and winningest TV-Western hero, with playful macho bravado. A fun-filled romp that works on enough levels to please all but the family curmudgeon, "The Adventures of Brisco County Jr." is part "Wild, Wild West," with a comical cliffhanger at every commercial break, and part Mel Brooks, peppered with sight gags, low puns and shameless double entendres....
>
> This is the kind of comic book caper that traffics in knockout gas, a mystical orb, trap doors in Chinese parlors and slapstick shootouts. You know, the good stuff.

Greg Dawson, whose review in the *Orlando Sentinel* (August 28, 1993) was distributed by the Associated Press, claimed that "anyone who sat stony-faced" through the two hour premiere "should apply immediately for a prosthetic funny bone":

> "The Adventures of Brisco County, Jr." is the sort of show that gives escapism a good name—and the resurgent cowboy genre a much-needed poke in the ribs. If the dreary "Dr. Quinn" and "Ned Blessing" are "Westerns," "Brisco County" is a Western omelette—a tantalizing combo of rousing, slapstick action, wry comedy, light romance and sci-fi fancy.

Jeff Jarvis of *TV Guide* (August 21-27, 1993) called *The Adventures of Brisco County, Jr.* "a western for people who don't like westerns":

> Not since "Maverick" have I seen a western with such a sense of humor.... What's great about "Brisco" is its light comic touch—so light it's hard to demonstrate the show's humor just quoting a joke. My favorite gag ends with this punch line: "Existential thought doesn't hold much water out in the territories." See: You had to be there. So be there. This is a western even people who don't like westerns could love. "Brisco" is a hoot—and one of the best shows of fall. My score: 9

Only Walter Goodman of the *New York Times* (August 27, 1993) had doubts about the series:

> The writers try everything, including some business involving raiders of a lost orb, without much of a payoff. Some of the characters, including an incompetent bounty hunter and a severely neurotic bad guy who fancies himself an art critic, are overdone; others, like a lawyer named Socrates Poole (another lame name joke), are underbaked....
>
> The evening is not without laughs.... But for most of the trek this show is like a would-be fast-drawer who has trouble getting his gun out of his holster, and when he manages that, the darned thing misfires.

The biggest problem faced by *Brisco County, Jr.*, was not John Bly's gang or even the magical orb, it was that evil nemesis of all television shows: ratings. The series had two strikes against it to begin with: because it was broadcast on the fledgling Fox Network, it had far fewer potential viewers; being scheduled on Friday evenings, one of the weakest viewing nights of the week limited its potential rating. By the fifth week it was ranked only eightieth out of 90 programs—one of Fox's lowest rated shows. Not surprisingly, at the end of the season Fox canceled it. It is unfortunate that it was not given a better opportunity to catch on. Exciting, funny, original and entertaining, *The Adventures of Brisco County, Jr.* was the best Western comedy to ride the video range since *Maverick*.

Harts of the West was a different kind of Western comedy. With more subtle humor and less slapstick, *Harts* tried to tug at the heartstrings almost as often as it tried to tickle the funny bone. The creation of writer Robert Moloney (who also created the Irish family comedy, *The Cavanaughs* for CBS in 1986), the show was based on an amusing, but not terribly original, premise. Dave Hart, a 41 year old lingerie salesman living in Chicago, has a "coronary episode." Because he has always wanted to be a cowboy, he answers a newspaper ad offering a ranch in Nevada for sale. After twisting his reluctant wife's arm, Dave packs up his three kids and heads for the wide open spaces. When they arrive in Showlo, Nevada (pop. 90), they find the ranch (formerly a dude ranch) is completely rundown. (There is no electricity, the roof leaks like a sieve and the stove does not work.) Furthermore, the salesman who sold them the property has died (his ashes are scattered out in front of "his favorite spot" on the ranch, the outhouse).

This basic concept has been effectively utilized in such plays as *George Washington Slept Here* (1942), novels and films like *The Egg and I* (1947), and television series like *Green Acres* (1965-1971) and an earlier comedy television Western, *Guestward Ho!* (1960-1961). The idea that a man can find his "inner self" in the freedom of the Western plains was also the theme of the 1991 box office hit *City Slickers*. What *Harts* had going for it was an outstanding cast playing a variety of interesting and sometimes wildly eccentric characters. Beau Bridges, who was also co-executive producer on the series, is near perfect as Dave. While Beau had extensive film experience in such highly acclaimed hits as *Norma Rae* (1978), *Heart Like a Wheel* (1983) and *The Fabulous Baker Boys* (1989), his television experience was more limited. He had won plaudits for his portrayal of James Brady in the made-for-television movie *Without Warning: The James Brady Story* (1991), but his attempts at series television were not very successful: *Ensign O'Toole*, a feeble imitation of *McHale's Navy*, in which Beau had a small supporting role, was cancelled after only one season; and *United States*, described by Brooks and Marsh as "often tedious, boring, and didactic,"[106] lasted less than two months.

Harley Jane Kozak is effective as the frustrated wife who genuinely loves her husband, and wants him to be happy, but finds it difficult to adjust to the primitive living conditions and her quirky new neighbors. Kozak's previous television experience included a supporting role on *Knightwatch*, the short-lived crime drama based on the Guardian Angels, and one of the leads in the acclaimed comedy series *Parenthood*.

Their three children, each named after one of their father's Western heroes, are all played by television newcomers: Meghann Haldeman is the unhappy teenager L'Amour who cannot wait to get back to the big city; Sean Murray plays the lovesick 15 year old Zane Gray Hart (who tells the 23 year old beauty he is "mooning" over that he is 18); and Nathan Watt portrays young John "Duke" Wayne Hart, who worships his dad and is the only sibling who really enjoys playing cowboy.

The characters they meet in Showlo are thinly drawn, but in some ways resemble the collection of eccentrics found on *Northern Exposure*. There is Augie, the resident

Indian with a face like weathered shoe leather, who has run the local store ("trading post") for the past 45 years (stoically played for laughs by Native American Saginaw Grant); Marcus St. Cloud, a black Wall Street lawyer who spent time in a "correctional facility" for insider trading and now just wants to learn how to rope horses and cows. (nicely played by *Homefront* alumnus Sterling Macer); Cassie Valasquez, a 23 year old Hispanic beauty who reads Susan Faludi's *Backlash: The Undeclared War Against Women* in her spare time (provocatively played by Talisa Soto); Garrol, a shiftless old codger who responds to every question he is asked by expectorating a stream of tobacco juice, but who can fly a "mean" airplane (an idiosyncratic portrayal by Dennis Fimple who did a similar character on *Matt Houston*); a gossipy but friendly waitress (a stand-out performance by O-Lan Jones) and the town's short-order cook, and sheriff, whose unlocked jail cell conjures up pleasant memories of Andy Taylor's gentle views on law and order in Mayberry (a promising role for Stephen Root).

Most memorable of all is Jake, the crusty old foreman of the Flying Tumbleweed Dude Ranch, who not only "knows everything there is to know about animals" but also "knows his limitations." Played by Beau's dad Lloyd, Jake steals every scene he is in. Comparable to the Jack Palance role in *City Slickers* (which won him an Oscar), Bridges may not be as grizzled, but is considerably more folksy and charming. (Lloyd, of course, practically qualifies as a television pioneer, with credits that go back to the mid-fifties—see Chapter V.)

The danger here is that the characters are so one dimensional that they sometimes tend to become stereotypes. For example, the fact that Augie sacrifices a live chicken once a month under a full moon for good luck does little to enhance the television image of the Native American. This is somewhat surprising, given Saginaw Grant's background. Grant is a Sac and Fox Indian from Cushing, Oklahoma, who was "discovered" in 1988 by artist Stanley J. Herd. Both attended the Haskell Powwow, a cultural exchange meeting held earlier that year at Haskell Indian Junior College in Lawrence, Kansas. Herd, who is white, was there taking photographs and was so impressed with Grant's face that he "created" his portrait in a 30-acre wheatfield near Lawrence with the aid of a plow and a lawn mower.[107] It is also doubtful that many feminists would approve of the sexy image presented by Cassie—even if she does read all the "right" books.

Still, all the prerequisites of the revisionist Western are present: a liberated woman, a black, an Hispanic, a Native American, and even a cause. Jake has been carrying on a one-man campaign against the District Land Office, whose agents have been killing off horses to control the wild horse population on the open range (so that the cattle barons can graze their cattle there).

The basic dilemma facing the Harts is nicely set up in a scene involving Dave and Jake about halfway through the pilot episode.

> JAKE: Everybody came out here to the Tumbleweed—the Hollywood crowd, politicians.
> DAVE: Ever since I was a kid, I loved the idea of the West.
> JAKE: Whole town worked out here.
> DAVE: Freedom—even named my children after my heroes—Zane Grey, Louis L'Amour and John Wayne...
> JAKE: It's all gone now—Shot to Hell! ... the Hollywood crowd are all goin' ta Betty Ford's and the politicians are goin' ta jail.

Of course, it is easy to figure out what comes next. Dave decides to fix up and reopen the dude ranch, Jake hires most of the town's eccentrics to help, and together they round up and save the wild horses. The rest of the Hart family is won over by the friendliness of the townspeople and decide to stay and try their hand at ranching. Jake will intermittently appear to teach them the tricks of the trade. It is unfortunate that Jake is only a recurring role because as Beau explains it: "My dad has carried series (like *Sea Hunt*) in the past and he knows how hard that is. At this stage in his career, he doesn't feel like busting his nut every week."[108]

Yet *Harts* is to some extent a family affair for the Bridges. Beau's mom, Dorothy, appears in the pilot's opening dream sequence (as a hangman, no less) and it was expected that Beau's little brother Jeff (who starred in an unrelated 1975 Western film called *Hearts of the West*) would make an appearance—maybe "as a wrangler with one line"[109]—if the show lasted long enough. *Harts* is also marked by a "laid-back" quality which is reflected in the words of the theme song written and performed under the opening credits by popular country singer Clint Black (and appropriately entitled "In a Laid-Back Way"). The background music (by John Debney in the pilot and Sam Winans in the series) is invigorating and folksy and a real asset to the show.

As *TV Guide* writers pointed out in their fall 1993 preview issue (September 18, 1993), the major problem facing *Harts of the West* is that it is "a comedy, not a straight Western drama—and Western comedy is a tricky mix, *City Slickers*, notwithstanding. On television it's rarely been done well since *Maverick*." However, their conclusion is, "If anybody can make it work, it's probably these guys." The network, CBS scheduled *Harts of the West* on Saturday nights at 9 P.M. Eastern time—between *Dr. Quinn, Medicine Woman* and *Walker, Texas Ranger*. According to executive producer Maloney: "'Dr. Quinn's' audience is primarily women 35 and older, which they feel we'll hold. We'll also introduce men into the mix. Then it's off to Chuck Norris, whose audience is almost exclusively male."[110]

At first it appeared that CBS's strategy had worked: the first week (September 25, 1993) each show won its time slot, with *Harts* finishing twentieth (*Dr. Quinn* was thirteenth, *Walker*, twenty-sixth), and CBS won Saturday night for the first time in years. Kozak had a rather simple explanation for this triumph: "I think the collective unconscious just decided this is the year of the Western. It's just one of those things that's in the air. Like pollen."[111] The critics had mixed feelings, however. Jeff Jarvis was almost ecstatic in his comments for *TV Guide* (September 25, 1993):

> It's "City Slickers" with light touches of "Green Acres" and "Middle Ages," plus real family charm. Beau Bridges, a fed-up underwear salesman, turns cowboy and drags his brood to a run-down ranch. Lloyd Bridges costars as a TV remake of Jack Palance.
> The kids and cowboys are quirky. And this is the most entertaining series in CBS's Saturday western revival. My score (0 to 10): 9

Matt Roush, *USA Today*'s critic, was more restrained, but liked the show nonetheless in his September 24, 1993, review:

> Think of it as "Western Exposure" with a broad family bent.... Beau Bridges plays daddy Dave Hart, "the Willy Loman of lingerie," who obviously digs the cowboy mystique. After a heart attack, Dave moves the clan out West to take over a dream ranch that's (big surprise) hardly a bargain.... [If] it starts moseying along more creatively, it could be a winner.

Only Ken Tucker of *Entertainment Weekly* (October 1, 1993) turned thumbs down:

> An hour-long laughless comedy, [which] stars Beau Bridges ... [who] drags his family (including this season's requisite three children, sullen little louts all) along with him ... [and] which will feature occasional appearances by Beau's dad, Lloyd, in the role of a crusty old rancher, is exceptionally unoriginal.... The small town near the Hart's ranch is populated by eccentrics who seem to be auditioning for a Bizarro World version of "Northern Exposure."

It was, of course, the viewers who decided the ultimate fate of television's first revisionist comedy Western, *Harts of the West*. As ratings steadily declined, CBS decided to cancel the series in midseason. Four new episodes, which had already been filmed, were aired in June (1994) and then *Harts of the West* disappeared from the video range without a whimper.

While the popularity of CBS's Saturday night block of Westerns might signify a modest revival of the genre, viewers needed to look no further than the trend in documentaries to realize that something significant was happening. Could it be that the Western documentary was the cowboys' next frontier? Early in 1992, Ken Burns, acknowledged master filmmaker, whose multipart documentary on the Civil War won critical raves and unprecedentedly high ratings, announced plans for a similar project that would focus on the history of the American West. Thus encouraged, other documentary producers hopped on the Old West bandwagon.

In September 1992, the Arts & Entertainment cable network premiered *The Real West*, a 13 week series hosted by popular country and western singer and actor Kenny Rogers. Using the Burns style to chronicle the men, the women, the Indians, and the events "that shaped and finally tamed the West," the program became one of A&E's highest rated series. It was so successful, in fact, that 26 additional episodes were ordered bringing the total in the first year of production to 39.

According to one critic, old paintings, photographs, diaries and comments from historians (like Dr. Paul A. Hutton of the University of New Mexico; Robert M. Utley; Mandell Plainfeather, Plains Indian historian for the National Park Service; and bestselling author Dee Brown) "were blended smoothly to form an impressive narrative."[112] The series also utilized a device not available to Burns in his film study of the Civil War—movie footage. The real West still existed when motion pictures became a reality in the 1890s. For example, real footage of Buffalo Bill and his troupe was utilized in "Buffalo Bill and his Wild West," one of the first episodes of *The Real West*. The music by Christopher L. Stone was also a plus. Stirring and uplifting, it was certainly superior to that in any of the other documentaries about the West.

Michael Cascio, director of documentary production of A&E, pointed out that the series tried to emphasize little-known events and people (like the "Mountain Meadows Massacre" about a rarely discussed massacre of a wagon train by Mormons and their Indian friends). Cascio elaborated in an interview:

> We've tried to bring the subject matter up a notch. We've tried to break the stereotypes. You learn things you didn't know and get a fresh look at the West....
>
> Like the Civil War, the interest [in the West] has always been there. It's just that with all those westerns in the 1950s and 1960s, we pretty much exhausted the old way of looking at the West.[113]

In recognition of the contributions of *The Real West* to the preservation and study of the American West, the series was honored with a 1993 Cowboy Hall of Fame Western Heritage Award.

A 10 hour miniseries, *The Wild West*, was developed by Warner Bros. Domestic Television for release during the spring of 1993. Utilizing the same techniques as *The Real West* (and many of the same experts for commentary), each episode focused on a different group who contributed to the settlement and development of the West—"The Cowboys," "The Indians," "The Settlers," "The Gunfighters," "The Searchers," etc. The series was lavishly illustrated with pictures gathered from more than 250 museums and collections. Eight historians and teams of researchers worked on it, and a companion book was published by Time-Life Books.

The narration was provided by Academy Award-winning actor Jack Lemmon and a host of other distinguished thespians were employed as readers to bring to life the words of both the great and the ordinary citizens who helped civilize the frontier. Included were Corbin Bernsen, Bruce Boxleitner, Lloyd Bridges, James Coburn, Richard Crenna, Brian Dennehy, Richard Farnsworth, Lee Grant, Mariette Hartley, Ken Howard, Brian Keith, Robert Morse, and Richard Thomas.

The Wild West is more focused around people—the people who lived in the West during the thirty-five years following the Civil War. They tell their own stories in their own, often moving, words. In the episode on "Indians," for example, the voices of such well-known Native American actors as George American Horse reading Geronimo, Floyd Red Crow Westerman as Sitting Bull, Rodney Grant as Red Cloud, Graham Greene as Black Elk, Buffy St. Marie as Sarah Winnemucca, and Wes Studi as Crazy Horse were used.

The Prime Time Arts & Entertainment Network syndicated the series in two-hour segments over five consecutive nights beginning on March 22, 1993. Series producer John Copeland explained in an *AP* press release (March 18, 1993):

> We wanted to tell about the West through the common elements of human experience, such as hopes, dreams, love, marriage, work and death. . . . It took one generation to fill up the land West of the Mississippi. We wanted to tell it in the words of the people, and we wanted it to be true to what happened. We didn't want the idealized West, the myth.[114]

The story of the West was close to Copeland's heart: His great grandfather, Elizah Simpson Hornoday, was a first sergeant in the 7th Cavalry with George Custer before the Battle of the Little Big Horn, and won the Medal of Honor with the 6th Cavalry at Sappa Creek, Kansas, in 1874.

Copeland and executive producer Douglas Netter had already tried their hand at producing Westerns for television. Their *The Sacketts* (1979) was a rambling saga based on two Louis L'Amour novels, *The Daybreakers* and *Sackett*, relating the adventures of the three Sackett Brothers, Tell, Orrin and Tyrel, in the post–Civil War West. It starred Sam Elliott, Tom Selleck, Jeff Osterhage, Glenn Ford, Ben Johnson, Gilbert Roland, Jack Elam and Mercedes McCambridge and was originally shown in two two-hour segments.

Copeland and Netter's *Wild Times* (1980) was an engaging version of Brian Garfield's book about a dime novel hero who becomes America's first Wild West Show impresario (very loosely based on the life of "Buffalo Bill") and starred Sam Elliott, Ben Johnson, Bruce Boxleitner, Penny Peyser, Dennis Hopper, Cameron Mitchell, Harry Carey, Jr., and Leif Erickson; it was also originally shown in two two-hour segments, and their *Buffalo Soldiers* was an unsuccessful pilot based on the black troopers of the 10th Cavalry.

The Wild West was, however, the first attempt by the two at a documentary. Still, it did not measure up to its predecessor in the eyes of the critics. Matt Roush of *USA Today* (March 22, 1993) wrote:

> Though it boasts all the tools of the trade—a collage of archival images, dramatic readings and scholarly commentary—"The Wild West" has none of the tricks of pure talent needed to bring the past to life.
>
> In the two random hours screened for preview, the only unifying thread is a scattershot approach to storytelling. Without a clear focus . . . the details drift by with the weightlessness of a tumbleweed. . . .
>
> With such a broad canvas, "The Wild West" screams for a raw poet's sensibilities, not twangy generalizations.

Both *The Wild West* and the much longer *Real West* were made available by their respective producers for sale to the general public on videocassettes. Historian Robert Utley, who contributed to several segments of both series, has stated:

> I think the 1990s are going to be the years of the West and (especially) the years of the Indian. "Dances with Wolves" had a lot to do with arousing an interest in Indians that did not exist before.[115]

Following close on the heels of these two documentary series was the Discovery Channel's excellent *How the West Was Lost* in May 1993 (see Chapter IX). During the summer of 1993, cable mogul Ted Turner announced plans for a series of movies and specials about Native Americans. Included in that programming was to be a three part documentary, *The Native Americans*, set to air on TBS late in 1994—an oral history supplemented with stills, artwork and atmospheric cinematography: Part I would examine the tribes of the Northeast; Part II, the tribes of the Far West and Southwest; and Part III, life on the plains before and after the arrival of the horse.

In advance of these documentaries, the Turner Broadcasting System aired two original fact-based films on Native Americans during the first two weeks of December 1993. The first, *Geronimo*, premiered on Sunday, December 5th, preceding the theatrical release of the big-budget, big-star *Geronimo, An American Legend* by five days. Unlike *American Legend*, which dealt primarily with the months before the Apache chief's final surrender, the television *Geronimo* dramatized the Indian leader's entire life. Produced by Norman Jewison (of *Moonstruck* fame), with an all Native American cast, Turner's film presented Geronimo as part avenging Superman (he believes bullets cannot stop him) and part Moses (he hears voices and sees visions which inspire him to lead his people into the wilderness). Reaction to the film was mixed. *TV Guide*'s Jeff Jarvis proclaimed (December 4–10, 1993):

> This is the best movie about Native Americans I've ever seen on TV.... Television has always portrayed Indians as bloody savages or as wax statues in museum dioramas. But here they are brought to life as lusty, angry, human characters led by Joseph Running Fox [as Geronimo].... "Geronimo" is exciting, fascinating, fresh. My score: 9.

On the other hand *Entertainment Weekly*'s Ken Tucker saw Turner's *Geronimo* as "a rather static docudrama" (December 10, 1993).

A week later (December 12) *The Broken Chain* was aired. In this made-for-cable film nearly all of the Indians were "good" and all but one of the whites (played by star Pierce Brosnan) were bad. *The Broken Chain* chronicled the failure of the Iroquois Confederation during the American Revolution. Directed and produced by Lamont Johnson (who brought *The Kennedys of Massachusetts* to the home screen) and written by Earl Wallace (who had scripted the highly acclaimed theatrical film *Witness*), the film focuses on the role of Joseph Brant, a Mohawk brave who is sent away to be educated by the British. When he returns, he finds that he is torn between his loyalty to his people and the whites who financed his schooling. Native American actor Eric Schweig (also seen in *The Last of the Mohicans*) plays Brant while Brosnan is cast as a British envoy. Other Indians in major roles include Buffy Sainte-Marie (from *Son of the Morning Star*) and J. C. White Shirt. The moral lesson of *The Broken Chain* is obvious: the competing French and English forces were so concerned with grabbing as much of America for themselves as they could that they totally ignored the claims of the land's native inhabitants.

Again critics could not agree on the film's merits. Jeff Jarvis writing in the December 11-17, 1993 issue of *TV Guide* judged it "not as good" as last week's *Geronimo*, explaining that it was about "politics, not people," and gave it a score of 6. This time Ken Tucker of *Entertainment Weekly* (December 10, 1993) is the one impressed. He found

"The Broken Chain," a work of historical fiction with emotions fully as engaging as the revisionist lessons it wants to teach....

This sort of information [the politics of imperialism] is left out of most pop entertainment about this period of our history, and "Broken Chain" does a good job of imparting its facts vividly while at the same time avoiding the sort of white-devil demonology that might make it too easy for some viewers to dismiss its arguments.

Tucker graded it "B+."

Actually, although both films presented credible dramatizations of American history from the perspective of the Native American, the "definitive" Native American television Western remains to be made.

As the nineties approached their mid-point the prospects for Westerns on television were hopeful. CBS had renewed both of its successful Saturday evening series, *Dr. Quinn, Medicine Woman* and *Walker, Texas Ranger* for third seasons. (*Walker* was renewed despite the fact that the Center for Media and Public Affairs placed that program in its top ten list of most violent shows.)

Kenny Rogers had completed work on his fifth "Gambler" miniseries: *Gambler V: Playing for Keeps* to be aired in late 1994. Based on a true story about Butch Cassidy, the Sundance Kid, and the "Hole-in-the-Wall" gang, the series was filmed around San Antonio, Galveston, and Big Bend National Park. The story begins with Brady Hawks (Rogers) setting out for Bolivia with the photo of a young man he believes to be his estranged son. Others in the cast included Bruce Boxleitner (in a cameo role), Dixie Carter, Loni Anderson and Marisa Hargitay (daughter of the late Jayne Mansfield).

Rob Ward, producer, developer and creator of the Wyatt Earp "featurizations," announced in the spring of 1994 plans for *Annie Oakley* and *Jim Bowie* "featurizations." Gail Davis, reprising her role as Annie Oakley, would be shown attending a wild west show while reminiscing about her earlier exploits. Flashbacks from the original series would be inserted using the same process as used in *Wyatt Earp: Return to Tombstone*. This method would also be employed in a revival of *The Adventures of Jim Bowie* which would include excerpts of the 1956–1958 series featuring such guest stars as Michael Landon and Chuck Connors.[116]

One of the most promising new Western series released for syndication in the fall of 1994 was *Hawkeye, the First Frontier*. Produced by Emmy–award winning writer and producer Stephen J. Cannell, *Hawkeye* was characterized by a careful attention to historic detail and stunning vistas of the North American wilderness. The adventures of *Hawkeye* were "inspired" by the hero of James Fenimore Cooper's classic novels, *The Leatherstocking Tales*, and were set in the mid-eighteenth century during the French and Indian Wars. It was a period of Anglo-French rivalry for control of the fur trading routes along the Hudson River and disputes between the various Indian tribes of the region, including the Delaware, Iroquois and Huron.

Paradise's Lee Horsley was cast in the title role with Lynda Carter as Elizabeth Shield, described in press releases as "a courageous woman who must face the rugged challenges of frontier life alone after the disappearance of her husband, William." Carter had gained fame as the star of ABC's *Wonder Woman* (1976–1981). The former Miss World–USA had appeared in such made-for-television movies as *The Last Song, Born to Be Sold*, in the title role of *Rita Hayworth: The Love Goddess*, and as a guest star on *Mickey Spillane's Mike Hammer*. In 1984 she had costarred with Loni Anderson in the short-lived but critically acclaimed NBC series, *Partners in Crime*. Carter had also delighted television audiences with her singing and dancing in such specials as the Emmy-winning *Lynda Carter Celebration, Lynda Carter: Body and Soul* and *Lynda Carter: Street Life*. After taking time out from her career, to raise a family, she had returned to television in NBC's *Daddy* and CBS's *Posing*.

Rounding out the cast of regulars on *Hawkeye* was the superb Native American actor Rodney A. Grant (of *Dances with Wolves* and *Son of the Morning Star*) as Chingachgook, a Mohican friend of Hawkeye. They had been "bonded together" since childhood "by their shared culture and connection to the natural world."

The storyline (at least for the scheduled first 22 episodes) would revolve around Elizabeth's search, with the assistance of Hawkeye, for her husband who had been kidnapped by the Iroquois. As the studio's press release explained:

> While the French and Indian War rages around them, a compelling love triangle develops among Hawkeye, Elizabeth and the vanished William. Although settlers rarely return after being taken by the Iroquois, Elizabeth's strong moral code requires her to remain true to her husband despite the mutual attraction growing between herself and Hawkeye. She sees in the handsome frontiersman many qualities that were lacking in her own husband: Hawkeye is completely self-sufficient, at peace with nature and wise in the ways of the local tribes, the Hurons, the Iroquois and the Mohicans. Beneath Hawkeye's strength and quick intelligence, Elizabeth also sees a kindness that touches her deeply.[117]

To bring the world of *Hawkeye* to life, Cannell and his production staff assembled an extraordinary team of designers, historians, and craftsmen. Production designer Phil Schmidt explained:

> While we're recreating life in the 1750s for the series, we're keeping in mind that James Fenimore Cooper wrote his novels nearly 100 years later. Cooper, as well as the Hudson River Valley school of painters in the mid-1800s, had romanticized vision of life on the frontier before the American Revolution. In reality, life during the French and Indian Wars was difficult, dirty and dark, but the art and literature of the next century portrays it with a sheen or glow, symbolizing the spirit of the 1700s and the heroism of the frontiersmen who helped forge a new nation. We're going to great lengths to create sets, costumes and props authentic to the Hudson River Valley region in the mid 1700s, but the series will also have a gorgeous, rich look in keeping with the heroic vision of Cooper and the other artists of his time.[118]

Fort Bennington, the British outpost that is the center of daily life in the series, was constructed according to authentic designs of the period by 20 carpenters in about 30 days. At the end of a winding road through the Greater Vancouver Regional District forest, in a clearing surrounded by mountains thick with evergreens, Fort Bennington was located, according to series Executive Producer David Levinson, "in one of the few places left on earth that remains as majestic and unspoiled as the vast wilderness of the Hudson River Valley encountered by North Amerian settlers in the 1750s."[119]

In a further attempt at authenticity, all Native American roles in *Hawkeye* were cast with Native American actors, many of whom were experts in the ancient arts of archery, hatchet throwing, canoeing and canoe building. In addition, Native American craftsmen were used to create props for the various tribes portrayed in the series, utilizing authentic methods. For example, hand-selected saplings were carved and soaked in water to make bows and wampum belts were created by a Native American expert who took 35 hours to hand-bead $200 worth of bone beads. Even the books used in filming were created using methods of that era: first folding the paper, then binding it and finally slicing the pages open. Firearms used in the series were also authentic to the period and actual flintlocks and black powder.

Attention to detail and accuracy was likewise employed in the selection of extras to play French and British soldiers. Cannell recuited men from historical recreation groups who had studied and reenacted life in the 1700s and were skilled in such crafts of the

Hawkeye **stars Lee Horsley (left) as Hawkeye, and Lynda Carter (center) as Elizabeth Shields, with series regular Rodney A. Grant (right) as Chingachgook.**

period as candlemaking, shoemaking, and fife playing. Furthermore, the French and British regiments featured in the series were trained according to actual drill manuals of the period and the military uniforms used were historically correct reproductions of the formal dress uniforms of the period including the officer's hat, coat, wig, walking stick and "gourget" (a small metal plate worn at the throat).

All this attention to detail surely made *Hawkeye* one of the most elaborately produced syndicated series (Western or otherwise) in television history. Whether it paid off with viewers only time would tell. Certainly with the appeal of the stars Horsley and Carter and the reputation of Cannell as known quantities, the chances were good that *Hawkeye* would be riding the video range for some time.

Historian Frederick Jackson Turner once said "each age writes the history of the past anew with reference to the conditions uppermost in its own time."[120] Television drama, more than any other dramatic form, is a product of its time and has been strongly influenced by historical events. And this has been especially true of the television Western.

From the cold war era, when Hoppy, Gene and Roy rode the video range showing viewers that they knew wrong from right and what to do about it, through the tumultuous sixties, when the Vietnam War brought death into everyone's home in living color and Matt Dillon had to deal with the psychological forces that motivated evildoers, to the eighties, when the Western seemed out of step with the sociological forces shaping American society and *Little House on the Prairie* was America's most popular Western, and the nineties, when Dr. Quinn provided a role model for the new liberated woman—television Westerns have closely reflected American cultural values. Some shows, while clearly a product of their time, like *The Outcasts* (born during the civil rights movement) and *Sara* (a result of the feminist movement), failed to attract a sufficient audience. Those shows, however, which proved to be most successful and enduring were those that evolved to mirror the changing times, like *Gunsmoke* and *Bonanza*.

Of all the forces shaping American culture, none has had more dramatic or far-reaching effects than the waning of the Communist threat and the dissolution of the Soviet Union. But while civil wars in Europe, Africa and Asia sprang up to replace the danger of nuclear confrontation, Westerns appeared again on the video range. Nearly half of the readers polled in a 1990 *TV Guide* survey indicated they would like to see more television Westerns (only movies and sitcoms scored higher among the dramatic options). Even when Westerns virtually disappeared from the home screen, Western themes and plot devices were still being employed by other genres. Such diverse programs as *Head of the Class* (sitcom), *MacGyver* (contemporary action-adventure), *Quantum Leap* (action and fantasy) and even *Star Trek: The Next Generation* (science fiction) featured episodes set in the mythic American West.

Contrary to earlier reports, the television Western was not dead—it had only been on sabbatical, gathering new strength. From *Lonesome Dove* to *Dr. Quinn* and *The Real West*, the Western still rode the video range. And as long as it continues to adapt to the changing times, this uniquely American genre never will ride into its last sunset.

Appendix

Individual Episodes Discussed in the Text

The following is essentially an index to specific episodes (subarranged chronologically) of various series (listed alphabetically). It is a specialized duplication of the main Index to this book (in which everything is simply alphabetical and there are no subarrangements). Series whose individual episodes were not titled (or, in a few cases, whose individual episode titles were not known) are not listed here; information on various episodes of such series can be found by looking up the series title in the main Index.

If an exact date is not known, the closest approximate date is given (e.g., 1/89 or fall 1978). A range of dates is used for series originally released in syndication.

The information in this appendix should not be considered an episode guide, but only as a handy way to find information on specific episodes of specific series.

Numbers in boldface are page numbers.

Bordertown (original air dates unknown)

Branded

Chapter Notes

I. Hoppy, The Ranger, Gene and Roy Ride In

1. J. Fred MacDonald, *Who Shot the Sheriff?* (New York: 1987), p. 15.
2. *Time Magazine* (March 30, 1959), p. 53.
3. William A. Henry III, "They Went Thataway!" *Memories* (December 1989/January 1990), p. 78.
4. James Horowitz in *They Went Thataway* (New York: 1976) gives 1898 in Cambridge, p. 118; so does Francis M. Nevins in *The Films of Hopalong Cassidy* (Waynesville, N.C.: 1988) p. 19; but Jane Wollman in "Hoppy at Last," *Memories* (June/July, 1989), p. 40 gives 1895 in Hedrysburg and she interviewed Boyd's widow, Grace, for her story.
5. Horowitz, *They Went Thataway*, p. 119.
6. Quoted in Bernard A. Drew, *Hopalong Cassidy: The Clarence E. Mulford Story* (Metuchen, NJ: 1991), p. 225.
7. Quoted in Wollman, "Hoppy," p. 42.
8. Quoted in Drew, *Hopalong Cassidy*, p. 220.
9. Quoted in *Ibid.*, p. 233.
10. Gabe Essoe, "One More Ride into the Sunset with Bill Boyd," *LA Times West Magazine* (May 4, 1969), p. 46.
11. Quoted in MacDonald, *Who Shot the Sheriff?*, p. 23.
12. For a complete video filmography see Francis N. Nevins' excellent *The Films of Hopalong Cassidy*, pp. 317–323.
13. *Ibid.*, p. 258.
14. Quoted in Adela Rogers St. Johns, "Hopalong Cassidy's Code," *The American Weekly* (June 17, 1951), p. 17.
15. F. Maurice Speed, *The Western Film and TV Annual* (MacDonald: London: 1957), p. 23.
16. MacDonald, *Who Shot the Sheriff?*, pp. 23–24.
17. See David Rothel, *Who Was That Masked Man?* (New York: 1976), Chapter 2; Fran Striker, Jr., *His Typewriter Grew Spurs* (privately printed: 1983), pp. 31–32.; David Holland, *From Out of the Past: A Pictorial History of the Lone Ranger* (Granada Hills, CA: 1988), p. 85.
18. Quoted in David W. Parker, *A Descriptive Analysis of the Lone Ranger as a Form of Popular Art* (Evanston, IL: 1955), pp. 213–214.
19. Striker, *His Typewriter*, p. 44
20. Quoted in *Ibid.* p. 47.
21. Quoted in Holland, *From Out of the Past*, p. 136.
22. J. Fred MacDonald, *Don't Touch That Dial! Radio Programming in American Life from 1920 to 1960* (Chicago: 1979), p. 197.
23. Quoted in Parker, *Descriptive Analysis*, p. 153.
24. Quoted in *Ibid.*, p. 183.
25. *Ibid.*, pp. 240–242.
26. Rothel, *Who Was...*, p. 145.
27. Quoted in Gary H. Grossman, *Saturday Morning TV* (New York: 1981), pp. 175–177.

28. *Ibid.*

29. See Striker, *His Typewriter*, pp. 137–143 for a complete list.

30. Quoted in *Los Angeles Times* (August 13, 1961), p. 39.

31. Quoted in Grossman, *Saturday Morning TV*, p. 179.

32. Quoted in Lee O. Miller, *Great Cowboy Stars of Movies and Television* (New York: 1979), p. 216. (The court order was lifted after the box-office failure of *The Legend of the Lone Ranger* in 1981.)

33. Gene Autry, *Back in the Saddle Again* (New York: 1978), p. 102.

34. Horowitz, *They Went Thataway*, p. 130.

35. David Rothel's *The Gene Autry Book* (Waynesville, NC: 1986) is the most comprehensive source of information about Autry's life and career.

36. Rothel, *The Gene Autry Book*, pp. 254–282.

37. Quoted in Grossman, *Saturday Morning TV*, p. 183.

38. Quoted in Dwight Whitney "Meanwhile, Back at Their Ranches...," *TV Guide* (August 8, 1959), p. 19.

39. Autry, *Back in the Saddle*, pp. 103–104.

40. *Ibid.*, pp. 184–185.

41. Quoted in Jeff Rovin, *The Great Television Series* (New York: 1977), p. 24.

42. Quoted in Grossman, *Saturday Morning TV*, p. 187.

43. Quoted in *Ibid.*, p. 190.

44. Quoted in Rovin, *The Great Television Series*, p. 39.

45. Quoted in Tim Brooks, *The Complete Directory to Prime Time TV Stars, 1946–Present* (New York: 1987), p. 232.

46. Rovin, *The Great Television Series*, p. 39.

47. Gene Autry, "Producing a Western," *Television Magazine* (October 1952), p. 25.

48. David Rothel, *The Roy Rogers Book* (Madison, NC: 1987), p. 26.

49. *Ibid.*, p. 27.

50. *Ibid.*, p. 171. (See pages 162–192 for a comprehensive examination of Rogers merchandise.)

51. Quoted in Carlton Stowers, *Happy Trails: The Story of Roy Rogers and Dale Evans* (Waco, TX: 1979), pp. 148–149.

52. *Ibid.*, pp. 168–169.

53. Ray White, "Adventure in Paradise Valley: The Roy Rogers Television Show," unpublished paper presented at the annual Popular Culture Association Convention in 1988, pp. 7–8.

54. Quoted in Grossman, *Saturday Morning TV*, p. 184.

55. Quoted in MacDonald, *Who Shot the Sheriff?*, p. 27.

56. White, "Adventure in Paradise Valley," pp. 8–9.

57. Quoted in Whitney, "Meanwhile," *TV Guide*, p. 18.

58. Quoted in Donald F. Glut and Jim Harmon, *The Great Television Heroes* (New York: 1975), p. 178.

59. Harry Castleman and Walter J. Podrazik, *Harry and Wally's Favorite TV Shows* (New York: 1989), p. 96.

60. Quoted in Grossman, *Saturday Morning TV*, p. 186.

61. Quoted in Brooks, *TV Stars*, p. 901.

62. Quoted in Grossman, *Saturday Morning TV*, p. 200.

63. Quoted in *Ibid.*, pp. 200, 204.

64. Quoted in *Ibid.*, pp. 317–318.

65. Quoted in *Ibid.*, pp. 321, 322, 325.

66. Quoted in "The Man in the Red Broadcloth Suit," *TV Guide* (February 17, 1956), pp. 6–7.

67. Don Miller, *Hollywood Corral* (New York: 1976), p. 242.

II. *Walt Disney Rides West*

1. Alex McNeil, *Total Television* (New York: 1984), p. 696.

2. Quoted in Leonard Maltin, *The Disney Films* (New York: 1973), p. 20.

3. *Ibid.*, p. 28.

4. Bob Thomas, *Walt Disney: An American Original* (New York: 1976), p. 223.

5. Tim Brooks and Earle Marsh, *The Complete Directory to Prime Time Network TV Shows, 1946–Present* (New York: 1992), p. 897.

6. Quoted in Maltin, *Disney Films*, p. 20.

7. Thomas, *Walt Disney*, pp. 255–256.

8. Glut and Harmon, *Television Heroes*, p. 116.

9. "The Ballad of Davy Crockett," copyright 1954 by Wonderland Music Company, Inc., and Walt Disney Productions.

10. Thomas, *Walt Disney*, p. 257.

11. MacDonald, *Who Shot the Sheriff?*, p. 39

12. Thomas, *Walt Disney*, pp. 257–258.

13. Charles Shows, *Walt: Backstage with Walt Disney* (La Jolla, CA: 1979), pp. 126–127.

14. Quoted in Thomas, *Walt Disney*, p. 258.

15. Quoted in Jeff Weingrad, "Crockett on Comeback Trail?" *Daily News* (January 2, 1987), p. 68.

16. MacDonald, *Who Shot the Sheriff?*, p. 41.

17. Thomas, *Walt Disney*, p. 258.

18. Quoted in Thomas, *Walt Disney*, p. 242.

19. Alan G. Barbour, *Days of Thrills and Adventure* (New York: 1970), p. 39

20. *Ibid.*

21. *Ibid.*, p. 40.

22. "Zorro Foiled His Rivals," *TV Guide* (April 26, 1958), pp. 24–26.

23. Gay Talese, "Zorro-TV Cut-Up," *New York Times* (April 13, 1958).

24. Kay Gardella, "Weight Tips Scale for TV's Sgt. Garcia," *NY Sunday News* (July 1, 1958), p. 8.

25. MacDonald, *Who Shot the Sheriff?*, p. 38.

26. Quoted in Talese, *New York Times* (April 13, 1958).

27. Thomas, *Walt Disney*, p. 285.

28. James K. Folsom, "Stewart Edward White," *The Reader's Encyclopedia of the American West* (New York: 1977), p. 1262.

29. Quoted in MacDonald, *Who Shot the Sheriff?*, p. 42.

30. Quoted in Thomas, *Walt Disney*, p. 285.

31. *Ibid.*, p. 286.

32. Marc Simmons, "Elfego Baca," *Reader's Encyclopedia*, p. 66.

33. Quoted in Maltin, *Disney Films*, p. 289.

34. Joe A. Stout, "John Slaughter," *Reader's Encyclopedia*, p. 1120.

35. Hedda Hopper, "Tom Tryon, New Shooting Sheriff," *The Pittsburgh Press* (November 16, 1958), p. 38.

36. Steven H. Scheuer, *Movies on TV* (New York: 1985), p. 90.

37. Quoted in Maltin, *Disney Films*, pp. 291–292.

38. Thomas, *Walt Disney*, p. 287.

39. MacDonald, *Who Shot the Sheriff?*, p. 43.

40. Douglas Brode, "Disneyland: The TV Westerns of Walt Disney," unpublished paper presented at the 18th annual meeting of the Popular Culture Association, March 25, 1988, New Orleans, La.

III. Television Westerns Grow Up

1. Ralph Brauer with Donna Brauer, *The Horse, the Gun and the Piece of Property: Changing Images of the TV Western* (Bowling Green, OH: 1975), p. 55.

2. MacDonald, *Who Shot the Sheriff?*, pp. 47–48.

3. "The Six-Gun Galahad," *Time* (March 30, 1959), pp. 52–53.

4. Martin Nussbaum, "Sociological Symbolism of the 'Adult Western'," *Social Forces* (October 1960), pp. 26–27.

5. John Crosby, "The Adult Western," *New York Herald Tribune* (January 5, 1957).

6. Quoted in Bob Lardine, "Granddaddy of All the Westerns," *NY Sunday News* (July 10, 1960), p. 8.

7. Quoted in MacDonald, *Don't Touch That Dial!* (Chicago: 1975), p. 218.

8. Quoted in Neil Summers, *The Official TV Western Book, Vol. #2* (Vienna, WV: 1989), p. 38.

9. Quoted in Jack Ross Stanley, *A History of the Radio and Television Western Dramatic Series "Gunsmoke," 1952–1973* (unpublished doctoral dissertation, University of Michigan, 1973), pp. 44–45.

10. Quoted in *Ibid.*, p. 48.

11. "Biography of Gunsmoke," WAMU-FM, Washington, D.C. (April 25, 1976).

12. Quoted in MacDonald, *Don't Touch That Dial!*, p. 224.

13. Quoted in Stanley, *A History*, p. 64.

14. An excellent comparison of the radio and television characters was written by Kathryn Esselman, "How Television Tamed 'Gunsmoke'" for the Popular Culture Association Convention in Louisville (unpublished, 1987).

15. "Biography of Gunsmoke," WAMU-FM.

16. Quoted in Stanley, *A History*, p. 59.

17. *Ibid.*, pp. 59–60.

18. *Ibid.*, p. 60.

19. SuzAnne and Gabor Barabas, *Gunsmoke: A Complete History* (Jefferson, NC: 1990), pp. 75–76.

20. Gerald Nachman, *New York Daily News* (March 27, 1978).

21. Favius Friedman, "The Case of the Runaway Giant," *Motion Picture Magazine* (Spring 1958), p. 62.

22. *Current Biography* (November 1978), p. 3.

23. Quoted in *Current Biography*, p. 4.

24. Quoted in Friedman, *Motion Picture*, p. 67.

25. Allen Eyles, *John Wayne* (New York: 1979), pp. 134–135.

26. Quoted in Friedman, *Motion Picture*, p. 67.

27. Friedman, *Motion Picture*, p. 67; *TV Guide*, December 2, 1961, p. 24–25. Robert deRoos, "Private Life of 'Gunsmoke' Star," *Saturday Evening Post* (April 12, 1958), p. 108; Dave Gelman, *New York Post* (December 3, 1957), p. M2.

28. Stanley, *A History*, p. 100.

29. Quoted in Friedman, *Motion Picture*, p. 68.

30. Quoted in deRoos, *Saturday Evening Post*, p. 33.

31. James Arness, "No Trick Horses for Me," *CBS Television Feature* (September 29, 1958), p. 2.

32. Quoted in Friedman, *Motion Picture*, p. 58.

33. Quoted in deRoos, *Saturday Evening Post*, pp. 108, 110.

34. Quoted in Friedman, *Motion Picture*, p. 68.

35. Quoted in Gelman, *New York Post*, p. M2.

36. Brauer, *The Horse*, pp. 166–169.

37. Quoted in Gelman, *New York Post*, p. M2.

38. James Arness, "Arness Likes 'Gunsmoke' Role," *New York Journal-American* (September 28, 1959).

39. Quoted in Stanley, *A History*, p. 129.

40. *Ibid.*

41. *Ibid.*

42. Nachman, *Daily News* (March 27, 1978).

43. Wallace Markfield, "A Fond Farewell to Matt Dillon, Dodge City and 'Gunsmoke'," *New York Times* (July 13, 1975), Sec. 2, p. 1.

44. Quoted in Stanley, *A History*, p. 110.

45. Barabas, *Gunsmoke*, p. 530.

46. Quoted in Miller, *Great Cowboy Stars*, p. 158.

47. Quoted in Barabas, *Gunsmoke*, p. 92.

48. Quoted in Stanley, *A History*, p. 114.

49. Quoted in *Ibid.*, pp. 114–116.

50. Barabas, *Gunsmoke*, p. 93.

51. Dee Phillips and Bev Copeland, "Riding High on the Waves of Indignation," *TV Guide* (June 12, 1965), p. 24.

52. Quoted in Barabas, *Gunsmoke*, p. 94.

53. Rita Parks, *The Western Hero in Film and Television* (Ann Arbor, MI: 1982), pp. 142–143.

54. Barabas, *Gunsmoke*, p. 95.

55. Quoted in "Mona Lisa of the Long Branch," *TV Guide* (December 13, 1960), p. 27.

56. Quoted in Joe Morheim, "She Who Never Gets Kissed," *TV Guide* (March 15, 1958), p. 9.

57. Quoted in Coyne Steven Sanders, "Miss Kitty and Gunsmoke," *Emmy Magazine* (July/August, 1985), pp. 90–92.

58. Quoted in "Mona Lisa," pp. 25–26.

59. Quoted in Kenneth Baily, ed., *The Television Annual for 1958* (Long Acre, London: 1958), pp. 39–41.

60. Parks, *Western Hero*, p. 142.

61. Quoted in "Mona Lisa," *TV Guide*, p. 25.

62. Quoted in Sanders, "Miss Kitty," p. 92.

63. Quoted in Stanley, *A History*, p. 141.

64. Quoted in Barabas, *Gunsmoke*, p. 116.

65. Quoted in "This Man Kissed a Girl!" *TV Guide* (June 26, 1964), p. 13.

66. *Ibid.*, p. 14.

67. Quoted in Stanley, *A History*, p. 146.

68. Quoted in "This Man...," *TV Guide*, p. 12.

69. Quoted in Stanley, *A History*, p. 148.

70. *Ibid.*, pp. 148–149.

71. Barabas, *Gunsmoke*, p. 118.

72. Quoted in *Ibid.*, pp. 173–174.

73. Quoted in *Ibid.*

74. Quoted in Leslie Raddatz, "Gunsmoke's Designated Hitter," *TV Guide* (December 8, 1973), p. 18.

75. *Ibid.*

76. Barabas, *Gunsmoke*, p. 147.

77. Brooks and Marsh, *Directory of TV Shows*, p. 979.

78. James Arness, "Why Westerns?" *Who's Who in Television* (No. 110, 1960–61), p. 13.

79. Barabas, *Gunsmoke*, p. 227.

80. Don Freeman, "Back in the Saddle Again," *TV Guide* (February 5, 1977), p. 14.

81. Quoted in *Ibid.*, p. 14.

82. Robert Lindsey, "Zeb Macahan Is More Fun Than Matt Dillon," *New York Times* (September 12, 1978), p. D32.

83. Lou Cameron, *How the West Was Won*, a novel based on the teleplays (New York 1977), p. 1.

84. MacDonald, *Who Shot the Sheriff?*, p. 123.

85. John Corry, "'Alamo: 13 Days to Glory,' on NBC," *New York Times* (April 10, 1988).

86. Jeff Jarvis, "James Arness Rides Again..." *TV Guide* (May 8, 1993), p. 49.

87. Brian Garfield, *Western Films* (New York: 1982), p. 266.

88. John J. O'Connor, "Why Bother Watching a Woeful Remake?," *New York Times* (April 10, 1988).

IV. Law and Order Arrive in the Video West

1. W. Eugene Hollon, "Law and Order," *Reader's Encyclopedia*, pp. 654–657.

2. Richard O'Connor, *Bat Masterson* (New York: 1957), p. 4.

3. Stuart N. Lake, *The Life and Times of Wyatt Earp* (Boston: 1931), p. vi.

4. Tedd Thomey, *The Glorious Decade* (New York: 1971), p. 186.

5. Quoted in "Last of the Swashbuckling Heroes," *TV Guide* (November 25, 1972), p. 27.

6. Quoted in *TV Western Roundup* (Vol I: 1957), p. 6.

7. Hugh O'Brian, "Marshal Earp," *TV Guide* (May 2, 1959), p. 8.

8. "The Real Wyatt Earp," *TV Guide* (May 2, 1959), p. 10.

9. Quoted in *Ibid.*

10. Thomey, *Glorious Decade*, p. 188.

11. Quoted in "Real Wyatt," p. 11.

12. Quoted in *Ibid.*

13. Quoted in "High in the Saddle," *Newsweek* (March 4, 1957), p. 65.

14. Quoted in Tom Ito, "From Wyatt Earp to the Unsung Heroism of HOBY," *Yesteryears* (Winter 1989), pp. 5–6.

15. Quoted in *Ibid.*, p. 5.

16. Quoted in *Ibid.*, p. 6.

17. Castleman and Podrazik, *Favorite TV Shows*, p. 556.

18. Quoted in "Dandiest Gun in the West," *TV Guide* (May 21, 1960), p. 19.

19. Quoted in *Ibid.*

20. Quoted in Robert Stahl, "The Facts Are Enough," *TV Guide* (March 7, 1959), p. 13.

21. O'Connor, *Bat Masterson*, Preface.

22. Gary L. Roberts, "Bat Masterson," *Reader's Encyclopedia*, p. 712.

23. Quoted in Stahl, "The Facts," p. 13.

24. *Ibid.*

25. Roberts, *Reader's Encyclopedia*, p. 712.

26. Castleman and Podrazik, *Favorite TV Shows*, p. 44.

27. Quoted in Stahl, "The Facts," p. 14.

28. Quoted in "'The Tall Man' Review," *TV Guide* (May 6, 1961) p. 23.

29. Gary L. Roberts, "John Ringo," *Reader's Encyclopedia*, p. 1019.

30. Larry James Gianakos, *Television Drama Series Programming: A Comprehensive Chronicle*, Vol IV (Metuchen, NJ: 1983), pp. 345–346.

31. Castleman and Podrazik, *Favorite TV Shows*, p. 549.

32. Quoted in "A Family Affair," *TV Guide* (March 1960), pp. 14–15.

33. Quoted in John Lackuk, "Culp the Perfectionist," *TV and Movie Western* (August 1958), p. 25.

34. *Ibid.*

35. Quoted in Brooks, *Directory of TV Stars*, p. 216.

36. Brooks, *Directory of TV Stars*, p. 915.

37. Quoted in Neil Summers, *The Official TV Western Book*, Vol III (Vienna, WV: 1991), p. 23.

38. Quoted in "Why 26 Men?" *TV Guide* (February 16, 1958), p. 30.

39. Neil Summers, *The First Official TV Western Book* (Vienna, WV: 1987), p. 48.

40. *Ibid.*, Vol III, p. 33.

41. Quoted in Robert Johnson, "He Has All the Expression of a Rock," *TV Guide* (July 25, 1959) pp. 17–18.

42. Quoted in "Peter Brown," *TV Guide* (July 9, 1960) p. 19.

43. Quoted in *Ibid.*

44. Quoted in Lynn Woolley, Robert W. Malsbary and Robert G. Strange, Jr., *Warner Bros. Television* (Jefferson, NC: 1985) p. 222.

45. Quoted in Johnson, "He Has All the Expression of a Rock," p. 19.

46. Quoted in Woolley et al., *Warner Bros.*, p. 225.

47. *Ibid.*, p. 231.

48. Quoted in "The Marshal's on the Level," *TV Guide* (April 1, 1960), p. 14.

49. Quoted in "Musical-Comedy Singer Goes West," *TV Guide* (August 9, 1960), p. 23.

50. Castleman and Podrazik, *Favorite TV Shows*, p. 123.

51. Summers, Vol II, p. 31.

52. Miller, *Great Cowboy Stars*, p. 178.

53. Quoted in *Ibid.*, p. 179.

54. Brooks and Marsh, *Directory of TV Shows*, p. 121; David Martindale, *Television Detective Shows of the 1970s* (Jefferson, NC: 1991), p. 64; Summers, Vol III, p. 101.

55. Martindale, *Ibid.*

56. Quoted in Joe Morhaim, "More Than Meets the Eye," *TV Guide* (June 7, 1958), p. 19.

57. Quoted in *Ibid.*

58. Quoted in Brooks, *Directory of TV Stars*, p. 275.

V. *Alone Against the Wild West*

1. Douglas Brode, "They Went Thataway," *Television Quarterly* (Summer 1982), p. 34.

2. Quoted in "Very Tall in the Saddle," *TV Guide* (August 19, 1956), p. 21.

3. Quoted in Walter Ames, "Clint Walker's Tall Tale," *Los Angeles Times* (November 25, 1956).

4. Quoted in Dave Gelman, "TV's Top Guns," *New York Post* (December 5, 1957), p. M2.

5. Woolley et al., *Warner Bros.*, p. 12.

6. Quoted in Gelman, "TV's Top Guns," p. M2.

7. Quoted in *Ibid.*

8. John Crosby, *NY Herald Tribune* (January 5, 1957).

9. Quoted in Gelman, "TV's Top Guns," p. M2.

10. Quoted in MacDonald, *Who Shot the Sheriff?*, p. 51.

11. Quoted in Gelman, "TV's Top Guns," p. M2.

12. Bob Anderson, "Cheyenne Will Be Gone by Mid-Season! (Part 1)," *Trail Dust* (Spring 1993), p. 18.

13. Quoted in Brooks, *Directory of TV Stars*, p. 872.

14. Woolley et al., *Warner Bros.*, p. 13.

15. Quoted in Bob Thomas, "Cheyenne Star Is Bowing Out," *N.Y. World-Tele. & Sun*, August 15, 1962.

16. Woolley et al., *Warner Bros.*, p. 205.

17. Episodes are listed by date in Larry James Gianakos, *Television Drama Series Programming: A Comprehensive Chronicle, Vol III, 1975*–1980, pp. 383–386; in Woolley, Malsbary, and Strange, Jr., *Warner Bros. Television*, pp. 205–219, episodes are divided into only two seasons for some reason.

18. W. Turentine Jackson, "Wells, Fargo & Co.," *Reader's Encyclopedia*, pp. 1250–1251.

19. Quoted in Robert Johnson "Looking a Gift Horse in the Mouth," *TV Guide* (July 26, 1958), p. 21.

20. Jon Tuska and Vicki Piekarski, *Encyclopedia of Frontier and Western Fiction* (New York: 1983), p. 138.

21. Quoted in *TV Guide* (July 20, 1957), p. 29. (Author and title unknown.)

22. Quoted in Johnson, *TV Guide* (July 26, 1958), p. 22.

23. Quoted in Marie Torre, "Dale Robertson Rides and Sings," *New York Herald Tribune* (October 13, 1958).

24. *TV Guide* (July 20, 1957), p. 29.

25. "The Horseman Who Became an Actor," *TV Guide* (October 24, 1959), p. 19.

26. Quoted in Torre, *New York Herald Tribune* (October 13, 1958).

27. Miller, *Great Cowboy Stars*, p. 188.

28. Gianakos, Vol. III, p. 368.

29. Quoted in "How to Be a TV Cowboy," *TV Guide* (January 18, 1958), p. 29.

30. Quoted in *Ibid.*

31. Gary L. Roberts, "William Preston Longley," *Reader's Encyclopedia*, p. 676.

32. Quoted in Dwight Whitney, "Smile When You Say That, Pardner," *TV Guide* (date unknown), p. 26.

33. Quoted in Summers, *The First Official TV Western Book*, p. 55.

34. Brooks and Marsh, *Directory of TV Shows*, p. 708.

35. Rovin, *Great Television Series*, pp. 72–73.

36. Quoted in "Do You Remember?" *The TV Collector* (July-August 1992), p. 16.

37. Quoted in "Man from Nanticoke," *TV Guide* (January 16, 1960), p. 15.

38. Cecil Smith, "Rebel Is Unique Western Fare with Timeless Quality," *Los Angeles Times* (October 11, 1959).

39. Quoted in *The TV Collector* (July-August 1992), p. 19.

40. Cecil Smith, "The TV Scene," *Los Angeles Times* (April 10, 1961).

41. *TV Guide* (December 31, 1960), p. 11.

42. Gianakos, *Television Drama*, Vol II, p. 37.

43. Summers, *The First TV Western Book*, p. 87.

44. Quoted in Garner Simmons, "Sam Peckinpah's Television Work," *Film Heritage* (Winter 1974-75), p. 7.

45. Quoted in *Ibid.*

46. *Ibid.*, p. 9.

47. Quoted in "An Autopsy Report," *TV Guide* (December 31, 1960), p. 11.

48. Quoted in Smith, "The TV Scene," Pt II, p. 11.

49. Quoted in *Ibid.*

50. Quoted in "Back to Civvies—the Hard Way," *TV Guide* (January 23, 1965), p. 8.

51. Quoted in *Ibid.*

52. Quoted in *Ibid.*

53. Quoted in *Ibid.*

54. Cleveland Amory, "Review," *TV Guide* (May 15, 1965), p. 28.

55. Castleman and Podrazik, *Favorite TV Shows*, p. 69.

56. Quoted in Fritz Goodwin, "How They Put a Skin Diver on a Horse," *TV Guide* (January 15, 1966), p. 9.

57. Castleman and Podrazik, *Favorite TV Shows*, p. 293.

58. Cleveland Amory, "Review," *TV Guide* (January 15, 1966), p. 2.

59. Quoted in Goodwin, *TV Guide*, p. 10.

60. Bill Davidson, "Bozo and Dan Are an Item!" *TV Guide* (June 11, 1977), pp. 26–27.

61. Quoted in Kay Gardella, "Grizzly Adams Started Out as Hollywood One-lioner," *NY Daily News* (September 2, 1977), p. 70.

62. Don Freeman, "The Computer Labored—and Brought Forth a Bear," *TV Guide* (January 28, 1978), p. 13.

63. Quoted in *Ibid.*, p. 14.

64. Quoted in *Ibid.*, p. 15.

65. Quoted in *Ibid.*

66. Brooks and Marsh, *Directory of TV Shows*, p. 448.

VI. Bounty Hunters, Gamblers and Hired Guns

1. Quoted in Harry Castleman and Walter J. Podrazik, *Watching TV: Four Decades of American Television* (New York: 1982), p. 116.

2. Mary Alice Money, *Evolutions of the Popular Western in Novels, Films, and Television, 1958–1974* (unpublished doctoral dissertation, University of Texas at Austin, 1975), pp. 78–79. Money points out that this incident is one of the few examples of the Civil War *not* being taken seriously, *Maverick* thereby reversing "even the convention of respect for the Lost Cause."

3. Quoted in Marion Hargrove, "This Is a Television Cowboy?" *Life* (January 19, 1959), pp. 73, 75.

4. Rovin, *Great Television Series*, p. 52.

5. Quoted in Hargrove, "This Is a Television Cowboy," p. 75.

6. John Javna, *Cult TV* (New York: 1985), p. 94.

7. Brooks and Marsh, *Directory of TV Shows*, p. 499.

8. Javna, *Cult TV*, p. 97.

9. Quoted in Raymond Strait, *James Garner* (New York: 1985), p. 59.

10. Quoted in Rovin, *Great Television Series*, p. 52.

11. Quoted in Liza Wilson, "Jim Garner ... Real Life Maverick," *The American Weekly* (August 10, 1958), p. 17.

12. Quoted in Miller, *Great Cowboy Stars*, p. 210.

13. Quoted in *Ibid.*, p. 211.

14. Quoted in *Ibid.*, p. 212.

15. Quoted in Woolley et al., *Warner Bros.*, p. 80.

16. Quoted in *Ibid.*, p. 81.

17. Quoted in Strait, *James Garner*, p. 59.

18. Quoted in Strait, *James Garner*, p. 343.

19. Quoted in *Ibid.*, p. 352 and (author unknown) *Maverick Annual* (London: 1981), p. 30.

20. Brooks and Marsh, *Directory of TV Shows*, pp. 105–106.

21. Castleman and Podrazik, *Favorite TV Shows*, p. 70.

22. Quoted in Strait, *James Garner*, p. 356.

23. Quoted in *Ibid.*, p. 357.

24. Quoted in *Ibid.*, p. 358.

25. *Ibid.*, p. 359.

26. Castleman and Podrazik, *Favorite TV Shows*, p. 70.

27. Ed Robertson, *Maverick, Legend of the West* (Los Angeles: 1994), p. xi.

28. Steven C. Smith, *A Heart at Fire's Center* (Los Angeles: 1991), p. 212.

29. Quoted in Rovin, *Great Television Series*, pp. 51–52.

30. Richard Gehman, "The Paradox of Paladin," *TV Guide* (January 7, 1961), p. 6.

31. Lee Edson, "TV's Rebellious Cowboy," *Saturday Evening Post* (August 6, 1960), p. 83.

32. Richard Schickel, "TV's Angry Gun," *Show* (November 1961), p. 53.

33. Quoted in Edson, "TV's Rebellious Cowboy," p. 82.

34. Castleman and Podrazik, *Favorite TV Shows*, p. 218.

35. Schickel, "TV's Angry Gun," p. 52.

36. This story is also related in Frank G. Roberton's exciting novel *A Man Called Paladin* (New York: 1963).

37. Dwight Whitney, "The Life and Good Times of Hollywood's Harry Julian Fink," *TV Guide* (February 27, 1960), p. 23.

38. Jack Smith, "Hero Today and Gone Tomorrow," *Los Angeles Times* (May 27, 1963), p. 27.

39. John Lachuk, "Steve McQueen's Gun," *TV and Movie Western* (June 1959), p. 12.

40. *Ibid.*, p. 13.

41. Quoted in William F. Nolan, *McQueen* (New York: 1984), p. 32.

42. Quoted in *Ibid.*, p. 30.

43. Quoted in Hal Humphrey, "Steve McQueen—The Thinking Man's Cowboy," *L.A. Mirror News* (June 24, 1959).

VII. Wagon Trains and Cattle Drives

1. Ralph Brauer, *The Horse*, p. 85.

2. *Ibid.*, pp. 97–100.

3. Andrew Sinclair, *John Ford: A Biography* (London, England: 1984), p. 155.

4. Quoted in *Ibid.*, p. 156.

5. Donald Shepherd and Robert Slatzer with Dave Grayson, *Duke: The Life and Times of John Wayne* (New York: 1985), p. 253.

6. Quoted in *The TV Collector* (March-April 1986), p. 10.

7. Quoted in *Newsweek* (March 27, 1960), p. 60.

8. Quoted in *The TV Collector* (October-November 1985), p. 12.

9. *The TV Collector* (December-January 1986), p. 18.

10. Quoted in *Ibid.*, p. 19.

11. Brauer, *The Horse*, pp. 97–99.

12. Brooks and Marsh, *Directory of TV Shows*, p. 652.

13. Richard K. Tharp, "Rawhide, Part 1," *Reruns: The Magazine of Television History* (April 1981), p. 6.

14. *Ibid.*

15. Quoted in Rovin, *Great Television Series*, p. 61.

16. Thomey, *Glorious Decade*, pp. 149–154.

17. Quoted in *Ibid.*

18. Quoted in *Ibid.*

19. Quoted in Boris Zmijewsky and Lee Pfeiffer, *The Films of Clint Eastwood* (Secaucus, NJ: 1982), p. 20.

20. Francois Guerif, *Clint Eastwood: The Man and His Films* (New York: 1984), p. 29.

21. Quoted in Arnold Hano, "How to Revive a Dead Horse," *TV Guide* (October 2, 1965), p. 20.

22. Quoted in *Ibid.*, p. 22.

23. *Ibid.*, p. 21.

24. Quoted in *Ibid.*, p. 21.

25. Brauer, *The Horse*, p. 91.

VIII. Single Parent Families on the Video Frontier

1. "Western Twist," *TV Guide* (September 27, 1958), p. 12.

2. Simmons, "Peckinpah's Television Work," pp. 2–3.

3. *Ibid.*

4. Quoted in "He Finally Made the Big Leagues," *TV Guide* (February 7, 1959), p. 27.

5. "Johnny Crawford," *TV Guide* (May 9, 1959), pp. 22–26.
6. Tim Lilley, "Paul Fix," *The Big Trail* (February 1987), p. 4.
7. Quoted in Simmons, "Peckinpah's Television Work," p. 4.
8. Quoted in "Chuck Connors on Target," *TV Guide* (February 24, 1962), p. 17.
9. Brauer, *The Horse*, p. 106.
10. Quoted in Dwight Whitney, "What a Bonanza!" *TV Guide* (September 8, 1962), p. 16.
11. Quoted in *Ibid.*
12. Quoted in John Poppy, "The Worldwide Lure of 'Bonanza,'" *Look* (December 1, 1964), p. 41.
13. Quoted in MacDonald, *Who Shot the Sheriff?*, p. 97.
14. Quoted in Parks, *Western Hero*, p. 163.
15. Quoted in Poppy, "The Worldwide Lure," p. 38.
16. Quoted in *Ibid.*, p. 149.
17. Richard K. Tharp, "Bonanza, Part I," *Reruns* (April 1982), p. 7.
18. Miller, *Cowboy Stars*, pp. 171–174.
19. Quoted in Dwight Whitney, "Patriarch of the Ponderosa," *TV Guide* (May 13, 1961), pp. 21–22.
20. Brauer, *The Horse*, p. 134.
21. Brooks, *Directory of TV Stars*, pp. 722–723.
22. Quoted in *Reruns* (April 1982), p. 7.
23. Quoted in "Togetherness — Western Style," *TV Guide* (June 25, 1960), p. 19.
24. Quoted in "A Petticoat for the Ponderosa," *TV Guide* (January 18, 1964), pp. 26–27.
25. Quoted in *Ibid.*, p. 27.
26. According to some sources, Roberts reluctantly *agreed* to a one year extension of his contract. See Marsha Daly, *Michael Landon: A Biography* (New York: 1987), pp. 74–78.
27. Melany Shapiro, *Bonanza: The Unofficial Story of the Ponderosa* (Las Vegas, NV: 1993), pp. 25–26.
28. Quoted in *Ibid.*, p. 31.
29. Dwight Whitney, "A Whale of a Hero," *TV Guide* (March 3, 1960), pp. 7–8.
30. Parks, *Western Hero*, p. 148.
31. Quoted in Dick Adler, "The Cartwrights Carry On," *TV Guide* (October 7, 1972), p. 40.
32. "Javelin Thrower on Horseback," *TV Guide* (January 6, 1962), p. 16.
33. *Ibid.*
34. Quoted in *Ibid.*, p. 15.
35. Quoted in *Ibid.*
36. Parks, *Western Hero*, p. 148.
37. Quoted in "Javelin Thrower," *TV Guide*, p. 16.
38. "Happiness Is a Slice of Salami," *TV Guide* (November 29, 1969), pp. 26–27.
39. Quoted in *Ibid.*, p. 27.
40. Dwight Whitney, "New Boy on 'Bonanza,'" *TV Guide* (March 2, 1968), pp. 22–23.
41. Melvin Durslay, "How Mitch Vogel Joined a Show Older Than His Pigeons, Rabbit and Chameleon Combined," *TV Guide* (March 27, 1971), pp. 28–30.
42. Brooks, *Directory of TV Stars*, p. 555.
43. Dick Hobson, "The Cartwrights Never Order Mandarin Duck," *TV Guide* (October 9, 1971), pp. 49–50.
44. Brooks, *Directory of TV Stars*, p. 833.
45. Quoted in Poppy, "Worldwide Lure," p. 43.
46. Quoted in Whitney, "What a Bonanza!" pp. 15–17.
47. Quoted in Adler, "Cartwrights Carry On," pp. 38–39.
48. " 'TV Guide' Presents 40 Years of the Best," *TV Guide* (April 17–23, 1993), p. 27.
49. Castleman and Podrazik, *Favorite TV Shows*, p. 65.
50. Quoted in Tim Appelo, "The Sons Also Ride," *Entertainment Weekly* (July 16, 1993), p. 33.
51. *Ibid.*
52. Dwight Whitney, "The Queen Goes West," *TV Guide* (February 22, 1966), pp. 6–7.
53. Al DiOrio, *Barbara Stanwyck* (New York: 1983), pp. 183–184.
54. Quoted in *Ibid.*, p. 202.
55. Quoted in Ella Smith, *Starring Miss Barbara Stanwyck* (New York: 1974), p. 293.
56. Quoted in DiOrio, *Barbara Stanwyck*, pp. 203–204.

57. Quoted in Smith, *Starring Miss*, p. 293.

58. Smith, *Starring Miss*, p. 294.

59. Charles Heckelmann, *The Big Valley* (Racine, WI: 1956), p. 25.

60. Brooks, *Directory of TV Stars*, p. 536.

61. "A New James Dean?" *TV Guide* (Feb. 19, 1966), pp. 30–31.

62. Heckelmann, *Big Valley*, p. 8.

63. Quoted in Woolley et al., *Warner Bros.*, p. 146.

64. Dwight Whitney, "Richard the Good," *TV Guide* (July 20, 1968), pp. 23–24.

65. Whitney, "Richard," *TV Guide* (July 20, 1968), p. 25.

66. Heckelmann, *Big Valley*, p. 27.

67. I am indebted to Marilyn Bieler, president of the Peter Breck Fan Club, for providing me with biographical information on Mr. Breck.

68. Heckelmann, *Big Valley*, p. 31.

69. Brooks, *Directory of TV Stars*, pp. 282–283; Leslie Raddatz, "Come Back in 1976," *TV Guide* (December 24, 1966), pp. 13–14.

70. Heckelmann, *Big Valley*, p. 36.

71. *Ibid.*, p. 38.

72. Smith, *Starring Miss*, p. 304.

73. Richard Warren Lewis, "Dammit, I *Am* Cochise," *TV Guide* (January 20, 1968), pp. 17–18.

74. Story by David Dortort, screenplay by Denne Bart Petitclerc, *Saguaro* (2nd draft, April 13, 1966), pp. 58–59.

75. Tim Kelly "The High Chaparral," *Arizona Highways* (September 1967), p. 30.

76. *Ibid.*

77. Quoted in *Ibid.*

78. Lewis, "Cochise," *TV Guide*, pp. 17–18.

79. Quoted in Kelly, "High Chaparral," p. 33.

80. All character descriptions are from the script by David Dortort and Denne Bart Petitclerc.

81. Dwight Whitney, "The Dusty Trail to the 'High Chaparral,'" *TV Guide* (August 23, 1969), p. 16.

82. Parks, *Western Hero*, p. 139.

IX. *Meanwhile Back on the Reservation*

1. Wayne Michael Sarf, *God Bless You, Buffalo Bill* (East Brunswick, NJ: 1983), pp. 194–195.

2. MacDonald, *Who Shot the Sheriff?*, p. 113.

3. Brauer, *The Horse*, pp. 177, 181–183.

4. Michael Hilger, *The American Indian in Film* (Metuchen, NJ: 1986), p. 1.

5. *Ibid.*, pp. 2–3.

6. Quoted in Sarf, *God Bless You*, p. 193.

7. Quoted in *New York Times*, June 26, 1960.

8. *Ibid.*

9. Holland, *From Out of the Past*, pp. 373–374.

10. James C. Jewell, "Jay Silverheels: Pride in Light of Prejudice," *Under Western Skies* (January 1981), p. 5.

11. Rovin, *Great Television Series*, p. 42.

12. Quoted in James Robert Parish and Michael K. Pitts, *The Great Western Pictures* (Metuchen, NJ: 1976), p. 38.

13. Quoted in Brooks, *Directory of TV Stars*, p. 30.

14. Quoted in *Ibid.*, p. 31.

15. Gianakos, *Television Drama*, Vol. II, p. 259.

16. Castleman and Podrazik, *Favorite TV Shows*, p. 281.

17. Summers, *First TV Western Book*, p. 83.

18. Brooks and Marsh, *Directory of TV Shows*, p. 995.

19. Quoted in *TV Guide* (May 22, 1959), p. 29. (Author, title unknown.)

20. Raymond William Stedman, *Shadows of the Indian* (Norman, OK: 1982), pp. 60–61.

21. Quoted in MacDonald, *Who Shot the Sheriff?*, p. 114.

22. Quoted in *Ibid.*, p. 118.
23. *Ibid.*
24. Quoted in Neil Summers, *The Official TV Western Book*, Vol. 4 (Vienna, WV: 1992), pp. 92–93.
25. Castleman and Podrazik, *Favorite TV Shows*, pp. 366–367.
26. Martindale, *Television Detective Shows*, p. 349.
27. Quoted in Summers, Vol 4, p. 93.
28. Grace Lichtenstein, "He Refuses to Be an 'Ugh-Tonto' Indian," *The New York Times* (June 6, 1976), p. 13.
29. Katrine Ames, "Big Will," *Newsweek* (July 26, 1976), p. 73.
30. Lichtenstein, "He Refuses to Be...," p. D13.
31. Quoted in Ames, "Big Will," p. 73.
32. Brooks and Marsh, *Directory of TV Shows*, p. 110.
33. Quoted in Stedman, *Shadows of the Indian*, p. 238.
34. Quoted in MacDonald, *Who Shot the Sheriff?*, p. 114.
35. Brauer, *The Horse*, pp. 179–180.
36. *Ibid.*, pp. 183–184.
37. *Ibid.*, p. 178.
38. Quoted in MacDonald, *Who Shot the Sheriff?*, p. 114.
39. See comments in Stedman, *Shadows of the Indian*, p. 238.
40. *Ibid.*
41. *Ibid.*, p. 239.
42. John J. O'Connor, "Historical Dramas—Fact or Fancy?" *The New York Times* (May 25, 1975), pp. D18–19.
43. Quoted in Michael J. Arlen, "White Man Speaks with Forked Tongue and Good Intentions," *The New Yorker* (May 19, 1975), p. 82.
44. *Ibid.*, pp. 86–87.
45. *Ibid.* pp. 88–89.
46. O'Connor, "Historical Dramas," pp. D18–19.
47. Stedman, *Shadows of the Indian*, pp. 224–225.
48. *Ibid.*, pp. 226–227.
49. Quoted in David Shaw, "Raquel Went on the Warpath—and Boy, Did the Casualties Mount," *TV Guide* (May 29, 1982), p. 22.
50. Quoted in *Ibid.*
51. *Ibid,*, p. 18.
52. *Ibid.*, p. 19.
53. Quoted in Hilger, *Indian in Film*, p. 160.
54. Quoted in Tony Schwartz, "An Indian Epic," *Newsweek* (April 16, 1979), p. 87.
55. Quoted in *Ibid.*, p. 86.
56. Quoted in Dwight Whitney, "The Warpath Runneth Over," *TV Guide* (May 19, 1984), p. 38.
57. Quoted in George Maksian, "Sioux Are Howling over 'Hanta Yo'." *NY Daily News* (May 8, 1980), p. 142.
58. Quoted in David Sheff and Jack Fincher, " A Growing War Over 'Hanta Yo'," *People* (June 23, 1980).
59. Quoted in Whitney, "The Warpath," p. 40.
60. Quoted in *Ibid.*
61. Quoted in *Ibid.*
62. Stephan Farber, "5-Hour TV Saga of the Sioux," *The New York Times* (May 17, 1984), p. C25.
63. Quoted in *Ibid.*
64. Quoted in *Ibid.*
65. Quoted in Whitney, "The Warpath," p. 42.
66. Quoted in *Ibid.*
67. Quoted in *Ibid.*
68. Quoted in Harry F. Waters, "The 'Roots' Indian Uprising," *Newsweek* (May 21, 1981), p. 76.
69. Quoted in John J. O'Connor, "Custer, Call Your Spin Doctor," *NY Times Magazine* (Feb. 3, 1991), p. 29.

70. *Ibid.*

71. *Ibid.*, p. 32.

72. Quoted in David Kronke, "The Warrior," *Entertainment Weekly* (February 1, 1991), p. 27.

73. Quoted in *Ibid.*, p. 26.

74. Quoted in *Ibid.*, p. 27.

75. Quoted in Stephen Galloway, "115 Years After Custer's Last Stand, Native Americans Are Back on the Warpath—Over Hollywood's Portrayal of Them," *TV Guide* (February 2, 1991), p. 12.

76. Quoted in *Ibid.*, p. 11.

77. Meredith Berkman, "How 'Dances' Got Real," *Entertainment Weekly* (March 8, 1991), p. 22.

78. Ken Tucker, "'Morning Star': The Review," *Entertainment Weekly* (February 1, 1991), p. 27.

79. Evan S. Connell, *Son of the Morning Star* (San Francisco: 1984), pp. 417–419.

80. Galloway, "... Back on the Warpath ...," pp. 10–11.

81. Paul Andrew Hutton, "Custer Legend Rises Again in 'Son'," *TV Guide* (February 2, 1991), p. 13.

82. Tucker, "Review," p. 27.

83. Edgar I. Stewart "Gall," *Reader's Encyclopedia*, pp. 427–428.

84. Quoted in Benjamin Svetkey, "Native Sons, Rising Stars," *Entertainment Weekly* (March 8, 1991), p. 20.

85. See Stedman, *Shadows of the Indian*, pp. 240–252.

X. *The Video Range Gets Bigger*

1. Quoted in Cleveland Amory, "Review," *TV Guide* (August 28, 1965), p. 27.

2. James K. Folsom, "Owen Wister," *Reader's Encyclopedia*, p. 1280.

3. Tuska and Piekarski, "Owen Wister," *Encyclopedia of Frontier and Western Fiction*, pp. 356–357.

4. Richard K. Doan, "TV Hits Trail Where the Westerns Began," *NY Herald Tribune* (March 11, 1962), p. 9.

5. Quoted in *Ibid.*

6. Folsom, "Owen Wister," *Reader's Encyclopedia*, pp. 1280–1281.

7. Quoted in Doan, "TV Hits Trail," p. 9.

8. Quoted in Parish and Pitts, *Great Western Pictures*, p. 384.

9. Quoted in *Ibid.*

10. *Ibid.*, p. 385.

11. Doan, "TV Hits Trail," pp. 8–9.

12. "Enter 'The Virginian'—Electronically," *TV Guide* (May 4, 1963), p. 22.

13. Quoted in *Ibid.*, p. 23.

14. Quoted in *Ibid.*

15. Peter Bogdanovich, "Where Seldom Is Heard an Encouraging Word," *TV Guide* (February 12, 1966), p. 30.

16. Quoted in Dwight Whitney, "The Garbo of the Sagebrush," *TV Guide* (December 8, 1962), pp. 19–20.

17. Amory, "Review," *TV Guide* (August 28, 1965), p. 27.

18. Bodganovich, "Where Seldom Is Heard...," pp. 28–29.

19. Quoted in Marian Dern, "Is It True Blond Cowboys Have More Fun?" *TV Guide* (July 18, 1964), pp. 7–9.

20. Bogdanovich, "Where Seldom Is Heard...," p. 29.

21. Quoted in Leslie Raddatz, "Rebirth of an Actor," *TV Guide* (October 26, 1963), pp. 19–20.

22. *Ibid.*, p. 20.

23. *Variety*, September 25, 1963.

24. Bogdanovich, "Where Seldom Is Heard...," p. 32.

25. Brooks, *Directory of TV Stars*, p. 388.

26. Brauer, *The Horse*, p. 119.

27. Richard Warren Lewis, "Stuart Whitman's 'Marshal Plan'," *TV Guide* (November 4, 1967), p. 20.

28. Quoted in Bill Davidson, "Grumbling, Hollering and Shocking Ladies," *TV Guide* (February 23, 1974), p. 30.

29. Cleveland Amory, "Review," *TV Guide* (February 24, 1973), p. 30.

30. Quoted in Miller, *Great Cowboy Stars*, pp. 165–166.

31. Dick Russell, "Neither Snow, Nor Thunder, Nor Hostile Indians...," *TV Guide* (September 30–October 6, 1978), p. 24.

32. Quoted in *Ibid.*, p. 25.

33. Quoted in Peter J. Boyer, "Strange Saga of NBC Special," *New York Post* (February 5, 1979), p. 28.

34. "Cheer Up, You Losers!," *City News* (September 24, 1978), p. 18R.

35. MacDonald, *Who Shot the Sheriff?*, p. 123.

XI. Spoofing the Television Western

1. Brauer, *The Horse*, p. 21.

2. Cleveland Amory, "Review," *TV Guide* (January 14, 1967), p. 36.

3. Michael Shain, "'Best' and Co. Spoofs the Wild West," *New York Post* (September 10, 1981), p. 77.

4. Castleman and Podrazik, *Watching TV*, p. 185.

5. Ronald Searle, "How the West Was Really Won," *TV Guide* (May 27, 1967), pp. 20–21.

6. Quoted in Leslie Raddatz, "Actors Should Act Like Actors," *TV Guide* (December 11, 1965) pp. 22–23.

7. Quoted in Tom Mackin, "Coming: 'McHale's Army'," *Newark Evening News* (July 25, 1965).

8. Quoted in Michael Fessier, Jr., "The World of Larry Storch," *TV Guide* (August 23, 1966), p. 16.

9. Quoted in Brooks, *Directory of TV Stars*, pp. 83–84.

10. Amory, "Review," *TV Guide* (January 14, 1967).

11. Searle, *TV Guide*, p. 22.

12. Castleman and Podrazik, *Watching TV*, p. 185.

13. Amory, "Review," *TV Guide* (April 1, 1967), p. 36.

14. Amory, "Review," *TV Guide* (May 6, 1967), p.29.

15. Joel Eisner and David Krinsky, *Television Comedy Series* (Jefferson, NC: 1984), p. 689.

16. Brooks and Marsh, *Directory of TV Shows*, p. 242.

XII. James Bond Goes West

1. Quoted in Javna, *Cult TV*, p. 141.

2. Susan E. Kesler, *The Wild Wild West: The Series* (Downey, CA: 1988), pp. 15–18.

3. Richard K. Tharp, "The Wild, Wild West, Part 2," *Reruns* (December 1980), p. 18.

4. Quoted in Elisabeth Lewis, "The Kid with the Golden Sandbox," *TV Guide* (December 4, 1965), pp. 14–15.

5. *Ibid.*, p. 16.

6. Leslie Raddatz, "The Wild, Wild Man from 'The Wild, Wild West'," *TV Guide* (May 21, 1966), pp. 15–17.

7. Quoted in Brooks, *Directory of TV Stars*, p. 551.

8. Quoted in Javna, *Cult TV*, p. 141.

9. Lorraine Beatty, "Gadgets and Guises" in James Van Hise, *The Wild Wild West Book* (Granada Hills, CA: 1988), pp. 46–57; Kesler, *Wild Wild West*, pp. 120–136.

10. Quoted in *Ibid.*, p. 139.

11. Quoted in *Ibid.*

12. Quoted in Dunn's obituary in *The New York Times*, August 31, 1973.

13. Quoted in Samuel J. Maronie, "An Interview with Robert Conrad," *Starlog* (January, 1981), p. 37.

14. Quoted in Kesler, *Wild Wild West*, pp. 166–175.

15. Tharp, "Part 2," p. 17.

16. Quoted in *Starlog* interview, p. 37.

17. Quoted in *Ibid.*, pp. 38, 63.
18. Quoted in *Ibid.*

XIII. Two by Two into the West

1. Quoted in Carolyn See, "An Old Actor Stands Fast in a Changing World," *TV Guide* (March 30, 1968) p. 11.
2. *Ibid.*
3. *Ibid.*, pp. 11–14.
4. Castleman and Podrazik, *Favorite TV Shows*, p. 209.
5. Quoted in Roberta Brandes Gratz, "The Outcasts," *New York Post* (Sept. 7, 1968), p. 33.
6. Quoted in *Ibid.*
7. Dick Hobson, "The Odyssey of a Black Man in 'White Man's Television'," *TV Guide* (March 1, 1969), p. 19.
8. Quoted in Gratz, "The Outcasts."
9. Quoted in Carolyn See, "How Can a Square Fit into the Hollywood Circle?" *TV Guide* (August 8, 1969), p. 26.
10. Steve Frazee, *The Outcasts* (Toronto: 1968), pp. 13–14.
11. Cleveland Amory, "Review," *TV Guide* (November 30, 1968), p. 8.
12. Quoted in Hobson, *TV Guide* (March 1, 1969), p. 18.
13. Quoted in *Ibid.*, pp. 19–20.
14. Quoted in *Ibid.*, pp. 20–21.
15. Quoted in *Ibid.*, p.21.
16. Quoted in *Ibid.*
17. Gratz,"The Outcasts," p. 33.
18. Quoted in *Ibid.*
19. See, "How Can a Square," p. 26.
20. Rovin, *Great Television Series*, p. 123.
21. Gianakos, *Television Drama*, Vol. II, p. 619.
22. Summers, *TV Western Book*, Vol. II, p. 129.
23. Castleman and Podrazik, *Favorite TV Shows*, p. 388.
24. Quoted in Parrish and Pitts, *Great Western Pictures*, p. 46.
25. Leonard Maltin, *TV Movies and Video Guide* (1991 edition), p. 154.
26. Arnold Hano, "The World's Greatest Lover," *TV Guide* (February 19, 1972), p. 22.
27. *Ibid.*
28. Quoted in *Ibid.*, p. 23.
29. Quoted in *TV Guide* (May 15, 1971), p. 30.
30. Quoted in *Ibid.*
31. Quoted in Kay Gardella, "Pete's Not Convinced He's Lucky," *Sunday News* (April 25, 1971), p. S20.
32. Quoted in *Ibid.*
33. Quoted in *Ibid.*
34. Quoted in *Ibid.*
35. Brooks, *Directory of TV Stars*, p. 244.
36. Quoted in *Variety* (August 16, 1972), p. 1, 40.
37. Quoted in Kay Gardella, "'The Quest' Is TV's Only Western," *NY Daily News* (May 7, 1976), p. 110.
38. Quoted in *Ibid.*
39. Quoted in *Ibid.*
40. Quoted in Kay Gardella, "Matheson Is of Relaxed New Breed," *NY Daily News* (July 22, 1976), p. 99.
41. MacDonald, *Who Shot the Sheriff?*, Table 11, p. 123.
42. UPI, December 16, 1976.
43. MacDonald, *Who Shot the Sheriff?*, p. 121.
44. Summers, *TV Western Book*, Vol II, p. 136.
45. Castleman and Podrazik, *Favorite TV Shows*, pp. 417–418.
46. Patricia Nelson Limerick, Clyde A Milner II, and Charles E. Rankin, *Trails: Toward a New Western History* (University Press of Kansas: 1991), preface, p. xi.

47. Undated, Screen Gems, Inc. press release entitled "'Two Faces' Star Faces One Redhead."

XIV. When East Met West

1. Howard Reid and Michael Crocher, *The Way of the Warrior* (New York: 1987), p. 63. This is an excellent source of information regarding the origin and development of the martial arts.
2. Quoted in "The Kung Fu Craze," *Newsweek* (May 7, 1973), p. 76.
3. Quoted in Bill Davidson, "Does Not the Pebble, Entering the Water, Begin Fresh Journeys?" *TV Guide* (January 26, 1974), pp. 22–24.
4. Quoted in Tom Burke, "David Carradine, King of 'Kung Fu'," *New York Times* (April 29, 1973).
5. Quoted in *Ibid.*
6. Quoted in "Would You Believe a Half-American Buddhist Monk in a Western?" *Fanfare* (May 11, 1973).
7. Scheuer, *Movies on TV*, p. 68.
8. Parish and Pitts, *Great Western Pictures*, p. 323.
9. Quoted in Leslie Raddatz, "No. 1 Son Is Now 'Master Po'," *TV Guide* (June 23, 1973), p. 32.
10. Quoted in *Ibid.*
11. Quoted in *Ibid.*, p. 28.
12. Quoted in Herbie J. Pilato, *The Kung Fu Book of Caine* (Boston: 1993), pp. 62–63.
13. Quoted in Burke, "King of 'Kung Fu'," (April 29, 1973).
14. Cleveland Amory, "Review," *TV Guide* (March 3, 1973), p. 42.
15. Bob Lardine, "I Say 'No!' to Everything and Everybody," *NY Sunday News* (February 10, 1974), magazine section, p. 14.
16. Quoted in *Ibid.*, p. 16.
17. Quoted in Burke, "King of 'Kung Fu'."
18. Quoted in Lardine, "I Say 'No!'," p. 14.
19. Quoted in Burke, "King of 'Kung Fu'."
20. Quoted in *Ibid.*
21. John M. Gourlie, "Kung Fu," paper presented at the annual meeting of the Popular Culture Association in New Orleans, La., March 24, 1988, pp. 1, 4–5, 9–10.
22. Brooks and Marsh, *Directory of TV Shows*, p. 427.
23. Castleman and Podrazik, *Favorite TV Shows*, p. 274.
24. MacDonald, *Who Shot the Sheriff?*, p. 115.
25. *Ibid.*
26. Quoted in Pilato, *The Book of Caine...*, p. 151.
27. AP Press release (January 23, 1993).
28. *Ibid.*
29. *Ibid.*

XV. The Saga of "Little House on the Prairie"

1. Roy Allen Billington and Martin Ridge, *Westward Expansion: A History of the American Frontier* (New York: 1982), p. 5.
2. Tuska and Piekarski, *Western Fiction*, p. 355.
3. Donald Zochert, *Laura: The Life of Laura Ingalls Wilder* (Chicago: 1976), p. xi.
4. Quoted in Bill Davidson, "Michael Landon, General Contractor," *TV Guide* (December 7, 1974), p. 38.
5. Leslie Raddatz, "Move Over, Lois Wilson, Irene Dunne, Jean Arthur and Debbie Reynolds," *TV Guide* (June 7, 1975), p. 23.
6. Daly, *Michael Landon*, p. 116.
7. John J. O'Connor, "Take One Covered Wagon, Add Sugar...," *The New York Times* (April 14, 1974).
8. Quoted in Arthur Unger, "In Love with a Time, a Place, a Way of Life," *Christian Science Monitor* (September 18, 1974).

9. Quoted in Daly, *Michael Landon*, p. 118.

10. Quoted in Davidson, "Michael Landon," p. 40.

11. Daly, *Michael Landon*, p. 120.

12. Cleveland Amory, "Review," *TV Guide* (January 4, 1975), p. 21.

13. Cleveland Amory, "Second Thoughts," *TV Guide* (June 7, 1975) p. 34.

14. Kay Gardella, "TV's Do-Gooders Arrive in Five New Shows Tonight," *Daily News* (September 11, 1974), p. 42.

15. Quoted in Daly, *Michael Landon*, p. 120.

16. Quoted in *Ibid.*, p. 121.

17. Unger, "In Love" (September 18, 1974).

18. Quoted in *Ibid.*

19. Quoted in Aileen Joyce, *Michael Landon, His Triumph and Tragedy* (New York: 1991), p. 100.

20. Castleman and Podrazik, *Favorite TV Shows*, p. 290.

21. Richard West, *Television Westerns* (Jefferson, NC: 1987), p. 1.

22. Brooks and Marsh, *Directory of TV Shows*, p. 453.

23. Brode, "They Went Thataway," p. 40.

24. Edward Buscombe, *BFI Companion to the Western* (New York: 1988), p. 412.

25. Buck Rainey, *The Shoot-Em-Ups-Ride Again* (Metuchen, NJ: 1990), p. 237.

26. Castleman and Podrazik, *Favorite TV Shows*, p. 290.

27. Brooks and Marsh, *Directory of TV Shows*, p. 453.

28. Quoted in Stephen Farber, "Prairie Set Is Dynamited for Final," *The New York Times* (February 6, 1984), p. C20.

29. Quoted in *Ibid.*

30. In "Letters," *Channels of Communication* (August/September 1981), p. 3.

31. Quoted in Joyce, *Michael Landon*, pp. 101–102.

32. *Current Biography* (July 1977), p. 27.

33. "The All-Time Best TV, Readers' Edition," *TV Guide* (June 19–25, 1993), pp. 14, 16.

34. Quoted in Daly, *Michael Landon*, p. 119.

35. John J. O'Connor, "TV: 'Father Murphy's a Western Series," *The New York Times* (November 3, 1981).

36. Quoted in *Current Biography* (July 1977), p. 27.

XVI. Which Way Did They Go?

1. Lee Margulies, "Television Westerns: Endangered Series," *Louisville Courier Journal & Times* (July 11, 1976), p. H9.

2. Quoted in *Ibid.*

3. Quoted in *Ibid.*

4. William A. Henry III, "They Went Thataway!" *Memories* (December 1989/January 1990), p. 83.

5. *Ibid.*

6. *Ibid.*

7. *Ibid.*

8. MacDonald, *Who Shot the Sheriff?*, p. 134.

9. Bill Cosford, "Where Have Westerns Gone?" *Denver-Post* (September 6, 1989), p. 2E.

10. *Ibid.*

11. Monica Collins, "Have Gun, Will Time-Travel," *USA Today* (December 26, 1986), p. 3D.

12. Leonard Maltin, *TV Movies* (1991 edition), p. 553.

13. *Ibid.*, p. 1282.

14. Quoted in Bob Anderson, "Davy Crockett, King of the Wild Frontier," *Trail Dust* (Fall 1992), p. 11.

15. Quoted in Paul Andrew Hutton, "Davy Crockett—He Was Hardly King of the Wild Frontier," *TV Guide* (February 4, 1989), p. 25.

16. Castleman and Podrazik, *Favorite TV Shows*, p. 117.

17. Glen Wonnacott, "Bordertown," *The Westerner* (March 1992), p. 12.

18. Donna S. Miller, "'Bordertown' Enforces All Those Cliches," *Chatelaine* (September 1989), p. 18.

19. Castleman and Podrazik, *Favorite TV Shows*, p. 66.

20. Wonnacott, *The Westerner*, p. 13.

21. Bill Yenne, *The Legend of Zorro* (Greenwich, CT: 1991), p. 98.

22. *Ibid.*, pp. 103–111.

23. Quoted in Janette Hyem Anderson, "Zorro . . . the Sign of the Z," *Trail Dust* (Fall 1992), p. 12.

24. Yenne, *The Legend of Zorro*, pp. 132–139.

25. Quoted in "The Old Gringo," *Entertainment Weekly* (February 23, 1990), p. 12.

26. Quoted in Stephen Farber, "New Western Series Stresses Family Drama," *New York Times* (October 26, 1988), p. C22.

27. Quoted in *Ibid.*

28. Quoted in Michael E. Hill, "Lee Horsley—Truly at Home on the Range," *Washington Post—TV Week* (March 11–17, 1990), p. 8.

29. Robert MacKenzie, "Review: 'Paradise'," *TV Guide* (May 13, 1989), p. 23.

30. Quoted in Matt Roush, "Loyal Fans Find a Cowboy 'Paradise'," *USA Today* (June 26, 1989), p. 3D.

31. Quoted in Jefferson Graham, "A Second Shot for 'Guns of Paradise'," *USA Today* (January 2, 1991), p. 3D.

32. For a further discussion of *Paradise*'s involvement in social issues see Bob Lamm's interesting column "A New Look at the Old West" in *The Village Voice* for May 15, 1990.

33. Michelle M. Sundin, "Paradise Regained," *The Westerner* (No. 11–no date), p. 22.

34. Castleman and Podrazik, *Favorite TV Shows*, p. 393.

35. Stephen Harrigan, "The Making of 'Lonesome Dove'," *Texas Monthly* (June 1988), p. 86.

36. Mervyn Rothstein, "A Texan Who Likes to Deflate the Legends of the Golden West," *New York Times* (November 1, 1988), p. C17.

37. Quoted in *Ibid.*

38. Quoted in *Ibid.*

39. Harrigan, "Making of 'Lonesome Dove'," p. 156.

40. Quoted in *Ibid.*

41. *Ibid.*

42. Quoted in Roy Reed, "A Hatful of Dust," *New York Times* (September 11, 1988), section 6, part 2, page 66.

43. Quoted in Harrigan, "Making of 'Lonesome Dove'," p. 156.

44. Quoted in Loren D. Estleman, "Star Robert Duvall Says: It's Going to Be Like a Western Godfather," *TV Guide* (February 4, 1989), p. 18.

45. Quoted in Jay Bobbin, "CBS Revives Western Drama. . .," *Chicago Tribune* TV Log (February 4, 1989), p. 3.

46. Harrigan, "Making of 'Lonesome Dove'," p. 158.

47. Quoted in "Western Kicks Off Sweeps," *TV Week* (February 5, 1989), p. 3.

48. Quoted in Bobbin, "CBS Revives. . .," p. 3.

49. Quoted in Reed, "Hatful of Dust," p. 70.

50. Quoted in Frank Sanello, "'Dove' Presents Gritty Flavor of the Old West" *Chicago Tribune TV Week* (February 4, 1989), p. 3.

51. Quoted in Estleman, "Robert Duvall Says. . .," p. 16

52. Quoted in Diane Haithman, "Television's Trail Twists and Turns for Robert Duvall," *Chicago Sun-Times* (February 5, 1989), p. 8(E).

53. Richard Zoglin, "Poetry on the Prairie," *Time* (February 6, 1989), p. 78.

54. Harrigan, "Making of 'Lonesome Dove'," p. 159.

55. Reed, "Hatful of Dust," p. 71.

56. Harrigan, "Making of 'Lonesome Dove'," p. 82.

57. Canadian Dove Productions, *Lonesome Dove: The Series—Synopsis*.

58. *Ibid.*

59. Castleman and Podrazik, *Favorite TV Shows*, p. 409.

60. Quoted in Norman Zollinger, "For the Western Serial, Time to Saddle Up Again," *New York Times* (September 17, 1989), Section 2, p. 33.

61. Quoted in AP Press release dated March 10, 1990, written by Mary Ann Townsend.

62. Quoted in Jae-Ha Kim, "'Young Riders' Star Says He's 'the Best' as Buffalo Bill," *Chicago Sun-Times* (November 6, 1989), p. 6.

63. Quoted in Townsend, AP Press release.

64. Quoted in Kay Gardella, "Buck Starts Here on 'Young Riders'," *N.Y. Daily News* (November 10, 1989), p. 2.

65. Quoted in Townsend, AP Press release.

66. Quoted in Brooks, *Directory of TV Stars*, p. 929.

67. Quoted in Zollinger, "For the Western Serial...," p. 40 H.

68. In most episodes no title is given in the screen credits. Where titles are known they are cited. The source of all second season titles is Frank Lovece, *The Television Yearbook* (New York: 1992), pp. 259–262.

69. Brooks and Marsh, *Directory of TV Shows*, p. 1001.

70. John Donahue, "Tuska's Classification of Westerns: Some Reflections on ABC's 'The Young Riders'," unpublished paper presented at the 22nd annual convention of the Popular Culture Association, April 20, 1992, in Louisville, Kentucky, pp. 7, 10.

71. Ron Miller, "'Bloody River' Suffers from Severe Anemia," *The Leader* (Corning, NY: March 15, 1991), p. 16D.

72. Summers, Vol. IV, p. 96.

73. Quoted in Bill Carter, "'Dr. Quinn' Cures CBS's Case of the Saturday Night Programming Blues," *NY Times* (January 25, 1993), p. D8.

74. Quoted in "Homespun Approach a Winner for Creator of CBS's 'Dr Quinn'," AP Press release (July 25, 1993).

75. Quoted in *Ibid.*

76. Quoted in *Ibid.*

77. Quoted in Carter, "'Dr. Quinn' Cures CBS's..."

78. Quoted in Stewart Weiner, "Jane Stakes Her Claim," *TV Guide* (February 20, 1993), p. 11.

79. Quoted in *Ibid.*

80. Carter, "'Dr Quinn' Cures CBS's..."

81. *Ibid.*

82. *Ibid.*

83. Connie Passalacqua, "'Dr. Quinn' Miracle Woman," *FanFare* (March 14, 1993), p. 32.

84. Quoted in Carter, "'Dr. Quinn' Cures CBS's..."

85. Quoted in "Homespun Approach," AP Press release.

86. Quoted in Passalacqua, "Miracle Woman," p. 20.

87. Quoted in Passalacqua, "Miracle Woman," p. 32.

88. *Ibid.*

89. Quoted in "Homespun Approach," AP Press release.

90. Quoted in Passalacqua, "Miracle Woman," p. 32.

91. MacDonald, *Who Shot the Sheriff?*, pp. 136–137.

92. Quoted in James Brady, "In Step With: Chuck Norris," *Parade Magazine* (June 6, 1993), p. 14.

93. Quoted in Frank Swertlow, "A Kick-Chop Texas Ranger," *TV Guide* (April 10, 1993), p. 22.

94. Quoted in *Ibid.*, p. 24.

95. Quoted in *Ibid.*, p. 23.

96. Quoted in *Ibid.*, p. 24.

97. Quoted in Brady, "Chuck Norris."

98. Quoted in Jay Bobbin, "'Ned Blessing' Rides Again on CBS," published in *The Leader* Television Supplement (Corning, NY: August 9, 1993), p. 4.

99. Quoted in *Ibid.*

100. Quoted in Jefferson Graham "'Brisco County Jr.' Is Fox's Big Gun for Fall," *USA Today* (July 2, 1993), p. 3D.

101. Quoted in *Ibid.*

102. Quoted in *Ibid.*

103. Quoted in Rick Marin, "This Season's Standout Stars," *TV Guide* (Sept. 25, 1993), p. 22.

104. Quoted in *Ibid.*

105. Quoted in Graham, "Brisco County Jr."

106. Brooks and Marsh, *Directory of TV Shows*, p. 937.

107. Bruce Weber, "Native Ground," *New York Times Magazine* (November 20, 1988), p. 118.

108. Quoted in Bruce Fretts, "Fall TV Preview," *Entertainment Weekly* (September 17, 1993), p. 66.

109. Quoted in *Ibid.*

110. Quoted in *Ibid.*

111. Quoted in *Ibid.*

112. Doug Nye, "'Real West' Returns to A&E," Knight-Ridder Newspapers (April 4, 1993).

113. Quoted in *Ibid.*

114. Quoted in Jerry Buck, "Story of West Told in People, Places of Era," AP Press release (March 18, 1993).

115. Quoted in *Ibid.*

116. Janette and Bob Anderson, "The Hitchin' Post," *Trail Dust* (Spring 1994), p. 30.

117. Stephen J. Cannell Productions, Inc., *Hawkeye: The First Frontier*, press release (7/94).

118. *Ibid.*

119. *Ibid.*

120. Quoted in Miriam Horn, "How the West Was Really Won," *U.S. News & World Report* (May 21, 1990), p. 56.

Bibliography

This bibliography is divided into three parts: Unpublished Sources, Published Sources—Books, and Published Sources—Periodicals.

Several directories were particularly useful in locating basic information about television shows: Brooks and Marsh's *Directory of TV Shows* provides broadcast dates, cast lists and a brief description of the premise on which each show is based. The information is easy to locate and reliable. Castleman & Podrazik's *Favorite TV Shows* also gives a brief critical assessment of each show. Brooks' *Directory of TV Stars* provides biographical information about the actors and actresses featured as continuing characters on series.

Neil Summers' four volume *Official TV Western Book* provides anecdotes about many of the shows in addition to basic background information. Nearly all but the most recent shows and miniseries are included and all four volumes are profusely illustrated with excellent photos.

Several shows have detailed published logs available: *Bonanza*, prepared by Melany Shapiro; *The Wild Wild West*, by Susan E. Kesler; *Kung Fu*, by Herbie J. Pilato; *Maverick*, by Ed Robertson; *The Lone Ranger*, by David Rothel, who also has published works on *The Gene Autry Show* and *The Roy Rogers Show*; and *Hopalong Cassidy*, by Francis M. Nevins. Logs of all the Warner Bros. Westerns can be found in Woolley, Malsbary and Strange's fine book; logs of comedy Westerns are included in Eisner and Krinsky's comprehensive volume; and, of course, the most exhausting and thorough study of any Western series yet published is SuzAnne and Gabor Barabas' work on *Gunsmoke*. Gianakos' six volume reference work is helpful in providing episode titles, dates and guest casts.

Among the many periodicals consulted in addition to *TV Guide*, special mention should be made of *The Westerner*, with interesting and useful information about all aspects of the West, published quarterly by Roger Crowley; *Trail Dust*, which specializes in articles about television and film Westerns and is published quarterly by Bob and Janette Hyem Anderson; and *The TV Collector*, which contains articles, interviews, book reviews, and extensive logs of television shows, and is published bimonthly by Stephen and Diane Albert.

Unpublished Sources

Brode, Douglas. "Disneyland: The TV Westerns of Walt Disney" (unpublished paper presented at the 18th annual meeting of the Popular Culture Association, New Orleans, La., 1988).

Donahue, John. "Tuska's Classification of Westerns: Some Reflections on ABC's 'The Young

Riders'" (unpublished paper presented at the 22nd annual meeting of the Popular Culture Association, Louisville, Ky., 1992).

Esselman, Kathryn. "How Television Tames 'Gunsmoke'" (unpublished paper presented at the 17th annual meeting of the Popular Culture Association, Louisville, Ky., 1987).

Gourlie, John M. "Kung Fu" (unpublished paper presented at the 18th annual meeting of the Popular Culture Association, New Orleans, La., 1988).

Money, Mary Alice. *Evolutions of the Popular Western in Novels, Films, and Television, 1958–1974* (unpublished doctoral dissertation, University of Texas at Austin, 1975).

Parker, David W. *A Descriptive Analysis of the Lone Ranger as a Form of Popular Art* (unpublished doctoral dissertation, Northwestern University, 1955).

Stanley, Jack Ross. *A History of the Radio and Television Western Dramatic Series "Gunsmoke," 1952– 1973* (unpublished doctoral dissertation, University of Michigan, 1973).

Striker, Fran, Jr. *His Typewriter Grew Spurs.* Privately printed, 1983.

White, Ray. "Adventure in Paradise Valley: The Roy Rogers Television Show" (unpublished paper presented at the 18th annual meeting of the Popular Culture Association, New Orleans, La., 1988).

Published Sources — Books

Autry, Gene. *Back in the Saddle Again.* New York: Doubleday, 1978.

Baily, Kenneth, editor. *The Television Annual for 1958.* London: Long Acre, 1958.

Barabas, SuzAnne, and Gabor Barabas. *Gunsmoke: A Complete History.* Jefferson, N.C.: McFarland, 1990.

Barbour, Alan G. *Days of Thrills and Adventure.* New York: Macmillan, 1970.

Beatty, Lorraine. "Gadgets and Guises" in James Van Hise, *The Wild Wild West Book.* Los Angeles: Shuster and Shuster, 1988.

Billington, Ray Allen, and Martin Ridge. *Westward Expansion: A History of the American Frontier.* New York: Macmillan, 1982.

Brauer, Ralph, with Donna Brauer. *The Horse, the Gun and the Piece of Property: Changing Images of the TV Western.* Bowling Green, Ohio: Bowling Green University Popular Press, 1975.

Brooks, Tim. *The Complete Directory to Prime Time TV Stars, 1946–Present.* New York: Ballantine, 1987.

_____, and Earle Marsh. *The Complete Directory to Prime Time Network TV Shows, 1946 to Present.* New York: Ballantine, 1992.

Buscombe, Edward. *BFT Companion to the Western.* New York: Atheneum, 1988.

Cameron, Lou. *How the West Was Won.* New York: Ballantine, 1977.

Castleman, Harry, and Walter J. Podrazik, *Harry and Wally's Favorite TV Shows.* New York: Prentice Hall, 1989.

_____, and _____. *Watching TV: Four Decades of American Television.* New York: McGraw-Hill, 1982.

Connell, Evan S. *Son of the Morning Star.* San Francisco: North Point, 1984.

Daly, Marsha. *Michael Landon: A Biography.* New York: St. Martin's, 1987.

DiOrio, Al. *Barbara Stanwyck.* New York: Coward-McCann, 1983.

Drew, Bernard A. *Hopalong Cassidy: The Clarence E. Mulford Story.* Metuchen, N.J.: Scarecrow, 1991.

Eisner, Joel, and David Krinsky. *Television Comedy Series.* Jefferson, N.C.: McFarland, 1984.

Eyles, Allen. *John Wayne.* New York: A.S. Barnes, 1979.

Folsom, James K. "Stewart Edward White," *The Reader's Encyclopedia of the American West.* New York: Harper & Row, 1977.

Folsom, "Owen Wister," *The Reader's Encyclopedia of the American West.* New York: Harper & Row, 1977.

Frazee, Steve. *The Outcasts.* Toronto: Popular Library, 1968.

Garfield, Brian. *Western Films.* New York: Rawson Associates, 1982.

Gianakos, Larry James. *Television Drama Series Programming: A Comprehensive Chronicle, Vol I., 1947– 1959;Vol II., 1959–1975;Vol. III., 1975–1980; Vol. IV 1980–.* Metuchen, N.J.: Scarecrow, 1978; 1981; 1983.

Glut, Donald F., and Jim Harmon. *The Great Television Heroes.* New York: Doubleday, 1975.

Grossman, Gary H. *Saturday Morning TV.* New York: Dell, 1981.

Guerif, Francois. *Clint Eastwood: The Man and His Films.* New York: St. Martin's Press, 1984.

Heckelmann, Charles. *The Big Valley.* Racine, Wis.: Whitman, 1956.

Hilger, Michael. *The American Indian in Film.* Metuchen, N.J.: Scarecrow, 1986.

Hitt, Jim. *The American West from Fiction (1823–1976) into Film (1909–1986).* Jefferson, N.C.: McFarland, 1990.

Holland, David. *From Out of the Past: A Pictorial History of the Lone Ranger.* Granada Hills, Calif.: Holland House, 1988.

Holland, Ted. *B Western Actors Encyclopedia: Facts, Photos and Filmographies for More than 250 Familiar Faces.* Jefferson, N.C.: McFarland, 1988.

Hollon, Eugene W. "Law and Order," *The Reader's Encyclopedia of the American West.* New York: Harper & Row, 1977.

Horowitz, James. *They Went Thataway.* New York: Ballantine, 1976.

Jackson, Turentine W. "Wells, Fargo & Co.," *The Reader's Encyclopedia of the American West*. New York: Harper & Row, 1977.

Javna, John. *Cult TV*. New York: St. Martin's, 1985.

Joyce, Aileen. *Michael Landon: His Truimph and Tragedy*. New York: Kensington, 1991.

Kesler, Susan E. *The Wild Wild West: The Series*. Downey, Calif.: Arnett Press, 1988.

Kulzer, Dina-Marie. *Television Series Regulars of the Fifties and Sixties in Interview*. Jefferson, N.C.: McFarland, 1992.

Lake, Stuart N. *The Life and Times of Wyatt Earp*. Boston: Houghton Mifflin, 1956.

Limerick, Patricia Nelson; Clyde A. Millner II, and Charles E. Rankin. *Trails: Toward a New Western History*. Manhattan: University Press of Kansas, 1991.

Lovece, Frank. *The Television Yearbook*. New York: Putnam, 1992.

MacDonald, J. Fred. *Don't Touch That Dial! Radio Programming in American Life from 1920 to 1960*. Chicago: Nelson-Hall, 1979.

_____. *Who Shot the Sheriff?* New York: Praeger, 1987.

McGhee, Richard D. *John Wayne: Actor, Artist, Hero*. Jefferson, N.C.: McFarland, 1990.

McNeil, Alex. *Total Television*. New York: Penguin, 1984.

Maltin, Leonard. *The Disney Films*. New York: Crown, 1973.

_____. *TV Movies and Video Guide*. New York: New American Library, 1991.

Martindale, David. *Television Detective Shows of the 1970s*. Jefferson, N.C.: McFarland, 1991.

Maverick Annual (author unknown). London: 1981.

Miller, Don. *Hollywood Corral*. New York: Barnes, 1976.

Miller, Lee O. *Great Cowboy Stars of Movies and Television*. New Rochelle, N.Y.: Arlington, 1979.

Nevins, Francis M. *The Films of Hopalong Cassidy*. Waynesville, N.C.: World of Yesterday, 1988.

Nolan, William F. *McQueen*. New York: Congdon & Weed, 1984.

O'Connor, Richard. *Bat Masterson*. New York: Bantam, 1957.

Parish, James Robert, and Michael K. Pitts. *The Great Western Pictures*. Metuchen, N.J.: Scarecrow, 1976.

Parks, Rita. *The Western Hero in Film and Television*. Ann Arbor: University of Michigan Press, 1982.

Pilato, Herbie J. *The Kung Fu Book of Caine*. Boston: Charles E. Tuttle, 1993.

Pitts, Michael R. *Western Movies: A TV and Video Guide to 4200 Genre Films*. Jefferson, N.C.: McFarland, 1986.

Rainey, Buck. *The Shoot-Em-Ups-Ride Again*. Metuchen, N.J.: Scarecrow, 1990.

Reid, Howard, and Michael Crocher. *The Way of the Warrior*. New York: Overlook, 1987.

Roberton, Frank G. *A Man Called Paladin*. New York: Macmillan, 1963.

Roberts, Gary L. "Bat Masterson," *The Reader's Encyclopedia of the American West*. New York: Harper & Row, 1977.

_____. "John Ringo," *The Reader's Encyclopedia of the American West*. New York: Harper & Row, 1977.

_____. "William Preston Longley," *The Reader's Encyclopedia of the American West*. New York: Harper & Row, 1977.

Robertson, Ed. *Maverick: Legend of the West*. Los Angeles: Pomegranate, 1994.

Rothel, David. *The Gene Autry Book*. Waynesville, N.C.: World of Yesterday, 1986.

_____. *The Roy Rogers Book*. Madison, N.C.: Empire, 1987.

_____. *Who Was That Masked Man?*. New York: A.S. Barnes, 1976.

Rovin, Jeff. *The Great Television Series*. New York: A.S. Barnes, 1977.

Sarf, Wayne Michael. *God Bless You, Buffalo Bill*. East Brunswick, N.J.: Fairleigh Dickinson University Press, 1983.

Scheuer, Steven H. *Movies on TV*. New York: Bantam, 1985.

Shapiro, Melany. *Bonanza: The Unofficial Story of the Ponderosa*. Las Vegas: Pioneer Books, 1993.

Shepherd, Donald, and Robert Slatzer, with Dave Grayson. *Duke: The Life and Times of John Wayne*. New York: Doubleday, 1985.

Shows, Charles. *Walt: Backstage with Walt Disney*. La Jolla, Calif.: Windsong Books, 1979.

Simmons, Marc. "Elfego Baca," *The Reader's Encyclopedia of the American West*. New York: Harper & Row, 1977.

Sinclair, Andrew. *John Ford: A Biography*. London: Dial Press/J. Wade, 1984.

Smith, Ella. *Starring Miss Barbara Stanwyck*. New York: Crown, 1974.

Smith, Steven C. *A Heart at Fire's Center*. Los Angeles: University of California Press, 1991.

Speed, F. Maurice. *The Western Film and TV Annual*. London: MacDonald, 1957.

Stedman, Raymond William. *Shadows of the Indian*. Norman: University of Oklahoma Press: Norman, 1982.

Stewart, Edgar I. "Gall," *The Reader's Encylopedia of the American West*. New York: Harper & Row, 1977.

Stout, Joe A. "John Slaughter," *The Reader's Encyclopedia of the American West*. New York: Harper & Row, 1977.

Stowers, Carlton. *Happy Trails: The Story of Roy Rogers and Dale Evans*. Waco, Texas: Word Book, 1979.

Strait, Raymond. *James Garner*. New York: St. Martin's, 1985.

Summers, Neil. *The First Official TV Western*

Kronke, David. "The Warrior." *Entertainment Weekly*. Feb. 1, 1991.

"The Kung Fu Craze." *Newsweek*. May 7, 1973.

Lachuk, John. "Culp the Perfectionist." *TV and Movie Western*. Aug. 1958.

_____. "Steve McQueen's Gun." *TV and Movie Western*. June 1959.

Lardine, Bob. "Granddaddy of All the Westerns." *New York Sunday News*. July 10, 1960.

_____. "I Say 'No' to Everything and Everybody." *New York Sunday News* (magazine section).

Feb. 10, 1974.

"Last of the Swashbuckling Heroes." *TV Guide*. Nov. 25, 1972.

Lewis, Elisabeth. "The Kid with the Golden Sandbox." *TV Guide*. Dec. 4, 1965.

Lewis, Richard Warren. "Dammit, I *Am* Cochise." *TV Guide*. Jan. 20, 1968.

_____. "Stuart Whitman's 'Marshal Plan'." *TV Guide*. Nov. 4, 1967.

Lichtenstein, Grace. "He Refuses to Be an 'Ugh-Tonto' Indian." *New York Times*. June 6, 1976.

Lilley, Tim. "Paul Fix." *The Big Trail*. Feb. 1987.

Lindsey, Robert. "Zeb Macahan Is More Fun Than Matt Dillon." *New York Times*. Sept. 12, 1978.

MacKenzie, Robert. "Review: 'Paradise'." *TV Guide*. May 13, 1989.

Mackin, Tom. "Coming: 'McHale's Army'." *Newark Evening News*. July 25, 1965.

Maksian, George. "Sioux Are Howling Over 'Hanta Yo'." *New York Daily News*. May 8, 1980.

"Man from Nanticoke." *TV Guide*. Jan. 16, 1960.

"The Man in the Red Broadcloth Suit." *TV Guide*. Feb. 17, 1956.

Margulies, Lee. "Television Westerns: Endangered Series." *Louisville Courier Journal & Times*. July 11, 1976.

Marin, Rick. "This Season's Standout Stars." *TV Guide*. Sept. 25. 1993.

Markfield, Wallace. "A Fond Farewell to Matt Dillon, Dodge City and 'Gunsmoke'." *New York Times*. July 13, 1975.

Maronie, Samuel J. "An Interview with Robert Conrad." *Starlog*. Jan. 1981.

"The Marshal's on the Level." *TV Guide*. April 1960.

"Michael Landon." *Current Biography*. July 1977.

Miller, Donna S. "'Bordertown' Enforces All Those Clichés." *Chatelaine*. Sept. 1989.

"Mona Lisa of the Long Branch." *TV Guide*. Dec. 13, 1960.

Morheim, Joe. "More Than Meets the Eye." *TV Guide*. June 7, 1958.

_____. "She Who Never Gets Kissed." *TV Guide*. March 15, 1958.

"Musical-Comedy Singer Goes West." *TV Guide*. Aug. 9, 1960.

Nachman, Gerald. "The Return of James Arness." *New York Daily News*. March 27, 1978.

"A New James Dean?" *TV Guide*. Feb. 19, 1966.

Nussbaum, Martin. "Sociological Symbolism of the 'Adult Western'." *Social Forces*. Oct. 1960.

Nye, Doug. "'Real West' Returns to A&E." *Knight-Ridder Newspapers*. April 4, 1993.

O'Brian, Hugh. "Marshal Earp." *TV Guide*. May 2, 1959.

O'Connor, John J. "Custer, Call Your Spin Doctor." *New York Times Magazine*. Feb. 3, 1991.

_____. "Historical Dramas—Fact or Fancy?" *New York Times*. May 25, 1975.

_____. "Take One Covered Wagon, Add Sugar...." *New York Times*. April 14, 1974.

_____. "TV: 'Father Murphy's' a Western Series." *New York Times*. Nov. 3, 1981.

_____. "Why Bother Watching a Woeful Remake?" *New York Times*. April 10, 1988.

"The Old Gringo." *Entertainment Weekly*. Feb. 23, 1990.

Passalacqua, Connie. "Dr. Quinn, Miracle Woman." *FanFare*. March 14, 1993.

"Peter Brown." *TV Guide*. July 9, 1960.

"A Petticoat for the Ponderosa." *TV Guide*. Jan. 18, 1964.

Phillips, Dee, and Bev Copeland. "Riding High on the Waves of Indignation." *TV Guide*. June 12, 1965.

Poppy, John. "The Worldwide Lure of 'Bonanza'." *Look*. Dec. 1, 1964.

Raddatz, Leslie. "Actors Should Act Like Actors." *TV Guide*. Dec. 11, 1965.

_____. "Come Back in 1976." *TV Guide*. Dec. 24, 1966.

_____. "Gunsmoke's Designated Hitter." *TV Guide*. Dec. 8, 1973.

_____. "Move Over, Lois Wilson, Irene Dunne, Jean Arthur and Debbie Reynolds." *TV Guide*. June 7, 1975.

_____. "No. 1 Son Is Now 'Master Po'." *TV Guide*. June 23, 1973.

_____. "Rebirth of an Actor." *TV Guide*. Oct. 26, 1963.

_____. "The Wild, Wild Man from 'The Wild, Wild West'." *TV Guide*. May 21, 1966.

"The Real Wyatt Earp." *TV Guide*. May 2, 1959.

Reed, Roy. "A Hatful of Dust." *New York Times* (section 6, part 2). Sept. 11, 1988.

Rothstein, Mervyn. "A Texan Who Likes to Deflate the Legends of the Golden West." *New York Times*. Nov. 1, 1988.

Roush, Matt. "Loyal Fans Find a Cowboy 'Paradise'." *USA Today*. June 26, 1989.

Russell, Dick. "Neither Snow, Nor Thunder, Nor Hostile Indians...." *TV Guide*. September 30-October 6, 1978.

St. Johns, Adela Rogers. "Hopalong Cassidy's Code." *American Weekly*. June 17, 1951.

Sanders, Coyne Steven. "Miss Kitty and Gunsmoke." *Emmy Magazine*. July/Aug., 1985.

Sarello, Frank. "'Dove' Presents Gritty Flavor of the Old West." *Chicago Tribune TV Week*. Feb. 4, 1989.

Schinckel, Richard. "TV's Angry Gun." *Show*. Nov. 1961.

Schwartz, Tony. "An Indian Epic." *Newsweek*. April 16, 1979.

Searle, Ronald. "How the West Was Really Won." *TV Guide*. May 27, 1967.

See, Carolyn. "How Can a Square Fit into the Hollywood Circle?" *TV Guide*. Aug. 8, 1969.

————. "An Old Actor Stands Fast in a Changing World." *TV Guide*. March 30, 1968.

Shain, Michael. "'Best' and Co. Spoofs the Wild West." *New York Post*. Sept. 10, 1981.

Shaw, David. "Raquel Went on the Warpath—and Boy, Did the Casualties Mount." *TV Guide*. May 29, 1982.

Sheff, David, and Jack Fincher. "A Growing War Over 'Hanta Yo'." *People*. June 23, 1980.

Simmons, Garner. "Sam Peckinpah's Television Work." *Film Heritage*. Winter, 1974-75.

"The Six-Gun Galahad." *Time*. March 30, 1959.

Smith, Cecil. "Rebel Is Unique Western Fare with Timeless Quality." *Los Angeles Times*. Oct. 11, 1959.

————. "The TV Scene." Part II. *Los Angeles Times*. April 10, 1961.

Smith, Jack. "Hero Today and Gone Tomorrow." *Los Angeles Times*. May 27, 1963.

Stahl, Robert. "The Facts Are Enough." *TV Guide*. March 7, 1959.

Sundin, Michelle. "Paradise Regained." *The Westerner*. No. 11 (no date).

Svetkey, Benjamin. "Native Sons, Rising Stars." *Entertainment Weekly*. March 8, 1991.

Swertlow, Frank. "A Kick-Chop Texas Ranger." *TV Guide*. April 10, 1993.

Talese, Gay. "Zorro-TV Cut-Up." *New York Times*. April 13, 1958.

"'The Tall Man' Review." *TV Guide*. May 6, 1961.

Tharp, Richard K. "Bonanza, Part I." *Reruns*. April 1982.

————. "Rawhide, Part 1." *Reruns*. April 1981.

————. "The Wild, Wild West, Part 2." *Reruns*. Dec. 1980.

"This Man Kissed a Girl!" *TV Guide*. June 26, 1964.

Thomas, Bob. "Cheyenne Star Is Bowing Out." *New York World-Telegram & Sun*. Aug 15, 1962.

"Togetherness-Western Style." *TV Guide*. June 25, 1960.

Torre, Marie. "Dale Robertson Rides and Sings." *New York Herald Tribune*. Oct. 13, 1958.

Townsend, Mary Ann. AP press release. March 10, 1990.

Tucker, Ken. "'Morning Star': The Review." *Entertainment Weekly*. Feb. 1, 1991.

"'TV Guide' Presents 40 Years of the Best." *TV Guide*. April 17, 1993.

TV Western Roundup. Vol I: 1957.

Unger, Arthur. "In Love with a Time, a Place, a Way of Life." *Christian Science Monitor*. Sept. 18, 1974.

"Very Tall in the Saddle." *TV Guide*. Aug. 19, 1956.

"Wagon Train," part I. *The TV Collector*. Oct.-Nov. 1985. Part II, Dec. 1985-Jan. 1986. Part III, Feb.-March 1986.

Waters, Harry F. "The 'Roots' Indian Uprising." *Newsweek*. May 21, 1984.

Weber, Bruce. "Native Ground." *New York Times Magazine*. Nov. 20, 1988.

Weiner, Stewart. "Jane Stakes Her Claim." *TV Guide*. Feb. 20, 1993.

Weingrad, Jeff. "Crockett on Comeback Trail?" *New York Daily News*. Jan. 2, 1987.

"Western Twist." *TV Guide*. Sept. 27, 1958.

Whitney, Dwight. "The Dusty Trail to the High Chaparral." *TV Guide*. Aug. 23, 1969.

————. "The Garbo of the Sagebrush." *TV Guide*. Dec. 8, 1962.

————. "The Life and Good Times of Hollywood's Harry Julian Fink." *TV Guide*. Feb. 27, 1960.

————. "Meanwhile, Back at Their Ranches...." *TV Guide*. Aug. 8, 1959.

————. "New Boy on 'Bonanza'." *TV Guide*. March 2, 1968.————. "Patriarch of the Ponderosa." *TV Guide*. May 13, 1961.

————. "The Queen Goes West." *TV Guide*. Feb. 22, 1966.

————. "Richard the Good." *TV Guide*. July 20, 1968.

————. "Smile When You Say That, Pardner." *TV Guide*. (date unknown).

————. "The Warpath Runneth Over." *TV Guide*. May 19, 1984.

————. "A Whale of a Hero." March 3, 1960.

————. "What a Bonanza!" *TV Guide*. Sept. 8, 1962.

"Why 26 Men." *TV Guide*. Feb. 16, 1958.

Wilson, Liza. "Jim Garner ... Real Life Maverick." *The American Weekly*. Aug. 10, 1958.

Wollman, Jane. "Hoppy at Last." *Memories*. June/July 1989.

Wonnacott, Glen. "Bordertown." *The Westerner*. March 1992.

"Would You Believe a Half-American Buddhist Monk in a Western?" *Fanfare*. May 11, 1973.

Zoglin, Richard. "Poetry on the Prairie." *Time*. Feb. 6, 1989.

Zollinger, Norman. "For the Western Serial, Time to Saddle Up Again." *New York Times* (section 2). Sept. 17, 1989.

"Zorro Foiled His Rivals." *TV Guide*. April 26, 1958.